THE HACHETTE LEARNING GUIDE TO
International Schools 2025/26

The authoritative guide to international education

Together we unlock every learner's unique potential

At Hachette Learning (formerly Hodder Education), there's one thing we're certain about. No two students learn the same way. That's why our approach to teaching begins by recognising the needs of individuals first.

Our mission is to allow every learner to fulfil their unique potential by empowering those who teach them. From our expert teaching and learning resources to our digital educational tools that make learning easier and more accessible for all, we provide solutions designed to maximise the impact of learning for every teacher, parent and student.

Aligned to our parent company, Hachette Livre, founded in 1826, we pride ourselves on being a learning solutions provider with a global footprint.

www.hachettelearning.com

Every effort has been made to trace all copyright holders, but if any have been inadvertently overlooked, the Publishers will be pleased to make the necessary arrangements at the first opportunity

Although every effort has been made to ensure that website addresses are correct at time of going to press, Hachette Learning cannot be held responsible for the content of any website mentioned in this book. It is sometimes possible to find a relocated web page by typing in the address of the home page for a website in the URL window of your browser

Hachette UK's policy is to use papers that are natural, renewable and recyclable products and made from wood grown in well-managed forests and other controlled sources. The logging and manufacturing processes are expected to conform to the environmental regulations of the country of origin

To order, please visit www.HachetteLearning.com or contact Customer Service at education@hachette.co.uk / +44 (0)1235 827827.

ISBN: 9781036019679

© Hachette Learning 2025

First published in 2025 by
Hachette Learning,
An Hachette UK Company
Carmelite House
50 Victoria Embankment
London EC4Y 0DZ
www.HachetteLearning.com

The authorised representative in the EEA is Hachette Ireland, 8 Castlecourt Centre, Dublin 15, D15 XTP3, Ireland (email: info@hbgi.ie)

All rights reserved. Apart from any use permitted under UK copyright law, no part of this publication may be reproduced or transmitted in any form or by any means, electronic or mechanical, including photocopying and recording, or held within any information storage and retrieval system, without permission in writing from the publisher or under licence from the Copyright Licensing Agency Limited. Further details of such licences (for reprographic reproduction) may be obtained from the Copyright Licensing Agency Limited, www.cla.co.u

A catalogue record for this title is available from the British Library

Typeset in the UK
Printed in the UK

Contents

Editorial
How to use this guide 5
Sparking genius all over the world
Dwight School, USA 6
Bilingualism: a foundation for success in Early Years and Primary
ICS Côte d'Azur, France 8
Beyond the classroom: cultivating well-being
Institut International Saint-Dominique, Italy 10
Exploring the French Riviera: a learning journey
The International School of Nice, France 12
Where Boarding Meets Global Citizenship
Jerudong International School, Brunei Darussalam 14
Grow, thrive, sustain: an outdoor learning ethos
Mougins British International School, France 16
United for the future: educating children for tomorrow's world
United Lisbon International School, Portugal 18
Citizens of the world: understanding Third Culture Kids
The American Overseas School of Rome, Italy 20
Shaping tomorrow's innovators
ICS Paris, France 22
The Impact Hub: a launchpad for tomorrow's innovators
International School of Lausanne, Switzerland 24
Education for greater good
Mulgrave School - The International School of Vancouver 26
Educating for purpose: the Round Square approach to enriched learning
The Hutchins School, Australia 28
The Transformative Power of Boarding
Hockerill Anglo-European College, UK 30
Classroom management: building a lasting positive learning environment
Stonehill International School, Bangalore 32
The questions you should ask 34

Profiles of international schools
Africa 39
Asia 43
Australasia 83
Europe 89
North America 219
South America 239

Directory of international schools
Africa D247
Asia D267
Australasia D337
Europe D345
North America D399
South America D425

Appendices
International school associations 439
Ministries of Education worldwide 449
International curricula, examinations and tests 467

Index 483

TEACHING WALKTHRUs

FIVE-STEP GUIDES TO INSTRUCTIONAL COACHING

WALKTHRUS.CO.UK

BOOKS

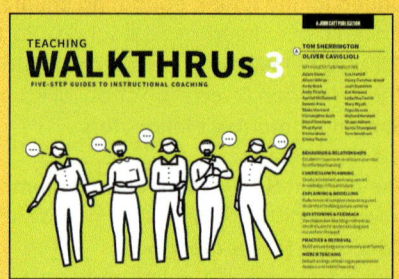

SCHOOLS CAN SIGN UP TO OUR PD RESOURCES PACK

GET STARTED

- Start planning your CPD programme
- Get going with Instructional Coaching
- Visit our website **walkthrus.co.uk**
- Email us **hello@walkthrus.co.uk**
- Visit **HachetteLearning.com/walkthrus**

How to use this guide

The Hachette Learning Guide to International Schools has been specifically designed with the reader in mind. Now in its 23rd year, this edition includes useful and informative information which is ideal for anyone looking for details of an international school, association, international curriculums, exams, tests and qualifications. There are clearly defined sections providing information for anyone looking at independent international education worldwide today.

Are you looking for help and advice? Take a look at our editorial section (see pages 6 to 35). Here you will find articles covering a wide variety of issues you are likely to come across when choosing a school for your child. Each year we try to find a differing range of topics to interest and inform you about the uniqueness of independent international education.

Perhaps you are looking for a school or college in a certain country? Then you need to look first in the directories (starting on page D245). Here you will find basic information about all the schools in each country (countries are featured in alphabetical order within their relevant continent), complete with contact details. From this section you will be directed to more detailed information in the guide, where this is available. An example of a typical directory entry is given at the end of this article. School profile information is written by the individual schools, outlining the reasons why you should choose their establishment.

Some of you may already be looking for a specific school or college. In which case, if you know the name of the school or college but are unsure of its location, simply go to the index at the back of the guide where you will find all the schools listed alphabetically. Page numbers prefixed with the letter D denote the directory section; those without, a full profile.

In the appendix you will find up-to-date information about international curriculums and the examinations, tests and qualifications available (see page 467), editorial about international schools associations (see page 439), and contact details for Ministries of Education worldwide (see page 449).

Key to directory

- Country
- Name of school or college
- Indicates that this school has a profile
- Address and contact number
- Head's name
- Age range
- Number of pupils. B = boys G = girls VIth = sixth form
- Fees per annum. Day = fees for day pupils. WB = fees for weekly boarders. FB = fees for full boarders.
- Curriculum
- Language of instruction
- Memberships/Accreditation

Whereford

College Academy

For further details see p.12

Which Street, Whosville, Wherofordshire AB12 3CD

Tel: 01000 000000

Head Master: Dr A Person

Age range: 11–18

No. of pupils: 660 B330 G330 VIth 200

Fees: Day £11,000 WB £16,000 FB £20,000

Curriculum: National, IBDP, ALevs

Language instr: English, French

(AISA) (COB) (EAR)

Key to icons

Key to symbols:
- Boys' school
- Girls' school
- Boarding accommodation

Member of:
- (AISA) Association of International Schools in Africa
- (CEE) Central and Eastern European Schools Association
- (EAR) East Asia Regional Council of Overseas Schools
- (ECIS) European Council of International Schools
- (RS) Round Square

Accreditation:
- (CIS) Council of International Schools
- (COB) Council of British International Schools

Sparking genius all over the world

Dwight School, USA, explores the importance of dialogue in the pursuit of academic excellence.

Since the founding of the flagship Dwight School in New York City in 1872, Dwight's network of schools has expanded to include campuses in London, Dubai, Shanghai, Seoul, Hanoi, and in the cloud with Dwight Global Online School. Dwight's role as a leader in education is steeped in academic tradition, but it remains a leader more than 150 years after its founding because of its willingness to dialogue and innovate in service of its mission of "finding the spark of genius" in every student.

That tradition of looking towards the future continues with *Sparking Genius*, the global network of Dwight Schools' original podcast. Host Dianne Drew, Head of School at Dwight New York and Global Education Director, sits down to dialogue with leaders and innovative thinkers to explore what the future of education holds. *Sparking Genius* dives into the most cutting-edge topics, and demonstrates firsthand how new strategies and fresh perspectives can inspire and enlighten parents, administrators, teachers and students.

"Anyone who has an interest in education, and children's development and well-being, would enjoy a listen — educators and parents alike," says Ms. Drew. *"This is such a thrilling project for Dwight, as it really highlights our thought leadership in the industry."*

Shortly after premiering its first episode on all podcasting platforms, including Spotify and Apple Podcasts, *Sparking Genius* garnered 5-star ratings and was in the Top 1% of podcasts in both the categories of Education and Technology.

Season 1 of *Sparking Genius* explored how Dwight Schools nurture each student's individual potential through personalized education, global citizenship, and innovative approaches to both learning and teaching. Specifically, across the six episodes, the series covered the IB curriculum, online learning, mental health and wellness, benefits of international education, and the evolving role of AI in the classroom.

On the second episode of Season 1, for example, Ms. Drew spoke with Nicole Bien, Chief Schools Officer at the International Baccalaureate Organization, and Marie Nieto, Head of Middle School Humanities at Dwight. Together, they had an important conversation about what makes the IB curriculum unique, and what the exciting future of technological advancements and AI holds for the IB.

Nicole Bien touched on what makes the IB stand out, especially in our evolving digital landscape. She said, *"We truly believe that with the changing world, and with the advancement of digital technology, students really need to have skills that prepare them for whatever their future professions might be, or the challenges that they need to tackle, as opposed to a very narrow focus on a specific area of knowledge."*

Thus far, Season 2 evaluated a range of topics — from athletics in an academically rich setting, to how education is changing in response to powerful forces like AI, systems thinking and shifting college admissions landscapes. Through meaningful conversations with leaders making a difference, the season offers fresh insight into how educators, students, and institutions can adapt and thrive in a rapidly changing environment.

Continuing to discover AI's potential in education, the first episode launched with experts Amanda Bickerstaff, CEO of AI for Education, and Christian Talbot, President of the Middle States Association (an organization that has been at the forefront of school accreditation and innovation) sharing their perspective on AI's advancements, drawn from extensive experience.

When discussing the Middle States Association's AI endorsement (which Dwight School is proud to have earned this past February), Mr. Taubman explained how the school's participation deepened students, teachers, and administrators' understanding of AI in education. Since AI tools are still in the "dial-up phase," as Ms. Bickerstaff said, and evolving quickly, it is important to keep an open mind and learn about what is possible for the future.

On another episode, Katie Korhonen, Director of Global Admissions, Evaluation, and Strategy at NYU, and Shellee Hendricks, Dwight's Global Director of College Counselling, gave valuable information regarding college admissions: test-optional policies, access to international opportunities, ethical concerns, and the impact of AI on admissions.

The episode also highlighted the need to maintain human interaction despite the technological advancements currently developing. *"We really need to help students … to put the counselling in college counselling. We need to help students understand themselves … [and] manage their emotions when things get tough,"* said Ms. Hendricks.

In the most recent episode, Ms. Drew and various guests talk about student-athletes, and the challenges they face, including maintaining high academic standards while committing to rigorous athletic schedules.

In discussion with John Pelin, Head of Athletics at Dwight School New York, and Dwight School New York student Kathryn McMahan '26, who impressively competes on three varsity teams — soccer, swimming, and softball — the podcast examines time management, motivation, dealing with pressure, and the impact sports can have on leadership and mental health.

Kathryn spoke about her own personal journey, heavily involved in Dwight Athletics, saying, *"I love the person that I am because of sports… the community, the people that I meet, the relationships that I make, it literally changed me. And so just showing up every day and just being with your friends … being with the community that it gives you, that's what makes it worth it. And that's what drives me to go every day."*

Sparking Genius continues to produce new and exciting content, aiming to illuminate the path forward by amplifying the expert voices that contribute to education — and ultimately shape its future. Whether you're a parent, educator, industry leader, or student, the podcast provides a powerful platform for new ideas, relevant conversation, and an unwavering commitment to igniting the spark in every learner all over the world.

Listeners can play episodes of *Sparking Genius* directly on the Dwight Global Network website or subscribe on their favourite platform.

For more information about Dwight School, see page 221

Bilingualism: a foundation for success in Early Years and Primary

ICS Côte d'Azur, France, explores the benefits of bilingualism in education and personal development.

At ICS Côte d'Azur, we believe that bilingualism is more than just the ability to speak two languages — it's a key to unlocking cognitive, academic, and social potential. We offer a bilingual education in both French and English, grounded in the principles of the International Baccalaureate (IB) Primary Years Programme (PYP). This innovative approach ensures that students not only develop language proficiency in both languages, but also acquire a deep understanding of the world through inquiry-based learning.

Our Early Years and Primary students are immersed in a dynamic bilingual environment where they thrive academically, socially, and emotionally. The IB PYP framework, which emphasises student agency, critical thinking, and international-mindedness, ensures that our learners are well prepared for the challenges and opportunities of the future.

Teaching methods that foster bilingualism

At ICS Côte d'Azur, we use a variety of innovative and engaging methods to support bilingualism. One of the most effective approaches in our Early Years and Primary classrooms is Total Physical Response (TPR), a method where students learn language through physical movement, responding to verbal instructions with actions.

This is especially effective for young learners, as it helps them associate words with actions, reinforcing their understanding of the language in a kinaesthetic way. TPR not only accelerates language acquisition but also makes learning fun and interactive, keeping students engaged while helping them develop both linguistic and motor skills.

Another key element of our bilingual approach is the use of bridging time to support vocabulary development. Bridging refers to planned moments within PYP units when students from the same year group — drawn from both the French and English classes — come together to connect their learning. During these sessions key vocabulary is shared and reinforced in both languages, enabling students to express ideas across French and English.

Rather than teaching the same content twice, we focus on building understanding once and then supporting it with vocabulary in both languages. This makes learning more meaningful and efficient.

For example, in the PYP unit Sharing the Planet, Year 2 students explored beehives in English and the lifecycle of a ladybird in French. While each class focused on different

ICS Côte d'Azur

content, related vocabulary was shared across both languages, enabling students to make connections and communicate their understanding more confidently.

Cognitive flexibility through mathematics in two languages

At ICS Côte d'Azur, we take the best elements from both the English and French national curricula, along with approaches such as White Rose Maths and Singapore Maths, to provide a balanced and flexible mathematics programme.

For instance, the French curriculum includes a strong focus on geometry, so students study this in French, while the English curriculum covers fractions at a more advanced level, so that topic is taught in English.

This dual approach helps students develop cognitive flexibility as they learn to solve problems using a variety of strategies. It also ensures they are well prepared for a smooth transition to secondary school — whether in France, the UK, or international institutions — where they can confidently engage with different educational systems.

A focus on daily reading and literacy development

At our school, daily reading in both French and English is a cornerstone of our literacy programme. This practice helps students build strong language skills, supporting their academic growth across all subjects.

Our classrooms are filled with a wide variety of bilingual books, giving students the chance to explore stories in both languages — broadening vocabulary, improving comprehension, and nurturing a love of literature.

Library activities are an integral part of our bilingual approach. We organise interactive storytelling sessions, book-related games, and group discussions in both languages, encouraging students to engage creatively with texts. These activities deepen their understanding while building connections between the two languages.

ICS Côte d'Azur also celebrates Book Week and hosts bilingual book fairs, further enriching our bilingual culture. Students take part in author visits, reading challenges, and creative projects — promoting exploration of new books and reinforcing the importance of bilingualism in both academic and personal development.

Our personalised language programmes

For students who join us at age 7 and beyond, ICS Côte d'Azur offers dedicated FLE (Français Langue Étrangère) and EAL (English as an Additional Language) programmes to help them thrive in a bilingual environment.

These programmes support language development through small-group pull-out sessions with a specialist teacher, offering personalised instruction tailored to each student's needs. In addition, students benefit from in-class support from the same specialist, helping them integrate smoothly into lessons.

This dual approach ensures that students not only build fluency in both languages but also gain the confidence to fully participate in the academic and social aspects of school life.

Preparing students for success in secondary school and beyond

By the time our students graduate from the Primary programme, they are not only academically prepared to enter secondary school, but also possess the social skills and confidence to succeed in a wide range of educational environments. Whether they continue their education in international schools, French schools, or boarding schools, our students are equipped with the language proficiency and cognitive skills to excel.

The bilingual education they receive at ICS Côte d'Azur provides them with a unique advantage — enabling them to adapt to diverse educational settings and thrive in multilingual environments.

Bilingualism at ICS Côte d'Azur is a cornerstone of our educational philosophy. Through a combination of innovative teaching methods, a strong focus on literacy, and a comprehensive curriculum that develops both languages in tandem, our students are prepared to take on the challenges of secondary school and beyond.

We believe that bilingualism isn't just an academic advantage — it's a gateway to a world of opportunities. At ICS Côte d'Azur, we are committed to helping our students develop the language skills, cognitive flexibility, and social confidence they need to thrive in an interconnected, multilingual world.

For more information about ICS Côte d'Azur, see page 121

Beyond the classroom: cultivating well-being

Institut International Saint-Dominique, Italy, focuses on the role of schools beyond academic achievement and how student well-being is nurtured.

In a world that often feels more complex and demanding than ever before, schools have a vital role to play in nurturing more than just academic excellence. At **Institut International Saint Dominique (ISD)**, this academic year has marked a significant turning point in our educational philosophy. We have placed a renewed and essential focus on **student well-being**, addressing growing concerns around anxiety, stress, and emotional health.

A response to modern-day challenges
The decision to prioritize well-being did not happen in isolation. Like many international schools, ISD is home to a wonderfully diverse student body navigating not only academic pressures but also global uncertainties, cultural transitions, and personal development in a fast-paced digital age. This year, our educators and administrators took a clear and meaningful step forward: to actively support students in managing their emotional and psychological challenges.

Our first initiative began with a **three-hour workshop led by a professional psychologist**, centered on managing exam-related stress and anxiety. Students learned to identify their emotional triggers, recognise signs of burnout, and most importantly, apply practical tools and techniques for self-regulation during exams. Breathing techniques, cognitive strategies, and small group reflections allowed students to understand that they are not alone in their experiences, and that stress is something that can be managed with the right support.

"I never thought I could control my anxiety during tests," said one student. *"But now I feel empowered instead of helpless."*

Connecting across cultures

One of the most impactful events this year was our **Cross-Cultural Well-being Workshop**, a special gathering that brought ISD students together with peers from another international school. The day was designed not just for learning, but for meaningful connection.

It began with a **professional yoga session**, where students explored mindfulness through movement and breath. The calm and focus created by the session set the tone for the rest of the day, which included small group activities and guided discussions on mental and emotional health. Students shared stories from their own educational journeys and reflected on the challenges they face both personally and academically.

What made this workshop truly special was the exchange of diverse perspectives. Coming from different cultural and educational backgrounds, students discovered shared emotions, common concerns, and new ways of looking at well-being. Together, they built friendships that crossed traditional boundaries and reminded us all that connection is one of the most powerful tools for emotional support.

"It felt amazing to realize that someone from another country feels the same things I do," one participant shared. *"We all understood each other, even though we had just met."*

Ongoing mindfulness and stress relief

Well-being is not something that can be achieved in a single day. It requires consistent attention and care. With that in mind, ISD introduced **monthly mindfulness and sound bath sessions** as a way for students to regularly pause, reflect, and recharge.

Led by trained professionals, these sessions are a moment of calm in the busy school schedule. Mindfulness practices help students bring awareness to the present moment, while sound baths use gentle vibrations and tones to ease tension and encourage relaxation. Many students have embraced these sessions as part of their monthly routine, describing them as a reset button that helps them feel more focused, calm, and clear-headed.

"It's like we press reset on our minds," said a student. *"I come out of the session feeling peaceful and focused."*

Educating the whole student

At ISD, we believe that true education means more than academic success. It means preparing young people to navigate life with confidence, compassion, and resilience. Our well-being initiatives reflect this belief by offering students not only the tools to succeed in school but also the mindset to thrive in all areas of life.

We are proud of the positive feedback from our students and excited about the direction this journey is taking us. Looking ahead, we plan to deepen this work with more collaborative workshops, nature-based retreats, and student-led wellness projects that reinforce our commitment to mental health and emotional balance.

At ISD, well-being is not an extra subject or an occasional event. It is part of who we are. We are committed to growing smarter, stronger, and more connected every day.

For more information about Institut International Saint-Dominique, see page 126

Exploring the French Riviera: a learning journey

The International School of Nice, France, considers how a learner's environment can contribute to a wider understanding and appreciation of community and culture.

Situated between the sea and the mountains, the International School of Nice (ISN) is uniquely placed to harness its local environment as an extension of the classroom. Here, learning is not confined to textbooks or whiteboards—it is lived, felt, and explored through the sights, sounds, and culture of the area. Whether students are building AI-powered smart gardens, designing wearable art from recycled materials, or mapping marine biodiversity along the coast, their education is infused with purpose and place.

Learning in context
At ISN, the French Riviera isn't just a beautiful location — it inspires curiosity, discovery, and learning. Our teachers use the environment to bring ideas to life. In Geography, and Environmental Sciences, students explore local habitats through fieldwork, including coastal walks and marine data collection. In Business and Model United Nations, students engage with the region's international conferences and pressing environmental issues. In the Creative Arts, they draw inspiration from Mediterranean culture and surroundings, while in Junk Kouture—a global competition that challenges students to design high-fashion garments entirely from recycled materials, the coastline and ocean conservation efforts become powerful sources of creative influence.

It nurtures a strong sense of belonging and personal responsibility to the local and global environment. And most importantly, it helps students make meaningful connections between their studies and the world they live in.

Whole school engagement through immersive learning
At ISN, immersive, hands-on learning is woven into the fabric of our educational approach. Across all age groups, students engage in projects that integrate sustainability, technology, and real-world relevance—ensuring consistent, meaningful learning experiences that go beyond the classroom.

One example is the **HiAi Sustainable Cities** project, part of the Globeducate initiative to explore how AI can support greener futures. Each year group engages in a series of progressive missions that build skills in data literacy, systems thinking, and environmental science.

In **Primary**, students create *Smart Terrariums*, build *AI-powered gardens*, and analyse environmental data through *Smart Microscopes*. They begin to see how natural ecosystems work—and how technology can support their health.

By **Secondary**, the focus shifts to urban sustainability. Students simulate city design through *3D-printing*, install *environmental sensors*, and use *AI vision systems* to analyse traffic and pollution patterns. The culmination of these efforts is a live *Ground Station Control Centre* where students manage real-time environmental data.

Through this experience, students not only learn STEAM and design skills—they explore what it means to be stewards of both nature and technology in the modern world.

Sustainability meets creativity: Junk Kouture
Another standout example of learning that draws from the local and global is ISN's participation in *Junk Kouture*.

ISN students transform discarded plastics from local beaches, used textiles, and old magazines into striking couture creations that make powerful artistic and ecological statements. The design process brings together science, fashion, environmental ethics, and performance, challenging students to think creatively and sustainably. Each year, the most outstanding designs are submitted to the Junk Kouture World Finals — and we're proud that for the past two years, an ISN design has earned a place on the global stage.

One team's dress, showcased at the **Nice Climate Summit**, turned heads not only for its aesthetic impact but for the student-led storytelling behind it. That same summit also saw students demo their **climate chatbot**, designed to answer common questions about environmental change, showcasing the fusion of tech, activism, and regional engagement.

Reflecting on the summit, Director of ISN Mel Curtis noted, *"Our students' involvement in the Nice Climate Summit reflects our deep commitment to sustainability and global citizenship. It was an invaluable experience for them to engage with international leaders and present their own projects. Receiving the Engaged for Ocean Label is a recognition of the hard work our students and staff have put into ocean conservation efforts."*

Local spaces, global ideas
ISN's facilities support this model of learning grounded in place. The **Marine Learning Hub, Teaching Kitchen**, and **Space Centre** each connect global competencies to local contexts.

In the Marine Hub, students might monitor local sea temperatures or assess biodiversity along the rocky coast. In the Teaching Kitchen, lessons explore nutrition through regional cuisine, such as the chemistry of making olive tapenade or the carbon footprint of imported produce. **In the Space Centre, students explore a wide range of STEAM and AI projects—tackling real-world challenges**

such as water purification, climate monitoring, and ethical technology use. The environment encourages innovation, collaboration, and critical thinking, empowering students to apply emerging technologies to issues that matter both locally and globally.

Beyond the classroom, into the community
Experiential learning at ISN goes beyond the classroom and into the community. Students take part in beach clean-ups, collaborate with the municipal government on local events, and lead initiatives through CAS (Creativity, Activity, Service) and MYP Service as Action. These projects often involve partnerships with local charities, environmental organisations, and civic leaders—fostering a strong sense of social responsibility and active citizenship.

These opportunities help students develop not only academic and technical skills but also empathy, cultural understanding, and ethical leadership. In every year group, students are supported to ask: *How can I use what I'm learning to help the people and places around me thrive?*

Place as a pathway to purpose
Ultimately, what sets ISN apart is not just that students learn about the world—but that they learn through it. The French Riviera becomes a co-teacher, offering lessons in creativity, ecological responsibility, global citizenship, as well as innovation.

At ISN, a strong emphasis on environmental and cultural context connects students to the world around them, providing a solid foundation as they prepare for futures that may lead them far from home. Whether designing smart cities, coding environmental bots, or sewing stories into recycled fabric, students are challenged to connect their knowledge with real-world impact.

This is what it means to learn on the Riviera—not just living nearby, but building a deep connection with the land, culture, and community that define the region.

For more information about International School of Nice, see page 145

Where Boarding Meets Global Citizenship

Jerudong International School, Brunei Darussalam, on how boarding can promote global citizenship, while striving for sustainable development

In today's ever-changing world, education extends far beyond exam results and university placements. Families increasingly seek environments where their children can grow into well-rounded individuals, resilient and confident to navigate the complexities of modern-day life. For many, international boarding schools provide exactly that.

Boarding can play a unique and powerful role in shaping this development. With a strong pastoral framework and a culture rooted in student wellbeing and inclusion, boarding provides the ideal environment for students to practise and live the school values every day.

At Jerudong International School (JIS), we believe in promoting holistic excellence that encompasses academic achievement, personal growth, empathy and leadership, leading to a transformational education for all.

Our Polio Points reward system, which is aligned with the UN's Sustainable Development Goals, encourages students to embody the school's core values of Challenge, Respect and Inspire. Whether through leadership, kindness or collaboration, students earn a Polio Point for behaviours that reflect the best of what JIS stands for. Polio Points are converted into a small donation towards the global effort to eradicate polio, with the support of local company Serikandi. For every six points collected, one for each of our school aims, $1 is put towards funding for polio vaccinations, creating a direct connection between students' actions and real-world impact.

In addition, our students are encouraged to take small yet significant actions known as 'Teaspoons of Change' that impact both local and global communities. Each year our students aim to earn over 10,000 Polio Points and often surpass it, showcasing that even the smallest steps can make a big difference.

So how exactly does boarding support this kind of development?

An integrated community
Boarding schools have evolved significantly from their traditional reputations. Instead of rigid discipline and isolation, most modern boarding environments prioritise student wellbeing, inclusion and a strong sense of community. Attention is paid to emotional health and

helping each individual find their place within the school.

One of the most important features of good boarding practice is the integration between boarding and day students. Encouraging these groups to mix naturally helps boarding students feel more included, while also promoting school-wide unity.

At Jerudong International School (JIS), for instance, this approach is a core part of the school's boarding ethos. Each boarding house is paired with a brother or sister day house, fostering regular interaction through shared events and collaboration. These partnerships help students feel connected to the wider school community, promoting a sense of continuity, camaraderie and mutual respect across the student body.

Building independence and responsibility
A significant advantage of the boarding experience is the opportunity to develop independence in a structured and supportive setting. With adult supervision on hand and a network of peers around them, students are gradually encouraged to take ownership of their routines, responsibilities and decisions.

Some schools go further by creating programmes specifically designed to prepare students for life after school. JIS, for example, launched an 'Independent Living' programme, where for over a two-week period, Year 13 boarders take full responsibility of running their own boarding house; budgeting, planning meals, cooking, cleaning and managing their daily routines. Led by Head of Boarding Mrs. Beenal Roberts, the initiative aimed to build essential life skills such as financial planning, time management and self-reliance.

Student reactions ranged from excitement to uncertainty, but the experience quickly fostered teamwork, resilience and mutual respect. *"Unique, intimidating yet exciting,"* is how Phoebe from Kingfisher House described the experience. *"I had a wonderful time getting to know other housemates who I may not have spoken with otherwise."* Nicholas from Ibis House agreed: *"The project has taught me valuable skills such as time management and budgeting and has helped me feel more prepared for what's to come after Sixth Form."*

Following the success of the pilot, JIS plans to expand the programme, reinforcing its commitment to nurturing well-rounded, confident individuals ready to thrive beyond the classroom and beyond school.

The role of pastoral care
Strong academic programmes are only one part of a successful school. Good boarding schools understand the importance of pastoral care; to focus on looking after each child's emotional and social wellbeing.

In a boarding environment, pastoral care goes far beyond occasional check-ins. Boarding staff often play a daily role in a student's life, providing consistency,

encouragement and a listening ear. In many cases, these staff members become trusted figures, guiding students through both academic pressures and personal growth. Providing the home environment, while away from home.

This close-knit care model ensures that no student is overlooked. Whether someone is thriving or facing challenges, they are known, understood and supported. It also provides a safety net for students as they develop independence, encouraging them to take risks and grow, knowing that help is never far away.

Looking to the future
At JIS, we believe that education is not just about preparing students for exams, but about future-proofing them for the world beyond school. In a rapidly evolving global landscape, students must develop more than academic knowledge. They need empathy, resilience and a deep understanding of their role in shaping a better future. Boarding, when done well, delivers exactly that.

This is why leadership and global citizenship are embedded into the culture of boarding life. Whether through service projects, leadership opportunities or the everyday interactions within a diverse, inclusive community, JIS boarders learn what it means to be thoughtful, compassionate changemakers. They are encouraged to see their actions, no matter how small, as part of a larger commitment to the world.

At Jerudong International School (JIS), boarding is more than a place to stay. It is where students grow and have a safe environment to embrace opportunities, take on new responsibilities, build friendships and find their voice. In every House, every student is valued and every achievement is celebrated. Whether it's succeeding in their classes, taking on leadership roles or volunteering for a meaningful cause, students should leave ready not just for university, but ready to contribute meaningfully to the world.

For more information about Jerudong International School, see page 58

Grow, thrive, sustain: an outdoor learning ethos

Mougins British International School, France, looks at how incorporating nature and the outdoors into a learner's education can benefit personal development.

At Mougins British International School, we believe that education extends beyond the confines of the classroom. Nestled in the heart of the French Riviera, our school takes full advantage of its natural surroundings to offer a learning experience that is as enriching as it is unique. By integrating outdoor learning and sustainability into the heart of our approach, we prepare students not just for exams, but for life.

Outdoor learning: a dynamic approach to education

Our approach to education in the Early Years and Primary stages places a strong emphasis on **outdoor learning**, providing children with dynamic, real-world opportunities to explore, discover, and apply what they've learned in the classroom.

Our **purpose-built outdoor classroom** serves as a natural extension of indoor learning spaces, enabling pupils to engage in interactive, hands-on experiences. Whether it's a maths lesson brought to life with chalk-drawn equations on the playground or a science class involving the search for minibeasts in the undergrowth, outdoor education helps students embed knowledge through context and experience.

Importantly, every outdoor lesson is **carefully designed to align with the British curriculum**, ensuring that time spent outside is not only enriching but academically rigorous. Teachers use the school's natural surroundings to deliver core subjects in innovative ways, such as setting up measuring stations in the school grounds.

One of our most exciting initiatives is the **'School in the Woods'** programme, introduced for Early Years and Key Stage 1 students. Each week, classes spend time in the beautiful woodland surrounding our campus, where they continue their learning through curriculum-based activities designed to engage their curiosity and develop critical thinking skills in a natural setting.

Nelly, a Year 6 student, shares: *"We do a lot of outdoor learning, where we bring our lessons from the classroom to outside. For example, we do painting, experiments, and activities with water. We have so much open space, you feel very, very free."*

Nelly's reflection perfectly captures the spirit of outdoor learning at Mougins: it's about freedom to explore, room to think creatively, and the joy of discovering that education can happen anywhere. By blending academic goals with experiential opportunities, we help students build confidence, independence, and a lifelong appreciation for the world around them.

Eco-School certification: a commitment to sustainability

Our outdoor philosophy goes hand in hand with our commitment to sustainability. For the past three years, Mougins British International School has proudly held Eco-School certification, an international recognition of our efforts to educate for a greener future.

Spearheaded by Carmen Burgues, our Eco Coordinator, and a dedicated team of Eco-Delegates, our programme empowers students to take real action for the environment. These delegates work collaboratively — and voluntarily — alongside their academic studies, leading initiatives that reduce waste, promote biodiversity, and raise awareness of global sustainability challenges.

This year, our focus has been on food sustainability, with a strong push to reduce food waste in the school canteen. Students conducted surveys, analysed waste patterns, and helped implement strategies to limit excess. Their findings contributed to a broader campaign that has meaningfully reduced waste and engaged the entire school community in change.

Growing knowledge from the ground up

At the heart of our sustainability programme is the school's organic vegetable garden — a vibrant, hands-on space where learning becomes life. Every class participates in planting, maintaining, and harvesting seasonal crops. Children learn not just about soil, seeds, and sun, but about the rhythms of nature, seasonal eating, and mindful consumption.

The harvest has a real impact too. Unsold produce is passed to our school's kitchen, where the chef incorporates it into student meals, ensuring that nothing goes to waste. In the process, children witness the full cycle of food — from earth to plate — and begin to understand sustainability not as an abstract idea, but as a tangible, everyday responsibility.

Eco leaders beyond the campus

Mougins students don't just think locally — they act globally. This year, our Eco-Delegates were invited to participate

in the 10th International Education and Sustainability Leadership Summit in Monaco, where they joined students from around the world to share ideas, challenges, and solutions for a sustainable future.

They also travelled to Rome, where they met peers at our Globeducate sister school, RIS Rome, to exchange best practices on making schools more environmentally friendly. These experiences build global citizenship, showing students that their voices matter — and that sustainability is a shared mission across borders and cultures.

At Mougins British International School, outdoor learning and sustainability are not just supplementary aspects of our curriculum; they are integral to our educational philosophy. By providing students with opportunities to learn in natural settings and engage in sustainability initiatives, we prepare them to be responsible global citizens who understand the importance of environmental stewardship.

Through our 'School in the Woods' programme, Eco-School certification, and various sustainability projects, we continue to foster an educational environment that values the interconnectedness of learning, nature, and sustainability. Our commitment to these principles ensures that our students are not only academically proficient but also environmentally conscious and prepared to contribute positively to the world around them.

For more information or to book a personalised tour, visit www.mougins-school.com

For more information about Mougins British International School, see page 170

United for the future: educating children for tomorrow's world

United Lisbon International School, Portugal, explores the importance of a multi-faceted education in shaping the learners of the future.

In a world increasingly defined by artificial intelligence, global disruption, and accelerating change, the future will not belong solely to those who can code, analyse data, or build machines. It will belong to those who understand people who can listen, question, empathise, and lead with emotional intelligence. At **United Lisbon International School** (ULIS), this human-centred vision of education is not just aspirational; it is foundational.

As a member of the Dukes Education family of schools, ULIS serves students aged 3 to 18 with a progressive international curriculum culminating in the International Baccalaureate Diploma Programme. Since its founding in 2020, the school has grown rapidly, attracting families from over 50 nationalities and building a reputation as one of Europe's most future-focused learning environments. But what truly defines ULIS is not only its academic ambition, it's the way it unites purpose, belonging, and innovation in every aspect of school life.

United by purpose: the ULIS pillars

From the outset, ULIS was founded on five core pillars: Technology, Global Citizenship, Entrepreneurism, Sports, and the Arts. These aren't extracurricular add-ons; they shape how learning unfolds across every age group, from Early Childhood to the senior years of high school.

Technology is embedded seamlessly throughout the school. As a Microsoft Showcase School, ULIS is committed to digital fluency but also to digital ethics and responsibility. Students explore everything from robotics to 3D printing in the school's Maker Space, not in isolation but as tools for creative problem-solving and collaborative thinking.

Meanwhile, the school's vibrant arts programme, expansive sports curriculum, and entrepreneurial initiatives provide platforms for expression, wellbeing, and real-world engagement. The result is an educational experience that equips students with a rich blend of competencies; intellectual, social, and emotional, that prepare them not only to perform, but to contribute meaningfully to life beyond school.

A school that understands belonging

One of the most powerful reflections on the future of education at ULIS hasn't come from a global expert or keynote speaker—but from one of its own Year 10 students. Writing about the human need to belong, the student argued that identity and group affiliation remain some of the strongest drivers of behaviour today. *"If we understood our need for belonging the way we understand economic systems or market patterns, we would see the mechanics behind so much of human behaviour."*

For the school's Executive Director, Martin Harris, this kind of reflection is exactly what schools should nurture. He says *"We talk a lot about preparing students for the future, but the future starts inside us. Yes, our young people need digital literacy, but they also need to know themselves. They need to understand why they think the way they do, and how to interact with others whose perspectives may be different."*

Empathy, intellectual humility, and critical thinking are central to this vision, alongside the school's fundamental values of Responsibility, Integrity, Curiosity, and Resilience. These are not soft skills; they are essential capabilities for leadership, adaptability, and social cohesion in a divided world. As the student so insightfully concluded, the goal is not to reject our need to belong, but to *"convert it into a force of unity."*

A connected learning environment

This commitment to connection is reflected not only in the ethos of the school, but in its everyday environment. The community at ULIS is truly international, with more than 600 students from around the world and a faculty with deep experience in global education.

The school's 6,500 sqm of outdoor space supports an extensive sports programme, while modern science labs and creative studios are equipped with cutting-edge tools that enable students to explore and experiment. Partnerships with leading extracurricular providers including the Lisbon Racket Centre and Sporting CP enrich the learning experience and build links between classroom learning and real-world pursuits.

Since 2024, United Lisbon International School has seen two cohorts of students graduate with excellent IB Diploma results, earning places at leading universities in the UK, US, Portugal, and across Europe; a testament to the school's academic strength and international outlook.

ULIS's collaboration with the United Lisbon Edu Hub also plays a key role in extending opportunity. Located in the heart of Lisbon's fast-growing Oriente innovation district, students benefit from accessibility to entrepreneurship

programmes, internships, and access to industries shaping tomorrow's economy from space tech to sustainable design.

More than an international school

While its facilities and curriculum are world-class, what distinguishes ULIS most is its guiding philosophy. This is a school that understands the future cannot be engineered purely through grades and qualifications. It must be cultivated through awareness, adaptability, and a sense of shared responsibility.

As Harris puts it: *"In the end, we're not just helping students prepare for university or the workforce. We're helping them prepare for life in all its complexity. That means learning to think for yourself but also learning to live well with others."*

In a world of shifting identities, polarisation, and rapid transformation, schools like ULIS are answering a critical call: to help young people build not only capability, but character; not only skills, but perspective.

A school united for what comes next

At United Lisbon International School, education is not seen as a linear journey from knowledge to outcome. It is a dynamic process of becoming: of learning to ask better questions, embracing complexity, and leading with empathy. In cultivating both confidence and connection, ULIS stands as more than just a school. It is a community united by values, vision, and the belief that the future belongs to those who understand what it means to belong.

For more information about United Lisbon International School, see page 214

Citizens of the world: understanding Third Culture Kids

The American Overseas School of Rome, Italy, considers how the unique perspectives of Third Culture Kids can benefit their learning and development

If you've witnessed a Third Culture Kid (TCK) hesitate to figure out how to answer the question, "Where are you from?" you know that it's not as easy as it sounds. TCKs are kids who have spent a significant part of their growing years outside of their parents' home country, fusing pieces from everywhere into this one hybrid identity.

It's a beautiful, sometimes strange dance of cultures, and for the students at the American Overseas School of Rome (AOSR), it's everyday life. AOSR was lucky enough to have Chris O'Shaughnessy visit the school campus. Chris is an author, speaker, and TCK himself with an incredible knack for taking the ups and downs of this unusual upbringing and putting them into perspective. His presentation resonated with our multicultural community, where nearly 40% of our students belong to families that reflect more than 55 nationalities.

Chris expressed that, *"Third Culture Kids and adults are the ones who know what it's like to be home everywhere and nowhere at the same time."*

TCKs are a fascinating bunch. They're the kids who've said as many goodbyes as hellos, who can order breakfast in three languages, and who've developed a deep appreciation for the peculiarity — as well as the universality — of human existence. They understand that home is not a location, but a collection of people, memories, and moments that don't always fit on a map.

During his visit to AOSR, Chris told a story that struck a chord in our community. He remembered going to a friend's wedding in Germany, glancing around the room and noticing that the guests represented over a dozen nations. He knew that each face was a melting pot of influences, each individual a mix of cultures.

"That's the TCK experience," he said. *"Where your friends are dispersed across time zones and friendships are formed on common experience instead of common geography."*

This isn't merely a poetic ideal. It's everyday life at AOSR, where our students are continually moving between cultures, switching from Italian to English (and often a third language) without skipping a beat. They're skilled at reading a room across cultures, seeking bridges where others would encounter walls. They're instinctive diplomats,

The American Overseas School of Rome

lunchroom conflict mediators, and expert adapters who can relate to just about anybody.

The challenges of belonging

Naturally, this existence of perpetual adjustment isn't all kittens and rainbows. Chris was quick to note that a lot of TCKs are chameleons, always changing to blend into their environment but occasionally having trouble truly knowing where they belong. It's a familiar theme in the TCK life — this feeling of being "at home" everywhere and nowhere simultaneously.

The inquiry, *"Where are you from?"* can be like a test with no correct answer.

At AOSR, we get this challenge. That's why we're dedicated to building a community in which TCKs can flourish. We provide professional pastoral care, support, and mentorship to help our students claim their multiple stories and learn to view the world through a multitude of different eyes. We know that although this identity can be difficult, it's also a tremendous strength.

Finding power in the in-between

Chris's message while visiting was straightforward: TCKs need to embrace this fluidity, not as a point of confusion, but as a source of strength.

"You are able to be the bridge in a world otherwise feeling very divided," he said to our students. *"You are able to bring together people who come from very different backgrounds. That's a superpower."*

As our students prepare to graduate and step into an interconnected world, Chris's words resonate deeply. It's a reminder that while TCKs might not always have a simple answer to the question of origin, they can confidently say, "I belong wherever I am."

Chris expressed this beautifully: *"Our gift to the world around us is hope — the kind that comes from staring pain and uncertainty in the face and refusing to believe that's all there is."*

It's a strong reminder not only for TCKs, but for anyone struggling to make sense of the world today. At AOSR, we're honoured to stand alongside these young world citizens as they author their own narratives, create their own paths, and define what belonging means to them. They're our diplomats, bridge-builders, and storytellers. They're the ones who will craft a more interdependent, compassionate world.

As the world shrinks and borders grow more porous, we are steadfast in our commitment to preparing our students not only for academic achievement, but for lives of purpose, connection, and global awareness. This is our pledge to them, and our gift to the world they will one day inherit.

For more information about The American Overseas School of Rome School, see page 101

Shaping tomorrow's innovators

ICS Paris, France, share how they are redefining 21st-century learning by looking beyond the classroom.

In an age where technology evolves rapidly and global challenges grow increasingly complex, education must go beyond traditional classroom methods. At ICS Paris, innovation, creativity, and academic excellence are woven into the very fabric of our learning philosophy. More than just preparing students for exams, we're preparing them to navigate, lead, and shape the world of tomorrow.

Located in central Paris, ICS Paris offers a transformative education experience designed for internationally minded families seeking more than conventional schooling. Through our robust STEAM (Science, Technology, Engineering, Arts, and Mathematics) curriculum, AI and robotics programmes, and our new state-of-the-art Innovation Centre, students are empowered to become adaptable, forward-thinking leaders of the future.

The Innovation Centre: a hub for hands-on discovery

A cornerstone of our progressive approach is the ICS Paris Innovation Centre, a newly inaugurated facility dedicated to experiential, hands-on learning. More than a physical space, the Innovation Centre serves as a launchpad for creativity, collaboration, and invention.

Within its walls, students find a fully equipped FabLab complete with 3D printers, laser cutters, robotics kits, coding workstations, and virtual reality technology. This environment inspires students to become makers and thinkers—developing prototypes, designing sustainable solutions, and experimenting with the same tools used by professionals in engineering and design.

"Our Innovation Centre is more than just a classroom—it's a launchpad for creativity, critical thinking, and global impact," says Angela Hollington, Head of School.

Whether building AI-powered robots that can detect obstacles or designing smart city models, students are not just learning theory—they're applying knowledge to real-world problems. This hands-on engagement cultivates a mindset of curiosity, resilience, and purpose.

STEAM: a foundation for future thinking

At ICS Paris, STEAM education is embedded across all year levels—from the Early Years Programme through to Secondary School. But more than a collection of subjects, STEAM represents a way of thinking. It equips students to ask bold questions, challenge assumptions, and solve complex problems creatively.

Robotics and artificial intelligence form a vital part of this integrated curriculum. As a proud member of Globeducate, ICS Paris hosts the annual Globeducate Robotics Challenge—an exciting international competition that brings together student teams to design and programme autonomous robots addressing real-world issues.

ICS Paris

The 2025 edition, held in our Innovation Centre, welcomed teams from across France and Europe. Students tackled sustainability-focused tasks, combining engineering skills with AI programming to develop innovative solutions. The event highlighted not only technical abilities, but also essential soft skills such as collaboration, perseverance, and creative thinking.

"The Robotics Challenge isn't just a competition—it's a celebration of innovation and the power of young minds to shape the future," noted Andrew Rhodes, Technology Coach.

Using platforms like LEGO® Mindstorms, Arduino, and Python, students are immersed in real-world coding, machine learning, and engineering—skills that are in growing demand across every industry.

Academic excellence meets innovation

At ICS Paris, a commitment to innovation is matched by a dedication to academic rigour. As an IB World School offering the full continuum of International Baccalaureate programmes (PYP, MYP, and IBDP), we deliver a well-rounded and globally relevant education.

The IB framework encourages inquiry-based learning and critical thinking, while ensuring a strong academic foundation. Our students are regularly assessed through projects, research, presentations, and reflective activities that go beyond rote learning. This ensures they develop both subject mastery and lifelong learning skills.

Our libraries—dedicated spaces for Primary and Secondary students—further enrich this balanced educational journey, supporting independent reading, research, and quiet study.

The International Baccalaureate Diploma Programme (IBDP), offered at ICS Paris for over 20 years, is known for its academic depth and international recognition. Our students consistently exceed global IB averages, demonstrating the school's strong teaching standards and excellent pastoral care.

"In a world where we don't yet know what the jobs of tomorrow will be, we focus on helping students 'learn how to learn'. We cultivate their ability to adapt, question, reflect, and act—with purpose," says Mrs. Boursin, IBDP Coordinator.

This holistic approach ensures our learners are not just technologically literate but are also confident communicators, critical thinkers, and compassionate global citizens.

Why families choose ICS Paris

Choosing the right school is a pivotal decision for families, particularly those who are internationally mobile. ICS Paris offers a distinctive educational experience rooted in global awareness, academic excellence, and innovation.

Here's why parents choose us:

- A central Paris location with a welcoming, inclusive school community
- A STEAM-powered curriculum integrated across all age levels
- A cutting-edge Innovation Centre and FabLab for hands-on learning
- Globeducate partnerships offering global learning experiences and competitions
- AI and robotics embedded into the learning journey
- Consistently high IB results, exceeding global benchmarks
- A balance of academic rigour and creative exploration
- An English-medium curriculum enriched with French language instruction

More than just a school, our campus is a vibrant environment where students are inspired to grow, invent, and thrive. Every child at ICS Paris is encouraged to discover their passions, strengths, and purpose—preparing them not just for the future, but to shape it.

For families seeking an education that's both forward-thinking and grounded in excellence, ICS Paris offers a truly unique opportunity.

To learn more or schedule a visit, please go to www.icsparis.fr.

For more information about ICS Paris School, see page 124

The Impact Hub: a launchpad for tomorrow's innovators

International School of Lausanne, Switzerland, on enabling learners to communicate, collaborate innovate throughout their education.

In a world that is changing at unprecedented speed, the ability to adapt, innovate, and lead is more important than ever. At the International School of Lausanne (ISL), education is not just about academic excellence—it is about preparing students to become confident, responsible global citizens. A shining example of this forward-thinking philosophy is the Impact Hub: a dynamic new space dedicated to fostering innovation, creativity, and entrepreneurship.

Officially inaugurated in January 2025, the Impact Hub has rapidly become a cornerstone of ISL's holistic educational offering. It serves as a vibrant incubator for students to turn ideas into action, collaborate with peers and professionals, and develop the real-world skills needed to thrive in the 21st century.

A vision beyond the classroom
Located in the heart of the school's modern campus in Le Mont-sur-Lausanne, in Switzerland, the Impact Hub is more than just a physical space—it is a mindset. Conceived to complement ISL's well-established International Baccalaureate (IB) curriculum, the Hub bridges academic learning with hands-on experience. Students from across the school are invited to engage in multidisciplinary projects, build prototypes, analyse real-world problems, and work alongside experts from global organisations.

According to Dr Frazer Cairns, Director of ISL, "The Impact Hub reflects our belief that learning goes beyond the walls of a classroom; it is about creating real opportunities for our students to become agents of change."

Whether designing solutions for sustainability challenges or exploring the frontiers of artificial intelligence, students at ISL are encouraged to think critically and act with purpose.

Inspiring projects and global competitions
The Impact Hub has already hosted a wide range of inspiring initiatives. One standout example is ISL's participation in **The Earth Prize**, a prestigious global competition focused on sustainability. This project challenges students to research, design, and pitch innovative solutions to environmental issues—skills that are increasingly vital in a world facing climate change and ecological degradation.

In addition, ISL has partnered with leading institutions such as EPFL (École polytechnique fédérale de Lausanne) to support student-led robotics projects and collaborate on interdisciplinary research. These partnerships provide

International School of Lausanne

invaluable exposure to cutting-edge science and technology and reinforce the relevance of classroom learning in real-world contexts.

The school also takes part in **Mission Zero**, an educational initiative run by the European Space Agency, which empowers young people to write code that runs on the International Space Station. Programmes like this not only spark curiosity but also highlight the boundless opportunities awaiting students with the right mindset and mentorship.

Learning by doing: a new approach
At the heart of the Impact Hub is a commitment to experiential learning. The space is designed to be flexible and adaptive, equipped with maker tools, collaborative workstations, and digital technologies that invite experimentation and iterative thinking.

Students are guided through a rich programme that includes:

- **Practical Skills Workshops:** Covering areas such as design thinking, artificial intelligence, sustainable product design, and project management.
- **Expert Mentorship:** With support from professionals at world-renowned companies including Nestlé, Medtronic, and EPFL, students gain direct insight into how innovative thinking is applied in business, science, and technology.
- **Interdisciplinary Collaboration:** Bringing together students from different year groups and subject areas to tackle complex challenges from multiple angles.

These experiences build confidence, nurture curiosity, and instil a growth mindset—preparing students not just to succeed in exams, but to make meaningful contributions in their future studies, careers, and communities.

A celebration of learning and impact
The official inauguration of the Impact Hub on 30 January 2025 marked a proud milestone for the ISL community. The evening brought together students, parents, faculty, and distinguished guests for a celebration of innovation in education. Attendees were treated to interactive displays of student work, presentations on ongoing projects, and discussions on the future of learning.

The keynote address was delivered by **Professor David Bach**, President of the International Institute for Management Development (IMD), a global leader in business education based in Lausanne. A respected voice on strategic leadership and innovation, Professor Bach spoke about the importance of equipping the next generation with the tools and mindsets to drive positive change on a global scale.

His insights echoed ISL's core mission: to empower young people to become principled, informed, and courageous leaders in an interconnected world.

A school with a global outlook
Founded in 1962, the International School of Lausanne is the largest private school in the canton of Vaud and a respected leader in international education. With around 850 students representing over 60 nationalities, ISL offers a bilingual (French and English) learning environment and a full IB continuum—from the Primary Years Programme (PYP) to the Diploma Programme (DP).

The school's diverse community is one of its greatest strengths. Whether families are relocating to Switzerland for professional opportunities or seeking a globally oriented education for their children, ISL provides a welcoming and inclusive environment where students feel seen, heard, and valued.

ISL's commitment to excellence goes hand-in-hand with its dedication to innovation and social responsibility. The Impact Hub is a natural extension of this ethos—an open invitation for students to dream big, take initiative, and leave a positive mark on the world.

Why the Impact Hub matters
For prospective parents considering ISL for their child, the Impact Hub is a compelling demonstration of the school's ability to prepare students not just for university, but for life. It answers the question many families are asking today: how can schools equip children to navigate complexity, act with empathy, and drive solutions to real-world problems?

By integrating experiential learning, cross-disciplinary projects, and industry partnerships, the Impact Hub helps students see themselves not only as learners but as changemakers.

As education evolves, ISL continues to set the pace—combining academic rigour with creativity, global awareness with local engagement, and tradition with transformation.

For more information about International School of Lausanne School, see page 139

Education for greater good

Craig Davis, Head of School at Mulgrave School - The International School of Vancouver, on the purpose of education

As an educator, I've asked myself many times over the years, in different institutions, "What is our purpose?" For leading international schools like ours that constantly seek the 'edge of excellence', the question of our 'ultimate goal' is crucial. Both research and common sense reveal that authentic reflections on mission and purpose are essential if we seek to keep our schools nimble, relevant, and inspiring.

Mulgrave has the luxury of being a maturing school. With just over 30 years of history, we have moved through rapid growth and are now an established institution with great strengths built on outstanding facilities and robust, competitive applicant pools. At this stage, schools typically focus on complexity, nuance, refinement, and operationalising the mission and vision. So now is the right time to ask...how do we achieve 'excellence' through teaching and learning? Additionally, we should also think of purpose in the greater sense...so what is the impetus of education at its core?

We have the benefit of being confident in our identity and mandate, so we can focus on how we can create greater, far-reaching impact. This is why Mulgrave's new strategic direction work pays attention to **both** the 'mechanisms of excellence' (fundamental components of teaching, learning, coaching, and learning experiences that deliver our stated aims) **and** how these experiences build student character, values, and skills to maximise the positive and purposeful difference they can make in the world.

And so, when we think about our purpose, we must dig deep into our intention. We must have a nuanced understanding, comfort in complexity, and a commitment to connecting research and data with real, concrete outcomes linked to solving global problems. In essence, this 'doubles down' on the original mission of the International Baccalaureate Organization. It is not our place to just impart knowledge and develop skills; as Tim Dacey of MIT says, *"In this new landscape (an AI-dominated world), human value will increasingly lie in wisdom-oriented skills such as critical and systems thinking, creativity, communication, and the ability to navigate complex, multifaceted problems."*

The rapid development of AI in education can be a positive force in supporting this goal, as we can already see the shifting learning goalposts. As AI outperforms

Mulgrave School - The International School of Vancouver

our abilities to replicate the 'mechanics' of learning, the deeper critical and dispositional components of education become more essential. We must challenge students to move beyond their own attainment, toward a mindset where they see the good they can do for others and how to make the world a better place.

This is one of the driving forces behind the IBO's new course, *IB Systems Transformation: Leadership for just and sustainable futures*. Mulgrave has been chosen as one of four pilot schools globally for this innovative approach to teaching and learning, and our first cohort will embark on the curriculum in the fall of 2025. It focusses on both the mindset and the skills needed to confront the global issues of the future, from climate change to emerging technologies and social inequities. Rather than teaching content in isolation by subject matter, the course weaves together knowledge from multiple disciplines, including the humanities, arts, social and physical sciences, and mathematics.

Central to Systems Transformation is a robust curriculum that pushes students to explore ideas like complex adaptive systems, the construction and deconstruction of narratives, ethics and ontologies, and the dynamics of power. Students are also introduced to ecopreneurial design and trained in processing and analysing real-world data. This transdisciplinary model reflects the reality that today's challenges don't fit neatly into subject boxes - they are interconnected, dynamic, and evolving.

This course represents a bold reimagining of what education can and should be: a tool not just for personal success, but for global transformation. By empowering students to think critically, act ethically, and lead courageously, the Systems Transformation course offers hope that the next generation will not only understand the world they inherit, but be ready to transform it for the better.

We will only remedy the societal polycrisis and increasing individualism by educating for the greater good. Drawing on the wisdom of elders globally and the foresight of Indigenous peoples of these lands, we must think about how our actions today will ripple over generations to come. It's only with this broader view that we can truly examine the essence of purpose.

For more information about Mulgrave School - The International School of Vancouver, see page 227

Educating for purpose: the Round Square approach to enriched learning

The Hutchins School, Australia, on equipping students with real-world skills.

At The Hutchins School, education is about more than academic achievement. It's about nurturing individuals of character—young people who live with kindness, humility, courage and respect. As a proud member of the Round Square global network, Hutchins brings this vision to life by connecting students with a world of opportunity, challenge and service.

Guided by Christian values and a commitment to developing the whole student—intellectually, spiritually, emotionally and socially—Hutchins provides an education that prepares students not only for success but for significance. Round Square enhances this mission through meaningful, real-world experiences that align powerfully with the school's guiding statements and core values.

A global network, a shared purpose

Round Square is a worldwide association of over 230 schools across 50 countries, united by a commitment to six key IDEALS: Internationalism, Democracy, Environmentalism, Adventure, Leadership and Service. These values complement Hutchins' own purpose—to provide an outstanding education that inspires students to make a positive difference.

Through global exchanges, collaborative projects and student-led conferences, Hutchins' students are immersed in diverse perspectives, global issues and opportunities to take action, growing as thoughtful, informed and responsible global citizens.

"Our involvement in Round Square allows us to offer students experiences that truly prepare them for the future," says Miss Samantha Judd, Co-ordinator of Gifted and Talented at Hutchins. *"They don't just learn about the world—they become active contributors to it."*

Courage and challenge beyond the classroom

Adventure, a core Round Square ideal, resonates deeply with the Hutchins approach to learning. Students are encouraged to push beyond their comfort zones through outdoor education, service learning, leadership programs and exchanges—experiences that cultivate courage, resilience and adaptability. These opportunities align with the school's goal to engage students in lifelong learning.

Global Learning Co-ordinator, Mr Erik Marr explains, *"Round Square enables students to put these values into practice, demonstrating that courage might mean leading a team, solving a difficult problem, or stepping into an unfamiliar cultural experience with curiosity and confidence. This helps students realise their potential and become their best selves."*

The Hutchins School

Leading with integrity and humility
At Hutchins, every student is encouraged to explore their leadership potential. Round Square provides authentic leadership experiences—locally and globally—that promote collaboration, ethical decision-making and reflection. Whether participating in student forums, planning community projects or attending leadership conferences, students are empowered to lead with purpose.

This reflects Hutchins' guiding statement to foster leadership and service that is courageous and humble, helping students understand that true leadership is about service to others, accountability and using their influence to make a meaningful impact.

Service with purpose
Service is integral to both Hutchins' values and the Round Square framework. Students are encouraged to contribute actively to their communities, from local outreach programs to international service initiatives. These experiences foster empathy, awareness, and a strong sense of social responsibility.

"We want our students to understand that service is not just something they do—it's a part of who they are," says Principal, Dr Rob McEwan. *"It's a mindset of compassion and action that continues well beyond school."*

By integrating service learning across the curriculum, Hutchins supports the development of global citizens who are grounded in values and committed to shaping a better world.

Environmental stewardship and responsibility
Round Square's focus on environmentalism offers students opportunities to engage with one of the most urgent issues of our time. At Hutchins, this commitment is reflected in sustainability initiatives, eco-leadership programs and curriculum offerings that empower students to act responsibly and creatively in response to environmental challenges.

This supports the school's guiding statement to foster stewardship of the natural and built environment, encouraging students to be accountable and innovative as they explore ways to preserve and protect the planet.

Internationalism and global citizenship
As the world becomes increasingly interconnected, it's essential that young people develop intercultural understanding and respect. Round Square provides students with exposure to different cultures, perspectives and voices through international exchanges, digital collaborations and forums.

Recently a group of Hutchins Years 11 and 12 students travelled to Oxford, UK to participate in Round Square Inspiring Voices – The Big Baraza. The Round Square event was held at The Oxford Union and the Sheldonian Theatre

at Oxford University, with 400 students from 46 different schools from around the world taking part.

This engaging forum provided students with the opportunity to participate in baraza groups, participate in healthy debates and to discuss many global issues facing their generation, whilst honing their ability to both confidently and respectfully articulate their thoughts and contribute their opinions to the conversations.

These global experiences help students grow in empathy, appreciation for diversity, and confidence in navigating complexity—echoing Hutchins' commitment to embrace diversity and promote equity, inclusion and respect for all.

Year 11 student, Otto Ford, who participated in a recent virtual Round Square conference shared, *"It opened my eyes to how many people around the world are working towards the same values we talk about at school—respect, compassion, courage. It made me feel part of something much bigger."*

The lasting impact
The impact of Hutchins' membership in Round Square is felt long after the school years are over. The program equips students with real-world skills: critical thinking, teamwork, ethical leadership and a strong sense of purpose. These experiences help shape well-rounded individuals ready to contribute meaningfully to society.

Through Round Square, students gain far more than knowledge—they develop the character, resilience and global perspective to lead with compassion and integrity. As the school's values affirm, they are guided by humility to serve, courage to lead and integrity to act.

At Hutchins, education is not just preparation for life—it is life. And through the opportunities that Round Square provides, that life is rich in learning, challenge and purpose.

For more information about The Hutchins School School, see page 87

The Transformative Power of Boarding

Alasdair Mackenzie, Principal of Hockerill Anglo-European College, UK, shares how the boarding experience equips students with vital skills for lifelong success.

Every parent hopes their child will grow into someone who understands their place in the world — curious about what lies ahead, ambitious for their future, and motivated to make a positive difference. While all schools strive to set young people on this path, boarding schools offer something unique: a fully immersive environment where learning continues beyond the classroom, equipping students with the mindset and skills they need to navigate the complexities of the future with confidence.

UNESCO identifies seven "macro-competencies" that are essential for young people to thrive in an ever-changing global landscape:

1. Lifelong learning – curiosity, creativity, and critical thinking
2. Self-agency – initiative, resilience, motivation, and responsibility
3. Use of diverse tools and resources – including digital fluency and responsible consumption
4. Interpersonal skills – teamwork, collaboration, and negotiation
5. Global engagement – balancing rights and responsibilities with respect and empathy
6. Transdisciplinarity – connecting knowledge across STEM, humanities, and social sciences
7. Multiliteracy – the ability to communicate and interpret information in a variety of forms

This competence-based framework combines knowledge, skills, values, ethics, and technological understanding—qualities that boarding schools foster naturally through community life, enriched experiences, and a culture of aspiration.

Hockerill Anglo-European College

For every young person to find their strengths and passions, they need access to a wide variety of experiences. Boarding schools are uniquely placed to provide this, offering a vibrant and diverse community where students, staff and families from around the world live and learn together. This daily immersion builds deep intercultural awareness and helps students develop essential life skills—such as collaboration, cooperation, and global engagement—three of UNESCO's key competencies for a successful future.

George H., an international boarder who joined the College in Year 10 and is now in the Sixth Form, reflects:

"Boarding has been an incredible experience. It's allowed me to meet people who share similar global experiences to mine—something I hadn't found anywhere else."

At boarding school, extra- and super-curricular opportunities are embedded into daily life. Whether before school, during the day, after lessons, or at weekends, students are constantly encouraged to explore, take part, and stretch themselves. When they discover a passion and are supported to pursue it, the confidence they gain often extends into every other area of their lives. In a boarding context, where the community is together round the clock, personal growth, resilience, and independent learning flourish—developing three more of UNESCO's competencies: lifelong learning, self-agency, and transdisciplinarity.

George also shared: "The friends I've made in boarding are incredible, and the experiences we've shared through living together assure me that these are friendships that will last long after school."

The final two UNESCO competencies—effective communication and fluency with tools and technologies—are likewise cultivated through the dynamic, interconnected nature of boarding life. Young people develop the confidence to communicate across cultures, work with diverse media, and adapt quickly to new challenges. With this toolkit, they are empowered to aim high and contribute meaningfully to their communities and beyond.

P. Lee, another international boarder who joined in Year 7 and is now in the Sixth Form, adds:

"The community is very integrated and welcoming. I instantly clicked with people, even those I didn't share interests with. It's easy to make friends and even easier to have an enjoyable but academic experience."

Boarding schools offer something truly distinctive: an environment that celebrates diversity, nurtures independence, and delivers a global education in its fullest sense. At Hockerill, we would be delighted to welcome you into our international community. To find out more or arrange a visit, please contact admissions@hockerill.com.

For more information about Hockerill Anglo-European College, see page 120

Classroom management: building a lasting positive learning environment

Kassandra Rieck, Learning Support Teacher at Stonehill International School, Bangalore, shares the importance of students taking an active role in their learning journey and how this encourages a sense of belonging

Creating a positive classroom climate: the power of modelling, agreements, and support
Good teachers understand that fostering appropriate student behaviour begins with modelling long before it is reinforced through rules and expectations. At the heart of effective teaching lies the creation of a positive classroom climate – an invaluable, preventative strategy that sets the stage for meaningful learning. When students feel safe, respected, and valued, they are more likely to engage, collaborate, and take ownership of their learning.

Classroom climate can be described through the dimensions offered by Trickett and Moos (1973): building interpersonal relationships, establishing order through rules and processes, and maintaining academic rigour. These dimensions ensure a balance of teacher and peer support, mutual respect, academic orientation, classroom culture, and a conducive physical environment. When these elements align, they foster a sense of belonging, encouraging students to grow socially, emotionally, and academically.

Essential learning agreements: a collective commitment
Students thrive in environments where they feel heard and empowered. Co-constructing classroom rules and expectations, known as Essential Learning Agreements, gives students a voice in shaping the norms that govern their learning space. These agreements emphasise motivation, achievement, and respect while reinforcing responsibility and accountability.

Establishing these agreements at the beginning of the academic year helps set a positive tone, but they can be introduced or revisited whenever needed to enhance the classroom climate. Crucially, the language used should be positive; for instance, instead of "We will not yell out in class," frame it as "We will listen carefully when someone is speaking." This approach fosters ownership and encourages students to uphold shared values.

Understanding student behaviour: an ecological approach
Student behaviour does not occur in a vacuum – it is shaped by relationships, home environments, and personal experiences. Effective teachers act as ecologists,

considering these influences and adapting their approach accordingly.

For example, a student who frequently disrupts the class may not be "difficult" but instead expressing an unmet emotional need. Rather than resorting to punitive measures, a more effective approach is to engage in a conversation, identify the root cause, and provide appropriate support. When teachers lead with empathy, they guide students toward meaningful behavioural change.

Strategies for maintaining a positive learning atmosphere
A structured and respectful learning environment requires deliberate strategies to foster consistency, engagement, and predictability. Clearly defined expectations, expressed in positive language, help students understand their role in maintaining a stable and supportive atmosphere.

Sometimes, a meaningful pause or a simple look can de-escalate potential disruptions before they escalate. Additionally, nurturing a strong classroom community fosters mutual accountability, respect, and collaboration. Effective classroom management is not about control but empowerment – ensuring students feel heard, valued, and invested in their education.

The evolving nature of classroom management
Achieving a positive classroom environment is an ongoing process, requiring continuous reflection and adaptation. A teacher's well-being directly impacts the classroom atmosphere; an educator experiencing stress may unknowingly project tension, whereas a mindful, self-regulated teacher brings patience and balance to the learning space. Prioritising self-care allows educators to be their best selves, ultimately benefiting their students.

When teachers thrive, classrooms become vibrant spaces for learning, growth, and respect. By fostering a climate of empathy, collaboration, and clear expectations, educators set the foundation for student success – both academically and personally.

Kassandra is an Australian international educator with over 15 years of experience teaching in Japan, China, South Korea, and India. She has studied at renowned Australian universities and has qualifications in International Business specialising in Economics and Marketing. She has been teaching English to Students of Other Languages (TESOL). Recently retrained in Learning Support, Kassandra completed post-graduate degrees in Psychological Science and Specialist Inclusive Education. She advocates for inclusive education, conducting workshops on differentiation and scaffolding strategies. Currently teaching at Stonehill International School in Bangalore, Kassandra writes articles on diverse learner needs that have been published on various platforms.

For more information about Stonehill International School School, see page 70

The questions you should ask

However much a school may appeal on first sight, you still need sound information to form your judgement

Schools, particularly independent schools, attract pupils by their reputations, so most go to considerable lengths to ensure that parents are presented with an attractive image. Modern marketing techniques try to promote good points and play down (without totally obscuring) bad ones. But every Head knows that, however good the school website/prospectus is, it only serves to attract parents through the school gates. Thereafter the decision depends on what they see and hear.

When you choose a school for your child, the key factor is that it will suit them. Many children and their parents are instinctively attracted (or otherwise) to a school on first sight. But even if it passes this test, and 'conforms' to what you are looking for in terms of location and academic, pastoral and extracurricular aspects, you will need to satisfy yourself that the school does measure up to what your instincts tell you.

Choosing an international school can prompt additional questions for parents and students alike. The international school's intake is not restricted by geographical or educational authority boundaries. International schools have the added benefit of being able to embrace a sense of national pride while encouraging a respect of and interest in international thinking, standards and cultures.

Research we have carried out over the years suggests that in many cases the most important factor in choosing a school is the impression given by the Head. As well as finding out what goes on in a school, parents need to be reassured by the aura of confidence that they expect from a Head. How they discover the former may help them form their opinion of the latter.

So how a Head answers your questions is important. Based on our research, we have drawn up a list of varied

The questions you should ask

points on which you may need to be satisfied. The order in which they appear below does not necessarily reflect their degree of importance to each parent, but how the Head answers them may help you draw your own conclusions:

- How accessible is the Head, whose personality is seen by most parents as setting the 'tone' of the school?
- Will the child fit in?
- What is the overall atmosphere?
- To which organisations does the school belong?
- How has it been accredited?
- What is the ratio of teachers to pupils?
- What are the qualifications of the teaching staff?
- How often does the school communicate with parents through reports, parent/teacher meetings or other visits?
- What are the school's exam results? What are the criteria for presenting them? Are they consistent over the years?
- How does the school cope with pupils' problems?
- What sort of academic advice is available?
- What is the school's attitude to discipline?
- Have there been problems with drugs or sex? How have they been dealt with?
- What positive steps are taken to encourage good manners, behaviour and sportsmanship?
- Is progress accelerated for the academically strong?
- How does the school cope with pupils who do not work?
- What is the attitude to religion?
- What is the attitude to physical fitness and games?
- What sports are offered and what are the facilities?
- What are the extracurricular activities?
- What cultural or other visits are arranged away from the school?
- What steps are taken to encourage specific talent in music, the arts or sport?
- What is the uniform?
- What steps are taken to ensure that pupils take pride in their personal appearance?
- What are the timetable and term dates?
- What are the boarding facilities like?
- Is there a dedicated person to look after new international students?
- Does the school have a recommended guardian service?
- Does the school have a dedicated and strong pastoral team?
- Is it possible to be put in contact with parents with children at the school to approach them for an opinion?
- Does the school have a dedicated teacher for Mother Tongue languages or ESL?

International school profiles

Schools in Africa 39
Schools in Asia 43
Schools in Australasia 83
Schools in Europe 89
Schools in North America 219
Schools in South America 239

International schools in Africa

Schools ordered A–Z by Name

Uganda

Acorns International School

Plot 328, Kisota Road, (Along) Northern Bypass, Kisaasi Roundabout,
Kampala, Uganda
Tel: +256 393 202 665
Email: admissions@acornskisaasi.com
Website: acornskisaasi.com
Head of School: Ameena Lalani

School type: Co-educational Day
Age range of pupils: 18 months–18 years
No. of pupils enrolled as at 01/09/2025: 800
Fees as at 01/09/2025:
$2,358–$11,090 per annum
Average class size: 20
Teacher/pupil ratio: 1:3 (2yrs) to 1:12 (13yrs)

Encapsulating the adage, 'A tree with strong roots laughs at storms', Acorns International School bears fruits that stand the test of time.

Nestled between the verdant folds of Kampala, the capital city of Uganda, Acorns is sprawled over a 5-acre state-of-the-art, purpose-built campus, that nurtures the balance between academics and extracurriculars.

Over two decades in the field of education, we have grown to represent more than 50 nationalities. The Acorns team strives to inspire and empower every student to achieve their personal best and become inquiring, knowledgeable, pluralists and lifelong learners, who create a better and peaceful world, through intercultural understanding and respect.

Admissions are open throughout the academic year, subject to availability. We have a limit to the number of students per classroom, for uncompromised quality. This interface gives teachers an edge to assess each student's area of strength, and improvement. Teachers are supported in this process, with timely professional development sessions, to ensure growth and excellence. Through an open-door policy, we ensure that our main stakeholders, our parents, are full partners in the decision-making process and voice concerns not only of their children, but their own too.

The language of instruction is English, with French and Kiswahili as part of our dynamic curriculum. Through our engaging and rigorous, inquiry-based environment, students reach their full academic potential and become responsible, caring, multilingual, and culturally-literate global learners.

Our teaching team is not just diverse, they epitomize academic excellence and have a penchant for pastoral care.

Acorns is a non-sectarian and co-educational institution, founded on strong partnerships between parents, teachers and learners.

A visit to Acorns allows your family to experience the school in a relaxed environment, meet with the administration, as well as visit homerooms, the science lab, performing arts rooms, libraries, swimming pool, auditorium, soccer fields and the basketball courts.

Acorns is an authorised International Baccalaureate (IB) Continuum World School, offering the Primary Years Programme (PYP), the Middle Years Programme (MYP) and the Diploma Programme (DP).

Acorns is an inclusive school that accepts students in the Early Childhood Department (Crèche to Reception Class), Primary (PYP1 to PYP6), and Secondary (MYP1 – DP2).

It is always onwards and upwards for us, and we would love for you to join us!

E.S.C.O.L.A. - English School Community of Luanda, Angola

Rua de Cambambe No. 21-23, Bairro Patrice Lumumba, Luanda, Angola
Tel: +244 935 929 501
Email: schooloffice@escolaangola.org

Website: escolaangola.org/escolateste
School type: Co-educational Day
Age range of pupils: 3–16 years

The English School Community of Luanda, Angola, (E.S.C.O.L.A.) is an English-medium, interdenominational, independent school catering for both boys and girls. For the past 21 years we have strived to offer every child who enters our school an education which will allow them to achieve to the best of their ability. There are currently 187 students at E.S.C.O.L.A.

The curriculum is based on the South African CAPS curriculum, which has been adapted to reflect a more international context.

We offer face-to-face classes from Pre-Primary 2 to Grade 9. E.S.C.O.L.A. has partnered with IVA Global Online School to allow students to continue after Grade 9 and complete their schooling with IGCSE, AS, and A levels. Students come to school but attend lessons online.

E.S.C.O.L.A. is a member of ISASA (Independent Schools Association of Southern Africa) who is a member of INISA (Network of Independent School Associations).

Mission Statement
The Mission of The English School Community of Luanda, Angola (E.S.C.O.L.A.) is to provide, through the medium of English, a student-centred education of the highest calibre that is holistically relevant in the southern African and international context.

E.S.C.O.L.A. is committed to:
- Providing education which promotes the growth of the complete person, in body, mind, and spirit;
- Developing the unique individuality of each student to their maximum potential in any given sphere;
- Encouraging communication and respect amongst students;
- Developing and maintaining effective communication and respect between and amongst the school administration, students, teachers, parents, and wider school community;
- Nurturing and developing the students' self-esteem, self-worth, self-control, self-discipline, self-motivation, and self-respect;
- Encouraging and developing self-directed and experiential learning skills;
- Encouraging and developing lifelong learning patterns;
- Fostering critical and creative thinking, problem solving, risk taking, and decision-making;
- Providing a firm base for students to become caring, principled, open-minded, and well-balanced citizens of the world;
- Developing self-motivated, successful, and knowledgeable students who will freely gain admission to other international educational institutions at all appropriate levels;
- Respecting and honouring the historical and cultural background of Angola by recognizing its heritage and public holidays

International schools in Asia

Schools ordered A–Z by Name

Indonesia

ACG School Jakarta

Jl Warung Jati Barat No.19, RW.5, Jati Padang, Kec. Ps. Minggu, Jakarta Selatan, DKI Jakarta 12540 Indonesia
Tel: +62 21 2978 0200 / +62 816 297800
Email: acgjkt@acgedu.com
Website: jakarta.acgedu.com
Principal: Mr Myles D'Airelle

School type: Co-educational Day
Age range of pupils: 3–17 years
No. of pupils enrolled as at 01/09/2025: 299
Fees as at 01/09/2025:
Day: IDR150,491,250–IDR357,761,250 per annum
Average class size: 16

Welcome to ACG School Jakarta, an exceptional educational institution providing a dynamic international education in the heart of South Jakarta. As a member of Inspired, a leading premium schools group with over 110 outstanding schools worldwide, ACG School Jakarta offers a comprehensive educational pathway from Kindergarten to Year 13.

We are renowned for our commitment to preparing students for success and providing a values-driven and diverse environment. Our world-class teaching faculty consists of specialist educators who deliver exceptional instruction tailored to meet the needs of each individual student. With a focus on personalised programmes of study that reflect students' abilities and backgrounds, we ensure that every child thrives academically.

ACG School Jakarta proudly offers globally recognised curricula that yield the best learning outcomes for our students. Through the International Baccalaureate Primary Years Programme (IBPYP) and Diploma Programme (IBDP), as well as Cambridge International Lower Secondary and IGCSE courses, we instill an international mindset and foster advanced critical thinking skills. Our emphasis on inquiry, investigation, and experiential discovery empowers students to be innovative problem solvers who are at the forefront of their own learning journey.

Beyond academic excellence, ACG School Jakarta places a strong emphasis on holistic development and well-being. Our well-established pastoral care system actively supports students socially, emotionally, and academically, ensuring they reach their full potential during their time with us and are well prepared for life beyond the classroom.

As a testament to our commitment to individual growth, ACG School Jakarta students have consistently achieved remarkable success on the global stage, with graduates gaining acceptance into top universities worldwide.

We believe that education extends beyond the confines of the classroom, which is why we offer a diverse range of co-curricular activities. From performing and fine arts to sporting and leadership opportunities, students have access to a plethora of pursuits that foster invaluable life skills such as persistence, commitment, and teamwork. In addition, cultural and service activities provide students with the opportunity to contribute to and develop a wider sense of community.

ACG School Jakarta is uniquely positioned to accommodate students holding passports from Indonesia and other parts of the world, making us an ideal choice for families employed by embassies and multinational corporations. Our central location ensures easy accessibility for all, further enhancing our appeal to both expatriate and local communities.

Join us at ACG School Jakarta, where exceptional education meets an unwavering commitment to individual growth. Experience first-hand how our internationally recognized curriculum, dedicated faculty, holistic learning approach, and vibrant co-curricular opportunities create an enriching environment for your child's educational journey.

Vietnam

Australian International School (AIS)

264 Mai Chi Tho Street, An Phu ward, Thu Duc City, Ho Chi Minh City, Vietnam
Tel: +84 28 3742 4040
Email: info@aisvietnam.com
Website: www.aisvietnam.com
Executive Principal: Mr Jon Standen

School type: Co-educational Day & Boarding
Age range of pupils: 18 months–18 years
No. of pupils enrolled as at 01/09/2025: 1330
Fees as at 01/09/2025:
Day: VND 295,600,000.00–860,700,000.00 per annum

Leading to a bright future
At Australian International School (AIS), every action we take is designed to lead our students towards a bright future. Since our establishment in 2006, we have continued to achieve this aim by delivering high-quality international education. We are dedicated to creating an environment where we stimulate inquiry, creativity and innovation, to help our students embrace all opportunities that life brings them and to become global citizens.

Providing the IB curriculum
Understanding the significance of all that the IB curriculum offers, AIS has long identified its ability to foster both academic and personal success while challenging students to excel in their studies and their individual development. AIS was one of the first schools in Vietnam to become an authorised IB World School, and as such, we are now among the most experienced educators in the country to provide this curriculum.

Currently, AIS offers the IB Primary Years Programme (PYP) for both our Kindergarten and Primary School students and the IB Diploma Programme as part of its Senior School education. The University of Cambridge Secondary Programme with the International General Certificate of Secondary Education (IGCSE) is provided for our Lower Secondary School students.

For the IB Diploma, AIS has an extensive background in supporting and preparing students to study this acclaimed curriculum and develop real-world skills that extend beyond the classroom. Consequently, AIS graduates consistently obtain results above the world average, and students have gone on to gain places at leading universities around the globe, many with full or partial scholarships.

Exceptional education with modern facilities
For almost 20 years, our team of highly-trained and experienced educators has been committed to delivering exceptional academic results. We strive to challenge, inspire, and support each and every student, tailoring our approach to meet their unique needs.

We support each child to reach their full academic potential, to nurture a love of arts, to become involved in and passionate about sport and to develop the resilience to overcome challenges. Our Australian values of fairness and a 'have a go' attitude, combined with a world-class curriculum, drive this ambition.

To aid our teaching staff, every classroom and learning environment is spacious, well-resourced, and technologically rich. Additionally, our students have access to an open garden style campus, swimming pools, a double gymnasium, an auditorium, soccer fields, a dedicated IB Centre, and much, much more.

Thailand

Bangkok Patana School

Bangkok Patana School
The British International School in Thailand
Established 1957

643 Lasalle Road (Sukhumvit 105), Bangna Tai, Bangna, Bangkok, 10260 Thailand
Tel: +66 2 785 2200
Email: admissions@patana.ac.th

Website: www.patana.ac.th
School type: Co-educational Day
Age range of pupils: 2–18 years

As the oldest British international school in Thailand, we are proud to embody the best of British values with an international outlook. The school has clear Guiding Statements that provide direction and purpose for the institution. Within our three values, Well-Being is intentionally first, followed by Learning and Global Citizenship. Our strong pastoral system supports student well-being and allows them to fulfil their potential.

Bangkok Patana is a not-for-profit school. The Board and management are the stewards of our organisation and they act on our core values of well-being, learning and global citizenship.

We are also a non-academically selective school, a fact that belies our history of excellent academic results and university matriculations.

Our curriculum is broad and balanced. From Nursery to Year 13, it links to the English National Curriculum with assessments taking place at key points. We are committed to the rigour of British education and emphasise hard work, integrity, strong moral principles and fairness. We provide diverse opportunities for our students to explore new areas and discover their passions. This includes more than 400 extra-curricular activities for students to choose.

We are a truly international school with a very diverse student body of students representing more than 65 nations. We develop global citizens and world perspectives are woven throughout the curriculum and extra-curricular programmes. We embrace the IB (International Baccalaureate) Learner Profile and students complete the IB Diploma Programme in their last two years at school. We are proud to see our students develop into respectful contributors to local and global communities.

At Bangkok Patana, we leverage our experience with the adoption of leading-edge pedagogical practices. More than 80% of our teachers are recruited from the UK or from British international schools. All our teachers are fully certified and we have a strong professional development culture to ensure they remain at the forefront of pedagogy. Our most recent CIS accreditors noted that, "The quality of learning at Bangkok Patana School is clearly a strength….

Parents and students were both highly complimentary about the teachers." Our teachers and students have been an integral part of campus development resulting in learning environments that are amongst the best in Asia.

Primary School children enjoy a 'neighbourhood', small-school environment within the larger community. They can feel confident and secure within their purpose-built "home", where their classrooms, collaborative learning spaces and playgrounds have been specially designed for their Year group. Secondary faculties also have purpose-built learning environments. The state-of-the-art Science Centre is well appointed, the Arts Centre boasts two theatres, sound-proofed music rooms, numerous Drama studios with mirrors and sprung floors and Art classes abundant in natural light. The Sports Complex has eight Tennis Courts and four full-size 11-a-side football pitches (in addition to the pitches on the school side).

Aside from the rigorous academic programme, the extra-curricular programme is second to none with more than 400 different activities being run each week. We have five academies: Swimming, Tennis, Gymnastics, Football and Dance and Drama. These academies offer specialised, focused training and competitive training. Our students benefit from this all-round development and supportive learning. Our graduates receive an incredible number of offers from top universities and programmes around the world. Our IGCSE and IB results are strong when compared with similar schools, and as a not academically selective school, this is the true test that shows we deliver on our mission to ensure that our students grow to their full potential as independent learners in a caring British international community.

Republic of Korea

Chadwick International

45, Art center-daero 97 beon-gil,
Yeonsu-gu, Incheon,
22002 Republic of Korea
Tel: +82 32 250 5000
Email: songdo-admissions@chadwickschool.org

Website: www.chadwickinternational.org
Head of School: Frederick T. "Ted" Hill
School type: Co-educational Day
Age range of pupils: 4–18 years
No. of pupils enrolled as at 01/09/2025: 1447
Teacher/pupil ratio: 1:8

Chadwick International is a PreK-G12 international school fully equipped with the state-of-the-art facility built in the Songdo International Business District, Incheon, Republic of Korea.

Chadwick International is the sister campus of Chadwick School, a K-12 school in the greater South Bay area of Los Angeles, which was founded by Margaret Lee Chadwick in 1935. The two campuses share the same mission that Chadwick Schools develop global citizens with keen minds, exemplary character, self-knowledge, and the ability to lead.

Chadwick International is an authorized four-programme International Baccalaureate (IB) World School, offering PYP, MYP, DP and CP. Chadwick International emphasizes experiential and inquiry-based learning both in and outside the classroom including Outdoor Education and Service Learning programs. The Outdoor Education allows students to develop conflict-resolution abilities and leadership skills through various outdoor experiences. Meanwhile, Service Learning program teaches students how to interact with both their local and international communities and problem solve on a deeper level. These fundamental programs assist students in transferring valuable lessons learned in the classroom and develop them as contributing members and leaders of tomorrow.

Physical Education plays an integral part of the Chadwick curriculum as it focuses on the promotion of good personal health and a holistic lifestyle for our students. Its activity-based program emphasizes the skill development that improves the fitness and well-being of the individual student as well as healthy and safe lifestyles.

Chadwick International has rich and diverse Visual and Performing Arts programs. In these classes, students develop their knowledge, skills, creativity and ability to respond to artistic ideas. Also, students are exposed to a variety of theatrical mediums to express themselves and heighten their awareness of themselves in relation to the people and culture around them.

Chadwick International helps to achieve its educational mission through recruiting and supporting highly experienced, dedicated, and diverse faculty members from around the world. With the support of the faculty, Chadwick International is capable of a low teacher to student ratio of 1:8.

Chadwick International's superior educational facilities include an aquatic center with scuba diving capabilities, two gymnasiums, two performing arts indoor theatres, a television studio that allows production up to eight channels, a working garden, purpose-built science laboratories and three design/maker spaces. These facilities permit the students to cultivate their intellectual, artistic and physical abilities based on Chadwick International's experience-based curriculum.

Chadwick International is accredited by Western Association of Schools and Colleges (WASC) and Council of International Schools (CIS).

Hong Kong, China

Discovery Bay International School

(Founded 1984)

Discovery Bay Road, Discovery Bay,
Lantau Island, Hong Kong, SAR,
Hong Kong, China
Tel: +852 2987 7331
Email: dbis@dbis.edu.hk
Website: www.dbis.edu.hk
Principal: Mr Marc Morris
School type: Co-educational Day
Age range of pupils: 3–18 years

No. of pupils enrolled as at 01/09/2025: 1000
Fees as at 01/09/2025:
Foundation Stage 1 & 2: HKD13,250.00 per annum
Year 1 – Year 6: HKD14,370.00 per annum
Year 7 – Year 11: HKD19,070.00 per annum
Year 12 – Year 13 (Sixth Form): HKD19,690.00 per annum
Average class size: 18-24

Located in the tranquil suburb of Discovery Bay, Discovery Bay International School (DBIS) offers an outstanding education for children aged three to eighteen. Just half an hour from Central and fifteen minutes from both Tung Chung and Sunny Bay, the school enjoys a prime location, with excellent transport links and direct access to the natural wonders of Lantau Island.

British Curriculum with an International Flair
DBIS follows the National Curriculum of England, tailored to the school's international setting. Students begin their learning journey in the Early Years Foundation Stage (EYFS), with teaching centred around the belief that all children are infinitely capable, creative and full of potential. Firm foundations are laid in EYFS, providing the building blocks for continued high-quality learning in the Primary and Secondary phases of the school.

Strong Academic Rigour
Small class sizes and individual attention from tutors and teaching staff support DBIS students in achieving excellent (I)GCSE, A Level and BTEC results, setting them up for continued success at world-class universities around the globe. The school's strong academic pedigree is underpinned by a truly holistic approach to education, nurturing balanced, well-rounded individuals, ready to take on the challenges of an ever-changing world. A wide variety of free-of-charge extracurricular activities are available to students.

Outstanding Facilities
With three exceptionally well resourced campuses, DBIS offers students access to first-class learning resources. Extensive indoor and outdoor facilities are found at the school's dedicated EYFS Campus, which is purposefully designed to support the intellectual, social and physical development of its youngest learners. Outdoor space is also abundant at the Primary and Secondary Campus, which boasts a swimming pool, gym, all-weather pitch, netball/basketball courts and playgrounds. Other facilities include state-of-the-art STEAM, Drama, Art and Music suites, Discovery, Design & Technology and Science labs, and an impressive library. Sixth Form students enjoy their own dedicated learning centre as well as access to the facilities at the Main Campus.

A True International Community
DBIS students hail from around the world, representing approximately 50 nationalities at any one time. This diversity is actively celebrated both in school and through a range of popular community events. The school has a very active Parent-Teacher-Student Association (PTSA), and parent involvement in school life is warmly welcomed. The oldest international school on Lantau Island, DBIS has been at the heart of the Discovery Bay community for over 40 years.

Dulwich College (Singapore)

DULWICH COLLEGE | SINGAPORE |

(Founded 2014)

71 Bukit Batok West Avenue 8,
Singapore, 658966 Singapore
Tel: +65 6890 1003
Email: admissions.singapore@dulwich.org
Website: singapore.dulwich.org
Headmaster: Mr. Nick Magnus
Head of Senior School: Ms. Melanie Ellis
School type: Co-educational Day & Boarding

Age range of pupils: 2–18 years
No. of pupils enrolled as at 01/09/2025: 3000
Fees as at 01/09/2025:
Day: S$20,270–S$56,220 per annum
Full Boarding: S$43,200 per annum
Average class size: 20
Teacher/pupil ratio: 1:4-22

Dulwich College (Singapore) is a leading international school founded on the ethos and values of a British international school system. The College proudly draws upon the rich heritage, excellence, innovation and values of the founding school in London. Part of the international network of schools, Dulwich College (Singapore) has a global outlook and contemporary approach, reflecting the diversity of the students from 2 to 18 years. The state-of-the-art green campus and rich academic, sports, arts and music curriculum are designed to help each individual child reach their potential and make a positive difference in the world.

Dulwich College (Singapore) believes in nurturing global citizens and well-rounded future leaders who are equipped to create solutions to the world's challenges. Students are encouraged to Live Worldwise – to make informed choices, take inspired action and create positive impact. The College's innovative and world-changing education is wellbeing-focused and balances academic excellence with a wealth of co-curricular opportunities that enable students to discover their individual talents and passions.

The College is academically selective and follows an enhanced version of the National Curriculum of England, adapted for the needs of our international student body.

Students follow the IGSCE curriculum in Years 9, 10 and 11 followed by the IB Diploma Programme and IB Career-related Programme in Years 12 and 13. Continuing the tradition of excellence started by the founding school, Dulwich College in London, Dulwich College International graduates go on to study at leading universities in the UK, USA and around the world.

The College's holistic education is complemented by rewarding co-curricular programmes. Students are encouraged to participate in sporting competitions and every child from the age of seven is taught a musical instrument. Drama and opportunities for public speaking feature heavily from an early age with students using the 742-seat Alleyn Theatre daily for assemblies, performances and more.

The College offers a dual language programme in English and Mandarin for students in Toddler to Year 2 (aged two to seven) and daily Mandarin classes, streamed according to ability from the age of four. Additional modern foreign languages are offered in the Senior School. The close collaboration among the network of Colleges gives our students unique opportunities to participate in events and benefit from the group's relationships with leading educational and artistic organisations. The network enjoys an ongoing and strong partnership with Dulwich College in London.

Vietnam

Dwight School Hanoi

The Manor Central Park, Hoang Mai District, Hanoi, Vietnam
Email: contact@dwighthanoi.org
Website: www.dwighthanoi.org
School type: Co-educational Day

Age range of pupils: 3–18 years
Fees as at 01/09/2025:
Day: VND: 325,000,000–845,000,000 per annum

Dwight School Hanoi is the newest member of the Dwight Schools global network of premier International Baccalaureate World Schools.

The inspiring campus, masterfully designed by the renowned Carlos Zapata Studio in New York, seamlessly blends advanced technology with open architecture to encourage collaboration and innovation. The 40,000-square-meter facility features: advanced learning studios, learning commons for all grades, three libraries to support our curriculum; design, technology, and engineering spaces; Spark Labs (Makerspaces) for all grades, supporting our commitment to problem-solving and innovation; specialty arts spaces dedicated to design, photography, and ceramics; an upcoming large performing arts center and a black box theater; as well as a music conservatory, recording studio, and rehearsal spaces. The school celebrates athletics with two large indoor multi-purpose sports halls, an advanced aquatics center, a fitness center, and specialty areas for activities, including martial arts, fencing, dance, and yoga. Outdoor spaces on the campus include a multipurpose, artificial turf sports field; terraced learning gardens and a greenhouse.

An additional standalone Early Childhood Division facility is designed for our youngest learners. This foundational educational experience values childhood and facilitates whole-body, transdisciplinary learning. ECD Learning Studios offer opportunities for preschoolers and kindergartners to practice fundamental academic skills in a safe and appropriately challenging environment. Outdoor and indoor play spaces allow for large motor play times, and the facility has its own custom-designed library.

As a member of the global network of Dwight Schools, students in Hanoi will also have the exclusive opportunity to access more than 50 cross-campus activities, exchanges, competitions, concerts, and tournaments, as well as travel and exchange options on any Dwight campus around the world.

Vietnam

European International School HCMC

730 Le Van Mien Street, Thao Dien Ward, Thu Duc City, Ho Chi Minh City, 70000 Vietnam
Tel: +8428 7300 7257
Email: info@eishcmc.com
Website: www.eishcmc.com
Co-Heads of School: Ms. Jo Roberts & Mr. Ben Armstrong

School type: Co-educational Day
Age range of pupils: 2–18 years
No. of pupils enrolled as at 01/09/2025: 750
Fees as at 01/09/2025:
VND 274,700,000.00–771,600,000.00 per annum

With possibly the most convenient location in Thao Dien, the European International School Ho Chi Minh City (EIS) is the only boutique international school, set in lush garden surroundings, offering the International Baccalaureate (IB) continuum of studies for children aged 2–18.

Our vibrant, unified campus is a place where students, teachers and parents of all grade levels and different backgrounds interact freely with each other within a home-away-from-home, tranquil village atmosphere. EIS offers a truly diverse 'melting pot' of 40+ nationalities and global cultures, where students are encouraged to find their unique voice, to pursue languages, and to contribute to all aspects of school life.

EIS teachers, with over 13 years' average experience, are well-practiced in individualized learning methods. With a very low student-to-teacher ratio, particularly in the middle-high school sections of the school, students benefit directly from more frequent access to teachers.

Graduating IB Diploma students consistently achieve well-above the world averages, and have achieved acceptances into prestigious universities worldwide, often with significant merit-based scholarships.

EIS provides an outstanding world-class education for students, evidenced by our full accreditation status with the Council of International Schools (CIS).

Being a medium-sized school, we are large enough to offer a wide range of educational opportunities, while also being intimate enough to provide the unique personal attention and care that each child deserves.

China

Hangzhou International School

(Founded 2002)

2190 Xiangbin Road, Binjiang District, Hangzhou, Zhejiang, 310052 China
Tel: +86 571 8669 0045
Email: admissions@hisdragons.org.cn
Website: www.his-china.org
Superintendent: Mr Jeffry Stubbs
Deputy Superintendent: Dr Aaron Ayers

Upper School Principal: Ms Cynthia Wissman
Lower School Principal: Mr Jeff Hart
School type: Co-educational Day
Age range of pupils: 2–18 years
No. of pupils enrolled as at 01/09/2025: 1100
Fees as at 01/09/2025:
Day: RMB222,500–RMB275,000 per annum

As an IB World School, Hangzhou International School (HIS) provides a rigorous, high-caliber academic program for all ages of students.

While HIS already has a highly reputed International Baccalaureate Diploma Programme (IB DP) for Grades 11–12, we are also authorized with the full IB Continuum of study, which includes delivering the Primary Years Programme (IB PYP) for Grades EY-5 and the Middle Years Programme (IB MYP) for Grades 6–10.

Upper School student participation in IB coursework is 100% and final results have been truly exceptional. Graduates have earned the highest scores on the SATs and IB Diploma, and each year since 2004 many will attend top-50 universities around the world.

HIS also continues to compete successfully in regional sporting events, such as ACAMIS, HISAC, SISAC, CISSA and SSL sporting leagues. HIS also hosts the regionally acclaimed West Lake Model UN conference each fall and continues to provide the city of Hangzhou with outstanding theater productions.

Overall, a hallmark of HIS has been our commitment to high standards of academic excellence as recognized by the Western Association of Schools and Colleges (WASC) accrediting organization.

HIS is the only internationally accredited school in Hangzhou and fully commits to the process of schoolwide self-study and external evaluation of our on-going school improvement processes. The latest WASC accreditation letter recognizes 'stellar' aspects of our school and congratulates HIS for the high quality of instruction offered.

A focus on curriculum and instruction as well as fine facilities and resources are, indeed, attributes of a good school. However, truly great educational institutions focus their efforts, time, and energy on our most treasured resource – people.

It is the people of Hangzhou International School that make it an outstanding school. Students, teachers, and parents are welcomed here, and know that their voice is heard and matters. HIS is a truly unique and truly international school.

Vietnam

Hoi An International School

24 Phan Ba Phien, Tan An, Hoi An, 510000 Vietnam
Tel: +84 235 651 8518
Email: admissions@hais.edu.vn
Website: www.hais.edu.vn

Principal: Brett Macdouall
CEO & Founder: Tran Hanh An
School type: Co-educational Day
Age range of pupils: 18 months–18 years
No. of pupils enrolled as at 01/09/2025: 300

Hoi An International School (HAIS) is the leading international school in Central Vietnam, located in the cultural and historic community of Hoi An.

HAIS meets and nurtures our students' individual needs in an intentional, supportive, community-minded environment. At HAIS, we teach with a long-term outlook for our students and thus, are committed to improving their academic and emotional outcomes, not just for tomorrow or the next five to ten years, but for lifelong success.

Hoi An International School adopts a unique curriculum that uses the Cambridge and Vietnamese National Curriculum as points of reference, allowing us to provide a holistic and balanced education for our learners, helping them thrive throughout their schooling and beyond. Our curriculum provides Vietnamese and international students with a strong foundation for further study.

HAIS is divided into three sectors: Early Years, Primary and Secondary (which includes Lower Secondary, IGCSE and the A Level programme). Each sector is developed as a springboard to the next level of education, with A Level preparing the students for university life after graduation.

Now entering its eighth year, HAIS is committed more than ever to being a truly child-centred, inclusive, small-scale school that delivers meaningful and engaging programmes, allowing all our students to find their passion and realise their dreams.

Hong Kong, China

Hong Kong Academy

(Founded 2000)

33 Wai Man Road, Sai Kung, Hong Kong, SAR, Hong Kong, China
Tel: +852 2655 1111
Email: admissions@hkacademy.edu.hk
Website: www.hkacademy.edu.hk
Head of School: Kasson Bratton
Primary School Principal: Virginia Hunt
Secondary School Principal: Joanna Crimmins
School type: Co-educational Day

Age range of pupils: 3–18 years
No. of pupils enrolled as at 01/09/2025: 550
Fees as at 01/09/2025:
PreK1 – PreK2: HK$116,570.00 per annum
K – G5: HK$221,800.00 per annum
G6 – G8: HK$244,100.00 per annum
G9 – G10: HK$254,400.00 per annum
G11 – G12: HK$2,264,700.00 per annum
Average class size: 18-24
Teacher/pupil ratio: 1:6

Founded in 2000, Hong Kong Academy (HKA) is a non-profit international school that provides a highly personalised and holistic education for students from 3-18 years old. HKA's educational programmes are designed to equip students with the skills and knowledge they need to thrive as thoughtful and successful individuals who meaningfully contribute to their local and global communities.

Three Diploma credentials
From our Early Childhood programme to the final years of Secondary School, teachers provide well rounded, student-centred experiences that encourage all learners to fulfill their greatest potential.

All HKA graduates can earn up to three Diploma credentials; the HKA Diploma, Global Citizen Diploma (GCD) certificate, and IB Diploma or IB course certificates. HKA's students consistently outperforming the IB Diploma Programme world pass rate and average total points, and we are the only school in Hong Kong to offer the GCD.

A unique international education
Small class sizes and a low student to teacher ratio allow for individualised attention; within our classrooms, we have the ability to meet the needs of accelerated learners as well as students requiring learner support. We offer a wealth of curricular and co-curricular programmes on our award-winning campus.

Award-winning campus
In recognition of our mission as an innovative and future-focussed school, our campus is rated Gold BEAM by the Green Building Council of Hong Kong. Designed to operate as a sustainable learning lab, the campus employs durable materials and data collection systems which enable students to connect their learning to their surroundings. We encourage students to see themselves as custodians of our world and they work alongside faculty and staff on sustainability projects, giving them a voice in operational decisions which benefit our social and natural world.

Highly engaged community
A warm and engaging community, HKA parents are integral to the school as volunteers. Whether serving on the board of trustees, reading in the classroom, sharing their experience as industry experts and mentors, leading community events, supporting the theatre or coaching HKA athletes, parents are partners who enrich our school in many ways.

Global alumni network
At the core of an HKA education is the belief that students should be encouraged to pursue their individual pathways to excellence. HKA graduates are able to effectively apply research, critical thinking and communication skills precisely, flexibly and intentionally. We are proud to be an inclusive and multicultural community, our graduates pursue post-secondary degrees in a diverse range of disciplines with the majority entering their first-choice universities and successfully securing employment in a wide variety of professions all over the world.

Singapore

International Community School

27A Jubilee Road, Singapore, 128575 Singapore
Tel: +65 6776 7435
Email: info@ics.edu.sg
Website: www.ics.edu.sg
Head of School: Mr. Darryl Harding

School type: Co-educational Day
Age range of pupils: 4–18 years
No. of pupils enrolled as at 01/09/2025: 400
Fees as at 01/09/2025:
Day: S$29,807–S$43,133 per annum
Average class size: 16

Founded over 30 years ago, the International Community School (Singapore) is a leading American curriculum school located in the heart of Singapore. ICS offers a rigorous K–12 education that combines academic excellence with personalized learning, leadership development, and community engagement in a culturally diverse setting.

ICS maintains a low student-teacher ratio and small class sizes, enabling teachers to provide tailored support and cultivate meaningful relationships with students. The school's Advanced Placement (AP) programme offers over 25 college-level courses and consistently exceeds global AP score averages. Graduates go on to attend top universities worldwide, including institutions in the Ivy League, Russell Group, and leading universities across Asia and Europe.

The school emphasizes real-world learning through inquiry-based instruction, interdisciplinary projects, and student-led initiatives. Students participate in a wide array of extracurriculars – from competitive sports and the arts to robotics, coding, and service learning. Character development and social responsibility are core to the ICS experience.

ICS is home to a vibrant international community, with students from more than 25 nationalities. Parents play an active role through a dynamic Parent-Teacher Fellowship, and the school's award-winning faculty are known for their commitment to student growth.

ICS has been recognized with eight major education awards, including Best Small School in Singapore (3 years running), Best American Curriculum, and Principal and Teacher of the Year honours, solidifying its reputation as a nurturing, future-focused school committed to excellence.

Brunei Darussalam

International School Brunei

(Founded 1964)

Jalan Utama Salambigar, Kampong Sungai Hanching, Berakas 'B' BC2115, Brunei Darussalam
Tel: +673 233 0608
Email: admission@ac.isb.edu.bn
Website: www.isb.edu.bn
Headteacher: Mr. Dominic Morley
School type: Co-educational Day & Boarding
Age range of pupils: 2–18 years

No. of pupils enrolled as at 01/09/2025: 1250
Fees as at 01/09/2025:
Early Years: BND$ 5,400–6,840 per annum
Primary - Secondary: BND$ 12,900–17,010 per annum
IB: BND$ 20,010 per annum
Boarding fees per annum: BND$ 16,500 (5 days)– 21,500 (7 days) per annum
Average class size: 20
Teacher/pupil ratio: 1:4

Established in 1964, ISB is one of Southeast Asia's most distinguished international schools, with over 60 years of academic excellence in Brunei Darussalam. With campuses in Bandar, Seria, and the Centre for Inclusive Learning in Panaga, ISB is an internationally accredited school known for its inclusive, eco-conscious approach and strong boarding and day school offerings.

ISB provides high-quality education for students aged 2 to 18, encompassing Early Years (Pre-Kindy to Reception), Primary (Years 1–6), Secondary (Years 7–11), and Pre-University (Years 12–13), offering the IGCSE and International Baccalaureate (IB) Diploma Programme.

Academic Excellence
ISB consistently achieves academic results above global averages. Its international curriculum combines the UK-based framework with IGCSE and IB, designed to support every student's cognitive, social, emotional, and physical growth. As an inclusive school, ISB welcomes students of all abilities and backgrounds, ensuring every learner has the opportunity to thrive.

The school's world-class teaching faculty from around the world delivers best practices in education. Students are encouraged to explore beyond the classroom with opportunities in performing arts, music, and sports.

World-Class Facilities
ISB's campuses feature modern, open-concept classrooms, a competition-standard swimming pool, a fully equipped multipurpose hall, a state-of-the-art theatre, and expansive sports fields. These facilities support a dynamic, inclusive learning environment that promotes creativity, collaboration, and excellence.

As a certified BCA Green Mark and Green Flag eco-school, ISB is committed to sustainability and environmental responsibility, embedding green practices into everyday learning.

ISB Residence – A Home Away from Home
Boarding at ISB offers a safe, structured, and inclusive environment where students thrive both academically and personally. With 5-day and 7-day options, boarders benefit from experienced pastoral care, world-class facilities, and weekend enrichment activities. Set on a secure green campus, ISB Residence supports students from over 40 nationalities, fostering independence, confidence, and global citizenship. This unique blend of care, challenge, and opportunity prepares students not only for academic success but for the demands of university life and beyond.

Brunei Darussalam

Jerudong International School

(Founded 1997)

Jalan Universiti, Kampong Tungku, Bandar Seri Begawan, BE2119 Brunei Darussalam
Tel: +673 241 1000 (Ext: 1205/1206/7100/1214)
Email: admissions@jis.edu.bn
Website: www.jerudonginternationalschool.com
Executive Principal: Mr Nicholas Sheehan BSc. Geography, PGCE
Appointed: August 2019
Head of Boarding: Mrs Beenal Roberts
School type: Co-educational Day & Boarding

Age range of pupils: 2–18 years (*Boarding from 8 years)
No. of pupils enrolled as at 01/09/2025: 1700
No. of boarders: 240
Fees as at 01/09/2025:
Day: B$18,048–B$28,896 per annum
Weekly Boarding: B$18,756–B$25,176 per annum
Full Boarding: B$24,108–B$31,620 per annum
Average class size: Years 7-9: 20; Years 10-13: 10-20
Teacher/pupil ratio: 1:20 (maximum), IBDP classes are typically 1:15 or less

About Jerudong International School

Jerudong International School (JIS) in Brunei is an outstanding British International, co-educational Day and Boarding School with a community of around 1700 students, aged 2–18 years old, from over 45 countries. JIS is recognised as one of the best international schools in Asia and is considered the premier school in Brunei, with recent nomination in the Spears Schools Indices as one of the top 100 leading international schools in the world and in the top 10 in Asia and the Pacific Region. JIS also made finalist in the BSA International School of the Year Award 2025, this recognition is testimony to the commitment of our dedicated community.

A world-class campus nestled on 120-acres of land with exceptional facilities, qualified teaching staff and excellent pastoral care, plus a large choice of co-curricular activities, enhance the overall holistic learning experience and provide a superior learning environment where JIS students are able to thrive and achieve excellence.

JIS is a leading member of the Federation of British Schools in Asia (FOBISIA), Council of British International Schools (COBIS), an international HMC School, an IB World School, an Eco Schools Green Flag Award recipient and is recognised by the prestigious Good Schools Guide.

JIS was honoured with the COBIS Patron's Accreditation and became the first international school worldwide to receive Beacon Status in three standards: Student Welfare, Boarding Provision and Extracurricular, Enrichment & Engagement.

Our core values of: Challenge, Respect and Inspire are woven into the fabric of our school and our students live by the school aims of: Communication, Engagement, Integration, Leadership, Resilience and Thinking.

All Round Excellence

At JIS, we are committed to providing a holistic education that supports students in every aspect of their development. Our curriculum is designed to cater to individual interests and strengths, offering a balanced approach that promotes personal growth.

By providing diverse curriculum options and personalised learning experiences, students consistently achieve outstanding results in their examinations and we are proud to see them enter into the best universities around the world every year.

Our specialist Higher Education team guides and prepares students for their university applications, facilitating over 1000 applications every year. Over 50% of our students who go to university in the UK attend a Russell Group University.

The top graduate destinations include but are not limited to: University of Oxford, Imperial College London, University College London, University of Toronto,

University of British Columbia, University of Melbourne, Monash University, University of Groningen, the National University of Singapore and Seoul National University of Science and Technology.

Exceptional Campus

We believe that education goes beyond the classroom. That's why we provide exceptional facilities that are fully connected to Wi-Fi, including 27 state-of-the-art science laboratories, an extensive Performing Arts Centre and music faculty, as well as art, design and technology studios. Our library provides a comfortable and modern learning space for our students. The Outdoor Discovery Centre – an eco-forestry initiative on the campus is regularly used for activities and as an Outdoor Classroom.

Our sports facilities are second to none, with two swimming pools (including an Olympic size – 50 metre pool), three air-conditioned sports halls, three covered netball/basketball courts and three football/rugby pitches. A bespoke Racquet Sports Centre includes four squash courts, two championship level tennis courts, and cricket practice nets.

Boarding Facilities

Our 'Home from Home' Boarding facilities for students cater to the needs of our weekly and full-time boarders. There are two girls' Houses (Osprey and Kingfisher House) and two boys' Houses (Eagle and Ibis House). Dedicated boarding staff provide comprehensive care for students, offering support and guidance and innovative initiatives specifically catered to the needs of our boarders.

Pastoral Care

All students and teachers in the school are members of a House, which is designed to provide pastoral care, foster competition and promote camaraderie among the students.

There are 16 Houses in the Senior School, all named after birds in Borneo, which are single-gendered. The brother and sister Houses collaborate for a range of events and social activities.

Each House has its own leadership team, including a House Captain and Deputy Captain, as well as other students in various unique leadership positions. House competitions take place weekly and include a variety of events such as sports, arts, talent shows, debates, spelling bees and quizzes.

Enriching Co-curricular Programme

At JIS, nurturing our students' talents and interests is important to us. We offer a strong co-curricular programme with almost 300 activities to choose from, including a wide range of sports and arts activities, the International Award (DoE) programme and the Model United Nations club. Encouraging engagement in co-curricular activities goes far beyond the confines of our campus. Our students are provided with enriching opportunities to participate in a range of local and international events, including FOBISIA competitions, UK Maths and Science Olympiads, Dive club, Music competitions across Asia. These all offer invaluable opportunities which will shape our students into well-rounded compassionate global citizens ready to inspire positive change and for success after JIS.

Vietnam

International School Ho Chi Minh City (ISHCMC)

28 Vo Truong Toan St., An Phu ward, Thu Duc City, Ho Chi Minh City, Vietnam
Tel: +84 28 3898 9100
Email: admissions@ishcmc.edu.vn
Website: www.ishcmc.com
Head of School: Mr. Marco Longmore
School type: Co-educational Day
Age range of pupils: 2–18 years

No. of pupils enrolled as at 01/09/2025: 1500
Fees as at 01/09/2025:
Early Years Tuition
VND 279,000,000-681,900,000
Primary Tuition
VND 681,900,000-747,100,000
Secondary Tuition
VND 849,400,000-959,000,000

At the International School Ho Chi Minh City (ISHCMC), we believe in nurturing the potential within every student. As HCMC's first IB continuum international school, ISHCMC boasts a proud 30-year legacy of academic excellence and student success. Our vibrant, diverse community, comprising over 60 nationalities, provides a holistic education empowering confident, compassionate, globally-minded individuals.

ISHCMC is the trusted choice for parents, drawn by our unwavering commitment to academic excellence, personalized learning, a culture of care, and rich opportunities. Our students consistently achieve outstanding academic results. 100% of graduates secure university offers in 2024 and 2025, with 98% getting offers from their top-choice universities. Our alumni gain admission to 7 of the top 10 QS ranked universities worldwide, including Harvard, Oxford, Yale, and more. In 2025, our students secured an impressive 1,187 offers from 22 countries and scholarships worth over 56M USD, celebrating their well-rounded accomplishments and readiness for the world.

Our dedicated team of over 170 teachers from 33 countries provides personalized holistic education. We offer multiple academic pathways, including the full IB Diploma, selected IB courses, or the ISHCMC High School Diploma, with tailored future pathway counseling. Our comprehensive Learning Support team ensures every student thrives, while our POSISH framework cultivates resilience, empathy, and integrity.

Education extends beyond the classroom with over 95 after-school activities, supported by state-of-the-art facilities like three gymnasiums and two heated 25-meter swimming pools. Our students excel in sports (760+ participants in SISAC) and the arts (ISHCMC Performing Arts Academy with 26+ programs and 24 teachers). We are also proud members of the Cognita global network, connecting us to 100+ schools across 17 countries, enriching learning with international perspectives.

We invite you to contact us today to explore how ISHCMC's renowned academic excellence can empower your child for a truly successful future.

Léman International School Chengdu

No. 1080 Da'an Road, Zheng Xing County, Tianfu New Area, Chengdu, Sichuan, 610218 China
Tel: +86 28 6703 8650
Email: admissions@lis-chengdu.com
Website: www.lis-chengdu.com
Principal: Tracy Connor
Head of Secondary: Paul Highdale
Head of Primary: Robert Dolan
School type: Co-educational Day
Age range of pupils: 2–18 years
No. of pupils enrolled as at 01/09/2025: 400
Fees as at 01/09/2025:
Day: RMB171,500.00–RMB279,500.00 per annum

Léman International School Chengdu (LIS) welcomes students from Pre-nursery to Year 13 on its 50-acre campus.

The Primary School follows the English National Curriculum for Maths, English, Computing, and PE, integrated with the International Primary Curriculum (IPC), used in over 1,000 schools worldwide. Secondary School (Years 7–11) follows the International Baccalaureate Middle Years Programme, with Year 12 and 13 following the International Baccalaureate Diploma Programme. LIS offers foreign languages including Mandarin and French. Korean and German are also offered to its native speakers.

LIS' extensive campus features modern classrooms, labs, art and music studios, IT rooms, maker spaces, a gym, a 25-meter indoor swimming pool, and outdoor sports facilities including two full-size football pitches, supporting rich extracurricular, sports, and arts programs.

We are proud that 3 out of 4 of our graduates gain admission to top 100 universities worldwide (QS ranking), including prestigious institutions such as Oxford, Johns Hopkins, The University of Hong Kong, UCL, Imperial College London, University of Toronto, Korea University, and Yonsei University. LIS holds full accreditation from the Council of International Schools (CIS), the New England Association of Schools and Colleges (NEASC), and the Council of British International Schools (COBIS), and is a proud member of the Association of China and Mongolia International Schools (ACAMIS).

As part of the global Nord Anglia Education family, LIS benefits from unique collaborations and global opportunities. We work closely with leading institutions like The Juilliard School in performing arts, MIT in higher education, and IMG Academy in sports education. Our partnership with UNICEF also helps raise students' social awareness and encourages a deeper care for the world and its people. Our innovative Global Campus platform connects over 90,000 Nord Anglia students worldwide, while the Nord Anglia University platform supports exceptional professional development for our staff.

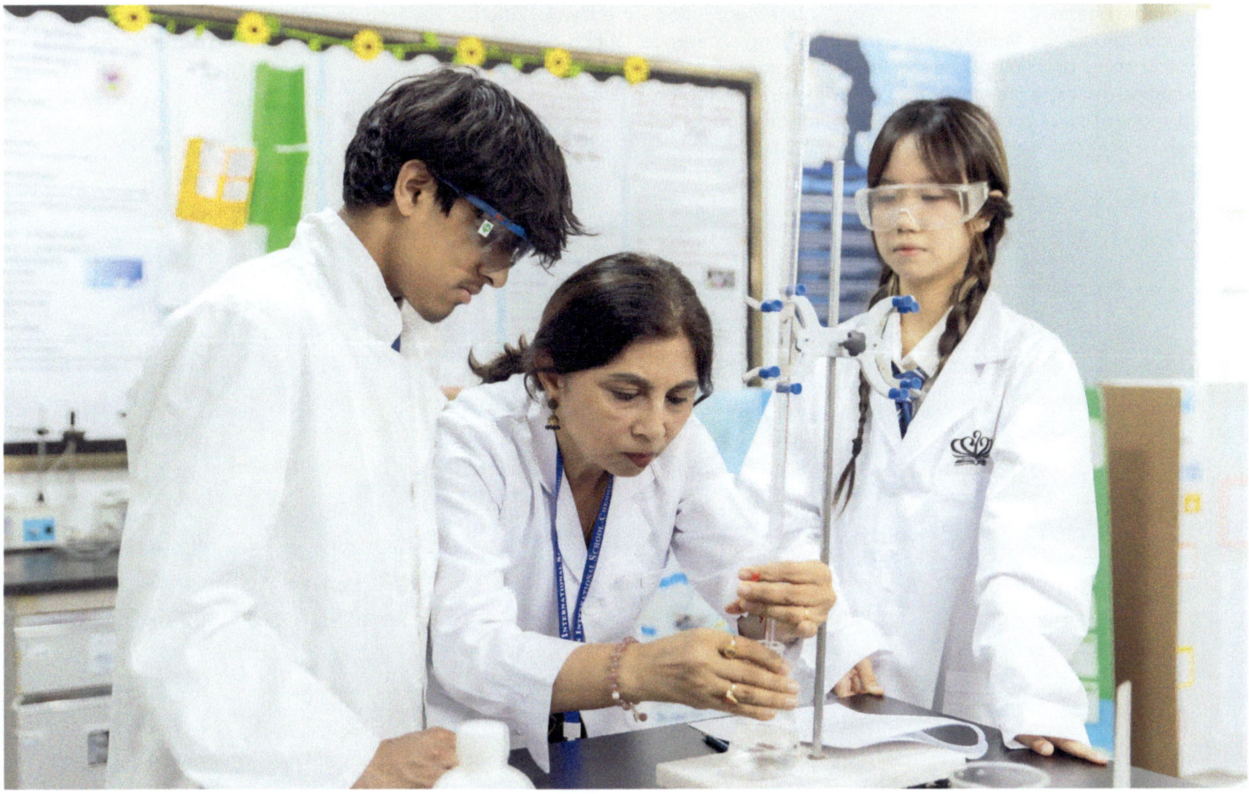

Malaysia

Marlborough College Malaysia

(Founded 2012)

Jalan Marlborough, 79200 Iskandar Puteri, Johor, Malaysia
Tel: +60 7 560 2200
Email: admissions@marlboroughcollege.my
Website: www.marlboroughcollegemalaysia.org
The Master: Mr Simon Burbury
School type: Co-educational Day & Boarding

Age range of pupils: 3–18 years (boarding from 9)
No. of pupils enrolled as at 01/09/2025: 1000
Fees as at 01/09/2025:
Day: RM60,000–RM159,000 per annum
Day Boarding: RM170,700–RM218,400 per annum
Full Boarding: RM195,900–RM247,800 per annum

Established in 2012 as a natural extension of one of the world's finest co-educational independent schools, Marlborough College Malaysia is a not-for-profit institution that provides a contemporary, challenging and enriching education, preparing pupils for a global future.

Recipient of the prestigious International School of the Year 2024 from the UK's Times Educational Supplement (TES), and more recently named International School of the Year by the Boarding Schools' Association (BSA), Marlborough College Malaysia is a leading co-educational, international school for boarding and day pupils aged 3 to 18 years, nestled in 92 acres of stunning Malaysian countryside just 15 minutes from the Singapore border.

Marlborough College Malaysia is a happy, flourishing, and vibrant community where friendships for life are made. Indeed, many of our pupils take the opportunity to develop independence and inter-reliance within the security and care of our outstanding boarding community. The space, facilities but above all, the community of a British international boarding school allows pupils to develop their talents and independence while still being close enough to maintain family bonds.

Guided by our principles of compassion, companionship and conversation, we want our pupils to be the best they can be, and we encourage them to embrace challenges with a sense of independence and determination. With our shared DNA and close links with Marlborough College, we value and instil a breadth of experience, intellectual curiosity, creative joy and sporting excellence. Our co-curricular programme is, quite possibly, second to none in the region, offering a staggering range of opportunities in sports, arts, service, and leadership.

In the Pre-Prep and Prep Schools (3–13 years), the curriculum is enriched and influenced by the international nature of our school, our pupils and our physical and cultural surroundings to include lessons such as Forest School, Ballet, Swimming, Mandarin and Drama.

In the Senior School (13–18 years) pupils prepare for IGCSEs, followed by the two year International Baccalaureate Diploma (IBDP). A rich co-curriculum, including societies, lectures, educational visits, debates, and concerts, ensures pupils experience more than academics, fostering well-rounded individuals. The timetable is designed with flexibility to fully integrate co-curricular activities such as sports, outreach, and other enriching experiences.

Thailand

NIST International School

(Founded 1992)

36 Sukhumvit Soi 15, Wattana, Bangkok, 10110 Thailand
Tel: +66 2 017 5888
Email: admissions@nist.ac.th
Website: www.nist.ac.th
Head of School: Dr James Dalziel
School type: Co-educational Day

Age range of pupils: 3–18 years
No. of pupils enrolled as at 01/09/2025: 1830
Fees as at 01/09/2025:
THB628,200–THB1,094,500 per annum
Average class size: 18-24
Teacher/pupil ratio: 1:12

NIST International School is a not-for-profit, full IB World School located in the heart of Bangkok's Sukhumvit district. Established in 1992 through efforts by United Nations families, NIST is widely regarded as one of Asia's leading international schools, offering a globally recognised IB education for students aged 3 to 18.

As a full IB World School, NIST delivers the complete International Baccalaureate continuum: the Primary Years Programme (PYP), Middle Years Programme (MYP), and Diploma Programme (DP). NIST students consistently achieve outstanding results in the IB Diploma Programme, with graduates accepted to leading universities around the world. More importantly, they leave NIST as principled, reflective individuals with the skills, mindset, and compassion to lead positive change – wherever life takes them.

With a student body representing over 77 nationalities, the school fosters a vibrant, inclusive community grounded in intercultural understanding and global citizenship. Language learning plays a vital role in supporting cultural identity and communication. NIST offers one of the most comprehensive World Languages programmes in Thailand, with over twelve home languages taught during the school day and additional languages offered after school. This commitment to multilingualism strengthens the school's focus on global awareness and personal identity.

At NIST, education is holistic by design. Learning extends beyond academics to include five interconnected elements: academics, service, wellbeing, activities, and expeditions. This unique model ensures that every student is nurtured intellectually, socially, and emotionally. Service is at the heart of this approach, developed through age-appropriate, intentional opportunities that build a mindset of empathy, action, and responsibility. Students are encouraged to think critically about the world around them, form meaningful connections, and take purposeful action to create a positive impact in their communities. Whether through sport, the arts, leadership, or experiential learning, students explore their interests, develop confidence, and build the skills to thrive in a dynamic world.

NIST is also a founding member of the Global Citizen Diploma (GCD), an innovative credential that recognises learning that takes place beyond the classroom. Through the GCD, students reflect deeply on their experiences and values, demonstrating their growth, purpose, and contributions to their communities. This complements the academic rigour of the IB and reinforces NIST's mission to inspire, empower, and enrich.

As a not-for-profit institution, every resource at NIST is reinvested directly into enhancing its programmes, professional development, and state-of-the-art facilities. The school is governed by the NIST International School Foundation, whose Board of Directors is elected by parents, ensuring strong community involvement and long-term sustainability.

NIST holds triple accreditation through the Council of International Schools (CIS), the New England Association of Schools and Colleges (NEASC), and Thailand's Office for National Education Standards and Quality Assessment (ONESQA) – a testament to its commitment to high standards and continuous improvement.

Through a future-ready learning experience and a deep commitment to values, NIST empowers students to thrive – not just in school, but throughout life.

Hong Kong, China

Nord Anglia International School, Hong Kong

(Founded 2014)
Pre-School Campus, 285 Hong Kin Road, Tui Min Hoi, Sai Kung, New Territories, Hong Kong, SAR, China
Primary Campus, 11 On Tin Street, Lam Tin, Kowloon, Hong Kong, SAR, China

Secondary Campus, 19 Yuet Wah Street, Kwun Tong, Kowloon, Hong Kong, SAR, China
Tel: +852 3958 1428
Email: admissions@nais.hk
Website: www.nais.hk
Principal: Mr Tim Richardson
School type: Co-educational Day
Age range of pupils: 3–18 years

Fees as at 01/09/2025:
Pre-school: HK$90,067–HK$189,020 per annum
Primary: HK$189,020 per annum
Secondary (Year 7–11): HK$211,441 per annum
Secondary (Year 12–13): HK$213,517 per annum
Teacher/pupil ratio: Nursery: 1:7, Reception 1:10, Primary/Secondary: 1:12

As a parent, you want the best for your child. So do we. That's why we enrich your child's learning experience with opportunities beyond traditional education and collaborate with world-leading organisations.

At Nord Anglia International School Hong Kong (NAISHK) we promise to support your child to be their very best and achieve more than they ever thought possible. We provide more than just teaching. We take education beyond the classroom to transform and enrich learning, enabling students to be ambitious and inspired to do more. Every child is unique, and by individually tailoring our approach to your child's education, we ensure that they will be confident and ready to take on any challenge that they may encounter in our ever-changing world.

NAISHK is part of a global family of over 80 premium international schools located in more than 30 countries across the world. Nord Anglia Education (NAE) teachers and school staff look after more than 80,000 students globally. Our global scale enables us to recruit and retain the best teachers in the world. The school's unique Global Campus allows students to connect with pupils from NAE's schools around the world through virtual learning and exchanges.

Nord Anglia holds exclusive collaborations with two of the world's most prestigious organisations, The Juilliard School – giving students a unique opportunity to learn about music through iconic works and regular connections with musicians; and the Massachusetts Institute of Technology (MIT) – bringing a new approach to learning the interdisciplinary subjects of Science, Technology, Engineering, Arts and Mathematics (STEAM). Groups of students visit MIT every year to meet leading researchers and take part in activities such as bio-engineering, coding and robotics. Furthermore, Nord Anglia's partnership with UNICEF enables students to take a leading role in the global discussion about key issues affecting our world.

NAISHK offers an all-round through-train education for students aged 3–18, with specialist teachers in Art, Music, Drama, PE and Mandarin from the very start of a child's educational journey. With a focus on individualised learning, teachers ensure that all students have a creative and transformational learning experience.

We are ambitious for our students, believing there is no limit to what they can achieve – our approach supports and nurtures every child to succeed academically, socially and personally,

Hong Kong, China

helping them go beyond what they thought possible. We encourage every student to love learning, to try something new, and, above all, to be ambitious.

All three campuses feature top-class facilities, including large multi-purpose indoor and outdoor spaces, outdoor play areas, library, and specialist music and art rooms. The Pre-school campus features specially-designed child-friendly furniture, purpose-built learning and play spaces, and amazing sea view of Sai Kung – sure to inspire learning and a love for nature.

Curriculum:
Early Years Foundation Stage framework, English National Curriculum, IGCSEs, IB Diploma Programme

Transport:
Comprehensive bus service available

Facilities (vary according to campus):
Multi-purpose hall, sports hall, performance hall, fitness suite, 25m swimming pool, large outdoor play areas, climbing walls, libraries, learning centre, drama and dance studios, Maker Space, space lab, science labs, music and art rooms, multi-media room, cafeteria.

Thailand

Regents International School Pattaya

(Founded 1994)

33/3 Moo 1, Pong, Banglamung, Chonburi, 20150 Thailand
Tel: +66 (0)93 135 7736
Email: admissions@regents-pattaya.co.th
Website: regents-pattaya.co.th
Principal: Ms. Amos Turner-Wardell

School type: Co-educational Day & Boarding
Age range of pupils: 2–18 years
No. of pupils enrolled as at 01/09/2025: 1210
Fees as at 01/09/2025:
THB459,000–THB873,000 per annum
Average class size at July 2025: 20

About Regents International School Pattaya - A Day and Boarding School

Regents is part of the Nord Anglia Education family, the world's leading premium schools' organization, with campuses located across 30+ countries in the Americas, Europe, China, India, Southeast Asia, and the Middle East. Together, our 80+ premium schools educate more than 80,000 students from kindergarten through to the end of secondary/high school.

At Regents International School Pattaya, we understand every student is different. We also know that your child will achieve more when they're happy and doing what they love. That's why we offer an unrivalled choice of subjects, two distinct pathways at sixth form, and a breadth of experiential adventures beyond the classroom. Combined with our award-winning wellbeing support, your child will benefit from a holistic education that takes them wherever they want to go in life – including their first-choice university.

Your child will love learning in our inclusive school community, where every student is empowered to create their own future. Their journey to success starts with our carefully considered blend of British and international curricula. We're one of the few schools in Thailand to offer a choice between A-levels and the International Baccalaureate Diploma Programme (IBDP) at 16. Your child will choose from the widest range of subject options in the region, too, as they create a personalised study programme that embraces their talents, passions, and future ambitions.

Behind every outstanding learning experience is an inspirational teacher, which is why we only recruit the most passionate, talented people. All our teachers are UK or internationally qualified. And at Secondary, each teacher is a genuine specialist in their subject field.

With an average of 13 years' experience in the classroom, our educators are adept at tailoring learning to different needs and preferences, as well as empowering students to take ownership of their entire educational experience. This not only improves academic performance, but also helps our students to think collaboratively, grow in confidence, and identify areas of interest and expertise.

We also make sure that learning is accessible to everyone. Our dedicated English as an Additional Language (EAL) team and expert learning support staff provide bespoke programmes of assistance to students who need specialist help.

For 30 years, this tailored approach has seen our students achieve remarkable exam results, which are consistently above the global average.

We are also a Boarding school and for our boarders, Regents is far more than a school - it's also a second home. Our safe and happy boarding environment is a place where each child gets the care, support, and attention they need to thrive. It's also a place where friendships, academic support, and exciting learning experiences happen every day.

At Regents International School Pattaya, we offer a range of boarding options for 8 to 18-year-olds. Our secure gated campus has 24/7 security, as well as modern dormitories, common areas, and access to all our facilities.

Qatar

SEK International School Qatar

(Founded 2013)

Onaiza 65, Doha, Qatar
Tel: +974 4012 7633
Email: info@sek.qa
Website: www.sek.qa

Head of School: Dr. Maripaz Augilera
School type: Co-educational Day
Age range of pupils: 3–18 years

SEK International School Qatar was founded in 2013 within the framework of the Outstanding Schools Programme of the Ministry of Education and Higher Education of the State of Qatar. The school today caters for students from over 60 nationalities. The teaching staff represents more than 25 different nationalities.

The school is an innovative coeducational, international and multilingual school in Qatar, with a cutting-edge learning campus located in the sophisticated West Bay district of Doha. English is the language of instruction, and the school also offers Spanish and Arabic courses for all students. Technology is embedded across the curriculum, supported by their staff as Microsoft Innovative Educators and a Bring your Own Laptop programme form Grade 4.

SEK-Qatar is an IB World School authorized to offer the IB Primary Years Programme (PYP), the Middle Years Programme (MYP) and the Diploma Programme (DP), from pre-school to grade 12. The IB offers high-quality and challenging educational programmes, with a reputation for their high academic standards. SEK-Qatar is also proud to be an accredited school by New England Association of Schools and Colleges (NEASC), one of the most prestigious international university and school accreditation agencies. It indicates that the school meets high standards of institutional quality through ongoing, independent, and objective process of peer-review.

Established in 1892, SEK International Schools are places where innovation and pedagogical leadership are combined with 120 years of tradition and history to offer educational programmes. The SEK Group has launched over a hundred pioneering initiatives introducing innovations such as the classrooms without walls, the SEKMUN Model United Nations and the International Baccalaureate Organisation programmes.

SEK-Qatar has a unique educational model, committed to offering quality education that promotes individualisation, places emphasis on learning rather than teaching, and fosters activity and effort, freedom, interaction and teamwork as well as transformational learning. Technology, sports, artistic and social activities also play a major role in the SEK educational model. The ultimate goal is for students to acquire skills, knowledge and understanding to become active citizens, committed and determined to build a better world.

SEK-Qatar has the infrastructure, digital devices and skilled staff to enable the delivery of online or blended learning depending on changing external scenarios, to which we are able to respond in a flexible and agile manner.

SEK International School Riyadh

(Founded 2021)

Al Toq Street, Ar Rabi, Riyadh, 13315 Saudi Arabia
Tel: +966 011 520 6170
Email: info@sek.sa

Website: www.sek.sa
Head of School: Ms. Sandra Ospina
School type: Co-educational Day
Age range of pupils: 2–15 years

SEK International School Riyadh opened its doors in September 2021, thereby establishing in the Middle East, the second international school from the prestigious SEK Education Group, which has 130 years of history and experience in national and international education in five countries.

SEK-Riyadh builds on the experience and legacy of our innovative group of schools. SEK Education Group has excelled in providing an outstanding international Education to the local and international communities in Spain, France, Ireland and Qatar, as will the new member of the group – SEK-Riyadh in Saudi Arabia.

We are a community of learners, working together to prepare young people for the challenges of tomorrow through a broad and engaging curriculum, effective use of learning technologies; an individualised programme to cover the educational needs of each student and challenging our students to think critically and independently. Our dedicated International and multicultural team of well trained teachers and support staff are highly motivated and engaged in helping each of our students reach their full potential.

The core of the SEK profile is to prepare our students to be capable of guiding their own futures and to becoming lifelong learners. To demonstrate our commitment towards this ambitious goal, SEK International School Riyadh is already an authorized IB Primary Years Programme (PYP) and Middle Years Programme (MYP) school, and a candidate school for the IB Diploma Programme (DP).

SEK-Riyadh has also started the process of International accreditation with the New England Association of Schools and Colleges (NEASC), to ensure we meet demanding international standards of education. NEASC accreditation is a highly valued globally recognized standard of excellence; we will be part of their network of over 2,000 schools, technical and career institutions, colleges and universities in New England and International schools spanning more than 65 countries.

Shanghai Community International School

(Founded 1996)

1161 Hongqiao Road, Shanghai, 200051 China
Tel: +86 21 6261 4338
Email: admissions@scis-china.org
Website: www.scis-china.org
Director of Schools: Daniel Eschtruth
Appointed: 2016

School type: Co-educational Day
Age range of pupils: 2–18 years
No. of pupils enrolled as at 01/09/2025: 1550
Fees as at 01/09/2025:
Day: RMB146,000–RMB324,500 per annum
Average class size: 20
Teacher/pupil ratio: 1:20

Established in 1996 as one of Shanghai's first international schools, Shanghai Community International School (SCIS) is a non-profit educational day school, governed by a self-perpetuating board of directors and overseen by the International Schools Foundation.

With over twenty years of rich tradition, SCIS offers a truly unique international experience. The SCIS community is unparalleled, consisting of a diverse mix of outstanding teachers, students, and parents representing over sixty nationalities and thirty-five languages, across six continents. SCIS leverages this unique community to provide a personalized approach to holistic education, ensuring all students have the opportunity to be successful.

SCIS is one of the first international schools in Shanghai to become fully authorized as an International Baccalaureate (IB) Continuum World School, a world class academic program aimed at rigorous critical thinking and global citizenship. This accreditation extends across all SCIS Campuses, including Hongqiao and Pudong, providing a seamless program for students aged 2–18, and comprised of the Primary Years Programme (PYP), Middle Years Programme (MYP), and Diploma Programme (DP).

Primary Years Programme (PYP) prepares students to become active, caring, lifelong learners who demonstrate respect for themselves and others and have the capacity to participate in the world around them. It focuses on the development of the whole child as an inquirer, both within and beyond the classroom. (Age 2–10)

Middle Years Programme (MYP) is a challenging framework that encourages students to make practical connections between their studies and the real world. The MYP is a five-year programme, which can be implemented in a partnership between schools. Students who complete the MYP are well-prepared to undertake the IB Diploma Programme (DP). (Age 11–15)

Diploma Programme (DP) is designed as an academically challenging and balanced program of education with final examinations that prepares students for success at university and life beyond. (Age 16–17).

India

Stonehill International School

(Founded 2008)

Near the International Airport, No.259/333/334/335, Tarahunise Post, Jala Hobli, Bengaluru, Karnataka, 562157 India
Tel: +91 80 4341 8300
Email: admissions@stonehill.in
Website: www.stonehill.in
Head of School: Joe Lumsden
Primary School Principal: Peter Spratling
Secondary School Principal: Manpreet Kaur

School type: Co-educational Day & Boarding
Religious Denomination: No religious affiliation
Age range of pupils: 3–18 years
No. of pupils enrolled as at 01/09/2025: 750
Average class size: 18
Teacher/pupil ratio: 1:7

Founded in 2008, Stonehill International School is one of the most widely reputed international schools in India today. We are an IB school and are accredited by the Council of International Schools (CIS), and the New England Association of Schools and Colleges (NEASC). Stonehill is also a member of the Australian Boarding Schools Association (ABSA). The expansive 34-acre lush green campus, near the International Airport, offers ample space and infrastructure for sporting, cultural, and leisure activities. Besides state-of-the-art classrooms, the world-class facilities include a 25-metre temperature-controlled swimming pool, synthetic turf football field, tennis and volleyball courts, dedicated buildings for the arts and STEM subjects, a state-of-the-art library, and a multi-purpose sports hall. Stonehill also prides itself on modern boarding houses and a fully equipped cafeteria that serves nutritious and healthy meals.

As a world-class educational institution, Stonehill is a dynamic, inclusive, and friendly day and boarding school. Our students and faculty comprise 35 different nationalities. We are dedicated to our mission statement – "To provide stimulating, engaging academics integrated with enhanced opportunities for technological innovation, sports, and the arts."

University Placement Programme
Our Career and College Counselling Department works with students from Grade 9 onwards to identify their aptitude, understand their interests, and guide them towards colleges that will help them meet their academic and personal goals. Stonehill graduates have been accepted to some of the most prestigious universities across the globe including, Carnegie Mellon University, London School of Economics, UC Berkeley, University of California, Los Angeles (UCLA), University of Toronto, University of St. Andrews, Imperial College London, Kings College London, University College London (UCL), University of Cambridge, National University of Singapore (NUS), Nanyang Technological University (NTU), University of Amsterdam, Stanford University, Massachusetts Institute of Technology (MIT), Dartmouth College, New York University (NYU), University of Melbourne, University of Michigan Ann Arbor, University of British Columbia, and many more.

English as an additional language (EAL)
Stonehill offers support to non-native English-speaking students. Individual

programmes are developed to enable English language acquisition in students.

Sports
Through our sports programme, importance is given to not just students' health and fitness, but also to develop skills, learning to work in teams and building leadership and personal growth. Stonehill students also compete regularly with teams from other schools in Bangalore, India, and Asia. Our students have made us proud by demonstrating commitment, great attitude and the spirit of teamwork. Swimming, tennis, equestrian sports, basketball, football, volleyball, and cricket are just a few of our sports offerings.

The Arts
Stonehill prides itself on a committed Arts department with a special focus on Visual Art, Drama, and Music. Stonehill uses the creative arts to promote attitudes such as empathy and appreciation, and skills such as analysis, that help see the uniqueness of each person as well as explore the commonalities that connect each other. We have a dedicated Arts Centre, that has purpose-built spaces for music, visual art, and drama. We also offer private music lessons for instruments such as piano, guitar, drums, violin and cello along with numerous opportunities to perform at concerts, assemblies and other gatherings.

Technology
At Stonehill, we have a 1:1 policy for devices and our students use a wide variety of tools to communicate, collaborate, research, and create.

In Primary School, the digital citizenship programme teaches students to be safe and responsible in the online world. They use an all-in-one digital platform for planning, assessments, portfolios, projects, and reports, which they can independently navigate. Learning is supported through the Makerspace where digitally enhanced Lego and robotics work alongside the traditional elements of design, sewing, and construction.

Technology in Secondary School is seamlessly integrated into all subjects. Additionally, Product Design, Digital Design, Design & Technology, and Computer Science are offered as subjects.

Boarding
Stonehill offers weekly and full-time boarding options to students. The residential programme at Stonehill is for students from Grade 6 onwards, and is designed to extend learning the IB way through academics, extracurricular

activities, and the social aspects of boarding. It offers students a home away from home, with spacious and comfortable living areas, and access to a host of extracurricular activities. The small number of boarding students provides a warm atmosphere and creates a sense of community. The boarding houses at Stonehill feature twin and quad-sharing rooms, a common lounge, and a study room. The houses are supported by a cafeteria, a fitness centre, and a 24-hour medical centre. Experienced House Parents, tutors, and service staff take care of children and their individual needs.

China

Shenzhen College of International Education

(Founded 2003)

No. 3, Sixth Antuoshan Road, Futian District, Shenzhen, Guangdong, China
Tel: +86 755 8349 5025
Email: info@scie.com.cn
Website: www.scie.com.cn
Headteacher: Neil Mobsby
Appointed: July 2018

School type: Co-educational Day & Boarding
Age range of pupils: 14–18 years
No. of pupils enrolled as at 01/09/2025: 1800+
Fees as at 01/09/2025:
Fees: RMB273,000 (regular stream) – RMB303,000 (Arts Academy) per annum

Founded in 2003, Shenzhen College of International Education (SCIE) was the first high school to offer an international curriculum in Shenzhen, China. It delivers (I)GCSE, AS, AL and AP courses to both day and boarding students who have undergone a rigorous and highly selective admissions process. In 2024, the Year 10 acceptance rate was 15%.

SCIE students are well-rounded, compassionate and highly-driven. They learn and thrive in an international and challenging environment, developing social responsibility, creativity, independence and enthusiasm during their four years at the College. Academically, their passion for learning, commitment and resilience have brought them the highest accolades in external examinations. In the Cambridge Assessment International Education IGCSE, AS and AL summer exams 2024, 35 SCIE students received 'Top in the World', 12 'Top in China' and 4 students received 'High Achievement'. In total, 51 students from SCIE received Outstanding Cambridge Learner Awards, accounting for one-fifth of the total awardees nationwide (265 individuals), outperforming all other CAIE schools in China. Over the 17 years, SCIE students have won 177 global firsts and 207 Chinese firsts in individual subjects and overall scores, and the total number of awards has reached 430.

Beyond the classroom, SCIE students have equally impressive achievements, especially in competitive events that challenge them to contribute to the wider community. In 2024, SCIE students achieved remarkable success in several prestigious international mathematics competitions. In the British Mathematical Olympiad BMO Round 1, the student earned a Global Gold Medal and a Global Bronze Medal, with 89 students advancing to Round 2. In the AMC 10/12, 49 students made the Honor Roll of Distinction, and 349 students qualified for the AIME. In the UKMT-SMC, 11 students won the Global Gold Medal, and 80 students received the same honor. Furthermore, our students have demonstrated their diverse talents in other academic fields such as chemistry and physics, securing numerous global awards in Olympiad competitions. Our iGEM team also delivered an outstanding performance, earning a top global award and recognition in specific categories. In addition to academics, SCIE students showcased exceptional skills and determination in both international and domestic sports events in Malaysia, Thailand, and Hainan, China. They achieved outstanding results in football, volleyball, basketball, and badminton, truly reflecting the breadth of interests and excellence of SCIE students across different fields and their continuous pursuit of excellence.

SCIE graduates attend leading universities in the world. With 41 Oxbridge offers this year, the College has maintained its position as the school in China with the highest number of Oxbridge offers for 20 consecutive years. Along with top US university offers including from Ivy League, SCIE celebrates another exceptional cohort that will join the alumni network: one that has been contributing to our world in both arts and sciences.

Singapore

Tanglin Trust School in Singapore

(Founded 1925)
95 Portsdown Road, 139299 Singapore
Tel: +65 67780771

Email: admissions@tts.edu.sg
Website: www.tts.edu.sg
CEO: Mr Craig Considine BA MA
School type: Co-educational Day
Age range of pupils: 3–18 years
No. of pupils enrolled as at 01/09/2025: approx. 2800
Fees as at 01/09/2025:
Infant School (Nursery – Year 2):
S$34,770–S$43,530 per annum
Junior School (Year 3 – 6):
S$45,570 per annum
Middle School (Year 7 – 9):
S$51,375 per annum
Upper School (Year 10 – 11):
S$53,760 per annum
Sixth Form (Year 12 – 13):
S$55,734 per annum
Average class size: Nursery: 20, Infants: 24, Junior School: 24, Sixth Form: 15

Established in 1925, Tanglin Trust School is the oldest British international school in Southeast Asia. The school provides the English National Curriculum with an international perspective to children from 3 to 18 years in Singapore.

Tanglin is a vibrant co-educational school of around 2,800 students representing over 50 nationalities and provides a unique learning environment for children from Nursery right through to Sixth Form. As a not-for-profit school, tuition fees are devoted to the provision of an outstanding education.

As the only school in Singapore to offer dual pathways of A Levels or the IB Diploma in Sixth Form, all of Tanglin's Sixth Formers study a programme that is tailored both to the subjects they are passionate about and to the style of learning that most suits them, ensuring they thrive and flourish.

Tanglin has an excellent academic reputation. Students' examination results consistently surpass Singapore and global averages, with around 96% of graduates typically receiving their first or second choice university, which are among the best in the world.

Tanglin is inspected within the British Schools Overseas (BSO) framework, recognised by Ofsted. All three schools have been awarded 'Outstanding', the highest possible grade in their latest inspections (2017, 2018, 2019 and 2022).

The Centenary Building which opened in 2023 is an inspirational addition to the campus. The building houses an olympic-standard gymnastics centre, an athletic development gym and physio hub, a 50m competition-standard swimming pool, and a 15m climbing wall. The building also houses the Music Department which stretches over two floors of the Centenary Building. Tanglin also offers the Centenary Music Scholarship. This academic award is an embodiment of the school's vision to nurture and inspire every individual to be the best they can be.

Located on the top floor is The Institute, a forum that provides thought leadership and encourages discourse to inspire, challenge and ultimately prepare its students for the future. The Institute also facilitates industry-led workshops as well as an entrepreneurship programme, both of which provide students with real-world experience and insights.

As part of its Centenary Celebrations in 2025, Tanglin has introduced the Highlands Programme. Described by Craig Considine as 'innovation in education' it will provide a 5–week experiential learning programme for Year 9 students located at the new 15–acre Tanglin Gippsland campus in Australia.

Tanglin has a thriving and energetic arts programme which plays an important part in school life. Students develop their skills in art, design, drama, music, and film-making, facilitating creative, social and intellectual development and the recent opening of the new Junior Arts Centre marks another exciting creative chapter for Tanglin. Throughout the year, there are many opportunities for students to participate in high-quality ensembles, recitals, performances and exhibitions.

Tanglin students are also encouraged to contribute actively to the local community, support service projects and participate in a wide variety of extra-curricular pursuits that stimulate and broaden student experience. These include 80 outdoor education trips, the International Duke of Edinburgh (DofE) Award, and the Creativity, Activity, Service (CAS) programme. Overall Tanglin is committed to providing a holistic education and its mission is to be the best school in the world with a dynamic learning community that nurtures and inspires every individual to be the best they can be.

What the students and alumni say
'At Tanglin, the dedication of the teachers to their students' success is unparalleled. There is an unwavering commitment to providing not just education, but also genuine care and guidance.'

China

The British School of Beijing, Sanlitun

THE BRITISH SCHOOL OF BEIJING, SANLITUN
A NORD ANGLIA EDUCATION SCHOOL

5 Xiliujie, Sanlitun Road, Chaoyang District, Beijing, 100027 China
Tel: +8610 8532 3088
Email: sltadmissions@bsbsanlitun.com
Website: www.bsbsanlitun.com

Principal: Jo Prabhu
School type: Co-educational Day
Age range of pupils: 1–11
No. of pupils enrolled as at 01/09/2025: 600

The British School of Beijing, Sanlitun is situated in the heart of the Embassy district, in downtown Beijing. It has been offering an education to international students for over 20 years and is part of the reputable Nord Anglia Education family, which has over 80 schools around the world.

With over 60% of teachers from the UK or Ireland, the students receive a truly British education in a very international setting, as the students represent over 50 different nationalities, making it one of the most diverse schools in Beijing.

BSB Sanlitun is a very special school, capturing the essence of a British prep school in a warm, welcoming and nurturing environment, where 91% of families are satisfied with the school overall.

Academic excellence
All children deserve the right to receive a high standard of education, delivered by passionate, experienced and qualified teachers, who differentiate their lessons to ensure all children reach their individual goals, and progress at their own speed.

At BSB Sanlitun our students are taught how to learn – resulting in students having a love of learning which can be attributed throughout their lives.

Providing English language lessons, and support to children with additional needs, means everyone can benefit from this exceptional education – no exception!

Students at the center
Happy, safe, secure and nurtured children thrive at school. At BSB Sanlitun, students are at the heart of every decision. Before any decision is made, we ask 'is it right for our students, how does it benefit our students' – it's back to the drawing board if it does not meet our expectations for our students.

The traditional house system, small classes, excellent teacher to student ratio and support teams ensure that every student matters and every student is known. Students are greeted by name by the Senior Team every morning outside the school, rain or shine!

Beyond the classroom

The Principal and her team have created space, time and resources for students to step out of the classroom – to learn new skills, find their passion and develop their personal skills – becoming independent, curious, resilient and kind individuals as they take part in sport, music, drama, art, academic pursuits, cooking and much more, as well as overnight residential trips for older children in China and internationally.

An environment for growth

BSB Sanlitun exudes warmth and joy. The school is an inviting and inspiring environment that goes far beyond the children. Parents are active, supportive and positive participants in the community. Teachers and staff care – this is not 'just a job'. Together we share the same goals and ambitions.

Developing future global citizens

It is our role to discover students' talents and to nurture and develop them further to ensure they have the skills and attributes to be prepared for the ever-changing world. We support and challenge students to achieve their best.

Progression

When students graduate from BSB Sanlitun they are automatically enrolled at their sister school, in Shunyi, on the outskirts of Beijing and just a short bus ride away. BSB Shunyi continues the British curriculum, as well as IGCSE in Year 10 and IBDP in Year 12.

We offer so many tangible parts to your child's education, but you'll only truly understand what a wonderful school BSB Sanlitun is when you visit us. Meet our students, observe them as they learn, play and grow. Our Admissions team would be delighted to hear from you.

Jordan

The International Academy - Amman

(Founded 2004)

PO Box 144255, King Hussein Parks, Sa'eed Khair Street, Amman, 11814 Jordan
Tel: +962 6550 2055
Email: info@iaa.edu.jo
Website: www.iaa.edu.jo
Director: Dr Hana Kanan
School type: Co-educational Day

Age range of pupils: 3–18 years
No. of pupils enrolled as at 01/09/2025: 1197
Boys: 630 **Girls:** 567
IB Grade 12: 74
Average class size: 22
Teacher/pupil ratio: 1:5 Early Years, 1:10 Primary, 1:18 Secondary

The International Academy - Amman is a place of vision, principle, and aspiration. Dedication to excellence propels it forward and upward, year after year. The four IAA Pillars, Leadership, Duty, Cultural Heritage, and Acceptance, are the basis of a clearly defined mission: to make our Learners of Today, our Leaders of Tomorrow.

IAA is an inclusive, non-profit, noncommercial educational institution offering an acclaimed curriculum at a world-class standard with focus on innovation and technology integration. It is an international, day school existing within a Jordanian context, promoting both global perspective and national heritage. This defining principle is reflected in the diversity of IAA staff, representing more than ten countries around the world and instilling a robust spirit of interculturalism within the school.

Accredited by the Council of International Schools (CIS) and the New England Association of Schools (NEASC), IAA now offers a comprehensive program beginning in Pre-K and culminating with Grade 12.

Most IAA graduates enjoy placement at competitive or top-tier universities throughout the United States, Britain, and Canada.

The IAA curriculum is a rigorous symbiosis of the finest curricula from around the globe, employing modern and holistic educational approaches. At the Primary level, IAA utilises an eclectic program based on the British curriculum for literacy and the Australian curriculum for mathematics. The curriculum is further enhanced by the International Primary Curriculum (IPC) that is used for an integrated approach to learning, covering a range of subjects. The Jordanian Ministry of Education curriculum is used for the Arabic Language. At the Secondary level, IAA is an International Baccalaureate (IB) World School authorised for the Middle Years Programme (MYP) and the IB Diploma Programme (DP). IAA also offers a myriad of extra-curricular activities, and rich opportunities to exercise leadership, athleticism, artistry, oratory, citizenship, and more, providing every student with a chance to explore his/her unique talents.

The sky is the limit at IAA.

For information, please visit www.iaa.edu.jo.

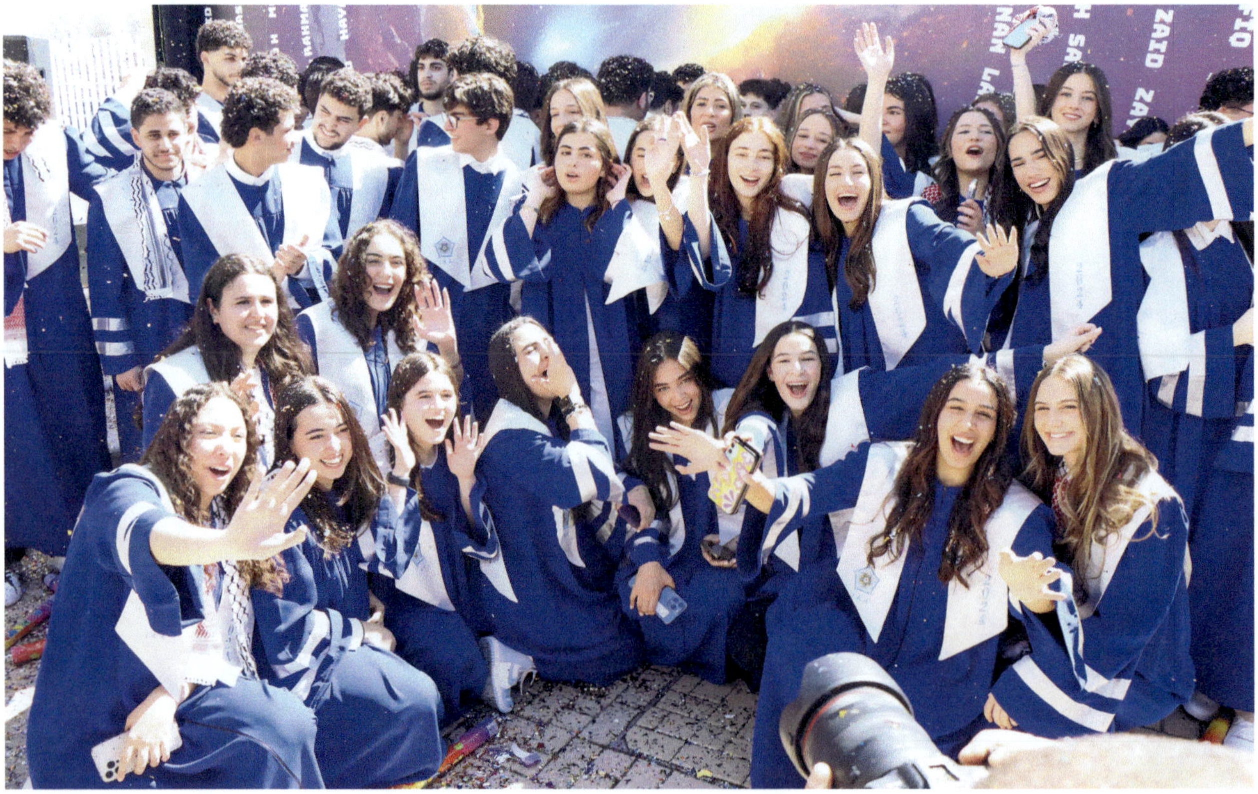

Malaysia

The International School of Kuala Lumpur (ISKL)

(Founded 1965)

No. 2 Lorong Kelab Polo Di Raja, Ampang Hilir, 55000 Kuala Lumpur, Malaysia
Tel: +60 3 4813 5000
Email: admissions@iskl.edu.my
Website: www.iskl.edu.my
Head of School: Mr Rami Madani , MA, BSc

School type: Co-educational Day
Age range of pupils: 3–18 years
No. of pupils enrolled as at 01/09/2025: 1800
Fees as at 01/09/2025:
Day: RM73,670–RM150,520 per annum

The International School of Kuala Lumpur (ISKL) believes that its success today is based on how well it prepares its students for their future. Offering a diverse academic and co-curricular program, ISKL supports learners in exploring and developing the passions, skills, and competencies they need to be future-ready, not only for university and their career but for life itself.

The school is located on a 25-acre, state-of-the-art campus in the heart of Kuala Lumpur and is home to students representing more than 70 nationalities. Students benefit from its robust international curriculum that combines leading North American educational frameworks with global best practices.

ISKL is a fully inclusive school and offers the International Baccalaureate Diploma Programme (IBDP) on a non-selective basis. As the longest-running World IB School in Malaysia, ISKL has seen more than 2,000 students graduate with an IB Diploma over the past 33 years.

ISKL is one of the only schools in Malaysia offering transdisciplinary pathways that are designed to enable every learner to choose a curriculum best suited to their abilities, interests, and aspirations. In addition to the IBDP, High School options include PRAXIS (Grade 9) and ISKL's Pursuits Program combining individual IB, Advanced Placement, and High School courses for students who want to deep-dive into a specific area.

ISKL is accredited internationally through the Council of International Schools (CIS) and in the United States through the Western Association of Schools and Colleges (WASC). ISKL has a strong focus on service and sustainability across its divisions and is a member of the Eco-Schools organization and the Green Schools Alliance.

Thailand

Wellington College International School Bangkok

WELLINGTON COLLEGE
INTERNATIONAL SCHOOL BANGKOK

18 Krungthep Kreetha Road, Saphan Sung District, Bangkok, 10250 Thailand
Tel: +66 2 087 8888
Email: admissions@wellingtoncollege.ac.th
Website: www.wellingtoncollege.ac.th

Master: Mr Christopher Nicholls
School type: Co-educational Day
Age range of pupils: 2–18 years
No. of pupils enrolled as at 01/09/2025: 1100

Wellington College International School Bangkok is part of the prestigious Wellington College Family of Schools, whose founding school was established in England over 160 years ago, receiving a royal charter from Queen Victoria. The school offers its students the chance to develop their zest for life. Our students are hungry to learn, willing to challenge and be challenged and are open to all that being a truly global citizen entails. We take a prestigious academic heritage, and we add something extra.

Situated on 28 acres of beautiful greenery, the campus is one of the finest in Thailand. It boasts individual Junior and Senior School buildings which have been specifically designed in great detail for outstanding learning. The school has numerous lawns, playgrounds and pitches where children can roam, play and compete. There are two swimming pools - one Olympic sized - and a huge Sports Hall where we host other schools in Thailand and internationally. We have a 600-seater theatre, two beautifully designed libraries, our own lagoon and so much more. Visitors often comment that they have never seen a school quite like it.

Our students will leave our school with moral values and social conscience to serve others and to do good. Our students embody 'the five Is'. They are -

- Inspired
- Intellectual
- Independent
- Individual
- Inclusive

Wellington College Bangkok is open to students aged 2 to 18. Children are welcome to join us in Pre-Nursery and stay until Year 13 when they will take A-Levels and move on to the world's best universities. We are absolutely focused on the individual child throughout. We work with parents to share the responsibility of guiding the children to academic, social and personal success. Every child is different, and every child will follow a different path. We find what is best for each child and we develop their passions and nurture their strengths. Whether a child is starting out on their first few phrases in Mandarin or preparing for Under 13 Basketball or taking IGCSE exams, they will be doing so the Wellington Way.

Our founding school has an exceptional academic record and we follow in their footsteps along with the other Wellington Schools globally. We teach the English National Curriculum from Early Years to IGCSE and A Level exams. The programme is enhanced to reflect Thai culture, to ensure an awareness of Thailand, of South East Asia, and of the Asian continent and its place in world history and politics. Our teachers are highly qualified and very experienced both in the UK and globally. They share a passion for teaching and for continuous professional development. They believe that learning is fun and that students should love every moment that they are in the classroom and beyond!

The learning spaces extend way beyond the walls of the classroom. Classrooms are linked to each other and set around collaborative learning and play spaces.

Thailand

The Junior School follows a journey from Pre-Nursery to Year 6 and the progression is marked not just in the change in spaces and the quality of the work on the walls but by the development of the students. They grow in confidence and ability until they are ready to progress to our amazing state-of-the-art Skylight Buildings, home to our Senior School.

Our Early Years have developed a wonderful reputation and a huge popularity in just seven years. We are determined to give our children the very best start on their journey. The teachers and leaders care enormously about the welfare and development of the children as they make those important first steps. We reassure our parents, we keep them abreast of their children's achievements and we work together in every way.

Our Senior School has a beautiful circular atrium around which sit classrooms, shared spaces and collaborative learning areas. The new Crowthorne Building opened in August 2025, showcasing world-class Design Technology, Music, Drama, IT and other classroom provision.

Students also have the chance to take part in every sport they could wish for. Our swimming teams and golf squads are very successful, boasting international level stars in the making. Our football, netball and basketball teams take on schools within Bangkok and across Asia. And children run, jump, play and experiment with each and every game, sport, pastime – because it's fun.

We run scholarship programmes in Academics, Sport and Music allowing the school to offer a first-class education to all. Our scholars inspire each and every student. They make us all proud. But every child here is a star. Every student is a champion. And every single one of us is a Wellingtonian and proud to be one.

Ploen, a Year 10 student sums it up – "*I feel proud of myself, being at Wellington and I really like it here. The teachers are really kind and take time to get to know you. The learning environment is very good and really helps me understand every topic. My school is filled with fun and laughter. I feel so lucky to be here.*"

Lebanon

Wellspring Learning Community

(Founded 2007)

Al Mathaf, Main Street, Near National Museum, PO Box 116-2134, Beirut, Lebanon
Tel: +961 1 423 444
Email: admissions@wellspring.edu.lb
Website: www.wellspring.edu.lb
Head of School: Kathleen Battah

Appointed: September 2010
School type: Co-educational Day
Age range of pupils: 3–19 years
No. of pupils enrolled as at 01/09/2025: 753
Average class size: 18-24
Teacher/pupil ratio: 1:5

Wellspring Learning Community is the First English Language IB Continuum World School in Lebanon and it is the realization of a belief that children of Lebanon deserve to study in a high quality learning environment that opens up space for developing their talents and intellectual potential, as well as their capacity for caring about the world around them.

Wellspring is a non sectarian community with no political affiliations. Depending on availability, enrollment is open throughout the year. Wellspring welcomes inquiries and visits from interested families.

Authorization/Accreditations
Wellspring is authorized for the IB Diploma, Middle Years Programme, and Primary Years Programme, Council of International Schools (CIS), New England Association of Schools and Colleges(NEASC). Wellspring is an IB Continuum World School.

Mission Statement
Wellspring Learning Community aims to establish an inquiry-based learning environment in which students from diverse backgrounds are given every opportunity to optimize their social, emotional and academic capacities and talents. Our students will become confident, resourceful, creative, caring, responsible global and local citizens prepared to use their education to contribute in meaningful ways towards improving society, both locally and internationally.

Teachers
Our 177 faculty members are highly qualified and experienced teachers; many are native English speakers. In addition to being IB trained, many teachers hold additional positions within the IB Educator Network (IBEN).

Students
Wellspring has a large international population, with 46 countries represented across our two campuses, in addition to our local students who come from diverse backgrounds within Lebanon.

Facilities
We are proud to offer two campuses in the vibrant area of Beirut. Both environments are attractive, technologically advanced, and continuously upgraded to keep pace with the demands of the educational program. Facilities include music and art rooms, science labs, computer labs, cafeteria(CCC), libraries, play areas and roof top sports spaces.

Western International School of Shanghai (WISS)

555 Lianmin Road, Xujing Town, Qingpu District, Shanghai, 201702 China
Tel: +86 (21) 6976 6015/6013
Email: enquiry@wiss.cn
Website: www.wiss.cn
Head of School: Jeremy Williams
School type: Co-educational Day

Age range of pupils: 2.5–18 years
No. of pupils enrolled as at 01/09/2025: 500
Fees as at 01/09/2025:
Day: ¥171,500–¥277,000 per annum
Early Bird Rate: ¥162,925–¥263,150 per annum

The Western International School of Shanghai (WISS) stands at the forefront of global education with a legacy of nearly 20 years of excellence. WISS is an IB World School, a member of the Council of International Schools, and is accredited by the Western Association of Schools and Colleges. The first full IB school in Shanghai and the first school in Mainland China to offer all four IB programmes, WISS has always been at the forefront of international education.

WISS takes pride in fostering high-caliber learning that nurtures student growth. Our educational philosophy is built upon four pillars: Academics, Sports, Arts, and Community Service. Education builds skill, character, promotes passion, and sets young people on course to make their dreams come true.

WISS integrates academic rigor with a blend of creative arts and athletics to create a nourishing and vibrant learning community. Home to a culturally rich student body representing dozens of nationalities, WISS offers an engaging international learning environment with a deep respect for China. Our rigorous Chinese programme allows our young people to be fully conversant in Chinese literature and culture.

Located in the New Hongqiao area, WISS has one of Shanghai's most extensive campuses, surrounded by lush greenery and conveniently accessible to the city's major commercial and tourist destinations. Spanning 18 acres, our purpose-built facilities cater to Early Years, Primary, and Secondary School students in a warm and welcoming atmosphere.

Our extensive Co-Curricular Programme features over 60 activities, elite academies, and a host of service projects. WISS provides unparalleled leadership opportunities through partnerships with the Global Alliance for Innovative Learning, the Duke of Edinburgh's International Award, and the Association of China and Mongolia International Schools.

Discover the exceptional journey that awaits at WISS, where students are not just educated but inspired to change our world for the better.

India

Woodstock School

(Founded 1854)

Mussoorie, Uttarakhand, 248179 India
Tel: +91 135 263 9000/+91 135 617 0500
Email: admissions@woodstock.ac.in
Website: www.woodstockschool.in
Principal: Mr Mark Windsor
School type: Co-educational Day & Boarding
Age range of pupils: 11–18 years
No. of pupils enrolled as at 01/09/2025: 500

Fees as at 01/09/2025:
Tuition Fee: INR2,164,000–INR2,404,000 per annum
Establishment Fee: INR475,000 (once off, non-refundable)
Security Deposit: INR450,000 (once off, refundable)
Teacher/pupil ratio: 1:15 (staff/pupil ratio: 1:6)

Woodstock is an accredited, co-educational, residential, international school located in the foothills of the Himalayas.

For 170 years Woodstock School has been transforming the lives of young people from around the world and from all walks of life coming to live and learn together. We are located at 7,000 feet above sea level, spread across a forested 250-acre campus.

Academics
Woodstock School offers the IB MYP (Middle Years Programme) for grades 6–10. For grades 11–12 we have a variety of graduation pathways, including IB DP, the Woodstock Diploma (Standard), and Woodstock Diploma Mastery Track. All students graduating from Woodstock receive a US-high school accredited diploma.

The WSDP-Standard track can be adapted to students' interests, and includes AP classes, DP classes, and electives. The resulting diploma is recognized and respected in the United States can be crafted to meet admission requirements for universities around the world.

The WSDP-Mastery track allows a student to focus in a specific area, for instance, STEM. Students build a program tailored to their goals. A WSDP-Mastery student's transcript will reflect their focus area, and they will receive diplomas stating that they have graduated 'with mastery' in the same.

Residential Life
At Woodstock School learning happens everywhere and not just in the classroom. Residential life hugely influences development, shaping students as they grow into confident individuals and global citizens. Woodstock School's dedicated Dorm Parents guide students as they develop into healthy, responsible, caring individuals.

Enrichment
Enrichment activities include music, drama, outdoor learning, badminton, tennis, basketball, TEDx, entrepreneurship, environmental sustainability, yearbook design, inter-national exposure through the Global Alliance for Innovative Learning, and much more.

"My favorite thing about Woodstock is that the sky is the limit. Do you have a pioneering project in mind? Go ahead. Do you want to plan a trip to take students for adventure sports? Go ahead. The amount of freedom and expression of creativity we get ensures that everyone can find their place here." – Aditi, Class of 2024

International schools in Australasia

Schools ordered A–Z by Name

Australia

International School of Western Australia

(Founded 2008)
193 St. Brigids Terrace, Doubleview, Perth, WA 6018 Australia
Tel: +61 8 9285 1144
Email: info@iswa.wa.edu.au
Website: www.iswa.wa.edu.au
Principal: Dr Caroline Brokvam

School type: Co-educational Day
Religious Denomination: Non-denominational
Age range of pupils: 3–18 years
No. of pupils enrolled as at 01/09/2025: 415
Fees as at 01/09/2025: Please see our website

The International School of Western Australia (ISWA) is a leading co-educational, non-denominational, independent international school offering a globally focused education from Kindergarten to Year 12. Nestled in Perth's northern suburbs, close to the ocean and city, our modern campus provides an inspiring environment where inquiry, curiosity, and excellence thrive.

At ISWA, we nurture students to become compassionate global citizens who lead lives of purpose, pursue excellence, and make a meaningful impact in the world. With a vibrant community representing over 60 nationalities, our school is a welcoming hub for local and international families. Our inclusive culture fosters a sense of belonging, warmth, and shared values, ensuring everyone feels at home.

Our curriculum emphasises international-mindedness, critical thinking, and social responsibility. Students explore local, national, and global issues, gaining a deep appreciation for diversity and the understanding that differing perspectives can coexist and hold value. This ethos underpins our co-educational, non-denominational approach, cultivating respectful collaboration and thoughtful debate.

As one of the select schools in Australia offering the International Baccalaureate Diploma Programme (IB DP) for Years 11 and 12, ISWA delivers a rigorous academic pathway tailored for the global stage. Our students consistently achieve exceptional results, performing above State and National averages in the National Assessment Program – Literacy and Numeracy (NAPLAN). Impressively, many of these achievements are from students for whom English is a second language.

At ISWA, education is more than academics – it's about inspiring inquiry, embracing diversity, and empowering students to excel in a dynamic and interconnected world.

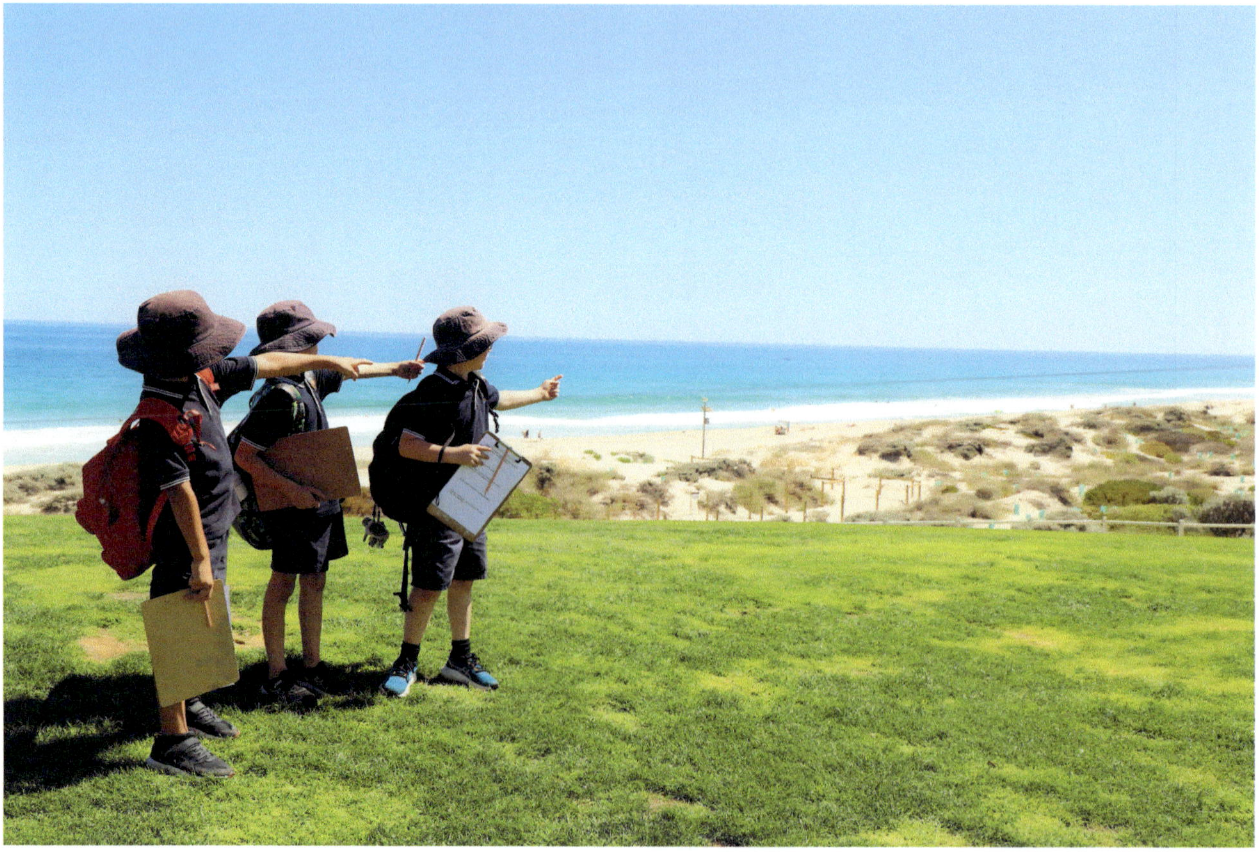

Australia

St Andrew's Cathedral School

ST ANDREW'S
CATHEDRAL SCHOOL

(Founded 1885)

Sydney Square, Sydney, NSW 2000 Australia
Tel: +61 2 9286 9500
Email: enrolments@sacs.nsw.edu.au
Website: www.sacs.nsw.edu.au
Head of School: Dr Julie McGonigle
School type: Co-educational Day

Religious Denomination: Anglican
Age range of pupils: 5–18 years
No. of pupils enrolled as at 01/09/2025: 1450
Fees as at 01/09/2025:
Day: AUS$25,306.00–AUS$44,525.00 per annum

Founded in 1885, St Andrew's Cathedral School is a coeducational, independent Anglican school, located in the heart of Sydney's CBD. Reflecting our Christian foundations, we are a strong and hopeful learning community that nurtures the individual strengths of each student in our care.

Originally founded as a Choral School in 1885, we are known for our outstanding performing arts programme with over 30 music ensembles, including our Cathedral choristers. With extensive sporting and co-curricular opportunities – we cater to a wide variety of interests. We also have an extensive outdoor education programme based in the NSW Southern Highlands.

As an International Baccalaureate (IB) World School, our middle school students are taught the NSW school curriculum through the IB Middle Years framework and Senior College students can choose to study either the HSC or the International Baccalaureate (IB) Diploma.

We are Sydney's quintessential city school, located in two high-rise buildings in the centre of Sydney's CBD. Our buildings are purposefully designed, light-filled learning spaces for Junior School, Middle School and a dedicated pre-tertiary environment for Senior College.

Our teachers are experts in their chosen fields who very much enjoy the relational nature of teaching and who engage in the character development of each child, both within and outside the classroom. They are also passionate about developing their practice and benefit from a progressive professional learning programme.

The School's commitment to genuine reconciliation and healing began in 2007 with the establishment of Gawura School, an award-winning, dedicated K-6 day school for First Nations students. Surrounded by language and culture, students are proud of their First Nations heritage. As a social justice initiative, Gawura School is an integral part of the broader school.

The academic performance of our Year 12 graduates is consistently impressive. To discover the latest St Andrew's Cathedral School IB Diploma and HSC results, please visit: www.sacs.nsw.edu.au/senior/about-us/our-results.

We have a growing number of international students, and our city location combines to ensure we have a diverse community of students with a global outlook, who are drawn from all over Sydney and beyond.

For further information, please contact our Enrolments Department on +61 2 9009 5439 or email enrolments@sacs.nsw.edu.au

Australia

The Friends' School

THE FRIENDS' SCHOOL

(Founded 1887)

23 Commercial Road, North Hobart, TAS 7002 Australia
Tel: +61 3 6210 2200
Email: enrol.office@friends.tas.edu.au
Website: www.friends.tas.edu.au
Principal: Esther Hill

School type: Co-educational Day & Boarding
Age range of pupils: 4–18 years
No. of pupils enrolled as at 01/09/2025: 1300
Fees as at 01/09/2025: AUS$12,080–AUS$23,560 per annum (includes GST)

The Friends' School, Tasmania, Australia
Situated in the heart of Hobart in Tasmania, The Friends' School is an independent, coeducational day and boarding school for students from Early Learning to Year 12.

A strong sense of community at the school provides a rich and stimulating environment for students. The school's philosophy aims to develop the whole person and for students to show a willingness to contribute to something greater than the individual. We offer a diverse range of co-curricular activities including sports, student-led committees, social functions and service opportunities. Our hope is that our students will leave the school with a broad understanding of and empathy for the Quaker testimonies of Simplicity, Peace, Integrity, Community, Equality and Stewardship.

Who We Are
Guided by Quaker values, The Friends' School thrives on an intrinsic spirit of warmth and friendliness, and its strong community atmosphere reflects the intentions of the founding Quakers whose original vision for the school in 1887 was an education for spiritual and intellectual growth.

We are proud of our consistently high academic results, varied curriculum and co-curricular opportunities, but we are prouder still of our students and all that they go on to achieve.

Our Location
The Friends' School is hidden in the picturesque city of Hobart in the heart of Tasmania, which has a worldwide reputation as a clean, safe and beautiful capital city, making it the perfect study destination.

Tasmania offers spectacular, unique mountain and coastal scenery, with extensive national parks and World Heritage Areas protecting the island's wilderness. Our enriching Outdoor Education program takes full advantage of our beautiful and diverse landscapes.

Our Learning Experience
Students of The Friends' School are offered high levels of flexibility and support so that they may pursue individual interests and passions. We encourage students to challenge themselves academically while exploring the many opportunities available to them through the school.

Students entering into Year 11 have three academic pathways available to them: The Tasmanian Certificate of Education (TCE), the International Baccalaureate Diploma Programme (IBDP) or varied Vocational Education and Training (VET) programs that they can complete alongside their TCE.

The Quaker Difference
The school celebrates the academic success of our students, while still valuing the individual strengths and abilities of each child in our care.

The commitment to connecting with the good in each person and nurturing their 'inner light' is a central aspect of what makes a Friends.' education so special. The Quaker commitment to equality is also core to The Friends' School and is demonstrated in the respectful relationships that develop between students and other members of the Friends' community.

Australia

The Hutchins School

(Founded 1846)

71 Nelson Road, Sandy Bay, Tasmania, TAS 7005 Australia
Tel: +61 3 6221 4200
Email: enrolment@hutchins.tas.edu.au
Website: www.hutchins.tas.edu.au
Principal: Dr Rob McEwan
School type: Boys' Day & Boarding

Age range of boys: 3–18 years
No. of pupils enrolled as at 01/09/2025: 1100
Fees as at 01/09/2025:
International Day Student: AU$28,880.00–AU$38,400.00 per annum
Boarding: AU$26,040.00 per annum
Teacher/pupil ratio: 1:4

The Hutchins School is an Anglican day and boarding school for boys from Pre-Kindergarten to Year 12, whose supportive learning community works together to nurture the character of boys. Established in 1846, we are one of Australia's most established schools and as a community we aspire to be people of integrity who act with humility, kindness, courage and respect.

Located in Australia's southernmost state, Tasmania, just five kilometres from the state's capital city, Hobart. Our Sandy Bay campus enjoys expansive grounds overlooking the picturesque River Derwent, allowing our students to make the most of a Tasmanian lifestyle.

The Hutchins School has modern classrooms, state-of-the-art science and computer laboratories, two libraries, a Performing Arts Centre with purpose-built dance studio, a chapel, Sailing Academy and a family orientated boarding house.

Our school continues to grow its advanced facilities and offers opportunities for senior students to extend their knowledge and learning into key co-curricular areas of interest such as Engineering Design, Environmental Science, Information Systems and Digital Technologies, Media Productions and Dance Choreography and Performance on top of our highly reputable academic curriculum.

As the only single-sex boys boarding school in Tasmania, we understand the importance of your child's formative years in the development of their identity. Every student is encouraged, nurtured and challenged to be the best version of themselves and given the opportunity to pursue their own individual talents, wherever their passions may lie. Inclusion and true belonging are at the core of Hutchins.

Fundamental to the Hutchins experience is the unique Power of 9 program. This program is designed to develop a strong sense of purpose in all students in Year 9 as they learn more about themselves. Students spend a full term away at a waterfront location where they prepare and experience outdoor challenges around Tasmania, Australia or overseas designed to extend each student as they take responsibility for their learning journey. Challenge locations include Port Davey and the wilderness of Southern Tasmania, Central Australia and overseas, most recently in Fiji.

International schools in Europe

Schools ordered A–Z by Name

Switzerland

Academia Schools
Academia Group Switzerland AG

Academia Group Switzerland AG, Binzmühlestrasse 15, 8050 Zürich ZH, Switzerland
Tel: +41 61 260 20 80
Email: info@academia-group.ch

Website: www.academia-schools.ch
Co-CEOs Academia Schools: Ludovic Allenspach, Roman Meier & Peter Petrin
School type: Co-educational Day
Age range of pupils: 3–18 years

Academia Schools: Forever Learning
At Academia, children and young people from pre-kindergarten to International A Level experience a close-knit yet cosmopolitan atmosphere, where they are treated as individuals and are able to develop as personalities. We take note of individual learning needs and develop flexible solutions. Our hand-picked, inspirational teachers deliver these solutions in thoughtfully designed learning settings. Our students are given full support throughout but are also encouraged to work intensively and expand their learning, subject knowledge, and social skills.

Academia Bilingual School: Naturally bilingual
Our bilingual schools in Basel (K–Y6), Küsnacht ZH (PreK–Y6) and Winterthur (K–Y8) offer a unique school experience in German and English, blending the national curriculum of Switzerland (Lehrplan 21) with the Cambridge International Curriculum.

What we stand for:
- We support each child individually: small classes with qualified mother tongue teachers.
- We convey more than knowledge: eloquence in two languages, promotion of self-reliance, capacity for teamwork, motivation and respect.
- We offer a variety of connecting options: targeted preparation for grammar school, exam free transition to Academia International School.
- We have an international orientation: consistent bilingual teaching, teachers and students from Switzerland and all over the world, promotion of cultural awareness.
- We can look after your child outside lesson times: flexible before and after school care, varied extracurricular and holiday programme.

Find out more:
www.academia-bilingual.ch

Academia International Schools: Globally recognized, holistic and innovative - your path to higher education
Our English schools in Basel (K–Y12), Winterthur (Y9–Y12) and Zurich (Y7–Y12) focus on the individual strengths of each student. We provide academic excellence in a cosy, caring environment.

What we stand for:
- We build on strengths: high flexibility, broad range of subjects, inclusive community.
- We are passionate about learning: holistic approach with innovative teaching and learning methods, highly qualified teachers with a great sense of care and commitment.
- We teach skills for life: critical thinking, metacognition, social skills, project work and a broad range of extracurricular activities.
- We are located in state-of-the-art school buildings: bright, well-equipped classrooms, various specialist rooms for science, art & design, music and spacious indoor and outdoor recreation areas.

Find out more:
www.academia-international.ch

Academia Schools – Forever Learning

Germany

accadis International School Bad Homburg

(Founded 2004)

SÜDCAMPUS Bad Homburg, Am Weidenring 2, 61352 Bad Homburg, Hesse, Germany
Tel: +49 61 72 984 141
Email: info@accadis-isb.com
Website: www.accadis-isb.com
Head of School: Mr. Maximilian Müllerleile
School type: Co-educational Day
Age range of pupils: 2–18 years

No. of pupils enrolled as at 01/09/2025: 725
Fees as at 01/09/2025:
Preschool: €3,360–€4,560 per annum
Elementary School: €9,240–€10,320 per annum
Secondary School: €12,600–€19,800 per annum

We are accadis ISB!
Our mission
accadis ISB aims to develop confident, knowledgeable and caring young people prepared to create a better future. We aim to build within each child a sense of responsibility, a love for learning, self-discipline, and respect for others. Challenging programs, combined with inter-cultural understanding and respect, enable our students to reach their potential and become compassionate and lifelong learners.

Who we are
Welcome to accadis International School, a family-run, non-profit educational institution, at SÜDCAMPUS Bad Homburg, close to the international metropolis of Frankfurt am Main. Under the umbrella of accadis Bildung GmbH, we offer a holistic educational concept that is unique in Germany, from early steps in the Kindergarten all the way to PhD studies at our own accadis Hochschule (University of Applied Sciences). At the co-educational accadis International School, students learn bilingually, some subjects are taught in English and others in German. accadis ISB is an official IB World School since January 2016 and accredited by Cambridge International Education for the two-year IGCSE courses taught in Grades 9 and 10.

Our students
The school provides a supportive and challenging environment where students are encouraged to become responsible and independent learners. accadis ISB caters for a wide range of students and is both a "local" school for families who live nearby and an international school for students who come to us from all over the world. We currently welcome approximately 600 students from 5–18 years of age in our Elementary and Secondary Schools as well as 125 children in our Bilingual Preschool, representing over 50 nationalities.

Our school
accadis ISB was founded in 2004 and is situated on a modern campus featuring its own sports hall with outdoor basketball court. Having added spaces and facilities gradually over the years to cater for the ever-increasing demand, including an inviting library, two Art rooms and a Music room for the Elementary School, we opened a new building exclusively for our Secondary School students in early 2023. It features more than 20 new classrooms, additional specialist spaces for Science, Art, Music and Drama as well as two libraries and a cafeteria. The new auditorium for up to 250 people is greatly appreciated and utilised by all parts of our organisation. The school focuses strongly on technology. The state-of-the-art learning environment includes interactive whiteboards in each classroom, Google Chromebook laptops, school-wide high-speed Wi-Fi and a 3D printer.

Andorra

Agora Andorra International School

(Founded 1999)

Carrer del Serrat del Camp 14, AD400 La Massana, Andorra
Tel: +376 838 366
Email: admissions@agorainternationalandorra.com
Website: www.agoraandorra.com

Head of School: Mrs. Clara Pintat Rossell
School type: Co-educational Day & Boarding
No. of pupils enrolled as at 01/09/2025: approx 450
Average class size: 20

Agora Andorra International School is a private school located in the heart of the Pyrenees. Our principal objective is to educate our students to be multilingual, responsible, ethical and capable young people, with the motivation to succeed in all areas of their lives. Our school offers full linguistic immersion and excellent educational standards, and we are authorised to teach the prestigious International Baccalaureate (IB) Diploma Programme (DP) at Post 16 level as well as the PYP since 2025. Moreover, we have excellent boarding facilities for international students. Agora Andorra International School is a private school, member of the Globeducate group which owns and operates in more than 65 schools worldwide.

The school is noted for its innovative curriculum and international outlook, focussing on full immersion in various languages and achieving excellent academic standards. Agora Andorra has first-rate boarding facilities welcoming children from all over the world. The three working languages are English, Spanish and French, with classes in Catalan, Andorra's official language. Students can obtain the International Baccalaureate (IB) Diploma Programme (DP), a prestigious degree recognized by the world's leading universities.

Location
Agora Andorra International School is located in the village of l'Aldosa (La Massana) at just 10 minutes from ski slopes. The school site offers good sports facilities, social and recreational activities, a swimming pool, and an art and music room. The international boarding house enables students from all over the world to study at Agora Andorra International School and comprises a three-storey building accommodating 50 students.

Boarders share rooms and the house incorporates two communal/recreational areas, a dining room, a study, and all the services necessary to make the residential students' lives happy and comfortable.

Foreign languages
Spanish (ELE) English (EAL) Catalan and French

IB World School
Agora Andorra International School is authorised to teach the International Baccalaureate® (IB) Diploma Programme (DP) at Post 16 level as well as the PYP since 2025. As an IB World School, it has created a learning environment that is proactive, innovative and reflective and is constantly striving to improve; the school's mission is to educate young people who can shape the world.

Spain

Agora Barcelona International School

(Founded 2008)

Carrer Puig de Mira, Sant Esteve Sesrovires, 08635 Barcelona, Catalonia, Spain
Tel: +34 93 779 89 28
Email: admissions@agoraisbarcelona.edu.es
Website: www.agorabarcelona.com

Headmaster: Mr. Marc Andreu
School type: Co-educational Day & Boarding
No. of pupils enrolled as at 01/09/2025: approx 500
Average class size: 18

Agora Barcelona International School is a private school, which offers the possibility of living in the boarding, integrated in the school and proud member of the Globeducate group, that owns and operates more than 65 schools worldwide.

Chosen by the Forbes list as one of the best schools in Spain, it is renowned for an innovative educational programme, excellent academic performance, and individualized attention, with a unique well-being programme, where students work both on mental and physical health projects. From Preschool onwards the students follow an enriched curriculum based on the Spanish model, with particular attention to Languages, Science, Music, and Sport. The school also has excellent boarding facilities for International students, welcoming children from 11 to 18 years old. Its language policy involves immersion in different languages and specific support for those international students who do not speak either English or Spanish.

The school's goal is to encourage a passion for excellence, social commitment, and critical thinking, helping students to achieve both academic and personal success.

IB World School
Agora Barcelona International School teaches the International Baccalaureate (IB) Diploma Programme (DP) at Post 16 level. As an IB World School, it has created a learning environment that is pro-active, innovative, and reflective and it is constantly striving to improve; Agora Barcelona's mission is to educate young people who can shape the world.

For senior students, the school also offers the Spanish National Baccalaureate, a complete Vocational Sports Training and the IB Career-related Programme for students aged 16–19.

High performance sport programme
20% of our students combine academic studies with high performance sport programmes including golf, football, tennis, paddle, chess, swimming or e-games.

Music
The school is affiliated with Barcelona's renowned music school, "Conservatori Liceu", which enables students to obtain official music diploma.

Foreign languages
English, German and French with official certifications.

Location
The school is located in Sant Esteve Sesrovires, 35 kilometres from the city of Barcelona.

The facilities are built to suit the requirements of each stage of the curriculum. The school site accommodates classrooms, libraries, laboratories, and a fully equipped Sports Centre that incorporates two football pitches, basketball, handball, tennis and paddle tennis courts, a gym and a 25-metre indoor swimming pool.

In September 2023, the school opened the Agora Barcelona International Boarding; Incorporated inside the main school building, it accommodates 50 places in shared rooms, as well as 3 common areas for studying and relaxing, a garden and everything needed to make its residential students feel happy and at home.

Spain

Agora Granada College International School

(Founded 1999)

Urbanización Llanos de Silva, 18230 Atarfe, Granada, Andalusia, Spain
Tel: +34 958 499 009
Email: admissions@granadacollege.es
Website: www.agoragranadacollege.com
Head of School: Mr Javier Jiménez Ortiz

School type: Co-educational Day
Age range of pupils: 0–18 years
No. of pupils enrolled as at 01/09/2025: approx 1050
Average class size: 22

Agora Granada College International School is a private, international, bilingual and secular school that offers a personalised education from 0 to 18 years of age. The principal objective is to provide an international education, oriented to the globalised world and with special attention to education in values. The school offers full linguistic immersion and excellent educational standards, and is authorised to teach the prestigious International Baccalaureate (IB) Diploma Programme (DP) a prestigious degree recognized by the world's leading universities.

Agora Granada College International School is a private school, member of the Globeducate group which owns and operates more than 65 schools worldwide.

The school focuses on achieving academic excellence, providing students with an outstanding academic education along with a strong ethical foundation so they become global citizens who can shape the world.

Location
Made up for two campuses, Agora Príncipes Infant School (Infant P0 to P4) located 5 minutes away from Granada and Agora Granada College (Infant P5 to Baccalaurate) located in an area surrounded by nature and tranquillity 15 minutes from Granada. Its facilities are designed to achieve the students' integral education, with complete facilities that promote a positive environment.

Agora Granada College International School has large classrooms, spacious and bright laboratory rooms, computer rooms, as well as digital classrooms with the latest advances in technology; it also has playgrounds, football pitches, basketball courts, swimming pool, a sports pavilion and a brand new athletics track.

Foreign languages
English, French and Mandarin Chinese

IB World School
In May 2025, the school received the MYP accreditation, consolidating its educational leadership by becoming the first school in Granada to offer the International Baccalaureate Continuum in its three academic stages.

Agora Lledó International School

(Founded 1989)

Camino Caminàs, 175, Castelló de la Plana, 12003 Castelló, Valencia, Spain
Tel: +34 964 72 31 70
Email: admissions@lledo.edu.es
Website: www.agoralledo.com

Headmaster: Mr. Luis Madrid
School type: Co-educational Day
No. of pupils enrolled as at 01/09/2025: approx 850
Average class size: 20

Agora Lledó International School is a private school in Castellón which places great importance on innovation, giving an all-round education and providing personalised attention for each of its pupils. The school is an official music conservatory as well as a sports centre and in 2011 it became the first school in Castellón to offer International Baccalaureate. In May 2024, the school received the MYP accreditation, consolidating its educational leadership by becoming the first school in Castellón and the second in the Valencian Community to offer the International Baccalaureate Continuum in its three academic stages.

Agora Lledó International School is part of the Globeducate international group of schools, which owns and operates more than 65 schools worldwide and meets the most demanding standards of education. With a 100% pass rate in University Entrance Exams the school provides an international education that focuses on our globalised world, with a special emphasis on values.

In addition to a language immersion programme with a wide range of foreign languages, Agora Lledó offers Spanish Baccalaureate and International Baccalaureate as well as comprehensive art, music and sports programmes. The objective is to awaken the students' desire to discover the world and help them to attain academic and personal success.

Location
The school is located in some wonderful natural surroundings full of orange groves and 200 metres from the neoclassical Lledó Basilica. The wide-open spaces are one of the keys to the educational project, which gives importance to learning through living. In addition, the school is an official music conservatory as well as a sports centre with facilities that adapt to every sporting need, such as a semiolympic swimming pool, basketball and tennis courts, two outdoor artificial turf football pitches and one indoor pitch.

Thanks to these facilities Agora Lledó International School excels in sports and takes part in gymnastics, swimming and football competitions on a national level.

Foreign languages
English, German, French.

IB World School
Agora Lledó International School is an IB World School offering the IB Continuum, with academic results that place it no. 1 in Spain and 5th in Europe over the last five years.

Spain

Agora Madrid International School

(Founded 1981)

Calle Duero, 35, Villaviciosa de Odón,
28670 Madrid, Spain
Tel: +34 91 616 71 25
Email: admissions@agoraism.com
Website: www.agoramadrid.com

Headmaster: Mr. Daniel García
School type: Co-educational Day
No. of pupils enrolled as at 01/09/2025: approx 600
Average class size: 20

Agora Madrid International School is a private, bilingual international school in Madrid. Our curriculum is designed to facilitate an English linguistic immersion and extends from Kindergarten to Pre-University. We focus on achieving educational excellence via an enriched curriculum tailored to meet the specific needs and requirements of each of our students.

Agora Madrid International School forms part of the highly renowned education group, Globeducate that owns and operates more than 65 schools worldwide. The school has been known as a hub for the creative arts, incorporating Performing Arts and integrating an official Music Conservatoire within the curriculum from Primary. The school also offers the unique International Baccalaureate specialized in Performing Arts and Film in Europe.

Senior students can follow the Spanish National and International Baccalaureates, having a 100% pass rate for the Spanish University Entrance Examinations. The school offers a broad and balanced curriculum, with a particular emphasis on co-curricular subjects such as Music, Sports and Arts, designed to help each student achieve their full academic and personal potential.

Location
Agora Madrid International School is located in the beautiful area El Bosque, in Villaviciosa de Odón to the west of Madrid, a quiet residential area surrounded by trees and with views towards the mountains. The excellent facilities are purpose-built to provide for the changing needs of the students at each stage of their education and are designed to create a calm and positive environment for both study and recreation. Agora Madrid International School has great sporting facilities, including an AstroTurf soccer pitch, a gymnasium and a fully equipped sports centre with basketball, handball, volleyball and paddle tennis courts.

Foreign languages
English immersion, German and French as a second language and Chinese extracurricular.

IB World School
Agora Madrid International School is authorized to teach the International Baccalaureate (IB) Diploma Programme (DP) at Post 16 level and in 2025 it has obtained the PYP accreditation for students from 3 to 12 years-old. Since 2023 Agora Madrid, along with Víctor Ullate Roche Sing and Dance Project, offers the first International Baccalaureate specialized in Performing Arts and Film that is unique in our country.

Spain

Agora Portals International School

(Founded 2008)

Carretera Vella Palma-Andratx, s/n,
Portals Nous, 07181 Mallorca,
Balearic Islands, Spain
Tel: +34 964 72 31 70
Email: admissions@agoraportals.edu.es
Website: www.agoraportals.com

Headmaster: Mr. Rafael Barea
School type: Co-educational Day
No. of pupils enrolled as at 01/09/2025: approx 1000
Average class size: 22

Agora Portals International School is a private international school in Majorca member of the Globeducate group which owns and operates more than 65 schools worldwide. The school is focused on achieving academic excellence, delivering a broad and balanced curriculum and meeting the individual needs of each student. The school incorporates an official Music Academy and, in 2011, Agora Portals International School became the first school in the Balearic Islands to offer the International Baccalaureate to senior school students.

Agora Portals is located on the island of Majorca at Portals Nous in Calvià. The school's mission is to provide students with an outstanding academic education along with a strong ethical foundation, and the curriculum is designed to facilitate linguistic zimmersion, particularly in English and Spanish.

Senior students can study for both the Spanish National and the International Baccalaureate and have a 100% pass rate for both the Spanish University Entrance Examinations and the IB Diploma. The school offers full programmes in Music, Sports and STEAM and aim to equip each student with the academic and personal skills that they need to become confident and responsible citizens who can shape the world.

With the aim of transmitting to students the value of preserving the seas and oceans, Agora Portals created the Aula del Mar, a project within the Agora Posidonia Experience. A unique project in the Balearic Islands and a pioneer in Spain.

Always working to innovate, in September 2023 Agora Portals inaugurated the Agora Innovation Centre, a benchmark classroom in Spain. This innovative space of more than 180sqm is equipped with state of the art tools that enrich the learning experience and spark imagination and creativity.

Location
Agora Portals International School is situated close to the sea and surrounded by nature, allowing students to study in a calm, focused and positive working environment, with all the facilities and resources that they need to succeed at every stage of their education. The school has an official Music Academy on site and excellent, purpose-built sporting facilities, including outdoor courts and pitches, a fully equipped indoor sports centre and indoor swimming pool.

Foreign languages
English, German, French, Chinese

IB World School
Agora Portals International School, after 10 years of implementing the IB Diploma programme, started teaching the IB methodology from the age of 3 (the Primary Years Programme) from September 2021 as well as the MYP since 2025 becoming an IB Continuum school.

Agora Portals is listed in the top 50 schools in Spain by FORBES and the unique in the Balearic Islands.

Spain

Agora Princess Margaret International School

(Founded 1967)

Passeig de la Fond d'en Fargas 15-17, 8032 Barcelona, Catalonia, Spain
Tel: +34 934 290 313
Email: admissions@agoraprincessmargaret.com
Website: www.agoraprincessmargaret.com

Headmaster: Alex Cerdá
School type: Co-educational Day
Age range of pupils: 3–15 years
No. of pupils enrolled as at 01/09/2025: approx 300
Average class size: 23

With over 55 years of experience, Agora Princess Margaret International School stands as a benchmark in educational innovation and the promotion of diversity. It's a private school, member of the Globeducate group which owns and operates in more than 65 schools worldwide.

The school is part of an international and diverse environment, committed to personalized education that adapts to the individual needs of each student. It is a pioneer in Barcelona for obtaining the official certification of the Middle Years Programme (MYP) and Primary Years Programme (PYP), highlighting its commitment to academic excellence and the holistic development of its students.

Location
Located in Barcelona, Agora Princess Margaret International School is a leading international school proud of its roots and well-integrated into the unique Barcelona neighbourhood. This approach allows the school to offer individualised, familiar, and accessible attention to students, understanding their needs and personalising their education.

The school creates optimal, close-knit environments for intensive, participative, and transdisciplinary learning. It is characterised by being a dynamic centre and constantly promotes new actions, such as the extracurricular English courses and the summer course, which provide a service to the community.

Foreign languages
Agora Princess Margaret International School prepares its students for an international future with a multilingual curriculum and linguistic immersion. The school offers the Cambridge programme for official qualifications from 2nd Primary to 4th ESO, and the Phonics programme, a synthetic phonetics program from ages 3 to 3rd Primary. To complement the school-based language programme, students are invited to participate in international events, exchanges, and trips to various overseas destinations.

IB World School
At Agora Princess Margaret International School, both the Primary Years Programme (PYP) and the Middle Years Programme (MYP) are taught. As an IB World School, it has created a learning environment that is proactive, innovative, and reflective. The school constantly strives for improvement with the mission to educate young people who are committed to enhancing their own futures and the future of the world around them.

Spain

Agora Sant Cugat International School

(Founded 1989)

Carrer Ferrer i Guàrdia, s/n, Sant Cugat del Vallès, 08174 Barcelona, Catalonia, Spain
Tel: +34 93 590 26 00
Email: ruth.sale@agorasantcugat.edu.es
Website: www.agorasantcugat.com
Headmaster: Mr. Jordi Ros

School type: Co-educational Day
Age range of pupils: 1–18 years
No. of pupils enrolled as at 01/09/2025: approx 1800
Average class size: 24

Agora Sant Cugat International School is ranked among Spain's top ten schools. It is a private school and a member of the Globeducate Group, which owns and operates more than 65 schools worldwide. Founded in 1989, it has become a prestigious private international school and its teaching methods are innovative with every student from Infant P0 to Baccalaureate receiving personalised attention.

Agora Sant Cugat is one of the few schools in Spain authorised to teach the International Baccalaureate Continuum at all levels.

The education is multilingual with English, Catalan and Spanish as the working languages and offers Mandarin Chinese, French and German. Teaching is mixed, plural and open and promotes respect for the beliefs of others in an atmosphere of dialogue and tolerance.

Agora Sant Cugat provides its students with the necessary tools for them to build their own learning by not only focusing on academic success but also on personal development and promoting healthy habits to achieve an all-round excellent physical, mental and emotional health and well-being.

This includes a very wide sporting offer, promoting arts and music, disciplines which provide them with key values such as perseverance, teamwork and self-improvement and a healthy meal programme designed by our nutrition specialists and School Chef.

Location
The Agora Sant Cugat Campus is located in Sant Cugat and has four separate buildings. Agora Sant Cugat International School, from Infant P1 to Baccalaureate, is on the outskirts of the city in Can Sant Joan) with two buildings. Agora Patufet Infant School, from Infant P0 to Infant P5, is located in the centre of Sant Cugat, and Agora Pipo, from Infant P0 to Infant P2 is located in the area of Volpelleres. A School Bus Service is offered and all three buildings have train stations nearby on the FGC train line.

Agora Sant Cugat has purpose-built classrooms, science laboratories, libraries, dining rooms, kitchens and a sports area with a full-size football pitch, two tennis padel courts and four multipurpose courts. The school has the Auditorium Josep Carreras that seats 380 people and is an ideal place for music activities, conferences, theatre performances, debates and educational events.

Foreign languages
English, German, French and Chinese, alongside Spanish and Catalan, are taught as foreign languages for international students.

IB World School
Agora Sant Cugat International School teaches the Diploma Programme (DP) of the International Baccalaureate® (IB) since 2012, which together with the Primary Years Programme (PYP) and the Middle Years Programme (MYP), makes the school one of the 20 schools in Spain authorised to teach what is known as the IB Continuum. The IBDP is taught in Spanish and English, and also offers a unique qualification in Cataluña that includes German as a language of teaching and learning. Since 2025 Agora Sant Cugat offers the first International Baccalaureate specialized in Performing Arts in Catalonia.

Austria

American International School Vienna

(Founded 1959)

Salmannsdorfer Strasse 47,
1190 Vienna, Austria
Tel: +43 1 401 32
Email: info@ais.at
Website: www.ais.at
Director: Kathryn Miner DEd
School type: Co-educational Day
Age range of pupils: 4–18 years

No. of pupils enrolled as at 01/09/2025: 800
Fees as at 01/09/2025:
Pre-Kindergarten: €15,325 per annum
Kindergarten-Grade 5: €23,931 per annum
Grades 6-8: €26,553 per annum
Grades 9-10: €27,618 per annum
Grades 11-12: €28,028 per annum
Teacher/pupil ratio: 1:8

Set within the rich cultural context of Austria, the American International School Vienna is one of the top international schools in the country. Founded in 1959 and having recently celebrated its 65th Anniversary, AIS Vienna today serves around 800 students, representing 80 countries, from Pre-Kindergarten through Grade 12 (International Baccalaureate (IB) or American diploma). AIS Vienna's core values – respect, aspire, and achieve – ensure that students develop intellectually and interculturally while internalizing the commitment and leadership necessary in today's globally-minded world.

AIS Vienna provides comprehensive opportunities for learners from around the world. Our students succeed academically, as well as in athletics, music, and visual arts. A variety of activities, including class trips to mountain ranges and service-oriented community projects, allow students to practice commitment, leadership, and meaningful self-reflection. We maintain a broad set of offerings to help us serve our students and be true to our mission.

Our tightly knit school community allows students to develop personal relationships with both their peers and highly qualified teachers. We maintain a culture of high expectations and close connection to the pulse of international education. Investments in the quality and skill of our staff are on-going, and recent enhancements to our facilities and technology resources are assuring our role as a vital partner and a leader in our city and region.

We welcome all to our community of learners; we work every day to assure learners understand the connections between learning and living. We make decisions based on the understanding that we are not only guiding children towards learning but building experiences and memories that will serve to inform futures not yet imagined. Our goal is to help each of our students define success in a nurturing environment that supports excellence. Ultimately, we prepare our students for the next step in their lives after AIS Vienna.

Italy

American Overseas School of Rome

(Founded 1947)

Via Cassia 811, 00189 Rome, Italy
Tel: +39 06 334 381
Email: admissions@aosr.org
Website: www.aosr.org/admissions
Head of School: Dr. Kristen DiMatteo
Appointed: July 2020
School type: Co-educational Day

Age range of pupils: 3–18 years
Fees as at 01/09/2025:
Pre-K – KG: €12,500–€17,000 per annum
Grades 1 – 5: €20,200–€21,000 per annum
Grades 6 – 10: €23,600–€26,700 per annum
Grades 11 – 12: €27,300–€27,700 per annum

Moving to a new country comes with major decisions – none bigger than finding the right school. At the American Overseas School of Rome (AOSR), we understand what families need when relocating: a strong academic program, a welcoming community, and the confidence that your child is safe, engaged, and happy from morning drop-off to the end of the day. We've been that place since 1947.

AOSR serves students aged 3 to 19 with a proven American-international curriculum. We offer both the Advanced Placement (AP) and International Baccalaureate (IB) Diploma Programme, ensuring students are prepared for university anywhere in the world.

Families often ask why AOSR offers both Advanced Placement (AP) courses and the full International Baccalaureate (IB) Diploma Programme. The answer is simple: not every student is the same. Some thrive in the depth and structure of the IB. Others benefit from the flexibility and subject choice that AP offers. We give students both pathways because we know the world they're heading into values agility and choice.

But we also know that academic quality isn't the only thing parents are looking for.

You want your child to enjoy going to school. To be excited about their day. To have meaningful friendships and feel supported, especially in a new environment. AOSR is known for its caring, international culture – with over 50 nationalities represented. About a third of our families are Italian, another third American, and the rest from all over. This diversity means your child will feel included, not isolated.

You also want a full day that works for your schedule. Our school day is structured to keep students active and engaged, with after-school activities, sports, arts, and clubs that run well into the afternoon. Whether it's robotics, soccer, debate, or theater, students can find something that keeps them learning and having fun.

For working parents, knowing your child is in good hands all day is essential. Our 6-acre campus in north Rome is safe, well-equipped, and fully supervised. Students have access to high-quality meals, nurse services, transportation options, and secure entry and exit systems. When you reunite at the end of the day, your child has stories to share – and you can focus on family time, knowing everything else was taken care of.

Our faculty are experienced, mostly native English-speaking educators who truly know their students. We focus on personal learning, strong relationships, and helping each child thrive academically and emotionally.

We know moving is stressful. School shouldn't be. AOSR gives you peace of mind and gives your child a place to grow, belong, and succeed.

Belgium

BEPS International School

(Founded 1972)

Avenue Franklin Roosevelt 21-23,
1050 Brussels, Belgium
Tel: +32 2 648 43 11
Email: admissions@beps.com
Website: www.beps.com
General Director: Pascale Hertay
Finance Director & Deputy General Director: Charlotte Van Brussel
School type: Co-educational Day
Age range of pupils: 2.5–18 years
No. of pupils enrolled as at 01/09/2025: 300
Fees as at 01/09/2025: Please see website: www.beps.com/admission/tuition-fees

Established in 1972, BEPS International School is situated in beautiful buildings in the heart of one of Brussels' most desirable areas, close to the Bois de la Cambre and the University (ULB).

The school offers an inquiry-based learning approach through the International Early Years Curriculum, the International Primary Curriculum, the Middle Years Programme, the IB Diploma Programme and the IB Career Related Programme from the International Baccalaureate® (IB).

In 2021, BEPS International School announced its expansion by acquiring the building attached to the BEPS Primary School campus. This allows the growing BEPS Secondary School to join the Early Years & Primary School at the same location where the BEPS adventure started in 1972. The transformation of the new building gives BEPS the opportunity to design spaces for innovative, authentic, and engaging learning which matches the BEPS approach to learning in the Middle and High School.

With the growth of the Secondary school, BEPS will cater for children between 2.5 – 18 years old. The school aims to achieve its full capacity of 450 students in the coming years.

Children learning English and children with learning needs receive additional support. French is taught as a second language from the Early Years and the development of the children's Mother Tongue is encouraged.

A wide range of After school clubs are available as well as a Garderie and holiday clubs. A door-to-door bus service also runs for most areas in Brussels.

Italy

Bilingual European School

Via Val Cismon 9, 20162 Milan, Italy
Via Resegone 1A, 20159 Milan, Italy
Tel: +39 02 6611 7449
Email: admissions@beschool.eu
Website: www.beschool.eu
Head of School: Mr. Francesco Masetti Placci

School type: Co-educational Day
Age range of pupils: 2–18 years
No. of pupils enrolled as at 01/09/2025: 546
Fees as at 01/09/2025:
Day: €12,250–€17,100 per annum

The British American Pre-School and the Bilingual European School prepare children aged 2 to 18 to be the travelers of the world, providing an outstanding educational journey that lays the groundwork to meet the challenges of tomorrow, developing their natural talents in both English and Italian.

BAPS, founded in 1987, offers a full immersion English programme that combines the inquiry-based and child-centered educational philosophy with the Early Years Foundation Stage curriculum (for the first three age groups) and Key Stage One (for Reception children). BAPS' play-based, learning-by-doing approach provides children with the knowledge and skills for a smooth transition to the BES bilingual programme.

BES, founded in 1999 as the first bilingual school in Milan, is an Italian Ministry-accredited bilingual Primary and Middle School, expanding to include a bilingual High School with its brand new campus from the 2025–2026 academic year. It integrates the Italian Ministerial curriculum with the IB Primary Years Programme, offering bilingual education of excellence with a global perspective.

All teachers are native speakers of either English or Italian, and students follow a dual curriculum that promotes critical thinking, creativity, and a deep understanding of both languages. Learning is hands-on, personalised, and aligned with a constructivist approach. The campuses – located in northern Milan – include over 13,000 sqm of space, recently redesigned by renowned architect Rosan Bosch.

The school hosts a permanent Bruno Munari® art lab and an accredited LEGO® Education Innovation Studio, and is recognised by Avanguardie Educative as a centre of excellence for innovation. BES also collaborates with Project Zero to shape future learning models and offers a new bilingual four-year Applied Sciences High School Programme, awarding both the Italian State Diploma and the Ontario Secondary School Diploma.

BAPS and BES joined Globeducate in 2021, combining the group's forward-thinking vision with the school's unique model of cognitive integrated bilingualism – recognised by Goethe University Frankfurt as a European and global benchmark. Globeducate connects students and teachers to international experiences, exchanges, and partnerships with organisations like WWF, LEGO, and Eco-Schools, and offers mobility across schools worldwide.

Bordeaux International School

(Founded 1987)

252 Rue Judaïque, 33000 Bordeaux, France
Tel: +33 5 57870211
Email: contact@bis33.com
Website: www.bordeaux-school.com
Principals: Mrs Bergey & Mme Bidalun
Appointed: September 2021
School type: Co-educational Day
Religious Denomination: Non-denominational

Age range of pupils: 3–19 years
No. of pupils enrolled as at 01/09/2025: 195
Fees as at 01/09/2025:
Day: €7,610.00–€16,060.00 per annum
Average class size: 12-15
Teacher/pupil ratio: 1:16 (Primary) 1:15 (Middle School) 1:10 (Upper School)

Located in the heart of Bordeaux, BIS has over 35 years experience in helping students achieve their potential by combining a bilingual education and an international learning environment. With students from over 25 different nationalities, our school community benefits from a wide range of cultural backgrounds. By keeping class sizes small (maximum 16 students), we create an environment where each student can fully engage in this multicultural setting.

BIS is the only institution in the region that is accredited as a 'school of excellence' by the Council of International Schools. Our unique approach to teaching and learning is based on a comprehensive and inclusive bilingual curriculum. Early Learning and Primary, under contract with the French Education Nationale, enables students to follow a fully bilingual programme. Our Middle School follows both the Education Nationale and the Cambridge International Lower Secondary programme. In Upper Secondary, we offer internationally recognised Cambridge IGCSE and A Levels.

At the heart of our mission to cultivate proactive, responsible global citizens lies a strong commitment to academic support. Our experienced, multinational teaching team provides a stimulating environment where active and differentiated learning empowers students to challenge themselves and reach their full potential. The internationally recognised qualifications our students earn open doors to universities around the world, reflecting our dedication to preparing them for global success.

We take pride in developing a school community grounded in understanding and mutual respect. To promote inclusivity and creativity, we offer a variety of activities, including international theme weeks, school shows, the International Award programme, and clubs such as Chinese, chess, and music band. Students also benefit from regular cultural excursions and additional sports activities at local venues. For those seeking a deeper cultural immersion, boarding with a French host family provides invaluable support and firsthand experience of French life.

Our students are encouraged to engage in a sustainable lifestyle, to develop a critical understanding of world issues and be inspired to become interculturally competent global citizens.

Spain

Cambridge House British International School

(Founded 1986)

Calle Profesorado Espanol 1, Santa Barbara, 46111 Rocafort, Valencia, Spain
Tel: +34 96 390 5019
Email: info@cambridgehouse.es
Website: www.cambridgehouse.es

Executive Head: Mr. Harry Ainscough
School type: Co-educational Day
No. of pupils enrolled as at 01/09/2025: approx 1700
Average class size: 25

Cambridge House British International School is a private, secular, independent school located in Valencia that follows the National Curriculum of England while meeting all Spanish schooling requirements. The school was the first school in Spain to obtain both the BSO distinction (British School Overseas) and NABSS accreditation (National Association of British Schools in Spain), seals that guarantee the educational excellence of this school founded in 1986.

Cambridge House joined Globeducate in September 2021, as part of the Globeducate British International Schools cluster with a clear goal: to be the first choice international school in Valencia, building a community of lifelong learners for a better future. They provide a system of learning designed to foster curiosity and confidence along with imparting all the necessary skills and knowledge required to succeed in exams and evaluations.

Its curriculum is designed to facilitate understanding of the world and the challenges young people will face. English is the vehicular language, and full immersion is achieved from the first day of school, in Early Years, although it is complemented with Spanish and French classes as the students progress through the school year.

Cambridge House offers an extensive educational programme for students aged 16–18 years old supporting student access to their first-choice university. The school offers a fully integrated curriculum of A Levels and Spanish Selectivo subjects to enable students to successfully gain access to local, national and international universities. The school also offers a vocational pathway for students at his level as an alternative to the academic pathway. This is in the form of an award-winning UK Btec programme of student. Students also benefit from extensive personalised advice and guidance from tutors to support their university applications.

Facilities

We have comprehensive, recently renovated facilities within a stunning natural setting. An abundance of trees provides an inspiring and tranquil environment for learning. The campus includes purpose-designed areas for Early Years, offering a safe and stimulating space for our youngest learners.

As students progress, they benefit from innovative spaces such as newness labs, green screen studios, and a fully equipped drama room, which foster creativity and exploration. Our music, art, and science classrooms are specially designed to enhance hands-on learning, while mini theatres and outdoor learning areas provide dynamic spaces for personal and academic growth. With sports courts and a gymnasium also on site, our students enjoy a well-rounded education in a vibrant and supportive environment.

Students as individuals

Educational success is key to its philosophy, but beyond pure academic success. The National Curriculum of England encourages students to explore the world around them, be curious about how things work, ask questions, apply critical thinking skills, and respect fellow students and teachers alike. Teamwork and communication skills form a key foundation to all its educational programmes. Additionally, all students are encouraged to become socially, ethically and environmentally aware.

The school aims to prepare students for life after school, teaching them skills that will help to succeed in secondary school, further education and the workplace. Learning experiences also take place outside the classroom; assemblies, cultural events and fun educational trips provide further opportunities to learn and develop.

More than just a school

At Cambridge House learning is not always about lessons. The school offers a wide range of extra-curricular activities to choose from, exchanges and a full programme of international events within Globeducate schools' network. The school also encourages Outdoor Learning and relies on a House System to foster collaboration between pupils of different ages, team spirit, leadership skills and a sense of pride in belonging to a strong and committed community.

Italy

Canadian School of Florence

Senior School - Florence Campus
Via Jacopo Nardi 18, 50132 Florence, Italy
Junior School - Lower Primary
Fiesole Campus: Via delle Fontanelle 2-4, 50014 Fiesole, Italy
Junior School - Upper Primary/ Middle School
Fiesole Campus: Piazza San Domenico 15, 50014 Fiesole, Italy

Tel: +39 055 098 2744
Email: info@csflorence.it
Website: www.csflorence.it
Head of School: Ms. Isabelle Leblanc
School type: Co-educational Day
Age range of pupils: 3–18 years
Fees as at 01/09/2025:
Day: €11,953–€20,940 per annum

The Canadian School of Florence (CSF) is a leading international school for students aged 3 to 18, with campuses in Florence and the hilltop town of Fiesole. Since opening its doors in 2017, CSF has quickly become known for its dynamic, values-driven approach to education, inspiring students to become confident, compassionate, and future-ready global citizens.

CSF offers the internationally recognized Ontario curriculum from kindergarten through Grade 12, alongside the Italian paritaria program. Beginning in September 2025, students entering high school will have the opportunity to pursue a Double Diploma – earning both the Ontario Secondary School Diploma and having the additional option of pursuing the Italian maturità diploma within four years. This dual pathway not only enhances academic opportunities in Italy and abroad but also reflects our school's commitment to bilingualism, academic excellence, and global citizenship.

At every level – Junior, Middle, and Senior School – learning is personalized and inclusive. Our small class sizes allow teachers to nurture each student's unique talents and strengths while fostering values such as trust, integrity, fairness, and compassion. Our approach blends rigorous academics with hands-on, experiential learning and an emphasis on wellbeing, creativity, and collaboration.

Rooted in the belief that schools should actively shape a better future, CSF is proud to be part of Globeducate, one of the world's leading international education groups. With over 65 schools across 11 countries, Globeducate schools share a common mission: to prepare students to become global citizens who can shape the world. This means providing real-world learning experiences, from sustainability initiatives to global forums on the UN Sustainable Development Goals, and opportunities for students to engage in arts, sports, and academic challenges with peers from across the globe.

Whether through cross-curricular projects, student-led initiatives, local excursions, or international collaborations, CSF students learn to lead with purpose, connect with others meaningfully, and meet the future with curiosity, courage, and heart.

Spain

Colegio San Patricio El Soto

(Founded 1958)
Calle Jazmin 148, El Soto de la Moraleja,
28109 Alcobendas, Madrid, Spain
Tel: +34 916 500 602
Email: infosoto@colegiosanpatricio.es

Website:
www.colegiosanpatriciomadrid.com
Head of School: Mr. Borja Díaz
School type: Co-educational Day
Age range of pupils: 12–18 years

For over 60 years, San Patricio School has successfully educated thousands of students on 3 different campuses in Madrid, empowering each one to achieve the most ambitious goals and pursue fulfilling careers: Serrano and La Moraleja for our Early Years and Primary students (1 to 11 years old), and El Soto, where students from the other two campuses can complete their San Patricio education through Secondary School and the Baccalaureate programmes (Spanish or IBDP).

Colegio San Patricio El Soto is a catholic coeducational secondary day school for children from ages 12 to 18 years old.

Our school is part of Inspired Education, the leading global premium group of schools that offer excellence in education to over 85,000 students worldwide.

From exchange programmes to exclusive camps, to leadership conferences and shared learning experiences, Inspired offers a range of enriching global opportunities which give students a chance to travel, meet peers from other countries and become a part of a vibrant international community.

Since its founding in 1958 our school has employed teaching methods that create a unique and comprehensive educational model. We have implemented strategies such as an inquiry-based approach to lessons and a multilingual approach to learning.

Our school has been recognised for this optimal learning environment: Colegio San Patricio was previously awarded the accolade of Best School in Spain in El Mundo's "100 Best schools in Spain" guide. PISA for schools, a project that assesses schools' prowess in Maths, Science and Reading has declared us the best school in Spain, and we are also ranked in the Top 5 of Forbes Magazine's best 50 schools in Spain.

Attending San Patricio means joining the SanPa family. Our community makes school a warm and welcoming place for all.

IB at Colegio San Patricio:
At the age of 16, students at our school have the option to choose between the Spanish National Baccalaureate and the IB. We have been an MYP candidate school for the past year and a half and will be offering the MYP in the coming academic year.

We believe that the IB provides a holistic educational experience, allowing students to maintain an education that is both broad and focused. The Diploma also consists of core elements - CAS programme, Extended Essay, and Theory of Knowledge. Overall, the IB creates a well-rounded, critically thinking learner.

In 2024, our average IB Diploma score was 34, with the top score being 42 points. Meanwhile, for the National Baccalaureate, the average score was an impressive 10.596 out of 14 and 24% of students achieved a score of 12+.

These outstanding results have meant that our students have been accepted by some of the best Universities in the world such as UCLA and Georgetown University in America and Imperial College and Bath University in the UK.

Collège Français Bilingue de Londres (CFBL)

(Founded 2011)

87 Holmes Road, Kentish Town,
London, NW5 3AX UK
Tel: 020 7993 7400
Email: info@cfbl.org.uk
Website: www.cfbl.org.uk
Head of School: Mr David Gassian
School type: Co-educational Day Preparatory, Senior & Nursery

Age range of pupils: 3–15 years
No. of pupils enrolled as at 01/09/2025: 700
Fees as at 01/09/2025:
Nursery: £15,440 per annum
Reception & Year 1: £18,306 per annum
Years 2 – 6: £15,882 per annum
Years 7 – 10: £16,162 per annum

Exceptional English-French bilingual education in the heart of London
Collège Français Bilingue de Londres (CFBL) provides exceptional English-French bilingual education to 700 boys and girls aged 3 to 15 years old (Nursery to Year 10).

Open to the world
Our pupils are nurtured in a warm and welcoming environment where they can discover the joys of learning, supported by attentive French and English teaching staff. CFBL is a multicultural environment with over 60 different nationalities, located in a central and cosmopolitan district of London where pupils grow into creative, open-minded individuals.

Choosing a bilingual education for your child is a smart choice for families of any nationality and language background and has been linked with a range of cognitive advantages and soft skills, from better focus to heightened empathy, open-mindedness and the ability to multitask.

Creativity and Kindness
Our pupils are encouraged to interact, be creative and take initiatives as well as responsibility in our international environment. They acquire a range of soft skills and robust academic knowledge, and develop into well-rounded adults, preparing them for a bright future anywhere in the world.

Ambition for all
With a focus on offering the best of French & British education, CFBL's unique curriculum gives our pupils the opportunity to choose to continue their studies in the British system, the French system, or any other.

We give them the tools and flexibility to adapt to whatever they decide to do next. The excellence of our bilingual teaching, our dedication to ensuring students' well-being, and our focus on providing a multicultural, international education make CFBL an attractive choice for families of any nationality.

Spain

Coruña British International School (A Coruña)

Coruña
BRITISH INTERNATIONAL SCHOOL
A CORUÑA

(Founded 2015)
Rúa Roma 1, 15008 A Coruña, Galicia, Spain
Tel: +34 981 28 67 99
Email: admissions@biscoruna.com
Website: www.biscoruna.com

Head of School: Mr. Dominic Abbott
School type: Co-educational Day
No. of pupils enrolled as at 01/09/2025: approx 450
Average class size: 20

Coruña British International School is a private, secular, independent school in A Coruña. The school follows the National Curriculum of England while meeting all Spanish schooling requirements, and it is approved and accredited by both the Galician government and the British Council Coruña British International School belongs to Globeducate British International Schools since 2017.

The education the school offers is high quality and individualised, with dedicated attention for each student. They aim to develop each child's full academic and personal potential and encourage their students to be curious, creative, self-disciplined and independent.

The school currently offers classes from Early Years up to Year 11. The school is progressively adding a new cohort each year until they offer the full range of schooling, from ages 3 to 18.

Our facilities
The school is located in the beautiful city of A Coruña, 10 minutes from the city centre with easy access by car. The school buildings and facilities are modern and designed with children in mind. In September 2026, the school is moving to its new, purpose-built campus in Culleredo in order to continue offering the best facilities as the school grows. This new campus contemplates warm, open and interconnected spaces that facilitate active learning and contribute to the development of the skills necessary to face the challenges of the 21st century.

Students as individuals
Educational achievement is key to school philosophy, but they think beyond pure academic success. The National Curriculum of England encourages students to explore the world around them, be curious about how things work, ask questions, apply critical thinking skills, and respect fellow students and teachers alike. Teamwork and communication skills form a key foundation to all their educational programmes. Additionally, all students are encouraged to become socially, ethically and environmentally aware.

The school aims to prepare students for life after school, teaching them skills that will help them to succeed in secondary school, further education and the workplace. Learning experiences also take place outside the classroom; assemblies, cultural events and fun educational trips provide further opportunities to learn and develop.

More than just a school
Life at Coruña British International School is not always about lessons. They have more than 30 extra-curricular activities to choose, exchanges and a full programme of international events with other Globeducate schools. They also encourage learning outside the classrooms through a unique Outdoor Learning programme, "The Journey", and rely on a House System to foster collaboration between pupils of different ages, team spirit, leadership skills and a sense of pride in belonging to a strong and committed community.

France

Ecole Jeannine Manuel - Lille

(Founded 1992)
418 bis rue Albert Bailly, Marcq-en-Baroeul, 59700 France

Tel: +33 3 20 65 90 50
Email: admissions-lille@ejm.net
Website: www.ecolejeanninemanuel.org
Head of School: Constance Devaux
School type: Co-educational Day & Boarding
Age range of pupils: 3–18 years
No. of pupils enrolled as at 01/09/2025: 980

Fees as at 01/09/2025:
International 10th grade (Day):
€13,085 per annum
11th & 12th grade IB (Day):
€25,475 per annum
11th & 12th grade IB (Boarding):
€53,300 per annum
Average class size: 25 (15 in IBDP)

École Jeannine Manuel Lille is a non-profit coeducational school founded in 1992 and welcomes students from nursery to 12th grade. As the sister campus of École Jeannine Manuel Paris, the school has the same educational project and mission: promoting international understanding through bilingual education. An associated UNESCO school, École Jeannine Manuel Lille is the only non-denominational independent school in Nord-Pas-de-Calais, with over 900 pupils representing 40 nationalities and every major cultural tradition. The school's academic excellence matches it diversity: École Jeannine Manuel Lille is regularly ranked among the best French high schools (ranked first for five consecutive years). The school is accredited by the French Ministry of Education, the International Baccalaureate Organization (IBO), the Council of International Schools (CIS), and the New England Association of Schools and Colleges (NEASC).

Ecole Jeannine Manuel Lille's campus extends over 8.5 acres. It includes a boarding house, a restaurant, and state-of-the-art sports facilities including a 1600 m2 gym with its own climbing wall, a 300m racing track, and two outdoor playing fields. The boarding house currently welcomes 120 pupils from 6th to 12th grade.

Each year, École Jeannine Manuel Lille welcomes non-French speaking students. These students integrate the school through the adaptation program, which provides intensive instruction in French, support in English as needed, help in understanding and adjusting to French culture, and differentiated coursework and assessment during their adaptation period. The lower and middle school follow the French national curriculum with several exceptions: in lower school, half of the day is taught in English, and in middle school, experimental sciences, history and geography are taught in English. The curriculum is enriched at all levels, not only with a more advanced English language and literature curriculum, but also, for example, with Chinese language instruction (compulsory in grades 3–4–5), an integrated science program in lower school, and independent research projects in middle school.

In upper school, tenth graders follow the French national curriculum, which is taught 50% in French and 50% in English. In 11th grade, pupils choose between the French track (*Baccalauréat Français International*, BFI) and the International Baccalaureate Diploma Programme (IBDP). Approximately 25% of our pupils opt for the IBDP.

Admission
Although admission is competitive, the school makes every effort to reserve space for international applicants, including children of families who expect to remain in France for a limited period of time and wish to combine a cultural immersion in French education with the ability to re-enter their own school systems and excel.

France

Ecole Jeannine Manuel - Paris

(Founded 1954)

70 rue du Théâtre, Paris, 75015 France
Tel: +33 1 44 37 00 80
Email: admissions@ejm.net
Website: www.ecolejeanninemanuel.org
Principal: Jérôme Giovendo
School type: Co-educational Day

Age range of pupils: 4–18 years
No. of pupils enrolled as at 01/09/2025: 2400
Fees as at 01/09/2025:
Day: €9,935.00–€10,830.00 per annum
IB: €31,565.00 per annum
Average class size: 25

École Jeannine Manuel is a non-profit PreK-12 coeducational school founded in 1954 with the mission to promote international understanding through bilingual (French/English) education. An associated UNESCO school, École Jeannine Manuel welcomes pupils representing 80 nationalities and every major cultural tradition. The school's academic excellence matches its diversity: École Jeannine Manuel is regularly ranked among the best French high schools (state and independent) for its overall academic performance (ranked first for ten consecutive years). The school is accredited by the French Ministry of Education, the International Baccalaureate Organization (IBO), the Council of International Schools (CIS) and the New England Association of Schools and Colleges (NEASC).

Each year, the school welcomes more than 100 new non-French speaking pupils. These students integrate the school through our adaptation program, which provides intensive instruction in French, support in English as needed, help in understanding and adjusting to French culture, and differentiated coursework and assessment during their adaptation period.

The lower and middle school follow the French national curriculum with several exceptions: in the lower school, half of the day is taught in English, and, in middle school, experimental sciences, history and geography are taught in English. The curriculum is enriched at all levels, not only with a more advanced English language and literature curriculum, but also, for example, with Chinese language instruction (compulsory in grades 3-4-5), an integrated science program in lower school, and independent research projects in middle school.

In upper school, tenth graders follow the French national curriculum, which is taught 50% in English and 50% in French. In 11th grade, pupils choose between the French track (*Baccalauréat Français International*, BFI) and the International Baccalaureate Diploma Programme (IBDP). Approximately 25% of our pupils opt for the IBDP.

Over the past three years, around 13% of our graduating students attended US colleges or universities, 41% chose to study in the UK, and 29% entered the French higher education system. Around 7% of graduating students go on to study in countries all over the world such as the Netherlands, Switzerland, Belgium, Germany, Spain, Italy, and Australia.

Admission:
Admission is competitive and applications typically exceed available spaces by a ratio of 7:1. The school nonetheless makes every effort to reserve space for international applicants, including children of families who expect to remain in France for a limited period of time and wish to combine a cultural immersion in French education with the ability to seamlessly re-enter the school system in their home country.

Netherlands

Elckerlyc International School

Klimopzoom 41, 2353 RE Leiderdorp, South Holland, Netherlands
Tel: +31 71 5896861
Email: international@elckerlyc.net
Website: www.elckerlyc-international.nl
Headteacher: Lesley de Quartel

School type: Co-educational Day
Age range of pupils: 3–11 years
No. of pupils enrolled as at 01/09/2025: 140
Fees as at 01/09/2025:
Day: €4,200 per annum

Learning together, growing together

We are a small local school where our aim is to help you and your child feel at home as quickly as possible. Knowing that every child is unique, we strive to help our students develop into valuable members of a global society. It is our task to identify how best to support them on this journey. Here at Elckerlyc, we believe education is much more than numeracy and literacy. It is also about responsibility, dealing with your own and other people's emotions, respect and communication.

Elckerlyc International is a member of The Dutch International Primary Schools (DIPS). This means that our school offers international education embedded in a Dutch context; as such we operate within the framework of the Dutch educational system. As we are partly funded by the Dutch government, we can ensure that education at our school remains affordable for expat families.

Italy

English Gate School

(Founded 2010)

Via Ginevrina da Fossano 38, 22063 Cantù, Como, Italy
Tel: +39 031 4896 941
Email: admissions@englishgate.it
Website: www.englishgate.it
Head of School:
Mr. Francesco Masetti Placci

School type: Co-educational Day
Age range of pupils: 1–14 years
No. of pupils enrolled as at 01/09/2025: 250
Fees as at 01/09/2025:
€9,000–€11,500 per annum

English Gate School
The English Gate School of Cantù is a private Innovative School catering for pupils from 1 to 14 years old, including Early Years, Primary and Middle School.

Our curriculum, where English is the main language of learning, is based on the British National Curriculum with an integration of the Italian Programma Ministeriale in order to keep and value the knowledge of the Italian culture and language.

EGS teachers are prepared to provide a wide range of learning strategies, catering for all learning styles and stimulating the students' multiple intelligences. EGS strives to inspire, motivate, and challenge all students to achieve their personal best, providing, if deemed necessary, customized programme and individual education plans to help students reach their full potential.

At English Gate, school means academics, discovery, hard work, responsibility, growth, but also community, amusement, friendship, and real life skills. Our didactics aims to develop a solid knowledge background, combined with experience-based approach, field trips, personal projects and engagements activities.

Our Values
At EGS we firmly believe that a welcoming and pleasant environment can enhance the quality of our educational intervention. Therefore, besides carefully selecting teachers and a rich and balanced curriculum, we are all committed to guaranteeing the happiness and wellbeing of our students through the following pillars that we teach and share:
- Respect
- Kindness
- Working together
- Helping each other
- Making mistakes.

Globeducate
EGS Cantù is a proud member of Globeducate, one of the world's leading premium K12 education organisations, with more than 50 schools located in Italy, France, Spain, United Kingdom, Portugal, Canada, Andorra, and India. A fundamental aim of Globeducate is preparing each student to shape the world and to understand their place in it as a global citizen. The bespoke gold standard school quality programme ensures that Globeducate's 31,000 students have the best start in life.

Spain

ES American School

(Founded 1999)

Autovia de Castelldefels C-31 Km 191, El Prat de Llobregat, 08820 Barcelona, Catalonia, Spain
Tel: +34 93 479 1611
Email: admin@es-school.com
Website: www.es-school.com
Head of School: Ms. Melanie Rose

School type: Co-educational Day
Age range of pupils: 6–18 years
No. of pupils enrolled as at 01/09/2025: 140
Fees as at 01/09/2025:
Day: €12,020–€20,485 per annum
Average class size: 5-20
Teacher/pupil ratio: 1:5

ES American School offers an independent, college preparatory American curriculum for 5 to 18 year olds (1st through 12th grades) located within the campus of the Emilio Sanchez Academy, Barcelona. Our Elementary is an authorized IB PYP school, offering the International Baccalaureate Primary Years Programme, a world-renowned curricular framework, where children learn to take ownership of their own learning, increasing confidence and self-motivation. In Middle School, the enrichment program supports students to have a broad range of learning experiences. The Advanced Placement (AP) program in High School offers students the opportunity to work at a more challenging level with the potential to earn university credit. Students who elect to take the Spanish program alongside the American curriculum are eligible to homologate their diploma.

With locations in Barcelona, Spain and Naples, Florida, USA, ES American School provides students with a truly international experience enabling them to excel both academically and athletically. All students receive individual attention, close academic guidance and personal counseling. The predominant language on campus is English.

Sports are an essential part of the curriculum and students benefit from the world-class tennis program and training facilities provided by Emilio Sanchez Academy. Our students have three distinct pathways with regards to sport: high-performance tennis (offered on-site), high-performance in other sports (offered off-site), including soccer, basketball, or horse riding OR our Physical Education Program for general fitness and well-being. ES American School, Barcelona is accredited by the Middle States Association of Colleges and Schools and is authorized by the Department of Education of the Catalan Government.

Haileybury

UK

Haileybury, Hertford, Hertfordshire SG13 7NU UK
Tel: +44 (0)1992 706353
Email: admissions@haileybury.com
Website: www.haileybury.com
The Master: Mr Eugene du Toit MA, MBA
Appointed: September 2024
School type: Co-educational Day & Boarding Senior & Sixth Form
Age range of pupils: 11–18 years (entry at 11+, 13+, 14+ and 16+)
No. of pupils enrolled as at 01/09/2025: 925

Boys: 476 **Girls:** 449 **Sixth Form:** 400
No. of boarders: 598
Fees as at 01/09/2025:
Senior Boarding: £56,796 per annum (incl. VAT)
Senior Day: £41,100 per annum (incl. VAT)
Lower School Boarding: £36,030 per annum (incl. VAT)
Lower School Day: £27,315 per annum (incl. VAT)
Teacher/pupil ratio: 1:7

Haileybury is a leading independent co-educational boarding and day school, situated on 500 acres of beautiful Hertfordshire countryside, just 20 miles north of London. Haileybury's spectacular grounds are home to outstanding facilities, excellent teaching and superb pastoral care for its community of pupils.

Academic excellence
The school offers a dedicated Lower School for Years 7 and 8 and a wide range of GCSEs and IGCSEs. In the Sixth Form, pupils can select to study for A levels or the International Baccalaureate (IB) Diploma. Haileybury is extremely proud of the excellent examination results achieved by its A Level, IB and (I)GCSE pupils and was named 'best UK fully co-educational IB independent school 2024' by The Times.

Boarding and day
Around two-thirds of pupils are boarders and boarding life is varied and fun. On joining Haileybury, boarding and day pupils are allocated to one of the Houses and are welcomed into their House community.

Exceptional opportunities
A key part of Haileybury's philosophy is empowering each child to follow their passions and build self-confidence. Beyond the academic curriculum, pupils benefit from a vast array of activities, including professional sports coaching for all and regular visits from speakers and performers from the arts, sporting and academic worlds. The co-curricular programme is packed with opportunities, from climbing and scuba diving to filmmaking and Model United Nations - and countless activities in between. Haileybury also encourages pupils to immerse themselves in the Creative Arts. Drama, Music, Dance, LAMDA and Art are at the heart of school life and the school takes pride in hosting spectacular

productions and multiple showcases each term. It is Haileybury's ambition to provide pupils with the very best facilities for all aspects of their education. The new Science and Technology buildings offer the latest technology to further challenge pupils and enhance their skills. It provides the space and opportunity for them to participate in innovative initiatives, such as the global Stan-X programme, a pioneering study of genetics. Working from purpose-built labs, Haileybury pupils are contributing to efforts to find cures for diseases such as pancreatic cancer and diabetes.

Supportive environment
At Haileybury, a caring environment is crucial to a pupil's happiness and fulfilment. There is an emphasis on pastoral care with around-the-clock support, as well as an on-site Health and Wellbeing centre providing a circle of care. The school is a home-from-home, with a warm and friendly feel.

Spain

Hamelin-Laie International School Barcelona

HAMELIN-LAIE INTERNATIONAL SCHOOL
BARCELONA
A NORD ANGLIA EDUCATION SCHOOL

(Founded 1989)

178-180 Ronda 8 de Març, 08390 Montgat, Barcelona, Catalonia, Spain
Tel: +34 935 55 67 17
Email: admissions@hamelinschool.com
Website: www.hamelinschool.com

Principal: Sarah Osborne-James
School type: Co-educational Day & Boarding
Age range of pupils: 4 months–18 years
No. of pupils enrolled as at 01/09/2025: 1475

Hamelin-Laie International School Barcelona is a thriving community of over 55 nationalities, where students learn in English as well as Spanish and Catalan. Part of the Nord Anglia Education family, we shape open-minded citizens who'll make their mark in our globalized world.

Our vibrant international community is a place where your child will embrace exciting learning experiences both in and outside the classroom. At our private international school, we'll also give them opportunities to connect with the world around them, ensuring they develop a truly global outlook.

Whatever your child wants to do or be in life, we'll ensure they have everything they need for success. Our talented teachers will guide them through their unique learning journey, encouraging their interests, passions, and talents.

Our history:
Hamelin-Laie International School Barcelona opened its doors in 1989. We were the first private school in Barcelona to offer learning in English, Spanish, and Catalan. Authorised by the Ministry of Education and Culture of Spain (MEC) – and the world-renowned International Baccalaureate – we continue to be the leading multilingual school in the region.

Since our founding, Hamelin-Laie has continued to grow, and we have added a premium boarding programme that's home to a diverse international community of up to 45 students.

We're proud to be part of the Nord Anglia family, an international schools' group with an outstanding reputation for academic and personal excellence worldwide.

Academic Excellence:
At Hamelin-Laie, our students immerse themselves in a bespoke academic programme adapted from the Spanish National Curriculum with many integrated global contexts, from our international learning environment. This is packed with engaging experiences, and project-based learning to foster emotional, social, listening, and critical thinking skills.

A Leading International Education Pathway
Our school is a fully accredited provider of the International Early Years Curriculum (IEYC), International Primary Curriculum (IPC), and International Middle Years Curriculum (IMYC). Our students begin their international learning journey in Nursery and Reception with the IEYC, progress to the IPC from Years 2 to 6, and transition into the IMYC for Years 7 to 10.

Spain

These curricula, developed by the International Curriculum Association (ICA) – a global leader in educational innovation since 1984 – promote inquiry-led, thematic learning rooted in international best practices.

In Years 10 and 11, students follow our bespoke Pre-Baccalaureate curriculum, designed to equip them with the academic, personal, and linguistic foundations required to thrive in the next stage of their education. This programme serves as a bridge to the next stage, depending on each student's goals.

From Years 12 to 13, students choose between two academically rigorous pathways:
- The IB Diploma Programme, a globally recognised qualification that nurtures critical thinking, global-mindedness, and academic excellence. Hamelin-Laie boasts a pass rate of 98% in recent years, significantly above the global average
- The Spanish National Baccalaureate, which offers an in-depth curriculum aligned with national university entry requirements.

At Hamelin, we are proud to offer a comprehensive international education that combines excellence, choice, and personalised careers guidance support to prepare students for success at top universities around the world.

Our Campus:
The Hamelin-Laie International School Barcelona campus is unlike any other. Situated in the safe and friendly town of Montgat, just 20 minutes from the historic heart of Barcelona, our modern, purpose-built school environment is surrounded by green spaces and natural beauty.

Our cleverly designed, free-flowing areas enable students to take in everything our extraordinary beachside location offers. Sweeping views of the Mediterranean Sea and local mountains inspire them, as they learn and play indoors and outside.

Boarding: An Exceptional Home Away from Home
Hamelin-Laie International School Barcelona is so much more than a school for our boarders. We're a second family, a thriving international community in Spain, and a place where 24/7 care, guidance, and friendship inspire our students to make their mark.

Your child will join a close-knit community of up to 50 secondary students, supported by our caring House parents and dedicated staff. They'll be guided throughout their time here by our boarding staff, who are available around the clock to provide invaluable support.

Living and studying in our international boarding house builds our students' confidence and independence, as they get ready to take on the world.

Global Awareness
At Hamelin-Laie, we want our students to have an open-minded worldview. Enhancing their global awareness becomes a key aspect of this, including how they connect with and help others.

We'd love to show you around our campus either in person or online, where we'll discuss how we can prepare your child for an extraordinary future. Contact us at **admissions@hamelinschool.com** or take our virtual tour: **guiap.com/360/hamelinschool/**

Switzerland

Haut-Lac International Bilingual School

(Founded 1993)
Ch. de Pangires 26, St-Légier-la Chiésaz,
CH-1806 Switzerland

Tel: +41 (0)21 555 51 29
Email: admissions@haut-lac.ch
Website: www.haut-lac.ch
Infant & Primary Head: Mr Renaud Milhoux
Secondary Head: Ms Rossella Cosso
School type: Co-educational Day & Boarding
Age range of pupils: 18 months–18 years

No. of pupils enrolled as at 01/09/2025: 650
Fees as at 01/09/2025:
Day: CHF24,900–CHF36,100 per annum
Full Boarding: CHF72,000–CHF88,000 per annum
Average class size: 12
Teacher/pupil ratio: 1:6

General
Haut-Lac is:
- Your Local International School

Haut-Lac means:
- Excellence in education for 3 to 18 year olds
- 30 years' experience in bilingual education
- 96% International Baccalaureate Diploma pass rate
- Higher education studies at top universities in Switzerland and worldwide
- Boutique boarding home for up to 30 international students and/or athletes

Haut-Lac values:
- Respect
- Resilience
- Open-mindedness
- Sense of belonging

Academics
Students develop the academic knowledge and soft skills required to succeed in the modern world.

Infant & Primary (3-11 y.o.)
- Bilingual French-English or predominantly English pathways
- Personalised programme combining Swiss, International & British curricula

Secondary
- Personalised bilingual, English-only or French-only pathways
- IB Middle Years Programme (11–16 y.o.)
- Swiss Option (11–14 y.o)
- IB Diploma Programme (16–19 y.o.)
- IB Career-Related Programme (16–19 y.o.)
  - Sustainable Management
  - Art & Design
  - Hospitality Management
  - International Sports Management
- US High School Diploma (16–19 y.o.)
- IB Sport & Study (11–19 y.o.)
  - Flexible and/or extended IBMYP, IBDP and IBCP programmes
  - Ski Racing Academy with Ski Zenit

Extra-Curricular
- 151 after-school clubs
- Out-of-hours care from 7:15 to 18:00, including lunchtime supervision
- Regular student and family events
- Bilingual Winter, Spring and Summer activity camps for 4 to 15 year olds
- Summer Residential Camps
  - Language & Adventure (10–16 year olds)
  - Leadership & Adventure (14–17 year olds)

Accreditations & Memberships
IB, CIS, WAoS Athlete-Friendly Education Centre, Eco-Schools, AVDEP, SGIS, FSEP

Italy

H-FARM International School

(Founded 1995)
Via Olivetti 1, 31056 Roncade (TV), Italy
Tel: +39 0422 789503
Email: info.ve@h-is.com
Website:
www.h-farm.com/en/h-farm-school/venezia

Head of School: Mr. Emiliano Cori
Appointed: September 2024
School type:
Co-educational Day & Boarding
Age range of pupils: 3–18 years

H-FARM International School is a day & boarding school offering three IB programmes (PYP, MYP, DP) within a stunning and innovative 50-hectare campus, located minutes away from Venice, Italy.

H-FARM International School, located just outside of Venice, Italy, empowers students to be internationally-minded citizens who are able to shape their own future in a rapidly changing global community. Through innovative learning environments and the development of relationships based on compassion and respect, we enable students to become confident, creative and collaborative. We are a community of active lifelong learners. H-FARM International School serves a diverse and growing community of students and families.

Our school uses English as the language of instruction and learning and aims to promote international mindedness and global citizenship.

We offer three of the International Baccalaureate Organization's educational programmes: Primary Years Programme (nursery / elementary school), Middle Years Programme (middle school + 1st two years of high school) and the world-renowned Diploma Programme (final two years of high school), an engaging curriculum that prepares students to access the most prestigious universities and colleges in the world.

Our school is located within the Campus of H-FARM, located just 10 minutes from Venice International Airport, an unparalleled center for innovation in Europe, with a strong DNA of digital technology, creativity and entrepreneurship. The sprawling campus boasts world class services for both its boarding and day students. H-FARM students have access to full-service Boarding facilities (which were recently certified by the BSA), an indoor and outdoor sports complex, a fully-equipped gymnasium, a coffee shop and restaurant, a library with communal study areas, a radio station, an astronomy observation station, innovative science and Virtual Reality laboratories.

This school year, we welcomed more than 170 new students and more than 100 Boarding students from 20 different countries and representing all 6 continents. Boarding students are cared for by Residence Life coordinators, who also facilitate weekend excursions and activities that allow students to enjoy the natural and cultural attractions of our stunning corner of Italy.

Hockerill Anglo-European College

(Founded 1980)

Dunmow Road, Bishops Stortford, Hertfordshire CM23 5HX UK
Tel: 01279 658451
Email: admissions@hockerill.com
Website: www.hockerill.com
Principal: Alasdair Mackenzie
Appointed: September 2020
School type: State Boarding & Day School

Age range of pupils: 11–18 years
No. of pupils enrolled as at 01/09/2025: 920
No. of boarders: 390
Fees as at 01/09/2025:
Residential Boarding: from £15,279 per annum
Average class size: 21
Teacher/pupil ratio: 1:13

Inspiring knowledgeable, enquiring and caring global citizens through excellence in education

Situated on a leafy campus in Bishop's Stortford, just 10 minutes from London Stansted Airport, Hockerill Anglo-European College is a leading UK state boarding school. Home to a strong, supportive community of around 900 students aged 11–18, including 400 boarders, all five boarding houses are located within the school grounds.

With a long-established reputation for academic excellence, Hockerill students consistently achieve strong results and progress to top universities in the UK and internationally. Many secure places at prestigious Russell Group institutions, and outcomes consistently compare favourably with those of leading independent schools.

The College offers a rigorous and broad curriculum. It is one of the UK's largest state providers of the prestigious International Baccalaureate programmes, offering both the Middle Years Programme (MYP) and the Diploma Programme (DP). Students study two foreign languages to GCSE from an extensive choice, reflecting the College's strong focus on languages and internationalism.

Main entry points are at ages 11 and 16, with some students joining at 13 or 14. After completing the MYP, students progress to GCSEs before embarking on the IB Diploma in the Sixth Form.

Life beyond the classroom is an essential part of the Hockerill experience. A wide-ranging co-curricular programme encourages students to explore new interests, express creativity and develop leadership. Each term, a refreshed roster of around 100 clubs and societies offers opportunities across music, sport, service and innovation – from choirs and orchestras to BMX, the CCF and debating.

The College's global outlook is brought to life through international trips and exchanges. From language immersions in Europe and Asia to biodiversity research in Croatia and outreach projects in Africa, students gain meaningful experiences that broaden horizons and build confidence.

Prospective families are warmly encouraged to visit and discover life at Hockerill.

France

ICS Côte d'Azur

(Founded 2006)

245 Route les Lucioles,
06560 Valbonne, France
Tel: +33 (0)4 93 64 32 84
Email: admissions@icscotedazur.com
Website: www.icscotedazur.com
Head of School: Ms. Gina Bianchi
Appointed: 2023

School type: Co-educational Day
Age range of pupils: 3–11 years
No. of pupils enrolled as at 01/09/2025: 200
Fees as at 01/09/2025:
Day: €12,480–€16,692 per annum
Average class size: 17

ICS Côte d'Azur is a bilingual, co-educational, non-sectarian IB World Primary School serving international and local families in the Sophia Antipolis region. The school offers Early Years and Primary Years education from KG1 (age 3) to PY6 (age 11) and is part of the Globeducate network.

Formerly known as EBICA, the school's multicultural community enjoys a modern, secure campus with outdoor learning and sports facilities in Valbonne, southwest of Nice. Recognised as an IB World School since 2018, ICS Côte d'Azur delivers an inquiry-based international education through the IB Primary Years Programme, while integrating aspects of the national curricula for England and France.

Students learn in both French and English from the early years onward. Within this bilingual environment, they develop global citizenship and an appreciation of French culture. Language support is offered from age 7 through French as a Foreign Language (FLE) and English as an Additional Language (EAL), helping learners build the confidence and skills to access the curriculum.

Through learner-centred teaching and a strong culture of care, students are encouraged to develop self-knowledge, independence and resilience. The attributes of the IB Learner Profile guide their academic and personal growth, preparing them to succeed in a diverse and connected world.

To foster creativity, critical thinking and collaboration, ICS Côte d'Azur offers a dynamic STEAM programme (Science, Technology, Engineering, Art and Maths), supported by a tinkering lab called The Hub and LEGO® Education Robotics. Outdoor Learning is also woven into the curriculum, offering hands-on experiences that inspire curiosity and connection to the natural world.

At ICS Côte d'Azur, every child is known, valued, and empowered to flourish in a bilingual setting that nurtures both academic and personal growth.

UK

ICS London

(Founded 1979)

7B Wyndham Place, London, W1H 1PN UK
Tel: +44 (0)20 729 88800
Email: admissions@icslondon.co.uk
Website: www.icslondon.co.uk
Head of School: Mona Taybi
School type: Co-educational Day Preparatory & Senior, Nursery & Sixth Form

Age range of pupils: 3–18 years
No. of pupils enrolled as at 01/09/2025: 150
Fees as at 01/09/2025:
Day: £22,890–£34,200 per annum
Average class size: Av 12, Max 16
Teacher/pupil ratio: 1:5

ICS London is an independent day school in the heart of central London. We offer the International Baccalaureate (IB) programme and iGCSE programme for learners aged 3 to 18 years.

Providing an inclusive and international community for early years, primary, secondary and high school students, our children and young people study on two close-by locations at our primary and secondary school sites in elegant Marylebone and Paddington.

With over 40 years' experience delivering globally-recognised education, today we serve our close-knit community of students and their families with the IB Primary Years Programme (PYP), the Middle Years Programme (MYP) and the Diploma Programme (DP). Within the MYP at Key Stage 4, the curriculum, including IGCSE qualifications, provides a solid foundation in preparation for the IBDP and a gateway for future studies. With instruction in English, we are a truly international school where diversity is celebrated with around 50+ different nationalities represented each year.

Quality is assessed, recognised and assured at ICS London through accreditation with the:
- IB World School: ICS London is authorised and accredited by the International Baccalaureate. This is subject to a strict accreditation process monitored by the IB which ensures our education provision is of the highest quality.
- Independent Schools Inspectorate: This is a government approved inspectorate for independent schools which ensures quality on behalf of the UK Department for Education (DfE).

ICS London also prides itself on offering a holistic and personalised learning experience:
- Class sizes: Between 6 and 18 students
- Teacher to student ratio: 1 to 5
- In Nursery and Reception there are 2 teachers in every class
- In Secondary School each student is assigned a mentor
- Individual study plans can be tailored to meet students' needs

As a rolling admissions policy is in place, students can join anytime throughout the year. Students can also easily transfer from other curriculums, such as the UK or US and join the IB programme at ICS London. For further information please visit www.icslondon.co.uk or call +44 (0)20 7298 8800.

ICS Milan

ICS Symbiosis, Viale Ortles, 46, 20139 Milano (MI), Italy

Tel: +39 02 36592694
Email: admissions@icsmilan.com
Website: www.icsmilan.com
Head of School: Mr Luke Osborne
Early Years & Primary Principal: Ms Jenny O'Fee

Secondary Principal: Mr. Robert Champion
School type: Co-educational Day
Age range of pupils: 1–18 years
No. of pupils enrolled as at 01/09/2025: 1000
Fees as at 01/09/2025:
Day: €15,000–€28,000 per annum

ICS Milan International School

ICS Milan is an IB World School dedicated to students aged 1–18 that offers an international curriculum enhanced by an innovative teaching approach based on experiential learning and a STEAM agenda (Science, Technology, Engineering, Arts and Maths). With three different campuses throughout the Milan area, ICS Milan is a school of innovation that helps children grow into citizens of the world.

ICS Milan serves a diverse community of students from a range of nationalities, cultures and backgrounds. The school offers a broad-based education that uses English as the main language of learning and caters for a range of student abilities. ICS Milan's vision is to inspire, motivate, and challenge all students to achieve their personal best by providing a rich, creative, and well-balanced educational experience.

International School with Italian Roots

As Scuola Paritaria (an officially recognised school), our school also adopts the national recommendations for the curriculum issued by MIM (the Ministry of Education). The Italian language and history programmes are designed for mother-tongue Italian speakers. A specific programme for Italian as an additional language is available for children of other nationalities.

ICS Values

ICS Milan teaches creativity, responsibility, respect, diversity, compassion and shared values. Students are invited to develop a sound knowledge base and to reflect on and reassess their surroundings from a variety of perspectives.

Our system fosters a balanced development of different personalities. It combines the importance of rules with a sense of expressive creativity, challenge and imagination, and it also provides the necessary tools for becoming "masters" of our own abilities.

Our teaching approach stimulates each developmental and learning phase of every child by placing respect for others and for ourselves at its centre.

Globeducate

ICS Milan is a proud member of Globeducate, one of the world's leading premium K12 education organisations, with more than 65 schools located in Italy, France, Spain, United Kingdom, Portugal, Canada, Andorra, and India. A fundamental aim of Globeducate is preparing each student to shape the world and to understand their place in it as a global citizen. The bespoke gold standard school quality programme ensures that Globeducate's 40,000 students have the best start in life.

France

ICS Paris

(Founded 1983)

23 rue de Cronstadt, 75015 Paris, France
Tel: +33 (0)1 56 56 60 31
Email: admissions@icsparis.fr
Website: www.icsparis.fr
Director: Mrs. Angela Hollington
School type: Co-educational Day

Age range of pupils: 3–18 years
No. of pupils enrolled as at 01/09/2025: 500
Fees as at 01/09/2025:
Day: €20,595–€31,260 per annum
Average class size: 20

ICS Paris has been ranked the #4 IB School in France and placed among the Top 65 IB Schools in Europe. This recognition is based on our exceptional International Baccalaureate Diploma Programme (IBDP) results. Established in 1983, ICS Paris is the only International Baccalaureate (IB) Continuum school in Paris that offers all three of the prestigious programmes – Primary Years Programme (PYP), Middle Years Programme (MYP) and Diploma Programme (DP) – on a single campus for students aged 3 to 18. We also offer the internationally recognised IGCSE curriculum for Grades 9 and 10, preparing students for a smooth transition into the IBDP. Officially authorised by the IB Organization (IBO), ICS Paris is an inclusive and intercultural educational community driven by a commitment to excellence.

Dedicated to developing global citizens and lifelong learners, we empower our students to shape a brighter future by preparing them for tomorrow's challenges today. We are proud of our vibrant multicultural environment, which welcomes students from over 70 countries, and we provide a high-quality education that equips them to thrive in the world, shape it and make a positive difference.

Located in the heart of Paris, we ensure that each of our students is immersed in many different aspects of French culture through outings in Paris and trips further afield in France, making for a rich learning experience. Our supportive, nurturing community cares about how our students grow into the generation of tomorrow. We expect our students to develop empathy, be kind to each other, and demonstrate resilience and perseverance when faced with difficult situations. Working together in groups, collaborating, and the many different approaches to learning that we use help to cultivate these crucial skills and contribute to developing responsible adults of the future.

At ICS Paris, our students are at the centre of everything we do. Our International Baccalaureate curriculum provides the framework for developing their thinking skills and empowering them to take ownership of their learning. Education at ICS Paris is rooted in the IB learning philosophy and is structured to equip students with the next generation's skills.

As an international school, we are building towards becoming a Bilingual Multilingual Learners (BML) smart school. With a research-based approach to learning languages and education, we are working on providing the knowledge, expertise, and facilities where children can learn their mother tongue language, and at the same time, follow a rigorous English-language curriculum. By providing opportunities for multiple language learning, we equip our students with the communication skills essential in an international environment while fostering an understanding and experience of French culture.

UK

Impington International College

New Road, Impington, Cambridge, Cambridgeshire CB24 9LX UK
Tel: 01223 200402
Email: international@ivc.tmet.org.uk
Website: www.impingtoninternational.org.uk
College Principal: Ms Johanna Sale

Appointed: 2025
School type: Co-educational Day & Boarding (in host families)
Age range of pupils: 16–19 years
No. of pupils enrolled as at 01/09/2025: 250
Average class size: 10-15
Teacher/pupil ratio: 1:15

A World Class IB education from Impington International College - your ticket to a world of opportunity
Why choose Impington International College?

1. **The quality of care is exceptional** - The tutor to student ratio is approximately 1 to 15, with a dedicated Student Manager for pastoral support and guidance. In lessons, the teacher to student ratio is, on average, 1 to 10.
2. **It delivers excellent outcomes** - The pass rate is 100% (international average: 80%) and the average International Baccalaureate (IB) point score is 35.
3. **Students go on to achieve great things** - In 2020, 90% of the students went on to study at university, with 25% offered Russell Group places (including Oxbridge). In addition to this, the remaining 10% of students were successful in their job applications and seamlessly moved into the world of work.
4. **Expert delivery of the International Baccalaureate** - for more than 30 years, Impington International College has offered the IB and was one of the first state schools in the UK to do so. The College is consistently rated 'Outstanding' by Ofsted.
5. **It is truly international** - around half of students attend Impington International College from overseas, creating a culturally diverse student cohort and unique opportunities for study and trips.

Impington International College offers the following programmes to students:
- IB Diploma Programme (DP)
- IB Career-related Programme (CP)
- Extended BTECs
- The Performance School
- Sports Scholarship Programmes

Impington International College bases its teaching on the IB's mission statement and ethos, aiming to develop "inquiring, knowledgeable and caring young people who help to create a better and more peaceful world". Not only do students gain a valuable breadth of skills through either the DP or the CP but IB higher level subjects also provide the same depth of knowledge as A Levels, so students can go on to achieve excellence in whichever path they choose.

The driven cohort achieve outstanding results and have gone on to attend renowned higher education institutions around the world, including: University of Cambridge, University of Oxford, London School of Economics and Political Science, University College London, King's College London, Loughborough University, Leiden University, UCLA, The Place, Italia Conti, International University of Japan, and many more. Many students from the College's Performance School go on to join professional companies, with a number starring in the West End. Students from the sports scholarship programme often go on to study coaching and management at university, or play semi-professionally for local teams.

Institut International Saint-Dominique

Via Igino Lega 5, 00189 Rome, Italy
Tel: +39 06 30 31 08 17
Email: info@institutsaintdominique.it
Website: www.institutsaintdominique.fr
Headmaster: Audren Séguillon
School type: Co-educational Day & Boarding

Age range of pupils: 18 months–18 years
No. of pupils enrolled as at 01/09/2025: 396
Fees as at 01/09/2025:
Day: €16,100 per annum
Weekly Boarding: €30,050 per annum
Full Boarding: €34,050 per annum

LEARN AND LIVE IN A UNIQUE FRENCH INTERNATIONAL SCHOOL IN ROME!
For over 60 years, the Institut International Saint-Dominique de Rome (ISD Rome) has welcomed students from around the world, from Nursery to High School, on an exceptional 6-hectare campus just outside the city. Rooted in French and international curricula, our educational approach combines academic excellence with individualized support, nurturing each student's unique potential.

A Truly International Education in the Eternal City
With a 100% success rate in the Baccalaureate, ISD Rome prepares students for entry into top universities worldwide. From an early age, students benefit from a multilingual learning journey, enriched by the opportunity to follow the International Baccalaureate (IB) pathway from Grade 9. "At St Dominique, the IB philosophy is not just an academic framework. It is a transformative journey. It empowers our students to think deeply, embrace diverse perspectives, and engage with the world around them in a meaningful way. I see them grow not only in knowledge, but in confidence, empathy, and purpose. As an educator, guiding them through this process is a true privilege. It is a daily reminder of how powerful education can be when it nurtures both the mind and the heart." – N. Hakmé, IBDP Coordinator at ISD Rome.

Life beyond the Classroom
ISD offers a varied afterschool program with a wide range of sports, artistic, and cultural activities throughout the year. Studying at St Dominique is also an opportunity to take part in bilingual Holiday Camps, combining learning

with fun activities. The school was founded by Dominican sisters who laid the foundations for a community of humanistic values. Students are free to participate in moments of spiritual activity.

A multicultural community
Joining ISD Rome means becoming part of a dynamic and diverse community shaped by over six decades of tradition and innovation. As a proud member of the Odyssey Education network, our students take part in international events such as the British Science Week, International Days, Francophonie celebrations, inter-school competitions, and educational trips – all enriching their global perspective.

A Home away from Home: our International Boarding School
Located in a city steeped in history and culture, our Boarding School provides a safe, welcoming, and well-equipped environment for students. Each room features a comfortable bed, private bathroom, study area, and ample storage. The ISD Boarding school offers cozy common spaces indoors and outdoors, ideal for socializing, studying, or relaxing. Boarding students enjoy full access to the campus facilities, including sports fields and a fitness room. Evening activities are organized daily, and weekend boarders have the chance to explore Rome through exciting outings led by our dedicated team.

Institut Le Châtelard

Route des Narcisses 80, 1833 Les-Avants-sur-Montreux, Switzerland
Tel: +41 21 989 8000
Email: info@lechatelard.com
Website: www.ecolechatelard.ch
Head of School: Mrs Federica Páez
School type: Girls' Boarding

Age range of girls: 13–17 (annual) & 12–15 (summer camps)
No. of pupils enrolled as at 01/09/2025:
Annual: 96
Summer Camps: 120
Fees as at 01/09/2025:
Full Boarding: CHF107,550.00–CHF124,400.00 per annum

Le Châtelard is a leading, prestigious, private, Catholic, international boarding school dedicated to the integral formation of young ladies all over the world, with more than 30 years of experience.

Located in the breathtaking Swiss Alps, our students live and grow in a safe environment that fosters their confidence, character, and purpose, guided by solid moral and faith values. Our mission is to nurture each student's potential – growing academically, socially and personally to become a confident, compassionate leader in today's world.

Program:
We believe in learning beyond the classroom. With French language immersion, our students explore, innovate, and grow through real-world international experience, following our innovative and competitive academic curriculum aligned with Swiss educational standards and our global Oak International Academies Network.

To ensure the highest educational standards, we provide students with recognised credentials that enhance their future opportunities, such as the DELF (French), Cambridge First Certificate (English), and our prestigious Le Cordon Bleu Diploma, which promotes knowledge, professional skills, culture, and the development of values and personal abilities. At the same time, our exclusive Savoir Vivre program nurtures self-awareness, emotional intelligence, and etiquette. Moreover, students thrive through our extensive sports program and incredible ski season.

Safe Environments and Facilities
We believe in the critical importance of a secure and well-being living environment. We ensure every student is heard, guided, and supported during her journey. Personal mentors and an emotional support team guide them beyond academics. Together with families, we build a community and an environment where our students feel at home.

Preserving the charm of a Belle Époque hotel from the late 1800s, our academy has been transformed into a modern boarding school balancing tradition and innovation. With comfortable en-suite rooms, sport and fitness areas, a Cordon Bleu kitchen room, theatre, and chapel, our students thrive in a safe and nurturing environment.

Institut Montana Switzerland

Schönfels 5, 6300 Zug ZG, Switzerland
Tel: +41 41 729 11 77
Email: admissions@montana-zug.ch
Website: www.montana-zug.ch
Director: Collective Leadership Model
School type: Co-educational Day & Boarding

Age range of pupils: 6–19 years
No. of pupils enrolled as of 01/09/2025: 360+
Fees as at 01/09/2025:
Day: CHF 32,900–CHF 36,800 per annum
Full Boarding: CHF 70,400–CHF 72,800 per annum
Average class size: 10

My Place to Grow. Since 1926.
We believe every child has talent. Our mission is to nurture this talent.

We are a Swiss international day and boarding school on the idyllic Zugerberg, on the doorstep of the vibrant city of Zug. Institut Montana Switzerland offers Swiss academic pathways (accredited by the Canton of Zug) as well as international programmes.

Currently, we host 360+ students from around 55 countries. They develop through our founding values: Internationalism, Individualism, Integration, and Innovation. Our dedicated teachers, small class sizes, high-quality teaching and co-curricular activities provide the optimal environment for our students to grow into strong, insightful, compassionate adults. This is the Montana Learning Experience.

Our Academic Pathways
- The Swiss Bilingual Primary School for grades 1–6 where students will learn half of the subjects in German and the other half in English based on the Swiss curriculum. Boarding is available from the age of 10.
- The Swiss Bilingual Secondary School for grades 7–9 is a bridge between primary and further education. With exceptional individual support the curriculum prepares students to transfer either to our Swiss Gymnasium (Schweizer Gymnasium) or to our International School.
- The Swiss Gymnasium for grades 7–12 where students learn in German and English as well as learn French based on the Swiss curriculum. The Matura grants direct entry to top Swiss universities (ETH, HSG) and is recognised by universities worldwide.
- The International School for grades 6–12 where students join the Cambridge Programmes (CLSP and IGCSE) and the IB Diploma Programme or the High School Diploma. With the IB Diploma, students can access universities in Switzerland and around the world.

Student well-being is a top priority throughout the entire campus – not only in the classroom but across all aspects of school life. A dedicated care team provides round-the-clock care and support, ensuring a smooth transition to life away from home.

We also offer a 2-week Summer Camp for students aged 10–16 years old in July where they will learn German or English alongside various activities and take field trips. As our summer motto goes, this is the place where students Learn. Grow. Move. Meet.

Switzerland

Inter-Community School Zurich

(Founded 1960)

Strubenacher 3, 8126 Zumikon, Switzerland
Tel: +41 44 919 8300
Email: contact@icsz.ch
Website: www.icsz.ch
School type: Co-educational Day
Age range of pupils: 24 months–18 years

No. of pupils enrolled as at 01/09/2025: 800
Fees as at 01/09/2025:
Day: CHF12,600–CHF39,700 per annum
Average class size: 12-20
Teacher/pupil ratio: 1:8

Founded in 1960, ICS is the oldest international school in the Greater Zurich Area and today, one of its most forward-looking.

We are the only school in Zurich to offer the full IB continuum (PYP, MYP, DP), educating students from Nursery to Grade 12 in a dynamic environment that celebrates self-discovery, global perspective, and deep-rooted community. Our approach is grounded in kindness, integrity, and respect – values that are embedded in the everyday rhythms of school life.

Nestled in the landscape of Canton Zurich, our campus and surroundings serve as a living classroom. From our pioneering Waldkinder programme to outdoor learning experiences across all ages, ICS connects education with the real world in meaningful, hands-on ways.

Our faculty are not only teachers, they are mentors and collaborators who shape learning experiences through a programme designed to support every student's journey. With 800 students representing more than 55 nationalities, ICS is a vibrant, inclusive community that reflects the world and prepares students to shape it.

Applications are welcome year-round. Learn more or schedule a personal tour at www.icsz.ch/prospective-students/enquire.

France

International Bilingual School of Provence

(Founded 1996)

500 Route de Bouc-Bel-Air, Domaine des Pins, Luynes, Aix en Provence, 13080 France
Tel: +33 (0)4 4224 0340
Email: info@ibsofprovence.com
Website: www.ibsofprovence.com
General Director: Jean-Marc Gobbi
School type: Co-educational Day & Boarding

Age range of pupils: 2–18 years
No. of pupils enrolled as at 01/09/2025: 1200
Fees as at 01/09/2025:
Day: €12,000–€18,000 per annum
Full Boarding: €25,000–€33,000 per annum
Average class size: 18
Teacher/pupil ratio: 1:6

The International Bilingual School of Provence, an independent coeducational school located near Aix-en-Provence in the south of France, owes its international character to the diversity of its student population. The school, established since 1984, has an annual enrolment of 1100 students from more than 76 different countries in its day and boarding sections. In addition to the French students who make up 50% of the student population, IBS welcomes pupils from the five continents desiring to pursue their education in English, French or both. A particularity of the school is that the international section is not dominated by any one nationality and new students are made to feel at home immediately. Committed to French-English bilingualism, the school offers both the International Baccalaureate Diploma Programme and the French Baccalaureate. The school offers eight first languages to ensure that the student maintains his/her own language skills.

Philosophy
Small classrooms, qualified teachers, modern facilities in a calm environment help ensure the success of each student. IBS offers its students six boarding houses and our campus includes: an amphitheatre, fully-equipped science laboratories, an outdoor and indoor dining hall, computer labs, library, swimming pool, fitness room, tennis courts, soccer field, gymnasium and dance/martial arts room. Involvement in various extracurricular activities is expected and enhances the development of each individual's character within the spirit of the school.

Politeness, respect and consideration for others are important values at IBS. Students leave IBS, the majority for university placements, as caring, responsible young citizens.

Spring and Summer Camps
During the spring and summer holidays, IBS offers French as a Foreign Language and English programmes. Over 600 students from all over the world join IBS every summer to develop their language skills while discovering the beauty of the Provence region.

Admissions
Admission applications are accepted throughout the year for interested students.

For more information, contact the Admissions Department at admissions www.ibsofprovence.com

Netherlands

International French School of Amsterdam

(Founded 2021)

Elementary: Anthonie van Dijckstraat 1 BG,
1077 ME Amsterdam,
North Holland, Netherlands
Secondary: Veerstraat 48,
1075 SW Amsterdam,
North Holland, Netherlands
Tel: +31 6 27 12 83 14
Email: admissions@internationalfrenchschool.com

Website: www.internationalfrenchschool.com
Director: Séverine Fougerol
Appointed: 2024
School type: Co-educational Day
Age range of pupils: 2–18 years
No. of pupils enrolled as at 01/09/2025: 360
Fees as at 01/09/2025:
Day: €11,000–€15,000 per annum
Average class size: 24

The International French School of Amsterdam is a reputable institution offering a rich and diverse educational experience in the heart of the vibrant city of Amsterdam, in a residential area of Amsterdam South. Catering to students from pre-school to high school, the school provides a rigorous and comprehensive curriculum grounded in the French National Education system.

The school's philosophy centres around fostering an inclusive and multicultural learning environment. The bilingual education we offer ensures that students think and study in both French and English, and we offer two hours additional language learning of Dutch. The curriculum is designed to promote academic excellence, personal development, and cultural awareness, enabling students to thrive in a dynamic and interconnected world. The international dimension of the school is a unique feature and this attracts families from a range of nationalities and different education systems.

IFS Amsterdam is a Globeducate school, sharing the network vision to prepare each student to become a global citizen who can shape the world and benefiting from Globeducate's international events and competitions, student exchange experiences and educational support on specialist areas such as Artificial Intelligence and safeguarding of students.

Our state-of-the-art facilities, including advanced science labs, a well-equipped library and creative arts spaces, make an exceptional learning environment. These resources support a broad range of academic and extracurricular activities, encouraging students to explore their interests and develop their talents.

Recognised by the French Ministry of Education, the school is part of the AEFE network (Agence pour l'Enseignement Français à l'Etranger). This affiliation ensures that the school adheres to high standards of educational quality and maintains a strong connection to French educational traditions while integrating international perspectives.

The school is staffed by highly qualified and dedicated international teachers. This ensures that students receive excellent instruction and support, fostering both their academic and personal growth. The school's commitment to excellence allows for individualised attention, helping each student to achieve their full potential and play an active role in their own learning.

Starting in September 2025, IFS Amsterdam will welcome its first Grade 12 class, thus offering a complete K–12 education – from nursery all the way to Grade 12.

Belgium

International Montessori School

(Founded 1993)

Hof Kleinenberg campus
Kleinenbergstraat 97-99, 1932 St. Stevens-Woluwe, Flemish Brabant, Belgium

Savoorke campus
Bergerstraat 24, 3080 Tervuren, Flemish Brabant, Belgium

Hot ten Berg campus
Hof ten Berg 22, 1200 Woluwe St. Lambert, Brussels, Belgium

Tel: +32 (0)2 669 90 80 / +32 (0)2 721 21 11
Email: woluwe@international-montessori.org; tervuren@international-montessori.org
Website: www.international-montessori.org
School type: Co-educational Day
Age range of pupils: 1–18 years
No. of pupils enrolled as at 01/09/2025: 350
Fees as at 01/09/2025:
€10,270–€35,500 per annum

Multilingual Montessori Education
Montessori education offers a holistic approach helping children develop all aspects of their personality. A well-balanced child is a happy child, ready to develop to his full potential and eventually make a difference for the greater good! We take into account that different ages have the ability to reach different developmental milestones in various ways. The principle in the toddler communities and pre-schools is to offer children the opportunity to develop in harmony with their own rhythm and pace, becoming independent, with respect for all. In Primary, a vast international curriculum is offered, allowing for personal interest, decision-making, autonomous learning and related responsibilities. Thereby developing ownership, joy in learning and self-esteem in a supported and stress-free environment.

IB World School
Between our four campuses, located in Woluwe and Tervuren, we offer a bilingual curriculum to children aged 0 to 18. The International Baccalaureate Middle Years Programme and Diploma Programme allow our oldest students to benefit from low student to teacher ratios, ensuring individualised education and mentorship at all stages of their development.

Aesthetic Learning Environments
Custom-renovated historical buildings offer attractive and stimulating environments to the children, helping them to develop whilst laying the academic foundations in all subjects. Respect for learning styles is important and emphasis is placed on the development of the different intelligences.

Individualised Education
Our highly qualified teachers offer a personal and warm atmosphere. Children and older students are allowed to be whom they are meant to be and are given assistance to develop the skills to balance their opportunities.

Aside from education on the cutting edge, the school offers a bus service with door to door pick up, musical instruments for all students and an After School Hours Programme till 18.30 including outdoor play, language immersion, cooking and lots of creative projects.

International School Edward Steichen

(Founded 2018)

1 Rue Edward Steichen,
9707 Clervaux, Luxembourg
Tel: +352 206 007-1
Email: info@lesc.lu
Website: www.lesc.lu
Principal: Max Wolff

School type: Co-educational Day
Age range of pupils: 4–19 years
No. of pupils enrolled as at 01/09/2025: 1400
Boys: 700 **Girls:** 700
Average class size: 12-25
Teacher/pupil ratio: 1:10

Lycée Edward Steichen (LESC) opened in September 2018 and as one of the international Accredited European Schools in the Grand Duchy of Luxembourg it gives students the option to follow the European curriculum or the Luxembourg national curriculum. LESC is a co-educational non-selective day school for students aged 4–19 with currently about 1400 students on roll which will be expanding to about 1700 students in total in the next few years.

Both the secondary and the primary school are located in Clervaux in the beautiful North of the Luxembourg Ardennes. We are easily accessible via public transport. Our primary school is located on a local primary school campus that is shared with a Luxembourg primary school. At primary school level, we follow the European Schools Curriculum. We offer an anglophone, a francophone and a German-speaking European section, which caters for all students from the age of 5 to the age of 11/12. In all sections, the curriculum is taught by experienced native speaker teachers of English, French or German.

As an international school operating in the heart of one of the world's most multilingual countries, the school teaches Luxemburgish (mother tongue and beginners) as well as German, French or English as an additional language from age 4.

At secondary school level, we currently have three European school strands (anglophone, francophone and German-speaking). In the German-speaking and the francophone strand, English is taught as a first foreign language. In the anglophone strand, English is taught by experienced native speakers and French or German as a first foreign language. In addition, we also include the traditional Luxemburg school strands within our institution ('section classique' and 'section générale') in order to give students the best possible choices for their education. We offer curricula that lead either to the European baccalaureate qualification or the equivalent Luxemburg national qualifications.

As an international school located in a multilingual region of Europe, we welcome about 50 different nationalities at our school. In order to help students to integrate in the region, we offer Luxemburgish lessons to all our non-Luxemburg students. All teaching staff are fully qualified and must have at least 5 years' professional experience. In addition, we support each student according to their individual needs via a one to one coaching programme, regular Pastoral-Social-Health Education sessions and an extracurricular programme of activities ranging from sports clubs, outdoor activities to the school choir, the school's own pop academy and voluntary work with local services.

As an international European school, our mission is to educate the whole child and to prepare them for the challenges of the 21st century. We aim to develop learners who become critical thinkers and well-rounded and educated students. For these reasons, in addition to offering traditional academic subjects, we also believe that the arts should play a major role in the life of the school; music, drama and dance are developed during lessons and via extracurricular activities.

The school has excellent facilities including a state-of-the-art design & technology workshop, Food & Nutrition workshops, purpose designed science, music and art classrooms and networked IT suites. At primary and secondary school, all students are supported in their learning via the use of iPads. Specialist rooms and facilities include science laboratories, art studios and modern languages and humanities classrooms, two fully equipped sports halls and a swimming pool plus a self-service restaurant and cafeteria.

A wide range of sports is offered, including football, climbing, swimming, gymnastics, athletics and basketball and the school participates successfully in sporting events. Extra-curricular activities are an integral part of the school day – we offer additional activities in sport, music and drama with opportunities for overseas travel and school trips and exchanges with national and international partner schools.

As our school continues to expand, we will continue to expand our school offer, but we will remain focused on providing all children with the best possible education in an ever-changing world.

International School Leiden

Van Vollenhovenkade 15, 2313 GG Leiden, South Holland, Netherlands
Tel: +31 71 5173464
Email: admissions@isleiden.nl
Website: isleiden.nl

Principal: Mr Deon du Plessis
School type: Co-educational Day
Age range of pupils: 4–11 years
Average class size: 22

International School Leiden is the first to offer international primary education within Leiden, ages 4–11. Our campus is situated a stones throw from the heart of Leiden, providing a warm and welcoming community feeling.

At ISL it is our mission to provide a safe learning environment for every student to become self-aware and develop a sense of responsibility towards themselves, respect for each other and their environment in order to become active global citizens. By embracing the International Primary Curriculum, the personal learning goals are embedded into our daily learning: Adaptable, Collaborator, Ethical, Communicator, Thinker, Resilient, Respectful and Empathetic.

We are very aware of the importance you place on your child's education. Your child, their learning, and their wellbeing is at the epicenter of all our decisions, planning, and practice.

We believe all children should receive an exemplary education in an environment that is safe and conducive to learning. Together we can help our children excel and grow individually.

ISL has a newly renovated and spacious campus which includes facilities such as:
- Collaborative Learning Spaces
- Specially designed sensory facilities for Early Years
- Library
- Playground and Outdoor Learning Spaces
- Specialist Subject Areas
- EAL learning environment

We are a member of The Dutch International Primary Schools (DIPS) partially funded by the Dutch government means we are able to offer international education at an affordable fee and fall in line with the framework of the Dutch educational system.

Beyond our academics, ISL offers a wide range of after school activities, available to all of our families. As well as providing an on site after school care facility. Offering our families options beyond the school day as well as piece of mind their children are safe.

The families within our school community play a crucial role in shaping the identity of our institution, contributing only positive aspects to its overall environment. ISL appreciates the participation of our students' parents and guardians

Italy

International School of Bergamo

Via Monte Gleno, 54, 24125 Bergamo, Italy
Tel: +39 035 213776
Email: info@isbergamo.com
Website: www.isbergamo.com
Head of School: Roberta Sana

Head of Primary: Roisin Cosgrove
Head of Secondary: Chiara Tabet
School type: Co-educational Day
Age range of pupils: 2–18 years
No. of pupils enrolled as at 01/09/2025: 420

Founded in 2011, the International School of Bergamo (IS Bergamo) is part of the Inspired Education group, a leading global schools group educating over 85,000 students across a network of more than 100 schools. From exchange programmes and exclusive camps to leadership conferences and shared learning experiences, Inspired offers a range of enriching global opportunities which give students a chance to travel, meet peers from other countries and become a part of a vibrant international community.

IS Bergamo is an IB Continuum school offering the Primary, Middle Years and Diploma Programmes. Committed to delivering high quality educational programmes, ISB strives to develop the intellectual, personal, emotional, and social skills needed to live, learn and work in a rapidly globalising world.

Joining the International School of Bergamo offers a fantastic opportunity to enter a safe and nurturing environment, where Italian culture is valued alongside the recognition and appreciation of a multicultural collective diversity. We are of the belief that technology can add much value to teaching and learning, thus, through our blended approach to learning, we have embedded technology into the school curriculum.

The school is located in a modern building in the Eastern part of Bergamo, in a green and peaceful environment. The area is rich in sporting facilities, including a modern football pitch situated just next to the school, as well as neighbouring athletics track and rugby fields.

Students can benefit from a newly refurbished building with specialised facilities including a dedicated Early Years area, an Art & Design Lab, a school library, an innovation hub, and an outdoor multipurpose sports facility, as well as a cafeteria and playgrounds. Recent additions to the facility also include a secondary school wing with specialized science laboratories, a music & dance studio, and a fully equipped indoor gym.

Thanks to an efficient bus service, the school welcomes pupils from all over the city of Bergamo and many of its the surrounding communities.

For more information, please visit our website or reach out via email.

Italy

International School of Como

Via Adda 25,
22073 Fino Mornasco (CO), Italy
Tel: +39 031 572289
Email: admissions.como@iscomo.com
Website: www.iscomo.com
Head of School: Philipa Smithson

Head of Primary: Phil Michaelides
Head of Secondary: Karen Lockett
School type: Co-educational Day
Age range of pupils: 2–18 years
No. of pupils enrolled as at 01/09/2025: 382

The International School of Como (ISC), founded in 2002 has grown into a school that stands for excellence and has contributed to the expansion of international education in Northern Italy. Today, ISC welcomes over 400 students from 2 to 18 years old of 30+ nationalities and an international staff of more than 60 qualified teachers and assistants.

Our school is part of Inspired Education, the leading global premium group of schools that offer excellence in education to over 75,000 students worldwide. From exchange programmes to exclusive camps, to leadership conferences and shared learning experiences, Inspired offers a range of enriching global opportunities which give students a chance to travel, meet peers from other countries and become a part of a vibrant international community.

ISC is committed to providing children with the best educational experience possible. We offer the IB (International Baccalaureate) Primary Years, Middle Years and Diploma Programmes and aspire to create an environment where students become ethical thinkers, creative problem-solvers, community-minded and individuals of global action.

Our state-of-the-art campus was designed and built to optimise our students' education. Over 10,000 square metres of internal and external spaces house our large classrooms, a robotics lab, two art studios, and indoor gym and outdoor multipurpose sports facility, cafeteria, and playgrounds. Our fully renovated secondary school wing, 3 fully equipped science laboratories, a drama studio, and primary and secondary school libraries complete the incredible experience. In 2025 the school will go through an expansion of its spaces with the addition of new state-of-the-art classrooms and an artificial turf football pitch.

A further expansion will also happen in 2025. Thanks to our efficient bus service, we welcome students from a considerable number of the surrounding communities - including Como, Cantù/Carimate, Lecco, Malgrate, Varese, and Ticino area (Switzerland).

At ISC we are driven by our mission statement: "International School of Como is a student-centred community of internationally minded learners. We offer a balanced and challenging curriculum, in a safe and nurturing environment, where we respect and value the Italian culture and our collective diversity. We empower all students to be active, reflective and responsible lifelong learners who can achieve their full potential and contribute to an ever-changing world."

For more information, please visit our website or reach out via email at admissions.como@iscomo.com.

Germany

International School of Düsseldorf e.V.

ISD
INTERNATIONAL SCHOOL OF DÜSSELDORF
SINCE 1968

(Founded 1968)

Niederrheinstrasse 323/336, 40489 Düsseldorf, North Rhine-Westphalia, Germany
Tel: +49 (0) 211-9406 6
Email: info@isdedu.de
Website: www.isdedu.de
School Director: Frank Tschan

Appointed: 2020
School type: Co-educational Day
Age range of pupils: 3–18 years
No. of pupils enrolled as at 01/09/2025: 1020
Fees as at 01/09/2025: please enquire
Average class size: 16-18
Teacher/pupil ratio: 1:8

Welcome to ISD – where no fitting in is required!

We're proud to say that at ISD, there is no 'one size fits all'. We welcome students with different interests, talents, and abilities into our school, and support each of them to become the very best version of themselves they can be.

Flexibility is therefore a hallmark of learning at ISD: our learning environments are adaptable and dynamic; our interdisciplinary units allow students to develop creative solutions outside the bounds of a single subject; our elective courses provide opportunities for students to forge their own path; and our Additional Learning Opportunities (ALOs) allow students the freedom to discover connections between their passions and their talents.

Crucial to this flexibility, is our teaching staff. Currently representing over 30 nationalities, they bring an abundance of knowledge, experience, and diversity to our classrooms. Working collaboratively, they provide a challenging and supportive environment for all students.

Families are another key partner in the learning journey. At ISD, parents enjoy ample opportunity to participate in all aspects of school life. We believe such broad community engagement exposes our students to more varied learning opportunities, and is an important part of what makes learning at our school rich and authentic.

In fact, the idea of the "ISD family" is a defining feature of the ISD culture. Newcomers are warmly welcomed, and carefully supported to integrate quickly into the school community. For many, ISD quickly becomes a home away from home, where lifelong friendships are forged.

This, in a nutshell, is ISD: a school committed to providing an education that is relevant, today and tomorrow; an education that sees our students flourish and inspires them to make a positive difference in their world.

Belgium

International School of Flanders

280 Chaussee de Waterloo,
1640 Rhode-St-Genese,
Flemish Brabant, Belgium
Tel: +32 2 358 56 06
Email: office@isfwaterloo.org
Website: www.isfwaterloo.org
Executive Head: Belinda Yates

Head of Primary School: Analida Anguizola
Head of Secondary School: Nadim Bayeh
School type: Co-educational Day
Age range of pupils: 2.5–18 years
No. of pupils enrolled as at 01/09/2025: 300
Fees as at 01/09/2025: Please see website

The International School of Flanders comprises of two campuses in two of the most green, liveable, family friendly suburbs outside of Brussels – Waterloo and Tervuren, we cater for children ages 2.5–18. We are accredited by CIS (Council of International Schools), COBIS (Council of British International Schools), BSO (British Schools Overseas) and are a registered Cambridge Online School and Exam Centre.

We offer small class sizes, individual attention and differentiated learning to all of our students. In our Primary sections, we follow the International Primary Curriculum, which is an internationally-minded, thematic based curriculum that encourages students to develop their ability to learn and acquire the skills needed to become life-long learners. In our Secondary section Years 7–9, students follow a curriculum based on the National Curriculum of England and Wales, Years 10–11 students follow a two-year IGCSE year programme from Cambridge, finally our Year 12–13 (A-Level) curriculum caters for students aged 17–18, preparing them for University entrance.

Our community is truly international, and we embrace individual differences, cultures, and religions. We foster in students the values of understanding, cooperation, honesty and respect. We believe that building a child's self-esteem and confidence is paramount. Our small class sizes provide a safe, caring and secure teaching environment where children receive individual attention and enjoy learning through exploration and discovery. ISF is a Google for Education school. All our students have access to Google learning resources using Chromebooks, Tablets and Interactive whiteboards. ISF is also working towards becoming a Green Flag school, and as such our students are involved in Eco-Friendly initiatives both in school and in the local community.

ISF has recently launched an Online School – Inventum International Online School. Here learners can access our future-focused coursework, resources and assessments in real time with the flexibility of allowing them to learn on their own schedule – anywhere, anytime.

Switzerland

International School of Lausanne

(Founded 1962)

Chemin de la Grangette 2,
1052 Le Mont-sur-Lausanne VD,
Switzerland
Tel: +41 21 560 02 02
Email: admissions@isl.ch
Website: www.isl.ch

Director: Frazer Cairns
School type: Co-educational Day
Age range of pupils: 3–18 years
No. of pupils enrolled as at 01/09/2025: 860
Fees as at 01/09/2025:
Day: CHF14,600–CHF38,600 per annum

The International School of Lausanne (ISL), a leading non-profit, independent school dedicated to delivering a world-class International Baccalaureate (IB) education, was established in 1962. ISL stands out for its exceptional academic track record, innovative and inclusive learning environment, and vibrant international community. Accredited by the Council of International Schools (CIS) and a member of the New England Association of Schools and Colleges (NEASC), ISL commits to providing a robust educational foundation.

At ISL, comprehensive education programmes from Early Childhood through to the Diploma Programmes for children aged 3-18 are offered. Its groundbreaking dual language programme, launched in 2021 within the Primary School, offers students a unique opportunity to enhance their French language skills alongside their English-medium studies.

In an increasingly interconnected world, the challenges faced require not only clear thinking but also effective dialogue and cooperation. ISL prepares students to navigate the complexities and uncertainties of our global society, empowering them to make meaningful contributions and thrive in a multicultural and interdependent world.

An education at ISL equips young individuals with:

1. A rigorous intellectual foundation that fosters critical thinking.
2. Opportunities for innovation and independent problem-solving.
3. Skills to effectively collaborate across diverse cultural boundaries.
4. A deep-rooted sense of community and care for the well-being of others.
5. Confidence and the courage to express their true selves.

Year after year, ISL students achieve exceptional results in the IB Diploma, consistently surpassing global averages. Join the International School of Lausanne, where academic excellence is nurtured along with the personal development of each student, preparing them to become leaders and changemakers of tomorrow.

Spain

International School of Madrid

(Founded 1971)

Calle Rosa Jardón 3, 28016 Madrid, Spain
Tel: +34 91 359 21 21
Email: info@internationalschoolofmadrid.com
Website: www.internationalschoolofmadrid.com
Heads of School: Mr. Rich Cook & Mr. Tom Davidson

School type: Co-educational Day
Age range of pupils: 2–18 years
No. of pupils enrolled as at 01/09/2025: 920
Boys: 433 **Girls:** 487 **Sixth Form:** 130
Average class size: 20
Teacher/pupil ratio: 1:9

We are a family school in the heart of Madrid, and since 1971, have been offering a quality British education to children aged 2 to 18 from all over the world. 50 years of academic excellence. Our motto is Respect, Loyalty and Friendship and these words form the foundation of everything we believe in. We are known for our child-centred approach, happy atmosphere and high standards of achievement – our pupils outperform their UK and international counterparts in official examinations and also excel in sports and the arts.

Many schools call themselves a family school but this is 100% the case here at ISM. The school has grown and developed like a family since 1971. The owners attended the school as children and now 8 children from the family are at the school. This family focus is not profit but the creation of a learning environment where students can thrive. Management decisions are solely focused on what is best for the learners in the school, not corporate offices nor investors demanding a return. Staff tenure is 10 years, staff come here and they stay. Children stay in the school too which creates a stable and supportive environment.

The extension of ISM being a settled, family school is that each child is known as an individual and their pathway to succeed, whatever it may be, is known and celebrated. Staff meet and greet each child by name as they arrive in the morning and depart in the afternoon. Our families also stay in the school. The recent parent satisfaction survey had a 50% participation rate with 92.2% satisfied or very satisfied with the quality of education and 97% feeling their child is safe and happy in school.

We follow the English National Curriculum throughout, in parallel with 20% for Spanish studies (Spanish language & literature and humanities). This means that students can validate their studies with the Spanish system and that all of our pupils have the opportunity to learn Spanish and English to a native level.

Students complete the IGCSE programme in Years 10–11 and then undertake A-Level studies in Years 12–13. Our unique mix of Advanced Level British and Spanish subjects in these final years mean that our students leave prepared to enter British, US and Spanish universities, as well as those from across the world. Our students achieve highly, with 100% usually going on to attend university at 18. Our students have been awarded 112 Outstanding Cambridge Learner Awards, in recognition of their phenomenal exam results and making us one of the most successful centres in Spain. The school's strength is its longevity. We are a founding member of NABSS, the association of 80+ British Schools in Spain. Our growth has also been considered and effectively managed and never with profit as a driver. We have grown and succeeded along with our families and our students leave us to the best universities in the world. Oxbridge, Russell Group, Ivy League and the best universities in Spain and the EU.

As a British school, we employ highly qualified, native-speaking teachers who provide an education to pupils just as if they were in a school in the UK. We encourage children in active rather than passive learning. No amount of book learning can make up for an equal period of first-hand experience. Our theme is not 'I teach, you learn'. No! We prefer 'We are all here together to learn from each other'.

We recognise that each student is unique and care passionately about their social and moral development. We are committed to providing the best possible start in life for every one of our pupils. Therefore, even more important than their academic success, we are proud of how well our students behave and of the good adults that they grow up to become.

Italy

International School of Milan

Via I Maggio, 20, 20021 Baranzate (MI), Italy
Tel: +39 02 872581
Email: admissions@ismilan.it
Website: www.internationalschoolofmilan.it
Executive Head: Rebecca Ruth Glover

School type: Co-educational Day & Boarding
Age range of pupils: 2–18 years (Boarding 14-18 years)
No. of pupils enrolled as at 01/09/2025: 850

Welcome to the International School of Milan. As the first established international school in the city, our school is supported by the strongest academic standards and most progressive and innovative education. This has allowed us to serve the international and Italian communities of Milan with a high quality of learning for over 60 years.

Our school is part of Inspired Education, the leading global premium group of schools, offering excellence in education to over 85,000 students worldwide. From exchange programmes to exclusive camps, to leadership conferences and shared learning experiences, Inspired offers a range of enriching global opportunities which give students a chance to travel, meet peers from other countries and become a part of a vibrant international community.

We are confident that our ethos, focused on achievement and underpinned by opportunity for all, will enable your children to develop their confidence and be ready to embrace the challenges of the future.

The IB curriculum (which runs throughout all years) follows a truly international approach to learning, perfectly fitting the needs of our student body, comprised of over 50 different nationalities. Our PYP, MYP and IB Diploma programmes thoroughly prepare our students for further study all around the world, including at the world's leading universities. We are proud of our position as the premier all-through IB school in Milan.

Our dedicated and skilled teachers ensure that all students are propelled and supported to achieve highly at the school, regardless of their ability. Our desire to challenge young minds is shaped by a growth mindset, ensuring that the focus is on every student accomplishing beyond their expectations. In short, we believe your child can grow to perform at their best at IS Milan.

In September 2018, we opened a brand-new boarding house that can accommodate up to approximately 42 students. With the care and attention given by our staff, boarding at IS Milan provides a truly transformative experience for 14 to 18-year-olds.

The International School of Milan is a place where learning is celebrated and where each of our students are valued and challenged to succeed. We work to create an educational environment where students are proud to belong to our school community and enthusiastic about the learning they take part in.

For more information, please visit our website or reach out via email at admissions@ism-ac.it

Italy

International School of Modena

Piazza Montessori, 1/A, 41051 Montale Rangone (MO), Italy
Tel: +39 059 530649
Email: admissions@ismodena.it
Website: www.internationalschoolofmodena.it

Head of School: Mr. Paul Barrie
School type: Co-educational Day
Age range of pupils: 3–18 years
No. of pupils enrolled as at 01/09/2025: 220

Welcome to the International School of Modena. ISM is a coeducational school that offers an IB continuum education to children aged 3 to 18 years old.

We are an international school with a student body representing approximately 33 different nationalities. ISM is one of only a handful of schools in Italy currently authorised to offer the IB programme. Therefore, we are well equipped with the standard of education to prepare your child for the next steps after graduation, including studying at some of the world's top universities.

Our school is part of Inspired Education, the leading global premium group of schools that offer excellence in education to over 85,000 students worldwide. From exchange programmes to exclusive camps, to leadership conferences and shared learning experiences, Inspired offers a range of enriching global opportunities which give students a chance to travel, meet peers from other countries and become a part of a vibrant international community.

The curriculum at ISM is carefully designed to reflect the ethos of the school and of the IB. We are committed to inquiry-based learning, encouraging every student to think for themselves and develop into confident, independent learners. Our dedicated, multinational teaching body ensures that our students are high achievers who are challenged to accomplish their best. We achieve excellent external examination results and our track record of success in the IB Diploma allows our graduating students to access the best universities around the Globe.

Our modern campus, surrounded by nature, is located 12km outside of the city of Modena. Resources have been built with our students in mind; for example, an innovative Early Years department features beautiful spaces and play structures specially designed to support the delivery of the IB PYP and Reggio-Inspired Early Years Curriculum.

We are certain that you will see that ISM is a place that celebrates learning and values each student, offering them a challenging, enjoyable education aimed at developing a range of skills required for future success.

For more information, visit our website or reach out via email.

Italy

International School of Monza

(Founded 1984)

Via Solferino 23, 20900 Monza (MB), Italy
Tel: +39 039 9357701
Email: admin@ismonza.it
Website: www.internationalschoolofmonza.it
Head of School: Mrs. Johanna Karen Urquhart

Appointed: September 2017
School type: Co-educational Day
Age range of pupils: 2.5–18 years
No. of pupils enrolled as at 01/09/2025: 300
Average class size: 17
Teacher/pupil ratio: 1:7

The International School of Monza is an International Baccalaureate continuum school and a member of the Inspired Education group, the leading global premium group of schools that offer excellence in education to over 85,000 students worldwide. From exchange programmes to exclusive camps, to leadership conferences and shared learning experiences, Inspired offers a range of enriching global opportunities which give students a chance to travel, meet peers from other countries and become a part of a vibrant international community.

We strive to deliver an education that embodies the IB learner profile and our school's Core Values. We are a community of curious learners, striving for a world without frontiers. Our learners are happy, experiential, ambitious, respectful and thoughtful.

With a 40-year long history, our record of success in the IB is well established as our students thrive all the way through our school from ages 2.5 to 18. As well as being well rooted in tradition, there's a fresh and unique approach to the way that we undertake teaching. The impressive results attained by our students in the cutting-edge MYP e-assessment and DP examinations, as well as their admission into a diverse range of some of the world's leading universities, is evidence of this.

Technology is harnessed in our classrooms through a blended approach – classrooms are fitted with smart TVs and students bring iPads or MacBooks to school. These carefully selected technologies, including Inspired AI, add value to both teaching and learning.

In addition to the IB Diploma, we also prepare our Italian students to sit their Quinta Elementare and Terza Media examinations. Every year they achieve truly exceptional results.

All this takes place in our city-centre campus designed to foster collaborative approaches to learning. Our science laboratories are fitted with state-of-the-art equipment, and we also boast on-site spaces which support the delivery of our Inspired Early Years Approach. We have beautiful libraries, a theatre, studios for visual and performative arts as well as a large indoor and outdoor sports complex just a three-minute walk away.

An active effort is also made to interact with the opportunities that lie beyond the walls of our school, as we seek to take advantage of being in such a culturally rich part of the world.

Our education prepares our students for the complex and interconnected world that lies ahead, whilst ensuring they are ever-curious and are instilled with the values to become exceptional global citizens.

Germany

International School of Neustadt

(Founded 2005)

Haardterstrasse 1, 67433 Neustadt an der Weinstrasse, Germany
Tel: +49 6321 8900 960
Email: info@is-neustadt.de
Website: www.is-neustadt.de
Principal: Vjeko Kovac

School type: Co-educational Day
Age range of pupils: 4–18 years
No. of pupils enrolled as at 01/09/2025: 95
Fees as at 01/09/2025:
Day: €9,000–€17,400 per annum

The International School Neustadt (ISN) is a coeducational, full-day international school for children aged 4-18 years. ISN was founded in 2005 by the Verband der Holz- und Kunststoffverarbeitenden Industrie Rheinland-Pfalz e.V together with the financial support of the "SBW Haus des Lernens" organisation (Switzerland). With around 95 students from over 20 nations, ISN offers a caring family atmosphere both for expatriates and local families. Expatriate families enjoy the social network at ISN which eases integration into a new location, while local German parents benefit from the innovative educational program and English language instruction.

ISN offers the Cambridge Primary, IGCSE (International General Certificate of Secondary Education) and A-level programs, and is an accredited examination center for Cambridge International Examinations, offering the full range of English examinations.

ISN offers all-day classes that meet the demand of today's workplace. Our school is open every day from 8am until 5pm. While the main language of instruction is English, German classes are also taught to all students from beginner to native speaker level. Before and after-school adult supervision is available each day, at no extra cost, to students from kindergarten up to grade 5. ISN also provides various after-school activities such as music, dancing, yoga, arts and crafts.

ISN is recognized by the state of Rhineland- Palatinate as an accredited supplementary school ("anerkannte Ergaenzungsschule").

The school is owned and managed by the famous Swiss education provider, SBW Haus des Lernens, which has over 40 years of experience in the field of private education, currently managing more than 10 schools throughout Switzerland and Germany. Some of the innovative approaches developed by SBW and implemented at ISN include personalized student coaching, autonomous learning and the development of learning skills.

For more information please contact the Admissions Office: info@is-neustadt.de

France

International School of Nice

(Founded 1977)

15 Avenue Claude Debussy,
06200 Nice, France
Tel: +33 (0)4 93 21 04 00
Email: admissions@isn-nice.com
Website: www.isn-nice.com
Director: Mrs. Mel Curtis
Appointed: 2020

School type: Co-educational Day
Age range of pupils: 3–18 years
No. of pupils enrolled as at 01/09/2025: 480
Fees as at 01/09/2025:
Day: €11,400–€24,885 per annum
Average class size: 22

The International School of Nice (ISN Nice) is known for its forward-thinking and inclusive approach to education. Catering to students aged 3 to 18, ISN offers a dynamic and supportive environment from Early Years through High School, preparing students for the academic, personal, and global challenges of the future. A truly international community, the school welcomes families from across the globe, with over 60 nationalities represented among the student body and faculty from more than 30 countries.

For nearly five decades, ISN has been a cornerstone of international education on the French Riviera. As an IB World School with both American and European accreditations, it provides a comprehensive and fully English-medium education, enhanced by daily French instruction. Located in the Cannes-Nice-Monaco region, ISN offers the full continuum of the International Baccalaureate: the Primary Years Programme (PYP), Middle Years Programme (MYP), and Diploma Programme (DP). Students also sit for the IGCSE examinations during their high school years.

ISN offers three graduation routes tailored to students' aspirations: the IB Diploma Programme, the High School Diploma accredited by the Middle States Association, and the High School Diploma with IB Courses – ensuring flexible pathways to university and beyond.

With the support of the Futureproof programme, over 95% of graduates progress directly to respected universities, mainly in the UK, France, and North America.

Recent campus renovations include modern learning hubs such as the innovative Space Centre and Marine Learning Hub, alongside a library, theatre, music studio, outdoor sports areas, and a fully equipped teaching kitchen. These facilities inspire collaboration, creativity, and digital literacy, while promoting teamwork and curiosity.

ISN Nice remains committed to empowering students to thrive in a rapidly changing world, fostering a sense of global citizenship and a passion for lifelong learning.

Italy

International School of Siena

Via del Petriccio e Belriguardo, 49/1, 53100 Siena, Italy
Tel: +39 0577 328103
Email: office@issiena.it
Website: www.internationalschoolofsiena.it

Principal: Mrs. Jennifer Tickle
School type: Co-educational Day
Age range of pupils: 3–18 years
No. of pupils enrolled as at 01/09/2025: 204

The International School of Siena, opened in 2010, is a school for children aged 3 to 18 years old and the only IB continuum school in Tuscany, fully authorised for the Primary Years Programme (PYP), Middle Years Programme (MYP) and Diploma Programme (DP).

Our school is a member of Inspired Education, the leading global premium group of schools that offer excellence in education to over 85,000 students worldwide. From exchange programmes to exclusive camps, to leadership conferences and shared learning experiences, Inspired offers a range of enriching global opportunities which give students a chance to travel, meet peers from other countries and become a part of a vibrant international community.

Learning at IS Siena is exciting and engaging, as students strive for excellence in a climate that is caring and responsive to individual needs and goals. Our global vision is coordinated by an outstanding team of educational leaders and implemented by our highly skilled and dedicated professional staff.

In January 2019, we relocated to a stunning new school building where we enjoy spacious classrooms, light, modern teaching spaces and a spacious gym, drama/dance studio, a library, music and art rooms and science laboratories fitted with equipment of the highest standards. Our Early Years spaces are also specially designed to complement the Reggio Inspired teaching approach.

Learning at the International School of Siena is an international experience with students from over 20 nationalities. It leads to a well-informed perception of the world and an education that merges understanding of our global context with the development of skills and attitudes that young people require to participate fully in the world of tomorrow, both as national and global citizens.

We deeply appreciate the diversity in our school community and aim to celebrate this diversity as well as supporting each student to appreciate and embrace Italian culture and become excellent in English. Our location in beautiful Tuscany provides us with access to this culture and to a variety of educational resources - we strive to incorporate our local community into the experience of the students, building connections between the classroom and the real world.

IS Siena's school community is welcoming to parents, students, and staff alike, as they work together to provide a stimulating and well-rounded education that engages its students and creates outstanding graduates.

For more information, please visit our website or reach out via email at admissions@issiena.it

Switzerland

International School of Ticino SA

Via Ponteggia, 23, Cadempino,
6814 Lugano, Switzerland
Tel: +41 919710344
Email: frontoffice@isticino.com
Website: www.isticino.com

Head of School: Mr. Mark Waldron
School type: Co-educational Day
Age range of pupils: 3–18 years
No. of pupils enrolled as at 01/09/2025: 280

The International School of Ticino is a coeducational day school for students aged 3 to 18 years old. As the first and only accredited International Baccalaureate (IB), Primary Years Programme (PYP) school and authorized Middle Years Programme (MYP) and Diploma Programme (DP) school in Ticino, our school is a special and exciting place to be.

Our school first was established as a Kindergarten in 2014 to offer the local and international residents of Ticino an IB education. As of 2017 the International School of Ticino joined Inspired Education, the leading global premium group of schools that offer excellence in education to over 85,000 students worldwide. From exchange programmes to exclusive camps, to leadership conferences and shared learning experiences, Inspired offers a range of enriching global opportunities which give students a chance to travel, meet peers from other countries and become a part of a vibrant international community.

This partnership with a leading education group has laid the foundations for the standard of learning and community that we see today in our new campus. The design and build of our impressive new campus draw upon our foundations – the IB mission and the vision of school: Inspiring the Extraordinary.

At the International School of Ticino, we strive to turn our students into lifelong learners by placing students at the centre of everything we do. We achieve this through our school culture, which is rooted in the IB mission statement that states: 'International Baccalaureate aims to develop inquiring, knowledgeable and caring young people who help to create a better and more peaceful world through intercultural understanding and respect'.

We place much emphasis on accommodating to the individual needs of our students - we acknowledge the potential, character, and unique talent of every student. Our innovative pedagogy encourages our students to respect each other, to respect the environment, to communicate through active dialogue and to create the foundations of a collaborative society. We achieve this within a safe, nurturing environment with a strong sense of community at its heart.

For more information, please visit our website or reach out via email at admission@isticino.com

Spain

International School San Patricio Toledo

(Founded 2006)

Juan de Vergara, 1, Urbanización La Legua, Toledo, Castilla-La Mancha, 45005 Spain
Tel: +34 925 280 363
Email: infotoledo@colegiosanpatricio.es
Website: colegiosanpatriciotoledo.com/en
Head of School: Mr. Simon Hatton-Burke

School type: Co-educational Day & Boarding
Age range of pupils: 1–18 years
No. of pupils enrolled as at 01/09/2025: 510
Average class size: 3-20 max

International School San Patricio Toledo is a prestigious day and boarding school offering the complete International Baccalaureate (IB) continuum, including the Primary Years Programme (PYP), Middle Years Programme (MYP), and Diploma Programme (DP), for students aged 1 to 18. Located on a stunning 30,000 m2 campus in the exclusive residential area of La Legua in Toledo, Spain, the school provides outstanding and unique educational opportunities in the region. Its IB curriculum is complemented by a multilingual approach, preparing students for a globalized future through a comprehensive and well-rounded education.

The school is proud of its strong academic achievements, highlighted by its excellent average Diploma scores in 2024, making it one of the schools with the highest average scores in Spain. As one of Spain's first official Google Education Reference Schools, San Patricio embraces cutting-edge technology to equip students with the skills and knowledge needed to thrive in a modern, interconnected world.

Situated in an exclusive residential area of Toledo, just one hour by car or 30 minutes by train from Madrid, the school spans over 30,000 square meters of spacious grounds. The purpose-built boarding facilities are located on campus, enabling seamless access to all amenities without the need for transportation. This ensures a secure, fully equipped, and self-contained environment for students.

The boarding community includes students from over 20 nationalities, offering a truly international experience in the culturally rich and historic city of Toledo. Boarding options include a complete educational program for students aged 14 to 18 and weekly boarding for those aged 12 to 18, fostering independence, communication, and social skills.

Each boarding student is assigned both a boarding house tutor and an academic tutor, ensuring comprehensive pastoral and academic support. A dedicated university counselor also guides students through higher education planning. The school meets the highest standards of safeguarding, accredited by leading organizations such as BSA and SACPA.

San Patricio offers instruction in English, Spanish, German, and French, as well as a variety of self-taught languages through the Diploma Programme. Boarding accommodations feature first-class facilities, with rooms arranged to promote diversity and inclusivity, housing 2, 3, or 4 students per room on separate male and female floors.

The school offers well-structured weekend activities designed to provide a balanced lifestyle, combining academic rigor with recreational and social opportunities, ensuring students flourish both academically and personally.

Germany

International School Westpfalz

(Founded 2017)

Nikolaus-von-Weis-Strasse 10,
66849 Landstuhl, Germany
Tel: +49 6371 980 930
Email: info@is-westpfalz.de
Website: www.is-westpfalz.de
Principal: Jodi Fillingame

School type: Co-educational Day
Age range of pupils: 4–18 years
No. of pupils enrolled as at 01/09/2025: 240
Fees as at 01/09/2025:
Day: €15,600–€17,700 per annum

Located in a beautifully restored former monastery in Landstuhl, Germany, the International School Westpfalz (ISW) is a full-day, coeducational international school for students aged 4–18. Founded in 2017 by the "SBW Haus des Lernens" (Switzerland), ISW currently serves around 240 students from over 34 nations, offering a supportive, family-like environment for both expatriate and local German families.

ISW follows the Cambridge International Curriculum, including Early Years, Primary, IGCSE, and A-level programs, and is an accredited Cambridge Examination Centre. English is the main language of instruction, while daily German, French and Spanish lessons ensure bilingual proficiency for native and non-native speakers.

School hours run from 08:30 to 15:30, with optional before- and after-school programs from 07:00 to 17:00, featuring activities such as music, drama, sports, and art. Recognized by the state of Rhineland-Palatinate as an accredited supplementary school (anerkannte Ergänzungsschule), ISW is committed to innovative, student-centered teaching and learning.

ISW benefits from the expertise of SBW Haus des Lernens, a Swiss educational group with over 40 years of experience managing 20+ schools across Switzerland and Germany. SBW's pioneering concepts – like personalised coaching, differentiated pathways igniting and fostering passions, autonomous self-directed learning, and the development of Future Skills™ – are integral to the ISW approach.

For more information contact Admissions:
info@is-westpfalz.de, www.is-westpfalz.de

Switzerland

International School Zurich North (ISZN)

Industriestrasse 50, 8304 Wallisellen ZH, Switzerland
Tel: +41 44 830 70 00
Email: info@iszn.ch
Website: www.iszn.ch
Headmaster: Mr James Stenning

School type: Co-educational Day
Age range of pupils: 3 months–18 years
No. of pupils enrolled as at 01/09/2025: 240
Fees as at 01/09/2025:
Day: CHF17,316–CHF38,280 per annum

Helping Young People Find Their Place in the World

In a fast-changing world, education should be more than academics. At International School Zurich North (ISZN), learning is about identity, confidence, and finding your place – within a community, and beyond.

Located in Zurich's dynamic Glattpark area, ISZN offers an international education for students from 3 months to 18 years. With a nurturing, personalised approach and a strong academic foundation, ISZN helps children grow into kind, capable, and curious global citizens.

From the earliest years, children at ISZN are supported in both English and German, laying the groundwork for strong communication and cultural awareness. In the Early Years programme – starting from just three months old – learning is play-based, caring, and inspired by the International Baccalaureate (IB) Primary Years Programme (PYP).

The IB PYP continues into Primary School, where students are encouraged to ask questions, explore big ideas, and develop both academic and emotional skills. ISZN's teachers don't just teach; they listen, guide, and celebrate each child's journey.

As students enter Middle School, they transition to the British curriculum. Early exposure to iGCSE-style learning helps students strengthen subject knowledge while building critical thinking and independence. This phase is designed to nurture confidence and stretch young minds in meaningful ways.

By Upper School, learners are prepared to pursue internationally respected iGCSEs and A-Levels – opening doors to top universities across the world. Throughout, ISZN balances academic rigour with the kind of personal attention that helps students feel seen, supported, and empowered to grow.

But education at ISZN goes far beyond the classroom. Students enjoy a vibrant co-curricular life that includes LEGO robotics, drama productions, Playball,

and award-winning sports teams. These activities spark creativity, build resilience, and strengthen friendships.

The school's modern, light-filled campus is designed with wellbeing in mind. Flexible classrooms, STEAM labs, outdoor learning areas, and a bright, welcoming library create a space where children feel calm, engaged, and inspired to learn.

As part of the global Cognita family of schools, ISZN students take part in cross-cultural projects and digital collaborations with peers around the world – experiences that deepen their understanding of international perspectives and empathy.

With over 36 nationalities represented among students and more than 25 among staff, diversity is part of everyday life at ISZN. The school's internationalism isn't just something it teaches – it's something it lives.

What truly sets ISZN apart is its people. Teachers bring global experience, creativity, and care to every classroom. They take the time to understand each child – not just as a learner, but as a person.

At every step, ISZN focuses on what really matters:

- Knowing each student as an individual
- Teaching skills for life, not just exams
- Encouraging voice, choice, and personal growth
- Building confidence through belonging

ISZN is more than a school. It's a place where young people are empowered to find their voice – and their place in the world.

Portugal

IPS Cascais

IPS Cascais
BRITISH INTERNATIONAL SCHOOL
PORTUGAL

(Founded 1982)

Rua da Lagoa 171, Bicesse, 2645-344 Alcabideche, Lisbon, Portugal
Tel: +351 214 570 149
Email: info@ipsschool.org
Website: www.ipsschool.org
Head of School: Christopher Starling
School type: Co-educational Day
Age range of pupils: 3–15 years (up to 18 in September 2028)

No. of pupils enrolled as at 01/09/2025: 400+
Fees as at 01/09/2025:
Average Tuition: €10,623–€20,251 per annum
Average class size: 22
Teacher/pupil ratio: 1:10

IPS Cascais British International School is located close to Lisbon. The school has been educating children for more than 40 years and has an international community of nearly 400 children from 38 nationalities. Offering the National Curriculum for England from Early Years (EYFS) to Secondary, pupils are working towards achieving their IGCSEs and A Levels.

This vibrant international community fosters a learning environment that promotes global understanding and cultural appreciation. The school is renowned for its high academic standards and encourages pupils to excel in all aspects of the curriculum.

The school was founded in 1982 and has been teaching the National Curriculum for England for 40 years. In 2010, the school moved to its sustainable, purpose-built facilities designed for primary education. This colourful campus includes playing fields, a library with over 22,000 books, and ample outdoor learning spaces. In September 2025, IPS will have Year 7 to 10 classes available in their secondary school, with a brand-new secondary campus set to open in 2026. Over the coming years, IPS Cascais will offer year groups from Early Years to Year 13.

The average class size at IPS Cascais is 22 pupils, with a teacher-student ratio of 1:10. The school places great importance on helping children become healthy, independent, and responsible members of society. The supportive school ethos encourages pupils' personal, social, and emotional development.

IPS Cascais is a proud member of Globeducate, one of the world's leading K12 education groups, with more than 65 premium bilingual and international schools in 11 countries, educating more than 40,000 pupils. Membership of Globeducate's British International Schools (GBIS) provides numerous benefits, including global events, partnerships, and learning communities focused on areas such as Artificial Intelligence, Outdoor Learning, STEAM, and Reading and Writing.

Pupils and teachers engage in collaborative projects through partnerships with organisations like LEGO® Education, WWF (World Wildlife Fund), and Eco-Schools. Globeducate's vision is to prepare each student to become a global citizen who can shape the world.

Jeannine Manuel School

(Founded 2015)

Bloomsbury, London, WC1B 3DN UK
Tel: 020 3829 5970
Email: admissions@jmanuel.uk.net
Website: www.ecolejeanninemanuel.org.uk
Head of School: Pauline Prévot
School type: Co-educational Day Preparatory & Senior, Nursery & Sixth Form

Age range of pupils: 3–18 years
No. of pupils enrolled as at 01/09/2025: 700
Fees as at 01/09/2025:
Day: £24,780–£35,208 per annum
Average class size: 15
Teacher/pupil ratio: 1:8

Jeannine Manuel School is a bilingual (English-French), international school in Bloomsbury, London. With 50 nationalities currently represented in our student body, we are proud to welcome pupils from all countries, cultural traditions and native languages.

Everything we do is driven by our mission: to *"promote international understanding through the bilingual education of a multicultural community of students, the fostering of pedagogical innovation, and the constant exploration of best practices in the context of an ever changing global environment."*

To achieve that, our curriculum is based on an enriched version of the international sections programmes of the French Ministry of Education. The English, Science and Chinese programmes were developed by our Paris sister school, a UNESCO associated school founded in 1954 and consistently recognised as a top French Lycée in national rankings. In History, the curriculum is complemented so pupils gain a coherent knowledge and understanding of Britain's past and that of the wider world.

Bilingualism is central to our identity. Classes are taught equally in English and French, and we welcome non-French speakers at all levels and beginners in English up to Year 7. Our aim is to bring pupils to a native proficiency – oral and written – in both languages.

Coherence and innovation drive our pedagogy. Inspired by current research in cognitive sciences and by best practices from around the world or designed by our school's pedagogues, our teaching methods aim to make pupils think, dare, share and care.

In Sixth Form, students take either the International French Baccalaureate ("BFI") or the International Baccalaureate ("IB"), leading them to receiving offers from top universities across the globe. Jeannine Manuel School is currently ranked the #1 French school abroad (among schools with 500–1,000 students) and #2 in the UK among small-cohort IB schools.

© Paul Riddle

Spain

Kensington School

(Founded 1968)
Avenida de Bularas No. 2, Pozuelo de Alarcón, 28224 Madrid, Spain
Tel: +34 91 7154 699
Email: kensington@kensingtonschool.net
Website: www.kensington-school.es

Head of School: Mr. Paul Murphy
School type: Co-educational Day
Age range of pupils: 18 months–18 years
No. of pupils enrolled as at 01/09/2025: 1300
Fees as at 01/09/2025:
Day: €6,875–€9,245 per annum

Kensington School is a British co-educational school for children aged 18 months to 18 years old. With our native British teachers and British curriculum, our education has been modelled in the image of the UK's education system.

Our school is a member of Inspired Education, the leading global premium group of schools that offer excellence in education to over 85,000 students worldwide. From exchange programmes to exclusive camps, to leadership conferences and shared learning experiences, Inspired offers a range of enriching global opportunities which give students a chance to travel, meet peers from other countries and become a part of a vibrant international community.

We aim to offer our students an excellent and well-rounded education, so that they leave our school as knowledgeable and socially conscious young adults. Our emphasis on multilingualism means that our students should graduate fluent in English, Spanish and French.

At our school students in Year 10 and 11 can opt to study principally either in English or Spanish; the students who opt for English will take the IGCSEs, internationally recognised qualifications, while alternatively they can opt to take 3º and 4º of ESO, the official Spanish curriculum, with reinforced studies in English and French.

During the last two years of school, we offer a choice between the International Baccalaureate Diploma programme, the internationally-recognised programme offered in English or the "Kensington Baccalaureate" in Spanish, with intensive emphasis on language reinforcement and a special preparation for the official University Entrance Exams (EvAU).

Pupils at Kensington achieve outstanding results in external examinations thanks to our system of individually tracking students' progress, needs and achievement; In the EvAU exam results of 2024, 32% of our students achieved a 12 or higher.

Our school values sport and the arts as key components of school life. We offer extracurriculars in music, art, and drama as well as all kinds of sports. Examples include judo, cookery class, music lessons and public speaking: the range of clubs on offer is extremely wide. With something for everyone, students are bound to find something that they enjoy. Through joining these clubs children can get the most out of their time and profit from forging new friendships built on shared interests and developing new skills and hobbies.

For more information, please visit our website or reach out via email.

Spain

King's College School Murcia

Calle Pez Volador s/n, Urbanización La Torre Golf Resort, 30709 Roldán, Murcia, Spain
Tel: +34 968 032 500
Email: murcia.info@kings.education
Website: www.murcia.kingscollegeschools.org

Head of School: Ms. Dawn Akyurek
School type: Co-educational Day
Age range of pupils: 18 months–18 years
No. of pupils enrolled as at 01/09/2025: 522

King's College School Murcia is part of the Inspired Education Group, stands as the only school in the region regularly undergoing external inspections accredited by the Department for Education (DfE) of the British Government. Located within the La Torre Golf Resort, the school offers the English National Curriculum to students from 18 months to 18 years old (Pre-Nursery to Year 13).

At King's College Murcia, students grow and develop from their early years into confident, well-rounded young adults with a global perspective. The school's first-class campus provides a stimulating environment to nurture their academic, artistic, and sporting talents. The educational experience is enhanced by dedicated teachers who deliver the English National Curriculum through inspiring teaching methods, ensuring each child's individual growth.

Since September 2022, King's College Murcia has been offering the prestigious International Baccalaureate (IB) Diploma Programme, becoming the only school in the region to provide this qualification entirely in English, with the opportunity to obtain a Bilingual Diploma. For the 2024-2025 academic year, the school is expanding its educational offer to include A-Levels and BTEC Business programs, making it one of the few schools in Spain to offer three distinct university entry routes.

Innovation is at the heart of King's College Murcia, with the incorporation of cutting-edge educational tools. Immersive virtual reality classes using MetaQuest 3 devices allow students to experience history and science in unique, interactive ways. The school also uses Inspired AI, an artificial intelligence platform that personalizes learning and significantly improves academic outcomes. These technological advancements are complemented by the use of Chromebooks and Google Classroom, equipping students with the essential digital skills needed for success in the future.

King's College Murcia, with the support of Inspired Education Group, is committed to offering a high-quality, forward-thinking education that prepares students for the challenges and opportunities of tomorrow.

Portugal

King's College School, Cascais

Rua Cesário Verde 395, Pampilheira, 2750-657 Cascais, Lisbon, Portugal
Tel: +351 215 966 634
Email: cascais@kingscollegeschool.pt
Website: www.kingscollegeschool.pt
Head of School: Adrian Frost
School type: Co-educational Day & Boarding

Age range of pupils: 1–13 years (18 years from Sep. 2026)
No. of pupils enrolled as at 01/09/2025: 720
Fees as at 01/09/2025:
Day: €10,431–€16,590 per annum

King's College School, Cascais is a co-educational school that opened in September 2022. The school is supported by a 50-year heritage of academic excellence from the King's College Schools Group, coupled with the expertise of Inspired Education group, the leading global premium group of schools that offer excellence in education to over 75,000 students worldwide. From exchange programmes to exclusive camps, to leadership conferences and shared learning experiences, Inspired offers a range of enriching global opportunities which give students a chance to travel, meet peers from other countries and become a part of a vibrant international community.

When complete in September 2024, King's College School, Cascais will offer state-of-the-art academic and sports facilities on an expansive, 40,000 m2 plot. With modern amenities designed to foster creativity, innovation, and excellence, our new campus will be a testament to our commitment to providing the best possible education for our students. We will offer boarding from September 2024 for students in Year 7 and above.

With subject-specialised teachers for all year groups, our education provides students with an international curriculum that aligns your child's perspective of the world with the increasingly global nature of our world. Students will benefit from Inspired education's approach to Early Years education that follows the world-renowned Cambridge International Primary Curriculum and offers a bilingual programme for students interested in following the Portuguese curriculum. In Secondary School, students will follow the Cambridge International Secondary Curriculum. Our school is a candidate school for the IB Diploma, pursing authorisation as an IB World School. These are schools that share a common philosophy - a commitment to a high quality, challenging education that our school believes is important for our students.

Technology is also a key part of our innovative curriculum, from the youngest learners utilising Beebots and Toughcams, to more senior students navigating 3D printers. Equally prevalent at our school is Sport and the performing arts, with extracurriculars such as dance and musical theatre on offer, as well as dedicated curriculum time for all students.

At King's College School, Cascais, we believe in creating out-of-the-box thinkers and spirited individuals, allowing our students to learn from first-hand experience, not just textbooks.

This curricular flexibility and strong commitment to ensuring that each student achieves their personal potential to thrive in a global world, places King's College School, Cascais at the forefront of international education.

For more information, please visit our website or reach out via email.

Spain

King's College Soto de Viñuelas

(Founded 1969)

Paseo de los Andes 35, Soto de Viñuelas, 28760 Madrid, Spain
Tel: +34 918 034 800
Email: kc.admissions@kingscollegeschools.org
Website: madrid-soto.kingscollegeschools.org
Headteacher: Mr. Chris Ramsey

School type: Co-educational Day & Boarding
Age range of pupils: 0 months–18 years
No. of pupils enrolled as at 01/09/2025: 1300
Fees as at 01/09/2025:
Day: €2,600–€6,630 per term
Full Boarding: €32,940–€39,390 per annum

King's College Madrid is a coeducational day and boarding school that offers a British education to children from the age of 20 months to 18 years (Pre-pre-nursery to Year 13).

Our school is part of Inspired Education, the leading global premium group of schools that offer excellence in education to over 85,000 students worldwide.

From exchange programmes to exclusive camps, to leadership conferences and shared learning experiences, Inspired offers a range of enriching global opportunities which give students a chance to travel, meet peers from other countries and become a part of a vibrant international community.

Since it's founding in 1969, King's College has gained a reputation for high academic standards. We pride ourselves on the fact that we are the only school in Madrid to offer both A Levels and the IB (International Baccalaureate) Diploma in English. This allows students to tailor their education to their own futures and preferred style of learning; students who prefer breadth tend to select the IB, whilst students seeking to dive into fewer subjects choose A levels. Our students excel no matter the chosen path, with our IB students receiving an average score of 36 points with the top score being 44 points in 2024 and 47% of A level students achieving an A*–A in 2023.

We are also fortunate to have a university entrance advisory department available to our students to guide and aid their admission into their dream destinations for high education. Every year our graduates go on to study at some of the best universities in the world (Russell Group, Ivy League & Oxbridge).

King's College is the only British curriculum school in Madrid accredited by the Department for Education in the UK as "Excellent".

Our 12-acre grounds, consisting of premium outdoor and indoor facilities, are located in the suburbs just 20 minutes away from Madrid's city centre.

Additionally, our boarding house, Tenbury House, opened in September 2011 and offers some of the best boarding accommodation in Europe.

Tenbury House is home to pupils from all over the world. The new facilities offer a 'home away from home' environment with single and double bedrooms with ensuite bathrooms, underfloor heating, and wireless internet. Students also have access to a dining room, common room, TV room, study room, and a kitchen with a laundry unit.

Our new additional boarding house is set to open in 2024, providing state-of-the-art living facilities or our students.

For more information, please visit our website or reach out via email.

King's College, The British School of Latvia

(Founded 2017)
Turaidas iela 1 Pinki, Babites novads,
LV2107 Latvia
Tel: +371 257 59 043
Email: latvia@kingscollegeschools.org
Website: latvia.kingscollegeschools.org

Head of School: Ms Adele Stanford
School type: Co-educational Day
Age range of pupils: 2–18 years
No. of pupils enrolled as at 01/09/2025: 500
Fees as at 01/09/2025:
Day: €9,900–€24,000 per annum

King's College, The British School of Latvia, is a coeducational school for students aged 2 to 18 years old. We provide a unique educational environment that puts children and their families at the heart of all we do. Our school in Latvia is located in the municipality of Marupe in Latvia's capital city, Riga.

Our school is a member of Inspired Education group, the leading global premium group of schools that offer excellence in education to over 85,000 students worldwide. From exchange programmes to exclusive camps, to leadership conferences and shared learning experiences, Inspired offers a range of enriching global opportunities which give students a chance to travel, meet peers from other countries and become a part of a vibrant international community.

At our school we take pride in offering inspiring teaching that draws on the best practices of the National Curriculum for England. This curriculum is designed to stimulate children and a desire to learn more through both an interdisciplinary approach and practical learning experiences inside and outside of the classroom. We offer the IBDP in Years 12 and 13.

Students gain an exemplary academic education while being equipped with the social and critical thinking skills to allow them to embrace the challenges of an ever-evolving world. At King's College Latvia children develop a rich ethical vocabulary, facilitating conversation and reflection. We believe in teaching values, and therefore our values permeate all we do.

As a King's College school, we have a 50-year heritage of academic excellence. Since 1969, pupils from King's College schools have gone on to continue their studies at some of the most prestigious universities in Europe and North America. A British education gives our alumni the best opportunities to work in challenging and interesting careers all over the world. We believe that the fundamental values that they learn while at King's College will also help them to have happy and fulfilling family lives.

In choosing King's, you can be assured your child's future is in safe hands.

For more information, please visit our website or reach out via email.

King's InterHigh

3 Burlington Gardens, London, W1S 3EP UK
Tel: +44 (0)1873 777 444
Email: contact@kingsinterhigh.co.uk
Website: www.kingsinterhigh.co.uk
Headteacher: Catriona Olsen
School type: Co-educational Day
Age range of pupils: 7–19 years

No. of pupils enrolled as at 01/09/2025: 6350
Fees as at 01/09/2025:
Primary: from £4,040 per annum
Lower secondary: from £5,500 per annum
GCSE: from: £6,670 per annum
A Level/IB Diploma: from £7,020 (A Levels)– £10,040 (IB Diploma) per annum

King's InterHigh is the leading British international online school, with 20 years' experience delivering the very best in innovative, personalised learning to students anywhere in the world.

An accredited Cambridge International school, King's InterHigh brings primary, secondary, IGCSE, and A-Level education to students aged 7–19, along with the world's first fully online IB Diploma Programme. Families can enrol at any time of year, with a choice of timetabled live lessons in three time zones and a school community spanning more than 100 nations.

At King's InterHigh, your child will learn in live, interactive online lessons each school day – where highly qualified and experienced teachers bring learning to life, combining traditional methods like class collaboration with cutting-edge tools such as immersive virtual reality (VR). With recordings of every lesson and a state-of-the-art personalised learning platform, students also enjoy the flexibility to fit school around their lifestyle or ambitions and master their learning at their own pace.

Part of Inspired Education, King's InterHigh brings together unparalleled online expertise and the academic excellence of King's College Schools. Since 2005, the school's well-rounded, future-ready approach to education has guided more than 12,500 alumni to bright futures across a vast range of successes: top universities and careers, sports and arts awards, entrepreneurship, and more.

Combining stellar academics with a vibrant school life, King's InterHigh also has lots happening outside the classroom. Your child can participate in online cocurricular clubs and events, join school trips and meetups, and take part in opportunities with over 121 Inspired schools worldwide. Students get guidance for university and future goals, and wellbeing is a top priority with comprehensive pastoral care and tailored support for SEN.

Exam results are outstanding for a nonselective online school, with students scoring above the national average at GCSE and across multiple A-Level subjects. In 2024, 20% of all A-Level grades achieved were A or A*, and 18% of our A-Level students were accepted to Russel Group Universities. Furthermore, 80% of all our IB students who applied for university in 2023–24 achieved their first-place offer.

With an innovative, personalised, supportive approach to learning and a diverse, thriving global community, King's InterHigh is the school that revolves around you. Find out more at kingsinterhigh.co.uk.

Spain

La Miranda - The Global Quality School

Carrer del Canigó 15, 08960 Sant Just Desvern, Barcelona, Catalonia, Spain
Tel: +34 93 371 73 58
Email: info@lamiranda.eu
Website: www.lamiranda.eu

Head of School: Ms. Debra Gregory
School type: Co-educational Day
Age range of pupils: 0–18 years
No. of pupils enrolled as at 01/09/2025: 1210

La Miranda, founded in 1967 in Sant Just Desvern, Barcelona, is a prestigious private, secular school within the renowned Inspired Education Group. With 1,210 students and 125 dedicated teachers, we are committed to providing an exceptional and innovative education. Our expansive campus spans over 13,500 square meters and includes 12 purpose-built buildings, offering a wide range of state-of-the-art facilities that create a nurturing and culturally diverse environment for students from ages 0 to 18.

At La Miranda, we place a strong emphasis on the individual growth of each student, fostering confidence and excellence. Our comprehensive curriculum is based on three core pillars: academics, the performing arts, and sports, ensuring the holistic development of well-rounded, thoughtful individuals who are fully equipped to thrive in a globalized world.

The school offers a range of academic programs, including the Spanish Bachillerato, the International Baccalaureate (IB) Diploma Programme, and the Dual Diploma Programme in collaboration with Academica International Studies (AIS). This innovative Dual Diploma Programme allows students to earn both the Spanish Bachillerato and the U.S. High School Diploma, providing them with a robust academic foundation and opening doors to universities worldwide.

As an Apple Distinguished School, La Miranda is recognized for its continuous innovation in teaching and learning. This prestigious designation highlights our commitment to leadership, creativity, collaboration, and critical thinking, all enhanced by the use of Apple products. These tools are integral to fostering academic excellence and enriching the overall learning experience.

Our campus is designed to support comprehensive student development, combining modern facilities with natural surroundings. Key features include play areas, a heated swimming pool, a sports center, gymnasiums, a football field, science laboratories, a robotics room, an art studio, a music room, an auditorium, a video recording studio, a library, and a cafeteria.

Innovative technologies such as Artificial Intelligence (AI) and the Metaverse are integrated into our educational programs. Our iTech Suite, dedicated to Virtual Reality (VR) projects, provides immersive learning experiences that foster collaboration and offer global perspectives.

La Miranda emphasizes multilingualism and project-based learning, encouraging critical thinking, creativity, and problem-solving from an early age. Our educational model nurtures intellectual, emotional, social, and physical growth, ensuring that students are well-prepared for the demands of the modern world.

As part of the Inspired Education Group, La Miranda benefits from a global network that promotes collaboration and offers access to world-class resources and best practices. This connection ensures our students receive an outstanding, future-focused education, preparing them to meet the challenges and opportunities of tomorrow.

Spain

Lady Elizabeth School

(Founded 1987)

Entrada Norte Cumbre del Sol s/n, 03726 Benitachell, Alicante, Valencia, Spain
Tel: +34 671 698 769
Email: info@les.edu.es
Website: ladyelizabethschool.com
Principal: Mr. Chris Akin
School type: Co-educational Day & Boarding

Age range of pupils: 3–18 years
Fees as at 01/09/2025:
Day: €6,580.00–€14,900.00 per annum
Weekly Boarding: €32,511.00–€34,801.00 per annum
Full Boarding: €38,010.00–€40,300.00 per annum

Lady Elizabeth School: A Community of Global Learners

Lady Elizabeth School (LES) has been delivering high-quality British international education for over 37 years. Located in an inspiring natural setting on Spain's Costa Blanca, LES welcomes students from age 2 to 18, offering a transformative educational experience where Confidence Grows.

At LES, education goes beyond academics. Our mission is to nurture confident, open-minded, lifelong learners who are prepared to thrive in an ever-evolving global world. Blending the British curriculum with international methodologies, we provide an immersive bilingual environment in English and Spanish. This dynamic and inclusive approach helps every student flourish academically, socially, and personally.

Multilingualism at the Core

A central pillar of the LES philosophy is multilingualism. With a vibrant learning community of over 60 nationalities, the school strongly supports language acquisition, offering full immersion in English alongside Spanish, French, and German. Additional mother tongue support is available to further enrich the linguistic experience. This commitment ensures that LES students not only communicate fluently across cultures but are also prepared to lead in a globalized world.

A Broad and Flexible Curriculum

LES offers a broad and balanced academic programme that encourages curiosity and caters to a wide range of interests and talents. From the International Primary Curriculum to GCSEs and A Levels, students can choose from over 20 subjects including Marine Science, Photography, Graphic Communication, Business, or Tourism. Each subject is supported by purpose-built facilities, from science laboratories and a professional recording studio to a photography room, sports courts, swimming pools, and a fully equipped theatre. The breadth of subjects and resources ensures that all learners, whether

Spain

creatively inclined or scientifically focused, find pathways that match their passions and future aspirations.

Beyond the Classroom
Life at LES is vibrant and fulfilling beyond academics. The school's Plus Clubs offer more than 40 extracurricular activities including robotics, Chinese, cheerleading, public speaking, theatre, sports, and film. Students participate in enriching international experiences through the International Schools Partnership programmes such as the ISP Model United Nations, ISP Chess Master, and ISP Filmmakers.

Personal development is also nurtured through leadership opportunities, community service, and globally recognised programmes like the Duke of Edinburgh Award. These experiences build resilience, teamwork, and independence, preparing students for life beyond school.

Exceptional Results and Global Futures
The 2023/24 academic year brought extraordinary achievements.
LES students earned:
- **Highest Mark in the World** – Graphic Communication
- **Highest Mark in Europe** – Photography (achieved by two students)
- **Highest Mark in Spain** – English Literature and Russian
- **Outstanding Achievement Award** – Marine Science
- Two A Level students received the **Higher Achiever Award** (Grade A or above in three subjects) and one GCSE student earned **Grade 9 in five subjects**

These outstanding results open doors to world-class universities. The graduating class of 2023/24 exemplifies LES's commitment to shaping future leaders and global citizens.

Recent graduates have gone on to pursue:
- **Aeronautical Engineering** at the University of Sydney
- **Theoretical Physics** at Lancaster University
- **Fashion Design** in Paris
- **Psychology** at UC San Diego

Such success reflects not only the academic rigour at LES but also the personal growth and confidence that students develop throughout their school journey.

Recognised Among the Best
In 2025, Lady Elizabeth School was recognised among the Best International Schools in Spain by El Mundo and included in the Top 100 Schools by Forbes. These accolades, along with national awards and consistently excellent academic outcomes, underscore the school's reputation as a leader in international education.

A Place to Belong, Learn, and Lead
At Lady Elizabeth School, every child is known, supported, and encouraged to achieve their full potential. Whether it's through a passion for science, creativity in the arts, linguistic fluency, or athletic talent, LES empowers students to discover their strengths and confidently pursue their goals.

As part of a truly international and multilingual community, our students don't just learn, they grow into thoughtful, adaptable individuals ready to make a difference. LES is more than a school; it's a place where young people from all backgrounds come together to learn, belong, and thrive.

UK

Loretto School

(Founded 1827)

Linkfield Road, Musselburgh,
East Lothian EH21 7RE UK
Tel: +44 (0)131 653 4455
Email: admissions@loretto.com
Website: www.loretto.com
Head of School: Mr. Pete Richardson
Appointed: 2024
School type: Co-educational Day & Boarding Prep & Senior, Nursery & Sixth Form
Age range of pupils: 3–18 years
No. of pupils enrolled as at 01/09/2025: 480

Fees as at 01/09/2025:
Day: £3,733–£11,274 per term (incl. VAT)
Weekly Boarding: £12,333–£15,226 per term (incl. VAT)
Full Boarding: £13,460–£16,544 per term (incl. VAT)
Flexi Boarding: £10,825–£13,909 per term (incl. VAT)
Average class size: Junior 14; Senior 17; Exam Years 15
Teacher/pupil ratio: 1:7

Our changing world is full of challenges and opportunities for young people. Finding a school that can provide an all-round education to prepare them for what lies ahead is vital. Loretto is that school.

Founded in 1827, Loretto is Scotland's first boarding school. Today an independent boarding, flexi and day school, it welcomes girls and boys from 3 to 18 years.

Set in a safe, leafy 85-acre campus just six miles from Edinburgh, Loretto enjoys all the advantages of this rural setting while being globally connected – the school is just nine kilometres from Scotland's capital city, its international airport, rail, and road networks.

The first thing you notice when you enter Loretto's campus is the warmth and energy of both pupils and staff. Relationships are marked by kindness, care and respect; a truly special environment for providing the confidence and know-how to thrive in life beyond Loretto.

With its superb location on Scotland's Golf Coast, the school has a strong tradition of top-level golf and established the Loretto Golf Academy in 2002 – the first of its kind within an independent school. Three distinct training programmes – Club, Team, and Reds – are delivered by top-class PGA Professional coaches within innovative facilities located on campus. The Academy continues to set the standard for excellence in golf education.

Loretto's founder was dedicated to blending academic excellence with a wealth of experiences beyond the classroom. The enormous range of extracurricular activities offered ensures that each pupil can grow and develop wherever their interests and talents may lie. The school's achievements in music, art, drama and its strong reputation in sporting endeavours – both in major team sports and other sports, are testament to that.

Ultimately, to really understand the warm and welcoming atmosphere that makes Loretto different, you have to experience the school in person. So please come along for a visit – you will soon see why our pupils are so proud to be called Lorettonians.

Poland

Lycée français de Varsovie (French School in Warsaw)

(Founded 1919)

Ul Walecznych 4/6, 03-916 Warsaw, Masovia, Poland
Tel: +48 22 616 54 00/01
Email: info@lfv.pl
Website: www.lfv.pl
Head of School: Anne Lesage

School type: Co-educational Day
Age range of pupils: 2–18 years
No. of pupils enrolled as at 01/09/2025: 700
Fees as at 01/09/2025:
Full Boarding: €7,700–€10,500 per term
Average class size: 20

Founded in 1919, the Lycée Français de Varsovie (French School in Warsaw – LFV) is an international school proposing the French national curriculum from Preschool to High School for children ages 2 to 18.

The school enrolls over 700 students from 45 nationalities in a true multicultural and multilingual environment. It is the only school in Poland accredited by the French Ministry of Education. The Lycée Français de Varsovie implements the same curricula as French public schools and prepares students for the same exams and diplomas. The accreditation ensures both compliance with the French model of education and high-quality teaching.

The teaching staff is composed of highly qualified, supportive and passionate teachers: all are certified by the Ministry of Education and 70% of them are native speakers.

The school is very well implemented in Warsaw (100 years of tradition and excellence) and the curricula are enhanced with Polish language classes and cultural projects. Also, the Lycée Français de Varsovie offers a large choice of over 40 extra-curricular activities for children of all ages.

Every year, the Lycée Français de Varsovie sends students to top American, British, Polish and French universities with a 100% success rate at the exam of Baccalauréat.

The school is located over two sites: Preschool and Primary school are in Sadyba/Mokotów and the Secondary and High Schools are in Saska Kepa.

The Lycée Français de Varsovie is also part of the AEFE Network (Agency For French Teaching Abroad), a global academic network that gathers more than 580 French schools around the world.

Learn more about the educational offer of LFV on our website: www.lfv.pl/en

Italy

Marymount International School Rome

(Founded 1946)

Via di Villa Lauchli, 180, 00191 Rome, Italy
Tel: +39 06 3629 1012
Email: admissions@marymountrome.com
Website: www.marymountrome.com
Head of School: Ms. Sarah Gallagher
Appointed: 2016
School type: Co-educational Day

Age range of pupils: 2–18 years
No. of pupils enrolled as at 01/09/2025: 950
Fees as at 01/09/2025:
Day: €13,700–€27,000 per annum
Average class size: 16
Teacher/pupil ratio: 1:6

One of Italy's top schools, Marymount International School Rome offers its students a long tradition of academic excellence. Over 85 nationalities and around 14 faiths contribute to its vibrant community life, and the School has championed social justice and intercultural understanding throughout its 78 year history in the footsteps of its founders, the Religious of the Sacred Heart of Mary.

An English-language program of studies from Early Childhood through Grade 12 (ages 2-18) prepares Marymount graduates for many of the world's best universities and colleges. Marymount's International Baccalaureate Diploma Program is complemented by an American High School Diploma and Advanced Placement courses.

The curriculum, regularly revised and updated to capture emerging technologies and global concerns, is fresh and meaningful. It features a wide array of languages including Ancient Greek, Arabic, Chinese, French, German, Italian, Latin and Spanish, in keeping with Marymount's deep commitment to an international education. With over 80 electives in High School, including a wide variety offered by the prestigious Global Online Academy, students have every opportunity to deepen their interests and expand their horizons.

Students are encouraged to think for themselves, and are equipped to do so from the Elementary School, where they develop logical argument, rhetorical skills and philosophical vocabulary to ensure that their engagement is supported by building solid critical foundations.

Students have access to a wide variety of bespoke individual and group academic, athletic and artistic enrichment plans such as grade-level clusters, JuniOrchestra, and Model United Nations, in addition to a well-rounded extracurricular activity program and a plethora of trips at home and abroad.

Marymount's 40-acre campus features multiple outdoor spaces which include a regulation-size soccer field, multi-purpose sports fields, tennis and basketball courts. The Forest School offers a unique learning environment that encourages curiosity, observation, and exploration from Early Childhood all the way through Grade 12.

Merchiston Castle School

(Founded 1833)

294 Colinton Road, Edinburgh, EH13 0PU UK
Tel: 0131 312 2200
Email: admissions@merchiston.co.uk
Website: www.merchiston.co.uk
Headmaster: Mr Huw Jones
Appointed: August 2025
Deputy Heads:
Mr Danny Rowlands (Wellbeing),
Dr Dale Cartwright (Learning and Teaching)
School type: Boys' Day & Boarding Senior & Sixth Form, Co-ed Prep & Nursery

Age range of boys: 3–18 years (boarding 12–18)
Age range of girls: 3–9 years
No. of pupils enrolled as at 01/09/2025: 350
No. of boarders: 197
Fees as at 01/09/2025:
Day: £18,000.00–£36,774.00 per annum
Full Boarding: £23,205.00–£48,276.00 per annum
Teacher/pupil ratio: 1:8

The Path to Excellence: Your Son's Journey at Merchiston

Nestled in peaceful woodlands just outside Edinburgh's vibrant city centre, Merchiston stands as a beacon of educational excellence where boys don't just receive an education – they discover their true potential. This is more than just a school; it provides a transformative journey where every boy's individual strengths are recognised, nurtured, and developed.

A tailored approach

What sets Merchiston apart is our unwavering commitment to understanding each boy as an individual. Within our intimate community, set across 100 acres of stunning Scottish landscape, we create an environment where every student is known, valued, and supported in pursuing his unique path to success. Whether your son dreams of academic achievement, sporting excellence, or a well-rounded education that encompasses both, our experienced educators work tirelessly to help him realise those aspirations.

Academic excellence

For academically-minded students, our track record speaks volumes. Our exceptional GCSE, A Level, and Higher results consistently open doors to prestigious universities. But these achievements aren't just numbers – they're the result of our dedicated approach to personal academic development. We take time to understand your son's learning style, identify areas for growth, and create tailored strategies that inspire him to reach his full potential.

Sporting achievements

For those with sporting ambitions, Merchiston's legacy of athletic excellence provides an unparalleled platform for development. With over 60 international rugby players and 24 international cricketers among our alumni, we understand what it takes to compete at the highest level.

Our specialised Tennis and Golf Academies offer elite training alongside customised academic programmes, ensuring talented athletes can excel both on and off the field. Yet even for those who play for enjoyment rather than competition, our diverse sporting programme – offering up to 30 different sports – instills valuable life skills and healthy habits that last a lifetime.

Co-curricular offering

Perhaps your son seeks a more diverse experience? Our rich co-curricular program opens doors to countless possibilities. From our acclaimed Choral Society to outdoor adventures in the surrounding countryside, every boy has the opportunity to discover new passions and develop hidden talents. We believe these experiences are crucial in forming well-rounded individuals ready to face future challenges with confidence.

Boarding life

At the heart of the Merchiston experience is our boarding community, where boys from diverse backgrounds forge lifelong friendships and develop essential life skills. The extended day allows both day and boarding students to fully immerse themselves in school life, participating in evening activities that range from indoor sports to cultural excursions.

Unique journey

What truly distinguishes Merchiston is our understanding that every boy's journey is unique. Our smaller school community enables us to forge meaningful connections with each student, ensuring we can provide the right balance of challenge and support. Whether your son is a budding scholar, a promising athlete, or an aspiring artist, we create an environment where he can thrive.

By the time your son leaves Merchiston, he will have achieved more than academic success or sporting accolades. He will have developed true integrity, character, and a deep understanding of his own potential. Most importantly, he will be thoroughly prepared for the next chapter of his life, equipped with the skills, confidence, and values needed to succeed in an ever-changing world.

At Merchiston, we don't just educate boys – we empower them to become the very best versions of themselves.

Portugal

Montalvo International School

(Founded 2023)

Avenida Marçal Pacheco 37, Loulé, Algarve, Faro, Portugal
Tel: +351 912 914 056
Email: admin@montalvoschools.com
Website: algarve.montalvoschools.com
Director: Mr Walter Mendonça
Exams Officer: Mr Andy Hargrave

School type: Co-educational Day
Age range of pupils: 14–19 years
Fees as at 01/09/2025:
Years 10 & 11: €13,255 per annum
Years 12 & 13: €9,800–€19,000 per annum (plus €500 non-refundable registration fee)
Average class size: Max 16

A young and new home for education, Montalvo International School, located in the picturesque town of Loulé, Portugal, offers a unique blend of traditional values and modern innovation in education. With a strong focus on providing a 21st-century learning experience, Montalvo is dedicated to nurturing well-rounded individuals prepared for the challenges of a globalized world while ensuring students are exposed to a cutting edge learning experience in and out of the classroom. We understand that even though the world is evolving and technology is becoming ever more important, there are values and ways of working that we believe should always have a place in educational institutions.

We aim to deliver bespoke education, thus our students benefit from one of our principles of small class sizes. With a maximum of 16 students per class, Montalvo ensures personalized attention and a supportive environment for each student. Our diverse teacher body represents a multitude of nationalities, fostering a rich multicultural atmosphere where students learn not just from books but from each other. Our supportive policies can be felt across the board where students that enrol to the school see themselves receiving benefits such as having their books provided, a set of 15 tuition lessons to be utilized and their exam fees covered for. At this stage, for iGCSEs

Portugal

and A Levels, students can pick from a selection of subjects such as, Psychology, Economics, Business, the 3 Core Sciences, Languages and Maths, among others. BTECs are set to be available from the start of 2025/2026 Academic year, providing a unique opportunity for a more vocational course where academics take a backstage in favor of practical experience.

Our upcoming center in Loulé is designed to be a hub of excellence for students in Years 10 to 13, focusing on iGCSEs and A Levels. With a capacity to accommodate approximately 128 students, it will not only be a place of learning but also an epicenter for academic excellence and personal growth.

In this building, we will have a small Lab dedicated to science classes and experiments in Biology, Chemistry and Physics. Students will be able to benefit from a library for their studies and peaceful relaxation during their downtime. Additionally our café and bar area will be finalized before the next academic school start, allowing us to deliver cooked meals to the students as well as providing an open space for teachers and parents to sit and socialize.

Being an integral part of our community is an important aspect for the school and those around us. To that effect we have developed the Montalvo Partnership Program, MPP. This program allows students, teachers and parents to take advantage of discounted items from select establishments in the town. We have chosen to associate with local businesses that have a similar image, positioning and attention to value and excellence to ensure a coherent group of partners in our program. In addition to supporting local businesses and promoting interaction between the school and its community, the MPP encourages those involved to communicate and interact in Portuguese - a perfect opportunity to put into practice what's covered in the classroom.

Following its initial Pilot year during 2023/2024, Montalvo International School will officially open its doors to the community in September 2024. Enrolments are open and we are accepting admissions for Years 10 to 13. Rigorous demands and requirements are in place for all candidates, especially students enrolling to Year 11 and 13 considering they are transitioning mid-curriculum. Montalvo holds high academic standards and we have the responsibility to ensure our current students continue to progress in their respective disciplines with as few disruptions and delays as possible.

We invite you to explore our website, understand our values and ethos as well as our goals for the future. Choosing the right school is a pivotal decision, and we wish you the best in your journey. Montalvo International School stands ready to be part of that journey, offering an exceptional education experience.

Spain

Mirabal International School

(Founded 1982)
Calle Monte Almenara, s/n, 28660 Boadilla del Monte, Madrid, Spain
Tel: +34 916 331 711
Email: mirabal@colegiomirabal.com
Website: www.colegiomirabal.com

Head of School:
Ms. Rosario de la Cruz López
School type: Co-educational Day
Age range of pupils: 0–18 years
No. of pupils enrolled as at 01/09/2025: 1678

Mirabal International School is a primary and secondary school that offers a multilingual approach to learning. Highly regarded for its exceptional academic standards, Mirabal has historically achieved world top positions in the annual PISA report for Schools, an educational evaluation promoted by the OECD.

Our school is a member of Inspired Education, the leading global premium group of schools that offer excellence in education to over 85,000 students worldwide. From exchange programmes to exclusive camps, to leadership conferences and shared learning experiences, Inspired offers a range of enriching global opportunities which give students a chance to travel, meet peers from other countries and become a part of a vibrant international community.

Founded in 1982, Mirabal International School is committed to instilling strong values in its students. We promote independence, tolerance, responsibility, diligence, generosity, and honour. The high standard of our learning continues to be facilitated by the integration of innovative teaching methodologies - such as the integration of iPads and inclusion of more modern subject material such as robotics. These techniques have meant that students learn research skills and become familiar with being met by a wide array of technology and information from a young age.

At our school students can choose to follow the Spanish National Curriculum, the International Baccalaureate (IB), or a double-honours program. The double-honours program is multilingual program offered by native teachers and is designed to stimulate intellectual, social, physical and artistic development.

Our approach to learning has generated fabulous exam results; in 2024, 38.3% of our students achieved a 12 or higher in the Spanish National Curriculum and in 2024, our IB students received an average score of 35.5 with the top score being 43 points.

Located in a suburban setting in the north of Madrid, Mirabal School, aware of the benefits of interactive and practical learning, also offers excellent facilities and resources. The school occupies a total of 45,000 m2 and offers a wide range of facilities - including tennis courts, athletics tracks, two swimming pools and several scientific laboratories.

In addition to its prowess in sport, Mirabal is a certified music school where students can obtain an official Music Elementary Degree in the instrument of their choice.

Overall, in addition to academics, we seek to promote emotional intelligence in our students. Through cooperative learning, the promotion of communication and community we strive to achieve this goal.

For more information, please visit our website or reach out via email.

Belgium

Montgomery International School - Brussels

Rue du Duc 133, 1200 Brussels, Belgium
Tel: +32 (0)2 733 63 23

Email: admissions@mischool.be
Website: www.mischool.be
Head of School: Danielle Franzén
School type: Co-educational Day
Age range of pupils: 5–19 years
No. of pupils enrolled as at 01/09/2025: 207
Fees as at 01/09/2025:
PYP 1 – PYP5 (Grades 1 to 5): €24,875 per annum
MYP 1 – MYP3 (Grades 6 to 8): €26,626 per annum
MYP 4 – 5 (Grades 9 and 10): €27,713 per annum
DP1 (Grade 11) – DP2 (Grade 12): €31,638–€32,292 per annum
Extra fees: €1,650 Administration Fee (annual)– €2,000 Registration Fee (one time)

Montgomery International School is an accredited IB (International Baccalaureate) school accepting students from primary education through the IB Diploma. Located in the centre of Brussels, our school is represented by a diverse and caring community that empowers students to achieve high academic standards through a holistic and engaging pedagogy. With a 100% success rate in the IB Diploma, and results exceeding the global average, Montgomery International School consistently ranks among the top international schools in Brussels.

Our vision
We strive for academic excellence while ensuring our students' well-being. With small class sizes and a dynamic, dedicated team of teachers, we aim to help our students reach their full potential in a supportive, inclusive, and open-minded environment.

Our guiding principles
- Innovative Curriculum
- Commitment to Academic Growth
- Knowing our students
- Student-teacher connection
- Culture of care

One School, Two Programmes
From primary all the way to secondary, we offer a programme entirely in English with French as a second language or a bilingual programme with French and English immersion courses. Moreover, we are the only school in Brussels which grants the Advanced Bilingual IB Diploma, a significant advantage when applying to universities.

A city school offering multiple opportunities
Montgomery International School is located in the heart of Brussels, close to NATO and European institutions. As a city school we have access to a wide range of resources and facilities. Every year we explore the city extensively, engaging with museums, theaters, sports clubs, and other enriching experiences beyond the confines of the school. Our location allows our students to commute to school easily and to develop a sense of independence.

Montgomery International School today
With over 200 students, our school has grown exponentially over the past few years. In September 2023, Montgomery International School officially joined the French educational group ERMITAGE. While this change opens up new opportunities, it remains perfectly aligned with our mission to offer students the very best in a caring environment where everyone finds their place.

France

Mougins British International School

Mougins BRITISH INTERNATIONAL SCHOOL

(Founded 1964)

615 Avenue Maurice Donat, CS 12180, 06252 Mougins CEDEX, France
Tel: +33 4 93 90 15 47
Email: admissions@mougins-school.com
Website: www.mougins-school.com
Director: Mr James Wellings
Appointed: 2021

School type: Co-educational Day
Age range of pupils: 3–18 years
No. of pupils enrolled as at 01/09/2025: 550
Fees as at 01/09/2025:
Day: €15,660–€24,768 per annum
Average class size: 19

Located in the heart of Nice Sophia-Antipolis, Mougins British International School offers an exceptional British school programme for students ages 3 to 18 and is a proud member of Globeducate. All lessons are taught in English, with a diverse student body of 550 children representing over 50 nationalities.

Since 1987, the school has flourished on a state-of-the-art, green, landscaped campus with peaceful shaded spots, as well as a theatre, a synthetic football pitch, sports court for games, science laboratories, a library, a canteen with an outdoor terrace, and the Millennium Building for classrooms and administration.

Mougins School's Early Learning Centre follows the English Early Years Foundation Stage (EYFS) curriculum, including Nursery and Reception classes, ideally preparing children for Key Stage 1. Young learners can explore the outdoor kitchen, investigate the sensory garden, and engage with the School in the Woods Programme, fostering a stimulating outdoor learning environment.

Following the British Curriculum, students in the Primary Section make excellent progress in oral comprehension and expression, literacy, numeracy and social skills. All subjects are taught in English and the practical methodology synonymous with the British curriculum means that different types of learners are able to progress at different rates.

Mougins School's Secondary Section provides a fantastic environment for fulfilling academic potential for students, where they are supported closely by teachers and tutors in preparation for their IGCSE and A Level examinations. They are encouraged to be keen, enthusiastic, independent learners and are given lots of opportunities to develop their interpersonal skills by working and cooperating with others. Through the curriculum they build their self-esteem and self confidence.

Mougins School is committed to enriching students' lives through a range of activities and programmes, including the THRIVE Enrichment Programme and LAMDA exams. Education is viewed as a nonlinear journey, where effort, perseverance, and embracing challenges shape learners to positively impact themselves, others, and the world around them. Through the integration of the STEAM approach, Mougins School ensures students develop interdisciplinary skills essential for the 21st century.

Mougins British International School is more than an academic institution – it's a launchpad for tomorrow's leaders, thinkers, and change-makers. By embracing the British International system, students are equipped not only with top-tier qualifications, but with the tools and values to shape their own path and contribute to the world around them.

From the early years at age three through to eighteen, Mougins School guides and supports each student on their journey, helping them find their path and follow their passions to build a meaningful future.

Portugal

Nobel Algarve British International School

(Founded 1972)

Lagoa Campus
EN 125, Porches, 8400-400 Lagoa, Portugal
Tel: +351 282 342 547
Email: admissions@nobelalgarve.com

Almancil Campus
Caminho das Pereiras, 8135-022 Almancil, Portugal
Tel: +351 282 342 547
Email: admissions.almancil David Jenkins

Website: www.nobelalgarve.com
Head of School: Ian Walker
School type: Co-educational Day
Age range of pupils: 3–18 years
No. of pupils enrolled as at 01/09/2025: 1000+
Fees as at 01/09/2025:
Average Tuition: €6,060–€18,560 per annum
Average class size: 13-25
Teacher/pupil ratio: 1:10

Nobel Algarve British International School has long been regarded as Southern Portugal's premier international school. Currently comprising two campuses in the Algarve: the flagship school in Lagoa, and the new state-of-the-art campus in Almancil, launched in 2020, the campuses educate more than 1,400 students from more than 50 nationalities, aged 3 to 18.

21st-century learning for a better future
Nobel Algarve British International School Lagoa offers a bilingual pre-school from 3 to 5 years old, following the British National Curriculum or the Portuguese Ministry of Education. Students in the international section follow a contextualised version of the British National Curriculum, sitting IGCSEs and A-Levels, with most of them going on to enrol in some of the world's leading higher-education institutions.

At Nobel Algarve British International School Lagoa learning goes beyond the classroom, offering an activity rich programme, and an outdoor learning programme called the Journey, which promotes environmental awareness and equips pupils to face challenges confidently, building character so they manage difficulties with tenacity and resilience.

The school has unveiled ambitious expansion plans, an impressive project branded 'Nobel Algarve – Shaping the Future', which is being developed in different phases. The current campus is being equipped with new buildings and classrooms, featuring state-of-the-art facilities, a new multi-purpose gymnasium/performance space, a bespoke pre-school, and a brand-new canteen. The new Early Years facilities and canteen building have already been launched, and over the coming months, the remaining buildings will be completed and the outdoor spaces enhanced, to provide a welcoming atmosphere for learning and growth.

GBIS School
Nobel Algarve British International School Lagoa is a proud member of Globeducate, one of the world's leading K12 education groups, with more than 65 premium bilingual and international schools in 11 countries, educating more than 40,000 students.

Membership of Globeducate's British International Schools (GBIS) provides numerous benefits, including global events, partnerships, and learning communities for areas such as Artificial Intelligence, Outdoor Learning, STEAM and Reading and Writing. Students and teachers collaborate with others on projects such as LEGO® Education, and through partnerships with WWF (World Wildlife Fund) and Eco-Schools. Globeducate's vision is to prepare each student to become a global citizen who can shape the world.

Spain

O Castro British International School (Vigo)

O Castro
BRITISH INTERNATIONAL SCHOOL
VIGO

(Founded 2008)

Camiño San Cosme 1, 36419 San Pedro de Cela (Mos), Pontevedra, Galicia, Spain
Tel: +34 986 20 00 28
Email: admissions@bisocastro.com
Website: www.bisocastro.com
Executive Head: Mr. Chis Long

School type: Co-educational Day
Age range of pupils: 3–18 years
No. of pupils enrolled as at 01/09/2025: approx 700
Average class size: 20

Located in Vigo, Galicia, O Castro British International School is a private, secular, international school for children ages 3 to 18. It is the only school in Galicia to offer a full National Curriculum of England from early years to sixth form. O Castro British International School belongs to Globeducate British International Schools and has been part of the Globeducate prestigious network since 2017. This allows the school to offer a diverse range of student international experiences and opportunities.

With a full English immersion programme, they aim to educate their students to become responsible members of society with the ability to understand and embrace the challenges of the world we live in today. Alongside being confident and effective communicators, they are also able to give their opinions and work effectively in teams.

The curriculum is designed to bring out the best in every student. The school follows the English National Curriculum, gaining qualifications that are accepted for entry at top universities across Spain, the UK, and the rest of the world. It is also certified by the Galician government and regulated by the British Council and NABSS (the National Association of British Schools in Spain) who conduct regular inspections in order to ensure that the school maintains the highest standards in all that they do.

Building skills to last a lifetime
They are dedicated to ensuring that every student is motivated toward their learning; each student is given individualised support to help realise their potential and to develop new skills and talents. As students move through the school they are taught how to research, study, and learn more independently, and their teachers employ a wide range of strategies to guide and direct each student's learning journey to ensure that they achieve their maximum potential.

The school offers a wide and balanced curriculum, both in the subjects taught and the delivery of these. Learning uses digital technologies combined with more traditional resources to help ensure students are ready for the next stage in their education or career.

School campus
Founded in September 2008, it was designed to meet the high standards expected of today's international private schools. The school is set in grounds of 33,000 m2, with modern, bright and spacious facilities, that have been carefully designed to meet each student's educational and social needs, both in terms of academic performance and extracurricular activities. It includes ICT and STEAM rooms, science labs, two libraries, a Black Box, recreational and wooded areas, including a Green Zone, a psychomotor skills suite for the little ones, a 2,000 m2 sports centre, basketball and a multi-purpose artificial grass pitch.

Life at O Castro goes beyond the classroom. The school offers a full programme of extra-curricular activities, exchanges and international events with other Globeducate schools. O Castro also provides their students with an exclusive outdoor learning programme, from the age of three upwards: "The Journey", a unique opportunity to build character, knowledge, skills, competencies and global perspectives as they embark on a personal journey of discovery and challenge. This programme, unique to Globeducate schools, lays the foundation for following the internationally recognised Duke of Edinburgh programme, aimed at students from Year 9 to Year 12.

As a British school, O Castro promotes the traditional House System to foster collaboration between students of different ages, team spirit, leadership skills and reinforce the sense of belonging to a community.

Portugal

PaRK International School

Estrada de Alfragide 94, 2610-015 Amadora, Lisbon, Portugal

Tel: +351 215 807 000
Email: admissions@park-is.com
Website: www.park-is.com
Executive Head of School: Samantha Gonçalves
School type: Co-educational Day

Age range of pupils: 1–18 years
No. of pupils enrolled as at 01/09/2025: 1450
Fees as at 01/09/2025:
Day: €7,680–€18,600 per annum
Enrolment Fee:: €800–€4,800 per annum

PaRK International School is a co-educational school with three different campuses in Lisbon. We are a part of Inspired Education, the leading global premium group of schools that offer excellence in education to over 85,000 students worldwide. From exchange programmes to exclusive camps, to leadership conferences and shared learning experiences, Inspired offers a range of enriching global opportunities which give students a chance to travel, meet peers from other countries and become a part of a vibrant international community.

An international school with Portuguese roots, PaRK IS welcomes students aged 1 to 18. Our mission is to educate and inspire students to have the skills to be happy and successful in their individually chosen path.

At PaRK IS, we teach children the skills and give them the tools to become bilingual, curious, collaborative, caring, autonomous and agile learners, to reach their full potential. Each age group is offered a demanding, dynamic, innovative and bespoke curriculum: a Bilingual Programme from Early Learning until Grade 4, an English stream in the Junior School starting from Grade 1, Cambridge from Grade 5 (including IGCSE in Grades 9 and 10), and the choice from the internationally acclaimed IB Diploma Programme or prestigious Cambridge Advanced Levels for Grades 11 and 12.

Alongside the strong academic curriculum, students receive a personalised and well-rounded education. Our Well-Being department guarantees that each student has their individual needs met, ensuring that school is a happy place for all. In the classroom, technology and innovation are fully integrated in the curriculum, and we offer exclusive arts and drama classes, in addition to PaRK Music Academy, where students can find a bridge between vocational and non-vocational music education. There is also a wide range of sporting activities, including PaRK Team, to participate in and compete against other international schools - all of this contributes to the development of students' personality, enriching their learning experience and broadening their interests.

Finally, we offer a unique sports programme to drive students, from Grade 5 to 12, who aspire to become accomplished athletes. This programme incorporates their sports into their academic and school life.

With a PaRK IS education, students will be prepared for academic excellence, proficient in more than one language and equipped with key life skills to be successful in an ever-changing world.

For more information, please visit our website or reach out via email.

Portugal

Prime School International

Estoril Campus
Rua Antoine de Saint-Exupéry, Alapraia, 2765-043 Estoril, Lisbon, Portugal
Lisbon Campus
Rua Carlos Lobo de Ávila, Alvalade, 1700-099 Lisbon, Portugal
Sintra Campus
Rua Mestre Neves 20, Portela de Sintra, 2710-422 Sintra, Lisbon, Portugal
Tel: +351 21 923 54 96
Email: info@primeschool.pt

Website: primeschool.pt
School type: Co-educational Day
Age range of pupils: 3–18 years
No. of pupils enrolled as at 01/09/2025: Approx. 450 across all campuses
Fees as at 01/09/2025:
Secondary & A-Levels: €15,500–€18,800 per annum
Early Years & Primary: €9,900–€12,500 per annum

Prime School, part of Group Prime Education, has been established in the Portuguese education market since 2008, with three campuses located in Lisbon, Estoril, and Sintra. We provide excellent international education based on the renowned Cambridge curriculum, including IGCSEs and A-Levels, for students aged 3 to 18.

Our key strength lies in our commitment to small class sizes, which allows for personalised attention to each student. This approach ensures that learners receive dedicated academic support and individual guidance, essential for their growth and success.

Classes are taught in English by highly qualified international teachers who focus on encouraging critical thinking, creativity, and practical engagement in learning. We value not only academic achievement but also students' emotional well-being, preparing them for the challenges of higher education and life beyond school.

Our campuses are equipped with modern facilities, including science laboratories, art studios, music rooms, and digital learning spaces. Beyond the academic curriculum, we offer opportunities in leadership, arts, sports, and community service to promote the holistic development of our students.

With a multicultural community representing over 52 nationalities, Prime School fosters an inclusive and enriching environment that promotes intercultural understanding and prepares students for a globalised world.

At Prime School, we believe education should be personalised and student-centred, ensuring every child is valued and supported to reach their full potential – not only academically but also as a global citizen.

UK

Queen Ethelburga's

(Founded 1912)
Thorpe Underwood Estate, York,
North Yorkshire YO26 9SS UK

Tel: +44 (0)1423 33 33 30
Email: admissions@qe.org
Website: www.qe.org
Principal: Daniel Machin
School type: Co-educational Day & Boarding Prep & Senior, Nursery & Sixth Form
Religious Denomination: Multi-Denominational

Age range of pupils: 3 months–19 years (boarding from 7)
No. of pupils enrolled as at 01/09/2025: 1100
Fees as at 01/09/2025:
Tuition (includes boarding for international students): £23,330 per term
Average class size: 15
Teacher/pupil ratio: 1:15

Set in more than 220 acres of North Yorkshire countryside, Queen Ethelburga's (QE) is a multi-award winning day and boarding school that welcomes girls and boys aged from three months to 19 years and boarders from Year 3. A through school, many students begin their QE journey in Chapter House Prep, King's Magna Middle School or at the start of GCSE or A level study in the senior school. QE's senior school also offers modern BTEC qualifications as well as performance sport and performing arts pathways.

The school places its emphasis on growing students into resilient, caring, compassionate and confident adults with an ethos of 'To be the best that I can with the gifts that I have' underpinning everything. QE takes pride in offering over 150 clubs onsite, making full use of its exceptional facilities with over 30 acres of elite grass and 3G artificial pitches, a 25-metre swimming pool, a 312 seat professional theatre, a new cricket pavilion and brand-new gym. Pupils can join the King's Academy for Performing Arts, Queen's Academy for Creative Arts, Performance Sport Pathway or Performing Arts (ADA) programme. They can partake in academically focused clubs and represent the school nationally in a variety of disciplines. QE strives to offer the most enriching activities for students, with large uptakes for QE Motorsports and QE sports teams.

QE's excellent pastoral team run a programme of activities to ensure student mental and physical health is a priority. In addition, a dedicated team of International Liaison Officers provide a specialist support role for students joining QE from across the globe. The international department help those students who have English as an additional language to develop their speaking and writing skills and to improve in listening and reading English. English as an Additional Language (EAL) is offered as a subject throughout the school.

QE is the first school in the UK to have achieved the Gold Award for Excellence in International Student Provision by QEGUK. QE has a boarding community unlike any other, a unique blend of cultures and nationalities, where friendships are formed that last a lifetime. Students in Years 6 to 13 have ensuite bedrooms and every boarding house includes a modern, well equipped common room for socialising. Younger students have specialised dorms and common rooms designed for little people. There are chill out spaces, a wellness room and study pods plus a communal open plan kitchen dining space.

In addition to term time boarding provision, during every half term and Easter holiday, an experienced team provides a comprehensive activity programme for boarding students who choose to stay on campus. Students can also join International Summer School and partake in a mix of learning, activities and trips. The aim for the whole student community is that QE feels like home.

Reddam House Berkshire

(Founded 2015)
Bearwood Road, Sindlesham, Wokingham, Berkshire RG41 5BG UK

Tel: +44 (0)118 974 8300
Email: registrar@reddamhouse.org.uk
Website: www.reddamhouse.org.uk
Principal: Mr Rick Cross
School type: Co-educational Day & Boarding Prep & Senior, Nursery & Sixth Form
Religious Denomination: Non-denominational

Age range of pupils: 3 months–18 years
No. of pupils enrolled as at 01/09/2025: 785
Fees as at 01/09/2025:
Day: £13,026–£20,883 per annum
Weekly Boarding: £32,769–£36,558 per annum
Full Boarding: £34,578–£38,310 per annum

About Reddam House Berkshire
Reddam House Berkshire is a co-educational, independent day and boarding school for pupils aged between 3 months and 18 years old. This truly majestic school, set in 125 acres of beautiful parkland, is conveniently located near Wokingham in the English county of Berkshire, a vibrant hub with easy access to the M3, M4, Heathrow and London.

The school is committed to focusing on the individual – to giving every student the personalised support they need to be their best selves in the classroom and beyond. From the world-class campus, they offer a future-focused curriculum that blends academics and the arts to create confident, independent-minded young people who are ready to excel and make a positive contribution to the world.

A future-focused, internationally respected curriculum balances academics, sports, and arts in a way that inspires all students. From the youngest early learners to the senior school students, they instil a love of learning that stays with them forever. The school was awarded 'Excellent' in every area in their ISI report 2022.

Exam Results
Reddam House Berkshire's Exam results were outstanding in 2022 with 76% of A-level grades awarded being A*/B and 50% A*/A, while 52% of GCSE results were level 9-7. More than 90% of graduates were offered places at their first choice of university.

Boarding
Reddam House offers a range of flexible boarding options for students from the age of 11 to 18 years old, including full and weekly boarding, extended days, and ad-hoc stays.

Students who board at Reddam House can expect to be part of an inclusive, respectful, and international community where independence and self-confidence are developed and celebrated.

Beyond the Classroom
The diverse programme of activities (over 80 clubs a week and a wide range of local, national and international trips) build resilience, courage, and versatility to thrive in life beyond school.

RIS Rome International School

(Founded 1988)

Via Guglielmo Pecori Giraldi n.137, 00135 Rome, Italy
Tel: +39 06 8448 2651
Email: office@romeinternationaschool.it
Website: www.romeinternationalschool.it
Head of School: Ms Niki Meehan
Early Years/Elementary Principal:
Ms Maria Palma Doriano
Middle/High School Principal:
Mr Francis McGuigan
School type: Co-educational Day
Religious Denomination: Non-denominational
Age range of pupils: 2–18 years
No. of pupils enrolled as at 01/09/2025: 400
Fees as at 01/09/2025:
Day: €10,395–€27,480 per annum

Rome International School (RIS) provides an exceptional international education, equipping students with the skills and mindset needed to tackle unforeseen challenges and excel in future careers yet to be envisioned.

We continue to be the only school in Rome authorised to offer both the International Baccalaureate (IB) Primary Years Programme and IB Diploma Programme. The school is an accredited centre for the Cambridge IGCSE thereby ensuring the quality and consistency of a true international education.

Highly qualified, caring and experienced staff motivate and inspire students to achieve their potential, both academically and personally.

We teach students to think for themselves and to understand the significance of what they are learning in global and local contexts. Our inquiry-based educational approach places students at the centre of the learning process and encourages them to be active participants in their education.

Students who complete the rewarding educational journey at RIS progress to attend universities of their choice worldwide. They will have established a personal set of values that will lay the foundation for international mindedness and critical thinking to develop and flourish.

From the Duke of Edinburgh's International Award to a sustainability education partnership with WWF and Eco Schools, our community of learners can participate in enriching co-curricular and extracurricular activities that take learning beyond the classroom and make real-life connections.

The school's state-of-the-art building has been purpose-built to meet every learning and teaching requirement. Nestled in almost four hectares of natural parkland in north-west Rome, close to the city centre, our campus offers students plenty of opportunities to play, discover and experiment.

Joining RIS means joining an extended international community.

RIS Rome belongs to the Globeducate family of schools, one of the world's leading K12 education groups with 55+ premium bilingual and international schools worldwide.

With a student intake of over 60 different nationalities, Rome International School is the ideal context for a rewarding and progressive educational experience.

Royal High Bath

(Founded 1865)

Lansdown Road, Bath, Bath & North-East Somerset BA1 5SZ UK
Tel: +44 (0)1225 313877
Email: admissions@rhsb.gdst.net
Website: www.royalhighbath.gdst.net
Head: Ms Heidi-Jayne Boyes
Head of Prep School: Ms Claire Lilley
School type: Girls' Day & Boarding Preparatory & Senior, Nursery & Sixth Form

Age range of girls: 3–18 years (boarding from 11)
No. of pupils enrolled as at 01/09/2025: 580
Fees as at 01/09/2025:
Day: £6,592 per term
Weekly Boarding: £13,549 per term
Full Boarding: £15,073 per term
Average class size: 14-18
Teacher/pupil ratio: 1:8

Royal High Bath, GDST is a leading independent day and boarding school in the south west of England. Part of the Girls' Day School Trust family of schools, RHB provides outstanding, contemporary, education for girls aged 3–18. The blend of academic rigour and an innovative curriculum combined with a supportive pastoral system means that students realise new talents, fulfil their potential and go on to have bright futures. Our Steinway Music School and Art School highlight our commitment to our students' creativity.

Academic
Built on the firm foundation of over 150 years of educating young women, we are an innovative, high-achieving school that provides a wonderful environment for girls to excel. From the very start of Year 7, girls are given a thorough grounding in the core subjects. This education is further enriched by Languages, PE, Arts and the Humanities, all taught by specialist teachers with a passion for their subjects. Sixth Form students follow a future-focused curriculum combining academic rigour of A Levels and an EPQ or AS Level and at least one elective subject as their pathway to university – students consistently achieve excellent grades and access to their first-choice university in the UK and overseas. The school's results are excellent, and consistently above the global average with students going on to study at prestigious universities in the UK and overseas, including Oxford, Cambridge, Imperial and UCL.

Community
The school is well-known for its friendliness and inclusivity. A school should be the heart of its community and we believe in organising initiatives that benefit our girls and their families as well as external charities and organisations.

Orientation
The school's expertise means the induction of students is quick and effective. A residential orientation experience helps students gain an understanding of the programme ahead and provides the space to plan their final years at school.

Boarding
With full and flexible boarding options, a diverse activities programme and excellent facilities, our girls can design their perfect home from home. Girls aged 11–16 board in School House, our stunning neo-Gothic main building while our Sixth Formers have their own dedicated house. House staff focus on creating a positive and secure atmosphere to ensure students quickly settle into a caring and supportive community. Each student is valued as an individual and their pastoral care and wellbeing are paramount.

Location
Situated in Bath, RHB has good transport links. Just 15 minutes from M4 motorway and with easy access to London, Bristol, Cardiff and Birmingham. Mainline rail links to London Paddington. Airports in Bristol, Southampton, Heathrow and Gatwick are easy to access and a shuttle to west London for weekly boarders can be arranged as required.

France

Sainte Victoire International School

(Founded 2011)

Domaine de Château l'Arc, Chemin de Maurel, 13710 Fuveau, France
Tel: +33 4 42 26 51 96
Email: contact@schoolsaintevictoire.com
Website: www.schoolsaintevictoire.com
Head of School: Frederic Fabre

School type: Co-educational Day & Boarding
Age range of pupils: 5–18 years
Fees as at 01/09/2025:
Day: €11,100–€20,350 per annum
Full Boarding: €25,400–€36,150 per annum

SVIS – Sainte Victoire International School is an IB World School located near Aix-en-Provence in the south of France. The school offers both the International Baccalaureate Diploma Programme and the Cambridge IGCSE examinations. SVIS provides education for students aged 5 years to 18 years from over 40 nationalities in our Primary, Middle, and High School. From the Primary school level, teaching is bilingual, allowing students to achieve their academic potential in English and French. SVIS also offers mother-tongue classes for several additional languages.

SVIS provides an innovative and rigorous approach to teaching and learning, incorporating cross-disciplinary subjects as well as a wide range of learning opportunities that take place off-campus. These include an extensive range of local and international trips, an abundant offering of after school activities, and an ecology park. SVIS integrates sustainability goals and service-learning into the curriculum to develop students as global citizens.

The school is situated in the heart of an international 18-hole golf course, facing the Sainte Victoire mountain and offers students a healthy and peaceful school environment. SVIS is a family-friendly environment focusing on the whole child and provides opportunities for students to explore their passions in athletics and the arts. Class sizes are limited to 15 maximum allowing for individualised education programs.

School Facilities
The school facilities include an amphitheater, a library with computers, a theatre/art room, a science laboratory, an indoor gym and outstanding outdoor facilities: an 18-hole golf course, a football/rugby grass pitch, a tennis court, a basketball court and ecology park where students can grow fruit and vegetables.

Boarding Facilities
The boarding house is located 20 meters from the entrance to the school. This facility offers an exceptional living environment, where students enjoy a healthy pace of life, conducive to academic success.

There is a maximum of 2 students per duplex. Each duplex is equipped with study rooms, a kitchen, 2 bathrooms, lounges, and a private terrace with outstanding views over the grounds.

Outstanding qualities of SVIS
- SVIS offers internationally renowned educational programs that are sought by leading universities.
- SVIS graduates have their first choice of leading universities.
- With more than 40 student nationalities, SVIS is a diverse and inclusive school.
- Each student receives individual support and guidance from teachers to achieve their maximum potential.
- The school provides students with opportunities to study a large variety of mother-tongue and foreign languages including English, Spanish, Russian, Chinese, Italian, German, Dutch, and Japanese.
- The school has an outstanding campus on an international 18-hole golf course in the south of France. The grounds are surrounded by pine forests.

Spain

SEK International School Alborán

(Founded 1999)

C/ Barlovento 141, Urb. Almerimar, El Ejido, 04711 Almería, Andalusia, Spain
Tel: +34 900 87 87 98
Email: sek-alboran@sek.es
Website: alboran.sek.es

Principal: Guadalupe Sánchez Ruiz
School type: Co-educational Day
Age range of pupils: 4 months–18 years
No. of pupils enrolled as at 01/09/2025: 735

Located on the seashore and adjacent to the Punta Entinas Natural Park, in Almería, SEK International School Alborán is regarded as a high quality international school in Andalusia. It is the only school in Almeria that offers three IB International Baccalaureate Programmes, from 3 to 18 years of age (Primary Years Programme Middle Years Programme – MYP and the Diploma Programme, either bilingually in English and Spanish or fully in English). These programmes are coordinated closely with the Spanish education system. We are also accredited by the New England Association of Schools and Colleges (NEASC).

For the SEK Education Group, to which SEK-Alborán belongs, physical fitness and respecting one's health are an essential element of the learning process. SEK-Alborán has extensive recreational areas, and 28,000m2 of outdoor spaces, as well as extensive sports facilities and a heated indoor pool. Its classrooms are equipped with cutting-edge technology (makerspace, video recording and editing spaces, radio, 3D printer, robotic tables). It is considered a model of educational innovation in Andalusia.

SEK-Alborán employs their own exclusive Future Learning Model, a learning method whose key objective is to develop intelligence and instil values in each of its students. The school has incorporated various units where students on the IB continuum will work with different AI tools in their teaching-learning process.

Social and emotional learning programmes are of particular importance in students' curricula to foster the social and personal awareness. In the Intelligent Classroom, each student progresses according to their potential, working in teams and having individual efforts rewarded. Teachers and tutors are afforded an open space for dialogue with students and parents both in-person and online. Students can take advantage of the Flipped Classroom to work on content and tackle issues from a broad perspective, solving doubts with their teachers, and learning by doing.

SEK-Alborán offers a bilingual Spanish-English education that is incorporated progressively over all educational stages (50% of the subjects are taught in English). It is the only school in Almeria authorized by Cambridge English Exams, Alliance Française and Goethe Institut in Almería. It also has an extensive program of exchanges and participations in United Nations Models.

In all SEK International Schools we are able to offer a quality online learning model in which students are able to continue their learning if necessary, with synchronous and asynchronous classes, and with personalized monitoring by teachers and tutors, which has proved successful with students and families.

Spain

SEK International School Atlántico

Rúa Illa de Arousa 4, Boavista. A Caeira, Poio, 36005 Pontevedra, Galicia, Spain
Tel: +34 900 87 87 98
Email: sek-atlantico@sek.es
Website: atlantico.sek.es

Principal: Jacobo Olmedo
School type: Co-educational Day
Age range of pupils: 4 months–18 years
No. of pupils enrolled as at 01/09/2025: 735

SEK International School Atlántico offers an outstanding international education to students, from 4 months to 18 years of age. SEK-Atlántico is authorised to teach the three International Baccalaureate Organisation programmes (PYP, MYP and IB). Sixth School in Spain with the best results in IBDP Exams in 2022 (31st in Europe).

SEK International Schools are committed to offering each student a learning experience focused on personal development and learning, preparing them for success in later life. Situated close to Pontevedra and Vigo, between the sea and the mountains, SEK-Atlántico boasts modern well-designed school spaces and buildings.

Students are afforded a bilingual education and learn to live with other cultures from an early age. The school places great importance on students' oral and written expression, fostering fluency in different languages. Considered a leader in educational innovation in Galicia, SEK-Atlántico offers learning in Galician, Spanish, English and French from year 3 of Primary.

The SEK education model allows students to play a leading role in their education. They explore and discover for themselves, and build and organise their own knowledge and skills, with expert support from teachers.

SEK-Atlántico students learn in facilities designed for their physical, social and creative development. They include: makerspaces, a psychomotor skills classroom for younger students, laboratories, music and art rooms, a library, language classrooms, a learning lab and large indoor and outdoor sports and recreational areas.

Technological spaces are integrated in the day to day lessons of the school and are designed to contribute fully to student learning. Devices have portability and compatibility enabling them to be used in any space.

From the second year of Primary to Baccalaureate, SEK-Atlántico students prepare for Cambridge University Examinations. In the Middle Years Programme and in Baccalaureate, students can also opt to take the Alliance Française Diplôme d'etude de langue française.

In all SEK International Schools we are able to offer a quality online learning model in which students are able to continue their learning if necessary, with synchronous and asynchronous classes, and with personalized monitoring by teachers and tutors, which has proved successful with students and families.

SEK International School Catalunya

(Founded 1995)

Av. del Tremolencs, 24, La Garriga, 08530 Barcelona, Catalonia, Spain
Tel: +34 900 87 87 98
Email: sek-catalunya@sek.es
Website: catalunya.sek.es

Principal: David Bauzá-Capart
School type: Co-educational Day & Boarding
Age range of pupils: 4 months–18 years
No. of pupils enrolled as at 01/09/2025: 1040

SEK International School Catalunya is located in a quiet and safe residential area spanning 100,000 m2, including a large expanse of Mediterranean forest. The school is in La Garriga, a picturesque town just 30 minutes from the centre of Barcelona, one of the most cosmopolitan cities in Europe.

SEK-Catalunya boasts modern facilities and innovative learning spaces and teaches the three International Baccalaureate Programmes. The Middle Years Programme is offered in Spanish and English and the Diploma Programme is offered entirely in English or in both languages. We are one of the leaders in the international rankings thanks to our excellent results in IB Diploma exams.

SEK-Catalunya is accredited by the New England Association of Schools and Colleges (NEASC), which is a process of external globally recognised quality assurance. NEASC accreditation allows SEK-Catalunya to offer the US High School Diploma, as a complement to the IB Diploma.

The school offers its Secondary School and Baccalaureate students the opportunity to take part in the prestigious Duke of Edinburgh's International Award, an all-round personal development scheme focused on the development and training of skills such as: leadership, autonomy, problem solving and teamwork.

The SEK-Catalunya Music School, in partnership with the Trinity College London, offers a complete curriculum for all students who wish to acquire the necessary skills to learn classical and modern music.

We also offer international boarding, housing students from Spain and abroad in modern, comfortable and functional facilities, designed for residents to live together, grow as individuals and develop their personal identity thanks to a multicultural environment and a rich offer of complementary activities.

SEK International School Catalunya has just joined ISTA, the International creative arts. The school has also launched the promotion of student lead projects in the EMPOWERMENT HUBS which give students the space and time in the school day to follow their interests and passions.

Spain

SEK International School Ciudalcampo

(Founded 1975)

Urb. Ciudalcampo, Paseo de las Perdices, 2, San Sebastián de los Reyes, 28707 Madrid, Spain
Tel: +34 900 87 87 98
Email: sek-ciudalcampo@sek.es

Website: ciudalcampo.sek.es
Principal: Cecilia Villavicencio
School type: Co-educational Day
Age range of pupils: 4 months–18 years
No. of pupils enrolled as at 01/09/2025: 1400

SEK International Schools are committed to offering each student a learning experience focused on personal growth, preparing for success in later life. SEK Schools are bilingual and pioneers in offering the IB programmes, boasting an educational model that has made a tradition of innovation, placing them among the best schools in Spain since their foundation in 1892. SEK International School Ciudalcampo is an IB continuum school, offering PYP, MYP, DP (in English and Spanish, or fully in English), and also our enriched programme of the Spanish Bachillerato, "Bachillerato +"; last two with outstanding examination results.

SEK-Ciudalcampo offers an innovative educational model based on early stimulation, immersion in English and the development of talent and creativity in a digital environment that favours the integral/holistic student development by providing a wide range of learning opportunities from High Artistic performance programme, with our "PlayMusic" project, the prestigious Duke of Edinburgh's Award, different sport schools or the enrichment projects in collaboration with the Camilo José Cela University, among others. Besides, we offer a high-performance sports programme that allows athletes to combine their academic studies with their training and competing schedules (we are the academic partner of important clubs as Real Madrid).

Through an active learning approach, SEK-Ciudalcampo turns the classrooms into a flexible learning space for all students. The student becomes an active agent, building learning for themselves. The Design Thinking methodology helps students to develop skills such as cooperation, creativity and innovation and, our linguistic immersion programme WIN opens our school to students with different linguistic profiles.

We believe that the way we learn has changed forever. As a result, SEK Future Learning Model is presented as a new opportunity to learn from new methodological formats, based on the Intelligent Classroom system, the use of new tools and the interaction between the different members of the educational community, offering enriched programmes for families such as the "Aula de Familias", sports, funky, the choir or the reading club.

SEK Ciudalcampo is accredited by NEASC in conjunction with IB with the CLP, focus on impactful learning processes. We are also the first Spanish school to be recognized as a global member of Round Square.

In all SEK International Schools we are able to offer a quality online learning model in which students are able to continue their learning if necessary, with personalized monitoring by teachers and tutors, which has proved successful with students and families.

Ireland

SEK International School Dublin

Belvedere Hall, Windgates, Greystones, Co. Wicklow, A63 EY23 Ireland
Tel: +35 31 287 41 75
Email: admissions-dublin@sek.ie
Website: www.sek.ie

Principal: Alberto Domínguez
School type: Co-educational Day & Boarding
Age range of pupils: 12–18 years

SEK International School Dublin is a leading IB school in Ireland. Small by design, with an emphasis on personalised learning, the school's unique teaching and learning model is built on inquiry-based learning to promote critical and creative thinking.

Located in a stunning natural setting, where the landscape of the Irish countryside meets the Atlantic coast, between the towns of Bray and Greystones. The latter was named one of the best towns in the world to live as a family, and is 30 km from Dublin. SEK-Dublin combines architectural tradition with cutting-edge technology, spanning over 250,000 m2 of grounds and boasting extensive green areas where our students can enjoy a diverse range of sports and outdoor activities, while enhancing their academic development.

SEK-Dublin is the first school in Ireland authorised by the International Baccalaureate Organisation to teach the Middle Years Programme (12–16 years) and the Diploma Programme (16–18 years), taught fully in English with optional languages, including German, French and Spanish.

SEK-Dublin opened its doors in 1981. The success of the school is based on several factors including: a multicultural team of highly trained teachers; the effective use of learning technologies; an individualised programme to cover the educational needs of each student; small class sizes; and an outstanding programme guaranteed by SEK schools' standards of excellence. Aware that education does not only take place in the classroom, for our boarding students we offer residential options with carefully selected local host families or in our on-campus high quality residential facilities, and diverse extracurricular and cultural activities. These aspects combine to nurture the holistic personal and academic development of our students. This all-round education serves them well for their future, enabling them to become mature and independent individuals, and providing them with lasting memories of their experiences at school.

In all SEK International Schools we are able to offer a quality online learning model in which students are able to continue their learning if necessary, with synchronous and asynchronous classes, and with personalized monitoring by teachers and tutors, which has proved successful with students and families.

Spain

SEK International School El Castillo

(Founded 1972)

Urb. Villafranca del Castillo, Castillo de Manzanares, s/n, Villanueva de la Cañada, 28692 Madrid, Spain
Tel: +34 900 87 87 98
Email: sek-castillo@sek.es
Website: madrid.sekinternationalschools.com

Head of School: Elvira Chiquero
School type: Co-educational Day & Boarding
Age range of pupils: 4 months–18 years
No. of pupils enrolled as at 01/09/2025: 1150

SEK International School El Castillo is a privileged place for coexistence and learning in the broadest sense of the word. The High Artistic Performance School (Music and Dance), the Artistic or the Research Baccalaureates, Sports academy programme or the enrichment projects in collaboration with the Camilo José Cela University, are some examples.

We have been authorised as an International Baccalaureate (IB) World School for over 40 years. The school offers the IB continuum for 3–19 year olds: The Primary Years Programme (PYP) for students aged 3 to 12, the Middle Years Programme (MYP) for students aged 11 to 16 and The Diploma Programme (DP) for students aged 16 to 19. For the Baccalaureate stage, students can take the Diploma Programme or the Spanish baccalaureate. The Middle Years and Diploma programmes are offered either in English or following an English-Spanish bilingual syllabus, with outstanding examination results. We are also accredited by the New England Association of Schools and Colleges (NEASC) in conjunction with IB with a process of quality assurance: the Collaborative Learning protocol with a focus on impactful learning processes and in 2023 have obtained recognition as a UNICEF Reference Center for Children's Rights and Global Citizenship.

We believe that the way we learn has changed forever. As a result, SEK Future Learning Model (FLM) is a learning method whose key objective is to develop intelligence and instil values in each of its students. It is an opportunity to learn from new methodological formats, based on design-thinking tools, the use of new educational technology and the interaction between the different members of the educational community, offering enriched programmes such as the Entrepeneurship hub and instrumental lessons for families in our Music School.

We boast first-rate sports facilities on campus and offer international boarders a professionally staffed, nurturing and safe environment. We provide linguistic immersion programmes in both our languages of instruction (English and Spanish) to ensure access to the curriculum for all our students. In addition, as part of our commitment to talent development, we offer a high-performance sports programme: SEK International Sports Academy (we are the academic partner of important sports clubs). This programme allows athletes to combine their academic studies with their training and competing schedules. Students can take advantage of our boarding facilities to enhance their time management. As part of our provision to develop engaged and active young adults, we offer students the opportunity to participate in the prestigious Duke of Edinburgh International Award.

In all SEK International Schools we offer a quality online learning model in which students are able to continue their learning if necessary, with synchronous and asynchronous classes, and with personalized monitoring by teachers and tutors, which is highly rated by students and families.

Spain

SEK International School Global Campus

(Founded 2023)

Urb. Villafranca del Castillo, Castillo de Manzanares, s/n, 28707 Ciudalcampo, Madrid, Spain
Email: sek-globalcampus@sek.online

Website:
sek.es/l/colegio-internacional/online
Head of School: Ana Karina
School type: Online School
Age range of pupils: 16–19 years

At SEK International School Global Campus we believe that education should not have borders. That is why we have launched a worldwide pioneering project to offer the IB Diploma Programme online. This will allow Baccalaureate students to pursue their dreams from anywhere in the world. Whether they travel frequently and need flexible study hours, are professional athletes or pursuing a career in the performing arts, live in a remote area, or face unique circumstances that require alternative access to face-to-face education, this programme is designed for all of them.

We are aware that, due to various circumstances, students may have to access lessons regardless of their location. A purpose-built platform ensures the freedom to complete activities and review materials when and where it suits them best. A typical week consists of 2–3 synchronous sessions per day (recording available for students who cannot attend) and asynchronous activities guided by a teacher, which students do according to their availability.

Our students thrive thanks to a dedicated network of mentors, educators, and university experts. This team collaborates to provide personalized guidance, offering support and inspiration to help each student realize their full potential. Each IBDP online student is paired with a dedicated faculty tutor who supports both academic progress and personal growth. Through meaningful events and experiences, students gain direction and encouragement on their journey of growth and exploration.

Language should never be a barrier to academic achievement. At SEK-Global Campus, the language of instruction is English, with access to Spanish as additional languages. Students may complete a bilingual diploma. In line with the SEK educational model, it is based on a dynamic learning experience, which revolves around discussion-based learning. Students will actively build knowledge and foster a sense of community with teachers and peers from around the world. Our state-of-the-art platform transforms any device into an interactive classroom, enabling students to join live sessions with teachers, collaborate with classmates in virtual spaces, access multimedia learning resources, and engage with immersive virtual labs and simulators. The comprehensive digital environment allows students to apply concepts, conduct experiments, and explore learning materials while staying connected with their educational community from anywhere.

France

SEK International School Les Alpes

195 Rue du Marteray, 73590 St Nicolas la Chapelle, France
Tel: +34 900 87 87 98
Email: sek-lesalpes@sek.es
Website: www.sek.es/l/colegio-internacional/les-alpes
School type: Boarding
Age range of pupils: 11–16 years

Experience education. Learn in freedom. Thrive without limits.
An international school in the heart of the Alps
Imagine waking each morning surrounded by mountains, breathing pure air, and learning in an environment where every corner inspires. Located in the idyllic Arly Valley, in the heart of the French Alps, SEK International School Les Alpes offers a unique educational experience for students aged 12 to 16.

An educational model that breaks boundaries
Aligned with the prestigious International Baccalaureate Middle Years Programme (MYP), SEK-Les Alpes presents a pioneering initiative:
- A six-week module each year, from Year 1 MYP to Year 5 MYP
- A shared experience with SEK students from all over the world.

A continuous development of knowledge, skills, and values, while maintaining alignment with the regular school calendar. Learning becomes natural – an in-depth inquiry unit developed in the heart of nature.

Learning Outside-In Methodology: where the environment educates
Here, nature is not simply a backdropo – it is a third educator.

Each module is delivered in English and integrates transdisciplinary units that redefine the classroom:
- Mountains as living laboratories
- Forests as spaces for exploration
- The natural setting as a catalyst for discovery, reflection and creativity in a truly breathtaking environment

A memorable experience that leaves a mark
- Independence and safety

Students learn to make decisions, overcome challenges, and grow in confidence – enhancing their personal well-being.
- Belonging and community

A rich culture of inclusion, mutual respect and lasting friendships.
- Curiosity and discovery

Students take an active role in their own learning and exploration of the world.
- * Authentic motivation

Learning becomes meaningful – connected to real life and driven by genuine interest.

International Boarding Residence: A home away from home
- A natural, safe and enriching environment
- Spaces designed to promote well-being, autonomy and community life
- Personalised care and healthy routines as the foundation for growth
- Ongoing monitoring and meaningful assessment
- Collaborative projects with real-world impact
- Continuous self-assessment and personal reflection
- Targeted feedback to support steady, personalised progress

Educators who guide and inspire
At SEK-Les Alpes, teachers serve as mentors and facilitators of unique learning experiences.

They design challenges, provide ongoing support, and engage in continuous professional learning to deliver vibrant, innovative and transformative education.

Can you imagine this experience for your child?
We invite you to discover SEK-Les Alpes, where education becomes an adventure – and every student is empowered to thrive.

SEK International School Santa Isabel

Calle San Ildefonso, 18, 28012 Madrid, Spain
Tel: +34 900 87 87 98
Email: sek-santaisabel@sek.es
Website: santaisabel.sek.es

Head of School: Nilce Morales
School type: Co-educational Day
Age range of pupils: 3–12 years
No. of pupils enrolled as at 01/09/2025: 324

With students representing more than 30 nationalities, SEK International School Santa Isabel offers a vibrant, multicultural environment in the heart of Las Letras, Madrid's historic cultural district. As the only school in central Madrid offering the International Baccalaureate Primary Years Programme, students learn through real-world experiences, with their classroom extending beyond school walls to include museums, theaters, galleries, neighborhood gardens, traditional markets, and Retiro Park.

SEK Santa Isabel offers Early Childhood and Primary Education (3–12). Our innovative educational model is grounded in concept exploration, inquiry-based learning, and the development of skills that promote critical thinking and creativity. We take pride in our engaging, close-knit learning community, and, we are deeply committed to providing personalized learning experiences in a safe, nurturing environment that supports the growth of emotional intelligence.

At SEK-Santa Isabel, an active learning approach transforms classrooms into flexible, dynamic learning environments where students take the lead in constructing their own knowledge. Through methodologies such as Design Thinking and Design for Change, students uncover their talents and develop key skills like collaboration, creativity, and innovation.

These approaches empower students to design and structure their own learning experiences, aligning goals, needs, and resources in projects that bridge academic content with real-world relevance. Two standout initiatives include: Passion Pursuits, whereby students discover and advance their own learning interests. Another is Learning Paths, named a best practice by Harvard's Project Zero project, where teachers and students design curricular learning activities using spaces and resources from the local community of the neighborhood and city.

We believe that learning has evolved for good. At SEK-Santa Isabel, we empower students with the skills they need to navigate future challenges, fostering global citizenship and international mindedness.

Students at SEK-Santa Isabel benefit from a wide range of activities linked to music, the arts, sports, and their individual learning needs. They can also choose from an extensive selection of extracurricular activities. The school features a spacious on-site gym and outdoor facilities for swimming, tennis, padel tennis, football, and basketball. Our Stellar Programme is designed to enrich the personal development of high-achieving students.

SEK Schools are pioneers in the implementation of International Baccalaureate Programmes, with an educational model rooted in a long-standing tradition of innovation. Since their founding in 1892, they have consistently ranked among the top schools in Spain.

Sevenoaks School

(Founded 1432)

High Street, Sevenoaks, Kent TN13 1HU UK
Tel: +44 (0)1732 455133
Email: admissions@sevenoaksschool.org
Website: www.sevenoaksschool.org
Head of School: Mr Jesse R Elzinga AB MSt FCCT
Appointed: September 2020
School type: Co-educational Day & Boarding Senior & Sixth Form

Age range of pupils: 11–18 years
No. of pupils enrolled as at 01/09/2025:
Total: 1245
Sixth Form: 500
Fees as at 01/09/2025:
Day: £35,925–£41,514 per annum
Full Boarding: £58,770–£64,257 per annum
Average class size: 8-24
Teacher/pupil ratio: 1:9

Sevenoaks is one of the leading schools in the UK, providing an outstanding modern education. All 450+ students in the sixth form study the IB Diploma Programme, which the school has taught since 1978. The leafy 100-acre campus is in the Kent countryside, just half an hour from Central London and Gatwick Airport. International students make up around 20 per cent of the student body and the school provides pupils with a balanced and intellectually stimulating education while promoting global understanding. Pastoral care is consistently excellent, enabling friendships between all members of a peer group to flourish.

Curriculum
A wide range of subjects is offered at GCSE and IGCSE. In the sixth form all pupils study the IB Diploma Programme. Academic results are outstanding. In 2025, the average IB Diploma score was 39.1 points, eight points above the world average. More than half of Sevenoaks' students earned 40 points or more, with 11 students earning 45 points. Virtually every student goes on to one of the world's best universities.

A wide range of sport is offered, and pupils achieve honours in cross country, rugby, football, hockey, netball, cricket, athletics, sailing, shooting, swimming and tennis. There is a strong emphasis on music, drama and art, with chamber music a particular strength. The school is proud of its strong tradition of community service and DofE Award participation.

Facilities
Facilities are first class. Recent developments include a striking, state-of-the-art boarding house, an award-winning performing arts centre, a Science & Technology Centre uniting the four core fields of science, and an innovative Sixth Form centre. There are eight boarding houses, including three boys' houses and three girls' houses (13–18), and two sixth form houses one for girls and one for boys (16–18).

Entrance
11+ or 13+ Early Decision January of Year 6 (closing date: 15 September of Year 6).

13+ Late Decision April of Year 7 (closing date: 1 October of Year 7).

16+ October of Year 11 (closing date: 1 August of year preceding entry).

All candidates are assessed through the school's entrance tests, references from candidate's current school, a group interview and reports.

Up to 50 scholarships are awarded annually at 11, 13 and 16, for academic excellence, music, sport, art and drama, and means-tested bursaries are available.

Sevenoaks School is a registered charity for purposes of education. Charity No. 1101358.

UK

Southbank International School

(Founded 1980)
Kensington: 36-38 Kensington Park Road, London, W11 3BU UK (Age 2*-11 years)
Hampstead: 16 Netherhall Gardens, London NW3 5TH (Age 2*-11 years)
Westminster: 63-65 Portland Place, London W1B 1QR (11-16 years)

Tel: +44 (0)20 3890 1969
Email: admissions@southbank.org
Website: www.southbank.org
Head of School:
David MacMorran (Kensington),
Stuart Bain (Hampstead),
Angela Liu (Westminster)
School type: Co-educational Day
Age range of pupils: 2*–18 years

Fees as at 01/09/2025:
Early Childhood: £6,724 (half day) – £10,721 (full day) per term
Kindergarten – Grade 2 (PYP) (5–8 years): £12,903 per term
Grades 3 – 5 (PYP) (8–11 years): £13,286 per term
Grades 6 – 10 (MYP) (11–16 years): £14,836 per term
Grades 11 & 12 (DP) (16–18 years): £15,446 per term

Southbank International School is an International Baccalaureate (IB) World School for 2*–18 year olds with campuses in Hampstead, Kensington and Westminster in Central London. We are the first school in the UK authorised to offer all three International Baccalaureate programmes. For over 40 years, Southbank has been at the forefront of providing internationally relevant, world class education.

We encourage our students to think critically and always challenge assumptions whilst ensuring they have an openness to the outside world and are ready to see other points of view. These qualities help our students develop to broaden their minds while excelling in their academic studies. We help them to develop as independent, confident, curious and lifelong learners who fulfil their academic potential and take the natural next step into the world's best universities.

With over seventy nationalities on our roll, we live and breathe the spirit of internationalism, as reflected in our three programmes of study and the many activities outside the classroom. Southbank uses London as our classroom, taking full advantage of the city's cultural riches, giving our students access to educational enrichment that is perhaps unparalleled anywhere else in the world.

Primary Years Programme (PYP) (2*–11 years old)

Based at our Hampstead and Kensington campuses, the Primary Years Programme focuses on the development of the whole child as an inquirer, both in the classroom and in the world outside. It is defined by six transdisciplinary themes of global significance, explored using knowledge and skills derived from six subject areas, with a powerful emphasis on inquiry-based learning.

Facilities at Hampstead include: A dedicated hands-on STEAM lab for science, technology, engineering, arts and maths activities; A music room with a range of

UK

percussion instruments and performance space; A bespoke art room with a wide range of materials for hands-on creativity; A multi-purpose hall for lunches, sport, school 'town meetings' and concerts; A vibrant, well-stocked library, which is regularly attended by students to develop literacy and research skills; An edible courtyard that offers a quiet space for vegetable and flower growing, as well as birdhouses and a bug hotel; An attractive, bright and spacious Early Childhood suite (for students aged 2*–5) with access to a dedicated outside play area with sand and climbing frame. Integral to the school's approach is the use of the 1:1 iPad programme to open up new pathways of learning, the school has gained recognition as an Apple Distinguished School.

Facilities at Kensington include: An IT lab featuring high-performance Macs; Interactive smartboards in all classrooms; A music room with a range of instruments and digital recording equipment; Two sound-proofed rooms for music practice; A bespoke art room with a wide range of materials for hands-on creativity; A multi-purpose hall that is used for lunches, sport, school 'town meetings' and concerts; A well-stocked library, which is regularly attended by students to develop literacy and research skills; A garden featuring a climbing frame, sandpit and wide range of educational toys and equipment; An attractive, bright and spacious Early Childhood suite (for students aged 2*–5) with access to a outside play area with sand and climbing frame.

Middle Years Programme (MYP) (11–16 years old)

Based at our Westminster campus on Portland Place, the Middle Years

Programme shares the PYP's commitment to learning through inquiry and continues to develop attributes of the IB learner profile. The MYP emphasises intellectual challenge, encouraging students to make connections between their studies in traditional subjects and the real world. At Southbank, we foster the development of skills for communication, intercultural understanding and global engagement – essential qualities for young people who are becoming global leaders.

Southbank Westminster is conveniently located near Regent's Park with good transportation links nearby. Facilities at Westminster include five science labs, a Design lab with desktop Macs to complement the 1:1 programme. Our Design labs include laser cutters, 3D printers, amongst other industry-level equipment. A hall/theatre, cafeteria, art and music rooms, and two libraries served by networked computers.

Diploma Programme (DP) (16–18 years old)

Based at Cleveland Street and Conway Street, the Diploma Programme encourages students to ask challenging questions, develop a strong sense of their own identity and culture, and develop the ability to communicate with and understand people from other countries and cultures. It prepares students for the next stage in their education and the qualification is widely-recognised by the world's leading universities.

Our 2024 IBDP students scored an average of 36 (world average 30.24). We achieved a 100% pass rate, with 21% of our students scoring 40 or more, putting them in the top 3% of students worldwide. 24.41% of our students obtained a bilingual diploma, showcasing their exceptional linguistic abilities.

Facilities at Conway Street include a science lab, library resource centre, art studio and language suite. Facilities at Cleveland St include a brand new art room, a large common room and a design technology lab.

Southbank also has dedicated university counsellors specialising in North American universities, the UK and the rest of the world. All counsellors are available for individual appointments and events are organised to inform parents about university planning.

Tours

We regularly host information mornings – a great opportunity to learn more about our school and community. To reserve your place, please visit: www.southbank.org/information-mornings-and-personal-tours We also offer personal tours led by our Admissions Managers. To arrange a tour, visit: https://www.southbank.org/information-mornings-and-personal-tours/ Prefer to explore from home? Take a virtual tour of any of our campuses for an initial look at life at Southbank: www.southbank.org/facilities-and-location/#virtual-tour We look forward to welcoming you to Southbank International School.

Spain

Sotogrande International School

(Founded 1978)

Avenida La Reserva SN,
Sotogrande, Cádiz,
Andalusia, 11310 Spain
Tel: +34 956 795 902
Email: info@sis.gl
Website: www.sis.ac
Head of School: Ms. Rachel Dent

School type:
Co-educational Day & Boarding
Religious Denomination:
Non-denominational
Age range of pupils: 4 months–18 years
No. of pupils enrolled as at 01/09/2025: 1300
Fees as at 01/09/2025:
€901–€2,595 per month

Sotogrande International School (SIS) is a day and boarding school for children from ages 4 months to 18 years old. It follows the IB (International Baccalaureate) programme throughout and is one of top 75 IB schools worldwide and top 5 IB schools in Spain.

Our school is a member of Inspired Education, the leading global premium group of schools that offer excellence in education to over 85,000 students worldwide. From exchange programmes to exclusive camps, to leadership conferences and shared learning experiences, Inspired offers a range of enriching global opportunities which give students a chance to travel, meet peers from other countries and become a part of a vibrant international community.

With more than 1,300 children coming from 54 different countries, Sotogrande's classrooms are brimming with culture and diversity; thus, our learning community can inspire and encourage intercultural understanding.

At Sotogrande International School, we are proud that our IB students demonstrate exceptional dedication to their studies. In 2023, entrants achieved a 100% pass rate in formal examinations with an average score of 34, 2 points above that of the world average.

Our school also offers a unique 'Elite Sports Programme' that combines our rigorous education with professional sport – including basketball, golf, tennis, swimming and more. This programme helps athletes to excel in their sport whilst also maintaining an elevated level of studies.

Technology also plays a significant role in our school, as it is embedded in the curriculum for all students. As an Apple Distinguished School, we leverage Apple's innovative technology to enhance learning experiences and empower both students and educators. The young engineers programme, F1 in Schools programme, and the Hyperbaric surfboard and hydrofoil challenge provide an exciting way for students to experience hands-on learning in STEM. We are encouraging our students to think critically and creatively, giving rise to the next generation of innovators.

Students who choose to board at our school are sure to benefit from the warm, and vibrant community with new and amazing resources and staff. The new boarding facility, Templeton House, has been designed with student comfort in mind. The cosy and modern furnishings will allow them to be as comfortable as possible. The ensuite rooms will be climate-controlled, with house-wide access to Wi-Fi. These facilities have been recognised as our school received the Boarding School of the Year at the Corporate LiveWire Global Awards 2023/24.

Ireland

St Andrew's College

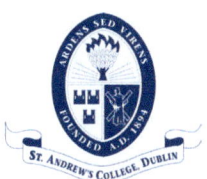

(Founded 1894)

Booterstown Avenue, Blackrock,
County Dublin, A94 XN72 Ireland
Tel: +353 1 288 2785
Email: information@st-andrews.ie
Website: www.sac.ie
College Principal: Ms Louise Marshall

School type: Co-educational Day
Religious Denomination: Presbyterian
Age range of pupils: 4–18 years
No. of pupils enrolled as at 01/09/2025: 1279
Average class size: 16
Teacher/pupil ratio: 1:12

St Andrew's College was founded by the Presbyterian community of Dublin in 1894 to provide a broadly-based, liberal education. From its inception, the College attracted students from a variety of backgrounds and strove to unite them through a shared experience of working, learning and playing together. Over the years the College has evolved in many ways, and is now a flourishing, interdenominational, co-educational school of over 1,270 pupils and over 150 teachers.

In 1982, St Andrew's College became the first school in Ireland to be authorised to offer the International Baccalaureate. It started teaching the IB Diploma Programme in 1983, and first held IBDP examinations in 1985. Over the last 28 years it has built up a well-deserved reputation for its excellent results and for its distinctive multicultural environment. The philosophy on which the College was founded and from which it draws its inspiration today is that a high-quality, rounded education is essential to the moral, social, spiritual, cultural and academic development and physical and mental well-being of the individual student. This philosophy is mirrored in the IB Learner Profile. The high quality of the education offered by the College and its commitment to continuous improvement are reflected in the fact that since 1982, St Andrew's College has been fully accredited by the European Council of International Schools and the New England Association of Schools and Colleges.

The IB Diploma Programme combines academic rigour with a strong extracurricular dimension and various community service projects. The IB students at St Andrew's College participate in a wide range of activities, representing their year on the Prefect Council, playing team sports such as hockey, rugby, tennis, basketball and badminton, taking part in activities such as the Model United Nations, being involved in environmental projects, assisting in the school library and local communities and helping various charities by fundraising and doing voluntary work. The IB Diploma Programme is the premier worldwide pre-university programme. Since 1985, St Andrew's College IB students have been accepted into many universities throughout the world. In recent years these have included all the top Irish universities; MIT, Yale, Stanford, Berkeley and Columbia (USA), Cambridge, Durham, Bristol, Edinburgh and the LSE (UK), the Universities of Tokyo and Keio (Japan). These students universally acknowledge the extent to which their studies in the IB Diploma Programme has given them invaluable help in their university careers.

The IB student profile at St Andrew's College is a truly international one, with students coming from all continents. This ethnic and cultural diversity enriches the school community in many ways and provides a wealth of knowledge and experience which is of great benefit to other students in the school.

Malta

St Edward's College, Malta

St Edward's College Malta

(Founded 1929)

Triq San Dwardu, Birgu (Vittoriosa), BRG 9039 Malta
Tel: +356 2788 1199
Email: admissions@stedwards.edu.mt
Website: www.stedwards.edu.mt
Headmaster: Mr Nollaig Mac an Bhaird
School type: Co-educational Day & Boarding

Religious Denomination: Roman Catholic
Age range of boys: 3–18 years (boarding from 11)
Age range of girls: 3–5 years (progressing annually to full co-ed)
Fees as at 01/09/2025:
Day: €2,500–€10,000 per annum
Full Boarding: €21,000–€33,000 per annum

Co-educational school from Nursery to IB Diploma
A Top Boarding School for the IB Diploma Programme

If you are looking for a top International boarding school, then look at the Mediterranean's secret gem – The St Edward's College in Birgu, Cottonera only a few minutes from Malta's Capital, Valletta. St Edward's was established in 1929, basing itself on British Public School ideals. It is a prestigious institution, foremost in the country for the formation of students who end up in top-tier leadership positions. This year, as part of its dynamic response to the needs of society, the college has gone fully co-educational. To avoid disruption to the students, the college is introducing co-ed in a different age cohort each year so that the transition to co-ed will be completed gradually.

Set in a historically protected building, formerly a military hospital approve by none other than the iconic Florence Nightengale, the campus has seen a number of additions, which include the Junior School building and the Kindergarten block. The College has also recently adjusted its facilities to begin accepting boarders from the ages of 11 to 18. Our boarding facilities are split over two floors where single and double rooms are available. At St Edward's College we strive to provide students with a seamless transition from Junior school up to Sixth Form level. We prepare the students for O'Level Matsec (local) and IGCSEs. O'Levels are available until Year 11 (age 15/16) followed by the two-year International IB Diploma programme which is recognised by both local and international universities. The College is an English speaking school so all the lessons are conducted in English. The College caters for students at all stages

of their studies from Nursery, through to Junior School, Secondary school and finally the International IB programme at Sixth Form level, which is the only stage besides nursery and kindergarten where girls are admitted both as day girls and as boarders. The complement of students is fairly international with local students as well as many others who are the sons of expats working in North Africa and the Middle East besides other areas like China, Russia and Italy. St Edward's offers a unique opportunity for parents seeking a boarding school:

- The school operates on British boarding school principles with high academic standards
- The location and environment are superb with year round sunshine on a Mediterranean island
- Malta is within three hours of any European capital city by air
- The IB Diploma is recognised by all top universities
- Our fees offer some of the best value of any European boarding schools

Come and join our students on the IB Diploma Programme!

St George's British International School, Rome

(Founded 1958)
Via Cassia, km 16, La Storta,
00123 Rome, Italy

Tel: +39 06 3086001
Email: admissions@stgeorge.school.it
Website: www.stgeorge.school.it
Principal: Dr John Knight
Appointed: September 2023
School type: Co-educational Day

Age range of pupils: 3–18 years
No. of pupils enrolled as at 01/09/2025: 1010
Fees as at 01/09/2025:
Day: €14,000–€26,500 per annum
Average class size: 18
Teacher/pupil ratio: 1:10

Established in 1958, St George's British International School is a leading independent, not-for-profit school offering a world-class education to internationally-minded families in Rome. With more than 100 nationalities represented, it is one of the most diverse international schools in Europe, providing a truly global learning environment.

The school delivers an enhanced version of the UK National Curriculum through to IGCSE, followed by two distinct Post-16 pathways: the International Baccalaureate Diploma Programme (IDBP) and A-Levels, both supported by the NEASC-accredited High School Diploma. Graduates progress to many of the world's top universities, including Cambridge, Imperial, UCL, Caltech, and NYU.

St George's is spread across two campuses. The La Storta campus (ages 3–18) is undergoing major development and has expanded to 25 acres, with dedicated Junior and Senior School facilities, state-of-the-art learning spaces, and a new indoor swimming pool. Its extensive infrastructure includes specialist science, art, and design studios, as well as two multi-sport AstroTurf pitches, courts, and an Olympic running track. The school is proud to be Newcastle United Foundation's first Football School Partner.

The City Centre campus, near the Vatican, offers a modern, purpose-built Junior School setting with a 25m pool, auditorium, and excellent cultural connections.

Creativity and personal development are strongly nurtured through music, drama, and performance. The school is an ABRSM centre, and pupils regularly achieve distinction in music examinations. Opportunities also include Model United Nations, sustainability projects, and a wide range of service activities. Teachers are predominantly UK-trained and native English speakers, ensuring academic rigour alongside a supportive and inclusive pastoral ethos.

Named among Europe's top international schools by the Spears and Carfax Schools Index, St George's continues to set the benchmark for excellence in British international education.

Spain

St. George's British International School (Bilbao)

St George's
BRITISH
INTERNATIONAL
SCHOOL
BILBAO

(Founded 1956)
Artazagane 51, 48940 Leioia, Biscay, Basque Country, Spain
Tel: +34 94 4633692
Email: admissions@bisstgeorges.com
Website: www.bisstgeorges.com

Head of School: Mr. Chris Long
School type: Co-educational Day
No. of pupils enrolled as at 01/09/2025: approx 330
Average class size: 20

St. George's British International School is a private school in Bilbao, proud member of Globeducate British International Schools cluster, and has been part of the prestigious Globeducate network since 2017. The school prepares their students for the world of tomorrow throughout a full English immersion from the age of 2, combining innovative methodologies and personalised attention to ensure that every one of our students reaches their full potential. Their students develop into well-rounded, socially responsible citizens with respect for one another. Music, sport, creative arts, and technology form an integral part of the curriculum.

Academic excellence since 1956

With a long heritage of education spanning more than half a century, the school has an educational philosophy based on four pillars, around which its ambitious and stimulating curriculum is structured: Enrich, Challenge, Shape and Achieve. St. George's British International has a clear goal: to enrich and challenge its students, so that each and every one of them can achieve success in their own way and do their bit to shape the world for the better.

St. George's British International School follows the National Curriculum of England, and it is accredited by both the British Council and the Basque Government. They are proud to be the first British school in Biscay to deliver the prestigious British education system at all stages of education, from two to 18 years of age. This transition began in 2021 and will complete the 2025–2026 academic year, when the school will have its first class of Sixth Form graduates.

The school is proud to be a part of Globeducate, which operates more than 60 schools worldwide. This international network provides their students with unique opportunities and international events to interact with students from a wide range of cultures and nationalities.

Beyond the classes

St. George's British International School provides its students with an exclusive outdoor learning programme, from the age of six upwards: "The Journey", a unique opportunity to build character, knowledge, skills, competencies and global perspectives as they embark on a personal journey of discovery and challenge. This programme, unique to Globeducate schools, lays the foundation for following the internationally recognised Duke of Edinburgh programme, aimed at students from Year 9 to Year 12.

The school also promotes the traditional House System to foster collaboration between students of different ages, team spirit, leadership skills and reinforce the sense of belonging to a community.

Switzerland

St. George's International School, Switzerland

(Founded 1927)

Chemin de St. Georges 19, CH-1815 Clarens/Montreux, Switzerland
Tel: +41 21 964 3411
Email: admissions@stgeorges.ch
Website: www.stgeorges.ch
Head of School: Dr. Ruth Norris

School type: Co-educational Day & Boarding
Age range of pupils: 1.5–18 years
No. of pupils enrolled as at 01/09/2025: 400
Fees as at 01/09/2025:
Please enquire

St. George's International School is a co-educational premium day and boarding school for children aged 1 to 18 years old, with a student body comprised of over 60 nationalities. In 2023, St. George's was ranked the #1 IB school in Switzerland and Top 100 Global IB Schools.

Our school is a member of Inspired Education group, the leading global premium group of schools that offer excellence in education to over 80,000 students worldwide. From exchange programmes to exclusive camps, to leadership conferences and shared learning experiences, Inspired offers a range of enriching global opportunities which give students a chance to travel, meet peers from other countries and become a part of a vibrant international community.

Since its founding in 1927 by two young graduates of Oxford University, our school has grown to become a well-recognised international school that provides its students with individual attention, career advice and structured pastoral care. Junior and Middle School pupils choose between an English-only or bilingual route through the Cambridge International Curriculum up to and including Year 9. In Senior School, pupils in Years 10 &11 choose between IGCSEs and the Pre Diploma qualification, and in Years 12 & 13 between the IB Diploma and the General Diploma.

Extensive English language acquisition tuition is available along with additional languages such as Spanish, German, Russian and Chinese that can also be learnt and practised daily. Through engaging in this multilingual and multicultural environment, we ensure that our students develop an understanding of a variety of different beliefs, religions, and lifestyles.

A great deal of focus is also put on sport and performing arts at St. George's. With access to outstanding sports facilities, pupils have extensive opportunities in individual and team sports throughout the seasons. Situated on the banks of Lake Geneva, with magnificent views of the Alps, the school occupies 12 acres of beautiful landscape and gardens. This setting promotes intellectual calm and a deep connection to the outdoors, with incomparable opportunities for hiking, skiing, water sports and more.

From a very young age students are encouraged to grow a mind of their own and explore their creativity through a range of performing and expressive arts in theatre, art, design, and music. Collaborations with NGOs are also very frequent and allow students to develop a social conscience.

The school motto "Levavi Oculos" ensures that St. George's International School is dedicated to lifting its students' eyes to embrace the exciting challenges and opportunities that await them.

Belgium

St. John's International School

(Founded 1964)
Drève Richelle 146, 1410 Waterloo,
Walloon Brabant, Belgium

Tel: +32 (0)2 352 06 10
Email: admissions@stjohns.be
Website: www.stjohns.be
Head of School: Mr. Kevin Foyle
School type: Co-educational Day & Boarding

Religious Denomination: Non-denominational
Age range of pupils: 12 months–18 years
No. of pupils enrolled as at 01/09/2025: 500
Fees as at 01/09/2025:
€13,750–€43,300 per annum

An Internationally trusted institution with an excellent reputation

Founded in 1964 in Waterloo, Belgium, St. John's International School has established itself as one of the leading international schools in Europe. For more than 60 years, St. John's has been a trusted institution, serving the expatriate and local communities of the greater area with a vibrant, inclusive, and welcoming community.

Our school is a member of Inspired Education, the leading global premium group of schools that offer excellence in education to over 85,000 students worldwide. From exchange programmes to exclusive camps, to leadership conferences and shared learning experiences, Inspired offers a range of enriching global opportunities which give students a chance to travel, meet peers from other countries and become a part of a vibrant international community.

Academic excellence and so much more

With over 50 years of teaching the International Baccalaureate, St. John's has a proud history of academic excellence with an experienced and dynamic teaching staff. Students are encouraged to balance high academic expectations with a fulsome commitment to unrivalled visual and performing arts and competitive sports programmes. St. John's prides itself in its ability to take the individual approach with smaller class sizes and outstanding pastoral care.

International in more than in name only

Our student body of 500, comprised of students between the ages of 12 months and 18 years from 67 nationalities, find themselves in a truly cosmopolitan atmosphere while pursuing their curricular ambitions and extra-curricular interest.

Here students are instilled with the open-mindedness to think globally and take individual responsibility for life-long learning, service, and achievement.

Learning without limits

As an International Baccalaureate (IB) World School, offering the Primary Years Programme (PYP), the Middle Years Programme (MYP) and the Diploma Programme (DP), and the only school in the Brussels area to offer the Advanced Placement (AP) testing, St. John's is the perfect springboard to top universities all over the world.

Flexible options

Fully flexible boarding options ensure that families who travel widely can continue their professional commitments whilst confident in the grounding of St. John's education combined with the nurturing environment of boarding at St John's Shannon house.

For more information, please visit our website or reach out via email.

Italy

St. Louis School

St. Louis Colonna:
Via Marco Antonio Colonna 24, 20149 Milan, Italy
St. Louis Caviglia:
Via Caviglia 1, 20139 Milan, Italy
St. Louis High School:
Via Olmetto 6, 20123 Milan, Italy
Tel: +39 02 55231235
Email: info@stlouisschool.com
Website: www.stlouisschool.com

Executive Principal High School:
Mrs. Kathy Crewe Read
Principal Colonna School:
Mrs. Kathleen Slocombe
Principal Caviglia School:
Mrs. Victoria Del Federico
School type: Co-educational Day
Age range of pupils: 2–18 years
No. of pupils enrolled as at 01/09/2025: 1750

Established in 1996 and based in the heart of Milan, St. Louis is a leading coeducational day international school that teaches over 1,600 students between the ages of 2 and 18 years old.

Our school is a member of Inspired Education, the leading global premium group of schools that offer excellence in education to over 85,000 students worldwide. From exchange programmes to exclusive camps, to leadership conferences and shared learning experiences, Inspired offers a range of enriching global opportunities which give students a chance to travel, meet peers from other countries and become a part of a vibrant international community.

Located across three different sites, our campuses are comprised of an Infant, Primary and Middle School, in the Caviglia and Colonna Campus, whilst our High School, located in Palazzo Archinto, neighbours the Duomo. St. Louis Caviglia is the founding campus, that haves incredible outdoor spaces to stimulate children's curiosity. The St. Louis Colonna is based in a former monastery in the north-east of Milan.

Once our students go to High school, they move to the historic grounds of Palazzo Archinto, designed in the 17th century by architect Francesco Maria Richini, that provides the students with the perfect learning environment, as it combines state-of-the-art facilities with a richness of craft and culture. The St. Louis School's academic programme is rigorous and challenging. The Infant School programme is based on the English Early Years Foundation Stage (EYFS) Curriculum. Primary and Middle School follow the English National Curriculum and, at the age of 6 onwards, also have the option to follow the Italian curriculum. High School is comprised of IGCSE examinations for Years 10-11 followed by the International Baccalaureate Diploma (IB) for Years 12-13.

This approach reinforces the importance of creative and critical thinking and allows for the development of independent learners who are well equipped to succeed in the IB and their journey beyond. St. Louis consistently achieves outstanding academic results with the highest average IB diploma score in continental Europe seven years running; our average score for the past 8 years of students is a 37 out of 45.

For more information, please visit our website or reach out via email.

Portugal

St. Peter's International School

(Founded 1993)
Quinta dos Barreleiros CCI 3952,
Volta da Pedra, 2950-201 Palmela,
Setúbal, Portugal
Tel: +351 21 233 6990
Email: admissions@stpeters.pt
Website: www.st-peters-school.com
Head of School: Ms. Abigail Lewis

School type: Co-educational Day & Boarding
Age range of pupils: 4 months–18 years
No. of pupils enrolled as at 01/09/2025: 1500
Fees as at 01/09/2025:
Day: €6,303–€14,146 per annum
Full Boarding: €17,792 per annum
(Plus tuition fees)

St. Peter's International school is a coeducational private school with three decades of experience in providing the best Portuguese and international education. It offers a competitive, high-quality education from nursery to secondary school, ensuring that students have access to the best opportunities and a high level of support to achieve their full academic and personal potential.

We are a part of Inspired Education, the leading global premium group of schools that offer excellence in education to over 85,000 students worldwide. From exchange programmes to exclusive camps, to leadership conferences and shared learning experiences, Inspired offers a range of enriching global opportunities which give students a chance to travel, meet peers from other countries and become a part of a vibrant international community.

Our guiding mission is to build self-reliant, critical, and creative students, who are prepared for academic, personal and professional success in an ever-changing world. We seek to promote the development of the skills and conceptual understandings that will help students to overcome whatever challenges they may face.

Our school offers the Portuguese National Curriculum and an International programme. In preschool we begin our bilingual education programme and students from Grade 1 to 4 may follow a bilingual education based on the Portuguese national curriculum or opt to join the Cambridge Primary Programme which is taught in English. From Grade 5 to 12, students are given the choice to follow the Portuguese National Curriculum or, they can choose an international pathway that offers continuity of the Cambridge Programme until completion of the IGCSE, followed by the IB Diploma Programme. St. Peter's is a school with outstanding academic results in both national and international exams, ensuring that students have access to top tier universities either in Portugal or further afield.

Located only 30 minutes from Lisbon, St. Peter's extensive 37,000 sqm campus has outstanding facilities for academics, arts, and sports, including dedicated music and drama rooms, a modern library, 4 fully equipped laboratories, 3 football pitches, a rugby pitch and 2 tennis courts. In addition, St. Peter's is home to the first boarding school in the Lisbon area, an extension of our commitment to excellence. Families living abroad can guarantee their children have access to an international, individualised education in a safe, comfortable, purpose-built environment. Boarding students have access to an extensive range of extracurricular and enrichment activities throughout the week and weekends.

UK

TASIS England

(Founded 1976)

Coldharbour Lane, Thorpe,
Surrey TW20 8TE UK
Tel: +44 (0)1932 582316
Email: ukadmissions@tasisengland.org
Website: www.tasisengland.org
Head of School: Mr Bryan Nixon
Appointed: July 2017
School type: Co-educational Day & Boarding Preparatory, Senior & Sixth Form

Religious Denomination: Non-denominational
Age range of pupils: 4–18 years (boarding from 13)
No. of pupils enrolled as at 01/09/2025: 650
Fees as at 01/09/2025:
Day: £15,600–£35,740 per annum
Full Boarding: £66,970 per annum
Average class size: 10-12
Teacher/pupil ratio: 1:8

TASIS England provides a truly international learning experience for day and boarding students aged 4 to 18. Our caring teachers are committed to providing the balance of academic challenge and support that will enable our students to realize their full potential and contribute to their community as they discover their passion and follow their own pathway.
- Average class size of 10–12 students
- American curriculum leading to an American High School Diploma
- Advanced Placement (AP) courses
- International Baccalaureate (IB) Diploma Programme
- Individualized four-year university counseling
- Bespoke learning experience, including more than 120 courses in Upper School
- Excellent university placement in the UK, US, and worldwide
- Over 70 nationalities and 30 languages spoken on campus
- 45 minutes from Central London
- 25 minutes from Heathrow Airport

Set in the beautiful Surrey countryside, our spacious 46-acre campus is close enough to London to take advantage of all the culture and excitement it offers for field trips and weekend activities. The TASIS boarding program provides a safe and welcoming home-away-from-home for students aged 13 to 18 (Grades 8–12) and won the ISA Boarding School of the Year Award in 2023.

In Upper School, our impressive academic offerings include Advanced Placement courses developed by the American College Board and the IB Diploma Programme. Both provide well-defined pathways to universities in the US, the UK, or anywhere in the world. A broad range of co-curricular, leadership, and service opportunities round out our students' learning.

TASIS England also offers an award-winning residential Summer Program for ages 11–17. Our program attracts bright and adventurous students from around the world who take one major academic course and one elective, complemented by sports, activities, and weekend excursions. We offer two three-week sessions starting in late June and ending in early August.

Switzerland

TASIS The American School in Switzerland

Via Collina d'Oro 15, 6926 Montagnola-Lugano, Switzerland
Tel: +41 91 960 5151
Email: admissions@tasis.ch
Website: www.tasis.ch
Head of School: Christopher Nikoloff

School type: Co-educational Day & Boarding
Age range of pupils: 3–19 years
No. of pupils enrolled as at 01/09/2025: 730
Fees as at 01/09/2025:
Day: CHF54,500 per annum
Full Boarding: CHF104,500 per annum

Founded by M. Crist Fleming in 1956, TASIS The American School in Switzerland is an international day and boarding school committed to creating global citizens through education, travel, and service. TASIS now welcomes more than 700 students in grades Pre-Kindergarten (starting at age 3) through 12 while also offering a Postgraduate program. The student body represents 60 nationalities and speaks more than 30 different mother tongues.

High School students can choose from individual Advanced Placement courses or pursue the International Baccalaureate (IB) Diploma, helping them receive offers from more than 400 universities in 20 different nations over the past five years. The School offers an extensive Fine Arts program that includes courses in Drama, Music, and the Visual Arts, enabling aspiring artists of any ilk to find their creative voice and nurture their talent.

The campus includes more than 25 buildings dating from the 17th century Villa De Nobili to the state-of-the-art Campo Science Center, which opened in 2014. Perched on a hillside in sunny southern Switzerland with commanding views of snow-capped mountains, palm trees, and Lake Lugano, the School's enviable location makes possible an impressive Academic Travel program. Travel experiences throughout the year bring students face-to-face with the rich cultural heritage of Europe and the spectacular natural beauty of the Alps and beyond.

The School's pioneering Global Service Program transforms lives by providing every High School student with a unique opportunity to connect across borders - whether geographic, economic, or social - through comprehensive experiences that build empathy and encourage personal responsibility. The Program awakens students to humanitarian needs; inspires them to build enduring, mutually beneficial relationships; and leads them toward a life of active service and committed service.

TASIS encourages physical fitness and healthy lifestyles. Varsity sports teams compete throughout Switzerland and Europe, and a variety of other fitness activities are offered to cater to all interests. Each year also brings many opportunities to ski and explore the breathtaking Alps.

Poland

Thames British School Mokotów High School Campus

ul. Domaniewska 50, 02-672 Warsaw, Masovia, Poland
Tel: +48 57 727 0477
Email: mokotowhigh@thamesbritishschool.pl
Website: thamesbritishschool.pl/campus/mokotow-high-school-campus

Head of School (Mokotów High School Campus): Ms Izabela Ryzak
Executive Head of Schools: Mr Berrin Schofield
School type: Co-educational Day
Age range of pupils: 15–19 years
Fees as at 01/09/2025:
Day: PLN: 48,500–98,000 per annum

Thames British School Warsaw is an international school offering the National Curriculum of English for children aged from 2.5 to 18 years (from Nursery/Kindergarten to IB diploma). The school implements English National Curriculum and IB Diploma Programme. The primary language of instruction is English, but students also learn Spanish and German. The school also offers additional Polish lessons twice a week.

Thames British School Warsaw operates on four modern and well-equipped campuses throughout Warsaw – Wlochy Campus, Ochota Campus, Mokotów Primary Campus and Mokotów High School Campus.

Teachers at Thames British School Warsaw are native speakers with British pedagogical experience. The school's aim is to create an environment where pupils can immerse themselves fully into learning by creating within them a set of core intrinsic values (Responsibility / Respect / Kindness / Honesty / Equality) which will motivate them to become life-long learners in an international community.

Extracurricular activities are treated as a key complement to school education. Classes conducted by teachers are free (included in tuition), while those provided by third-party organizations are paid extra. The school also provides bus transport for students and a meals program.

Applications and admissions are accepted year-round. Children applying into the Nursery and Reception levels do not need to know any English. From Year 3 onwards, a written exam is required, as well as previous school report cards and a letter of recommendation from the previous teacher.

If you are interested in our offer at any of our campuses:
- 1) Check out the admissions procedure: thamesbritishschool.pl/admissions/admission-procedure
- 2) Arrange an on-site visit to our schools (we have 4 campuses): thamesbritishschool.pl/admissions/arrange-a-school-visit
- 3) Arrange a virtual meeting with our staff and admissions team: thamesbritishschool.pl/admissions/virtual-meeting
- 4) Contact us anytime via email: admissions (+48) 574 797 778, or via our contact form on the website: thamesbritishschool.pl/contact
- 5) Arrange a free trial session anytime: thamesbritishschool.pl/admissions/free-trial-session

Thames British School Mokotów Primary Campus

ul. Józefa i Jana Rostafinskich 1, 02-593 Warsaw, Masovia, Poland
Tel: +48 53 091 7566
Email: mokotowprimary@thamesbritishschool.pl
Website: thamesbritishschool.pl/campus/mokotow-primary-campus

Acting Head of School / Mokotów Primary
National Head: Ms Katarzyna Kurzac
Executive Head of Schools: Mr Berrin Schofield
School type: Co-educational Day
Age range of pupils: 3–11 years
Fees as at 01/09/2025:
Day: *PLN:* 48,500–98,000 per annum

Thames British School Warsaw is an international school offering the National Curriculum of English for children aged from 2.5 to 18 years (from Nursery/Kindergarten to IB diploma). The school implements English National Curriculum and IB Diploma Programme. The primary language of instruction is English, but students also learn Spanish and German. The school also offers additional Polish lessons twice a week.

Thames British School Warsaw operates on four modern and well-equipped campuses throughout Warsaw – Wlochy Campus, Ochota Campus, Mokotów Primary Campus and Mokotów High School Campus.

Teachers at Thames British School Warsaw are native speakers with British pedagogical experience. The school's aim is to create an environment where pupils can immerse themselves fully into learning by creating within them a set of core intrinsic values (Responsibility / Respect / Kindness / Honesty / Equality) which will motivate them to become life-long learners in an international community.

Extracurricular activities are treated as a key complement to school education. Classes conducted by teachers are free (included in tuition), while those provided by third-party organizations are paid extra. The school also provides bus transport for students and a meals program.

Applications and admissions are accepted year-round. Children applying into the Nursery and Reception levels do not need to know any English. From Year 3 onwards, a written exam is required, as well as previous school report cards and a letter of recommendation from the previous teacher.

If you are interested in our offer at any of our campuses:
- 1) Check out the admissions procedure: thamesbritishschool.pl/admissions/admission-procedure
- 2) Arrange an on-site visit to our schools (we have 4 campuses): thamesbritishschool.pl/admissions/arrange-a-school-visit
- 3) Arrange a virtual meeting with our staff and admissions team: thamesbritishschool.pl/admissions/virtual-meeting
- 4) Contact us anytime via email: admissions (+48) 574 797 778, or via our contact form on the website: thamesbritishschool.pl/contact
- 5) Arrange a free trial session anytime: thamesbritishschool.pl/admissions/free-trial-session

Thames British School Ochota Campus

ul. Wawelska 66/74, 02-034 Warsaw, Masovia, Poland
Tel: +48 22 822 15 75
Email: ochota@thamesbritishschool.pl
Website: thamesbritishschool.pl/campus/ochota-campus

Head of School (Ochota Campus): Mr Christian Rosser
Executive Head of Schools: Mr Berrin Schofield
School type: Co-educational Day
Age range of pupils: 5–11 years
Fees as at 01/09/2025:
Day: PLN: 48,500–98,000 per annum

Thames British School Warsaw is an international school offering the National Curriculum of English for children aged from 2.5 to 18 years (from Nursery/Kindergarten to IB diploma). The school implements English National Curriculum and IB Diploma Programme. The primary language of instruction is English, but students also learn Spanish and German. The school also offers additional Polish lessons twice a week.

Thames British School Warsaw operates on four modern and well-equipped campuses throughout Warsaw – Wlochy Campus, Ochota Campus, Mokotów Primary Campus and Mokotów High School Campus.

Teachers at Thames British School Warsaw are native speakers with British pedagogical experience. The school's aim is to create an environment where pupils can immerse themselves fully into learning by creating within them a set of core intrinsic values (Responsibility / Respect / Kindness / Honesty / Equality) which will motivate them to become life-long learners in an international community.

Extracurricular activities are treated as a key complement to school education. Classes conducted by teachers are free (included in tuition), while those provided by third-party organizations are paid extra. The school also provides bus transport for students and a meals program.

Applications and admissions are accepted year-round. Children applying into the Nursery and Reception levels do not need to know any English. From Year 3 onwards, a written exam is required, as well as previous school report cards and a letter of recommendation from the previous teacher.

If you are interested in our offer at any of our campuses:
- 1) Check out the admissions procedure: thamesbritishschool.pl/admissions/admission-procedure
- 2) Arrange an on-site visit to our schools (we have 4 campuses): thamesbritishschool.pl/admissions/arrange-a-school-visit
- 3) Arrange a virtual meeting with our staff and admissions team: thamesbritishschool.pl/admissions/virtual-meeting
- 4) Contact us anytime via email: admissions (+48) 574 797 778, or via our contact form on the website: thamesbritishschool.pl/contact
- 5) Arrange a free trial session anytime: thamesbritishschool.pl/admissions/free-trial-session

Poland

Thames British School Wlochy Campus

ul. Gladka 31, 02-172 Warsaw, Masovia, Poland
Tel: +48 510 161 597
Email: wlochy@thamesbritishschool.pl
Website: thamesbritishschool.pl/campus/wlochy-campus
Head of School (Wlochy Campus): Ms Katarzyna Wisniewska

Executive Head of Schools: Mr Berrin Schofield
School type: Co-educational Day
Age range of pupils: 2.5–14 years
Fees as at 01/09/2025:
Day: PLN: 48,500–98,000 per annum

Thames British School Warsaw is an international school offering the National Curriculum of English for children aged from 2.5 to 18 years (from Nursery/Kindergarten to IB diploma). The school implements English National Curriculum and IB Diploma Programme. The primary language of instruction is English, but students also learn Spanish and German. The school also offers additional Polish lessons twice a week.

Thames British School Warsaw operates on four modern and well-equipped campuses throughout Warsaw – Wlochy Campus, Ochota Campus, Mokotów Primary Campus and Mokotów High School Campus.

Teachers at Thames British School Warsaw are native speakers with British pedagogical experience. The school's aim is to create an environment where pupils can immerse themselves fully into learning by creating within them a set of core intrinsic values (Responsibility / Respect / Kindness / Honesty / Equality) which will motivate them to become life-long learners in an international community.

Extracurricular activities are treated as a key complement to school education. Classes conducted by teachers are free (included in tuition), while those provided by third-party organizations are paid extra. The school also provides bus transport for students and a meals program.

Applications and admissions are accepted year-round. Children applying into the Nursery and Reception levels do not need to know any English. From Year 3 onwards, a written exam is required, as well as previous school report cards and a letter of recommendation from the previous teacher.

If you are interested in our offer at any of our campuses:
- 1) Check out the admissions procedure: thamesbritishschool.pl/admissions/admission-procedure
- 2) Arrange an on-site visit to our schools (we have 4 campuses): thamesbritishschool.pl/admissions/arrange-a-school-visit
- 3) Arrange a virtual meeting with our staff and admissions team: thamesbritishschool.pl/admissions/virtual-meeting
- 4) Contact us anytime via email: admissions (+48) 574 797 778, or via our contact form on the website: thamesbritishschool.pl/contact
- 5) Arrange a free trial session anytime: thamesbritishschool.pl/admissions/free-trial-session

Netherlands

The British School of Amsterdam

(Founded 1978)

Havenstraat 6, 1075 PR Amsterdam, North Holland, Netherlands
Tel: +31 (0)20 679 7840
Email: info@britams.nl
Website: www.britams.nl
Principal: Ciaran Harrington
Appointed: August 2025

School type: Co-educational Day
Age range of pupils: 3–18 years
No. of pupils enrolled as at 01/09/2025: 1050
Fees as at 01/09/2025:
Day: €18,750–€21,528 per annum
Average class size: 22

Who we are:
At The British School of Amsterdam (The BSA), we see ourselves as a bridge - an empowering connection, an inspiring portal, and a nurturing link for your child's future. For us it is about where you wish to go in life more than where you have come from. It is about desired outcomes. It is about your future, and we are the bridge to that future.

We set out not just to offer the highest standard of academic teaching through the acknowledged National Curriculum used in England leading to GCSE and A Level qualifications, but to do much more. Our aim is to provide, as well, the practical life skills that will help our students get to where they need and want to go – to the world's top universities and to satisfying careers.

We are the only school in Amsterdam to offer the full British Curriculum, which is accredited in all countries, and by the world's finest universities, thanks to its breadth and depth. Our high-quality and stable staff body provides not just superb teaching but also the level of pastoral care which allows each child to feel recognised as an individual - only then can they give of their best and be enthused by their learning.

What we offer:
We have three school sections, the Early Years School for children aged 3 to 6 years old, the Junior School for 6 to 11 year olds and the Senior School for 11 to 18 year olds. Each has their own distinctive character that offers a stimulating environment where students benefit from small class sizes and truly talented teaching staff. Classes for the Early Years and Junior Schools do not exceed 24 and for the Senior School, we do not exceed 22 in a class. In 2024, 48% of students at A Level achieved A* or A grades (20% above the UK national average) and at GCSE, 53% of students achieved 9–7 / A* or A grades (42% above the UK national average).

Our school building has some of the finest educational facilities in Amsterdam including a large sports hall, designated outdoor playgrounds, a theatre hall, as well as fully equipped science laboratories and music rooms. The school is located in Amsterdam Oud-Zuid near several green spaces, and is easily accessible for families commuting from different parts of the city and surrounding areas.

Belgium

The British School of Brussels (BSB)

(Founded 1969)

Pater Dupierreuxlaan 1,
3080 Tervuren, Belgium
Tel: +32 (0)2 766 04 30
Email: admissions@britishschool.be
Website: www.britishschool.be
Principal & CEO: Mr James Penstone
Head of Post-16: Mr James Willis
School type: Co-educational Day

Age range of pupils: 1–18 years
No. of pupils enrolled as at 01/09/2025: 1333
Fees as at 01/09/2025:
Day: €35,600–€45,550 per annum
Average class size: 14-21
Teacher/pupil ratio: 1:9

Welcome to the British School of Brussels (BSB), an award-winning international educational institution catering to 1,333 students from 70 different nationalities, spanning ages 1 to 18. Distinguished as the sole school in Belgium offering three distinct pre-university pathways – A Levels, the International Baccalaureate (IB) Diploma, and BTEC vocational courses – BSB ensures a diverse range of academic opportunities for its students.

At BSB, diversity is celebrated and embraced through our French-English bilingual programme, commencing from age 4 in Primary School until age 14 (Year 9) in Secondary School. Additionally, support is readily available for students with English as an additional language and those with Additional Educational Needs.

Our Early Childhood Centre (ECC) provides a nurturing environment for children aged 1 to 3, fostering a happy and stimulating atmosphere conducive to early development. Recognised for its exceptional indoor and outdoor learning spaces, ECC sets the foundation for a lifelong love of learning.

In the Primary School, students benefit from a tailored curriculum that blends the warmth of a small school community with the resources of a larger institution. Rooted in a bespoke, inquiry-driven approach inspired by the UK national curriculum, our Primary education caters to the diverse needs of our student body.

Transitioning to Secondary School, BSB offers a harmonious blend of British and international educational standards, culminating in three pre-university pathways: English A Levels, BTEC qualifications, and the prestigious IB Diploma. Our commitment to academic excellence is evident in our students' outstanding achievements, with a remarkable average pass rate of 98% in the IB Diploma Programme and a 99% pass rate at A Level over the past four years.

Beyond academics, BSB encourages students to explore their interests and hone their talents through a rich array of extracurricular activities. From sports to arts, our school fosters holistic development, supported by state-of-the-art facilities including our own swimming pool and a modern sports centre, equipped with world-class amenities such as gymnastics spaces, a dance studio, and a fitness arena.

At BSB, we are dedicated to nurturing well-rounded individuals equipped with the skills, knowledge, and confidence to thrive in an ever-changing world. Join us on a journey of academic excellence and personal growth at the British School of Brussels.

The British School of Milan (Sir James Henderson)

(Founded 1969)

Via Carlo Alberto Pisani Dossi, 16,
20134 Milan, Italy
Tel: +39 02 210941
Email: info@bsm.school
Website: www.britishschoolmilan.com
Principal: Simon Lockyer

School type: Co-educational Day
Age range of pupils: 3–18 years
No. of pupils enrolled as at 01/09/2025: 780
Fees as at 01/09/2025:
€14,000–€22,700 per annum
Teacher/pupil ratio: 1:17

Mission: To inspire learning within a caring, creative and international community, to pursue excellence, and to enable students to fulfil their ambitions.

The British School of Milan, founded in 1969, is the only school in Milan rated 'Excellent' by UK Government Inspectors (ISI). It has been identified as one of the top 10 British Schools in the world and leading IB school in Italy.

The BSM is a not-for-profit school which provides world-class education to 780 students aged 3 to 18 of over 40 different nationalities. The school values cultural diversity and offers a rich international experience while rigorously following the UK National Curriculum.

In the Primary School, students follow the English National Curriculum, culminating in the Senior School with public exams at (I)GCSE. In Years 12 and 13 (the Sixth Form), students pursue the International Baccalaureate (IB) Diploma – considered the gold standard of world education and the best preparation for universities and the globally competitive world of work.

Academic results are outstanding and students progress to top universities around the globe. In the last few years they have gained places at Oxford, Cambridge, Yale, Columbia, LSE, Imperial, University College London, The University of Edinburgh, Trinity College Dublin, Università Bocconi, Sciences Po and many other leading universities.

There is a strong emphasis on co-curricular activities with over 100 options available. The school is particularly proud of its exceptional music, art and drama departments. In addition, the school acts as the Italian centre for the UK-based ABRSM, the exam board of the Royal Schools of Music. The school nourishes a strong tradition of community service, with its involvement in the International Duke of Edinburgh's Award Scheme and three IB scholarships offered annually.

High quality teaching and learning is at the core of what we do at the BSM. The style of teaching is modern and progressive. BSM staff are almost all British-trained and mother-tongue teachers. Our teachers are professionally qualified, highly experienced and annually appraised. Languages are taught almost exclusively by native language speakers including Italian, French and Spanish.

The BSM is situated just outside the centre of Milan, close to the metro and on several bus routes. Linate airport and the popular Milano 2 residences are just minutes from the school.

Admission applications are accepted throughout the year.

Poland

The British School Warsaw

THE BRITISH SCHOOL WARSAW
A NORD ANGLIA EDUCATION SCHOOL

(Founded 1992)

Limanowskiego 15, 02-943 Warsaw, Masovia, Poland
Tel: +48 22 842 32 81
Email: admissions@thebritishschool.pl
Website: www.thebritishschool.pl
Principal: Mr John Brett
Appointed: 2024
Deputy Principal: Dr Jacek Latkowski
School type: Co-educational Day
Age range of pupils: 2.5–18 years
Average class size: 20
Teacher/pupil ratio: 1:11

The British School Warsaw was established in 1992 by Iwona Thomas in partnership with Nord Anglia Education. It opened its doors with a total of 35 students wishing to follow an English curriculum. At present, we are proud to be educating over 1000 students from the international community in Warsaw.

At The British School Warsaw, your child will receive the very best of British academics, delivered by outstanding teachers in an international environment that promotes respect, discipline and hard work. Your child will leave our school with everything they need for success – whatever they choose to be or do in life. Your family will be part of a vibrant, international community that promotes well-being and social responsibility, whilst developing cultural awareness.

Our students learn using the the world's most respected curricula, enabling a life-long love of learning and academic results that opens pathways to the world's best universities.

For Primary students, we offer a perfect blend of English National Curriculum and International Primary Curriculum (IPC) which provides young, globally minded students with a skillset enabling them to smoothly transition to the next stages of international education through iGCSE and IBDP. For our Senior students, we offer the internationally-recognised and highly regarded IB Diploma Programme. The skills and attributes developed through this programme provide outstanding preparation for higher education giving our students the best opportunity to access the world's top universities.

We are unique in Warsaw in that we are part of a family of 81 schools with Nord Anglia Education (NAE) which allows us to leverage international collaborations. Our students have the opportunity to travel to our expedition based snow-sports centre in Switzerland; renovate schools in Tanzania; perform with over 500 talented musicians at the Juilliard School, New York; attend Space camp and STEAM festival at MIT University and take over UNICEF Headquarters in NY.

Our teacher standards are second to none, partly thanks to a global Education Team that drives success in academics, quality assurance, accreditation and safeguarding across our schools.

Spain

The Global College

(Founded 2022)

C. de Castellón de la Plana 8,
28006 Madrid, Spain
Tel: +34 915 689 937
Email: info@theglobalcollege.com
Website: theglobalcollege.com

Principal: Mr. Barry Cooper
School type: Co-educational Day & Boarding
Age range of pupils: 15–18 years

The Global College is a co-educational day and boarding school for 15 to 18-year-olds, offering an innovative 2 years IB Diploma Programme, fully in English, in the city center of Madrid, Spain.

The Global College holds a strategic partnership with IE University, one of the world's leading higher education institutions that shapes leaders with a global vision, an entrepreneurial spirit, and a human-centered approach. This partnership gives the school unique insight into the skills needed in a world characterized by technological advancements and constant change.

Through a highly inspiring curriculum and superb mentoring, the college prepares students from all over the world for access to leading universities in the US, UK, and Europe. The school offers a wide range of IB courses at both HL and SL which allow personalization, and expert professors that foster intellectual curiosity, critical thinking, and a lifelong passion for learning. The school embraces the concept of international-mindedness, equipping students to make meaningful contributions to a diverse global community. Each year, the campus comes alive with around 50 different nationalities, creating a rich tapestry of cultures. For international students, there's a newly refurbished boarding house available, situated just a pleasant stroll away from the campus. This inviting residence offers a cozy and secure environment, allowing students to feel at home while also being close to the city's dynamic cultural and social attractions.

The college offers a vibrant, student-centered campus in the heart of Madrid. Designed to support modern teaching methods, it features specialized laboratories for both individual study and collaborative work. These facilities enhance learning while fostering creativity and teamwork. Facilities have been designed to provide students with their first pre-university experience, rather than their last two school years. The campus welcomes students and supports academic success by staying

open on weekends and beyond regular hours. This access allows students to utilize resources, seek faculty help, and engage in group study sessions to complete their Baccalaureate and prepare for future educational goals. To support its mission of fostering a diverse and inclusive learning environment, the school offers a scholarship and financial aid initiative for students from all socioeconomic backgrounds.

In addition to academic excellence, The Global College offers a wide range of extracurricular activities. These activities span creativity, sports, and community service, ensuring students can explore their interests, develop emotional balance, and contribute positively to their surroundings.

Italy

The New School Rome

(Founded 1972)
Via Della Camilluccia 669, 00135 Rome, Italy
Tel: +39 06 329 4269
Email: info@newschoolrome.com
Website: www.newschoolrome.com

Headteacher: Mr Norman Doyle
School type: Co-educational Day
Age range of pupils: 3–18 years
Fees as at 01/09/2025:
Day: €10,700–€19,800 per annum

About Us
The New School was founded in 1972 by parents and teachers who wanted to create a school where academic excellence would be combined with attention to the individual and the development of personal and social responsibility. Over 50 years on, this vision continues to thrive and serve the needs of the international community in Rome.

Our students follow an enhanced English National Curriculum that places learning in both a local and global context and culminates in the 'Gold Standard' A-Level examinations that provide entry pathways to Universities across the world. Students take part in a wide range of extra curricular activities including the Duke of Edinburgh Award and the Model UN. Our Academic outcomes are excellent and our pastoral care second to none.

As an Association, we have a unique democratic structure where teachers, students and parents work together in partnership through the two decision making bodies that drive the school development plan.

All of our teachers are native English speakers, qualified and trained in the UK and Ireland with an average tenure of over 12 years. This brings continuity and stability to the learning environment and is testimony to the strong family community that makes us a distinct school.

The School Environment
Situated on the leafy, residential north side of the city, The New School is just 15 minutes from Piazza del Popolo and the historic centre of Rome.

The school buildings are set in a beautiful garden with a large villa. New buildings provide bespoke science laboratories, primary classrooms and a well stocked library run by a full time librarian.

Onsite we have football, basketball and volleyball facilities, a Performing Arts studio and Art Studio. The Physical Education curriculum is augmented by the use of extensive facilities and qualified coaches available in a local sports club.

The Royal Masonic School for Girls

(Founded 1788)
Rickmansworth Park, Rickmansworth, Hertfordshire WD3 4HF UK

Tel: 01923 725354
Email: admissions@rmsforgirls.com
Website: www.rmsforgirls.com
Headmaster: Mr Kevin Carson M.Phil (Cambridge)
Appointed: January 2017
School type: Girls' Day & Boarding Preparatory & Senior, Nursery & Sixth Form
Religious Denomination: Non-denominational

Age range of boys: 2–3 years
Age range of girls: 2–18 years (boarding from 8)
No. of pupils enrolled as at 01/09/2025: 901
Fees as at 01/09/2025:
Day: £5,685–£9,674 per term (incl. VAT)
Weekly Boarding: £12,776–£16,135 per term (incl. VAT)
Full Boarding: £14,050–£17,340 per term (incl. VAT)

An introduction
Founded in 1788, RMS for Girls is one of England's oldest girls' schools. RMS embraces a distinctive approach, challenging pupils daily to be committed learners who also support others. In return, staff continually stretch and support them, instilling the importance of preparation, effort, and self-belief. This empowers RMS pupils to leave with the confidence to make a difference in the world.

Location
Set within 315 acres of parkland, RMS enjoys a safe and wonderful location just 22 minutes from central London and 25 minutes from Heathrow.

Community
RMS welcomes pupils aged 2 to 18, with boarding from age eight. Their broad curriculum and over 100 co-curricular activities ensure every girl discovers her niche and thrives. RMS is particularly proud of the strong integration between its cosmopolitan boarding community and day pupils, fostering a comfortable and supportive 21st-century boarding environment.

Facilities
RMS boasts exceptional facilities, including a planetarium and an observatory. Their sports centre features a gymnasium, sports hall, fitness suite, yoga studio, and squash courts, alongside an Astroturf pitch, and a six-hole golf course. School facilities include multiple tennis, netball, and cricket facilities and an indoor heated swimming pool.

Creative pursuits thrive in separate Art, Textiles, and Photography departments, plus a top of the range Food & Nutrition classroom as we well as a dedicated Performing Arts Centre with a recital suite, green room, and recording studio.

Why RMS?
The decision of where to educate your daughter is an important one; arguably one of the most important decisions you will make on behalf of your child. Learning at RMS inspires pupils to explore what matters to them and to see themselves in futures they may not have imagined. As experts in girls' education, we understand how girls prefer to learn. Pupils at RMS are guided and supported and given the opportunity to expand their horizons. They are encouraged to think critically, creatively and collaboratively. Above all, RMS girls are happy, balanced and will become the best version of themselves.

Portugal

United Lisbon International School

Avenida Marechal Gomes da Costa 9,
1800-255 Lisbon, Portugal
Tel: +351 211 161 110
Email: info@unitedlisbon.school
Website: www.unitedlisbon.school
Executive Director: Mr Martin Harris

School type: Co-educational Day
Age range of pupils: 3–18 years
No. of pupils enrolled as at 01/09/2025: 600+
Fees as at 01/09/2025:
€11,000–24,000 per annum

United Lisbon International School (ULIS) is a world-class international English language school in the heart of Lisbon and part of the Dukes Education Group.

Located in the Park of Nations – Lisbon's emerging "technology hub", ULIS offers English-medium academic programmes from Early Childhood (age 3) to Grade 12, with a rigorous curriculum culminating in the International Baccalaureate Diploma Programme (IBDP). The school prepares students for top universities and life beyond, with a strong focus on global citizenship and 21st-century competencies.

Now in its fifth year, ULIS continues to expand its facilities and educational vision. Recent developments include 7,300 sqm of new classrooms, labs, sports spaces, lounges, and a 250-seat auditorium, adding to 6,500 sqm of outdoor space. A Microsoft Showcase School, ULIS integrates technology across all learning.

The School's Mission
ULIS nurtures individual learners through a student-centred, values-led environment focused on curiosity, resilience, empathy, and integrity. With over 50 nationalities on campus, students grow into compassionate and capable global citizens.

Curriculum
ULIS provides a personalised academic journey. In the Middle School "Golden Years" (Grades 6–8), students study core subjects alongside performing arts, coding, AI, leadership, financial literacy, and service learning. This broad foundation supports deeper academic focus in later years.

Grades 9 and 10 offer flexible pathways, allowing students to build around their strengths – whether in sciences, arts, humanities, or technology – preparing them for the IB Diploma Programme in Grades 11 and 12. The approach blends academic rigour with inquiry-led learning, digital fluency, and future-readiness.

United Lisbon Advantage
ULIS offers a vibrant co-curricular programme and strong local partnerships with institutions such as Sporting FC, Lisboa Racket Centre and STAT Martial Arts. The school fosters leadership, sustainability, creativity, and personal growth through all areas of school life.

From Early Childhood to graduation, ULIS equips students with the knowledge, values, and skills needed to thrive in a rapidly changing world.

Italy

UWC Adriatic

COLLEGIO DEL MONDO UNITO DELL'ADRIATICO O.N.L.U.S.

(Founded 1982)

Località Duino 29, 34011 Duino-Aurisina TS, Italy
Tel: +39 040 3739111
Email: uwcad@uwcad.it
Website: www.uwcad.it
Head of College: Dr. Khalid El-Metaal
Appointed: August 2022
School type: Co-educational Boarding
Religious Denomination: Non-denominational

Age range of pupils: 16–19 years
No. of pupils enrolled as at 01/09/2025: 186
Fees as at 01/09/2025:
Two-year Fee: €26,000 per annum (scholarships available)
Average class size: 14
Teacher/pupil ratio: 1:7

UWC Adriatic (UWCAD) is part of the United World Colleges (UWC), which currently includes 18 schools and colleges worldwide. Established in 1982, Adriatic was the first UWC in a non-English-speaking country. Located on an open campus in Duino, a picturesque village overlooking the Adriatic Sea, the college lies at the crossroads of diverse cultures. This setting, influenced by the complexities of post-war Europe, provides a rich backdrop for its mission to promote peace and international understanding through education.

UWC Adriatic operates a policy of deliberate diversity central to its mission. Its nearly 200 students come from over 80 countries and a wide range of socio-economic backgrounds. In 2023–24, 90% of the student body benefited from a full or partial scholarship, with 70% of students receiving full financial support.

The College's educational programme places equal emphasis on academic excellence, co-curricular activities, and informal learning through residential life, providing students with a truly holistic and values-driven education. The rigorous International Baccalaureate (IB) curriculum, taught in English, is complemented by a vibrant co-curricular programme and ample opportunities for students to explore their passions and talent, serve the local community, take initiative, and engage with real-world issues, building essential skills along the way. Since 2024, the College has run the UWC Impact Programme, where alumni with relevant expertise teach first-year students to design and implement social entrepreneurial projects. The College also partners with leading institutions, including international research centres in Trieste, to offer additional opportunities such as internships.

UWCAD's educational experience draws inspiration from Italy's rich cultural heritage, sparking creativity and personal reflection. All students study Italian, as part of the Diploma programme or as an additional subject, to encourage full integration into the local culture. The College's coastal location in Northeast Italy and proximity to the Alps allow students to take part in outdoor activities like sailing, kayaking, climbing, hiking, downhill and cross-country skiing, and snowshoeing.

UWC Adriatic's seven student residences are spread throughout Duino, alongside well-equipped facilities, including science laboratories, an art centre, and a music school. Medical staff are available 24 hours a day.

Admissions
Applications to UWCAD take place through the different UWC national committees.

Netherlands

UWC Maastricht

(Founded 2009)

Discusworp 65, 6225 XP Maastricht, Limburg, Netherlands
Tel: +31 432 410 410
Email: admissions@uwcmaastricht.nl
Website: www.uwcmaastricht.nl
Head of College: Viki Stiebert
Director of Primary School: Nilde Pais
Director of Secondary School: Position currently being filled

School type: Co-educational Day & Boarding
Age range of pupils: 4–19 years
No. of pupils enrolled as at 01/09/2025: 980
Fees as at 01/09/2025:
Ranging from: €7,890 in primary school – €30,000 in the residential programme (scholarships available)

UWC Maastricht (UWCM) in the Netherlands is part of United World Colleges, a global network of 18 international schools and colleges working for peace and a sustainable future (see all UWC schools at uwc.org/schools). The school is part of the Dutch public education system and receives funding from the Dutch government.

Inside the Classroom
This holistic and connected approach across all year levels helps students grow into reflective thinkers ready to shape their own future and that of the world around them." to "This holistic and connected approach across all year levels helps students grow into reflective thinkers, ready to shape their own future and contribute to the world around them.

Outside the Classroom
In addition to academics, UWC Maastricht emphasises social impact. Students take part in action-oriented courses, social entrepreneurship and community service. They learn how to recognise problems and injustices and how to take initiative. They also organise and lead events and conferences to engage more deeply with local and global issues. With over 100 nationalities represented on campus, there are always diverse perspectives and vibrant discussions.

Campus and Facilities
The UWCM campus is near the city centre and is bordered by sports fields, a nature reserve and modern housing. Residential students live in three buildings with three floors each and every floor has six rooms. Each room houses four students from different countries. Shared spaces include a common room, study room, laundry and kitchenette. Each floor is supported by a Residence Mentor who lives nearby.

Admission
We look forward to your application via uwcmaastricht.nl

Italy

Vittoria International School

(Founded 2008)

Via delle Rosine 14, 10123 Turin, Italy
Tel: +39 011 889870
Email: infovis@vittoriaweb.it
Website: www.vittoriaweb.it
Head of School: Marcella Margaria Bodo
School type: Co-educational Day
Age range of pupils: 3–19 years

Fees as at 01/09/2025:
Nursery School: €5,900 per annum
Cambridge Primary: €6,850 per annum
Cambridge Lower Secondary:
€7,950 per annum
Cambridge IGCSE: €11,100 per annum
IBDP: €12,200 per annum

Founded in 1975 as one of the first linguistic high schools in Italy, the Vittoria International School Torino offers bilingual education from elementary school through to the IB diploma. Located in the heart of Turin's city centre, the school provides a modern and innovative learning environment for students of all ages and nationalities.

From the school's inception, we have leveraged the best of tradition and innovation both in the choice of educational pathways and teaching methods. Fully certified by the Italian Ministry of Education, the school offers bilingual Primary and Lower Secondary programs, in addition to two separate high school courses: the traditional Italian program, and an international curriculum in English. An authorized IB World School since 2008, we have offered the IBDP (grades 11–12) and a Cambridge Upper Secondary School IGCSE (grades 9–10) since 2010. In September 2018 we began welcoming students in the Primary (grades 1–5) and Lower Secondary (grades 6–8) years as well.

Our range of study pathways and programs is constantly expanding and is progressively adapted to the individual needs of our students. The final scores and completion rates of our students are consistently above the international average. We provide professional, personalized career and university guidance, and our students go on to study at world-class universities around the globe. We support our student's pursuit of excellence in extracurricular activities, and many have excelled nationally and internationally in sports and the arts.

A low student-teacher classroom ratio allows for individual attention as part of a socially and academically rich formative experience.

Our teachers are all graduates – IB and Cambridge trained. They are passionate about their subjects and dedicated to their students.

A vibrant discussion of global issues begins in our classrooms and extends into CAS projects. Students experience world issues as they play out in our local community and abroad. We also have an ongoing relationship with important international organizations located in Turin.

International schools in North America

Schools ordered A–Z by Name

British International School of Chicago, Lincoln Park

BRITISH INTERNATIONAL SCHOOL OF CHICAGO, LINCOLN PARK
A NORD ANGLIA EDUCATION SCHOOL

(Founded 2001)

814 & 821 W Eastman Street,
Chicago, IL 60642 USA
Tel: +1 773 907 5000
Email: admissions@bischicagolp.org
Website: www.bischicagolp.org
Principal: Mr. John Biggs
School type: Co-educational Day

Age range of pupils: 15 months–11 years
No. of pupils enrolled as at 01/09/2025: 675
Fees as at 01/09/2025:
Day: $11,380–$38,400 per annum
Average class size: 20
Teacher/pupil ratio: 1:10

British International School of Chicago, Lincoln Park is a private international school for student's ages 15 months to 11 years old offering individualized, global and innovative hands-on learning experiences through the English National Curriculum and the International Primary Curriculum. Every student in our school reaches their potential through differentiated instruction delivered by highly trained faculty. Our high number of specialist teachers and specialist classrooms provide even our youngest students a breadth of environments and experiences.

Located in the attractive Lincoln Park neighborhood of Chicago, we offer our students a more than 74,000 square foot urban campus with state of the art facilities and learning extending beyond the classrooms in Chicago's leading academic, cultural and arts institutions. Our students also benefit from collaborations with world renowned institutions through our Julliard-Nord Anglia Performing Arts Programme, which prepares them for the world's stage and our MIT STEAM curriculum which focuses on transferrable skills in an evolving world. Additionally, our students are gaining global perspective on sustainability through work with UNICEF and the 17 sustainable development goals.

We connect our students, representing over 40 nationalities, with their peers in our network of Nord Anglia schools worldwide, and these meaningful interactions and collaborations provide a truly international education. Our online Global Campus provides learning opportunities and challenges for the students which gives direct links to other Nord Anglia students around the world. Our extensive enrichment programs give our students opportunities to build on their passions and strengths in over 30 after school clubs and sports.

We have a vibrant school life with an actively engaged parent community, social interactions, house system and many cultural celebrations. Our values curriculum focuses on the personal, social and emotional development of our students, preparing them not only academically but developing their character and moral compass. Our students continue their secondary education at our second campus located in the South Loop.

USA

Dwight School

(Founded 1872)

291 Central Park West, New York, NY 10024 USA
Tel: +1 212 724 6360
Email: admissions@dwight.edu
Website: dwight.edu/newyork
Chancellor: Stephen H. Spahn
Vice Chancellor: Blake Spahn

Head of School: Dianne Drew
School type: Co-educational Day
Age range of pupils: 2–18 years
No. of pupils enrolled as at 01/09/2025: 910
Fees as at 01/09/2025:
Kindergarten: US$63,900 per annum
Grades 1-12: US$67,900 per annum

Dwight is a global network of leading private international schools committed to educating the next generation of innovative global leaders. For over 150 years, we've been dedicated to crafting a personalized journey for every student based on individual interests and passions. We call this "igniting the spark of genius in every child." Personalized learning, together with community and global vision, are the three pillars upon which a Dwight world-class education rests.

Innovation is an integral part of daily life on campus and takes many forms, from being the first school in the Americas to offer all four International Baccalaureate (IB) programs, to having Makerspaces for each age level and empowering student entrepreneurs to translate their novel ideas into reality through our unique Spark Tank incubator program, supported by The Dwight School Foundation. Dwight has also embraced AI as a tool for learning and is one of the "Founding 50" schools to receive the only K–12 accreditation in AI: the RAIL (Responsible Use of AI License).

Dwight's inspiring faculty – master teachers from all corners of the globe – encourage students to believe in their own talents and take intellectual risks through the academically challenging IB. No two student journeys are the same. Offering one of the lowest student-faculty ratios among independent schools in New York City, Dwight provides one-on-one attention and ample opportunities for students to excel within and beyond the classroom through extensive language, design, and technology instruction; rich visual and performing arts programs; championship-winning athletic teams; and global leadership training.

Dwight has been an accredited IB World School since 1980, and no other curriculum fits better with Dwight's vision of educating innovative global leaders poised to succeed in today's rapidly changing workplace. The academic breadth and depth of the IB are unparalleled; it is the

"gold standard" worldwide in pre-university preparation.

With a global network of brick-and-mortar Dwight Schools in New York, London, Seoul, Shanghai, Dubai, and Hanoi, students have numerous opportunities to travel and participate in cross-campus cultural and curricular exchange programs beginning in grade 5. These shared, enriching experiences prepare students for a future as leaders on the global stage, and the connections they forge will last a lifetime.

Dwight Global Online School, our campus in the cloud, ranked the #2 best online high school in the U.S. by *Newsweek*, offers students in grades 6-12 the flexibility to pursue their passions beyond the classroom. Students can take IB or AP online classes from anywhere, and come to Dwight's campus in New York for in-person experiences a few times a year.

Dwight's college counseling team provides expertise and guidance for students in grade 9. Our graduates attend top colleges and universities, including Harvard, Yale, Princeton, MIT, Stanford, Columbia, Dartmouth, Cornell, McGill, Oxford, and the University of Edinburgh, among others. Upon graduation, they join a vibrant Dwight alumni network that stretches across the globe.

México

Greengates School

GREENGATES SCHOOL MEXICO
A NORD ANGLIA EDUCATION SCHOOL

(Founded 1951)

Av. Circunvalación Pte. 102, Balcones de San Mateo, Naucalpan, Estado de México, C.P. 53200 México
Tel: +52 55 5373 0088
Email: admissions@greengates.edu.mx
Website: www.greengates.edu.mx

General Director: Mr Eamonn Mullally
School type: Co-educational Day
Age range of pupils: 3–18 years
No. of pupils enrolled as at 01/09/2025: 1200
Fees as at 01/09/2025:
Please contact the school

Greengates School, founded in 1951, is the premier British international school of Mexico with nearly 1200 students. The school is private, selective, K-12 and coeducational. It is the most international school by percentage of students and the highest scoring IB Diploma Programme school in the country. As a member of the Nord Anglia Education family of schools, we are committed to providing an exceptional educational experience that fosters character development, self-discipline, respect, and reflection within a challenging learning environment.

At Greengates, we prioritise academic excellence on the world stage. Our team of highly qualified teachers brings together the best of British and international academics, ensuring that our students receive an exceptional standard of education. Through the world-renowned International Baccalaureate Diploma Programme (IBDP), we equip our students with the necessary skills and knowledge to thrive in their future. Whether they aspire to attend the best universities or pursue promising career paths, our students are prepared to excel on a global scale.

We take pride in the achievements of our multicultural community, which resonates around the world. Our international curriculum opens doors to a myriad of opportunities for growth and accomplishment, laying a strong foundation for success in a globally connected future. By embracing diversity and promoting a global perspective, we empower our students to broaden their horizons and develop a deep understanding of different cultures and viewpoints.

Greengates has been held in high esteem for over 70 years. It is recognised in Mexico and the world for its high academic standards, respectful treatment of all and for being a truly international and multi-cultural community. It is a self-sustained day school set in the metropolitan area of Mexico City just 20 minutes away from the prestigious Polanco neighbourhood. The campus covers an area of over 20,000 square metres, with purpose-built facilities that include state-of-the-art library, nine science laboratories, computer media centres, four art studios, a theatre, a spacious and modern 700-seat auditorium, a large multi-purpose gymnasium, basketball and volleyball courts, an indoor swimming pool, an organic learning garden, a new STEAM Makerspace, a cafeteria, an all-weather field and an adventure playground.

At Greengates we act with integrity and seek to motivate our students to become socially responsible citizens while achieving academic excellence. Most of our students come from the diplomatic and business communities in Mexico City. Over 50 different nationalities are represented, and we receive students from different educational systems and academic calendars year-round and while there is a significant population of long-term locally

México

based students, newcomers are ever present and warmly embraced.

The faculty at Greengates is comprised of almost 120 teachers from a wide variety of backgrounds. Alongside the many British teachers, highly qualified and experienced educators come from around the world; Australia, Brazil, Canada, France, Ireland, Mexico, South Africa, and the USA. Teachers bring an array of different skills and modern methods to the classroom and beyond.

As a British International school, our language of instruction is English, though all students from the age of six study Spanish at the appropriate level, and some +50 percent of students who require Mexican educational qualifications take a limited number of courses in Spanish. Support in both languages is given as required. Furthermore, French is taught in the Secondary School and can be taken at IGCSE and IB Diploma. Korean and Japanese are also available as options of the Diploma Programme.

The Primary School is the first fully accredited International Early Years Curriculum (IEYC) and International Primary Curriculum (IPC) School in Latin America with aspects of mastering in its practice. Learning with the IEYC and IPC means that children focus on a combination of academic, personal and international learning that is exciting, engaging and challenging.

The Secondary School prepares students for the International General Certificate of Secondary Education

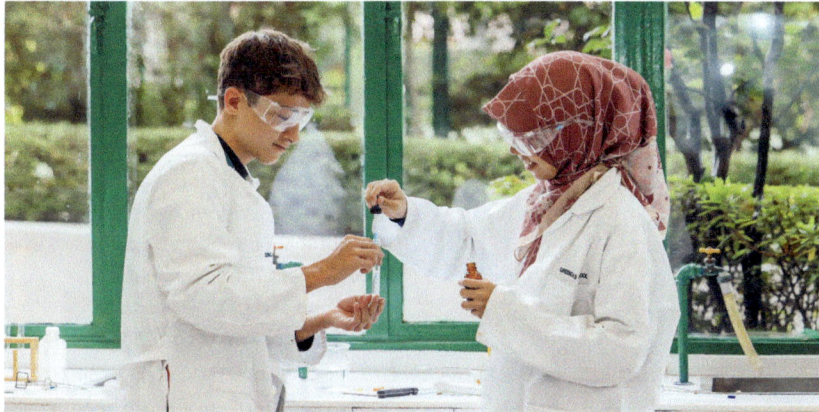

(IGCSE) administered by Cambridge Assessment International Education. We offer a wide range of IGCSE subjects. Our IGCSE results are always above the world average. The IGCSE two-year course is studied prior to embarking on the IB Diploma Programme.

In Years 12 and 13 all students follow the International Baccalaureate Diploma Programme (IBDP) with cohorts between 45 to 60 students. Greengates is the only school in Mexico to require all these students to complete and graduate with the IBDP and not an alternate pathway. We expect the highest standard of academic excellence from our students and prepare them for the rigour of the IBDP. The Secondary School has been accredited to offer the Diploma Programme since 1986, obtaining a pass rate of 98-100 percent during each of the last five years, with overall points scores consistently well above the world average. Greengates is the highest IBDP scoring school in Mexico. Whilst the world average for academic year 23/24 dropped by nearly 2 points, Greengates maintained its high average.

Greengates has a remarkable track record of sending students to prestigious colleges and universities worldwide, while also securing an extraordinary sum of over 6 million USD in scholarships and financial aid within the past 5 years supported by a comprehensive and personalised university counselling programme. This achievement stands as a testament to our exceptional educational standards, ensuring our students are well-prepared to thrive and succeed at recognised and esteemed institutions globally. The academic excellence and international diversity of Greengates make us both unique in Mexico and renowned worldwide.

USA

International School of Denver

(Founded 1977)

7701 E. 1st Pl, Unit C, Denver, CO 80230 USA
Tel: +1 303 340 3647
Email: info@isdenver.org
Website: www.isdenver.org
Head of School: Roberto d'Erizans
School type: Co-educational Day
Age range of pupils: 3-15 years
No. of pupils enrolled as at 01/09/2025: 679

Fees as at 01/09/2025:
ECE and Primary School (K1–G5):* US$28,100.00 per annum
Middle School (G6–G8): US$30,300.00 per annum
High School (Grade 9): US$34,000.00 per annum

The International School of Denver is a dynamic, inclusive community that has delivered a world-class education for nearly 50 years. Located in central Denver, we offer a bilingual, International Baccalaureate (IB) education beginning at age 3—and starting Fall 2025, we are expanding through the launch of our high school and Grade 9 founding class.

Our students engage in immersive learning in French, Spanish, or Chinese alongside a globally focused curriculum that emphasizes inquiry, critical thinking, and compassion. By Grade 8, they are bilingual and well-prepared for the most rigorous academic challenges.

ISDenver is the only school in the region offering a continuous IB pathway from preschool through high school. Our new high school will build on this foundation, offering a forward-thinking, globally minded education that prepares students to lead, innovate, and thrive in an interconnected world. Students enrolling now in Grades 9 and 10 enter an environment filled with unique opportunities for leadership, growth, and meaningful contributions to shape our high school's identity.

Our diverse student body—representing more than 30 nationalities—benefits from a rich international perspective both in and out of the classroom. Whether through multilingual storytelling in early years, international exchanges in middle school, or real-world impact projects in high school, students gain the tools to navigate a complex, global future.

Grounded in nearly five decades of excellence and innovation, ISDenver offers an education that goes far beyond academics. We empower students to become kind, curious, and confident changemakers—fluent in more than one language and culture, and ready to shape the future.

International School of Los Angeles

(Founded 1978)

1105 W. Riverside Drive,
Burbank, CA 91506 USA
Tel: +1 626 695 5159
Email: admissions@lilaschool.com
Website: www.internationalschool.la
Head of School: Ms Anneli Harvey

School type: Co-educational Day
Age range of pupils: 2–18 years
No. of pupils enrolled as at 01/09/2025: 1060
Fees as at 01/09/2025:
Day: $22,925.00–$31,580.00 per annum

The International School of Los Angeles is an independent, international school that offers both a French immersion program from preschool through 12th grade and the English-language International Baccalaureate® in middle and high school.

Students study a common bilingual program from preschool through elementary, after which they choose one of two rigorous programs that culminates in the International Baccalaureate® Diploma (taught in English) or the French baccalauréat (taught in French). With an education delivered in an intimate, nurturing, and diverse environment, our students become caring global citizens prepared to thrive in a changing world.

LILA has offered the IB Diploma Programme for more than 20 years. Possessing such a robust bilingual background, many of our students pursue the prestigious Bilingual Diploma, demonstrating their proficiency by completing the requirements in both English and French at Literature level. This highly sought-after credential has become another mark of distinction for the International School of Los Angeles' IB students.

The International School of Los Angeles is committed to the values of respect, excellence, and diversity, and to preparing students of all backgrounds to excel in and contribute to a global world. Since 1978, the School has been instilling the love of learning in all its students through small classes and low student-to-teacher ratios. With over 65 nationalities and 40 spoken languages represented on the campuses, students at the International School of Los Angeles truly speak and think globally.

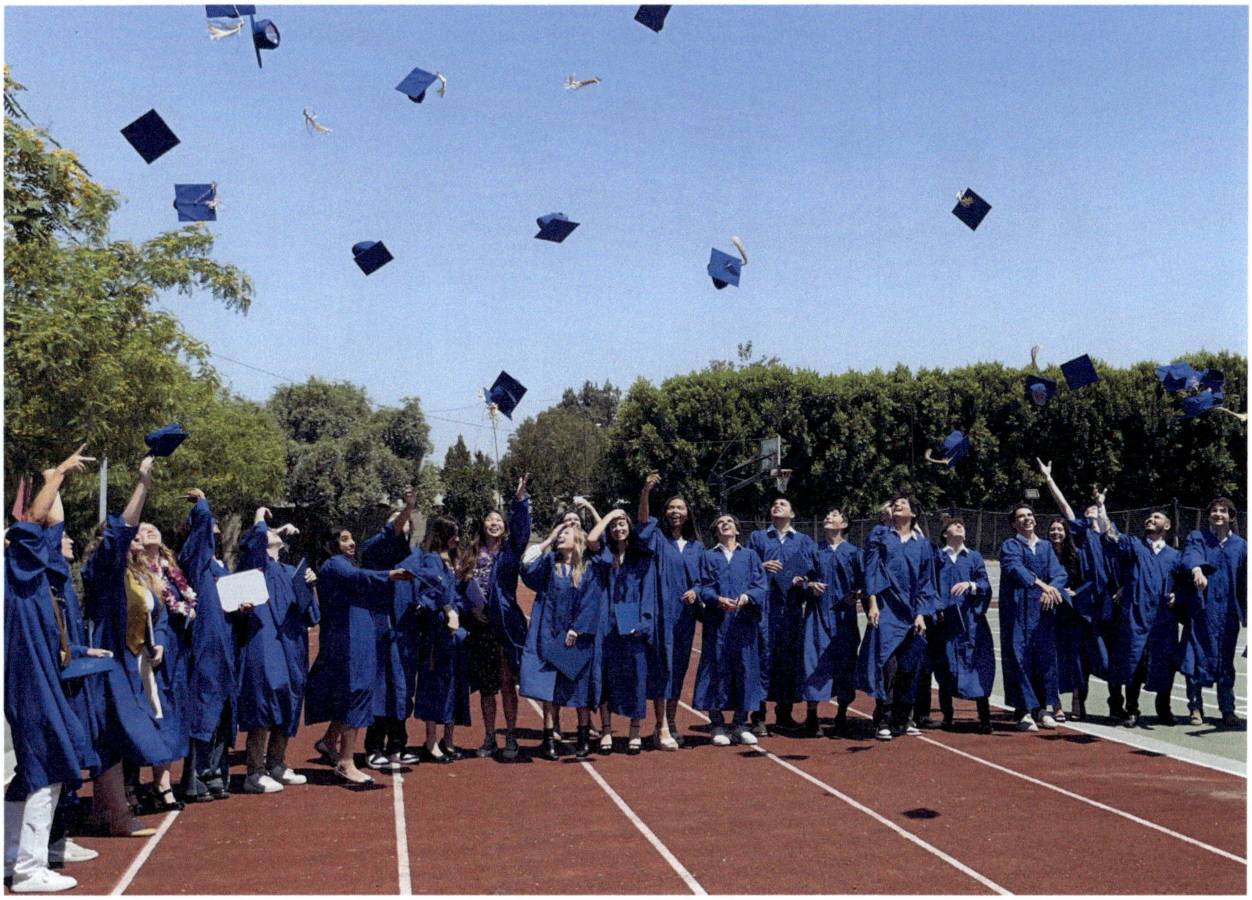

USA

Le Lycée Français de Los Angeles

Le Lycée Français de Los Angeles

3261 Overland Avenue, Los Angeles, CA 90034 USA
Tel: +1 310 836 3464
Email: generalinfo@LyceeLA.org
Website: www.lyceela.org
President: Mrs. Clara-Lisa Kabbaz
Admissions Director: Mrs. Sophie Darmon
School type: Co-educational Day

Age range of pupils: 2–18 years
No. of pupils enrolled as at 01/09/2025: 680
Boys: 300 **Girls:** 380
Fees as at 01/09/2025:
Day: $22,000–$40,780 per annum
Average class size: 1:15
Teacher/pupil ratio: 1:8

Celebrating 60 Years of Excellence in Education

Founded in 1964, Le Lycée Français de Los Angeles is an international, independent, coed school providing a global education with dual curriculums to students from junior preschool to 12th grade. It is located on 5 unique and age-appropriate campuses in the West Los Angeles area. The school offers the choice of an English-language college prep program and another entirely taught in French, both of which nurture the mind, body and character of every student.

In addition to strong academics, athletics, arts, and music, many clubs/extracurricular activities ensure a balanced education and encourage every child to develop their full potential. Le Lycée Français de Los Angeles' student body is made up of approximately 700 pupils from over 45 countries, 65 percent of whom are U.S. citizens. The diverse and engaging community of students, parents and teachers fosters a caring and nurturing environment, creating globally-minded world citizens.

Over the last six decades Le Lycée Français de Los Angeles graduates have enrolled in the most prestigious colleges and universities in the world, and proceeded to distinguish themselves in the arts, humanities and sciences.

Le Lycée Français de Los Angeles is accredited by the Western Association of Schools and Colleges, as well as being fully recognized by the French Ministry of Education.

Diplomas:
College Board AP Capstone
Classic Baccalaureate (BAC)
Baccalauréat Français International (BFI)
U.S. High School Diploma

Tradition - Innovation - Excellence
No French knowledge required to enroll

We Teach the World.

Canada

Mulgrave School, The International School of Vancouver

(Founded 1993)

2330 Cypress Bowl Lane,
West Vancouver BC, V7S 3H9 Canada
Tel: +1 604 922 3223
Email: admissions@mulgrave.com
Website: www.mulgrave.com
Head of School: Craig Davis
Appointed: 2023

School type: Co-educational Day
Age range of pupils: 3–18 years
No. of pupils enrolled as at 01/09/2025: 1030
Fees as at 01/09/2025:
Day: CND$28,850.00–CND$32,560.00 per annum
Average class size: PYP: 20, MYP: 18, DP:13

Mulgrave, The International School of Vancouver, is a gender-inclusive, multicultural International Baccalaureate World School offering Preschool (for three and four year olds) to Grade 12. Our campus, at the base of Cypress Mountain, provides students and faculty with breathtaking ocean views and access to nature. Purpose-built spaces inspire our diverse community to develop interpersonal and intercultural skills, attitudes, and values that allow our students to thrive, contribute, and be happy anywhere in the world. Our graduates have been accepted at post-secondary institutions around the globe, including UBC and McGill in Canada, NYU and UC Berkeley in the United States, and Amsterdam and Oxford internationally.

A Focus on Learner Confidence
As a maturing international school, Mulgrave reflects deeply on its purpose, moving beyond excellence in teaching and learning to education that drives meaningful impact and fosters confident learners. With a strong foundation, we now focus on how to best develop character, values, and wisdom-oriented skills that are vital in an AI-driven world. When every student knows they are consistently making progress, self-esteem also flourishes, which is foundational in nurturing young people as good human beings. This development is supported by our outstanding teaching and learning principles and practices linked to the best global research.

A Future-Facing Model for Education
Our strategic direction embraces complexity and global insight to guide students toward solving real-world

problems and serving the greater good, ensuring our school's purpose remains relevant, enduring, and transformative.

In support of this effort and the evolution of the IB Diploma Programme, Mulgrave is one of the four pilot schools around the world tasked by the International Baccalaureate Organization to co-develop and pilot IB Systems Transformation: Leadership for just and sustainable futures. This transdisciplinary, experiential, project-based course will be available to Mulgrave students starting in the 2025–26 school year.

Our Culture: A warm, vibrant, supportive community
Developing a strong aptitude for learning, service, and leadership is inherent to our school's ethos, as is a strong culture of care and support. Mulgrave is highly valued for our positive community spirit, enriched by the diversity of families from around 40 countries, and our vibrant learning atmosphere. Experienced teachers from around the world provide a comprehensive, appropriately challenging, and personalised IB curriculum to an equally ambitious and capable student body.

Accreditations
Mulgrave is proud to be an accredited member of the Council of International Schools (CIS), the Independent Schools Association of British Columbia (ISABC), and Canadian Accredited Independent Schools (CAIS), and is also authorised by the International Baccalaureate Organization as an IB Continuum School.

USA

Nord Anglia International School, New York

NORD ANGLIA INTERNATIONAL SCHOOL NEW YORK

111 E 22nd Street, New York, NY 10010 USA
Tel: +1 212 600 2010
Email: info@ny.nae.school
Website: www.naisny.com
Principal: Jimmy Frawley

School type: Co-educational Day
Age range of pupils: 2–14 years
No. of pupils enrolled as at 01/09/2025: 150
Fees as at 01/09/2025:
Average Tuition: US$49,100 per annum

Nord Anglia International School, New York isn't like any other school in NYC. Situated in the heart of Gramercy, close to Flatiron and Madison Square Park. At NAISNY your child will always be ahead of the curve, as we shape learning around their personal interests, goals, and needs – and encourage them to connect their understanding to the world, so they're empowered to go after an ambitious path.

We start children on the road to learning as young as 2 years old, and by the time they graduate from NAISNY in 8th grade, they have plans to attend the best high schools in NYC and beyond, including Packer, LaGuardia, Columbia Prep, and Stuyvesant.

Building on the British International Curriculum, we take a tailored approach to learning, encouraging differentiated instruction across NAISNY, so our students can flourish in their strengths and feel fulfilled. Our exceptional teachers and subject specialists know how to support and challenge your child, as they follow a personalized learning plan that helps your child exceed their targets. All students, even our youngest learners, will be taught by specialist teachers in dance, drama, music, art, Spanish, and physical education.

With unique collaborations with The Juilliard School, MIT, and UNICEF our students learn from world-renowned leaders in STEAM, the creative arts, and global impact. Students will become critical thinkers and become skilled problem solvers thanks to these curricula.

Class trips provide our students with rich opportunities to visit the best organizations in New York City and beyond. This year, students have ventured to The Juilliard School, Broadway stages, the Ashokan Center upstate, and the Red Bull Arena for a soccer tournament. We also offer transformative trips within the Nord Anglia international family for further travel. Middle School students have an opportunity to attend annual, Olympic-style sports camps hosted by Nord Anglia schools in Florida and Costa Rica.

At NAISNY, there's something different for everyone. What motivates your child isn't necessarily going to be the same as what compels their classmate. No matter what fascinates or excites your child, we'll boost their growth through exciting challenges and meaningful activities beyond the classroom.

We are proud to offer one-to-one, in-person tours, as well as rolling admissions. Please do not hesitate to reach out, we would be thrilled to help your child create their future.

Costa Rica

Pan-American School

PAN-AMERICAN SCHOOL

(Founded 1971)

632-4005 San Antonio de Belen, Heredia, Costa Rica
Tel: +506 2298 5700
Email: info@panam.ed.cr
Website: www.panam.ed.cr
Head of School: Alan Wrafter
Appointed: July 2019

School type: Co-educational Day
Age range of pupils: 6 months–18 years
No. of pupils enrolled as at 01/09/2025: 512
Fees as at 01/09/2025:
Day: US$10,200–US$20,250 per annum
Teacher/pupil ratio: 1:6

Our Story
Pan-American School: Cultivating excellence, inspiring purpose, and empowering learners to thrive – today and tomorrow.

Founded in 1971, Pan-American School is an IB World School offering a transformative education that blends academic excellence with purpose-driven learning. Located on a lush, 35,000 m2 campus just west of San José, our learning environment is intentionally designed to nurture curiosity, wellbeing, and connection with nature. We serve an inclusive, globally minded community, including families working in Costa Rica's vibrant innovation hubs and international sectors.

Academic Excellence
We proudly offer the full International Baccalaureate Continuum – PYP, MYP, and DP – infused with Costa Rican context and culture. Our students can graduate with:
- The IB Diploma
- A US High School Diploma
- The Costa Rican Bachillerato

Learning at Pan-American School is anchored in a dynamic curriculum that emphasizes:
- Early Learning: Purposeful play and foundational development from 6 months
- Future-Ready Skills: Critical thinking, creativity, and collaboration
- Wellbeing & Belonging: Social, emotional, and physical development
- Creative Expression: Visual arts, music, design, and performance
- Global Citizenship: Service learning, sustainability, and ethical action

Beyond the Classroom
Service in Action: Every student and staff member engages in meaningful service projects each year, ensuring our values make a lasting impact within and beyond the school.

Sports & Wellness:
- Daily sports and wellness programs from PreKinder onward
- Competitive athletics in soccer, basketball, volleyball, and track
- Secondary morning fitness program supporting healthy, focused learning
- Pan-American School teams have achieved top rankings in Central America (AASCA champions in basketball and volleyball), and earned podium finishes in soccer, swimming, tennis, ultimate frisbee, and chess.

Our Students
Pan-American School graduates are principled, capable, and future-ready. They are guided by strong values, embrace multiple perspectives, and lead with empathy, integrity, and a commitment to the common good in a rapidly changing world.

Our Community
We believe that each individual brings unique strengths and perspectives that enrich our learning community. Our students thrive in an environment built on inclusive practices, personalized support, and a shared commitment to growth. Guided by our core value of excellence, we strive to achieve our personal best in all that we do – academically, socially, and ethically. With expert educators, learning specialists, emotional support staff, and language acquisition professionals, every student is known, valued, and empowered to reach their full potential.

Rochambeau, The French International School

9600 Forest Road, & 9650 Rockville Pike, Bethesda, MD 20814 USA
Tel: +1 301 530 8260
Email: admissions@rochambeau.org
Website: www.rochambeau.org
Head of School: Mr Xavier Jacquenet
Appointed: September 2020
School type: Co-educational Day

Age range of pupils: 2–18 years
No. of pupils enrolled as at 01/09/2025: 1272
Fees as at 01/09/2025:
Grade 5: US$26,890 per annum
Grades 6-9: US$27,765 per annum
Grades 10-12: US$32,505 per annum
Average class size: 18
Teacher/pupil ratio: 1:13

Are you looking for an exceptional multi-cultural learning experience for your child? Perhaps you want to increase his or her cognitive development and linguistic ability with a bilingual education. If so, look no further than Rochambeau, The French International School of Washington DC. The school has been in existence since 1955. It started with 11 students and has grown to 1272 students in 2025, representing over 80 nationalities. As part of the French Network of School Abroad (AEFE) students can seamlessly move to and from other schools within the network around the world.

Rochambeau has two campuses all located in Bethesda and welcomes students from age 2 through 12th grade.

The maternelle (preschool) program, noted as the "crown jewel of the French school system," emphasise play, written and oral skills, and learning to live in a community. Students appreciate the holistic approach implemented in this well-balanced comprehensive program. Motor skills, expression, and movement are also taught to these young minds.

Children can enroll in the school without any knowledge of French until the first grade. In addition to French, students have the option of learning a number of languages, including Arabic, German, Latin, and Spanish. Students at Rochambeau participate in a number of extracurricular activities, including soccer, theater, basketball, and rock climbing. Students receive their US high school diploma at the end of 11th grade and the French Baccalaureate or the International Baccalaureate at the end of 12th grade. Indeed, Rochambeau also offers the IB program as of 9th grade. Graduates of Rochambeau go on to study in both the US and internationally, attending some of the top universities around the world.

For more information, please see Rochambeau's website: www.rochambeau.org. Explore everything the school has to offer to broaden your child's horizons and increase his or her linguistic ability. Check it out today!

Canada

Stratford Hall

(Founded 2000)
3000 Commercial Drive, Vancouver BC,
V5N 4E2 Canada

Tel: +1 604 436 0608
Email: info@stratfordhall.ca
Website: www.stratfordhall.ca
Head of School: Richard Kassissieh
Interim Senior School Principal: Andy Wong
Junior School Principal: Smita Karam

School type: Co-educational Day
Age range of pupils: 5–18 years
No. of pupils enrolled as at 01/09/2025: 545
Fees as at 01/09/2025:
Day: CAD$29,490–CAD$34,450 per annum
Average class size: 22

Stratford Hall is an independent, gender-inclusive, non-denominational, university preparatory day school with a student population of 545 ranging from Kindergarten to Grade 12. Our location in a vibrant, urban setting in East Vancouver, British Columbia reflects our diverse community of students. Through the continuum of International Baccalaureate (IB) programmes, the Primary Years Programme (Kindergarten – Grade 5), Middle Years Programme (Grades 6–10) and Diploma Programme (Grades 11 & 12) the School provides a level of individual challenge and academic rigour beyond the norm. Equally important is our commitment to the IB Learner Profile as a guide, fostering international-mindedness in students and adults alike.

At Stratford Hall, every child will be given the opportunity to learn and to thrive; to discover their unique strengths, and to explore the diverse opportunities our rapidly changing world offers. Under the guidance of our staff and faculty, they will grow and mature, while equipping themselves with intellectual tools, strength of character, and a global perspective.

Stratford Hall is a not-for-profit school operating under the authority of the Ministry of Education of British Columbia.

Our Mission:
Empowering a diverse community of learners to passionately steward our changing world
Our Vision:
Inspiring minds through innovation and ingenuity
Our Values:
Integrity | Curiosity | Belonging

TFS - Canada's International School

(Founded 1962)

306 Lawrence Avenue East, Toronto ON, M4N 1T7 Canada
Tel: +1 416 484 6533
Email: admissions@tfs.ca
Website: www.tfs.ca
Head of School: Norman Gaudet
Appointed: 2021
School type: Co-educational Day

Religious Denomination: Non-denominational
Age range of pupils: 2–18 years
No. of pupils enrolled as at 01/09/2025: 1500
Fees as at 01/09/2025:
Day: CAD$24,230–CAD$40,830 per annum
Average class size: Max 22
Teacher/pupil ratio: Varies

TFS' mission is to develop multilingual critical thinkers who celebrate difference, transcend borders and strive for the betterment of humankind and the planet. As the pioneer of French immersion in Canada, our education is unparalleled in its excellence, preparing students for success in today's global world.

Bilingual and co-ed since 1962, TFS teaches the curricula of France and Ontario through the framework established by the IB programs (PYP, MYP and bilingual IB Diploma Programme). We want our students to exude academic ambition, benefit from an all-round development as individuals and citizens, and view the world from an international perspective. TFS students master French and English, while balancing rigorous science, arts and humanities programs.

No prior knowledge of French is necessary, but all students are bilingual when they graduate due to our successful Intro program, offered until Grade 7. TFS students are well-rounded, inquisitive learners, forming friendships for life within our supportive community. Co-curricular programs include competitive sports, robotics, and music, visual and dramatic arts. Students benefit from exceptional facilities, a 26-acre ravine, and a diverse, non-denominational environment. TFS has campuses in Toronto and Mississauga.

In addition to being authorized by the IB, TFS is accredited by the Ministry of Education of Ontario, the French Ministry of Education, and Canadian Accredited Independent Schools (CAIS). TFS is also a member of the Conference of Independent Schools of Ontario (CIS), the Council of International Schools, and Agence pour l'enseignement français à l'étranger (aefe).

Please visit us at www.tfs.ca.

USA

The Biltmore School

(Founded 1926)

1600 S. Red Road, Miami, FL 33155 USA
Tel: +1 305 266 4666
Email: info@biltmoreschool.com
Website: www.biltmoreschool.com
Principal: Gina C. Duarte-Romero M.Ed.
Assistant Principal: Ana V. Seoane

School type: Co-educational Day
Age range of pupils: 1–14 years
No. of pupils enrolled as at 01/09/2025: 200
Fees as at 01/09/2025:
US$18,575–US$29,575 per annum

Originally founded in Coral Gables in 1926, The Biltmore School is one of the oldest operating schools in Miami Dade County. Our school boasts a tradition of educational excellence that has provided guidance to children for over 90 years.

Our Director, Gina Romero and our Biltmore Faculty members are actively involved in the Project Zero research initiative sponsored by Harvard University that promotes creative thinking, encourages children to be self-reliant, and empowers them to think "outside the box" through a challenging curriculum that incorporates instruction maximizing multiple intelligences, individual learning styles and modalities. Through participation in ongoing professional development workshops in partnership with Florida International University, our staff under the guidance of our director actively explore Visible Thinking strategies that promote the highest levels of intelligences, abstract, and critical thinking in children of all ages.

During the 2007-2008 school year our school was awarded accreditation by AISF (Association of Independent Schools of Florida), NCPSA (National Council on Private School Accreditation), MSA–CESS (Middle States Association of Colleges and Schools – Commissions of Elementary and Secondary Schools), COGNIA, and NIPSA (National Independent Private School Association). The Biltmore School has also been an IB World School since March 2012 and offers the IB Primary Years Programme.

The Biltmore School believes that students are capable and knowledgeable agents of their learning. We feel that it is the responsibility of the educator to be both the partner and guide in the growth and development of the child. It is through much research and collaboration that our school has embraced and synthesized diverse educational views and practices to best benefit our students.

The Biltmore School offers a comprehensive program for students from age one through eighth grade.

USA

The École

The École Elementary & Middle School
115 East 22nd Street, New York, NY 10010 USA
The École Maternelle
206 Fifth Avenue, New York, NY 10010
Phone 1: +1 646 766 18432
Tel: +1 646 410 2238
Email: bonjour@theEcole.org

Website: www.theecole.org
Head of School: Jean-Yves Vesseau
School type: Co-educational Day
Age range of pupils: 2–14 years
No. of pupils enrolled as at 01/09/2025: 360+
Fees as at 01/09/2025:
From $44,700 per annum

The École: Where Bilingual Education Creates World Citizens

Nestled in the heart of Manhattan's Flatiron District, The École stands out as a nurturing, innovative, and international independent school committed to bilingual and bicultural excellence. Guided by its mission statement – WE CARE – The École blends the best of French and American education to foster intellectual curiosity, emotional intelligence, and global citizenship in students from Pre-Nursery through 8th Grade.

Since its founding in 2009, The École has evolved into a dynamic educational community. Its bilingual program is thoughtfully designed, immersing students in both French and English from their earliest years. Native-speaking educators lead rigorous and engaging instruction aligned with the French Ministry of Education and New York State standards, seamlessly integrating cultural perspectives and pedagogical practices.

The school's two-building Flatiron campus includes the Maternelle Building at 206 Fifth Avenue for Pre-Nursery through Kindergarten and the Elementary & Middle School Building at 115 East 22nd Street for 1st though 8th Grade. In 2022, The École launched a High School Track in partnership with Léman Manhattan Preparatory School, allowing students to continue their bilingual journey toward the prestigious International Baccalaureate (IB) diploma. High school placement guidance ensures graduates are prepared for top-tier public and private schools in New York, France, and beyond.

At every stage, The École emphasizes personal growth, adaptability, and creativity. From early Mandarin and Spanish instruction to after-school programs in art, coding, and athletics, students enjoy a holistic learning experience.

Supported by affiliations with AEFE, MLF, NAIS, and AFSA, The École is deeply connected to a global educational network. Families benefit from tuition assistance, flexible programs, and a warm, inclusive school culture.

At The École, students are more than bilingual – they are bi-literate, culturally agile, and inspired to lead with care and confidence in an ever-changing world.

USA

The Village School

13051 Whittington Drive,
Houston, TX 77077 USA
Tel: +1 281 496 7900
Email: admissions@thevillageschool.com
Website: www.thevillageschool.com

Head of School: Mr. Bill Delbrugge
School type: Co-educational Day & Boarding
Age range of pupils: 2–18 years

One World. One Village.
The Village School, a pre-k through 12th grade private day and boarding school in Houston, delivers a global perspective, exceptional learning experiences, and access to world-class teachers. Voted the #1 most diverse private school in Houston, #1 boarding school in Texas and amongst the top 20 best private schools in the United States, Village is home to a collaborative, supportive and global community. Recognized for excellence in STEAM education, world-class internships and differentiated programs, they offer a rigorous but nurturing individualized environment. The Village School offers a rich selection of academics, arts, and athletics providing a 100% matriculation rate to the best colleges and universities worldwide.

Exceptional Learning Experiences
The Village School offers a unique and enriched approach inclusive of entrepreneurship, internships, and experiential learning, along with collaborations with world-leading institutions. Visionary teachers inspire learners to excel and foster a thirst for knowledge. This unique approach to teaching and learning enables students to gain a better grasp of concepts, think more creatively and allow for greater reflection on experiences.

Five Diploma Options
Village is proud to offer five rigorous diploma options: the International Baccalaureate, Pre-Medical Science, Entrepreneurship, Computer Science and The Village School U.S. Diploma programs. To prepare for their college of choice, students can also take Advanced Placement (AP) courses.

Cultivating a Global Perspective
The Village School student body represents over 90 different countries across six continents, offering students the opportunity to interact with and learn from peers across the world. This culturally rich environment helps cultivate a global perspective and provides interaction with people from other ethnicities, cultures, schools of thought, and viewpoints.

Preparing for the Future
Students have access to experienced college advisors who know the complexities of the application process and university requirements for schools both nationally and abroad. The college counseling team helps Village students gain acceptance into top colleges and universities. In addition, our recent graduating class earned more than $50 million in scholarships toward higher education institutions around the world.

Premier Collaborations
Village students benefit from collaborations with esteemed institutions such as the Massachusetts Institute of Technology (MIT), The Juilliard School, UNICEF, and Space Center Houston.

Visit Village!
Inquire online at www.thevillageschool.com or find out more by emailing our Admissions Team at admissions@ thevillageschool.com or by calling (281) 491-7900. Take a virtual tour at www.nordangliaeducation.com/ village-houston/virtual-tour.

USA

THINK Global School

(Founded 2010)

960 Madison Avenue Fifth Floor, New York, NY 10021 USA
Tel: +1 646 504 6924
Email: info@thinkglobalschool.org
Website: thinkglobalschool.org
Principal: Jen Buchanan
School type: Co-educational Boarding

Age range of pupils: 16–18 years
No. of pupils enrolled as at 01/09/2025: 31
Fees as at 01/09/2025:
Full Boarding: $94,000 per annum (with sliding-scale tuition available to all students)
Teacher/pupil ratio: 1:4

THINK Global School (TGS) stands as the world's first and only traveling high school, offering an unparalleled educational experience for students aged 16–18. Founded in 2010 by visionary Joann McPike, TGS brings together 35 exceptional students from 20 countries to embark on a transformative two-year journey that redefines international education. Uniquely positioned as "A School for the Bravely Curious," the nomadic community travels to four countries each academic year, with students and faculty living, learning, and growing together in an immersive global classroom that spans continents.

THINK Global School's vision is to envision a future where learning is real, relevant, and deeply relational – where TGS sparks curiosity and forges connections to reveal a world of possibility. Rather than confining education to traditional classroom walls, the school leverages the entire world as its campus, creating authentic learning opportunities that connect academic study to real-world experiences. The small student body ensures unprecedented individualized attention, with a remarkable 4:1 student-to-teacher ratio.

Academic Excellence Through Innovation

At the heart of TGS's educational philosophy lies the award-winning Changemaker Curriculum, a groundbreaking approach that seamlessly blends experiential learning with project-based education. Students don't simply read about the world's challenges; they investigate them firsthand, developing innovative solutions through hands-on projects that

USA

address real issues in the communities they visit. This methodology has produced over 2,000 student projects to date, each contributing meaningful impact to local communities while developing essential 21st-century skills.

The academic program is fully accredited by the Western Association of Schools and Colleges, ensuring that the innovative approach meets the highest educational standards. With 70% of faculty holding advanced degrees, students receive instruction from passionate educators who serve as mentors and collaborators in the learning journey. The results speak for themselves: TGS maintains a 100% graduation rate and an impressive 94% university matriculation rate, with graduates gaining admission to prestigious institutions worldwide including Oxford, Harvard, MIT, and other top-tier universities.

Global Values and Learning Environment
Central to the TGS experience are eight core values, each drawn from wisdom traditions around the world and lived through immersive cultural experiences. Students embody values including Kaizen (continuous improvement), Meraki (giving fully with soul and creativity), Satya (living with integrity), and Ubuntu (connecting to community wholeness). These values become lived experiences as students travel, offering a lens through which they see, engage, and grow while grounding them in their humanity.

The "campus" spans the globe, with students experiencing diverse learning environments from bustling international cities to ancient cultural sites, from innovative technology hubs to natural wonders worldwide. Each location is carefully selected to provide unique learning opportunities that align with the curriculum objectives and offer students exposure to different cultures, languages, and perspectives. TGS also maintains state-of-the-art technology resources that travel with the community, ensuring seamless integration of technology into the learning experience.

Graduate Profile and Future Readiness
TGS graduates emerge as curious, courageous, and connected individuals, prepared to shape the future with vision, joy, and care. The Graduate Profile reflects five core competencies: Thinks Critically & Curiously, Communicates with Purpose, Lives with Integrity, Designs Solutions that Matter, and Understands Systems & Interdependence. Students

develop these competencies through real-world problem-solving, cultural immersion, and collaborative innovation.

Graduation requirements include a comprehensive portfolio showcasing the full TGS experience, a year-long Mastery Project demonstrating deep inquiry and purpose-driven learning, meaningful Service Learning experiences, and demonstrated competency mastery across disciplines. Graduates don't just leave with academic credentials – they step into their futures with the curiosity to ask beautiful questions, the skills to navigate rapid change, and the compassion to lead lives of integrity and meaningful contribution to the interconnected world.

The Wingate School

An inspired school
(Founded 2016)

Carr. Huixquilucan Río Hondo Km 14, Col. San Bartolomé Coatepec, Huixquilucan, Estado de México, C.P. 52770 México
Tel: +52 55 8288 0982
Email: office@wingate.edu.mx

Website: www.wingate.edu.mx
Head Teacher: Mr Tom Wingate
School type: Co-educational Day
Age range of pupils: 2–18 years

The Wingate School, part of the Inspired Education Group, is a leading British International School in Mexico City, committed to developing critical thinkers with a global outlook who are prepared to contribute meaningfully to society.

A significant part of our community is composed of international expatriate families residing in Mexico City who seek a high-quality education for their children. Wingate offers an academic pathway grounded in the British tradition, beginning with the Cambridge Lower Secondary Curriculum and progressing through the IGCSEs, culminating in the prestigious International Baccalaureate Diploma Programme. This structure provides students with the academic rigour and international perspective required to succeed at top universities around the world.

Inspired Education Group is a global leader in premium private education, with over 90,000 students across 119 schools in 27 countries. Its educational model is built on three core pillars: academic excellence, sports, and the creative arts – fostering holistic development in every student. With international recognition and the integration of cutting-edge technologies, including AI-driven learning tools, Inspired ensures students receive a personalised education that reflects both local and global standards.

At Wingate, we are committed to offering a comprehensive learning experience that extends beyond academic performance. Our diverse student body creates an inclusive environment where intercultural understanding and global citizenship are central to daily life.

A cornerstone of our educational approach is the School of Character programme, a fundamental pillar in the formation of well-rounded individuals. At its core is the value of Respect, which guides students in their personal and social development, helping them grow with integrity, empathy, and a sense of responsibility.

The Wingate School provides a supportive and inspiring environment where every student is empowered to reach their full potential and become a confident, compassionate, and engaged global citizen.

International schools in South America

Schools ordered A–Z by Name

Brazil

Escola do Futuro - São Paulo

R. Dr. Francisco Pati 40, Cidade São Francisco, São Paulo, SP 05352-120 Brazil
Tel: +55 (11) 2168 4100
Email: visitas@escoladofuturo.com.br
Website: www.escoladofuturo.com.br

Headmaster: Ivonne Betsabé Muniz
School type: Co-educational Day
Age range of pupils: 2–18 years
No. of pupils enrolled as at 01/09/2025: 600

Bringing World Leaders Together

Escola do Futuro does not have this name by chance. The institution offers a Cognia accredited bilingual curriculum developed on the basis of multicultural and Christian values from Preschool to Grade 12. The students experience a learning environment of total immersion in English where they acquire the cultural knowledge needed to gain proficiency in the target language, as well as preparing to face future challenges as leaders who can change the world into a better place. Escola do Futuro's goal is to bring together world citizens. The students acquire full proficiency in additional languages, such as English and Spanish and also build the necessary cultural references and values which will allow them to interact naturally and consciously wherever they are. The students learn to accept and welcome diversity. The educational philosophy is based on a skill-driven curriculum focused on the development of autonomy and critical thinking; so students become aware of their transforming role in making a better world. The School's vision is clearly reflected in its environment, where the purpose built facilities integrate the learning process. The classrooms, common areas, such as the cafeteria, patio, and courts, invite the students to interact socially, while allowing them to respect each other's individuality. The international program provides students with the opportunity to pursue higher education abroad; anchored in the education of professionals that face the challenges of tomorrow, as citizens of the world.

Chile

Santiago College

(Founded 1880)

Av. Camino Los Trapenses 4007,
Lo Barnechea, Santiago, Chile
Tel: +56 2 27338800
Email: master@scollege.cl
Website: www.scollege.cl
Head of School: Mr Alan Lorenzini

Appointed: 2025
School type: Co-educational Day
Age range of pupils: 4–18 years
No. of pupils enrolled as at 01/09/2025: 2044
Average class size: 25
Teacher/pupil ratio: 1:8

Santiago College is a prestigious, well-regarded private school with more than 145 years of innovation and tradition. It is uniquely placed to provide a high quality, holistic and bilingual programme to over 2000 boys and girls.

Santiago College was the first school in the country to adopt the International Baccalaureate and is currently offering three programmes: PYP, MYP and DP. The educational programmes meet the full requirements of the Chilean Ministry of Education, and the school is also accredited by CIS and NEASC. The school year begins in March and ends in December.

Santiago College shares an understanding with the IB that at the centre of education are students who come to the school with combinations of unique and shared values, knowledge, skills and experiences of the world and their place within it. The school's educational programmes grow from an understanding that people work together to construct meaning and make sense of the world.

Along with intellectual and creative development, the school programmes address spiritual, personal, social, emotional and physical well-being. Santiago College seeks to support, challenge and inspire personal excellence by removing barriers to learning and wellbeing, and by encouraging students to become confident and self-directed, lifelong learners.

Brazil

The British College of Brazil

THE BRITISH COLLEGE OF BRAZIL
A NORD ANGLIA EDUCATION SCHOOL

CF Campus
Rua Álvares de Azevedo, 50, Chácara Flora, São Paulo, SP 04671-040 Brazil

CJ Campus
Av. Engenheiro Oscar Americano, 630, Cidade Jardim, São Paulo, SP 05673-050 Brazil

Tel: +55 11 5547 3030
Email: admissions-bcb@britishcollegebrazil.org

Website: www.britishcollegebrazil.org
Headteacher: Mr. Maurice Hartnett
School type: Co-educational Day
Age range of pupils: 2–18 years
No. of pupils enrolled as at 01/09/2025: 600+
Fees as at 01/09/2025:
R$92,000–138,000 per annum
Average class size: 18
Teacher/pupil ratio: 1:10

The British College of Brazil (BCB), a Nord Anglia Education school, is São Paulo's school of choice for expatriate families looking to provide their children with an international education. We offer engaging learning environments to students in Early Years, Primary and Secondary school in a warm and supportive atmosphere where they can thrive. Our schools and the one-of-a-kind opportunities we create inside and outside the classroom enrich learning, instill lifelong memories and a deep sense of achievement. We welcome your family to become a valued member of our community.

At the British College of Brazil, we teach the English National Curriculum adapted to an international environment, the International Primary Curriculum, the IGCSE in Year 10 and 11 followed by the IB Diploma Programme in Years 12 and 13. Throughout our core curricula and programs we help your child to develop a global mindset and nurture essential skills such as creativity, collaboration, and resilience. We want every student to become lifelong learners, to try something new and, above all, to be ambitious.

We are part of the Nord Anglia Education family of 87 international schools, boarding schools and private schools located in 33 countries around the world. Together we can enrich your child's learning experience with opportunities beyond the ordinary. From online debates and challenges, Global Campus connects our students around the world to learn together every day. Our unique international programs provide our students a great opportunity to broaden their horizons, expand cultural knowledge and foster connections.

They can either opt for summer camps in exciting locations from Oxford to Florida, to Switzerland, or choose spending a year in one of our boarding schools – Windermere Preparatory School, The Village School, or North Broward Preparatory School, through our Study Abroad Program. Through our Global expeditions in Tanzania and Switzerland or participating in our Performing Arts Festival in Miami or in the Global Games in Orlando, Nord Anglia's students grow up with a well-rounded view of the world, a passion for learning and discovery, and lifelong memories of achievement and leadership.

Additionally, our collaborations with world leading institutions such as The Juilliard School, The Massachusetts Institute of Technology (MIT), IMG Academy and UNICEF enhance the curriculum and offer exceptional professional development for teachers. This approach results in high academic outcomes and equips students with the skills that are essential to thrive in the 21st century.

We believe that there is no limit to what our students, our people, and our communities can achieve. We encourage your child to set their sights higher by fostering a global perspective together with our school's personalised approach to learning – helping every child to succeed, thrive and love learning.

Brazil

The British School, Rio de Janeiro

A caring community, striving for excellence, where every individual matters.

(Founded 1924)

Rua Real Grandeza 99, Botafogo, Rio de Janeiro, RJ 22281-030 Brazil
Tel: +55 21 2539 2717
Email: edu@britishschool.g12.br
Website: www.britishschool.g12.br
Directors: Steve Lang, Fernanda Reis & Isadora Guise
School type: Co-educational Day

Age range of pupils: 2–18 years
No. of pupils enrolled as at 01/09/2025: 2300
Boys: 1100 **Girls:** 1200
Fees as at 01/09/2025:
Day: R115,000 approx per annum
Average class size: 12-24
Teacher/pupil ratio: 1:7.3

Founded in 1924, we are a non-profit, independent and coeducational day school offering a complete and coherent curriculum for students of all nationalities from ages 2–18. Our school aims to give students a broad, balanced and relevant educational experience. The educational Philosophy and practice are primarily British in nature with international and Brazilian elements incorporated, where appropriate. The programmes of study are: Early Years Foundation Stage (EYFS) and International Primary Curriculum (IPC) for 2 to 11 year olds; Key Stage 3 (Middle Years) of the UK National Curriculum for 11 to 14 year olds; Cambridge IGCSE for 14 to 16 year olds; and the International Baccalaureate (IB) Diploma for 16 to 18 year olds.

Over 82% of our students are from Brazilian families and the remainder are from over 48 different countries, with British and other European nationals being the biggest proportion. English is the main language of instruction with Portuguese, French and Spanish also being taught.

The school is an IB World School accredited by the Council of International Schools (CIS) and by Council of British International Schools (COBIS). The Director is a member of the Latin American Heads Conference (LAHC). It has approximately 2300 students located on three sites. The Zona Sul Unit – Botafogo Site houses a primary school; the secondary school is based at the Zona Sul Unit – Urca Site, close to the Sugar Loaf. The Barra Unit is a full unit located in the Barra suburb area, with a full school with students from age 2 (Pre-Nursery) to age 18 (Year 13).

Classes are generally small and the school environment is pleasant, well-resourced and stimulating, with a strong focus on health, safety and security. Performing arts, sports, Model United Nations, Duke of Edinburgh's Award Scheme and work experience provide a wide range of co-curricular opportunities. Experiences beyond the school include numerous local day visits and national or international residential trips for most year groups from Primary Year 5 upwards.

Our teachers are well-qualified (some 30% being recruited from overseas) and supported by a robust and effective programme of continuing professional development.

Our school provides a caring and friendly, yet demanding, learning environment and makes every effort to ensure that each individual has the opportunity to develop their particular abilities and talents to the full. The emphasis on academic achievement is also balanced by our concern to meet our students' physical, emotional and social needs. Personal development and social responsibility are an integral part of our educational programme. We place a high value on good social behavior and ethical standards, with respect for the individual and the environment. We want our students to be happy in school and we hope that their school experience will be fondly and warmly remembered for life. We believe that this can be achieved through high expectations; clear guidelines and limits; constant encouragement; and addressing individual needs.

Extracurricular Activities
Football, capoeira, volleyball, basketball, ballet, artistic gymnastics, judo, choir, music (instruments and singing), cooking, drama and arts are available.

Facilities
Air-conditioned classrooms, interactive Whiteboards, computers, laptops, tablets, science and computer & technology & robotics labs, libraries, gymnasiums and open spaces for sports and games, playgrounds with a variety of toys, auditoriums for Drama classes, presentations and art exhibitions, sickbays (first-aid – nurses), and dining halls.

Directory of international schools

Schools in Africa D247
Schools in Asia D267
Schools in Australasia D337
Schools in Europe D345
Schools in North America D399
Schools in South America D425

International schools in Africa

Schools ordered A–Z by Country

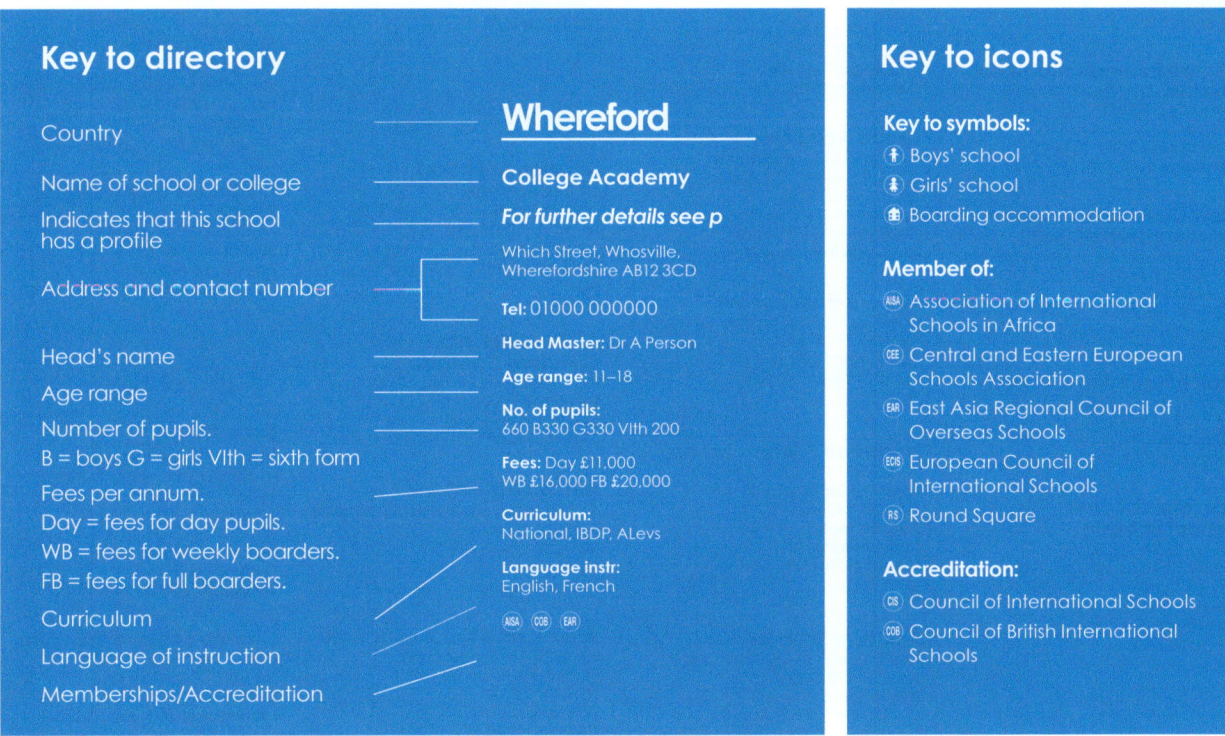

Key to directory

- Country
- Name of school or college
- Indicates that this school has a profile
- Address and contact number
- Head's name
- Age range
- Number of pupils. B = boys G = girls VIth = sixth form
- Fees per annum. Day = fees for day pupils. WB = fees for weekly boarders. FB = fees for full boarders.
- Curriculum
- Language of instruction
- Memberships/Accreditation

Whereford

College Academy

For further details see p

Which Street, Whosville, Wherefordshire AB12 3CD

Tel: 01000 000000

Head Master: Dr A Person

Age range: 11–18

No. of pupils: 660 B330 G330 VIth 200

Fees: Day £11,000 WB £16,000 FB £20,000

Curriculum: National, IBDP, ALevs

Language instr: English, French

(AISA) (COB) (EAR)

Key to icons

Key to symbols:
- Boys' school
- Girls' school
- Boarding accommodation

Member of:
- (AISA) Association of International Schools in Africa
- (CEE) Central and Eastern European Schools Association
- (EAR) East Asia Regional Council of Overseas Schools
- (ECIS) European Council of International Schools
- (RS) Round Square

Accreditation:
- (CIS) Council of International Schools
- (COB) Council of British International Schools

Please note: Schools are coeducational day schools unless otherwise indicated

Africa

ANGOLA

E.S.C.O.L.A. - ENGLISH SCHOOL COMMUNITY OF LUANDA, ANGOLA
For further details see p. 41
Rua de Cambambe No. 21-23, Bairro Patrice Lumumba, Luanda
Tel: +244 935 929 501
Email: schooloffice@escolaangola.org
Website: escolaangola.org/escolateste
Age range: 3–16 years
Language instr: English

Luanda International School
Via S6, Bairro de Talatona, Município de Belas, Luanda
Tel: +244 932 337 056
Age range: 3–18 years
No. of pupils: 620
Curriculum: IBDP, IBMYP, IBPYP
Language instr: English
(AISA) (CIS)

Lycée Français Alioune Blondin Beye
Zona escolar 1° de Maio (Baïrro), Luanda CP 5332
Tel: +244 924 946 151
Age range: 3–16 years
Language instr: French, Portuguese

BENIN

EFE Montaigne
No. 655, Rue 12.052, Les Cocotiers, Cotonou 01 BP 679
Tel: +229 21 30 17 28
Age range: 4–16 years
Curriculum: FrenchBacc
Language instr: French

English International School
Haie Vive, Cotonou 08 BP 0430
Tel: +229 21 30 92 87
Age range: 3–18 years
Curriculum: IGCSE, ALevs
Language instr: English

New Covenant American School International
Lot 1283, Rue 517, Cotonou 08 BP 909
Tel: +229 97 64 08 32
Age range: 3–16 years
Curriculum: USA
Language instr: English

Oak International School
Lot 4-6 PLM, Akpakpa, Cotonou
Tel: +229 64 93 11 11
Curriculum: IBMYP
Language instr: English, French

QSI International School of Benin
Lot No. 126 & 127, Zone Residentielle de la Radio, Camp Guezo, Cotonou 02 BP 1087
Tel: +229 66 62 12 46
Age range: 3–16 years

BOTSWANA

Broadhurst Primary School
Private Bag BR 114, 8578 Lenyaphiri Road, Gaborone
Tel: +267 3971 221

Daystar Primary School
PO Box 2899, Flower Town, Mahalapye
Tel: +267 471 1801

Delta Waters International School
Private Bag 0153, Boseja, Maun
Tel: +267 6860 560

Enko Botho International School
Plot 60114, Block 7, near Botswana Qualifications Authority and HRDC, Gaborone
Tel: +267 396 0044
Curriculum: IBDP
Language instr: English

Gaborone International School
P.O. Box AD 590 ADD, Post Net Kgale View, Gaborone
Tel: +267 316 2230
Age range: 3–18 years
Curriculum: IGCSE, ALevs

Kgaswe International School
PO Box 75, Palapye
Tel: +267 492 0441
Age range: 3–18 years
Curriculum: IGCSE, ALevs

Kopano School
Plot Number 1107, Kopano Road, Selebi-Phikwe
Tel: +267 261 0552
Age range: 3–16 years
Curriculum: IGCSE

Legae Academy
PO Box 750, Mogoditshane, 19893 Katjiratjira, Gaborone
Tel: +267 392 4313
Age range: 11–18 years
Curriculum: IGCSE, ALevs
Language instr: English

Maru-a-Pula School
Plot 4725, Maruapula Way, Gaborone
Tel: +267 391 2953
Age range: 11–18 years
Curriculum: IGCSE, ALevs

Northside Primary School
PO Box 897, Plot 2786, Tshekedi Crescent Ext 9, Gaborone
Tel: +267 395 2440
Age range: 4–11 years
Curriculum: IBPYP
Language instr: English
(CIS)

Rainbow Schools
Namutupeka Road, Gaborone
Tel: +267 393 6932
Age range: 3–18 years
Curriculum: IGCSE, ALevs

Thornhill Primary School
PO Box 163, Gaborone
Tel: +267 395 2490
Age range: 4–16 years

Westwood International School
Phase 4, Plot 22978, Mmankgwedi Road, Gaborone
Tel: +267 390 6736
Age range: 4–19 years
Curriculum: IBDP, IBMYP, IBPYP, IGCSE
Language instr: English
(AISA) (CIS)

BURKINA FASO

African American Academy, Ouagadougou Campus
Ouaga 2000, Ouagadougou
Tel: +226 61 79 72 72
Age range: 4–18 years
Curriculum: IGCSE

Enko Ouaga International School
Zogona, venant du Boulevard Charles de Gaulle, premier six-mètres après la mosquée de Zogona à gauche, Ouagadougou
Tel: +226 25 36 01 77
Age range: 11–18 years
Curriculum: IBDP
Language instr: French, English

International School of Ouagadougou
01 BP 1142, Ouagadougou
Tel: +226 25 36 21 43
Age range: 3–19 years
Curriculum: IBDP, SAT
Language instr: English
(AISA)

CAMEROON

Academic School of Excellence
4323 Yaoundé
Tel: +237 2 22 20 03 23
Curriculum: IBDP
Language instr: English, French

ACE Leadership School, Bonaberi Campus
B.P. 3069, Bonaberi, Douala
Tel: +237 6 99 96 45 44
Age range: 3–18 years
Curriculum: AP, USA, IGCSE, ALevs

African American Academy, Bonanjo Campus
B.P. 3909, Douala
Tel: +237 6 74 63 52 92
Age range: 4–18 years
Curriculum: IGCSE

American School of Douala
B.P. 1909, 771 Avenue de L'independence, Douala
Tel: +237 2 33 42 14 37
Age range: 4–18 years
Curriculum: AP, USA
Language instr: English

American School of Yaoundé
B.P. 7475, Rue Martin Samba, Yaoundé
Tel: +237 2 22 22 04 21
Age range: 3–18 years
Curriculum: IBDP, IBMYP, IBPYP, USA
Language instr: English
(AISA) (CIS)

Enko Bonanjo International School
Rue 1.171, No. 414, In front of Camwater, Bonanjo, Douala
Tel: +237 6 93 06 82 98
Age range: 11–19 years
Curriculum: IBDP, IGCSE

Enko La Gaiete International School
B.P 14853, Nouvelle Route Bastos (échangeur simplifié), Yaoundé
Tel: +237 6 97 26 59 00
Age range: 2–19 years
Curriculum: IBDP, IGCSE
Language instr: English

Rain Forest International School
Near Petite Marche Odza, Yaoundé
Tel: +237 6 77 93 71 62
Age range: 12–19 years
Curriculum: AP, SAT, USA, IGCSE
Language instr: English

Rousseau International School
P.O. Box 5321, Hotel de l'air Bonapriso, 34 Avenue de L'indépendance 2351,
Tel: +237 2 33 42 12 69
Curriculum: IBDP
Language instr: English, French

Russian International School Galaxy
Monté Ste Monique, Makepé, Douala
Tel: +237 690 58 00 08
Curriculum: IBDP
Language instr: English, Russian

The Bridge International School
P.O. Box 4157, Douala
Tel: +237 6 98 87 60 19
Age range: 4–18 years
Curriculum: IPC, UK, IGCSE, ALevs
(COB)

COTE D'IVOIRE

Enko Riviera International School
Riviera Golf, Carrefour M'Pouto/Sol Béni, Next to the Embassy of Lebanon, Abidjan
Tel: +225 27 22 54 1098
Age range: 11–16 years
Curriculum: IBDP, IBMYP
Language instr: English, French

Groupe Scolaire L'Ardoise
Cocody Riviera III, Abidjan
Tel: +225 07 08 41 0101
Curriculum: IBMYP
Language instr: English, French

Africa

International Community School of Abidjan
Off Boulevard Arsène Usher Assouan Road, Riviera III, Abidjan 06 BP 544
Tel: +225 27 22 47 1152
Age range: 4–18 years
Curriculum: AP, IBDP, SAT, USA
Language instr: English
(AISA) (CIS)

International University Demonstration School (IUDS)
1km from Abidjan Mall / 2.6km from CNPS Angré, Cocody, Riviera Bonoumin, Abidjan 06 BP 2556
Tel: +225 27 22 49 7090
Age range: 3–18 years
Curriculum: USA
Language instr: English

DEMOCRATIC REPUBLIC OF THE CONGO

Complexe Scolaire Les Calinours
617 Avenue Kamina, Kolwezi, Lualaba
Tel: +243 97 24 33289
Curriculum: IBDP
Language instr: English, French

Ecole Internationale Bilingue Le Cartésien (EIBC)
34 7ème Rue, Q. Industriel, Limete, Kinshasa
Tel: +243 99 82 22800
Age range: 3–19 years
Curriculum: IBDP, IBPYP
Language instr: French, English

English-Speaking School of Lubumbashi
476 Av. Le Verger, Quartier GOLF (opposite the Golf course), Lubumbashi
Tel: +243 82 59 16993
Language instr: English

Institut Aurora
8 Avenue Kalemie, Commune de la Gombe, Kinshasa
Tel: +243 97 17 44509
Age range: 3–18 years
Curriculum: IBMYP
Language instr: English, French

Jewels International School of Kinshasa
6705 Av. de l'O.U.A., Commune de Ngaliema, Kinshasa
Tel: +243 81 88 88839
Age range: 3–18 years
Curriculum: IBDP, IBMYP, IBPYP
Language instr: English

Saint Marcel Academy International School
Corner Mwela and Marcel Senga, Golf Meteo, Lubumbashi
Tel: +243 82 97 09605
Curriculum: IBPYP
Language instr: English, French

The American School of Kinshasa
Route de Matadi, Ngaliema, Kinshasha
Tel: +243 81 88 46619
Age range: 3–18 years
Curriculum: IBDP, IBMYP, IBPYP, USA
(AISA) (CIS)

EGYPT

Al Afak Al Gadeda International School
First settlement, Behind Police Academy, Infront of Gehaz Al Tagamoa Al Awal, New Cairo City, Cairo
Tel: +20 12 7101 1900
Age range: 4–18 years
Curriculum: USA

Al Bashaer International School
Lot 3, Al Shatr District 13, Zahraa El Maadi, Cairo
Tel: +20 2 2517 8305
Age range: 4–18 years
Curriculum: UK, USA, IGCSE, ALevs

Alexandria House of English
KM 8 Alexandria/Cairo Agricultural Road, Alexandria
Tel: +20 12 7170 3888
Age range: 4–18 years
Curriculum: UK, USA, IGCSE, ALevs

Alexandria International Academy
Plots 2 & 3 Section 1, Abis, Alexandria
Tel: +20 12 8621 5550
Age range: 3–18 years
Curriculum: IBDP, IBPYP, USA
Language instr: English, Arabic

Alwaha Schools
Marriotia, Alharam, Behind Cataract Hotel, Giza
Tel: +20 2 3770 0108
Age range: 4–18 years
Curriculum: USA

Amal Language Schools
18 Street 105, Maadi Al Khabiri Al Wasti, Al Maadi, Cairo

American City International School
6 Mohamed Thakeb Street, Zamalek, Cairo
Tel: +20 12 2720 0099
Age range: 4–18 years
Curriculum: USA, IGCSE

American International School in Egypt - Main Campus
P.O. Box 8090, Masaken, Nasr City, Cairo 11371
Tel: +20 2 2618 8400
Age range: 3–18 years
Curriculum: IBDP, USA

American International School in Egypt - West Campus
P.O. Box 12588, Greens compound, Sheikh Zayed City, Giza 12588
Tel: +20 2 3854 0600
Age range: 4–18 years
Curriculum: IBDP, USA

American School Beverly Hills Cairo
Beverly Hills Compound, Sheikh Zayed City, 6th of October City, Giza 12588
Tel: +20 10 0005 0431
Age range: 4–18 years
Curriculum: USA

American School of Alexandria
Gamila Abu Hereid Street, Seouf, Alexandria
Tel: +20 3 331 1306
Age range: 4–18 years
Curriculum: SAT, USA

Amgad International School
Ezbet Fahmy, El Basatin, Cairo 4234330
Tel: +20 2 2516 6619
Curriculum: UK

Bedayia International School
1st Urban Distrcit, El Banafseg Zone, New Cairo City, Cairo 11865
Tel: +20 11 1900 9727
Age range: 4–18 years
Curriculum: IBDP, USA
Language instr: English

British Columbia Canadian International School - East
5th Settlement, Section 34, Suez Road Entrance, P.O Box 98, El Sherouk City, Cairo
Tel: +20 1 0021 28112
Age range: 4–18 years

British Columbia Canadian International School - West
O West Compound, 6th of October City, Giza
Tel: +20 10 2898 1999
Age range: 4–18 years

Cairo American College
1 Midan Digla, Maadi, Cairo 11431
Tel: +20 2 2755 5555
Age range: 4–18 years
Curriculum: IBDP, IBPYP, USA
Language instr: English

Cairo Covenant School
Cairo
Age range: 4–18 years
Curriculum: USA

Cairo English School
P.O. Box 8020, Masaken, Nasr City, Cairo 11371
Tel: +20 2 2249 0200
Age range: 4–18 years
Curriculum: IBDP, UK, IGCSE, ALevs
Language instr: English
(CIS)

Cairo Modern International School
1st Compound, Al Rehab City, Main Road, Cairo
Tel: +20 2344 2859
Age range: G3–18 years
Curriculum: SAT, USA

Carleton College International School
Greenland ElShorouk, Cairo 11837
Tel: +20 11 1245 3338
Age range: 2.5–14 years
Curriculum: IBPYP
Language instr: English, Arabic

Collège Saint Marc, Alexandria
El Shatby, Alexandria
Age range: B4–18 years

Creative International School
Korneish El Nil, Imababa, Qanater Road, Giza, Cairo
Tel: +20 2 3891 1037
Age range: 4–18 years
Curriculum: USA

Dar El Tarbiah - IGCSE Agouza
64 Abdel Moniem Riad Street, Agouza, Giza
Tel: +20 10 0126 2759
Curriculum: IGCSE

Dar El Tarbiah - IGCSE Zamalek
24 Ismail Mohamed Street, Zamalek, Cairo
Tel: +20 12 2219 4862
Curriculum: IGCSE

Delta American School
Mansoura-Domyat Highway, Talkha, Dakahlia 35681
Tel: +20 10 9070 0727
Curriculum: USA

Deutsche Evangelische Oberschule Kairo
P.O. Box 131, Orman, Cairo
Tel: +20 2 3748 1475
Age range: 4–18 years

Deutsche Schule Beverly Hills Kairo
Beverly Hills, 16th District, Beverly Hills Road, Giza
Tel: +20 3857 8070
Age range: 3–18 years
Curriculum: Abitur, IBDP
Language instr: English, German

Deutsche Schule der Borromäerinnen Alexandria
32 Rue Salah-El-Dine, Alexandria 21131
Tel: +20 3398 0145
Age range: 3–18 years
Curriculum: Abitur

Deutsche Schule der Borromäerinnen Kairo
8 Mohamed Mahmoud Street, Bab El Louk, Cairo 11111
Tel: +20 2 2790 0088
Age range: G4–18 years
Curriculum: Abitur

Deutsche Schule Hurghada
Bowling Street, Qesm Hurghada, Hurghada, Red Sea 84511
Tel: +20 10 0461 2747
Age range: 4–18 years
Curriculum: IBDP
Language instr: Arabic, German

Africa

Dover International School
Street 10, Hamza Ibn Abdel-Motaleb, Zone (9) El- Shorouk City, Cairo
Tel: +20 2 2479 6120
Age range: 4–18 years
Curriculum: USA

Dr. Nermien Ismail Schools (NIS) - 6th of October City
6th of October City, Giza
Curriculum: FrenchBacc, UK, USA

Dr. Nermien Ismail Schools (NIS) - El Shorouk City
In front of Banque Misr, El Shohadaa Road, Al Shorouk City, Cairo
Curriculum: FrenchBacc, UK, USA

Dr. Nermien Ismail Schools (NIS) - First Settlement
El-Tagammoe El-Awwal, Extension of Zaker Hussein Street, Beside the Police Academy, Cairo
Curriculum: IBDP, FrenchBacc, UK, USA
Language instr: English

Dr. Nermien Ismail Schools (NIS) - Nasr City
Mostafa el-Nahhas Street, District11, Area 15-16, Nasr City, Cairo
Curriculum: FrenchBacc, UK, USA

Dr. Nermien Ismail Schools (NIS) - New Capital All Girls International School
New Capital, Cairo
Curriculum: FrenchBacc, UK, USA

Dr. Nermien Ismail Schools (NIS) - New Capital National School
In front of Paris Mall, New Capital, Cairo
Curriculum: FrenchBacc, UK, USA

Dr. Nermien Ismail Schools (NIS) - Porto Said
International Coastal Road, Al Manasrah, Port Said
Curriculum: FrenchBacc, UK, USA

Dream International School
Champs Elysee Street, Dream Land, Gate 2, Wahat Road, 6th of October City, Giza
Tel: +20 2 3858 0661
Age range: 4–18 years
Curriculum: National, USA

Ecole Oasis Internationale
Zahraa El Maadi, Quarter No. 3 & No. 7, Part A & B, Cairo 11435
Tel: +20 2 2516 2608
Age range: 3–18 years
No. of pupils: 1554
Curriculum: IBDP, IBMYP, IBPYP, IBCP
Language instr: French

Egypt British International School (EBIS)
1st Urban District, El Banafseg Zone, Area 1, New Cairo City, Cairo
Tel: +20 10 0008 4843
Age range: 3–18 years
Curriculum: UK, IGCSE

Egyptian American International School (EAIS) 6th October
El-Tawba Mosque, 6th of October City, Giza 3233863
Tel: +20 12 0067 3934
Age range: 4–18 years
Curriculum: USA

Egyptian American International School (EAIS) El Shorouk
El Shorouk, Cairo
Tel: +20 12 8195 2665
Age range: 4–16 years
Curriculum: USA

Egyptian American International School (EAIS) New Cairo
62-60 Street 24, New Cairo City, Cairo 4722280
Tel: +20 12 8303 0151
Age range: 4–18 years
Curriculum: USA

Egyptian American School
Ring road behind Nozha Airport, Alexandria 21522
Age range: 4–18 years
Curriculum: ACT, AP, IBDP, USA
Language instr: English

Egyptian British International School (EBIS) 6th October
El-Tawba Mosque, 6th of October City, Giza 3233863
Age range: 4–16 years
Curriculum: UK

Egyptian British International School (EBIS) El Shorouk
El Shorouk, Cairo
Tel: +20 12 8195 2665
Age range: 4–16 years
Curriculum: UK

Egyptian British International School (EBIS) New Cairo
62-60 Street 24, New Cairo City, Cairo 4722280
Tel: +20 12 2734 3587
Age range: 4–18 years
Curriculum: UK

Egyptian English Language Schools (EELS)
Mostafa Kamel Street, Behind Fire Station, El Mandara, Alexandria
Tel: +20 3537 2959
Age range: 4–18 years
Curriculum: National, UK, USA, IGCSE

Egyptian Language School (ELS) New Cairo
62-60 Street 24, Katameya, New Cairo City, Cairo 4722280
Tel: +20 12 2733 3955
Age range: 4–18 years
Curriculum: National
Language instr: English

El Alsson British and American International Schools - NewGiza
P.O. Box 16, KM 22 Cairo-Alex Road, Smart Village, Cairo 12577
Tel: +20 2 3827 0800
Age range: 3–18 years
Curriculum: IBDP, UK, USA, IGCSE, ALevs
Language instr: English

El Gouna International School
Downtown El Gouna, Near Hurghada, Red Sea 84513
Tel: +20 6 5358 0080
Age range: 3.5–18 years
Curriculum: National, UK, IGCSE, ALevs

El Mokatam International Language School
9 El Mokattam, El Khalifa, Cairo
Tel: +20 2 2508 2082
Curriculum: UK, IGCSE
Language instr: English, Arabic

El Rowad College
8 Mostafa El Nahhas Street, 8th District, Nasr City, Cairo
Tel: +20 2 2472 3271
Curriculum: National, UK, USA, IGCSE

El-Fouad International School
El-Ahrar Road, Kafr Mohammed Hussein, El-Shaheed Ahmed Fouar Bakr Street, Zagazig, Sharqia

Elite International School
Airport Road, off Ring Road, Behind Nozha Airport, Abees 10th, Alexandria
Tel: +20 10 9330 7078
Age range: 3–18 years
Curriculum: IBDP, IBMYP, IBPYP
Language instr: English, Arabic

El-Massira Integrated School
N.B 7, 10th of Ramadan City, Sharqia
Tel: +20 10 2333 7437

El-Quds Language Schools
Mostafa Kamel Street, Off 45 St Miami, Alexandria
Tel: +20 3962 5553
Curriculum: National, UK, USA, IGCSE

Europa-Schule Kairo
Abdel Malik Ben Marwan Street, Tagamoa El Khames, New Cairo City, Cairo
Tel: +20 2 2537 3301
Age range: 4–18 years
Curriculum: Abitur

Evolution International School
New Giza Campus, Km 22, Cairo/Alex desert Road, 6th of October City, Giza 12588
Tel: +20 10 0366 6223
Age range: 3–18 years
Curriculum: IBDP
Language instr: English

FES Futures British School
Al-Othman Street, from the extention of Hassan El Maamoun Street, Nasr City, Cairo
Tel: +20 11 5884 6099
Age range: 2.5–18 years
Curriculum: UK

FES Futures International School
Behind Shooting Club, Investors Land, Kattemeya, Cairo
Tel: +20 12 7579 3041
Age range: 2.5–18 years
Curriculum: USA

FES L'Ecole de l'Avenir
Omar Ibn Alkhattab Square, Gate 13, El Rehab, Cairo
Tel: +20 2 2607 5044
Age range: 2.5–18 years
Curriculum: FrenchBacc

Gateway International Montessori School
Katameya Gardens, 5th Settlement, New Cairo City, Cairo
Tel: +20 11 1310 2222
Age range: 3–18 years
Curriculum: IBDP, IBMYP, USA
Language instr: English, Arabic

GEMS Academy Alexandria
Kilo 13 Alexandria-Cairo Agricultural Road, Alexandria
Tel: +2 03 5190 800
Curriculum: IBDP, IBMYP, IBPYP, FrenchBacc, UK
Language instr: English, French

GEMS British International School - Madinaty
Talaat Mostafa Road, Suez Road, Madinaty, Cairo 19511
Tel: +20 10 2223 0014
Age range: 3–18 years
Curriculum: UK
Language instr: English

GEMS British School - Al Rehab
Talaat Mostafa Road, Al Rehab City, New Cairo City, Cairo 11841
Tel: +20 2 2607 0291
Age range: 3–18 years
Curriculum: UK
Language instr: English

GEMS International School - Cairo
Al Rehab Extension, Zone 8, New Cairo City, Cairo
Tel: +20 10 6161 8302
Age range: 3–14 years
Curriculum: IBDP, IBMYP, IBPYP, USA
Language instr: English

Genesis International Schools
29Km. Misr Ismailia Road, Cairo
Tel: +20 12 1140 2252
Curriculum: UK, USA

Global Paradigm Baccalaureate School
ASR2 Mostakbal City, New Cairo City, Cairo 11477
Tel: +20 127 601 2219
Curriculum: IBDP, IBMYP, IBPYP
Language instr: English, Arabic

Africa

Global Paradigm International School
First Settlement, Block K1, Sector 8, New Cairo City, Cairo 16834
Tel: +20 222 461 809/10/12
Age range: 3–18 years
Curriculum: IBDP
Language instr: English

Green Heights International School
First District, Alamn Alaam Compound, Behind Mirage City, New Cairo City, Cairo
Tel: +20 2 2328 5069
Age range: 4–18 years
Curriculum: UK, USA

Green Land - Pré Vert International Schools - GPIS-Egypt
405 Geziret Mohammad, Bashtil, Cairo
Tel: +20 2 01002226053/50/54
Age range: 3–18 years
No. of pupils: 1550
Curriculum: IBDP, IBMYP, IBPYP
Language instr: French, English

Hayah International Academy
South of Police Academy, 5th District, New Cairo 11835
Tel: +202 25373000/3333
Age range: 3–18 years
No. of pupils: 1713
Curriculum: IBDP, IBPYP
Language instr: English

Heritage International School
Al-Yasmine Greenland, Second Touristic Village, 6th of October City, Giza
Tel: +20 10 6858 3873
Curriculum: USA

Integrated Thebes American College in Cairo (ITACC)
Km. 27 Ismailia Desert Road, Cairo
Tel: +20 2 2477 2311
Curriculum: USA

International American School of Alexandria
Agriculture Road, 2k pass abees Gate, Alexandria
Tel: +20 3955 4334
Age range: 4–18 years
Curriculum: SAT, USA

International Arab Egyptian School
Kilo 4.5, Ezz El Din, Ismailia
Tel: +20 26 4331 2327
Age range: 3–18 years
Curriculum: UK, IGCSE, ALevs

International New Future School (Neue Deutsche Schule Alexandria)
El Prince Street, off Moustafa Kamel Street, Mandara Kebly, Alexandria
Tel: +20 3 958 6481
Curriculum: IBDP
Language instr: English

International School of Elite Education
5th Settlement, off Road 90, behind Masraweya Compound, New Cairo City, Cairo
Tel: +20 11 1114 3225
Age range: 4–18 years
Curriculum: IBDP, UK, USA, IGCSE, ALevs
Language instr: English

International Schools of Egypt - Alexandria
Agricultural Road, 500 meters past Abees Gate, Alexandria
Tel: +20 12 2598 5579
Age range: 3–18 years
Curriculum: UK, IGCSE, ALevs

International Schools of Kenana - American Division
30th KM Cairo Ismalia Road, Cairo
Tel: +20 12 2794 0075
Curriculum: USA

Irish School Cairo
Cairo
Age range: 6 months–11 years

Jana Dan International School
Beside the new shooting club at El Katameya, Nasr City Maadi ring road, Cairo
Tel: +20 11 1330 1111
Age range: 4–18 years
Curriculum: USA

Kaumeya Language School
8 Mokarar Takseem El Madares, Ring Road, Abees, Alexandria
Tel: +20 12 8637 7990
Curriculum: IBDP, IBPYP, UK, IGCSE
Language instr: English

King's School The Crown
The Crown, Palm Hills, 6th of October City, Giza 12566
Tel: +20 10 2277 7269
Age range: 3 months–18 years
Curriculum: UK, IGCSE, ALevs
Language instr: English

Leaders International College
21 El Narges Services Region, Off 90th Road, 5th Settlement, New Cairo City, Cairo 11835
Tel: +20 12 7292 4777
Age range: 3–18 years
Curriculum: IBDP, IBMYP, IBPYP, USA
Language instr: English

Lycée Français du Caire - Maadi
7 Rue 12, Maadi, Cairo 11431
Tel: +20 2 2726 0900
Age range: 4–11 years
Curriculum: FrenchBacc

Lycée Français du Caire - Mearag
Land No. 5, El Mearag City Division, 2nd Megawra, Cairo
Tel: +20 2 2726 0900
Age range: 11–18 years
Curriculum: FrenchBacc

Lycée Français du Caire - New Cairo
5th Settlement, El Banafseg Area, New Cairo City, Cairo
Tel: +20 12 8561 5169
Age range: 4–11 years
Curriculum: FrenchBacc

Lycée Français du Caire - Zamalek
8 Ibn Zanki Street, Zamalek, Cairo
Tel: +20 2 2738 4085
Age range: 4–11 years
Curriculum: FrenchBacc

Lycée International Balzac
N Teseen, New Cairo City, Cairo 4731101
Tel: +20 2 2537 9358
Age range: 4–18 years
Curriculum: FrenchBacc
Language instr: Arabic, French

Maadi British International School
4th District, Zahraa El Maadi, Cairo
Tel: +20 2 2517 8288
Age range: 3–17 years
Curriculum: UK
Language instr: English

Maadi Community Study Centre (MCSC)
Building 10, Road 77, Maadi, Cairo 11431
Tel: +20 2 2358 5911
Age range: 4–14 years
Curriculum: UK

Madinaty Integrated Language Schools (MILS)
Wadi Road, Behind South Park, Opposite to B6, Madinaty, Cairo
Tel: +20 10 2805 0305
Age range: 3–18 years
Language instr: English

Madinaty Language School
Talaat Mostafa Road, Opposite to B2, Madinaty, Cairo
Tel: +20 2 2110 9877
Age range: 3–18 years
Language instr: English

Majesty International Schools
Plot (1-2), Al Khamayel Phase III, Gate 6, 26th of July Corridor, 6th of October City, Giza
Tel: +20 10 3050 3000
Age range: 4–18 years
Curriculum: UK, USA, IGCSE
Language instr: English

Malvern College Egypt
B2-B3 South Ring Road, Investment Zone Kattameya, Cairo
Tel: +202 26144400
Age range: 2.6–18 years
No. of pupils: 920
Curriculum: IBDP, IGCSE, ALevs
Language instr: English

Manarat El Mostaqbal International School
Opposite Carrefour, City Center, off the Qattamiya Ring Road, Mokattam, Cairo
Tel: +20 10 0966 6700
Curriculum: USA

Manaret Heliopolis International School
Hazem Salah Street, Ext. Mostafa El Nahas, Nasr City, Cairo 11351
Tel: +20 2 2471 3332
Age range: 3–13 years
No. of pupils: 700
Curriculum: IBDP, IBMYP, IBPYP
Language instr: English

Manor House American & IGCSE School
Heliopolis, Cairo
Tel: +20 2 565 3434
Age range: 3–18 years
Curriculum: UK, USA, IGCSE

Manor House American School
59 El Hussein Street, Dokki, Cairo
Tel: +20 33371067
Age range: 4–18 years
Curriculum: USA

Manor House International School - British Division
7 Abdel Rahman El Rafie Street, Off Mohie El Din Aboul Ezz Street, Mohandessin, Cairo
Tel: +20 3760 8797
Age range: 4–18 years
Curriculum: UK, IGCSE

Mansoura College
Educational Campus, Mansoura Damietta High Way, Mansoura, Dakahlia
Tel: +20 5 0258 8888
Age range: 4–18 years
Curriculum: National, UK, USA, IGCSE
Language instr: English

Memphis International School
K 36 Masr-Ismalia Desert Road, Infront of El Sherouk City, Gate 1, Cairo
Tel: +20 10 2538 9021
Curriculum: USA

Misr Language Schools
Cairo-El Fayoum Desert Road, Giza
Tel: +20 2337 6306
Age range: 3–18 years
Curriculum: National, FrenchBacc, UK, USA, IGCSE

Modern Education Schools
Street 2, 1st District, Area No 4, 5th Settlement, New Cairo City, Cairo 11835
Tel: +20 2 2541 6291
Age range: 4–18 years
Curriculum: National, UK, USA, IGCSE

Modern English School Cairo
P.O. Box 5, South of Police Academy, New Cairo City, Cairo 11835
Tel: +202 2618 9600
Age range: 3.5–18 years
Curriculum: IBDP, UK, USA, IGCSE, ALevs
Language instr: English

Africa

Narmer American College
20 El-Narguis Service Area,
El-Tagamoa El Khames,
New Cairo City, Cairo
Tel: +20 2 2587 4000
Age range: 4–18 years
Curriculum: IBDP, IBMYP, UK, USA, IGCSE
Language instr: English

Nefertari International School
Km 22 Cairo-Ismailia Desert Road,
Nefertari Street, Cairo 11341
Tel: +20 1026604040
Age range: 3–18 years
Curriculum: IBDP, IBPYP, National, FrenchBacc, UK, USA, IGCSE
Language instr: English, Arabic

Nefertari International School - 6th of October
Gamal Abd El-Naser Street, Gardenia Buildings, El-Shams Project, Behind Mall of Arabia, 6 October City
Curriculum: IBPYP, UK, USA
Language instr: English, French

New Cairo British International School
Road 17, 1st District, 3rd Zone, 5th Settlement, New Cairo City, Cairo
Tel: +20 2 2565 7115
Age range: 3–18 years
Curriculum: IBDP, UK, IGCSE, ALevs
Language instr: English

New Castle International School
Al Bashair District, In Al Bashair Service Center, 6th of October City, Giza
Tel: +20 10 2368 0517
Age range: 4–18 years
Curriculum: IBDP, National, UK, USA, IGCSE
Language instr: English, Arabic

New Future International School
El Prince Street, Off Moustafa Kamel Street, Behind ElMontaza 3rd Police Station, Alexandria 5522151
Tel: +20 15 0821 4710
Curriculum: IBPYP
Language instr: English, German

New Generation International Schools
27th KM Cairo-Ismailia Road, Cairo
Tel: +20 10 0606 9977
Age range: 4–18 years
Curriculum: AP, USA

New Horizon International School
8 Al Ofouk Street, Zahraa Al Maadi City, Sector No. 3, Maadi, Cairo
Tel: +20 2 2733 2058
Age range: 4–16 years
Curriculum: National, UK, IGCSE

New Ramses College
P.O. Box 2035, 14 Lofty El Saied Street, Ghamra, Cairo
Tel: +20 2 2445 3444
Age range: 4–16 years
Curriculum: National, UK, IGCSE

New Vision International Schools
P.O. Box 120, Beverly Hills, Sheikh Zayed Road, Giza 12588
Tel: +20 12 0426 5778
Age range: 3–18 years
Curriculum: IBDP, IBMYP, IBPYP, USA
Language instr: English, Arabic

Nile International College
Beside Qibaa, Street 44, Fifth District, New Cairo City, Cairo 11853
Tel: +20 10 6100 0526
Curriculum: IBMYP, IBPYP
Language instr: English

Notion International School
Gamal Eldin Albana Street, Almariotya, Haram, Giza
Tel: +20 2 3746 5406
Age range: 3–18 years
Curriculum: IBDP, IBMYP, IBPYP
Language instr: English

Orouba Language School - Dokki
8 Hussein Wassef Street, Dokki, Giza
Tel: +20 3 748 4496
Age range: 4–18 years
Curriculum: National, UK, IGCSE, ALevs

Orouba Language School - Maadi
1 Amr Street, District 6, New Maadi, Cairo
Tel: +20 2516 8091
Age range: 4–18 years
Curriculum: National, UK, USA, IGCSE, ALevs

Own Heliopolis Schools
Street 12, Sheraton Al Matar, El Nozha, Cairo
Tel: +20 12 0637 3794
Age range: 4–18 years
Curriculum: National, UK, USA, IGCSE

Pakistan International School Cairo
29 Taha Hussein, Mohammed Mazhar, Zamalek, Cairo 4271151
Tel: +20 2 2737 2417
Age range: 4–18 years
Curriculum: UK, IGCSE, ALevs

Pioneers International School
El Qasem, As Soyouf Qebli, (Include Izbat Derbanah), Montaza 2, Alexandria
Tel: +20 3537 1820
Curriculum: USA

Port Said International Schools
Mohamed Aly Street (In front of Golf), El Dawahy District, El Sharq, Port Said 8555136
Tel: +20 6 6372 9644
Age range: 4–18 years
Curriculum: National, USA

Princeton International School
Zizinia, 5th Settlement, Close to AUC Gate 4, New Cairo City, Cairo
Tel: +20 10 9149 7999
Age range: 3–18 years
Curriculum: IBDP, IBMYP, IBPYP, USA
Language instr: English, French

Rahn Schulen Kairo
Plot 15A, Al-Istethmar Region, El-Kattamia, Cairo 11371
Tel: +20 2 2725 2555
Age range: 4–18 years
Curriculum: Abitur, IBDP
Language instr: German

Rajac Language Schools
Km 30 Cairo-Ismailia Desert Road, Cairo
Tel: +20 12 2396 9364
Curriculum: National, FrenchBacc, UK, USA

Regent British School - New Mansoura
Phase 1, Service area, New Mansoura City, Dakahlia
Tel: +20 12 7605 0231
Age range: 3–18 years
Curriculum: UK

Regent British School - West
Cosmic Village, 6th of October City, Giza
Tel: +20 10 6677 5060
Age range: 3–18 years
Curriculum: UK

Royal Canadian School - Cairo
DC-SC-3, Land R2, The Residential Neighbourhood, New Cairo City, Cairo
Tel: +20 1 2898 3111
Curriculum: IBDP
Language instr: English, Arabic

Salahaldin International School
Ja'far ibn Abi Talib, New Cairo City, Cairo
Tel: +20 10 3333 7291
Age range: 4–18 years
Curriculum: IBDP
Language instr: English, Arabic

SAMA International School
P.O. Box 37, Al Mokattam, Maadi, Kattameya Ring Road, Opposite Carrefour, Cairo
Tel: +20 2730 4070
Age range: 4–18 years
Curriculum: National, USA

Schutz American School
P.O. Box 1000, 51 Schutz Street, Alexandria
Tel: +20 3 576 2205
Age range: 3–18 years
Curriculum: IBMYP, IBPYP, USA
Language instr: English, Arabic

Sharm International British School
Block 16, Halomy Street, Naama Bay, Qesm Sharm El Sheikh, South Sinai
Tel: +20 10 0347 0241
Age range: 4–18 years
Curriculum: UK, IGCSE, ALevs
Language instr: English

Sheraton Heliopolis Language Schools
2 Khaled Ibn El Walid Street, Sheraton District, Cairo
Tel: +20 2 2266 2090
Age range: 3–18 years
Curriculum: National, USA

SKILLS - Suad Kafafi International Language Learning Schools
Giza
Tel: +20 10 2664 4419
Age range: 4–18 years
Curriculum: Abitur, National, UK, USA, IGCSE, ALevs

Smart International Schools
Abeess 4th, School Complex, Alexindria
Tel: +20 12 7003 9367
Curriculum: UK, USA
Language instr: English

St. Fatima Schools - Badr
Al-Salam 2, Attaka District, End of Cairo Suez Road, Next to Watanya Petrol Station, Suez
Age range: 4–18 years
Curriculum: National, UK, USA, ALevs

St. Fatima Schools - Nasr City
66 Ismail Al Kabbani Street, Nasr City, Cairo
Tel: +20 2 2260 0961
Age range: 4–18 years
Curriculum: National, UK, USA, ALevs

St. John American School
KM 30 Cairo - Suez Road, Patmos, Cairo
Tel: +20 12 2010 0046
Curriculum: USA

St. Joseph's International School
Banks Street, Hadaba, Sharm El Sheikh, South Sinai
Tel: +20 10 0210 8164

St. Peter's School
3 Abdel Rahman El Rafei, Heliopolis, Cairo 11351
Tel: +20 2 2180 5497
Age range: 4–18 years
Curriculum: National, UK, USA

Sunrise International School
Mubarak 1, Behind Nile Hospital, Hurghada, Red Sea
Tel: +20 65351 3692

The British International School, Cairo
P.O. Box 137, Gezira, Cairo
Tel: +20 2 3827 0444
Age range: 3–18 years
Curriculum: IBDP, UK, GCSE, IGCSE
Language instr: English

Africa

The British School in Cairo
D3 Cairo to Kattameya Ring Road, Maadi, Cairo
Tel: +20 10 0250 6708
Age range: 4–18 years
Curriculum: National, UK, IGCSE, ALevs

The British School of Egypt
9th Zone Service Centre, Dahshour Route, Sheikh Zayed City, Giza
Tel: +20 12 0878 7015
Age range: 2.5–18 years
Curriculum: UK, IGCSE, ALevs

The British School, Alexandria
7 Kafr Abdou Street, Kafr Abdou, Alexandria
Tel: +20 3544 5426
Age range: 3–18 years
Curriculum: UK, GCSE, IGCSE, ALevs
Language instr: English

The International School of Choueifat - Cairo
P.O. Box 2760, Fifth Urban Community, Al Horreya, Heliopolis, New Cairo City, Cairo
Tel: +20 2 2542 8777
Age range: 4–18 years
Curriculum: ACT, AP, SAT, TOEFL, UK, USA, IGCSE, ALevs
Language instr: English

The International School of Choueifat - City of 6 October
6th October City, Giza
Tel: +20 10 0606 9001
Age range: 4–18 years
Curriculum: AP, SAT, TOEFL, UK, USA, IGCSE, ALevs

The International School of Egypt
5th Settlement, 2nd District, Street 68, New Cairo City, Cairo
Tel: +20 2 2564 7038
Age range: 4–18 years
Curriculum: IBDP, USA
Language instr: English

Uptown International School
Al Abageyah, El Mukkatam, Cairo
Tel: +20 12 2584 7419
Curriculum: IBMYP, IBPYP
Language instr: English, Arabic

Windrose Academy
Ring Road - Ain Sukhna Exit, Katameya, Cairo
Tel: +20 2 2749 8700
Age range: 3–18 years
Curriculum: UK, IGCSE, ALevs
Language instr: English

ERITREA

Asmara International Community School (AICS)
Asmara
Tel: +291 1 161705
Age range: 3–18 years
Language instr: English

ESWATINI

Lilima Montessori High School
P.O. Box 8832, Mbabane H100
Tel: +268 24 10 0580
Curriculum: IBMYP
Language instr: English

Sifundzani School
Mbabane
Age range: 4–18 years

UFS International
Jabula Crescent, Mhlambanyatsi
Tel: +268 78 08 1061
Age range: 4–18 years
Curriculum: IGCSE, ALevs
Language instr: English

Waterford Kamhlaba UWC of Southern Africa
Waterford Park, Mbabane H100
Tel: +268 24220867
Age range: 11–20 years
No. of pupils: 627
Curriculum: IBDP, IGCSE
Language instr: English

ETHIOPIA

Andinet International School
P.O. Box 1289, Addis Ababa
Tel: +251 11 647 9986
Age range: 4–18 years
Curriculum: IPC

Bingham Academy
Kolfe, Addis Ababa
Tel: +251 11 279 1791
Age range: 4–18 years
Curriculum: IPC, IGCSE, ALevs
Language instr: English

British International School, Addis Ababa
P.O. Box 5583, Addis Ababa
Tel: +251 11 663 0707
Age range: 3–18 years
Curriculum: IGCSE, ALevs
Language instr: English

German Embassy School Addis Ababa
P.O. Box 1372, Addis Ababa
Tel: +251 11 553 4465
Age range: 4–18 years
Curriculum: IBDP
Language instr: English, German

International Community School of Addis Ababa
Mauritania Road, Addis Ababa
Tel: +251 11 371 1544
Age range: 4–18 years
Curriculum: IBDP, IBPYP
Language instr: English

International School of Africa
Near Italian Base, Nagad, Djibouti
Tel: +253 77 22 4848
Curriculum: USA

Kelem International School
Kazanchis in front of Meles foundation, Addis Ababa
Tel: +251 91 152 7301
Age range: 5–16 years

Lycée Franco-Éthiopien Guébré-Mariam
P.O. Box 1496, Churchill Avenue, Addis Ababa
Tel: +251 11 155 1603
Age range: 4–18 years

One Planet International School
P.O. Box 3115, Code 1250, Addis Ababa
Tel: +251 11 618 1010
Age range: 4–18 years
Curriculum: IGCSE, ALevs

QSI International School of Djibouti
P.O. Box 2384, Lotissement Haramous, Djibouti
Tel: +253 2134 0709
Age range: 3–19 years
Curriculum: ACT, SAT, TOEFL

Sandford International School
P.O. Box 30056 MA, Addis Ababa
Tel: +251 111 233 892
Age range: 2–18 years
Curriculum: IBDP, IPC, IGCSE
Language instr: English

GABON

American International School Libreville
BP 2243, Libreville
Tel: +241 0174 3332
Age range: 4–18 years
Language instr: English

Lycée Franco-Britannique Ecole Internationale
Batterie IV, B.P. 159, Libreville
Tel: 00241 1 17 37 117
Age range: 3–18 years
No. of pupils: 200
Curriculum: IBDP, IBMYP, IBPYP
Language instr: French, English

The International School of Gabon Ruban Vert
Batterie IV, Libreville, Gabon 2144
Tel: +241 11 44 26 70
Age range: 2–19 years
Curriculum: IBDP, IBPYP
Language instr: English, French

GHANA

Accra Grammar School
VVU 54, Oyibi, Accra
Tel: +233 27 700 0034
Curriculum: USA

Akosombo International School
Akosombo
Tel: +233 55 324 8000
Age range: 4–18 years
Curriculum: UK, IGCSE

Alpha Beta Education Centres - Pre-School, Primary & Christian College
Sahara, Dansoman
Tel: +233 30 230 8002
Age range: 18 months–18 years
Curriculum: UK

Al-Rayan International School
P.O. Box AC-84, Accra
Tel: +233 54 189 7254
Age range: 2–19 years
Curriculum: IBDP, IBMYP, IBPYP, IBCP, UK, IGCSE, ALevs
Language instr: English, French

American International School
Nii Klu Osae Avenue, Otinshie Road, East Legon, Accra
Tel: +233 28 954 7951
Age range: 4–18 years
Curriculum: AP, IBDP, USA
Language instr: English, French

Association International School
6 Patrice Lumumba Road, Airport Residential Area, Accra
Tel: +233 30 277 7735
Age range: 2–18 years
Curriculum: IBDP, IBMYP, IBPYP
Language instr: English, French

Aves International Academy
VRA Road Community 25, Tema
Tel: +233 26 615 3097
Age range: 1–18 years
Curriculum: IBDP, UK, IGCSE
Language instr: English

Beacon International School
Peduase Village Avenue, Peduase Lodge, Akuapem Ridge, Aburi
Tel: +233 50 145 4327
Age range: 3–18 years (boarding from 12)
Curriculum: National, UK, IGCSE, ALevs

Cornerstone International Academy
No. 2 Harare Street, Off Mensah Wood Avenue, East Legon, Accra
Tel: +233 30 255 0425
Age range: 3–16 years
Curriculum: IBPYP
Language instr: English, French

Datus International School
P.O. Box 8001, Fraiser Street, Tema
Curriculum: IBPYP
Language instr: English

Africa

Dayspring International Academy
Otano / Adjiriganor before Ability Square Ghana, Adenta
Tel: +233 27 777 7172
Age range: 2–18 years
Curriculum: UK, IGCSE, ALevs

Delhi Private School (DPS) International Ghana
Community 25, Tema
Tel: +233 55 662 0540
Age range: 4–18 years
Curriculum: IBDP, National, UK, IGCSE, ALevs
Language instr: English

Galaxy International School
No. 734 Ashale Botwe Sraha CT 70, Cantonments, Accra
Tel: +233 30 291 1646
Age range: 4–18 years
Curriculum: National, UK, IGCSE, ALevs
Language instr: English

German International School Accra
P.O. Box 30526, Ring Road Central, Accra
Tel: +233 30 222 3522
Age range: 4–18 years
Curriculum: Abitur

Ghana Christian International High School
P.O. Box DD 66, Dodowa
Tel: +233 30 707 9798
Age range: 11–18 years
Curriculum: National, UK, IGCSE, ALevs

Ghana International School
P.O. Box GP 2856, 2nd Circular Road, Cantonments, Accra
Tel: +233 30 397 9588
Age range: 3–18 years
Curriculum: UK, IGCSE, ALevs
Language instr: English

Healthy-Mind International School
P.O. Box GP2066, Boundary Road, Madina, Accra
Tel: +233 55 139 9944
Age range: 3–11 years
Curriculum: IBMYP, IBPYP
Language instr: English, French

International Community College
BAE 29, Baatsona Community 19, off the Spintex Road, Tema
Tel: +233 26 729 3200
Age range: 6 months–18 years
Curriculum: UK, IGCSE, ALevs

International Community School Ghana - Accra
Ogbojo, East Legon, Accra
Tel: +233 54 853 8043
Age range: 2–18 years
Curriculum: IPC, UK, IGCSE, ALevs

International Community School Ghana - Kumasi
P.O. Box KS10631, Pakyi No. 1, Kumasi
Tel: +233 32 209 1443
Age range: 2–18 years
Curriculum: IPC, UK, IGCSE, ALevs
Language instr: English

International School of Accra
Borstal Avenue, Accra
Tel: +233 24 258 6062
Curriculum: IBDP
Language instr: English

International School of Ahafo
Mensah Kumta Village, Newmont Ghana Gold Ltd, Ahafo Mine, Kenyasi
Tel: +233 50 301 7826
Age range: 2–13 years
Curriculum: UK

Learning Skills International School
Adjiringanor Campus, Near Buildaf Estates, Accra
Tel: +233 54 688 4146
Age range: 3–13 years
Curriculum: IBPYP
Language instr: English

Liberty American School (LAS)
32 Liberty Road, Near CSRI Park - American House, East Legon, Accra
Tel: +233 28 954 7951
Age range: 3 months–18 years
Curriculum: USA
Language instr: English

Lincoln Community School
#126/21 Reindolf Road, Abelemkpe, Accra
Tel: +233 30 221 8100
Age range: 4–18 years
No. of pupils: 560
Curriculum: IBDP, IBMYP, IBPYP
Language instr: English

Lycée Français International Jacques Prévert d'Accra
P.O. Box 1813, Cantonments, 6 Bathur Street, East Legon, Accra
Tel: +233 30 254 4067
Age range: 3–18 years
Curriculum: FrenchBacc

Merton International School
No. 1 Merton School Close, Hilla Limann Hwy, Accra
Tel: +233 26 444 4405
Age range: 4–18 years
Curriculum: UK, IGCSE, ALevs

Morgan International Community School
Gomoa Manso, Agona Swedru
Tel: +233 20 641 2859
Age range: 4–18 years
Curriculum: IBDP, UK, IGCSE
Language instr: English

SOS-Hermann Gmeiner International College
Private Mail Bag, Community 6, Tema
Tel: +233 30 320 2907
Age range: 11–18 years
Curriculum: IBDP, IBMYP
Language instr: English

Takoradi International School
Box TD 453, Off Ama Akroma Street, Takoradi
Tel: +233 31 202 5681/709 0621
Age range: 4–18 years
Curriculum: UK, IGCSE

Tema International School
P.O. Box CO864, Off Tema-Akosombo Road (Opposite Afariwaa Farms), Tema
Tel: +233 30 330 5134
Age range: 3–18 years
Curriculum: ACT, IBDP, IBMYP, IBPYP, SAT
Language instr: English

The Hilltop International British School of Kumasi
Cecilia Agyei-Amoako Road, Kumasi
Tel: +233 32 229 9229
Age range: 2–18 years
Curriculum: UK, IGCSE, ALevs

The Owl's Nest International School (ONIS)
4 Shippi Close, East Cantonments, Accra
Tel: +233 24 511 3227
Age range: 16 months–11 years
Curriculum: UK

The Roman Ridge School
P.O. Box GP21057, No. 14 Onyasia Crescent, Roman Ridge, Accra
Tel: +233 30 278 0456
Age range: 4–18 years
Curriculum: UK, IGCSE, ALevs
Language instr: English

Vilac International School
P.O. Box MS444, Mile 7, Maple Leaf Hotel Road, Kingsby Junction, New Achimota, Accra
Tel: +233 24 425 3985

GUINEA

American International School of Conakry
Near Nongo Stadium, Nongo, Conakry
Tel: +224 6542 84530
Age range: 4–18 years
Language instr: English

The English Speaking Community School of Guinea
Kaporo Beach Road, Ruelle face du Marché Kaporo Avant le Centre de Santé, Conakry
Tel: +224 6645 17282
Age range: 1–18 years

KENYA

Braeburn Garden Estate School
Garden Estate Road, Nairobi
Tel: +254 20 501 8000
Age range: 2–18 years
Curriculum: IBDP, IBCP, UK, IGCSE, ALevs
Language instr: English

Braeburn Imani International School
P.O. Box 750, Mang'u Road (Exit 16A off Thika Highway), 00100 Thika
Tel: +254 72 137 4858
Age range: 3–18 years
Curriculum: UK, IGCSE, ALevs
Language instr: English

Braeburn Kisumu International School
P.O. Box 1276, 4010 Kisumu
Tel: +254 72 065 5200
Age range: 2–16 years
Curriculum: UK, IGCSE

Braeburn Mombasa International School
P.O. Box 83009, Malindi Road, off Cement Factory/Vescon Road, JCC Road, 80100 Mombasa
Tel: +254 72 384 6878
Age range: 2–18 years
Curriculum: UK, IGCSE, ALevs
Language instr: English

Braeburn Nanyuki International School
P.O. Box 1537, 10400 Nanyuki
Tel: +254 72 048 6604
Age range: 2–13 years
Curriculum: UK

Braeburn School
P.O. Box 45112, Gitanga Road, Lavington, 00100 Nairobi
Tel: +254 72 268 5575
Age range: 3–18 years
Curriculum: UK, IGCSE, ALevs
Language instr: English

Braeside School
P.O. Box 25578, Off Muthangari Road, Lavington, 00603 Nairobi
Tel: +254 20 501 8000
Age range: 3–18 years
Curriculum: UK, IGCSE, ALevs

Brookhouse School, Karen
Magadi Road, Nairobi
Tel: +254 72 220 4413
Age range: 1–18 years
Curriculum: National, UK, IGCSE, ALevs
Language instr: English

Africa

Brookhouse School, Runda
Off Kiambu Road, Nairobi
Tel: +254 70 439 2000
Age range: 1–18 years
Curriculum: National, UK, IGCSE, ALevs
Language instr: English

Cavina School
Elgeyo Marakwet Road, Nairobi
Age range: 2–13 years
Curriculum: UK
Language instr: English

Coast Academy
Kaunda Avenue, Mombasa
Tel: +254 20 210 7788
Age range: 3–18 years
Curriculum: UK, IGCSE, ALevs

German School Nairobi (Michael Grzimek Schule)
P.O. Box 978, Limuru Road, Gigiri (across from Village Market), 00621 Nairobi
Tel: +254 721 258 417
Age range: 18 months–18 years
Curriculum: Abitur

Greensteds International School
Private Bag, Nakuru
Tel: +254 50 50770
Age range: 3–18 years
Curriculum: UK

Hillcrest Preparatory School
P.O. Box 24819, 00502 Karen, Nairobi
Tel: +254 72 425 6173
Age range: 18 months–13 years
Curriculum: UK

Hillcrest Secondary School
P.O. Box 24819, 00502 Karen, Nairobi
Tel: +254 71 060 0359
Age range: 13–18 years
No. of pupils: 570
Curriculum: UK, IGCSE, ALevs
Language instr: English

International School of Kenya
P.O. Box 14103, 00800 Nairobi
Tel: +254 202 091 308
Age range: 4–18 years
Curriculum: IBDP, USA
Language instr: English

Kenton College Preparatory School
P.O. Box 25406, Gichugu Road, 00603 Nairobi
Tel: +254 203 541 513
Age range: 6–13 years
Curriculum: UK
Language instr: English

Light Academy Mombasa
P.O. Box 1835, Nyali, 80100 Mombasa
Tel: +254 731 395 162
Age range: 3–18 years
Curriculum: UK, IGCSE, ALevs
Language instr: English

Light International School - Malindi
P.O. Box 1835, 80100 Malindi
Tel: +254 716 839 822
Age range: 3–18 years
Curriculum: UK, IGCSE, ALevs

Light International School - Mombasa
P.O. Box 1835, Nyali, 80100 Mombasa
Tel: +254 784 777 771
Age range: 3–18 years
Curriculum: UK, IGCSE, ALevs

Light International School - Nairobi
P.O. Box 1799, Karen, 00502 Nairobi
Tel: +254 788 185 595
Age range: 4–18 years (boarding from 11)
Curriculum: UK, IGCSE, ALevs

Lycée Français International Denis Diderot
Argwings Kodhek Road, Kilimani (Near Yaya Center), Nairobi
Tel: +254 202 437 714
Age range: 2–18 years
Curriculum: FrenchBacc
Language instr: English, French

Mombasa Academy
P.O. Box 86487, 80100 Mombasa
Tel: +254 414 471 629
Age range: 3–18 years
Curriculum: UK, IGCSE, ALevs

M-PESA Foundation Academy
P.O. Box 7954, 01000 Thika
Tel: +254 703 200 000
Age range: 13–18 years
No. of pupils: 588
Curriculum: IBDP, IBMYP, IBCP
Language instr: English

Mustard Seed International Schools
16105 Kiamunyi, Along the main Nakuru-Eldoret Highway, Nakuru
Tel: +254 721 300 121
Age range: 2–18 years
Curriculum: UK, IGCSE, ALevs

Nairobi Jaffery Academy
Naushad Merali Drive, Nairobi
Tel: +254 727 441 218
Age range: 2–18 years
Curriculum: UK, IGCSE, ALevs

Nairobi Waldorf School
Miotoni Road, Karen, Nairobi
Tel: +254 722 823 463
Age range: 4–18 years
Curriculum: IBDP
Language instr: English

Naisula School
Off Nairobi-Namanga Road, Kajiado
Tel: +254712 245 702
Age range: 13–18 years
Curriculum: IBDP, UK, IGCSE, ALevs
Language instr: English, Swahili

Oshwal Academy Mombasa
Off Beach Road West, Nyali, Mombasa
Tel: +254 722 207 785
Age range: 2–18 years
Curriculum: IPC, UK, IGCSE, ALevs
Language instr: English

Oshwal Academy Nairobi
First Parklands Avenue, Off Mpaka Road, Parklands, Nairobi
Tel: +254 725 529 622
Age range: 2–18 years
Curriculum: UK, IGCSE, ALevs

Pembroke House School
P.O. Box 31, Nyahururu Road, 20116 Gilgil
Tel: +254 711 875 972
Age range: 2–13 years
Curriculum: UK

Peponi House
P.O. Box 23203, Lower Kabete, 00604 Nairobi
Tel: +254 202 585 710
Age range: 3–13 years (boarding from 11)
Curriculum: UK
Language instr: English

Peponi School
P.O. Box 236, 00232 Ruiru
Tel: +254 203 546 456
Age range: 13–18 years
Curriculum: UK, IGCSE, ALevs
Language instr: English

Premier Academy
Prof. Wangari Maathai Road, Nairobi
Tel: +254 722 205 855
Age range: 2.5–19 years
Curriculum: UK, IGCSE, ALevs

Rift Valley Academy
P.O. Box 80, 00220 Kijabe
Tel: +254 713 000 700
Age range: 4–18 years
Curriculum: USA, IGCSE

Rosslyn Academy
P.O. Box 14146, 00800 Nairobi
Tel: +254 202 635 294
Age range: 4–18 years
Curriculum: AP, USA

Rusinga Schools
P.O. Box 25088, Lavington, 00603 Nairobi
Tel: +254 709 554 101
Age range: 2–19 years
Curriculum: UK, IGCSE, ALevs

SABIS International School - Runda
P.O. Box 111, Two Rivers, 00627 Nairobi
Tel: +254 743 162 670
Age range: 4–18 years
Curriculum: UK, USA

Sandpiper International School
Off Lamu Road, Along Golf Course Drive, Opposite Africa Pearl Hotel, Malindi
Tel: +254 788 062 618
Age range: 18 months–18 years
Curriculum: UK
Language instr: English

St Andrew's Turi Prep School
Private Bag 20106, Molo
Tel: +254 722 209 750
Age range: 3–13 years
Curriculum: UK
Language instr: English

St Andrew's Turi Senior School
Private Bag 20106, Molo
Tel: +254 735 337 736
Age range: 13–18 years
Curriculum: UK, GCSE, IGCSE, ALevs
Language instr: English

St. Austin's Academy
P.O. Box 25138, James Gichuru Road, Nairobi
Tel: +254 202 165 653
Age range: 2–18 years
Curriculum: UK, IGCSE, ALevs

St. Christopher's Schools
P.O. Box 21378, 00505 Nairobi
Tel: +254 723 318 833
Age range: 18 months–18 years
Curriculum: UK, IGCSE, ALevs

St. Mary's School - Nairobi
P.O. Box 40580, 00100 Nairobi
Tel: +254 721 490 140
Age range: 3–18 years
Curriculum: IBDP, IGCSE, ALevs
Language instr: English

Still I Rise International School - Nairobi
Off Huruma Road, Mathare, Nairobi
Curriculum: IBMYP
Language instr: English, Swahili

The Aga Khan Academy Mombasa
P.O. Box 90066-80100, Mbuyuni Road, Kizingo, Mombasa
Tel: +254 735 931 144
Age range: 6–18 years
Curriculum: IBDP, IBMYP, IBPYP
Language instr: English, Swahili

The Aga Khan Academy, Nairobi
P.O. Box 44424-00100, 1st Parklands Avenue, off Limuru Road, Nairobi
Tel: Junior: +254 0733 758 510, Senior: +254 736 380 101
Age range: 3–19 years
No. of pupils: 1020
Curriculum: IBDP, IBMYP, IBPYP
Language instr: English

Africa

The Aga Khan High School, Nairobi
P.O. Box 42171-00100,
Waiyaki Way, Nairobi
Tel: +254 736 801 580
Age range: 11–18 years
Curriculum: National,
UK, IGCSE, ALevs

The Aga Khan Nursery School, Nairobi
PO Box 14998, Nairobi 00800
Tel: +254 020 374 2114
Age range: 3–4 years
Curriculum: IBPYP

The Banda School
P.O. Box 24722, Magadi Road,
Langata, 00502 Nairobi
Tel: +254 709 951 000
Age range: 1–13 years
Curriculum: UK
Language instr: English

The Nairobi Academy
P.O. Box 24817, Langata Road, Next to Mamba Village, 00502 Nairobi
Tel: +254 722 208 365
Age range: 2–19 years
Curriculum: IBDP, UK, IGCSE, ALevs
Language instr: English, Swahili

The Vale School Muthaiga
Muthaiga Road, Nairobi
Tel: +254 708 191 397
Age range: 1–9 years
Curriculum: IBPYP
Language instr: English

West Nairobi School
P.O. Box 1333, 18 Miotoni Lane,
Karen, 00502 Nairobi
Tel: +254 709 331 000
Age range: 4–18 years
Curriculum: USA

LESOTHO

American International School of Lesotho
P.O. Box 333, Old Europa, Maseru 100
Tel: +266 22 322 987
Age range: 3–14 years
Language instr: English

Machabeng College, International School of Lesotho
P.O. Box 1570, Maseru 100
Tel: +266 22 313 224
Age range: 11–19 years
Curriculum: IBDP, IGCSE, ALevs
Language instr: English

Maseru Preparatory School
Cnr Caldwell & Tona-Kholo
Road, Maseru 100
Tel: +266 22 312 276
Age range: 2–11 years
Language instr: English

LIBERIA

American International School of Monrovia
P.O. Box 1625, Old Road,
Congo Town, Monrovia
Tel: +231 777 818 775
Age range: 3–18 years
Curriculum: AP, SAT, USA

Our Lady of Grace International School
15th Street, Sinkor, Monrovia 1000
Tel: +231 880 30 00 02
Curriculum: IBDP
Language instr: English, French

LIBYA

Benghazi European School
P.O. Box 300, Benghazi
Tel: +218 61 223 3188
Age range: 11–18 years
Curriculum: IGCSE, ALevs

Canadian Academy of Libya
Serraj Area, Tripoli
Tel: +218 92 463 4628
Age range: 4–18 years

International School Benghazi
Al Hawaree, Benghazi
Tel: +218 61 470 0005
Age range: 4–18 years
Curriculum: UK, IGCSE, ALevs
Language instr: English

ISM International School
Hai Andalus, Janzur, Gurgi, Tripoli
Tel: +218 91 668 7834

The British School of Benghazi
P.O. Box 536, Benghazi
Tel: +218 61 222 5822
Language instr: English

MADAGASCAR

Ambatovy International School
Management Housing Village,
Takapala, Toamasina
Tel: +261 32 33 667 74
Age range: 4–18 years
Curriculum: AP, USA

The American School of Antananarivo
Lotissement Le Park Alarobia,
Antananarivo 101
Tel: +261 20 22 420 39
Age range: 3–18 years
Curriculum: IBDP, IBMYP, IBPYP, USA
Language instr: English

MALAWI

Bambino Schools
Area 15, Lilongwe
Tel: +265 990 929 001
Age range: 3–16 years

Bishop Mackenzie International School
Barron Avenue, Lilongwe
Tel: +265 1 756 631
Age range: 4–18 years
Curriculum: IBDP, IBMYP, IBPYP
Language instr: English

Hillview International School
P.O. Box 5809, Hetherwick
Road, Limbe
Tel: +265 21 211 4477
Age range: 3–16 years
Curriculum: IGCSE

Kamuzu Academy
Private Bag 1, Mtunthama
Tel: +265 1 259 246
Age range: 11–18 years
Curriculum: IGCSE, ALevs
Language instr: English

Mzuzu International Academy
P.O. Box 20165, Mzuzu
Tel: +265 887 572 177
Age range: 4–16 years
Language instr: English

Sir Harry Johnston International School
P.O. Box 52, Kalimbuka Road, Zomba
Tel: +265 1 525 280
Age range: 2–16 years
Curriculum: IGCSE

Southend Secondary School
P.O. Box 2764, Chikawa
Road, Blantyre
Tel: +265 1 638 058
Age range: 11–16 years

St Andrew's International High School
Private Bag 211, Brereton Drive,
Nyambadwe, Blantyre
Tel: +265 891 000 437
Age range: 11–18 years
Curriculum: IGCSE, ALevs
Language instr: English

St Andrew's International Primary School
P.O. Box 593, Blantyre
Tel: +265 999 970 998
Age range: 4–11 years

MALI

American International School of Bamako
Rue 90, Port 134, Bougouba,
Sotuba, Bamako
Tel: +223 6530 0909
Age range: 3–18 years
Curriculum: AP, USA
Language instr: English

Ecole Les Lutins
Sotuba ACI, Bamako
Tel: +223 7799 4747
Age range: 4–11 years
Curriculum: FrenchBacc

Enko Bamako International School
B.P. 104, Quartier du Fleuve, Avenue
De L'yser, Porte 510, Bamako
Tel: +223 9369 5283
Age range: 11–19 years
Curriculum: IBDP
Language instr: English, French

Lycée Français Liberté de Bamako
B.P. 910, Boulevard du
Peuple, Bamako
Tel: +223 4498 0180
Age range: 4–18 years
Curriculum: FrenchBacc

MAURITANIA

American International School of Nouakchott
B.P. 3107, Nouakchott
Tel: +222 4525 2967
Age range: 4–18 years
Curriculum: USA
Language instr: English

Lycée Français Théodore Monod
B.P. 4911, Nouakchott
Tel: +222 4525 1850
Curriculum: FrenchBacc

TLC International School
55 E. Nord, Nouakchott
Tel: +222 4604 1532
Age range: 4–18 years
Curriculum: USA
Language instr: English

MAURITIUS

Alexandra House School
King George V Avenue, Floreal
Tel: +230 696 4108
Age range: 4–11 years
Curriculum: UK
Language instr: English

Clavis International Primary School
Mount Ory, Moka
Tel: +230 433 4439
Age range: 4–11 years
Curriculum: IBPYP
Language instr: English

Africa

École du Centre - Collège Pierre Poivre
Helvetia, Saint Pierre 81405
Tel: +230 433 2475
Age range: 3–18 years
Curriculum: FrenchBacc

Ecole du Nord
Village Labourdonnais, Mapou 31803
Tel: +230 266 3009
Age range: 3–16 years
Curriculum: FrenchBacc

International Preparatory School
Route Royale, Labourdonnais Village, Mapou
Tel: +230 266 1973
Age range: 3–11 years
Curriculum: IBPYP
Language instr: English, French

Le Bocage International School
Mount Ory, Moka
Tel: +230 433 9900
Age range: 11–19 years
Curriculum: IBDP, IBMYP, IBCP, IGCSE
Language instr: English

Lycée La Bourdonnais
Ramdenee Building, Rue Rochecouste, Forest Side, Curepipe 74438
Tel: +230 6706 097
Age range: 4–16 years
Curriculum: FrenchBacc

Northfields International School
Main road, Labourdonnais Village, Mapou 31803
Tel: +230 266 9448
Age range: 18 months–18 years
Curriculum: IBDP, IBMYP, IGCSE
Language instr: English

Westcoast International Primary School
Flic en Flac Road, Cascavelle 90203
Tel: +230 452 9193
Age range: 4–11 years
Curriculum: IPC
Language instr: English

Westcoast International Secondary School
Flic en Flac Road, Cascavelle 90203
Tel: +230 489 2034
Age range: 11–18 years
Curriculum: IBDP, IGCSE
Language instr: English

MOROCCO

Al Akhawayn School of Ifrane (ASI)
Al Akhawayn University, Ifrane
Tel: +212 535 862349
Age range: 3–18 years
Curriculum: USA
Language instr: English

American Academy Casablanca
RN 3020 Ville Verte, Casa Green Town, Bouskoura 27182
Tel: +212 529 039112
Age range: 4–18 years
Curriculum: AP, IBDP, USA
Language instr: English, French

American School of Marrakesh
B.P. 6195, Route de Ouarzazate (km 9), Marrakesh 40000
Tel: +212 524 329860
Age range: 2–18 years
Curriculum: IBDP, USA
Language instr: English

American School of Tangier
149 Rue Christophe Colomb, Tangier
Tel: +212 539 939827
Age range: 3–18 years
Curriculum: USA
Language instr: English, French, Arabic

British International School of Casablanca
P3020 Route Sidi Messoud, Casablanca 20000
Tel: +212 520 500200
Age range: 3–18 years
Curriculum: IGCSE, ALevs

Casablanca American School
Route de la Mecque, Lotissement Ougoug, Quartier Californie, Casablanca 20150
Tel: +212 522 793939
Age range: 3–18 years
Curriculum: IBDP, IPC
Language instr: English

College Anatole France
Rue Vouziers, Casablanca 20300
Tel: +212 522 242936

Dar Essalaam American School
Avenue Haj Mohamed Bahraoui, Rabat 10220
Tel: +212 538 050080
Curriculum: IBDP
Language instr: English

Ecole André Chénier
32 Bd Lyazidi, Quartier Hassan, Rabat 10000
Tel: +212 537 724521
Age range: 3–11 years
Curriculum: FrenchBacc

Ecole Paul Cézanne
Place Jean Courtin, (près du lycée Descartes), Rabat 10080
Tel: +212 537 672637
Age range: 3–11 years
Curriculum: FrenchBacc

Écoles Al Madina, Site Ain Sebaa
Km 9, route de Rabat, Hay Chabab, Ain sébàa, Casablanca
Tel: +212 522 756969
Age range: 3–18 years
Curriculum: IBMYP
Language instr: French, Arabic

Écoles Al Madina, Site Californie
Lotissement Bellevue 2, Rue 3 Californie, Casablanca
Tel: +212 522 505097
Age range: 3–18 years
Curriculum: IBMYP
Language instr: French, Arabic

Écoles Al Madina, Site Polo
52 Boulevard Nador, Polo, Casablanca
Tel: +212 522 210505
Age range: 3–18 years
Curriculum: IBMYP
Language instr: French, Arabic

George Washington Academy
Bd. Abdelhadi Boutaleb, (ex km 5.6 Route d'Azemmour), Casablanca 20220
Tel: +212 522 953000
Age range: 3–18 years
Curriculum: IBDP, USA
Language instr: English, French, Arabic

Groupe Scolaire Al Karaouiyine
350 Boulevard Sebta, Lotisement Anfa, Mohammedia
Tel: +212 523 314770
Language instr: Arabic, French

Groupe Scolaire La Résidence
87-89 Avenue 2 mars, Casablanca
Tel: +212 522 809050/51
Age range: 2–20 years
Curriculum: IBMYP
Language instr: French

Institut Scolaire les Palmiers
Ain Sebaa 76 Rue Abdelhamid Bnou Badiss, Casablanca 20590
Tel: +212 522 343757
Age range: 3–18 years
Language instr: Arabic, English, French

Institution El Yakada
Route de Méhdia, Lotissement Koutoubia (Avant Hay Chemaou), Salé
Tel: +212 537 844844
Age range: 4–18 years
Curriculum: IBMYP
Language instr: English, French

International School of Morocco
3 Impasse Jules Gros, Quartier Oasis, Casablanca
Tel: +212 522 993987
Age range: 2–7 years
Curriculum: IBPYP
Language instr: English

Khalil Gibran School
4 Avenue Bir Kacem, Souissi, Rabat
Tel: +212 661 959067
Age range: 3–18 years
Curriculum: National, UK, IGCSE, ALevs
Language instr: English, French, Arabic

Lycée Français Guy de Maupassant
Quartier Almaz, Rocade Sud-Ouest, Casablanca
Tel: +212 5 22 65 43 00
Age range: 2–18 years
No. of pupils: 2276
Curriculum: FrenchBacc
Language instr: Arabic, English, French

Lycée Lyautey
260 Boulevard Ziraoui, Casablanca 20040
Tel: +212 522 436900
Age range: 3–18 years
Curriculum: FrenchBacc

Newton International School
Rue Ibn Khafaja, Anfa, Mohammedia
Tel: +212 523 316552
Age range: 11–18 years
Curriculum: IBMYP
Language instr: French

Planete Montessori International School
Site Agdal: Lotissement Palm Tree Paradise No. 5, Mechouar Essaid, Marrakesh
Tel: +212 623 861429
Age range: 3–12 years
Curriculum: IBPYP
Language instr: English, French

Rabat American School
Fath 1, Ave. Al Mohit Al Hadi, Almanzeh-Yacoub Al Mansour, Rabat 10052
Tel: +212 537 758590
Age range: 4–18 years
Curriculum: IBDP
Language instr: English

Saudi School in Rabat
10 Rue Abda, Rabat
Tel: +212 537 636155

MOZAMBIQUE

American International School of Mozambique
P.O. Box 2026, Rua de Rio Raraga 266, Maputo
Tel: +258 822 255247
Age range: 4–18 years
Curriculum: IBDP, IBMYP, IBPYP
Language instr: English

Benga Riverside International School
Moatize
Tel: +258 847 175447
Age range: 3–16 years
Curriculum: IBPYP
Language instr: English

Africa

Enko Riverside International School
Rua José Macamo 175, Polana, Maputo
Tel: +258 845 409151
Age range: 11–19 years
Curriculum: IBDP, UK, IGCSE
Language instr: English

Enko Sekeleka International School
Complexo Residencial de Nhamacunda, Vilankulo
Tel: +258 829 922112
Age range: 2–19 years
Curriculum: UK, IGCSE, ALevs

Grandeur International School
1463 Ave. Dos Martires da Machava, Maputo
Tel: +258 826 555550
Age range: 4–18 years
Curriculum: UK, IGCSE, ALevs

Lycée Français International Gustave Eiffel
Rio Raraga No. 203, Polana Caniço, Maputo
Tel: +258 823 126410
Age range: 4–18 years
Curriculum: FrenchBacc

Maputo International School
C.P. 4152, 389 Rua da Nachingwea, Maputo
Tel: +258 21 492131
Age range: 3–18 years
Curriculum: UK, IGCSE, ALevs

The Aga Khan Academy Maputo
Av. Zimbabwe, 212 Matola 'A', Maputo
Tel: +258 853 016339
Age range: 3–13 years
Curriculum: IBDP, IBMYP, IBPYP
Language instr: English, Portuguese

NAMIBIA

Deutsche Höhere Privatschule Windhoek
P.O. Box 78, 11-15 Church Street, Windhoek
Tel: +264 61 373100
Age range: 4–18 years

St George's Diocesan School
17-21 Sinclair Road, Windhoek
Tel: +264 61 234133
Age range: 4–18 years
Curriculum: IGCSE, ALevs
Language instr: English

St Paul's College
P.O. Box 11736, Windhoek
Tel: +264 61 227783
Age range: 4–18 years
Language instr: English

The International School of Walvis Bay
P.O. Box 487, 86 Hage Geingob Street, Walvis Bay
Tel: +264 64 203995
Age range: 4–18 years
Curriculum: UK, IGCSE, ALevs

Windhoek International School
P/Bag 16007, Scheppmann Street, Pioneers Park Ext. 1, Windhoek
Tel: +264 61 241783
Age range: 3–18 years
Curriculum: IBDP, IBMYP, IBPYP, IGCSE
Language instr: English

NIGER

American International School of Niamey
P.O. Box 11201, c/o US Embassy, Rue des Ambassades Kouara Kano, Niamey
Tel: +227 20 723942
Age range: 3–18 years
Curriculum: USA

Lycée Enoch Olinga
B.P. 12255, Quartier Dar-es-Salam, Niamey 8001
Tel: +227 94 959872
Age range: 11–18 years
Curriculum: IBDP
Language instr: French

NIGERIA

Abuja Capital International College
352/352 Sunny Ade Street, off Road 35, off Pa. Michael Imoudu Ave, Gwarinpa Estate, Abuja, FCT
Tel: +234 906 566 8535
Age range: 3–18 years
Curriculum: IGCSE

Access International School
P.O. Box 13582, Magboro Akeran, Lagos-Ibadan Expressway, Ikeja, Lagos
Tel: +234 803 442 2420
Age range: 3–16 years

Acorns and Oaks Academy
11 Ambrose Ogbonna Avenue, Off Stadium Road, Port Harcourt, Rivers
Tel: +234 704 489 3886
Age range: 3–11 years
Language instr: English

Aduvie International School
1 Aduvie Close, Off Aduvie Way, Jahi, Abuja, FCT
Tel: +234 808 939 4474
Age range: 3–18 years
Curriculum: IGCSE

American Christian Academy
PO Box 19629, 2, 4, 6, Shell Close, Onireke, Ibadan, Oyo
Tel: +234 809 981 4312
Age range: 4–18 years
Curriculum: IGCSE, ALevs

American International School of Abuja
Plot 346, Cadastral Zone B 02, Durumi District, Abuja, FCT
Tel: +234 703 215 3798
Age range: 3–18 years
Curriculum: AP, USA
Language instr: English

American International School of Lagos
Behind 1004 Estates, Victoria Island, Lagos
Tel: +234 818 663 2769
Age range: 3–18 years
Curriculum: IBDP, USA
Language instr: English

American University of Nigeria Schools
99 Lamido Zubairu Way, Yola Bypass, Yola, Adamawa
Tel: +234 706 778 9426
Age range: 6 months–16 years
Curriculum: National, USA

Atlantic Hall School
Epe, Lagos
Tel: +234 706 421 5003
Age range: 11–18 years
Curriculum: UK, IGCSE

Attwool School
Awoyaya, Lagos
Tel: +234 814 886 0745
Age range: 4–18 years

Avi-Cenna International School
6 Harold Shodipo Crescent, Ikeja, Lagos
Tel: +234 1 342 6271
Age range: 2.5–16 years
Curriculum: UK, IGCSE
Language instr: English

Bridge House College
Plot 8, Block II, Royal Palm Avenue, Osborne Phase II Foreshore, Ikoyi, Lagos
Tel: +234 802 842 7208
Age range: 16–18 years
Curriculum: SAT, TOEFL, UK, USA, ALevs

British International School Nigeria
1 Landbridge Avenue, Oniru Private Estate, Victoria Island, Lagos
Tel: +234 1 291 5022
Age range: 11–18 years
Curriculum: UK, ALevs
Language instr: English

British Nigerian Academy
Drive 6, Prince & Princess Estate, Duboyi District, P.M.B 5285, Wuse, Abuja, FCT
Tel: +234 703 414 5537
Age range: 11–18 years
Curriculum: IBDP, IGCSE
Language instr: English

Brookstone School International
No.1 Brookstone Close, GRA Phase 3, Port Harcourt, Rivers
Tel: +234 703 402 2088
Age range: 15 months–18 years
Language instr: English

Buckswood School Nigeria
Lords Estate, Ago-Oko Titun, Sagamu / Abeokuta Express Way, Abeokuta, Ogun
Tel: +234 803 335 8283
Curriculum: SAT, TOEFL, UK, USA, IGCSE, ALevs

Caleb British International School
Caleb Adebogun Crescent, Abijo GRA, Lekki, Lagos
Tel: +234 901 161 8109
Age range: 3–18 years
Curriculum: UK, IGCSE

Cedar Court British International School
10 Imgbi Road, Amarata, Yenagoa Bayelsa State
Age range: 3–11 years

Cedarwood School
6 Olaribigbe Street, 5th Avenue, Rumuibekwe, Port Harcourt, Rivers
Tel: +234 803 312 2894
Curriculum: UK
Language instr: English

CEDEC International Schools
14 Alhaji Yusuf Street, Olodi Apapa, Lagos
Tel: +234 906 000 7498
Age range: 4–16 years

Children's International School
Plot 8, Amore Street, Lekki Phase 1, Lagos
Tel: +234 903 848 5768
Age range: 3–18 years
Curriculum: UK, IGCSE, ALevs
Language instr: English

Chrisland Schools
P.M.B. 21614, 26 Opebi Road, Ikeja, Lagos
Tel: +234 906 313 5544
Age range: 4–18 years
Curriculum: National, UK, IGCSE, ALevs

Africa

City of Knowledge Academy
P.M.B. 2144, Itanrin Ososa Junction, Benin-Sagamu Expressway, Ijebu-Ode, Ogun
Tel: +234 706 903 9881
Age range: 11–18 years
Curriculum: National, UK

Corona School Gbagada
2/10 Olujobi Crescent, Gbagada Anthony Behind Bertola Machinery, Lagos
Tel: +234 903 111 0444
Age range: 3 months–11 years
Curriculum: IPC, National, UK

Corona School Ikoyi
No. 6 Mekunwen Road, off Bourdillon Road, Ikoyi, Lagos
Tel: +234 809 056 5468
Age range: 3 months–18 years
Curriculum: IPC, National, UK, IGCSE, ALevs

Corona School Lekki
Block 35 Corona Drive, Abijo GRA Scheme 2, Lagos
Tel: +234 809 056 5472
Age range: 3 months–11 years
Curriculum: IPC, National, UK

Corona School Victoria Island
P.M.B. 1963, Waziri Ibrahim Crescent, Off Adeola Odeku Street, Victoria Island, Lagos
Tel: +234 903 111 0222
Age range: 3 months–11 years
Curriculum: IPC, National, UK

Cradle to Crayon School
37 Lake Chad Crescent, Maitama, Abuja, FCT
Tel: +234 703 595 4101
Age range: 9 months–5 years
Language instr: English

CTC International School
23 Sobo Arobiodu Street, Ikeja, Lagos
Tel: +234 1 493 6874

Day Waterman College
Asu Village Road, Off Abeokuta-Sagamu Expressway, Abeokuta, Ogun
Tel: +234 705 678 0016
Age range: 11–16 years
Curriculum: National, SAT, UK, IGCSE

Debiruss School
Debiruss Drive, Behind Golden Park Estate, Lekki-Epe Express Way, Lekki, Lagos
Tel: +234 818 669 3218
Age range: 3–18 years
Curriculum: National, UK

Delightsome Land School
229A & 229B Muri Okunola Street, Victoria Island, Lagos
Tel: +234 1270 1223
Age range: 1–11 years
Curriculum: National, UK

Deutsche Schule Abuja
Gwarinpa, Abuja, FCT
Tel: +234 803 906 7000
Age range: 3–13 years
Curriculum: Abitur, UK

Divine Royal International College
Along Nkpor-Umuoji Road, Nkpor, Anambra
Tel: +234 703 863 8417
Age range: 13–18 years
Curriculum: National, UK

D-Ivy College
153 Ilo-Awela Road, Toll Gate, Ota, Ogun
Tel: +234 807 975 3320
Age range: 4–18 years
Curriculum: National, SAT, TOEFL, UK
Language instr: English

Doregos Private Academy
Bernardino Doregos Street, off BO/BQ Street, Federal Housing Estate, Akinogun, Ipaja, Lagos
Tel: +234 909 877 1453
Age range: 11–18 years
Curriculum: National, SAT, TOEFL, UK, IGCSE, ALevs

Dowen College
18 Adebayo Dohery Road, Lekki Phase 1, Lagos
Tel: +234 906 000 1032
Age range: 13–18 years
Curriculum: National, SAT, TOEFL, UK, IGCSE
Language instr: English

Ebenezery Heights International Schools
007-013 Soji Olagunju Street, Off Alpha Beach Road, Lekki, Lagos
Tel: +234 802 800 0440

École Française de Kano
4 Hospital Road, Kano
Tel: +234 64972779
Curriculum: UK

École Française Marcel Pagnol d'Abuja
After Prince and Princess Estate, Kaura, Abuja, FCT
Tel: +234 916 441 7221
Age range: 2–18 years
Curriculum: FrenchBacc

Edgewood College
13 Sule Onabiyi Street, Off Christ Avenue, Off Admiralty Way (By Tantalizers), Lekki Phase 1, Lekki, Lagos
Tel: +234 812 580 5503
Age range: 11–18 years
Curriculum: UK, IGCSE, ALevs

Emerald Schools
c/o 8/10 Olawale Daodu Street, Ifako Gbagada, Lagos
Tel: +234 909 663 0728
Age range: 4–18 years
Curriculum: TOEFL
Language instr: English

FAMAKS British Schools
8 Adekunle Fajuyi Close, Off Ajayi Crowther Street, Asokoro, Abuja, FCT
Tel: +234 913 059 9552
Age range: 4 months–18 years
Curriculum: UK, IGCSE
Language instr: English

Funtaj International School
No. 6 Nelson Mandela Street, Off Kwame Nkruma Crescent, Off Thomas Sankara Street, Asokoro, Abuja, FCT
Tel: +234 705 792 8066
Age range: 1–18 years
Curriculum: National, UK, IGCSE

Glisten International Academy
Plot 1457 Cadastrial Zone B8, Jahi District, Abuja, FCT
Tel: +234 90 3888 2824
Age range: 3–17 years
Curriculum: National, UK
Language instr: English

Global International Secondary School & College
Block 12 31A Admiralty way, Lekki Phase 1, Lagos
Tel: +234 802 314 5132
Age range: 11–18 years
Curriculum: UK, USA, IGCSE, ALevs

Grange School
Harold Shodipo Crescent, Ikeja, Lagos
Tel: +234 1 295 7630
Age range: 2.5–16 years
Curriculum: UK, IGCSE
Language instr: English

Greenoak International School
St. Michael's Crescent, Off Tombia Road Extension, GRA Phase 3, Port Harcourt, Rivers
Tel: +234 1 295 0946
Age range: 4–18 years
Curriculum: IPC, National, SAT, UK, USA, IGCSE, ALevs
Language instr: English

Greensprings School, Lagos
P.O. Box 4801K Ikeja Headquarters, Ikeja, 32 Olatunde Ayoola Avenue, Anthony, Lagos
Tel: +234 877 6874
Age range: 3 months–18 years
Curriculum: IBDP, IPC, UK, IGCSE
Language instr: English

Grenville Primary School
18 Ladoke Akintola Road, Ikeja, Lagos
Tel: +234 906 287 1313
Age range: 3–11 years

Grenville Secondary School
15 Joel Ogunnaike Street, Ikeja, Lagos
Tel: +234 906 287 1313
Age range: 11–18 years

Halifield Schools
2-6 Oki Lane, Maryland, Lagos
Tel: +234 815 090 4600
Age range: 1–18 years
Curriculum: National, UK, IGCSE

Hillcrest School (Jos)
P.O. Box 652, 13 Old Bukuru Road, Jos, Plateau
Tel: +234 803 719 0351
Age range: 4–18 years
Curriculum: AP, USA
Language instr: English

Ibadan International School
24 Jibowu Crescent, Iyaganku, Ibadan, Oyo
Tel: +234 2 291 8483
Age range: 2–18 years
Curriculum: IBPYP, UK, IGCSE, ALevs
Language instr: English

Inspire Academy
Plot 1482, Juba Street, Katampe District, Abuja, FCT
Tel: +234 802 458 0118
Age range: 4–11 years
Curriculum: National, UK
Language instr: English

International Community School, Abuja
Plot 75, ICS Drive, Off Citec Road, Dakibiyu, Abuja, FCT
Tel: +234 803 349 8741
Age range: 2–18 years
Curriculum: ACT, AP, SAT, USA, IGCSE
Language instr: English

James Hope College
Twin Lakes Estate, Lekki, Lagos
Tel: +234 708 366 2229
Curriculum: National, UK, IGCSE
Language instr: English

KAD Academy
No. 5 Rock Close,, Malali,, Kaduna
Tel: +234706 258 1020
Curriculum: UK

Kaduna International School
PO Box 2947, 1 Wurno Road, Kaduna
Tel: 002348166481918
Age range: 3–12
No. of pupils: 154 B79 G75
Curriculum: National, UK

Africa

Lagos Preparatory & Secondary School
36/40 Glover Road, Ikoyi, Lagos
Tel: +234 818 953 7887
Age range: 3 months–18 years
Curriculum: UK, IGCSE
Language instr: English

LauraStephens School
Laurastephens Road, Lekki Scheme II, Lekki- Epe Express Road, Lekki, Lagos
Tel: +234 813 702 2005
Curriculum: National, UK

Lead British International School
Aliyu Mustdafa Street (Opp Trafford Hotel), Off Wole Soyinka Avenue, Gwarinpa, P.M.B 5334, Wuse, Abuja, FCT
Tel: +234 9291 4098
Age range: 4–18 years
Curriculum: National, UK, IGCSE

Lead-Forte Gate Schools
1 Insha-Alla Street, Off Ramat Cresent, Ogudu GRA, Lagos
Tel: +234 802 778 5366
Age range: 3–11 years
Curriculum: National, UK

Lekki British School
Victoria Arobieke Street, Lekki Phase 1, Lagos
Tel: +234 01 906 0000
Age range: 15 months–18 years
Curriculum: UK, IGCSE, ALevs
Language instr: English

Lifeforte International Schools
#1 Lifeforte Boulevard, Awotan GRA, Ibadan, Oyo
Tel: +234 802 301 7324
Age range: 3–18 years
Curriculum: National, UK, IGCSE, ALevs
Language instr: English

Lifespring Montessori School
CMD Road, Magodo, Lagos
Tel: +234 803 367 3067

Lycée Français Louis Pasteur
P.O. Box 72172, 16 Younis Bashorun Street, Victoria Island, Lagos
Tel: +234 1 270 0545/46
Age range: 4–18 years
Curriculum: FrenchBacc

Meadow Hall Education
Meadow Hall Way, Alma Beach Estate, Lekki-Epe Express Way, Lekki, Lagos
Tel: +234 807 300 0556
Age range: 3 months–18 years
Curriculum: National, UK

Netherlands International School Lagos (NISL)
4 Onitana Road, Off Mobolaji Johnson Avenue, Ikoyi, Lagos
Tel: +234 808 221 1745
Age range: 2–12 years
Curriculum: IPC, National, UK

Nigerian Tulip International College - Abuja
Monrovia Street, Wuse II, Abuja 900288
Tel: +234 805 190 8030
Age range: 4–18 years
Curriculum: National, SAT, UK, IGCSE, ALevs

Nigerian Tulip International College - Kaduna
10 Inuwa Wada Road, Unguwan Rimi GRA, Kaduna
Tel: +234 703 341 6566
Age range: 4–18 years
Curriculum: National, SAT, UK, IGCSE, ALevs

Nigerian Tulip International College - Kano
Hadeja Road by Pass by Ring Road, Yankaba, Kano
Tel: +234 809 835 5663
Age range: 4–18 years
Curriculum: National, SAT, UK, IGCSE, ALevs

Nigerian Tulip International College - Lagos
4A Agbaoku Street, Off Odepi Road, Ikeja, Lagos
Tel: +234 814 686 2641
Age range: 4–18 years
Curriculum: National, SAT, UK, IGCSE, ALevs

Nigerian Tulip International College - Ogun
Banku, Ogun
Tel: +234 704 536 0794
Age range: 4–18 years
Curriculum: National, SAT, UK, IGCSE, ALevs

Nigerian Tulip International College - Yobe
Mamudoo, Potiskum, Yobe
Tel: +234 803 597 0890
Age range: 4–18 years
Curriculum: National, SAT, UK, IGCSE, ALevs

Noble Hall Leadership Academy for Girls
Plot 273, Institutes & Research District, By Idu Yard, Jabi-Airport Road, Off Coca Cola Junction, Abuja, FCT
Tel: +234 807 729 9329
Age range: G10–16 years
Curriculum: National, UK, IGCSE
Language instr: English

Norwegian International School
11 Rotimi Amaechi Drive, GRA Phase 3, Port Harcourt, Rivers
Tel: +234 708 188 8098
Age range: 2–16 years
Curriculum: UK, IGCSE
Language instr: English

Oakland International British School
15 Tennesse Crescent, Off Panama Street, Ministers Hill, Maitama, Abuja, FCT
Tel: +234 905 623 8659
Age range: 6 months–11 years
Curriculum: UK
Language instr: English

Ocean Crest School
T.F. Kuboye Road, Lekki, Lagos
Tel: +234 816 000 0580
Age range: 3 months–16 years
Curriculum: National, UK, IGCSE

Olashore International School
P.M.B. 5059, Oba Oladele Olashore Way, Iloko-Ijesa 233116
Tel: +234 807 712 4311
Age range: 11–18 years
Language instr: English

Oxbridge Tutorial College
49 Sobo Arobiodu Street, GRA, Ikeja, Lagos
Tel: +234 817 052 6734
Age range: 16–18 years
Curriculum: SAT, UK, USA, ALevs
Language instr: English

Pampers Private School Lekki
Plot 12, Block 88, Otunba Adedoyin Ogungbe Crescent, off Admiralty Road, Lekki Phase 1, Lekki, Lagos
Tel: +234 817 984 0785
Age range: 1–11 years
Curriculum: National, UK
Language instr: English

Pampers Private School Surulere
99 Owukori Crescent, Alaka Estate, Surulere, Lagos
Tel: +234 813 002 7220
Age range: 1–11 years
Curriculum: National, UK
Language instr: English

Pegasus Schools, Eket
North End of St. Gregory Street, Eket, Akwa Ibom
Tel: +234 802 499 7603
Age range: 3–18 years
Curriculum: National, UK, IGCSE
Language instr: English

Pinefield School
Christ Avenue, Off Admiralty Road, Lekki Phase 1, Victoria Island, Lagos
Tel: +234 802 315 8055
Age range: 1–16 years
Curriculum: UK

Premier International School
P.M.B. 5043, 26 N'djamena Crescent, Wuse II, Abuja, FCT
Tel: +234 806 978 1274
Age range: 3 months–18 years
Curriculum: National, UK, IGCSE, ALevs

Premiere Academy
Premiere Academy Street, Federal Housing Estate, Lugbe, Airport Road, Abuja, FCT
Tel: +234 903 387 0155
Age range: 11–18 years
Curriculum: National, SAT, TOEFL, UK

Primegate Academy
A234, Off Ibrahim Aliyu Street, Phase 11 Brick City Estate, Kubwa, Abuja, FCT
Tel: +234 813 070 8831
Age range: 3–18 years
Curriculum: National, UK
Language instr: English

RA International School (RAIS)
Nigeria LNG Residential Area, Bonny Island, Rivers
Language instr: English

Rainbow College
51 Johnson Street, Off Bode Thomas Street, Surulere, Lagos
Tel: +234 818 049 2228
Age range: 11–18 years

Redeemer's International School
4 Otigba Crescent, GRA, Onitsha, Anambra
Tel: +234 703 495 7216
Language instr: English

Sacred Heart Primary School
Independence Way, PO Box 620, Kaduna
Tel: +234 803 701 7488
Age range: 5–12
No. of pupils: 296 B159 G137

St Saviour's School
54 Alexander Avenue, Ikoyi, Lagos
Tel: +234 913 900 1113/4
Age range: 4–11 years
Curriculum: UK

St. Bernadette School Akoka
73 Community Road, Akoka, Lagos
Tel: +234 909 877 1418
Age range: 4–11 years
Curriculum: IPC, National, UK

St. Bernadette School Ipaja
3rd Avenue, 32nd Road, Gowon Estate, Ipaja, Lagos
Tel: +234 909 877 1437
Age range: 4–11 years
Curriculum: IPC, National, UK

Start-Rite International School
Plot 1036 Adesoji Aderemi Street, Off Samuel Jereton Mariere Road, After Zone "E" Gate, National Assembly Quarters, Gudu +, Abuja, FCT
Tel: +234 810 633 4006
Age range: 2–18 years

Africa

Surefoot International School
1 Surefoot International School Drive, Off Murtala Muhammed Highway (Opp. Zone 6 Police Stati+, Calabar, Cross River
Tel: +234 807 254 8185
Age range: 1–18 years
Curriculum: UK, IGCSE

Temple Primary School
1 Temple Drive, Off Olusoji Idowu Street, Ilupeju, Lagos
Tel: +234 817 874 3503
Age range: 3–11 years
Curriculum: UK

Temple Secondary School
4-6 Odegbami Street, Off Aba Johnston Street, Adeniyi Jones, Ikeja, Lagos
Tel: +234 908 155 0288
Age range: 11–18 years
Curriculum: UK, IGCSE
Language instr: English

The Centagon International School
29/31 Mississippi Street, Maitama, Abuja, FCT
Tel: +234 805 728 0323
Age range: 3–18 years
Curriculum: National, UK, USA, IGCSE

The Childville
8/10 Bola Sonoiki Avenue, Ramat, Ogudu GRA, Lagos
Tel: +234 1 453 8675
Age range: 3–16 years
Curriculum: National, UK, IGCSE

The International School of IITA
Oyo Road, Ibadan, Oyo
Tel: +234 803 437 9697
Age range: 3–13 years
Curriculum: IBPYP, UK
Language instr: English

The Mervyn Academy
Sabon Lugbe, Cadastral Zone 07-07, off Airport road, Abuja, FCT
Tel: +234 913 403 4731
Curriculum: National, UK

The Priory Preparatory School
1 Sikiru Alade Oloko Crescent, Off Admiralty Way, Lekki Peninsula Phase 1, Lekki, Lagos
Tel: +234 809 720 4149
Curriculum: UK

The Regent Primary School, Abuja
No. 1 Euphrates Crescent, Maitama, Abuja, FCT
Tel: +234 703 779 3222
Age range: 2–11 years
Curriculum: UK
Language instr: English

The Regent Secondary School, Abuja
Plot 858, Mabushi, Abuja, FCT
Tel: +234 807 229 3289
Age range: 11–16 years
Curriculum: UK, IGCSE

The RiverBank School
2 COD Road, RCCG City of David, Oniru Estate, Victoria Island, Lagos
Tel: +234 808 581 0478
Age range: 2–13 years
Curriculum: UK

Thomas Adewumi International College (TAICO)
P.O.Box 1050, Omu-Aran, Kwara
Tel: +234 803 824 5006
Age range: 11–16 years
Curriculum: National, UK

Vivian Fowler Memorial College for Girls
Plot 5 Billingsway, Oregun, Ikeja, Lagos
Tel: +234 806 155 0543
Age range: G11–16 years
Curriculum: National, SAT, TOEFL, UK, IGCSE

Whiteplains British School
Plot 528 Cadastral Zone B4, Jabi, Abuja, FCT
Tel: +234 803 345 3454
Age range: 4–18 years
Curriculum: National, UK, IGCSE, ALevs

REPUBLIC OF THE CONGO

American International School of Brazzaville
P.O. Box 1780, Bacongo, Brazzaville
Tel: +242 06 868 0804
Age range: 4–18 years
Curriculum: IBDP, IBMYP, IBPYP, USA
Language instr: English

Connie's Academy International British Primary School
26 Rue Tchicaya U'Tamsi, Mpita, Pointe-Noire
Tel: +242 06 814 2308
Age range: 2–18 years
Curriculum: UK
Language instr: English

RWANDA

Cubahiro International School
P.O. Box 2073, Avenue du large, Kinindo, Bujumbura, Burundi
Tel: +257 22 28 0288
Age range: 1.5–19 years
Curriculum: IBDP, IBMYP, UK, IGCSE, ALevs
Language instr: English, French

Green Hills Academy
P.O. Box 6419, KG 278 Street, Nyarutarama, Kigali
Tel: +250 735 832 348
Age range: 3–18 years
Curriculum: IBDP, IBMYP, IBPYP, IBCP
Language instr: English

International School of Kigali
KG 307 Street, Kibagabaga, Kigali
Tel: +25 786 725 369
Age range: 3–18 years
Curriculum: USA

Kigali International Community School
Kigali
Tel: +250 784 741 277
Age range: 3–18 years
Curriculum: ACT, AP, SAT, USA
Language instr: English

SENEGAL

Cours Sainte Marie de Hann
Route Des Peres Maristes, BP 98, Dakar
Tel: +221 33 832 14 87
Curriculum: IBDP
Language instr: English, French

Dakar Academy
B.P. 3189, Dakar 10200
Tel: +221 78 547 13 73
Age range: 3–18 years
Curriculum: USA
Language instr: English

Enko Keur Gorgui International School
Cité Keur Gorgui, Mermoz-Sacré-Cœur, Dakar
Tel: +221 33 821 30 64
Age range: 3–19 years
Curriculum: IBDP, IBMYP

Enko Waca International School
BP 24340, Ouakam, Dakar
Tel: +221 33 820 49 29
Age range: 11–19 years
Curriculum: IBDP
Language instr: French, English

Institution Bilingue Montessori
Yoff virage Villa n 6 et 7, Dakar
Tel: +221 77 187 06 99
Curriculum: IBDP
Language instr: English, French

International School of Dakar
B.P. 5136, Fann, Dakar 10700
Tel: +221 33 825 08 71
Age range: 3–18 years
Curriculum: IBDP, IBMYP, IBPYP, USA
Language instr: English

IQRA Bilingual Academy
2 Voies Liberté 6 derrière Numero Uno, Dakar
Tel: +221 33 827 56 23
Age range: 3–18 years
Language instr: English, French, Arabic

Le Collège Bilingue de Dakar
No. 53 Sacré-Coeur, Pyrotechnie, Dakar
Tel: +221 33 860 60 10
Age range: 11–18 years
Curriculum: IBDP
Language instr: English, French

Lycée Billes
Commune de Plan Jaxaay-Cité, Gendarmerie–Niacoulrab, Dakar
Tel: +221 77 413 73 55
Curriculum: IBDP
Language instr: English, French

SEYCHELLES

Independent School Seychelles
Union Vale, Ile Du Port, Mahé
Tel: +248 432 23 37
Age range: 3–18 years
No. of pupils: 1017
Curriculum: UK, IGCSE, ALevs
Language instr: English

International School Seychelles
P.O. Box 315, Mont Fleuri Victoria, Mahé
Tel: +248 467 9800
Age range: 4–18 years
Curriculum: UK, IGCSE, ALevs
Language instr: English

Vijay International School
Baie St Anne, Praslin
Tel: +248 423 6116
Age range: 3–18 years
Curriculum: IGCSE, ALevs

SIERRA LEONE

American International School of Freetown
24 Hillcot Brow Hill Station, Freetown
Tel: +232 76 622 453
Age range: 3–18 years
Curriculum: AP, IPC, USA

British International School and Montessori Education Freetown
No. 7/8 Hill Cot Road, Freetown
Tel: +232 76 567 509
Age range: 16 months–16 years
Curriculum: UK, IGCSE

Africa

SOMALIA

Hilal International Academy
Jaziira Road, Wadajir District,
Banadir, Mogadishu
Tel: +252 613 661 515
Age range: 3–16 years
Curriculum: IBMYP, IBPYP
Language instr: English, Arabic

SOUTH AFRICA

Academia Private School
24 Ludorf Street, 0480
Bela-Bela, Limpopo
Tel: +27 14 736 5881
Age range: 0–18 years
Curriculum: UK, IGCSE, ALevs

ACE Leadership School, Midrand Campus
53 West Road, Glen Austin AH,
1685 Midrand, Gauteng
Tel: +27 74 077 8070
Age range: 3–18 years

Alma Mater International School
1 Coronation Street,
Krugersdorp, Gauteng
Tel: + 27 11 660 7567
Age range: 3 months–18 years
Curriculum: UK, IGCSE, ALevs

Amazing Grace Private School
359 Pretoria Avenue,
Ferndale, Randburg, 2195
Johannesburg, Gauteng
Tel: +27 73 212 7905
Age range: 4–18 years

American International School of Cape Town
42 Soetvlei Avenue, Constantia,
7806 Cape Town, Western Cape
Tel: 27 21 713 2220
Age range: 2–18 years
Curriculum: AP, USA
Language instr: English

American International School of Johannesburg
Private Bag X4, Bryanston, 2021
Johannesburg, Gauteng
Tel: +27 11 464 1505
Age range: 4–18 years
Curriculum: IBDP, USA
Language instr: English

Bishops Diocesan College
Campground Road, Rondebosch,
7700 Cape Town, Western Cape
Tel: +27 21 659 1000
Age range: B5–18 years

Blouberg International School
74 Ringwood Drive, Parklands,
7441 Cape Town, Western Cape
Tel: +27 21 557 9071
Age range: 2–16 years
Curriculum: UK, IGCSE

Bridge House School
P.O. Box 444, 7690 Franschhoek,
Western Cape
Tel: +27 021 874 8100
Age range: 2–18 years
(boarding from 11)
Language instr: English

British International College - Bryanston
130 Bryanston Drive, Bryanston,
Johannesburg, Gauteng
Tel: +27 11 706 7775
Age range: 13–18 years
Curriculum: UK, IGCSE, ALevs

British International College - Pretoria
Cnr Stanza Popape & East Street,
Eastcliff, Pretoria, Gauteng
Tel: +27 11 706 7775
Age range: 13–18 years
Curriculum: UK, IGCSE, ALevs

British International Preparatory School
82 Selbourne Road, Fourways,
Johannesburg, Gauteng
Tel: +27 11 706 7775
Age range: 4–13 years
Curriculum: UK

Charter College International High School
2 Johan Road, Ambot
AH, Honeydew, 2040
Roodepoort, Gauteng
Tel: +27 11 794 7132
Age range: 13–18 years
Curriculum: IGCSE, ALevs

Charterhouse Schools
10 Erasmus Road,
Radiokop, Honeydew, 2040
Roodepoort, Gauteng
Tel: +27 11 475 6809
Age range: 3–13 years
Curriculum: UK

Cornwall Hill College
Nellmapius Drive, Centurion,
0062 Irene, Gauteng
Tel: +27 12 667 1360
Age range: 3–18 years
(boarding from 13)
Curriculum: National
Language instr: English

Courtney House International School
47 Charles Bramley Street, Bailey's
Muckleneuk, Pretoria, Gauteng
Tel: +27 12 346 4051
Age range: 4–18 years
Curriculum: UK, IGCSE, ALevs

Crawford International Bedfordview
7 Marais Road, Bedfordview,
2008 Johannesburg, Gauteng
Tel: +27 87 350 4633
Age range: 3–15 years
Curriculum: IBPYP
Language instr: English, Afrikaans

Crawford International Bryanston
6 Hobart Road, Bryanston, Sandton,
2191 Johannesburg, Gauteng
Tel: +27 11 706 6609
Age range: 2–6 years
Language instr: English, Afrikaans

Crawford International Fourways
16 Campbell Road, Craigavon,
Fourways, Sandton, 2191
Johannesburg, Gauteng
Tel: +27 11 465 4418
Age range: 3–13 years
Curriculum: IBPYP
Language instr: English, Afrikaans

Crawford International La Lucia
79 Armstrong Avenue, La Lucia,
4001 Durban, KwaZulu-Natal
Tel: +27 31 562 9444
Age range: 2–18 years
Curriculum: IBPYP
Language instr: English, Afrikaans

Crawford International Lonehill
17 Lonehill Boulevard, Lonehill,
2062 Johannesburg, Gauteng
Tel: +27 11 467 0936/5
Age range: 1.5–18 years
Curriculum: IBPYP
Language instr: English, Afrikaans

Crawford International North Coast
Watson Highway, 4399
Tongaat, KwaZulu-Natal
Tel: +27 32 943 3240
Age range: 3–18 years
Curriculum: IBPYP
Language instr: English, Afrikaans

Crawford International Pretoria
555 Sibelius Street, Lukasrand,
0181 Pretoria, Gauteng
Tel: +27 12 343 5903
Age range: 2–18 years
Curriculum: IBPYP
Language instr: English, Afrikaans

Crawford International Ruimsig
Cnr Peter and Kuilstock Roads,
Ruimsig, 1724 Roodepoort, Gauteng
Tel: +27 11 958 0707
Age range: 1.5–18 years
Curriculum: IBPYP
Language instr: English, Afrikaans

Crawford International Sandton
Crawford Estate Waterstone Drive (off
Benmore Road), Benmore, Sandton,
2196 Johannesburg, Gauteng
Tel: +27 11 784 3447
Age range: 2–18 years
Curriculum: IBPYP
Language instr: English, Zulu

Dainfern College
96 Broadacres Drive, Dainfern,
2055 Johannesburg, Gauteng
Tel: +27 11 469 0635
Age range: 2–18 years
Curriculum: ALevs

Greenwood Bay College
Piesang Valley Road, 6600
Plettenberg Bay, Western Cape
Tel: +27 44 533 2549
Age range: 2–18 years
Curriculum: UK, IGCSE, ALevs

Helderberg International School
Hazelden Drive, Heritage Park,
Somerset West, 7130 Cape
Town, Western Cape
Tel: +27 21 851 6290/1
Age range: 2–19 years
Curriculum: UK, IGCSE, ALevs

Hilton College
Hilton, 3245 Pietemaritzburg,
KwaZulu-Natal
Tel: +27 33 383 0100
Age range: B14–18 years

Horizon High School
7 Pieter Wessels Street, Stafford,
2197 Johannesburg, Gauteng
Tel: +27 11 434 5234
Age range: B13–18 years
Language instr: English

Hout Bay International School
61 Main Road, Hout Bay, 7806
Cape Town, Western Cape
Tel: +27 21 791 7900
Age range: 2–18 years
No. of pupils: 530
Curriculum: IBDP, IBMYP, IBPYP, IGCSE
Language instr: English

International School of Cape Town
Woodland Heights, Edinburgh
Close, Claremont, 7806 Cape
Town, Western Cape
Tel: +27 21 761 6202
Age range: 3.5–18 years
Curriculum: National,
UK, IGCSE, ALevs
Language instr: English

International School of South Africa
Cnr. William Dick Avenue &
Nelson Mandela Drive, Libertas,
2745 Mahikeng, North West
Tel: +27 18 381 1102
Age range: 4–18 years
Curriculum: UK, IGCSE, ALevs
Language instr: English

Jacaranda Academy
37 Van Tonder Road, Eden
Glen, Edenvale, 1609
Johannesburg, Gauteng
Tel: +27 11 609 6218
Age range: 4–13 years

Lycée Jules Verne
Cnr Bauhinia & Cestrum,
Morningside Ext 40, Sandton,
2196 Johannesburg, Gauteng
Tel: +27 11 884 8936
Age range: 3–18 years
Curriculum: FrenchBacc

Africa

Michaelhouse
R103, 3275 Balgowan, KwaZulu-Natal
Tel: +27 33 234 1000
Age range: B13–18 years
Language instr: English

Mokopane Destiny Academy
Cnr Geyser & Fourie Street, RET Centre, 0601 Mokopane, Limpopo
Tel: +27 15 491 2049
Curriculum: IBMYP, IBPYP
Language instr: English

North American International School
431 Atterbury Road, Menlo Park, Pretoria, Gauteng
Tel: +27 12 346 2530
Age range: 2–18 years
Language instr: English

Penryn College
Boschrand Farm, R40, 1200 Mbombela, Mpumalanga
Tel: +27 13 758 9000
Age range: 3–18 years
Language instr: English

Reddam House Atlantic Seaboard
20 Cavalcade Road, Green Point, 8051 Cape Town, Western Cape
Tel: +27 21 433 0105
Age range: 1–18 years
Language instr: English

Reddam House Ballito
Hills Drive, Ballito,, Dolphin Coast, KwaZulu-Natal
Tel: +27 31 140 8808
Age range: 1–18 years
Language instr: English

Reddam House Bedfordview
28 Smith Road, Bedfordview, 2007 Johannesburg, Gauteng
Tel: +27 11 615 6710
Age range: 1–18 years
Language instr: English

Reddam House Constantia
Reddam Avenue, Steenberg Boulevard, Constantia, 7806 Cape Town, Western Cape
Tel: +27 21 702 2322
Age range: 1–18 years
Language instr: English

Reddam House Durbanville
Clara Anna Fontein Estate, Shamwari Close, Durbanville, 7550 Cape Town, Western Cape
Tel: +27 21 975 6649
Age range: 1–18 years
Curriculum: UK, ALevs
Language instr: English

Reddam House Helderfontein
1 Chattan Road, Glenferness, Fourways, 407 Johannesburg, Gauteng
Tel: +27 10 060 4232
Age range: 1–18 years
Language instr: English

Reddam House Umhlanga
21 Preston Drive, Prestondale, 4021 Umhlanga, KwaZulu-Natal
Tel: +27 31 566 5736
Age range: 1–18 years
Language instr: English

Reddam House Waterfall
Country Estate Road, Midrand, 1682 Johannesburg, Gauteng
Tel: +27 10 060 0107
Age range: 1–18 years
Language instr: English

Reddford House Blue Hills
Blue Hills Estate, 5 Mopani Road, Blue Hills, Midrand, 1685 Johannesburg, Gauteng
Tel: +27 10 060 0761
Age range: 3 months–18 years
Language instr: English

Reddford House Northcliff
14th Avenue, Fairlands, Randburg, Johannesburg, Gauteng
Tel: +27 10 060 4234
Age range: 3 months–18 years
Language instr: English

Reddford House The Hills
Garsfontein Road, 0057 Pretoria, Gauteng
Tel: +27 10 060 0757
Age range: 3 months–18 years
Language instr: English

Redhill School
20 Summit Road, Morningside, Sandton, 2057 Johannesburg, Gauteng
Tel: +27 11 783 4707
Age range: 4–18 years
Curriculum: IBDP, IBMYP, National
Language instr: English

Roedean School
Princess of Wales Terrace, Parktown, 2193 Johannesburg, Gauteng
Tel: +27 11 647 3200
Language instr: English

Silver Oaks International
40 Pinaster Avenue, Hazelwood, Pretoria, Gauteng
Tel: +27 12 346 4770
Curriculum: GCSE, ALevs

St Andrew's College
1 Somerset Street, Makhanda (Grahamstown), Eastern Cape
Tel: +27 46 603 2300
Age range: B13–18 years
Curriculum: ALevs
Language instr: English

St Cyprian's School
Gorge Road, Oranjezicht, 8001 Cape Town, Western Cape
Tel: +27 21 300 6500
Language instr: English

St John's College
St David Road, Houghton, 2198 Johannesburg, Gauteng
Tel: +27 11 645 3000
Age range: B3–18 years
G3–4 & 16 - 18 years

St Stithians College
40 Peter Place, Lyme Park, Sandton, 2191 Johannesburg, Gauteng
Tel: +27 11 577 6000
Age range: 4–18 years
Curriculum: IGCSE, ALevs

Stanford Lake College
A22, off the R71, 0730 Magoebaskloof, Limpopo
Tel: +27 15 276 6103
Age range: 13–18 years
Language instr: English

Star College Bridgetown
126 Tarentaal Road, Bridgetown, 7764 Cape Town, Western Cape
Tel: +27 21 699 0606
Age range: B4–18 years G4–13 years
Language instr: English

Star College Cape Town
22 Elgin Road, Sybrand Park, Rondebosch, 7700 Cape Town, Western Cape
Tel: +27 21 697 0194
Age range: B4–13 years G4–18 years
Language instr: English

Star College Durban Boys High
20 Kinloch Avenue, Westville North, 3630 Durban, KwaZulu-Natal
Tel: +27 31 262 7190
Age range: B13–18 years
Language instr: English

Star College Durban Girls High
20 Kinloch Avenue, Westville North, 3630 Durban, KwaZulu-Natal
Tel: +27 31 262 7191
Age range: G13–18 years
Language instr: English

Star College Durban Primary
20 Kinloch Avenue, Westville North, 3630 Durban, KwaZulu-Natal
Tel: +27 31 262 7190
Age range: 3–13 years
Language instr: English

Star College Pretoria
25 Meadow Avenue, Equestria (14.89 km), 0184 Pretoria, Gauteng
Tel: +27 12 807 2346
Age range: 4–18 years
Language instr: English

The Mountain Cambridge School
Portion 2 of Plot 21, Beethoven Road, 0216 Hartbeespoort, North West
Tel: +27 63 482 6822
Age range: 4–18 years
No. of pupils: 300
Curriculum: IGCSE, ALevs

SUDAN

Cambridge International School - Bahry
Kafoury Block 6, Bahri
Tel: +249 85 235799
Age range: 4–16 years
Curriculum: IGCSE

Cambridge International School - Khartoum
Taief - Nakheel Street/ Block 22, Khartoum
Tel: +249 83 253669
Age range: 4–16 years
Curriculum: IGCSE

Cambridge International School - Omdurman
Almulazmeen/ Nile Street, Omdurman
Tel: +249 87 563499
Age range: 4–16 years
Curriculum: IGCSE

Confluence International School of Khartoum
Greek Community School Campus, Building No.5, Gamhouria Avenue, Khartoum
Tel: +249 960099970
Age range: 4–18 years
Curriculum: IBDP, IBMYP, IBPYP
Language instr: English, Arabic

Khartoum American School
Mohamed Najeeb Street, Khartoum
Tel: +249 15 577 0105
Age range: 3–18 years
Curriculum: SAT, TOEFL, USA

Khartoum International Community School
P.O. Box 1840, Madani Street, Khartoum
Tel: +249 183 215 000
Age range: 4–18 years
Curriculum: IBDP, IBPYP
Language instr: English

Unity High School
Al Qasr Street, Khartoum
Tel: +249 844 663 6692
Age range: 11–18 years
Curriculum: UK, IGCSE, ALevs

TANZANIA

Academic International School
P.O. Box 63333, Dar es Salaam
Age range: 3–18 years
Curriculum: UK, IGCSE, ALevs
Language instr: English

Africa

Al Muntazir Schools
United Nations Road, Dar es Salaam
Tel: +255 78 8300964
Age range: 3–18 years
Curriculum: UK, IGCSE, ALevs

Braeburn Dar es Salaam International School
P.O. Box 31158, Africana/Mbezi Beach, off Bagamoyo Road at the African+, Dar es Salaam
Tel: +255 76 3086646
Age range: 2–16 years
Curriculum: UK, IGCSE
Language instr: English
(AISA) (CIS)

Braeburn International School Arusha
P.O. Box 14268, Kisongo, 14km west of Arusha, Arumeru District, Arusha
Tel: +255 75 9123124
Age range: 2–18 years
Curriculum: UK, IGCSE, ALevs
Language instr: English
(AISA) (CIS)

Canon Andrea Mwaka School
P.O. Box 228, Shule Avenue, Uzunguni, Dodoma
Tel: +225 26 2323220
Age range: 3–16 years
Curriculum: UK, IGCSE
Language instr: English

Cheka School
Kiranyi, Sakina, Arusha
Age range: 3–7 years
Language instr: English, Swahili

Dar es Salaam Independent School
P.O. Box 32391, Dar es Salaam
Tel: +255 77 2111228
Age range: 4–18 years
Language instr: English

Dar es Salaam International Academy
P.O. Box 23282, Manara Road, Ada Estate, Dar es Salaam
Tel: +255 75 8828300
Age range: 4–18 years
Curriculum: IBDP, IBMYP, IBPYP
Language instr: English
(AISA) (CIS)

École française Arthur Rimbaud de Dar es Salaam
P.O. Box 2183, Plot 282, Mawenzi Road, Masaki, Dar es Salaam
Tel: +255 76 5562235
Age range: 2–18 years
Curriculum: FrenchBacc
Language instr: French

Feza Schools
P.O. Box 77965, Dar es Salaam
Tel: +255 71 2339239
Age range: 3–18 years
Curriculum: IGCSE, ALevs

Genesis Schools
P.O. Box 105792, Dar es Salaam
Tel: +255 78 4612222
Age range: 3–19 years

Haven of Peace Academy
Kunduchi Junction, Bagamoyo Road, Dar es Salaam
Tel: +255 78 6845135
Age range: 4–18 years
Curriculum: UK, USA, IGCSE, ALevs
(AISA)

Hope International School
P.O. Box 7640, Moshi
Tel: +255 76 3270467
Age range: 3–16 years
Curriculum: IGCSE
Language instr: English

International School of Tanganyika
P.O. Box 2651, Dar es Salaam
Tel: +255 67 7002444
Age range: 3–18 years
Curriculum: IBDP, IBMYP, IBPYP
Language instr: English
(AISA) (CIS)

International School of Zanzibar
P.O. Box 1787, Zanzibar
Tel: +255 77 7477053
Age range: 2–18 years
No. of pupils: 175
Curriculum: IPC, UK, IGCSE, ALevs
Language instr: English

Iringa International School
P.O. Box 912, Iringa
Tel: +255 26 2702018
Age range: 3–16 years
Curriculum: IGCSE
Language instr: English
(AISA)

Isamilo International School Mwanza
P.O. Box 42, Balewa Road, Mwanza
Tel: +255 28 2500497
Age range: 3–18 years
Curriculum: UK, IGCSE, ALevs
Language instr: English

Kennedy House International School
P.O. Box 350, Usa River
Tel: +255 68 9119788
Age range: 2–13 years
Curriculum: UK
Language instr: English

Kwanza International School
P.O. Box 34133, Dar es Salaam
Tel: +255 75 4000144
Age range: 1–11 years

Laureate International School
Warioba Street, Dar Es Salaam
Tel: +255 77 3288888

Morogoro International School
Msamvu Area, (Near Mambo Club), Morogoro
Tel: +255 71 5794864
Age range: 2–19 years
Curriculum: UK, IGCSE, ALevs
Language instr: English

St. Constantine's International School
P.O. Box 221, Dodoma Road, Arusha
Tel: +255 75 3871855
Age range: 3–18 years
Curriculum: IGCSE, ALevs
Language instr: English
(AISA)

The Aga Khan Mzizima Secondary School, Dar es Salaam
P.O. Box 21563, Fire Road, Upanga, Dar es Salaam
Tel: +255 22 2151253
Age range: 11–18 years
Curriculum: IBDP, IBPYP, IGCSE, ALevs
Language instr: English

The Aga Khan Nursery and Primary School, Dar es Salaam
PO Box 10263, Dar es Salaam
Tel: +255 22 2152484
Age range: 2–11 years
Language instr: English

The Latham School
P.O. Box 23119, Dar es Salaam
Tel: +255 76 7528426
Age range: 4–11 years
Curriculum: UK

UWC East Africa, Arusha Campus
P.O. Box 2691, Dodoma Road, Kisongo, Arusha
Tel: +255 78 4490133
Age range: 3–19 years
Curriculum: IBDP, IBMYP, IBPYP
Language instr: English
(AISA) (CIS)

UWC East Africa, Moshi Campus
P.O. Box 733, Lema Road, Moshi, Kilimanjaro
Tel: +255 75 6446777
Age range: 3–19 years
Curriculum: IBDP, IBMYP, IBPYP
Language instr: English
(AISA) (CIS)

THE GAMBIA

Banjul American International School
Atlantic Boulevard, Fajara, Serrekunda
Tel: +220 219 3800
Age range: 2–18 years
Curriculum: USA
(AISA)

École Française de Banjul
P.O. Box 4682, Bakau
Tel: +220 438 3619
Age range: 3–18 years
Curriculum: FrenchBacc

Marina International School
P.O. Box 717, Banjul
Tel: +220 449 4376
Age range: 3–18 years
Curriculum: UK, IGCSE, ALevs
Language instr: English

Shiloh Bilingual Education Centre (SBEC) International School
Serrekunda
Age range: 2–18 years
Curriculum: FrenchBacc, UK, IGCSE, ALevs
Language instr: English, French

TOGO

American International School of Lomé
10mn from US Embassy, Near Kegue Stadium, Lomé
Tel: +228 22 61 18 96
Age range: 2–18 years
Curriculum: USA
Language instr: English

Arc-en-Ciel International School
B.P. 2985, Lomé BP: 2985
Tel: +228 22 22 03 29
Age range: 1–18 years
Curriculum: IBDP, IBMYP, IBPYP
Language instr: French, English

Cours Lumière
Rue Alissutin, Agbalépédogan, Lomé
Tel: +228 91 77 99 03
Age range: 4–18 years
Curriculum: IBDP
Language instr: English, French

École Pilote Innovante Alpha
Tokoin - Agoè, Lomé
Tel: +228 99 11 11 11
Curriculum: IBDP
Language instr: English, French

International Christian School of Lomé
Lomé
Tel: +228 97 07 97 69
Age range: 3–18 years
Language instr: English, French

The British School of Lomé
B.P. 20050, Résidence du Bénin, Lomé
Tel: +228 22 26 46 06
Age range: 18 months–18 years
Curriculum: IBDP, UK, IGCSE, ALevs
Language instr: English

TUNISIA

American Cooperative School of Tunis
B.P. 150, Cite Taeib M'hiri, Laouina, 2045 Tunis
Tel: +216 71 760 905
Age range: 3–18 years
Curriculum: IBDP, USA
Language instr: English

Africa

British Academy of Tunis
Boulevard de l'Environnement,
Les Berges du Lac1, Tunis
Tel: +216 29 849 000
Age range: 3–18 years
Curriculum: IBDP, IBMYP, IBPYP
Language instr: English, French

British International School of Tunis
49 Rue du Parc, La Soukra, 2036 Tunis
Tel: +216 70 240 880
Age range: 3–18 years
Curriculum: UK, IGCSE, ALevs
Language instr: English

École Canadienne de Tunis
Rue de l'énergie solaire, 2035 Tunis
Tel: +216 71 206 035
Age range: 3–18 years
Curriculum: IBDP, IBMYP, IBPYP
Language instr: French

École Robert Desnos
92 bis route de l'hôpital militaire,
El Omrane, 1005 Tunis
Tel: +216 70 014 999

Groupe Scolaire International Les Nouvelles Générations
Km 5, Route Ajim-Houmt Souk,
Bousmayel, 4135 Djerba, Medenine
Tel: +216 70 279 340
Age range: 5–18 years
Curriculum: IBDP, IBMYP, IBPYP
Language instr: French, Arabic

International School of Carthage
Les Jardins de Carthage, Ain Zaghouan, 2046 Tunis
Tel: +216 71 777 722
Age range: 3–18 years

John Dewey School de Sousse
Sahloul, 4054 Sousse
Tel: +216 70 286 900
Curriculum: IBPYP
Language instr: Arabic, French

La Joconde de Carthage
Les Jardins de Carthage, 1090 Tunis
Tel: +216 27 584 447
Curriculum: IBPYP
Language instr: Arabic, French

Les écoles Idéales - Lycee Nabeul
Avenue El-Margheb El-Arabi, 8000 Nabeul
Age range: 12–18 years
Curriculum: IBMYP
Language instr: Arabic, French

Les écoles Idéales - Primaire/Maternelle Nabeul
Rue El-Akhtal Dar Chaâbene Plage, 8075 Nabeul
Tel: +216 72 360 214
Age range: 3–12 years
Curriculum: IBPYP
Language instr: Arabic, French

Lycée Pierre Mendès France
B.P. 125, 9 rue Pierre Mendes France, El Mahrajene, 1082 Tunis
Tel: +216 70 014 900
Curriculum: FrenchBacc

UGANDA

ACORNS INTERNATIONAL SCHOOL
For further details see p. 40
Plot 328, Kisota Road, (Along) Northern Bypass, Kisaasi Roundabout, Kampala
Tel: +256 393 202 665
Email: admissions@acornskisaasi.com
Website: acornskisaasi.com
Head of School: Ameena Lalani
Age range: 18 months–18 years
No. of pupils: 800
Fees: $2,358–$11,090
Curriculum: IBDP, IBMYP, IBPYP
Language instr: English

Ambrosoli International School
Plot 10-12 Binayomba Street, Bugolobi, Kampala
Tel: +256 414 220416
Age range: 3–11 years
Curriculum: IPC, UK
Language instr: English

École Française Les Grands Lacs
P.O. Box 7212, Lugogo By-Pass, Kampala
Tel: +256 414 341 660
Age range: 2–18 years
Curriculum: FrenchBacc
Language instr: English, French

Galaxy International School Uganda
Plot 1077 Lubowa Estate, Entebbe Road, P.O. Box 11119, Kampala
Tel: +256 781 468 000
Age range: 4–18 years
Curriculum: UK, IGCSE, ALevs

GEMS Cambridge International School - Kampala
Plot 102/104 Butabika Road, Before Royal Palms Estate, Luzira, Kampala
Tel: +256 755 177 982
Age range: 2.5–18 (boarding from 7)
Curriculum: UK, IGCSE
Language instr: English

International School of Uganda
272 Entebbe Road, Kampala
Tel: +256 414 200 374
Age range: 2.5–19 years
Curriculum: IBDP, IBMYP, IBPYP
Language instr: English

Kampala International School Uganda (KISU)
P.O.Box 34249, Bukoto, Kampala
Tel: +256 752 711 882
Age range: 2–18 years
Curriculum: IBDP
Language instr: English

Rainbow International School Uganda
P.O. Box 7632, Kampala
Tel: +256 312 266 696/7
Age range: 2–18 years
Curriculum: UK, IGCSE, ALevs
Language instr: English

The Aga Khan High School, Kampala
P.O. Box 6837, Muammar Gaddafi Road, Kampala
Tel: +256 414 308 245
Age range: 13–18 years
No. of pupils: 550
Curriculum: IBDP, UK, IGCSE, ALevs
Language instr: English

The Aga Khan Primary School, Kampala
P.O. Box 21533, Kampala
Tel: +256 414 308 232
Age range: 4–13 years
No. of pupils: 300
Curriculum: IPC, UK
Language instr: English

ZAMBIA

Trident College Solwezi
P.O. Box 110506, Solwezi
Tel: +260 962 555 363
Age range: 11–18 years
Curriculum: UK, IGCSE, ALevs
Language instr: English

Acacia School
P.O. Box 60719, Sub B Lot 5379/M, Nakatindi Road, Livingstone
Tel: +260 950 318 656
Age range: 3–13 years
Curriculum: UK
Language instr: English

American International School of Lusaka
P.O. Box 320176, 487 A/F/3 Leopards Hill Road, Lusaka
Tel: +26 978 772 600
Age range: 3–18 years
Curriculum: IBDP, IBMYP, IBPYP, USA
Language instr: English

Banani International School
Plot #2161/B, Chisamba, Lusaka
Tel: +260 966 737 770
Age range: G6–18 years (boarding from 11)
Curriculum: UK, IGCSE, ALevs
Language instr: English

Baobab College
P.O Box 350099, Kafue Road, Lilayi Lusaka, Chilanga
Tel: +260 966 876 804
Age range: 2–18 years
Curriculum: UK, IGCSE, ALevs
Language instr: English

International School of Lusaka
P.O. Box 50121, Ridgeway, Lusaka
Tel: +260 211 252 291
Age range: 2–18 years
Curriculum: IBDP, IBPYP, IGCSE
Language instr: English

Lechwe School
P.O. Box 20830, Kitwe
Tel: +260 212 227 040
Age range: 3–18 years
Curriculum: IPC, SAT, UK, IGCSE, ALevs

Lusaka International Community School
P.O. Box 30528, 242A Kakola Road, Roma, Lusaka
Tel: +260 211 292 447
Age range: 2–18 years
Curriculum: UK, IGCSE, ALevs

Lycée Français of Lusaka (LFL)
Plot 22725, Alick Nkhata Avenue, Longacres, Lusaka 10101
Tel: +260 975 010 203
Age range: 2–18 years
Curriculum: FrenchBacc

Martin House Trust School
Kalundu Farm, Chisamba Road, Chisamba
Tel: +260 962 143 920
Age range: 3–18 years
Curriculum: UK, IGCSE, ALevs

Musikili Primary School
P.O. Box 670370, Mazabuka
Tel: +260 966 861 242
Age range: 4–13 years
Curriculum: UK

Pestalozzi Education Centre
Off Twin Palm Road, Ibex Hill, Lusaka 10101
Tel: +260 978 950 599
Curriculum: IBDP
Language instr: English

Sentinel Kabitaka School
Old Chingola Road, Solwezi
Tel: +260 968 037 679
Age range: 3–18 years
Curriculum: IPC, IGCSE

Simba International School
P.O. Box 240216, Ndola
Tel: +260 21 2 613 674
Age range: 3–18 years
Curriculum: UK, IGCSE, ALevs

Africa

The Italian School of Lusaka
Stand No. 4919, Lubu Road, Lusaka
Tel: +260 211 254 181
Age range: 3–18 years
Curriculum: UK, IGCSE, ALevs

Trident Prep School
P.O. Box 110506, George Grey Way,
Kansanshi Golf Estate, Solwezi
Tel: +260 961 188 683
Age range: 4–11 years

ZIMBABWE

Divaris Makaharis
Corner Lavenham Drive/
Northolt Road, Bluffhill, Harare
Tel: +263 772 952 598

Falcon College
51 Livingstone Avenue, Corner
12th Avenue, Suburbs, Bulawayo
Tel: +263 086 770 04566
Age range: 13–18 years
No. of pupils: 450
Curriculum: UK, IGCSE, ALevs
Language instr: English

Harare International School
66 Pendennis Road, Mount
Pleasant, Harare
Tel: +263 242 870 514
Age range: 3–18 years
Curriculum: IBDP, IBMYP, IBPYP, USA
Language instr: English

Peterhouse Boys School
P Bag 3741, Marondera
Tel: +263 65 2322200
Age range: B11–18 years

Peterhouse Girls School
P Bag 3774, Marondera
Tel: +263 65 2323599
Age range: G11–18 years

Peterhouse Group of Schools
Private Bag 3741, Marondera
Tel: +263 652 323 598
Age range: 12–18
No. of pupils: 915 B515 G400
Curriculum: UK, IGCSE, ALevs
Language instr: English

Ruzawi School
Private Bag 3713, Marondera
Tel: +263 778 283 840
Age range: 6–12 years

Springvale House
Marondera
Tel: +263 65 2323598
Age range: 6–12 years

St George's College
Private Bag 7727, Causeway,
3 Borrowdale Road,
Borrowdale, Harare
Tel: +263 242 704 064
Age range: B12–18 years G16–18 years
Curriculum: UK, IGCSE, ALevs
Language instr: English

St John's College
179 Fisher Avenue, Rolf
Avenue, Harare
Tel: +263 242 870 942
Age range: B12–18 years
Language instr: English

St John's Preparatory School
179 Fisher Avenue, Rolf
Avenue, Harare
Tel: +263 242 885 121
Age range: B5–12 years
Language instr: English

The Heritage School Zimbabwe
Heritage Drive, Borrowdale
Brooke, Harare
Tel: +263 242 861 989
Age range: 1–18 years
Curriculum: UK

International schools in Asia

Schools ordered A–Z by Country

Key to directory

- Country
- Name of school or college
- Indicates that this school has a profile
- Address and contact number
- Head's name
- Age range
- Number of pupils.
  B = boys G = girls VIth = sixth form
- Fees per annum.
  Day = fees for day pupils.
  WB = fees for weekly boarders.
  FB = fees for full boarders.
- Curriculum
- Language of instruction
- Memberships/Accreditation

Whereford

College Academy
For further details see p

Which Street, Whosville,
Wherefordshire AB12 3CD

Tel: 01000 000000

Head Master: Dr A Person

Age range: 11–18

No. of pupils:
660 B330 G330 VIth 200

Fees: Day £11,000
WB £16,000 FB £20,000

Curriculum:
National, IBDP, ALevs

Language instr:
English, French

(AISA) (COB) (EAR)

Key to icons

Key to symbols:
- Boys' school
- Girls' school
- Boarding accommodation

Member of:
- (AISA) Association of International Schools in Africa
- (CEE) Central and Eastern European Schools Association
- (EAR) East Asia Regional Council of Overseas Schools
- (ECIS) European Council of International Schools
- (RS) Round Square

Accreditation:
- (CIS) Council of International Schools
- (COB) Council of British International Schools

Please note: Schools are coeducational day schools unless otherwise indicated

Asia

BAHRAIN

Abdul Rahman Kanoo International School
P.O. Box 2512, Manama
Tel: +973 17875055
Age range: 3–18 years
Curriculum: IBDP, IGCSE
Language instr: English, Arabic

Ahlia School
Building 166, Street. 45, Block 545, Al Qurayya
Tel: +973 77476666
Age range: 6–18 years
Curriculum: IBDP, USA
Language instr: English, Arabic

Al Hekma International School
Building No. 1962, Road 4363, Block 743, Sanad
Tel: +973 17620820
Age range: 4–18 years
Curriculum: AP, IBDP, SAT, TOEFL
Language instr: English

Al Mahd School, Riffa
Building No. 471, Road No. 4114, Riffa
Tel: +973 17792422
Age range: 4–16 years
Curriculum: IGCSE

Al Mahd School, Saar
Road No. 1727, Saar
Tel: +973 17792422
Age range: 4–16 years
Curriculum: IGCSE

Al Mahd School, Samaheej
Samaheej Avenue, Samaheej
Tel: +973 17792422
Age range: 4–16 years
Curriculum: IGCSE

Al Noor International School
P.O. Box 85, Manama
Tel: +973 17736773
Age range: 3–18 years
Curriculum: National, UK, IGCSE, ALevs

Al Raja School
P.O. Box 1, Manama
Tel: +973.17254414
Age range: 5–18 years
Curriculum: AP, USA
Language instr: English, Arabic

Al Rawabi School
Building 689, Road 3514, Block 435, P.O. Box 18575, Jablat Hebshi
Tel: +973 17595252
Age range: 4–18 years
Curriculum: IBDP, UK, USA, IGCSE
Language instr: English

American School of Bahrain
Building 1528, Road 3429, Block 934, North Riffa (Riffa Alshamali), Riffa
Tel: +973 17211800
Age range: 3–18 years
Curriculum: IBDP, USA
Language instr: English, Arabic

Arabian Pearl Gulf (APG) School
Bldg 1786, Rd 6306, Blk 363, Bilad AlQadeem, Manama
Tel: +973 17 403 666
Age range: 3–17 years
No. of pupils: 1440
Curriculum: IBDP, IGCSE
Language instr: English, French, Arabic

Bahrain Bayan School
Bldg 230, Road No. 4111, P.O. Box 32411, Isa Town 841
Tel: +973 7712 2244
Age range: 4–18 years
No. of pupils: 1313
Curriculum: IBDP
Language instr: English, Arabic

Bahrain Capital School
Road 5755, Block 457, Bu Quwah
Tel: +973 17008880
Age range: 3–18 years
Curriculum: UK, IGCSE, ALevs

Bahrain School
Al Ghurafaiyah Building 540, Area 342, Road 4225, Juffair, Manama
Tel: +973 17727828
Age range: 4–18 years
Curriculum: AP, USA
Language instr: English

Beacon Private School
Building 101, Avenue 14, Block 109, P.O. Box 52030, Al Hidd
Tel: +973 66000088
Age range: 4–18 years
Curriculum: IBDP
Language instr: English, Arabic

Britus International School, Bahrain
Building 208, Road 408, Block 704, P.O. Box 18041, Salmabad Manama
Tel: +973 17598444
Age range: 3–18 years
Curriculum: IBDP, UK, USA, IGCSE
Language instr: English

Creativity Private School
P.O. Box 24176, Muharraq
Tel: +973 17243855
Age range: 4–18 years
Curriculum: USA
Language instr: English, Arabic

Hawar International School
Building 22, Road 42, Block 910, P.O. Box 38338, Riffa
Tel: +937 13666555
Age range: 4–14 years
Curriculum: IBDP, IGCSE
Language instr: English

Ibn Khuldoon National School
Building 161, Road 4111, Area 841, P.O. Box 20511, Isa Town
Tel: +973 17780661
Age range: 4–18 years
No. of pupils: 1818
Curriculum: IBDP, IBMYP, IBPYP, National, SAT, TOEFL, USA
Language instr: English, Arabic

Lycée Français International de Bahreïn
P.O. Box 24447, Muharraq
Tel: +973 17323770
Age range: 4–18 years
Curriculum: FrenchBacc
Language instr: English, French, Arabic

Modern Knowledge Schools
Building 515, Road 4209, Juffair, Manama
Tel: +973 17727712
Age range: 4–18 years
Curriculum: IBDP, USA
Language instr: English

Nadeen School Bahrain
Block 337, Road 3748, House 1969, Manama
Tel: +973 17728886
Age range: 3–18 years
Curriculum: UK
Language instr: English

Naseem International School
P.O. Box 28503, Riffa
Tel: +973 17782000
Age range: 3–18 years
Curriculum: IBDP, IBMYP, IBPYP, IBCP, National, USA
Language instr: English, Arabic
CIS ECIS

Quality Education School
Building 63, Road 83, Block 505, Muqabah, Budaiya
Tel: +973 17692917
Age range: 3–18 years
Curriculum: National, UK, IGCSE

Riffa Views International School
Building 407, Road 4303, Block Al Mazrowiah 943, P.O. Box 3050, Riffa
Tel: +973 16565000
Age range: 3–18 years
Curriculum: IBDP, USA
Language instr: English
CIS

Sacred Heart School
P.O. Box 388, Isa Town, Manama
Tel: +973 17684367
Age range: 4–18 years
Curriculum: IGCSE
Language instr: English

Shaikha Hessa Girls' School
Riffa
Tel: +973 17756111
Age range: G3–18 years
Curriculum: IBDP, IGCSE
Language instr: English
CIS

St Christopher's School
Building 119, Road 4109, P.O. Box 32052, Isa Town
Tel: +973 17605301
Age range: 3–18 years
No. of pupils: 2400
Curriculum: IBDP, IGCSE, ALevs
Language instr: English
COB

Talent International & The Infant School (Manama Branch)
Road No. 5641, Salihiya, Manama
Tel: +973 17252346
Age range: 3 months–18 years
Curriculum: UK, IGCSE, ALevs
Language instr: English

Talent International & The Infant School (Riffa Branch)
Road No. 2506, Riffa
Tel: +973 17770078
Age range: 3 months–18 years
Curriculum: UK, IGCSE, ALevs
Language instr: English

The Asian School
P.O. Box 1143, Manama
Tel: + 973 17722886
Age range: 4–18 years
Curriculum: National

The British Preparatory School
Villa 12-14, Entrance 300, Saar Avenue, Al Markh
Tel: +973 17792010
Age range: 0–6 years
Curriculum: UK
Language instr: English

The British School of Bahrain
PO Box 30733 - Budaiya, Building 1080, Road 1425, Block 1014, Hamala
Tel: +973 1 761 0920
Age range: 3–18 years
Curriculum: UK, IGCSE, ALevs
Language instr: English

The Children's Academy, Bahrain
Building 22, Avenue 42, Block 910, Riffa
Tel: +973 17613234
Age range: 4–16 years
Curriculum: IPC, UK, IGCSE

The Indian School
P.O. Box 558, Isa Town
Tel: +973 17684166
Age range: 4–18 years

The International School of Choueifat - Manama
P.O. Box 50559 Arad, Bldg. 110, Road 59, Area 257, Choueifat Avenue, Manama, Amwaj Islands
Tel: +973 160 33 333
Age range: 3–18 years
Curriculum: AP, IGCSE

BANGLADESH

Abdul Kadir Molla International School
16/8 Baghdi (Dhaka-Sylhet Highway), Narsingdi Sadar, Narsingdi 1600, Dhaka
Tel: +880 961 750 6070
Age range: 3–18 years
Curriculum: IBDP, IBPYP, IGCSE, ALevs
Language instr: English, Bengali

Asia

American International School, Dhaka
12 United Nations Road, 1212 Dhaka
Tel: +880 24 108 1837
Age range: 3–18 years
Curriculum: IBDP, IBPYP, USA
Language instr: English

American Standard International School
House No. 20B, Road No. 79/82, Gulshan, 1212 Dhaka
Tel: +880 175 671 0196
Curriculum: SAT, UK, USA, IGCSE, ALevs
Language instr: English

Aurora International School
House NE (A) 3A, Road 74, Gulshan, 1212 Dhaka
Tel: +880 222 228 3251
Age range: 2–13 years
Curriculum: IBPYP
Language instr: English

Australian International School, Dhaka
Joarshahara, Khilkhet, 1229 Dhaka
Tel: +880 171 156 7236
Age range: 3–18 years
Curriculum: IBDP, IBMYP, IBPYP
Language instr: English

Bangladesh International Tutorial School
Plot No. 13, Road No.1/A, Sector No. 14, Uttara Model Town, 1230 Dhaka
Tel: +880 5 508 7116
Age range: 4–18 years
Curriculum: UK, IGCSE, ALevs
Language instr: English

British Standard School
13 Larmini Street, Wari, Dhaka
Tel: +880 24 711 5628
Age range: 2–18 years
Curriculum: UK

Canadian International School Bangladesh
Senior Campus: Plot No. 110, Road No. 27, Block A, Banani 1213, Dhaka
Tel: +880 184 146 1999
Age range: 4–18 years
Curriculum: IBDP
Language instr: English

Chittagong Grammar School (CGS)
321/11 Sarson Road, Chittagong
Tel: +880 3 162 2472
Age range: 2–18 years
Curriculum: National, SAT, UK, GCSE, ALevs
Language instr: English

Chittagong Grammar School (CGS) Dhaka
Block-B, House No. 83, Road No. 4, Banani, 1213 Dhaka
Tel: +880 132 443 9783
Age range: 2–18 years
Curriculum: National, SAT, UK, GCSE, ALevs
Language instr: English

Crans-Montana International School
Rahaman Housing Family Estate, 1492, C D A Avenue, East Nasirabad, Chittagong
Tel: +880 163 155 5222
Age range: 3–16 years
Curriculum: IBPYP
Language instr: English, Bengali

East West International School & College
265/1 West Shewrapara, Mirpur, 1216 Dhaka
Tel: +880 173 301 1222
Age range: 3–16 years
Curriculum: IGCSE
Language instr: English

EFID - French International School of Dhaka
Plot 13, Embassy Road, Baridhara, 1212 Dhaka
Tel: +880 171 309 0457
Age range: 3–11 years
Curriculum: FrenchBacc

Grace International School
House-6B, Road 02, Gulshan 1, Dhaka
Tel: +880 171 330 3468
Age range: 2–18 years
Curriculum: UK, IGCSE, ALevs

Hurdco International School
Ka-19/1, Bashundhara Main Gate, 1229 Dhaka
Tel: +880 2 841 5034
Age range: 3–18 years
Curriculum: UK, IGCSE, ALevs

International School Dhaka (ISD)
Plot 80, Block E, Bashundhara R/A, (Opposite Apollo Hospitals Dhaka), 1229 Dhaka
Tel: +880 2 843 1101
Age range: 2–19 years
Curriculum: IBDP, IBMYP, IBPYP
Language instr: English

Oxford International School - Banasree Campus
House No. 7 & 8, Block A, Banasree, Rampura, 1219 Dhaka
Tel: +880 192 600 0751
Age range: 3–16 years
Curriculum: UK, IGCSE

Oxford International School - Dhamnondi Main Campus
House No. 34, Road No. New 16, Dhanmondi R/A, 1209 Dhaka
Tel: +880 176 585 5555
Age range: 3–18 years
Curriculum: UK, IGCSE, ALevs

Oxford International School - Gulshan Campus
Plot No. Ga 25/5/1, Shahjadpur, Progoti Swarani, Gulshan, 1212 Dhaka
Tel: +880 192 600 0737
Age range: 3–16 years
Curriculum: UK, IGCSE

Oxford International School - Old Dhaka Campus
House No. 91/1 A, Swamibagh, New Doyagonj Road, Wari, Gandaria, 1100 Dhaka
Tel: +880 192 600 0749
Age range: 3–16 years
Curriculum: UK, IGCSE

Oxford International School - Uttara Campus
House No. 40, Gausul Azam Avenue, Sector-13, Uttara, 1230 Dhaka
Tel: +880 192 600 0738
Age range: 3–16 years
Curriculum: UK, IGCSE

Pledge Harbor International School
Singer Dighi, Maona, Gazipur 1741, Dhaka
Tel: +880 967 880 0404
Age range: 3–19 years
Curriculum: IBDP, IBMYP, IBPYP, IBCP
Language instr: English

RISE Royal Institute of Smart Education
1 Lovely Road, Shubidbazar, Sylhet
Tel: +880 173 070 0877
Age range: 4–18 years
Curriculum: UK, IGCSE, ALevs

Scholastica Schools
Plot 2, Road 8 & 9, Sector 1, Uttara Model Town, 1230 Dhaka
Tel: +880 181 924 3499
Age range: 3–18 years
Curriculum: UK, IGCSE, ALevs

Springdale International School
Road 55, House 11/A, Gulshan 2, 1212 Dhaka
Tel: +880 140 707 6610
Curriculum: IBPYP
Language instr: English, Bangla

Sunnydale School
Plot No. 19A, Road No. 13, Block G, Bashundhara, 1229 Dhaka
Tel: +880 132 443 0197
Age range: 3–18 years
Curriculum: UK, IGCSE, ALevs

Sunshine Grammar School and College
House 11, Road 1, Nasirabad H/S, 4000 Chittagong
Tel: +880 171 310 2143
Age range: 3–18 years
Curriculum: SAT, UK, IGCSE, ALevs
Language instr: English

Sylhet Khananchibari International School and College
Nayasarak Road, 3100 Sylhet
Tel: +880 082 171 9487
Age range: 3–18 years
Curriculum: National, UK, IGCSE, ALevs
Language instr: English

The Aga Khan Academy Dhaka
Ka-65/1, Kuratoli, 1229 Dhaka
Tel: +880 963 811 1222
Curriculum: IBDP, IBMYP, IBPYP
Language instr: English

The Aga Khan School, Dhaka
Road 6A, Sector 4, Uttara Model Town, 1230 Dhaka
Tel: +880 2 4895 9722
Age range: 3–18 years
Curriculum: IBDP, IGCSE, ALevs
Language instr: English

William Carey Academy
G.P.O. Box 96, 1986/A Zakir Hossain By-Lane, East Nasirabad, 4000 Chittagong
Tel: +880 24 135 5731
Age range: 4–18 years
Curriculum: SAT, USA
Language instr: English

BRUNEI DARUSSALAM

Bright Jigsaw International School
No. 675, Km 13.5, Kampong Salambigar, Jalan Muara, Bandar Seri Begawan BC 1515
Tel: +673 234 1035

INTERNATIONAL SCHOOL BRUNEI
For further details see p. 57
Jalan Utama Salambigar, Kampong Sungai Hanching, Berakas 'B' BC2115
Tel: +673 233 0608
Email: admission@ac.isb.edu.bn
Website: www.isb.edu.bn
Headteacher: Dominic Morley
Age range: 2–18 years
No. of pupils: 1250
Fees: 5,400–6,840
Curriculum: IBDP, National, SAT, UK, IGCSE
Language instr: English

JERUDONG INTERNATIONAL SCHOOL
For further details see p. 58
Jalan Universiti, Kampong Tungku, Bandar Seri Begawan BE2119
Tel: +673 241 1000 (Ext: 1205/1206/7100/1214)
Email: admissions@jis.edu.bn
Website: www.jerudong internationalschool.com
Executive Principal: Nicholas Sheehan
Age range: 2–18 years (*Boarding from 8 years)
No. of pupils: 1700
Fees: Day B$18,048–B$28,896 WB B$18,756–B$25,176 FB B$24,108–B$31,620
Curriculum: IBDP, SAT, UK, GCSE, IGCSE, ALevs
Language instr: English

Asia

Seri Mulia Sarjana International School
Spg. 340 Kg. Mata-Mata, Jalan Gadong, Bandar Seri Begawan, Negara BE1718
Tel: +673 242 1311
Age range: 5–11 years
Curriculum: UK

CAMBODIA

Abundant Life International School
House 94, ST 315, Tuol Kouk, Phnom Penh
Tel: +855 88 690 1111
Age range: 2–18 years
Curriculum: National, USA
Language instr: Khmer, English, Chinese

Asian Hope International School
168 Chres Village Road, Sen Sok Khan, Phnom Penh Thmey, Phnom Penh
Tel: +855 23 885 170
Age range: 3–18 years
Curriculum: National, UK, IGCSE, ALevs
Language instr: English

Australian International School Phnom Penh
No. 76 Angkor Boulevard, Sangkat Toul Sangke 2, Khan Russey Keo, Phnom Penh 120707
Tel: +855 92 111 136
Age range: 3–18 years
Curriculum: IBDP, IBMYP, IBPYP, IBCP
Language instr: English, Khmer

Bluebird British International School
No. 25, Street 71, Sangkat Beong Keng Kang 1, Khan Beong Keng Kang, Phnom Penh
Tel: +855 23 215 421
Age range: 2–13 years
Curriculum: IPC, National

Canadian International School of Phnom Penh
Koh Pich (Diamond Island), Elite Town Street, Phnom Penh
Tel: +855 23 900 399
Age range: 3–18 years
Curriculum: IBDP
Language instr: English, French

CIA FIRST International School
839, Street Doung Ngeab III, Khan Sen Sok, Phnom Penh
Tel: +855 95 200 011
Age range: 4–18 years

East-West International School
131 Street 143, Boeung Keng Kang 3, Phnom Penh
Tel: +855 23 998 244
Age range: 2–18 years
Curriculum: IPC, IGCSE, ALevs
Language instr: English, Khmer

Footprints International School
No. 84, Street 135, (at the intersection of Street 470), Phnom Penh
Tel: +855 17 222 084
Age range: 1.5–18 years
Curriculum: National
Language instr: English

Golden Gate American School
No. 846 Street 1003, Sen Sok District, Phnom Penh 12101
Tel: +855 99 777 550
Curriculum: IBDP
Language instr: English

HOPE International School
P.O. Box 2521, Phnom Penh 3 12000
Tel: +855 12 550 522
Age range: 3–18 years
Curriculum: IBDP, IGCSE
Language instr: English

iCAN British International School
15 Ke Nou Street 9, Sangkat Tonle Bassac, Phnom Penh 120101
Tel: +855 23 222 416-8
Age range: 2–11 years
Curriculum: IPC, UK

International School of Phnom Penh
P.O. Box 138, Hun Neang Boulevard, Phnom Penh
Tel: +855 23 425 088
Age range: 3–18 years
Curriculum: IBDP, IBMYP, IBPYP
Language instr: English
(CIS) (EAR)

International School of Siem Reap
Ring Road, Kor Kranh Village, Siem Reap Commune, Siem Reap District, P.O. Box 93169, Siem Reap 171209
Tel: +855 12 878 782
Age range: 2.5–18 years
Curriculum: UK, IGCSE, ALevs

Invictus International School Phnom Penh
144C Preah Norodom Boulevard (Street 41), Sangkat Tonle Bassac, Khan Chamkarmon, Phnom Penh
Tel: +855 23 723 212
Age range: 3–18 years
Curriculum: IPC, UK, IGCSE, ALevs

Jay Pritzker Academy
P.O. Box 93298, Tachet Village, Samroang Yea Commune, Puok District, Siem Reap
Tel: +855 (0)92 655 322
Age range: 4–18 years
Curriculum: AP

Lycée Français René Descartes
Rue Christopher Howes (rue 96), Phnom Penh 10000
Tel: +855 92 437 464
Age range: 4–18 years
Curriculum: FrenchBacc

Northbridge International School Cambodia
Street 2004, Trapang Chhouk Village, Teuk Thlar Commune, Sen Sok District, Phnom Penh 12102
Tel: +855 23 900 749
Age range: 2–18 years
No. of pupils: 1000
Curriculum: IBDP, IBMYP, IBPYP
Language instr: English

Paragon International School Cambodia - Primary Campus
No. 39, St. 315, Boeng Kok 1 Toul Kork, Phnom Penh
Tel: +855 23 884 040
Age range: 2–11 years
Curriculum: National, UK
Language instr: English

Paragon International School Cambodia - Secondary Campus
No. 2843, St. 3, Sangkat Tonle Basak Khan Chamkar Morn, Phnom Penh
Tel: +855 23 214 040
Age range: 11–18 years
Curriculum: National, SAT, UK, IGCSE, ALevs
Language instr: English

SGIS International School
93 Thmor Meas Road, Salakamreuk Commune, Siem Reap
Tel: +855 92 590 033
Age range: 4–18 years
Curriculum: National

The Giving Tree International School
N4A1, Street 398, Beoung Keng Kang 1, Phnom Penh
Tel: +855 17 997 112
Age range: 6 months–12 years
Curriculum: IBPYP
Language instr: English, French

Western International School
No. 20, St. 598C, Phnom Penh
Tel: +855 16 699 192
Age range: 3–18 years
Curriculum: USA
Language instr: English, Khmer

CHINA

Access International Academy Ningbo
No1 Ai Xue Road, Beilun District, Ningbo, Zhejiang 315800
Tel: +86 574 8686 9999
Age range: 4–18
Curriculum: USA
Language instr: English
(EAR)

Achieve Xiamen International School (AXIS School)
No. 877 Fanghu North 2nd Road, Huli District, Xiamen, Fujian
Tel: +86 59 2666 8099
Curriculum: IBPYP
Language instr: English, Chinese

Affiliated School of JNU for Hong Kong and Macao Students - Dongguan
No. 19 Guangchang North Road, Gaobu Town, Dongguan, Guangdong 523270
Tel: +86 769 8878 5333
Curriculum: IBPYP
Language instr: English

Affiliated School of JNU for Hong Kong and Macao Students - Guangzhou
No. 18 Huilong Road, Longdong Street, Tianhe District, Guangzhou, Guangdong 510630
Tel: +86 20 8708 5090
Curriculum: IBDP, IBMYP, IBPYP
Language instr: English, Chinese

AISB-Hope International
Building 5, Dayu, Yard 4, Chaoyang Farm, Chaoyang District, Beijing 100018
Tel: +86 10 8431 2141
Age range: 5–18 years
Curriculum: AP
Language instr: English

AISL Harrow Haikou
No. 15 Linhai No. 3 Road, Meilan, Haikou
Tel: +86 898 6616 9981
Age range: 2–18 years
Curriculum: UK, IGCSE, ALevs

AISL Harrow School Beijing
Harrow Beijing City Campus, No. 5, 4th Block, Anzhen Xili, Chaoyang, Beijing 100029
Tel: +86 10 6444 8100
Age range: 3–18 years
Curriculum: UK, IGCSE, ALevs

Alcanta International College
14 Guang Sheng Road, Nansha District, Guangzhou City, Guangdong 511458
Tel: +86 20 8618 3999/3666
Age range: 12–19
Curriculum: IBDP
Language instr: English, Mandarin

American International School of Guangzhou
No 3 Yan Yu Street South, Ersha Island, Yuexiu District, Guangzhou, Guangdong 510105
Tel: +86 20 8735 3392
Age range: 3–18 years
No. of pupils: 1100
Curriculum: IBDP, IBPYP
Language instr: English
(EAR)

Ardingly College Zhongshan Kindergarten
No. 233 Haojiang Road, East District, Zhongshan, Guangdong 528400
Curriculum: IBPYP
Language instr: English, Chinese

Asia

Bade Intercultural Academy, Chengdu
168 Zhongli Road, Banzhuyuan Town, Xindu District, Chengdu, Sichuan
Tel: +86 130 7600 8225
Language instr: English, Chinese

Baowei Kindergarten
No.4 Baiyun Road, Xicheng District, Beijing 100045
Tel: +86 13716522908
Language instr: Chinese, English

Beanstalk International Bilingual School (BIBS) - Changying
No. 1 Yaojiadian Street, Chaoyang District, Beijing
Tel: +86 10 8456 2808
Curriculum: IBPYP
Language instr: English, Chinese

Beanstalk International Bilingual School (BIBS) - Chengdu
No. 351 Honghe Road, Longquanyi district, Chengdu, Sichuan
Tel: +86 28 8481 0088
Curriculum: AP, IBDP, IBMYP, IBPYP, IGCSE, ALevs
Language instr: English, Chinese

Beanstalk International Bilingual School (BIBS) - Haidian Academy
Yanxitai, Jushan Road, Sijiqing, Haidian District, Beijing
Tel: +86 10 6576 0906
Curriculum: AP, IBPYP, IGCSE, ALevs
Language instr: English, Chinese

Beanstalk International Bilingual School (BIBS) - Huairou
No. 13 Yanqi North Second Street, Huairou District, Beijing
Tel: +86 176 0165 9138
Curriculum: AP, IGCSE, ALevs
Language instr: English, Chinese

Beanstalk International Bilingual School (BIBS) - Kunming
No. 986 Yongzheng Street, Chenggong District, Kunming, Yunnan
Tel: +86871 6747 8668
Curriculum: IBDP, IBMYP, IBPYP, IGCSE, ALevs
Language instr: English, Chinese

Beanstalk International Bilingual School (BIBS) - Shunyi
No. 15 Liyuan Street, TianZhu County, Shunyi District, Beijing
Tel: +86 10 6518 9081
Curriculum: IBDP, IBMYP, IBPYP
Language instr: English, Chinese

Beanstalk International Bilingual School (BIBS) - Upper East Side
No. 6 North East 4th Ring Road, Chaoyang District, Beijing
Tel: +86 10 5130 7951
Curriculum: IBPYP
Language instr: English, Chinese

Beanstalk International Bilingual School (BIBS) - Weihai
Agile Weihai Champion Sports Town, NanHai New District, Weihai, Shandong
Tel: +86 63 1885 6118
Curriculum: IGCSE, ALevs
Language instr: English, Chinese

Beijing Bacui Bilingual School
No 1 Bacui Road, Chaoyang District, Beijing 100025
Tel: +86 10 6549 8092

Beijing BISS International School
No 17, Area 4, An Zhen Xi Li, Chaoyang District, Beijing 100029
Tel: +86 10 64 433151
Age range: 2–19 years
Curriculum: IBDP, IBMYP, IBPYP
Language instr: English

Beijing Chaoyang KaiWen Academy
No.46 Baoquansan Street, Chaoyang District, Beijing
Tel: +86 108 302 8199
Curriculum: IBDP
Language instr: English, Chinese

Beijing City International School
77 Baiziwan Nan Er Road, Chaoyang District, Beijing 100022
Tel: +86 10 8771 7171
Age range: 3–18
No. of pupils: 1029 B428 G601
Curriculum: IBDP, IBMYP, IBPYP, SAT
Language instr: English

Beijing Concord College of Sino-Canada
Conglin, Zhuangyuan, Tongzhou District, Beijing 101118
Tel: +86 108 959 1234
Language instr: English

Beijing Enlighten School
No. 300 Shunbai Road, Chaoyang District, Beijing
Tel: +86 10 6431 9970
Curriculum: IBPYP
Language instr: English, Chinese

Beijing Haidian Foreign Languages Tengfei School
No. 368-2 Hanhe Road, Haidian District, Beijing 100195
Tel: +86 10 8843 8003
Curriculum: IBDP
Language instr: English

Beijing Huijia Kindergarten, Beiou Campus
No.80 Maliandao Road, Xicheng District, Beijing 100085
Tel: +86 10 63354580
Curriculum: IBPYP
Language instr: Chinese, English

Beijing Huijia Kindergarten, Wanquan Campus
No. 35 Bagou South Road, Wanquan Xinxin Jiayuan Building 14, Haidian District, Beijing 100089
Tel: +86 10 8255 1751
Age range: 2–6
No. of pupils: 110
Language instr: Chinese

Beijing Huijia Kindergarten, Xibahe Dongli Campus
No.103 Xibahe Dongli, Chaoyang District, Beijing 100028
Tel: +86 (10) 64655212
Age range: 2–6
No. of pupils: 120
Curriculum: IBPYP
Language instr: Chinese

Beijing Huijia Private School
157 Changhuai Road, Changping District, Beijing 102200
Tel: +86 (10) 608 49399
Age range: 3–19
No. of pupils: 2100
Curriculum: IBDP, IBMYP, IBPYP
Language instr: Chinese, English

Beijing Hurston Kindergarten
Room 2-1, Building 2, No. 145, Jiukeshu, Tongzhou District, Beijing
Tel: +86 40 0855 1958
Curriculum: IBPYP
Language instr: English, Chinese

Beijing International Bilingual Academy
No. 1 Yumin Road, Houshayu, Shunyi, Beijing 101300
Tel: +86 10 80410390
Age range: 1–18 years
Curriculum: IBDP, IBMYP
Language instr: English

Beijing Royal Foreign Language School
No. 11 Wangfu Street, Changping District, Beijing 102209
Tel: +86 10 81 785 511
Curriculum: IBMYP, IBPYP
Language instr: Chinese, English

Beijing Royal Kindergarten
No. 11, Wangfu Street, Changping District, Beijing 102209
Tel: +86 10 81 785 511
Curriculum: IBPYP
Language instr: English, Chinese

Beijing Royal School
No. 11 Wangfu Street, Changping District, Beijing 102209
Tel: +86 10 81 785 511
Age range: 14–19
No. of pupils: 200
Curriculum: IBDP, USA
Language instr: English, Chinese

Beijing Shuren-Ribet Private School
Beijing Tongzhou District, Songzhuang Xiaopu South # 1, Beijing 101118
Tel: +86 10 80856787
Age range: 4–18
Curriculum: ACT, SAT, USA

Beijing World Youth Academy
18 Hua Jia Di Bei Li, Chao Yang District, Beijing 100102
Tel: +86 10 6470 6336
Age range: 11–18
No. of pupils: 685
Curriculum: IBDP, IBMYP
Language instr: English

Beijing Xin Fuxue International Academy
No. 99 Jingshun Road, Shunyi District, Beijing
Tel: +86 10 8942 0199
Curriculum: IBDP, IBMYP
Language instr: English, Chinese

Beijing Zhongshan International School
No. 137 MoShiKou Village, Shijingshan District, Beijing
Tel: +86 10 8890 1988
Language instr: English, Chinese

Boren Sino Canadian School
No. 20, Shuanglong Avenue, Jiangmen City, Guangdong
Tel: +86 750 3218848
Curriculum: National

Boston International School
9 Jinghui West Road, New District, Wuxi, Jiangsu 214000
Tel: +86 400 032 8000
Age range: 2–18
No. of pupils: 133 B65 G68
Curriculum: IBDP, IBMYP, IBPYP
Language instr: English

Boya International Academy - Kindergarten
No. 2756 Qunxian Middle Road, Jinghe New District, Shaoxing, Zhejiang
Curriculum: IBPYP
Language instr: English, Chinese

Bright Academy
Building 39#, ShiFoYing XiLi, Chaoyang District, Beijing 100025
Curriculum: IBPYP
Language instr: English, Chinese

Brilliant International School
No. 5 Building of Guanyang Mingdi, Chongchuan District, Nantong, Jiangsu 226000
Curriculum: IBPYP
Language instr: English

Asia

British School of Beijing, Shunyi
South Side, No. 9 An Hua Street,
Shunyi District, Beijing 101318
Tel: +8610 8047 3558
Age range: 18 months–18 years
No. of pupils: 1100
Curriculum: IBDP, UK, IGCSE
Language instr: English, German

Bubble Kingdom International Kindergarten
No. 431, Linjiang Avenue, Zhujiang New Town, Tianhe District, Guangzhou, Guangdong 510620
Tel: +86 20 6622 2520
Curriculum: IBPYP
Language instr: English, Chinese

Buena Vista Concordia International School
BaoAn exit, GuangShen HighWay, XiCheng (Buena Vista) BaoAn, Shenzhen, Guangdong
Tel: +86 755 2823 8166
Curriculum: National, USA

Cade International Kindergarten
No. 188 Lianchuang Road, Yuhang District, Hangzhou, Zhejiang
Tel: +86 571 8909 9666
Curriculum: IBPYP
Language instr: English, Chinese

Canada British Columbia International Schools - Hefei
5th Floor, International Department, Hefei No.1 High School, 2356 Xizang Road, Binhu New District, Hefei, Anhui
Tel: +86 199 5605 8176
Curriculum: IBDP
Language instr: English, Chinese

Canadian Foreign Language School- Cambridgeshire
Inside Agile Cambridgeshire, Nancun Town, Panyu District, Guangzhou, Guangdong 511442
Tel: +86 186 2078 9095
Curriculum: IBMYP, IBPYP
Language instr: English, Chinese

Canadian International School of Beijing
38 Liangmaqiao Lu, Chaoyang District, Beijing 100125
Tel: +86 10 6465 7788
Age range: 18 months–18 years
No. of pupils: 1093 B547 G546
Curriculum: IBDP, IBMYP, IBPYP, SAT
Language instr: English

Canadian International School of Beijing - Jianguomen DRC Campus
No.1 Xiushui Street, Chaoyang District, Beijing 100600
Tel: +86 10 85315312
Language instr: Chinese, English

Canadian International School of Guangzhou
122 Dongyi Road, Panyu District, Guangzhou, Guangdong
Tel: +86 020 3993 9920
Age range: 2–18 years
Curriculum: IBPYP
Language instr: English, Chinese

Canadian International School of Hefei
Fuxing Rd., High-Tech Zone, Hefei, Anhui 230088
Tel: +86 551 6267 6776
Curriculum: IBDP, IBMYP, IBPYP
Language instr: English

Canadian International School of Shenyang
No.301 Hui Shan Road, Hunnan District, Shenyang, Liaoning 110167
Tel: +86 24 66675379
Curriculum: IBDP, IBMYP, IBPYP
Language instr: Spanish, Chinese

CATS College China
No. 3039 Pan Jing Road, Bao Shan District, Shanghai
Tel: +86 21 5432 5279
Age range: 15–16+ years
Curriculum: UK, USA, ALevs

CBIS Bilingual School
Citic Lake Community, Lishui Town, Nanhai District, Foshan, Guangdong 528244
Curriculum: IBMYP, IBPYP
Language instr: English

Changchun American International School
2899 Dong Nan Hu Road, Changchun, Jilin 130033
Tel: +86 431 8458 1234
Age range: 3–18
No. of pupils: 400
Curriculum: IBDP, IBMYP, IBPYP
Language instr: English

Changsha WES (Bilingual) Academy
No. 58 Beidou Road, Changsha National Economic & Technical Development Zone, Changsha, Hunan 410100
Tel: +86 731 8275 8900
Curriculum: IBPYP
Language instr: English, Chinese

Changsha WES Academy
8 Dongyi Road, Xingsha, Changsha National Economic & Technical Development Zone, Changsha, Hunan 410100
Tel: +86 731 8275 8900
Age range: 3–19 years
Curriculum: IBDP, IBPYP, IBCP, IGCSE, ALevs
Language instr: English

Changwai Bilingual School
No.66 Hengshan Road, Changzhou, Jiangsu 213022
Tel: +86 519 86921160
Age range: 4–14
No. of pupils: 2100
Curriculum: IBDP, IBMYP, IBPYP, IPC

Changzhou Wujin Qingying Foreign Language School
No. 5 Xihu Road, Wujin District, Changzhou, Jiangsu 213100
Curriculum: IBPYP
Language instr: English, Chinese

Chengdu International School
68 Tong Gui Road, Jin Jiang District, Chengdu, Sichuan 61066
Tel: +86 28 6517 522 8/9

Chengdu Jinjiang Jiaxiang Foreign Languages High School
International Building, Jiaxiang Foreign Languages ??Senior High Scho+, No. 6 Chenhui North Road, Jinjiang District, Chengdu, Sichuan
Tel: +86 28 8666 6501
Curriculum: IBDP
Language instr: English

Chengdu Meishi International School
1340 Middle Section of Tianfu Avenue, Chengdu, Sichuan 610042
Tel: +86 028 8533 0653
Age range: 6–18
Curriculum: IBDP, IBMYP, IBPYP
Language instr: English, Chinese

Chengdu Parkview PYP Kindergarten
Yidu Road Longchengyihao, Chengdu, Sichuan 610101
Tel: +86 28 8464 9066
Curriculum: IBPYP
Language instr: Chinese, English

Chenshan School
QiYunXiDaDao, XiuNing District, Huangshan, Anhui 245400
Tel: +86 559 7511878
Curriculum: IBDP
Language instr: English, Chinese

China World Academy Changshu
No.8 Yijia Road, Changshu, Jiangsu 215500
Tel: +86 185 0152 9096
Curriculum: IBDP
Language instr: English, Chinese

Chiway Repton School Xiamen
No. 388 Xibin Road, Jimei District, Xiamen, Fujian 361022
Tel: +86 59 2210 0886
Curriculum: IBMYP, IBPYP
Language instr: English, Chinese

Chongqing Bachuan International High School
666 Tashan East Street, Tongliang District, Chongqing 402560
Curriculum: USA

Chongqing Nankai Liangjiang Secondary School
No. 209 Yujiang Avenue, Longxing, Yubei District, Chongqing 401135
Curriculum: IBDP
Language instr: English, Chinese

Clifford School
Panyu, Guangzhou, Guangdong 511495
Tel: +86 20 8471 1441

Cogdel Cranleigh School, Changsha
No. 117 Lixin Street (Langli Block), Changsha Economy and Technology Zone, Changsha, Hunan
Tel: +86 731 8406 1777
Age range: 3–18 years
Curriculum: AP, IBDP, IBMYP, IBPYP, IGCSE, ALevs
Language instr: English, Chinese

Cogdel Cranleigh School, Wuhan
No. 9 Tianyu Road, Panlongcheng Economic Zone, Huangpi District, Wuhan, Hubei
Tel: +86 27 8591 9666
Curriculum: IBDP
Language instr: English, Chinese

Concordia International School Shanghai
999 Ming Yue Road, JinQiao, Pudong, Shanghai 201206
Tel: +862 1 5899 0380
Age range: 3–18 years
No. of pupils: 1200
Curriculum: USA
Language instr: English

Country Garden Silver Beach School
Country Garden Silver Beach, Renshan Town, Huidong County, Huizhou, Guangdong 516347
Tel: +86 139 2910 2096
Curriculum: IBDP, IBMYP, IBPYP
Language instr: English, Chinese

Dalian American International School
No. 2 Dianchi Road, Golden Pebble Beach National Resort, Dalian Development Area, Jinzhou District, Dalian, Liaoning 116650
Tel: +86 411 8757 5788
Age range: 4–18 years
Language instr: English

Asia

Dalian Maple Leaf Foreign Nationals School
78 Caiyun Road, Xigang, Dalian, Liaoning
Tel: +86 411 6760187
Age range: 3–15 years
No. of pupils: 200

Dalian Maple Leaf International High School
Fushun Street, Jinzhou, Dalian, Liaoning
Tel: +86 400 655 6877
Age range: 14–19

Daystar Academy
No. 2, Shunbai Road, Chaoyang District, Beijing
Tel: +86 (0)10 64337366
Curriculum: IBDP, IBMYP, IBPYP
Language instr: English

Daystar Academy Sanlitun
No.13 East 4th Street, Sanlitun, Chaoyang, Beijing 100600
Curriculum: IBPYP
Language instr: English, Chinese

Dehong Beijing International Chinese School
Block #1, Luneng Grassetown, Bifu Road, Tongzhou District, Beijing 101100
Tel: +86 10 8083 6983
Curriculum: IBDP
Language instr: English, Chinese

Dehong Shanghai International Chinese School
1935 Shuguang Road, Maqiao, Minhang District, Shanghai 201111
Tel: +86 21 3329 9458
Curriculum: IBDP
Language instr: English, Chinese

Deutsche Botschaftsschule Peking
Liangmaqiao Lu 49 A, Chaoyang District, Beijing 100125
Tel: +86 10 6532 2535

Deutsche Schule Shanghai Pudong
1100 Jufeng Lu, Shanghai 201206
Tel: +86 (21) 68 97 55 08

Dongguan Hanlin Experimental School
Chuangye Road No.5, Wanjiang District, Dongguan, Guangdong 523000
Tel: +86 769 2277 6456
Age range: 3–18 years
Curriculum: IBMYP, IBPYP
Language instr: English, Chinese

Dulwich College Beijing
89 Capital Airport Road, Shunyi District, Beijing 101300
Tel: +86 10 6454 9000
Age range: 3–18 years
No. of pupils: 1610
Curriculum: IBDP, IGCSE
Language instr: English

Dulwich College Kindergarten, Shanghai
425 LanAn Road, JinQiao, Pudong, Shanghai 201206
Tel: +86 21 5899 9910
Age range: 2–7
Curriculum: UK

Dulwich College Shanghai Pudong
266 Lan An Road, Jinqiao, Pudong, Shanghai 201206
Tel: +8621 3896 1200
Age range: 2–18 years
No. of pupils: 1600
Curriculum: IBDP, UK, IGCSE
Language instr: English

Dulwich College Shanghai Puxi
2000 Qianpujing Road, Maqiao, Minhang District, Shanghai 201111
Tel: +86 21 3329 9310
Age range: 2–18 years
No. of pupils: 500
Curriculum: IBDP, UK, IGCSE
Language instr: English, Mandarin, Spanish

Dulwich College Suzhou
360 Gang Tian Road, Suzhou Industrial Park, Suzhou, Jiangsu 215021
Tel: +86 512 6295 9500
Age range: 2–18 years
No. of pupils: 900
Curriculum: IBDP, IBCP, IGCSE
Language instr: English

Dulwich International High School Suzhou
Fangzhong Street, Near East Zhong Xin Avenue, Suzhou, Jiangsu 215021
Tel: +86 512 6787 5003
Age range: 14–19 years
No. of pupils: 750
Curriculum: IGCSE, ALevs
Language instr: English

Dulwich International High School Zhuhai
No. 29 Hongjing Road, Guangdong-Macao in-depth cooperation zone in Hengqin, Zhuhai, Guangdong 519060
Tel: +86 756 8693133
Age range: 14–18 years
No. of pupils: 300
Curriculum: IGCSE, ALevs
Language instr: English

Eaglebridge International School
9 Guoqiang Road, Zhengxing New District, Dandong, Liaoning
Tel: +86 415 228 3333
Curriculum: USA

Ecole Francaise Internationale de Canton
Caibin Middle Road, Shangshui Street 62-70, Jinshazhou, Baiyun District, Guangzhou, Guangdong
Tel: +86 20 3879 7324
Curriculum: FrenchBacc
Language instr: French, English, Chinese

École francaise internationale de Wuhan
Campus international 10-1 Bo Xue Lu, Wuhan, Hubei 430056
Tel: +86 27 8473 9018

EL Genesis Kindergarten
No. 8 Ruichang Road, Hi-Tech Zone, Ningbo, Zhejiang 315048
Tel: +86 40 0801 8000
Curriculum: IBPYP
Language instr: English, Chinese

EtonHouse International School Suzhou
102 Kefa Road, Suzhou Science & Technology Town, Suzhou, Jiangsu 215163
Tel: +86 512 6825 5666
Age range: 2–18 years
No. of pupils: 236
Curriculum: IBDP, IBMYP, IBPYP
Language instr: English

EtonHouse International School Times Residence, Chengdu
180 Zhiquan Section, East Avenue, Times Residence, Chengdu, Sichuan 610061
Tel: +86 28 8477 7977
Curriculum: IBPYP
Language instr: English

EtonHouse International School, Foshan
32 Fufeng Square, 1st Foping No.4 Road, Guicheng, Nanhai, Foshan, Guangdong
Tel: +86 757 6668 8333
Curriculum: IBPYP, UK, IGCSE, ALevs
Language instr: English

EtonHouse International School, Nanjing
10 South Qing'ao Rd, Jianye District, Nanjing, Jiangsu 210019
Tel: +86 25 8669 6778
Curriculum: IBPYP

EtonHouse International School, Riverside
AddressSouth Pudong Road 1570, Pudong, Shanghai
Tel: +86 21 5068 9695
Language instr: English, Chinese

Etu King's Kindergarten of Wuhan
Building 1, Phase 5, Tongan Home, Houhu Avenue, Houhu Street, Wuhan, Hubei
Tel: +86 27 8228 6677
Curriculum: IBPYP
Language instr: English, Chinese

Exploratory Model Primary School
Chongqing BI Academy, No. 766 Konggang East Road, Yubei District, Chongqing 401120
Tel: +86 186 2076 5920
Curriculum: IBPYP
Language instr: English, Chinese

Fettes College Guangzhou
No. 2 Xinxue Road, Phoenix City, Nan'an Village, Xintang Town, Zengcheng District, Guangzhou, Guangdong 511340
Tel: +86 20 8299 8816
Curriculum: IBMYP, IBPYP
Language instr: English, Chinese

FLS Personalized Innovative Education Preschool
No. 2 Science Avenue, Science City, Huangpu District, Guangzhou, Guangdong 510665
Tel: +86 20 8985 2080
Curriculum: IBPYP
Language instr: English, Chinese

Fuzhou International Preschool @ 1 Park Avenue
1 Park Avenue, Jinju Road 826, Jinshan District, Fuzhou, Fujian 350000
Tel: +86 0591 83505222
Curriculum: IBPYP
Language instr: English, Chinese

Fuzhou Lakeside International School
No.72 North Meng Shan Road, Gulou District, Fuzhou, Fujian
Tel: +86 591 2806 6277
Curriculum: IBMYP
Language instr: English, Chinese

GDUFS International School Guangzhou
No. 599 Guanghua 1st Road, Baiyun District, Guangzhou, Guangdong 510450
Tel: +86 180 2634 2734
Curriculum: IBDP
Language instr: English, Chinese

Golden Apple International Preschool and Kindergarten
No. 7 Chuangrui Road, Hi-tech District, Chengdu, Sichuan 610041
Tel: +86 28 8523 7403
Curriculum: IBPYP
Language instr: Chinese, English

Golden Apple Jincheng No. 1 Secondary School
No. 99 Xianglong 3rd Street, High-tech Zone, Chengdu, Sichuan 610041
Tel: +86 28 6010 9299
Curriculum: IBDP
Language instr: English, Chinese

Golden Apple New Montessori Kindergarten (Jincheng Lake)
No. 900 Jincheng Avenue, High Tech Zone, Chengdu, Sichuan 610041
Tel: +86 28 8523 1763
Curriculum: IBPYP
Language instr: Chinese

Asia

Golden Apple Tianfu International Preschool and Kindergarten
No. 187 Shengxing Street, Jiannan Street North, Hi-tech District, Chengdu, Sichuan 610041
Tel: +86 28 8517 1648
Curriculum: IBPYP
Language instr: English

Grand Canadian Academy (GCA Jiaxing)
288 Zhenxing Donglu, Tongxiang, Zhejiang 314500
Tel: +86 573 8810 7576

Green Oasis School
No.4030, Shennan Middle Road, Tianmian, Futian District, Shenzhen, Guangdong 518026
Tel: +86 755 8395 9000
Age range: 5–16
Curriculum: IGCSE

Guangdong Country Garden School
Beijiao Town, Shunde District, Foshan City, Guangdong
Tel: +86 757 2667 7888
Age range: 2–18 years
No. of pupils: 4800
Curriculum: IBDP, IBMYP, IBPYP
Language instr: Chinese, English

Guangdong Shunde Desheng School
Minxing Road, New District, Daliang, Shunde, Guangdong 528300
Tel: +86 0757 22325121
Age range: 12–18 years
No. of pupils: 560
Curriculum: IBDP
Language instr: English

Guangzhou Huamei International School
No. 23 Huamei Road, Tianhe District, Guangzhou, Guangdong 510520
Tel: +86 20 8721 0178
Curriculum: IBPYP, USA
Language instr: English

Guangzhou International Kindergarten Huangpu ZWIE
No. 438 Fengle South Road, Huangpu District, Guangzhou, Guangdong 510700
Tel: +86 20 6298 6871
Curriculum: IBPYP
Language instr: Chinese

Guangzhou International Middle School Huangpu ZWIE
No. 438 Fengle South Road, Huangpu District, Guangzhou, Guangdong 510700
Tel: +86 40 0780 2003
Curriculum: IBMYP
Language instr: English, Chinese

Guangzhou International Primary School Baiyun ZWIE
No. 998 Tonghe Road, Baiyun District, Guangzhou City, Guangdong 510515
Tel: +86 20 3724 8716
Curriculum: IBPYP
Language instr: English, Chinese

Guangzhou International Primary School Huangpu ZWIE
No. 188 Huangpu East Road, Huangpu District, Guangzhou, Guangdong 510700
Tel: +86 40 0780 2003
Curriculum: IBPYP
Language instr: English, Chinese

Guangzhou SCA School
No. 2 Ciji Road, China-Singapore Knowledge City, Huangpu District, Guangzhou, Guangdong
Tel: +86 16 6020 1230
Curriculum: IBDP
Language instr: English, Chinese

Guiyang Huaxi Country Garden International School
Country Garden Community, Mengguan Town, Huaxi District, Guiyang, Guizhou 550026
Tel: +86 (0)851 83651885
Curriculum: IBPYP
Language instr: English, Chinese

Hailiang Foreign Language School
Hailiang Educational Park, No.199 West 3rd Ring Road, Taozhu Street, Zhuji, Zhejiang
Tel: +86 575 8900 3866
Curriculum: IBDP, IBMYP, IBPYP, UK, USA, ALevs
Language instr: English, Chinese

Hainan Micro-City Future School
Chengmai County, Hainan 571900
Curriculum: IBDP
Language instr: English, Chinese

Hangzhou Binjiang Wickham Kindergarten
No.525 Weiye Road, Binjiang District, Hangzhou, Zhejiang 31500
Curriculum: IBPYP
Language instr: English, Chinese

Hangzhou Dipont School of Arts and Science
No. 1 Guowen Road, Hangzhou, Zhejiang 310000
Tel: +86 571 5639 5678
Curriculum: IBDP
Language instr: English, Chinese

Hangzhou Future Sci-Tech City Wickham Kindergarten
No. 968-8, Gaojiao, Road, Yuhang District, Hangzhou, Zhejiang 311100
Tel: +86 571 88665991
Curriculum: IBPYP
Language instr: English, Chinese

Hangzhou Greentown Yuhua Qinqin School
2 Zhujia Road, Yuhang District, Hangzhou, Zhejiang 311112
Curriculum: IBPYP
Language instr: English, Chinese

Hangzhou Greentown Yuhua School
No. 532 Wenyi West Road, Hangzhou, Zhejiang 310012
Tel: +86 571 88477561
Curriculum: IBMYP
Language instr: Chinese, English

Hangzhou Huamei Wickham Kindergarten
No. 5, 289 Lane, Daguan Road, Gongshu District, Hangzhou, Zhejiang
Curriculum: IBPYP
Language instr: English, Chinese

HANGZHOU INTERNATIONAL SCHOOL
For further details see p. 53
2190 Xiangbin Road, Binjiang District, Hangzhou, Zhejiang 310052
Tel: +86 571 8669 0045
Email: admissions@hisdragons.org.cn
Website: www.his-china.org
Superintendent: Jeffry Stubbs
Age range: 2–18 years
No. of pupils: 1100
Fees: Day RMB222,500–RMB275,000
Curriculum: IBDP, IBMYP, IBPYP
Language instr: English

Hangzhou Shanghai World Foreign Language School
167 Li Shui Road, Hangzhou, Zhejiang 310015
Tel: +86 571 8998 1588
Curriculum: IBPYP
Language instr: English

Hangzhou Victoria Kindergarten (Jiarun)
4th Tower, Jiarun Mansion, Jinji Road, Xiaoshan District, Hangzhou, Zhejiang
Tel: +86 571 8380 3939
Curriculum: IBPYP
Language instr: English, Chinese

Hangzhou Victoria Kindergarten (Landscape Bay)
Hongyi Road, Jinghai Bay Community, Xiaoshan District, Hangzhou, Zhejiang
Tel: +86 571 8351 5277
Language instr: English, Chinese

Hangzhou Weiyou Guotai Preschool
Linping District, Hangzhou, Zhejiang
Curriculum: IBPYP
Language instr: English, Chinese

Hangzhou Wesley School (Binjiang Campus)
1426 Wentao Road, Binjiang District, Hangzhou, Zhejiang 310000
Tel: +86 571 8791 6660
Curriculum: IBPYP
Language instr: English, Chinese

Hangzhou Wesley School (Early Education Center)
269 Gongfa Road, Gongshu District, Hangzhou, Zhejiang 311231
Tel: +86 571 8882 8880
Curriculum: IBPYP
Language instr: English, Chinese

Hangzhou Wesley School (Gongshu/Blue Peacock Campus)
60 Chunque Street, Gongshu District, Hangzhou, Zhejiang 310000
Tel: +86 571 8882 8880
Curriculum: IBPYP
Language instr: English, Chinese

Hangzhou Wesley School (Shangcheng/Jianggan Campus)
162 Yanjia Road, Jianggan District, Hangzhou, Zhejiang 310000
Tel: +86 571 8680 6660
Curriculum: IBPYP
Language instr: English, Chinese

Hangzhou Wickham International School
533 Jingchang Road, Yuhang District, Hangzhou, Zhejiang
Tel: +86 0571 88665901
Curriculum: IBPYP
Language instr: Chinese

Hangzhou World Foreign Language School
66 Muge Road, Banshan Street, Gongshu District, Hangzhou, Zhejiang 310000
Tel: +86 189 5814 3128
Age range: 6–18 years
No. of pupils: 110
Curriculum: IBDP
Language instr: English, Chinese

Happykids Kindergarten
No. 218, Lane 2488, Wenchuan Road, Baoshan District, Shanghai
Tel: +86 21 5678 7887
Curriculum: IBPYP
Language instr: English, Chinese

Harrow Innovation Leadership Academy Chongqing
Liangjiang Avenue, Yubei, Chongqing 401147
Tel: +86 6595 2888
Age range: 3–18 years (boarding from 11)
Curriculum: UK, IGCSE, ALevs

Asia

Harrow Innovation Leadership Academy Nanning
No.6, Xintan Road, Yongning, Nanning, Guangxi Zhuang AR 530200
Tel: +86 77 1577 8866
Age range: 2–18 years
Curriculum: UK, IGCSE, ALevs

Harrow Innovation Leadership Academy Zhuhai (Hengqin)
No. 168, Yiwen 2nd Avenue, Hengqin, Zhuhai, Guangdong 519000
Tel: +86 75 6272 1688
Age range: 2–18 years
Curriculum: National, UK, IGCSE, ALevs

Harrow International School Shanghai
No. 588 Gaoxi Road, Pudong, Shanghai 200137
Tel: +86 21 6881 8282
Age range: 18 months–18 years
Curriculum: UK, IGCSE, ALevs

Harrow International School Shenzhen (Qianhai)
Northwest Corner Tinghai Road, No.3 Qianwan Road, Nanshan, Shenzhen 518054
Tel: +86 755 8898 7618
Age range: 2–18 years
Curriculum: UK, IGCSE, ALevs

HD Beijing School
No.1 East Jinzhan Forest Park, Chaoyang District, Beijing
Tel: +86 10 8539 8568
Age range: 3–16 years
Curriculum: IBDP
Language instr: English, Chinese

Hefei Run'an Boarding School
292 Fanhua West Road, Economic & Technology Development Zone, Hefei, Anhui 230601
Tel: +86 551 6982 1861
Age range: 6–12
No. of pupils: 150
Curriculum: IBMYP, IBPYP
Language instr: Chinese, English

Hefei Shanghai World Foreign Language School
Jinxiu Avenue & Heilongjiang Road intersection, Baohe District, Hefei, Anhui
Tel: +86 551 6288 7969
Curriculum: IBPYP
Language instr: English, Chinese

Hefei Xinhua Academy
No.7888 Changjiang West Road, Hefei, Anhui 230088
Tel: +86 551 6558 6888
Curriculum: IBPYP
Language instr: English, Chinese

Henan Jianye Little Harvard Bilingual School
No.31, East Section of Weisi Road, Jinshui District, Zhengzhou, Henan
Tel: +86 371 8655 0161
Age range: 6–12
No. of pupils: 780
Curriculum: IBPYP
Language instr: English, Chinese

Hengyang Royal Kindergarten
No. 8 Changfeng Avenue, Huaxin, Hengyang, Hunan
Tel: +86 73 4841 7888
Curriculum: IBPYP
Language instr: English, Chinese

Hong Qiao International School
218 South Yi Li Road, Shanghai 201103
Tel: +86 21 62682074
No. of pupils: 460
Curriculum: IBPYP

Hongwen School, Qingdao Campus
No. 232 Songling Road, Laoshan District, Qingdao, Shandong 266100
Tel: +86 400 622 0900
Age range: 4–18 years
Curriculum: IGCSE, ALevs
Language instr: English, Chinese

Hongwen School, Shanghai Campus
No. 318 Chuanda Road, Pudong, Shanghai
Tel: +86 21 2036 2318
Age range: 4–18 years
Curriculum: IBDP, IGCSE, ALevs
Language instr: English, Chinese

Huanan Country Garden International Kindergarten
Huanan Country Garden, Nancun Town, Panyu District, Guangzhou, Guangdong 511442
Curriculum: IBPYP
Language instr: English, Chinese

Huawai-Tongman Foreign Language School (SCNUFL-TM)
No. 2 Science Avenue, Science City, Huangpu District, Guangzhou, Guangdong 510633
Tel: +86 20 3205 1890
Curriculum: IBMYP, IBPYP
Language instr: English, Chinese

Hübschmann Zhan International School
No. 2-1 Hun He Shi Street, Economic & Technological Development Area, Shenyang, Liaoning 110027
Tel: +86 24 3120 0049
Age range: 5–18 years
Curriculum: Abitur, IBDP, IGCSE, ALevs
Language instr: English, German

Huili School Shanghai
No. 235 Linyao Road, Pudong, Shanghai 200126
Tel: +86 21 3177 5088
Curriculum: IBDP
Language instr: English, Chinese

Innova Early Years Center, Yizhuang Campus
Floor 1, Building B, Zhaolin Plaza, Yizhuang, Beijing 100026
Curriculum: IBPYP
Language instr: English, Chinese

International Montessori School of Beijing
Building 8, 2A, Xiang Jiang Bei Lu, Chao Yang District, Beijing 100103
Tel: +86 (10) 6432 8228
Age range: Co-ed 18 months–12 years
Language instr: English, Chinese

International School of Beijing-Shunyi
No 10 An Hua Street, Shunyi District, Beijing 101318
Tel: +86 10 8149 2345 ext 1001
Age range: 3–18 years
No. of pupils: 1750
Curriculum: IBDP
Language instr: English

International School of Dongguan
#11 Jin Feng Nan Road, Dongguan, Guangdong 523000
Tel: +86 769 2882 5882
Age range: 3–18
No. of pupils: 361
Curriculum: IBDP
Language instr: English

International School of Nanshan Shenzhen
11 Longyuan Road, Taoyuan Sub-District, Nanshan District, Shenzhen, Guangdong 518052
Tel: +86 755 2666 1000
Age range: 3–19
Curriculum: IBDP, IBMYP, IBPYP
Language instr: English

International School of Qingdao
26 Tianshui Road, Licang District, Qingdao, Shandong 266041
Tel: +86 532 8881 5668
Age range: 3–18 years
Curriculum: USA
Language instr: English

International School of Tianjin
Weishan Road, Shuanggang, Jinnan District, Tianjin 300350
Tel: +86 22 2859 2001
Age range: 3–18
No. of pupils: 470
Curriculum: ACT, IBDP, IBMYP, IBPYP, SAT
Language instr: English

ISA International Academy
66 Yushu South Road, Science City, Huangpu District, Guangzhou, Guangdong
Tel: +86 20 3171 2906
Language instr: English, Chinese

ISA Liwan International School
Hailong Road, Liwan District, Guangzhou, Guangdong
Tel: +86 20 3172 6802
Age range: 2–18 years
Curriculum: AP, IBMYP, IGCSE, ALevs
Language instr: English, Chinese

ISA Science City International School
66 Yushu South Road, Science City, Huangpu District, Guangzhou, Guangdong
Tel: +86 20 3736 2580
Age range: 2–18 years
Curriculum: IBDP, IBMYP, IBPYP
Language instr: English, Chinese

ISA Tianhe International School
Block C2-2 Redtory, No.128 Siheng Road, Yuan Village, Tianhe District, Guangzhou, Guangdong 510655
Tel: +86 20 8890 0909
Age range: 2–11 years
Curriculum: IBPYP, UK
Language instr: English, Chinese

ISA Wenhua International Centre for A Level
66 Yushu South Road, Science City, Huangpu District, Guangzhou, Guangdong
Tel: +86 185 2068 6218
Age range: 16–18 years
Curriculum: ALevs
Language instr: English, Chinese

ISA Wenhua Liwan School
Hailong Road, Liwan District, Guangzhou, Guangdong
Tel: +86 20 3171 3140
Age range: 3–18 years
Curriculum: IBDP, IBMYP, IGCSE, ALevs
Language instr: English, Chinese

ISA Wenhua Wuhan School
Fenglin Road, Junshan New Town, Wuhan Economic & Technological Development Zone, Wuhan, Hubei
Tel: +86 27 5065 1675
Age range: 2–18 years
Curriculum: IBDP
Language instr: English, Chinese

ISA Wuhan International School
Fenglin Road, Junshan New Town, Wuhan Economic & Technological Development Zone, Wuhan, Hubei
Tel: +86 27 5065 1675
Age range: 2–18 years
Curriculum: IBDP, IBMYP, IBPYP
Language instr: English, Chinese

Asia

Ivy Academy
East Lake Villas, No 35
Dongzhimenwai Street, Suite
D-102, Beijing 100027
Tel: +86 10 8451 1380
Age range: 2–6
Language instr: English, Chinese

IVY Kindergarten of Tongzhou District, Beijing
Hebin Road No.1, Yongshun Town,
Tongzhou District, Beijing 101100
Tel: +86 10 8969 6628
Curriculum: IBPYP
Language instr: English, Chinese

Jianye International School
No. 88 Jianye Road, Jinshui District,
Zhengzhou, Henan 450000
Curriculum: IBMYP
Language instr: English, Chinese

Jianye Xie He Cheng Bang Kindergarten
Minhang Road, Zhongzhou Avenue,
Zhengzhou, Henan 450003
Curriculum: IBPYP
Language instr: English, Chinese

Jinan Tianshan Experimental School
Huixin Road, Jiyang District,
Jinan, Shandong 251400
Tel: +86 531 5560 9377
Curriculum: IBDP
Language instr: English, Chinese

Jurong Country Garden School
No.2 Oiuzhi Road, Jurong
Economic Development Zone,
Zhengjiang City, Jiangsu 212400
Tel: +86 511 8078 0326
Curriculum: IBDP, IBMYP, IBPYP
Language instr: English

Kang Chiao International School (East China Campus)
No.500, Xihuan Rd., Huaqiao
Economic Development Zone,
Kunshan City, Jiangsu 215332
Tel: +86 512 3686 9833
Curriculum: IBDP, IBMYP, IBPYP
Language instr: English, Chinese

Keystone Academy
11 Anfu Street, Houshayu, Hou Sha Yu
Town, Shunyi District, Beijing 101318
Tel: +86 10 8049 6008
Curriculum: IBDP, IBMYP
Language instr: English, Chinese

Kids 'R' Kids Nanjing
No. 101-1 Huanling Road, Qixia
District, Nanjing Jiangsu 210000
Curriculum: IBPYP
Language instr: English, Chinese

King's Kindergarten Shenzhen
Jingtian North 5th Street,
Lianhua Street, Futian District,
Shenzhen, Guangdong
Tel: +86 188 2333 5566
Curriculum: IBPYP
Language instr: English, Chinese

Kunming International Academy
Yan Jia Di Xiao Qu, Kunming,
Yunnan 650034
Tel: +86 871 412 6887
Age range: 4–16
No. of pupils: 200
Curriculum: USA
Language instr: English

Kunming World Youth Academy
Building 2, No.3 High School
Dianchixingcheng Campus,
Chenggong District,
Kunming, Yunnan 650500
Tel: +86 871 6745 1511
Curriculum: IBDP
Language instr: English, Chinese

Lady Eleanor Holles International School Foshan (LEH Foshan)
26 Jingping Road, Chancheng
District, Foshan City,
Guangdong 528000
Tel: +86 757 2992 8101
Age range: 6–18 years
No. of pupils: 850
Curriculum: UK, IGCSE, ALevs
Language instr: English

Lanzhou Country Garden School
Qingbaishi Street, Chengguan
District, Lanzhou, Gansu 730000
Tel: +86 931 8790000
Curriculum: IBDP, IBPYP
Language instr: English, Chinese

Le Petit Lotus Bleu
Shanghai Aiju Primary
School, No. 247 Anfu Lu, Xuhui
District, Shanghai 200031
Tel: +86 21 54043697 (Ext:636)

LÉMAN INTERNATIONAL SCHOOL CHENGDU
For further details see p. 61
No. 1080 Da'an Road, Zheng
Xing County, Tianfu New Area,
Chengdu, Sichuan 610218
Tel: +86 28 6703 8650
Email: admissions@lis-chengdu.com
Website: www.lis-chengdu.com
Principal: Tracy Connor
Age range: 2–18 years
No. of pupils: 400
Fees: Day RMB171,500–RMB279,500
Curriculum: IBDP, IBMYP, IPC
Language instr: English

Lycee Francais de Shanghai-Qingpu Campus
350 Gao Guang Lu, Qingpu
District, Shanghai 201702
Tel: +86 21 3976 0555
Curriculum: FrenchBacc

Lycée Français International Charles de Gaulle de Pekin
3 Xinjin Lu, Beijing 100015
Tel: +86 10 8474 7088
Age range: 4–18 years
No. of pupils: 850
Curriculum: FrenchBacc
Language instr: Chinese, English, French

Macau Anglican College
109-117 Avenida Padre Tomas
Pereira, Taipa, Macau SAR
Tel: +853 2885 0000
Curriculum: UK, IGCSE

Malvern College Chengdu
Zhi Wu Yuan South Gate,
Tianhui Town, Jinniu District,
Chengdu, Sichuan 610083
Tel: +86 28 68937366
Curriculum: UK, IGCSE, ALevs
Language instr: English

Malvern College Qingdao
No. 77 Xifu Cavalry Mountain
Town, Cheng Yang District,
Qingdao, Shandong
Tel: +86 532 5865 9999
Age range: 11–18
Curriculum: UK, IGCSE, ALevs
Language instr: English

Manila Xiamen International School
No 735 Long Hu Shan Lu,
Zeng Cuo An, Si Ming District,
Xiamen, Fujian 361005
Tel: +86 592 2516373
Curriculum: IBDP, IBMYP
Language instr: English

MOK Kindergarten
Huatang Golf Villa comprehensive
Business Building, Yanjiao, Sanhe,
Langfang, Hebei 065201
Curriculum: IBPYP
Language instr: English, Chinese

Morgan Henry Bilingual Kindergarten
567 Jinfeng Road, Huacao Town,
Minhang District, Shanghai 201107
Tel: +86 21 6091 3366
Curriculum: IBPYP
Language instr: English, Chinese

Nanchang International School
1122 Phoenix Centre Road,
Hong Gu Tan District,
Nanchang, Jiangxi 330038
Tel: +86 791 83855352
Curriculum: IBPYP
Language instr: English

Nanjing Eternal Sea Kindergarten
No. 8 Huitong Road, Qixia District,
Nanjing, Jiangsu 210000
Tel: +852 25 5870 6268
Curriculum: IBPYP
Language instr: English

Nanjing International School
No. 8 Xueheng Road,
Nanjing, Jiangsu 210023
Tel: +86 25 85899111
Age range: 3–18
No. of pupils: 670
Curriculum: IBDP, IBMYP, IBPYP
Language instr: English

Nansha College Preparatory Academy
180 Gang Qian Boulevard, Nansha,
Guangzhou, Guangdong 511458
Tel: +86 20 3468 3339
Curriculum: USA

Nanshan Chinese International College Immersion
33 Shizhou Zhong Road,
Nanshan District, Shenzhen,
Guangdong 518053
Tel: +86 755 3320 9088

Nantong Stalford International School
No. 46 Hongxing Road, NETDA,
Nantong, Jiangsu 226015
Tel: +86 4008 4008 63
Curriculum: IBDP, IBPYP
Language instr: English, Chinese

New Oriental Academy
101 Manbai Road, Machikou Town,
Changping District, Beijing 102206
Tel: +86 40 0688 1000
Curriculum: IBDP
Language instr: English, Chinese

New Oriental Stars Kindergarten
Room 506, 5th Floor, Building F,
Phoenix Plaza, No. A5, Shuguangxili,
Chaoyang District, Beijing 100028
Tel: +86 40 0066 5030
Curriculum: IBPYP
Language instr: English

Nexus Preschool
No. 1108 Huamu Road, Pudong
New Area, Shanghai 201204
Curriculum: IBPYP
Language instr: English, Chinese

Ningbo Huamao International School
No 2 Yinxian dadao (Middle),
Ningbo, Zhejiang 31519
Tel: +86 574 8821 1160
Age range: 2–18
No. of pupils: 730 B441 G300 VIth16
Curriculum: IBDP, IBMYP, IBPYP, IBCP
Language instr: English

Asia

Ningbo Zhicheng School
No 377 Jiangbei Road, Jiangbei District, Ningbo, Zhejiang 315033
Tel: +86 574 8756 4017

Nord Anglia Chinese International School, Shanghai
1399 Jinhui Road, Minhang, Shanghai 201107
Tel: +86 (021) 2403 8800
Curriculum: IBDP
Language instr: Chinese, English

Nord Anglia International School Shanghai, Pudong
2888 Junmin Road, Pudong New District, Shanghai 201315
Tel: +86 (0)21 5812 7455 (Ext:1015)
Age range: 2–18 years
Curriculum: IBDP, UK, IGCSE
Language instr: English

Nord Anglia School Beijing, Fangshan
No. 236 Beiliuzhuang Village, Qinglonghu Town, Fangshan District, Beijing
Tel: +86 10 8865 8000
Curriculum: IBDP
Language instr: English, Chinese

Nord Anglia School Foshan
No. 55 Dongxi Avenue, West Bank, Xiqiao Town, Nanhai District, Foshan, Guangdong
Tel: +86 757 8121 7688
Curriculum: IBDP
Language instr: English

Nord Anglia School Jiaxing
No. 353 Qingze Road, Economic Development Zone, Jiaxing, Zhejiang 314000
Tel: +86 189 6734 1988
Curriculum: IBDP
Language instr: English, Chinese

Nord Anglia School Nantong
No. 99, Jiangcheng Road, Sutong Park, Nantong, Jiangsu 226000
Tel: +86 513 8918 3800
Curriculum: IBDP
Language instr: English, Chinese

Nord Anglia School Ningbo, Fenghua
No. 88 Wenbo Road, Xiaowangmiao Street, Fenghua District, Ningbo, Zhejiang 315500
Tel: +86 574 8720 3280
Curriculum: IBDP
Language instr: English, Chinese

Nord Anglia School Suzhou, Xiangcheng
No. 8 Liu Jue Road, Xiangcheng District, Suzhou, Jiangsu 215134
Tel: +86 512 6580 5800
Curriculum: IBDP
Language instr: English, Chinese

Olive Tree International Academy, BFSU
No.136 Xincheng Road, Nanyuan Street, Yuhang District, Hangzhou, Zhejiang
Tel: +86 571 8610 0011
Curriculum: IBMYP, IBPYP
Language instr: English, Chinese

Oriental Cambridge International School (Shenyang/Benxi Campus)
No 23, Mulan Road, Xihu District, Benxi, Liaoning 117000
Curriculum: IBDP
Language instr: English, Chinese

Oriental English College, Shenzhen
No 10 Xuezi Road, Education Town, Bao'an, Shenzhen, Guangdong 518128
Tel: +86 755 2751 2624
Age range: 6–18 years
Curriculum: IBDP, IBPYP
Language instr: Chinese, English

Oujing International Kindergarten
Beicun Road, Yiwu, Zhejiang 322000
Tel: +86 159 8561 7777
Curriculum: IBPYP
Language instr: English

Overseas Chinese Academy Suzhou
208 Zhong Nan Street, Suzhou Industrial Park, Jiangsu 215021
Tel: +86 (512) 65001600
Curriculum: IBDP, IBMYP, IBPYP
Language instr: Chinese, English

Oxford International College, Chengdu
185 Taoqi Road, Bali District, Chengdu, Sichuan 610051
Tel: +86 28 8351 7000
Curriculum: UK, IGCSE, ALevs

Oxstand International School, Shenzhen
No.2040, BuXin Road, Luohu District, Shenzhen, Guangdong
Tel: +86 755 2580 5707
Curriculum: IBDP
Language instr: English

PeyJoy Kindergarten
No.7-99 Yayuan Road, Bantian Street, Longgang District, Shenzhen, Guangdong 518000
Curriculum: IBPYP
Language instr: English, Chinese

Phoenix City International Kindergarten
No. 1 Yaxi Road, Phoenix City, Yongnin Street, Zengcheng District, Guangzhou, Guangdong 511340
Tel: +86 20 3298 8186
Curriculum: IBPYP
Language instr: English, Chinese

Phoenix City International School
Xintang Town, Zengcheng City, Guangzhou, Guangdong 511340
Tel: +86 20 6228 6902
Curriculum: IBMYP, IBPYP
Language instr: Chinese, English

Pingtan Saier Bilingual School
No. 2 Tianshan North Road, Beicuo Town, Pingtan Comprehensive Experimental Zone, Fuzhou, Fujian 350400
Tel: +86 591 6288 8633
Curriculum: IBPYP
Language instr: English, Chinese

Princeton SkyLake International Kindergarten
No. 7010 Beihuan Avenue, Futian District, Shenzhen, Guangdong
Tel: +86 180 3342 4827
Curriculum: IBPYP
Language instr: English, Chinese

Qingdao Academy
No 111 Huazhong Road, Gaoxin District, Qingdao, Shandong 266111
Tel: +86 532 5875 3788
Curriculum: IBDP
Language instr: English, Chinese

Qingdao Amerasia International School
68 Shandongtou Lu, Qingdao, Shandong 266061
Tel: +86 532 8388 9900
Curriculum: IBDP, IBMYP, IBPYP
Language instr: English

Qingdao Chaoyin Primary School
No. 2 Zhenjiang Minor Road, Qingdao, Shandong 266000
Curriculum: IBPYP
Language instr: English, Chinese

Qingdao MINGDE School
No. 111 Gongjian Road, Huangdao District, Qingdao, Shandong
Tel: +86 532 5558 5997
Curriculum: IBDP, IBPYP
Language instr: English, Chinese

Qingdao No.1 International School of Shangdong Province (QISS)
232 Songling Road, Qingdao, Shandong 266061
Tel: +86 532 6889 8888
Age range: 3–17
Curriculum: UK
Language instr: English

QSI International School of Chengdu
American Garden, 188 South 3rd Ring Road, Chengdu, Sichuan 610041
Tel: +86 28 8511 3853
Age range: 3–18 years
No. of pupils: 200
Curriculum: ACT, AP, IBDP, SAT, USA
Language instr: English

QSI International School of Dongguan
2nd Floor, Block A2, Dong Cheng Center, Dongguan City, Guangdong 523000
Tel: +86 769 2230 0131
Age range: 2–17
No. of pupils: 117
Curriculum: USA
Language instr: English

QSI International School of Shenyang
Fuli Segovia, The Phoenix Street 77, 8-1, Dongling District, Shenyang, Liaoning
Tel: +86 024 2379 7530

QSI International School of Shenzhen
5th Floor, Bitao Building, 8 Tai Zi Road, Shekou, Shenzhen, Guangdong 518067
Tel: +86 755 2667 6031
Age range: 2–18 years
No. of pupils: 1100
Curriculum: AP, IBDP, SAT, USA
Language instr: English

QSI International School of Zhuhai
No. 168 Anning Road, Xianzhou District, Zhuhai, Guangdong 519000
Tel: +86 756 815 6134
Age range: 2–18
No. of pupils: 39 B21 G18
Curriculum: USA
Language instr: English

Saint Paul American School
18 Guan Ao Yuan, Qinghe, Haidian District 100192
Tel: 86-10-80703429
Curriculum: USA

Sanya Foreign Language School
No. 38 Luhuitou Road, Serenity Coast, Jiyang District, Sanya, Hainan
Tel: +86 898 3188 3111
Curriculum: IBPYP, National, UK, IGCSE, ALevs
Language instr: English, Chinese

Asia

Sanya Foreign Language School Kindergarten (SLSK)
No. 38 Luhuitou Road, Serenity Coast, Jiyang District, Sanya, Hainan
Tel: +86 898 3188 0700
Curriculum: IBPYP
Language instr: English, Chinese

Sanya Overseas Chinese School - Nanxin Campus
Shang Bao Po Road, Lizhi District, Sanya, Hainan
Tel: +86 89 8886 9023
Curriculum: IBDP
Language instr: English, Chinese

School of the Nations
Rua de Minho, Taipa, Macau SAR
Tel: +853 2870 1759
Age range: 3–18
Curriculum: IBDP, IGCSE
Language instr: English

Seven Star Kindergarten Xiamen
No. 146 Qixing West Road, Siming District, Xiamen, Fujian
Tel: +86 59 2766 6678
Curriculum: IBPYP
Language instr: English, Chinese

Shanghai American School (Pudong Campus)
Shanghai Links Executive Community, 1600 Lingbai Road, Sanjiagang, Pudong, Shanghai 201201
Tel: +86 21 6221 1445 (Ext:2000)
Age range: 4–18
No. of pupils: 2950
Curriculum: AP, IBDP, SAT
Language instr: English

Shanghai American School (Puxi Campus)
26 Jinfeng Road, Huacao Town, Minhang District, Shanghai 201107
Tel: +86 21 6221 1445
Age range: 3–18
No. of pupils: 2853
Curriculum: AP, IBDP, SAT
Language instr: English

Shanghai Arete Bilingual Kindergarten
1 Nan An De Road, Shanghai 201805
Tel: +86 13 5246 94182
Curriculum: IBPYP
Language instr: English, Chinese

Shanghai Arete Bilingual School
569 Anchi Road, Jiading District, Shanghai 201805
Tel: +86 400 920 6698
Curriculum: IBDP
Language instr: English

Shanghai BeiBeiJia Olion Kindergarten
No. 377 Baoju Road, Shanghai
Tel: +86 137 6467 7623
Curriculum: IBPYP
Language instr: English, Chinese

Shanghai Changning International School
No 79, Lane 261, Jiangsu Lu, Shanghai 200050
Tel: +86 21 6252 3688
Age range: 3–15
No. of pupils: 510 B260 G250

SHANGHAI COMMUNITY INTERNATIONAL SCHOOL - HONGQIAO CAMPUS
For further details see p. 69
1161 Hongqiao Road, Shanghai 200051
Tel: +86 21 6261 4338
Email: admissions@scis-china.org
Website: www.scis-china.org
Director of Schools: Daniel Eschtruth
Age range: 2–18 years
No. of pupils: 1550
Fees: Day RMB146,000–RMB324,500
Curriculum: AP, IBDP, IBMYP, IBPYP, USA
Language instr: English

Shanghai Community International School - Pudong Campus
198 Hengqiao Road, Zhoupu, Pudong, Shanghai 201315
Tel: +86 21 5812 9888
Age range: 2–18
No. of pupils: 650
Curriculum: IBDP, IBMYP, IBPYP
Language instr: English

Shanghai Ivy School
No. 816 Xiuyan Road, Pudong New Area, Shanghai 200000
Tel: +86 40 0050 5553
Curriculum: IBPYP
Language instr: English, Chinese

Shanghai Liaoyuan Bilingual School
No. 150 Pingyang Road, Minhang District, Shanghai
Tel: +86 21 6480 6128
Curriculum: IBDP, IBMYP, IBPYP
Language instr: English, Chinese

Shanghai Livingston American School
No. 580 Gan Xi Road, Changning District, Shanghai 200335
Tel: +86 21 62383511

Shanghai Pinghe School
261 Huang Yang Road, Pudong, Shanghai
Tel: +86 21 5031 0791
Age range: 5–18
No. of pupils: 1550
Curriculum: IBDP
Language instr: English, Chinese

Shanghai Qibao Dwight High School
Physical Campus, 3233 Hongxin Road, Minhang District, Shanghai 201101
Tel: +86 21 6461 0367
Curriculum: IBDP
Language instr: English

Shanghai Qingpu World Foreign Language Kindergarten
639 Panwen Road, Qingpu District, Shanghai 201702
Tel: +86 21 3988 6958
Curriculum: IBPYP
Language instr: English, Chinese

Shanghai Qingpu World Foreign Language School
Longlian Road 915, Qingpu District, Shanghai 201700
Tel: +86 21 6928 0977
Curriculum: IBPYP
Language instr: English, Chinese

Shanghai Shangde Experimental School
No 1688 Xiu Yan Road, Pudong New District, Shanghai 201315
Tel: +86 21 6818 0001 or +86 21 6818 0191
Curriculum: IBDP, IBMYP, IBPYP
Language instr: English

Shanghai Singapore International School
301 Zhujian Road, Minhang District, Shanghai 201106
Tel: +86 21 62219288
Age range: 2–18
No. of pupils: 1400
Curriculum: IBDP, IBCP, IGCSE
Language instr: English

Shanghai United International School, Gubei/Hongqiao Campus
248 Hong Song Road (E), Gubei, Minhang District, Shanghai 201103
Tel: +8621 51753030
No. of pupils: 1985
Curriculum: IBDP, IBPYP
Language instr: English

Shanghai United International School, Jiaoke
No. 55, Wan Yuan Road, Minhang District, Shanghai
Tel: +86 21 64807218

Shanghai United International School, Pudong
48 Xueye Road, Pudong District, Shanghai
Tel: +86 21 58869990

Shanghai United International School, Shangyin
No. 185, Long Ming Road, Minhang District, Shanghai
Tel: +86 21 54178143

Shanghai United International School, Wanyuan
No. 509 Pingji Road, Minhang District, Shanghai
Tel: +86 21 64980188

Shanghai United International School, Wenzhou
No.1, Chuitai Road, Louqiao Industrial Park, Ouhai District, Wenzhou, Zhejiang
Tel: +86 577 8629 9077

Shanghai United International School, Xiamen
No. 850 Honglianbeier Road, Siming District, Xiamen, Fujian
Tel: +86 592 5205850

Shanghai Victoria Kindergarten (Gumei)
No. 300 Gumei Road, Minhang District, Shanghai
Tel: +86 21 6401 1084
Curriculum: IBPYP
Language instr: English, Chinese

Shanghai Victoria Kindergarten (Pudong)
38-39 Yinxiao Road, Pudong District, Shanghai
Tel: +86 21 5045 9084
Curriculum: IBPYP
Language instr: English, Chinese

Shanghai Victoria Kindergarten (Qibao)
No. 1225 Xinzhen Road, Minhang District, Shanghai
Tel: +86 21 5415 0469
Curriculum: IBPYP
Language instr: English, Chinese

Shanghai Victoria Kindergarten (Xuhui)
71-1 Huating Road, Xuhui District, Shanghai
Tel: +86 21 5403 6901
Curriculum: IBPYP
Language instr: English, Chinese

Shanghai World Foreign Language Middle School
380 Pu Bei Road, Xu Hui District, Shanghai 200233
Tel: +8621 6436 3556
Curriculum: IBDP, IBMYP
Language instr: Chinese

Shanghai World Foreign Language Primary School
No 380 Pubei Road, Xu Hui District, Shanghai 200233
Tel: +86 21 5419 2245
Curriculum: IBPYP
Language instr: English, Chinese

Shekou International School
Jingshan Villas, Nanhai Boulevard, Shekou, Nanshan, Shenzhen, Guangdong
Tel: +86 755 2669 3669
Age range: 2–18 years
No. of pupils: 1140
Curriculum: IBDP, IBPYP, SAT
Language instr: English

Asia

Shen Wai International School
29 Baishi 3rd Road, Nanshan District, Shenzhen, Guangdong 518053
Tel: +86 755 8654 1200
Age range: 4–19
No. of pupils: 1040
Curriculum: IBDP, IBMYP, IBPYP
Language instr: English

Sheng Kung Hui Choikou School
Avenida Dr Franscisco V Machado S/N, Macau SAR
Tel: +853 2834 1791

Shenghua Zizhu Academy
No. 155 Tanjiatang Road, Minhang District, 200241
Tel: +86 21 6145 7950
Curriculum: AP, IBDP, IGCSE, ALevs
Language instr: English, Chinese

Shenyang No.2 Sino-Canadian High School
198 Shenbei Road, Shenbei New District, Shenyang, Liaoning 110164
Tel: +86 024 88043958
Curriculum: National

Shenzhen American International School
No. 82, Gongyuan Rd, Shekou, Nanshan, Shenzhen, Guangdong 518067
Tel: +86 755 8619 4800
Curriculum: USA

SHENZHEN COLLEGE OF INTERNATIONAL EDUCATION
For further details see p. 72
No. 3, Sixth Antuoshan Road, Futian District, Shenzhen, Guangdong
Tel: +86 755 8349 5025
Email: info@scie.com.cn
Website: http://www.scie.com.cn
Headteacher: Neil Mobsby
Age range: 14–18 years
No. of pupils: 1800
Fees: RMB273,000–RMB303,000
Curriculum: AP, UK, USA, IGCSE, ALevs
Language instr: English

Shenzhen Concord College of Sino-Canada
166 Nanguang Road, Nanshan District, Shenzhen, Guangdong
Tel: +86 755 2656 8886
Language instr: Chinese

Shenzhen Elite International Academy
No. 9310 Binhe Avenue, next to Xiasha Tairan Plaza, Futian District, Shenzhen, Guangdong
Tel: +86 755 3336 0102
Curriculum: IBPYP
Language instr: English, Chinese

Shenzhen Foreign Languages GBA Academy
No. 30 Xiangtang Road, Bantian Street, Longgang District, Shenzhen, Guangdong
Tel: +86 755 2939 5900
Age range: 4–18 years
Curriculum: IBDP, IBMYP, IBPYP
Language instr: English, Chinese

Shenzhen Futian Funful Bilingual School
Goldfield Seaview Gardens, South Xinzhou Road, Futian District, Shenzhen, Guangdong
Tel: +86 755 2381 0830
Age range: 3–12
Language instr: English, Putonghua

Sias International School
Longhu Middle Ring Road & Chaoyang Road Intersection, Zhengdong New District, Zhengzhou, Henan 450000
Tel: +86 371 8890 8999
Curriculum: IBMYP, IBPYP
Language instr: English, Chinese

SMIC Private School
No. 169, Qing-Tong Road, Pudong New Area, Shanghai 201203
Tel: +86 21 2033 2515
Curriculum: USA

Soochow Foreign Language School
No. 188, Yucheng Road, Xiangcheng District, Suzhou, Jiangsu
Tel: +86 512 8918 0556
Curriculum: IBDP, IBPYP
Language instr: English, Chinese

Soong Ching Ling School
No 2 Ye Hui Road, Zhao Xiang, Qing Pu District, Shanghai 201703
Tel: +86 21 6975 6670
No. of pupils: 900

Springboard International Bilingual School
Gucheng Village, 15 Huosha Road, Houshayu Town, Shunyi District, Beijing 101318
Tel: +86 10 80490307
Age range: 3–18 years
Curriculum: AP, IBDP, IBMYP, IBPYP
Language instr: English, Chinese

St Bees Dongguan
121 Gedi Xinnan Road, Nancheng Street, Dongguan, Guangdong
Tel: +86 40 0686 2268
Age range: 15–18 years
Curriculum: UK, IGCSE, ALevs

St Bees Shijiazhuang
No. 19 Huayang Road, Zhengdingxin District, Shijiazhuang, Hebei
Age range: 4–13 years
Curriculum: UK

Suzhou Foreign Language School
No.201, Zhuyuan Road, Suzhou, Jiangsu
Tel: +86 512 8718 8009
Curriculum: IGCSE, ALevs

Suzhou Industrial Park Foreign Language School
No.89, Suzhou Industrial Park, Suzhou, Jiangsu 215021
Tel: +86 512 6289 7710
Curriculum: IBDP
Language instr: English

Suzhou Innovation Academy
100 Xiangcheng Ave, Xiangcheng District, Suzhou, Jiangsu
Tel: +86 (0)512 65490211
Curriculum: IBDP
Language instr: English

Suzhou North America High School
268 Tian E Dang Road, Wuzhong District, Suzhou, Jiangsu 215000
Tel: +86 512 6625 8897
Curriculum: IBDP
Language instr: English, Chinese

Suzhou Science and Technology Town Foreign Language School
No. 180, Jialing River Road, High-tech Zone, Suzhou, Jiangsu 215163
Tel: +86 512 69370111
Curriculum: IBMYP, IBPYP
Language instr: English, Chinese

Suzhou Singapore International School
208 Zhong Nan Street, Suzhou Industrial Park, Jiangsu 215021
Tel: +86 512 6258 0388
Age range: 2–18 years
No. of pupils: 1000
Curriculum: IBDP, IBMYP, IBPYP
Language instr: English

Suzhou Victoria Kindergarten
Bay Garden Community, Phase 3, 1 Linglong Street, Suzhou Industrial Park, Suzhou, Jiangsu
Tel: +86 512 8081 1610
Curriculum: IBPYP
Language instr: English, Chinese

Teda International School
72 Third Avenue, Teda, Tianjin 300457
Tel: +86 22 6622 6158
Age range: 3–18
No. of pupils: 326 B166 G160
Curriculum: AP, SAT, USA
Language instr: English

The Affiliated International School of Shenzhen University
A105, No.101, Qianhai Rd, Nanshan District, Shenzhen, Guangdong 518054
Tel: +86 755 2606 0520
Curriculum: IGCSE, ALevs

The British International School Shanghai, Puxi
111 Jinguang Road, Huacao Town, Minhang District, Puxi, Shanghai 201107
Tel: +86 (0)21 62217542
Age range: 2–18
Curriculum: IBDP, UK, IGCSE
Language instr: English

THE BRITISH SCHOOL OF BEIJING, SANLITUN
For further details see p. 74
5 Xiliujie, Sanlitun Road, Chaoyang District, Beijing 100027
Tel: +8610 8532 3088
Email: sltadmissions@bsbsanlitun.com
Website: www.bsbsanlitun.com
Principal: Jo Prabhu
Age range: 1–11
No. of pupils: 600
Curriculum: UK

The British School of Guangzhou
983-3 Tonghe Road, Baiyun District, Guangzhou, Guangdong 510515
Tel: +86 20 8709 4788
Age range: 1–18
No. of pupils: 1450
Curriculum: UK, IGCSE, ALevs
Language instr: English

The British School of Nanjing
No.16 Hanfu Road, Jiangning District, Nanjing, Jiangsu
Tel: +86 25 5210 8987
Age range: 2–18 years
No. of pupils: 400
Curriculum: UK, IGCSE, ALevs

The Garden International School
Agile Cambridgeshire, Panyu District, Guangzhou, Guangdong 511400
Tel: +86 (0)20 3482 3833
Curriculum: IBPYP
Language instr: English

The International School of Macao
Macau University of Science and Technology (Block K), Avenida Wai Long, Taipa, Macau SAR
Tel: +853 2853 3700
Age range: 3–17
No. of pupils: 840 B420 G420
Curriculum: IBDP
Language instr: English

The Kindergarten of Hefei Run'an Boarding School
No. 268 Cui Wei Road, Economic and Technogical Development Zone, Hefei, Anhui 230601
Tel: +86 (0)551 63821888
Curriculum: IBPYP
Language instr: English

Asia

The MacDuffie School, Shanghai
No. 799 North Hui Feng Road, Fengxian District, Shanghai 201403
Tel: +86 21 400 600 2260
Curriculum: IBDP
Language instr: English

The Royal Grammar School Guildford, Nanjing
No. 17 Kangjian Road, Jiangbei New Area, Nanjing, Jiangsu 211800
Tel: +86 25 5667 8333
Curriculum: IBPYP
Language instr: English, Chinese

Tianjin International School
1 Sishui Dao, Hexi District, Tianjin 300222
Tel: +86 22 8371 0900
Curriculum: USA
Language instr: English

Tianjin Yinghua International School
Yongyang West Road, Wuqing District, Tianjin
Tel: +86 22 5961 1161

Times College
18 Shennong Road, Qixia District, Nanjing, Jiangsu
Tel: +86 25 85539090
Curriculum: IBDP, IBMYP, IBPYP
Language instr: English, Chinese

Tongwen School, Jiaxing
No. 2339 Huayuan Road, Jiaxing, Zhejiang 314000
Curriculum: IBPYP
Language instr: English, Chinese

Tsinghua International School
Campus of Tsinghua High School, Zhongguancun North Street, Haidian District, Beijing 100084
Tel: +86 10 62797000
Curriculum: UK

Tungwah Wenzel International School
No. 17 Keyuan Road, Songshan Lake High-Tech Industrial Zone, Dongguan, Guangdong
Tel: +86 769 2289 0858
Curriculum: IBDP, IBMYP, IBPYP
Language instr: English

ULink College Guangzhou
180 Gang Qian Boulevard, Nansha, Guangzhou, Guangdong 511458
Tel: +86 20 3909 0100
Curriculum: IGCSE, ALevs

Ulink College of Shanghai
No. 559 Laiting South Road, Jiuting, Songjiang District, Shanghai 201615
Tel: +86 21 3373 7900
Curriculum: IBDP, IGCSE, ALevs
Language instr: Chinese, English

Utahloy International School Guangzhou (UISG)
800 Sha Tai Bei Road, Bai Yun District, Guangzhou, Guangdong 510515
Tel: +8620 8720 2019
Age range: 2–18
No. of pupils: 900
Curriculum: IBDP, IBMYP, IBPYP, TOEFL
Language instr: English

Utahloy International School Zengcheng (UISZ)
San Jiang Town, Zeng Cheng City, Guangdong 511325
Tel: +86 20 8291 3201
Age range: 2–18
No. of pupils: 200
Curriculum: IBDP, IBMYP, IBPYP
Language instr: English

UWC Changshu China
No. 88 Kunchenghuxi Road, Changshu, Jiangsu 215500
Tel: +86 512 5298 2602
Age range: 15–19 years
No. of pupils: 620
Curriculum: IBDP
Language instr: English

Vanke Bilingual School
No. 3568 Qixin Road, Minhang District, Shanghai
Tel: +86 21 6459 9759
Age range: 7–16 years
Curriculum: National
Language instr: English, Chinese

Vanke School Pudong
No. 1700-2-4 Kangqiao Road, Pudong, Shanghai 201315
Tel: +86 21 3463 3623
Age range: 4–18 years
Curriculum: IBDP, IBMYP, IBPYP, IBCP
Language instr: English, Chinese

Victoria Kindergarten Shenzhen (Futian)
No.2135 Fuqiang Road, Futian District, Shenzhen, Guangdong
Tel: +86 755 8296 1010
Curriculum: IBPYP
Language instr: English, Chinese

Victoria Kindergarten Shenzhen (Le Parc)
317 Fuzhong Road, Futian District, Shenzhen, Guangdong
Tel: +86 755 8328 2004
Curriculum: IBPYP
Language instr: English, Chinese

Victoria Kindergarten Shenzhen (Lilin)
7 LongChuanTang Street, DongBin Road, Nanshan District, Shenzhen, Guangdong
Tel: +86 130 5815 8907
Curriculum: IBPYP
Language instr: English, Chinese

Victoria Kindergarten Shenzhen (Shenzhen Bay)
Shenzhen Bay Science & Technology Ecological Park, Building 5, Floor 3, Nanshan District, Shenzhen, Guangdong
Tel: +86 755 8653 7070
Curriculum: IBPYP
Language instr: English, Chinese

Victoria Park Academy
No. 8 Longchuantang Street, Dongbin Road, Nanshan District, Shenzhen, Guangdong
Tel: +86 181 2380 6799
Curriculum: IBPYP
Language instr: English, Chinese

Wahaha International School
5 Yaojiang Road, Shangcheng District, Hangzhou, Zhejiang 310008
Tel: +86 571 8780 1933
Curriculum: IBMYP, IBPYP
Language instr: English, Chinese

Walton Foreign Language School, Taicang
No. 200 Suzhou Middle Road, Economic Development Zone, Taicang, Jiangsu 215400
Tel: +86 512 3306 2220
Age range: 4–18 years
Curriculum: ALevs
Language instr: English, Chinese

Weihai IVY International School
Jingzi Scenic Area, Huancui District, Weihai, Shandong
Tel: +86 400 886 1771
Curriculum: IGCSE, ALevs

Weihai Zhongshi International School (WZIS)
42 East Jiang Su Road, New Industrial District, Weihai, Shandong 264211
Tel: +86 63 1599 6381
Age range: 5–18
No. of pupils: 340
Curriculum: UK

Wellington College International Hangzhou
2399 Xue Zhi Road, Xiaoshan District, Hangzhou, Zhejiang 311231
Tel: +86 (571) 8239 6366
Age range: 2–18 years
Curriculum: UK, IGCSE, ALevs
Language instr: English, Mandarin

Wellington College International Shanghai
No.1500 Yao Long Road, Pudong, Shanghai 200124
Tel: +86 21 5185 3866
Age range: 2–18 years
No. of pupils: 1600
Curriculum: IBDP, UK, IGCSE
Language instr: English

Wellington College International Tianjin
No 1 Yide Dao, Hong Qiao District, Tianjin 300120
Tel: +86 22 8758 7199
Age range: 2–18
Curriculum: UK, IGCSE, ALevs

Western Academy Of Beijing
PO Box 8547, 10 Lai Guang Ying Dong Lu, Chao Yang District, Beijing 100102
Tel: +86 10 5986 5588
Age range: 3–18
No. of pupils: 1362
Curriculum: IBDP, IBMYP, IBPYP
Language instr: English

WESTERN INTERNATIONAL SCHOOL OF SHANGHAI (WISS)
For further details see p. 81
555 Lianmin Road, Xujing Town, Qingpu District, Shanghai 201702
Tel: +86 (21) 6976 6015/6013
Email: enquiry@wiss.cn
Website: www.wiss.cn
Head of School: Jeremy Williams
Age range: 2.5–18 years
No. of pupils: 500
Fees: *Day* ¥171,500–¥277,000 ¥162,925–¥263,150
Curriculum: IBDP, IBMYP, IBPYP
Language instr: English

Whittle School & Studios - Shenzhen Campus
8 Hai Cheng Road, Nanshan District, Shenzhen, Guangdong 518067
Tel: +86 755 8785 1818

Wuhan Aoxin Elite School
No. 322 Luoshi Road, Hongshan District, Wuhan, Hubei 430067
Curriculum: IBPYP
Language instr: Chinese

Wuhan Britain-China School
No. 10 Gutian Ce Road, Qiaokou District, Wuhan, Hubei
Tel: +86 27 8361 1201
Curriculum: IBDP, IBMYP, IBPYP, ALevs
Language instr: English, Chinese

Wuhan Yangtze International School
Wuhan International Educational Center, Bo Xue Road, Wuhan Economic & Technology Development Zone, Wuhan, Hubei 430056
Tel: +86 27 8423 8713
Curriculum: USA
Language instr: English

Wuxi Dipont School of Arts and Science
No. 188 Qingyuan Road, Wuxi Economic Development District, Wuxi, Jiangsu
Tel: +86 510 8883 9188
Curriculum: IBDP
Language instr: English, Chinese

Asia

Wuxi Foreign Language School
1 Xifeng Road, Taihuxincheng, Wuxi, Jiangsu 214131
Curriculum: IBPYP
Language instr: Chinese

Wuxi United International School
No. 8, Wenjing Road, Xishan District, Xidong New Town, Wuxi, Jiangsu 214104
Tel: +86 510 8853 7700
Curriculum: IBDP
Language instr: English

Wycombe Abbey International School
No.9 Huanhu North Road, Wujin Economic Zone, Changzhou, Jiangsu 213149
Tel: +86 0519 8888 0686
Age range: 3–18
Curriculum: UK

X.L.X. Kindergarten (Qingcheng Campus)
No.5, Building 7, Lane 2501, Guyang North Road, Songjiang District, Shanghai
Tel: +86 21 6029 1140
Curriculum: IBPYP
Language instr: English, Chinese

X.L.X. Kindergarten (Tangzhen Campus)
No. 58 Hongya Road, Pudong New District, Shanghai
Tel: +86 21 6070 2623
Curriculum: IBPYP
Language instr: English, Chinese

Xiamen Flair Kindergarten
No. 6 Houbinlu, Siming District, Xiamen, Fujian
Curriculum: IBPYP
Language instr: English, Chinese

Xiamen International School
262 Xing Bei San Lu, Xinglin, Jimei District, Xiamen, Fujian 361022
Tel: +86 592 625 6581
Age range: 3–18
No. of pupils: 450 B250 G220
Curriculum: ACT, IBDP, IBMYP, IBPYP, SAT
Language instr: English

Xi'an Hanova International School
188 Yudou Road, Yanta District, Xian, Shaanxi 710077
Tel: +86 29 88693780
Curriculum: IBDP, IBMYP, IBPYP
Language instr: English

Xi'an Liangjiatan International School (XLIS)
International Community, Xi'an, Shaanxi 710100
Tel: +86 29 85915100-8000
Age range: 3–18 years
Curriculum: IBDP, IBMYP, IBPYP
Language instr: English

Xiaomiao Kindergarten (Luoxiu Campus)
No. 1977 Luoxiu Road, Minhang District, Shanghai 201104
Tel: +86 21 5481 6417
Curriculum: IBPYP
Language instr: English, Chinese

Xiaomiao Kindergarten (Xinsong Campus)
No. 47, Lane 499, Xinli Road, Minhang District, Shanghai
Tel: +86 21 6492 0495
Curriculum: IBPYP
Language instr: English, Chinese

Xining International Academy
Tianjin Lu, Xining, Qinghai 810003
Tel: +86 97 1630 7721
Curriculum: USA

Yang Guang Qing School of Beijing
2 Tianbao North Street, Daxing District, Beijing
Tel: +86 10 6787 1129
Curriculum: National

Yantai American School
No. 8 San Lei Lu, Laishan District, Yantai, Shandong 264003
Tel: +86 535 214 3762
Curriculum: USA

Yantai Huasheng International School
100 Jinshajiang Lu, Development Area, (Intersection of Jinshajiang Lu and Tianshan Lu), Yantai, Shandong 264000
Tel: +86 53 5610 1166
Curriculum: USA

Yew Chung International School of Beijing
Honglingjin Park, 5 Houbalizhuang, Chaoyang District, Beijing 100025
Tel: +86 10 8585 1836
Age range: 2–18 years
No. of pupils: 750
Curriculum: IBDP, UK, IGCSE
Language instr: Chinese, English

Yew Chung International School of Chongqing
No 2 Huxia Street, Yuan Yang Town, New Northern Zone, Chongqing 401122
Tel: +86 23 8879 1600
Age range: 3–18 years
Curriculum: IBDP, SAT, UK, IGCSE, ALevs
Language instr: English, Chinese

Yew Chung International School of Qingdao
72 Tai Hang Shan Lu, Qingdao West Coast New Area, Huangdao, Shandong 266555
Tel: +86 532 8699 5551
Age range: 2–18 years
No. of pupils: 331
Curriculum: IBDP, UK, ALevs
Language instr: English

Yew Chung International School of Shanghai - Century Park Campus
1433 Dong Xui Road, Pudong, Shanghai 200127
Tel: +86 21 2226 7666
Age range: 10–18 years
Curriculum: IBDP, National, UK, IGCSE
Language instr: English, Chinese

Yew Chung International School of Shanghai - Gubei Campus
18 West Rong Hua Road, Gubei New Area, Puxi, Shanghai 201103
Tel: +86 21 2226 7666
Age range: 2–18 years
No. of pupils: 2500
Curriculum: UK, IGCSE
Language instr: English, Chinese

Yew Chung International School of Shanghai - Hongqiao Campus
11 Shui Cheng Road, Puxi, Shanghai 200336
Tel: +86 21 2226 7666
Age range: 2–18 years
No. of pupils: 2500
Curriculum: IBDP, National, UK
Language instr: English, Chinese (Mandarin)

Yew Chung International School of Shanghai - Regency Park Campus
1817 Hua Mu Road, Pudong, Shanghai 201204
Tel: +86 21 2226 7666
Age range: 2–9 years
Curriculum: National, UK
Language instr: English, Chinese

YK Pao School
1800, Lane 900, North Sanxin Road, Songjiang District, Shanghai 201602
Tel: +86 21 61671999
Curriculum: IBDP
Language instr: English

Yuwen Princeton Kindergarten
Qingshan Distict, Qingdongdonglu, Baotou, Inner Mongolia AR 014030
Curriculum: IBPYP
Language instr: English, Chinese

Zhuhai International School
Qi ' Ao Island, Tang Jia Wan, Zhuhai, Guangdong 519080
Tel: +86 756 331 5580
Curriculum: IBDP, IBMYP, IBPYP
Language instr: English

Ziling Changxing Kindergarten
No. 1099 Qishan Road, Huzhou, Zhejiang
Tel: +86 57 2623 5173
Curriculum: IBPYP
Language instr: English, Chinese

EAST TIMOR

Dili International School
14 Rue Avenue de Portugal, Pantai Kelapa, Dili
Tel: +670 773 39030
Age range: 4–18 years
Curriculum: IBPYP

QSI International School of Dili
Aldea 04 Marconi, Suco Fatuhada, Sub Distrito Dom Alexio, Dili
Tel: +670 332 2389
Age range: 5–18 years
Curriculum: AP, USA
Language instr: English

HONG KONG, CHINA

American International School Hong Kong
125 Waterloo Road, Kowloon Tong, Kowloon, Hong Kong, SAR
Tel: +852 2336 3812
Age range: 3–18
No. of pupils: 840
Curriculum: AP, SAT, USA
Language instr: English

American School Hong Kong
6 Ma Chung Road, Tai Po, New Territories, Hong Kong, SAR
Tel: +852 3919 4100
Curriculum: IBDP
Language instr: English

Anfield School
No. 1, Lung Pak Street, Tai Wai, Shatin, Hong Kong, SAR
Tel: +852 2692 8823
Curriculum: UK

Australian International School Hong Kong
3A Norfolk Road, Kowloon Tong, Hong Kong, SAR
Tel: +852 2304 6078
Age range: 4–18
No. of pupils: 1125 B564 G561
Curriculum: IBDP
Language instr: English

California School
3/F, Front Block, 550 Nathan Road, Lung Ma Building, Yau Ma Tei, Kowloon, Hong Kong SAR
Tel: +852 2388 9844
Curriculum: UK, IGCSE, ALevs

Canadian International School of Hong Kong
36 Nam Long Shan Road, Aberdeen, Hong Kong, SAR
Tel: +852 2525 7088
Age range: 3–18
No. of pupils: 1835
Curriculum: IBDP, IBMYP, IBPYP
Language instr: English

Asia

Carmel School
460 Shau Kei Wan Road, Shau Kei Wan, Hong Kong, SAR
Tel: +852 3665 5388
Age range: 1–18
No. of pupils: 398 B187 G211
Curriculum: IBDP, IBMYP, IBPYP
Language instr: English

Causeway Bay Victoria International Kindergarten
32 Hing Fat Street, Causeway Bay, Hong Kong, SAR
Tel: +852 2578 9998
Curriculum: IBPYP

Chinese International School
1 Hau Yuen Path, Braemar Hill, Hong Kong, SAR
Tel: +852 2 510 7288
Age range: 4–18
No. of pupils: 1479
Curriculum: ACT, IBDP, IBMYP, SAT
Language instr: English

Christian Alliance International School
33 King Lam Street, Lai Chi Kok, Kowloon, Hong Kong, SAR
Tel: +852 3699 3899
Curriculum: IBDP

Concordia International School
68 Begonia Road, Yau Yat Chuen, Kowloon, Hong Kong, SAR
Tel: +852 2789 9890
Age range: 12–19
No. of pupils: 100
Curriculum: AP, SAT, USA

Creative Primary School
2A Oxford Street, Kowloon Tong, Kowloon, Hong Kong, SAR
Tel: +852 2336 0266
No. of pupils: 660
Curriculum: IBPYP

Delia School Of Canada
Tai Fung Avenue, Taikoo Shing, Hong Kong, SAR
Tel: +852 3658 0338
Age range: 4–20
No. of pupils: 897

Diocesan Boys' School
131 Argyle Street, Mong Kok, Kowloon, Hong Kong, SAR
Tel: +852 2711 5911
Age range: B12–18
No. of pupils: 1420
Curriculum: IBDP
Language instr: English

DISCOVERY BAY INTERNATIONAL SCHOOL
For further details see p. 49
Discovery Bay Road, Discovery Bay, Lantau Island, Hong Kong, SAR
Tel: +852 2987 7331
Email: dbis@dbis.edu.hk
Website: www.dbis.edu.hk
Principal: Marc Morris
Age range: 3–18 years
No. of pupils: 1000
Fees: HKD13,250
Curriculum: UK, IGCSE, ALevs
Language instr: English

Discovery Mind Primary School - Discovery Bay Campus
1/F, Shop 102, 92 Siena Avenue, Discovery Bay North Plaza, Lantau Island, Hong Kong, SAR
Tel: +852 2914 2202
Age range: 2–11
No. of pupils: 78
Curriculum: IPC

Discovery Mind Primary School - Tung Chung Campus
G/F, Shop A-D, Seaview Crescent, 8 Tung Chung Waterfront Road, Tung Chung, Hong Kong, SAR
Tel: +852 2915 0666
Age range: 2–11
No. of pupils: 100
Curriculum: IPC

Discovery Montessori Academy
Block1, Discovery Bay North, Lantau Island, Hong Kong SAR
Tel: +852 2812 9668
Curriculum: IBPYP
Language instr: English, Chinese

ELCHK Lutheran Academy
25 Lam Hau Tsuen Road, Yuen Long, New Territories, Hong Kong, SAR
Tel: +852 8208 2092
Age range: 6–18 years
No. of pupils: 1207
Curriculum: IBDP, IBMYP, IBPYP
Language instr: English, Mandarin, Cantonese

ESF Abacus International Kindergarten
Mang Kung Uk Village, Clearwater Bay Road, Hong Kong SAR
Tel: +852 27195712
Age range: 3–5 years
No. of pupils: 190
Curriculum: IBPYP
Language instr: English, Mandarin

ESF Beacon Hill School
23 Ede Road, Kowloon Tong, Hong Kong SAR
Tel: +852 2336 5221
Age range: 5–11 years
No. of pupils: 540
Curriculum: IBPYP, UK
Language instr: English

ESF Bradbury School
43C Stubbs Road, Hong Kong SAR
Tel: +852 2574 8249
Age range: 5–11 years
No. of pupils: 720
Curriculum: IBPYP
Language instr: English

ESF Clearwater Bay School
DD229, Lot 235, Clearwater Bay Road, New Territories, Hong Kong SAR
Tel: +852 2358 3221
Age range: 5–11 years
No. of pupils: 720
Curriculum: IBPYP, UK
Language instr: English

ESF Discovery College
38 Siena Avenue, Discovery Bay, Lantau Island, Hong Kong SAR
Tel: +852 3969 1000
Age range: 5–18 years
No. of pupils: 1400
Curriculum: IBDP, IBMYP, IBPYP, IBCP
Language instr: English

ESF Glenealy School
7 Hornsey Road, Mid Levels, Hong Kong SAR
Tel: +852 2522 1919
Age range: 5–11 years
No. of pupils: 360
Curriculum: IBPYP
Language instr: English

ESF Hillside International Kindergarten
43B Stubbs Road, Hong Kong SAR
Tel: +852 2540 0066
Age range: 3–5 years
No. of pupils: 366
Curriculum: IBPYP
Language instr: English

ESF Island School
20 Borrett Road, Hong Kong SAR
Tel: +852 2524 7135
Age range: 11–18 years
No. of pupils: 1200
Curriculum: IBDP, IBMYP, IBCP, UK, IGCSE
Language instr: English

ESF Jockey Club Sarah Roe School
2B Tin Kwong Road, Homantin, Kowloon, Hong Kong SAR
Tel: +852 2761 9893
Age range: 5–19
No. of pupils: 70
Curriculum: UK
Language instr: English

ESF Kennedy School
19 Sha Wan Drive, Pokfulam, Hong Kong SAR
Tel: +852 2579 5600
Age range: 5–11 years
No. of pupils: 900
Curriculum: IBPYP, UK
Language instr: English

ESF King George V School
2 Tin Kwong Road, Homantin, Kowloon, Hong Kong SAR
Tel: +852 2711 3029
Age range: 11–18 years
No. of pupils: 1846
Curriculum: IBDP, IBMYP, IBCP, IGCSE
Language instr: English

ESF Kowloon Junior School
20 Perth Street, Homantin, Kowloon, Hong Kong SAR
Tel: +852 3765 8700
Age range: 5–11 years
No. of pupils: 900
Curriculum: IBPYP, UK
Language instr: English

ESF Peak School
20 Plunkett's Road, The Peak, Hong Kong SAR
Tel: +852 2849 7211
Age range: 4–11 years
No. of pupils: 360
Curriculum: IBPYP
Language instr: English

ESF Quarry Bay School
6 Hau Yuen Path, Braemar Hill, North Point, Hong Kong SAR
Tel: +852 2566 4242
Age range: 5–11 years
No. of pupils: 720
Curriculum: IBPYP
Language instr: English

ESF Renaissance College
5 Hang Ming Street, Ma On Shan, New Territories, Hong Kong SAR
Tel: +852 3556 3556
Age range: 5–18 years
No. of pupils: 2100
Curriculum: IBDP, IBMYP, IBPYP, IBCP
Language instr: English

ESF Sha Tin College
3 Lai Wo Lane, Fo Tan, Sha Tin, New Territories, Hong Kong SAR
Tel: +852 2699 1811
Age range: 11–18 years
No. of pupils: 1200
Curriculum: IBDP, IBMYP, IBCP, IGCSE
Language instr: English

ESF Sha Tin Junior School
3A Lai Wo Lane, Fo Tan, Sha Tin, New Territories, Hong Kong SAR
Tel: +852 2692 2721
Age range: 5–11 years
No. of pupils: 900
Curriculum: IBPYP, UK
Language instr: English

ESF South Island School
50 Nam Fung Road, Hong Kong SAR
Tel: +852 2555 9313
Age range: 11–18 years
No. of pupils: 1430
Curriculum: IBDP, IBMYP, IBCP, IGCSE
Language instr: English

Asia

ESF Tsing Yi International Kindergarten
Maritime Square, 33 Tsing King Road, Tsing Yi, New Territories, Hong Kong SAR
Tel: +852 2436 3355
Age range: 3–5 years
No. of pupils: 352
Curriculum: IBPYP
Language instr: English

ESF Tung Chung International Kindergarten
1/F, Commercial Accommodation, The Visionary, 1 Ying Hong Street, Tung Chung, Lantau, New Territories, Hong Kong SAR
Tel: +852 3742 3500
Age range: 3–5 years
No. of pupils: 312
Curriculum: IBPYP
Language instr: English

ESF West Island School
250 Victoria Road, Pokfulam, Hong Kong SAR
Tel: +852 2819 1962
Age range: 11–18 years
No. of pupils: 1220
Curriculum: IBDP, IBMYP, IBCP, UK, IGCSE
Language instr: English

ESF Wu Kai Sha International Kindergarten
599 Sai Sha Road, Ma On Shan, Sha Tin, Hong Kong SAR
Tel: +852 2435 5291
Age range: 3–5 years
No. of pupils: 343
Curriculum: IBPYP
Language instr: English

French International School
165 Blue Pool Road, Happy Valley, Hong Kong, SAR
Tel: +852 25776217
Age range: 3–17 years
No. of pupils: 2700
Curriculum: IBDP, IPC, FrenchBacc, IGCSE
Language instr: English

Funful Sear Rogers International School
1 Cumberland Road, Kowloon Tong, Hong Kong, SAR
Tel: +852 2408 6683
Age range: 5–11
Language instr: English

G. T. (Ellen Yeung) College
10, Ling Kong Street, Tiu Keng Leng, Tseung Kwan O, Hong Kong, SAR
Tel: +852 2535 6867
Curriculum: IBDP
Language instr: English, Chinese

Galilee International School
G/F & 1/F, Peace Garden, 2 Peace Avenue, Ho Man Tin, Kowloon, Hong Kong, SAR
Tel: +852 2390 3000
Age range: 2–6 years
No. of pupils: 80
Curriculum: IBPYP
Language instr: English, Mandarin, Cantonese

German Swiss International School
11 Guildford Road, The Peak, Hong Kong, SAR
Tel: +852 2849 6216
Age range: 3–18 years
Curriculum: Abitur, IBDP, IGCSE
Language instr: English, German

Hamilton Hill International Kindergarten
2/F Tang Kung Mansion, 31 Tai Koo Shing Road, Tai Koo, Hong Kong SAR
Tel: +852 2567 5454
Language instr: English, Chinese

Han Academy
G/F - 2/F, 33-35 Wong Chuk Hang Road, Aberdeen, Hong Kong, SAR
Tel: +852 3998 6300
Curriculum: IBDP
Language instr: English, Chinese

Harrow International School Hong Kong
38 Tsing Ying Road, Tuen Mun, Hong Kong, SAR
Tel: +852 2824 9099
Age range: 3–18 years
Curriculum: UK, IGCSE, ALevs

HKCA Po Leung Kuk School
62 Tin Hau Temple Road, Hong Kong, SAR
Tel: +852 3465 8400
Age range: 3–12 years
Curriculum: IBPYP
Language instr: English, Putonghua

HKMA David Li Kwok Po College
8 Hoi Wang Road, Mongkok West, Kowloon, Hong Kong, SAR
Tel: +852 2626 9100
Age range: 12–20
No. of pupils: 850
Curriculum: National
Language instr: English, Cantonese, Putonghua

> **HONG KONG ACADEMY**
> *For further details see p. 55*
> 33 Wai Man Road, Sai Kung, Hong Kong, SAR
> **Tel:** +852 2655 1111
> **Email:** admissions@hkacademy.edu.hk
> **Website:** www.hkacademy.edu.hk
> **Head of School:** Kasson Bratton
> **Age range:** 3–18 years
> **No. of pupils:** 550
> **Fees:** HK$116,570
> **Curriculum:** ACT, IBDP, IBMYP, IBPYP
> **Language instr:** English

Hong Kong International School
1 Red Hill Road, Tai Tam, Hong Kong, SAR
Tel: +852 3149 7001
Age range: 4–18
No. of pupils: 2700
Curriculum: AP, USA
Language instr: English

International Christian School
1 On Muk Lane, Shek Mun, Sha Tin, Hong Kong, SAR
Tel: +852 3920 0000

International College Hong Kong
60 Sha Tau Kok Road, Shek Chung Au, Sha Tau Kok, New Territories, Hong Kong, SAR
Tel: +852 2655 9018
Age range: 11–18 years
Curriculum: IBDP, National, UK, IGCSE
Language instr: English

International College Hong Kong - Hong Lok Yuen
3 Twentieth Street, Hong Lok Yuen, Tai Po, New Territories, Hong Kong, SAR
Tel: +852 3955 3000
Age range: 3–11 years
No. of pupils: 380
Curriculum: IBPYP, National, UK
Language instr: English

Invictus School Hong Kong
G27 Monterey Place, 23 Tong Chun Street, Tseung Kwan O, New Territories, Hong Kong, SAR
Tel: +852 3643 1868
Age range: 3–11 years
Curriculum: IPC, UK

Invictus Secondary School
188 Tai Tam Road, Hing Man Shopping Complex, Chai Wan, Hong Kong, SAR
Tel: +852 3852 7200
Age range: 11–18 years
Curriculum: UK, IGCSE, ALevs

Island Christian Academy
70 Bridges Street, Sheung Wan, Hong Kong, SAR
Tel: +852 2537 2552
Curriculum: IPC

Japanese International School
4663 Tai Po Road, Tai Po, New Territories, Hong Kong, SAR
Tel: +852 2834 3531
Age range: 4–11
No. of pupils: B85 G84
Curriculum: IBPYP
Language instr: English

Kellett School
7 Lam Hing Street, Kowloon Bay, Hong Kong, SAR
Tel: +852 3120 0700
Age range: 4–18 years
No. of pupils: 1500
Curriculum: UK, IGCSE, ALevs
Language instr: English

Kiangsu & Chekiang Primary School
30 Ching Wah Street, North Point, Hong Kong, SAR
Tel: +852 2570 4594
Age range: 3–12
No. of pupils: 290
Curriculum: UK

Kiangsu-Chekiang College, International Section
20 Braemar Hill Road, North Point, Hong Kong, SAR
Tel: +852 2570 1281
Age range: 3–18
Curriculum: IBDP, UK, IGCSE
Language instr: English, Mandarin

Kingston International Kindergarten
12-14 Cumberland Road, Kowloon Tong, Hong Kong, SAR
Tel: +852 2337 9049
Curriculum: IBPYP
Language instr: English, Putonghua

Kingston International School
113 Waterloo Road, Kowloon Tong, Hong Kong, SAR
Tel: +852 2337 9031
Age range: 1–11 years
No. of pupils: 420
Curriculum: IBPYP
Language instr: English, Mandarin

Lantau International School - Pui O Campus
House 19, South Lantau Road, Lo Wai Village, Lantau Island, Hong Kong, SAR
Tel: +852 2984 0302
Curriculum: UK

Logos Academy
1 Kan Hok Lane, Tseung Kwan, Hong Kong, SAR
Tel: +852-23372123
Age range: 6–18
No. of pupils: 2100
Curriculum: IBDP
Language instr: English

Malvern College Hong Kong
3 Fo Chun Road, Pak Shek Kok, Hong Kong, SAR
Tel: +852 3898 4688
Age range: 5–18 years
No. of pupils: 1200
Curriculum: IBDP, IBMYP, IBPYP
Language instr: English

> **NORD ANGLIA INTERNATIONAL SCHOOL, HONG KONG**
> *For further details see p. 64*
> 11 On Tin Street, Lam Tin, Kowloon, Hong Kong, SAR
> **Tel:** +852 3958 1428
> **Email:** admissions@nais.hk
> **Website:** https://www.nais.hk
> **Principal:** Tim Richardson
> **Age range:** 3–18 years
> **Fees:** HK$90,067–HK$189,020
> **Curriculum:** IBDP, UK, IGCSE
> **Language instr:** English

Norwegian International School Hong Kong
170 Kam Shan Road, Kam Shan Village, Tai Po, Hong Kong, SAR
Tel: +852 2658 0341
Curriculum: IPC

Asia

Parkview International Pre-school
Tower 18 Parkview, 88 Tai Tam Reservoir Road, Hong Kong, SAR
Tel: +852 2812 6023
Age range: 1–5
Curriculum: IBPYP
Language instr: English, Putonghua

Parkview International Pre-School (Kowloon)
Podium Level, Kowloon Station, 1 Austin Road West, Kowloon, Hong Kong, SAR
Tel: +852 2812 6801
Age range: 1–6
No. of pupils: 450
Curriculum: IBPYP
Language instr: English

Po Leung Kuk Choi Kai Yau School
6 Caldecott Road, Piper's Hill, Kowloon, Hong Kong, SAR
Tel: +852 2148 2052
Curriculum: IBDP

Shrewsbury International School Hong Kong
10 Shek Kok Road, Tseung Kwan O, Hong Kong, SAR
Tel: +852 2480 1500
Age range: 3–11
Curriculum: UK
Language instr: English

Singapore International School (Hong Kong) - Preparatory Years & Primary Section
23 Nam Long Shan Road, Aberdeen, Hong Kong, SAR
Tel: +852 2872 0266
Age range: 4–12

Singapore International School (Hong Kong) - Secondary Section
2 Police School Road, Wong Chuk Hang, Hong Kong, SAR
Tel: +852 2919 6966
Age range: 3 years 8 months–18 years
No. of pupils: 1400
Curriculum: IBDP, IGCSE
Language instr: English

St. Paul's Co-educational College
33 MacDonnell Road, Central, Hong Kong, SAR
Tel: +852 2523 1187
Age range: 11–18
No. of pupils: 1300
Curriculum: IBDP

Stamford American School Hong Kong
25 Man Fuk Road, Ho Man Tin, Kowloon, Hong Kong, SAR
Tel: +852 3467 4500
Age range: 5–18 years
Curriculum: IBDP, USA
Language instr: English

Tai Kwong Hilary College (TKHC)
No. 178 Kam Shan, Tai Po, N.T., Hong Kong SAR
Curriculum: IBDP
Language instr: English, Chinese

The Harbour School
332 Ap Lei Chau Bridge Road, Ap Lei Chau, Hong Kong, SAR
Tel: +852 3905 0180
Curriculum: USA
Language instr: English

The Independent Schools Foundation Academy
1 Kong Sin Wan Road, Pokfulam, Hong Kong, SAR
Tel: +852 2202 2000
Age range: 5–18
No. of pupils: 1650 B830 G820 VIth80
Curriculum: ACT, IBDP, IBMYP, SAT
Language instr: English, Chinese

Think International School
117 Boundary Street, Kowloon Tong, Hong Kong, SAR
Tel: +852 2338 3949
Curriculum: IBPYP, IGCSE

Victoria (Belcher) International Kindergarten
Portion of Level 3 (Kindergarten Area), The Westwood, 8 Belchers Street, Hong Kong, SAR
Tel: +852 2542 7001
Age range: 2–6
Curriculum: IBPYP
Language instr: English, Mandarin, Cantonese

Victoria (Harbour Green) International Kindergarten
8 Sham Mong Road, G/F., Harbour Green, Kowloon, Hong Kong SAR
Tel: +852 2885 1928
Curriculum: IBPYP
Language instr: English

Victoria (Homantin) International Nursery
1/F., Carmel-on-the-Hill, 9 Carmel Village Street, Homantin, Kowloon, Hong Kong, SAR
Tel: +852 2762 9130
Curriculum: IBPYP
Language instr: English

Victoria (South Horizons) International Kindergarten
Podium Level 2, Phase 2, South Horizons, Ap Lei Chau, Hong Kong, SAR
Tel: +852 2580 8633
Curriculum: IBPYP
Language instr: Cantonese, English, Mandarin

Victoria Kindergarten
G/F., 2-8 Hong On Street, Kornhill, Hong Kong, SAR
Tel: +852 2885 3331
Curriculum: IBPYP
Language instr: English

Victoria Nursery
Ko Fung Court, Harbour Heights, 5 Fook Yum Road, North Point, Hong Kong, SAR
Tel: +852 2571 7888
Age range: 2–6
Curriculum: IBPYP
Language instr: Cantonese, English, Mandarin

Victoria Shanghai Academy (VSA)
19 Shum Wan Road, Aberdeen, Hong Kong, SAR
Tel: +852 3402 1000
Age range: 5 yrs 8 mths–18 yrs
No. of pupils: 1800
Curriculum: IBDP, IBMYP, IBPYP
Language instr: English, Putonghua

Yew Chung International School of Hong Kong
3 To Fuk Road, Kowloon, Hong Kong, SAR
Tel: +852 2338 7106
Age range: 6 months–18 years
Curriculum: IBDP, UK, IGCSE
Language instr: English, Chinese

Yew Chung International School of Hong Kong - Early Childhood Education
3 Somerset Road, Kowloon Tong, Hong Kong, SAR
Tel: +852 2336 3443
Age range: 6 months–5 years
Curriculum: UK
Language instr: English, Chinese

Yew Chung International School of Hong Kong - Primary Section
2 Kent Road, Kowloon Tong, Hong Kong SAR
Tel: +852 2336 7292
Age range: 5–11 years
Curriculum: UK
Language instr: English, Chinese

YMCA of Hong Kong Christian College
2 Chung Yat Street, Tung Chung, Lantau Island, Hong Kong, SAR
Tel: +852 2988 8123
Age range: 11–21
Curriculum: National, UK, IGCSE, ALevs

INDIA

10X International School
Billapura Cross, Attibele Road, Sarjapur, Bengaluru, Karnataka 562125
Tel: +91 98 8632 0014
Curriculum: IBDP, IBMYP
Language instr: English, Spanish

Aarth Universal School
Block 148, Surat-Bhesan-Barbodhan Road, Malgama, Surat, Gujarat 395005
Tel: +91 81 5592 2000
Curriculum: IBPYP
Language instr: English

Adani International School
Opposite Belvedere Golf & Country Club, Shantigram, Near Vaishnodevi Circle, S.G. Highway, Ahmedabad, Gujarat 382421
Tel: +91 79 2555 6888
Age range: 3–18 years
Curriculum: IBDP, IBPYP
Language instr: English

Aditya Birla World Academy
Vastushilp Annexe, Gamadia Colony, J D Road, Tardeo, Mumbai, Maharashtra 400034
Tel: +91 22 2352 8400
Curriculum: IBDP
Language instr: English

Ahlcon Public School
Mayur Vihar Ph 1, New Delhi, Delhi 110091
Tel: +91 11 4634 7777
Curriculum: IBCP
Language instr: English

Ahmedabad International School
Opp Rajpath Row Houses, Behind Kiran Motors, Judges Bungalow Road, Bodakdev, Ahmedabad 380015
Tel: +91 79 2687 2459
Age range: 3–17
No. of pupils: 1200
Curriculum: IBDP, IBPYP, IGCSE, ALevs
Language instr: English

Ajmera Global School
Yogi Nagar, Eksar Road, Borivali West, Mumbai, Maharashtra 400092
Tel: +91 22 32401053
Curriculum: IBPYP
Language instr: English

Akal Academy Baru Sahib
Via Rajgarh, Teh. Pachhad, Distt. Sirmore, Himachal Pradesh 173101
Tel: +91 9816400538
Curriculum: IBPYP
Language instr: English

Akshar Árbol International School - ECR Campus
Bethel Nagar, North 9th Street, Injambakkam, Chennai, Tamil Nadu 600115
Tel: +91 9444973275
Curriculum: IBDP, IBPYP
Language instr: English

Al Fajr International School
No. 7 & 8, II Main Road, Nehru Nagar, Perungudi, Chennai 600 096
Tel: +91 044 455 72228
Curriculum: UK, IGCSE

Al Qamar Academy
14 Kalyani Nagar, Opp Journalist's Colony, Kottivakkam, Chennai, Tamil Nadu 600041
Tel: +91 44 2451 1226
Age range: 12–16
No. of pupils: 300
Curriculum: IGCSE

Asia

All Saints' College
Nainital, Uttarakhand 263002
Tel: +91 5942 235121
Age range: G5–18
No. of pupils: 800
Curriculum: National

Alliance World School
C-54/A, Sector-56, Noida,
Uttar Pradesh 201301
Tel: +91 12 0258 9073
Age range: 4–19
No. of pupils: 100
Curriculum: IGCSE

aLphabet School
178 St. Mary's Road, Alwarpet,
Chennai, Tamil Nadu 600018
Tel: +91 44 4211 2025
Curriculum: IBDP, IBMYP, IBPYP
Language instr: English

American Embassy School
Chandragupta Marg, Chanakyapuri,
New Delhi, Delhi 110021
Tel: +91 11 2688 8854
No. of pupils: 1200
Curriculum: ACT, AP, IBDP, SAT
Language instr: English

American International School - Chennai
100 Feet Road, Taramani,
Chennai 600113
Tel: +91 44 2254 9000
Age range: 3–18
No. of pupils: 226 B116 G110
Curriculum: IBDP
Language instr: English

American School of Bombay
SF 2, G-Block, Bandra Kurla
Complex Road, Bandra East,
Mumbai, Maharashtra 400051
Tel: SS: +91 22 6772 7272
ES: +91 22 6131 3600
Age range: 3–18 years
No. of pupils: 610
Curriculum: AP, IBDP, IBPYP, SAT, USA
Language instr: English

Amity Global School, Gurgaon
Main Sector Road 4, Sector 46,
Gurgaon, Haryana 122002
Tel: +91 84 4848 1410
No. of pupils: 60
Curriculum: IBDP, IBPYP
Language instr: English

Amity Global School, Noida
A Block, C Block, Sector 44,
Noida, Uttar Pradesh 201301
Tel: +91 12 0243 2959
Curriculum: IBPYP
Language instr: English

Amity International School Saket
M Block, Saket, New
Delhi, Delhi 110017
Tel: +91 11 29561606
Age range: 4–12

Amrita International Vidyalayam
Choodasandra, Huskur P.O.,
Bengaluru, Karnataka 560099
Tel: +91 90 1920 2583
Curriculum: IBPYP
Language instr: English

Apeejay School International, South Delhi
Sheikh Sarai-Phase I, Panchsheel
Park, New Delhi, Delhi 110017
Tel: +91 11 26016935
Curriculum: IBDP, IBMYP, IBPYP
Language instr: English

APL Global School
Survey No 104/8C3, Foundry
Road, Okiiam Thoraiopakkam,
Chennai, Tamil Nadu 600097
Tel: +91 44 4282 3272
Curriculum: UK, IGCSE, ALevs

Ascend International School
5 'F' Block, Opp. Govt. Colony,
Bandra Kurla Complex (Bandra E),
Mumbai, Maharashtra 400051
Tel: +91 22 7122 2000
Age range: 3–13
No. of pupils: 280
Curriculum: IBDP, IBMYP, IBPYP
Language instr: English

ASIS Chennai
Parvathi Avenue Madanandapuram,
Udhaya Nagar Main Road, Porur,
Chennai, Tamil Nadu 600116
Tel: +91 80 1213 7777
Age range: 2–19 years

Aspee Nutan Academy
Marve Road, Malad West,
Mumbai, Maharashtra 400064
Tel: +91 70 9800 9090
Curriculum: IBCP
Language instr: English

Baldwin Boys' High School
14 Hosur Road, Richmond Town,
Bengaluru, Karnataka 560025
Tel: +91 804 936 3866
Age range: B6–18 years
Curriculum: National

Bangalore International School
Geddalahalli, Hennur Bagalur
Road, Kothanur Post, Bengaluru,
Karnataka 560077
Tel: +91 80 2846 5060/2844 5852
Age range: 3–18
No. of pupils: 502
Curriculum: AP, IBDP, UK,
USA, IGCSE, ALevs
Language instr: English

BD Somani International School
625 GD Somani Marg, Cuffe Parade,
Mumbai, Maharashtra 400005
Tel: +91 22 2216 1355
Age range: 13–17 years
No. of pupils: 190
Curriculum: IBDP, IGCSE
Language instr: English

BGS International Academia School
BGS Knowledge City, Nityanandha
Nagar, K.Gollahalli, Bengaluru,
Karnataka 560074
Tel: +91 96 0626 3332
Curriculum: IBDP
Language instr: English

Billabong High International (Santa Cruz)
Ajivasan, Off. Juhu Tara Road,
Opp. Lido Cinema, Next to
SNDT College, Santa Cruz West,
Mumbai, Maharashtra 400049
Tel: +91 22 26613389
Curriculum: UK, IGCSE

Birla Open Minds International School
Survey No. 192 & 193, Outer
Ring Road, Gachibowli, Kollur,
Hyderabad, Telangana 502300
Tel: +91 84 9999 3928
Age range: 4–18 years
Curriculum: IBCP, National, UK, IGCSE
Language instr: English

Bishop Cotton School
Shimla Bypass, Near Khalini, Shimla,
Himachal Pradesh 171002
Tel: +91 17 7262 0880
Age range: B7–18 years

BLiSS Edify International School, Pune
38 Phase 1, Rajiv Gandhi
Infotech Park, Hinjawadi,
Pune, Maharashtra 411057
Tel: +91 77 4185 0000
Curriculum: IBDP, IBMYP, IBPYP
Language instr: English

Bloomingdale International School
Municipal Employee Colony,
Main Road, Vijayawada,
Andhra Pradesh 520010
Tel: +91 7799787827
Curriculum: IBDP, IBMYP, IBPYP
Language instr: English

Bluebells School International
Kailash (Opp) Lady Shriram
College, New Delhi, Delhi 110048
Tel: +91 011 29232963
Age range: 4–18
No. of pupils: B976 G893
Curriculum: National
Language instr: English

Bodhi International School
Shikargarh Enclave, Near Mini
Market, Jodhpur, Rajasthan 342015
Tel: +91 291 2970100-1
Curriculum: IBPYP
Language instr: English

Bombay International School
Gilbert Building, 2nd Cross
Lane, Babulnath, Mumbai,
Maharashtra 400007
Tel: +91 22 2364 8206
Curriculum: IBDP, IBPYP

Bright Start Fellowship International School
Fellowship Society Campus,
Near August Kranti Maidan,
Gowalia Tank, 400036
Tel: +91 22 23803388
Curriculum: UK, IGCSE, ALevs

British Oak Tree Nursery
Site No-4 Mayfield Garden
Sector 57, Opp Orchid Islands,
Gurugram, Haryana
Tel: +91 95 8294 8440
Curriculum: UK

Buddhi School
1&2 Dasarahalli Extension, HA Farm
Post, (Next to Legacy Apartments),
Opposite to Shoba Moonsto+,
Bengaluru, Karnataka 560024
Tel: +91 92420 20302
Curriculum: UK, IGCSE, ALevs

Bunts Sangha's S.M. Shetty International School & Jr. College
Hiranandani Gardens, Powai,
Mumbai, Maharashtra 400076
Tel: +91 22 61327346
Curriculum: IBDP
Language instr: English

C P Goenka International School - Borivali
Spring Buds International - Gorai
Swami, Link Road, Borivali West,
Mumbai, Maharashtra 400091
Tel: +91 22 2891 1473
Age range: 3–18 years
Curriculum: National

C P Goenka International School - Oshiwara
A-21, Near Income Tax Quarters,
Oshiwara, Andheri (West),
Mumbai, Maharashtra 400053
Tel: +91 22 4749 0748
Age range: 3–18 years
Curriculum: IBDP, IGCSE, ALevs
Language instr: English

C P Goenka International School - Pune
Behind Hotel Mapple Adhwryou,
Ubale Nagar, Nagar-Pune
Highway Road, Wagholi,
Pune, Maharashtra 412207
Tel: +91 20 6736 9600
Age range: 3–18 years
Curriculum: IBCP, National,
IGCSE, ALevs
Language instr: English

C P Goenka International School - Thane
Kapurbawdi Junction, Off
Ghodbunder Road, Next to
Lake City Mall, Thane (West),
Maharashtra 400607
Tel: +91 22 4885 5555
Age range: 3–18 years
Curriculum: IGCSE, ALevs

Asia

C P Goenka International School - Ulwe
Plot 18, Sector 05, Near Jio Institute, Ulwe, Navi, Mumbai, Maharashtra 410206
Tel: +91 97 0209 4984
Age range: 3–11 years
Curriculum: National

C P Goenka's Spring Buds International Preschool - Juhu
C/O. Gulmohar Cross Road No. 1, Sweta Apartment, JVPD, Vile Parle (W), Mumbai, Maharashtra 400049
Tel: +91 22 6128 6900
Language instr: English

C P Goenka's Spring Buds International Preschool - Lamington Road
Diamond Plaza 391, Swastik Cinema Compound, Lamington Road, Mumbai, Maharashtra 400004
Tel: +91 99 2027 5633
Language instr: English

Calcutta International School
724 Anandapur, E M Bypass, Kolkata, West Bengal 700107
Tel: +91 33 2443 2054
Age range: 3–18
No. of pupils: 642 B360 G282
Curriculum: IBDP, UK, IGCSE, ALevs
Language instr: English

Caledonian International School
Near Power Gym, Saili Road, Pathankot, Punjab 145001
Tel: +91 98 7883 3613
Age range: 1.5–18 years
Curriculum: IBMYP, IBPYP
Language instr: English

Calorx Olive International School
Besides Ahmedabad Dental College, Near Arjun Farm, Ranchodpura - Bhadaj Road, Ahmedabad, Gujarat 380058
Tel: +91 90 9993 3804
Curriculum: IBDP, IBMYP, IBPYP
Language instr: English

Cambridge International School
Choti Baradari, Phase II, Jalandhar, Punjab 144001
Tel: +91 181 462 3955
Curriculum: IBDP, IBPYP

Cambridge International School, Dasuya
Hazipur Road, Dasuya, Hoshiarpur, Punjab 144205
Tel: +91 18 8350 2108
Age range: 3–18 years
Curriculum: IGCSE, ALevs

Campion International School
River Side Avenue, Shalbari, West Bengal
Tel: +91 99335 39999
Age range: 4–19
Curriculum: UK, IGCSE, ALevs

Canadian International School
Survey No 4 & 20, Manchenahalli, Yelahanka, Bengaluru, Karnataka 560064
Tel: +91 80 6759 4444
Age range: 3–19+
No. of pupils: 420 B220 G200
Curriculum: IBDP, SAT
Language instr: English

Candor International School
Koppa-harapanhalli Road, Hullahalli, Off, Bannerghatta Main Rd, near Electronic City, Bengaluru, Karnataka 560105
Tel: +91 77 6029 9992
Age range: 3–17
No. of pupils: 600
Curriculum: IBDP, IBPYP
Language instr: English

Chaman Bhartiya School
Thanisandra Main Road, Bhartiya City, Chokkanahalli, Bangalore, Karnataka 560064
Curriculum: IBMYP
Language instr: English, Kannada

Chatrabhuj Narsee School
Valley of Flower, Next to Gundecha Premiere Tower, off. Western Express Highway, Kandivali East, Mumbai, Maharashtra 400101
Tel: +91 22 2886 6677
Curriculum: IBDP
Language instr: English

Children's Academy International School
BL Murarka Marg, Bachani Nagar, Malad East, Mumbai, Maharashtra 400097
Tel: +91 22 2883 5014
Curriculum: IBCP
Language instr: English

Chinmaya International Residential School
Nallur Vayal Post, Siruvani Road, Coimbatore, Tamil Nadu 641114
Tel: +91 422 261 3300/3303
Age range: 10–19
No. of pupils: 500 B320 G180
Curriculum: IBDP, National
Language instr: English

Chinmaya International Vidyalaya
P-125, Warangade, Maan, Taluka and Dist: Palghar, Boisar, Maharashtra 401501
Tel: +91 73 7848 9121
Curriculum: IBPYP
Language instr: English, Hindi

CHIREC International
Survey No 73, Behind Candure Marketing Office, Sudarshan Nagar, Gachibowli, Serlingampally, Hyderabad, Telangana 500133
Tel: +91 5498 4903
Age range: 2.5–18 years
Curriculum: IBDP, IBCP, National
Language instr: English

Choithram International
Choithram Hospital Campus, 5 Manik Bagh Road, Indore, Madhya Pradesh 452014
Tel: +91 731 2360345/6
Age range: 3–19
No. of pupils: 500
Curriculum: IBDP, IBMYP, IBPYP
Language instr: English

Christ Church School
Clare Road, Byculla, Mumbai, Maharashtra 400008
Tel: +91 22 2309 9892
Curriculum: IBDP
Language instr: English

Christ Junior College
Hosur Road, Bhavani Nagar, Suddagunte Palya, Bengaluru, Karnataka 560029
Tel: +91 804 012 9292
Age range: 16–18 years
Curriculum: IBDP
Language instr: English

Christ Junior College - Residential
Mysore Road, Kanmanike, Kumbalgodu, Bengaluru, Karnataka 560074
Tel: +91 804 012 9870
Age range: 16–18 years
Curriculum: IBDP
Language instr: English

Cochin International School
18/431A Vayanashala Chemmalapady Road, Pukkattupady, Malayidamthuruth P.O, Ernakulam, Kochi, Kerala 683561
Tel: +91 97 7841 2991
Curriculum: IBPYP
Language instr: English

CPS Global School - Anna Nagar Campus
A 80, IIIrd Avenue, Annanagar, Chennai, Tamil Nadu 600102
Tel: +91 44 4351 5121
Curriculum: IBDP
Language instr: English

CPS Global School - Thirumazhisai Campus
SH 50, Thiruvallur High Road, Thirumazhisai, Chennai, Tamil Nadu 600124
Tel: +91 44 3500 3800
Curriculum: IBDP
Language instr: English

Crossroads International School
11-12 Modern Complex, Devendra Dham Ki Gali, Opposite Celebration Mall, Udaipur, Rajasthan 313001
Tel: +91 29 4298 0215
Curriculum: IBPYP
Language instr: English, Hindi

Cygnus World School
Besides Motnath Mahadev Temple, Harni, Vadodara, Gujarat 390022
Tel: +91 90 9913 0334
Curriculum: IBDP
Language instr: English, Hindi

D Y Patil International College
DY Patil Knowledge City, Charholi(BK), Via. Lohegaon, Pune, Maharashtra 412105
Tel: +91 20 30612700/752/753
Age range: 3–18 years
Curriculum: IGCSE
Language instr: English

D Y Patil International School, Lohagaon
Charoli Bd., Lohagaon, Pune, Maharashtra 412105
Tel: +91 020 30612 714

D Y Patil International School, Nagpur
MIHAN Project Area, Village Khapri (Railway), Nagpur, Maharashtra 441108
Tel: +91 22 3928 5999
Language instr: English

D Y Patil International School, Nerul
Dr D Y Patil Vidhyanagar, Sector 7, Nerul, Navi Mumbai, Maharashtra 400706
Tel: +91 22 47700840
Curriculum: IBDP

D Y Patil International School, Worli
Opp MIG Colony A, Worli, Mumbai, Maharashtra 400025
Tel: +91-22 69047999
Curriculum: IBDP, IBPYP, IBCP, IGCSE
Language instr: English

Daly College
Residency Area, Indore, Madhya Pradesh 452001
Tel: +91 731 271 9000
Age range: 4–18 years
Curriculum: National, IGCSE, ALevs
Language instr: English

De Paul International Residential School
Belagola, Srirangapatna, Taluk, Avverahalli, Karnataka 571606
Tel: +91 9535187506
Age range: 4–18
Curriculum: IGCSE

Asia

Delhi Public School Bangalore East (DPSBE)
Survey No. 43, Dommasandra Post, 1B & 45, Kodati Sulikunte Road, Sulikunte, Bangalore, Karnataka 562125
Tel: +91 96 6311 5148
Curriculum: IBCP
Language instr: English

Delhi Public School Bangalore North (DPSBN)
Survey No 35/1A, Sathnur Village, Bagalur Post, Off Bellary Road, Jalla Hobli, Bangalore, Karnataka
Tel: +91 80 2972 4864
Curriculum: IBCP
Language instr: English

Delhi Public School Bangalore South (DPSBS)
11th KM, Bikaspura Main Road, Kanakapura Road, Konanakunte, Bangalore, Karnataka 560062
Tel: +91 80 2666 8581
Curriculum: IBCP
Language instr: English

Delhi Public School Ghaziabad (DPSG) International
P.O. Dasna, Hindon Nagar, Dasna, Kallu Garhi, Ghaziabad, Uttar Pradesh 201303
Tel: +91 11 4734 2000
Curriculum: IBPYP
Language instr: English

Delhi Public School Ghaziabad (DPSG) Meerut Road
Site No. 3, Meerut Road Industrial Area, Ghaziabad, Uttar Pradesh 201001
Tel: +91 11 4734 2000
Curriculum: IBDP, IBPYP
Language instr: English

Delhi Public School Ghaziabad (DPSG) Palam Vihar
I Block, Palam Vihar, Gurugram, Haryana 122017
Tel: +91 11 4734 2000
Curriculum: IBPYP
Language instr: English

Delhi Public School Ghaziabad (DPSG) Vasundhara
Sector 9, Vasundhara, Ghaziabad, Uttar Pradesh 201012
Tel: +91 11 4734 2000
Curriculum: IBPYP
Language instr: English

Deutsche Schule New Delhi
EP16/17 Chandragupta Marg, Chanakyapuri, New Delhi, Delhi 110021
Tel: +91 11 2611 2193

Dhirubhai Ambani International School
Bandra-Kurla Complex, Bandra (East), Mumbai, Maharashtra 400098
Tel: +91 22 3563 7000
Age range: 3–18 years
Curriculum: IBDP, IBMYP, IBPYP, National, IGCSE
Language instr: English

Diamond Stone International School
Nallur Road, Madivallam Cross, Hosur, Tamil Nadu 635109
Tel: +91 766 731 2999
Language instr: English, Hindi, Tamil

Don Bosco International School
Nathalal Parekh Marg, Matunga (E), Mumbai, Maharashtra 400019
Tel: +91 22 2412 7474
Curriculum: IBDP, IBPYP
Language instr: English

DPS International, Gurgaon
HS-01, Block W, South City II, Gurugram, Haryana 122001
Tel: +91 8377000164
Curriculum: IBDP, IBMYP, IBPYP
Language instr: English

DPS International, Saket
P-37 MB Road, Sector VI, Pusph Vihar, Saket, New Delhi, Delhi 110057
Tel: +91 11 2956 1187
Age range: 11–18
Curriculum: National, IGCSE, ALevs
Language instr: English

Dr Pillai Global Academy
Plot No 1, RSC 48, Gorai - II, Borivali (W), Mumbai, Maharashtra 400092
Tel: +91 22 2868 4467/87
Age range: 3–18
Curriculum: IBDP, IGCSE, ALevs
Language instr: English

Dr Pillai Global Academy, New Panvel
Sector-7, Khanda Colony, New Panvel, Navi Mumbai, Maharashtra 410206
Tel: +91 22 2748 1737
Age range: 3–17 years
No. of pupils: 508
Curriculum: IBDP
Language instr: English

DRS International School
Survey No. 523, Opp. Apparel Park, Gundla Pochampally, Medchal Mandal, Telangana, Hyderabad 500100
Tel: +91 93 9142 2060
Curriculum: IBDP, IBMYP, IBPYP
Language instr: English

DSB International School
Urmi Estate 95, Ganpatrao Kadam Marg, Opposite Peninsula Business Park, Mumbai, Maharashtra 400013
Tel: +91 73 0459 7529
Age range: 3–18 years
No. of pupils: 210
Curriculum: IBDP, UK, IGCSE
Language instr: English, German

Dwarkibai Gangadhar Khetan International School
Krishna Realties, Behind Sunder Nagar, Off. S.V. Road & Link Road, Malad (West), Mumbai, Maharashtra 400064
Tel: +91 22 28785360
Curriculum: UK, ALevs

Eastern Public School
Ward 1, Abbas Nagar, Bhopal, Madhya Pradesh 462036
Tel: +91 755 2805695
Curriculum: IBDP, IBPYP

Ecole Mondiale World School
Gulmohar Cross Road No. 9, J.V.P.D. Scheme, Juhu, Mumbai, Maharashtra 400049
Tel: +91 22 26237265/66
Age range: 2–18 years
Curriculum: IBDP, IBMYP, IBPYP
Language instr: English

Edubridge International School
Wadilal A. Patel Marg, Grant Road (East), Mumbai, Maharashtra 400007
Tel: +91 22 238 999 11
Curriculum: IBDP, IBMYP, IBPYP
Language instr: English

Ela Green School
No.1 Karambur Village, Chengalpattu Taluk, Kandchipuram District, Urapakkam, Maraimalai Nagar, Chennai, Tamil Nadu 603209
Tel: +91 89 3995 8989
Curriculum: IBDP, IBMYP, IBPYP
Language instr: English

Elpro International School
Elpro compound, Entrance from Shridhar Nagar road, Pimpri-Chinchwad Link Road, Pune, Maharashtra 411033
Tel: +91 20 6733 3500
Curriculum: IBDP, IBCP
Language instr: English

European International School
7A, Wisecy House, 14/15 Nanchundaroa Road, Injambakkam, Chennai, Tamil Nadu 600115
Tel: +91 44 24492562

Excelsior American School
Sector 43 behind Dell Building, C-2 Block, Sushant Lok, Phase 1, Gurugram, Haryana 122001
Tel: +91 1 124 4049342
Curriculum: IBDP, UK, IGCSE, ALevs
Language instr: English

Fazlani L'Académie Globale
Shiv das Chapsi Marg, Opp. Wallace Flour Mills, Mazagaon, Mumbai, Maharashtra 400009
Tel: +91 222 373 2730
Curriculum: IBPYP
Language instr: English

Finland International School (FIS) Thane
Road no. 27, Shreenagar, Wagle Estate, Thane West, Thane, Maharashtra 400604
Tel: +91 5203 9926
Age range: 3–18 years
Curriculum: IBDP, National, UK, IGCSE
Language instr: English, Hindi

FirstSteps School
Opp. Blind Girls Hostel, Sector 26, Chandigarh, Punjab 160019
Tel: +91 172 2793992
Age range: 2–15
No. of pupils: 265 B151 G114
Curriculum: IBPYP, IGCSE
Language instr: English

Fountainhead School
Opp Ambetha Water Tank, Kunkni, Rander-Dandi Road, Surat, Gujarat 395005
Tel: +91 800 0130 031
Age range: 3–17 years
No. of pupils: 1900
Curriculum: IBDP, IBMYP, IBPYP
Language instr: English

Fravashi International Academy
Adjacent to Gangapur Dam Rest House, Gangapur - Dugaon Road, Dugaon Village, Nashik, Maharashtra 422203
Tel: +912532215000
Curriculum: UK, IGCSE, ALevs

G D Goenka Global School
S-3130, DLF 3, Near Neelkanth Hospital, Gurugram, Haryana 122010
Curriculum: IBPYP
Language instr: English, Hindi

G D Goenka World School
G D Goenka Education City, Sohna-Gurgaon Road, Sohna, Haryana 122103
Tel: +91 95 1363 1471
Curriculum: IBDP, IBPYP
Language instr: English

G Global School
29A, Rajagoundampalayam 2nd Street, Pallipalayam Road, Tiruchengodu, Tamil Nadu 637211
Tel: +91 42 8825 0999
Curriculum: IBPYP
Language instr: English, Tamil

Garodia International Centre for Learning
153, Garodia Nagar, Ghatkopar East, Mumbai, Maharashtra 400077
Tel: +91 22 25061133/3157
No. of pupils: 365
Curriculum: IBDP
Language instr: English

Gateway International School
TOD Ashram, Jabakadal Street, Padur, Kazhipattur Post, Kelambakkam, Chennai, Tamil Nadu 603103
Tel: + 91 860 811 7700
Curriculum: IBDP, IBMYP, IBPYP
Language instr: English

Asia

GEMS Akademia International School
Bakrahat Road, Thakurpukur,
P.O. Rasapunja, Kolkata,
West Bengal 700104
Tel: +91 33 2498 0671
Age range: 2–18 years
Curriculum: IGCSE, ALevs

GEMS Cambridge International School, Batala
Amritsar Road, Batala, Punjab 143505
Tel: +91 87 2889 2400

GEMS Cambridge International School, Hoshiarpur
Jalandhar - Phagwara, ByPass Road, Hoshiarpur, Punjab 146111
Tel: +91 97 7988 9306
Age range: 3–16 years
Curriculum: IGCSE

GEMS Genesis International School
Near Viashnovedi Circle, SP Ring Road, Ahmedabad, Gujarat 382421
Tel: +91 927 4 022333
Curriculum: UK, IGCSE, ALevs

GEMS International School, Gurgaon
Block C-2, Palam Vihar, Gurugram, Haryana 122017
Tel: +91 95 8219 9008
Language instr: English

GEMS Modern Academy - Kochi
Plot B1-4, Smart City Kochi, Opp. Infopark Phase II, Brahmapuram, Kochi, Kerala 682303
Tel: +91 48 4258 7800
Curriculum: IBPYP
Language instr: English

GEMS Modern Academy, Gurgaon
Block E, South City II, Sector 49, Gurugram, Haryana 122018
Tel: +91 95 6079 3697
Language instr: English

Genesis Global School
A1 & A12, Sector 132, Noida Expressway, Uttar Pradesh 201304
Tel: +91 9711 000626
Age range: 2 years 6 months–18 years
Curriculum: IBDP, IBMYP, IBPYP, IBCP
Language instr: English

German International School Chennai
4/391 Ram Garden Anna Salai, Palavakkam, Chennai, Tamil Nadu 600041
Tel: +91 44 2451 2504
Age range: 5–18
No. of pupils: 300

GJR International School
1/1 & 1/2 Chinnappanahalli, Bangalore, Karnataka 560037
Tel: +91 96 0648 9500
Age range: 3–11 years
No. of pupils: 360
Language instr: English

Glendale Academy, Sun City
Don Bosco post, Bandlaguda Jagir, Rajender Nagar, Hyderabad, Telangana 500086
Tel: +91 75 0500 0600
Age range: 3–18 years
Curriculum: IBDP, National, UK, IGCSE
Language instr: English

Glendale International School, Tellapur
Plot A, Road No. 20, HMDA Layout, Tellapur, Hyderabad, Telangana 502032
Tel: +91 90 3000 1128
Age range: 3–12 years
Curriculum: IBPYP
Language instr: English

Global City International School
135, 5th Main, 6th Cross, Malleshpalya, New Thippasandra Post, Near CV Raman Nag+, Bengaluru, Karnataka 560075
Tel: +91 80 25349199
Age range: 4–16
Curriculum: IGCSE

Global English School - Calicut
Kaimpalam, Pantheerankavu-Mankavu Road, Pantheerankavu, Calicut, Kerala
Tel: +91 495 243 5511
Age range: 5–16
No. of pupils: 300
Curriculum: IGCSE

Global Indian International School (GIIS) Uppal Campus
Survey No. 8 & 9, Peerjadiguda, Uppal Mandal, Hyderabad, Telangana

Global Indian International School (GIIS) Ahmedabad Campus
Godrej Garden City, Jagatpur, Ahmedabad, Gujarat 382470
Tel: +91 80 0572 2810

Global Indian International School (GIIS) Balewadi Campus
Kul Echoloch', Near Balewadi Sports Complex, Nande–Balewadi Road, Mahalunge, Pune, Maharashtra 411045
Tel: +91 80 0572 2810

Global Indian International School (GIIS) Bannerghatta Campus
Bannerghatta Main Road, Gollahalli, Bannerghatta, Bangalore, Karnataka 560083
Tel: +91 80 0572 2810

Global Indian International School (GIIS) Hadapsar Campus
Leisure Town, Behind Amanora Fire Station, Malwadi, Hadapsar, Pune, Maharashtra 411028
Tel: +91 80 0572 2810

Global Indian International School (GIIS) Noida Campus
D-5, Sector 71, (2 Km from Noida City Centre Metro Station), Noida, Uttar Pradesh 201301
Tel: +91 80 0572 2810

Global Indian International School (GIIS) Surat Campus
Chalthan (Next to Chokhi Dhani), Kadodara–Palsana Highway, Surat, Gujarat 394305
Tel: +91 80 0572 2810

Global Indian International School (GIIS) Whitefield Campus
No-5, 6, 8 Heggondahalli Village, Whitefield Sarjapur Main Road, Gunjur Post, Bangalore, Karnataka 560087
Tel: +91 80 0572 2810

Goldcrest International
Sector 29, Plot No: 59, Near Rajiv Gandhi Park, Navi Mumbai, Maharashtra 400703
Tel: +91 22 2789 2261
Curriculum: IBDP

Good Shepherd International School
Good Shepherd Knowledge Village, M Palada PO, Ootacamund, Tamil Nadu 643 004
Tel: +91 423 2550371
Age range: 8–17
No. of pupils: 1000
Curriculum: IBDP, IBMYP, IBPYP, IGCSE
Language instr: English

GPS Brookes Kochi
P.O. via Chottanikkara Ernakulam Kerala, Purackal Joseph Memorial Auditorium, Thiruvaniyoor, Kerala 682308
Tel: +91 48 4271 2748
Curriculum: IBDP, IBPYP
Language instr: English

Grassroots Global School
7/4, Lynwood Avenue, Mahalingpuram, Chennai, Tamil Nadu 600034
Tel: +91 44 2825 5969

Greenwood High International School
No.8-14, Chickkawadayara Pura, Near Heggondahalli, Gunjur Post, Varthur via, Bengaluru, Karnataka 560087
Tel: +91 80 22010500
Age range: 6–19 years
Curriculum: IBDP

Harrow International School Bengaluru
National Highway 648, (Devanahalli - Doddaballapur Road), Bangalore, Karnataka 562110
Tel: +91 966 301 1616
Age range: 11–18 years
Curriculum: IBDP, UK, IGCSE, ALevs
Language instr: English

Harvest International School
Jassowal-Kular, Tehsil Jagraon, Ludihana, Punjab 141023
Tel: +91 98 76500635
Age range: 11–18
No. of pupils: 190
Curriculum: IGCSE, ALevs

Harvest International School
Carmalaram post silk farm, Kodathi village, Off sarjapur road, near Kodathi village, Bangalore, Karnataka 560035
Tel: +91 80 6733 1884
Curriculum: IBMYP, IBPYP
Language instr: English, Hindi

Hebron School
Lushington Hall, Ootacamund, Tamil Nadu 643001
Tel: 0091 423 2225820
Age range: 5–19
No. of pupils: 373 B194 G179
Curriculum: UK, IGCSE, ALevs
Language instr: English

Heritage Xperiential Learning School, Gurgaon
Sector 62, Gurugram, Haryana 122011
Tel: +91 124 2855124
Curriculum: IBDP, IBPYP
Language instr: English, Hindi

HFS International Powai
Richmond Street, Hiranandani Gardens, Powai, Mumbai, Maharashtra 400076
Tel: +91 22 2576 3001
Curriculum: IBDP
Language instr: English

Hill Spring International School
C Wing, NSS Educational Complex, MP Mill Compound, Tardeo, Mumbai, Maharashtra 400034
Tel: +91 22 2355 6201
No. of pupils: 600
Curriculum: IBDP, IBPYP
Language instr: English

Hillside Academy
Road No 46, Jubilee Hills, Hyderabad, Telangana 500033
Tel: +91 40 2354 6113

Himalayan International Residential School
P. O. Rajganj, Dist Jalpaiguri, West Bengal 735134
Tel: +91 98008 72984
Curriculum: National, UK, IGCSE, ALevs

Himali Boarding School
Doomaram, P.O. Kurseong, Dist Darjeeling, West Bengal 734203
Tel: +913542332529
Curriculum: UK, IGCSE, ALevs

Hindustan International School
40 GST Road, St Thomas Mount, Guindy, Chennai, Tamil Nadu
Tel: +91 44 2234 2020
Age range: 4–18
Curriculum: IGCSE

Asia

HLC International - Chennai
Wing Haven Gardens, Karanai,
Chennai, Tamil Nadu 603103
Tel: +91 99628 05259
Age range: 5–18
No. of pupils: 300
Curriculum: IGCSE

HUS International School
5/63 Old Mahabalipuram Ro, Egattur Village, Padur PO, Kelambakkam, Chennai, Tamil Nadu 600130
Tel: +91 9500 118651
Age range: 2 years 6 months–18 years
Curriculum: IBDP, IBMYP, IBPYP
Language instr: English

HVB Global Academy
79 Marine Drive, F Road, Mumbai, Maharashtra 400020
Tel: +91 22 6143 6000
Age range: 3–18 years
No. of pupils: 750
Curriculum: UK, IGCSE, ALevs
Language instr: English

India International School
Kshipra Path, Opp VT Road, Mansarovar, Jaipur, Rajasthan 302020
Tel: +91 141 2786401
Age range: 6–18
No. of pupils: 2182 B1330 G852
Curriculum: IBDP, National, UK, ALevs
(ISA)

India International School
26/1, Sarjapur Road, Chikkabellandur, Bengaluru, Karnataka 560035
Tel: +91 080 2843 9001

India Kids School
Opp. H.P. Petrol Pump, Omara Morh, Udhampur, Jammu & Kashmir 182101
Tel: +91 70 5198 7388
Curriculum: IBPYP
Language instr: English, Hindi

Indus International Primary School
Plot No. 186, Road No. 13, Jubilee Hills, Hyderabad, Telangana 500033
Tel: +91 99 4937 1545
Curriculum: IBPYP
Language instr: English

Indus International School (Bangalore)
Billapura Cross, Sarjapur, Bengaluru, Karnataka 562125
Tel: +91 80 2289 5900
Age range: 6–18 years
No. of pupils: 1000
Curriculum: IBDP, IBMYP, IBPYP, IBCP
Language instr: English

Indus International School, Hyderabad
Survey No 424 & 425, Kondakal Village, Near Mokila (M), Shankarpally, Hyderabad, Telangana 501203
Tel: +91 8417 302100
Age range: 5–18 years
No. of pupils: 350
Curriculum: IBDP, IBMYP, IBPYP, IBCP
Language instr: English

Indus International School, Pune
576 Bhukum, Near Manas Resort, Tal Mulshi, Pune, Maharashtra 411042
Tel: +91 80 2289 5900
Curriculum: IBDP, IBMYP, IBPYP, IBCP

International Fateh Academy
Academy Road, Jandiala Guru, Amritsar, Punjab 143001
Tel: +91 18 3243 0205
Curriculum: IBPYP
Language instr: English, Punjabi

International School Aamby
Aamby Valley City, Ambavene, Pune, Maharashtra 410401
Tel: +91 20 3910 2500
Age range: 8–18
No. of pupils: 100
Curriculum: IPC, IGCSE
Language instr: English

International School Kashmir (ISK)
Baghat Chowk, Srinagar, Jammu & Kashmir
Tel: +91 9419038733
Language instr: English

International School of Hyderabad
ICRISAT Main Entrance Gate, Patancheru, Ramachandrapuram, Hyderabad, Telangana 502324
Tel: +91 4030713865
Age range: 3–18 years
No. of pupils: 400
Curriculum: IBDP, USA, IGCSE
Language instr: English

International Village School Chennai
33A, Clasic Farms Road, Sholinganallur, Chennai, Tamil Nadu 600119
Tel: +91 44 4860 3757
Age range: 2–11
No. of pupils: 40
Curriculum: IBPYP
Language instr: English

Inventure Academy
Whitefield - Sarjapur Road, Chikkavaderapura, Near Dommasandra Circle, Bengaluru, Karnataka 562125
Tel: +91 80 27822101
Curriculum: National, UK, IGCSE, ALevs

Ithaka International School
Near Kanuparthipadu, Golagamudi Road, Nellore, Andhra Pradesh
Tel: +91 861 6521 111
Age range: 5–18
No. of pupils: 300

Ivy World Play School, Jalandhar
180-A, Civil Lines, Opposite Aveda Kamal Hotel, Jalandhar, Punjab 144001
Tel: +91 84 3709 6800

Ivy World School, Jalandhar
Hoshiarpur Road, Rama Mandi, Jalandhar, Punjab 144007
Tel: +91 18 1241 0803
Age range: 4–18 years

Jain International Residential School
Jakkasandra Post, Kanakpura Road, Ramanagara District, Bengaluru, Karnataka 562112
Tel: +91 80 2757 7750
Age range: 9–18
No. of pupils: B500 G250
Curriculum: IBDP, National, SAT, TOEFL, IGCSE, ALevs
Language instr: English

Jamnabai Narsee International School
Narsee Monjee Bhavan, N.S. Road No.7, J.V.P.D Scheme, Vile Parle (West), Mumbai, Maharashtra 400049
Tel: +91 (0)22 26187575/ 7676
Age range: 3–19
No. of pupils: 660
Curriculum: ACT, AP, IBDP, IBMYP, IBPYP, National, SAT, TOEFL, IGCSE
Language instr: English

Jayshree Periwal High School
3, Adjoining Stadium, Ajmer Road, Chitrakoot, Jaipur, Rajasthan 302021
Tel: +91 141 4132222

Jayshree Periwal International School
Mahapura, SEZ Road, Ajmer Road, Jaipur, Rajasthan 302026
Tel: +91 97827 44444/44445
Age range: 12–18
No. of pupils: 800 B500 G300
Curriculum: IBDP, IBPYP
Language instr: English

JBCN International School - Borivali
Plot CTS No. 96, Remison Towers, Near Bhagwati Hospital, Baburao Ranade Marg, Opp. Union Bank Staff Quarters, B+, Mumbai, Maharashtra 400103
Tel: +91 22 2892 7089
Curriculum: IGCSE, ALevs

JBCN International School - Chembur
Yogi Tower, Chembur Education Society, CTS No. 1284 (Chembur), R.C. Marg, Chembur (E), Mumbai, Maharashtra 400071
Tel: +91 86 5797 6711
Curriculum: IBPYP, IGCSE
Language instr: English

JBCN International School - Oshiwara
Survey No. 41, CTS No. 1, Off Andheri Link Road, Behind Tarapore Towers, Mhada Colony, Oshiwara, Andher+, Mumbai, Maharashtra 400058
Tel: +91 22 2630 2398
Curriculum: IBDP, IBPYP, IGCSE
Language instr: English

JBCN International School - Parel
Yogi Mansion, CTS No. 244, Dr Vinay Walimbe Road, Off Dr S.S. Rao Marg, Parel East, Mumbai, Maharashtra 400012
Tel: +91 22 2411 4627
Age range: 3–18 years
Curriculum: IBDP, IBPYP, UK, IGCSE
Language instr: English

JG International School
JG Campus of Excellence, JG Campus Road, Ahmedabad, Gujarat 380061
Tel: +91 79 65411315
Age range: 3–18
No. of pupils: 1000
Curriculum: IBDP
Language instr: English

Johnson Grammar School ICSE&IBDP
Street No 3, Kakatiya Nagar, Habsiguda, Hyderabad, Andhra Pradesh 500007
Tel: +91 81064 72685
No. of pupils: 5500
Curriculum: IBDP
Language instr: English

Jyotirmay International School
Opp Wageshwar Temple, Gat No 2188 A, Pl No. 8 & 9 A, Bhd. Rambhau Moze Engineering College, BAIF Rd, Wagholi, Pune, Maharashtra 412207
Tel: +91 20 65100784
Curriculum: UK, IGCSE

K.R. Mangalam Global School
N-Block, Nandi Vithi Road, Greater Kailash-1, New Delhi, Delhi 110048
Tel: +91 97 1885 8181
Curriculum: IBDP, IBMYP, IBPYP, IBCP
Language instr: English, Hindi

K.R. Mangalam Global School, Gurugram
Opp. D Block, near Patio Club, Block K, South City I, Sector 41, Gurugram, Haryana 122001
Tel: +91 95 1363 2642
Curriculum: IBPYP
Language instr: English, Hindi

Kai Early Years
66/2, 2nd Main Road, Nallurhalli, Whitefield, Bangalore, Karnataka 560066
Tel: +91 97 4048 0123
Age range: 2–6 years
Curriculum: IBPYP
Language instr: English, Hindi

Kanakia International School Chembur
Ghatkopar - Mankhurd Link Road, ACC Nagar, Chedda Nagar, Mumbai, Maharashtra 400043
Tel: +91 77 3834 9697
Age range: 3–18 years
Curriculum: IBDP, IBMYP, IBPYP, UK, IGCSE
Language instr: English

Asia

KC High
Olympia Panache, Navalur, OMR, Chennai, Tamil Nadu 600130
Tel: +91 93 848 27992
Age range: 4–18 years
Curriculum: IBDP, UK, IGCSE
Language instr: English

Kennedy High - The Global School
Bachupally, Miyapur-Medchal Highway, Hyderabad, Telangana 500090
Tel: +91 40 64646477
Age range: 5–18
No. of pupils: 300

KiiT International School
KiiT Campus 9, Patia, Bhubaneswar, Odisha 751024
Tel: +91 674 2725805
Age range: 3.5–19 years
No. of pupils: 2000
Curriculum: IBDP, National, IGCSE
Language instr: English

King's College India
A1 Sector 5, Rohtak, Haryana 124001
Tel: +91 708 200 5414
Age range: 3–18
Curriculum: UK, IGCSE
Language instr: English

Knowledgeum Academy
44/4 District Fund Road, Jayanagar 9th Block, Bangalore, Karnataka 560069
Tel: +91 73 5301 2391
Curriculum: IBDP, IBCP
Language instr: English

Kodaikanal International School
PO Box 25, Seven Roads Junction, Kodaikanal, Tamil Nadu 624101
Tel: +91 4542 247500
Age range: 3–18
No. of pupils: 393
Curriculum: ACT, IBDP, IBMYP, IBPYP, IBCP, SAT, USA
Language instr: English

Kohinoor American School
Old Mumbai - Pune Highway, Near to The Dukes Retreat, Khandala, Maharashtra 410301
Tel: +91 9324323003
Age range: 12–18
No. of pupils: 120
Language instr: English

Kunskapsskolan Gurgaon
Site No. 1122, Block A, DLF Phase-I, Gurugram, Haryana 122002
Tel: +91 12 4441 9999
Curriculum: IBMYP
Language instr: English, Hindi

L'Ecole Française Internationale de Bombay
Ashishwang Bungalow, Plot No.72, Pochkhanwala Road, Worli, Mumbai, Maharashtra 400030
Tel: + 91 (0)22249 08801
Curriculum: FrenchBacc

Lady Andal Venkatasubba Rao Matriculation School
Shenstone Park, No.7 Harrington Road, Chennai, Tamil Nadu 600031
Tel: +91 44 2836 3404
Curriculum: IBPYP
Language instr: English

Lakshmipat Singhania Academy
12B Alipore Road, Kolkata, West Bengal 700027
Tel: +91 33 2479 3600

Lalaji Memorial Omega International School
79, Omega School Road (Pallavaram Road), Kolapakkam, Kovur Post, Chennai, Tamil Nadu 600128
Tel: +91 44 66241127
Age range: 3–18
No. of pupils: 4252
Curriculum: IBDP, GCSE, IGCSE, ALevs
Language instr: English

Lancers International School
DLF Phase V, Sector 53, Gurugram, Haryana 122001
Tel: +91 124 423 8753
Age range: 18 months–18 years
No. of pupils: 900
Curriculum: IBDP, IBMYP, IBPYP, IBCP
Language instr: English

Learners International School
Knowledge Park-III, Greater Noida, Uttar Pradesh 201308
Tel: +91 12 0518 9101
Curriculum: IBPYP
Language instr: English

Learning Panorama School
Plot no 25c, Old MHB Colony, OPP Vaidya Kumar Gdn, Nr Don Bosco School, Gorai Link Road, Borivali(W), Mumbai, Maharashtra 400092
Tel: +91 22 6553 9224

Legacy School, Bangalore
6/1 A, 6/2 Byrathi Village, Bidarahalli Hobli, East Taluk, Bengaluru, Karnataka 560077
Tel: +91 70222 92405
Age range: 2.5–18 years
No. of pupils: 766
Curriculum: IBDP, UK, IGCSE, ALevs
Language instr: English

Lycée français de Pondichéry
12 rue Victor Simonel, Pondicherry, Tamil Nadu 605001
Tel: +91 413 233 58 31

M Ct M Chidambaram Chettyar International School
179, Luz Church Road, Mylapore, Chennai, Tamil Nadu 600004
Tel: +91 44 2467 0120
Age range: 11–19
No. of pupils: 39 B21 G18
Curriculum: IBDP, IGCSE
Language instr: English

Mahatma Gandhi International School
Sheth Motilal Hirabhai Bhavan, Opp. Induben Khakhrawala, Mithakali, Navrangpura, Ahmedabad, Gujarat 380006
Tel: +91 79 2 646 3888
No. of pupils: 180
Curriculum: IBDP, IBMYP, IBCP
Language instr: English

Mahindra International School
P26, Rajeev Gandhi Infotech park, Phase 1, Hinjewadi, Pune, Maharashtra 411057
Tel: +91 2042954444
Age range: 3–18
No. of pupils: 342
Curriculum: IBDP, IBMYP, IBPYP
Language instr: English

Mainadevi Bajaj International School
Plot No: 23-A, 24-28 Swami Vivekanand Road, Malad (West), Mumbai, Maharashtra 400064
Tel: +91 22 28733807

Mallya Aditi International School
Yelahanka New Town, Bengaluru, Karnataka 560106
Tel: +91 80 40447000
Age range: 5–18
No. of pupils: 592
Curriculum: National

Manav Rachna International School
Sector 14 (Gate No. 2), Faridabad, Haryana 121002
Tel: +91 90 9899 1000
Age range: 3–18 years
Curriculum: IBDP, IBMYP, IBPYP
Language instr: English

Manchester International School
SF 29/3A, Hudco Colony, Vellakinar, Coimbatore, Tamil Nadu 641029
Tel: +91 422 655 5551
Curriculum: IBDP, IBMYP, IBPYP
Language instr: English

Manthan International School Kompally
1150 Ayyappa Society Main Road, Madhapur, Hyderabad, Telangana 500081
Tel: +91 4220 6060
Curriculum: IBCP, UK, IGCSE

Maple Bear Canadian School
4-7 C DDA Shopping Centre, New Friends Colony, New Delhi, Delhi 110025
Tel: +91 9711165900

Mayo College
Srinagar Road, Ajmer, Rajasthan 305001
Tel: +91 145 266 1154
Age range: B8–18 years
Curriculum: National, IGCSE
Language instr: English

Mayo College Girls' School
Mayo Link Road, Ajmer, Rajasthan 305007
Tel: +91 145 263 6000
Age range: G8–18 years
Curriculum: National, IGCSE
Language instr: English

Meluha International School
Adj to Central Forensic Lab, Near VIF College of Engineering & Techno+, Osman Sagar X Roads, Aziz Nagar, Gandipet, Hyderabad, Telangana 500075
Tel: +91 81 4237 6666
Curriculum: IBCP
Language instr: English

Meridian School, Banjara Hills
#8-2-541, Road No.7, Banjara Hills, Hyderabad, Telangana 500034
Tel: +91 80 9691 8857
Curriculum: IBPYP
Language instr: English, Hindi

Meridian School, Madhapur
#11/4 & 11/5, Opp: Hitech City, Kukatpally Bypass Road, Khanamet Village, Sherlingampally Mandal, Hyderabad, Telangana 500081
Tel: +91 99 4804 3440
Curriculum: IBPYP
Language instr: English, Hindi

MET Rishikul Vidyalaya - Bhujbal Knowledge Centre, Mumbai
Bandra Reclamation, Bandra (West), Mumbai, Maharashtra 400050
Tel: +91 22 2644 0446
Age range: 5–18
No. of pupils: 2200
Curriculum: IGCSE

Metro Delhi International School
AIPF Campus, Mission Hospital Road, Sat Bari, Chattarpur, New Delhi, Delhi 110074
Tel: +91 8860150178
Curriculum: USA

MGD Girls' School
Tonk Rd, Ashok Nagar, Jaipur, Rajasthan 302001
Tel: +91 1412 364478
Language instr: English

Miri Piri Academy
Guru Ki Wadali, Chheharta, Amritsar, Punjab 143105
Tel: +91 805 401 8906
Curriculum: UK, IGCSE, ALevs

MM International School
MM Educational Complex, Mullana, Ambala, Haryana 133003
Tel: +91 1731 275400
Age range: 2–19

MM International School
Patan By Pass Road, Behind Global College,, Jabalpur, Madhya Pradesh 482004
Tel: +91 8109000157

Asia

Modern High School for Girls
78, Syed Amir Ali Avenue,
Kolkata, West Bengal 700019
Tel: +913322875326
Age range: 3–18
No. of pupils: 3000
Curriculum: IBDP
Language instr: English

Modern Public School
B-Block, Shalimar Bagh,
New Delhi, Delhi 110088
Tel: +91 11 4142 7627
Age range: 4–18 years
Curriculum: IBPYP, National
Language instr: English, Hindi

Modern School
Sector E, Aliganj, Lucknow,
Uttar Pradesh 226024
Tel: +91 955 493 3337
Curriculum: IBPYP

Mody School
Mody Institute of Education
& Research, Lakshmangarh,
Rajasthan 332311
Tel: +91 91 16637196
Language instr: English

Motilal Nehru School of Sports
Grand Trunk Road, Rajiv
Gandhi Education City, Rai,
Sonipat, Haryana 131029
Tel: +91 1302 366201
Language instr: English

Mount Abu Public School
Sector-5, Pocket B-8,
Rohini, Delhi 110085
Tel: +91 11 2704 1516
Curriculum: IBPYP, National
Language instr: English, Hindi

Mount Litera School International (MLSI)
GN Block, Behind Asian Heart
Hospital, Near UTI Buildings, Bandra
Kurla Complex, Bandra East,
Mumbai, Maharashtra 400051
Tel: +91 22 6229 6000
Age range: 3–18 years
No. of pupils: 500
Curriculum: IBDP, IBMYP, IBPYP
Language instr: English

Mussoorie International School
Sri Nagar Estate, Polo Ground,
Charleville, Mussoorie,
Uttarakhand 248179
Tel: +91 98 3746 0408
Age range: G5–18 years
Curriculum: IBDP, IBMYP, IBPYP, National, IGCSE, ALevs
Language instr: English

Nahar International School
Nahar's Amrit Shakti, Chandivali Farm
Road, Off Saki Vihar Road, Andheri
East, Mumbai, Maharashtra 400072
Tel: +91 (0)22 6838 5500
No. of pupils: 1200
Curriculum: IBDP
Language instr: English

National Centre for Excellence - CV Raman Nagar
154/1, Vijay Kiran Knowledge
Park, 5th Main, Malleshpalya,
Bangalore, Karnataka 560075
Tel: +91 80 6945 5100
Curriculum: IBCP
Language instr: English

Navrachana International School
Vasna Bhayali Road, Bhayali,
Vadodara, Gujarat 391410
Tel: +91 265 225 3851/2/3/4
Curriculum: IBDP, IBMYP, IBPYP
Language instr: English

Neerja Modi School
Shipra Path, Near Building
Technology Park, Mansarovar,
Jaipur, Rajasthan 302020
Tel: +91 141 2785 484
Curriculum: IBDP

Neev Academy - North Campus
No. 14, Park Road, Tasker Town,
Bengaluru, Karnataka 560001
Tel: +91 80 41144285
Language instr: English

Neev Academy - Yemalur Campus
No. 16, Yemalur-Kempapura
Main Road, Opp. Sai Garden
Apartments, Yemalur, Bengaluru,
Karnataka 560037
Tel: +91 80 71101700
No. of pupils: 350
Curriculum: IBDP, IBMYP, IBPYP
Language instr: English

NES International School Dombivli
Sankara Nagar, Kalyan-Shil Road,
Opp. DNS Bank, Sonarpada,
Dombivli (E), Thane, Mumbai,
Maharashtra 421203
Tel: +91 88 2880 1008
Age range: 3–16 years
Curriculum: IBMYP, IBPYP, IGCSE
Language instr: English, Hindi

NES International School Mumbai
Malabar Hill Road, Vasant
Garden, Mulund(W), Mumbai,
Maharashtra 400082
Tel: +91 22 25911478
Curriculum: IBDP, IBMYP, IBPYP
Language instr: English

NEXT School
Park Road, Off Devi Dayal
Road, Mulund W, Mumbai,
Maharashtra 400080
Tel: +91 22 25600036
Curriculum: IBDP, IBMYP, IBPYP, IBCP
Language instr: English

Niraj International School
Kandlakoya, 5 km from Dhola-ri-
Dhani, Hyderabad, Telangana 132133
Tel: +91 84 18200476
Language instr: English

Oakridge International School, Bachupally
Survey No 166/6, Bowrampet
Village, Near Bachupally,
Hyderabad, Telangana 500043
Tel: +91 720 764 8111
Curriculum: IBDP, IBPYP, IGCSE

Oakridge International School, Bengaluru
Varthur Road, Near Dommassandra
Circle, Sarjapur Hobli, Bengaluru,
Karnataka 562125
Tel: +91 0802 254 3600
Age range: 3–18
No. of pupils: 891
Curriculum: IBDP, IBMYP, IBPYP
Language instr: English

Oakridge International School, Gachibowli
Khajaguda, Nanakramguda
Road, Cyberabad, Hyderabad,
Telangana 500008
Tel: +91 7207 648 111
Age range: 2–18
Curriculum: IBDP, IBMYP, IBPYP
Language instr: English

Oakridge International School, Mohali
Next to Thunderzone Amusement
Park, Mohali, Punjab 140307
Tel: +91 752 701 3370
Curriculum: IBDP, IBPYP, IGCSE
Language instr: English

Oakridge International School, Visakhapatnam
NH 5 Road, Behind HP Petrol
Bunk, Maharajpeta Junction,
Tagarapuvalasa, Visakhapatnam,
Andhra Pradesh 531162
Tel: +91 773 081 6999
Curriculum: IBDP, UK, IGCSE
Language instr: English

Oasis International School
No. 29, 1st Stage, 1st Block, HBR
Layout, Bengaluru, Karnataka 560043
Tel: +91 8025433053
Curriculum: IBPYP, UK, IGCSE

Oberoi International School
Oberoi Garden City, Off Western
Express Highway, Goregaon (E),
Mumbai, Maharashtra 400063
Tel: +91 22 4236 3131
Age range: 3–18 years
No. of pupils: 1616 B816 G800
Curriculum: IBDP, IBMYP, IBPYP, IGCSE
Language instr: English

Oberoi International School - JVLR Campus
Jogeshwari Vikroli Link Road,
Jogeshwari East, Mumbai,
Maharashtra 400060
Curriculum: IBDP, IBMYP, IBPYP
Language instr: English

One World International School (OWIS) Sarjapur
188/3 & 188, Dommasandra, Sarjapur
Road, Bengaluru, Karnataka 562125
Tel: +91 180 0309 9875
Age range: 3–18 years
Curriculum: IBDP, IBMYP, IBPYP, National
Language instr: English

One World International School (OWIS) Whitefield
Goravigere, Kannamangala
Post Whitefield, Bengaluru,
Karnataka 560067
Tel: +91 180 0309 9875
Age range: 3–16 years
Curriculum: IBPYP, National
Language instr: English

P P Savani Cambridge International School
Mota varaccha, Abrama Road,
At & Po Abrama Tah-Kamrej,
Surat, Gujarat 394150
Tel: +912616503388
Curriculum: UK, IGCSE

Panbai International School
Guru Narayan Rd, Sen Nagar,
Near.B.M.C office, Santacruz (East),
Mumbai, Maharashtra 400055
Tel: +91 22 2617 7771
Curriculum: UK, IGCSE

Pathways School Gurgaon
Baliawas, Off Gurgaon Faridabad
Road, Gurugram, Haryana 122003
Tel: +91 124 487 2000
Curriculum: IBDP, IBMYP, IBPYP, IBCP
Language instr: English

Pathways School Noida
Sector 100, Noida, Uttar
Pradesh 201301
Tel: +91 120 461 7000
Age range: 3–18 years
Curriculum: IBDP, IBMYP, IBPYP, IBCP
Language instr: English

Pathways World School, Gurgaon
Aravali Retreat, Off Gurgaon Sohna
Road, Gurugram, Haryana 122102
Tel: +91 124 451 3000
Curriculum: IBDP, IBMYP, IBPYP
Language instr: English

Pinnacle High International School
Sunder lane, Orlem, Malad (w),
Mumbai, Maharashtra 400064
Tel: +91 22 2844 9155
Curriculum: UK, IGCSE, ALevs

Podar International School
Ramee Emerald Building, Near
Shamrao Vithal Bank, S.V.Road, Khar
(West), Mumbai, Maharashtra 400052
Tel: +91 22 2648 7321
Age range: 3–18
No. of pupils: 1013 B500 G513
Curriculum: IBDP, IBPYP, IBCP
Language instr: English

Asia

Podar International School (Kalyan)
H/N 9, Next to Union Cricket Ground, Gandhari Viilage, Khadakpada, Kalyan, Maharashtra 421301
Tel: +91 251 2203028
Curriculum: IBCP, UK, IGCSE

Podar O.R.T International School, Worli
PODAR-ORT School Building, 68, Worli Hill Estate, Worli, Mumbai, Maharashtra 400018
Tel: +91 7506112200
Curriculum: IBDP, IBMYP, IBPYP
Language instr: English

Primus Public School
Post Box 21, Chikanayakanahalli Village, Off. Sarjapur Road, Bengaluru, Karnataka 560035
Tel: +91 80 2574 1450
Curriculum: UK, IGCSE, ALevs

Prometheus School
I-7, Jaypee Wishtown, Sector 131, Noida, Uttar Pradesh 201304
Tel: +91 99 9987 6583
Curriculum: IBDP, IBMYP, IBPYP
Language instr: English, Hindi

Punjab Public School
Nabha, District Patiala, Punjab 147201
Tel: +91 01765 220675
Age range: 4–18 years
Curriculum: National, UK, ALevs

Queen Mira International School
Melakkal Road, Kochadai, Madurai, Tamil Nadu 625016
Tel: +91 96557 77000
Curriculum: National

Rajkumar College Raipur
Gate 2, G.E Road, Near Rajkumar College Road, Mukut Nagar, Raipur, Chhattisgarh 492013
Tel: +91 771 470 1051
Age range: 5–18 years
Curriculum: National

Rasbihari International School
Vrindavan, Nashik-Ozar Road, Nashik, Maharashtra 422003
Tel: +91 253 230 4622
Age range: 3–14
Curriculum: IBPYP, IGCSE
Language instr: English

RBK International School, Bhayandar
Indralok Phase 6, Panchamratna Park, Bhayandar (E), Maharashtra
Tel: +91 74 0009 5434
Age range: 3–18 years
Curriculum: UK, IGCSE, ALevs

Redbridge International Academy
#114, S Bingipura Village, Hulimangala Post, Begur-Koppa Road, Bangalore, Karnataka 560105
Tel: +91 9620863456
Curriculum: IBDP
Language instr: English

RIMS International School and Junior College
New Link Road, Near Fun Republic, Andheri West, Mumbai, Maharashtra 400049
Tel: +91 22 6699 4333
Age range: 11–19
No. of pupils: 200
Curriculum: IGCSE

Riverside International School
c/o Project India, Project India Educational Center, Mori, Godavari 533250
Tel: +91 8862226492
Age range: 5–18
No. of pupils: 418
Curriculum: USA

Rockwell International School
Sy No.160(p), Gandipet Main Rd, Kokapet, Hyderabad, Telangana 500075
Tel: +91 9618662201
Curriculum: IBDP
Language instr: English

Ruh Continuum School
Sf No. 71/1 Vaigai Nagar, Pattanam Singanallur to Vellalore Road, Coimbatore, Tamil Nadu 641016
Tel: +91 63 8463 1313
Age range: 4–18 years
Curriculum: IBDP, IBCP, IGCSE
Language instr: English

Rungta International School
Near Nandan Van, Veer Savarkar Nagar, Raipur, Chhattisgarh 492099
Tel: +91 98261 45333
Curriculum: IBDP, IBMYP, IBPYP
Language instr: English

Ryan Global School, Andheri
Yamuna Nagar, Near Pizza Hut Circle, Andheri West, Mumbai, Maharashtra 400053
Tel: +91 22 2632 0205
Curriculum: IBPYP, IGCSE
Language instr: English, Hindi

Ryan Global School, Chembur
Marwali Village, Mahul Road, Aziz Baugh, Chembur, Mumbai, Maharashtra 400074
Tel: +91 22 2554 5485
Curriculum: IGCSE
Language instr: English, Hindi

Ryan Global School, Kharghar
Plot No. 1, 2 & 3, Sector 11 Road, Block G, Sector 11, Kharghar, Navi Mumbai, Maharashtra 410210
Tel: +91 22 2774 5898
Curriculum: IBCP, IGCSE
Language instr: English, Hindi

Ryan Global School, Kundalahalli
Behind Hindustan Lever Ltd, M. H. Colony, Ryan School Road, Kundalahalli, Brookefield, Bengaluru, Karnataka 560037
Tel: +91 80 2847 6963
Curriculum: IGCSE
Language instr: English, Hindi

Sai International School
Plot -5A, Infocity, Chandrasekharpur, Bhubaneswar, Odisha 751024
Tel: +91 93 3816 9966
Curriculum: IBCP

Sanatan High School
D-Block, Ranjeet Nagar, Bharatpur, Rajasthan 321001
Tel: +91 95 2119 1522
Curriculum: IBPYP
Language instr: English, Hindi

Sancta Maria International School - Faridabad
Sector 93, Faridabad, Haryana 121002
Tel: +91 99991 16900
Age range: 5–18 years
Curriculum: IBDP
Language instr: English

Sancta Maria International School - Hyderbad
Survey No 106/107, Serilingampally, Hyderbad, Telangana 500019
Tel: +91 40 2301 1222
Age range: 3–19 years
Curriculum: IGCSE, ALevs

Sangam School of Excellence
N.H. 79, Atun, Bhilwara By Pass, Chittorgarh Highway, Bhilwara, Rajasthan 311001
Tel: +91 1482 249 700
Age range: 4–19 years
Language instr: English

Sanjay Ghodawat International School
Gat No. 555, Kolhapur - Sangli Highway, Atigre, Maharashtra
Tel: +91 231 2689700
Age range: 16–18 years (boarding from 6)
Curriculum: IBDP
Language instr: English

Sanskar School
117-121, Vishwamitra Marg, Hanuman Nagar Ext., Sirsi Road, Jaipur, Rajasthan 302012
Tel: +91 0141 2246189
Age range: 4–17
No. of pupils: 2302 B1502 G800
Curriculum: IBDP, IBPYP
Language instr: English

Sarala Birla Academy
Bannerghatta PO, Jigni Road, Bengaluru, Karnataka 560083
Tel: +91 80 41348200/03
Age range: 10–18
No. of pupils: 426
Curriculum: IBDP
Language instr: English

Satya School
Block E, South City II, Sector 49, Gurugram, Haryana 122018
Tel: +91 83 7603 0644
Curriculum: IBPYP
Language instr: English

SCAD World School
SCAD Knowledge City, Palladam - Pollachi Highway, Palladam, Tamil Nadu 641664
Tel: +91 8012551468
Curriculum: UK, IGCSE, ALevs

Scindia Kanya Vidyalya
Moti Mahal Road, Gwalior, Madhya Pradesh 474009
Tel: +91 751 232 2137

Scottish High International School
G-Block, Sector 57, Sushant Lok-II, Gurugram, Haryana 122011
Tel: +91 124 4112781-90
Age range: 3–17 years
Curriculum: IBDP, IBPYP, IBCP, National, IGCSE
Language instr: English

Seedling International Academy
Sector-4, Park Lane, Jawahar Nagar, Jaipur, Rajasthan 302004
Tel: +91 141 2653377
Language instr: English

SelaQui International School
PO Sela Kui, Chakrata Road, Dehradun, Uttarakhand 248197
Tel: +91 7669 04 04 04
Language instr: English

Shambhu Dayal Global School
Dayanand Nagar, Opp. Nehru Stadium, Ghaziabad, Uttar Pradesh 201001
Tel: +91 70 4234 1944
Curriculum: IBMYP, IBPYP, National
Language instr: English, Hindi

Shantiniketan International School
35-25, GKColony, Ramakrishnapuram, Secunderabad, Telangana 500056
Tel: +91 73311 95555
Curriculum: IBPYP
Language instr: English

Asia

Sharanya Narayani International School
#232/1, Thoranahalli, Byranahalli post, Near Hoskote, Bengaluru, Karnataka 563130
Tel: +91 80 46629500
Age range: 2.8–18
Curriculum: IBDP, IBMYP, IBPYP
Language instr: English

Shigally Hill International Academy
P.O.Box No. 239, Doon Valley, Shigally Estate, Mussoorie Road, Via Malsi Deer Park, Guniyal Gaon, Dehradun, Uttarakhand 248001
Tel: +91 98370 98368
No. of pupils: 200

Shiv Nadar School Chennai
Besant Avenue Road, Adyar, Chennai, Tamil Nadu 600020
Tel: +91 99 9003 5642
Language instr: English

Shiv Nadar School Faridabad
Sector 82, Naharpar, Faridabad, Haryana 121002
Tel: +91 12 9461 5000
Curriculum: IBDP
Language instr: English

Shiv Nadar School Gurgaon
DLF City, Phase -1 Block -E, Pahari Road, Gurugram, Haryana 122011
Tel: +91 124 4549200
Curriculum: IBDP
Language instr: English

Shiv Nadar School Noida
Plot No -SS -1, Expressway Sector 168, Noida, Uttar Pradesh 201305
Tel: +91 9773725551
Age range: 2.5–18 years
No. of pupils: 6500
Curriculum: IBDP
Language instr: English

Shree Swaminarayan Gurukul Vishwavidya Pratishthanam SGVP
Nr. SGVP Circle, SG Highway, Chharodi, Ahmedabad, Gujarat 382481
Tel: +91 2717 242138/9
Curriculum: National, UK, IGCSE

Silver Oaks International School, Hyderabad
Miyapur-Dindigal Road, Bachupally, Hyderabad, Telangana 500090
Tel: +91 40 23047777
Age range: 3–18 years
Curriculum: IBPYP, National
Language instr: English

Silver Oaks International School, Visakhapatnam
Adj Gitam Medical College, Yendada Road, Rushikonda, Visakhapatnam, Andhra Pradesh 530045
Tel: +91 76 6197 8999
Age range: 3–16 years
Curriculum: IBPYP, National
Language instr: English

Singapore International School, Mumbai
On National Highway No. 8, Post Mira Road, Dahisar, Mumbai, Maharashtra 401104
Tel: +91 222 828 5200
Age range: 4–18
No. of pupils: 501
Curriculum: IBDP, IBPYP, UK
Language instr: English

Skill Stork International School
#55-1-219, SVS Campus, Bheemaram, Hasanparthy(m), Hanamkonda, Warangal, Telangana 506015
Tel: +91 80 0888 0011
Age range: 2–18 years
Curriculum: IBDP, IBPYP, UK, IGCSE, ALevs
Language instr: English

Smt. Sulochanadevi Singhania School
Pokharan Road No.1, J K Gram, Thane (West), Maharashtra 400606
Tel: +91 22 4036 8410/1
Curriculum: IBDP
Language instr: English

South City International School
375 Prince Anwar Shah Road, Kolkata, West Bengal 700068
Tel: +91 33 4007 2000
Age range: 5–19
No. of pupils: 300

Sreenidhi International School
Near Appa Junction, Moinabad, Hyderabad, Telangana 500075
Tel: +91 9912244409
Age range: 3–18 years
No. of pupils: 900
Curriculum: IBDP, IBMYP, IBPYP, SAT
Language instr: English

SRV International School
Marappan Thottam, 4/3 Gandhi Salai, Pattanam Road, Rasipuram, Namakkal, Tamil Nadu 637408
Tel: +91 96 5562 4458
Curriculum: IBPYP
Language instr: English

St. Xavier's High School
Rosewood City, Sector-49-50, Main Golf Course, Extension Road, Gurugram, Haryana
Tel: +91 99 1023 8318/19
Curriculum: IBCP
Language instr: English

Step by Step School
Plot A 10, Sector 132 Taj Expressway, Noida, Uttar Pradesh 201303
Tel: +91 12 0508 7300
Curriculum: IBDP
Language instr: English

Still I Rise International School - Mumbai
Mumbai, Maharashtra
Language instr: English

STONEHILL INTERNATIONAL SCHOOL
For further details see p. 70
Near the International Airport, No.259/333/334/335, Tarahunise Post, Jala Hobli, Bengaluru, Karnataka 562157
Tel: +91 80 4341 8300
Email: admissions@stonehill.in
Website: www.stonehill.in
Head of School: Joe Lumsden
Age range: 3–18 years
No. of pupils: 750
Curriculum: IBDP, IBMYP, IBPYP
Language instr: English

Strawberry Fields High School
Sector 26, Chandigarh, Punjab 160019
Tel: +91 172 279 5903/5904
Age range: 5–18
No. of pupils: 1722 B955 G767 VIth135
Curriculum: IBDP
Language instr: English

Suncity School
Suncity Township, Sector 54, Gurugram, Haryana 122002
Tel: +91 (0)124 4845300 (Ext:302)
Curriculum: IBDP
Language instr: English

Sunflower English School
Sunflower House, 80 Feet Road, Near Bhaktinagar Circle, Rajkot, Gujarat 360002
Tel: +91 93772 12341
Language instr: English

Sunshine Worldwide Secondary School
20/1-B, Bainguinim, Off NH-748 By-pass Kadamba Road, Old Goa, Goa 403402
Tel: +91 98 5032 3818
Curriculum: IBPYP
Language instr: English, Hindi

SVKM JV Parekh International School
CNM School Campus, Dadabhai Road, Off. S.V. Road, Vile Parle (West), Mumbai, Maharashtra 400056
Tel: +91 22 4233 3030
Curriculum: IBDP

Swami Vivekanand International School - Gorai
RSC-16, Gorai 1, Borivali (W), Mumbai, Maharashtra 400091
Tel: +91 22 3501 9555
Curriculum: National

Swami Vivekanand International School - Kandivali
MG Road, Parekh Nagar, Kandivali (W), Mumbai, Maharashtra 400067
Tel: +91 86 5702 4001
Curriculum: National

Symbiosis International School
Symbiosis Viman nagar Campus, Off. New AirPort road, Viman Nagar, Pune, Maharashtra 411014
Tel: +91 20 2655 7300
Curriculum: IBDP, IBPYP
Language instr: English

Taktse International School
PO Box 90, Gangtok, Sikkim 737101
Tel: +91 3592 237081
Age range: 4–19

TCIS
Survey no. 215/3, Varthur Sharjapur, Whitefield Main Road, Bangalore, Karnataka
Tel: +91 78 9902 5222
Curriculum: IBPYP
Language instr: English, Hindi

Thakur International School
C.T.S. No. 1299 Shivaji Road, Off M.G. Road, Kandivali (W), Mumbai, Maharashtra 400067
Tel: +91 22 2802 1333
Age range: 2–19
Curriculum: IGCSE, ALevs

The Aga Khan Academy Hyderabad
Survey No 1/1 Hardware Park, Maheshwaram Mandal, Rangareddy District, Hyderabad, Telangana 501510
Tel: +91 40 66291313
Age range: 6–18 years
No. of pupils: 630
Curriculum: IBDP, IBMYP, IBPYP
Language instr: English

The Assam Valley School
P.O. Balipara, Dist. Sonitpur, Balipara, Assam 784101
Tel: +91 9678074320

The Bombay Suburban Grain Dealers' Junior College of Commerce, Arts & Science
Road No.1, Bhadran Nagar, S V Road, Malad (W), Mumbai, Maharashtra 400064
Tel: +91 22 2808 5424
Curriculum: IBCP
Language instr: English

The British School
Dr Jose P Rizal Marg, Chanakyapuri, New Delhi, Delhi 110021
Tel: +91 11 4066 4166
Age range: 3–18
No. of pupils: 1134 B555 G579 VIth148
Curriculum: IBDP, IGCSE
Language instr: English

The British School, Sector 8, Panchkula
Panchkula, Haryana 134109
Tel: +91 172 4646246
Age range: 2–11
No. of pupils: 300
Curriculum: IGCSE

Asia

The Cambridge School
7& 7/1 Satyendra Nath, Majumder Sarani, Kolkata, West Bengal 700026
Tel: +91 33 82320 42019
Curriculum: UK

The Cathedral & John Connon School
6 Purshottamdas Thakurdas Marg, Mumbai, Maharashtra 400001
Tel: +91 22 2200 1282
Age range: 3–18 years
No. of pupils: 2072
Curriculum: IBDP, National, UK, USA, IGCSE
Language instr: English

The Choice School, Tripunithura
Nadama East, Tripunithura, Kochi, Kerala 682301
Tel: +91 48 4277 5692
Curriculum: IBDP
Language instr: English

The Doon School
Mall Road, Dehradun, Uttarakhand 248001
Tel: +91-135 2526 400
Age range: B12–18
Curriculum: IBDP, National, IGCSE
Language instr: English

The Emerald Heights International School
Opposite Akashwani, A. B. Road, Rau, Indore, Madhya Pradesh 453331
Tel: +91 872 000 9992/3
Age range: 4–19
Curriculum: IGCSE
Language instr: English

The Galaxy School
C/o S N Kansagra School Akashwani Chowk, University Road, Rajkot, Gujarat 360005
Tel: +91 635 879 1118
Curriculum: IBDP
Language instr: English

The Gaudium School
Survey No. 148, Nanakramguda Village, Serilingampally, Nanakramguda, Hyderabad, Telangana 500008
Tel: +91 73370 00200
Curriculum: IBDP, IBMYP, IBPYP
Language instr: English, Hindi

The Heritage School, Kolkata
994 Maduraha, Chowbaga Road, Anandpur, PO East Kolkata Township, Kolkata, West Bengal 700107
Tel: +91 33 2443 0448
Curriculum: IBDP

The International School Bangalore
Whitefield-Sarjapur Road, Near Dommasandra Circle, Bengaluru, Karnataka 562125
Tel: +91 80 6723 5900
Age range: 3–18
No. of pupils: 1100
Curriculum: IBDP, IGCSE
Language instr: English

The Lawrence School
Sanawar, MDR 10, Solan, Himachal Pradesh 173202
Tel: +91 1792 261208
Language instr: English

The NEST School
363 Arcot Road (NSK Salai), Kodambakkam, Chennai, Tamil Nadu 600024
Tel: +91 99 4010 6358
Curriculum: IBPYP
Language instr: English

The New Tulip International School
Sterling City, Bopal, Ahmedabad, Gujarat 380058
Tel: +91 27 17 329210
Age range: 5–18

The Pupil, Saveetha Eco School
4/68, Thiruverkkadu Road, Behind Saveetha Dental College, Poonamallee, Chennai, Tamil Nadu 600056
Tel: +91 44 2680 2013
Curriculum: IBDP, IBMYP, IBPYP
Language instr: English, Tamil

The Rajkumar College Rajkot
Dr. Radhakrishnan Road, Rajkot, Gujarat 360001
Tel: +91 281 246 6064
Age range: 5–18 years
Curriculum: National
Language instr: English

The Riverside School
307 Behind C.S.D Depot, Off Airport Road, Cantonment, Ahmedabad, Gujarat 380004
Tel: +91 79 22861321
Age range: 4–16

The Sanskaar Valley School
Chandanpura, Bhopal, Madhya Pradesh 462016
Tel: +91 888 953 3346/7/8/9
Language instr: English

The Scindia School
The Fort, Gwalior, Madhya Pradesh 474008
Tel: +91 751 248 0750
Age range: B11–18 years
Curriculum: National
Language instr: English

The Shri Ram Academy
Beside Srija Hospital, Padmasree Gardens, Gowlidoddy, Hyderabad, Telangana 500032
Tel: +91 75 6989 1111
Curriculum: IBPYP
Language instr: English

The Shri Ram School
Moulsari Avenue DLF Phase-3, Gurugram, Haryana 122002
No. of pupils: 227
Curriculum: IBDP
Language instr: English

The Shriram Millennium School, Faridabad
Sector 81, Faridabad, Haryana 121002
Tel: +91 999 959 4838
Age range: 4–18 years
Curriculum: National

The Shriram Millennium School, Gurugram
Sector 64, Opposite M3M Urbana, Adjacent to Orana Convention Centre, Gurugram, Haryana 122002
Tel: +91 844 700 0281
Age range: 4–18 years
Curriculum: National

The Shriram Millennium School, Noida
Plot S-1, Sector 135, off Greater NOIDA Expressway, Noida, Uttar Pradesh 201301
Tel: +91 999 917 6666
Age range: 4–18 years
Curriculum: IBDP, IGCSE
Language instr: English

The Universal School
Plot No. 17, Near Lion's Garden, Tilak Road, Ghatkopar (E), Mumbai, Maharashtra 400077
Tel: +91 773 8146 123
Age range: 4–19
Curriculum: IBDP, IGCSE
Language instr: English, Hindi

The White School International
HiLITE Knowledge Village, Parammal, Perumanna, Kozhikode, Kerala 673019
Tel: +91 95260 777 78
Curriculum: IBDP, IBMYP, IBPYP
Language instr: English, Malayalam

TIPS Bengaluru
HBR Layout, Nagawara, Bangalore, Karnataka 560045
Tel: +91 77 082 95959

TIPS Chennai
No. 50/51, First Main Road, Perungudi Industrial Estate, Perungudi, Chennai, Tamil Nadu 600069
Tel: +91 44 7118 8011
Curriculum: IBDP, IBPYP
Language instr: English

TIPS Coimbatore
193 Sathy Road, S.S.Kulam P.O., Coimbatore, Tamil Nadu 641107
Tel: +91 42 2236 6666
Age range: 2.6–17 years
Curriculum: IBDP, IBPYP, IGCSE
Language instr: English

TIPS Erode
Chennimalai Road, Senapathipalayam, Goundachi palayam post, Erode, Tamil Nadu 638112
Tel: +91 967745 8888
Age range: 4–18 years
Curriculum: IBPYP, IGCSE, ALevs
Language instr: English

TIPS Karur
S.F.No. 371 & 379/1, Pazhamapuram, Poolampalayam (Post), Punnam Village, Karur, Tamil Nadu 639163
Tel: +91 75 5815 9111

TIPS Kochi
Edachira, Thengode(Post), Kakkanad, Kochi, Kerala 682030
Tel: +91 48 4485 4850
Curriculum: IBPYP
Language instr: English

TIPS Madurai
No.3, VP Rathnasamy Nadar Street, BB Kulam, Madurai, Tamil Nadu 625002
Tel: +91 97 8944 1188

TIPS Salem
No 2, Mangayarkarasi Street, Off Advitha Ashram Road, Fairlands, Salem, Tamil Nadu 636016
Tel: +91 92 8258 8888
Curriculum: IBPYP
Language instr: English, Tamil

TIPS Tirupur
No.10/720, Arulpuram, Arulpuram (P.O.), Palladam Road, Tirupur, Tamil Nadu 641605
Tel: +91 75 5817 9111

TIPS Trichy
49/3, K.Kallikudi (North), Dindigul Main Road, Ramji Nagar, Srirangam Tk, Trichy, Tamil Nadu 620009
Tel: +91 73 3911 1777

Treamis
Hulimangala Post, near Electronics City, Bengaluru, Karnataka 560105
Tel: +91 99723 99046
Age range: 4–19
Curriculum: IBDP, IBPYP, IGCSE, ALevs
Language instr: English, Kannada

Trinity International School
Plot No 247-248, Near Gokul Hall, Sion (E), Mumbai, Maharashtra 400022
Tel: +91 22 24094344
Age range: 14–19
Curriculum: IGCSE

Trio World Academy
3/5 Kodigehalli Main Road, Sahakar Nagar, Bengaluru, Karnataka 560092
Tel: +91 80 40611222
Curriculum: IBDP, IBPYP

Trivandrum International School
Edackcode, PO Korani, Trivandrum, Kerala 695104
Tel: +91 471 2619051
Curriculum: IBDP, IBPYP

Udgam School for Children
Opp. Sardar Patel Institute, Thaltej, Ahmedabad, Gujarat 380054
Tel: +91 79 7101 2345
Curriculum: IBCP
Language instr: English

Asia

UNICOSMOS School
Site 2, Sector 55, Off Golf Course Road, Gurugram, Haryana 122011
Tel: +91 95 6080 3800
Curriculum: IBPYP
Language instr: English, Hindi

Unison World School
Mussoorie Diversion Road, Dehradun, Uttarakhand 248009
Tel: +91 135 7113000
Age range: G9–16
No. of pupils: 450
Curriculum: UK, IGCSE, ALevs
Language instr: English

United World Academy (UWA)
Sy No. 1/1 and 62, Chikkawadayerapura, Sarjapur Hobali, Anekal Taluk, Bengaluru, Karnataka 560087
Tel: +91 7624 981 603
Age range: 4–18 years
Curriculum: IBDP
Language instr: English

Utpal Shanghvi Global School
East West Road No. 3, JVPD Scheme, Juhu, Mumbai, Maharashtra
Tel: +91 84 3395 1863
Curriculum: IBPYP
Language instr: English

Uttpal Shanghvi School
East West Road No.3, J.V.P.D. Scheme, Juhu, Mumbai, Maharashtra 400049
Tel: +91 22 2620 7413
Age range: 4–19
No. of pupils: 300

UWC Mahindra College
Village Khubavali, PO Paud, Taluka Mulshi, Pune, Maharashtra 412108
Tel: +91 97644 42751-54
Age range: 16–19 years
No. of pupils: 240
Curriculum: IBDP, IBCP
Language instr: English

Vaels International School
Pon Vidhyashram Gardens, Off East Coast Road, Injambakkam, Chennai, Tamil Nadu 600115
Tel: +91 44 6565 2992
Curriculum: National, UK, IGCSE, ALevs

Vedanya International School
Central Park Resorts, Sector 48, Gurugram, Haryana 122018
Tel: +91 74 2869 7080
Curriculum: IBPYP
Language instr: English

Vibgyor High School, Pune (NIBM Road)
Dorabjee Paradise, Near Palace Orchard, Off. Corinthian Club Road, Extn NIBM Road, Mohammedwadi, Hadapsar, Pune, Maharashtra 411060
Tel: +91 20 3044 6000
Age range: 14–19
Curriculum: National, IGCSE

Vibgyor High, Mumbai (Goregagon)
Motilal Nagar - 1, Srirang Sabde Marg, Off. Link Road, Goregaon, Mumbai, Maharashtra 400104
Tel: +91 22 3957 7070
Age range: 14–19
Curriculum: National, IGCSE

Vibgyor High, Vadodara
Opp Banco Product, Padra Road, B/H Bhayali Railway Station, Vadodara, Gujurat 391410
Tel: +91 265 3076 101
Age range: 14–19
Curriculum: IGCSE, ALevs

Victorious Kidss Educares
Survey No. 53, 54 & 58, Hissa No. 2/1A, Off. Shreeram Society, Nagar Road, Kharadi, Pune, Maharashtra 411014
Tel: +91 20-67116300/1/2
Age range: 6 weeks–19 years
No. of pupils: 960
Curriculum: IBDP, IBMYP, IBPYP
Language instr: English

Vidhyashram International School
Ahead of Shikargarh Mini Market, Defence Lab Road, Jodhpur, Rajasthan 342015
Tel: +91 291 222 7976
Age range: 4–19
No. of pupils: 300
Curriculum: UK, IGCSE

Vidya Global School
Vidya Knowledge Park, Baghpat Road, Meerut, Uttar Pradesh 250002
Tel: +91 92 6868 4400
Age range: 4–16
Curriculum: IBMYP, IBPYP, National, IGCSE

Vidyanjali International School
20/1, Ram Mohon Dutta Road, Kolkata, West Bengal 700020
Tel: +91-33-2486 1771
Curriculum: UK

Vikaasa World School
Ponnagaram Compound, New Jail Road, Madurai, Tamil Nadu 625014
Tel: +91 9597607888
Curriculum: IGCSE, ALevs

Vishwashanti Gurukul
Rajbaug, off Pune-Solapur Highway, Loni, Pune, Maharashtra 412201
Tel: +91 20 39210000
Age range: 5–18
No. of pupils: 350 B200 G150
Curriculum: IBDP, IBMYP, IBPYP, UK, IGCSE
Language instr: English

Vista International School
Next to Wipro SEZ - Gopanapalli Campus, Vattingula Palli, Lingampalli - Khanapur Road, Gachibowli Financial Dist+, Hyderabad, Telangana 500046
Tel: +91 70 3213 2222
Curriculum: IBPYP, National
Language instr: English

VIVA The School
Beside VVIT college campus, NAMBUR village, Pedakakani Mandal, Nambur, Guntur, Andhra Pradesh 522508
Tel: +91 73 3114 2336
Curriculum: IBPYP
Language instr: English, Telugu

Vivek High School
Vidya Path, Sector 38-B, Chandigarh, Punjab 160036
Tel: +91 172 269 8988
Language instr: English

Welham Boys' School
5 Circular Rd, Dalanwala, Dehradun, Uttarakhand 248001
Tel: +91 976 054 4755

Wisdom High International School
Rameshwar Nagar, Anandwali, Gangapur Road, Nashik, Maharashtra 422007
Tel: +91 70 3090 1255
Age range: 11–19
Curriculum: IGCSE

Witty International School Bhilwara
7 D 8, Ahead Shreenath Circle, RC Vyas Colony, Bhilwara, Rajasthan 311001
Tel: +91 1482 239153
Age range: 5–18

Witty International School Malad
Ramchandra Lane, Malad (W), Mumbai, Maharashtra 400064
Tel: +91 22 28882310
Age range: 5–18
No. of pupils: 300
Curriculum: IGCSE

Witty International School Udaipur
1 Witty Lane, Gaurav Path, Nathdwara Road, Opp Sukher Thana, Udaipur, Rajasthan 313004
Tel: +91 92142 55667
Age range: 5–18

Witty World Goregaon
Plot No 165, Near Ayappa Temple, Bangur Nagar, Goregaon, Mumbai, Maharashtra 400062
Tel: +91 92230 11704
Age range: 5–11

Wockhardt Global School
Dr Habil Khorakiwala Education and Health Foundation, E-1/NP-1, SEZ, Five Star Industrial Estate, MIDC, Shen+, Aurangabad, Maharashtra 431154
Tel: +91 240 6662888
Curriculum: IBDP, IBMYP, IBPYP
Language instr: English

WOODSTOCK SCHOOL
For further details see p. 82
Mussoorie, Uttarakhand 248179
Tel: +91 135 263 9000
Email: admissions@woodstock.ac.in
Website: www.woodstockschool.in
Principal: Mark Windsor
Age range: 11–18 years
No. of pupils: 500
Fees: INR2,164,000–INR2,404,000
Curriculum: ACT, AP, IBDP, IBMYP, SAT, UK, USA
Language instr: English

Yadavindra Public School
New Lal Bagh, Patiala, Punjab
Tel: +91 1752 215634
Language instr: English

INDONESIA

ACG SCHOOL JAKARTA
For further details see p. 44
Jl Warung Jati Barat No.19, RW.5, Jati Padang, Kec. Ps. Minggu, Jakarta Selatan, Jakarta, DKI 12540
Tel: +62 21 2978 0200 / +62 816 297 7800
Email: acgjkt@acgedu.com
Website: jakarta.acgedu.com
Principal: Myles D'Airelle
Age range: 3–17 years
No. of pupils: 299
Fees: Day IDR150,491,250–IDR357,761,250
Curriculum: IBDP, IBPYP
Language instr: English

ACS Jakarta
Jl Bantar Jati, Kelurahan Setu, Jakarta Timur, DKI 13880
Tel: +62 21 8459 7175
Age range: 3–18 years
Curriculum: IBDP, IGCSE
Language instr: English

Al Firdaus World Class Islamic School
Jl. Al Kautsar, Mendungan, Pabelan, Kec. Kartasura, Kabupaten Sukoharjo, Surakarta, Jateng 57169
Curriculum: IBMYP, IBPYP
Language instr: English, Indonesian

Al Jabr Islamic School
Jl. Bango II No.38, RT.6/RW.3, Pondok Labu, Cilandak, Jakarta Selatan, DKI 12450
Tel: +62 21 7591 3675
Age range: 3–18 years
Curriculum: IBMYP, IBPYP, IBCP
Language instr: English, Indonesian

Australian Independent School, Bali
Jl. Imam Bonjol No. 458A, Denpasar, Bali 80119
Tel: +62 36 1845 20000
Age range: 3–18 years
Curriculum: IBDP
Language instr: English

Asia

Australian Independent School, Jakarta
Jl. Pejaten Barat No. 68, Jakarta Selatan, DKI 12510
Tel: +62 21 782 1141
Age range: 3–18 years
Curriculum: IBDP
Language instr: English
(CIS)

Bali Island School
Jl. Danau Buyan IV No. 15, Sanur, Denpasar, Bali 80228
Tel: +62 36 128 8770
Age range: 3–18 years
Curriculum: IBDP, IBMYP, IBPYP
Language instr: English
(CIS) (EAR)

Bandung Alliance Intercultural School
Jl. Bujanggamanik Kav 2, Kota Baru Parahyangan, Bandung, Jabar 40553
Tel: +62 22 2101 2247
Age range: 3–18 years
Curriculum: USA
(EAR)

Bandung Independent School
Jl. Prof. Drg. Surya Sumantri No. 61, Bandung, Jabar 40164
Tel: +62 22 201 4995
Age range: 3–18 years
Curriculum: IBDP, IBMYP, IBPYP
Language instr: English
(CIS)

Beacon Academy
Jl. Pegangsaan Dua No. 66, Kelapa Gading, Jakarta Utara, DKI 14250
Tel: +62 21 460 3480
Age range: 4–18 years
Curriculum: IBDP, IBPYP
Language instr: English

Bina Bangsa School
Jl. Arjuna Sel. No.87, RT.4/RW.4, Kebon Jeruk, Jakarta Barat, DKI 11530
Tel: +62 21 532 8833
Age range: 2–18 years
Curriculum: UK, IGCSE, ALevs

Binus School Bekasi
Jl. Saraswati No. 1, Bumiwedari Vida, Bekasi, Jabar 17156
Tel: +62 21 8261 7799
Age range: 3–18 years
Curriculum: National, UK, ALevs

Binus School Semarang
POJ Avenue Kav. 3, Tawangsari, Semarang Barat, Semarang, Jateng 50144
Age range: 3–18 years
Curriculum: National, UK, ALevs

Binus School Serpong
Jl. Lengkong Karya - Jelupang No. 58, Lengkong Karya, Serpong, Tangerang, Banten 15322
Tel: +62 21 538 0400
Age range: 3–18 years
Curriculum: National, UK, ALevs

Binus School Simprug
Jl. Sultan Iskandar, Muda Kav G-8, Simprug, Jakarta Selatan, DKI 12220
Tel: +62 21 724 3663
Age range: 3–18 years
Curriculum: IBDP, IBMYP, IBPYP
Language instr: English

Blossom International School
Citra Garden 3 Extension Block F No. 1, Kalideres, Jakarta Barat, DKI 11830
Tel: +62 21 5595 5756
Curriculum: IBPYP
Language instr: English, Chinese

British School Jakarta
Bintaro Jaya Sektor 9, Jl. Raya Jombang, Ciledug, Pondok Aren, Tangerang, Banten 15427
Tel: +62 21 745 1670
Age range: 2–18 years
Curriculum: IBDP, IBMYP, IBCP, IPC, UK
Language instr: English
(CIS) (COB) (EAR)

BTB School (Sekolah Bina Tunas Bangsa)
Jl. Pluit Tumur Blok MM, Jakarta Utara, DKI 14450
Tel: +62 21 669 8888
Age range: 4–18 years
Curriculum: IBDP
Language instr: English

Bunda Mulia School
Jl. Lodan Raya No. 2, Jakarta Utara, DKI 14430
Tel: +62 21 690 9742
Age range: 2–18 years
Curriculum: UK, IGCSE, ALevs

Canggu Community School
Jl. Subak Sari, Banjar Tegal Gundul, Tibubeneng, Kuta Utara, Badung, Canggu, Bali 80361
Tel: +62 36 1844 6391
Age range: 3–18 years
Curriculum: IBDP, IGCSE
Language instr: English
(CIS)

Cita Hati Christian School - East Campus
Jl. Kejawan Putih Barat 28-30, Pakuwon City (Laguna Indah), Surabaya, Jatim 60112
Tel: +62 3 1742 5470
Age range: 3–18 years
Curriculum: IBDP, IGCSE
Language instr: English

Cita Hati Christian School - Samarinda Campus
Aminah Syukur 32, Samarinda, Kaltim 75242
Tel: +62 54 1777 7691
Curriculum: IBDP
Language instr: English, Indonesian

Cita Hati Christian School - West Campus
Jl. Bukit Golf L2 No. 1, Citra Raya, Surabaya, Jatim 60211
Tel: +62 812 4901 5181
Age range: 3–18 years
Curriculum: IBDP, IGCSE
Language instr: English

Deutsche Schule Jakarta
Jl. Puspa Widya No. 8, Lengkong Wetan, Serpong, Tangerang, Banten 15322
Tel: +62 21 537 8080
Age range: 2–18 years
Curriculum: Abitur

Elyon Christian School
Raya Sukomanunggal Jaya No. 33A, Surabaya, Jatim 60187
Tel: +62 31 732 5999
Age range: 1.5–18 years
Curriculum: National, UK, IGCSE

Gandhi Memorial Intercontinental School, Bali
Jl. Tukad Yeh Penet No. 8A Renon, Denpasar, Bali 80235
Tel: +62 877 5833 2234
Age range: 3–18 years
Curriculum: IBDP, IBMYP, IBPYP, IBCP, IGCSE
Language instr: English

Gandhi Memorial Intercontinental School, Jakarta
Jl. HBR Motik No. Kav 1 Block D6, Kemayoran, Jakarta Pusat DKI 14410
Tel: +62 21 6586 5667
Age range: 3–18 years
Curriculum: IBDP, IBMYP, IBPYP, IBCP, IGCSE, ALevs
Language instr: English

Global Jaya School
Emerald Boulevard, Bintaro Jaya Sektor IX, Tangerang, Banten 15224
Tel: +62 21 745 7562
Age range: 4–18 years
Curriculum: IBDP, IBMYP, IBPYP
Language instr: English
(EAR)

Global Sevilla - Pulo Mas Campus
Jl. Pulo Mas Jaya No. 1, Pacuan Kuda Pulo Mas, Jakarta Timur, DKI 13210
Tel: +62 21 4788 2288
Age range: 1.5–18 years
Curriculum: IPC, IGCSE, ALevs

Global Sevilla - Puri Indah Campus
Jl. Kembangan Raya Blok JJ No. 1, Puri Indah, Jakarta Barat, DKI 11610
Tel: +62 21 580 6699
Age range: 1.5–18 years
Curriculum: IPC, IGCSE, ALevs

Green School Bali
Jalan Raya Sibang Kaja, Abiansemal, Badung, Bali 80352
Tel: 0062 361 469875
Age range: 3–18 years
No. of pupils: 375
Language instr: English, Bahasa

Hillcrest School
Jl. Sekolah Internasional No. 1, Hinekombe, Sentani, Jayapura, Papua 99352
Tel: +62 96 759 1460
Age range: 4–18 years
Curriculum: AP, USA
Language instr: English
(EAR)

Hope Academy
Puri Indah CBD, Jl. Puri Indah Raya Blok U 1, Kembangan Selatan, Jakarta Barat, DKI 11610
Tel: +62 895 4262 88800
Age range: 2–12 years
Curriculum: IBPYP
Language instr: English

Ichthus School - West Campus
Jl Surya Mandala 3 Blok N2 No 11, Sunrise Garden, Jakarta Barat, DKI 11520
Tel: +62 21 581 2228
Age range: 5–18
No. of pupils: 300
Curriculum: IGCSE

IPEKA Integrated Christian School
Komplek Taman Meruya Ilir, Jalan Batu Mulia Blok K, RT.11/RW.7, Meruya Utara, RT.11/RW.7, Meruya Utara, Kem+, Jakarta Barat, DKI 11620
Tel: +62 21 58905890
Curriculum: IBDP
Language instr: English, Indonesian

Islamic Village School
Jl. Islamic Raya No.1, Komplek Islamic Village, Kelapa Dua, Tangerang, Banten 15810
Tel: +62 21 547 0787
Curriculum: IBMYP, IBPYP
Language instr: English, Indonesian

Jakarta Intercultural School
Jalan Terogong Raya No. 33, Cilandak, Jakarta Selatan, DKI 12430
Tel: +62 21 50989555
Age range: 3–18 years
Curriculum: IBDP, IBCP
Language instr: English
(CIS)

Jakarta Montessori School
Jl. Durian 10, Jagakarsa, Jakarta Selatan, DKI 12620
Tel: +62 21 727 2162
Curriculum: IBDP
Language instr: English, Indonesian

Jakarta Multicultural School
Jl. Pisangan Raya No. 99 (Taman Wisata Situ Gintung), Cirendeu, Ciputat Timur, Banten 15419
Tel: +62 21 744 4864
Age range: 1.5–18
Curriculum: IBDP

Jakarta Nanyang School
Jl. Sekolah Foresta No. 1, Foresta, BSD City, Tangerang, Banten 15331
Tel: +62 21 50 555 999
Curriculum: UK, IGCSE, ALevs

Kanaan Global School
Taman Surya, Jl. Boulevard blok L2, Perumahan Taman Surya 3, Jakarta Barat, DKI 11830
Tel: +62 21 6197205
Curriculum: National, UK

Asia

Kinderstation Primary
Jl. Adisucipto Km 9 No 9B,
Maguwo, Yogyakarta, DIY 55282
Tel: +62 274 489671
Age range: 2–11

Kingston School
Kompleks Graha Metropolitan,
Jln. Kapten Sumarsono Blok E
25/26, Medan, Sumut 20124
Tel: +62 61 8458555
No. of pupils: 450
Curriculum: IPC, National, UK, IGCSE

Lycée Français de Bali
76 Jalan Umalas Kauh,
Kerobokan, Bali 80117
Tel: +62 361 4732 314
Curriculum: FrenchBacc

Lycée Français Louis-Charles Damais
Jl. Cipete Dalam No. 32,
Jakarta Selatan, DKI 12410
Tel: +62 21 750 30 62
Curriculum: FrenchBacc

Madania
Telaga Kahuripan, Parung,
Bogor, Jabar 16330
Tel: +62 251 602777
Curriculum: IBPYP
Language instr: English

Makassar Independent School
Botolempangan 17/19,
Makassar, Sulsel 90125
Tel: +62 411 315 889
Age range: 5–13
No. of pupils: 26
Curriculum: UK

Manado Independent School
Jl. Walanda Maramis, North Minahasa, Sulut 95371
Tel: +62 431 893300
Curriculum: UK

Medan Independent School
Jl. Jamin Ginting Km. 10 / Jl. Tali Air No.5, Medan, North Sumatra 20141
Tel: +62 61 836 1816
Age range: 3–18 years
No. of pupils: 80
Curriculum: IBDP, IBMYP, IBPYP
Language instr: English

Mentari Intercultural School Bintaro
Jalan Perigi Baru No.7A,
Tangerang, Pd. Aren, Tangerang Selatan, Banten 15228
Tel: +62 21 745 8418
Curriculum: IBDP
Language instr: English

Mentari Intercultural School Jakarta
Jl. H. Jian No.2, RT.4/RW.3,
North Cipete, Kby. Baru,
Jakarta Selatan, DKI 12150
Tel: 21 727 94 870
Age range: 5–17
Curriculum: IBDP, IBMYP, IBPYP, National, UK
Language instr: English

Mountainview Christian School
Jl. Nakula Sadewa Raya No 55, Salatiga, Jateng 50711
Tel: +62 298 311673
Age range: 5–19
No. of pupils: 230
Curriculum: ACT, AP, SAT, USA
Language instr: English

Mt Zaagkam School
Tembagapura Raya Street No. 605,
Tembagapura, Papua 99967
Tel: +62 901 408 767
Age range: 3–12
Curriculum: IBPYP
Language instr: English

Mutiara Harapan Islamic School
Jl. Pondok Kacang Raya No. 2,
Pondok Kacang Timur, Pondok Aren, Tangerang, Banten 15426
Tel: +62 (0)21 74860451
Curriculum: IBPYP
Language instr: English

Nassa School
Jl Bojong Nangka II/38, Jati Rahayu-Pondok Melati, Bekasi, Jabar 17414
Tel: +62 21 846 3229
Curriculum: IBPYP
Language instr: English, Indonesian

New Zealand Independent School
Jl Kemang Selatan I no 1A, Kemang, Jakarta Selatan, DKI 12730
Tel: +62 21 7183222
Curriculum: IGCSE, ALevs
Language instr: English

Nord Anglia School Jakarta
Jalan NIS 1, Kenanga Terusan,
Ampera Raya-Cilandak,
Jakarta Selatan, DKI 12560
Tel: +62 811 9727 979
Age range: 18 months–12 years
No. of pupils: 300
Curriculum: IPC, UK

North Jakarta Intercultural School
PO Box 6759/JKUKP, Jalan Raya Kelapa Nias, Kelapa Gading Permai, Jakarta Utara, DKI 14250
Tel: +62 21 4586 5222;
+62 21 36 700 770
Age range: 4–16
Curriculum: IBDP, IBMYP, IBPYP, SAT, USA
Language instr: English, Indonesian

Pelangi School (Yayasan Cahaya Pelangi Bali)
Br. Kumbuh, Mas, Bali
Tel: +62 821 4524 7146
Curriculum: IPC

Penabur Secondary Tanjung Duren (PSTD)
Jl. Tanjung Duren Raya no.4, building D, Grogol, Jakarta Barat, DKI 11470
Tel: +62 21 560 2042
Age range: 11–18

PSKD Mandiri
PO Box 6013, Menteng,
Jakarta Pusat, DKI 10310
Tel: +62 21 392 4384

Raffles Christian School
Jl Gedung Hijau Raya 1 No 1, Pondok Indah, Jakarta Selatan, DKI 12310
Tel: +62 21 7590 3342
Curriculum: UK, ALevs

Rama School
Kemban Kuning, Ubrug, Jatiluhur,
PO Box 60, Purwakarta, Jabar 41011
Tel: +62 264 207052
Age range: 3–15
No. of pupils: 240
Curriculum: National

Saint Peter's School
Boulevard Timur Raya No. 8, Kelapa Gading, Jakarta Utara, DKI 14240
Tel: +62 21 452 4246
Age range: 4–19
No. of pupils: 300
Curriculum: GCSE

Sampoerna Academy, Jakarta Campus
L'Avenue Campus, Jln.
Raya Pasar Minggu, Kav. 16
Pancoran, Jakarta 12780
Tel: +62 (0)21 5022 22 34
Curriculum: IBDP
Language instr: English, Indonesian

Sampoerna Academy, Medan Campus
Jln. Jamin Ginting, Kompleks Citra Garden, Medan
Tel: +62 (0)61 821 27 15
Curriculum: IBDP
Language instr: English, Indonesian

SDK BPK Penabur Banda
Jl Bahureksa No 26,
Bandung, Jabar 40115
Tel: +62 22 4210787
Curriculum: IBPYP
Language instr: English

Sekolah Bogor Raya
Perumahan Danau Bogor Raya, Bogor, Jabar 16143
Tel: +62 251 837 8873
No. of pupils: 500
Curriculum: IBDP, IBPYP
Language instr: English

Sekolah Buin Batu
Sekongkang, Buin Batu,
West Sumbawa, NTB
Tel: +62 37 2635 318
Age range: 3–18 years
Curriculum: IBDP, IBMYP, IBPYP, National
Language instr: English, Indonesian

Sekolah Cikal Jakarta
Jalan Setu Raya No.3, Cipayung,
Jakarta Selatan, DKI 13880
Age range: 3–18 years
Curriculum: IBDP, IBMYP
Language instr: English, Indonesian

Sekolah Cikal Lebak Bulus
Jl. Lebak Bulus I, RT. 006/RW.004,
Cilandak Barat Village, Cilandak District, Jakarta Selatan, DKI 12440
Age range: 3–18 years
Curriculum: IBDP, IBPYP
Language instr: English, Indonesian

Sekolah Cikal Surabaya
Jl. Raya Lontar No. 103, Lontar Village, Sambikerep District,
Surabaya, Jatim 60216
Tel: +62 815 7595 7599
Age range: 3–18 years
Curriculum: IBPYP
Language instr: English

Sekolah Ciputra, Surabaya
Puri Widya Kencana, Citraland,
Surabaya, Jatim 60213
Tel: +62 31 741 5018
Age range: 1–18
No. of pupils: 1300
Curriculum: IBDP, IBMYP, IBPYP
Language instr: English

Sekolah Cita Buana
Jl Paso No 84, Jagakarsa,
Jakarta Selatan, DKI 12620
Tel: +62 21 7820088
Age range: 3–13
No. of pupils: 270

Sekolah Djuwita Batam
Komplek Anggrek Mas 1 Batam Center, Batam, Kepri 29432
Tel: +62 778 464 005
Curriculum: UK, IGCSE

Sekolah Global Indo-Asia
Jalan Raya Batam Centre Kav SGIA,
Batam Centre, Batam Island, Kepri
Tel: +62 778 467333
Age range: 2.5 Yrs–17 Yrs
Curriculum: IBDP, IBPYP
Language instr: English

Sekolah Monte Sienna
Jl. Yos Sudarso, Sungai Jodoh,
Kecamatan Batu Ampar,
Batam, Kepri 29453
Tel: +62 77 8741 8817
Age range: 3–18 years
Curriculum: IBMYP, IBPYP, National, IGCSE, ALevs
Language instr: English, Indonesian

Sekolah Mutiara Nusantara
Jl. Sersan Bajuri - Setiabudi, Km 1.5,
RT 3 RW 1, Bandung, Jabar 40559
Tel: +62 22 201 7773
Age range: 3–18 years
Curriculum: IBDP
Language instr: English

Sekolah Paradisa Cendekia
Jalan Pulo, Leuwinanggung,
Kalimanggis, Cibubur, DKI
Tel: +62 21 28671700
Curriculum: IBPYP
Language instr: English, Indonesian

Sekolah Pelita Harapan, Kemang Village
Jl. Pangeran Antasari 36, Kemang Village, Jakarta Selatan, DKI 12150
Tel: +62 21 290 56 789
Curriculum: IBDP

Asia

Sekolah Pelita Harapan, Lippo Cikarang
Jl. Dago Permai No.1 Komp. Dago Villas, Lippo Cikarang, Bekasi, Jabar 17550
Tel: +62 21 897 2786 87
Age range: 3–18
Curriculum: IBDP
Language instr: English

Sekolah Pelita Harapan, Lippo Village
2500 Boulevard Palem Raya, Lippo Village, Tangerang, Banten 15810
Tel: +62 21 546 0234
Age range: 1–18
No. of pupils: 2145
Curriculum: IBDP, IBMYP, IBPYP, SAT
Language instr: English

Sekolah Pelita Harapan, Sentul City
Jl. Babakan Madang, Sentul City, Bogor, Jabar 16810
Tel: +62 21 8796 0234
Age range: 4–20
No. of pupils: 380 B190 G190
Curriculum: IBDP, IBMYP, IBPYP, National
Language instr: English

Sekolah Pilar Indonesia
Jl Dewa 9, Ciangsana, Kawasan Cibubur, Bogor, Jabar 16968
Tel: +62 21 84936222
Age range: 3–17
No. of pupils: 320
Curriculum: IBPYP

Sekolah Tunas Bangsa
Jalan Arteri Supadio, (Achmad Yani II) Km 2, Pontianak, Kalbar 78391
Tel: +62 561 725555
No. of pupils: 377
Curriculum: IBPYP
Language instr: English

Sekolah Victory Plus
Jl Kemang Pratama Raya, AN 2-3 Kemang Pratama, Bekasi, Jabar 17116
Tel: +62 21 8240 3878
Curriculum: IBDP, IBMYP, IBPYP, National, UK
Language instr: English

Semarang Multinational School
Jalan Jangli Raya 37, Candisari, Semarang, Jateng 50254
Tel: +62 24 8311424
Age range: 1–11
No. of pupils: 72 B32 G40
Language instr: English

Sinarmas World Academy
Jl TM Pahlawan Seribu, CBD Lot XV, BSD City, Tangerang, Banten 15322
Tel: +62 21 5316 1400
Age range: 3–18
No. of pupils: B261 G239
Curriculum: IBDP, IBMYP
Language instr: English, Chinese

Sinarmas World Academy Thamrin
Gedung CHUBB Square, Thamrin Nine Podium, 8th Floor, Jl. MH. Thamrin No. 10, Jakarta Pusat, DKI 10230
Tel: +62 21 29937234 (Ext:300)
Curriculum: UK

SIS Cilegon
Jl. Raya Merak No. 49, Bonakarta, Cilegon, Banten 42414
Tel: +62 254 394 460
Age range: 2–12 years

SIS Kelapa Gading
Jl. Pegangsaan Dua No. 83, Kelapa Gading, Jakarta Utara, DKI 14250
Tel: +62 21 460 8888
Age range: 2–19 years
Curriculum: IBDP
Language instr: English

SIS Medan
Royal Sumatra Complex, Jl. Letjen Jamin Ginting Km. 8,5, Medan, Sumut
Tel: +62 61 836 2880
Age range: 2–19 years
Curriculum: IBDP

SIS Palembang
199 Kelurahan Duku Kecamatan Ilir Timur III, Palembang, Sumsel 30114
Tel: +62 711 562 6778
Age range: 2–16 years

SIS Pantai Indah Kapuk
Jl. Mandara Indah 4, Pantai Indah Kapuk, Jakarta Utara, DKI 14460
Tel: +62 21 588 3835
Age range: 2–19 years
Curriculum: IBDP

SIS Semarang
Jl. Bukit Candi Golf No. 20, Graha Candi Golf Residence, Semarang, Jateng 50274
Tel: +62 24 850 9108
Age range: 2–19 years

SIS South Jakarta
Jl. Bona Vista Raya, Lebak Bulus, Jakarta Selatan, DKI 12440
Tel: +62 21 759 14414
Age range: 2–18 years
Curriculum: IBDP
Language instr: English

SMA Islam Al-Azhar 3 Jakarta
Jl. Sisingamangaraja, RT.2/RW.1, Selong, Kec. Kby. Baru, Jakarta Selatan, DKI 12110
Tel: +62 21 726 9935
Curriculum: IBDP
Language instr: English, Indonesian

SMA Pradita Dirgantara
Jl. Cendrawasih No.4. Adi Sumarmo Airport Complex, Surakarta, Jateng 57375
Tel: +62 71 7467 569
Curriculum: IBDP
Language instr: English

Springfield School - Permata Buana 1 Campus
Pulau Sebaru Blok L4/1, Taman Permata Buana, Jakarta Barat, DKI 11610
Tel: +62 21 58357830
Age range: 2–18
Curriculum: USA

Stella Maris School
Sektor 8A, Vatican Cluster, Gading Serpong, Tangerang, Banten 15310
Tel: +62 21 54 212 999
Curriculum: IBDP
Language instr: English

Surabaya European School
At Pakuwon Golf & Family Club, Villa Bukit Regensi, Pakuwon Indah, Surabaya, Jatim 60123
Tel: +62 31 739 17 51
Age range: 3–16
Curriculum: IPC, UK, IGCSE

Surabaya Intercultural School
Citra Raya, Lakarsantri, Tromol Pos 2/SBDK, Surabaya, Jatim 60225
Tel: +62 31 741 4300
Age range: 3–18 years
Curriculum: ACT, IBPYP, SAT

Taman Rama School
Jl. Cokroaminoto No. 382 Ubung Kaja, Denpasar Utara, Bali 80116
Tel: +62 361 414849
Curriculum: National, UK, IGCSE, ALevs

The Independent School Batam
Complex Rosedale Blok E 123-124, Batam, Kepri 24893
Tel: +62 778 461696
Age range: 4–19
No. of pupils: 70
Curriculum: UK

The Intercultural School of Bogor
Jalan Papandayan No 7, Bogor, Jabar 16151
Tel: +62 251 8324 360
Age range: 2–13
Language instr: English

Tunas Muda School Kedoya
Jl Angsana Raya D8/2, Taman Kedoya Baru, Jakarta Barat, DKI 11520
Tel: +62 21 581 8766
No. of pupils: 274
Curriculum: IBPYP
Language instr: English, Indonesian

Tunas Muda School Meruya
Jl. Meruya Utara No. 71, Kembangan, Jakarta Barat, DKI 11620
Tel: +62 (0)21 587 0329
Age range: 1–18
No. of pupils: 1130
Curriculum: IBDP, IBMYP, IBPYP
Language instr: English, Bahasa Indonesia

Tunas Unggul
Jl. Pasir Impun No. 94, Kel. Pasir Impun, Kec. Mandalajati, Bandung, Jabar 40195
Tel: +62 81 1226 9420
Curriculum: IBPYP
Language instr: English

Tzu Chi School, Pantai Indah Kapuk
Jl. Pantai Indah Kapuk Boulevard, Tzu Chi Centre, Kelurahan Kamal Muara, Kecamatan Penjaringan, Jakarta Utara, DKI 14470
Tel: +62 21 5055 6668
Curriculum: IBDP, IBMYP
Language instr: English

Wesley School
Kotak Pos 275, Malang, Jatim 65101
Tel: +62 341 586410
Age range: 5–18
No. of pupils: 110 B55 G55
Curriculum: AP, SAT, USA
Language instr: English

Yogyakarta Independent School
Jl. Tegal Mlati No. 1, Jombor Lor, Sinduadi, Mlati, Sleman, Yogyakarta, DIY 55284
Tel: +62 274 530 5147
Age range: 3–16
Curriculum: IBDP, IBMYP, IBPYP, IPC, IGCSE, ALevs
Language instr: English

YPJ School Kuala Kencana
Jalan Irian Jaya Barat No.1, Kuala Kencana, Timika, Papua 99910
Curriculum: IBMYP, IBPYP
Language instr: English

YPJ School Tembagapura
Jalan Raya Tembagapura No. 605, PO Box 14, Tembagapura, Papua 99910
Curriculum: IBMYP, IBPYP
Language instr: Indonesian

IRAN

École Française de Téhéran
1623 Shariati Avenue, Tehran
Tel: +98 21 2261 5456-8
Age range: 4–18 years
Curriculum: FrenchBacc

German Embassy School Tehran (DBST)
Shariati, under the Sadr Bridge, Shahid Keshani Street (Mahale Darbdowom), Tehran
Tel: +98 212 260 4902
Age range: 3–18 years
Curriculum: Abitur, IBPYP
Language instr: English

Mehr-e-Taban International School
Ghasredasht Avenue, Shiraz
Tel: +98 713 635 9983
Age range: 6–18 years
No. of pupils: 200
Curriculum: IBDP, IBMYP, IBPYP, USA
Language instr: English

Asia

Shahid Mahdavi Educational Foundation
Kouh-Daman, Mina, Zanbagh, Ejazi, Zafaranie Street, Tehran
Tel: +98 212 243 5550 (Ext:190)
Age range: 4–18 years
Curriculum: IBDP, IBPYP
Language instr: English, Persian

Soodeh Educational Complex
End of Arabshahi Avenue, Ashrafi Isfahani Highway, Tehran
Tel: +98 214 424 9702-4
Age range: G4–16 years
Curriculum: IBMYP
Language instr: English

IRAQ

British International Schools in Kurdistan
Mosul Road, Erbil, Kurdistan
Tel: +964 750 251 914
Age range: 4–18 years
Curriculum: AP, SAT, USA

Canadian International School - Erbil
Permam Street, Near Kurdistan TV, Erbil, Kurdistan
Tel: +964 750 568 1313
Age range: 3–18 years
Language instr: English, Arabic, Kurdish

Cedars Interdisciplinary School
Baharka's Road, next to the Lebanese Village, Erbil
Tel: +964 750 591 9000
Curriculum: IBMYP, IBPYP
Language instr: English

Da Vinci School International Duhok
Maf Street, Malta Sari Qr., Zone 99450, Duhok, Kurdistan 42001
Tel: +964 750 757 4333
Age range: 4–18 years
Curriculum: IBDP, IBMYP, IBPYP
Language instr: English

Da Vinci School International Erbil
Close to West Emergency Hospital, Erbil, Kurdistan 44001
Tel: +964 751 933 2323
Curriculum: IBPYP
Language instr: English, Kurdish

Deutsche Schule Erbil
Postfach 67, Post Office Newroz, 100-Meter-Street, Erbil, Kurdistan
Tel: +964 750 335 9848
Age range: G4–18 years
Curriculum: Abitur, IBDP
Language instr: German

Eastwood International School Erbil
Baharka Road, Opposite 150m Roundabout, Erbil
Tel: +964 751 157 1313
Age range: 3–16 years
Curriculum: IBPYP, USA
Language instr: English

Global United School
Al-Masafi Intersection, First Branch On The Right, Behind Al-Hayat Mall, Before Dijlah College, Al-Doura +, Baghdad
Tel: +964 782 714 9199
Age range: 6–16 years
Curriculum: IBPYP
Language instr: English

International College University School (ICUS) Baghdad
ICUS Road, Baghdad
Tel: +964 773 222 1115
Age range: 4–12 years
Curriculum: IBPYP, National
Language instr: English

International Maarif Schools Erbil
P.O. Box No. 43/0383, Mardin District, 120m Street, Opposite to Toreq Village, Erbil, Kurdistan
Tel: +964 751 741 7879
Age range: 4–18 years
Curriculum: IBDP, IBMYP, IBPYP
Language instr: Arabic, English, Kurdish, Turkish

Mar Qardakh School
P.O. Box 34, Mar Qardakh Street, Ankawa, Erbil, Kurdistan 1065
Tel: +964 750 144 5021
Age range: 4–16 years
Curriculum: IBMYP, IBPYP
Language instr: English

Meltho International School
Area 128, near Umm Al-Nour Church Ankawa, Erbil, Kurdistan
Tel: +964 750 506 4040
Age range: 4–18 years
Curriculum: AP, SAT, UK, USA, IGCSE

The International School of Choueifat - Dream City
100 Meter Street, Dream City, Erbil, Kurdistan
Tel: +964 750 373 9444
Age range: 4–10 years

The International School of Choueifat - Erbil
Massif Road, Khanzad Area, Erbil, Kurdistan
Tel: +964 750 416 4444
Age range: 4–18 years

The International School of Choueifat - Sulaimani
Qasimlu Street, Sulaimani, Kurdistan
Tel: +964 53 328 5412
Age range: 4–18 years

ISRAEL

Anglican International School Jerusalem
82 Rechov Hanevi'im, 91001 Jerusalem
Tel: +972 2 567 7200
Age range: 2–18 years
Curriculum: IBDP, IBMYP, UK, USA
Language instr: English

Collège Français de Tel-Aviv Marc Chagall
24 Rehov Chelouch, 61500 Tel-Aviv
Tel: +972 3 517 2429
Curriculum: FrenchBacc

Jerusalem American International School
24 Sderot Shai Agnon Street, San Simon, Goldstein Youth Village, Jerusalem
Tel: +972 2 679 9611
Age range: 3–13 years
Curriculum: USA

King Solomon School
HaKfar HaYarok, 47100 Ramat Hasharon
Tel: +972 73 234 2030
Curriculum: IBDP, UK
Language instr: English, Hebrew

La Salle Beit Hanina
P.O. Box 60076, 24 Taha Hussein, Beit Hanina, 9160102 Jerusalem
Tel: +972 2 585 5764
Curriculum: IBDP
Language instr: English, Arabic

Lycée Français de Jérusalem
B.P. 1731, 66 Haneviim Street, 9514117 Jerusalem
Tel: +972 2 538 4102
Age range: 4–18 years
Curriculum: FrenchBacc

Tabeetha School
P.O. Box 8710, 21 Jeffet Street, 61081 Jaffa
Tel: +972 3 6821581/19357
Age range: 4–18 years
Curriculum: UK, GCSE, IGCSE, ALevs
Language instr: English

Talitha Kumi School
P.O. Box 7, Beit Jala
Tel: +972 2 274 1247
Age range: 3–18 years
Curriculum: Abitur, National

TreeHouse International School (T.H.I.S.)
Wingate 70 / Ramat Yam 55, Herzliya Pituah, Herzliya
Tel: +972 52 256 5059
Age range: 1–18 years
Curriculum: IBDP, USA
Language instr: English

Walworth Barbour American International School
P.O. Box 484, 65 Hashomron Street, 4051765 Even Yehuda
Tel: +972 9 890 1000
Age range: 4–18 years
Curriculum: USA

JAPAN

ABC International School
2-11-8 Moto-Azabu, Minato-ku, Tokyo, Kanto 106-0046
Tel: +81 36 812 6737
Age range: 1–7 years

Abroad International School - Okayama
Yanagimachi 1-10-9, Kita-ku, Okayama, Chugoku 700-0904
Tel: +81 86 221 0144
Age range: 1–7 years
Curriculum: IBPYP
Language instr: English, Japanese

Abroad International School - Osaka
1-3-2 2-Chome-14-3, Hayashiji, Ikuno Ward, Osaka, Kansai 544-0023
Tel: +81 06 6716 3381
Age range: 1–13 years
Curriculum: IBMYP, IBPYP
Language instr: English, Japanese

AIC World College of Hiroshima Elementary School
13-13 Osugacho, Minami-ku, Hiroshima, Chugoku 732-0821
Curriculum: IBPYP
Language instr: English, Japanese

Aichi International School
Nijigaoka 3-4, Meito-ku, Nagoya, Aichi, Chubu 465-0078
Tel: +81 52 788 2255
Age range: 3–11 years
Curriculum: National
Language instr: English, Japanese

AICJ Junior & Senior High School
3-1-15 Gion, Asaminami-ku, Hiroshima, Chugoku 731-0138
Tel: +81 82 832 5037
Curriculum: IBDP
Language instr: English

AIE International High School
1-48 Hama, Awaji, Hyogo, Kansai 656-2304
Tel: +81 79 974 0020
Curriculum: IBDP
Language instr: English

Angel Kindergarten
80-6 Ojiri Shimonagakubo, Nagaizumi, Shizuoka, Chubu 411-0934
Tel: +81 55 987 5323
Curriculum: IBPYP
Language instr: English, Japanese

Aoba-Japan Bilingual Preschool - Harumi Campus
Harumi Triton Square 2F, 1-8-2 Harumi, Chuo-ku, Tokyo, Kanto 104-0053
Tel: +81 36 228 1811
Age range: 1–7 years
Curriculum: IBPYP
Language instr: English, Japanese

Asia

Aoba-Japan Bilingual Preschool - Mitaka Campus
4-15-41 Shimorenjaku, Mitaka, Tokyo, Kanto 181-0013
Tel: +81 42 229 8977
Age range: 1–7 years
Curriculum: IBPYP
Language instr: English, Japanese

Aoba-Japan Bilingual Preschool - Nakano Campus
2F Imasu Nakano Minamidai, Crystal Court 88, 3-6-17 Minamidai, Nakano-ku, Tokyo, Kanto 164-0014
Tel: +81 36 380 3218
Age range: 1–7 years
Curriculum: IBPYP
Language instr: English, Japanese

Aoba-Japan Bilingual Preschool - Shimomeguro Campus
5-29-6 Shimomeguro, Meguro-ku, Tokyo, Kanto 153-0064
Tel: +81 35 734 1640
Curriculum: IBPYP
Language instr: English, Japanese

Aoba-Japan Bilingual Preschool - Waseda Campus
Chiyoda Building No. 2, 1-14-8 Takadanobaba, Shinjuku-ku, Tokyo, Kanto 169-0075
Tel: +81 36 385 2818
Age range: 1–7 years
Curriculum: IBPYP
Language instr: English, Japanese

Aoba-Japan International School
7-5-1 Hikarigaoka, Nerima-ku, Tokyo 179-0072
Tel: +81 3 4578 8832
Age range: 2–19 years
No. of pupils: 800
Curriculum: IBDP, IBMYP, IBPYP
Language instr: English

Asahijuku Secondary School
2590 Mitsushitori, Kita-ku, Okayama, Chugoku 709-2136
Tel: +81 86 726 0111
Curriculum: IBDP, IBMYP
Language instr: English, Japanese

Beyondia International School Ikebukuro
9th Floor, Higashi-Ikebukuro Center Building, 4-41-24 Higashi-Ikebukuro, Toshima-ku, Tokyo, Kanto 170-0013
Tel: +81 36 912 6912
Curriculum: IBPYP
Language instr: English, Japanese

Bright Kids Garden International School Kokura
3-2-27 Muromachi Glocal Building 5F, Kokurakita-ku, Kitakyushu, Fukuoka, Kyushu 803-0812
Tel: +81 93 583 8555
Age range: 3–6 years
Language instr: English

Canadian Academy
4-1 Koyo-Cho Naka, Higashinada-ku, Kobe, Hyogo, Kansai 658-0032
Tel: +81 78 857 0100
Age range: 3–18 years
Curriculum: IBDP, IBMYP, IBPYP
Language instr: English

Canadian International School Tokyo
5-8-20 Kitashinagawa, Shinagawa-ku, Tokyo, Kanto 141-0001
Tel: +81 35 793 1392
Age range: 3–18 years
Curriculum: AP, IBPYP
Language instr: English

CGK International School
2F, 6-75 Otamachi, Naka-ku, Yokohama, Kanagawa, Kanto 231-0011
Tel: +81 45 228 9397
Curriculum: IBPYP
Language instr: English, Japanese

Christian Academy in Japan
1-2-14 Shinkawa-cho, Higashikurume, Tokyo, Kanto 203-0013
Tel: +81 42 471 0022
Age range: 4–18 years
Curriculum: USA
Language instr: English

Chuo International School
VORT Shintomicho Building 4F, 3-5-10 Minato, Chuo-ku, Tokyo, Kanto 104-0043
Age range: 4 months–12 years

Columbia International School
153 Matsugo, Tokorozawa, Saitama, Kanto 359-0027
Tel: +81 42 946 1911
Age range: 4–18 years
Language instr: English

Deutsche Schule Kobe International (DSKI)
3-2-8 Koyochonaka, Higashinada-ku, Kobe, Hyogo, Kansai 658-0032
Tel: +81 78 857 9777
Age range: 2–11 years
Curriculum: Abitur, IBPYP
Language instr: English, German, Japanese

Deutsche Schule Tokyo Yokohama
2-4-1 Chigasaki Minami, Tsuzuki-ku, Yokohama, Kanagawa, Kanto 224-0037
Tel: +81 45 941 4841
Age range: 4–18 years

Doshisha International Academy (DIA) Elementary School
7-31-1 Kizugawadai, Kizugawa, Kyoto, Kansai 619-0225
Tel: +81 77 471 0810
Curriculum: IBPYP
Language instr: English

Doshisha International School, Kyoto
7-31-1 Kizugawadai, Kizugawa, Kyoto, Kansai 619-0225
Tel: +81 77 471 0810
Age range: 11–18 years
Curriculum: IBDP
Language instr: English

Eisugakkan School
980-1 Hikino-cho, Fukuyama, Hiroshima, Chugoku 721-8502
Tel: +81 84 941 4115
Age range: 4–18 years
Curriculum: IBDP, IBPYP
Language instr: English, Japanese

Enishi International School
2-12-32 Kikui Nishi Ward, Nagoya, Aichi 451-0044
Tel: +81 52 581 0700
Age range: 1–18 years
Curriculum: IBDP, IBMYP, IBPYP
Language instr: English, Japanese

Everest International School, Japan
1-19-10 Ogikubo, Suginami-ku, Tokyo, Kanto 167-0051
Tel: +81 35 335 7379
Age range: 3–18 years

Fukuoka Daiichi High School
22-1 Tamagawa-cho, Minami-ku, Fukuoka, Kyushu 815-0037
Tel: +81 92 541 0165
Curriculum: IBDP
Language instr: English, Japanese

Fukuoka International School
3-18-50 Momochi, Sawara-ku, Fukuoka, Kyushu 814-0006
Tel: +81 92 841 7601
Age range: 3–18 years
Curriculum: IBDP, IBMYP, IBPYP
Language instr: English

Global Indian International School (GIIS) Higashi Kasai Campus
9-3-6 Higashikasai, Edogawa-ku, Tokyo, Kanto 134-0084
Tel: +81 35 676 5081
Age range: 11–18 years
Curriculum: IBDP, IBPYP, IGCSE
Language instr: English, Japanese

Global Indian International School (GIIS) Nishi Kasai Campus
8-3-13 Nishikasai, Edogawa-ku, Tokyo, Kanto 134-0088
Tel: +81 35 696 7141
Age range: 4–11 years

Global Indian International School (GIIS) Seishincho Campus
2-10-1 Seishincho, Edogawa-ku, Tokyo, Kanto 134-0087
Tel: +81 33 686 3055
Age range: 3–6 years

Green Hills Elementary School/Junior High School
1-531 Tomita, Nagano, Chubu 380-0882
Tel: +81 26 239 0571
Curriculum: IBPYP
Language instr: English, Japanese

GREGG International School
1-14-6 Jiyugaoka, Meguro-ku, Tokyo, Kanto 152-0035
Tel: +81 33 725 8000
Age range: 3–11 years

Gunma Kokusai Academy
1361-4 Uchigashima-cho, Ota, Gunma, Kanto 373-0813
Tel: +81 27 647 7711
Curriculum: IBDP, IBMYP
Language instr: English, Japanese

Harrow International School Appi
180-8 Appikogen, Hachimantai, Iwate 028-7306
Tel: +81 19 573 5377
Age range: 11–18 years
No. of pupils: 250
Curriculum: UK, IGCSE, ALevs
Language instr: English

Hiroshima International School
3-49-1 Kurakake, Asakita-ku, Hiroshima, Chugoku 739-1743
Tel: +81 82 843 4111
Age range: 3–18 years
Curriculum: IBDP, IBMYP, IBPYP
Language instr: English

Hokkaido International School
1-55 5-jo, 19-chome, Hiragishi, Toyohira-ku, Sapporo, Hokkaido 062-0935
Tel: +81 11 816 5000
Age range: 3–18 years
Curriculum: AP, IPC

Hokkaido International School, Niseko
12 Aza Fujimi, Niseko, Hokkaido 048-1501
Tel: +81 13 655 5252
Age range: 3–13 years
Curriculum: IPC

Horizon Academy Sendai Campus
4-2-540 Takamori, Izumi-ku, Sendai, Miyagi, Tohoku 981-3203
Tel: +81 22 739 9622
Age range: 3–11 years
Curriculum: IBPYP
Language instr: English, Japanese

Horizon Japan International School
1-24 Onocho, Kanagawa-ku, Yokohama, Kanagawa, Kanto 221-0055
Tel: +81 45 624 8717
Age range: 3–18 years
Curriculum: IBDP, IBMYP, IBPYP
Language instr: English, Japanese

Asia

Hosei University Kokusai High School
1-13-1 Kishiya, Tsurumi-ku, Yokohama, Kanagawa, Kanto 230-0078
Tel: +81 45 571 4482
Curriculum: IBDP
Language instr: English, Japanese

Ikuei Nishi Jr. & Sr. High School
4-637-1 Mimatsu, Nara, Kansai 631-0074
Tel: +81 74 247 0688
Curriculum: IBMYP
Language instr: English, Japanese

India International School in Japan
3-1-4 Sengoku, Koto-ku, Tokyo, Kanto 135-0015
Tel: +81 35 875 5435
Age range: 4–18 years
Curriculum: IBDP
Language instr: English

International School of Nagano
7779-1 Shimauchi, Matsumoto, Nagano, Chubu 390-0851
Tel: +81 26 387 5971
Age range: 0–13 years
Curriculum: IBPYP
Language instr: English

International School of the Sacred Heart
4-3-1 Hiroo, Shibuya-ku, Tokyo, Kanto 150-0012
Tel: +81 33 400 3951
Age range: B4–6 years G4–18 years
Curriculum: AP
Language instr: English

Joy to the World American International School
Koishikawa 5-11-17 2F, Bunkyo-ku, Tokyo, Kanto 112-0002
Tel: +81 35 684 0247
Age range: 1–11 years
Curriculum: USA

K. International School Tokyo (KIST)
1-5-15 Shirakawa, Koto-ku, Tokyo, Kanto 135-0021
Tel: +81 33 642 9993
Age range: 3–18 years
Curriculum: IBDP, IBPYP
Language instr: English

Kagoshima Shugakukan Junior & Senior High School
2-9-1 Nagayoshi, Kagoshima, Kyushu 890-0023
Tel: +81 99 258 2211
Curriculum: IBMYP
Language instr: English, Japanese

Kaichi Junior & Senior High School
186 Tokuriki, Iwatsuki-ku, Saitama, Kanto 339-0004
Tel: +81 48 795 0777
Curriculum: IBDP
Language instr: English, Japanese

Kaichi Nihonbashi Gakuen Junior & Senior High School
2-7-6 Bakurocho, Nihonbashi, Chuo-ku, Tokyo, Kanto 103-8384
Tel: +81 33 662 2507
Age range: 11–18 years
Curriculum: IBDP, IBMYP
Language instr: English, Japanese

Kaichi Nozomi Primary & Secondary School
3400 Tsutsudoaza-suwa, Tsukubamirai, Ibaraki, Kanto 300-2435
Tel: +81 29 738 6000
Age range: 6–18 years
Curriculum: IBDP, IBMYP, IBPYP
Language instr: English, Japanese

KAIS International School
3-10-60 Kami-Osaki, Shinagawa-ku, Tokyo, Kanto 141-0021
Tel: +81 35 421 0127
Age range: 4–18 years
Curriculum: AP, USA
Language instr: English

Kansai Christian School
282-2 Oaza Misato, Heguri-cho, Ikoma-gun, Nara, Kansai 636-0904
Tel: +81 74 545 6422
Age range: 6–18 years
Curriculum: USA

Kansai International Academy
Abeno Lucius 7F, 1-5-1 Abenosuji, Abeno-ku, Osaka, Kansai 545-0052
Age range: 0–18 years
Curriculum: IBDP, IBMYP, IBPYP
Language instr: English, Japanese

Karugamo English School
987-7 Mimuro, Midori-ku, Saitama, Kanto 336-0911
Tel: +81 48 873 8558
Age range: 1–6 years
Curriculum: IBPYP
Language instr: English

Katoh Gakuen Gyoshu Junior & Senior High School
1361-1 Okanomiya, Numazu, Shizuoka, Chubu 410-0011
Tel: +81 55 924 3322
Age range: 3–18 years
Curriculum: IBDP, IBMYP
Language instr: English, Japanese

Keiki Intercultural Preschool
4-5-8 Nakamachi, Setagaya, Tokyo, Kanto 158-0091
Tel: +81 33 703 8778
Age range: 1–8 years
Curriculum: IBPYP
Language instr: English

Kensington School
Noguchi Building 3F, 2-3-3 Sanno, Ota-ku, Tokyo, Kanto 143-0023
Tel: +81 33 774 8686
Language instr: English

Kids Tairiku Frontown Ikuta
1-1-1 Ikuta, Tama-ku, Kawasaki, Kanagawa, Kanto 214-0038
Tel: +81 44 819 6613
Age range: 1–6 years
Curriculum: IBPYP
Language instr: English, Japanese

Kindai University High School
5-3-1 Wakaenishishinmachi, Higashiosaka, Osaka, Kansai 578-0944
Tel: +81 66 722 1261
Curriculum: IBDP
Language instr: English, Japanese

Kobe Bilingual School
7-1-25 Momoyamadai, Tarumi-ku, Kobe, Hyogo 655-0854
Tel: +81 78 742 7101
Age range: 3–12 years
Curriculum: IBPYP
Language instr: English, Japanese

Korea International School
2-13-35 Toyooka, Ibaraki, Osaka, Kansai 567-0057
Tel: +81 72 643 4200
Curriculum: IBDP
Language instr: Korean, Japanese

Kouhoku School Corporation - Certified Child Center Ainosato
4-jo 6-2-5 Ainosato, Kita-ku, Sapporo, Hokkaido 002-8074
Tel: +81 11 778 7272
Age range: 2–6 years
Curriculum: IBPYP
Language instr: English, Japanese

Kumamoto International School
2-18-8 Nishihara, Higashi-ku, Kumamoto, Kyushu 861-8029
Tel: +81 96 285 3938
Age range: 6–11 years
Curriculum: IBPYP
Language instr: English, Japanese

Kyoto International School
317 Kitatawara-cho, Kamigyo-ku, Kyoto, Kansai 602-8247
Tel: +81 75 451 1022
Age range: 4–18 years
Curriculum: IBMYP, IBPYP
Language instr: English

Learning Tree International School
5-6-30 Kiba, Koto-ku, Tokyo, Kanto 135-0042
Tel: +81 35 809 8900
Age range: 6 months–11 years
Curriculum: USA

Liberty International School
342-16 Shimohiratsuka, Tsukuba, Ibaraki, Kanto 305-0813
Tel: +81 29 855 0177
Age range: 4–18 years
Curriculum: SAT, USA

Linden Hall High School
3-10-1 Futsukaichikita, Chikushino, Fukuoka, Kyushu 818-0056
Tel: +81 92 929 4558
Age range: 12–18 years
No. of pupils: 80
Curriculum: IBDP
Language instr: English, Japanese

Lycée français international de Kyoto
411 Motoshinmeicho, Tominokojidori Gojo agaru, Shimogyo-ku, Kyoto, Kansai 600-8065
Tel: +81 75 354 5240
Age range: 3–18 years
Curriculum: FrenchBacc
Language instr: French, Japanese

Lycée français international de Tokyo
5-57-37 Takinogawa, Kita-ku, Tokyo, Kanto 114-0023
Tel: +81 36 823 6580
Age range: 3–18 years
Curriculum: FrenchBacc
Language instr: French, Japanese

Machida Kobato Kindergarten
2904 Honmachida, Machida, Tokyo, Kanto 194-0032
Tel: +81 42 723 1494
Age range: 0–6 years
Curriculum: IBPYP
Language instr: English, Japanese

Makuhari International School
3-2-9 Wakaba, Mihama-ku, Chiba, Kanto 261-0014
Tel: +81 43 296 0277
Age range: 3–12 years
Curriculum: National
Language instr: English, Japanese

Malvern College Tokyo
3-2-1 Josuiminamicho, Kodaira, Tokyo, Kanto 187-0021
Tel: +81 42 312 4008
Age range: 3–18 years
Curriculum: IBMYP, IBPYP
Language instr: English, Japanese

Marist Brothers International School
1-2-1 Chimori-cho, Suma-ku, Kobe, Hyogo, Kansai 654-0072
Tel: +81 78 732 6266
Age range: 3–18 years
Curriculum: IBDP, USA
Language instr: English

Matsumoto Kokusai High School
3-6-25 Minami, Murai-cho, Matsumoto, Nagano, Chubu 399-0036
Tel: +81 26 388 0033
Age range: 13–18 years
Curriculum: IBDP
Language instr: English, Japanese

Meikei High School
1-1 Inarimae, Tsukuba, Ibaraki, Kanto 305-8502
Tel: +81 29 851 6611
Age range: 12–18 years
Curriculum: IBDP
Language instr: English, Japanese

Miura Gakuen High School
3-80 Kinugasa-sakaecho, Yokosuka, Kanagawa 238-0031
Tel: +81 46 852 0284
Curriculum: IBDP
Language instr: English, Japanese

Asia

Mizuho School
3-2-25, Shakujiidai, Nerima-ku, Tokyo, Kanto 177-0045
Tel: +81 35 372 1525
Age range: 1–6 years
Curriculum: IBPYP
Language instr: English

Musashino University Chiyoda High School
11 Yonbancho, Chiyoda-ku, Tokyo, Kanto 102-0081
Tel: +81 33 263 6551
Curriculum: IBDP
Language instr: English, Japanese

Nagano Nihon University School of Education
253 Higashiwada, Nagano, Chubu 381-0038
Tel: +81 26 243 1079
Curriculum: IBDP
Language instr: English, Japanese

Nagoya International School
2686 Minamihara, Nakashidami, Moriyama-ku, Nagoya, Aichi, Chubu 463-0002
Tel: +81 52 736 2025
Age range: 3–18 years
Curriculum: IBDP, IBMYP, IBPYP
(CIS)

New International School of Japan
3-18-32 Minami-Ikebukuro, Toshima-ku, Tokyo, Kanto 171-0022
Tel: +81 33 980 1057
Age range: 3–18 years
Language instr: English, Japanese

Nishimachi International School
2-14-7 Moto Azabu, Minato-ku, Tokyo, Kanto 106-0046
Tel: +81 33 451 5520
Age range: 4–14 years
Language instr: English
(CIS) (EAR)

NUCB International College
4-4 Sagamine Komenoki, Nisshin, Aichi, Chubu 470-0193
Tel: +81 56 173 8181
Age range: 15–18 years
No. of pupils: 100
Curriculum: IBDP
Language instr: English, Japanese

NUCB International Junior & Senior High School
1-16 Hiroji Honmachi, Showa-ku, Nagoya, Aichi, Chubu 466-0841
Tel: +81 52 858 2200
Age range: 13–18 years
Curriculum: IBDP, IBMYP
Language instr: English

Okayama University of Science High School
1-1 Riomachi, Kita-ku, Okayama, Chugoku 700-0005
Tel: +81 86 256 8511
Curriculum: IBDP
Language instr: English, Japanese

Okinawa Christian School International
1835 Zakimi, Yomitan, Nakagami-cho, Okinawa, Kyushu 904-0301
Tel: +81 98 958 3000
Age range: 3–18 years

Okinawa International School
143 Tamagusukufusato, Nanjo, Okinawa, Kyushu 901-0611
Tel: +81 98 948 7711
Age range: 3–14 years
Curriculum: IBDP, IBMYP, IBPYP
Language instr: English, Japanese

Okinawa Shogaku School
747 Kokuba, Naha, Okinawa, Kyushu 902-0075
Tel: +81 98 832 1767
Age range: 12–18 years
Curriculum: IBDP
Language instr: English, Japanese

One World International School (OWIS) Osaka
3-1-39 Shariji, Ikuno-ku, Osaka, Kansai 544-0022
Tel: +81 66 715 6855
Age range: 3–18 years

One World International School (OWIS) Tsukuba
1400 Kunimatsu, Tsukuba, Ibaraki, Kanto 300-4354
Age range: 3–18 years

Osaka International High School
1-28 Matsushita-cho, Moriguchi-shi, Osaka, Kansai 570-8787
Tel: +81 66 992 5931
Curriculum: IBDP
Language instr: English, Japanese

Osaka International School of Kwansei Gakuin
4-4-16 Onohara-nishi, Minoh, Osaka, Kansai 562-0032
Tel: +81 72 727 5050
Age range: 4–18 years
Curriculum: IBDP, IBMYP, IBPYP
Language instr: English
(CIS) (EAR)

Osaka Jogakuin Senior High School
2-26-54 Tamatsukuri, Chuo-ku, Osaka, Kansai 540-0004
Tel: +81 66 761 4451
Age range: 12–18 years
Curriculum: IBDP, National
Language instr: English, Japanese

Osaka YMCA International School
6-7-34 Nakatsu, Kita-ku, Osaka, Kansai 531-0071
Tel: +81 66 345 1661
Age range: 4–18 years
Curriculum: IBDP, IBMYP, IBPYP
Language instr: English
(EAR) (ECIS)

Phoenix House International School
3-7 Yonban-cho, Chiyoda-ku, Tokyo, Kanto 102-0081
Tel: +81 35 530 7406
Age range: 5–11 years
Curriculum: UK
Language instr: English

Ritsumeikan Uji Junior and Senior High School
33-1 Hachikenyadani, Hirono-cho, Uji, Kyoto, Kansai 611-0031
Tel: +81 774 41 3000
Age range: 12–17 years
No. of pupils: 1749
Curriculum: IBDP
Language instr: English, Japanese

Rugby School Japan
6-2-5 Kashiwanoha, Kashiwa, Chiba, Kanto 277-0882
Tel: +81 471 68 0536
Age range: 11–18 years
No. of pupils: 140 VIth15
Curriculum: IGCSE, ALevs

Sai Sishya International School
2-12-8 Naka Kasai, Edogawa-ku, Tokyo, Kanto 134-0083
Tel: +81 36 808 9230
Curriculum: IBPYP
Language instr: English, Japanese

Saint Maur International School
83 Yamate-cho, Naka-ku, Yokohama, Kanagawa, Kanto 231-0862
Tel: +81 45 641 5751
Age range: 2.5–18 years
Curriculum: IBDP, SAT, IGCSE
Language instr: English, French
(CIS)

Sapporo Nihon University High School
5-7-1 Nijigaoka, Kitahiroshima, Hokkaido 061-1103
Tel: +81 11 375 5311
Age range: 13–18 years
Curriculum: IBDP
Language instr: English, Japanese

Seirei Gakuen
3453 Mikatabara, Chuo-Ku, Hamamatsu, Shizuoka, Chubu 433-8558
Tel: +81 53 436 5311
Curriculum: IBPYP
Language instr: English, Japanese

Seisen International School
1-12-15 Yoga, Setagaya-ku, Tokyo, Kanto 158-0097
Tel: 81 33 704 2661
Age range: B2–5 years G2–18 years
Curriculum: IBDP, IBMYP, IBPYP, SAT
Language instr: English

Sendai Ikuei Gakuen High School
2-4-1 Miyagino, Miyagino-ku, Sendai, Miyagi, Tohoku 983-0045
Tel: +81 22 256 4141
Age range: 12–18 years
No. of pupils: 3150
Curriculum: IBDP, IBMYP
Language instr: English, Japanese

Senri International School of Kwansei Gakuin
4-4-16 Onohara-nishi, Minoh, Osaka, Kansai 562-0032
Tel: +81 72 727 5050
Age range: 12–18 years
Curriculum: National
Language instr: English

Seta International School
27-12, Seta 1-chome, Setagaya-ku, Tokyo, Kanto 158-0095
Tel: +81 35 717 6769
Age range: 3–6 years

Shinagawa International School
3-6-21 Minamishinagawa, Shinagawa, Tokyo, Kanto 140-0004
Tel: +81 36 433 1531
Age range: 3–18 years
Curriculum: IBDP, IBMYP, IBPYP
Language instr: English
(CIS)

Shizuoka Salesio School
3-2-1 Nakanogo, Shimizu-ku, Shizuoka, Chubu 424-8624
Tel: +81 54 345 2296
Age range: 4–18 years
Curriculum: IBDP, IBMYP, IBPYP
Language instr: English, Japanese

Shohei Junior & Senior High School
851 Shimono, Sugito, Saitama, Kanto 345-0044
Tel: +81 48 034 3381
Age range: 12–18 years
Curriculum: IBDP, IBMYP
Language instr: English, Japanese

Shukou Junior High School
2-4-1 Miyagino, Miyagino-ku, Sendai, Miyagi, Tohoku 985-0853
Tel: +81 22 256 4141
Age range: 12–16 years
Curriculum: IBMYP
Language instr: English, Japanese

St Michael's International School
3-17-2 Nakayamatedori, Chuo-ku, Kobe, Hyogo, Kansai 650-0004
Tel: +81 78 231 8885
Age range: 3–11 years
Curriculum: IPC
Language instr: English
(CIS) (COB)

St. Joseph's Junior High & Senior High School
11-1 Higashterao Kitadai, Tsurumi-ku, Yokohama, Kanagawa, Kanto 230-0016
Tel: +81 45 581 8808
Curriculum: IBMYP
Language instr: English, Japanese

Asia

St. Joseph's Primary School
11-1 Higashterao Kitadai, Tsurumi-ku, Yokohama, Kanagawa, Kanto 230-0016
Tel: +81 45 581 8808
Age range: 6–11 years
Curriculum: IBPYP
Language instr: English, Japanese

St. Mary's International School
1-6-19 Seta, Setagaya-ku, Tokyo, Kanto 158-8668
Tel: +81 33 709 3411
Age range: B4–18 years
Curriculum: IBDP
Language instr: English

Summerhill International School
2-13-8 Moto-Azabu, Minato-ku, Tokyo, Kanto 106-0046
Tel: +81 35 453 0811
Age range: 15 months–6 years
Curriculum: IBPYP
Language instr: English, Japanese

Sunnyside International School
4-10-25 Iwai, Gifu, Chubu 501-3101
Tel: +81 58 241 1000
Age range: 4–11 years
Curriculum: IBPYP
Language instr: English, Japanese

Sunshine Kids Academy
VORT Shintomicho Building 4F, 3-5-10 Minato, Chuo-ku, Tokyo, Kanto 104-0043
Age range: 4 months–12 years

Tamagawa Academy K-12 & University
6-1-1 Tamagawa Gakuen, Machida, Tokyo, Kanto 194-8610
Tel: +81 42 739 8111
Age range: 4–18 years
Curriculum: IBDP, IBMYP
Language instr: English

Teikyo University Kani Junior & Senior High School
1-1 Katsuragaoka, Kani, Gifu, Chubu 509-0237
Tel: +81 57 464 3211
Age range: 12–18 years
Curriculum: IBDP
Language instr: English, Japanese

The American School in Japan
1-1-1 Nomizu, Chofu, Tokyo, Kanto 182-0031
Tel: +81 42 234 5300
Age range: 3–18 years
Curriculum: AP, USA
Language instr: English

The British School in Tokyo
1-3-3 Azabudai, Minato-ku, Tokyo, Kanto 106-0041
Tel: +81 35 544 9160
Age range: 3–18 years
Curriculum: IBDP, UK, GCSE, IGCSE, ALevs
Language instr: English

The Montessori School of Tokyo
3-5-13 Minami Azabu, Minato-ku, Tokyo, Kanto 106-0047
Tel: +81 35 449 7067
Age range: 2–15 years

Tohoku International School
7-101-1 Yakata, Izumi-ku, Sendai, Miyagi, Tohoku 981-3214
Tel: +81 22 348 2468
Age range: 4–18 years
Curriculum: IBDP, IBPYP
Language instr: English, Japanese

Tokai Gakuen High School
2-901 Nakahira, Tenpaku-ku, Nagoya, Aichi, Chubu 468-0014
Tel: +81 52 801 6222
Language instr: English, Japanese

Tokyo International School
2-13-6 Minami Azabu, Minato-ku, Tokyo, Kanto 106-0047
Tel: +81 35 484 1160
Age range: 4–16 years
Curriculum: IBMYP, IBPYP
Language instr: English

Tokyo West International School
185 Umetsubo-machi, Hachioji, Tokyo, Kanto 192-0013
Tel: +81 42 691 1441
Age range: 2–16 years
Curriculum: IBPYP
Language instr: English

Torisawa Kindergarten
1973-1 Torisawa, Otsuki, Yamanashi, Chubu 409-0502
Curriculum: IBPYP
Language instr: English, Japanese

Tsukuba International School
Kamigo 7846-1, Tsukuba, Ibaraki, Kanto 300-2645
Tel: +81 29 886 5447
Age range: 3–18 years
Curriculum: IBDP, IBMYP, IBPYP
Language instr: English

UIA International School of Tokyo
3-14-4 Kiba, Koto-ku, Tokyo 135-0042
Tel: +81 35 646 5280
Age range: 4–18 years
Curriculum: UK, IGCSE, ALevs

UPBEAT International School - Atsuta Campus
2-3-18 Hachiban, Atsuta-ku, Nagoya, Aichi, Chubu
Tel: +81 52 661 3155
Age range: 0–12 years
Curriculum: IBPYP
Language instr: English, Japanese

UPBEAT International School - Nakagawa Campus
1-5-1 Kohoncho, Nakagawa-ku, Nagoya, Aichi, Chubu
Tel: +81 52 398 6015
Age range: 0–12 years
Language instr: English, Japanese

UPBEAT International School - Tempaku Campus
201 Shimadagaoka, Tempaku-ku, Nagoya, Aichi, Chubu
Tel: +81 12 080 3768
Age range: 0–12 years
Language instr: English, Japanese

Urawagakuin High School
172 Daiyama, Midori Ward, Saitama City, Saitama, Kanto 336-0975
Tel: +81 48 878 2101
Curriculum: IBDP
Language instr: English, Japanese

UWC ISAK Japan
5827-136 Nagakura, Karuizawa-machi, Kitasaku-gun, Nagano, Chubu 389-0111
Tel: +81 26 746 8623
Age range: 15–18 years
Curriculum: IBDP
Language instr: English

Wakakusa Kindergarten
3-15-4 Yoshida, Nagano, Chubu 381-0043
Tel: +81 26 241 4151
Age range: 2–6 years
Curriculum: IBPYP
Language instr: English, Japanese

Willowbrook International School
2-14-28 Moto-azabu, Minato-ku, Tokyo, Kanto 106-0046
Tel: +81 33 449 9030
Age range: 1.5–6 years
Curriculum: IBPYP
Language instr: English, Japanese

Yamanashi Gakuin School
3-3-1 Sakaori, Kofu, Yamanashi, Chubu 400-0805
Tel: +81 55 233 1111
Age range: 2–18+ years
Curriculum: IBDP, IBPYP
Language instr: English, Japanese

Yamata Kindergarten
351-1 Higashiyamatacho, Tsuzuki-ku, Yokohama, Kanagawa, Kanto 224-0024
Tel: +81 45 592 4850
Age range: 1.5–6 years
Curriculum: IBPYP
Language instr: Japanese

Yokohama International School
2-100-1 Kominato-cho, Naka-ku, Yokohama, Kanagawa, Kanto 231-0802
Tel: +81 45 622 0084
Age range: 3–18 years
Curriculum: IBDP, IBMYP, IBPYP
Language instr: English

Yoyogi International School
5-67-5 Yoyogi, Shibuya-ku, Tokyo, Kanto 151-0053
Tel: +81 35 478 6714
Age range: 4–13 years
Curriculum: IBPYP, UK, USA
Language instr: English

JORDAN

Abdul Hamid Sharaf School
P.O. Box 6008, Amman 11118
Tel: +962 6 592 4188
Age range: 4–18 years
Curriculum: ACT, UK, USA, GCSE, IGCSE
Language instr: English, Arabic

Ahliyyah & Mutran
13 Rifa'ah Al Tahtawi Street, Amman
Tel: +962 6 222 1100
Age range: G4–18 years
Curriculum: IBDP, IBMYP, IBPYP, IBCP
Language instr: English, Arabic

Al Assriya Schools
P.O. Box 1002, Amman 11821
Tel: +962 6 533 7267
Age range: 3–18 years
Curriculum: National, UK, IGCSE

Al Ittihad International School
Aws bin Hajar Street, Opp. Princess Tharwat College, Sports City area, Amman
Tel: +962 6 565 8000 (Ext:4)
Age range: 4–18 years
Curriculum: UK, USA, IGCSE

Al-Ra'ed Al-Arabi School
Ahmad Orabi Street, Amman
Tel: +962 6 566 6449
Age range: 4–18 years
Curriculum: National, UK, IGCSE

American Community School Amman
P.O. Box 310, Amman 11831
Tel: +962 6 581 3944
Age range: 3–18 years
Curriculum: USA
Language instr: English

Amman Academy
P.O. Box 840, Khalda, Amman 11821
Tel: +962 6 537 4444
Age range: 4–18 years
Curriculum: IBDP, IBMYP, IBPYP
Language instr: English, Arabic

Amman Baccalaureate School
Al Hijaz Street, Dabouq, PO Box 441, Sweileh 11910, Amman
Tel: +962 6 541 1191
Age range: 4–18 years
Curriculum: IBDP, IBMYP, IBPYP, IBCP
Language instr: English, Arabic

Asia

Amman Baptist School
P.O.Box 17033, Amman 11195
Tel: +962 6 551 6907
Age range: 3–18 years
Curriculum: IBDP
Language instr: English, Arabic

Amman National School
P.O.Box 140565, Amman 11814
Tel: +962 6 541 1067
Age range: 4–18 years
Curriculum: IBDP, IBMYP
Language instr: English

Aqaba International School
P.O. Box 529, Palm Area, Aqaba 77110
Tel: +962 3 203 9922
Age range: 3–18 years
Curriculum: UK, IGCSE, ALevs
Language instr: English, Arabic

Asamiah International School
Khalda - Taqi El-Din al-Sabki, Amman
Tel: +962 6 5335 301
Age range: 3–18 years
No. of pupils: 916
Curriculum: IBDP, IBMYP, IBPYP
Language instr: English, Arabic

British International Academy (BIA)
P.O. Box 829, Amman 11831
Tel: +962 79 0222450
Age range: G4–18 years
Curriculum: IBDP, IBMYP, IBPYP
Language instr: English, Arabic

Cambridge High School
Al Rabia, Abdel Kareem, Al Dabbas Street, Amman 11185
Tel: +962 6 551 2556
Age range: 4–18 years
Curriculum: IBDP, IBMYP
Language instr: English, Arabic

Canadian International School - Amman
20 Al Mikyal Street, Deir Ghbar, Amman
Tel: +962 6 593 9370
Age range: 3–18 years
Curriculum: IBDP, IBMYP, IBPYP
Language instr: English

Collège De La Salle Frères
Ar-Razi Street, Amman 11110
Tel: +962 6 563 4555
Curriculum: IBDP, IBMYP
Language instr: English, Arabic

English Talents School
P.O.Box 18082, Amman 11195
Tel: +962 6 537 0201
Age range: 4–18 years
Curriculum: IBDP, IBMYP, IBPYP
Language instr: English

French international School of Amman
Al-Yadudeh, Airport Road, B.P. 830059, Amman 11183
Tel: +962 6 430 0600
Age range: 2–18 years
Curriculum: FrenchBacc

IBN Rushd National Academy
P.O. Box 940397, Amman 11194
Tel: +962 79 896 1810
Age range: 4–18 years
Curriculum: IBDP, IBMYP, IBPYP
Language instr: English, Arabic

International Community School
P.O. Box 2002, Amman 11181
Tel: +962 6 479 0666
Age range: 3–18 years
Curriculum: SAT, UK, USA, IGCSE, ALevs
Language instr: English

International Independent Schools IIS
P.O. Box 499, Marj Al-Hamam, Airport Road, Next to Petra University, Amman 11732
Tel: +962 6 573 3377
Age range: 4–18 years
Curriculum: AP, National, UK, USA, IGCSE, ALevs

Islamic Educational College
Al-Hakem An-Nisabouri Street, Amman
Tel: +962 6 464 1331
Age range: 4–18 years
Curriculum: ACT, AP, IBDP, IBMYP, UK, USA, IGCSE
Language instr: English, Arabic

Jordanian International Schools
12 Usamah Bin Munqeth Street, Amman
Tel: +962 6 562 3777
Age range: 4–18 years
Curriculum: ACT, National, SAT, UK, USA, IGCSE

Jubilee Institute
P.O. Box 830578, Amman 11183
Tel: +962 6 523 8216
Age range: 14–18 years
Curriculum: IBDP, National, UK, IGCSE
Language instr: English

King's Academy
P.O. Box 9, Madaba-Manja 16188
Tel: +962 6 430 0230
Age range: 12–18 years
Curriculum: AP, USA
Language instr: English

Mashrek International School
P.O. Box 1412, Amman 11118
Tel: +962 79 957 7771
Age range: 3–18 years
Curriculum: IBDP, IBMYP, IBPYP, National
Language instr: Arabic, English

Modern American School
P.O. Box 950553, Sweifieh, Amman 11195
Tel: +962 6 586 2779
Age range: 3–18 years
Curriculum: AP, IBDP, SAT, USA
Language instr: English, Arabic

Modern Montessori School
P.O. Box 1941, Khilda, Amman 11821
Tel: +962 6 553 5190
Age range: 3–18 years
No. of pupils: 1655
Curriculum: IBDP, IBMYP, IBPYP
Language instr: English, Arabic

National Orthodox School Shmaisani
P.O. Box 941502, 5 Al-Hajjaj Al-Sahmi Street, Shmaisani, Amman 11194
Tel: +962 6 560 8500
Age range: 4–18 years
Curriculum: IBDP, National, IGCSE, ALevs
Language instr: Arabic, English

New English School
P.O. Box 154, Amer Bin Malek Street, Amman 11821
Tel: +962 6 55 17 111
Age range: 2–18 years
Curriculum: UK, USA, IGCSE, ALevs

Oxford Schools
P.O. Box 960628, Amman 11196
Tel: +962 79 515 4199
Age range: 2–18 years
Curriculum: ACT, SAT, UK, USA, IGCSE, ALevs
Language instr: English, Arabic

Pearl International Academy
Affash Aalawi Shudayfat Street, Al-Rawnaq, Bayader Wadi Al-Seer, Amman
Tel: +962 77 077 7705
Age range: 4–18 years
Curriculum: National, UK, IGCSE

RAMS (Rawdat Al-Maaref Schools & College)
PO Box 676, Khalda, Amman 11821
Tel: +962 6 552 8599
Age range: 4–18 years
Curriculum: National, SAT, UK, USA, IGCSE

Rosary Sisters School - Aqaba
Othman Bin Affan Street, Services District, Aqaba
Tel: +962 3 201 4262
Age range: 4–18 years

THE INTERNATIONAL ACADEMY - AMMAN
For further details see p. 76
PO Box 144255, King Hussein Parks, Sa'eed Khair Street, Amman 11814
Tel: +962 6550 2055
Email: info@iaa.edu.jo
Website: www.iaa.edu.jo
Director: Hana Kanan
Age range: 3–18 years
No. of pupils: 1197 B630 G567
Curriculum: IBDP, IBMYP, IPC, National
Language instr: English

The International School of Choueifat - Amman
P.O. Box 316, Wadi Essir, Amman 11810
Tel: +962 6 429 1133
Age range: 4–18 years
Language instr: English

The Little Academy
12 Al Iftikhar Street, Amman
Tel: +962 6 585 8282
Age range: 18 months–8 years
Curriculum: IBPYP
Language instr: English

Whitman Academy
12 Al Hajeab Street, Amman
Tel: +962 77 536 6610
Age range: 4–18 years
Curriculum: AP, SAT, USA

KAZAKHSTAN

Astana Garden School
A. Bokeikhanov 34, Astana 010000
Tel: +7 701 272 55 88
Curriculum: IBPYP, IBCP
Language instr: English, Russian

Dostyk American International School
TCO, Dostyk Village, 37 Vladimirskaya Street, Atyrau 060011
Tel: +7 712 220 92 03
Age range: 3–13 years
Curriculum: USA
Language instr: English

Galaxy International School
4th Microdistrict 9, Almaty 050063
Tel: +7 727 243 77 80
Age range: 4–18 years
Curriculum: UK, IGCSE, ALevs
Language instr: English

Haileybury Almaty
112 Al-Farabi Avenue, Almaty 050040
Tel: +7 727 355 01 00
Age range: 4–18 years
Curriculum: UK, IGCSE, ALevs
Language instr: English

Haileybury Astana
Ivan Panfilov bldg. 4, Astana 010000
Tel: +7 717 255 98 55
Age range: 2–18 years
Curriculum: IBDP, UK, IGCSE
Language instr: English

International College of Continuous Education, Almaty
69A Zheltoksan Street, Almaty 480004
Tel: +7 727 279 97 36
Age range: 4–16 years
Curriculum: IBMYP, IBPYP
Language instr: English, Russian

International College of Continuous Education, Astana
8/4 Tashenov Street, Astana 010000
Tel: +7 717 242 55 54
Age range: 4–16 years
Curriculum: IBMYP, IBPYP
Language instr: English, Russian

Asia

International School of Almaty
40b Satpayev Street, Almaty 050057
Tel: +7 727 274 48 08
Curriculum: IBMYP, IBPYP
Language instr: Russian, English

International School of Astana
Turkistan Street 32/1, Astana 010000
Tel: +8 717 291 61 77
Age range: 4–18 years
Curriculum: IBDP, IBMYP, IBPYP
Language instr: English, Russian
(CIS)

Kazakhstan International School
Al-Farabi Avenue 118/15, Almaty 050000
Tel: +7 727 356 50 00
Age range: 2–18 years
Curriculum: IBDP, IBMYP, IBPYP
Language instr: English

Lyceum School Nurorda
Kassym Amanzholov Street 34, Astana 020000
Tel: +8 717 242 78 29
Age range: 4–18 years
Curriculum: AP, USA
(CIS)

Miras International School, Almaty
190 Al-Farabi Avenue, Almaty 050043
Tel: +7 727 227 69 42
Age range: 3–18 years
Curriculum: IBDP, IBMYP, IBPYP
Language instr: English, Kazakh, Russian
(CIS) (ECIS)

Miras International School, Astana
Kuishi Dina Street 34, Astana 010009
Tel: +7 717 236 98 67
Age range: 2–18 years
Curriculum: IBDP, IBMYP, IBPYP
Language instr: English, Russian, Kazakh

QSI Almaty International School
185 Baiken Ashimov Street, Kalkaman 2 Micro-District, Nauryzbay District, Almaty 050006
Tel: +7 727 381 87 10
Age range: 3–18 years
Curriculum: AP, USA
Language instr: English

QSI International School of Astana
17 Bayan-Sulu Street, Komsomolskiy Village, Astana 010000
Tel: +7 717 227 77 60
Age range: 3–18 years
Curriculum: AP, USA
Language instr: English

QSI International School of Atyrau
473 Sultan Beibarys Prospect, Atyrau 060011
Tel: +7 712 251 83 97
Age range: 3–18 years
Curriculum: SAT, USA
Language instr: English

Spectrum International School
Kasym Amanzholov Street 34, South-East (right side) m-n, Astana
Tel: +7 707 926 36 46
Age range: 6–18 years
Curriculum: UK, IGCSE, ALevs
(CIS) (ECIS)

Tien Shan International School
Karasai District, Raimbek Rural District, South of the village Dolan, Almaty 040922
Tel: +7 727 344 12 66
Age range: 4–18 years

KUWAIT

Al Amal Indian School
Al Khansa Street, Block 5, 22062 Salmiya, Hawalli
Tel: +965 2571 2971
Age range: 4–18 years

Al Ghanim Bilingual School
288 Al-Mutanabi Street, Salwa, Block 6, Kuwait City, Hawalli
Tel: +965 2564 4953
Age range: 4–18 years
(CIS)

Al Ru'ya Bilingual School
Block 2, Street 3, Parcel 94, 44230 Sabah Al Salem, Mubarak Al-Kabeer
Tel: +965 2552 9781
Age range: 4–18 years
Language instr: English, Arabic
(CIS)

Al-Bayan Bilingual School
Beirut Street, 32004 Hawally, Hawalli
Tel: +965 2227 5000
Age range: 3–18 years
Curriculum: AP, National
Language instr: English, Arabic
(CIS)

Alrashid School
Block 5, Kuwait City, Farwaniya
Tel: +965 5173 5171
Age range: 4–18 years
(CIS)

American Baccalaureate School
Street 59, Block 6, Ibn Zuhair Street, Abraq Khaitan, Kuwait City, Farwaniya
Tel: +965 2479 1791
Age range: 3–18 years
Curriculum: USA

American Creativity Academy
P.O. Box 1740, 32018 Hawally, Hawalli
Tel: +965 2267 3333
Age range: 3–18 years
No. of pupils: 6600
Curriculum: IBDP, USA
Language instr: English

American International School of Kuwait
P.O. Box 3267, 22033 Salmiya, Hawalli
Tel: +965 1 843 247
Age range: 4–18 years
No. of pupils: 2799
Curriculum: IBDP, IBMYP, IBPYP, SAT, USA
Language instr: English

American United School
Street 101, Block 1, Sabah Al Salem, Mubarak Al-Kabeer
Tel: +965 2553 0100
Age range: 3–18 years
Curriculum: USA
(CIS)

A'Takamul International School
P.O. Box 2975, Block 1, Road 4, 32030 Sabah Al Salem, Mubarak Al-Kabeer
Tel: +965 2552 2204
Age range: 4–18 years
Curriculum: USA

Danah Universal School of Kuwait
Salem Al-Daway Street, Block 1, Salwa, Hawalli
Tel: +965 2221 8123
Age range: 3–18 years
Curriculum: USA

Dasman Bilingual School
Bin Misbah Street, Kuwait City, Al-Asimah
Tel: +965 2227 7377
Age range: 3–21 years
Curriculum: USA
Language instr: English, Arabic

Fahaheel Al Watanieh Indian Private School
P.O. Box 9951, 49 South Street, Block 9, 61010 Ahmadi
Tel: +965 2221 3145
Age range: 3–18 years

Future Bilingual Schools
Street 16, Off Makkah Street, Behind Ahmadi Educational Area, Block 9, Fahaheel, Ahmadi
Tel: +965 2392 4243
Age range: 3–18 years
Language instr: English, Arabic
(CIS)

Gulf British Academy
Saba Street, Block 10, Salmiya, Hawalli
Tel: +965 2225 6777
Age range: 3–13 years
Curriculum: UK

Gulf English School
P.O. Box 33106, Al Dimanah Street, Block 4, Salmiya, Hawalli
Tel: +965 2575 7022
Age range: 4–18 years
Curriculum: UK

Ideal Education School
Hilalli Street, Sharq, 13136 Kuwait City, Al-Asimah
Tel: +965 240 3668
Age range: 5–21 years

Indian Central School
Street 100, Abbasiya School Complex, Block 1, Kuwait City, Farwaniya
Tel: +965 5535 7199
Age range: 3–18 years

Indian Educational School
Jleeb Al Shyoukh-School Street, Opposite Fire Station & Jleeb Cinema, Kuwait City, Farwaniya
Tel: +965 2434 0882
Age range: 2–18 years

International Academy of Kuwait
Uhud Street, Salmiya, Hawalli
Tel: +965 2209 7280
Age range: 3–18 years
Curriculum: UK, IGCSE, ALevs

International British School
Ibn Taimiya Street, Block 9, Fahaheel, Ahmadi
Tel: +965 2221 9245
Age range: 3–18 years
Curriculum: UK
Language instr: English

Iqra'a Bilingual School
Street 25, Block 4, Jleeb Al Shuyoukh, Kuwait City, Farwaniya
Tel: +965 2221 9900
Age range: 4–18 years
Curriculum: USA
Language instr: English

Khalifa School
Al Dimnah Street, Area 4, Salmiya, Hawalli
Tel: +965 2370 0000
Age range: 6–21 years
(CIS)

Kuwait American School
P.O. Box 5150, Belagat Street, Block 3, Street 3, 22062 Salmiya, Hawalli
Tel: +965 2572 0920
Age range: 4–18 years
Curriculum: USA
(CIS)

Kuwait Bilingual School
P.O. Box 3125, Al-Jahra, 01033 Al Jahra City, Jahra
Tel: +965 2458 1118
Age range: 3–18 years
Curriculum: IBDP, IBMYP, IBPYP, USA
Language instr: English, Arabic

Kuwait English School
P.O. Box 8640, Salwa, Area 11, Street 9, 22057 Salmiya, Hawalli
Tel: +965 2239 0100
Age range: 3–18 years
Curriculum: UK, ALevs
Language instr: English
(COB) (ECIS)

Kuwait International English School
Al Hassan Al Bassry Street, Block 10, Hawally, Hawalli
Tel: +965 2221 9228
Age range: 3–18 years
Curriculum: UK, IGCSE, ALevs

Asia

Kuwait National English School
P.O. Box 44273, Mousa Bin Nussair Street, Block 2, 32057 Hawally, Hawalli
Tel: +965 2265 6904/5/6
Age range: 3–18 years
Curriculum: UK, GCSE, IGCSE, ALevs

Little Land Nursery & Montessori Centre
House 7, Street 40, Block 4, Faiha, Kuwait City, Al Asimah
Curriculum: IBPYP
Language instr: English, Arabic

Lycee Francais De Koweit
P.O. Box 9450, Hamad Al-Mubarak Street, 22095 Salmiya, Hawalli
Tel: +965 2224 0666
Age range: 3–18 years
Curriculum: FrenchBacc

Manarat School - Kuwait (MSK)
Salem Mubarak Street, Behind American University of Kuwait, Salmiya, Hawalli
Tel: +965 2572 2083
Age range: 6–18 years
Curriculum: SAT, TOEFL, USA
Language instr: English

New English School
P.O. Box 6156, Street 1, Block 12, 32036 Jabriya, Hawalli
Tel: +965 2531 8060/1
Age range: 3–18 years
Curriculum: UK, IGCSE, ALevs
Language instr: English

New Pakistan International School
Suraqah Bin Malik Street, Block 8, Hawally, Hawalli
Tel: +965 2221 3153/4
Age range: 4–18 years
Curriculum: UK, IGCSE, ALevs

Oxford Academy
Street 1, Block 7, Salwa, Hawalli
Tel: +965 2209 7274
Age range: 3–18 years
Curriculum: UK, IGCSE, ALevs

Reborn Kids Education Academy (RKEA)
Street 507, Block 5, Al-Siddiq
Tel: +965 6900 6521
Age range: 3–6 years
Curriculum: IBPYP
Language instr: English

Salmiya School
Abo Thar Al Ghafari Street, Block 12, Salmiya, Hawalli
Age range: 4–11 years
Curriculum: UK
Language instr: English, Arabic

Salwa School
Street 2, Block 7, Salwa, Hawalli
Age range: 9 months–18 years
Curriculum: UK, IGCSE, ALevs
Language instr: English, Arabic

The American Academy for Girls
P.O. Box 6087, Building 288, Street 1, Block 5, 32035 Salwa, Hawalli
Tel: +965 9800 8179
Age range: G3–18 years
Curriculum: USA

The American School of Kuwait
P.O. Box 6735, Al Muthanna Street, 32042 Hawally, Hawalli
Tel: +965 2266 4341
Age range: 3–18 years
Curriculum: AP, USA

The British School of Kuwait
Street 1, Area 1, Salwa, Hawalli
Tel: +965 183 0456
Age range: 4–18 years
Curriculum: UK, GCSE, IGCSE, ALevs
Language instr: English

The English Academy
Ahmad Ibn Tolon Street, Area 8, Hawally, Hawalli
Tel: +965 2265 1195
Age range: 4–18 years
Curriculum: UK, IGCSE, ALevs
Language instr: English, Arabic

The English School Fahaheel
P.O. Box 7209, Fahaheel, 64003 Kuwait City, Al-Asimah
Tel: +965 2371 1070
Age range: 3–18 years
Curriculum: UK, IGCSE, ALevs
Language instr: English

The English School for Girls
Street 1, Block 7, Salwa, Hawalli
Tel: +965 9222 1086
Age range: 3–18 years
Curriculum: UK, IGCSE, ALevs

The English School, Kuwait
P.O. Box 379, Safat, 13004 Kuwait City, Al-Asimah
Tel: +965 2227 1385
Age range: 3–13 years
Curriculum: UK
Language instr: English

The Indian Community School Kuwait
Essa Al Qatami Street, Jiddah 8, Block 10, Salmiya, Hawalli
Tel: +965 2562 9583
Age range: 4–18 years

Universal American School
P.O. Box 17035, Khaldiya, 72451 Kuwait City, Al-Asimah
Tel: +965 1822 827
Age range: 3–18 years
Curriculum: AP, SAT, USA
Language instr: English

KYRGYZSTAN

Bishkek International School
67A Bronirovannaia Street, Bishkek 720044
Tel: +996 3122 14406
Age range: 2–18 years
Curriculum: IBDP, IBMYP, IBPYP, IGCSE
Language instr: English

Hope Academy of Bishkek
127B Gogol Street, Bishkek 720011
Tel: +996 3126 81079
Age range: 3.5–18 years
Curriculum: AP, USA

Oxford International School
Mira Avenue 153/1, Bishkek 720040
Tel: +996 5585 51155
Age range: 4–18 years
Curriculum: IBDP, UK, IGCSE, ALevs
Language instr: English, Russian

QSI International School of Bishkek
14A Tynystanova Street, Bishkek 720055
Tel: +996 3125 63139
Age range: 3–18 years
Curriculum: AP, USA
Language instr: English

Silk Road International School
Microregion 11, Aytieva 7A, Bishkek 720049
Tel: +996 3125 20290
Age range: 5–19 years
Curriculum: UK, IGCSE, ALevs

LAOS

Diamond International School
Donghanghin Village, Xaythany District, Vientiane
Tel: +856 205 528 8668
Curriculum: IBPYP
Language instr: English, Lao

French International High School Vientiane
B.P. 2526, route de Thadeua, Vientiane
Tel: +856 2122 7227
Age range: 4–18 years
Curriculum: FrenchBacc
Language instr: French

Kiettisack International School
Lao-Thai Friendship Road, Sokpaluang Village, Sisattanak District, Vientiane
Tel: +856 21 314979
Age range: 2–18 years
Curriculum: UK, IGCSE, ALevs

Panyathip International School
Saphanthong Neua Village, Sisattanak District, Vientiane
Tel: +856 30 9818999
Age range: 4–18 years
Curriculum: IPC, UK, IGCSE

The Australian International School
Ban Nondouang Tai, Sikkhotabong District, Vientiane
Tel: +856 20 22220526
Age range: 4–18 years

Vientiane International School
P.O. Box 3180, Phonesavanh Road, Saphanthong Tai Village, Sisattanak District, Vientiane
Tel: +856 21 31 8100
Age range: 3–18 years
No. of pupils: 480
Curriculum: IBDP, IBMYP, IBPYP
Language instr: English

LEBANON

Ahliah School
Wadi Abou Jmil, Downtown, Beirut
Tel: +961 1 372960
Age range: 3–18 years
Curriculum: National, USA

Al-Hayat International School
Ras Al-Zaytoun, Aramoun
Tel: +961 5 806306
Age range: 3–16 years
Curriculum: IBDP, IBMYP, IBPYP
Language instr: English, Arabic

American Community School Beirut
P.O. Box 11 - 8129, Riad El Solh, Beirut
Tel: +961 1 374370
Age range: 3–18 years
Curriculum: IBDP, National, USA
Language instr: English

Antonine International School
Zone 7, Street 4, Ajaltoun
Tel: +961 9 230967
Age range: 2 months–18 years
Curriculum: IBDP, National, SAT
Language instr: English

Brummana High School
P.O. Box 36, Brummana
Tel: +961 2 4960430
Age range: 4–18 years
Curriculum: IBDP, National, SAT, UK, USA, IGCSE, ALevs
Language instr: English

Cadmous College
Jwar al Nakhel, Tyre
Tel: +961 7 380391
Age range: 3–18 years
Curriculum: IBDP, National, SAT
Language instr: English

Christian Teaching Institute (CTI)
Mar Maroun Street, Horsh Tabet, Sin el Fil, Beirut
Tel: +961 1 497974
Age range: 4–18 years
Curriculum: IBDP, National, SAT
Language instr: English, Arabic

Asia

Collège des Frères Maristes Champville
B.P. 70540, Dik el-Mehdi (Metn), Antélias
Tel: +961 4 913327
Age range: 4–18 years
Curriculum: FrenchBacc

Collège Notre Dame de Nazareth
Nasra Road, Achrafieh, Beirut
Tel: +961 1 327150
Curriculum: FrenchBacc

Collège Notre Dame des Soeurs Antonines (Hazmieh-Jamhour)
B.P. 45201, Place Mar Tacla, Jamhour, Baabda
Tel: +961 5 769027
Curriculum: IBDP
Language instr: English, Arabic

Collège Notre-Dame de Jamhour
B.P. 45-151, Hazmieh
Tel: +961 5 924151
Curriculum: FrenchBacc

Collège Protestant Français
B.P. 13-6283, Rue Madame Curie, Chouran, Beirut
Tel: +961 1 811892

Collège Protestant Français Montana
Rue 4, Dik El Mehdi
Tel: +961 4 914006
Curriculum: IBDP, IBPYP
Language instr: English, Arabic

Eastwood College Kafarshima
Old Saida Road, Kafarshima
Tel: +961 5 431525
Curriculum: IBDP
Language instr: English, Arabic

Eastwood International School Beirut
Sami Solh Street, Mansourieh El Metn, Beirut
Tel: +961 4 409307
Curriculum: IBDP, IBMYP, IBPYP
Language instr: English

German International School Beirut
PO Box 11-3888, Bliss Street, Ras Beirut, Beirut
Tel: +961 1 740523
Age range: 3–18 years
No. of pupils: 800
Curriculum: IBDP
Language instr: English

Grand Lycée Franco-Libanais Beyrouth
P.O. Box 165-636, Rue Beni Assaf, Achrafieh, Beirut
Tel: +961 1 420700
Age range: 4–18 years
Curriculum: National, FrenchBacc

Greenfield College
Al Mourouj Street - Bir Hassan, Beirut
Tel: +961 1 834 838
Age range: 4–18 years
Curriculum: IBDP, National, FrenchBacc, USA
Language instr: English

Hariri High School II
Rue Abdul Kader, Batrakiyyeh, Beirut
Tel: +961 1 373310
Age range: 4–18 years
Curriculum: IBDP
Language instr: English, Arabic

Houssam Eddine Hariri High School
P.O. Box 67, Saida
Tel: +961 7 739898
Age range: 3–18 years
Curriculum: IBDP, IBPYP, National, FrenchBacc
Language instr: Arabic, English, French

International College Lebanon, Ain Aar
P.O. Box 113-5373, Mount Lebanon, Ain Aar
Tel: +961 4 928468
Age range: 3–14 years
Curriculum: IBPYP, National, FrenchBacc, USA
Language instr: Arabic, English, French

International College Lebanon, Ras Beirut
P.O. Box 113-5373, Hamra, Bliss Street, Beirut
Tel: +961 1 362500
Age range: 3–18 years
Curriculum: IBDP, IBPYP, National, FrenchBacc, USA
Language instr: Arabic, English, French

Jesus & Mary School
Rabweh, Cornet Chahwan
Tel: +961 4910531/2/3/4/5
Curriculum: IBDP
Language instr: English, Arabic

Leila C. Saad SABIS School El-Metn
El-Mtein
Tel: +961 4 297 666

LWIS DT Beirut-City International School
Zokak Al Blat, Hussein Beyhum Street, Downtown, Beirut
Tel: +961 1 369500
Age range: 3–18 years
Curriculum: IBDP
Language instr: English, Arabic

LWIS Keserwan-Adma International School
Mar Nohra, Fatqa, Keserwan
Tel: +961 9 740225
Age range: 3–18 years
No. of pupils: 470
Curriculum: IBDP, USA
Language instr: English

LWIS Koura-Universal School of Lebanon
Bterram Al-Koura
Tel: +961 6 930964
Age range: 3–18 years
No. of pupils: 660
Curriculum: IBDP, National, USA
Language instr: English, Arabic

Lycée Abdallah Rassi
P.O. Box 03, Halba-Akkar
Tel: +961 6 690642
Age range: 4–18 years
Curriculum: National, FrenchBacc

Lycée Français International Elite
Mousaytbe, rue Yazbeck, Beirut
Tel: +961 1 818810
Age range: 4–18 years
Curriculum: National, FrenchBacc

Lycée Français International Institut Moderne du Liban
Rue 11-D, Fanar
Tel: +961 1 680160/1/2
Age range: 3–18 years
Curriculum: IBDP, IBMYP
Language instr: Arabic, French

Lycée Franco-Libanais Abdel Kader
P.O. Box 11-8464, Rue Boutros Boustani Quartier, Zuqaq El Blat, Beirut
Tel: +961 1 365429
Age range: 4–18 years
Curriculum: National, FrenchBacc

Lycée Franco-Libanais Alphonse De Lamartine
P.O. Box 130, Tripoli
Tel: +961 6 417082
Age range: 4–18 years
Curriculum: National, FrenchBacc

Lycée Franco-Libanais Habbouche-Nabatieh
Rue Interne, quartier Chrayfeh, Habbouche, Nabatieh
Tel: +961 7 530712
Age range: 4–18 years
Curriculum: National, FrenchBacc

Lycée Franco-Libanais Nahr Ibrahim
P.O. Box 1589, Jounieh
Tel: +961 9 446457
Age range: 4–18 years
Curriculum: National, FrenchBacc

Lycée Franco-Libanais Verdun
Rue Rachid Karamé, Beirut
Tel: +961 1 771500
Age range: 4–18 years
Curriculum: National, FrenchBacc

Lycée Montaigne
Quartier Baydar Chouar, Beit Chabab
Tel: +961 4 983845
Age range: 4–18 years
Curriculum: National, FrenchBacc

Monsif International School
Monsif Main Road, Monsif
Tel: +961 9 790170
Age range: 4–18 years
Curriculum: IBDP, National, USA
Language instr: English, Arabic

Rafic Hariri High School
Kneissat, Saida
Tel: +961 7 723551
Age range: 4–18 years
Curriculum: IBDP, IBPYP, National, USA
Language instr: English, Arabic

SABIS International School - Adma
Orange Zone, Adma
Tel: +961 9 854 154
Age range: 4–18 years

Sagesse High School
Ain Saadeh, Matn, Beirut
Tel: +961 1 872145
Age range: 3–18 years
Curriculum: IBDP, National, USA
Language instr: English

Saint Joseph School
Metn, Cornet Chahwan
Tel: +961 4 925005
Age range: 4–14 years
Curriculum: IBDP
Language instr: English, Arabic

Stars College
Abbasiyeh
Tel: +961 07 380 444
Age range: 3–18 years
Curriculum: National, USA
Language instr: Arabic, English, French

The International School of Choueifat - Choueifat
Charles Saad Street, Amrosioeh, Choueifat
Tel: +961 5 430 430
Age range: 4–18 years

The International School of Choueifat - Koura
Fih Village, Koura
Tel: +961 6 930 740
Age range: 4–18 years

Universal College - Aley
P.O. Box 284, Jamia Al Watnia, Facing Druze Court, Aley
Tel: +961 2 5556665
Age range: 4–18 years
Curriculum: National, USA

WELLSPRING LEARNING COMMUNITY
For further details see p. 80
Al Mathaf, Main Street, Near National Museum, PO Box 116-2134, Beirut
Tel: +961 1 423 444
Email: admissions@wellspring.edu.lb
Website: www.wellspring.edu.lb
Head of School: Kathleen Battah
Age range: 3–19 years
No. of pupils: 753
Curriculum: IBDP, IBMYP, IBPYP, National
Language instr: English

Asia

MALAYSIA

Alice Smith School
2 Jalan Bellamy, 50460 Kuala Lumpur
Tel: +60 3 2148 3674
Age range: 3–18 years
No. of pupils: 1550
Curriculum: GCSE, ALevs
Language instr: English

Asia Pacific International School
No. 1, Persiaran A, Off Jalan Lapangan, Terbang Subang, 47200 Subang, Selangor
Tel: +60 3 7847 1000
Age range: 4–18
No. of pupils: 342

Aspiration International School
Bangunan AHP, Jalan Tun Mohd Fuad 3, Taman Tun Doktor Ismail, 60000 Kuala Lumpur
Tel: +60 3 2856 2477
Curriculum: IBPYP
Language instr: English

Australian International School Malaysia
22 Jalan Anggerik, The Mines Resort City, 43300 Seri Kembangan, Selangor
Tel: +60 3 8949 5000
Age range: 3–18
Language instr: English

Beaconhouse-Newlands, Kuala Lumpur International School
823 & 984 Batu 9, Jalan Cheras, 43200 Kuala Lumpur
Tel: +60 3 9075 1662/63

Brighton International School (BIS)
Bangunan Sri Impian, No 24-31, Jalan Setiawangsa 8, Taman Setiawangsa, 54200 Kuala Lumpur
Tel: +60 3 4265 7962
Age range: 5–18 years
Curriculum: UK, IGCSE, ALevs

BXCL International School Penang
No. 2, Persiaran Mutiara 5, Pusat Komersial Bandar Tasek Mutiara, 14120 Simpang Ampat, Penang
Tel: +60 4 509 7000
Age range: 3–18 years
Curriculum: UK, GCSE, IGCSE
Language instr: English

Cempaka International Ladies' College
Persiaran Timur Kampong L.B. Johnson, 71760 Seremban, Negeri Sembilan
Age range: G11–18
Language instr: English

Cempaka International School
No 19, Jalan Setiabakti 1, Damansara Heights, Kuala Lumpur
Tel: +60 3 2094 0623

Charterhouse Malaysia
62 Jalan Sri Hartamas 1, Taman Sri Hartamas, 50480 Kuala Lumpur
Tel: +60 3 2702 5270
Curriculum: UK, IGCSE, ALevs

Dalat International School
Jalan Tanjung Bungah, 11200 Tanjung Bungah, Penang
Tel: +60 4 899 2105
Age range: 3–18
No. of pupils: 400 B200 G200
Curriculum: ACT, SAT, USA
Language instr: English

Destiny Academy
No. 4 Taman Mas Ria, Jalan Junid Dalam, 84000 Muar, Johor
Tel: +60 6 959 2059
Curriculum: USA

Deutsche Schule Kuala Lumpur
Lot 5, Lorong Utara B,, Off Jalan Utara, 46200 Petaling Jaya, Selangor
Tel: +60 3 7956 6557

DISTED College
340 Macalister Road, 10350 George Town, Penang
Tel: +60 4 2296579
Curriculum: UK, ALevs

Eaton International School
Persiaran Puncak Utama, Jade Hills, 43000 Kajang, Selangor
Tel: +60 3 87414965
Curriculum: UK, IGCSE

elc International School
3664, Jalan Sierramas Barat, Sierramas, 47000 Sungai Buloh, Selangor
Tel: +60 3 6156 5001/2
Age range: 3–16
No. of pupils: 650
Curriculum: UK
Language instr: English

ELC International School Cyberjaya
Lingkaran Cyber Point Barat, 63000 Cyberjaya, Selangor
Tel: +60 3 8319 1641
Age range: 4–16 years
No. of pupils: 350
Curriculum: UK, IGCSE

Epsom College in Malaysia
Persiaran Kolej, 71760 Bandar Enstek, Negeri Sembilan
Tel: +60 6 2404 188
Age range: 3–18 years
No. of pupils: 400
Curriculum: UK
Language instr: English

Fairview International School Ipoh (FISI)
Hala Lapangan Suria, Medan Lapangan, Suria, 31350 Ipoh, Perak
Tel: +60 5 313 6888
Age range: 3–16 years
Curriculum: IBMYP, IBPYP
Language instr: English

Fairview International School Johor Bahru (FISJB)
Lot PTD 168450, Jalan Dato' Onn Utama, Bandar Dato' Onn, Mukim Tebrau, 81100 Johor Bahru, Johor
Tel: +60 7 364 3378
Age range: 3–16 years
Curriculum: IBMYP, IBPYP

Fairview International School Kuala Lumpur (FISKL)
Lot 4178, Jalan 1/27D, Section 6, Wangsa Maju, 53300 Kuala Lumpur
Tel: +60 3 4142 0888
Age range: 3–19 years
Curriculum: IBDP, IBMYP, IBPYP
Language instr: English, Mandarin

Fairview International School Penang (FISP)
Tingkat Bukit Jambul 1, Bukit Jambul Indah, 11900 Bayan Lepas, Penang
Tel: +60 4 640 6633
Age range: 3–16 years
Curriculum: IBMYP, IBPYP

Fairview International School Subang Jaya (FISJ)
2A, Jalan TP 2, Sime UEP Industrial Park, 47600 Subang Jaya, Selangor
Tel: +60 3 8023 7777
Age range: 3–16 years
Curriculum: IBMYP, IBPYP

Garden International School
16 Jalan Kiara 3, Off Jln Bukit Kiara, 50480 Kuala Lumpur
Tel: +60 3 6209 6888
Age range: 3–18
No. of pupils: 2000
Curriculum: UK, IGCSE, ALevs
Language instr: English

Garden International School Kuantan
A6230 Jalan Tengku Muhamad, Taman Pantai Chempedak, 25050 Kuantan, Pahang
Tel: +60 3 6209 6888
Curriculum: UK, IGCSE

Global Indian International School (GIIS) Kuala Lumpur Campus
242 Lorong Abdul Samad, off Jalan Sultan Abdul Samad, Brickfields, 50470 Kuala Lumpur
Tel: +60 1 9616 0075
Curriculum: UK, IGCSE

HELP International School HIS
No 2 Persiaran Cakerawala, Subang Bestari, Seksyen U4, 40150 Shah Alam, Selangor
Tel: +60 3 7809 7000
Curriculum: IPC, UK, IGCSE, ALevs

HIBISCUS International School
No 2 Jalan Udang Harimau 3, Taman Sri Segambut, 52000 Kuala Lumpur
Tel: +60 3 6242 5544
Age range: 4–18
No. of pupils: 139
Curriculum: IGCSE

IGB International School
Jalan Sierramas Utama, Sungai Buloh, Kuala Lumpur, Selangor 47000
Tel: +60 3 6145 4688
Age range: 3–19
Curriculum: IBDP, IBMYP, IBPYP, IBCP
Language instr: English

International Islamic School
Batu 8, Jalan Sungai Pusu, Gomback, 53100 Kuala Lumpur
Tel: +60 3 6188 4400
Age range: 4–11
No. of pupils: 800

International School of Kuantan
Jalan IM 7/9, Bandar Indera Mahkota, 25200 Kuantan, Pahang
Tel: +60 9573 6010
Curriculum: AP, USA
Language instr: English

Invictus Horizon Hills
No. 3 Persiaran Selatan, Horizon Hills, 79100 Iskandar Puteri, Johor
Tel: +60 7 233 0800
Age range: 3–18 years
Curriculum: UK, IGCSE, ALevs

Kelantan International School
5376B, Jalan Telipot, 15150 Kota Bharu, Kelantan
Tel: +60 9 744 6991

Kinabalu International School
PO Box 12080, 88822 Kota Kinabalu, Sabah
Tel: +60 88 224526
Age range: 3–18
No. of pupils: 460

King Henry VIII College - Malaysia
Persiaran Bestari, Cyber 11, 63000 Cyberjaya, Selangor
Tel: +60 (03) 8800 9888
Age range: 3–18

Kingsley International School
Persiaran Kingsley, Kingsley Hills, Putra Heights, 47650 Subang Jaya, Selangor
Tel: +60 3 5481 6090
Curriculum: UK, IGCSE, ALevs

Kolej Tuanku Ja'afar
71700 Mantin, Negeri Sembilan
Tel: +60 6 7582561
Age range: 3–19 years
Curriculum: IPC, UK, IGCSE, ALevs
Language instr: English

Asia

Kolej Yayasan UEM
Lembah Beringin, PO Box 62,
35900 Tanjung Malim, Perak
Tel: +60 3 6460 1234
Curriculum: UK, ALevs

Labuan International School
Lot 11334, Kampung Tanjung Aru,
Jalan Tanjung Aru, 87008 Labuan
Tel: +6 087 597300
Curriculum: National, UK

Lodge Group of Schools
Lorong Keranji 4E, Jalan
Keranji 4, Tabuan Desa,
93350 Kuching, Sarawak
Tel: +60 8 2363554

Lycée Français de Kuala Lumpur
34, Jalan Dutamas Raya,
51200 Kuala Lumpur
Tel: +60 (03) 6250 4415
Curriculum: FrenchBacc

Malacca Expatriate School
No 2-12, Jalan Siakap 1A,
Taman Permatang Pasir
Perdana, 75460 Malacca
Tel: +60 6 269 3300
Age range: 4–16
No. of pupils: 200
Curriculum: SAT, UK, IGCSE

MARLBOROUGH COLLEGE MALAYSIA
For further details see p. 62
Jalan Marlborough, 79200
Iskandar Puteri, Johor
Tel: +60 7 560 2200
Email: admissions@marlboroughcollege.my
Website: www.marlboroughcollegemalaysia.org
The Master: Simon Burbury
Age range: 3–18 years
(boarding from 9)
No. of pupils: 1000
Fees: RM60,000–RM159,000
Curriculum: IBDP, UK, IGCSE
Language instr: English

Matrix Global Schools
PT 12652, Sendayan, Merchant
Square, Persiaran 1, Sendayan
Utama, Pusat Dagangan
Sendayan, 71950 Bandar Sri
Sendayan, Negeri Sembilan
Tel: +60 6 781 9888
Age range: 3–17
No. of pupils: 730
Curriculum: National, IGCSE
Language instr: English, Bahasa Melayu

MAZ International School
No. 1 MAZ House, Jalan 20/19,
Paramount Gardens, 46300
Petaling Jaya, Selangor
Tel: +60 3 78742930
Curriculum: UK, IGCSE, ALevs

Methodist College
Off Jalan Tun Sambanthan 4,
Brickfields, 50470 Kuala Lumpur
Tel: +60 3 2274 1851
Age range: 16–19

Mont'Kiara International School
22 Jalan Kiara, Mont'Kiara,
50480 Kuala Lumpur
Tel: +60 3 2093 8604
Age range: 3–18
No. of pupils: 600
Curriculum: IBDP, IBMYP, IBPYP, SAT, USA
Language instr: English

Mutiara International Grammar School
Lot 707, Jalan Kerja Ayer
Lama, Ampang Jaya, 68000
Ampang, Selangor
Tel: +60 3 4257 5036
Age range: 3–17 years
Curriculum: UK, IGCSE
Language instr: English

Nexus International School Malaysia
No 1 Jalan Diplomatik 3/6,
Presint 15, 62050 Putrajaya
Tel: +60 3 8889 3868
Age range: 3–18 years
Curriculum: IBDP, IPC, UK, GCSE, IGCSE
Language instr: English

Prince of Wales Island International Primary School (POWIIS Primary)
Sunrise Tower, Mezzanine Floor, 190-192 Persiaran Gurney, 10250 Penang
Tel: +60 4 828 9999
Age range: 3–11

Prince of Wales Island International School (POWIIS)
1 Jalan Sungai Air Putih 6,
Bandar Baru Air Putih, 11000
Balik Pulau, Penang
Tel: +60 4 8689999
Curriculum: UK
Language instr: English

R.E.A.L Schools, Cheras Campus
Lot 217, Batu 13, Jalan Hulu Langat,
43100 Hulu Langat, Selangor
Tel: +60 3 9021 3601

R.E.A.L Schools, Johor Bahru Campus
Lot 2361, Jalan Persiaran Sri
Plentong, Bandar Baru Permas
Jaya, 81750 Masai, Johor
Tel: +60 7 3864468

R.E.A.L Schools, Shah Alam Campus
Lot No. 5, Jalan Merah Saga U9/5,
40250 Shah Alam, Selangor
Tel: +60 3 7842 3228

Raffles American School Johor
Raffles K12 Sdn Bhd, Jalan Raffles,
79050 Iskandar Puteri, Johor
Tel: +60 7 213 2638
Age range: 4–18 years
Curriculum: AP, IBDP, SAT
Language instr: English

Rafflesia International School Kajang Campus
Jalan Kajang 2 Utama, Seksyen
2,, 43000 Kajang, Selangor
Tel: +603 8741 7099
Curriculum: IPC, UK, IGCSE

Rafflesia International School Puchong Campus
Persiaran Sierra 2, Bandar 16
Sierra, 47100 Puchong, Selangor
Tel: +60 3 8953 9088
Curriculum: IPC, UK, IGCSE

Repton International School (Invictus Spring Hills)
No. 8, Jalan Purnama, Bandar Seri
Alam, 81750 Johor Bahru, Johor
Tel: +60 7 888 999
Curriculum: IBDP
Language instr: English

Sayfol International School
No. 261 Jalan Ampang,
50450 Kuala Lumpur
Tel: +60 3 4256 8791
Age range: 4–18
No. of pupils: 1000
Curriculum: UK

Sekolah Sri KDU (Kota Damansara)
No. 5 & 7, Jalan Teknologi
2/1, Kota Damansara, 47810
Daerah Petaling, Selangor
Tel: +60 3 6145 3888
Age range: 4–16 years
Language instr: English

Sri Ara International School
23 Jalan Straits View, 80200
Johor Bahru, Johor
Tel: +6 07 222 2089/223 0089
Age range: 4–18 years
Curriculum: IGCSE

Sri Emas International School
Lot 1214, Seksyen 40, Batu 10,
Lebuhraya Persekutuan, Off Jalan SS
7/2, 47300 Petaling Jaya, Selangor
Tel: +60 3 7865 5787
Age range: 11–16
No. of pupils: 700
Curriculum: GCSE

Sri KDU International School (Klang)
PT 4194, Jalan Tampin 1/KU1, Off
Jalan Goh Hock Huat, Sungai
Pinang, 41050 Klang, Selangor
Tel: +60 3 3082 6888
Age range: 3–18 years
Language instr: English

Sri KDU International School (Kota Damansara)
No. 3, Jalan Teknologi 2/1,
Kota Damansara, 47810
Daerah Petaling, Selangor
Tel: +60 3 6145 3888
Age range: 6–17 years
Curriculum: IBDP
Language instr: English

Sri KDU International School (Subang Jaya)
Jalan MP2, Tropicana Metropark,
47500 Subang Jaya, Selangor
Tel: +60 3 5036 8900
Age range: 3–18 years
No. of pupils: 700
Curriculum: UK, IGCSE, ALevs
Language instr: English

Sri Kuala Lumpur School
No 1 Jalan SS 15/7A, 47500
Subang Jaya, Selangor
Tel: +60 3 56343491
Age range: 6–17
Curriculum: UK, IGCSE

St Christopher's International Primary School
10 Nunn Road, 10350
George Town, Penang
Tel: +60 4 226 3589
Age range: 3–11
No. of pupils: 580 B291 G289
Curriculum: IPC, UK
Language instr: English

St. Joseph's Institution International School Malaysia (Tropicana PJ Campus)
No. 1, Jalan PJU 3/13, 47410
Petaling Jaya, Selangor
Tel: +60 3 8605 3605
Curriculum: IBDP
Language instr: English

Stella Maris Medan Damansara
7, Lorong Setiabistari 2, Bukit
Damansara, 50490 Kuala Lumpur
Tel: +60 3 20830025
Age range: 5–19
No. of pupils: 822
Curriculum: IBDP, IGCSE, ALevs
Language instr: English

Straits International School
No.2, Lilitan Sungai Tiram, 11900
Bayan Lepas, Penang
Tel: +60 4 643 1815
Curriculum: UK, IGCSE

Sunway International School, Bandar Sunway
No. 3, Jalan Universiti, Bandar
Sunway, 47500 Selangor
Tel: +60 3 7491 80/0
Curriculum: IBDP

Sunway International School, Sunway Iskandar
Jalan Persiaran Medini 3,
Sunway Iskandar, 79250 Johor
Tel: +60 7 533 8070
Age range: 4–18
No. of pupils: 244
Curriculum: IBDP, IBMYP, IBCP
Language instr: English

Tanarata International Schools
Kajang-Serdang Road,
43000 Selangor
Tel: +60 3 8737 7366
Curriculum: UK, IGCSE, ALevs

Asia

Taylor's College Sri Hartamas
No.1, Jalan Taylor's, 47500 Subang Jaya, Selangor
Tel: +60 3 5629 5000
Curriculum: ALevs
Language instr: English

Taylor's College Subang Jaya
No 1 Jalan SS15/8, 47500 Subang Jaya, Selangor
Tel: +60 3 5636 2641
Age range: 16–19
No. of pupils: 100
Curriculum: ALevs

Taylor's International School, Kuala Lumpur
No 9 Jalan 1/75C, Off Jalan Pria Taman Maluri, 55100 Kuala Lumpur
Tel: +60 3 9200 9898
Age range: 4–16
No. of pupils: 1550
Curriculum: UK, IGCSE

Tenby Schools Ipoh
16 Persiaran Meru Utama, Bandar Meru Raya, 30020 Ipoh, Perak
Tel: +60 5 5252628
Language instr: English

Tenby Schools Miri
Lot 10700, Block 5, Jalan Desa Senadin, Kuala Baram District, Miri, Sarawak
Tel: +60 8 5491526
Language instr: English

Tenby Schools Penang
No. 2, Lintang Lembah Permai 1, 11200 Tanjung Bungah, Penang
Tel: +60 4 892 7777
Language instr: English

Tenby Schools Setia Eco Gardens
7, Jalan Laman Setia Utama, Taman Setia Utama, 81550 Johor Bahru, Johor
Tel: +60 7 5588812
Age range: 3–16
No. of pupils: 344 B172 G172
Curriculum: IPC, UK, IGCSE
Language instr: English

Tenby Schools Setia Eco Hill
No. 6, Jalan Ecohill 1, Setia Ecohill, 43500 Semenyih, Selangor
Tel: +60 3 8725 5625

Tenby Schools Setia Eco Park
No.1, Jalan Setia Tropika U13/18T, Seksyen U13, 40170 Shah Alam, Selangor
Tel: +60 3 3342 1535
Language instr: English

The British International School of Kuala Lumpur
No 1 Changkat Bukit Utama, Bandar Utama, 47800 Petaling Jaya, Selangor
Tel: +60 3 7727 7775
Age range: 2–18 years
No. of pupils: 1200
Curriculum: UK, IGCSE, ALevs

The International School @ Park City Kuala Lumpur
No 1 Jalan Intisari, Desa Park City, 52200 Kuala Lumpur
Tel: +60 3 6280 8880
Age range: 3–18
No. of pupils: 1100
Curriculum: UK, IGCSE, ALevs
Language instr: English

THE INTERNATIONAL SCHOOL OF KUALA LUMPUR (ISKL)
For further details see p. 77
No. 2 Lorong Kelab Polo Di Raja, Ampang Hilir, 55000 Kuala Lumpur
Tel: +60 3 4813 5000
Email: admissions@iskl.edu.my
Website: www.iskl.edu.my
Head of School: Rami Madani
Age range: 3–18 years
No. of pupils: 1800
Fees: Day RM73,670–RM150,520
Curriculum: AP, IBDP, SAT
Language instr: English

The International School of Penang (Uplands)
Jalan Sungai Satu, Batu Feringgi, 11100 Penang
Tel: +604 8819 777
Age range: 4–18 years
No. of pupils: 660
Curriculum: IBDP, IBMYP, IBPYP, GCSE, IGCSE
Language instr: English

TIPS Kuala Lumpur
TIPS Valley International School, 55 Jalan Thamby Abdullah, 50470 Kuala Lumpur
Tel: +60 3 2859 2522

Tunka Putra School
Jalan Stadium, Petra Jaya, 93050 Kuching, Sarawak
Tel: +60 82 539 800
Curriculum: IPC, National, UK, IGCSE

UCSI International School
1 Persiaran UCSI International School, 71010 Port Dickson, Negeri Sembalan
Tel: +60 6653 6888
Curriculum: IBDP, IBMYP, IBPYP
Language instr: English

Wadi Sofia College
Binjai, Kubang Kerian, 16150 Kota Bharu, Kelantan
Tel: +60 9 764 1724
Age range: 14–19
No. of pupils: 300
Curriculum: UK

Westlake International School
Lot 18662, Jalan Universiti, Taman Bandar Barat, 31900 Kampar, Perak
Tel: +60 5 467 2222
Curriculum: UK, IGCSE, ALevs

Woodlands International School
No.1 Jalan Teku, 96000 Sibu, Sarawak
Tel: +60 84 239761
Curriculum: IPC, UK, IGCSE, ALevs

Zenith International School
126, Jalan S2 B4, Uptown Avenue, 70300 Seremban, Negeri Sembilan
Tel: +60 1300 222 188
Curriculum: IPC, UK, IGCSE

MONGOLIA

American School of Ulaanbaatar
P.O. Box 2365, Central Post Office, Zaisan Hill 11, Khan Uul District, Ulananbaatar
Tel: +976 1 1348888
Age range: 4–18 years
Curriculum: USA

British School of Ulaanbaatar
P.O. Box 80, ?Naadamchidiin Road 50, Ulaanbaatar 17081
Tel: +976 7 0047788
Age range: 3–18 years
Curriculum: UK, GCSE, IGCSE, ALevs
Language instr: English

Human International School
122/4 Ar Zaisan Street, Khan-Uul District, 11th Khoroo, Ulaanabatar 17025
Tel: +976 7277 3111
Curriculum: IBDP
Language instr: English, Mongolian

International School of Ulaanbaatar
P.O. Box 36/10, Four Seasons Garden, Khan-Uul District, 18 Khoroo, Ulaanbaatar 17032
Tel: +976 7 0160010
Age range: 3–18 years
Curriculum: IBDP, IBMYP, IBPYP
Language instr: English

Olonlog Academy
IBDP School Building, Ikh Khuree Street-339, Bayanzurkh District-26, Ulaanbaatar 13312
Tel: +976 9 4999029
Age range: 15–18 years
No. of pupils: 112
Curriculum: IBDP
Language instr: English

Orchlon International School
Capital Region 67, Post Office Branch 36, Khan-Uul District, District 15, Ulaanbaatar 17011
Tel: +976 7 7114433
Age range: 3–18 years
Curriculum: UK, IGCSE, ALevs
Language instr: English, Mongolian

Shine Ue School
UNESCO Street 12, Khoroo 1, Sukhbaatar District, Ulaanbaatar 14220
Tel: +976 7 0128044
Age range: 4–18 years
Curriculum: IBDP, IGCSE
Language instr: English, Mongolian

The English School of Mongolia
Tokyo-89, 1st Khoroo, Bayanzurkh District, Ulaanbaatar 13380
Tel: +976 1 1451230
Age range: 3–18 years
Curriculum: IBDP, IBPYP, UK, IGCSE, ALevs
Language instr: English, Mongolian

Ulaanbaatar Elite International School
Seoul Street, 2nd Khoroo, Sukhbaatar District, Ulaanbaatar 14523
Tel: +976 7 0105010
Age range: 3–18 years
Curriculum: National, UK, IGCSE, ALevs
Language instr: English

MYANMAR

Ayeyarwaddy International School
No. 25(B), 52nd Street, Between 33rd & 34th Street, Chan Aye Tharzan Township, Mandalay
Tel: +959 26 545 9667
Age range: 3–18 years
Curriculum: AP, USA

Bahan International Science Academy
No. 25 Po Sein Road, Bahan Township, Yangon
Tel: +95 1 548452
Age range: 3–16 years
Curriculum: IBDP, UK, IGCSE
Language instr: English

Brainworks Total International Schools Yangon
No. 1 Thumingalar Street, 16/4 Quarter, Thingangyun Township, Yangon
Tel: +95 1 855 1360
Age range: 2–18 years
Curriculum: IBDP, UK, IGCSE, ALevs
Language instr: English, Burmese

ILBC IGCSE & A Level School
51-G/2, Taw Win Pale, Taw Win Pale Housing, Kyaikkasan, Yangon
Tel: +95 1 542 982
Age range: 3–18 years
Curriculum: UK, IGCSE, ALevs

International School of Myanmar
W-22, Mya Kan Thar Main Road, Mya Kan Thar Housing, 5th Quarter, Hlaing Township, Yangon
Tel: +95 1 530 082
Age range: 4–18 years
Curriculum: AP, USA
Language instr: English

Asia

Mandalay International Science Academy
58 Street, Between 27 & 28 Street, Kan Kauk Quarter, Chan Aye Tharzan Township, Mandalay
Tel: +95 2 407 2753
Age range: 3–14 years
Curriculum: UK
Language instr: English

Myanmar International School
No. 20 Pyin Nya Waddy Street, Yankin Township, Yangon
Age range: 2–18 years
Curriculum: UK, IGCSE, ALevs

Myanmar International School Yangon (MISY) Mandalay
No. 23 48th Street, Between 109 x 110, Chan Mya Thar Si Township, Mandalay
Tel: +95 2 80926
Age range: 3–18 years
Curriculum: UK, IGCSE, ALevs
Language instr: English
(CIS)

Myanmar International School Yangon (MISY) Yangon
No. 24 Sae Myaung Street, 11th Quarter, Yankin Township, Yangon
Tel: +95 1 657885
Age range: 3–18 years
Curriculum: UK, IGCSE, ALevs
Language instr: English
(CIS)

Nay Pyi Taw International Science Academy
No. 14 Oattara Thiri Myo Thit, (Near Sinma Living Mall), Nay Pyi Taw
Tel: +95 6 743 3134
Age range: 2–14 years
Curriculum: UK

Pride International School Myanmar (PISM)
Aung Chan Thar 4th Street, Aung Myay Thar Zi, Kamayut Township, Yangon
Age range: 3–18 years
Curriculum: UK, IGCSE, ALevs

Royal British International School Yangon
15 Thukhitar Street, Moe Kaung Road, Yankin Township, Yangon
Tel: +95 157 9492
Age range: 3–18 years
Curriculum: UK, IGCSE, ALevs

SIS Yangon
29 Quarter Thuwunna Villa, Previous(1)/Present (6A) Paw San Hmwe Road, Thingangyun Township, Yangon
Tel: +95 9 426 888 100
Age range: 2–16 years
Curriculum: National, UK, IGCSE

SKT International College
No. 235 Shu Khinn Thar Myo Pat Road, Thaketa Township, Yangon
Tel: +95 145 0396
Age range: 3–16 years
Curriculum: IBDP, IGCSE

Taunggyi International School
24/12 Kan Baw Za Street (Wun Gyi Street), Yae Aye Quin Quarter, Taunggyi
Tel: +95 8 120 6765
Age range: 3–18 years
Curriculum: IBDP, UK, IGCSE, ALevs
Language instr: English, Burmese

Thalun International School
108 Hnin Si Street, Saw Yan Paing (South) Ward, Ahlone Township, Yangon
Tel: +95 997 628 5050
Age range: 18 months–18 years
Curriculum: AP, USA

The British School Yangon
Taw Win Street, Mayangone, Yangon
Tel: +95 925 073 98 73
Age range: 2–18 years
Curriculum: UK, IGCSE, ALevs

The International School Yangon
20 Shwe Taungyar Street, Bahan Township, Yangon
Tel: +95 9 880 441 040
Age range: 4–18 years
Curriculum: IBDP, USA
Language instr: English

Yangon Academy International School
35B, University Avenue Housing, New University Avenue Road, Bahan Township, Yangon 11201
Tel: +959 7707 9999 4
Age range: 3–18 years
Curriculum: AP, SAT, USA

Yangon American International School
No. 2A Yangon-Insein Road, Building (2), No. 9 Ward, Hlaing Township, Yangon
Tel: +95 997 701 2100
Age range: 2–18 years
Curriculum: AP, IBPYP, USA
Language instr: English, Burmese

Yangon International School
No. 117 Thumingalar Housing, Thingangyun Township, Yangon
Tel: +95 1 578171
Age range: 3–18 years
Curriculum: AP, IBDP, USA
Language instr: English

NEPAL

Cosmos International College
Gairapatan Road, Pokhara 33700
Tel: +977 6 1522 376
Curriculum: UK, IGCSE, ALevs

Delhi Public School - BPKIHS
Ghopa, Dharan, Sunsari 56700
Tel: +977 2 5523 308
Age range: 3–18 years

Ecole Française Internationale de Katmandou
P.O. Box 452, Lazimpat, Kathmandu
Tel: +977 1 4001 673
Age range: 4–18 years
Curriculum: National, FrenchBacc
Language instr: French, English, Nepali

Gandaki Boarding School
Ward No. 16, Lamachaur, Pokhara
Tel: +977 6 1440 414
Age range: 9–18 years
Curriculum: National, UK, ALevs

Genius School Lalitpur
Mahalaxmi Municipality, Lubhu, Lalitpur 44700
Tel: +977 1 5582 564
Age range: 3–16 years
Curriculum: IBPYP
Language instr: English

Himalayan WhiteHouse IB World School
Subidhanagar, Tinkune-32, Kathmandu 44604
Tel: +977 980 1268 579
Curriculum: IBPYP
Language instr: English, Nepali

Kathmandu Euro School
Gongabu, Baniyatar, Kathmandu
Tel: +977 984 3430 945
Curriculum: IBPYP
Language instr: English, Nepali

Kathmandu International Study Centre (KISC)
P.O. Box 2714, Thecho, Lalitpur
Tel: +977 1 5570 142
Age range: 4–18 years
Curriculum: AP, UK, USA, IGCSE, ALevs
Language instr: English

Lincoln School
P.O. Box 2673, Rabi Bhawan, Kathmandu
Tel: +977 1 5370 482
Age range: 3–18 years
Curriculum: USA
Language instr: English

Lumbini International College
P.O. Box 8975, Mahalaxmisthan, Lagankhel, Lalitpur 5666
Curriculum: UK, ALevs

Machhapuchchhre School
Lalitpur Metropolitan-13, Lalitpur
Tel: +977 1 5193 144
Curriculum: IBPYP
Language instr: English, Nepali

Malpi International College (MIC)
Narayan Gopal Chowk, Chakrapath, Kathmandu 44600
Tel: +977 1 4372 986

Modern Indian School
G.P.O. Box No: 1497, Chobhar, Kathmandu
Tel: +977 1 4330 088
Age range: 4–18 years
Curriculum: National
Language instr: English, Hindi, Nepali

Novel Academy
Pokhara 33700
Tel: +977 6 1585 629
Curriculum: UK, ALevs

Orient College
Basundhara, Kathmandu
Tel: +977 1 4362 218
Curriculum: National, UK, ALevs

Premier International School
Khumaltar Height, Satdobato, Lalitpur
Tel: +977 1 5528 032
Age range: 3–18 years
Curriculum: IBDP, IBMYP, IBPYP
Language instr: English, Nepali

Rato Bangala School
Shree Durbar Tole, Patan Dhoka, Lalitpur
Tel: +977 1 5447 618
Age range: 3–18 years
Curriculum: National, UK, ALevs

Saipal Academy
G.P.O. Box 11774,
Tel: +977 01 4009054
Age range: 3–18 years
Curriculum: National, UK, ALevs

Swostishree Gurukul
Sanobharyang, Kathmandu
Tel: +977 1 4890 314
Age range: 4–18 years
Curriculum: IBMYP, IBPYP, National
Language instr: English, Nepali

The British School Kathmandu
P.O. Box 566, Jhamsikhel, Patan
Tel: +977 1 5421 794
Age range: 3–18 years
Curriculum: National, UK, IGCSE, ALevs
Language instr: English, Nepali
(COB)

Ullens School
G.P.O. Box 8975, Khumaltar, Lalitpur 15, Kathmandu 1477
Tel: +977 1 5230 944
Age range: 3–18 years
Curriculum: IBDP, National
Language instr: English

OMAN

ABA Oman International School
P.O. Box 372, Madinat Al Irfan, 115 Muscat
Tel: +968 2495 5801
Age range: 3–18 years
No. of pupils: 940
Curriculum: IBDP, IBMYP, IBPYP, USA
Language instr: English
(CIS)

Asia

ABQ Azzan Bin Qais International School
P.O. Box 32, Bareeq Al Shatti Mall, 103 Muscat
Tel: +968 2421 0200
Age range: 3–18 years
Curriculum: National, UK, IGCSE, ALevs
Language instr: English, Arabic

Al Batinah International School
P.O. Box 193, Muweilah, 321 Sohar
Tel: +968 2685 0001
Age range: 3–18 years
Curriculum: IBDP, IBMYP, IBPYP

Al Injaz International Private School
P.O. Box 2111, 133 Al Khuwair
Tel: +968 2458 5299
Age range: 4–18 years
Curriculum: UK, IGCSE, ALevs

Al Sahwa Schools
Building No. 592, Way No. 3052, Shatti Al Qurum, Muscat
Tel: +968 2460 7620
Age range: 4–18 years
Curriculum: IBDP, IBMYP, IBPYP, National
Language instr: English, Arabic

Al Shomoukh International School
P.O. Box 938, Al Azaibah, 130 Muscat
Tel: +968 2428 4756
Age range: 3–18 years
Curriculum: National, UK, IGCSE, ALevs
Language instr: English

A'Soud Global School
P.O. Box 2598, Al Bahia Street, Al Seeb, 130 Muscat
Tel: +968 2442 3970
Age range: 4–18 years
Curriculum: IPC, UK, IGCSE, ALevs
Language instr: English

Assafwah Private School
P.O. Box 27, Al Khoudh, 132 Muscat
Tel: +968 254 6929
Age range: 3–18 years
Curriculum: UK, IGCSE, ALevs

Bangladesh School Muscat
18 November Street,
Tel: +968 2449 7127
Curriculum: UK, IGCSE, ALevs

British School Muscat - BSM
P.O. Box 1907, Al Nadhayer Street, 112 Muscat
Tel: +968 2460 0842
Age range: 3–18 years
Curriculum: UK
(COB)

British School Salalah - BSS
Al Rakha Street, Way 33023, Building 44, 214 Salalah
Tel: +968 2323 5242; +968 7930 6983
Age range: 3–18 years
Curriculum: UK

Digital Private School
Bausher Street, Behind MCBS, Bausher
Tel: +968 2458 3561
Curriculum: IBPYP
Language instr: English, Arabic

Ellesmere Muscat
Al Salam Street, Opposite Al Khoudh Police Station, Seeb, Muscat
Tel: +968 2455 4711
Age range: 3–18 years
Curriculum: IBDP, IBMYP, IBPYP
Language instr: English, Arabic

Hay Al Sharooq International School
P.O. Box 888, 411 Sur
Tel: +968 2524 0100
Age range: 3–16 years
Curriculum: National, UK, IGCSE

Indian School Al Buraimi
P.O. Box 388, 512 Al Buraimi
Tel: +968 2564 3220
Age range: 4–18 years

Indian School Al Ghubra
P.O. Box 1887, Seeb, 111 Muscat
Tel: +968 2449 1587
Age range: 4–18 years

Indian School Muscat
P.O Box 2470, Ruwi, 112 Muscat
Tel: +968 2470 2567
Age range: 4–18 years

Indian School Rustaq
P.O. Box 475, 318 Rustaq
Tel: +968 2687 6833
Age range: 4–18 years

Indian School Thumrait
P.O. Box 105, 222 Thumrait
Tel: +968 9246 4670
Age range: 4–18 years

Knowledge Gate International School
Way 2947, Al Marafah Street, Al Hail, Muscat
Tel: +968 24 07 35 00
Age range: 3–18 years
Curriculum: National, UK, IGCSE, ALevs
Language instr: English

Madinat Al Sultan Qaboos Private School (MSQPS)
P.O. Box 412, 116 Muscat
Tel: +968 2469 9739
Age range: 4–18 years
Curriculum: National, UK
Language instr: English, Arabic

Muscat International School
Muscat Expressway, Qurum
Tel: +968 2265 0100
Age range: 3–18 years
Curriculum: National, UK, IGCSE, ALevs
Language instr: English

MySchool Oman
Al Hail South, Al Seeb, Al Huda Street, Way No. 2933, Building No. 3344, Muscat
Tel: +968 2455 5171
Age range: 3–18 years
Curriculum: IBDP, IBMYP, IBPYP
Language instr: English, Arabic

OurPlanet International School Muscat
Al-Inshirah Street, Building No. 205, Plot No. 95, Block No. 221, 111 Muscat
Tel: +968 2200 5642
Age range: 3–16 years
No. of pupils: 237
Curriculum: IBMYP, IBPYP
Language instr: English

Pakistan School Muscat
P.O. Box 987, Ruwi, 112 Muscat
Tel: +968 9238 7848
Age range: 4–18 years
Curriculum: UK, IGCSE

PDO School
P.O. Box 81, Kauther Street, 100 Muscat
Tel: +968 2467 7279
Age range: 3–11 years
Curriculum: IPC, UK

Royal Flight School
P.O. Box 301, 111 Muscat
Tel: +968 2425 3660
Age range: 3–11 years
Curriculum: UK

The American International School of Muscat (TAISM)
P.O. Box 584, 130 Azaiba
Tel: +968 2459 5180
Age range: 3–18 years
Curriculum: AP, USA

The International School of Choueifat - Muscat
P.O. Box 1104, Postal Code 111 C.P.O, Muscat
Tel: +968 2453 4000
Age range: 3–18 years
Curriculum: AP, SAT, TOEFL, UK, USA, IGCSE, ALevs

The Sri Lankan School Muskat
P.O. Box 2433, 112 Ruwi
Tel: +968 2481 1005
Age range: 3–18 years
Curriculum: UK, IGCSE

The Sultan's School
P.O. Box 665, Seeb, 121 Muscat
Tel: +968 2453 6777
Age range: 4–18 years
Curriculum: IBDP, UK, IGCSE
Language instr: English, Arabic
(CIS)

PAKISTAN

Aitchison College
The Mall, Lahore 54000
Tel: +92 42 6363063
Age range: B4–18
Curriculum: ALevs

Angels International College
Faisal Town, Near Faisal Valley, West Canal Road, Faisalabad, Punjab 38000
Tel: +92 41 8850012
Curriculum: IBDP, IBMYP, IBPYP
Language instr: English

Beaconhouse College Campus Gulberg
3-C, Zafar Ali Road, Lahore 54000
Tel: +92 42 3588 6239
Curriculum: IBDP
Language instr: English

Beaconhouse Newlands Islamabad
Hill View Road, Mohra Noor, Islamabad 44000
Tel: +92 51 261 3935/6/7
Curriculum: IBDP, IBMYP, IBPYP, IBCP
Language instr: English

Beaconhouse Newlands Lahore
632/1 Street 10, Phase VI DHA, Lahore 54000
Tel: +92 (42) 111 111 020
Curriculum: IBMYP, IBPYP
Language instr: English

Beaconhouse Newlands Multan
4A, Officers Colony, Khanewal Road, Multan, Punjab 60000
Tel: +92 61 111 111 020
Curriculum: IBMYP, IBPYP
Language instr: English, Urdu

Beaconhouse School System, Clifton Campus
Frere Town 2/3 McNeil Road, Clifton, Karachi 75600
Tel: +92 21 35659190
Curriculum: IBPYP
Language instr: English

Beaconhouse School System, Defence Campus
207 A, Saba Avenue, Phase VIII, DHA, Karachi, Sindh 75500
Tel: +92 2135847083 84
Curriculum: IBDP
Language instr: English

Beaconhouse School System, Margalla Campus
Pitras Bukhari Rd, H-8/4, Islamabad 44000
Tel: +92 3345501113
Curriculum: IBDP
Language instr: English

Beaconhouse School System, PECHS Campus
35P/1, Block 6 Extension, PECHS, Karachi 75100
Tel: +92 21 34380045
Curriculum: IBDP
Language instr: English

Bloomfield Hall Schools
Head Office, 13 - A, Block S,, Gulberg II,, Lahore
Tel: +92 42 35764687
Curriculum: UK, ALevs

Asia

British Overseas School
AL 7/8, 14th/15th Lane, Off Khayaban-e-Hilal, DHA Phase VII, Karachi
Tel: +922 13 584 2307
Age range: 3–18

EMS High School
House # 33, Street #60, F 11/4, Islamabad 44000
Tel: +92 51 346 5286644
Curriculum: UK, IGCSE

Foundation Public School
A Level Campus, 42 B, Block 6, PECHS, Dr Mahmood Hussain Road, Karachi
Tel: +92 3452 5413
Age range: 16–18
Curriculum: UK, ALevs

Foundation Public School - O Level Defence Campus
PN Shifa Road, Behind Tooba Masjid, Defence Phase II, Karachi
Tel: +92 3539 0634
Age range: 14–16
No. of pupils: 550

Froebel's International School
Street 13, Sector F 7/2, Islamabad 44000
Tel: +92 51 265 2164
Curriculum: UK, IGCSE, ALevs

Happy Home School- O Level Maryam Faruqi Campus
5/3 Modern Housing Society, Shaheed-e-Millat Road, Karachi
Tel: +92 4557603
Age range: 2.5–18
Curriculum: National, UK, ALevs

Headstart School, Kuri Campus
Kuri Road, Off Park Rd, Near CDA/Park Enclave, Islamabad 44000
Tel: +92 51 8435 473
Age range: 2–19 years
No. of pupils: 2500
Curriculum: IBDP, IBMYP, IBPYP, IGCSE, ALevs
Language instr: English

Ilmesters Academy
B-31, PECHS, Block-6, Near Progressive Center, Karachi 75400
Tel: +92 21 34524423
Age range: 2.5–19 years
No. of pupils: 250
Curriculum: IBDP, IBMYP, IBPYP
Language instr: English, Urdu

International School of Islamabad
Sector H-9/1, Johar Road, P.O. Box 1124, Islamabad 44000
Tel: +92 51 443 4950
Age range: 2–19 years
No. of pupils: 321
Curriculum: IBDP, IBPYP, SAT, USA
Language instr: English

Karachi American School
Amir Khusro Road, Karachi 75350
Tel: +92 21 3453 9196
Age range: 3–18
No. of pupils: 336 B189 G147
Curriculum: USA
Language instr: English

Kingston College
1 Canal Road, Khaira, Lahore, Punjab
Tel: +92 42 3652 6047
Curriculum: IBPYP
Language instr: English

LACAS School - Gujranwala Campus
Their Sansi, Near Judicial Colony, Canal Bank Road, Gurjranwala
Tel: +92 55 4001 591
Age range: 5–18
No. of pupils: 300

Lahore American School
15 Upper Mall Canal Bank, Lahore 54000
Tel: +92 42 576 2406
Age range: 4–18
No. of pupils: 410 B310 G100

Lahore Grammar School Defence (Phase 1)
136 - E, Phase 1 Defence Housing Authority (DHA), Lahore Cantt, Punjab, Lahore 54810
Tel: +92 (42) 358 94306
Curriculum: IBPYP
Language instr: English

Lahore Grammar School Defence (Phase V)
#483/4, Block G, Education City, Phase V, Defence Housing Authority (DHA), Lahore Cantt, Lahore, Punjab 54810
Tel: +92 42 37176005/6/7
Curriculum: IBPYP
Language instr: English

Lahore Grammar School International
32/3, Sector J, DHA Phase VIII, Lahore 54972
Tel: +92 42 37175751
Curriculum: IBDP, IBMYP, IBPYP
Language instr: English

Lahore Grammar School Islamabad
Plot # 86, Faiz Ahmad Faiz Road, Sector H-8/1, Islamabad 44000
Tel: +92 51 4922092
Curriculum: IBPYP
Language instr: English

Lahore Grammar School Johar Town International
254 F1 Johar Town, Lahore, Punjab
Curriculum: IBDP
Language instr: English, Urdu

Lawrence College
Ghora Gali, Murree
Tel: +92 51 3751004
Curriculum: UK

Learning Alliance
32/1 J block, DHA Phase VIII, Lahore 54000
Tel: +92 42 111 66 66 33
Curriculum: IBDP, IBMYP, IBPYP, ALevs
Language instr: English

L'école Mondiale
Block B2, Block B 2, Phase 1, Johar Town, Lahore, Punjab 54600
Tel: +92 42 111 532653
Curriculum: IBPYP
Language instr: English, Urdu

Links School
D-101/1, Block 4, Clifton, Karachi
Tel: +92 215874322
Age range: 3–11

Pak Turk International School - Islamabad Girls Campus
Plot # 87 and 88, Sector H-8/1, Islamabad 44000
Tel: +92 51 4442713

Roots International Schools Islamabad Pakistan
Campus # 66, Street 7, Wellington Campus H-8/4, Islamabad
Tel: +92 51 8439001-7
Curriculum: SAT, IGCSE, ALevs
Language instr: English

Roots IVY International School - Chaklala Campus
Walayat Homes, Chakalala Scheme 3, Rawalpindi
Tel: +92 51 578 8380
Curriculum: IBPYP
Language instr: English

Roots Ivy International School - DHA Phase V Lahore
Plot #550/1, Sector G, DHA, Phase V (6,192.65 km), Lahore 54000
Tel: +92 302 6274309
Curriculum: IBPYP
Language instr: English, Urdu

Roots IVY International School - Faisalabad Campus
Opposite Guttwala Park, Faisalabad
Tel: +92 321 8912555
Curriculum: IBPYP
Language instr: English

Roots IVY International School - Riverview Campus
Main GT Road, Rawalpindi
Tel: +92 (0)51 4917302/3
Language instr: English

Roots Millennium Schools, Flagship Campus
No. 308, Street No. 3, Sector I-9/3, Islamabad 44000
Tel: +92 51 8439981-6
Language instr: English

Roots Millennium Schools, One World Campus
Head Office, No.80, Street 1, Sector E-11/4, Islamabad 44000
Tel: +92 51 111 111 193
Curriculum: IBMYP
Language instr: English

Rupani Academy
Riaz Road, Jutial, Gilgit, Gilgit-Baltistan
Tel: +92 58 114 58926
Curriculum: IBMYP, IBPYP
Language instr: English, Urdu

Sadiq Public School
Ahmedpur Road, Bahawalpur 63100
Tel: +92 621 2877692
No. of pupils: 2045
Curriculum: UK, ALevs

Schole International Academy
273/1/1A, Adjacent Ilma University, Near Suzuki Showroom, Korangi Creek, Karachi, Sindh
Tel: +92 (21) 350 93330
Curriculum: IBMYP, IBPYP
Language instr: English, Urdu

Sheikh Zayed International Academy
Street 8, Sector H-8/4, Islamabad
Tel: +92 51 4939298
Age range: 2–18 years
Curriculum: IBDP, IBMYP, IBPYP, UK, GCSE, IGCSE, ALevs
Language instr: English

SICAS DHA Phase VI
310/2F DHA, Phase 6, Lahore, Punjab 54770
Tel: +92 4237338361-3
Curriculum: IBPYP
Language instr: English

Springfield Public School & College
15-C Main Harley Street, Rawalpindi, Punjab 46000
Tel: +92 51 111 777 464
Age range: 11–19

St Mary's Academy
Tulsa Road, Lalazar, Rawalpindi 46000
Tel: +92 51 5178321
Curriculum: UK, GCSE

The Avicenna School - Tipu Sultan Road (Girls Campus)
17 Al-Hamra CHS, Block 7/8, Main Tipu Sultan Road, Karachi
Tel: +92 3453/414
Curriculum: ALevs

The Avicenna School - Tipu Sultan Road Campus (Boys and Girls)
36 Modern Housing Society, Main Tipu Sultan Road, Karachi
Tel: +92 21 3453 3760
Age range: 16–19
Curriculum: ALevs

The City School - A Level Campus
30-E, Industrial Area, Gurumangat Road, Gulberg-III, Lahore
Tel: +92 42 35773321
Age range: 16–19
Curriculum: ALevs

Asia

The City School, Capital Campus Islamabad
Pitras Bokhari Road, Sector H-8/1, Islamabad
Tel: +92 051 4939280
Age range: 5–19
Curriculum: IGCSE
Language instr: English

The City School, Kohat Campus
Near OTS Bypass, Bowana Road, Kohat
Tel: +92 922 861105 7
Age range: 6–16
No. of pupils: 100

The Democratic School
Masjid Ismail Road, Sitara Sapna City, Sidhupura, Faisalabad, Punjab 38001
Tel: +92 33 030 00275
Age range: 3–16 years
Curriculum: IBMYP, IBPYP
Language instr: English, Urdu

The Educational World (FB Area Senior Chapter)
D 16, Block 4, FB Area, Karachi 75950
Tel: +92 21 3636 8127
Age range: 8–16
No. of pupils: 200
Curriculum: UK

The International School (TIS)
Executive, 51-C Old Clifton, Near Mohatta Palace, Karachi 75600
Tel: +92 21 35835805-6
Age range: 3–18
No. of pupils: 250 B130 G120 VIth50
Curriculum: IBDP, IBMYP, IBPYP, UK, IGCSE
Language instr: English

The International School of Choueifat - Lahore
662-G/1, Abdul Haque Road, Johar Town, Lahore 54700
Tel: +92 423 530 0028
Age range: 4–18 years

The Learning Tree
F-8, Khayaban-e-Saadi, Block 5, Clifton, Karachi, Sindh 75600
Tel: +92 213 587 0001
Language instr: English

The Lyceum School
78 Clifton, Karachi 75600
Tel: +92 213 582 1741
Curriculum: ALevs
Language instr: English

The Peace Attitude Schools
Aurora Knowledge Park, Labmeel, Tehsil Taxila, Hazara Road, near AWC Colony, Wah, Punjab
Tel: +92 30 511 11021
Curriculum: IBPYP
Language instr: English, Urdu

Think and Grow
Plot No. 3, Green Drive, 10 km Raiwind Road, Lahore, Punjab
Tel: +92 30 011 15922
Curriculum: IBPYP
Language instr: English, Urdu

TNS Beaconhouse Defence
483/3 Sector G, Phase 5, DHA, Lahore, Punjab
Tel: +92 42 371 762 41 - 43
Age range: 3–19 years
Curriculum: IBDP, IBMYP, IGCSE
Language instr: English

TNS Beaconhouse Gulberg
1-H Jail Road, Gulberg II, Lahore, Punjab
Tel: +92 42 111 867 867
Curriculum: IBMYP
Language instr: English, Urdu

PALESTINE

Al Mustaqbal School
P.O. Box 2422, Al-Tireh, Ramallah
Tel: +970 2 296 1583
Age range: 3–18 years
Curriculum: UK, IGCSE, ALevs

Ramallah Friends School (Lower School)
P.O. Box 66, Ramallah
Tel: +970 2 295 6240
Age range: 4–11 years
Curriculum: IBPYP
Language instr: English

Ramallah Friends School (Upper School)
P.O. Box 66, Ramallah
Tel: +970 2 295 6230
Age range: 11–18 years
Curriculum: IBDP, IBMYP
Language instr: English

The American International School in Gaza
Nazareth Street, Rinal, Gaza
Tel: +972 8 288 0440
Age range: 3–18 years
Curriculum: USA

PHILIPPINES

Assumption College San Lorenzo
San Lorenzo Drive, San Lorenzo Village, 1223 Makati City, Metro Manila
Tel: +63 2 8817 0757
Curriculum: IBDP
Language instr: English, Filipino

Australian International School, Manila
8428 Dr. A. Santos Avenue (Sucat Road), Brgy. BF Homes 1, 1720 Paranaque City, Metro Manila
Tel: +63 91 7525 8109
Age range: 3–16
No. of pupils: 147 B75 G72
Language instr: English

Bannister Academy
Circulo Verde, Calle Industria, Bagumbayan, Quezon City, Metro Manila
Tel: +63 0998 575 7448
Curriculum: IBDP
Language instr: English, Pilipino

Benedictine International School
Capitol Hills Drive, Matandang Balara, Quezon City, Metro Manila
Tel: +63 917 193 2363
Age range: 4–16
Language instr: English

Brent International School Baguio
Brent Road, 2600 Baguio City, Cordillera
Tel: +63 74 442 4050
Curriculum: IBDP
Language instr: English

Brent International School Manila
Brentville Subdivision, Mamplasan, 4024 Biñan, Calabarzon
Tel: +63 2 8779 5140
Curriculum: IBDP
Language instr: English

Brent International School Subic
Building 6601 Binictican Drive, Subic Bay Freeport Zone, Zambales, 2222 Subic, Central Luzon
Tel: +63 47 252 6871/72
Curriculum: IBDP
Language instr: English

Brentwood College of Asia International School
Naga City, Bicol
Tel: +63 54 472 6345
Language instr: English

Britesparks International School
#15 Metropoli Drive, C5-Bagumbayan, 1110 Quezon City, Metro Manila
Tel: +63 917 324 1706
Age range: 2–15

British School Manila
36th Street, University Park, Bonifacio Global City, 1634 Taguig City, Metro Manila
Tel: +63 2 8860 4800
Age range: 3–18 years
Curriculum: IBDP, UK
Language instr: English

Cebu International School
Pit-os, 6000 Cebu City, Central Visayas
Tel: +63 32 342 7788
Age range: 3–18 years
Curriculum: IBDP, IBMYP, IBPYP
Language instr: English

Chiang Kai Shek College
1274 Padre Algue Street, Tondo, 1012 Manila, Metro Manila
Tel: +63 2 252 6161
Curriculum: IBDP, IBMYP, IBPYP
Language instr: English, Pilipino

Chinese International School Manila
Upper McKinley Road, McKinley Hill, Fort Bonifacio, 1634 Taguig City, Metro Manila
Tel: +63 2 8743 8134
Curriculum: IBDP
Language instr: English

CIE British School
168 President Magsaysay Street, Kasambagan, 6000 Cebu City, Central Visayas
Tel: +63 917 322 5444

Domuschola International School
#13 J. Cruz Street, Ugong, 1609 Pasig City, Metro Manila
Tel: +63 2 8635 2002
Curriculum: IBDP, IBPYP
Language instr: English, Filipino

Eton International School
CCP Complex, Roxas Boulevard, Pasay, Metro Manila
Tel: +63 917 631 4547
Language instr: English

Faith Academy
Penny Lane Street, Valley Golf Subdivision, San Juan, 1900 Cainta, Calabarzon
Tel: +63 2 8651 7100
Age range: 3–18 years

Fountain International School
#1 Goverment Center Cor Col. Bonny Serrano, 1500 San Juan, Metro Manila
Tel: +63 2 8723 7307
Age range: 4–18 years
Curriculum: IGCSE, ALevs
Language instr: English

German European School Manila
75 Swaziland Street, Better Living Subdivision, 1711 Paranaque City, Metro Manila
Tel: +63 2 8776 1000
Age range: 3–18 years
Curriculum: IBDP, IBPYP, IBCP
Language instr: English

Hope Christian High School
1242 Benavidez Street, Santa Cruz, 1003 Manila, Metro Manila
Tel: +63 2 5310 8071
Curriculum: IBPYP
Language instr: English, Chinese

Immaculate Conception Academy
10 Grant Street, Greenhills, San Juan, Metro Manila
Tel: +63 2 8723 7041
Curriculum: IBDP
Language instr: English, Tagalog

Asia

International British Academy
KM25 General Aguinaldo Highway, Anabu 2D, 4103 Imus City, Calabarzon
Tel: +63 46 471 5922
Age range: 3–17 years
Curriculum: UK, IGCSE
Language instr: English

International School Manila
University Parkway, Fort Bonifacio Global City, 1634 Taguig City, Metro Manila
Tel: +63 2 8840 8400
Age range: 3–18 years
No. of pupils: 2450
Curriculum: IBDP
Language instr: English

Keys School Manila
951 Luna Mencias Street, corner Araullo Street, Addition Hills, 1550 Mandaluyong City, Metro Manila
Tel: +63 2 8727 9357
Age range: 2–18 years
Curriculum: IBDP
Language instr: English

Kids International Learning Academy
#4 Cobra Street Village East, 1900 Cainta, Calabarzon
Tel: +63 2 8655 9841
Language instr: English

La Salle Green Hills
343 Ortigas Avenue, 1550 Mandaluyong, Metro Manila
Tel: +63 2 8721 2000
Curriculum: IBDP
Language instr: English, Pilipino

Learning Links Academy
Alcalde Street, Tibig, Silang, 4118 Cavite, Calabarzon
Tel: +63 917 305 8574
Language instr: English

Life Academy International
CCF Center, Ortigas East, Ortigas Avenue cor. C-5 Road, Ugong, Pasig City, Metro Manila
Tel: +63 917 777 5433
Curriculum: IBDP
Language instr: English

MGC New Life Christian Academy
14th Drive, University Parkway, Bonifacio Global City, Fort Bonifacio, 1634 Taguig City, Metro Manila
Tel: +63 2 8816 4233
Curriculum: IBPYP
Language instr: English, Pilipino

MIT International School
Alabang-Zapote Road, corner Don Manolo Boulevard, Alabang, 1770 Muntinlupa City, Metro Manila
Tel: +63 2 8809 1616
Language instr: English

Mother Goose Lipa
City Park Avenue, corner of Gladiola Street, City Park Subd., Sabang, 4217 Lipa City, Calabarzon
Tel: +63 43 702 9630
Curriculum: IBPYP
Language instr: English, Pilipino

Multiple Intelligence International School
4 Escaler Street, Loyola Heights, 1108 Quezon City, Metro Manila
Tel: +63 920 927 3664
Age range: 3–18 years

Noblesse International School
Circumferential Road, Friendship Highway, Cutcut, Santo Domingo, 2009 Angeles City, Central Luzon
Tel: +63 45 459 9000
Age range: 3–18 years
Curriculum: IBDP, IBMYP, IBPYP
Language instr: English

Nord Anglia International School Manila
Bradco Avenue, Aseana, Paranaque City, Metro Manila 1701
Tel: +63 2 7987 7878
Age range: 2–18 years
No. of pupils: 200
Curriculum: UK, IGCSE, ALevs
Language instr: English

ONE International School Philippines
Atmosphere Resorts & Spa, 6217 Maayong Tubig, Central Visayas
Tel: +63 917 312 0517
Curriculum: UK

Our Lady of Victories Catholic School of Quezon City
6 Cannon Road Street, 1112 Quezon City, Metro Manila
Tel: +63 2 998 886 5809
Age range: 3–18 years
Curriculum: IBMYP, IBPYP
Language instr: English, Pilipino

Reedley International School
J. Cruz Street, Ugong, 1604 Pasig City, Metro Manila
Tel: +63 917 507 9306
Language instr: English

Saint Jude Catholic School
327 Ycaza Street, San Miguel, 1005 Manila, Metro Manila
Tel: +63 2 8735 6386
Curriculum: IBDP
Language instr: English

Singapore School Cebu
Zuellig Avenue, North Reclamation Area, Mandaue City, 6014 Cebu, Central Visayas
Tel: +63 32 236 5772
Age range: 3–18 years
Curriculum: IBDP
Language instr: Chinese, English

Singapore School Clark
D'Heights (Sunvalley) Golf and Resort, Jose Abad Santos Avenue, Clark Freeport Zone, Pampanga, Central Luzon
Tel: +63 908 885 3848
Age range: 3–18 years
Curriculum: IGCSE

Singapore School Manila
Lots 1 & 40, Block 2 East Street, East District, Asena City, Paranaque City, Metro Manila
Tel: +63 2 7500 4672
Age range: 3–18 years
Curriculum: IBDP
Language instr: English

Singapore School Manila Green Campus
Balite 2, Silang, Cavite, Calabarzon
Tel: +63 917 547 1717
Age range: 3–18 years

Southville International School & Colleges (SISC)
1281 Luxembourg Street, corner Tropical Avenue, B.F. Homes International, 1740 Las Pinas City, Metro Manila
Tel: +63 2 8825 6374
Age range: 3–18 years
Curriculum: IBDP
Language instr: English

Stonyhurst Southville International School - Batangas City Campus
Gov. Antonio Carpio Road, Gulod Itaas, Batangas City, Calabarzon
Tel: +63 43 723 3595

Stonyhurst Southville International School - Malarayat Campus
Mahogany Avenue, Dagatan, 4217 Lipa City, Calabarzon
Tel: +63 43 757 4878

The Beacon Academy
Cecilia Araneta Parkway, 4024 Binan, Calabarzon
Tel: +63 2 425 1326
Curriculum: IBDP, IBMYP
Language instr: English

The Beacon School
PCPD Building, 2332 Chino Roces Avenue Extension, Taguig City 1630
Tel: +632 840 5040 loc 105
Age range: 5–14
No. of pupils: 269 B144 G125
Curriculum: IBMYP, IBPYP
Language instr: English

The Manila Times College of Subic
George Dewey Complex, Subic Bay Gateway District II, Subic Bay Freeport Zone, Zambales, 2222 Subic, Central Luzon
Tel: +63 927 365 8270
Curriculum: IBPYP
Language instr: English, Pilipino

Victory Christian International School
339 Robinson Circle, Capt. Henry Javier Drive, Oranbo, 1600 Pasig City, Metro Manila
Tel: +63 2 8671 8505
Language instr: English

Westfields International School
21-2 Friendship Highway, Cutcut, 2009 Angeles City, Central Luzon
Tel: +63 917 510 0002
Age range: 2–18 years
Language instr: English

Xavier School
64 Xavier Street, Greenhills West, 1500 San Juan, Metro Manila
Tel: +63 2 8723 0481
Age range: B3–18 years
Curriculum: IBDP
Language instr: English

QATAR

ACS Doha International School
Building No. 10, Street No. 161, Area number/Zone 70, Al Kheesa, Doha
Tel: +974 4474 9000
Age range: 3–18 years
Curriculum: IBDP, IBMYP, IBPYP, IBCP
Language instr: English

Al Bayan Educational Complex for Girls
PO Box 23533, Doha
Tel: +974 44591791
Age range: G3–18
Language instr: English

Al Jazeera Academy
PO Box 22250, Mesaimeer, Doha
Tel: +974 4469 3777
Age range: 3–19
No. of pupils: 1340
Curriculum: UK
Language instr: English

Al Khor International School
Al Khor Community, PO Box 22166, Doha
Tel: +974 4473 4666
Age range: 4–18
No. of pupils: 1650 B950 G700
Curriculum: SAT, UK
Language instr: English

Alpha Cambridge School
P.O. Box 8055, Street 300 Zone 91, Al Mashaf, Al Wukhair
Tel: +974 4463 7494

American School of Doha
PO Box 22090, Doha
Tel: +974 4459 1500
Age range: 4–18
No. of pupils: 2250 B1275 G1275
Curriculum: ACT, AP, IBDP, SAT, USA
Language instr: English

Arab International Academy
Al Sadd Area, Sports Roundabout, Doha 15810
Tel: +974 40414999
Curriculum: IBDP, IBMYP, IBPYP
Language instr: Arabic, English

Asia

Awfaz Global School
PO Box 6303, Doha
Tel: 974 44814331
Age range: 2–12
No. of pupils: 405

AWSAJ Academy
PO Box 6639, Doha
Tel: +974 4454 2111
Age range: 7–16
No. of pupils: 181
Curriculum: USA

Beta Cambridge School
Building 9, Street 91, Zone 81, Al Meshaf, Al Wukair, Al Wakrah, Doha
Tel: +974 4494 1200
Curriculum: AP, IBDP, IBMYP, IBPYP
Language instr: English, Arabic

Cambridge International School for Girls
PO Box 23018, Al Nuaija East, Doha
Tel: +974 446 59106
Age range: 4–18
No. of pupils: 300
Curriculum: UK

Cardiff International School
No 40 Universty Road, Near Qatar University, Dafna, Doha
Tel: +974 4411 4683
Age range: 5–9
No. of pupils: 100
Curriculum: UK

Compass International School Doha, Gharaffa
P.O. Box 22463, 13 Al Waab Al Abareeq Street, Building 55, Street No. 670 Al Abareeq, Zone 51, Doha
Tel: +974 4034 9666
Age range: 3–18 years
Curriculum: UK, IGCSE, ALevs
Language instr: English

Compass International School Doha, Madinat Khalifa
P.O. Box 22463, Al Baihaqi Street, Building 34, Street 926, Zone 32, Doha
Tel: +974 4034 9888
Age range: 3–18 years
Curriculum: IBDP, UK, IGCSE, ALevs
Language instr: English

Compass International School Doha, Themaid
P.O. Box 22463, Al Themaid, Building 16, Street 1457, Zone 51, Doha
Tel: +974 4034 6801
Age range: 3–18 years
Curriculum: UK, IGCSE, ALevs
Language instr: English

Deutsche Internationale Schule Doha
Ibn Seena School Street No. 30, Doha
Tel: +974 4451 6836
Age range: 3–18
No. of pupils: 320
Curriculum: IBDP
Language instr: English, German

Doha British School - Ain Khaled
Rawdat Al Sagah Street, Doha
Tel: +974 4019 8000
Age range: 3–18 years
Curriculum: IBDP, UK, IGCSE, ALevs
Language instr: English

Doha British School - Al Wakrah
Al Jamiyah Street, Al Wakrah
Tel: +974 4019 8080
Age range: 3–18 years
Curriculum: UK, IGCSE, ALevs
Language instr: English

Doha British School - Rawdat Al Hamama
Street 1107, Zone 70, Rawdat Al Hamama, Doha
Tel: +974 4019 8008
Age range: 3–16 years
Curriculum: UK, IGCSE
Language instr: English

Doha College
P.O. Box 7506, Al Niser Street, Doha
Tel: +974 4407 6777
Age range: 3–18 years
No. of pupils: 2600
Curriculum: UK, IGCSE, ALevs
Language instr: English

Doha English Speaking School (DESS)
Al Maarri Street, Fereej Kalaib, Doha
Tel: +974 4459 2750
Age range: 3–13 years
No. of pupils: 850
Curriculum: UK
Language instr: English

Doha Modern Indian School
P.O. Box 47391, Abu Hamour, Doha
Tel: +974 4458 3121

Dukhan English Speaking School
PO Box 100,001, Dukhan
Tel: +974 4471 6231/147
Age range: 4–16
No. of pupils: 602 B296 G306
Curriculum: SAT, UK

Education City High School
P.O. Box: 1129, Luqta Street, Doha
Tel: +974 44540973
Age range: 14–18 years
No. of pupils: 328
Language instr: Arabic, English

Etqan Global Academy
Zone 70, Street 120, Property #345, Umsuwiya street, Al Khisa
Tel: +974 4435 0475
Curriculum: IBPYP
Language instr: English, Arabic

GEMS American Academy - Qatar
Mian Street, Al Wukair, Al Wakra
Tel: +974 4 032 9000
Curriculum: USA
Language instr: English

GEMS Wellington School - Qatar
Mian Street, Al Wukair, Al Wakra
Tel: +974 4 041 7445
Age range: 3–18 years
Curriculum: UK
Language instr: English

Global Academy International
PO Box 23161, Doha
Tel: 00 974 4465 5001
Age range: 4–18
No. of pupils: 1460

Hamilton International School
Mesaimeer Area, (near the Religious Complex), Doha
Tel: +974 4492 4343
Curriculum: IBDP
Language instr: English, Arabic

Hayat Universal School (HUBS)
PO Box: 6124, Doha
Tel: +974 4468 7171
Curriculum: UK

International School of London (ISL) Qatar
PO Box 18511, North Duhail, Doha
Tel: +974 4433 8600
Age range: 3–18 years
No. of pupils: 1190
Curriculum: IBDP, IBMYP, IBPYP, USA
Language instr: English

Iqra English Girls School
PO Box 22786, Doha
Tel: +974 4451 0053
Age range: 5–11
No. of pupils: 100
Curriculum: UK

King's College, Doha
Building 14, Umm Al Shuwail Street, Zone 47, Al Thumama, Doha
Tel: +974 4496 5888
Age range: 3–18 years
No. of pupils: 731
Curriculum: UK
Language instr: English

Loydence Academy
PO Box 4524, Doha
Tel: 00974 44918111
Age range: 4–11
Curriculum: UK

Loyola International School
Al Andalus Street, Al Nasr, Doha
Tel: 00974 44311390
Age range: 4–11

Lycée Bonaparte
Al Intisar Street, PO Box 6110, Doha
Tel: +974 44 96 03 00
Age range: 4–18
Curriculum: National
Language instr: French

Lycee Franco-Qatarien Voltaire
P.O. Box 12634, Zone 55, street Al Daoudiya no. 201, Doha
Tel: +974 4035 4015
Age range: 3–18 years
No. of pupils: 1711
Curriculum: IBDP
Language instr: French, English, Arabic

Middle East International School
PO Box 269, Doha
Tel: +974 4444 9892
Age range: 4–18
No. of pupils: 500
Curriculum: USA

Newton British Academy AlDafna
Al Dafna, Doha
Tel: +974 441 422 94
Age range: 3–12
No. of pupils: 540
Curriculum: UK, IGCSE
Language instr: English

Newton British Academy Barwa City
Barwa City, Doha
Tel: +974 400 615 01
Age range: 2–14
No. of pupils: 300

Newton British School Al Waab
Al Waab, Doha
Tel: +974 444 724 27
Age range: 3–12 years
No. of pupils: 700
Curriculum: UK
Language instr: English

Newton International School
D-Ring Road, Doha
Tel: +974 446 662 46
Age range: 3–13
Curriculum: UK

Newton International School Lagoon
PO Box 8449, Doha
Tel: +974 441 222 54
Age range: 4–19
Curriculum: IGCSE
Language instr: English

Newton International School West Bay, Doha
West Bay, Doha
Tel: +974 449 355 07
Age range: 3–11
Curriculum: UK

Noor Al Khaleej International School
PO Box 24550, Doha
Tel: +974 4 466 6110
Age range: 3–19
Curriculum: UK, IGCSE

Asia

Nord Anglia International School, Al Khor
Building 3, Taimiyah Street,
Zone 74, Al Khor
Tel: +974 44379600

Olive International School - Doha
Nuaija, Doha
Tel: +974 4417 1734
Age range: 5–10

Oryx International School
Mesaimeer Campus, Barwa City Street, Mesaimeer, Doha
Tel: +974 403 600 63
Curriculum: UK, GCSE, IGCSE
(CIS)

Pak Shamaa School
P.O. Box 22579, Mesaimeer Bldg.
No. 142, Street 1011, Area 56, Doha
Tel: +974 4416 3712
Age range: 4–18 years
Curriculum: National

Park House English School
PO Box 23512, Doha
Tel: +974 4468 3800
Age range: 3–18
No. of pupils: 973 B474 G499
Curriculum: SAT, UK

Pearling Season International School of Doha
P.O. Box 47021, 46 Al Khudari Street (810), Bin Dirham (25), Al Mansou+, Doha
Tel: +974 4032 2408
Age range: 4–18 years
Curriculum: UK, IGCSE, ALevs

Philippine School Doha
Saad Bin Surara Old Murror, Al Messilah Area, PO Box 19664, Doha
Tel: +974 4440 9888
Age range: 4–18
No. of pupils: 3000

Qatar Academy Al Khor
P.O.Box: 60774, Mowasalat Street, Al Khor
Tel: +974 44546775
Age range: 3–18 years
No. of pupils: 1243
Curriculum: ACT, IBDP, IBMYP, IBPYP
Language instr: Arabic, English

Qatar Academy Al Wakra
P.O. Box: 2589, Al Farazdaq Street, street No.: 1034, Zone: 90, Doha
Tel: +974 44547418
Age range: 3–17 years
No. of pupils: 1400
Curriculum: IBDP, IBMYP, IBPYP
Language instr: Arabic, English

Qatar Academy Doha
P.O. Box: 1129, Luqta Street, Doha
Tel: +974 44542000
Age range: 3–18 years
No. of pupils: 1869
Curriculum: IBDP, IBMYP, IBPYP
Language instr: Arabic, English
(CIS)

Qatar Academy Msheireb
Msheireb Downtown Doha
Tel: +974 44542116
Age range: 3–10 years
No. of pupils: 400
Curriculum: IBPYP
Language instr: English, Arabic
(CIS)

Qatar Academy Sidra
P.O. Box: 34077, Doha
Tel: +974 44542322
Age range: 3–18 years
No. of pupils: 856
Curriculum: IBDP, IBMYP, IBPYP, IBCP
Language instr: English, Arabic
(CIS)

Qatar International School
PO Box 5697, Doha
Tel: +974 4483 3456
Age range: 3–18
Curriculum: UK
Language instr: English

Qatar Leadership Academy
PO Box 24421, Al Khor Street, Al Khor
Tel: +974 445422222
Age range: B11–18
No. of pupils: 111
Curriculum: SAT, TOEFL
Language instr: English

SEK INTERNATIONAL SCHOOL QATAR
For further details see p. 67
Onaiza 65, Doha
Tel: +974 4012 7633
Email: info@sek.qa
Website: www.sek.qa
Head of School: Maripaz Augilera
Age range: 3–18 years
Curriculum: IBDP, IBMYP, IBPYP
Language instr: Arabic, English, Spanish

Sherborne Qatar
PO Box 1108, Doha
Tel: +974 4459 6400
Age range: 3–18
No. of pupils: B400 G400 VIth80
Curriculum: UK, IGCSE, ALevs
Language instr: English

Stafford Sri Lankan School Doha
P.O. Box: 30220, Doha
Tel: +974 44694869
Age range: 4–18 years
Curriculum: SAT, UK, IGCSE, ALevs
Language instr: English

Step One International School
Musa Bin Omair St, Doha
Tel: +974 44772228
Curriculum: UK
(CIS)

Sunbeam Kindergarten
Al Bayyan Gardens Compound, (Near Al Saad Sports Stadium), PO Box 19612
Tel: +974 4444 0108
Age range: –12
Curriculum: UK

Swiss International School Qatar
Al Hashimaya Street, Al Luqta, Doha
Tel: +974 40363131
Curriculum: IBDP, IBMYP, IBPYP
Language instr: English

Tariq Bin Ziad School
Al Dafaf Street, Street 893, Al Sadd Area, Doha
Tel: +974 44542005
Age range: 3–13 years
No. of pupils: 736
Curriculum: IBPYP
Language instr: English, Arabic

The Cambridge School
PO Box 22580, Al Madeed Street, Mamoura Area
Tel: +974 4469 6590
Age range: 14–19
No. of pupils: 1500
Curriculum: UK, ALevs

The English Modern School
PO Box 875, Doha
Tel: +974 44883806/07
Age range: 3–18
No. of pupils: 2300 B1212 G1088 VIth105
Curriculum: IGCSE, ALevs
Language instr: English

The Gulf English School
PO Box 2440, Doha
Tel: +974 4457 8777
Age range: 3–18 years
Curriculum: UK
Language instr: English
(CIS)

The International School of Choueifat - Doha
P.O. Box 22085, Aba Al Erhayyat Street #915 Building #50, Legtaifiya A+, Doha
Tel: +974 4 495 9595
Age range: 4–18 years
Curriculum: AP, UK, USA, IGCSE, ALevs

The Pearl School
Al Hadara Street, Al Rowdah, Doha
Tel: +974 44442555
Age range: 5–18
No. of pupils: 40

The Royal Grammar School Guildford, Doha
Um Salal Mohamed, Street No. 631, Building No. 17, Zone No. 71, Doha
Tel: +974 4 036 0450
Age range: 3–18 years
Curriculum: UK, IGCSE, ALevs

The Scholars' International School
PO Box 201308, Doha
Tel: +974 44336336
Age range: 3–14

Vision International School - Qatar
Majilis Al Taawon Street, Almuftah Village, Al Wakra
Tel: +974 4487 0995
Age range: 3–18

REPUBLIC OF KOREA

Asia Pacific International School
820 wolgye 2-dong Nowon-gu, Seoul 139-724
Tel: +82 (0)2 907 2747
Age range: 4–18
Curriculum: AP, National, USA
Language instr: English
(EAR)

Atherton International School (AIS) Geoje
9-8 Seogando-gil, Okpo-dong, Geoje, South Gyeongsang 53227
Tel: +82 55 680 5000
Age range: 3–18 years
Curriculum: IPC, UK, IGCSE, ALevs
Language instr: English
(CIS)

Branksome Hall Asia
234 Global edu-ro, Daejeong-eup, Seogwipo-si, Jeju-do 63644
Tel: +82 64 902 5000
Age range: 3–19 years
Curriculum: IBDP, IBMYP, IBPYP
Language instr: English

British Education Korea
The British Prep, 244 Yeoksam-ro,, Gangnam-gu, South Korea 06226
Tel: 82-2-6203-9500
Curriculum: UK
(COB)

British International Academy
24, Deokpo 3-gil, Geoje 53213
Tel: +82 055 688 5154
Curriculum: IBDP, IBMYP, IBPYP

Busan Foreign School
45, Daecheon-ro 67 beon-gil, Haeundae-gu, Busan 48084
Tel: +82 (0)51 747 7199
Age range: 3–18 years
No. of pupils: 252
Curriculum: AP, SAT, USA
(EAR)

CHADWICK INTERNATIONAL
For further details see p. 48
45, Art center-daero 97 beon-gil, Yeonsu-gu, Incheon 22002
Tel: +82 32 250 5000
Email: songdo-admissions@chadwickschool.org
Website: www.chadwickinternational.org
Head of School: Frederick T. Ted Hill
Age range: 4–18 years
No. of pupils: 1447
Curriculum: IBDP, IBMYP, IBPYP
Language instr: English

Chung Nam Samsung Academy
77 Samseong-ro, Tangjeong-myeon, Asan-si, Chungcheongnam-do
Tel: +82 41 339 3000
Curriculum: IBDP
Language instr: English, Korean

Asia

Daegu Daegun Middle School
46 Wolgok-ro 94-gil, Dalseo-gu, Daegu, North Gyeongsang
Tel: +82 53 234 8808
Curriculum: IBMYP
Language instr: Korean

Daegu International School (DIS)
22, Palgong-ro 50-gil, Dong-gu, Daegu, North Gyeongsang 41021
Tel: +82 53 980 2100
Age range: 4–18 years
No. of pupils: 350
Curriculum: AP

Dulwich College Seoul
6 Sinbanpo-ro 15-gil, Seocho-gu, Seoul 06504
Tel: +82 2 3015 8500
Age range: 3–18 years
No. of pupils: 700
Curriculum: IBDP, UK, IGCSE
Language instr: English

Dwight School Seoul
21 World Cup Buk-ro 62-gil, Mapo-gu, Seoul 03919
Tel: +82 2 6920 8600
Age range: 3–18 years
Curriculum: IBDP, IBMYP, IBPYP, SAT
Language instr: English
(CIS) (EAR)

Gyeonggi Academy of Foreign Languages
30, Gosan-ro 105 Beon-gil, Uiwang-si, Gyeonggi-do 16075
Tel: +82 (0)31 361 0500
Age range: 15–18
Curriculum: IBDP
Language instr: English

Gyeonggi Suwon International School
451 YeongTong-Ro, YeongTong-Gu, Suwon City, Gyeonggi-Do 16706
Tel: +82 31 695 2800
Curriculum: IBDP, IBMYP, IBPYP
Language instr: English
(EAR)

Gyeongnam International Foreign School
49-22, Jodong-gil, Sanam-myeon, Sacheon-si, Gyeongnam 52533
Tel: +82 (0)55 853 5125
No. of pupils: 115
Curriculum: IBDP, IBMYP, IBPYP
Language instr: English

Hyundai Foreign School
3rd Floor, Hanmaeum Community Center, 30 Badeurae 1-gil, Dong-Gu, Ulsan 44033
Tel: +82 52 252 2851
Age range: 3–14 years
No. of pupils: 50
Language instr: English

International Christian School Pyeongtaek
53 Shindaegojan-gil, Pyeongtaek, Gyeonggi 17830
Tel: +82 31 651 1376
Age range: 5–18 years
Curriculum: AP, USA
Language instr: English

International Christian School Uijeongbu
Jindeung-ro 28, Uijongbu 11608
Tel: +82 31 855 1276
Language instr: English
(EAR)

International School of Busan
50 Gijang-daero, Gijang-eup, Gijang-gun, Busan 46081
Tel: +82 51 742 3332
Age range: 2–18
No. of pupils: 310
Curriculum: IBDP, IBMYP, IBPYP, IGCSE
Language instr: English

Korea Foreign School
7-16, Nambusunhwan-ro 364-gil, Seocho-gu, Seoul 06739
Tel: +82 2 571 2917/18
Curriculum: IBPYP
Language instr: English
(CIS) (EAR)

Korea International School
373-6 Baekhyun-dong, Bundang-gu, Seonhnam-si, Gyeonggi-do 463-420
Tel: +82 31 789 0505
Age range: 4–18
(EAR)

Korea Kent Foreign School
13 Jayang-Ro 35-Gil, Gwangjin-Gu, Seoul, 04993
Tel: +82 2 2201 7091
Curriculum: USA
(EAR)

Kwangju Foreign School
106 Samso-ro, Geonguk-dong, Buk-gu, Gwangju, South Jeolla
Tel: +82 62 575 0900
Age range: 4–18 years
Curriculum: USA

Namsung Elementary School
Joong-gu Samgil 14, Busan, South Gyeongsang 48926
Curriculum: IBPYP
Language instr: English, Korean

North London Collegiate School Jeju
33, Global edu-ro 145beon-gil, Daejeong-eup, Seogwipo-si, Jeju-do 63644
Tel: +82 64 793 8004
Age range: 4–18 years
No. of pupils: 1320
Curriculum: IBDP, IGCSE
Language instr: English

Seoul Foreign British School
39 Yeonhui-ro 22 gil, Seodaemun-gu, Seoul 120-823
Tel: +82 2 330 3100
Age range: 3–14
No. of pupils: 300
Curriculum: SAT, UK
Language instr: English

Seoul Foreign School
39 Yeonhui-ro 22-gil, Seodaemun-gu, Seoul 03723
Tel: +82 2 330 3100
Age range: 2–18 years
No. of pupils: 1600
Curriculum: ACT, IBDP, IBMYP, IBPYP, SAT, UK, USA, IGCSE
Language instr: English
(EAR)

Seoul International School
388-14 Bokjeong-dong, Sujeong-gu, Seongnam, Gyeonggi-do, Seoul 461-200
Tel: +82 31 750 1200
Age range: 4–19
No. of pupils: 999 B490 G509
Curriculum: USA
(EAR)

SIS Gwangju
2~6F, SIS Bldg, 17 Obang-ro, Nam-gu, Gwangju
Tel: +62 21 759 14414

Taejon Christian International School
77 Yongsan 2 Ro, Yuseong Gu, Daejeon 305-500
Tel: +82 42 620 9000
Age range: 3–18 years
No. of pupils: 400
Curriculum: IBDP, IBMYP, IBPYP
Language instr: English
(EAR)

Westminster Canadian Academy
36 Dolmugae-Gil,, Gwacheon-City, Gyeonggi-Do
Tel: +82 (0) 2 504 7200
Curriculum: National

Yongsan International School of Seoul
285 Itaewon-ro, Yongsan-gu, Seoul 04347
Tel: +82 2 797 5104
Age range: 5–18
Curriculum: AP, SAT, USA
Language instr: English
(EAR)

REPUBLIC OF MALDIVES

Billabong High International School
EPSS Building, Ameenee Magu, Malé 20371
Tel: +960 302 2040
Age range: 3–18 years
Curriculum: UK, IGCSE, ALevs

Lale Youth International School
Reethigas Hingun, Hulhumale 23000
Tel: +960 335 0029
Age range: 3–18 years
Curriculum: UK, IGCSE, ALevs

SAUDI ARABIA

Abdulaziz International School - Al Sulaimaniah
Prince Turki Bin Abdullah Al Saud Street, Riyadh 11537
Tel: +966 11 473 8555
Age range: 4–18 years
Curriculum: AP, UK, USA, IGCSE, ALevs

Abdulaziz International School - Al Wadi
P.O. Box 68629, Exit 6, Al Wadi, Riyadh 11537
Tel: +966 50 189 4546
Age range: 4–14 years

Advanced Generations School - Elementary Boys
Al Nahdah District, Jeddah 23437
Tel: +966 420 2432
Age range: 4–12

Advanced Generations School - Elementary Girls
Al Nahdah District, Jeddah 23437
Tel: +966 420 2283
Age range: 4–12

Advanced Learning Schools
PO Box 221985, Riyadh 11311
Tel: +966 1 207 0926
Age range: 4–18
No. of pupils: 465
Curriculum: IBDP, IBMYP, IBPYP
Language instr: English
(CIS)

Ajial Aseer International School
PO Box 43, Khamis Mushayt
Tel: +966 7 223 1967
Age range: 4–15
No. of pupils: 180 B100 G80
Language instr: English

Al Alia International Indian School
PO Box 281025, Riyadh 11392
Tel: +966 4128884
Age range: 5–18
No. of pupils: 300

Al Andalus Private Schools
Batarji Street, Azzahra Dist, Jeddah 21443
Tel: +966 556 645 532
Curriculum: IBPYP
Language instr: English, Arabic

Al Anjal Private School
PO Box 849, Hofuf 31982
Tel: +966 2 683 0551
Age range: 5–18
No. of pupils: 1628
Curriculum: USA

Asia

Al Bayan Model School Girls
PO Box 13949, Jeddah 21414
Tel: +966 6611004
Curriculum: USA

Al Faris International School
Tawaan Area, Imam Saud Road, Khan Younes Street, Riyadh 9483
Tel: +966 011 454 9358
Age range: 3–18
No. of pupils: 2439
Curriculum: IBDP, IBMYP, IBPYP
Language instr: English

Al Hussan International Academy
PO Box 297, Dammam 31411
Tel: +966 13 858 0500
Age range: 3–18 years
No. of pupils: 1655
Curriculum: IBDP, IGCSE, ALevs

Al Hussan International Grammar School
16th Street, Madinat Al Umal, Al Khobar 34442
Tel: +966 882 1845

Al Hussan International School Jubail
P.O. Box 10957, Jubail 31961
Tel: +966 13 341 5561

Al Hussan International School Riyadh
P.O. Box 259777, Riyadh 11351
Tel: +966 011 248 9338

Al Hussan International School Yanbu
Prince Sultan Road, Radwa 3, Yanbu 46452
Tel: +966 14 392 1121

Al Isra International School
P.O Box 145333, Yanbu
Tel: +04 3908412
Curriculum: UK, IGCSE

Al Kawthar International Schools
7983 King Abdulaziz Branch Road, Al Mohammadiyyah, Jeddah 23618
Tel: +966 50 656 1717
Curriculum: IBMYP, IBPYP
Language instr: Arabic, French

Al Majd International School
PO Box 76240, Al Khobar 31952
Tel: +966 13 858 0383/0380/0277
Age range: 5–18
No. of pupils: 500

Al Omam International School
4283 Tal Al Asfar, Al Rihab District, Jeddah
Tel: +966 2 6746557
Age range: 5–18
No. of pupils: 300
Curriculum: USA

Al Reeyada International School
PO Box 5282, Al Hasa 31982
Tel: +966 1 3599 3961
Curriculum: UK, IGCSE, ALevs

Al Rissalah International School
Sulemaniah Street, East of Jazirah Supermarket, PO Box 250905, Riyadh 11391
Tel: +966 1 465 79 90
Age range: 4–18
Curriculum: USA, IGCSE

Al Waha International School
P.O. Box 12491, Jeddah 21473
Tel: +966 12 619 9181
Age range: 4–18 years
Curriculum: UK, IGCSE, ALevs

Al-Afaq International School
Hail Street, Al Hamra District, PO Box 9717, Jeddah 21423
Tel: +966 12 665 2423
Age range: 4–19
Curriculum: USA

Al-Bassam International School
Dammam
Tel: +966 013 843 4999
Curriculum: IBMYP, IBPYP
Language instr: English, Arabic

Al-Bassam School - Girls Section
PO Box 945, Dammam 31421
Tel: +966 3 8094040
Age range: 4–18
No. of pupils: 300

Aldenham Prep Riyadh
Al Noura, As Sahafah, Riyadh 13321
Age range: 3–11 years

Al-Faisal International School
Al-Moalifeen Street, Jeddah
Tel: +966 2 6761955
Age range: 3–15
No. of pupils: 100
Curriculum: UK

Al-Oruba International School
Ahmed Bin Roshed Street, Fasil Bin Fahd Road, Al Rafeeah Zone Riyadh 23661, Riyadh 11553
Tel: +4153264
Age range: 4–19
No. of pupils: 3020
Curriculum: SAT, USA

Al-Rowad International Schools
P.O. Box 93354, Al-Nuzha, Riyadh 11673
Tel: +966 11 281 3003
Curriculum: SAT, UK, USA, IGCSE, ALevs

American International School - Riyadh
PO Box 990, Riyadh 11421
Tel: +966 11 459 7500
Age range: 4–18
No. of pupils: 1355
Curriculum: IBDP, USA
Language instr: English

American International School of Jeddah
P.O. Box 127328, Jeddah 21352
Tel: +966 12 232 8668
Age range: 3–18 years
Curriculum: IBDP
Language instr: English

American School Dhahran
PO Box 31677, Al-Khobar 31952
Tel: +966 (0)13 330 0555
Curriculum: IBDP

Andalus International School, Jeddah
Zayd Ibn Alkhattab Street, Ash Shati, Jeddah 23614
Tel: +966 55 506 3771
Curriculum: IBMYP, IBPYP
Language instr: English, Arabic

Andalus International School, Mecca
Al Hamra Umm Al Jud, Al-Tahkasosy, Mecca
Tel: +966 55 506 3771
Language instr: English, Arabic

Aqeeq International Academy
2644 Abi Al Hasan Al Husari, Al Aqeeq Dist. Unit No 1, Riyadh 13511-6812
Tel: +966 920 00 304
Age range: 3–18
Language instr: English, Arabic

Bangladesh International School, Jeddah (Bangla Section)
Nuzlah Sharqia, Kilo-3, Post Box 31598, Jeddah 21418
Tel: +966 02 6800520

Bangladesh International School, Jeddah (Bangla Section) Riyadh
Office No. 107 & 116, First Floor Babtain building, Olayah Street 11351
Tel: +966 05 46888648

Baraem RAIS - Dhahran - Al-Dana
Afif St, Dana Al Janubiyah, Dhahran 34453
Tel: +966 581865531

Baraem RAIS - Riyadh - Al-Sahafa
6965 Prince Abdullah Bin Saud Bin Abdullah Snatan Al Saud, Al Yasmin, Riyadh 13325 3800
Tel: +966 2145475

Bayan Gardens School
PO Box 180, Al Khobar 31952
Tel: +966 3 882 2645
Age range: 3–13
No. of pupils: 350
Curriculum: USA
Language instr: Arabic, English

Bright Life International School
6704 Jibal As Sarwat, Al Mathar Ash Shamali, behind Saco Altakhasosi, Riyadh 12312
Tel: +966 53 330 0485
Curriculum: National

Bright Minds International School
Pr. Sultan Street, Behind Haram Center, An Naim District, Jeddah
Tel: +966 (0)12 654 2505
Curriculum: IBPYP
Language instr: English, Arabic

British International School of Al Khobar
PO Box 4359, Al Khobar 31952
Tel: +966 13 882 5425
Age range: 3–18
No. of pupils: 750 B400 G300 VIth50
Curriculum: UK, GCSE, IGCSE, ALevs
Language instr: English

British International School Riyadh
PO Box 85769, Al Hamra, Riyadh 11612
Tel: +966 11 520 9050
Age range: 3–18 years
Curriculum: IBDP, UK, GCSE, IGCSE, ALevs
Language instr: English

Britus International School, Al Olaya
3505 Prince Abdulaziz Ibn Musaid Ibn Jalawi Street, Al Olaya 6430, Riyadh 12221
Tel: +966 55 583 7660
Age range: 4–18 years
Curriculum: USA

Coral International School
Alrawdah District, PO Box 9864, Jeddah 21423
Tel: +966 2 683 2002
Age range: 4–18
No. of pupils: 783
Curriculum: USA

Dar Al Fikr Schools
PO Box 14279, Jeddah 21424
Tel: +966 2 631 1118
Age range: 3–19
No. of pupils: 643
Curriculum: AP, USA

Dar Jana International School-Rawda Campus
PO Box 118149, Jeddah 21312
Tel: +966 2 664 8310
Curriculum: USA

Deutsche Internationale Schule Jeddah
P.O. Box 7510, Jeddah 21472
Tel: +966 12 691 3584
Curriculum: IBDP
Language instr: English

Dhahran Ahliyya Schools
P.O.Box 39333, Dhahran 31942
Tel: +966 138919222
Age range: B3–18
Curriculum: IBMYP, IBPYP, SAT, USA
Language instr: English, Arabic

Asia

Dhahran British Grammar School
PO Box 31677, Al-Khobar 31952
Tel: +966 13 330 0555
Age range: 4–18
No. of pupils: 700 B350 G350 VIth37
Curriculum: UK, GCSE, IGCSE, ALevs
Language instr: English
(CIS)

Dhahran Elementary/ Middle School
PO Box 31677, Al-Khobar 31952
Tel: +966 13 330 0555 (Ext:2353)

Dunes International School
King Saud Road (Al-Qashla Road),
PO Box 8627, Al-Andalus 34437
Tel: +966 3 8145850
Age range: 3–14

Ecole Internationale Arc de Triomphe
PO Box 32546, Jeddah 21438
Tel: + 966 12 6065 421
Curriculum: FrenchBacc

Education Castle International School
Al Iqtisad, Alfayhaa, Riyadh 14253
Tel: +966 54 412 1160
Age range: 4–18 years

Education Gate International School, Al Murraba
P.O. Box 24804, Al Murraba, Riyadh 11456
Tel: +966 56 994 6993
Age range: 4–16 years
Curriculum: National

Education Gate International School, Al Rawdah
4245 Zaidal khyr, Ar Rawdah, Riyadh 13211
Tel: +966 59 472 5599 / +966 55 521 6601
Age range: 4–16 years
Curriculum: National

Green Hills International School
PO Box 118707, Jeddah 21312
Tel: +966 12 6063959
Age range: 4–19
No. of pupils: 800

Hala International School
Al Khwarazmi Street, Al Aziziya District, Jeddah, KSA
Tel: +966 12 6715543
Curriculum: IGCSE, ALevs

Horizon International School
Abdullah Alanqari Street, Al Wurud, Riyadh
Tel: +966 11 460 4646
Age range: 5–18
Curriculum: USA

International Indian School - Jeddah
PO Box 14861, Jeddah 21434
Tel: + 966 6751536
Age range: 4–19

International Programs School
Prince Sultan Road, Qurtoba, Al Khobar 34236
Tel: +966 13 857 5603
Age range: 4–18 years
Curriculum: IBDP, IBPYP
Language instr: English

International Schools Group (ISG) Dammam
PO Box 31677, Al-Khobar 31952
Tel: +966 13 808 4676

International Schools Group (ISG) Jubail
PO Box 10059, Jubail 31961
Tel: +966 13 341 7550
Age range: Pre-K–Grade 12
No. of pupils: 410 B210 G200
Curriculum: IBDP, USA
Language instr: English

Italian School
North Cornich Road, Jeddah 21434
Tel: +966 2 606 4335
Age range: 14–19

Jeddah International Academy
P.O. Box 23445, Al Makarunah Street, Al Faisaliyya District, Jeddah
Tel: +966 92 003 3255
Age range: 4–18 years
Curriculum: ACT, AP, SAT, TOEFL, IGCSE

Jeddah Knowledge International School
Al Salamah District, Mohammed Mosaud St. (Behind Iceland), PO Box 7180, 21462 Jeddah
Tel: +966 2 691 7367
Age range: 3–18
No. of pupils: 2014
Curriculum: IBDP, IBMYP, IBPYP, National, USA
Language instr: English, Arabic
(CIS) (ECIS)

Jeddah Prep and Grammar School
PO Box 6316, Jeddah 21442
Tel: +966 2 654 2354
Age range: 3–18 B3–18 G3–18
No. of pupils: 593 B450 G450 VIth83
Curriculum: UK, IGCSE, ALevs
Language instr: English
(COB)

Jeddah Private International School
Jeddah
Tel: +966 126 064 309
Age range: 4–11

Jubail International School
PO Box 10957, Jubail 31961
Tel: +966 3 341 8710
Age range: 3–18
No. of pupils: 357 B181 G176
Curriculum: UK, USA
(CIS)

King Abdulaziz School
Ali Ibn Abi Taleb Road, P.O. Box 43111, Medina 41561
Tel: +966 553 039 300/+966 503 454 420
No. of pupils: 160
Curriculum: IBDP, IBMYP, IBPYP
Language instr: English
(♿)

King Faisal Boys School
P.O. Box 94558, Riyadh 11614
Tel: +966 11 482 0802
Age range: 3–6 years B6–18 years
Curriculum: IBDP, IBMYP, IBPYP, USA
Language instr: English, Arabic
(♿)

King Faisal Girls School
P.O. Box 94558, Riyadh 11614
Tel: +966 11 482 0802
Age range: 3–6 years G6–18 years
Curriculum: IBDP, IBMYP, IBPYP, USA
Language instr: English, Arabic
(♿)

Kingdom Schools
Ar Rabi, Riyadh
Tel: +966 11 275 5555
Age range: 3–18 years
Curriculum: USA
Language instr: English

Learning Caravan International School
PO Box 295160, Riyadh 11351
Tel: +966 1 463 45 73
Age range: 3–11
Curriculum: UK

Learning Oasis International National School
Umar Ibn Zaid, An Nafal, Riyadh 13312
Curriculum: IBPYP
Language instr: English, Arabic

MADAC Schools
P.O.Box 444, Jabla bin Thour Street, Abu Kubir District, Medina
Tel: +966 555261230
Curriculum: IBMYP, IBPYP
Language instr: English, Arabic

Manarat Jeddah International School - Boys
PO Box 40513, Jeddah 21511
Tel: +966 12 2678 3215
Age range: 11–19

Manarat Jeddah International School - Girls
PO Box 40513, Jeddah 21511
Tel: +966 12 6730 225
Age range: 11–19

Multinational School - Riyadh
Al Barkah x7, Al Falah District, Othman Bin Affah Main Road
Tel: +966 1 2751751
No. of pupils: 1600
Curriculum: IGCSE, ALevs

Nada International School
PO Box 1065, Al-Ahsa 30150
Tel: +966 1 3532 3338
Language instr: English
(ECIS)

Najd International School
Intersection of Imam Road, with Eastern Ring Road, Riyadh
Tel: +96614563922
Age range: 4–18
No. of pupils: 3800

NEOM Community School
Al Khraibah, Tabuk
Curriculum: IBDP, IBMYP, IBPYP, IBCP
Language instr: English, Arabic

New Middle East International School
PO Box 250377, Riyadh 11391
Tel: +966 1 4161201
Age range: 3–16
No. of pupils: 3500

New World International School
PO Box 3682, Dammam 31481
Tel: +966 13 814 4801
Age range: 4–19
No. of pupils: 300
Curriculum: IGCSE, ALevs

Nobles International School
PO Box 51868, Al Rawdah District, Jeddah
Tel: +966 02 664 3288
Age range: 3–18
No. of pupils: 800

Nün Academy
7639 Omair Ibn Abi Waqqas, Al Murjan District, Al Murjan District, Jeddah 23715
Tel: +966 509 939 702
Curriculum: UK
(CIS)

One World International School (OWIS) Riyadh
Al Muruj, Olaya Street, Mann Street, Riyadh 13334
Tel: +966 011 442 6021
Age range: 3–18 years
Curriculum: AP, IBPYP, USA
Language instr: English

Orbit International School Khobar
P.O. Box 31153, Al-Khobar 31952
Tel: +966 13 847 5555

Pakistan International School (English Section) Jeddah
PO Box 4690, Al-Rehab District, Jeddah 21412
Tel: +966 12 673 8670
Age range: 3–18
Curriculum: UK, IGCSE, ALevs

Pakistan International School (English Section) Riyadh
PO Box 6891, Riyadh 11452
Tel: +966 11 8805327
Age range: 3–18
No. of pupils: 300
Curriculum: IGCSE

Qodrat Alajyal School
Al-Qaswaa District, Medina
Tel: +966 56 927 2700
Language instr: Arabic, French

Qurtubah Private Schools
Prince Sultan Street, North-West
Al-Tareekh Square, Jeddah 21581
Tel: +966 551757472
Curriculum: IBPYP
Language instr: Arabic

Radhwa International School Yanbu
P.B.No. 32006, Yanbu 41912
Curriculum: IBMYP, IBPYP
Language instr: English

RAIS - Dammam - AlZahour for Boys
Anas Ibn Malik St, Az Zuhur, Dammam 32423
Tel: +966 138307890

RAIS - Dammam - AlZahour for Girls
Anas Ibn Malik St, Az Zuhur, Dammam 32423

RAIS - Dammam - Hamra International for Girls
6350 Anas Ibn Malik St, Al Hamra, Dammam 32422 3411
Tel: +966 591415477

RAIS - Jeddah - Abhor for Girls
Jeddah

RAIS - Riyadh - Mogharazat for Boys
Prince Muqrin Ibn Abdulaziz St, Al Mughrizat, Riyadh 12481
Tel: +966 920033433

RAIS - Riyadh - Mogharazat for Girls
Prince Muqrin Ibn Abdulaziz St, Al Mughrizat, Riyadh 12481

RAIS - Riyadh - Qurtoba for Girls
2590 Al Bayt Al Atiq, Qurtubah, Riyadh 13245 6874
Tel: +966 920033099

Rand International School
PO.box 9712, Dammam 31423
Tel: +966 13 8504488
Curriculum: IBPYP
Language instr: Arabic, English

Riyadh Schools
An Namudhajiyah, Prince Fahd bin Salman Road, Riyadh
Tel: +966 11 402 8411
Language instr: English, Arabic

Saad National School
PO Box 30531, Al Khobar 31952
Tel: +966 13 858 0055
Age range: 4–19
Curriculum: National

Sands International School
Shuraih Ibn Al Arith, Sulaimaniyah, Riyadh 12223
Tel: +966 11 4634124
Age range: 1–16
No. of pupils: 800

Saud International School
Hamdan Street, Sulaimaniyah, Riyadh
Tel: +966 920002877
Age range: 2–18
No. of pupils: 844
Curriculum: USA

SEK INTERNATIONAL SCHOOL RIYADH
For further details see p. 68
Al Toq Street, Ar Rabi, Riyadh 13315
Tel: +966 011 520 6170
Email: info@sek.sa
Website: www.sek.sa
Head of School: Sandra Ospina
Age range: 2–15 years
Curriculum: IBMYP, IBPYP
Language instr: English, Arabic, Spanish

Thamer International School
PO Box 52799, Jeddah
Tel: +966 12 6977033
Age range: 5–18
Curriculum: IGCSE

The British International School of Jeddah
PO Box 6453, Jeddah 21442
Tel: +966 12 283 4600
Age range: 3–18
No. of pupils: 1531 B843 G688 VIth140
Curriculum: IBDP, IGCSE
Language instr: English

The KAUST School
4700 KAUST, Thuwal, Western Province 23955-6900
Tel: +966 12 808 6803
Curriculum: IBDP, IBMYP, IBPYP
Language instr: English

The World Academy
King Abdullah Economic City, P.O. Box 8299, Jeddah 21482
Tel: +966 55 471 2325
Age range: 3–18 years
Language instr: English

Waad Academy
Obhur, Jeddah 23828
Tel: +966 1223 99710

Zahrat Al Sahraa International School
Hassan Basalma Street, PO Box 13259, Jeddah 21493
Tel: +966 12 6671199
Age range: 3–18
No. of pupils: 1050
Curriculum: USA

SINGAPORE

ACS (International), Singapore
61 Jalan Hitam Manis, Singapore 278475
Tel: +658 6472 1477
Age range: 11–19
No. of pupils: 960
Curriculum: IBDP, IGCSE
Language instr: English

Anglo-Chinese School (Independent)
121 Dover Road, Singapore 139650
Tel: +65 6773 1633
Age range: B13–18 G17–18
No. of pupils: 2898 B2664 G234
Curriculum: IBDP, UK
Language instr: English

Ascensia International School
Blk 106A Henderson Crescent, #01-01 Henderson Area Office, Singapore 151106
Tel: +65 6466 5505
Curriculum: IGCSE, ALevs
Language instr: English

Australian International School, Singapore
1 Lorong Chuan, Singapore 556818
Tel: +65 6664 8127
Age range: 2 months–18 years
Curriculum: IBDP, IBPYP, National, IGCSE
Language instr: English

Brighton College Signapore
1 Chuan Lane, Singapore 554299
Tel: +65 6505 9790
Age range: 1–11 years
Curriculum: UK
Language instr: English

Canadian International School, Lakeside Campus
7 Jurong West Street 41, Singapore 659414
Tel: +65 6743 8088
Age range: 2–18
No. of pupils: 3000
Curriculum: IBDP, IBMYP, IBPYP
Language instr: English

Chatsworth International School
72 Bukit Tinggi Road, Singapore 289760
Tel: +65 6463 3201
Age range: 3–18 years
No. of pupils: 800
Curriculum: IBDP, IBMYP, IBPYP, USA
Language instr: English

Chatsworth International School - Orchard Campus
37 Emerald Hill, Singapore 229313
Tel: +65 6737 5955
Age range: 2–11
Language instr: English

Dover Court International School Singapore
301 Dover Road, Singapore 139644
Tel: +65 6775 7664
Age range: 3–18 years
No. of pupils: 2000
Curriculum: IBDP, UK
Language instr: English

DPS International School
36 Aroozoo Avenue, Singapore 539842
Tel: +65 6285 6300
Age range: 2–18
Curriculum: UK, IGCSE, ALevs

DULWICH COLLEGE (SINGAPORE)
For further details see p. 50
71 Bukit Batok West Avenue 8, Singapore 658966
Tel: +65 6890 1003
Email: admissions.singapore@dulwich.org
Website: singapore.dulwich.org
Headmaster: Nick Magnus
Age range: 2–18 years
No. of pupils: 3000
Fees: Day S$20,270–S$56,220 FB S$43,200
Curriculum: IBDP, IGCSE
Language instr: English, Mandarin

EtonHouse International School, Broadrick
51 Broadrick Road, Singapore 439501
Tel: +65 6346 6922
Age range: 3–11 years
No. of pupils: 375
Curriculum: IBPYP
Language instr: English

EtonHouse International School, Claymore
15 Claymore Road, Singapore 229542
Tel: +65 6737 3322

EtonHouse International School, Islander
35 Allanbrooke Road, Singapore 099982
Tel: +65 6274 2211

EtonHouse International School, Mountbatten 223
223 Mountbatten Road #01-18, Singapore 398008
Tel: +65 6440 5100

EtonHouse International School, Mountbatten 717
717 Mountbatten Road, Singapore 437737
Tel: +65 6440 0777

EtonHouse International School, Mountbatten 718
718 Mountbatten Road, Singapore 437738
Tel: +65 6846 3322
Curriculum: IBPYP
Language instr: English

Asia

EtonHouse International School, Newton
39 Newton Road, Singapore 307966
Tel: +65 6352 3322
Curriculum: IBPYP
Language instr: English

EtonHouse International School, Orchard
10 Tanglin Road, Singapore 247908
Tel: +65 6513 1155
Curriculum: IBDP, IBPYP
Language instr: English, Spanish

EtonHouse International School, Robertson Walk
Robertson Walk, 11 Unity Street, #02-20, Singapore 237995
Tel: +65 6221 1050

EtonHouse International School, Sentosa
33 Allanbrooke Road, Sentosa, (5 mins from Sentosa Cove and Harbourfront), Singapore 099981
Tel: +65 6377 3322

EtonHouse International School, Thomson
8 Thomson Lane, (5 mins from Newton/Novena & 10 mins from Orchard), Singapore 297743
Tel: +65 6252 3322
Language instr: English, Mandarin

EtonHouse International School, Upper Bukit Timah
215 Upper Bukit Timah Road, Singapore 588184
Tel: +65 6762 3322

EtonHouse International School, Vanda
1 Vanda Road, Singapore 287771
Tel: +65 6468 7880

EtonHouse International School, Zhong Hua
681 Bukit Timah Road #01-03, Singapore 269782
Tel: +65 6467 3322

German European School Singapore (GESS)
2 Dairy Farm Lane, Singapore 677621
Tel: +65 6461 0881
Age range: 2–18 years
Curriculum: Abitur, IBDP, IBMYP, IBPYP, IBCP, National
Language instr: English, German

Global Indian International School (GIIS) East Coast Campus
82 Cheviot Hill, Singapore 459663
Tel: +65 6914 7100
Age range: 2.5–18 years
Curriculum: IBDP, IBPYP, IGCSE
Language instr: English

Global Indian International School (GIIS) SMART Campus
27 Punggol Field Walk, Singapore 828649
Tel: +65 6914 7100
Age range: 3–18 years
No. of pupils: 3000
Curriculum: IBDP, IBPYP, IGCSE
Language instr: English

Hollandse School Singapore
65 Bukit Tinggi Road, Singapore 289757
Tel: +65 64 66 0662
Age range: 2–12
No. of pupils: 410
Curriculum: IPC
Language instr: Dutch, English

Hwa Chong International School
663 Bukit Timah Road, Singapore 269783
Tel: +65 6464 7077
Age range: 13–18 years
No. of pupils: 1000
Curriculum: IBDP
Language instr: English

HWA International School
6 Raffles Boulevard, Marina Square #02-100/101, Singapore 039594
Tel: +65 6254 0200
Age range: 3–18 years
Curriculum: IBDP, IBMYP, IBPYP
Language instr: English, Chinese

Insworld Institute
100 Victoria Street, #08-02 National Library Building, Singapore 188064
Tel: +65 6732 1728
Age range: 12–21 years
No. of pupils: 100
Curriculum: UK, IGCSE, ALevs
Language instr: English

INTERNATIONAL COMMUNITY SCHOOL
For further details see p. 56
27A Jubilee Road, Singapore 128575
Tel: +65 6776 7435
Email: info@ics.edu.sg
Website: www.ics.edu.sg
Head of School: Darryl Harding
Age range: 4–18 years
No. of pupils: 400
Fees: Day S$29,807–S$43,133
Curriculum: AP, SAT, USA

ISS International School
21 Preston Road, 109355
Tel: +65 6475 4188
Age range: 4–19 years
Curriculum: IBDP, IBMYP, IBPYP, USA
Language instr: English

Madrasah Aljunied Al-Islamiah
30 Victoria Lane, Singapore 198424
Tel: +65 6391 5970/1
Curriculum: IBDP
Language instr: English, Malay

Nexus International School (Singapore)
1 Aljunied Walk, Singapore 387293
Tel: +65 6536 6566
Age range: 3–18 years
No. of pupils: 1200
Curriculum: IBDP, IBPYP, UK, IGCSE, ALevs
Language instr: English

North London Collegiate School Singapore
130 Depot Road, Singapore 109708
Tel: +65 6989 3000
Curriculum: IBDP, IBMYP
Language instr: English

NPS International School
11 Hillside Drive, Singapore 548296
Tel: +65 6294 2400
Age range: 3–18 years
No. of pupils: 1400
Curriculum: IBDP, IGCSE
Language instr: English

Odyssey The Global Preschool - Dempsey Campus
29 Harding Road, Singapore 249537
Tel: +65 6333 5888
Language instr: English, Chinese

Odyssey The Global Preschool - Fourth Avenue Campus
20 Fourth Avenue, Singapore 268669
Tel: +65 6781 8800
Curriculum: IBPYP
Language instr: English, Chinese

Odyssey The Global Preschool - Loyang Campus
191 Jalan Loyang Besar, Singapore 506996
Tel: +65 6781 8800
Curriculum: IBPYP
Language instr: English, Chinese

Odyssey The Global Preschool - Orchard Campus
50A Lloyd Road, Singapore 239128
Tel: +65 6781 8800
Language instr: English, Chinese

Odyssey The Global Preschool - Still Road Campus
25 Still Road South, Singapore 423934
Tel: +65 6781 8800
Curriculum: IBPYP
Language instr: English, Chinese

Odyssey The Global Preschool - Wilkinson Campus
101 Wilkinson Road, Singapore 436559
Tel: +65 6781 8800
Curriculum: IBPYP
Language instr: English, Chinese

One World International School (OWIS) Digital Campus Punggol
#01-02, Global Campus Village, 27 Punggol Field Walk, Singapore 828649
Tel: +65 6914 6700
Age range: 3–15 years
Language instr: English

One World International School (OWIS) Nanyang
21 Jurong West Street 81, Singapore 649075
Tel: +65 69146700
Age range: 3–18 years
No. of pupils: 1600
Curriculum: IBDP, IBPYP, IGCSE
Language instr: English

One World International School (OWIS) Suntec
1 Raffles Boulevard, Singapore 039593
Tel: +65 6914 6700
Age range: 3–11 years

Overseas Family School
81 Pasir Ris Heights, Singapore 519292
Tel: +65 6 738 0211
Age range: 2–18 years
Curriculum: IBDP, IBMYP, IGCSE
Language instr: English

Pegasus International College (Singapore)
331 North Bridge Road, #11-01 Odeon Towers, Singapore 188720
Tel: +65 6392 3850

Rosemount International School
25 Ettrick Terrace, Siglap 458588
Tel: +65 6446 4636

Singapore American School
40 Woodlands Street 41, Singapore 738547
Tel: +65 6363 3403
Age range: 3–21
No. of pupils: 2196
Curriculum: ACT, AP, SAT, TOEFL, USA

Singapore Chinese Girls School
190 Dunearn Road, 309437
Tel: +65 6252 7966
Age range: 6–16
Curriculum: National

Singapore Korean School
71 Bukit Tinggi Road, Singapore 289759
Tel: +65 6741 0778
Age range: 4–19

Sir Manasseh Meyer International School
3 Jalan Ulu Sembawang, Singapore 758932
Tel: +65 6331 4633

St Francis Methodist School
492 Upper Bukit Timah Road, 678095
Tel: +65 6760 0889
Age range: 12–20
Curriculum: IBDP
Language instr: English

St. Joseph's Institution International
490 Thomson Road, Singapore 298191
Tel: +65 6353 9383
Age range: 4–18 years
No. of pupils: 2000
Curriculum: IBDP, IPC, IGCSE
Language instr: English

Asia

Stamford American International School
1 Woodleigh Lane, 357684
Tel: +65 6653 2949
Age range: 2 months–18 years
No. of pupils: 3000
Curriculum: IBDP, IBMYP, IBPYP, USA
Language instr: English

Swiss School in Singapore
38 Swiss Club Road, Singapore 288140
Tel: +65 64 68 21 17
Age range: 2–12
No. of pupils: 250
Language instr: French/German, English

TANGLIN TRUST SCHOOL IN SINGAPORE
For further details see p. 73
95 Portsdown Road, 139299
Tel: +65 67780771
Email: admissions@tts.edu.sg
Website: www.tts.edu.sg
CEO: Craig Considine
Age range: 3–18 years
No. of pupils: 2800
Fees: S$34,770–S$43,530
Curriculum: IBDP, UK, IGCSE, ALevs
Language instr: English

The Little Skool-House International (By-the-Vista)
170 Ghim Moh Road, Ulu Pandan Community Club, #03-01, Singapore 279621
Tel: +65 6468 3725
Curriculum: IBPYP
Language instr: English

UWC South East Asia, Dover Campus
1207 Dover Road, 139654
Tel: +65 6775 5344
Age range: 4–18 years (Boarding from 13)
No. of pupils: 3008
Curriculum: IBDP, IGCSE
Language instr: English

UWC South East Asia, East Campus
1 Tampines Street 73, 528704
Tel: +65 6305 5344
Age range: 4–18 years (Boarding from 13)
No. of pupils: 2608
Curriculum: IBDP, IGCSE
Language instr: English

Westbourne College Singapore
491B River Valley Road, No. 16-03 Valley Point, Singapore 248371
Tel: +65 6235 1538
Curriculum: IBDP
Language instr: English, Chinese

XCL World Academy
2 Yishun Street 42, Singapore 768039
Tel: +65 6871 8835
Age range: 2–18 years
Curriculum: IBDP, IBMYP, IBPYP, UK
Language instr: English

SRI LANKA

Adventist International School
103/A, St. Jude Mawatha Mahahunupitiya, Negombo 11500
Tel: +94 31 2 237 181
Age range: 3–18 years
Curriculum: National

British School in Colombo
63 Elvitigala Mawatha, Colombo 08
Tel: +94 11 7 603 400
Age range: 2–18 years
Curriculum: UK, IGCSE, ALevs
Language instr: English

Cambridge International School
148 Aluththmawatha Road, Colombo 15
Tel: +94 11 2 423 162
Curriculum: National, USA

Colombo International School
28 Gregory's Road, Colombo 7
Tel: +94 11 2 697 587
Age range: 2.5–18 years
Curriculum: UK, IGCSE, ALevs
Language instr: English

Colombo International School Kandy
175 Paranagantota Road, Mawilmada, Kandy
Tel: +94 81 2 234 298
Age range: 2.5–18 years
Curriculum: UK, IGCSE, ALevs
Language instr: English

Elizabeth Moir School
4/20 Thalakotuwa Gardens, Colombo 5
Tel: +94 11 2 512 275
Age range: 2–18 years
Curriculum: UK, IGCSE, ALevs
Language instr: English

Gateway College Colombo
185 Koswatta Road, (Via Parliment Road, Off Royal Gardens), Rajagiriya
Tel: +94 11 2 888 288
Age range: 4–18 years
Curriculum: UK, IGCSE, ALevs

Gateway College Dehiwala
No. 285/1 Galwihara Road, Dehiwala
Tel: +94 11 2 720 290
Age range: 4–18 years
Curriculum: UK, IGCSE, ALevs

Gateway College Kandy
80 Wariyapola Sri Sumangala Mawatha, Asgiriya, Kandy
Tel: +94 81 2 200 300
Age range: 4–18 years
Curriculum: UK, IGCSE, ALevs

Gateway College Negombo
No. 62 Negombo Road, Kurana
Tel: +94 31 2 227 772
Age range: 4–18 years
Curriculum: UK, IGCSE, ALevs

Ilma International Girl's School
4/100 Thalakotuwa Gardens, Colombo 05
Tel: +94 11 4 362 212
Age range: 4–18 years
Curriculum: National, UK, IGCSE, ALevs

Jennings International College
Nainamadama
Tel: +94 31 2 254 187

NICE International School
31/2 School Lane, Wester Seaton Estate, Kadirana North, Demanhandiya, Negombo
Tel: +94 70 3 234 512
Age range: 2–18 years
Curriculum: UK

Royal Institute International School
Havelock Town, Colombo 05
Tel: +94 77 7 701 557
Age range: 2–18 years
Curriculum: National, UK, IGCSE, ALevs

Stafford International School
37 Guildford Crescent, Colombo 7
Tel: +94 11 2 694 592
Age range: 3–18 years
Curriculum: UK, IGCSE, ALevs

The Overseas School of Colombo
P.O. Box 9, Pelawatte, Battaramulla 10120
Tel: +94 11 2 784 920-2
Age range: 3–18 years
No. of pupils: 340
Curriculum: IBDP, IBMYP, IBPYP
Language instr: English

Wycherley International School Gampaha
No. 05 Mudungoda, Miriswatta, Gampaha
Tel: +94 77 0 037 037
Age range: 3–18 years
Curriculum: UK, IGCSE, ALevs

SYRIAN ARAB REPUBLIC

Pakistan International School of Damascus
P.O. Box 9787, Yaa'four, Damascus
Tel: +963 11 392 1479
Age range: 3–18 years
Curriculum: UK, IGCSE, ALevs

The International School of Choueifat - Damascus
Achrafieh Sahnaya, Amman Road, Daraa Highway, Damascus
Tel: +963 11 673 0800
Age range: 3–18 years

TAIWAN

American School in Taichung
21-1 Chu Yuan Lane, Beitun, Taichung 406051
Tel: +886 4 2239 7532
Age range: 4–18 years
Curriculum: USA
Language instr: English

Dominican International School
76 Tah Chih Street, Taipei 10464
Tel: +886 2 2533 8451
Age range: 3–18 years
Curriculum: USA
Language instr: English

Hong Wen Senior High School
No. 100 Hongwen Street, Tanzi District, Taichung City 427009
Tel: +886 4 2534 0011
Age range: 12–18 years
Curriculum: IBDP
Language instr: English, Chinese

Hsinchu International School
No. 290 Niu Pu East Road, Hsinchu 30091
Tel: +886 9 6332 1167
Age range: 4–18 years
Curriculum: AP, USA
Language instr: English

I-Shou International School
No 6, Sec 1, Xuecheng Road, Dashu District, Kaohsiung 840302
Tel: +886 7 657 7115
Age range: 3–18 years
Curriculum: IBDP, IBMYP, IBPYP, National
Language instr: English, Chinese

Ivy Collegiate Academy
320, Lane 165, Section 1 Tan-Hsing Road, Tan-Tzu District, Taichung 427
Tel: +886 4 2539 5011
Age range: 12–18 years
Curriculum: AP, SAT, TOEFL, USA

Juntou International School
No. 48 Shuitou Road, Puli
Tel: +886 4 9242 0272
Curriculum: IBPYP
Language instr: English, Chinese

Kang Chiao International School, Xiugang Campus
No. 800 Huacheng Road, Xindian District, New Taipei City 231308
Tel: +886 2 2216 6000
Age range: 11–18 years
Curriculum: AP, IBDP, IBMYP, National, USA
Language instr: Chinese, English

Asia

Kaohsiung American School
889 Cueihua Road, Zuoying District, Kaohsiung 81354
Tel: +886 7 586 3300
Age range: 3–18 years
Curriculum: IBDP, IBMYP, USA
Language instr: English

Mingdao High School
497 Sec. 1, Zhongshan Road, Wuri District, Taichung 41401
Tel: +886 4 2337 2101
Age range: 11–18 years
Curriculum: AP, IBDP, IBMYP, IBCP, National
Language instr: English, Chinese

Morrison Academy Kaohsiung
42 Jiacheng Road, Dashe District, Kaohsiung 81546
Tel: +886 7 356 1190
Age range: 4–18 years
Curriculum: AP, USA

Morrison Academy Taichung
216 Si Ping Road, Taichung 40679
Tel: +886 4 2292 1171
Age range: 4–18 years
Curriculum: AP, USA
Language instr: English

Morrison Academy Taipei
1 Donghu Road, Linkou District, New Taipei City 24449
Tel: +886 2 2602 6502
Age range: 4–18 years
Curriculum: AP, USA
Language instr: English

Pacific American School
No. 307, Sec 1, Xinglong Road, Zhubei
Tel: +886 3 558 6688
Age range: 4–18 years
Curriculum: AP, USA

Starlight International Kindergarten - Feng Yuan Campus
No. 569, Section 7, Fengyuan Boulevard, Shengang District, Taichung
Tel: +886 4 2520 8466
Curriculum: IBPYP
Language instr: English, Chinese

Starlight International Kindergarten - Hui Wen Campus
No. 8, Section 1, Huilai Road, Nantun District, Taichung
Tel: +886 4 2251 4007
Curriculum: IBPYP
Language instr: English, Chinese

Taichung City Starlight Experimental Education
No. 23 Daguan Road, Nantun District, Taichung 408
Tel: +886 4 2389 1626
Curriculum: IBMYP, IBPYP
Language instr: English, Chinese

Taipei Adventist American School
No. 64, Lane 80, Zhuang Ding Road, Shihlin District, Taipei 111
Tel: +886 2 2861 6400
Age range: 6–13 years
Curriculum: USA
Language instr: English

Taipei American School
800 Zhongshan North Road, Section 6, Taipei 11152
Tel: +886 2 7750 9900
Age range: 3–18 years
Curriculum: AP, IBDP, USA
Language instr: English

Taipei European School
Swire European Campus, 31 Jian Ye Road, Yang Ming Shan, Shihlin District, Taipei 11193
Tel: +886 2 8145 9007
Age range: 3–18 years
Curriculum: Abitur, IBDP, IBMYP, IBCP, FrenchBacc, UK
Language instr: English, French, German

Taipei Kuei Shan School
200 Mingde Road, Taipei 11280
Tel: +886 2 2821 2009
Age range: 4–18 years
No. of pupils: 700
Curriculum: IBDP, IBMYP, IBPYP
Language instr: English

Taiwan Adventist International School
555 No. 39 Qiongwen Lane, Inside Sanyu Christian College, Yuchi Township, Nantou County
Tel: +886 4 9289 9778
Age range: 12–18 years
Curriculum: National, USA

Tung Der High School
No. 8 Peiying Lane, Zhongzheng Road, Caotun, Nantou 542018
Tel: +886 4 9255 3109
Curriculum: IBDP
Language instr: English, Chinese

Victoria Academy
1110 Jhen-Nan Road, Douliu, Yun-Lin 640
Tel: +886 5 5378 899 (Ext: 2202)
Age range: 12–18 years
Curriculum: IBDP, National, UK, IGCSE
Language instr: Chinese, English

TAJIKISTAN

Contofield International School
Bukhora 2 Street, Dushanbe
Tel: +992 9383 97006
Age range: 4–18 years
Curriculum: UK
Language instr: English

Dushanbe International School
Bofanda Street, Dushanbe
Tel: +992 372 211 104
Age range: 4–18 years
Curriculum: IGCSE, ALevs

Modern International School
Dushanbe N. Ganjavi Str. 377/1, 734013 Dushanbe
Tel: +992 900 550 105
Age range: 5–18 years
Curriculum: UK

QSI International School of Dushanbe
Turakul Zehni 3 Street, 734001 Dushanbe
Tel: +992 939 906 906
Age range: 3–18 years
Curriculum: AP, USA
Language instr: English

THAILAND

AIT International School
Km. 42, Phaholyothin Highway, Klong Luang, Patumthani 12120
Tel: +66 (0)2 524 5984
Age range: 3–12
No. of pupils: 285
Curriculum: National

American Pacific International School
158/1 Moo 3, Hangdong-Samoeng Road, Banpong, Hangdong, Chiang Mai 50230
Tel: +66 53 365 303/5
Age range: 2–18
No. of pupils: 380
Curriculum: AP, IBDP, IBMYP, IBPYP, USA
Language instr: English

Amnuay Silpa School
304/1 Sri Ayutthaya Road, Ratchathewee, Bangkok 10400
Tel: +66 2 354 5267
Age range: 3–18
No. of pupils: 920
Curriculum: GCSE

Anglo Singapore International School
341 Sukhumvit 31 (Soi Si Yak Sawatdee), Klongtan, Wattana, Bangkok 10110
Tel: +66 02 662 3105 6
Age range: 3–12
No. of pupils: 211 B107 G104
Curriculum: National, UK
Language instr: English, Thai, Chinese

Ascot International School
80/82 Ramkhamhaeng Soi 118, Sapansung, Bangkok 10240
Tel: +66 2 373 4400
Age range: 2–18 years
No. of pupils: 400
Curriculum: IBDP, IBPYP, IBCP, UK, IGCSE
Language instr: English

Assumption Commercial College
141 Soi Sathorn 13, Sathorn Rd Sathorn, Bangkok 1012
Tel: +662 2113744
Curriculum: National

Bangkok Adventist International School
P.O. Box 234 Prakhanong, Klongtan Nua, Wattana, Bangkok 10110
Tel: +66 2 381 9406
Age range: 4–17
No. of pupils: B54 G46
Curriculum: USA
Language instr: English

Bangkok Christian College
35 Pramoan Road, Silom Bangrak, Bangkok 10500
Tel: +66 2 637 1852
Curriculum: USA

Bangkok Christian International School
53 Soi 44 Pattanakarn Road, Suan Luang, Bangkok 10250
Tel: +662 322 1979
Age range: 4–18
No. of pupils: 300
Curriculum: AP, USA

Bangkok Grace International School
79/3-12 Latphrao Soi 112, Wangthonglang, Bangkok 10310
Tel: +66 2 539 4516/7/8
Age range: 2–18
No. of pupils: 42 B23 G19
Curriculum: USA
Language instr: English

BANGKOK PATANA SCHOOL
For further details see p. 46
643 Lasalle Road (Sukhumvit 105), Bangna Tai, Bangna, Bangkok 10260
Tel: +66 2 785 2200
Email: admissions@patana.ac.th
Website: www.patana.ac.th
Age range: 2–18 years
Curriculum: IBDP, IGCSE
Language instr: English

Bangkok Prep International School
23 Sukhumvit 53, Vadhana District, Bangkok 10110
Tel: +66 2 700 5858
Age range: 3–18 years
No. of pupils: 1300
Curriculum: UK, ALevs
Language instr: English

Beaconhouse Yamssard International School - Pattankarn
166/1 Pattanakarn Soi 78, Prawet, Bangkok 10250
Tel: +66 2 722 2571
Age range: 2–11

Asia

Berkeley International School
123 Bangna-Trad Road,
Bangna, Bangkok 10260
Tel: +662(0)2 747 4788
(EAR)

Bloomsbury International School Hatyai
2119 Moo 6, Airport-Lopburirames Road, Kuanlung, Hatyai, Songkhla 90110
Tel: +66 74 251 255/6
Curriculum: UK
(CIS)

Brighton College International School Bangkok
8/8 Krungthep Kreetha Soi 15 Yaek 4 (Surao Yai), Hua Mak, Bang Kapi, Bangkok 10240
Tel: +66 (0)2 136 7898
Age range: 2–18
Curriculum: UK, GCSE, ALevs
Language instr: English

British Columbia International School
608/1 Kalapapruk Road, Bangwar, Phasicharoen, Bangkok 10160
Tel: +66 2 802 1188
Age range: 12–18
Curriculum: National

British International School, Phuket
59 Moo 2, Thepkrasattri Road, T. Koh Kaew, A. Muang, Phuket 83000
Tel: +66 (0) 76 335 555
Age range: 2–18 years
No. of pupils: 1150
Curriculum: IBDP, IGCSE
Language instr: English
(圖) (CIS)

British School Bangkok Ltd
36 Sukhumvit Soi 4, Soi Nana, Bangkok 10110
Tel: +66 2 656 7734
Age range: 2–11
No. of pupils: 178 B102 G76
Curriculum: SAT, UK
Language instr: English
(CIS)

Bromsgrove International School Early Years Campus
344 Mu 12, Ramkamhaeng 164 Road, Minburi, Bangkok 10510
Tel: +66 2540 7122 3
Age range: 2–7
No. of pupils: 40

Bromsgrove International School Primary and Secondary Campus
555 Mu 9, Windsor Park and Golf Club,, Suwinthawong Road, Minburi, Bangkok 10510
Tel: +66 2989 4873
Age range: 2–18
No. of pupils: 400 B200 G200
Curriculum: UK, IGCSE, ALevs
Language instr: English
(圖) (CIS)

California Prep International School (CPIS)
9 Moo 11, A Banpa, Kaeng Khoi, Saraburi
Tel: +66 (0)36 358714
Curriculum: USA
(圖)

Canadian International School of Thailand
1001 Charan Sanitwong 46, Bangyeekhan, Bang Phlat, Bangkok 10700
Tel: +66 02 886 9464
Curriculum: IBMYP, IBPYP
Language instr: English, Thai
(圖)

Charter International School
36 Chalermprakiat Ror 9 Road, Pravate, Bangkok 10250
Tel: +66 2 7268283/4
Age range: 3–18
No. of pupils: 345 B175 G170
Curriculum: IGCSE, ALevs
Language instr: English
(CIS)

Chiang Mai International School
PO Box 38, 13 Chetupon Road, Chiang Mai 50000
Tel: +66 (53) 306152-3
Age range: 4–18
Curriculum: AP, USA
(EAR)

Christian German School Chiangmai
PO Box 12, Chiangmai 50140
Tel: +66 53 816 624

Concordian International School
918 Moo 8, Bangna-Trad Highway Km 7, Bangkaew, Bangplee Samutprakarn 10540
Tel: +66 2 706 9000
Age range: 2–18
No. of pupils: B361 G309
Curriculum: IBDP, IBMYP, IBPYP
Language instr: English, Chinese
(CIS) (EAR)

Crescent International School
72 Soi Sribumphen, Rama 4 Road, Tungmahamek, Sathon 1 10120
Tel: +66 2679 8777
Curriculum: National, UK, IGCSE

D-PREP International School
38, 38/1-3, 39, Moo 6, Bangna Trad Rd., Km. 8, Bang Kaeo, Bang Phli District, Samut Prakan 10540
Tel: +66 95 879 4944
Age range: 4–18 years
Curriculum: IBPYP
Language instr: English, Thai

Ekamai International School
57 Ekamai 12 (Soi Charoenjai), Sukhumvit 63 Road, Klongtan Neua, Wattana, Bangkok 10110
Tel: +66 023 913 593
Language instr: English
(EAR)

Garden International School (Bangkok campus)
2/1 Yen Akart Soi 2, Yen Akart Road, Sathorn, Bangkok 10120
Tel: +66 2249 1880
Age range: 2–18 years
No. of pupils: 236 B118 G118
Curriculum: UK, IGCSE
Language instr: English

Garden International School (Rayong Campus)
188/24 Moo 4, Pala-Ban Chang Road, Tambol Pala, Ban Chang, Rayong 21130
Tel: +66 3803 0808
Age range: 3–18 years
No. of pupils: 475
Curriculum: IBDP, UK, IGCSE
Language instr: English
(圖) (CIS)

Global Indian International School (GIIS) Bangkok Campus

Grace International School
88 Muu 3 T.Harn Kaew A. Hang Dong, Chiang Mai 50230
Tel: +66 53 131 175
Age range: 5–19
No. of pupils: 558
Curriculum: USA
(EAR)

Harrow International School Bangkok
45 Soi Kosumruamchai 14, Kosumruamchai Road, Don Mueang Subdistrict, Don Mueang District, Bangkok 10210
Tel: +66 02 503 7222
Age range: 18 months–18 years
No. of pupils: 1735
Curriculum: UK, IGCSE, ALevs
(圖) (CIS)

Heathfield International School
10/22 Moo 4, Sukhapiban 3 (Rakhambaeng Road), Saphansung, Bangkok
Tel: +662 372 2678
Age range: 2–15
No. of pupils: 154 B74 G80
Curriculum: UK
(CIS)

Hua Hin International School
549 Moo 7, Hin Lek Fai, Hua Hin, Prachuap Khiri Khan 77110
Tel: +66 32 900 632
Curriculum: IBDP
Language instr: English, Thai

International Christian School Nonthaburi (ICSN)
145/1 Pracharat Road Moo 6, Muang Nonthaburi, Nonthaburi 11000
Tel: +66 2 525 1302
Age range: 4–18 years
Curriculum: USA

International Community School
1225 The Parkland Road, Bangna, Bangkok 10260
Tel: +66 2 338 0777
(EAR)

International Pioneers School
20 Radruam Charoen, Charoen Nakorn Soi 14, Charoen Nakorn Road,, Klongsan 10600
Tel: +66 2 862 3030
Age range: 3–18
Curriculum: UK, IGCSE, ALevs

International School Bangkok
39/7 Soi Nichada Thani, Samakee Road, Pakkret, Nonthaburi 11120
Tel: +66 2 963 5800
Age range: 3–18 years
No. of pupils: 1800
Curriculum: IBDP, USA
Language instr: English
(EAR)

International School Eastern Seaboard
282 Moo 5 T. Bowin, SriRacha, Chonburi 20230
Tel: +66 38 372 591
Age range: 3–18
No. of pupils: 260
Curriculum: IBDP
Language instr: English
(EAR)

International School of Chonburi
315 Moo 1 Banglamung Soi 39, Nongprue Banglamung, Chonburi 20150
Tel: +66 38 241 085
Age range: 2–11
No. of pupils: 50
Curriculum: UK

Kevalee International School
90 Hathairaj 37 Road, Klongsamwa District, Bangkok 10510
Tel: +66 2 9066427
Age range: 2.5–17 years
No. of pupils: 105
Curriculum: USA
Language instr: English

Kiddykare International Kindergarten
59/34 Sukhumvit 26, Klongton, Bangkok 10110
Tel: +66 2665 6777
Age range: 18 months–6 years
No. of pupils: B11 G29
Curriculum: UK
Language instr: English

Kids Academy International Pre-School
52/1-2 Sukhumvit 63, Soi 2, Bangkok 10110
Tel: +66 2 714 3636
Age range: 18 months–6 years
No. of pupils: 181
Curriculum: UK
Language instr: English

Asia

Kincaid International School of Bangkok
205/73-74, Pasooksanti3, Pattanakarn 69, Pravej, Bangkok 10250
Tel: +66 2 321 7010
Age range: 4–17

KIS International School
999/123-124 Pracha Utit Road, Samsennok, Huay Kwang, Bangkok 10310
Tel: +66 (0)2 2743444
Age range: 3–19 years
No. of pupils: 750
Curriculum: IBDP, IBMYP, IBPYP, IBCP
Language instr: English

Krabi International School
188 Moo 6, Nong Thale, Muang, Krabi 81180
Tel: +66 (0)75 656 900
Age range: 5–18 years
No. of pupils: 150
Curriculum: UK, IGCSE, ALevs
Language instr: English

Ladybird International Kindergarten
21 Soi Promsri 2, Sukhumvit 39, Bangkok 10110
Tel: +66 2382 3338
Age range: 18 months–5
Curriculum: UK, USA
Language instr: English

Lanna International School Thailand
166 Moo 10 Baan Waen, Hang Dong, Chiang Mai 50230
Tel: +66 52 000 838
Age range: 2–18 years
No. of pupils: 900
Curriculum: UK, IGCSE, ALevs
Language instr: English

Lertlah School, Phetkasem Road
45 Petkasem Road, Soi Phetkasem 77, Nongkhaem District, Bangkok 10160
Tel: +66 2 809 9081 5
Age range: 2–12
No. of pupils: 1300

Lycee Francais International de Bangkok
498, soi Rhamkhamhaeng 39 (Thep Leela 1), Wangthonglang, Bangkok 10310
Tel: +66 2 934 8008
Language instr: French

Magic Years International School
22/122, Moo 3, Soi Prasoet Islam, Bang Talat, Pakkret, Nonthaburri 11120
Tel: +66 2156 6222
Age range: 1–12 years
No. of pupils: 150
Curriculum: IBPYP
Language instr: English

Modern International School Bangkok
125-135 Soi Phobmitr, Sukhumvit 39 Road, Wattana 10110
Tel: +66 2258 8222
Curriculum: UK, IGCSE, ALevs

Montfort International College
19/1 Montfort Rd, T.Tasala A.Muang, Chiang Mai 50000
Tel: +66 5324 5570-5
Age range: 4–19

Mulberry House International Pre-school
7 Soi Tonson, Ploenchit Road, Lumpini Sub-district, Pathumwan District, Bangkok 10330
Tel: +66 2010 5620
Age range: 2–6
Curriculum: UK
Language instr: English

Nakornpayap International School (NIS)
240 Moo 6 San Phi Sua, Muang Chiang Mai 50300
Tel: +66 5 311 0680
Age range: 3–18 years
No. of pupils: 700
Curriculum: AP, USA
Language instr: English

New Sathorn International School
289/2, 289/5 Soi Naradhiwas Rajanakharindra 24, Naradhiwas Rajanakarindra Rd, Chongnonsri, Yannawa, Bangkok 10120
Tel: +66 26 722 100-1
Age range: 2–17
Curriculum: UK, USA
Language instr: English

NIST INTERNATIONAL SCHOOL
For further details see p. 63
36 Sukhumvit Soi 15, Wattana, Bangkok 10110
Tel: +66 2 017 5888
Email: admissions@nist.ac.th
Website: www.nist.ac.th
Head of School: James Dalziel
Age range: 3–18 years
No. of pupils: 1830
Fees: THB628,200–THB1,094,500
Curriculum: IBDP, IBMYP, IBPYP
Language instr: English

Niva International School
18 Soi Phokaew 3 Yeak 9, Ladprao 101, Bangkapi, Bangkok 10240
Tel: +66 2 948 4605 7
Age range: 3–18
No. of pupils: 327

Norwich International School, Bangkok
233/131 Nusasiri Villages Rama 2 Road, Moo 1, Bang Nam Chuet, Muang Samut Sakhon, Samut Sakhon, Bangkok 74000
Tel: +66 2 451 1100/1/2
Curriculum: IBDP
Language instr: English

Pan-Asia International School
100 Moo 3, Charaemprakiat, Rama 9 St, Soi 67, Kwang Dokmai Prawet District, Bangkok 10250
Tel: +66 2 726 6273-4
Curriculum: IBDP, IBMYP
Language instr: English

Panyaden International School
218 Moo 2, T.Namprae, A.Hang Dong, Chiang Mai 50230
Tel: +66 80 078 5115
Curriculum: IBDP, UK
Language instr: English

Patanadek School
144/1 Sri Chan Rd, T Naimueang, A Mueang 40000
Tel: +66 43 222 869
Age range: 4–19

Phuket Thaihua ASEAN Wittaya School
103/5 Wichitsongkram Road, Talad Nuea, Mueang, Phuket 83000
Tel: +66 7 652 2567
Curriculum: IBMYP, IBPYP
Language instr: English, Chinese

Prem Tinsulanonda International School
234 Moo 3, Huay Sai, Mae Rim, Chiang Mai 50180
Tel: +66 53 301 500
Age range: 3–19
No. of pupils: 500
Curriculum: IBDP, IBMYP, IBPYP, IBCP
Language instr: English

QSI International School of Phuket
81/4 Moo1, Chalermprakiat r.9 Road, T. Kathu, A. Kathu, Phuket 83120
Tel: +66 76 304 312
Age range: 3–16
No. of pupils: 126
Curriculum: USA
Language instr: English

Raffles American School Bangkok
15 Moo. 15, Bangna-Trad Road, Bangkaew, Bangplee, Samutprakarn, Bangkok
Tel: +66 2 034 0700
Curriculum: IBDP
Language instr: English

Ramkhamhaeng Advent International School
1 Soi Ramkhamhaeng 119, Sukhapibal 3, Huamark, Bangkapi, Bangkok 10240
Tel: +66 2 370 0316
Age range: 3–18
No. of pupils: 700
Curriculum: USA

Rasami British International School
48/2 Soi Rajavithi 2, Rajavithi Road, Samsennai, Phayathai 10400
Tel: +66 2644 5291
Age range: 2–17
No. of pupils: 200
Curriculum: UK

RC International School
25/3-4 Ruamrudee Soi 1, Ploenchit Road, Bangkok 10330
Tel: +66 2 254 4380
Age range: 18 months–13
No. of pupils: 150
Curriculum: UK

REGENTS INTERNATIONAL SCHOOL PATTAYA
For further details see p. 66
33/3 Moo 1, Pong, Banglamung, Chonburi 20150
Tel: +66 (0)93 135 7736
Email: admissions@regents-pattaya.co.th
Website: regents-pattaya.co.th
Principal: Amos Turner-Wardell
Age range: 2–18 years
No. of pupils: 1210
Fees: THB459,000–THB873,000
Curriculum: IBDP, UK, ALevs
Language instr: English

RIS Swiss Section-Deutschsprachige Schule Bangkok
6/1 Ramkamhaeng Road, Minburi 10510
Tel: +66 2 5180 340
Age range: 2–18
No. of pupils: 310
Curriculum: National

Roong Aroon International School
391/5 Soi 33 Rama 2 Road (Soi Wat Yai Rom), Bang Khunthien, Bangkok 10150
Tel: +66 (0)2 870 7512 3
Curriculum: IBDP, IBMYP, IBCP
Language instr: English, Thai

Ruamrudee International School
6 Ramkhamhaeng 184, Minburi, Bangkok 10510
Tel: +66 (0)2 791 8900
Age range: 2–18 years
No. of pupils: 940
Curriculum: AP, IBDP, SAT, TOEFL, USA
Language instr: English

Sarasas Extra School
336/7 Soi Satupradit 20 Rd, Bangkok 10120
Tel: +66 2212 0157
Age range: 3–17
No. of pupils: 2500

Satit Bilingual School of Rangsit University
52/347 Muang Ake, Phahonyothin Road., Lak Hok, Mueang, Pathum Thani 12000
Tel: +66 2 792 7500 4
Curriculum: IBPYP, IGCSE
Language instr: English

Shrewsbury International School
1922 Charoen Krung Road, Wat Phrayakrai, Bang Kholame, Bangkok 10120
Tel: +66 2 675 1888
Age range: 3–18
No. of pupils: 1600
Curriculum: UK, GCSE, IGCSE, ALevs

Asia

Siam International School
55/5 Moo 1, Klong 3, Rangsit-Nakhonnayok Road, T.Bungyeetho, Thanyaburi Pathumthani, Bangkok 12130
Tel: +66 85 009 9059
Age range: 4–19
No. of pupils: 250

Silver Fern International School
16 Moo 21 Airport Road, Tambon Neua Muang, Amphoe Muang, Roi-Et 45000
Tel: +66 994 671 222
Curriculum: IBPYP
Language instr: English

Singapore International School of Bangkok
Pracha Utit Campus, 498/11 Soi Ramkhamhaeng 39 (Tepleela 1), Wangthonglang, Bangkok 10310
Tel: +66 2 158 9191
Age range: 2–18
Curriculum: IBDP, IGCSE, ALevs
Language instr: English, Chinese, Thai
(EAR)

Srithammarat Suksa School
1 Rajadamnurn Road, Nakon Sri Thammarat 80000
Tel: +66 75 313 717
Age range: 4–19

St Andrews International School Bangkok
1020 Sukhumvit Road, Phra Khanong, Khlong Toei, Bangkok 10110
Tel: +662 056 9555
Age range: 2–18 years
No. of pupils: 2200
Curriculum: IBDP, IBCP, IGCSE
Language instr: English
(CIS)

St Andrews International School, Dusit Campus
253/1 Sawankhaloke Road, Dusit, Bangkok 10300
Tel: +66 2 668 5920
Age range: 2–11 years
Curriculum: UK
Language instr: English

St Andrews International School, Green Valley Campus
Moo 7, Ban Chang-Makham Koo Road, Ban Chang, Rayong 21130
Tel: +66 3 803 0611
Age range: 2–18 years
Curriculum: IBDP, IBPYP, UK, IGCSE
Language instr: English
(CIS)

St Andrews International School, Sathorn Campus
9 Sathorn Soi 4, North Sathorn Road, Bangrak 10500
Tel: +66 2 632 1995
Age range: 2–11 years
Curriculum: UK
Language instr: English

St Andrews International School, Sukhumvit Campus
7 Sukhumvit 107 Road, Bangna, Bangkok 10260
Tel: +66 2 393 3883
Age range: 2–18 years
Curriculum: IBDP, IBCP, UK, IGCSE
Language instr: English

St Andrews Samakee International School
43 Soi Tiwanond 48, Nonthaburi 11000
Tel: +66 2952 4003
Age range: 1–14

St Mark's International School
900 New Rama 9 Road, Suanluang, Bangkok 10250
Tel: +662 300 5463 4
Age range: 4–16
No. of pupils: 60

St Stephen's International School
998 Viphavadi-Rangsit Road, Lad Yao, Chatuchak, Bangkok 10900
Tel: +66 (0)2 513 0270
Age range: 3–18
No. of pupils: 457 B227 G230 VIth30
Curriculum: IPC, UK, IGCSE, ALevs
Language instr: English
(CIS)

St Stephen's International School, Khao Yai
49/1-3 Moo 4, Thanarat Road, Nongnamdaeng, Pak Chong, Nakhon Ratchasima 30130
Tel: +66 (0)864688040
Age range: 3–16
No. of pupils: 140 B70 G70
Curriculum: IPC, UK, IGCSE
Language instr: English
(⚜)

Thai Sikh International School
1799 Rim Thang Rod Fai Kao, Moo 1 Samrong Nua, Samut Prakarn 10270
Tel: +66 2 743 5049 - 52
Age range: 5–16
No. of pupils: 342
(CIS)

Thai-Chinese International School
101/177 Moo 7 Soi Mooban Bangpleenives, Prasertsin Road, Bangplee Yai, Samutprakarn 10540
Tel: +66 2 751 1201
Curriculum: USA
Language instr: English
(EAR)

The American School of Bangkok - Green Valley Campus
900 Moo 3 Bangna-Trad Road Km. 15 Bangplee, Samutprakarn, Bangkok 10540
Tel: +66 (0)2026 3518
Age range: 4–18 years
Curriculum: IBDP, USA
(⚜)

The American School of Bangkok - Sukhumvit Campus
59-59/1 Sukhumvit Road Soi 49/3 Wattana, Bangkok 10110
Tel: +66 (0)2620 8600
Age range: 4–18 years
Curriculum: USA

The British International School of Northern Thailand
Located Near Wat Baan Ta Tempel, Municipal Bridge, Baan Ta Mor Som, A.Maung 52000
Tel: +66 54 324596
Age range: 2–18
No. of pupils: 300
Curriculum: UK

The City School
18 Soi Sukhumvit 49/4, Khlong Tan Nuea, Watthana, Bangkok 10110
Tel: +66 2 381 2919
No. of pupils: 200
(CIS)

The International School of Samui
141/21 Moo 6, Bophut, Koh Samui, Surat Thani 84320
Tel: +66 (0)77 48 45 48
Age range: 2–16
No. of pupils: 250 B121 G114
Curriculum: UK, IGCSE
Language instr: English
(COB)

The Regent's School, Bangkok
601/99 Pracha-Uthit Road, Wangthonglang, Bangkok 10310
Tel: +66 (0)2 957 5777
Curriculum: IBDP
Language instr: English
(⚜)(CIS)

Traill International School
36 Soi 18, Ramkangheng Road, Huamark, Bangkok
Tel: +66 2718 8779
Age range: 5–16
No. of pupils: 160
Curriculum: UK
(ECIS)

Udon Thani International School (UDIS)
222/2 Moo. 2 Mittrapab Road, Tumbonkudsra, Aumpearmuang, Udon Thani 41000
Tel: +66 (0)42 110 379
Curriculum: IBDP, IBMYP, IBPYP
Language instr: English, Thai

UWC Thailand International School
115/15 Moo 7 Thepkasattri Road, Thepkasattri, Thalang, Phuket 83110
Tel: +66 76 336 076
Age range: 2–18 years
No. of pupils: 580
Curriculum: IBDP, IBMYP, IBPYP
Language instr: English
(⚜)

Varee Chiangmai International School
59 Moo 6, Mahidol Road, Nonghoi, Muang, Chiang Mai 50000
Tel: +66 5314 0233
Age range: 4–19
No. of pupils: 200
Curriculum: UK

WELLINGTON COLLEGE INTERNATIONAL SCHOOL BANGKOK
For further details see p. 78
18 Krungthep Kreetha Road, Saphan Sung District, Bangkok 10250
Tel: +66 2 087 8888
Email: admissions@wellingtoncollege.ac.th
Website: www.wellingtoncollege.ac.th
Master: Christopher Nicholls
Age range: 2–18 years
No. of pupils: 1100
Curriculum: UK, IGCSE, ALevs
Language instr: English

Wells International School - Bang Na Campus
10 Srinakarin Soi 62, Nong Bon, Prawet, Bangkok 10250
Tel: +66 02 746 6060 1
Curriculum: IBPYP
Language instr: English, Thai

Wells International School - On Nut Campus
2209 Sukhumvit Road, Bangchak, Prakanong, Bangkok 10260
Tel: +66 097 920 8511
Age range: 5–19
No. of pupils: 520
Curriculum: AP, IBDP, SAT, USA
Language instr: English
(EAR)

TURKMENISTAN

QSI Ashgabat International School
Berzengi, Ataturk Street, Ashgabat
Tel: +993 12 48 90 27
Age range: 2–18 years
Curriculum: AP, USA
Language instr: English

UNITED ARAB EMIRATES

Abu Dhabi International (Pvt) School
Karamah Street, PO Box 25898, Abu Dhabi
Tel: +971 2 443 4433
Age range: 3–18
No. of pupils: 3225
Curriculum: IBDP
Language instr: English

Ajman Academy
Sheikh Ammar Road, Mowaihat 2, Ajman
Tel: +971 6 731 4444
No. of pupils: 990
Curriculum: IBMYP, IBPYP, IGCSE
Language instr: English

Asia

Ajman Modern School
PO Box 1778, Ajman
Tel: +971 6 7431 168
Age range: 3–15
No. of pupils: 800

Ajyal International School
Behind Sheukha Fatma Mosque, 10 Minutes from Mazyad Mall, Mohammad Bin Zayed City
Tel: +971 2552 2668
Age range: 4–18
Curriculum: UK

Al Adab Iranian Private School for Boys
Behind Al Bustan Center, Al Nahda 1, Qusais, Dubai
Tel: +971 42633405
Age range: 5–19
No. of pupils: 600
Curriculum: IBDP
Language instr: English

Al Adhwa Private School
PO Box 64997, Falai Hazza'a, Al Ain
Tel: +971 3 7828870
Age range: 4–18
No. of pupils: 536
Curriculum: USA

Al Ain American School
PO Box 100774, Al Ain
Tel: +971 3 7675030
Age range: 3–14 years
Curriculum: USA

Al Ain British Academy
Al Salam Street, Sarooj, Al Ain
Tel: +971 3 715 1000
Age range: 3–18 years
Curriculum: UK, GCSE, IGCSE, ALevs

Al Ain English Speaking School
PO Box 17939, Al - Ain
Tel: +971 3 7678636
Age range: 3–18
No. of pupils: 440

Al Ain International School
PO Box 88228,, Salam Street, Al Ain
Tel: +971 3 7151000
Curriculum: UK

Al Amana Private School
PO Box 27194, Sharjah
Tel: +971 6 5676783
Age range: 3–18
No. of pupils: 800
Curriculum: IGCSE

Al Ansar International School
PO Box 43114, Sharjah
Tel: +971 6 545 9441
Curriculum: IGCSE, ALevs

Al Basma British School
PO Box No 45994, Behind Deerfields Mall, Abu Dhabi
Tel: +971 2 562 3454

Al Bustan Private School
PO Box 7443, Opp Madinat Zayed Market, Abu Dhabi
Tel: + 971 2 6330036
Curriculum: USA

Al Dhafra Private School
PO Box 25801, Abu Dhabi
Tel: +971 2 610 8400/1
Age range: 3–18
Curriculum: National, UK, USA

Al Diyafah High School
PO Box 24023, Dubai
Tel: + 971 4 2671115
Curriculum: UK, IGCSE, ALevs

Al Ittihad Private School Jumeirah
PO Box 37090, Jumeirah-Dubai
Tel: +971 43 945 111
Curriculum: USA
Language instr: English

Al Ittihad Private School Mamzar
Cairo Road, Mamzar-Dubai
Tel: +971 42 966 314
Curriculum: USA
Language instr: English

Al Maali International School
PO Box 42007, Abu Dhabi
Tel: +971 2 559 1000
Curriculum: USA

Al Maaref Private School
PO Box 87823, Dubai
Tel: +971 4 2988881
Age range: 4–18 years

Al Ma'Arifa Private School
Box 7190, Al Yarmook, Sharjah
Tel: +971 6 5014444
Curriculum: UK, USA, IGCSE

Al Maharat Private School
P.O. Box 126534, Plot No. 1, Street No. 1, Community No. 80, Shakbout City, Khalifa City-B, Abu Dhabi
Tel: +97122059000
Age range: 4–17 years
Curriculum: UK
Language instr: English

Al Manhal International School
P.O.Box:3110,
Tel: 00971 2-4998777
Curriculum: UK, USA

Al Mawakeb School - Al Barsha
PO Box 35001, Dubai
Tel: +971 4 3478288

Al Mawakeb School - Al Garhoud
PO Box 10799, Dubai
Tel: +971 4 2851415
Age range: 3–18
Curriculum: National, SAT, TOEFL, USA

Al Murooj English School
Al Azra Area, Sharjah
Tel: 00 971 6 527 3720
Age range: 4–11
Curriculum: UK

Al Murooj Scientific Private School
Kalidiyah Khalifa Bin Shakhbun St, PO Box 42275, Abu Dhabi
Tel: +971 2 6669229

Al Nahda International Schools
PO Box 815, Abu Dhabi
Tel: +971 2 445 4200/2984
Age range: 4–18
No. of pupils: 3500 B1200 G3300
Curriculum: SAT, TOEFL, ALevs

Al Nahda National Schools
PO Box 815, Abu Dhabi
Tel: +971 2 4477600
Curriculum: SAT, TOEFL, UK, USA, IGCSE

Al Najah Private School (ANPS)
9 Near Al Safir Mall, Mohammed Bin Zayed City, Abu Dhabi
Tel: +971 2 553 0935
Age range: 4–18 years
Curriculum: IBDP, UK, IGCSE, ALevs

Al Rabeeh School
PO Box 41807, Abu Dhabi
Tel: +971 2 4482856
Age range: 3–12
No. of pupils: 798 B425 G373
Curriculum: National, UK
Language instr: English, Arabic

Al Resalah School of Science
PO Box 1250, Sharjah
Tel: +971 6 522 1222
Curriculum: USA

Al Salam Private School and Nursery
Al Nahda 2, Al Ghusais, PO Box 5251, Dubai
Tel: +971 4 267 9594
Age range: 4–18
No. of pupils: 600

Al Sanawbar School
PO Box 1781, Al Ain
Tel: + 971 3 7679 889
Curriculum: USA

Al Shohub School
PO Box 31515, Abu Dhabi
Tel: +971 2 5559995
Age range: B3–9 G3–18
No. of pupils: 913 B197 G716 VIth11
Curriculum: UK, IGCSE, ALevs
Language instr: English

Al Yasat Private School
Abu Dhabi 25586
Tel: +971 2 641 2300
Age range: 3–8
No. of pupils: 500
Curriculum: USA

Al-Mizhar American Academy for Girls
PO Box 78484, Dubai
Tel: +971 4 288 7250
Age range: G4–19
No. of pupils: 650
Curriculum: USA

Ambassador International Academy
Al Khail Gate, Al Quoz, Plot No. 3653942, Dubai
Tel: +971 4 580 6999
Curriculum: IBDP, IBMYP, IBPYP, IBCP
Language instr: English

Ambassador School
PO Box 126924, Plot No 317-278, 41 A Street, Mankhool, Bur Dubai, Dubai
Tel: +971 4 379 9333
Age range: 6–18
No. of pupils: 602

American Community School of Abu Dhabi
P.O. Box 42114, Abu Dhabi
Tel: +971 2 681 5115
Age range: 4–18 years
Curriculum: IBDP, USA
Language instr: English

American Gulf School
Al Rahmaniya Shaghrafah 4, Sharjah
Tel: +971 6 506 1111
Curriculum: IBDP, IBMYP, IBPYP
Language instr: English, Arabic

American International School Dubai
PO Box 87727, Dubai
Tel: +971 4 2988666

American International School in Abu Dhabi
P.O. Box 5992, Abu Dhabi
Tel: +971 2 4444 333
Age range: 4–18 years
No. of pupils: 1300
Curriculum: IBDP, IBPYP, USA
Language instr: English

American School of Dubai
PO Box 7118, Dubai
Tel: +971 4 395 0005
Age range: 4–18
No. of pupils: 1850
Curriculum: AP, SAT, USA

Apple International School
PO Box 33963, Dubai
Tel: +971 4 263 8989
Age range: 4–14
No. of pupils: 2020

Arab Unity School
PO Box 10563, Rashidiya, Dubai
Tel: +971 4 2886226/7
Age range: 3–18
No. of pupils: 3321 B1742 G1579
Curriculum: UK, IGCSE, ALevs

Arcadia School
District 9, Orchid Street, Jumeirah Village Triangle, Dubai
Tel: +971 4 552 2600

Asia

Asian International Private School - Madinat Zayed (Western Zone)
PO Box 50251, Zayed City, Abu Dhabi
Tel: +971 2 88 47470
Age range: 4–19
No. of pupils: 300

Asian International Private School - Ruwais (Western Zone)
ADNOC Building, PO Box 12000, Ruwais, Abu Dhabi
Tel: +971 2 8778789

Aspen Heights British School
P.O. Box 137352, Al Bahya, Abu Dhabi
Tel: +971 2 564 2229
Curriculum: IBDP
Language instr: English

Australian International School
PO Box 43364, Sharjah
Tel: +971 6 558 9967
No. of pupils: 1200
Curriculum: IBDP
Language instr: English

Australian School of Abu Dhabi
Khalifa City B, PO Box 36044, Abu Dhabi
Tel: +971 2 5866980
Curriculum: IBDP, IBMYP, IBPYP
Language instr: English

Bateen World Academy
Khalifah Bin Shakahbout Street, Al Manaseer Area, Abu Dhabi
Tel: +971 2 813 2000
Age range: 3–18 years
Curriculum: IBDP, IBPYP, IBCP, UK, GCSE, IGCSE, ALevs
Language instr: English

Bloom World Academy
Between Hessa Street & Umm Suqeim Street, Al Barsha South, Dubai
Tel: +971 4 371 4777
Age range: 3–18 years
Curriculum: IBDP, IBMYP, IBPYP, IBCP
Language instr: English

Bradenton Preparatory Academy
PO Box 111123, Dubai Sports City, Dubai
Tel: +971 4 818 3600
Age range: 5–18
No. of pupils: 206

Brighton College Abu Dhabi
PO Box 129444, Abu Dhabi
Tel: +971 2 815 6500
Curriculum: UK
Language instr: English
(COB)

Brighton College Al Ain
PO Box 14000, Al Ain
Tel: +971 (0)3 7133 999
Curriculum: UK
Language instr: English
(COB)

Canadian International School Abu Dhabi
PO Box 3976, Khalifa A City, Abu Dhabi
Tel: +971 2 556 4206
Age range: 4–19
No. of pupils: 300

Capital School
PO Box 236498, Baghdad Street, Al Qusais
Tel: +971 4 2381 888
Age range: 4–11

Central School Dubai
PO Box 90697, Dubai
Tel: +971 4 2674433
Age range: 3–18
No. of pupils: 2789

Clarion School
P.O. Box 2819, Dubai
Tel: +971 04 457 4321

Collegiate International School
50 Al Maydar Street, Umm Suqeim 2, P.O. Box: 121306, Dubai
Tel: +971 4 427 1400
Curriculum: IBDP, IBMYP, IBPYP, IBCP

Cranleigh Abu Dhabi
PO BOX 51072, Abu Dhabi
Tel: +971 (0)2 497 0000
Age range: 3–18
Curriculum: UK, GCSE, IGCSE, ALevs
Language instr: English

Crescent English High School Dubai
PO Box 923, Al Qusais, Dubai
Tel: +971 4 29 888 66
Age range: 3–18
No. of pupils: 1432

Dar Al Marefa Private School
P.O.Box: 112602, Dubai 112602
Tel: +971 42885782
Curriculum: IBDP, IBMYP, IBPYP

Dawha High School
PO Box 5914, Orouba Street Khalidiya, Sharjah
Tel: +971 6 522 6500
No. of pupils: 2000
Curriculum: USA

Deira International School
PO Box 79043, Dubai
Tel: +9714 2325552
Age range: 3–18
No. of pupils: 1750
Curriculum: IBDP, IBCP, UK, IGCSE
Language instr: English
(CIS)

Deira Private School
Al Twar 3, PO Box 231959, Dubai
Tel: +971 4 2641595
Age range: 4–11
No. of pupils: 111
Curriculum: National
Language instr: English

Delhi Private School Dubai
PO Box 38321, The Gardens, Jebel Ali, Dubai
Tel: +971 4 882 1848
Age range: 3–18
No. of pupils: 3274

Delhi Private School Sharjah
PO Box 26005, Sharjah
Tel: +971 6 5345352
Curriculum: National

Delta English School
PO Box 20121, Sharjah
Tel: 00 971 6 5359244
Age range: 3–16

Dubai British Foundation
Jumeirah Islands,
Tel: +971 (0)4 558 7308
Curriculum: UK

Dubai British School
Springs 3, Emirates Hills, PO Box 37828, Dubai
Tel: +971 4361 9361
Age range: 3–18
No. of pupils: 1039 B531 G508
Curriculum: GCSE, IGCSE, ALevs
Language instr: English
(CIS) (COB)

Dubai British School Jumeirah Park
Al Warood St 1, Jumeirah Park Dubai,
Tel: +971 (0)4 552 0247
Age range: 3–18
Curriculum: UK, GCSE, IGCSE, ALevs

Dubai Carmel School
PO Box 51977, Dubai
Tel: + 971 4 267 5424
Age range: 4–11
No. of pupils: 830
Curriculum: IGCSE

Dubai College
PO Box 837, Al Sufouh, Dubai
Tel: +971 4 399 9111
Age range: 11–18
No. of pupils: 885
Curriculum: UK, GCSE, IGCSE, ALevs
Language instr: English
(COB)

Dubai English Speaking College
PO Box 125814, Dubai
Tel: +971 (0) 4360 4866
Age range: 11–18
No. of pupils: 350

Dubai English Speaking School
PO Box 2002, Dubai
Tel: +971 4 3371457
Age range: 3–11
No. of pupils: 875 B450 G425
Curriculum: UK
Language instr: English
(COB)

Dubai International Academy, Al Barsha
P.O. Box: 118111, Al Barsha, Dubai
Tel: +971 4 524 4800
Curriculum: IBDP, IBMYP, IBPYP, IBCP
Language instr: English

Dubai International Academy, Emirates Hills
P.O. Box: 118111, First Al Khail Street, Emirates Hills, Dubai
Tel: +971 4 368 4111
Age range: 3–18
No. of pupils: 1660 B830 G830
Curriculum: IBDP, IBMYP, IBPYP, IBCP
Language instr: English, Arabic

Dubai International School - Al Garhoud
PO Box 15495, Dubai 16029
Tel: +971 4 282 3513
Age range: 3–19

Dubai International School - Al Qouz Branch
PO Box 125676, Dubai
Tel: +971 4 3385530
Age range: 3–18
No. of pupils: 2010

Dubai Modern Education School
PO Box 61720, Dubai
Tel: +971 4 2885115
Age range: 4–18
No. of pupils: 2470

Dubai National School - Al Barsha Branch
PO Box 24060, Al Barsha, Dubai
Tel: + 971 4 3474 555
Age range: 4–18
No. of pupils: 2579
Curriculum: SAT

Dubai Scholars Private School
PO Box 2819, Dubai
Tel: + 971 4 2988892

Dunecrest American School
P.O. Box 624265, Wadi Al Safa 3 (next to Al Barari), Dubai
Tel: +971 4 508 7444
Curriculum: IBDP
Language instr: English

Dwight School Dubai
Dubai Sports City, Dubai
Tel: +971 8003 94448
Age range: 3–18 years
No. of pupils: 700
Curriculum: IBDP, IBMYP, IBPYP, USA
Language instr: English

Elite English School
PO Box 51212, Near Century Mall, Al Wuheida Road, Deira
Tel: +971 4 2688244
Curriculum: National

Elite Private School
Mohammed Bin Zayed City, P.O.Box 41231, Opposite of Al Ain University,, ME9 P14, Abu Dhabi
Tel: + 971 2 4475800
Curriculum: USA

Emirates Future International Academy
PO Box 128576, Abu Dhabi
Tel: +971 2 5525 188
Age range: 4–19
No. of pupils: 2700
Curriculum: USA

Asia

Emirates International School - Jumeirah
PO Box 6446, Dubai
Tel: +971 4 3489804
Age range: 3–18
No. of pupils: 2013
Curriculum: IBDP, IBMYP, IBPYP, IBCP
Language instr: English

Emirates International School - Meadows
PO Box 120118, Dubai
Tel: +971 4 362 9009
Age range: 3–18
No. of pupils: 1500 B800 G700
Curriculum: IBDP, IBMYP, IBPYP, IGCSE
Language instr: English

Emirates National School - Abu Dhabi City Campus
P.O. Box 44759, Abu Dhabi
Tel: +971 2 642 5993
Curriculum: IBDP, IBMYP
Language instr: English, Arabic

Emirates National School - Al Ain City Campus
PO Box 69392, Al Ain
Tel: +971 3 761 6888
No. of pupils: 2149
Curriculum: IBDP, IBMYP, IBPYP
Language instr: English, Arabic

Emirates National School - Branch 3
P.O. Box 44759, Khalifa Bin Shakhbout Street, Abu Dhabi
Curriculum: IBPYP
Language instr: English

Emirates National School - Dubai Campus
Al Khawaneej, Dubai
Tel: +971 4 562 8888
Age range: 4–11 years
Curriculum: IBPYP
Language instr: English, Arabic

Emirates National School - Mohammed Bin Zayed Campus
PO Box 44321, Mussafah, Abu Dhabi
Tel: +971 2 559 00 00
Age range: 3.8–17
No. of pupils: 3544
Curriculum: IBDP, IBMYP, IBPYP, National
Language instr: Arabic, English

Emirates National School - Ras Al Khaimah Campus
Ras Al-Khaimah
Tel: +971 7 203 3333
Curriculum: IBDP, IBMYP, IBPYP
Language instr: English

Emirates National School - Sharjah Campus
Al Rahmaniya, Sharjah
Tel: +971 6 599 0999
Curriculum: IBDP, IBMYP, IBPYP
Language instr: English

Emirates Private School Abu Dhabi
PO Box 2564, Abu Dhabi 2564
Tel: +971 2444 8863
Age range: 3–18
No. of pupils: 1150
Curriculum: USA

Emirates Private School Al Ain
PO Box 17549, Al Ain
Tel: + 971 3 7679322
Age range: 4–18
Curriculum: ACT, UK, USA, ALevs

English School in Kalba
PO Box 17555, Sharjah
Tel: +971 9 2778199
Age range: 4–11
No. of pupils: 100
Curriculum: GCSE

Fairgreen International School
PO Box 392024, The Sustainable City, Dubai
Tel: +971 4 875 4999
Age range: 3–18 years
Curriculum: IBDP, IBMYP, IBPYP, IBCP, UK
Language instr: English

Far Eastern Private School
PO Box 29047, Sharjah
Tel: +971 6 568 0888
Curriculum: National

First Steps School and Nursery
PO Box 32283, Abu Dhabi
Tel: +971 2 4454920
Age range: 18 months–4 years
Curriculum: National, UK

Foremarke School Dubai
P.O. Box 391984, Al Barsha South, Dubai
Tel: +971 4 818 8600
Curriculum: UK

Fujairah Private Academy
PO Box 797, Fujairah
Tel: +971 9 2224001
Age range: 3 –18

Future International Academy
P.O. Box 90167, New Sarooj Street, Al Ain, Abu Dhabi
Tel: +971 3 764 6888
Age range: 3–18 years
Curriculum: IBDP
Language instr: English, Arabic

GEMS Al Barsha National School
Al Barsha South 2, Dubai
Tel: +971 4 506 9222
Age range: 3–17 years
Curriculum: UK
Language instr: English

GEMS Al Khaleej International School
Al Warqa'a 4, Dubai
Tel: +971 4 217 3900
Age range: 3–18 years
Curriculum: IBDP, USA
Language instr: English, Arabic

GEMS American Academy - Abu Dhabi
Khalifa City A, Abu Dhabi
Tel: +971 2 201 9555
Age range: 3–18 years
No. of pupils: 1800
Curriculum: IBDP, IBPYP, USA
Language instr: English

GEMS Cambridge International Private School - Sharjah
Muwailih School Zone, Sharjah
Tel: +971 6 502 4800
Age range: 4–18 years
Curriculum: UK
Language instr: English

GEMS Cambridge International School - Abu Dhabi
Baniyas City, Abu Dhabi
Tel: +971 2 510 4343
Age range: 4–17 years
Curriculum: UK
Language instr: English

GEMS Cambridge International School - Dubai
Al Twar 1, Dubai
Tel: +971 4 282 4646
Age range: 3–18 years
Curriculum: UK
Language instr: English

GEMS Dubai American Academy
Al Barsha, Dubai
Tel: +971 4 704 9777
Age range: 3–18 years
Curriculum: IBDP, USA
Language instr: English

GEMS FirstPoint School
The Villa Dubai, Dubai
Al Ain Road, Dubai
Tel: +971 4 278 9700
Age range: 3–18 years
Curriculum: UK
Language instr: English

GEMS Founder School - Mizhar
Al Mizhar, Dubai
Tel: +971 4 210 3555
Age range: 3–16 years
Curriculum: UK
Language instr: English

GEMS Founders School - Dubai
Al Barsha South, Dubai
Tel: +971 4 519 5222
Age range: 3–18 years
Curriculum: UK
Language instr: English

GEMS International School - Al Khail
Dubai Hills, Dubai
Tel: +971 4 339 6200
Age range: 3–19 years
Curriculum: IBDP, IBMYP, IBPYP, IBCP
Language instr: English

GEMS Jumeirah College
Al Wasl Road, Dubai
Tel: +971 4 395 5524
Age range: 11–18 years
Curriculum: UK

GEMS Jumeirah Primary School
Al Safa 1, Dubai
Tel: +971 4 394 3500
Age range: 4–11 years
Curriculum: UK
Language instr: English

GEMS Legacy School
Garhoud, Dubai
Tel: +971 4 282 4090
Age range: 4–12 years
Language instr: English

GEMS Metropole School - Al Waha
Al Waha, Dubai
Tel: +971 4 573 5565
Age range: 4–12 years
Curriculum: UK
Language instr: English

GEMS Metropole School - Dubai
Honsho Road, Motor City, Dubai
Tel: +971 4 550 7200
Age range: 3–18 years
Curriculum: UK
Language instr: English

GEMS Millennium School - Sharjah
Sharjah School Zone Area, Sharjah
Tel: +971 6 535 8176
Age range: 3–18 years
Language instr: English

GEMS Modern Academy - Dubai
PO Box 53663, Nad al Sheeba 3,4, Dubai
Tel: +971 4 326 3339
Age range: 4–18 years
No. of pupils: 2312
Curriculum: IBDP, IBMYP, IBPYP
Language instr: English

GEMS New Millennium School - Al Khail
Al Khail Road, Dubai
Tel: +971 4 445 2900
Age range: 3–18 years
Curriculum: UK
Language instr: English

GEMS Our Own English High School - Al Ain
Al Ain
Tel: +971 3 767 9747
Age range: 3–18 years
Curriculum: UK
Language instr: English

GEMS Our Own English High School - Boys
Juwaiza'a, Sharjah
Tel: +971 6 535 5227
Age range: B4–17 years
Language instr: English

Asia

GEMS Our Own English High School - Dubai
41 Street, Al Warqa'a 3, Dubai
Tel: +971 4 236 1335
Age range: 3–17 years
Language instr: English

GEMS Our Own English High School - Girls
Industrial Area-6, Sharjah
Tel: +971 6 538 6486
Age range: 4–17 years
Language instr: English

GEMS Our Own High School - Al Warqa'a
P.O. Box 35519, Al Warqa'a 1, Dubai
Tel: +971 4 280 0077
Age range: 5–17 years
Language instr: English

GEMS Our Own Indian School - Dubai
Al Quoz, Dubai
Tel: +971 4 339 1188
Age range: 4–17 years
Language instr: English

GEMS Royal Dubai School
Al Mizhar 1, Dubai
Tel: +971 4 288 6499
Age range: 3–11 years
Curriculum: UK
Language instr: English

GEMS United Indian School
P.O. Box 10996, 42nd Street, Baniyas West, Abu Dhabi
Tel: +971 2 205 9777
Age range: 4–18 years
Language instr: English

GEMS Wellington Academy - Al Khail
Exit 18, Al Marabea Street, Dubai
Tel: +971 4 512 9100
Age range: 2–18 years
Curriculum: UK
Language instr: English

GEMS Wellington Academy - Silicon Oasis
P.O. Box 49746, Silicon Oasis, Dubai
Tel: +971 4 515 9000
Age range: 2–18 years
Curriculum: IBDP, IBCP, UK
Language instr: English

GEMS Wellington International School
Al Sufouh Area, Sheikh Zayed Road, Dubai
Tel: +971 4 307 3000
Age range: 3–18 years
Curriculum: IBDP, IBCP, UK
Language instr: English

GEMS Westminster School - Ras Al Khaimah
Seih Al Uraibi, Ras Al Khaimah
Tel: +971 7 203 5999
Age range: 3–18 years
Curriculum: UK
Language instr: English

GEMS Westminster School - Sharjah
Muweilah, Sharjah
Tel: +971 6 542 6323
Age range: 4–17 years
Curriculum: UK
Language instr: English

GEMS Winchester School - Abu Dhabi
Madinat Zayed, Abu Dhabi
Tel: +971 2 403 5499
Age range: 4–14 years
Curriculum: UK
Language instr: English

GEMS Winchester School - Dubai
Dubailand, near IMG Worlds of Adventure, Dubai
Tel: +971 4 337 4112
Age range: 3–17 years
Curriculum: UK
Language instr: English

GEMS Winchester School - Fujairah
Fujairah
Tel: +971 9 201 4000
Age range: 3–18 years
Curriculum: UK
Language instr: English

GEMS World Academy - Abu Dhabi
Najmat, Al Reem Island, Abu Dhabi
Tel: +971 2 659 5959
Age range: 3–12 years
Curriculum: IBMYP, IBPYP, UK
Language instr: English

GEMS World Academy - Dubai
Al Barsha South, Dubai
Tel: +971 4 373 6373
Age range: 2–19 years
Curriculum: IBDP, IBMYP, IBPYP, IBCP
Language instr: English

German International School Dubai
PO Box 391162, DIAC, Dubai
Tel: +971 4 456 2718
Age range: 3–19
No. of pupils: 506

German International School Sharjah
Al Abar, Sharjah
Tel: +971 6 5676014
Age range: 3–19
No. of pupils: 200
Curriculum: IBDP
Language instr: English

German School Abu Dhabi
PO Box 4150, Abu Dhabi
Tel: +971 2 6668668

Global Indian International School (GIIS) Abu Dhabi Campus
Street 12, Plot 17, Behind Lulu Hypermarket, Baniyas East, Abu Dhabi
Tel: +971 02 5079555

Global Indian International School (GIIS) Dubai Campus
Near Al Manar Islamic Center, Al Meydan Road, Dubai
Tel: +971 800 444 7392

Global Indian School, Ajman
P.O. Box: 1382, Al Jurf 2, Ajman
Tel: +971 6 743 7477
Age range: 4–19

Goodwill Children Private School
ME-10, Muhammad Bin Zayed City, Mussafah
Tel: +971 2 553 4277
Age range: 4–11
No. of pupils: 200

Greenfield International School
Dubai Investments Park, Dubai
Tel: +971 (0)4 885 6600
Age range: 3–18 years
No. of pupils: 1397
Curriculum: IBDP, IBMYP, IBPYP, IBCP
Language instr: English

Greenwood International School
PO Box 79595, Dubai
Tel: +971 4 2888 000
Age range: 3–18
No. of pupils: 836

Gulf Asian English School
PO Box 3406, Sharjah
Tel: +971 6 5340000
Age range: 4–18
No. of pupils: 273

Gulf Model School
PO Box 13683, Dubai
Tel: +971 4 2544222
Curriculum: National, UK

Hartland International School
Sobha Hartland,, Nad Al Sheba, Mohammed Bin Rashid Al Maktoum City,,
Tel: +971 4 407 9444
Curriculum: UK, IGCSE, ALevs

HH Shaikh Rashid Al Maktoum Pakistan School, Dubai
Baghdad Street, Dubai
Tel: +971 4298 8303
Age range: 3–18
No. of pupils: 1348

Horizon English School
P.O. Box 6749, 30B Street, Off Al Wasl Road, Dubai
Tel: +971 4342 2891
Age range: 3–11 years
Curriculum: UK
Language instr: English

Horizon International School
Street 9A, Off Al Wasl Road, Umm Al Sheif, Dubai
Tel: +971 4348 3314
Age range: 3–18 years
Curriculum: UK, IGCSE, ALevs
Language instr: English

iCademy Middle East
PO Box: 502981, Block 12, Floor 1, Unit F12, Dubai, Knowledge Village
Tel: +971 444 01212
Age range: 5–12

Indian High School
Oud Metha Rd, Dubai
Tel: +971 4 337 7475
Language instr: English

Indian School Ras Al Khaimah
PO Box 4943, Ras Al Khaimah
Tel: +971 7 2288346
Age range: 4–11

Institute of Applied Technology
Abu Dhabi
Tel: +971 2 8131 555

International Academic School
P.O Box: 300165, Al Warqa 1, Dubai
Tel: +971 4 2800 993
No. of pupils: VIth1200
Curriculum: National, USA

International Community School (ICS) Al Falah
Al Farah Street, Al Falah, Abu Dhabi
Tel: +971 2 633 8181
Age range: 4–11 years
Curriculum: USA

International Community School (ICS) City Centre
Al Najda Street, City Centre, Abu Dhabi 5710
Tel: +971 2 644 4003
Age range: 3–16 years
Curriculum: UK, GCSE, IGCSE

International Community School (ICS) Khalidiya
PO BOX 2977, Al Khalidiya Area, Abu Dhabi
Tel: +971 2 444 1400
Age range: 4–11 years
Curriculum: UK

International Community School (ICS) Khalifa
P.O. Box 3456, SE 38, Khalifa City A, Abu Dhabi
Tel: +971 2 559 5566
Age range: 4–14 years
Curriculum: USA

International Community School (ICS) Mushrif
24th Street, Al Mushrif Area, Abu Dhabi 55022
Tel: +971 2 633 0444
Age range: 3–18 years
No. of pupils: 1500
Curriculum: IBDP, USA
Language instr: English, Arabic

International Concept for Education (ICE Dubai)
Meydan Street, Nad al Sheba 1, Next to the Meydan Hotel, Meydan, Dubai
Tel: +971 4 337 7818
Curriculum: IBDP, IBPYP
Language instr: English, French

Asia

International School of Creative Science
PO Box 25779, Sharjah
Tel: +971 6 534 4444
Age range: 5–18
No. of pupils: 1200
Curriculum: GCSE, IGCSE

Iqraa International School
PO Box 3598, Sharjah
Tel: +971 6 535 1166
Age range: 4–18
Curriculum: USA

Japanese School
PO Box 8120, Abu Dhabi
Tel: +971 2 446104
Age range: 4–19
No. of pupils: 78

Japanese School in Dubai
PO Box 7149, Dubai
Tel: +971 4 3449119
Age range: 4–16
No. of pupils: 148

Jebel Ali School
PO Box 17111, Dubai
Tel: +971 4 884 6485
Age range: 4–16
No. of pupils: 650
Curriculum: UK
(COB)

JSS International School
671-1431 Al Barsha South,
PO Box 37232, Dubai
Tel: +971 4 325 6886
Age range: 4–15
No. of pupils: 1380

Jumeira Baccalaureate School
53 B Street, off Al Wasl Road,
Jumeira 1, Dubai
Tel: +971 (0)4 344 6931
Age range: 3–19 years
No. of pupils: 1270
Curriculum: IBDP, IBMYP, IBPYP, IBCP
Language instr: English

Jumeirah English Speaking School (JESS), Arabian Ranches
Main entrance of Arabian Ranches community, PO Box 24942, Dubai
Tel: +971 4 3619019
Age range: 3–18
No. of pupils: 1378
Curriculum: IBDP, UK, IGCSE
Language instr: English
(COB) (ECIS)

Jumeirah English Speaking School (JESS), Jumeirah
PO Box 24942, Dubai
Tel: +971 4 3619019
Age range: 3–11
Curriculum: UK

Kent College Dubai
PO Box 334022, Dubai
Tel: +971 4343 0987
Age range: 3–18
Curriculum: IBDP, IBCP, UK, GCSE, ALevs
Language instr: English
(COB)

Kings' School Al Barsha
PO Box 38199, Dubai
Tel: +971 4 356 6900
No. of pupils: 1700
Curriculum: UK, GCSE, ALevs
(COB)

Kings' School Dubai
PO Box 38199, Dubai
Tel: +971 4 348 3939
Age range: 3–11 years
No. of pupils: 940
Curriculum: National, UK

Kings' School Nad Al Sheba
PO Box 38199, Dubai
Tel: +971 4 237 5555
No. of pupils: 550
Curriculum: UK

Latifa School for Girls
PO Box 11533, Dubai
Tel: +971 4 3361065
Age range: G3–18
Curriculum: UK, GCSE, IGCSE, ALevs
Language instr: English

Leaders Private School
PO Box 45094, Sharjah
Tel: +971 6 522 55 60
Age range: 3–16
No. of pupils: 1700

Liwa International School
PO Box 81685, Al Ain
Tel: +971 3 7810444
Age range: 4–18
No. of pupils: 1404
Curriculum: USA

Lycee Francais International
PO Box 2226, Dubai
Tel: +971 4 336 8552
Age range: 3–16
No. of pupils: 1428

Lycée Français International Georges Pompidou - École de Sharjah
PO Box 294471, Dubai
Tel: +971 65673430
Curriculum: FrenchBacc

Lycee Libanais Francophone Prive
PO Box 28759, Dubai
Tel: +971 4 264 0800
Age range: 3–15
No. of pupils: 783

Lycee Louis Massignon
PO Box 2314, Abu Dhabi
Tel: +971 2 444 80 85
Age range: 4–18
No. of pupils: 1470
Curriculum: National

MADAR International School
PO Box 15658, Al Ain
Tel: +971 3 76 11 330
Age range: 4–17
No. of pupils: 2012
Curriculum: USA

Mamoura British Academy
Al Nahyan Camp, behind Al Mamoura buildings, Abu Dhabi
Tel: +971 2 885 7100
Age range: 3–18 years
Curriculum: UK, GCSE, IGCSE, ALevs

Mirdif American School
P.O. Box 79195, Algeria Street -11A- Mizhar 1, Dubai
Tel: +971 4 288 3303
No. of pupils: 895
Curriculum: USA

MSB Private School
PO Box 94550, Dubai
Tel: +971 4 2677100
Age range: 3–16
No. of pupils: 496

Muna British Academy
Al Danah, Abu Dhabi
Tel: +971 2 501 4777
Age range: 3–18 years
Curriculum: UK, GCSE, IGCSE, ALevs

New Academy School
PO Box 11439, Dubai
Tel: +971 4 398 8873
Age range: 3–18
No. of pupils: 710

New Indian Model School
PO Box 3780, Sharjah
Tel: +971 6 5228035
Age range: 4–19
No. of pupils: 300

New Indian Model School (Dubai)
PO Box 3100, Dubai
Tel: +971 4 2824313
Age range: 3–19

New World Private School
PO Box 56988, Dubai
Tel: +971 42610033
Age range: 3–18

Nord Anglia International School, Dubai
off Hessa Street, Dubai
Tel: +971 (0)4 2199 999
Curriculum: IBDP
(COB)

North London Collegiate School Dubai
Nad Al Sheba, Mohammed Bin Rashid Al Maktoum City, Dubai
Tel: +971 (0)4319 0888
Age range: 2–18
Curriculum: IBDP, IBMYP, IBPYP
Language instr: Arabic, English

Our Own English High School - Fujairah
P.O. Box 967, Al Faseel, Fujairah
Tel: +971 9 222 4855
Age range: 4–18 years
Curriculum: IGCSE

Pakistan Education Academy
PO Box 621, Dubai
Tel: +971 4 3370126
Age range: 4–8
No. of pupils: 1682

Pakistan Islamia Higher Secondary School
Post Box No 1493, Sharjah
Tel: +971 (0)6 5670700
Age range: 14–19
No. of pupils: 2200

Pearl British Academy
Al Dhafrah, Abu Dhabi
Tel: +971 2 641 8887
Age range: 3–11 years
Curriculum: UK

Philadelphia Private School Dubai
PO Box 185020, Dubai
Tel: +971 4 26 46 202
Age range: 4–19
No. of pupils: 792

Pristine Private School
PO Box 60830, Dubai
Tel: +971 4 2674299
Age range: 3–18
No. of pupils: 600

Providence English Private School
PO Box 25532, Sharjah
Tel: +971 6 5340443
Age range: 3–18
Curriculum: National, UK, IGCSE

Raffles International School
Al Baghla Street, Umm Suqeim 3, PO Box 122900, Dubai
Tel: +971 4 4271200
Curriculum: UK
(CIS)

Raffles World Academy
Al Marcup Street, Umm Suqeim 3, P.O. Box 122900, Dubai
Tel: +971 4 4271351/2
Age range: 3–18+
Curriculum: IBDP, IBMYP, IBPYP, IBCP, SAT, IGCSE
Language instr: English

Raha International School - Gardens Campus
Khalifa City 'A', Al Raha Gardens, Abu Dhabi
Tel: +971 2 556 1567
Age range: 3–18 years
Curriculum: IBDP, IBMYP, IBPYP
Language instr: English

Raha International School - Khalifa City Campus
11 Al Mutafani Street, Khalifa City, Sector 13, Abu Dhabi
Tel: +971 2 5505 271
Age range: 3–16 years
Curriculum: IBDP, IBMYP, IBPYP
Language instr: English
(CIS)

Rajagiri International School
PO Box 62012, Al Warqaa 1, Dubai
Tel: +971 4 2800691
Age range: 3–12
No. of pupils: 1163

Asia

Ranches Primary School
P.O. Box 644818, Arabian Ranches 2, Dubai
Tel: +971 4442 9765
Age range: 1–11 years
Curriculum: UK
Language instr: English

Ras Al Khaimah Academy
PO Box 975, Ras Al Khiamah
Tel: +971 7 236 2441
Age range: 2.5–18
No. of pupils: 1300 B700 G600
Curriculum: IBDP, IBPYP, SAT, UK
Language instr: English

Ras Al Khaimah American Academy
Sheikh Saqr Bin Khalid Road, Seih Al Uraibi, Ras Al Khaimah
Tel: +971 7 2047999
Age range: 4–7 years B8–18 years G8–18 years
Curriculum: National, USA
Language instr: English

Rashid School for Boys
PO Box 2861, Dubai
Tel: +971 4 3361300
Age range: B3–18
No. of pupils: 650
Curriculum: SAT, TOEFL, UK, ALevs
Language instr: English, Arabic

Redwood Center of Excellence
Corner Road 43 & 36 B Street, Dubai
Tel: +971 50 452 3865
Curriculum: IBPYP
Language instr: English, Arabic

Regent International School
The Greens, Emirates Living Community, PO Box 2487, Dubai
Tel: +971 4 360 8830
Age range: 3–18
Curriculum: UK, ALevs

Repton Abu Dhabi
P.O. Box 45016, Al Reem Island, Abu Dhabi
Tel: +971 2 508 1900
Age range: 3–18 years
Curriculum: UK, IGCSE, ALevs
Language instr: English

Repton Al Barsha
P.O. Box 391984, Al Barsha South, Dubai
Tel: +971 4818 8600
Age range: 3–18 years
Curriculum: UK, IGCSE, ALevs
Language instr: English

Repton Dubai
P.O. Box 300331, Nad Al Sheba 3, Dubai
Tel: +971 4426 9393
Age range: 3–18 years
Curriculum: IBDP, IBCP, UK, IGCSE, ALevs
Language instr: English

SABIS International School - Aljada
Madar Street, Al Jada Center, Sharjah
Tel: +971 6 502 2111
Age range: 4–18 years
Curriculum: AP, UK, USA, IGCSE

SABIS International School - Ruwais
P.O. Box 11845, Ruwais Housing Complex - Phase 4, Abu Dhabi
Tel: +971 2 807 5000
Age range: 4–19 years
Curriculum: AP, SAT, TOEFL, UK, USA, IGCSE, ALevs

SABIS International School - Yas Island
P.O. Box 113495, Yas East, Yas Island, Abu Dhabi
Tel: +971 2 565 0065
Age range: 4–18 years

Safa British School
PO Box 71091, Dubai
Tel: +971 4 388 4300
Age range: 3–11

Safa Community School
PO Box 71091, Dubai
Tel: +971 4 385 1810
Age range: 3–14
No. of pupils: 750

Scholars Indian School RAK
PO Box 3659, Ras Al Khaimah
Tel: +971 7 222 7600
Age range: 14–19
No. of pupils: 1000

Scholars International Academy
PO Box 47425, Sharjah
Tel: +971 6 5355033
Age range: 4–11
No. of pupils: 800
Curriculum: UK

School of Modern Skills
PO Box: 57475, Dubai
Tel: +971 42887765
Language instr: English

Sharjah American International School
P.O. Box 47755, Al Warqa 1, Dubai
Tel: +971 4 280 1111
Age range: 4–18 years
Curriculum: AP, SAT, USA

Sharjah British International School
PO Box 681, Sharjah
Tel: +971 6 5347722
Age range: 4–18
No. of pupils: 400
Curriculum: ALevs

Sharjah English School
P.O. Box 1600, Sharjah
Tel: +971 6 558 9304
Age range: 3–18 years
Curriculum: UK

Sharjah Public School
PO Box 20268, Sharjah 20268
Tel: +971 6 5221244
Age range: 3–17
No. of pupils: 800

SKBZ Bangladesh Islamia School & College
P.O. Box: 8174, Abu Dhabi
Tel: +971 2 4446904
Age range: 3 years 8 months–18 years
Curriculum: National

Springdale Indian School
Al Azra Area, PO Box 27060, Sharjah
Tel: +971 6 524 3335
Curriculum: National

St Mary's Catholic High School
PO Box 1665, Fujairah
Tel: +971 70 9 2282828
Curriculum: GCSE, ALevs

St Mary's Catholic High School
PO Box 52232, Dubai
Tel: +971 4 3370252
Age range: 5–19
No. of pupils: 1966
Curriculum: IGCSE

Star International School
PO Box 51008, Dubai
Tel: +971 4288 4644
Age range: 3–13

Star International School, Mirdif
24B Street, Mirdif, Dubai
Tel: +971 4 288 4644
Age range: 3–12
No. of pupils: 304

Sunmarke School
District 5 (Behind Limitless Building on Al Khail Road), Jumeirah Village Triangle, Dubai
Tel: +971 4 423 8900
Curriculum: IBDP, IBCP
Language instr: English

Sunrise English Private School
PO Box 71356, Mussafah, Abu Dhabi
Tel: +971 2 5529989
Age range: 14–19
No. of pupils: 1240

Swiss International Scientific School in Dubai
Dubai Healthcare City, Phase 2, Al Jaddaf, PO Box 505002, Dubai
Tel: +971 4 375 0600
Age range: 3–18
No. of pupils: 1200
Curriculum: IBDP, IBMYP, IBPYP, IBCP
Language instr: English, French, German

Taaleem
PO Box 76691, 1st Floor Century Plaza, Jumeira Road
Tel: +971 4 349 8806
Age range: 3–19
No. of pupils: 4280 B1828 G2452
Curriculum: IBDP, IBMYP, IBPYP, National, UK, USA, IGCSE, ALevs
Language instr: English

The Aquila School
Opposite Skycourts Tower A, Dubailand Residence Complex, Wadi Al Safa 5, Dubai
Tel: +971 4 586 2700
Age range: 3–18 years
Curriculum: IBDP, IBCP
Language instr: English

The Arbor School
Al Furjan, PO Box 413898, Dubai
Tel: +971 (0) 4 581 4100
Age range: 3–11
Curriculum: UK

The British International School, Abu Dhabi
PO Box 60968, Abu Dhabi
Tel: +971 2 510 0176
Age range: 3–18
No. of pupils: 1800
Curriculum: IBDP, UK, IGCSE
Language instr: English

The British School - Al Khubairat
PO Box 4001, Abu Dhabi
Tel: +971 2 4462280
Age range: 3–18
No. of pupils: 1284 B673 G611
Curriculum: UK

The Cambridge High School - Abu Dhabi
ME 9, Shabia (Near Safeer Mall), Mussafah, Mohammed Bin Zayed City, Abu Dhabi
Tel: +971 2552 1621
Age range: 4–19 years
Curriculum: UK
Language instr: English

The English College
Al Safa 1, off Sheikh Zayed Road, opp. Oasis Mall, P.O. Box 11812, Dubai
Tel: +971 4 394 3465
Age range: 3–18 years
Curriculum: UK, GCSE, ALevs
Language instr: English

The Indian Academy, Dubai
Behind Madina Mall, Al Muhaisnah - 4, P.O: 55510, Plot No: 245-703, Dubai
Tel: +971 4264 6733
Age range: 3–18
Curriculum: National

The International School of Choueifat - Abu Dhabi
P.O. Box 7212, Mushrif Area, Abu Dhabi
Tel: +971 2 446 1444
Age range: 3–18 years

Asia

The International School of Choueifat - Abu Dhabi Khalifa City
P.O. Box 502, Khalifa City, Abu Dhabi
Tel: +971 2 556 2555
Age range: 4–18 years

The International School of Choueifat - Ajman
P.O. Box 16666, Al Tallah 2, South Sector, Ajman
Tel: +971 6 742 1111
Age range: 4–18 years

The International School of Choueifat - Al Ain
P.O. Box 15997, Bldg. #103, Saeed Ibn Shakhboot Street, Ugdat Al Mutawaa, Al Muwaiji, Al Ain
Tel: +971 3 767 8444
Age range: 4–18 years

The International School of Choueifat - Dubai
Hessa Street, Al Sufouh 2 area, Jumeirah, Dubai
Tel: +971 4 399 9444
Age range: 4–18 years

The International School of Choueifat - Dubai Investments Park
P.O. Box 643581, Dubai Investments Park 1, Dubai
Tel: +971 4 884 7884
Age range: 4–18 years

The International School of Choueifat - Ras Al Khaimah
P.O. Box 1644, Ras Al Khaimah
Tel: +971 7 235 3446
Age range: 4–18 years

The International School of Choueifat - Sharjah
P.O. Box 2077, University City Road, Industrial Area 6, Sharjah
Tel: +971 6 558 2211
Age range: 4–18 years
Curriculum: AP, UK, USA, IGCSE, ALevs
Language instr: English

The International School of Choueifat - Umm Al Quwain
P.O. Box 3142, Khalifa City, Umm Al Quwain
Tel: +971 6 766 5888
Age range: 4–18 years

The Millennium School - Dubai
Al Baghdad Street, Behind Lulu Hypermarket, Al Qusais, Dubai
Tel: +971 4 298 8567
Age range: 4–17 years
Language instr: English

The Model School
PO Box 25723, Abu Dhabi
Tel: +971 2 5527200
Age range: 4–19
No. of pupils: 300

The Oxford School Dubai
PO Box 50091, Dubai
Tel: +971 4 2543666
Age range: 3–18
No. of pupils: 1828
Curriculum: ALevs

The Royal Grammar School Guildford, Dubai
D 61 - Tilal Al Ghaf, Dubai
Tel: +971 4 446 4333
Age range: 3–18 years
Curriculum: UK, GCSE, ALevs
Language instr: English, Arabic

The School of Research Science
44 Baghdad Street, Dubai
Tel: +971 4 6011011
Age range: 3–18
Language instr: English, Arabic

The Sheffield Private School
Al Nahda 2, Dubai
Tel: +971 4 267 8444
Age range: 3–18 years
Curriculum: UK, ALevs
Language instr: English

The Sheikh Zayed Private Academy for Boys
P.O. Box 812, Abu Dhabi
Tel: +971 2 203 3333
Age range: B4–18 years
Curriculum: USA

The Sheikh Zayed Private Academy for Girls
P.O. Box 42989, Abu Dhabi
Tel: +971 2 619 5555
Age range: G4–18 years
Curriculum: USA

The WellSpring School
34B St, Ras Al-Khaimah
Tel: +971-07-2362446
Curriculum: USA

The Westminster School - Dubai
Al Qusais, Dubai
Tel: +971 4 298 8333
Age range: 3–18 years
Curriculum: UK
Language instr: English

The Winchester School - Dubai
The Gardens, Jebel Ali, Dubai
Tel: +971 4 882 0444
Age range: 3–17 years
Curriculum: UK
Language instr: English

Towheed Iranian School
Al Meydan Road, Al Quoz 1, Dubai
Tel: +971 4 338 9953
Curriculum: IBDP
Language instr: English

United International Private School
PO Box 60817, Dubai
Tel: +971 4 2543888
Age range: 5–16
No. of pupils: 1000

Universal American School, Dubai
PO Box 79133, Al Rashidiya, Dubai
Tel: +971 4 232 5222
Age range: 3–18
No. of pupils: 1100 B616 G484
Curriculum: IBDP, IBPYP, SAT, USA
Language instr: English, Arabic

Uptown International School
Corner of Algeria Road & Tripoli Street, Mirdif, PO Box 78181, Dubai
Tel: +971 (0)4 2515001
Age range: 6 months–18 years
No. of pupils: 1230
Curriculum: IBDP, IBMYP, IBPYP, IBCP
Language instr: English

Victoria English School
PO Box 25549, Sharjah
Tel: +971 6 5227770
Age range: 2–18
No. of pupils: 582 B309 G273
Curriculum: UK
Language instr: English

Victoria International School of Sharjah
PO Box 68600, Al Mamzar, Sharjah
Tel: +971 6 577 1999
Curriculum: IBDP

Victory Heights Primary School
PO Box 454959 Dubai
Tel: (+971) 4 423 1100
Curriculum: UK

Wesgreen International School - Sharjah
Al Muweilah Commercial, Sharjah
Tel: +971 6 506 2999
Age range: 3–18 years
Curriculum: UK
Language instr: English

Yas American Academy
Al Tahaddur Street, Yas Island, Abu Dhabi
Tel: +971 2 885 7000
Age range: 3–18 years
Curriculum: AP, USA

Yasmina British Academy
Khalifa City A, Abu Dhabi
Tel: +971 2 508 9500
Age range: 3–18 years
Curriculum: UK, GCSE, IGCSE, ALevs

UZBEKISTAN

International Talent Academy
30A Hamid Alimjan Street, Mirzo-Ulugbek District, 100072 Tashkent
Tel: +998 78 113 28 28
Curriculum: IBMYP
Language instr: English, Russian

INVENTO the Uzbek International School
Furqat street 4A, 100021 Tashkent
Tel: +998 71 210 99 99
Curriculum: IBDP, IBMYP, IBPYP
Language instr: English, Russian

Oxbridge International School
Oymarik Street 10, Mirzo Ulug'bek District, Tashkent
Tel: +998 71 263 00 15
Age range: 4–18 years
Curriculum: IBDP, IBMYP, IBPYP
Language instr: English, Russian

Smart School
Amir Temur Avenue 33, Mirabad District, Tashkent
Tel: +998 71 231 99 55
Age range: 4–18 years
Curriculum: IBDP, National, UK
Language instr: English, Russian

Tashkent International School
38 Sarikulskaya Street, Tashkent
Tel: +998 55 501 96 70
Age range: 3–18 years
Curriculum: IBDP, IBMYP, IBPYP
Language instr: English

Tashkent Ulugbek International School
3A Rakat Street, Tashkent
Tel: +998 71 280 56 81

The British School of Tashkent
Building 3, Kalandar Street, Mirzo Ulugbek District, Tashkent
Tel: +998 71 262 60 20
Age range: 1.5–18 years
Curriculum: National, UK, IGCSE, ALevs
Language instr: English

Vosiq International School
Domrosa Street, 4th Drive, Chilanzar District, Tashkent
Tel: +998 71 207 00 88
Curriculum: IBPYP
Language instr: English, Russian

VIETNAM

American International School of Vietnam
220 Nguyen Van Tao, Nha Be District, Ho Chi Minh City
Tel: +84 28378 00808
Curriculum: IBDP, IBMYP, IBPYP, SAT, USA
Language instr: English, Vietnamese

Asian International School Primary School
(Caothang Campus 1), 177 bis Caothang Street, Ward 12, District 10 848
Tel: +84 8 38680259
Curriculum: USA

Asia

AUSTRALIAN INTERNATIONAL SCHOOL (AIS)
For further details see p. 45
264 Mai Chi Tho Street,
An Phu ward, Thu Duc
City, Ho Chi Minh City
Tel: +84 28 3742 4040
Email: info@aisvietnam.com
Website: www.aisvietnam.com
Executive Principal: Jon Standen
Age range: 18 months–18 years
No. of pupils: 1330
Fees: 295,600,000–860,700,000
Curriculum: IBDP, IBPYP, IGCSE

British International School Ho Chi Minh City
246 Nguyen Van Huong Street, Thao Dien, Thu Duc City, Ho Chi Minh City
Tel: +84 (0)28 3744 2335
Age range: 2–18 years
No. of pupils: 2400
Curriculum: IBDP, IPC, UK, IGCSE
Language instr: English

British International School, Hanoi
Hoa Lan Road, Vinhomes Riverside, Long Bien District, Hanoi 100000
Tel: +84 24 3946 0435
Age range: 2–18 years
No. of pupils: 1100
Curriculum: IBDP, IPC, UK, IGCSE

British Vietnamese International School, Hanoi
72A Nguyen Trai Street, Thanh Xuan District, Hanoi
Tel: +84 24 6266 8800

British Vietnamese International School, Ho Chi Minh City
44-46 Street 1, Binh Hung, Binh Chanh, Ho Chi Minh City
Tel: +84 83 758 0717 Ext:211

Canadian International School - Vietnam
No. 86, Road 23, Phu My Hung, Tan Phu Ward, District 7, Binh Chanh District, Ho Chi Minh City
Tel: +84 28 54 123 456
Curriculum: IBDP
Language instr: English

Concordia International School Hanoi
Van Tri Golf Compound, Kim No, Dong Anh, Hanoi
Tel: +84 (0) 24 3795 8878
Age range: 3–18 years
No. of pupils: 380
Curriculum: AP
Language instr: English

DWIGHT SCHOOL HANOI
For further details see p. 51
The Manor Central Park, Hoang Mai District, Hanoi
Email: contact@dwighthanoi.org
Website: www.dwighthanoi.org
Age range: 3–18 years
Fees: 325,000,000–845,000,000

English French School (EFS)
So 3 Duong 46, Thao Dien, Quan 2, Ho Chi Minh City
Age range: 5–11 years
No. of pupils: 20
Curriculum: FrenchBacc, UK
Language instr: English, French

EUROPEAN INTERNATIONAL SCHOOL HCMC
For further details see p. 52
730 Le Van Mien Street, Thao Dien Ward, Thu Duc City, Ho Chi Minh City 70000
Tel: +8428 7300 7257
Email: info@eishcmc.com
Website: www.eishcmc.com
Co-Heads of School: Ms. Jo Roberts & Mr. Ben Armstrong
Age range: 2–18 years
No. of pupils: 750
Fees: 274,700,000–771,600,000
Curriculum: IBDP, IBMYP, IBPYP
Language instr: English

Fosco International School (FIS)
40 Ba Huyen Thanh Quan, Ward 6, District 3,, Ho Chi Minh City
Tel: +84 28 3930 5930
Age range: 18 months–11 years
Curriculum: USA

Global Indian International School (GIIS) Vietnam Campus
Ho Chi Minh City

Hanoi Academy
D45 - D46, Ciputra International City, Hanoi
Tel: +84 43 7430135
Age range: 2–18
Curriculum: National

Hanoi International School
48 Lieu Giai Street, Ba Dinh District, Hanoi
Tel: +84 4 3832 8140
Age range: 4–18
No. of pupils: 270 B130 G140
Curriculum: IBDP, IBMYP, IBPYP
Language instr: English

HOI AN INTERNATIONAL SCHOOL
For further details see p. 54
24 Phan Ba Phien, Tan An, Hoi An 510000
Tel: +84 235 651 8518
Email: admissions@hais.edu.vn
Website: www.hais.edu.vn
Principal: Brett Macdouall
Age range: 18 months–18 years
No. of pupils: 300
Curriculum: National, IGCSE, ALevs
Language instr: English, French, Vietnamese

Horizon International Bilingual School - Hanoi Campus
98 To Ngoc Van St, Villa 1, 2,, District Tay Ho, Hanoi
Tel: +84 3719 49 53
Age range: 14–17
No. of pupils: 207 B135 G72
Curriculum: National
Language instr: English, Vietnamese

Horizon International Bilingual School - HCMC Campus
6-6A-8, Duong 44, Thao Dien Ward, District 2
Tel: +84 8 5402 2482
Age range: 5–18
No. of pupils: 286
Curriculum: SAT, UK, IGCSE, ALevs

International German School HCMC
12 Vo Truong Toan, An Phu Ward, District 2, Ho Chi Minh City
Tel: +84 (0)28 37 44 63 44
Curriculum: IBDP
Language instr: English, German

INTERNATIONAL SCHOOL HO CHI MINH CITY (ISHCMC)
For further details see p. 60
28 Vo Truong Toan St., An Phu ward, Thu Duc City, Ho Chi Minh City
Tel: +84 28 3898 9100
Email: admissions@ishcmc.edu.vn
Website: www.ishcmc.com
Head of School: Marco Longmore
Age range: 2–18 years
No. of pupils: 1500
Fees: 279,000,000–681,900,000
Curriculum: IBDP, IBMYP, IBPYP
Language instr: English

International School Ho Chi Minh City (ISHCMC) - American Academy
16 Vo Truong Toan Street, An Phu Ward, Thu Duc City (District 2), Ho Chi Minh City
Tel: +84 283 898 9098
Age range: 11–18 years
Curriculum: AP, USA
Language instr: English

International School of Vietnam
No. 6-7 Nguyen Cong Thai Street, Dai Kim Urban area, Hoang Mai, Hanoi
Tel: +84 (0)435 409 183
Curriculum: IBDP, IBPYP
Language instr: English

International School Saigon Pearl
92 Nguyen Huu Canh Street, Ward 22, Binh Thanh District, Ho Chi Minh City
Tel: +84 282 222 7788
Age range: 1.5–11 years
Curriculum: IBPYP, USA
Language instr: English, Vietnamese

International Schools of North America
Street 20, Him Lam Residential Area, Binh Chanh District, Ho Chi Minh City
Tel: +84 28 730 197 99
Age range: 5–19
No. of pupils: 425
Curriculum: IBDP, IBMYP, IBPYP
Language instr: English

KinderWorld International Kindergarten (KIK) @ Hanoi Towers
3rd Floor, 49 Hai Ba Trung Street, Hoan Kiem District, Hanoi
Tel: +84 4 3934 7243

KinderWorld International Kindergarten (KIK) @ The Manor (Hanoi)
C5-C11, 1st Floor, The Manor Building, My Dinh, Me Tri New Urban, Tu Liem District, Hanoi
Tel: +84 4 3794 0209

KinderWorld International Kindergarten (KIK) @ The Manor (HCMC)
The Manor Building, 91 Nguyen Huu Canh Street, Binh Thanh District, Ho Chi Minh City
Tel: +84 8 3514 3036

Lycée Français Alexandre Yersin
12 Nui Truc, Ba Dinh, Hanoi
Tel: +844 3843 67 79
Curriculum: FrenchBacc

Odyssey International School
Lot A1, urban area 7B Sentosa City, Dien Ngoc Ward, Dien Ban Town, Quang Nam Province
Tel: +84 235 371 1678
Age range: 3–14 years
Curriculum: IPC
Language instr: English

Pegasus International College - Da Nang
Vung Trung 3, Phu My New Urban Area, Hoa Hai Ward, Ngu Hanh Son District, Da Nang City
Tel: +84 023 6730 1555

Pegasus International College - Hanoi
No. 2/2C, Doan Van Phuc Diplomatic Area, Kim Ma Street, Ba Dinh District, Hanoi
Tel: +84 024 7304 1555

QSI International School of Haiphong
Lot CC2, Me Linh Village, Anh Dung Ward, Duong Kinh District, Haiphong
Tel: +84 31 381 4258
Age range: 2–18 years
Curriculum: IBDP, USA
Language instr: English

Asia

Renaissance International School Saigon
74 Nguyen Thi Thap Street, Binh Thuan Ward, District 7, Ho Chi Minh City
Tel: +84 283 7733 171
Age range: 2–18
No. of pupils: 560
Curriculum: IBDP, IBPYP, UK, IGCSE
Language instr: English
(RS)

Saigon South International School
78 Nguyen Duc Canh, Tan Phong Ward, District 7, Ho Chi Minh City 70000
Tel: +84 28 5413 0901
Age range: 3–18
No. of pupils: 1005 B486 G519 VIth74
Curriculum: AP, IBDP, SAT, USA
Language instr: English
(EAR)

Singapore International School (SIS) @ BDNC
Lot F7, Le Loi Street, Binh Duong New City, Hoa Phu Ward, Thu Dau Mot City, Binh Duong Province
Tel: +84 27 4730 0777
Age range: 3–17 years

Singapore International School (SIS) @ Can Tho
Nguyen Van Cu Street, An Binh Ward, Ninh Kieu District, Can Tho City
Tel: +84 29 2730 1777
Age range: 3–17 years

Singapore International School (SIS) @ Ciputra
Block C3 (NT III B) Ciputra Hanoi International City, Phu Thuong Ward, Tay Ho District, Hanoi
Tel: +84 24 7304 3777
Age range: 3–11 years

Singapore International School (SIS) @ Da Nang
SIS Building, Vung Trung 3 Street, Phu My An New Urban Area, Hoa Hai Ward, Ngu Hanh Son District, Da Nang City
Tel: +84 23 6730 1777
Age range: 3–17 years

Singapore International School (SIS) @ Gamuda Gardens
Gamuda Gardens 2 Road, Gamuda Gardens, Km 4.4 Phap Van, Hoang Mai District, Hanoi
Tel: +84 24 7304 1777
Age range: 3–16 years

Singapore International School (SIS) @ Ha Long
Hung Thang Urban and Service Area, Hung Thang Ward, Halong City, Quang Ninh Province
Tel: +84 20 3655 8811
Age range: 3–17 years

Singapore International School (SIS) @ Saigon South
No. 29, Road No. 3, Trung Son Residential Area, Hamlet 4, Binh Hung Ward, Binh Chanh District, Ho Chi Minh City
Tel: +84 236 730 1777
Age range: 18 months–18 years
Curriculum: National, IGCSE, ALevs
Language instr: English

Singapore International School (SIS) @ Van Phuc
2D Van Phuc Diplomatic Compound, 46 Van Bao Street, Ba Dinh District, Hanoi
Tel: +84 24 7304 2777
Age range: 3–11 years

Singapore International School (SIS) @ Vung Tau
Dai An Residential, Ward 9, Vung Tau City
Tel: +84 25 4730 1777
Age range: 3–17 years

Singapore Vietnam International School (SVIS) @ Nha Trang
Vinh Diem Trung Residential Area, Nha Trang City
Tel: +84 25 8730 1777

St. Paul American School Hanoi
Splendora New Urban, Km 10 + 600 Thang Long Highway, Hoai Duc, Hanoi
Tel: +84 24 3399 6464
Curriculum: AP, USA
(EAR)

Tesla Education - Tan Binh Campus
171B Hoang Hoa Tham Street, Ward 13, Tan Binh District, Ho Chi Minh City
Tel: +84 98 494 8080
Age range: 18 months–18 years
Curriculum: IBPYP
Language instr: English, Vietnamese

TH School
6 Chua Boc, Quang Trung, Dong Da, Hanoi
Tel: +84 24 7309 2255
Age range: 2–18
No. of pupils: 170 B90 G80
Curriculum: ACT, IPC, SAT, IGCSE, ALevs
Language instr: English

The ABC International School
#2 1E Street, Khu Dan Cu, Trung Son, Binh Hung, Binh Chanh, Ho Chi Minh City
Tel: +84 28 5431 1833
Age range: 2–18
No. of pupils: 750
Curriculum: AP, UK, IGCSE, ALevs
Language instr: English
(COB)

The Asian International School
177 Bis 2 Cao Thang, Phuong 12, Quan 10 (6,272.60 mi), Ho Chi Minh City 72510
Tel: +84 28 3868 0270
Curriculum: USA
(CIS)

The International School @ Park City Hanoi
Le Trong Tan Road, Ha Dong District, Hanoi
Tel: +84 93 44 55 228
Age range: 3–18 years

The Olympia Schools
Trung Van New urban area, South Tu Liem, Hanoi
Tel: +84 24 6267 7999
Curriculum: IBDP
Language instr: English, Vietnamese

United Nations International School of Hanoi
G9 Ciputra, Tay Ho, Hanoi
Tel: +84 24 7300 4500
Age range: 3–18
No. of pupils: 1130
Curriculum: IBDP, IBMYP, IBPYP
Language instr: English
(CIS) (EAR) (ECIS)

Vietnam-Finland International School
01, D1 Street, Tan Phong Ward, District 7, Ho Chi Minh City
Tel: +84 28 37 755 110
Curriculum: IBDP
Language instr: English, Vietnamese

Wellspring International Bilingual School - Hanoi
No. 95, Ai Mo Town, Bo De ward, Long Bien District, Hanoi
Tel: +84 24 3766 3838
Age range: 5–18
Curriculum: IGCSE
Language instr: English, Vietnamese

Wellspring Saigon International Bilingual School
92 Nguyen Huu Canh Street, Ward 22, Binh Thanh District, Ho Chi Minh City
Tel: +84 28 3840 9292
Age range: 5–18
Curriculum: IGCSE
Language instr: English, Vietnamese

Western Australian Primary and High School
157 Ly Chinh Thang Street, Vo Thi Sau Ward, District 3, Ho Chi Minh City
Tel: +84 28 7109 5077
Age range: 2–18 years
No. of pupils: 2500
Curriculum: IBDP
Language instr: English

Westlink International School
Gia Vinh Road, Tay Ho Tay urban area, Xuan Tao Ward, Bac Tu Liem District, Hanoi
Tel: +(84) 86 577 7900
Curriculum: IBPYP
Language instr: English

Wisdomland Diamond Island
Block Hawaii, Diamond Island, Binh Trung Tay Ward, Thu Duc City, Ho Chi Minh City
Tel: +84 28 6287 19 74
Curriculum: IBPYP
Language instr: English, Vietnamese

YEMEN

Hadhramaut International Schools
Main Street (next to Bin Jribah Brothers), Mukalla
Tel: 05321250/1
Age range: 4–16 years
Curriculum: UK, IGCSE

Sana'a British School
Nouakchott Street, Sana'a
Tel: +967 1 203 950
Age range: 3–18 years
Curriculum: UK, IGCSE, ALevs
Language instr: English

International schools in Australasia

Schools ordered A–Z by Country

Key to directory

Country

Name of school or college

Indicates that this school has a profile

Address and contact number

Head's name

Age range

Number of pupils.
B = boys G = girls VIth = sixth form

Fees per annum.
Day = fees for day pupils.
WB = fees for weekly boarders.
FB = fees for full boarders.

Curriculum

Language of instruction

Memberships/Accreditation

Whereford

College Academy
For further details see p

Which Street, Whosville,
Wherefordshire AB12 3CD

Tel: 01000 000000

Head Master: Dr A Person

Age range: 11–18

No. of pupils:
660 B330 G330 VIth 200

Fees: Day £11,000
WB £16,000 FB £20,000

Curriculum:
National, IBDP, ALevs

Language instr:
English, French

(AISA) (COB) (EAR)

Key to icons

Key to symbols:
- Boys' school
- Girls' school
- Boarding accommodation

Member of:
- (AISA) Association of International Schools in Africa
- (CEE) Central and Eastern European Schools Association
- (EAR) East Asia Regional Council of Overseas Schools
- (ECIS) European Council of International Schools
- (RS) Round Square

Accreditation:
- (CIS) Council of International Schools
- (COB) Council of British International Schools

Please note: Schools are coeducational day schools unless otherwise indicated

AUSTRALIA

Adelaide High School
West Terrace, Adelaide SA 5000
Tel: +61 8 8231 9373
Age range: 12–18 years
Curriculum: National
Language instr: English

Adelaide Secondary School of English
253 Torrens Road, West Croydon SA 5008
Tel: +61 8 8340 3733
Age range: 12–18 years
Curriculum: National

Al Zahra College
3-5 Wollongong Road, Arncliffe NSW 2205
Tel: +61 2 9599 0161
Age range: 3–18 years
Curriculum: IBDP, IBMYP, IBPYP
Language instr: English

All Saints' College
Ewing Avenue, Bull Creek WA 6149
Tel: +61 8 9313 9333
Age range: 3–18 years
Curriculum: National

Anglican Church Grammar School
Oaklands Parade, East Brisbane QLD 4169
Tel: +61 7 3896 2200
Age range: B4–18 years
Curriculum: IBDP, IBPYP, National
Language instr: English

Annesley Junior School
28 Rose Terrace, Wayville SA 5034
Tel: +61 8 8422 2288
Age range: 2–11 years
Curriculum: IBPYP
Language instr: English

Aquinas College
46 Great Ryrie Street, (PO Box 190), Ringwood VIC 3134
Tel: +61 3 9259 3000
Age range: 11–18 years
Curriculum: National
Language instr: English

Ascham School
188 New South Head Road, Edgecliff NSW 2027
Tel: +61 2 8356 7000
Age range: G4–18 years (boarding from 11)
Curriculum: National

Australian International Academy - Caroline Springs Campus
183-191 Caroline Springs Boulevard, Caroline Springs, Melbourne VIC 3023
Tel: +61 3 8372 5446
Age range: 4–18 years
Curriculum: IBDP, IBPYP, National
Language instr: English

Australian International Academy - Kellyville Campus
2 Foxall Road, North Kellyville, Sydney NSW 2155
Tel: +61 2 8801 3100
Age range: 4–18 years
Curriculum: IBDP, IBMYP, IBPYP, National
Language instr: English

Australian International Academy - King Khalid Coburg Campus
653 Sydney Road, Coburg, Melbourne VIC 3058
Tel: +61 3 9354 0833
Age range: 4–11 years
Curriculum: National
Language instr: English

Australian International Academy - Strathfield Campus
420 Liverpool Road, Strathfield South, Sydney NSW 2135
Tel: +61 2 9642 0104
Age range: 4–18 years
Curriculum: IBDP, IBMYP, IBPYP, National
Language instr: English

Australian International Academy of Education
Melbourne Senior Campus, 56 Bakers Road, North Coburg VIC 3058
Tel: +61 3 9350 4533
Age range: 5–18 years
No. of pupils: 2127
Curriculum: IBDP, IBMYP, IBPYP, National
Language instr: English

Ballarat Grammar
201 Forest Street, Wendouree VIC 3355
Tel: +61 3 5338 0700
Age range: 6 months–18 years
Curriculum: IBPYP, National
Language instr: English

Banksia Park International High School
610 Milne Road, Banksia Park SA 5091
Tel: +61 8 8264 8122
Age range: 13–18 years
Curriculum: National
Language instr: English

Barker College
91 Pacific Highway, Hornsby NSW 2077
Tel: +61 2 8438 7999
Age range: 3–18 years
Curriculum: IBPYP
Language instr: English

Bendigo Senior Secondary College
P.O. Box 545, Bendigo VIC 3552
Tel: +61 3 5443 1222
Age range: 16–18 years
Curriculum: National
Language instr: English

Bendigo South East College
56 Ellis Street, Flora Hill VIC 3550
Tel: +61 3 5443 4522
Age range: 11–18 years
Curriculum: National
Language instr: English

Billanook College
197-199 Cardigan Road, Mooroolbark VIC 3138
Tel: +61 3 9725 5388
Age range: 3–18 years
Curriculum: National
Language instr: English

Bribie Island State High School
65-101 First Avenue, Bongaree, Bribie Island QLD 4507
Tel: +61 7 3400 2444
Age range: 11–18 years
Curriculum: National
Language instr: English

Brighton Grammar School
90 Outer Crescent, Brighton VIC 3186
Tel: +61 3 8591 2200
Age range: B3–18 years
Curriculum: National
Language instr: English

Brisbane Grammar School
Gregory Terrace, Brisbane QLD 4000
Tel: +61 7 3834 5200
Age range: B9–18 years
Curriculum: National
Language instr: English

Camberwell Grammar School
55 Mont Albert Road, Canterbury VIC 3126
Tel: +61 3 9835 1777
Age range: B4–18 years
Curriculum: National
Language instr: English

Cambridge Primary School
29 Carruthers Drive, Hoppers Crossing VIC 3029
Tel: +61 3 9748 9011
Age range: 4–11 years
Curriculum: National
Language instr: English

Canberra Girls Grammar School
Melbourne Avenue, Deakin ACT 2600
Tel: +61 2 6202 6400
Age range: B3–8 G3–18 years
Curriculum: IBDP, IBPYP, National
Language instr: English

Canberra Grammar School
40 Monaro Crescent, Red Hill, Canberra ACT 2603
Tel: +61 2 6260 9700
Age range: 3–18 years
Curriculum: IBDP, IBPYP
Language instr: English

Carey Baptist Grammar School
349 Barkers Road, Kew VIC 3101
Tel: +61 3 9816 1222
Age range: 3–18 years
No. of pupils: 2704
Curriculum: IBDP, National
Language instr: English

Caulfield Grammar School - Caulfield Campus
217 Glen Eira Road, St Kilda VIC 3183
Tel: +61 3 9524 6300
Age range: 12–18 years
Curriculum: IBMYP
Language instr: English

Caulfield Grammar School - Malvern Campus
5 Willoby Avenue, Glen Iris VIC 3146
Tel: +61 3 9805 9300
Age range: 3–11 years
Curriculum: IBPYP
Language instr: English

Caulfield Grammar School - Wheelers Hill Campus
74-82 Jells Road, Wheelers Hill VIC 3150
Tel: +61 3 8562 5300
Age range: 3–18 years
Curriculum: IBMYP, IBPYP
Language instr: English

Caulfield Junior College
186 Balaclava Road, Caulfield North VIC 3161
Tel: +61 3 9509 6872
Age range: 4–11 years
Curriculum: National
Language instr: English, French

Charles Campbell College
3 Campbell Road, Paradise SA 5075
Tel: +61 8 8165 4700
Age range: 4–18 years
Curriculum: National
Language instr: English

Christ Church Grammar School
Queenslea Drive, Claremont WA 6010
Tel: +61 8 9442 1555
Age range: B4–18 years
Curriculum: National
Language instr: English

Concordia College, Concordia Campus - Highgate
24 Winchester Street, Highgate SA 5063
Tel: +61 8 8272 0444
Age range: 11–18 years
Curriculum: IBMYP, IBPYP
Language instr: English

Concordia College, St Peter's Campus - Blackwood
71 Cumming Street, Blackwood SA 5051
Tel: +61 8 8278 0800
Age range: 4–11 years
Curriculum: IBPYP
Language instr: English

Australasia

Cornish College
65 Riverend Road,
Bangholme VIC 3175
Tel: +61 3 9781 9000
Age range: 3–18 years
Curriculum: IBPYP
Language instr: English

Cranbrook School
5 Victoria Road, Bellevue
Hill NSW 2023
Tel: +61 2 9327 9000
Age range: B3–18 years (Co-ed senior from 2026)
No. of pupils: 1800
Curriculum: IBDP, IBMYP, IBPYP, National
Language instr: English

Creek Street Christian College
91 Creek Street, Bendigo VIC 3550
Tel: +61 3 5442 1722
Age range: 4–18 years
Curriculum: IBDP
Language instr: English

Elonera Montessori School
21 Mount Ousley Road,
Mount Ousley NSW 2519
Tel: +61 2 4225 1000
Age range: 2–18 years
Curriculum: IBDP, IBCP
Language instr: English

Encounter Lutheran College
64 Adelaide Road, Victor
Harbor SA 5211
Tel: +61 8 8552 8880
Age range: 4–18 years
Curriculum: IBMYP, IBPYP
Language instr: English

Faith Lutheran College
130 Magnolia Road, Tanunda SA 5352
Tel: +61 8 8561 4200
Age range: 3–18 years
Curriculum: IBMYP, IBPYP
Language instr: English

Fintona Girls' School
79 Balwyn Road, Balwyn VIC 3103
Tel: +61 3 9830 1388
Age range: G3–18 years
Curriculum: National

Firbank Grammar School - Brighton Campus
Middle Crescent, Brighton,
Melbourne VIC 3186
Tel: +61 3 9591 5141
Age range: 3–11 years
Curriculum: IBPYP
Language instr: English

Firbank Grammar School - Sandringham Campus
45 Royal Avenue,
Sandringham VIC 3191
Tel: +61 3 9533 5711
Age range: 3–11 years
Curriculum: IBPYP
Language instr: English

Geelong Grammar School - Bostock House
139 Noble Street, Newtown VIC 3220
Tel: +61 3 5221 7760
Age range: 3–9 years
Curriculum: IBPYP
Language instr: English

Geelong Grammar School - Corio Campus
50 Biddlecombe Avenue,
Corio VIC 3214
Tel: +61 3 5273 9200
Age range: 11-13 & 16–18 years
Curriculum: IBDP, IBPYP
Language instr: English

Geelong Grammar School - Timbertop
Private Mail Bag, Mansfield VIC 3722
Tel: +61 3 5733 6777
Age range: 14–15 years
Language instr: English

Geelong Grammar School - Toorak Campus
14 Douglas Street, P.O. Box
530, Toorak VIC 3142
Tel: +61 3 9829 1444
Age range: 3–11 years
Language instr: English

Genazzano FCJ College
301 Cotham Road, Kew VIC 3101
Tel: +61 3 8862 1000
Age range: G3–18 years
Curriculum: IBPYP
Language instr: English, Italian

Geraldton Grammar School
134 George Road,
Geraldton WA 6530
Tel: +61 8 9965 7800
Age range: 3–18 years
Curriculum: National
Language instr: English

German International School Sydney
33 Myoora Road, Terrey Hills NSW 2084
Tel: +61 2 9485 1900
Age range: 3–19 years
No. of pupils: 380
Curriculum: IBDP, National
Language instr: English, German

Golden Grove Lutheran Primary School
21-23 Richardson Drive,
Wynn Vale SA 5127
Tel: +61 8 8282 6000
Age range: 4–11 years
Curriculum: IBPYP
Language instr: English

Good News Lutheran College
580 Tarneit Road, Tarneit VIC 3029
Tel: +61 3 8742 9000
Curriculum: IBMYP, IBPYP
Language instr: English

Good Shepherd Lutheran College - Howard Springs Campus
Corner of Whitewood
Road & Kundook Place,
Howard Springs NT 0835
Tel: +61 8 8983 0300
Age range: 3–18 years
Curriculum: IBMYP, IBPYP
Language instr: English

Good Shepherd Lutheran College - Leanyer Campus
95 Leanyer Drive, Leanyer NT 0812
Tel: +61 8 8983 0300
Age range: 3–11 years
Curriculum: National
Language instr: English

Good Shepherd Lutheran College - Noosa
115 Eumundi Road,
Noosaville QLD 4566
Tel: +61 7 5455 8600
Age range: 3–18 years
Curriculum: National

Good Shepherd Lutheran College - Palmerston Campus
Cnr Temple Tce & Emery
Avenue, Palmerston NT 0830
Tel: +61 8 8983 0300
Age range: 3–11 years
Curriculum: National

Good Shepherd Lutheran School - Angaston
7 Neldner Avenue, Angaston SA 5353
Tel: +61 8 8564 2396
Age range: 3–11 years
Curriculum: IBPYP, National
Language instr: English

Grace Christian College
20 Kinchington Road, Leneva,
Mellboune VIC 3691
Tel: +61 2 6056 2288
Age range: 4–18 years
Curriculum: IBDP
Language instr: English

Haileybury
855 Springvale Road,
Keysborough VIC 3173
Tel: +61 3 9904 6000
Age range: 3–18 years
Curriculum: National
Language instr: English

Haileybury Rendall School
6057 Berrimah Road,
Berrimah NT 0828
Tel: +61 8 8922 1611
Age range: 3–18 years
Curriculum: National
Language instr: English

Hills Grammar
43-53 Kenthurst Road,
Kenthurst NSW 2156
Tel: +61 2 9654 2111
Age range: 3–18 years
Curriculum: National
Language instr: English

Hills International College
105-111 Johanna Street,
Jimboomba QLD 4280
Tel: +61 7 5546 0667
Age range: 4–18 years
Curriculum: IBPYP, National
Language instr: English

Holy Trinity Primary School
18-20 Theodore Street,
Curtin ACT 2605
Tel: +61 26281 4811
Age range: 4–12 years
No. of pupils: 390
Curriculum: IBPYP
Language instr: English

Humanitas High School
42 Amelia Street, Fortitude
Valley QLD 4006
Curriculum: IBDP, IBCP
Language instr: English

Hunter Valley Grammar School
42 Norfolk Street,
Ashtonfield NSW 2323
Tel: +61 2 4934 2444
Age range: 3–18 years
No. of pupils: 1150
Curriculum: IBDP, IBMYP, IBPYP, IBCP
Language instr: English

IES College
495 Boundary Street,
Spring Hill QLD 4004
Tel: +61 7 3832 7699
Curriculum: IBDP
Language instr: English

Immanuel College
32 Morphett Road, Novar
Gardens SA 5040
Tel: +61 08 8294 3588
Curriculum: IBMYP, National
Language instr: English

Immanuel Gawler
11 Lyndoch Road, Gawler
East SA 5118
Tel: +61 8 8522 5740
Curriculum: National

Immanuel Primary School
Saratoga Drive, Novar
Gardens SA 5040
Tel: +61 8 8294 8422
Age range: 3–12
No. of pupils: 670
Curriculum: IBPYP
Language instr: English

INTERNATIONAL SCHOOL OF WESTERN AUSTRALIA
For further details see p. 84
193 St. Brigids Terrace,
Doubleview, Perth WA 6018
Tel: +61 8 9285 1144
Email: info@iswa.wa.edu.au
Website: www.iswa.wa.edu.au
Principal: Caroline Brokvam
Age range: 3–18 years
No. of pupils: 415
Curriculum: IBDP, IBMYP, IBPYP
Language instr: English

Australasia

Islamic College of Melbourne (ICOM)
83 Wootten Road, Tarneit VIC 3029
Tel: +61 3 8742 1739
Curriculum: IBDP
Language instr: English

Ivanhoe Grammar School
PO Box 91, The Ridgeway, Ivanhoe VIC 3079
Tel: +61 3 9490 3501
Age range: 3–18
No. of pupils: 2220
Curriculum: IBDP, National
Language instr: English

John Paul College
John Paul Drive, Daisy Hill QLD 4127
Tel: +61 7 3826 3333
Age range: 6 weeks–18 years
No. of pupils: 1950
Curriculum: IBPYP
Language instr: English

John Wollaston Anglican Community School
Centre Road, Camillo WA 6111
Tel: +61 (08) 9495 8100
Age range: 3–18 years
No. of pupils: 1200
Curriculum: IBPYP
Language instr: English

Kambala
794 New South Head Road, Rose Bay, Sydney NSW 2029
Tel: +612 93886777
No. of pupils: 1050
Curriculum: IBDP
Language instr: English

Kardinia International College
29-31 Kardinia Drive, Bell Post Hill, Geelong VIC 3215
Tel: +61 3 5278 9999
Age range: 3–18 years
Curriculum: IBDP, IBPYP
Language instr: English

Kingswood College
355 Station Street, Box Hill, Melbourne VIC 3128
Tel: +61 3 9896 1700
Curriculum: IBPYP
Language instr: English

Launceston Church Grammar School
10 Lyttleton Street, East Launceston TAS 7250
Tel: +61 3 6336 5900
Curriculum: IBPYP
Language instr: English

Lauriston Girls' School
38 Huntingtower Road, Armadale VIC 3143
Tel: +61 3 9864 7555
Age range: G3–18
No. of pupils: 920
Curriculum: IBDP
Language instr: English

Loreto College
316 Portrush Road, Marryatville SA 5068
Tel: +61 8 8334 4200
Language instr: English

Lycée Condorcet - The International French School of Sydney
758 Anzac Parade, Maroubra, Sydney NSW 2035
Tel: +61 2 9344 8692
Age range: 3–18 years
No. of pupils: 1150
Curriculum: IBDP
Language instr: English

Mansfield Steiner School
91 Highett Street, Mansfield VIC 3722
Tel: +61 3 57791445
Curriculum: IBDP
Language instr: English

Mater Christi College
28 Bayview Road, Belgrave, Melbourne VIC 3160
Tel: +61 3 9754 6611
Age range: 12–18
No. of pupils: 720
Curriculum: IBMYP
Language instr: English

Melbourne Grammar School
355 St Kilda Road, Melbourne VIC 3004
Tel: +61 3 9865 7555
Age range: B11–18 years

Melbourne Grammar School - Grimwade House
67 Balaclava Road, Caulfield VIC 3161
Tel: +61 3 9865 7800
Age range: 4–11 years

Melbourne Montessori School
741 Hawthorn Road, Brighton East VIC 3187
Tel: +61 3 9131 5200
Age range: 2–12 years
No. of pupils: 450
Curriculum: IBDP
Language instr: English

Mentone Girls' Grammar School
11 Mentone Parade, Mentone VIC 3194
Tel: +61 3 9581 1200
Age range: G3–18
No. of pupils: 800
Curriculum: IBPYP, National
Language instr: English

Mercedes College
540 Fullarton Road, Springfield SA 5062
Tel: +61 8 8372 3200
Age range: 5–18 years
Curriculum: IBDP, IBMYP, IBPYP
Language instr: English

Merici College
Wise Street, Braddon ACT 2612
Tel: +61 2 6243 4100
Age range: 11–18 years
No. of pupils: 850
Curriculum: IBDP, IBMYP
Language instr: English

Methodist Ladies' College (MLC)
207 Barkers Road, Kew VIC 3101
Tel: +61 3 9274 6316
Age range: B6 weeks–4 years G6 weeks–18 years
No. of pupils: 2100
Curriculum: IBDP, National
Language instr: English

MLC School
Rowley Street, Burwood, Sydney NSW 2134
Tel: +61 2 9747 1266
Age range: G4–18 years
No. of pupils: 1380
Curriculum: IBDP
Language instr: English

Monte Sant' Angelo Mercy College
PO Box 1064, 128 Miller Street, North Sydney NSW 2059
Tel: +61 2 9409 6200
Age range: G12–18
No. of pupils: 1170
Curriculum: IBDP, IBMYP
Language instr: English

Montessori International College
880-932 Maroochydore Road, Forest Glen QLD 4556
Tel: +61 7 5442 3807
Language instr: English

Moreton Bay Boys' College
302 Manly Road, Manly West QLD 4179
Tel: +61 07 3906 9444
No. of pupils: 530
Curriculum: IBPYP

Moreton Bay College
450 Wondall Rd, Manly West QLD 4179
Tel: +61 7 3390 8555
No. of pupils: 1200 G1200
Curriculum: IBPYP
Language instr: English, French, Japanese

Mosman Church of England Preparatory School
PO Box 950, Spit Junction NSW 2088
Tel: +61 2 9968 4044
Age range: B4–11
No. of pupils: 290
Curriculum: National

Mount Scopus Memorial College
245 Burwood Highway, Burwood VIC 3125
Tel: +61 3 9834 0000
Age range: 3–18 years
Curriculum: IBPYP
Language instr: English, Hebrew

Navigator College
PO Box 3199, Port Lincoln SA 5606
Tel: +61 8 86825099
Age range: 4–18
Curriculum: IBMYP, IBPYP

New England Girls' School
Uralla Road, Armidale NSW 2350
Tel: +61 2 6774 8700
Age range: G4–18
No. of pupils: 400 B40 G360

Newington College - Lindfield
26 Northcote Road, Lindfield, New South Wales NSW 2070
Tel: +61 2 9416 4280
Age range: 5–12 years
Curriculum: IBPYP
Language instr: English

Newington College - Stanmore
200 Stanmore Road, Stanmore NSW 2048
Tel: +61 2 9568 9333
Age range: 3–18 years
No. of pupils: 2142
Curriculum: IBDP, TOEFL
Language instr: English

Norwood International High School
505 The Parade, Magill SA 5072
Tel: +61 8 8364 2299
Age range: 12–18 years
Curriculum: IBDP, IBMYP
Language instr: English

Oakleigh Grammar
77-81 Willesden Road, Oakleigh VIC 3166
Tel: +61 3 9569 6128
Age range: 2–18
No. of pupils: 904
Curriculum: IBMYP
Language instr: English

Our Lady of the Nativity
29 Fawkner Street, Aberfeldie VIC 3040
Tel: +61 3 9337 4204
Curriculum: IBPYP
Language instr: English

Our Saviour Lutheran School
28 Taylors Road West, Aberfoyle Park SA 5159
Tel: +61 8 8270 5488
Language instr: English

Pembroke School
342 The Parade, Kensington Park SA 5068
Tel: +61 8 8366 6200
Age range: 4–18
No. of pupils: 1550 B800 G750
Curriculum: IBDP, IBPYP, National
Language instr: English

Australasia

Penrhos College
6 Morrison Street, Como,
Perth WA 6152
Tel: +61 8 9368 9500
Curriculum: IBPYP
Language instr: English

Penrith Anglican College
PO Box 636, Kingswood NSW 2747
Tel: +61 247 36 8100
Age range: 5–18
No. of pupils: 1300 B650 G650
Curriculum: National
Language instr: English

Plenty Valley Christian College
840 Yan Yean Road, Doreen VIC 3754
Tel: +61 3 9717 7400
Age range: 5–12
Language instr: English

Presbyterian Ladies' College - Perth
14 McNeil Street, Peppermint Grove, Perth WA 6011
Tel: +61 8 9424 6444
Age range: G3–18 years
Curriculum: IBDP, IBPYP
Language instr: English

Presbyterian Ladies' College Melbourne
141 Burwood Highway, Burwood VIC 3125
Tel: +61 3 9808 5811
Age range: G6 months–18 years
No. of pupils: 1550
Curriculum: IBDP
Language instr: English

Preshil - The Margaret Lyttle Memorial School
395 Barkers Road, Kew, Melbourne VIC 3101
Tel: +613 9817 6135
Age range: 3–18
No. of pupils: 275
Curriculum: IBDP, IBMYP, IBPYP

Prince Alfred College
P.O. Box 571, Kent Town SA 5071
Tel: +61 8 8334 1200
Age range: B2–18 years
Curriculum: IBDP
Language instr: English

Queenwood
Locked Bag 1, Mosman NSW 2088
Tel: +61 2 8968 7777
Age range: G5–18 years
No. of pupils: 900
Curriculum: IBDP
Language instr: English

Radford College
College Street, Bruce, Canberra ACT 2617
Tel: +61 2 6162 5332
Curriculum: IBDP, IBPYP

Ravenswood
10 Henry Street, Gordon, Sydney NSW 2072
Tel: +612 9498 9898
Age range: G4–18 years (boarding from 13)
No. of pupils: 1476
Curriculum: IBDP, IBPYP
Language instr: English

Reddam ELS Lindfield
15a Treatts Road, Lindfield NSW 2070
Tel: +61 2 9415 8099
Age range: 1–5 years

Reddam ELS St Leonards
80 Christie Street, St Leonards NSW 2065
Tel: +61 2 9439 8434
Age range: 1–5 years

Reddam ELS Woollahra
70 Edgecliff Road, Woollahra NSW 2025
Tel: +61 2 9369 4096
Age range: 1–5 years

Reddam House Sydney
56 Mitchell Street, Bondi NSW 2026
Tel: +61 2 9300 8200
Age range: 12 months–18 years
Language instr: English

Redeemer Lutheran School, Nuriootpa
Box 397, Nuriootpa SA 5355
Tel: +61 885 621655
Curriculum: IBPYP
Language instr: English

Redlands
272 Military Road, Cremorne NSW 2090
Tel: +61 2 9908 6479
Age range: 3–19 years
Curriculum: IBDP
Language instr: English

Rivercrest Christian College
Gate 6, 500 Soldiers Road, Clyde North VIC 3978
Tel: +61 3 9703 9777
Age range: 3–18 years
No. of pupils: 673
Curriculum: IBDP, IBMYP, IBPYP
Language instr: English

Roseville College
Locked Bag 34, 27 Bancroft Avenue, Roseville NSW 2069
Tel: +61 2 9884 1100
Curriculum: IBPYP
Language instr: English

Sacred Heart College Geelong
Retreat Road, Newtown VIC 3220
Tel: +61 3 52214211
Age range: G11–16
Curriculum: IBMYP
Language instr: English

Santa Maria College
50 Separation Street, Northcote, Melbourne VIC 3070
Tel: +61 3 9488 1600
Curriculum: IBMYP

Santa Sabina College
90 The Boulevarde, Strathfield, Sydney NSW 2135
Tel: +61 2 9745 7000
Age range: B4–10 years G4–19 years
Curriculum: IBDP
Language instr: English

Scotch College
76 Shenton Road, Swanbourne, Perth WA 6010
Tel: +61 8 9383 6800
Age range: B3–18
No. of pupils: 1450
Curriculum: IBDP, IBMYP, IBPYP
Language instr: English

Scotch Oakburn College
85 Penquite Road, Newstead TAS 7250
Tel: +61 363 363 300
Language instr: English

Serpell Primary School
Tuckers Rd, Templestowe VIC 3106
Tel: +61 398 428 182

Seymour College
546 Portrush Road, Glen Osmond, Adelaide SA 5064
Tel: +61 8 8303 9000
Curriculum: IBDP
Language instr: English

Somerset College
Somerset Drive, Mudgeeraba QLD 4213
Tel: +61 (0)7 5559 7100
Age range: 3–18 years
Curriculum: IBMYP, IBPYP
Language instr: English

Sophia Mundi Steiner School
St. Mary's Abbotsford Convent, 1 St Heller's Street, Abbotsford, Melbourne VIC 3067
Tel: +61 3 9419 9229
Age range: 5–18
No. of pupils: 200
Curriculum: IBDP, National
Language instr: English

Southern Christian College
150 Redwood Road, Kingston, Tasmania TAS 7050
Tel: +613 6229 5744
Age range: 4–18 years
Curriculum: IBPYP
Language instr: English

ST ANDREW'S CATHEDRAL SCHOOL
For further details see p. 85
Sydney Square, Sydney NSW 2000
Tel: +61 2 9286 9500
Email: enrolments@sacs.nsw.edu.au
Website: www.sacs.nsw.edu.au
Head of School: Julie McGonigle
Age range: 5–18 years
No. of pupils: 1450
Fees: *Day* AUS$25,306–AUS$44,525
Curriculum: IBDP, IBMYP
Language instr: English

St Andrews Lutheran College
PO Box 2142, Burleigh BC QLD 4220
Tel: +61 7 5568 5900
Age range: 5–18 years
Curriculum: IBPYP
Language instr: English

St Andrew's School
22 Smith Street, Walkerville SA 5081
Tel: +61 8 81685555
Age range: 3–11 years
Curriculum: IBPYP

St Brigid's College
200 Lesmurdie Road, Lesmurdie, Perth WA 6076
Tel: +61 8 9290 4200
Age range: B3–12 G3–17
No. of pupils: 1300
Language instr: English

St Dominic's Priory College
139 Molesworth Street, North Adelaide SA 5006
Tel: +61 8 8267 3818
Language instr: English

St Gregory's College Campbelltown
100 Badgally Road, Gregory Hills NSW 2557
Tel: +61 2 4629 4222
Curriculum: IBPYP
Language instr: English, Spanish

St John's Anglican College
College Avenue, Forest Lake QLD 4078
Tel: +61 (0)7 3372 0111
Curriculum: IBPYP
Language instr: English

St John's Lutheran School, Eudunda, Inc.
8 Ward Street, Eudunda SA 5374
Tel: +61 8 8581 1282
Age range: 5–13
No. of pupils: 107
Curriculum: IBPYP
Language instr: English, Japanese

St Leonard's College
163 South Road, Brighton East, Melbourne VIC 3187
Tel: +61 3 9909 9300
Age range: 3–18
No. of pupils: B750 G750
Curriculum: IBDP, IBPYP, National
Language instr: English

St Margaret's Berwick Grammar
27-47 Gloucester Avenue, Berwick, Melbourne VIC 3806
Tel: +61 3 9703 8111
Age range: 3–18 years
Curriculum: IBPYP, National
Language instr: English

St Mary Star of the Sea College
15 Harbour Street, Wollongong NSW 2500
Tel: +61 2 4228 6011
Age range: G11–18 years
Language instr: English

Australasia

St Michael's Lutheran School
6 Balhannah Rd, Hahndorf SA 5250
Tel: +61 8 8388 7228
No. of pupils: 290
Curriculum: IBPYP
Language instr: English

St Paul's Grammar School
Locked Bag 8016, Penrith NSW 2751
Tel: +61 2 4777 4888
Age range: 4–18
No. of pupils: 840 B420 G420 VIth100
Curriculum: IBDP, IBMYP, IBPYP
Language instr: English

St Paul's School Brisbane
34 Strathpine Rd, Bald Hills QLD 4036
Tel: +61 732 611 388
Language instr: English

St Peter's Anglican Primary School
Howe Street, Campbelltown NSW 2560
Tel: +61 (2) 4627 2990
Curriculum: IBPYP
Language instr: English

St Peter's College
Hackney Road, Hackney, Adelaide SA 5069
Tel: +61 8 8404 0400
Age range: B3–18
Curriculum: IBDP
Language instr: English

St Peter's Girls' School
Stonyfell Road, Stonyfell SA 5066
Tel: +61 88 334 2200
Curriculum: IBDP, IBPYP

St Peters Lutheran College
66 Harts Road, Indooroopilly QLD 4068
Tel: +61 7 3377 6222
Age range: 5–18
No. of pupils: 2038 B1045 G993 VIth188
Curriculum: IBDP, IBPYP
Language instr: English

St Peter's Woodlands Grammar School
39 Partridge Street, Glenelg, Adelaide SA 5045
Tel: +61 (8) 8295 4317
Age range: 2–13

St Philips College, Australia
Schwarz Crescent, Alice Springs NT 0870
Tel: +61 889 504 511
Language instr: English

St Ursula's College Kingsgrove
69 Caroline Street, Kingsgrove NSW 2208
Tel: +61 2 9502 3300
Curriculum: IBDP
Language instr: English

Tara Anglican School for Girls
Masons Drive, North Parramatta, Sydney NSW 2151
Tel: +61 2 9630 6655
Curriculum: IBMYP, IBPYP
Language instr: English

The Armidale School
Locked Bag 3003, 87 Douglas Street, Armidale NSW 2350
Tel: +61 2 6776 5800
Age range: B4–18 G4–11
Curriculum: IBPYP, National

The Essington School
PO Box 42321, Casuarina NT 0811
Tel: +61 8 8985 0100
Age range: 3–16
No. of pupils: 3087 B2811 G276
Curriculum: National
Language instr: English

THE FRIENDS' SCHOOL
For further details see p. 86
23 Commercial Road, North Hobart TAS 7002
Tel: +61 3 6210 2200
Email: enrol.office@friends.tas.edu.au
Website: www.friends.tas.edu.au
Principal: Esther Hill
Age range: 4–18 years
No. of pupils: 1300
Fees: AUS$12,080–AUS$23,560
Curriculum: IBDP, IBPYP
Language instr: English

THE HUTCHINS SCHOOL
For further details see p. 87
71 Nelson Road, Sandy Bay, Tasmania TAS 7005
Tel: +61 3 6221 4200
Email: enrolment@hutchins.tas.edu.au
Website: www.hutchins.tas.edu.au
Principal: Rob McEwan
Age range: B3–18 years
No. of pupils: 1100
Fees: AU$28,880–AU$38,400

The Illawarra Grammar School
10-12 Western Ave, Wollongong NSW 2500
Tel: +61 2 4220 0200
Age range: 3–18
No. of pupils: 900
Curriculum: IBPYP
Language instr: English

The King's School
87-129 Pennant Hills Road, North Parramatta NSW 2151
Tel: +612 9683 8555
Age range: 3–18 years
Curriculum: IBDP, IBPYP
Language instr: English

The King's School, Tudor House
6480 Illawarra Highway, Moss Vale NSW 2577
Tel: +61 2 4868 0000
Age range: B4–12
Curriculum: IBPYP

The Montessori School Kingsley
P.O. Box 194, Landsdale WA 6065
Tel: +61 8 9409 9151
Age range: 3–18 years
Curriculum: IBDP, IBCP
Language instr: English

The Riverina Anglican College
127 Farrer Road, Wagga Wagga NSW 2650
Tel: +61 (0)2 6933 1811
Curriculum: IBDP
Language instr: English

The Scots College
Locked Bag 5001, Bellevue Hill, Sydney NSW 2023
Tel: +61 2 9391 7600
Age range: B3–18
Language instr: English

The Scots School Albury
393 Perry Street, Albury NSW 2640
Tel: +61 (0)2 6022 0000
No. of pupils: 491 B244 G247
Curriculum: IBPYP
Language instr: English

The Southport School
2 Winchester Street, Southport QLD 4125
Tel: +61 755 319 911
Language instr: English

Thomas Mitchell Primary School
Thomas Mitchell Drive, Endeavour Hills VIC 3802
Tel: +61 397 062 254

Toorak College
PO Box 150, Mount Eliza VIC 3930
Tel: +61 3 9788 7200
Age range: 3–18
Language instr: English

Townsville Grammar School
45 Paxton Street, North Ward QLD 4810
Tel: +61 7 4722 4900
Age range: 4–18
No. of pupils: 1400 B700 G700 VIth160
Curriculum: IBDP
Language instr: English

Treetops Montessori School
PO Box 59, Darlington WA 6076
Tel: +61 8 9299 6725
No. of pupils: 130
Curriculum: IBDP
Language instr: English

Trinity Anglican School
200-212 Progress Rd, White Rock, Queensland QLD 4868
Tel: +61 7 4036 8111
No. of pupils: 850
Language instr: English

Trinity Grammar School Preparatory School
115-125 The Boulevarde, Strathfield NSW 2135
Tel: +61 2 8732 4600
Curriculum: IBPYP

Trinity Grammar School, Kew
40 Charles Street, Kew VIC 3101
Tel: +61 3 9854 3600
Curriculum: IBPYP
Language instr: English

Trinity Grammar School, Sydney
119 Prospect Road, Summer Hill NSW 2130
Tel: +61 2 9581 6000
No. of pupils: 2071
Curriculum: IBDP, IBPYP
Language instr: English

Trinity Lutheran College
PO Box 322, Ashmore City QLD 4214
Tel: +61 7 5556 8200
Age range: 4–18
Curriculum: IBPYP, National
Language instr: English

Trinity Lutheran College
920 Fifteenth Street, Mildura VIC 3500
Tel: +61 3 5023 7013
Curriculum: IBMYP, IBPYP
Language instr: English

Unity College Murraylands
P.O. Box 5141, Owl Drive, Murray Bridge SA 5253
Tel: +61 8 8532 0100
Age range: 4–18 years
Curriculum: IBMYP, IBPYP
Language instr: English

Waikerie Lutheran Primary School
16 McCutcheon Street, Waikerie SA 5330
Tel: +61 8 8541 2344
Age range: 5–13
No. of pupils: 100
Language instr: English

Walford Anglican School for Girls
316 Unley Road, Hyde Park SA 5061
Tel: +61 8 8272 6555
Age range: G1–18
No. of pupils: G720
Curriculum: IBDP, IBPYP
Language instr: English

Wenona School
176 Walker Street, North Sydney NSW 2060
Tel: +61 2 9409 4400
Curriculum: IBPYP
Language instr: English

Australasia

Wesley College Melbourne - Elsternwick Campus
5 Gladstone Parade, Elsternwick VIC 3185
Tel: +61 3 8102 6808
Age range: 3–15
No. of pupils: 402
Curriculum: IBMYP, IBPYP
Language instr: English

Wesley College Melbourne - Glen Waverley Campus
620 High Street Road, Glen Waverley VIC 3150
Tel: +61 3 8102 6508
Age range: 3–18
No. of pupils: 1230
Curriculum: IBMYP, IBPYP
Language instr: English

Wesley College Melbourne - St Kilda Road Campus
577 St Kilda Road, Melbourne VIC 3004
Tel: +613 8102 6508
Age range: 3–18
No. of pupils: 3300
Curriculum: IBDP, IBMYP, IBPYP, National
Language instr: English

Westminster School, Adelaide
1/23 Alison Avenue, Marion SA 5043
Tel: +61 882 760 276
Language instr: English

Woodcroft College
Bains Road, Morphett Vale SA 5162
Tel: +61 8 8322 2333
Age range: 4–18
No. of pupils: 1300
Curriculum: IBPYP
Language instr: English

Woodleigh School
485 Golf Links Road, Langwarrin South VIC 3911
Tel: +61 3 5971 6100
Age range: 3–18 years
Curriculum: IBMYP, IBPYP
Language instr: English

Xavier College, Kostka Hall Campus
47 South Road, Brighton, Melbourne VIC 3186
Tel: +61 3 9519 0600
Curriculum: IBPYP

Xavier College, Senior Campus
135 Barkers Road, Kew VIC 3101
Tel: +61 3 9854 5411

FIJI

Champs International School
P.O. Box 11587, Nadi Airport, Nadi, Ba, Viti Levu
Tel: +679 998 5614
Age range: 5–11 years
Curriculum: IBPYP
Language instr: English, Fijian

International School Nadi
P.O. Box 9686, Nadi Airport, Nadi, Ba, Viti Levu
Tel: +679 776 2960
Age range: 3–18 years
Curriculum: IBDP, IBMYP, IBPYP
Language instr: English

International School Suva
Lot 59, Siga Road, Laucala Beach Estate, Suva, Rewa, Viti Levu
Tel: +679 339 3300
Age range: 3–18 years
Curriculum: IBDP, IBPYP
Language instr: English

Pacific Harbour Multi-Cultural School
Great Harbour Drive, Pacific Harbour, Serua, Viti Levu
Tel: +679 345 0005

Port Vila International School
P.O. Box 302, Port Vila, Shefa, Vanuatu
Tel: +678 23837
Age range: 3–18 years
Language instr: English, French

GUAM

St. John's School
911 North Marine Corps Drive, Upper Tumon, Tamuning 96913
Tel: +1 671 646 8080
Age range: 3–18 years
Curriculum: AP, IBDP, USA
Language instr: English

NEW ZEALAND

ACG Parnell College
2 Titoki Street, Parnell, Auckland 1052
Age range: 4–18 years
Curriculum: IGCSE, ALevs
Language instr: English

ACG Penguins Early Learning
197 Whitford Road, Shamrock Park, Auckland 2016
Tel: +64 9 537 4970
Age range: 1–5 years

ACG Queenstown Early Learning
7 Henry Street, Queenstown 9300
Tel: +64 3 409 0441
Age range: 1–5 years

ACG Remuera Early Learning
27 Ohinerau Street, Remuera, Auckland 1050
Tel: +64 9 523 0177
Age range: 1–5 years

ACG Strathallan
50 Hayfield Way, Karaka, Auckland 2113
Age range: 3–18 years
Curriculum: IGCSE, ALevs
Language instr: English

ACG Sunderland
6 Waipareira Avenue, Henderson, Auckland 0610
Tel: +64 9 838 7070
Age range: 3–18 years
Curriculum: IGCSE, ALevs
Language instr: English

ACG Tauranga
6 Keenan Road, (off Pyes Pa Road), Tauranga 3173
Tel: +64 7 213 0100
Age range: 3–18 years
Curriculum: IGCSE, ALevs
Language instr: English

ATEA College
21 Domain Road, Panmure, Auckland 1072
Tel: +64 9 570 5873
Age range: 4–18 years
Curriculum: IGCSE, ALevs

Chilton Saint James School
124 Waterloo Road, Lower Hutt, Wellington 5010
Tel: +64 4 566 4089
Age range: B2–5 years G2–18 years
Curriculum: National, IGCSE, ALevs
Language instr: English

City Impact Church School
794 East Coast Road, Oteha, Auckland 0630
Tel: +64 9 477 0302
Age range: 1–18 years
Curriculum: IGCSE, ALevs

Destiny School
25 Druces Road, Manukau City, Wiri 2104
Tel: +64 9 527 7312
Age range: 4–18 years
Curriculum: IGCSE, ALevs

Diocesan School for Girls
Clyde Street, Epsom, Auckland 1051
Tel: +64 9 520 0221
Age range: G3–18 years
Curriculum: IBDP, IBPYP, National
Language instr: English

Eden Christian Academy
LaValla Estate, 131 Dominion Road, Tuakau 2121
Tel: +64 9 237 8228
Age range: 4–18 years
Curriculum: IGCSE, ALevs

Huanui College
328 Ngunguru Road, Glenbervie RD 3, Whangarei 0173
Tel: +64 9 459 1930
Age range: 11–18 years
Curriculum: IGCSE, ALevs
Language instr: English

King's College, Auckland
41 Golf Avenue, Otahuhu, Auckland 1062
Tel: +64 9 276 0600
Age range: 14–18 years
Curriculum: National, IGCSE, ALevs
Language instr: English

Kristin School
360 Albany Highway, Albany, Auckland 0632
Tel: +64 9 415 9566
Age range: 6 months–18 years
No. of pupils: 1800
Curriculum: IBDP, IBMYP, IBPYP, National
Language instr: English

Manukau Christian School
77 Rogers Road, Manurewa, Auckland 2102
Tel: +64 9 269 1050
Age range: 4–18 years
Curriculum: IGCSE, ALevs

Nga Tawa Diocesan School
164 Calico Line, Calico Line, Marton 4787
Tel: +64 6 327 6429
Age range: G11–18 years
Curriculum: National

Pinehurst School
75 Bush Road, Albany, Auckland 0632
Tel: +64 9 414 0960
Age range: 5–18 years
Curriculum: IGCSE, ALevs

Pukekohe Christian School
82 Yates Road, Pukekohe 2677
Tel: +64 9 238 6449
Age range: 5–18 years
Curriculum: IGCSE, ALevs

Queen Margaret College
53 Hobson Street, Thorndon, Wellington 6011
Tel: +64 4 473 7160
Age range: G3–18 years
Curriculum: IBDP, IBMYP, IBPYP
Language instr: English

Saint Kentigern Boys' School
82 Shore Road, Remuera, Auckland 1050
Tel: +64 9 520 7682
Age range: B5–12 years

Saint Kentigern College
130 Pakuranga Road, Pakuranga, Auckland 1021
Tel: +64 9 577 0749
Age range: 11–18 years
No. of pupils: 2325
Curriculum: IBDP
Language instr: English

Saint Kentigern Girls' School
82 Shore Road, Remuera, Auckland 1050
Tel: +64 9 520 1400
Age range: G5–12 years

Scots College
PO Box 15064, Strathmore, Wellington 6243
Tel: +64 4 388 0850
Age range: 5–18 years
No. of pupils: 1150
Curriculum: IBDP, IBMYP, IBPYP
Language instr: English

Australasia

Selwyn House School
122 Merivale Lane, Merivale,
Christchurch 8014
Tel: +64 3 355 7299
Age range: G5–13 years
Curriculum: IBPYP
Language instr: English

Shirley Boys' High School
209 Travis Road, North New
Brighton, Christchurch 8083
Tel: +64 3 375 7057
Age range: B14–18 years
Curriculum: National

Springbank School
?78 Waimate North
Road, Kerikeri 0293
Tel: +64 9 407 5236
Age range: 5–18 years
Curriculum: IGCSE, ALevs

St Cuthbert's College
122 Market Road, Epsom,
Auckland 1051
Tel: +64 9 520 4159
Age range: G5–18 years
Curriculum: IBDP
Language instr: English

St Margaret's College
12 Winchester Street, Merivale,
Christchurch 8014
Tel: +64 3 379 2000
Age range: G5–18 years
(boarding 11-18)
No. of pupils: 850
Curriculum: IBDP
Language instr: English

St Mark's School
13 Dufferin Street, Basin
Reserve, Wellington 6021
Tel: +64 4 385 9489
Age range: 2–13 years
Curriculum: IBPYP
Language instr: English

St Patrick's Silverstream
207 Fergusson Drive,
Silverstream, Upper Hutt 5018
Tel: +64 4 939 4224
Age range: B13–18 years
No. of pupils: 720
Curriculum: National

St Paul's Collegiate School
77 Hukanui Road, Hamilton 3240
Tel: +64 7 957 8899
Age range: B13–18 years G16–18 years
Curriculum: National, ALevs

St Peter's College
23 Mountain Road, Epsom,
Auckland 1023
Tel: +64 9 524 8108
Age range: B11–18 years
Curriculum: IGCSE, ALevs

St Peter's School, Cambridge
1716 Cambridge Road,
Cambridge 3283
Tel: +64 7 827 9899
Age range: 11–18 years
(boarding from 13)
Curriculum: IBDP, National
Language instr: English

Te Hihi School
767 Linwood Road, RD 1
Papakura, Auckland 2580
Tel: +64 9 292 7706
Curriculum: National
Language instr: English

Wentworth College & Primary
65 Gulf Harbour Drive, Gulf
Harbour, Auckland 0930
Tel: +64 9 424 3273
Age range: 4–18 years
Curriculum: IGCSE, ALevs

PAPUA NEW GUINEA

Alotau International School
P.O. Box 154, Section 58,
Lot 15, Charles Able Road,
Alotau, Milne Bay 211
Tel: +675 641 1078
Age range: 4–14 years
Curriculum: National

Bava International School
Corner Turua Avenue & Taurama
Road, (opposite Manu Autoport),
Boroko, Port Moresby, NCD
Tel: +675 325 8715
Age range: 2–12 years

Ela Murray International School
P.O. Box 1137, Port Moresby, NCD 111
Tel: +675 302 3800
Age range: 4–14 years
Curriculum: National

Gordon International School
P.O. Box 1825, Boroko, NCD 111
Tel: +675 325 4088
Age range: 4–14 years
Curriculum: National

Goroka International School
P.O. Box 845, Section 14, Lot
11, Griffiths Street, Goroka,
Eastern Highlands 441
Tel: +675 532 1452
Age range: 4–14 years
Curriculum: National

Highlands Lutheran International School
P.O. Box 363, Wabag, Enga
Tel: +675 7201 6641
Age range: 3–18 years
Curriculum: National

Kamarau International School
P.O. Box 756, Katsin Kuri,
Buka, Bougainville 355
Tel: +675 973 9033
Age range: 4–14 years
Curriculum: National

Kimbe International School
P.O. Box 307, Section 30, Lot 5,
Kimbe, West New Britain 621
Tel: +675 983 5078
Age range: 4–18 years
Curriculum: National

Kiunga International School
P.O. Box 109, Sare Corner,
Kiunga, Western 335
Tel: +675 649 1110
Age range: 4–14 years
Curriculum: National

Koroboro International School
P.O. Box 1319, Section 70,
Lot 01, Gagoma Street,
Korobosea, Boroko NCD 121
Tel: +675 7476 9616
Age range: 4–12 years
Curriculum: National

Kundiawa International School
P.O. Box 165, Section 007, Lot
003, Kundiawa, Simbu 461
Tel: +675 535 1263
Age range: 4–14 years
Curriculum: National

Lae International School
P.O. Box 2130, Bumbu Road,
Eriku, Lae, Morobe 411
Tel: +675 479 1422
Age range: 4–18 years
Curriculum: ACT, National,
UK, USA, IGCSE

Lihir International School/ School to Mine
Newcrest Townsite, Lihir
Island, New Ireland
Tel: +675 986 4233
Age range: 4–16 years

Madang International School
P.O. Box 306, Section 31, Lot 2,
Bahunia Avenue, Madang 511
Tel: +675 422 2472
Age range: 4–14 years
Curriculum: National

Mount Hagen International School
P.O. Box 945, Mount Hagen,
Western Highlands 281
Tel: +675 542 1964
Age range: 4–14 years
Curriculum: National

Popondetta International School
P.O. Box10, Bambusi Street,
Popondetta, Oro 241
Tel: +675 629 7180
Age range: 4–14 years
Curriculum: National

Port Moresby Grammar School
P.O. Box 1149, Port Moresby, NDC 121
Tel: +675 323 6577
Age range: 5–18 years

Port Moresby International School
P.O. Box 276, Corner Bava Street,
Boroko Drive, Boroko, NCD 111
Tel: +675 325 6690
Age range: 13–18 years
Curriculum: ACT, IBDP,
National, UK, USA, IGCSE
Language instr: English

Rabaul International School
P.O. Box 855, Takubar Industrial
Centre, Tokua Road, Kokopo,
East New Britain 611
Tel: +675 982 8770
Age range: 4–14 years
Curriculum: National

St Joseph's International Catholic College
P.O. Box 5784, Section 21, Allotment
45, Vaivai Avenue, Boroko, NCD 111
Tel: +675 325 3733
Age range: 3–18 years
Curriculum: National

Tabubil International School
P.O. Box 408, Newman Street,
Tabubil, Western 332
Tel: +675 649 9233
Age range: 4–16 years
Curriculum: National

The Australian International School (AISPNG)
P.O. Box 800, Goroka,
Eastern Highlands 441
Tel: +675 7810 1415
Age range: 2–18 years

Ukarumpa International School
P.O. Box 1 (406), Ukarumpa,
Eastern Highlands 444
Tel: +675 537 3544 (Ext: 4970)
Age range: 3–18 years
Curriculum: USA
Language instr: English

Wewak International School
P.O. Box 354, Section 20, Lot 1,
Wewak Hill, Wewak, East Sepik 531
Tel: +675 456 3576
Age range: 4–14 years
Curriculum: National

SOLOMON ISLANDS

Woodford International School
P.O. Box R44, Kukum
Highway, Honiara
Tel: +677 30186
Age range: 3–18 years
Curriculum: IBPYP, UK, IGCSE, ALevs
Language instr: English

TONGA

Ocean of Light International School
P.O. Box 2878, Nuku'alofa
Tel: +676 25 332
Age range: 3–18 years
Curriculum: UK, IGCSE, ALevs

International schools in Europe

Schools ordered A–Z by Country

Key to directory

- Country
- Name of school or college
- Indicates that this school has a profile
- Address and contact number
- Head's name
- Age range
- Number of pupils.
  B = boys G = girls VIth = sixth form
- Fees per annum.
  Day = fees for day pupils.
  WB = fees for weekly boarders.
  FB = fees for full boarders.
- Curriculum
- Language of instruction
- Memberships/Accreditation

Whereford

College Academy

For further details see p

Which Street, Whosville,
Whereferdshire AB12 3CD

Tel: 01000 000000

Head Master: Dr A Person

Age range: 11–18

No. of pupils:
660 B330 G330 VIth 200

Fees: Day £11,000
WB £16,000 FB £20,000

Curriculum:
National, IBDP, ALevs

Language instr:
English, French

(AISA) (COB) (EAR)

Key to icons

Key to symbols:
- Boys' school
- Girls' school
- Boarding accommodation

Member of:
- (AISA) Association of International Schools in Africa
- (CEE) Central and Eastern European Schools Association
- (EAR) East Asia Regional Council of Overseas Schools
- (ECIS) European Council of International Schools
- (RS) Round Square

Accreditation:
- (CIS) Council of International Schools
- (COB) Council of British International Schools

Please note: Schools are coeducational day schools unless otherwise indicated

D345

Europe

ALBANIA

Albanian College Durres
Lagjia Nr. 1, Rruga Anastas Durrsaku, Durres 2001
Tel: +355 44 513 471
Language instr: English

GDQ International Christian School
c/o AEP (Box 89), K.P. 119, Tirana
Tel: +355 (0)4 244 8113
Age range: 5–19
Curriculum: UK, USA, IGCSE

Memorial International School of Tirana
Rruga Dritan Hoxha, Nr.1, Tirana
Tel: +355 4 223 7375
Age range: 6–17
No. of pupils: 161 B71 G90
Curriculum: National, UK
Language instr: English

QSI Tirana International School
Rruga Gilson, Fshati Mullet, Kutia Postare 1527, Tirana
Tel: +355 4 236 5239
Age range: 2–18 years
No. of pupils: 491
Curriculum: IBDP
Language instr: English

Shkolla Udha e Shkronjave
rr. Qemal Stafa, nr.226, (pranë shkollës, Tirana
Tel: +355 4 226 7048

World Academy of Tirana
Rruga e Rezervave, Lunder, Tirane
Tel: +355 69 6056 123
Age range: 3–18 years
Curriculum: IBDP, IBMYP, IBPYP
Language instr: English

ANDORRA

AGORA ANDORRA INTERNATIONAL SCHOOL
For further details see p. 92
Carrer del Serrat del Camp 14, AD400 La Massana
Tel: +376 838 366
Email: admissions@agorainternationalandorra.com
Website: www.agoraandorra.com
Head of School: Clara Pintat Rossell
No. of pupils: 450
Curriculum: IBDP
Language instr: English, Spanish, French, Catalan

The British College of Andorra
Ctra. de la Comella i de la Plana S/N, AD500 Andorra la Vella
Tel: +376 720 220
Curriculum: IBDP, UK
Language instr: English, Spanish

ARMENIA

Ohanyan Educational Complex
Isahakyan 5/6, Yerevan 0060
Tel: +374 106 17684
Curriculum: IBPYP
Language instr: English, Armenian

QSI International School of Yerevan
PO Box 82, Astarak Highway 49/15, Yerevan 0088
Tel: +374 10 349130
Age range: 3–13
No. of pupils: 61
Curriculum: USA
Language instr: English

Quantum College
Bagratuniats 23/2, Shengavit, Yerevan 0046
Tel: +374 10 422217
Curriculum: IBDP
Language instr: English

Shirakatsy Lyceum International Scientific-Educational Complex
35 Artem Mikoyan Street, Yerevan 0079
Tel: +374 10 680 102
Age range: 2–18
No. of pupils: 1010
Curriculum: IBDP, IBMYP, IBPYP
Language instr: Armenian

UWC Dilijan
7 Getapnya Street, Dilijan 3903
Tel: +44 (0)1446 799000
Age range: 16–18
No. of pupils: 219
Curriculum: IBDP
Language instr: English

AUSTRIA

AMADEUS International School Vienna
Bastiengasse 36-38, 1180 Vienna
Tel: +43 1 470 30 37 00
Age range: 3–18 years
No. of pupils: 530
Curriculum: IBDP, IBMYP, IBPYP, IBCP
Language instr: English

American International School – Salzburg
Moosstrasse 106, 5020 Salzburg
Tel: +43 662 824617
Age range: 13–19
No. of pupils: 84
Curriculum: AP, SAT, USA

AMERICAN INTERNATIONAL SCHOOL VIENNA
For further details see p. 100
Salmannsdorfer Strasse 47, 1190 Vienna
Tel: +43 1 401 32
Email: info@ais.at
Website: www.ais.at
Director: Kathryn Miner
Age range: 4–18 years
No. of pupils: 800
Fees: €15,325
Curriculum: AP, IBDP, National, SAT, USA
Language instr: English

Anton Bruckner International School (ABIS)
Bruckner Tower, Wildbergstrasse 18, 4040 Linz, Upper Austria
Tel: +43 7327 11691
Curriculum: IBMYP, IBPYP
Language instr: English, German

Campus Wien West
Seuttergasse 29, 1130 Vienna
Tel: +43 680 5577 573
Curriculum: IBDP
Language instr: English

Danube International School Vienna
Josef-Gall Gasse 2, 1020 Vienna
Tel: +43 1 7203110
Age range: 3–18
No. of pupils: 500
Curriculum: IBDP, IBMYP, IBPYP
Language instr: English

European High School BRG 15
Henriettenplatz 6, 1150 Vienna
Tel: +43 1 8936743
Age range: 14–19

European Middle School
Neustiftgasse 100, 1070 Vienna
Tel: +43 1 526 19 78
Age range: 10–14

International Christian School of Vienna
Wagramer Strasse 175, Panethgasse 6a, 1220 Vienna
Tel: +43 1 25122 0
Age range: 5–18 years
No. of pupils: 350
Curriculum: IBDP, USA
Language instr: English

International Highschool Herzogberg
Herzogbergstraße 230, 2380 Perchtoldsdorf, Lower Austria
Tel: +43 6991 7750 055
Curriculum: IBDP
Language instr: English, German

International School Carinthia
Rosentaler Straße 15, 9220 Velden Am Worthersee, Carinthia
Tel: +43 4274 52471 10
Age range: 6–15 years
Curriculum: IBDP, IBMYP, IBPYP
Language instr: English, German

International School Kufstein Tirol
Andreas-Hofer-Strasse 7, 6330 Kufstein, Tyrol
Tel: +43 5372 21990
Age range: 10–18 years
Curriculum: IBDP, IBMYP
Language instr: English

Junior High School Neue Mittelschule
Carlbergerstrasse 72, 1230 Vienna
Tel: +43 1 869 76 23
Age range: 14–19

Lycèe Français de Vienne
Liechtensteinstrasse 37 A, 1090 Vienna
Tel: +43 1 317 22 41
Age range: 4–18
No. of pupils: 1950
Language instr: French

Marie Jahoda School Vienna
Herbststraße 86, 1160 Vienna
Tel: +43 1 492 43 23
Age range: 4–11
No. of pupils: 380

Schloss Krumbach International School
Schloss 1, 2851 Krumbach, Lower Austria
Tel: +43 6765 409630
Age range: 12–19 years
No. of pupils: 25
Curriculum: IBDP, ALevs
Language instr: English, German

St. Gilgen International School GmbH
Ischlerstrasse 13, 5340 St. Gilgen
Tel: +43 62 272 0259
Age range: 9–18 years
No. of pupils: 220
Curriculum: IBDP, IBMYP, IGCSE
Language instr: English

Theresianische Foundation Academy
Favoritenstraße 15, 1040 Vienna
Tel: +43 1 505 15 71 0

VBS Vienna Bilingual School
Scheibenbergstrasse 63, 1180 Vienna
Tel: +43 1 470 63 69
Age range: 4–11
No. of pupils: 250
Language instr: English, German

Vienna International School
Strasse der Menschenrechte 1, 1220 Vienna
Tel: +43 1 203 5595
Age range: 3–18
No. of pupils: B743 G657
Curriculum: IBDP, IBMYP, IBPYP
Language instr: English

Europe

AZERBAIJAN

Azerbaijan British College
20/41 Mikayil Aliyev str., Baku
Tel: +994 50 844 85 67
Curriculum: UK, IGCSE, ALevs

Baku International Education Complex
Metbuat pr 54, Yasamal, Baku 1001
Tel: +994 50 423 49 10
Curriculum: IBPYP
Language instr: English, Russian

Baku Modern Educational Complex
218 Aliyar Aliyev Street, Narimanov District, Baku
Tel: +994 12 404 12 82
Curriculum: IBDP
Language instr: English, Azerbaijani

Baku Talents Education Complex
Sabail District, Salyan Highway (New Bibiheybet mosque), Baku 1023
Tel: +994 50 292 22 95
Language instr: English, Azeri

British School in Baku
13 Koroglu Ragimov Str, Baku AZ1072
Tel: +99412 465 80 86
Age range: 4–18
No. of pupils: 500 B250 G250
Curriculum: UK
Language instr: English

CET Gunar - Baku Oxford School
8 A Abbaszadeh Str., AZ 1073, Baku
Tel: +994 12 510 80 01
Age range: 4–18
Curriculum: National, UK, IGCSE, ALevs

Dunya School
Ajami Nakhchivani 9, Baku AZ1130
Tel: +994 12 563 59 40/47/48
Curriculum: IBDP, IBMYP, IBPYP
Language instr: English

European Azerbaijan School
A. Abbaszadeh str., 1128 Baku
Tel: +994 12 499 89 39
Age range: 3–18 years
Curriculum: IBDP, IBMYP, IBPYP, IBCP
Language instr: English

Idrak Lyceum
2 Samad Vurghun, Sumqayit 5001
Tel: +994 18 655 59 73
Curriculum: IBDP, IBPYP
Language instr: English

Istak Lyceum
Fatalikhan khoyski 109, Baku AZ1052
Tel: +994 12 4658410
Curriculum: AP, SAT, IGCSE
Language instr: English, Azerbaijani

Kaspi International School
Natig Aliyev 26, Khatai, Baku
Tel: +994 12 310 55 12
Curriculum: IBPYP
Language instr: English

QSI Baku International School
Darnagul Qasabasi, Str Ajami Nakhchivani, Block 3097, Baku 1108
Tel: +994 12 440 66 16
Age range: 2–18
No. of pupils: 151
Curriculum: AP, SAT, USA
Language instr: English

SABIS SUN International School - Baku
Zigh Highway, 22km towards H. Aliyev Int. Airport, Dreamland, Baku
Tel: +994 55 212 20 28
Age range: 4–18 years
Curriculum: SAT

The International School of Azerbaijan, Baku
Yeni Yasamal, Stonepay, Royal Park, Baku AZ1070
Tel: +994 12 404 01 12
Age range: 2–17
No. of pupils: 630 B335 G295
Curriculum: IBDP, IBMYP, IBPYP
Language instr: English

XXI Century International Education and Innovation Center
30 Inshaatchilar Avenue, Baku 1065
Tel: +994 12 510 0205

BELARUS

QSI International School of Minsk
Perioluk Bogdanovicha, 15, 220040 Minsk
Tel: +375 17 280 66 00
Age range: 3–18
No. of pupils: 154
Curriculum: USA
Language instr: English

BELGIUM

Agnès School
Rue Louis Hap 143, B-1040 Brussels
Tel: +32 2736 13 86
Age range: 2–17 years
Curriculum: UK
Language instr: English, French, Dutch

Antwerp International School
Veltwijcklaan 180, Ekeren, 2180 Antwerp
Tel: +32 (0)3 543 93 00
Age range: 2–18
No. of pupils: 392 B188 G192
Curriculum: IBDP, IBMYP, IBPYP

BEPS INTERNATIONAL SCHOOL
For further details see p. 102
Avenue Franklin Roosevelt 21-23, 1050 Brussels
Tel: +32 2 648 43 11
Email: admissions@beps.com
Website: www.beps.com
General Director: Pascale Hertay
Age range: 2.5–18 years
No. of pupils: 300
Curriculum: IBDP, IBMYP, IPC
Language instr: English

Bogaerts International School - North Campus
Bessenveldstraat 25, 1831 Diegem, Flemish Brabant
Tel: +32 488 44 83 07
Curriculum: IBDP
Language instr: English, French

Bogaerts International School - South Campus
Rue Engeland 555, 1180 Uccle, Brussels
Tel: +32 2 230 03 39
Curriculum: IBDP, IBMYP, IBPYP
Language instr: English, French

Brussels International Catholic School
Rue Général Leman 86, 1040 Brussels
Tel: +32 223 002 18
Age range: 2–18
No. of pupils: 625
Curriculum: IGCSE, ALevs
Language instr: English, French

Da Vinci International School Antwerp
Verbondstraat 67, 2000 Antwerp
Tel: +32 3216 12 32
Age range: 2.5–18 years
Curriculum: IBDP, IBMYP, IBPYP
Language instr: English

European School Brussels I
Avenue du Vert Chasseur 46, 1180 Bruxelles
Tel: +32 2 373 8611
Age range: 4–18
No. of pupils: 3100

European School Brussels II
Avenue Oscar Jespers 75, 1200 Brussels
Tel: +32 2 774 22 24
Age range: 6–18
No. of pupils: 2900

European School Brussels III
Boulevard du Triomphe 135, 1050 Brussels
Tel: +32 2 629 4700
Curriculum: IBCP

European School of Bruxelles-Argenteuil
Square d'Argenteuil 5, 1410 Waterloo, Brussels
Tel: +32 2 357 06 70
Age range: 3–18 years
Curriculum: IBDP
Language instr: English, French

European School of Mol
Europawijk 100, 2400 Mol, Antwerp
Tel: +32 14 563 111
Age range: 3–18
No. of pupils: 750
Language instr: English, French, German, Dutch

INTERNATIONAL MONTESSORI SCHOOL
For further details see p. 132
Kleinenbergstraat 97-99, 1932 St. Stevens-Woluwe, Flemish Brabant
Tel: +32 (0)2 669 90 80 / +32 (0)2 721 21 11
Email: woluwe@international-montessori.org; tervuren@international-montessori.org
Website: www.international-montessori.org
Age range: 1–18 years
No. of pupils: 350
Fees: €10,270–€35,500
Curriculum: IBDP, IBMYP
Language instr: English, French

International School Ghent
De Pintelaan 258, 9000 Ghent, East Flanders
Tel: +32 9 221 23 00
Age range: 2.5–12
No. of pupils: 93
Curriculum: IPC, UK
Language instr: English

International School of Belgium
Kontichsesteenweg 40, 2630 Aartselaar, Antwerp
Tel: +32 3 271 0943
Age range: 3–18 years
No. of pupils: 240
Curriculum: IBDP, IPC, IGCSE
Language instr: English

INTERNATIONAL SCHOOL OF FLANDERS
For further details see p. 138
280 Chaussee de Waterloo, 1640 Rhode-St-Genese, Flemish Brabant
Tel: +32 2 358 56 06
Email: office@isfwaterloo.org
Website: www.isfwaterloo.org
Executive Head: Belinda Yates
Age range: 2.5–18 years
No. of pupils: 300
Language instr: English

International School of Flanders (Tervuren Campus)
Stationsstraat 3, 3080 Tervuren, Flemish Brabant
Tel: +32 2 767 3098
Age range: 2.5–11 years
No. of pupils: 80
Language instr: English

International School of Leuven
Geldenaaksebaan 335, 3001 Heverlee, Flemish Brabant
Tel: +32 16 375 790
Age range: 2–11
Curriculum: IPC

Europe

Internationale Deutsche Schule Brüssel
Lange Eikstraat 71, Wezembeek-Oppem, 1970 Brussels
Tel: +32 2 785 01 30
Age range: 2–19
No. of pupils: 600
Curriculum: Abitur, GCSE, ALevs
Language instr: German, English

Le Verseau International School
Rue De Wavre 60, 1301 Wavre, Walloon Brabant
Tel: +32 10 23 17 17
Curriculum: IGCSE
Language instr: French

Lycée Français International Anvers
Lamorinièrestraat 168A, 2018 Antwerp
Tel: +32 3 239 18 89
Age range: 2.5–19
No. of pupils: 175
Curriculum: FrenchBacc

Lycee Francais Jean Monnet
9 Avenue Lycee Francais, 1180 Brussels
Tel: +32 2 374 58 78
Curriculum: FrenchBacc

MONTGOMERY INTERNATIONAL SCHOOL - BRUSSELS
For further details see p. 169
Rue du Duc 133, 1200 Brussels
Tel: +32 (0)2 733 63 23
Email: admissions@mischool.be
Website: www.mischool.be
Head of School: Danielle Franzén
Age range: 5–19 years
No. of pupils: 207
Fees: €24,875
Curriculum: IBDP, IBMYP, IBPYP
Language instr: English, French

Shape International School
SHAPE, Rue Grande, 7010 Mons, Hainaut
(ECIS)

ST. JOHN'S INTERNATIONAL SCHOOL
For further details see p. 198
Drève Richelle 146, 1410 Waterloo, Walloon Brabant
Tel: +32 (0)2 352 06 10
Email: admissions@stjohns.be
Website: www.stjohns.be
Head of School: Kevin Foyle
Age range: 12 months–18 years
No. of pupils: 500
Fees: €13,750–€43,300
Curriculum: AP, IBDP, IBMYP, IBPYP
Language instr: English

The British International School of Brussels
163 Av Emile Max, 1030 Brussels
Tel: +32 2 736 8981
Age range: 3–11 years
Curriculum: UK
Language instr: English

The British Junior Academy of Brussels
83 Boulevard St Michel, Etterbeek, 1040 Brussels
Tel: +32 2 732 5376
Age range: 3–13 years
Curriculum: UK

THE BRITISH SCHOOL OF BRUSSELS (BSB)
For further details see p. 208
Pater Dupierreuxlaan 1, 3080 Tervuren
Tel: +32 (0)2 766 04 30
Email: admissions@britishschool.be
Website: www.britishschool.be
Principal & CEO: James Penstone
Age range: 1–18 years
No. of pupils: 1333
Fees: Day €35,600–€45,550
Curriculum: IBDP, UK, GCSE, IGCSE, ALevs, CSFS
Language instr: English, French (bilingual programme ages 4-14)

The Courtyard International School of Tervuren
Stationsstraat 49a, 3080 Tervuren
Curriculum: IBDP, IBMYP, IBPYP, IBCP
Language instr: English, French

The International School of Brussels (ISB)
Kattenberg 19, 1170 Brussels
Tel: +32 2 661 4211
Age range: 3–18
No. of pupils: 1500
Curriculum: AP, IBDP, IBCP, SAT, USA
Language instr: English

BOSNIA & HERZEGOVINA

Maarif Schools of Sarajevo
Ul. Hasiba Brankovica 2A, 71000 Sarajevo
Tel: +387 33 257 260
Curriculum: IBDP
Language instr: English, Bosnian

QSI International School of Sarajevo
Omladinska #16, 71320, Vogosca-Sarajevo
Tel: +387 33 424450
Age range: 3–17
No. of pupils: 136
Curriculum: USA
Language instr: English

Richmond Park International School, Bihac
Dacka 42, 77000 Bihac
Tel: +387 37 941 170
Age range: 3–18
Language instr: English

Richmond Park International School, Sarajevo
Francuske revolucije bb, 71000 Ilid a - Sarajevo
Tel: +387 33 944 130
Age range: 3–19
Language instr: English

Richmond Park International School, Tuzla
Slavinovickog odreda bb, 75000 Tuzla
Tel: +387 35 951 315
Age range: 3–19
Language instr: English

UWC Mostar
Spanski trg 1, Mostar 88000
Tel: +387 36 320 601
Age range: 16–19
No. of pupils: 200
Curriculum: IBDP
Language instr: English

BULGARIA

American College Arcus
16 Dragoman Str., 5000 Veliko Tarnovo
Tel: +359 62 619959
Age range: 14–19
No. of pupils: 189 B82 G107
Curriculum: IBDP, IBMYP, National
Language instr: English

American College of Sofia
P.O. Box 873, 1000 Sofia
Tel: +359 2 434 10 08
Age range: 13–19 years
No. of pupils: 800
Curriculum: AP, IBDP, SAT, USA
Language instr: English

American English Academy Sofia
1 Orlova Krusha Str., Lozen Area, 1151 Sofia
Tel: +359 2 973 12 22
Curriculum: USA
Language instr: English

Anglo American School of Sofia
1 Siyanie St., 1137 Sofia
Tel: +359 2 923 88 10
Age range: 4–18
No. of pupils: 580
Curriculum: IBDP
Language instr: English

BRITANICA Park School
27 Momino Venche Street, Dragalevtsi Quarter, Sofia
Tel: +359 2 4887877
Curriculum: IBDP
Language instr: English, Bulgarian

British International School Classic
7 Lady Strangford Street, 4000 Plovdiv
Tel: +359 886 902 295
Age range: 6–19
Curriculum: IBDP, National, UK, IGCSE
Language instr: English, Bulgarian

British School of Sofia
18, Radi Radev Street, Lozenets, 1700 Sofia
Tel: +359 886 510 510
Curriculum: IBDP, IBCP, UK
Language instr: English, Bulgarian

Bulgarsko Shkolo Private Secondary School
ul. General-Mayor Vasil Delov No. 10, Mladost 2, 1799 Sofia
Tel: +359 8 84256736
Curriculum: IBMYP
Language instr: Bulgarian

Discover (Otkrivatel) Montessori School
6 Bolgrad Str., 1421 Sofia
Tel: 0885 500155
Curriculum: IBPYP
Language instr: English, Bulgarian

Lycée Français de Sofia Victor Hugo
complexe MAXI, 110 Simeonovsko chaussée, quartier Vitosha, 1700 Sofia
Tel: +359 2 9632964
Age range: 4–18
No. of pupils: 625

Meridian 22 Private High School
Mladost 2 bl.227, 1799 Sofia
Tel: +359 2 8876 423; +359 2 8840 238
Curriculum: IBDP
Language instr: English

Private Primary School 'Progressive Education'-Sofia
107 Nishava Str., Sofia 1408
Tel: +359 882 741 944
Curriculum: IBPYP
Language instr: English

Simeon Radev School
Blagoy Gebrev 17, 25/11A, 2304 Pernik
Tel: +359 76670140
Age range: 14–19

St. George International School and Preschool
47 Nikola Vaptsarov blvd., Lozenetz, 1407 Sofia
Tel: +359 2 414 44 14
Curriculum: National, UK, IGCSE, ALevs

Uwekind International School
136 Voivodina Mogila Street, Knyajevo, 1619 Sofia
Tel: +359 885 614 724
Age range: 3–18 years
Curriculum: IBDP, IBMYP, IBPYP
Language instr: Bulgarian

Zlatarski International School
49 Kliment Ohridski Boulevard, 1756 Sofia
Tel: +359 2 876 67 67
Age range: 13–19
No. of pupils: 300 B150 G150
Curriculum: IBDP, National
Language instr: English

Europe

CROATIA

Adria International School
Stubi te Miroslava Krle e
1, 51000 Opatija
Tel: +385 91 4925 555
Age range: 3–19 years
Curriculum: IBPYP
Language instr: English

American International School of Zagreb
Damira Tomljanovica
Gravrana 3, 10020 Zagreb
Tel: +385 1 7999 300
Age range: 3–18
No. of pupils: 211 B108 G103
Curriculum: AP, IBDP, SAT, USA
Language instr: English
(CEE) (ECIS)

Bright Horizons - International School of Zagreb
Sveti Duh 122, 10000 Zagreb
Tel: +385 1 37 45 146
No. of pupils: 105
Curriculum: UK
Language instr: English
(COB)

British International School of Zagreb
Dedici 102, 10000 Zagreb
Tel: +385 1 4611 007
Curriculum: IPC, UK
(COB)

École Française Internationale de Zagreb
Fratrovac ulica 36, 10000 Zagreb
Tel: +385 1 234 7710

Harfa International School
Poljudsko setaliste 4, 21000 Split
Tel: +385 99 532 1462
Curriculum: IBPYP
Language instr: English, Croatian

Split International School
Bihacka ul. 2, 21000 Split
Tel: +385 91 6182877
Curriculum: IBDP, IBPYP
Language instr: English

CYPRUS

American Academy Larnaca
PO Box 40112, Gregoris Afxentiou Avenue, Larnaca 6301
Tel: +357 24 815400
Age range: 4–19
No. of pupils: 937 B470 G467 VIth116
Curriculum: GCSE, ALevs

American Academy Primary School
7 Lefkas Street, 3070, Limassol
Tel: +357 25 382782
Age range: 4–11
No. of pupils: 390
Curriculum: UK

American Academy Secondary School
24 Despinas Pattichi Str, 3071, Limassol
Tel: +357 2533 7054
Age range: 2–19
No. of pupils: 750
Curriculum: UK, GCSE, IGCSE, ALevs
Language instr: English

American International School in Cyprus
PO Box 23847, 11 Kassos Str, Nicosia 1686
Tel: +357 22 316345
Age range: 3–19
No. of pupils: 315
Curriculum: IBDP, SAT, USA
Language instr: English
(ECIS)

école Franco-Chypriote
P.O. Box 22091, Nicosia 1517
Tel: +357 22 66 53 18
Curriculum: FrenchBacc

Foley's Grammar and Junior School
40 Homer Street, Limassol 3095
Tel: +357 25 582191
Age range: 4–18
No. of pupils: 530 B255 G275 VIth55
Curriculum: UK, GCSE, IGCSE, ALevs
Language instr: English

Forum Private Institute and Language Centre
PO Box 25567, Nicosia 1310
Tel: 00 357 22 446 344
Age range: 11–17

Girne American University
University Drive, PO Box 5, 99428 Karmi Campus, Karaoglanoglu, Kyrenia, TRNC
Tel: +90 850 650 20 00
Age range: 2–18
No. of pupils: 854 B447 G407
Curriculum: National, UK, IGCSE, ALevs
Language instr: English
(ECIS)

Highgate Private School
5 Irinikou, Agioi Trimithias, PO Box 20748, Nicosia 2670
Tel: +357 22 780527
Age range: 2–18
No. of pupils: 300
Curriculum: UK

KES School of Languages
5, Kallipolis Avenue, 1055 Nicosia
Tel: +357 22 875737

Logos School of English Education
33-35 Agialousa Street, PO Box 51075, Limassol 3501
Tel: +357 253 36061
Age range: 3–18
No. of pupils: 290
Curriculum: UK, IGCSE, ALevs
Language instr: English

Lumio Private School
Academias Street, Acheleia, Paphos 8503
Tel: +357 26 44 3003
Age range: 6–18 years
No. of pupils: 384
Language instr: English

PASCAL Private English School - Larnaka
2, Polytechniou Street, Larnaka, 7103 Aradippou
Tel: +357 22509300
Age range: 12–18
No. of pupils: 620
Curriculum: IBDP, UK, IGCSE, ALevs
Language instr: English

PASCAL Private English School - Lefkosia
177, Kopegchagis Street, Lefkosia, 2306 Lakatamia
Tel: +357 22509000
Age range: 12–18
No. of pupils: 300
Curriculum: IBDP, National, IGCSE, ALevs
Language instr: English

The American Academy Nicosia
PO Box 21967, Nicosia 1515
Tel: +357 22 664 266
Curriculum: USA

The English Learning Centre
138 Vasileos Canstantinou, Limassol 3080
Tel: + 357 2538 7674
Age range: 7–18
No. of pupils: 500
Curriculum: IGCSE

The English School of Kyrenia
Bilim Sokak, Bellapais, Kyrenia, North Cyprus
Tel: +90 392 444 0375
Age range: 2–18 years
No. of pupils: 1250
Curriculum: IBDP, GCSE, ALevs
Language instr: English
(COB)

The English School, Cyprus
P.O. Box: 23575, 1684 Nicosia
Tel: +357 22 799 300
Age range: 11–18 years
Curriculum: UK, GCSE, IGCSE, ALevs
Language instr: English

The Falcon School
P.O. Box: 23640, 1685 Nicosia 1685
Tel: +357 22 424 781
Age range: 4–18 years
Curriculum: UK, GCSE, IGCSE, ALevs
Language instr: English

The G C School of Careers
96 Steliou Hadjipetri Street, Nicosia 2057
Tel: +357 224 64400

The Grammar School Limassol
Katinas Paxinou Panthea Hill, PO Box 51340, Limassol 3504
Tel: +357 25727933
Age range: 11–19
No. of pupils: 682

The Grammar School Limassol - Junior School
Manoli Kalomiri & Theklas street, PO Box 51340, Limassol 3504
Tel: +357 25352141

The Grammar School, Nicosia
PO Box 22262, Anthoupolis Highway, Pano Deftera 1519
Tel: + 357 22 695 695

The Heritage Private School
Palodina, Limassol CY-4549
Tel: +357 25 367 018
Age range: 2–18

The International School of Paphos
100 Aristotelous Savva Avenue, Anavargos, 8025 Paphos
Tel: +357 26 821700
Age range: 2.6–19 years
No. of pupils: 1150
Curriculum: UK, IGCSE, ALevs
Language instr: English

The Island Private School of Limassol
Vangeriotissas 95A, Palodia, Limassol
Tel: +357 25 75 25 75
Age range: 3–18 years
Curriculum: IBDP, IBMYP, IBPYP
Language instr: English

The Junior & Senior School
P O Box 23903, Kyriakou Matsi Avenue, Ayioi Omoloyites, 1687 Nicosia
Tel: +357 22664855
Age range: 3–18
Curriculum: SAT, UK
Language instr: English

The Senior School
PO Box 25445, 2237 Nicosia
Tel: +357 22660156
Age range: 14–19
No. of pupils: 583
Curriculum: UK, IGCSE

Xenion Education
55, 1st April Avenue, PO Box 33900, 5281 Paralimni
Tel: +357 23811080
Age range: 4–19
No. of pupils: 560
Curriculum: UK, IGCSE, ALevs

CZECH REPUBLIC

1st International School of Ostrava
Gregorova 3, 702 00 Ostrava
Tel: +420 723 332 653
Curriculum: IBDP
Language instr: English

Christian International School of Prague (CISP)
Legerova 5, 120 00 Prague 2
Tel: +420 272 730 091
Age range: 6–18
No. of pupils: 160
Curriculum: AP, USA
Language instr: English

Europe

Deutsche Schule Prag
Schwarzenberská 1/700,
158 00 Prague 5
Tel: +420 235 311 725

Dino High School s.r.o.
Bellova 352, 109 00 Prague 10
Tel: +420 240 200 082
Curriculum: IBDP
Language instr: Czech, English

Gymnasium Evolution
Jizni Mesto, Tererova 2135
/ 17, 149 00 Prague 4
Tel: +420 267 914 553
Curriculum: IBDP
Language instr: English, Czech

Gymnázium Duhovka
Ortenovo náměstí 34, Hole
ovice, 170 00 Prague 7
Tel: +420 241 404 217
Curriculum: IBDP
Language instr: English, Czech

International Montessori School of Prague
Hrudickova 2107/16, 148 00 Prague 4
Tel: +420 272 937 758
Age range: 1.5–12

International School of Brno
Cejkovicka 10, 628 00 Brno-Vinohrady
Tel: +420 544 212 313
Age range: 3–19 years
No. of pupils: 160
Curriculum: IBDP, IBPYP, National
Language instr: English

International School of Prague
Nebusicka 700, 164 00 Prague 6
Tel: +420 220 384 111
Age range: 3–19
No. of pupils: 851 B432 G419
Curriculum: AP, IBDP, IBMYP, IBPYP, IBCP, SAT
Language instr: English

International School Olomouc
Rooseveltova 101, 779 00 Olomouc
Tel: +420 585 754 880
Curriculum: UK
Language instr: English

Leonardo da Vinci Academy
Dlouhá 34, 110 00 Prague 1
Tel: +420 251 554 848
Curriculum: IBDP
Language instr: English, Czech

Lycee Francais De Prague
Drtinova 7, 150 00 Prague 5
Tel: +420 222 550 000
Age range: 4–19
No. of pupils: 680

Meridian International School
Frydlantska 1350/1, 182 00 Prague 8
Tel: +420 286 581 805
Curriculum: UK
Language instr: English

Open Gate School
Babice 5, 251 01 Rícany
Tel: +420 724 730 512
Curriculum: IBDP
Language instr: English

Ostrcilova International School
Ostrcilova 1/2557, 702 00 Ostrava
Tel: +420 596 113 411
Age range: 3–11
No. of pupils: 200

Park Lane International School - Prague 1
Vald tejnská 151/6a, 118 01 Prague 1
Tel: +420 257 316 182
Age range: 10–18
Curriculum: IBDP, UK, IGCSE
Language instr: Czech, English

Park Lane International School - Prague 6
Norbertov 3, 162 00 Prague 6
Tel: +420 220 512 653
Age range: 3–10
Curriculum: UK, IGCSE

PORG International School - Ostrava
Rostislavova 7, 703 00 Ostrava
Tel: +420 597 071 020
Curriculum: IBDP
Language instr: English

PORG International School - Prague
Pod Krcskym lesem 1300/25,
142 00 Prague 4
Tel: +420 244 403 650
Curriculum: IBDP

Prague British International School
Brunelova 960/12, 142 00 Prague 4
Tel: +420 272 181 911
Age range: 2–19 years
Curriculum: SAT, UK
Language instr: English

PRIGO Language and Humanities Grammar School
Mojmirovcu 1002/42, Mariánské Hory, 709 00 Ostrava
Curriculum: IBDP
Language instr: English

Riverside International School
Roztocka 9/43, Sedlec,
160 00 Prague 6
Tel: +420 2 24315336
Age range: 3–18
No. of pupils: 290
Curriculum: AP, IBDP, National, IGCSE, ALevs
Language instr: English

Sunny Canadian International School
Straková 522, 252 42 Jesenice, Osnice
Tel: +420 734 827 106

The Ostrava International School
Gregorova 2582/3, 702 00 Ostrava
Tel: +420 724 142 287
Age range: 3–18
No. of pupils: 250
Curriculum: IBDP, IBMYP, IBPYP, UK
Language instr: English

The Prague British School - Kamyk Site
K Lesu 558/2, 142 00 Prague 4
Tel: +420 226 096 200
Age range: 1–18
No. of pupils: 650 B320 G330
Curriculum: IBDP, IBCP, SAT
Language instr: English

The Prague British School - Vlastina Site
Vlastina 19, 161 00 Prague 6
Tel: +420 22 609 6200

Townshend International School
Hradcany 1070, 373 41 Hluboka
Tel: +420 387 688 113
Age range: 3–18
Curriculum: UK, IGCSE, ALevs
Language instr: English

Zakladni Skola a Materska Skola Klas s.r.o
kolní náměstí 37, 533 51
Rosice nad Labem
Tel: +420 774 305 011
Language instr: Czech, English

Zakladni Skola Buresova
Zernosecká 3/1597, 182 00 Prague 8
Age range: 6–15

DENMARK

Aarhus International School
Dalgas Avenue 12, 8000
Aarhus, Midtjylland
Tel: +45 8672 6060
Curriculum: IBMYP, IBPYP
Language instr: English

Bernadotte Skolen
Hellerupvej 11, Hellerup, 2900
Copenhagen, Hovedstaden
Tel: +45 3962 1215
Age range: 6–16
No. of pupils: 560 B270 G290

Bjorn's International School
Gartnerivej 5, 2100
Copenhagen, Hovedstaden
Tel: +45 3929 2937
Age range: 6–16
No. of pupils: 165
Curriculum: National, IGCSE
Language instr: English, Danish

Copenhagen International School
Levantkaj 4-14, 2150
Copenhagen, Hovedstaden
Tel: +45 3946 3300
Age range: 2 years 10 months–18 years
No. of pupils: 930
Curriculum: IBDP, IBMYP, IBPYP, SAT, USA
Language instr: English

Esbjerg International School
Guldager Skolevej 4, 6710
Esbjerg, Syddanmark
Tel: +45 7610 5399
Age range: 3–16 years
No. of pupils: 298
Curriculum: IBMYP, IBPYP
Language instr: English

Herlufsholm Skole
Herlufsholm Allé 170, 4700
Naestved, Sjaelland
Tel: +45 5575 3500
Age range: 15–20
No. of pupils: 643
Curriculum: IBDP, National
Language instr: English

Institut Sankt Joseph
Dag Hammarskjölds Allé 17, 2100
Copenhagen, Hovedstaden
Tel: +45 3538 4735

International School Ikast-Brande
Bøgildvej 2, 7430 Ikast, Midtjylland
Tel: +45 9715 6465
Curriculum: National, UK, IGCSE

International School of Aarhus
Engtoften 22, 8260
Aarhus, Midtjylland
Tel: +45 8611 4560
Age range: 5–16
Curriculum: UK

International School of Billund
Skolevej 24, 7190 Billund, Syddanmark
Tel: +45 2632 7800
Age range: 3–14 years
No. of pupils: 450
Curriculum: IBMYP, IBPYP
Language instr: English

International School of Hellerup
Rygårds Allé 131, 2900
Hellerup, Hovedstaden
Tel: +45 7020 6368
Age range: 3–19 years
No. of pupils: 600
Curriculum: IBDP, IBMYP, IBPYP
Language instr: English

Lycée Français Prins Henrik
Frederiksberg Allé 22A, 1820
Frederiksberg, Hovedstaden
Tel: +45 3355 0064

Europe

North Zealand International School
Christianshusvej 16, 2970 Hørsholm, Hovedstaden
Tel: +45 4557 2616
Age range: 4–16
No. of pupils: 220
Curriculum: IBDP, IGCSE
Language instr: English

Ranum Efterskole College
Kaervej 6/8, 9681 Ranum, Nordjylland
Tel: +45 9666 4400
Age range: 5–12
No. of pupils: 121

Rygaards School
Bernstorffsvej 54, 2900 Hellerup, Hovedstaden
Tel: +45 3962 1053
Age range: 4–16
No. of pupils: 460
Curriculum: UK, IGCSE
Language instr: English

Sankt Petri Skole
Larslejsstraede 5, 1451 Copenhagen, Hovedstaden
Tel: +45 3313 0462
Age range: 4–18
No. of pupils: 600

Skt. Josef's International School
Frederiksborgvej 10, 4000 Roskilde, Sjaelland
Tel: +45 4635 2526
Age range: 5–16
Curriculum: UK
Language instr: English

Sønderborg International School
Agervang 14, 6400 Sønderborg, Syddanmark
Tel: +45 7443 0110
Age range: 6–16 years
Curriculum: UK, IGCSE

VpR International
Trekronervej 10-14, 8800 Vlborg, Midtjylland
Tel: +45 8662 0888
Curriculum: UK, IGCSE

ESTONIA

Audentes School
Tondi str 84, 11316 Tallinn, Harju
Tel: +372 699 6591
Age range: 2–18
No. of pupils: 520
Curriculum: IBDP

International School of Estonia
Juhkentali 18, 10132 Tallinn, Harju
Tel: +372 666 4380
Age range: 3–19
No. of pupils: 130 B62 G68
Curriculum: IBDP, IBMYP, IBPYP
Language instr: English

International School of Tallinn
Keevise 2, 11415 Tallinn, Harju
Tel: +372 5066 080
Curriculum: IBDP, IBMYP, IBPYP
Language instr: English, Estonian

Tallinn European School
Tehnika 18, 10149 Tallinn, Harju
Tel: +372 735 0550
Age range: 4–18
Language instr: English, French

Tallinna Saksa Gümnasium
J. Sütiste tee 20, 13411 Tallinn, Harju
Tel: +372 6 522 240
Age range: 11–18
No. of pupils: 1280

Tartu International School
J. Liivi 2d, 50409 Tartu
Tel: +372 742 4241
Curriculum: IBPYP
Language instr: English

FINLAND

Aalto University School of Business
Mikkeli Campus, Lönnrotinkatu 5, 50100 Mikkeli, South Savo
Tel: +358 (0)50 4389837
Age range: 16–19
No. of pupils: 4000

Deutsche Schule Helsinki
Malminkatu 14, 00100 Helsinki, Uusimaa
Tel: +358 9 685065-0
Language instr: German, Finnish

Ecole Français Jules Verne
Ratakatu 6A, 00120 Helsinki, Uusimaa
Tel: +358 9 565 19 26

European School of Helsinki
Bulevardi 18, 00120 Helsinki, Uusimaa
Tel: +358 295 332 451

Helsingin Suomalainen Yhteiskoulu
Isonnevantie 8, 00320 Helsinki, Uusimaa
Tel: +358 9 4774 1814
Age range: 9–19
No. of pupils: 1200 B600 G600
Curriculum: IBDP, National

International School Cygnaeus
Tasavallankatu 1, 28100 Pori, Satakunta
Tel: +358 2 621 5227
Age range: 4–11
No. of pupils: 50

International School of Helsinki
Selkämerenkatu 11, 00180 Helsinki, Uusimaa
Tel: +358 9 686 6160
Age range: 4–18
No. of pupils: 320
Curriculum: IBDP, IBMYP, IBPYP, SAT
Language instr: English

International School of Vantaa
Hagelstamintie 1, 01520 Vantaa, Uusimaa
Tel: +358 9 8392 4810
Age range: 6–16
No. of pupils: 350
Language instr: English

Kotkansaari School
The Central Street, 28 Centre Street, 48100 Kotka, Kymenlaakso
Tel: +358 234 4531
Age range: 13–15
No. of pupils: 411

Maunula Primary School
Maunulanmaki 5, 00630 Helsinki, Uusimaa
Tel: +358 9 310 82484
Age range: 6–12
No. of pupils: 340

Mussalon ala-asta
Rajakalliontie 10, 48310 Kotka, Kymenlaakso
Tel: +358 234 5802
Age range: 4–19

Myllytullin Koulu
Kirkkokatu 1, 90100 Oulu, North Ostrobothnia
Tel: +358 8 44 703 9633
Age range: 5–13
No. of pupils: 70

Oulu International School
Kasarmintie 4, 90130 Oulu, North Ostrobothnia
Tel: +358 50 371 6977
No. of pupils: 280
Curriculum: IBMYP, IBPYP
Language instr: English

Rajala School
Sammakkolammentie 14, 70200 Kuopio, North Savo
Tel: +358 44 718 4356

The English School
Mäntytie 14, 00270 Helsinki, Uusimaa
Tel: +358 10 321 7920

FRANCE

American School of Paris
41 rue Pasteur, 92210 Saint-Cloud
Tel: +33 01 41 12 86 55
Age range: 3–18 years
No. of pupils: 830
Curriculum: ACT, AP, IBDP, SAT, USA
Language instr: English

Antonia International School (École Antonia)
2 rue Patrice Lumumba, 34000 Montpellier
Tel: +33 4 11 93 09 87
Curriculum: IBDP
Language instr: English, French

Apex2100 Academy
Le Rosset, 73320 Tignes
Curriculum: IBDP, IBCP
Language instr: English, French

BORDEAUX INTERNATIONAL SCHOOL
For further details see p. 104
252 Rue Judaïque, 33000 Bordeaux
Tel: +33 5 57870211
Email: contact@bis33.com
Website: www.bordeaux-school.com
Principals: Mrs Bergey & Mme Bidalun
Age range: 3–19 years
No. of pupils: 195
Fees: Day €7,610–€16,060
Curriculum: National, UK, IGCSE, ALevs
Language instr: English, French, Spanish

Chavagnes International College
96 Rue du Calvaire, 85250 Chavagnes-en-Paillers
Tel: +33 2 51 42 39 82
Age range: 11–18
No. of pupils: 200

Cite Scolaire Internationale de Lyon
Section Anglophone, 2 Place de Montreal, 69361 Lyon
Tel: +33 4 7869 6006
Age range: 6–18
No. of pupils: 1600
Curriculum: SAT

Collège de Niki de St Phalle - Anglophone Section
Chemin du Darbousson, Sophia Antipolis, 06905 Valbonne
Tel: +33 4 92915130
Age range: 11–15
No. of pupils: 200
Curriculum: National

College Hauts Grillets
10 Bd Hector Berlioz, 78100 Saint-Germain-en-Laye
Tel: +33 1 30 87 46 20
Age range: 11–18

College International de Fontainebleau
Anglophone Section, 48 Rue Geurin, 77300 Fontainblau
Tel: +33 1 6422 1177
Age range: 6–18
No. of pupils: 450 VIth44
Curriculum: FrenchBacc, UK, IGCSE

College Marcel Roby (American Section)
2 bis rue du Fer a Cheval, 78100 Saint Germain en Laye
Tel: +33 1 34 51 74 85
Age range: 11–15
Curriculum: USA

College Sainte Clotilde
9 rue de Bel Orme, 33000 Bordeaux
Tel: +33 5 56 48 29 06
Age range: 14–19

Europe

Collège-Lycée Saint François-Xavier
3 rue Thiers, 56000 Vannes
Tel: +33 (0)2 97 47 12 80
Curriculum: IBDP
Language instr: English, French

Cours Moliere
2-4 Boulevard Soult, 75012 Paris
Tel: +33 1 43 43 44 96
Age range: 5–18
No. of pupils: 300
Curriculum: FrenchBacc, IGCSE

Deutsche Schule Toulouse
Eurocampus 2, 2 Allée de l'Herbaudiére, Colomiers, 31770 Toulouse
Tel: +33 5 67 73 29 20
Age range: 4–18
No. of pupils: 210

Don Bosco Landser
1 Rue Don Bosco, 68440 Landser
Tel: +33 3 89 81 31 03
Age range: 4–19

Ecole Active Bilingue
Administration, 117 Boulevard Malesherbes, 75008 Paris
Tel: +33 1 45 63 62 22
Age range: 3–18
No. of pupils: 3000
Curriculum: AP, IBDP, SAT, ALevs

École at Montessori - Babylone
24 rue de Babylone, 75007 Paris
Tel: +33 (0)7 49 94 83 93
Age range: 2–6 years
Language instr: English, French

École at Montessori - Ranelagh
49 rue du Ranelagh, 75016 Paris
Tel: +33 (0)7 49 94 83 93
Age range: 3–6 years
Language instr: English, French

Ecole des Francs Bourgeois
21 rue St Antoine, 75004 Paris
Tel: +33 1 44 59 20 90
Age range: 11–19
Language instr: French

Ecole Des Roches
295 avenue Edmond Demolins, 27130 Verneuil d'Avre et d'Iton
Tel: +33 (0) 232 6040 00
Age range: 11–18 years
No. of pupils: 320
Curriculum: IBDP
Language instr: English, French

Ecole Européenne de Strasbourg
2 Rue Peter Schwarber, CS 60014, 67015 Strasbourg
Tel: +33 (0)3 88 34 82 20

ECOLE JEANNINE MANUEL - LILLE
For further details see p. 110
418 bis rue Albert Bailly, Marcq-en-Baroeul 59700
Tel: +33 3 20 65 90 50
Email: admissions-lille@ejm.net
Website: www.ecolejeanninemanuel.org
Head of School: Constance Devaux
Age range: 3–18 years
No. of pupils: 980
Fees: €13,085
Curriculum: IBDP, National, FrenchBacc
Language instr: French, English

ECOLE JEANNINE MANUEL - PARIS
For further details see p. 111
70 rue du Théâtre, Paris 75015
Tel: +33 1 44 37 00 80
Email: admissions@ejm.net
Website: www.ecolejeanninemanuel.org
Principal: Jérôme Giovendo
Age range: 4–18 years
No. of pupils: 2400
Fees: *Day* €9,935–€10,830 €31,565
Curriculum: IBDP, IGCSE
Language instr: English, French

École Montessori Bilingue de Levallois-Perret
6 rue Barbès, 92300 Levallois-Perret
Tel: +33 (0)7 49 94 83 93
Age range: 2–6 years
Language instr: English, French

Ecole Privée Bilingue Internationale
Domaine de massane, 34670 Baillargues
Tel: +33 4677 07844
Curriculum: IBDP, IBMYP
Language instr: English, French

Ecole Privée Val Saint André
19, Av Henri Malacrida, 13100 Aix-en-Provence
Tel: +33 442 271 447
Curriculum: FrenchBacc, UK, IGCSE

EIB de La Jonchère
Sente de Bournival, 78170 La Celle-Saint-Cloud
Tel: +33 1 61 30 30 19
Age range: 3–15 years
No. of pupils: 320
Curriculum: UK, IGCSE
Language instr: English, French

EIB Etoile High School
9 rue Villaret de Joyeuse, 75017 Paris
Tel: +33 1 45 63 30 73
Age range: 13–18 years

EIB Grenelle
176 rue de Grenelle, 75007 Paris
Tel: +33 1 45 01 18 50
Age range: 3–11 years
No. of pupils: 130

EIB Lamartine
123 Rue de la Pompe, 75116 Paris
Tel: +33 1 45 53 89 36
Age range: 3–11 years

EIB Monceau Middle School (Collège EIB Monceau)
16 Rue Margueritte, 75017 Paris
Tel: +33 1 46 22 40 20
Age range: 11–13 years

EIB Monceau Primary School
6 Avenue Van Dyck, 75008 Paris
Tel: +33 1 46 22 14 24
Age range: 3–11 years

Ellipse Montessori Academy
3 rue Amélie, 75007 Paris
Tel: +33 1 45 00 66 25
Age range: 2–18 years
Language instr: English, French

Ermitage International School
46 Avenue Eglé, 78600 Maisons-Laffitte
Tel: +33 139 62 81 75
Age range: 3–18 years
No. of pupils: 1500
Curriculum: IBDP, IBMYP
Language instr: English, French

Eurecole
5 rue de Lubeck, 75116 Paris
Tel: +33 1 40 70 12 81
Age range: 2–15
No. of pupils: 190
Curriculum: National

Forest International School
28 Chemin du Tour d'Echelle du Mur, de Cloture de la Foret de Marly, 78750 Mareil Marly
Tel: +33 1 39 16 87 35
Language instr: English

Franklin St Louis De Gonzague
12 Rue Benjamin Franklin, 75116 Paris
Tel: +33 1 44 30 45 50
Age range: 6–18
No. of pupils: 1500
Curriculum: GCSE

Hattemer Bilingue Paris 16e
43 rue Decamps, 75116 Paris
Tel: +33 (0)1 84 79 29 99
Age range: 2.5–11 years
No. of pupils: 129
Language instr: English, French

Hattemer Bilingue Paris 8e
52 rue de Londres, 75008 Paris
Tel: +33 (0)1 43 87 59 14
Age range: 2.5–11 years
No. of pupils: 160
Curriculum: IBDP
Language instr: English, French

ICS CÔTE D'AZUR
For further details see p. 121
245 Route les Lucioles, 06560 Valbonne
Tel: +33 (0)4 93 64 32 84
Email: admissions@icscotedazur.com
Website: www.icscotedazur.com
Head of School: Gina Bianchi
Age range: 3–11 years
No. of pupils: 200
Fees: *Day* €12,480–€16,692
Curriculum: IBPYP, IGCSE
Language instr: English, French

ICS PARIS
For further details see p. 124
23 rue de Cronstadt, 75015 Paris
Tel: +33 (0)1 56 56 60 31
Email: admissions@icsparis.fr
Website: www.icsparis.fr
Director: Angela Hollington
Age range: 3–18 years
No. of pupils: 500
Fees: *Day* €20,595–€31,260
Curriculum: IBDP, IBMYP, IBPYP, IPC, IGCSE
Language instr: English

INTERNATIONAL BILINGUAL SCHOOL OF PROVENCE
For further details see p. 130
500 Route de Bouc-Bel-Air, Domaine des Pins, Luynes, Aix en Provence 13080
Tel: +33 (0)4 4224 0340
Email: info@ibsofprovence.com
Website: http://www.ibsofprovence.com
General Director: Jean-Marc Gobbi
Age range: 2–18 years
No. of pupils: 1200
Fees: *Day* €12,000–€18,000 *FB* €25,000–€33,000
Curriculum: AP, IBDP, FrenchBacc, TOEFL, UK, IGCSE
Language instr: English, French

International School 33
47 Avenue de la Poterie, 33170 Gradignan
Tel: +33 6 51 27 98 19
Age range: 3–18 years
Curriculum: IBDP, IBMYP, IBPYP
Language instr: English, French

International School of Béarn
200 Boulevard du Cami Salié, 64000 Pau
Tel: +33 559 09 94 74
Age range: 2–18
No. of pupils: 265
Curriculum: SAT, UK
Language instr: English, French, Spanish

International School of Lyon
80 Chemin du Grand Roule, 69110 Sainte-Foy-lès-Lyon
Tel: +33 4 78 86 61 90
Age range: 3–18 years
No. of pupils: 335
Curriculum: IBDP, IBPYP, UK, IGCSE
Language instr: English

Europe

International School of Marseille
27 Boulevard de la Corderie, 13007 Marseille
Tel: +33 491 53 00 00
Age range: 2–11
No. of pupils: 65
Curriculum: National
(ECIS)

INTERNATIONAL SCHOOL OF NICE
For further details see p. 145
15 Avenue Claude Debussy, 06200 Nice
Tel: +33 (0)4 93 21 04 00
Email: admissions@isn-nice.com
Website: www.isn-nice.com
Director: Mel Curtis
Age range: 3–18 years
No. of pupils: 480
Fees: Day €11,400–€24,885
Curriculum: ACT, AP, IBDP, IBMYP, IBPYP, SAT, UK, USA, IGCSE, ALevs
Language instr: English, French
(CIS) (ECIS)

International School of Paris
6 rue Beethoven, 75016 Paris
Tel: +33 1 42 24 09 54
Age range: 3–18
No. of pupils: 700
Curriculum: IBDP, IBMYP, IBPYP
Language instr: English
(CIS) (ECIS)

International School of Toulouse
2 Allee De L'Herbaudiere, Route de Pibrac, 31770 Colomiers
Tel: +33 5 62 74 26 74
Age range: 3–18 years
No. of pupils: 500
Curriculum: IBDP, IBPYP, IGCSE
Language instr: English
(CIS) (ECIS)

International School Strasbourg
7 rue de Soultz, 67100 Strasbourg
Tel: +33 9 78 80 94 10
Curriculum: IBDP
Language instr: English, French

Internationale Deutsche Schule Paris (iDSP)
18 Rue Pasteur, 92210 Saint-Cloud
Tel: +33 (0)146028568
Age range: 3–18
No. of pupils: 360
Curriculum: Abitur
Language instr: German, French

La Villa Blanche - Notre Dame du Sacre Coeur
3 rue Pasteur, 6500 Menton
Tel: +33 4 92 10 56 10
Age range: 14–19

Lab School Paris
38 rue Parmentier, 93100 Montreuil
Tel: +33 6 51 84 56 74
Age range: 6–18 years
No. of pupils: 180
Curriculum: IBDP
Language instr: English, French

Lennen Bilingual School - Primary Campus
176 rue de Grenelle, 75007 Paris
Tel: +33 1 44 42 99 00

Les Petits Polyglottes
15 Chemin de Vireloup, 01210 Ferney-Voltaire
Tel: +33 4 50 42 49 57
Curriculum: IBPYP
Language instr: English, French

Lindenwood International School
Centre Ville, 78124 Mareil-sur-Mauldre
Tel: +33 6 13 47 77 89
Age range: 3–16 years
Language instr: English, French

Lycee de Sevres, International Sections
Rue Lecocq, 92310 Sevres
Tel: +33 1 46 23 9635
Age range: 11–18
No. of pupils: 620

Lycée International de Saint Germain-en-Laye, American Section
2 bis rue du Fer à Cheval, 78100 Saint-Germain-en-Laye
Tel: +33 1 34 51 74 85
Age range: 4–18 years
No. of pupils: 700
Curriculum: National, FrenchBacc, USA
Language instr: French, English

Lycee International Des Pontonniers
1 Rue des Pontonniers, 67081 Strasbourg
Tel: +33 3 88 37 15 25
Age range: 5–18
No. of pupils: 870
Curriculum: IGCSE

Lycée International François 1ER
11 rue Victor Hugo, 77300 Fontainebleau
Tel: +33 1 60 74 58 30
Age range: 14–19

Lycee Internationale de Saint Germain-en-Leye - British Section
BP 70107, 78101 Saint Germain En Laye
Tel: +33 757072358
Age range: 5–18
No. of pupils: 680
Curriculum: UK, IGCSE

Lycee Louis de Foix
4 Avenue Jean Rostand, BP 331, 64103 Bayonne
Tel: +33 5 59 63 31 10
Age range: 14–19

Lycee Notre Dame
Rue Principale, 49310 La Salle de Vihiers
Tel: +33 2 41 49 02 50
Age range: 11–19
No. of pupils: 300

Lycee Notre Dame du Grandchamp
97 rue Royale, RP 934, 78000 Versailles
Tel: +33 1 39 24 12 80
Age range: 14–19
No. of pupils: 200

Lycee Pierre de Coubertin
320 Boulevard du 8 Mai, 62225 Calais
Tel: +33 3 21 46 88 00
Age range: 14–19

Malherbe International School
19-21 Rue du 11 Novembre, 78110 Le Vésinet
Tel: +33 1 39 76 47 37
Age range: 2–11 years
No. of pupils: 140
Curriculum: FrenchBacc, UK
Language instr: English, French, Spanish

Marymount International School Paris
72, boulevard de la Saussaye, 92200 Neuilly-sur-Seine
Tel: +33 (0)1 46 24 93 25
Age range: 2–14 years
No. of pupils: 330
Curriculum: USA
Language instr: English
(CIS) (ECIS)

Massillon - Ecole Bilingue Internationale
5 Rue Bansac, 63000 Clermont-Ferrand
Tel: +33 4 73 98 09 73
Age range: 3–18 years
No. of pupils: 1500
Curriculum: FrenchBacc, SAT, IGCSE
Language instr: English, French

MOUGINS BRITISH INTERNATIONAL SCHOOL
For further details see p. 170
615 Avenue Maurice Donat, CS 12180, 06252 Mougins CEDEX
Tel: +33 4 93 90 15 47
Email: admissions@mougins-school.com
Website: www.mougins-school.com
Director: James Wellings
Age range: 3–18 years
No. of pupils: 550
Fees: Day €15,660–€24,768
Curriculum: UK, GCSE, IGCSE, ALevs
(COB)

Notre Dame International High School
106 Grande-Rue, 78480 Verneuil-sur-Seine
Tel: +33 9 70 40 79 22
Age range: 15–18 years
No. of pupils: 40
Curriculum: IBDP, USA
Language instr: English, French

Ombrosa, Lycée Multilingue de Lyon
95 Quai Clemenceau, 69300 Caluire
Tel: +33 4 78 23 22 63
Age range: 2–18
No. of pupils: 1007 B528 G479
Curriculum: AP, IBDP, National
Language instr: English, Spanish

SAINTE VICTOIRE INTERNATIONAL SCHOOL
For further details see p. 179
Domaine de Château l'Arc, Chemin de Maurel, 13710 Fuveau
Tel: +33 4 42 26 51 96
Email: contact@schoolsaintevictoire.com
Website: www.schoolsaintevictoire.com
Head of School: Frederic Fabre
Age range: 5–18 years
Fees: Day €11,100–€20,350 FB €25,400–€36,150
Curriculum: IBDP, IGCSE
Language instr: English, French

Saudi School in Paris
60 bis avenue d'Iéna, 75016 Paris
Tel: +33 1 40 73 80 40
Language instr: English

Sections Internationales de Sèvres
1 Parvis Charles De Gaulle, 92310 Sevres
Tel: +33 1 72 77 70 43
Age range: 3–19
No. of pupils: 262
Curriculum: FrenchBacc

SEK INTERNATIONAL SCHOOL LES ALPES
For further details see p. 187
195 Rue du Marteray, 73590 St Nicolas la Chapelle
Tel: +34 900 87 87 98
Email: sek-lesalpes@sek.es
Website: www.sek.es/l/colegio-internacional/les-alpes
Age range: 11–16 years

The Bilingual Montessori School of Paris - Auteuil
53 rue Erlanger, 75016 Paris
Tel: +33 (0)7 49 94 83 93
Age range: 2–6 years
Language instr: English, French

The Bilingual Montessori School of Paris - George V
23 avenue George V, 75008 Paris
Tel: +33 (0)7 49 94 83 93
Age range: 2–6 years
Language instr: English, French

The Bilingual Montessori School of Paris - Orsay
65 quai d'Orsay, 75007 Paris
Tel: +33 (0)7 49 94 83 93
Age range: 2–12 years
Language instr: English, French

Europe

The British School of Paris
38 Quai De L'Ecluse, 78290
Croissy-sur-Seine
Tel: +33 1 34 80 45 96
Age range: 3–18
No. of pupils: 800 B400 G400 VIth100
Curriculum: GCSE, ALevs
Language instr: English
(COB)

Trillium International School
9 rue de la Sabotte,
78160 Marly-le-Roi
Tel: +33 1 80 83 93 61
Age range: 18 months–10 years
Curriculum: FrenchBacc, UK
Language instr: English, French

GEORGIA

British Georgian Academy
Leo Kvatchadze 17, Tbilisi 0186
Tel: +995 322 251 253
Curriculum: IBDP
Language instr: English, Georgian

British International School of Tbilisi
Leo Kvachadze 17 (Lisi Lake Area), Tbilisi 0186
Tel: +995 322 251 253
Curriculum: IPC, UK, IGCSE, ALevs
(CIS)

Buckswood International School Tbilisi
156 Rustaveli Street, Tskneti 0181
Tel: +955 577 992 993
Age range: 5–18 years
Language instr: English, Russian

European School
2 Irine Skhirtladze Street, Tbilisi 0177
Tel: +995 322 144 244
Age range: 3–18 years
Curriculum: IBDP, IBMYP, IBPYP, IBCP, USA
Language instr: English

New School, International School of Georgia
35 Tskneti Highway, Bagebi, Tbilisi 0162
Tel: +995 511 190 809
Age range: 5–18 years
Curriculum: IBDP, IBMYP, IBPYP
Language instr: English, Georgian

Newton Free School
Anna Politkovskaya Street
N30, Tbilisi 0186
Tel: +995 570 705 080
Age range: 3–19 years
Curriculum: IBDP, IBMYP, IBPYP
Language instr: English

QSI International school of Tbilisi
Village Zurgovani, Tbilisi 0126
Tel: +995 322 537 670
Age range: 4–18 years
Curriculum: SAT, USA
Language instr: English

St George's British Georgian School
M. Aleksidze II Lane 6 (By Sports Palace), Tbilisi
Tel: +995 322 609 989
Age range: 4–18 years
Curriculum: GCSE, IGCSE, ALevs
Language instr: English

GERMANY

ACCADIS INTERNATIONAL SCHOOL BAD HOMBURG
For further details see p. 91
SÜDCAMPUS Bad Homburg,
Am Weidenring 2, 61352
Bad Homburg, Hesse
Tel: +49 61 72 984 141
Email: info@accadis-isb.com
Website: www.accadis-isb.com
Head of School: Maximilian Müllerleile
Age range: 2–18 years
No. of pupils: 725
Fees: €3,360–€4,560
Curriculum: IBDP
Language instr: English, German

Aloisiuskolleg
Elisabethstraße 18, 53177 Bonn,
North Rhine-Westphalia
Tel: +49 228 82003 (101)
Curriculum: IBDP
Language instr: English, German

Bavarian International School gAG (BIS) - City Campus
Leopoldstrasse 208, 80804
Munich, Bavaria
Tel: +49 89 89655 203
Curriculum: IBPYP
Language instr: English

Bavarian International School gAG (BIS) - Haimhausen Campus
Hauptstrasse 1, 85778
Haimhausen, Bavaria
Tel: +49 (0)81 33 917 203
Age range: 3–19 years
No. of pupils: 1250
Curriculum: IBDP, IBMYP, IBPYP, IBCP
Language instr: English
(CIS) (ECIS)

BBIS Berlin Brandenburg International School
Schopfheimer Allee 10, 14532
Kleinmachnow, Brandenburg
Tel: +49 33 203 8036 0
Age range: 3–19 years
No. of pupils: 860
Curriculum: IBDP, IBMYP, IBPYP
Language instr: English

Berlin British School
Dickensweg 17-19, 14055 Berlin
Tel: +49 (0)30 35109 180
Age range: 2–18
No. of pupils: 480
Curriculum: IBDP, IBPYP, UK, IGCSE
Language instr: English
(COB) (ECIS)

Berlin Cosmopolitan School
Rückerstrasse 9, 10119 Berlin
Tel: +49 30 688 33 23 0
Curriculum: IBDP, IBPYP

Berlin International School
Lentzeallee 8/14, 14195 Berlin
Tel: +49 (0) 30 8200 7790
Age range: 6–18
No. of pupils: 825 B410 G415
Curriculum: IBDP, IBPYP, SAT, IGCSE
Language instr: English, German
(CIS) (ECIS)

Berlin Metropolitan School
Linienstrasse 122, 10115 Berlin
Tel: +49 30 8872 7390
Age range: 5–11
No. of pupils: 424 B192 G232
Curriculum: IBDP, IBPYP, National
Language instr: English, German
(ECIS)

Bertolt-Brecht-Gymnasium Dresden
Lortzingstrasse 01, 01307
Dresden, Saxony
Tel: +49 351 449040
Curriculum: IBDP
Language instr: English

Black Forest Academy
Postfach 1109, 79396 Kandern,
Baden-Württemberg
Tel: +49 7626 91610
Age range: 10–19
No. of pupils: B160 G164
Curriculum: ACT, AP, SAT, USA
Language instr: English

Bonn International School e.V.
Martin-Luther-King Strasse 14, 53175
Bonn, North Rhine-Westphalia
Tel: +49 228 30854 0
Age range: 3–19
No. of pupils: 730
Curriculum: IBDP, IBMYP, IBPYP, SAT
Language instr: English
(CIS) (ECIS)

Cecilien Gymnasium
Schorlemerstrasse 99, 40547
Düsseldorf, North Rhine-Westphalia
Tel: +49 211 892 33 11

Cologne International School
Rudi-Conin-Strasse 10, 50829
Cologne, North Rhine-Westphalia
Tel: +49 221 310 634-0
Curriculum: IBDP, IBPYP
Language instr: English, German

Dresden International School e.V
Annenstrasse 9, 01067
Dresden, Saxony
Tel: +49 351 440070
Age range: 1–19 years
No. of pupils: 498 B257 G240
Curriculum: IBDP, IBMYP, IBPYP, USA
Language instr: English
(CIS) (ECIS)

Ecole Élémentaire Franco-Allemande de Stuttgart - Sillenburch
Silberwaldstrasse 22, 70619
Stuttgart, Baden-Württemberg
Tel: +49 711 216 20 860
Age range: 6–11
No. of pupils: 500

École française de Sarrebruck et Dilling
Halbergstrasse 112, 66121
Saarbrücken, Saarland
Tel: +49 68 162 624

École française Pierre et Marie Curie
Wieblinger Weg 9, 69123
Heidelberg, Baden-Württemberg
Tel: +49 62 21840 983

École Grundschule Voltaire
Kurfürstenstrasse 53, 10785 Berlin
Tel: +49 30 4110015

Erasmus International School
Flotowstrasse 10, 14480
Potsdam, Brandenburg
Tel: +49 331 237 2790
Age range: 4–18
No. of pupils: 80 B37 G43
Curriculum: UK, IGCSE
Language instr: English

European School Karlsruhe
Aldert Schweitzerstrasse 1, 76139
Karlsruhe, ?Baden-Württemberg
Tel: +49 7 21 6 80 09 0
Age range: 3–19
No. of pupils: 950

European School Munich
Elise-Aulinger Strasse 21,
81739 Munich, Bavaria
Tel: +49 89 62 8160
Age range: 3–19
No. of pupils: 1345

European School of Frankfurt
Praunheimer Road 126,
60439 Frankfurt, Hesse
Tel: +49 69 92 88 74 0
Age range: 4–19
No. of pupils: 1080

European School RheinMain gGmbH
Theodor-Heuss-Strasse 65,
61118 Bad Vilbel, Hesse
Tel: +49 61 015056 60
Curriculum: IBDP, IBMYP
Language instr: English, German

Franconian International School
Marie-Curie-Strasse 2, 91052
Erlangen, Bavaria
Tel: +49 9131 940390
Age range: 3–18 years
No. of pupils: 650
Curriculum: IBDP, IBMYP, IPC
Language instr: English
(CIS) (ECIS)

Europe

Frankfurt International School
An der Waldlust 15, 61440 Oberursel, Hesse
Tel: +49 6171 2024 0
Age range: 3–18 years
No. of pupils: 1800
Curriculum: IBDP, IBPYP
Language instr: English

Frankfurt International School (Wiesbaden Campus)
Rudolf-Dietz-Strasse 14, Naurod, 65207 Wiesbaden, Hesse
Tel: +49 6127 99400
Age range: 3–14
No. of pupils: 220 B110 G110
Language instr: English, German

Groupe Scolaire Jean de la Fontaine
Meckenheimer Strasse 45, Mehelm, 53179 Bonn, North Rhine-Westphalia
Tel: +49 228 9538031
Age range: 4–18
No. of pupils: 190

Gymnasium im Stift Neuzelle
Stiftsplatz 7, 15898 Neuzelle, Brandenburg
Tel: +49 341 3939 2810
Curriculum: IBDP
Language instr: English, German

Hansa-Gymnasium, Hamburg-Bergedorf
Hermann-Distel-Strasse 25, 21029 Hamburg
Tel: +49 (0)40 724 18 60
Age range: B10–19 G10–19
No. of pupils: VIth185
Curriculum: Abitur, IBDP, TOEFL
Language instr: German, English

Heidelberg International School
Wieblinger Weg 7, 69123 Heidelberg, Baden-Württemberg
Tel: +49 6221 75 90 600
Age range: 4–18 years
No. of pupils: 300
Curriculum: AP, IBDP, IBMYP, IBPYP
Language instr: English

HPC International School
Slevogtstraße 3-5, 69126 Heidelberg, Baden-Württemberg
Tel: +49 62 2170501 864
Curriculum: IBDP, IBMYP, IBPYP
Language instr: English

IBSM - International Bilingual School Munich gGmbH
Lerchenauerstrasse 197, 80935 Munich, Bavaria
Tel: +49 89 41 11 49 550
Language instr: English, German

Independent Bonn International School
Tulpenbaumweg 42, 53177 Bonn, North Rhine-Westphalia
Tel: +49 228 323 166
Age range: 3–13
No. of pupils: 225 B110 G115
Curriculum: UK
(CIS) (COB) (ECIS)

International Gymnasium Geithain
Friedrich-Fröbel-Strasse 1, 04643 Geithain, Saxony
Tel: +49 34 34146 012
Curriculum: IBDP
Language instr: English

International Gymnasium Reinsdorf
Mittlerer Schulweg 13, 08141 Reinsdorf, Saxony
Tel: +49 37 5212 595
Curriculum: IBDP
Language instr: English, Spanish

International Kids Campus
Lerchenauerstrasse 197, 80935 Munich, Bavaria
Tel: +49 89 411149 550
Age range: 2.5–6 years
Curriculum: IBPYP
Language instr: English, German

International School Augsburg (ISA)
Wernher-von-Braun-Strasse 1a, 86368 Gersthofen, Bavaria
Tel: +49 821 45 55 60 0
Age range: 3–18
No. of pupils: 350
Curriculum: IBDP, IBPYP
Language instr: English
(CIS)

International School Braunschweig-Wolfsburg
Helmstedter Strasse 37, 38126 Braunschweig, Lower Saxony
Tel: +49 531 889210-0
Age range: 4–19 years
No. of pupils: 250
Curriculum: IBDP, IGCSE
Language instr: English

International School Hannover Region
Bruchmeisterallee 6, 30169 Hannover, Lower Saxony
Tel: +49 511 270 416 50
Age range: 3–18 years
No. of pupils: 591 B287 G304
Curriculum: IBDP, IBMYP, IBPYP
Language instr: English
(CIS) (ECIS)

International School Mainfranken e.V.
Kalifornienstrasse 1, 97424 Schweinfurt, Bavaria
Tel: +49 9721 53861-80
Age range: 6–18
No. of pupils: 105
Curriculum: IBDP, IBMYP, IBPYP
Language instr: English

International School of Bremen
Badgasteiner Strasse 11, 28359 Bremen
Tel: +49 421 5157790
Age range: 3–18
No. of pupils: 345
Curriculum: ACT, IBDP, IPC, SAT, IGCSE
Language instr: English
(ECIS)

> **INTERNATIONAL SCHOOL OF DUSSELDORF E.V.**
> *For further details see p. 137*
> Niederrheinstrasse 323/336, 40489 Düsseldorf, North Rhine-Westphalia
> **Tel:** +49 (0) 211-9406 6
> **Email:** info@isdedu.de
> **Website:** www.isdedu.de
> **School Director:** Frank Tschan
> **Age range:** 3–18 years
> **No. of pupils:** 1020
> **Curriculum:** IBDP, IBMYP, IBPYP, USA
> **Language instr:** English

International School of Hamburg
Hemmingstedter Weg 130, 22609 Hamburg
Tel: +49 (0)40 8000 500
Age range: 3–18 years
No. of pupils: 740
Curriculum: IBDP, IBMYP, IBCP, IPC
Language instr: English

> **INTERNATIONAL SCHOOL OF NEUSTADT**
> *For further details see p. 144*
> Haardterstrasse 1, 67433 Neustadt an der Weinstrasse
> **Tel:** +49 6321 8900 960
> **Email:** info@is-neustadt.de
> **Website:** www.is-neustadt.de
> **Principal:** Vjeko Kovac
> **Age range:** 4–18 years
> **No. of pupils:** 95
> **Fees:** Day €9,000–€17,400
> **Curriculum:** IGCSE, ALevs
> **Language instr:** English

International School of Stuttgart, Degerloch Campus
Sigmaringestrasse 257, 70597 Stuttgart, Baden-Württemberg
Tel: +49 71 17696 000
Age range: 3–10 years
No. of pupils: 850
Curriculum: IBDP, IBMYP, IBPYP
Language instr: English

International School of Stuttgart, Sindelfingen Campus
Hallenserstrasse 2, 71065 Sindelfingen, Baden-Württemberg
Tel: +49 70 316859 780
Age range: 4–16 years
No. of pupils: 850
Curriculum: IBMYP, IBPYP
Language instr: English

International School of Ulm/Neu Ulm
Schwabenstraße 25, 89231 Neu-Ulm, Bavaria
Tel: +49 731 379 353-0
Age range: 3–18
No. of pupils: 290
Curriculum: IBDP, IBPYP, IGCSE
Language instr: English
(ECIS)

International School Ruhr
Moltkeplatz 1 + 61, 45138 Essen, North Rhine-Westphalia
Tel: +49 (0)201 479 104 09
Age range: 3–19
No. of pupils: 153
Curriculum: IBDP, IBPYP, IGCSE
Language instr: English

> **INTERNATIONAL SCHOOL WESTPFALZ**
> *For further details see p. 149*
> Nikolaus-von-Weis-Strasse 10, 66849 Landstuhl
> **Tel:** +49 6371 980 930
> **Email:** info@is-westpfalz.de
> **Website:** www.is-westpfalz.de
> **Principal:** Jodi Fillingame
> **Age range:** 4–18 years
> **No. of pupils:** 240
> **Fees:** Day €15,600–€17,700
> **Curriculum:** IGCSE, ALevs
> **Language instr:** English

Internationales Stiftungsgymnasium Magdeburg
Agnetenstrasse 14, 39106 Magdeburg-Neustadt, Saxony-Anhalt
Tel: +49 39 179293 340
Curriculum: IBDP
Language instr: English, French

ISF International School Frankfurt Rhein-Main
Strasse zur Internationalen Schule 33, 65931 Frankfurt, Hesse
Tel: +49 69 954319 710
Age range: 3–18 years
Curriculum: Abitur, AP, IBDP, SAT, IGCSE
Language instr: English
(CIS) (ECIS)

ISR International School on the Rhine – NRW
Konrad-Adenauer-Ring 2, 41464 Neuss, North Rhine-Westphalia
Tel: +49 2131 40388-0, -11
Age range: 3 (Kindergarten)/5-6 (Primary)–18 years (Middle and Upper School)
No. of pupils: 700
Curriculum: AP, IBDP, SAT, IGCSE
Language instr: English
(ECIS)

Josef-Schwarz-Schule (JSS)
Georg-Ohm-Strasse 15, 74235 Erlenbach, Baden-Württemberg
Tel: +49 71 324884 980
Age range: 5–11
Curriculum: National
Language instr: English, German

Europe

Kämmer International Bilingual School
Paderbornerstrasse 1, 30539 Hannover, Lower Saxony
Tel: +49 51 12200 890
Age range: 1–18
No. of pupils: 400
Language instr: German, English

Leibniz Privatschule Elmshorn
Ramskamp 64B, 25337 Elmshorn, Schleswig-Holstein
Tel: +49 41 212610 40
Age range: 6–19
No. of pupils: 1000
Curriculum: IBDP
Language instr: English, German

Leipzig International School
Könneritzstrasse 47, 04229 Leipzig, Saxony
Tel: +49 34 139377 634
Age range: 1–18 years
No. of pupils: 1078
Curriculum: IBDP, IPC, IGCSE
Language instr: English

Leonardo Da Vinci Campus
Zu den Luchbergen 13, 14641 Nauen, Brandenburg
Tel: +49 33 217487 820
Curriculum: IBDP
Language instr: English, Spanish

Lycée Antoine-de-Saint-Exupéry de Hambourg
Antoine de Saint Exupéry, Hartsprung 23, 22529 Hamburg
Tel: +49 (0)40 790147 0
Curriculum: FrenchBacc

Lycée Français
Derfflingerstrasse 7, 10785 Berlin
Tel: +49 30 257589 51
Age range: 12–18
No. of pupils: 558

Lycée français de Düsseldorf
Graf-Recke-Straße 220, 40237 Düsseldorf, North Rhine-Westphalia
Tel: +49 21 16107 950
Age range: 3–18
No. of pupils: 570
Curriculum: National, FrenchBacc
Language instr: French, German, English

Lycée Français Jean Renoir
Berlepschstrasse 3, 81373 Munich, Bavaria
Tel: +49 89 72100 70
Curriculum: FrenchBacc

Lycée Français Victor Hugo
Gontardstrasse 11, 60488 Frankfurt am Main
Tel: +49 (0)69 74 74 98 149

Lycée français Victor-Hugo
Gontardstrasse 11, 60488 Frankfurt, Hesse
Tel: +49 69 74 74 98 0
Curriculum: National, FrenchBacc
Language instr: French, German

Main Taunus International School
Hugenottenstrasse 119, 61381 Friedrichsdorf, Hesse
Tel: +49 (0)6172 76465-0
Language instr: English, German

Metropolitan International School (MIS Heidelberg)
Mozartstrasse 4, 69120 Heidelberg, Baden-Württemberg
Tel: +49 6221 726 7900
Age range: 10 months–6 years

Metropolitan International School (MIS Mannheim)
SoHo TURLEY, Turley-Strasse 12, 68167 Mannheim, Baden-Württemberg
Tel: +49 6214 458 8282
Age range: 10 months–6 years

Metropolitan International School (MIS Viernheim)
Walter-Gropius-Allee 3, 68519 Viernheim, Hesse
Tel: +49 6204 7087 796
Age range: 4–18 years
Curriculum: IBDP
Language instr: English, German

Metropolitan School Frankfurt
Eschborner Landstrasse 134-142, 60489 Frankfurt, Hesse
Tel: +49 69 96 86 405-0
Age range: 3–18 years
No. of pupils: 620
Curriculum: IBDP, IBPYP
Language instr: English

Munich International School e.V.
Schloss Buchhof, Percha, 82319 Starnberg, Bavaria
Tel: +49 8151 366 0
Age range: 4–18 years
No. of pupils: 1250
Curriculum: IBDP, IBMYP, IBPYP
Language instr: English

Netzaberg Middle School
Unit 28130, 09144 Munich, Bavaria
Tel: +49 96 459179 229

Nymphenburger Schulen
Sadelerstrasse 10, 80638 Munich, Bavaria
Tel: +49 89 159 120
Age range: 10–18
Curriculum: IBDP, National
Language instr: German, English

Phorms Campus Berlin Mitte
Ackerstrasse 76, 13355 Berlin
Tel: +49 30 467 986 303/0/9
Age range: 3–19
No. of pupils: 570 B280 G290
Curriculum: Abitur, National, UK
Language instr: English, German

Phorms Campus Berlin Süd
Harry-S.-Truman-Allee 3, 14167 Berlin
Tel: +49 30 916 849 90
Age range: 1–18
No. of pupils: 500
Curriculum: AP, UK, ALevs

Phorms Campus Hamburg
Wendenstrasse 35-43, 20097 Hamburg
Tel: +49 40 325 370 50

Phorms Campus Munich
Maria-Theresia-Straße 35, 81675 Munich, Bavaria
Tel: +49 89 324 9337 00
Curriculum: IBDP
Language instr: English

Phorms Frankfurt City
Fürstenbergerstraße 3-9, 60322 Frankfurt, Hesse
Tel: +49 69 173 92 550

Phorms Taunus Campus
Waldstrasse 91, 61449 Steinbach, Hesse
Tel: +49 6171 206 02 70

Prälat-Diehl-Schule Oberstufe
Darmstädter Strasse 90A, 64521 Gross Gerau, Hesse
Tel: +49 6152 93350
No. of pupils: 1400
Curriculum: UK

Private Herder-Schule
Luisenstrasse 134-135, 42103 Wuppertal, North Rhine-Westphalia
Tel: +49 202 313170
Age range: 10–20
No. of pupils: 150
Curriculum: Abitur, National, TOEFL
Language instr: German

QSI International School of Münster
Lettisches Centrum Münster e.V., Salzmannstrasse 152, 48159 Münster, North Rhine-Westphalia
Tel: +49 251 38349446

Schule Birklehof
Birklehof 1, 79856 Hinterzarten, Baden-Württemberg
Tel: +49 7652 1220
Language instr: German

Schule Schloss Salem
Schlossbezirk 1, 88682 Salem, Baden-Württemberg
Tel: +49 7553 919 352
Age range: 10–19
No. of pupils: 600
Curriculum: Abitur, IBDP, National
Language instr: English, German

SIS Swiss International School Berlin
Heerstrasse 465, 13593 Berlin
Tel: +49 30 3643 9820
Age range: 3–16 years
Curriculum: IBDP
Language instr: English, German

SIS Swiss International School Frankfurt
An den drei Hasen 34-36, 61440 Oberursel, Hesse
Tel: +49 6171 8875 8011
Age range: 4–16 years
Language instr: English, German

SIS Swiss International School Friedrichshafen
Fallenbrunnen 1, 88045 Friedrichshafen, Baden-Württemberg
Tel: +49 7541 954 370
Age range: 3–16 years
Curriculum: IBDP
Language instr: English, German

SIS Swiss International School Ingolstadt
Stinnesstrasse 1, 85057 Ingolstadt, Bavaria
Tel: +49 841 981 446 0
Age range: 3–16 years
Curriculum: IBDP
Language instr: English, German

SIS Swiss International School Kassel
Johanna-Waescher-Strasse 15, 34131 Kassel, Hesse
Tel: +49 561 316 68 30
Age range: 4–16 years
Curriculum: IBDP
Language instr: English, German

SIS Swiss International School Regensburg
Klosterackerweg 1, 93049 Regensburg, Bavaria
Tel: +49 941 9925 9300
Age range: 3–16 years
Curriculum: IBDP
Language instr: English, German

SIS Swiss International School Stuttgart-Fellbach
Schmidener Weg 7/1, 70736 Stuttgart-Fellbach, Baden-Württemberg
Tel: +49 711 4691 9410
Age range: 3–16 years
Curriculum: IBDP
Language instr: English, German

St. George's The British International School Cologne
Husarenstrasse 20, 50997 Cologne, North Rhine-Westphalia
Tel: +49 2233 808 870
Age range: 2–18 years
Curriculum: IBDP, IBCP, IGCSE
Language instr: English

St. George's The British International School Munich
Heidemannstrasse 182, 80939 Munich, Bavaria
Tel: +49 8972 469 330
Age range: 2–18 years
Curriculum: IBDP, IBCP, IGCSE
Language instr: English

Europe

St. George's The British International School, Düsseldorf Rhein-Ruhr
Am Neuen Angerbach 90, 47259 Duisburg, North Rhine-Westphalia
Tel: +49 203 456 860
Age range: 2–18 years
Curriculum: IBDP, IBCP, IGCSE
Language instr: English

Stiftung Landheim Schondorf am Ammersee
Country Home 1-14, 86938 Schondorf am Ammersee, Bavaria
Tel: +49 8192 8090
Language instr: German

Stiftung Louisenlund
Louisenlund 9, 24357 Güby, Schleswig-Holstein
Tel: +49 (0)4354 999 333
No. of pupils: 500
Curriculum: IBDP, IBMYP
Language instr: English

Strothoff International School Rhein-Main Campus Dreieich
Frankfurterstrasse 160-166, 63303 Dreieich, Hesse
Tel: +49 6103 8022 500
Age range: 3–18
Curriculum: ACT, IBDP, IBMYP, IBPYP, SAT
Language instr: English

Taunus International Montessori School
Zimmersmuehtenweg 77, 61440 Oberursel, Hesse
Tel: +49 6171 913310
Age range: 1–6
No. of pupils: 60

UWC Robert Bosch College
Kartäuserstrasse 119, 79104 Freiburg, Baden-Württemberg
Tel: +49 761 708 395 00
Age range: 16–19
No. of pupils: 200
Curriculum: IBDP
Language instr: English

GIBRALTAR

Loreto Convent School
13 Europa Road, GX11 1AA
Tel: +350 200 75781
Age range: 1–12 years
No. of pupils: 422 B193 G229
Curriculum: UK
Language instr: English

Prior Park School
Sacred Heart Terrace,
Tel: 00350 200 62006
Curriculum: UK

St Anne's Middle School
St Anne's Road,
Tel: +350 20077161
Age range: 8–12
No. of pupils: 450

GREECE

American Community Schools of Athens
129 Aghias Paraskevis Str., Halandri, 152 34 Athens
Tel: +30 210 639 3200
Age range: 3–18 years
No. of pupils: 1100
Curriculum: IBDP
Language instr: English

American Farm School
Marinou Antipa 54, PO Box 23, Thessaloniki 551 02
Tel: +30 23104 92700
Curriculum: USA

Anatolia High School
PO Box 21021, 60 John Kennedy Avenue, 555 35 Pylea
Tel: +30 2310 398 200
Curriculum: IBDP, IBMYP
Language instr: English (IBDP), Greek (MYP)

Byron College
7 Filolaou Street, 15344 Gerakas
Tel: +30 210 60 47 722 - 5
Age range: 3–18
Curriculum: UK, GCSE, IGCSE, ALevs
Language instr: English

Campion School Athens
PO Box 674 84, Pallini 153 02
Tel: +30 210 607 1700
Age range: 3–18
No. of pupils: 510
Curriculum: IBDP
Language instr: English

Costeas-Geitonas School
Pallini - Attikis, Athens 15351
Tel: +30 210 6030 411
Curriculum: IBDP, IBMYP, IBPYP
Language instr: English

Deutsche Schule Athen
Dimokritou 6 & Germanikis Scholis Athinon, GR 151 23 Maroussi
Tel: +30 210 6199260-5

Deutsche Schule Thessaloniki - DST
PO Box 51, Thessaloniki-Thermi km 9, GR-55102 Thessaloniki-Fin
Tel: +30 2310 475 900

European Interactive School (DES)
Barakos Hill, Ribas 19400
Tel: +30 210 8974143
Curriculum: IBPYP
Language instr: English, Greek

Geitonas School
T.TH. 74128, 166 02 Vari Attikis 166 02
Tel: +30 210 9656200
Curriculum: IBDP
Language instr: English

HAEF, Athens College
15 Stephanou Delta Street, Psychico, Athens 15452
Tel: +30 2106798100
Curriculum: IBMYP, IBPYP
Language instr: English, Greek

HAEF, Athens College Elementary
Paleopanagias Avenue, Kantza 15351
Tel: +30 2106798100
Language instr: English, Greek

HAEF, John M. Carras Kindergarten
15 Stephanou Delta Street, Psychico, Athens 15452
Tel: +30 2106798100
Curriculum: IBPYP
Language instr: English, Greek

HAEF, Psychico College
15 Stephanou Delta Street, Psychico, Athens 15452
Tel: +30 2106798100
Curriculum: IBDP, IBMYP, IBPYP
Language instr: English, Greek

HAEF, Psychico College Elementary
Paleopanagias Avenue, Kantza 15351
Tel: +30 2106798100
Language instr: English, Greek

I.M. Panagiotopoulos School
Milisi 3, Pallini, Athens 153 51
Tel: +30 21 0666 6117
Age range: 3–18
Curriculum: National
Language instr: English

Institut Français de Thessalonique
Leoforos Stratou 2A, Thessaloniki
Tel: +30 23 10 821 231
Age range: 4–18
No. of pupils: 70

International Metropolitan School
Ypsilanti 9, 164 52 Argyroupoli, Athens
Tel: +30 21 0 996 9866
Age range: 3–15 years
Curriculum: IBPYP
Language instr: English, Greek

International School of Athens
PO Box 51051, Kifissia, Athens 14510
Tel: +30 210 6233 888
Age range: 3–18
No. of pupils: 324 B189 G135 VIth25
Curriculum: AP, IBDP, IBMYP, IBPYP, SAT
Language instr: English

International School of Larissa
Tyrnavos 40100, Larissa 40100
Tel: +30 24920 22233
Age range: 4–18
No. of pupils: 300
Curriculum: USA

International School of Piraeus
66-70 Praxitelous street, Piraeus 18532
Tel: +30 210 417 5580
Curriculum: IBPYP
Language instr: English

Ionios School
PO Box 13622, Filothei 15202
Tel: +30 210 6857130
Curriculum: IBDP

Lampiri Schools
Metamorphosis 155 and Ilissou, Moschato, Athens
Tel: +30 210 9480530
Curriculum: IBDP
Language instr: English

Lycée Franco-Hellénique Eugène Delacroix
B.P. 60050, Rues Chlois & Trikalon, 153 54 Aghia Paraskevi-Athènes
Tel: +30 211 300 91 00
Curriculum: FrenchBacc, IGCSE

Mary N. Raptou School SA
Karditsis 21, Larissa 41335
Tel: +30 2410 625724
Language instr: English

Moraitis School
A Papanastasiou & Ag Dimitriou, Paleo Psychico, Athens 15452
Tel: +30 210 679 5000
Age range: 4–18
No. of pupils: 1800
Curriculum: IBDP, National, SAT, TOEFL
Language instr: English

Pierce - The American College of Greece
6 Gravias Street, Aghia Paraskevi, Athens 153 42
Tel: +30 210 600 9800 (Ext:1060)
Curriculum: IBDP
Language instr: English, Greek

Pinewood American International School
60 John Kennedy Avenue, 555 35 Pylea
Tel: +30 23 1 030 1221
Age range: 4–18 years
Curriculum: AP, IBDP, IBMYP, IBPYP
Language instr: English

Platon School
Eleytheriou Venizelou Street, Glyka Nera, Attika 15354
Tel: +30 210 6611 793
Curriculum: IBDP, IBMYP, IBPYP

St Catherine's British School
Leoforos Venizelou 77, Lykovrissi, Athens 141 23
Tel: +30 210 2829 750
Age range: 3–18
No. of pupils: 1060
Curriculum: IBDP, UK
Language instr: English

Europe

St Lawrence College
PO Box 7422, 16602
Varkiza Attiki, Athens
Tel: +30 21 0891 7000
Age range: 3–19
No. of pupils: 755 B372 G383
Curriculum: UK, IGCSE, ALevs
Language instr: English
(COB)

HUNGARY

American International School of Budapest
Nagykovácsi út 12, Nagykovácsi 2094
Tel: +36 26 556 000
Age range: 3–20
No. of pupils: B434 G429
Curriculum: IBDP, SAT, USA
Language instr: English
(CEE) (CIS) (ECIS)

BME International Secondary School
Egry Jozsef utca 3-11, Budapest 1111
Tel: +36 12094983
Curriculum: IBDP
Language instr: English

Britannica International School
Kakukk Way 1-3, 1121 Budapest
Tel: +36 1 466 9794
Age range: 5–18
No. of pupils: B150 G140
Curriculum: National, UK, IGCSE, ALevs
Language instr: English
(COB)

Budapest British International Academy
1025 Budapest,, Berkenye utca 13-15,
Tel: +36 30 563 55 28
Curriculum: UK
(COB)

Budapest British International School
4 Zsolna utca, Budapest 1125
Tel: +36 70 425 5225
Curriculum: IBDP, IBMYP, UK
Language instr: English

Deutsche Schule Budapest Thomas Mann Gymnasium
Cinege út 8/C, Budapest CH-1121
Tel: +36 1 39191 00

Greater Grace International School of Budapest
Szilagyi Erzsebet Fasor 22/B, Budapest 1125
Tel: + 36 1 275 4795

International Christian School of Budapest
H-2049 Diosd, Ifjusag 11
Tel: +36 23 381 986
Age range: 5–18
No. of pupils: 225
Curriculum: USA
Language instr: English
(CEE)

International School of Budapest
Konkoly Thege M u 21, Budapest 1121
Tel: +36 1 395 6543
Age range: 5–18 years
No. of pupils: 400
Curriculum: IBDP, National
Language instr: English

International School of Debrecen (ISD)
Heltai Gáspár Street 1, 4002 Debrecen
Tel: +36 20 404 4822
Curriculum: IBDP, IBMYP, IBPYP
Language instr: English, Hungarian

QSI International School of Pápa
Komáromi út 12, 8500 Pápa
Tel: +36 89 777 999

REAL School Budapest
Záhony utca 7, Budapest 1031
Tel: +36 21 262 0380
Age range: 5–14 years
Curriculum: UK
Language instr: English
(COB)

SEK Budapest International School
Hűvösvölgyi út 131, Budapest 1021
Tel: +36 1 394 2968
Age range: 3–18 years
Curriculum: IBDP
Language instr: English

Szeged International Primary School
Lidicei tér 1, Szeged 6727
Tel: +36 70 799 8256
Age range: 5–13 years

The British International School
Kiscelli Köz 17, Budapest 1037
Tel: +36 1 200 9971
Age range: 3–18
No. of pupils: 800
Curriculum: IBDP, UK, GCSE
Language instr: English
(COB) (ECIS)

ICELAND

International School of Iceland
órsmörk vi Ægisgrund, 210 Gar abœr
Tel: +354 594 3100
Age range: 5–15 years
Curriculum: IBMYP
Language instr: English, Icelandic
(ECIS)

IRELAND

Castle Park School
Castle Park Road, Dalkey, Co Dublin
Tel: +353 1 280 3037
Age range: 3–12
No. of pupils: 286 B162 G124
Language instr: English

Cistercian College
Mount St. Joseph Abbey, Roscrea
Tel: + 353 505 23344
Age range: B12–19
Curriculum: National
Language instr: English

Headfort School
Kells, Co Meath
Tel: +353 4692 40065
Age range: 7–13
No. of pupils: 105 B65 G40

International School of Dublin
Synge Street, Dublin D08 PW64
Tel: +353 087 329 1417
Age range: 3.5–12 years
No. of pupils: 50
Curriculum: IBPYP
Language instr: English, Spanish

John Scottus School
Old Conna, Ferndale Road, Rathmichael, Co. Dublin
Tel: +353 (1) 668 0828

Lycée Français d'Irlande - Collège et Lycée
Eurocampus Dublin, Roebuck Road, Clonskeagh, Dublin 14
Tel: +353 1 288 4834
Age range: 11–18
No. of pupils: 490
Curriculum: FrenchBacc

Nord Anglia International School Dublin
South County Business Park, Leopardstown, Dublin 18
Tel: +353 1 5442323
Age range: 3–18 years
Curriculum: IBDP, IBMYP, IBPYP
Language instr: English

Sandford Park School
Ranelagh, Dublin 6
Tel: +353 1 4971417
Age range: 12–18
No. of pupils: 350
Language instr: English

SEK INTERNATIONAL SCHOOL DUBLIN
For further details see p. 184
Belvedere Hall, Windgates, Greystones, Co. Wicklow A63 EY23
Tel: +35 31 287 41 75
Email: admissions-dublin@sek.ie
Website: www.sek.ie
Principal: Alberto Domínguez
Age range: 12–18 years
Curriculum: IBDP, IBMYP
Language instr: English

ST ANDREW'S COLLEGE
For further details see p. 193
Booterstown Avenue, Blackrock, County Dublin A94 XN72
Tel: +353 1 288 2785
Email: information@st-andrews.ie
Website: www.sac.ie
College Principal: Louise Marshall
Age range: 4–18 years
No. of pupils: 1279
Curriculum: ACT, IBDP, National, SAT
Language instr: English
(AISA) (CIS) (ECIS)

St Columba's College
Kilmashogue Lane, Whitechurch, Dublin 16
Tel: +353 1 4906791
Age range: 11–18
No. of pupils: 295 B159 G136 VIth137
Curriculum: National
Language instr: English

Sutton Park School
St Fintan's Road, Sutton, Dublin 13
Tel: +353 1 8322940
Age range: 4–18
No. of pupils: 278 B167 G111
Curriculum: SAT
(CIS)

The King's Hospital
Palmerstown, Dublin 20
Tel: +353 1 643 6564
Age range: 12–18 years
No. of pupils: 740 B400 G340
Curriculum: National

Villiers School
North Circular Road, Limerick V94 F983
Tel: +353 61 451447
Age range: 12–18 years
No. of pupils: 600
Curriculum: IBDP
Language instr: English

ITALY

Acorn International School
Via della Giustiniana 1200, 00189 Rome
Tel: +39 068 7462 195
Curriculum: IBDP
Language instr: English, Italian

Ambrit International School
Via F Tajani 50, 00149 Rome
Tel: +39 06 5595 305/301
Age range: 3–14
No. of pupils: 450 B225 G225
Curriculum: IBMYP, IBPYP, National
Language instr: English

Europe

AMERICAN OVERSEAS SCHOOL OF ROME
For further details see p. 101
Via Cassia 811, 00189 Rome
Tel: +39 06 334 381
Email: admissions@aosr.org
Website: www.aosr.org/admissions
Head of School: Kristen DiMatteo
Age range: 3–18 years
Fees: €12,500–€17,000
Curriculum: AP, IBDP, National, SAT, USA
Language instr: English

American School of Milan
Via K. Marx, 14, 20073 Noverasco di Opera (MI)
Tel: +39 02 5300 001
Age range: 3–18 years
No. of pupils: 860
Curriculum: IBDP, SAT
Language instr: English

Andersen International School
Via Don Carlo, San Martino 8, 20133 Milan
Tel: +39 02 7000 6580
Age range: 3–18 years
Curriculum: IBDP, UK
Language instr: English, Italian

Bilingual British School
Via Pietro Piccinelli 10, 24020 Scanzorosciate BG
Tel: +39 035 6591 406
Age range: 6 months–18 years
Curriculum: IBDP
Language instr: English, Italian

BILINGUAL EUROPEAN SCHOOL
For further details see p. 103
Via Val Cismon 9, 20162 Milan
Via Resegone 1A, 20159 Milan
Tel: +39 02 6611 7449
Email: admissions@beschool.eu
Website: www.beschool.eu
Head of School: Francesco Masetti Placci
Age range: 2–18 years
No. of pupils: 546
Fees: Day €12,250–€17,100
Curriculum: IBPYP
Language instr: English, Italian

Britannia International School of Rome
Via Ernesto Parisi 11, 00134 Rome
Tel: +39 06 713 54252
Age range: 2–11
No. of pupils: 135
Curriculum: UK

British School Genova
Piazzale dei Traghetti, Iqbal 5, 16123 Genoa
Tel: +39 010 540903
Age range: 4–19

Cabella International Sahaja School CISS
Via Martiri della Libertà 11, Cabella Ligure, 15060 Alessandria
Tel: +39 0143 919805
Curriculum: IPC, UK

Canadian College Italy (CCI - The Renaissance School)
Via Cavour 13, Lanciano, 66034 Chieti
Tel: +39 872 714969
Age range: 15–19

CANADIAN SCHOOL OF FLORENCE
For further details see p. 106
Via Jacopo Nardi 18, 50132 Florence
Tel: +39 055 098 2744
Email: info@csflorence.it
Website: www.csflorence.it
Head of School: Isabelle Leblanc
Age range: 3–18 years
Fees: Day €11,953–€20,940

Canadian School of Milan
Via Melchiorre Gioia 42, 20124 Milan
Tel: +39 02 67074775
Age range: 3–18 years
No. of pupils: 400
Curriculum: IBDP, IBMYP
Language instr: English

Castelli International School
Via Degli Scozzesi 13, Grottaferrata, 00046 Rome
Tel: +39 06 94315779
Age range: 5–14 years
No. of pupils: 125
Curriculum: National, UK, IGCSE

Collegio San Carlo
Corso Magenta 71, 20123 Milan
Tel: +39 02 43 06 31
Age range: 2–19 years
No. of pupils: 1891
Curriculum: IBDP
Language instr: English, Italian

Core International School
Via Crati 19, 00199 Rome
Tel: +39 068411137
Curriculum: UK

Deledda International School
Corso Mentana 27, 16128 Genoa
Tel: +39 010 5536268
No. of pupils: 770
Curriculum: IBDP, IBMYP
Language instr: English

Deutsche Schule Genua
Scuola Germanica di Genova, Via Mylius 1, 16128 Genoa
Tel: +39 010 564 334

Deutsche Schule Mailand
Scuola Germanica di Milano, Via Legnano 24, 20121 Milan
Tel: +39 (0)2 6597614

Ecole Française de Naples Alexandre Dumas
Via Francesco Crispi no 86, 80121 Naples
Tel: +39 (0)81 66 89 36

ENGLISH GATE SCHOOL
For further details see p. 113
Via Ginevrina da Fossano 38, 22063 Cantù, Como
Tel: +39 031 4896 941
Email: admissions@englishgate.it
Website: www.englishgate.it
Head of School: Francesco Masetti Placci
Age range: 1–14 years
No. of pupils: 250
Fees: €9,000–€11,500
Curriculum: IPC

European School of Varese
Via Montello 118, 21100 Varese
Tel: +39 332 806 111
Age range: 4–18
No. of pupils: 1350

Florence Bilingual School
V.le Spartaco Lavagnini 11, 50129 Florence
Tel: +39 055 495061
Age range: 1–13 years
Curriculum: National
Language instr: English, Italian

German School of Rome
Via Aurelia Antica 397-403, 00165 Rome
Tel: +39 06 663 8776
Age range: 4–18
No. of pupils: 700

GIS The International School of Monza srl
Via Federico Confalonieri 18, 20900 Monza (MB)
Tel: +39 039 2287034
Curriculum: IBPYP
Language instr: English, Italian

Gonzaga International School
Via Piersanti Mattarella 38/42, 90141 Palermo
Tel: +39 91 302093
Age range: 18 months–18 years
No. of pupils: 190
Curriculum: IBDP, IBMYP, IBPYP
Language instr: English

Greenwood Garden School
Via Vito Sinisi 5, 00189 Rome
Tel: +39 06 3326 6703
Age range: 2–6
No. of pupils: 44 B22 G22
Curriculum: USA
Language instr: English

H-FARM INTERNATIONAL SCHOOL
For further details see p. 119
Via Olivetti 1, 31056 Roncade (TV)
Tel: +39 0422 789503
Email: info.ve@h-is.com
Website: www.h-farm.com/en/h-farm-school/venezia
Head of School: Emiliano Cori
Age range: 3–18 years
Curriculum: IBDP, IBMYP, IBPYP
Language instr: English

H-International School Rosà
Via Segafredo 50, 36027 Rosà
Tel: +39 0424 582191
Age range: 4–14
No. of pupils: 276 B137 G139
Curriculum: National, TOEFL
Language instr: English, Italian

H-International School Vicenza
Borgo Santa Lucia, 51 Vicenza, 36100 Vicenza
Tel: +39 444 54 50 07
Age range: 18 months–16 years
No. of pupils: 213
Curriculum: IBDP, IBMYP, IBPYP, National, UK
Language instr: English

ICS MILAN
For further details see p. 123
ICS Symbiosis, Viale Ortles, 46, 20139 Milano (MI)
Tel: +39 02 36592694
Email: admissions@icsmilan.com
Website: www.icsmilan.com
Head of School: Luke Osborne
Age range: 1–18 years
No. of pupils: 1000
Fees: Day €15,000–€28,000
Curriculum: IBDP, IBMYP, IPC
Language instr: English, Italian

INSTITUT INTERNATIONAL SAINT-DOMINIQUE
For further details see p. 126
Via Igino Lega 5, 00189 Rome
Tel: +39 06 30 31 08 17
Email: info@institutsaintdominique.it
Website: www.institutsaintdominique.fr
Headmaster: Audren Séguillon
Age range: 18 months–18 years
No. of pupils: 396
Fees: Day €16,100 WB €30,050 FB €34,050
Curriculum: IBDP, FrenchBacc
Language instr: English, French

International School Brescia
Via Benaco 34/B, Bedizzole, 25080 Brescia
Tel: +39 030 2191182
Age range: 3–19 years
No. of pupils: 206
Curriculum: IBDP, IBMYP, IBPYP
Language instr: English

INTERNATIONAL SCHOOL OF BERGAMO
For further details see p. 135
Via Monte Gleno, 54, 24125 Bergamo
Tel: +39 035 213776
Email: info@isbergamo.com
Website: www.isbergamo.com
Head of School: Roberta Sana
Age range: 2–18 years
No. of pupils: 420
Curriculum: IBDP, IBMYP, IBPYP
Language instr: English

Europe

International School of Bologna
Via della Libertà 2, 40123 Bologna
Tel: +39 051 6449954
Age range: 3–18
No. of pupils: 270
Curriculum: IBDP, IBMYP, IBPYP
Language instr: English

INTERNATIONAL SCHOOL OF COMO
For further details see p. 136
Via Adda 25, 22073 Fino Mornasco (CO)
Tel: +39 031 572289
Email: admissions.como@iscomo.com
Website: www.iscomo.com
Head of School: Philipa Smithson
Age range: 2–18 years
No. of pupils: 382
Curriculum: IBDP, IBMYP, IBPYP
Language instr: English, Italian

International School of Florence
Via del Carota 23/25, Bagno a Ripoli, 50012 Florence
Tel: +39 055 6461 007
Age range: 3–18
No. of pupils: 439 B216 G223 VIth28
Curriculum: IBDP, IBPYP, National, SAT, USA
Language instr: English, Italian

International School of Lago Patria
Via 1a Marenola, 17, 80014 Giugliano in Campania
Tel: +39 081 5096452
Language instr: English

INTERNATIONAL SCHOOL OF MILAN
For further details see p. 141
Via I Maggio, 20, 20021 Baranzate (MI)
Tel: +39 02 872581
Email: admissions@ismilan.it
Website: www.internationalschoolofmilan.it
Executive Head: Rebecca Ruth Glover
Age range: 2–18 years (Boarding 14-18 years)
No. of pupils: 850
Curriculum: IBDP, IBMYP, IBPYP
Language instr: English

INTERNATIONAL SCHOOL OF MODENA
For further details see p. 142
Piazza Montessori, 1/A, 41051 Montale Rangone (MO)
Tel: +39 059 530649
Email: admissions@ismodena.it
Website: www.internationalschoolofmodena.it
Head of School: Paul Barrie
Age range: 3–18 years
No. of pupils: 220
Curriculum: IBDP, IBMYP, IBPYP
Language instr: English

INTERNATIONAL SCHOOL OF MONZA
For further details see p. 143
Via Solferino 23, 20900 Monza (MB)
Tel: +39 039 9357701
Email: admin@ismonza.it
Website: www.internationalschoolofmonza.it
Head of School: Johanna Karen Urquhart
Age range: 2.5–18 years
No. of pupils: 300
Curriculum: IBDP, IBMYP, IBPYP
Language instr: English, Italian

International School of Rimini
Via Santa Chiara 40, 47921 Rimini RN 47921
Tel: +39 054 1786 129
Curriculum: IBPYP
Language instr: English

INTERNATIONAL SCHOOL OF SIENA
For further details see p. 146
Via del Petriccio e Belriguardo, 49/1, 53100 Siena
Tel: +39 0577 328103
Email: office@issiena.it
Website: www.internationalschoolofsiena.it
Principal: Jennifer Tickle
Age range: 3–18 years
No. of pupils: 204
Curriculum: IBDP, IBMYP, IBPYP
Language instr: English, Italian

International School of Talents - Multicampus (IST)
Via degli Alpini, 28/5, 31046 Oderzo, Treviso
Tel: +39 0422 789 503

International School of Trieste
Via Conconello 16, 34151 Trieste
Tel: +39 040 211 452
Age range: 2–18
No. of pupils: 335 B165 G170
Curriculum: AP, USA
Language instr: English

International School of Turin
Strada Pecetto 34, 10023 Chieri, Turin
Tel: +39 011 645 967
Age range: 3–18 years
Curriculum: IBDP, IBMYP, IBPYP
Language instr: English

International School of Venice
Via Bissagola 25, 30173 Mestre, Venezia
Tel: +39 041 983 711
Language instr: English, Italian

International School of Verona
Aleardo Aleardi, Via Segantini 20, 37138 Verona
Tel: +39 04557 8200
Age range: 3–18
No. of pupils: 730
Curriculum: IBDP, National, IGCSE
Language instr: English

ISE Kiddy English
Via Antonio Bordoni 2, 20124 Milan
Tel: +39 02 87258880
Age range: 2–6 years
Language instr: English

Kendale International Primary School
86 Via Gradoli, Tombe di Nerone, 00189 Rome
Tel: +39 06 3326 7608
Age range: 3–11
No. of pupils: 100 B48 G52
Curriculum: UK
Language instr: English

Kinder College
Via Osservanza 88, 40136 Bologna BO
Tel: +39 051 581344
Age range: 2–14 years
Curriculum: IBPYP
Language instr: English, Italian

Little Genius International
Via di Grotte Portella 28, 00044 Frascati, Rome
Tel: +39 06 97245148

Livorno Elementary/Middle School
Unit 31301, Box 66, 09613-0005 Livorno
Tel: +39 050 54 7573
Age range: 4–14
No. of pupils: 150
Curriculum: USA

Lonati Anglo American School
Via Bormioli 60, 25135 Brescia
Tel: +39 03 02 35 73 60
Age range: 5–12
No. of pupils: 121
Curriculum: IBPYP
Language instr: English

Lycée Chateaubriand de Rome
PATRIZI/Malpighi, Via di Villa Patrizi 9, 00161 Rome
Tel: +39 06 441 604 1
Curriculum: FrenchBacc

Lycée français Jean Giono de Turin
Corso Casale 324, 10132 Torino
Tel: +39 011660 29 55
Curriculum: FrenchBacc

Lycée Victor Hugo
Palazzo Venturi Ginori, Via della Scala 85, 50123 Florence
Tel: +39 055 266 991
Curriculum: FrenchBacc

MARYMOUNT INTERNATIONAL SCHOOL ROME
For further details see p. 164
Via di Villa Lauchli, 180, 00191 Rome
Tel: +39 06 3629 1012
Email: admissions@marymountrome.com
Website: www.marymountrome.com
Head of School: Sarah Gallagher
Age range: 2–18 years
No. of pupils: 950
Fees: Day €13,700–€27,000
Curriculum: AP, IBDP
Language instr: English

O.M.C. - Collegio Vescovile Pio X
Borgo Cavour 40, 31100 Treviso
Tel: +39 0422 411725
Curriculum: IBDP
Language instr: English

QSI International School of Brindisi
Via Benvenuto Cellini 25, 72100 Brindisi
Tel: +39 0831 518764
Age range: 3–13
No. of pupils: 34
Curriculum: USA
Language instr: English

RIS ROME INTERNATIONAL SCHOOL
For further details see p. 177
Via Guglielmo Pecori Giraldi n.137, 00135 Rome
Tel: +39 06 8448 2651
Email: office@romeinternationaschool.it
Website: www.romeinternationalschool.it
Head of School: Niki Meehan
Age range: 2–18 years
No. of pupils: 400
Fees: Day €10,395–€27,480
Curriculum: IBDP, IBPYP, UK, GCSE, IGCSE
Language instr: English

Scuola Svizzera di Catania
Via M.R Imbriani 32, 95128 Catania
Tel: +39 095 447116
Age range: 3–15
No. of pupils: 70

Scuola Svizzera di Milano
Via Appiani 21, 20121 Milan
Tel: +39 02 655 57 23
Age range: 2–18
No. of pupils: 360

SIS Swiss International School Milano-Basiglio
Via don Silvio Coira 45, 20080 Basiglio MI
Tel: +39 024 6517 699
Age range: 4–12 years
Curriculum: National
Language instr: English, German

Europe

Smiling International School
Via Roversella 2, 44121 Ferrara
Tel: +39 05 32209416
Age range: 2–18 years
Curriculum: IBDP
Language instr: English, Italian

ST GEORGE'S BRITISH INTERNATIONAL SCHOOL, ROME
For further details see p. 195
Via Cassia, km 16, La Storta, 00123 Rome
Tel: +39 06 3086001
Email: admissions@stgeorge.school.it
Website: www.stgeorge.school.it
Principal: John Knight
Age range: 3–18 years
No. of pupils: 1010
Fees: Day €14,000–€26,500
Curriculum: IBDP, UK, GCSE, IGCSE
Language instr: English
(CIS) (COB) (ECIS)

St. Francis International School
Via delle Benedettine, 50/b, 00135 Rome
Tel: +39 (0)6 35 5110 23
Curriculum: UK, USA

St. Louis Archinto
Via Olmetto 6, 20123 Milan
Tel: +39 02 36723970
Age range: 13–18 years

St. Louis Colonna
Via Marco Antonio Colonna 24, 20149 Milan
Tel: +39 02 33007523
Age range: 2–13 years

ST. LOUIS SCHOOL
For further details see p. 199
SLS S.P.A., Via E. Caviglia, 1, 20139 Milan
Tel: +39 02 55231235
Email: info@stlouisschool.com
Website: www.stlouisschool.com
Executive Principal High School: Kathy Crewe Read
Age range: 2–18 years
No. of pupils: 1750
Curriculum: IBDP, UK, IGCSE
Language instr: English, Italian

St. Stephen's School
Via Aventina 3, 00153 Rome
Tel: +39 06 575 0605
Age range: 14–19 years
Curriculum: ACT, AP, IBDP, SAT, USA
Language instr: English

St. Thomas's International School
Via San Giovanni Decollato 1, 01100 Viterbo
Tel: +39 0761 1767857
Curriculum: IBPYP
Language instr: English, Italian

The Anglo-Italian School, Montessori Division
Ex NATO Base, Building H Viale della Liberazione, 1, 80124 Bagnoli, Naples
Tel: +39 081 570 6587
Age range: 2–15
No. of pupils: 346 B180 G166
Curriculum: National, USA
(ECIS)

THE BRITISH SCHOOL OF MILAN (SIR JAMES HENDERSON)
For further details see p. 209
Via Carlo Alberto Pisani Dossi, 16, 20134 Milan
Tel: +39 02 210941
Email: info@bsm.school
Website: www.britishschoolmilan.com
Principal: Simon Lockyer
Age range: 3–18 years
No. of pupils: 780
Fees: €14,000–€22,700
Curriculum: IBDP, UK, IGCSE
Language instr: English
(COB)

The English International School of Padua
Via Forcellini 168, 35128 Padova
Tel: +39 049 80 22 503
Age range: 2–18
No. of pupils: 759 B398 G361
Curriculum: IBDP, National, SAT, UK, IGCSE, ALevs
Language instr: English
(ECIS)

The International School in Genoa
Via Romana Della Castagna 11A, 16148 Genova
Tel: +39 010 386528
Age range: 3–17 years
Curriculum: IBDP, IBMYP, IBPYP, National
Language instr: English, Italian
(CIS)

The International School of Naples
Viale della Liberazione, 1, 80125 Bagnoli, Naples
Tel: +39 081 762 8429
Age range: 4–18
No. of pupils: 242 B120 G122
Curriculum: National, SAT, USA
(CIS) (ECIS)

THE NEW SCHOOL ROME
For further details see p. 212
Via Della Camilluccia 669, 00135 Rome
Tel: +39 06 329 4269
Email: info@newschoolrome.com
Website: www.newschoolrome.com
Headteacher: Norman Doyle
Age range: 3–18 years
Fees: Day €10,700–€19,800
Curriculum: UK, GCSE, ALevs
(COB)

Udine International School
Via Martignacco 187, 33100 Udine
Tel: +39 043 2541 119
Age range: 2–18 years
Language instr: English
(CIS)

UWC ADRIATIC
For further details see p. 215
Località Duino 29, 34011 Duino-Aurisina TS
Tel: +39 040 3739111
Email: uwcad@uwcad.it
Website: www.uwcad.it
Head of College: Khalid El-Metaal
Age range: 16–19 years
No. of pupils: 186
Fees: €26,000
Curriculum: IBDP
Language instr: English

Villa Grimani International School
Via Leonardo da Vinci 4, 35027 Noventa Padovana
Tel: +39 049 8933833
Age range: 3–13
(ECIS)

VITTORIA INTERNATIONAL SCHOOL
For further details see p. 217
Via delle Rosine 14, 10123 Turin
Tel: +39 011 889870
Email: infovis@vittoriaweb.it
Website: www.vittoriaweb.it
Head of School: Marcella Margaria Bodo
Age range: 3–19 years
Fees: €5,900
Curriculum: IBDP, IGCSE
Language instr: English

World International School of Torino
Via Traves 28, 10151 Torino
Tel: +39 0111972111
Curriculum: IBDP, IBMYP, IBPYP
Language instr: English

YIES Your Italian English School
Via Monte Grappa 17, 20854 Vedano al Lambro (MB)
Tel: +39 345 834 7521
Curriculum: IBPYP
Language instr: English, Italian

KOSOVO

Finnish Schools International
Magjistralja Prishtine, Ferizaj, Tek rrethi i QMI-së,
Tel: 00381 45 235650
Age range: 3–18

International Learning Group School - ILG School
Veternik 1, 10000 Prishtina
Tel: +386 38 722 893
Curriculum: IBDP, IBMYP, IBPYP
Language instr: English

International School of Prishtina
Preoc, Marigona Residence, Gracanica 10000
Tel: +386 49 770513 / +386 49 425216
Age range: 6–18
No. of pupils: 425
Curriculum: National
(ECIS)

Kindergarten & Primary School 'Yllka'
Rr. Fan Noli Nr: 1, Prizren
Tel: +377 44 669665 / +381 29 233237

Mehmet Akif College - Gjakova
Rr. Zidi Sadikagas, ish TMK, Gjakovë
Tel: +386 49 773 775

Mehmet Akif College - Lipjan
Banullë, Lipjan
Tel: +38138581999 / +38649770514
No. of pupils: 563
(ECIS)

Mehmet Akif College - Prizren
Korishë, Prizren
Tel: +38129233441 / +37744140900

QSI International School of Kosovo
24 Maji-ARBERIA Street #15, 10000 Pristina
Tel: +386 49 775 731

LATVIA

Exupery International School
Jauna iela 8, Pinki, Babites pagasts LV-2107
Tel: +371 266 22 777
Age range: 2.5–18 years
No. of pupils: 370
Curriculum: IBDP, IBPYP, IGCSE
Language instr: English
(CIS)

International School of Latvia
Meistaru 2, Pinki, Babites pag., Babites nov., LV-2107
Tel: +371 6775 5146
Age range: 3–18
No. of pupils: 363
Curriculum: IBDP, IBMYP, IBPYP, SAT
Language instr: English
(CEE) (CIS)

International School of Riga
Zvejnieku iela 12, Riga 1048
Tel: +371 6762 4622
Age range: 2–14
Curriculum: IBDP, IBPYP
Language instr: English
(CIS)

International School Premjers
1 Lomonosova Str., Bld. 7, Riga 1019
Tel: +371 67218501
Curriculum: IBDP, IBMYP
Language instr: English, Russian

Europe

KING'S COLLEGE, THE BRITISH SCHOOL OF LATVIA
For further details see p. 157
Turaidas iela 1 Pinki,
Babites novads LV2107
Tel: +371 257 59 043
Email: latvia@kingscollegeschools.org
Website: latvia.kingscollegeschools.org
Head of School: Adele Stanford
Age range: 2–18 years
No. of pupils: 500
Fees: Day €9,900–€24,000
Curriculum: IBDP, UK, IGCSE, ALevs
Language instr: English

RTU International School of Science & Technology
Kronvalda Boulevard 1, Riga LV1010
Tel: +371 6708 9998
Age range: 16–18 years
Curriculum: ALevs
Language instr: English

LITHUANIA

Erudito Licejus, Kaunas
J. Gruodzio g. 9, 44293 Kaunas
Tel: +370 65 788 820
Curriculum: IBDP
Language instr: English, Lithuanian

Erudito Licejus, Vilnius
Aludariu g. 3, 01113 Vilnius
Tel: +370 66 719 972
Curriculum: IBDP
Language instr: English, Lithuanian

Kaunas Jesuit High School
Rotuses a. 9, 44280 Kaunas
Tel: +370 8 37 28 05 25
Age range: 11–19
No. of pupils: 780 B322 G358
Curriculum: IBDP
Language instr: Lithuanian, English

Klaipeda Universa Via International School
Baltikalnio street 11, Klaipeda
Tel: +370 8 46 38 34 65
Curriculum: IBPYP
Language instr: English, Lithuanian

The American International School of Vilnius
Subaciaus 41, 11350 Vilnius
Tel: +370 5 212 1031
Age range: 3–16
No. of pupils: 171 B25 G34
Curriculum: IBDP
(CEE) (CIS) (ECIS)

The British School of Vilnius
Nemencines pl. 48, 10103 Vilnius
Tel: +370 52 338 855
Age range: 2–18 years
Curriculum: UK, IGCSE
(COB)

Vilniaus Karalienes Mortos mokykla
Luksines g. 29, 11332 Vilnius
Tel: +370 63 007 474
Curriculum: IBDP
Language instr: English, Lithuanian

Vilnius International Meridian School (VIMS)
M.Dauk os g. 7, 02101 Vilnius
Tel: +370 5 2 728 725
Curriculum: UK, IGCSE, ALevs

Vilnius International School
Turniskiu Str 21, Rusu Str 3, 01125 Vilnius
Tel: +370 5 276 1564
Curriculum: IBMYP, IBPYP

Vilnius Private Gymnasium
V. Grybo street 7, 10313 Vilnius
Tel: +370 69 854 808
Curriculum: IBDP
Language instr: English, Lithuanian

LUXEMBOURG

Ecole Privee Over the Rainbow
5, rue d'Orval, Luxembourg L 2270
Tel: +352 26 09 45 42
Age range: 4–11
Curriculum: IPC

European School of Luxembourg
Boulevard Konrad Adenauer 23, Kirchberg, Luxembourg L-1115
Tel: +352 43 20 82 1
Age range: 4–18
No. of pupils: 3008

Fräi-Ëffentlech Waldorfschoul Lëtzebuerg
45 rue de l'Avenir, Luxembourg 1147
Tel: +352 466932
No. of pupils: 349
Curriculum: IBDP
Language instr: French

INTERNATIONAL SCHOOL EDWARD STEICHEN
For further details see p. 133
1 Rue Edward Steichen,
9707 Clervaux
Tel: +352 206 007-1
Email: info@lesc.lu
Website: www.lesc.lu
Principal: Max Wolff
Age range: 4–19 years
No. of pupils: 1400 B700 G700
Language instr: English, French, German

International School of Luxembourg
36 Boulevard Pierre Dupong, 1430 Luxembourg
Tel: +352 26 04 40
Age range: 3–18
No. of pupils: 1357 B727 G630
Curriculum: ACT, IBDP, IBPYP, SAT, IGCSE
Language instr: English
(CIS) (ECIS)

OTR International School Luxembourg
7 Rue Val Ste Croix, 1371 Luxembourg
Tel: +352 2609 45 42
Age range: 3–18 years
Curriculum: IBDP, IBMYP
Language instr: English, French

St George's International School Luxembourg
11 Rue des Peupliers, L-2328 Luxembourg
Tel: +35 242 32 24
Age range: 3–18 years
Curriculum: UK, IGCSE, ALevs
Language instr: English
(CIS) (COB) (ECIS)

VAUBAN, Ecole et Lycée Français de Luxembourg
1-3 rue Albert Einstein, 1484 Luxembourg
Tel: +352 28 10 14 00
Curriculum: FrenchBacc

MACEDONIA

American High School Skopje
Treta Makedonska Brigada No. 60, 1000 Skopje
Tel: +389 2 2469 993
Curriculum: IBDP
Language instr: English, Macedonian

International School Maximilian
Bul. 8mi Septemvri No. 14, 1000 Skopje
Tel: +389 2 3099 925
Curriculum: IBPYP
Language instr: English

IPS Macedonia
Skupi 11, 1000 Skopje
Tel: +389 (0)2 3070 723
Age range: 3–18 years
No. of pupils: 370
Curriculum: IBDP, IBMYP, IBPYP
Language instr: English

NOVA International Schools
Praska 27, 1000 Skopje
Tel: +389 2 3061 907
Age range: 16–18
No. of pupils: 606 B306 G300
Curriculum: IBDP, IBMYP, IBPYP
Language instr: English

QSI International School of Skopje
Zenevska #51, 1000 Skopje
Tel: +389 2 305 1844
Age range: 5–13
No. of pupils: 103
Curriculum: USA
Language instr: English

MALTA

QSI International School of Malta
Triq Durumblat, Mosta 4815
Tel: +356 21 423067
Age range: 5–18
Curriculum: USA
Language instr: English

San Andrea School
L-Imselliet, Zebbiegh MST 11
Tel: +356 21 43 88 00
Age range: 4–16
No. of pupils: 800
Curriculum: IGCSE

San Anton School
L-Imselliet, Zebbiegh MGR2850
Tel: +356 2158 1907
Age range: 3–16
No. of pupils: 1000
Curriculum: UK, GCSE

ST EDWARD'S COLLEGE, MALTA
For further details see p. 194
Triq San Dwardu, Birgu (Vittoriosa) BRG 9039
Tel: +356 2788 1199
Email: admissions@stedwards.edu.mt
Website: www.stedwards.edu.mt
Headmaster: Nollaig Mac an Bhaird
Age range: B3–18 years (boarding from 11) G3–5 years (progressing annually to full co-ed)
Fees: Day €2,500–€10,000 FB €21,000–€33,000
Curriculum: IBDP, National, IGCSE
Language instr: English

Theresa Nuzzo (Marsa) School
Balbi Street, Marsa HMR 14
Tel: +356 7924 0391
Age range: 5–10
No. of pupils: 320

Verdala International School
Fort Pembroke, Pembroke PBK 1641
Tel: +356 21375133
Age range: 3–18
No. of pupils: 520
Curriculum: IBDP, IBMYP, IBCP, IPC, SAT, IGCSE
Language instr: English
(ECIS)

MOLDOVA

QSI International School of Chisinau
48/2 Nicolae Costin Street, Chisinau MD 2051
Tel: +373 22 588 346
Age range: 3–13
No. of pupils: 47
Curriculum: USA
Language instr: English

MONACO

International School of Monaco
43 Avenue Princesse Grace, Monte Carlo 98000
Tel: +377 9325 6820
Age range: 3–18 years
No. of pupils: 830
Curriculum: IBDP, IBMYP, IBPYP, IBCP, IGCSE
Language instr: English, French
(CIS) (ECIS)

Lycée Albert 1er
4 Place de la Visitation, Monaco 98000
Tel: +377 98 98 80 54
Age range: 15–18
No. of pupils: 825

Europe

MONTENEGRO

Adriatic College
13 Rozino, 85312 Budva
Tel: +382 69 324 101
Curriculum: IBDP
Language instr: English

Arcadia Academy
Ljesevici bb, 85330 Kotor
Tel: +382 32 662 662
Language instr: English

Knightsbridge Schools International Montenegro (KSI Montenegro)
Seljanovo bb, Porto Montenegro, 85320 Tivat
Tel: +382 32 672 655
Age range: 3–18 years (boarding from 11)
Curriculum: IBDP, IBMYP, IBPYP
Language instr: English

QSI International School of Montenegro
Ul. Romanovih 33, Zabjelo, 81000 Podgorica
Tel: +382 20 641 734
Age range: 5–13
No. of pupils: 42 B20 G22
Language instr: English

United Kids International Montenegro
Kotorska 3, Podgorica
Curriculum: IBPYP
Language instr: English

NETHERLANDS

AFNORTH International School
Ferdindand Bolstraat 1, 6445 EE Brunssum, Limburg
Tel: +31 45 5278221
Age range: 4–19
No. of pupils: 1000
Curriculum: ACT, AP, SAT, UK, USA
Language instr: English, German, French

American School of The Hague
Rijksstraatweg 200, 2241 BX Wassenaar
Tel: +31 70 512 1060
Age range: 3–18 years
No. of pupils: 1089
Curriculum: ACT, AP, IBDP, SAT, TOEFL, USA
Language instr: English

Amity International School Amsterdam
Amsterdamseweg 204, 1182 HL Amsterdam, North Holland
Tel: +31 20 3454181
Curriculum: IBDP, IBMYP, IBPYP
Language instr: English

Amsterdam International Community School
Prinses Irenestraat 59, 1077 WV Amsterdam, North Holland
Tel: +31 20 5771240
Age range: 4–19
Curriculum: IBDP, IBMYP, IBPYP, IBCP, IPC
Language instr: English

Amsterdam Liberal Arts & Sciences Academy (ALASCA)
Geertje Wielemaplein 1, 1095 MM Amsterdam, North Holland
Tel: +31 20 2623240
Curriculum: IBDP
Language instr: English, Dutch

College Den Hulster
PO Box 60, 5900 AB Venlo, Limburg
Tel: +31 77 3590300
Age range: 12–18
No. of pupils: 1500

Deutsche Internationale Schule Den Haag
van Bleiswijkstraat 125, 2582 LB The Hague, South Holland
Tel: +31 70 3549454
Age range: 3–18
No. of pupils: 220

Eerde International Boarding School Netherlands
Kasteellaan 1, 7731 PJ Ommen, Overijssel
Tel: +31 52 9451452
Age range: 4–19 years
No. of pupils: 100
Curriculum: IBDP, USA, IGCSE
Language instr: English

ELCKERLYC INTERNATIONAL SCHOOL
For further details see p. 112
Klimopzoom 41, 2353 RE Leiderdorp, South Holland
Tel: +31 71 5896861
Email: international@elckerlyc.net
Website: www.elckerlyc-international.nl
Headteacher: Lesley de Quartel
Age range: 3–11 years
No. of pupils: 140
Fees: Day €4,200
Curriculum: IPC, National
Language instr: English

European School Bergen
Molenweidtje 5, 1862 BC Bergen, North Holland
Tel: +31 72 5890109
Age range: 4–18
No. of pupils: 600 B300 G300
Language instr: French, Dutch, English, German

Gifted Minds International School
c/o Corporate Office, Landtong 18, 1186 GP Amstelveen, North Holland
Tel: +31 23 888 8874
Curriculum: IBPYP, USA
Language instr: English

HSV International Primary School - KSS Location
Koningin Sophiestraat 24a, 2595 TG The Hague, South Holland
Tel: +31 70 3243453
Age range: 4–11
No. of pupils: 540
Curriculum: IPC
Language instr: English

HSV International Primary School - NSL Location
Nassaulaan 26, 2514 JT The Hague, South Holland
Tel: +31 70 3184950
Age range: 4–11
Curriculum: IPC
Language instr: English

HSV International Primary School - VNS Location
Van Nijenrodestraat 16, 2597 RM The Hague, South Holland
Tel: +31 70 3281441
Age range: 4–11
No. of pupils: 100
Curriculum: IPC
Language instr: English

INTERNATIONAL FRENCH SCHOOL OF AMSTERDAM
For further details see p. 131
Anthonie van Dijckstraat 1 BG, 1077 ME Amsterdam, North Holland
Tel: +31 6 27 12 83 14
Email: admissions@internationalfrenchschool.com
Website: www.internationalfrenchschool.com
Director: Séverine Fougerol
Age range: 2–18 years
No. of pupils: 360
Fees: Day €11,000–€15,000
Curriculum: FrenchBacc
Language instr: Dutch, English, French

International Primary School GSV
Rijksstraatweg 24, 9752 AE Haren
Tel: +31 50 5270818
Age range: 4–12
No. of pupils: 100
Curriculum: IPC

International School Delft
Colijnlaan 2, 2613 VZ Delft
Tel: +31 15 8200208
Age range: 4–18 years
No. of pupils: 540
Curriculum: IBDP, IBMYP, IBPYP
Language instr: English

International School Eindhoven
Oirschotsedijk 14b, 5651 GC Eindhoven, North Brabant
Tel: +31 40 2519437
Age range: 4–18 years
No. of pupils: 1400
Curriculum: IBDP, IBMYP, IPC
Language instr: English, Dutch

INTERNATIONAL SCHOOL LEIDEN
For further details see p. 134
Van Vollenhovenkade 15, 2313 GG Leiden, South Holland
Tel: +31 71 5173464
Email: admissions@isleiden.nl
Website: isleiden.nl
Principal: Deon du Plessis
Age range: 4–11 years
Curriculum: IPC

International School of Amsterdam
Sportlaan 45, 1185 TB Amstelveen, North Holland
Tel: +31 20 347 1111
Age range: 2–18 years
No. of pupils: 1184
Curriculum: IBDP, IBMYP, IBPYP
Language instr: English

International School The Rijnlands Lyceum Oegstgeest
Apollolaan 1, BA 2341 Oegstgeest, South Holland
Tel: +31 71 5193555
Age range: 11–18
No. of pupils: 1200
Curriculum: IBDP, IBMYP
Language instr: English

International School Twente
Tiemeister 20, 7541 WG Enschede, Overijssel
Tel: +31 53 482 11 30
Curriculum: IBDP, IBPYP
Language instr: English

International School Utrecht
Van Bijnkershoeklaan 8, 3527 XL Utrecht
Tel: +31 30 8700400
Age range: 4–18 years
No. of pupils: 900
Curriculum: IBDP, IBMYP, IBPYP
Language instr: English

Laar & Berg
Langsakker 4, 1251 GB Laren, North Holland
Tel: +31 35 5395422
Age range: 11–18
No. of pupils: 800 B406 G394
Curriculum: IBMYP, National
Language instr: English, Dutch

Lycee Francais Vincent Van Gogh
Scheveningseweg 237, 2584 AA The Hague, South Holland
Tel: +31 70 3066920
Curriculum: FrenchBacc

Maartenscollege & International School Groningen
Hemmenlaan 2, 9751 NS Haren, Groningen
Tel: +31 50 5340084
Age range: 11–18
No. of pupils: 200
Curriculum: IBDP, IBMYP
Language instr: English

D363

Europe

Marcanti College
Jan van Galenstraat 31, 1051 KM
Amsterdam, North Holland
Tel: +31 20 6069000

Montessori Lyceum Amsterdam
Pieter de Hoochstraat 59, 1071
ED Amsterdam, North Holland
Tel: +31 20 6767855
Age range: 11–18
No. of pupils: 1600

Nord Anglia International School Rotterdam
Verhulstlaan 21, 3055 WJ
Rotterdam, South Holland
Tel: +31 10 4225351
Age range: 3–18 years
No. of pupils: 250
Curriculum: IBDP, IPC
Language instr: English
(CIS) (ECIS)

OBS Dubbeldam
Eikenlaan 25, 3319 SC
Dordrecht, South Holland
Tel: +31 78 6160151
Age range: 4–11

Rivers International School Arnhem
Groningensingel 1245, 6835
HZ Arnhem, Gelderland
Tel: +31 26 3202840
Age range: 12–18
No. of pupils: 155 B80 G75
Curriculum: IBDP, IBMYP
Language instr: English
(ECIS)

Rotterdam International Secondary School
Bentincklaan 294, 3039 KK
Rotterdam, South Holland
Tel: +31 (0)10 890 77 44
Age range: 12–18 years
No. of pupils: 380
Curriculum: IBDP, IBCP, IGCSE
Language instr: English
(CIS) (ECIS)

Stedelijk Gymnasium Nijmegen
Kronenburgersingel 269, 6511
AS Nijmegen, Gelderland
Tel: +31 24 3220606
Age range: 14–19
No. of pupils: 1320

The British School in the Netherlands - Leidschenveen
Vrouw Avenweg 422, 2496 WX
The Hague, South Holland
Tel: +31 70 3154077
Age range: 3–18 years
No. of pupils: 2000
Curriculum: IBDP, IBCP,
UK, GCSE, ALevs
Language instr: English
(COB) (ECIS)

The British School in the Netherlands - Vlaskamp
Vlaskamp 19, 2592 AA The
Hague, South Holland
Tel: +31 70 3154077
Age range: 3–11 years
Curriculum: UK
Language instr: English
(COB) (ECIS)

The British School in the Netherlands - Voorschoten
Jan van Hooflaan 3, 2252 BG
Voorschoten, South Holland
Tel: +31 70 3154077
Age range: 11–18 years
No. of pupils: 2100
Curriculum: IBDP, IBCP,
UK, GCSE, ALevs
Language instr: English
(COB) (ECIS)

> **THE BRITISH SCHOOL OF AMSTERDAM**
> *For further details see p. 207*
> Havenstraat 6, 1075 PR
> Amsterdam, North Holland
> **Tel:** +31 (0)20 679 7840
> **Email:** info@britams.nl
> **Website:** www.britams.nl
> **Principal:** Ciaran Harrington
> **Age range:** 3–18 years
> **No. of pupils:** 1050
> **Fees:** Day €18,750–€21,528
> **Curriculum:** UK, GCSE,
> IGCSE, ALevs
> **Language instr:** English
> (COB)

The International School of The Hague
Wijndaelerweg 11, 2554 BX
The Hague, South Holland
Tel: +31 70 328 1450
Age range: 4–18 years
No. of pupils: 1840
Curriculum: IBDP, IBMYP, IBCP
Language instr: English
(CIS) (ECIS)

Theodore International Startup Academy (TISA) Leiden
Lorentzkade 15a, 2313 GB
Leiden, South Holland
Tel: +31 64 3283316
Age range: 3–12 years
Curriculum: IBPYP
Language instr: English, Dutch

> **UWC MAASTRICHT**
> *For further details see p. 216*
> Discusworp 65, 6225 XP
> Maastricht, Limburg
> **Tel:** +31 432 410 410
> **Email:** admissions@uwcmaastricht.nl
> **Website:** www.uwcmaastricht.nl
> **Head of College:** Viki Stiebert
> **Age range:** 4–19 years
> **No. of pupils:** 980
> **Fees:** €7,890–€30,000
> **Curriculum:** IBDP, IBMYP,
> IBPYP, IGCSE
> **Language instr:** English
> (CIS) (ECIS)

Violenschool International Primary School - Frans Hals Location
Frans Halslaan 57, 1213 BK
Hilversum, North Holland
Tel: +31 35 6930641
Age range: 4–8
No. of pupils: 135

NORWAY

Aalesund International School
Borgundvegen 418, 6015
Aalesund, Møre og Romsdal
Tel: +47 908 69 948
Age range: 5–15
Curriculum: IBMYP, IBPYP
Language instr: English

Arendal International School
Julius Smiths vei 40, 4817 His, Agder
Tel: +47 370 18 550
Curriculum: IBMYP, IBPYP
Language instr: English

Birralee International School
Bispegata 9c, 7012
Trondheim, Trøndelag
Tel: +47 73 87 02 60
Age range: 4–16
No. of pupils: 250 B121 G129
Curriculum: UK, IGCSE
Language instr: English

British International School of Stavanger (BISS) Gausel
Gauselbakken 107, Gausel,
4032 Stavanger, Rogaland
Tel: +47 519 50 250
Age range: 2–19
No. of pupils: 530
Curriculum: IBDP, IBMYP, IBPYP, IBCP
Language instr: English
(COB)

Children's International School Fredrikstad
Torsnesveien 5-7, 1630 Gamle
Fredrikstad, Østfold
Tel: +47 690 02 500
Age range: 6–16
No. of pupils: 231
Curriculum: IBMYP, IBPYP
Language instr: English

Children's International School Moss
Moss Verk 1, 1534 Moss, Østfold
Tel: +47 400 01 128
Age range: 6–16
No. of pupils: 268
Curriculum: IBMYP, IBPYP
Language instr: English

Children's International School Sarpsborg
Tuneveien 20, 1710 Sarpsborg, Østfold
Tel: +47 400 02 607
Curriculum: IBMYP, IBPYP
Language instr: English, Norwegian

Deutsche Schule Oslo - Max Tau
Sporveisgata 20, 0354 Oslo
Tel: +47 22 93 12 20

Gjøvikregionen International School
Studieveien 17, 2815 Gjøvik, Innlandet
Tel: +47 240 76 141
Curriculum: IBMYP, IBPYP
Language instr: English, Norwegian

International School of Bergen
Sandslihaugen 30, 5254
Bergen, Vestland
Tel: +47 55 30 63 30
Age range: 3–16
No. of pupils: 180
Curriculum: IBMYP, IBPYP, National
Language instr: English
(CIS) (ECIS)

International School of Stavanger
Treskeveien 3, 4043
Hafrsfjord, Rogaland
Tel: +47 51 55 43 00
Age range: 3–18
No. of pupils: 630
Curriculum: ACT, IBDP,
SAT, UK, USA, IGCSE
Language instr: English, Dutch
French, German, Norwegian, Spanish
(CIS) (COB) (ECIS)

International School Telemark
Hovet Ring 7, 3931
Porsgrunn, Telemark
Tel: +47 35291400
Age range: 6–16
No. of pupils: 133 B73 G60
Curriculum: IBMYP, IBPYP
Language instr: English

Kristiansand International School
Kongsgård alle 20, 4631
Kristiansand, Agder
Tel: +47 95826601
Age range: 6–16 years
No. of pupils: 194
Curriculum: IBMYP, IBPYP
Language instr: English

Lycée Français René Cassin
Skovveien 9, 0257 Oslo
Tel: +47 22 92 51 20
Curriculum: FrenchBacc

Norlights International School
Skådalsveien 33, 0781 Oslo
Tel: +47 40 07 35 50
Curriculum: IBDP, IBMYP, IBPYP
Language instr: English

Oslo International School
PO Box 53, 1318 Bekkestua, Akershus
Tel: +47 67 8182 90
Age range: 3–18
No. of pupils: 600 B320 G280
Curriculum: IBDP, IPC, SAT
Language instr: English
(CIS) (ECIS)

Skagerak International School
Framnesveien 7, 3222
Sandefjord, Vestfold
Tel: +47 334 56 500
Age range: 4–18 years
Curriculum: IBDP, IBMYP, IBPYP
Language instr: English

Europe

The Children's House
Åsenvegen 100, 4055 Sola, Rogaland
Tel: +47 47 48 22 92
Age range: 2–7
No. of pupils: 158 B86 G72

Tromsø International School
4 Breiviklia, 9019 Tromsø, Troms
Tel: +47 99200780
Curriculum: IBMYP, IBPYP
Language instr: English

UWC Red Cross Nordic
Hauglandsvegen 304,
6968 Flekke, Vestland
Tel: +47 5773 7000
Age range: 16–19
No. of pupils: 200
Curriculum: IBDP, SAT
Language instr: English

POLAND

2 Spoleczne Liceum Ogolnoksztalcace STO im. Pawla Jasienicy (2SLO)
ul. Nowowiejska 5, 00-643 Warsaw, Masovia
Tel: +48 22 825 11 99
Curriculum: IBDP
Language instr: English

Akademeia High School in Warsaw
ul. Ledóchowskiej 2, 02-972 Warsaw, Masovia
Tel: +48 22 299 8787
Curriculum: UK, IGCSE, ALevs
Language instr: English

American Elementary School
ul Lowicka 41, 81-504 Gdynia, Pomerania
Tel: +48 58 664 69 71

American School of Warsaw
Bielawa, ul Warszawska 202, 05-520 Konstancin-Jeziorna, Masovia
Tel: +48 22 702 8500
Age range: 3–18
Curriculum: ACT, AP, IBDP, IBMYP, IBPYP, SAT
Language instr: English

American School of Wroclaw
Partynicka 29-37, 53-031 Wroclaw, Lower Silesia
Tel: +48 51 616 1113
Age range: 1–18 years
Curriculum: IBDP, IBMYP
Language instr: English, Polish

ATUT Bilingual Primary School
ul. Raclawicka 101, 53-149 Wroclaw, Lower Silesia
Tel: +48 71 782 26 25
Curriculum: IBMYP
Language instr: English

British International School of Cracow
ul.Smolensk 25, 31-108 Kraków, Lesser Poland
Tel: +48 1229 264 78
Age range: 3–19
No. of pupils: 230
Curriculum: IBDP
Language instr: English

British International School of the University of Lodz
ul Matejki 34a, 90-237 Lodz
Tel: +48 42 635 60 06
Age range: 5–19
Curriculum: IBDP, UK, IGCSE, ALevs
Language instr: English

British International School Wroclaw
Al Akacjowa 10/12, 53-134 Wroclaw, Lower Silesia
Tel: +48 71 7966861
Age range: 3–18
No. of pupils: B55 G54
Curriculum: National, UK, IGCSE, ALevs
Language instr: English

British Primary School of Wilanow
ul. Hlonda 12, 02-972 Warsaw, Masovia
Tel: +48 22 111 0062
Curriculum: UK
Language instr: English

Da Vinci's International Schools
Pilotów 4c Street, 31-362 Kraków, Lesser Poland
Tel: +48 608 322 388
Age range: 3–18 years
Curriculum: IBDP, IBMYP
Language instr: English, Polish

Edison Primary School
ul. Królewicza Jakuba 69, 02-956 Warsaw, Masovia
Tel: +48 22 858 81 60
Curriculum: UK

International American School
Ul Dembego 18, 02-796 Warsaw, Masovia
Tel: +48 22 649 1442
Curriculum: IBDP
Language instr: English

International British School Vocandus
ul. Woronicza 16, 91-030 Lodz
Tel: +48 696 050 078
Age range: 5–18
No. of pupils: 24 B14 G10
Curriculum: National, UK, IGCSE

International European School Warsaw
ul. Wiertnicza 140, 02-952 Warsaw, Masovia
Tel: +48 22 842 44 48
Curriculum: IBDP
Language instr: English

International High School of Wroclaw
ul. Raclawicka 101, 53-149 Wroclaw, Lower Silesia
Tel: +48 71 782 26 26
Curriculum: IBDP, IBMYP
Language instr: English

International Primary School
52 Drukarska St, 53-312 Wroclaw, Lower Silesia
Tel: +48 503 188 843
Curriculum: IBPYP
Language instr: English

International School of Gdansk
ul. Sucha 29, 80-531 Gdansk, Pomerania
Tel: +48 58 342 31 00
Age range: 5–18
No. of pupils: 300
Curriculum: IBPYP, USA
Language instr: English, Polish

International School of Krakow
ul Sw Floriana 57, Lusina, 30-698 Krakow, Lesser Poland
Tel: +48 12 270 1409
Age range: 3–18
No. of pupils: 160 B76 G84
Curriculum: AP, IBDP, SAT
Language instr: English

International School of Poznan
Ul Taczanowskiego 18, 60-147 Poznan, Greater Poland
Tel: +48 61 646 37 60
Curriculum: IBDP, IBPYP
Language instr: English

Kolegium Europejskie
ul. Slusarska 9, 30-710 Kraków, Lesser Poland
Tel: +48 73 388 31 21
Age range: 12–18 years
No. of pupils: 300
Curriculum: IBDP, National
Language instr: English

LYCÉE FRANÇAIS DE VARSOVIE (FRENCH SCHOOL IN WARSAW)
For further details see p. 163
Ul Walecznych 4/6, 03-916 Warsaw, Masovia
Tel: +48 22 616 54 00/01
Email: info@lfv.pl
Website: www.lfv.pl
Head of School: Anne Lesage
Age range: 2–18 years
No. of pupils: 700
Fees: FB €7,700–€10,500
Curriculum: FrenchBacc
Language instr: French

Monnet International School
ul. Abramowskiego 4, 02-659 Warsaw, Masovia
Tel: +48 22 852 31 10
No. of pupils: 67
Curriculum: IBDP, IBMYP, IBPYP
Language instr: English

Open Future International School
ul. Kwiecista 25, 30-389 Kraków, Lesser Poland
Tel: +48 123 524 525
Curriculum: IBDP, IBMYP, IBPYP
Language instr: English, Polish

Paderewski Private Grammar School
ul Symfoniczna 1, 20-853 Lublin
Tel: +48 81 740 7543
Age range: 13–19
No. of pupils: 220
Curriculum: IBDP, IBMYP, IBPYP, ALevs
Language instr: English

Polish British Academy of Warsaw
ul. Wiertnicza 75, ul. Wiertnicza 43, 02-952 Warsaw, Masovia
Tel: +48 501 115 114
Curriculum: UK

Poznan British International School
ul Darzyborska 1a, 61-303 Poznan, Greater Poland
Tel: +48 61 870 97 30
Age range: 2–15
Curriculum: IPC, National

Private High School Gaudium et Studium
ul. st. Michala 50 M, 61-118 Poznan
Tel: +48 60 892 1887
Curriculum: IBDP
Language instr: English, Polish

Private Primary School 97
Abramowskiego Street 4, 02-659 Warsaw, Masovia
Tel: +48 22 853 36 60
Curriculum: IBPYP
Language instr: English

Prywatne Liceum Ogolnoksztalcace im.M.Wankowicza
ul. Witosa 18, 40-832 Katowice, Silesia
Tel: +48 32 254 9194
Age range: 15–19
Curriculum: IBDP, National
Language instr: Polish, English

Sokrates International High School
St. Torunska 55-57, 85-023 Bydgoszcz, Kuyavia-Pomerania
Tel: +48 51 984 1530
Curriculum: IBDP
Language instr: English, Polish

Europe

Szczecin International School
ul Starzynskiego 3-4, 70-506
Szczecin, West Pomerania
Tel: +48 91 4240 300
Curriculum: IBDP, IBMYP, IBPYP
Language instr: English

Szczecinska Szkola Witruwianska SVS
Wojska Polskiego, 164, 71-335
Szczecin, West Pomerania
Tel: +48 512 868 176
Curriculum: IBPYP
Language instr: English, Polish

Szkola Europejska - Gimnazjum / Liceum
ul Tuszynska 31, 93-020 Lódz
Tel: +48 42 682 3696
Language instr: English

THAMES BRITISH SCHOOL MOKOTÓW HIGH SCHOOL CAMPUS
For further details see p. 203
ul. Domaniewska 50, 02-672 Warsaw, Masovia
Tel: +48 57 727 0477
Email: mokotowhigh@thamesbritishschool.pl
Website: thamesbritishschool.pl/campus/mokotow-high-school-campus
Head of School (Mokotów High School Campus): Izabela Ryzak
Age range: 15–19 years
Fees: 48,500–98,000
Curriculum: IBDP, UK, IGCSE, ALevs
Language instr: English

THAMES BRITISH SCHOOL MOKOTÓW PRIMARY CAMPUS
For further details see p. 204
ul. Józefa i Jana Rostafinskich 1, 02-593 Warsaw, Masovia
Tel: +48 53 091 7566
Email: mokotowprimary@thamesbritishschool.pl
Website: thamesbritishschool.pl/campus/mokotow-primary-campus
Acting Head of School / Mokotów Primary National Head: Katarzyna Kurzac
Age range: 3–11 years
Fees: 48,500–98,000
Curriculum: UK
Language instr: English

THAMES BRITISH SCHOOL OCHOTA CAMPUS
For further details see p. 205
ul. Wawelska 66/74, 02-034 Warsaw, Masovia
Tel: +48 22 822 15 75
Email: ochota@thamesbritishschool.pl
Website: thamesbritishschool.pl/campus/ochota-campus
Head of School (Ochota Campus): Christian Rosser
Age range: 5–11 years
Fees: 48,500–98,000
Curriculum: UK
Language instr: English

THAMES BRITISH SCHOOL WLOCHY CAMPUS
For further details see p. 206
ul. Gladka 31, 02-172 Warsaw, Masovia
Tel: +48 510 161 597
Email: wlochy@thamesbritishschool.pl
Website: thamesbritishschool.pl/campus/wlochy-campus
Head of School (Wlochy Campus): Katarzyna Wisniewska
Age range: 2.5–14 years
Fees: 48,500–98,000
Curriculum: UK
Language instr: English

THE BRITISH SCHOOL WARSAW
For further details see p. 210
Limanowskiego 15, 02-943 Warsaw, Masovia
Tel: +48 22 842 32 81
Email: admissions@thebritishschool.pl
Website: www.thebritishschool.pl
Principal: John Brett
Age range: 2.5–18 years
Curriculum: IBDP, IPC, UK, IGCSE
Language instr: English
(COB) (ECIS)

The Canadian School of Warsaw
Kanadyjska Szkola Podstawowa, Ul. Belska 7, 02-638 Warsaw, Masovia
Tel: +48 22 646 92 89
Curriculum: IBPYP
Language instr: English

The Nazareth Middle and High School in Warsaw
ul. Czerniakowska 137, 00-720 Warsaw, Masovia
Tel: +48 22 841 3854/+48 601 644 102
Age range: G13–19
Curriculum: IBDP
Language instr: English, Polish

Towarzystwo Edukacyjne Vizja
Okopowa 59, 01-043 Warsaw, Masovia
Tel: +48 57 775 5001
Curriculum: IBDP
Language instr: English, Polish

VIII Prywatne Akademickie Liceum Ogólnoksztalcace
ul Karmelicka 45, 31-128 Krakow
Tel: +48 12 632 93 13
Age range: 6–18 years
No. of pupils: 830
Curriculum: IBDP, National
Language instr: English

Warsaw Montessori High School
ul. Pytlasinskiego 13a, 00-777 Warsaw, Masovia
Tel: +48 787 095 835
Curriculum: IBDP
Language instr: English, Polish

Wroclaw International School
ul. Raclawicka 101, 53-149 Wroclaw, Lower Silesia
Tel: +48 71 782 26 24
Curriculum: IBMYP, IBPYP
Language instr: English

Zespól Szkól Ogólnoksztalcacych im. Pawla z Tarsu
ul Poezji 19, 04-994 Warsaw, Masovia
Tel: +48 22 789 14 02
No. of pupils: 75
Curriculum: IBDP
Language instr: English

PORTUGAL

Carlucci American International School of Lisbon
Rua Antonio dos Reis, 95, 2710-301 Linhó, Lisbon
Tel: +351 219 239 800
Age range: 3–18
No. of pupils: 600
Curriculum: IBDP, SAT, USA
Language instr: English

CLIB - The Braga International School
Rua da Igreja Velha – Gualtar, 4710-069 Braga
Tel: +351 253 679 860
Age range: 3–18
No. of pupils: 249 B124 G125
(ECIS)

CLIP - Oporto International School
Rua de Vila Nova 1071, 4100-506 Porto
Tel: +351 226 199 160
Age range: 5–18
No. of pupils: 497 B282 G215
(CIS) (ECIS)

Colégio Atlântico
Av. da Ponte It 356/A, Pinhal de Frades, 2840-167 Seixal, Lisbon
Tel: +351 212 247 828
Curriculum: IBDP
Language instr: English, Portuguese

Colégio Internacional de Vilamoura (Vilamoura International School)
Sitio das Quintinhas, 8125-406 Vilamoura, Faro
Tel: +351 289 303 280
Age range: 3–18 years
No. of pupils: 770
Curriculum: IBDP, National, UK
Language instr: English, Portuguese

Colégio Luso-Internacional do Centro
Rua D João Pereira Venâncio, 2430-291 Marinha Grande, Leiria
Tel: +351 244 503 710
Age range: 3–18
Curriculum: UK
Language instr: English, Portuguese

Colégio Mira Rio
Estrada de Telheiras 113, 1600-768 Lisbon
Tel: +351 213 030 480
Curriculum: IBDP
Language instr: English, Portuguese

Colegio Planalto
Rua Armindo Rodrigues 28, 1600-414 Lisbon
Tel: +351 217 541 530
No. of pupils: 550
Curriculum: IBDP, National
Language instr: English

Colégio Santiago Internacional
Praça Zacarias Guerreiro 29, 8800-391 Tavira, Faro
Tel: +351 281 328 677
Age range: 4–18
Curriculum: IGCSE

Escola da APEL
Caminho dos Saltos 6 ou Rua do Til 69, 9050-219 Funchal, Madeira
Tel: +351 291 740 470
Curriculum: IBDP
Language instr: English

Greene's College Oxford, Estoril
Rua D. Afonso Henriques no. 1614, 2765-576 Estoril, Lisbon
Tel: +351 211 165 450
Age range: 14–18
No. of pupils: VIth60
Curriculum: IGCSE, ALevs
Language instr: English

International Christian School of Cascais
Av. de Sintra 1154, 2755-322 Cascais, Lisbon
Tel: +351 214 842 279
Age range: 4–18
No. of pupils: B23 G22
Curriculum: SAT, USA
Language instr: English

International School of Palmela
Av. Vila Amélia, Lote 171-172, Cabanas, 2950-805 Quinta do Anjo, Setúbal
Tel: +351 966 216 593
Language instr: English, Portuguese
(ECIS)

International Sharing School - Madeira
Caminho dos Saltos 6, 9050-219 Funchal, Madeira
Tel: +351 291 773 218
Age range: 3–16 years
No. of pupils: 250
Curriculum: IBDP, IBMYP, IBPYP, National, UK
Language instr: English

Europe

International Sharing School - Taguspark
Avenida Dr. Mário Soares 14, 2740-119 Oeiras, Lisbon
Tel: +351 214 876 140
Age range: 1–18 years
No. of pupils: 700
Curriculum: IBDP, IBMYP, IBPYP
Language instr: English

IPS CASCAIS
For further details see p. 151
Rua da Lagoa 171, Bicesse, 2645-344 Alcabideche, Lisbon
Tel: +351 214 570 149
Email: info@ipsschool.org
Website: www.ipsschool.org
Head of School: Christopher Starling
Age range: 3–15 years (up to 18 in September 2028)
No. of pupils: 400
Fees: €10,623–€20,251
Curriculum: UK, IGCSE, ALevs
Language instr: English

KING'S COLLEGE SCHOOL, CASCAIS
For further details see p. 155
Rua Cesário Verde 395, Pampilheira, 2750-657 Cascais, Lisbon
Tel: +351 215 966 634
Email: cascais@kingscollegeschool.pt
Website: www.kingscollegeschool.pt
Head of School: Adrian Frost
Age range: 1–13 years (18 years from Sep. 2026)
No. of pupils: 720
Fees: Day €10,431–€16,590

L'École Trilingue
Avenida do Restelo 21, 1400-314 Lisbon
Tel: +351 910 335 102
Age range: 2–6 years
No. of pupils: 45
Curriculum: FrenchBacc
Language instr: English, French

Lisbon Montessori School
Rua de Santana 1696, Alto do Cobre, 2750-833 Cascais, Lisbon
Tel: +351 939 016 234
Age range: 2.5–12
Language instr: English

Lycée Français International de Porto
R. Gil Eanes 27, 4150-348 Porto
Tel: +351 226 153 030
Age range: 4–18
No. of pupils: 921
Curriculum: FrenchBacc

MONTALVO INTERNATIONAL SCHOOL
For further details see p. 166
Avenida Marçal Pacheco 37, Loulé, Algarve, Faro
Tel: +351 912 914 056
Email: admin@montalvoschools.com
Website: algarve.montalvoschools.com
Director: Walter Mendonça
Age range: 14–19 years
Fees: €13,255
Curriculum: IGCSE, ALevs

Nobel Algarve British International School - Almancil
Caminho das Pereiras, 8135-022 Almancil
Tel: +351 282 342 547
Age range: 3–16 years
No. of pupils: 400
Curriculum: UK, GCSE, IGCSE, ALevs
Language instr: English

NOBEL ALGARVE BRITISH INTERNATIONAL SCHOOL - LAGOA
For further details see p. 171
EN 125, Porches, 8400-400 Lagoa
Tel: +351 282 342 547
Email: admissions@nobelalgarve.com
Website: www.nobelalgarve.com
Head of School: Ian Walker
Age range: 3–18 years
No. of pupils: 1000
Fees: €6,060–€18,560
Curriculum: UK, GCSE, IGCSE, ALevs
Language instr: English

Oeiras International School
Rua Antero de Quental 7, 2730-013 Barcarena, Oeiras, Lisbon
Tel: +351 211 935 330
Age range: 6–19 years
No. of pupils: 460
Curriculum: IBDP, IBMYP, IBPYP
Language instr: English

Oporto British School
Rua da Cerca 338, Foz do Douro, 4150-201 Porto
Tel: +351 226 166 660
Age range: 3–18 years
No. of pupils: 550
Curriculum: IBDP, UK, IGCSE
Language instr: English
(CIS) (COB) (ECIS)

PARK INTERNATIONAL SCHOOL
For further details see p. 173
Estrada de Alfragide 94, 2610-015 Amadora, Lisbon
Tel: +351 215 807 000
Email: admissions@park-is.com
Website: www.park-is.com
Executive Head of School: Samantha Gonçalves
Age range: 1–18 years
No. of pupils: 1450
Fees: Day €7,680–€18,600 €800–€4,800
Curriculum: IBDP

PaRK International School - Cascais
Rua Cesário Verde 395, Pampilheira, 2750-657 Cascais, Lisbon
Tel: +351 214 831 211

PaRK International School - Praça de Espanha
Av. Columbano Bordalo Pinheiro 52, 1070-064 Lisbon
Tel: +351 215 855 000

PaRK International School - Restelo
Av. das Descobertas 21, 1400-091 Lisbon
Tel: +351 213 026 316
Curriculum: UK, IGCSE

PRIME SCHOOL ESTORIL
For further details see p. 174
Rua Antoine de Saint-Exupéry, Alapraia, 2765-043 Estoril, Lisbon
Tel: +351 21 923 54 96
Email: info@primeschool.pt
Website: primeschool.pt
Age range: 3–18 years
No. of pupils: 450
Fees: €15,500–€18,800
Curriculum: IGCSE, ALevs

Prime School Lisbon
Rua Carlos Lobo de Ávila,
Tel: +351 21 923 54 96
Age range: 3–18 years

Prime School São Pedro do Estoril
Av. Marginal 435, 02765-315 Estoril, Lisbon
Tel: +351 966 155 909

Prime School Sintra
Rua Mestre Neves 20, Portela de Sintra, 2710-422 Sintra, Lisbon
Tel: +351 21 923 54 96
Age range: 3–11 years
Curriculum: IGCSE

Queen Elizabeth's School
Rua Filipe Magalhaes 1, Alvalade, 1700-194 Lisboa
Tel: +351 21 841 0140
Age range: 3–10 years
Curriculum: UK

Saint Dominic's International School, Portugal
Rua Maria Brown, Outeiro de Polima, 2785-816 S Domingos de Rana, Lisbon
Tel: +351 21 444 0434
Age range: 3–18 years
No. of pupils: 700
Curriculum: IBDP, IBMYP, IBPYP
Language instr: English
(CIS) (ECIS)

St James' Primary School
Rua dos Depósitos de Água 339, 2750-561 Cascais Lisbon
Tel: +351 214 864 754
Age range: 6–10

St Julian's School
Quinta Nova, 2775-588 Carcavelos e Parede, Lisbon
Tel: +351 214 585 300
Age range: 3–18 years
No. of pupils: 1280
Curriculum: IBDP, National, SAT, UK
Language instr: English
(CIS) (COB) (ECIS)

ST. PETER'S INTERNATIONAL SCHOOL
For further details see p. 200
Quinta dos Barreleiros CCI 3952, Volta da Pedra, 2950-201 Palmela, Setúbal
Tel: +351 21 233 6990
Email: admissions@stpeters.pt
Website: www.st-peters-school.com
Head of School: Abigail Lewis
Age range: 4 months–18 years
No. of pupils: 1500
Fees: Day €6,303–€14,146 FB €17,792
Curriculum: IBDP
Language instr: English, Portuguese

TASIS Portugal
Estrada Nacional No. 9, Quinta da Beloura II, 2710-697 Sintra, Lisbon
Tel: +351 219 241 004
Age range: 3–18 years
Curriculum: IBDP, IGCSE
Language instr: English

The British School of Lisbon
Rua de S. Paulo 89, 1200-427 Lisbon
Tel: +351 211 511 942
Age range: 3–14 years
Curriculum: UK

Theodore International Startup Academy (TISA) Lisbon
R. São Sebastião da Pedreira 27, 1050-010 Lisbon
Tel: +351 913 516 545
Age range: 3–12 years

UNITED LISBON INTERNATIONAL SCHOOL
For further details see p. 214
Avenida Marechal Gomes da Costa 9, 1800-255 Lisbon
Tel: +351 211 161 110
Email: info@unitedlisbon.school
Website: www.unitedlisbon.school
Executive Director: Martin Harris
Age range: 3–18 years
No. of pupils: 600
Fees: €11,000–€24,000
Curriculum: IBDP, IPC
Language instr: English
(CIS)

Vale Verde International School
Apartado 125, 8601-927 Luz, Lagos, Faro
Tel: +351 282 697 205
Age range: 11–18
Curriculum: UK, IGCSE, ALevs
(ECIS)

ROMANIA

Acorns British Style Nursery
63 Popa Soare Street, Sector 2, 031122 Bucharest
Tel: +40 788 418 186
(COB)

Europe

American International School of Bucharest
Sos Pipera-Tunari 196, Voluntari,
Jud Ilfov, 077190 Bucharest
Tel: +40 (21) 204 4300
Age range: 2–19
No. of pupils: 830 B448 G382
Curriculum: IBDP, IBMYP, IBPYP, SAT
Language instr: English

British International School of Timisoara
8 Aurora Street, 300291 Timisoara
Tel: +40 726 241 438
Curriculum: IBDP
Language instr: English

British School of Bucharest
42 Erou Iancu Nicolae Street,
077190 Bucharest
Tel: +40 21 267 89 19
Age range: 2–18
No. of pupils: 500 B250 G250 VIth38
Curriculum: UK, GCSE, IGCSE, ALevs
Language instr: English

Bucharest - Beirut International School
Sos.Vergului, nr.14, District
2, 022448 Bucharest
Tel: +40 (0)744 309 199
Curriculum: IBDP, IBMYP, IBPYP
Language instr: English

Cambridge School of Bucharest
Strada Erou Iancu Nicolae Nr.
126 C, 077190 Voluntari, Ilfov
Tel: +40 21 210 2131
Age range: 2–19 years
No. of pupils: 700
Curriculum: IBDP, IGCSE
Language instr: English

Cambridge School of Constanta
No. 3 Capidava Street, Constanta
Tel: +40 241 647745
Age range: 4–18
No. of pupils: 250
Language instr: English

Centrul Gifted Education
Strada Berzei 22, Bucharest

Colegiul German Goethe
Strada Cihoschi nr. 17,
Sector 1, Bucharest
Tel: +40 21 211 34 25
Age range: 11–18
No. of pupils: 1450

Genesis College
Straulesti Street, 89A
District 1, Bucharest
Tel: +40 73 310 7914
Curriculum: IBDP, IBMYP, IBPYP
Language instr: English, Romanian

Gradinita BritAcademy Sector 2
Olimpiadei, nr.36, sect.2, Bucharest
Tel: +40 740329105
Curriculum: UK

Hermann Oberth International German School
34E Pipera Blvd, Voluntari, Ilfov
Tel: +4 021 231 20 45
Age range: 2–18 years
No. of pupils: 250
Curriculum: IBDP
Language instr: English, German

International British School of Bucharest
21-25 Agricultori St. District
2, 021481 Bucharest
Tel: +40 21 253 1698
Age range: 3–18
No. of pupils: 340 VIth45
Curriculum: UK, GCSE, IGCSE, ALevs
Language instr: English

International School of Bucharest
1R Gara Catelu Str., Sector
3, Bucharest 032991
Tel: +40 21 3069530
Age range: 2–18 years
No. of pupils: 650
Curriculum: IBDP, SAT, UK, IGCSE, ALevs
Language instr: English

King's Oak British International School
72 Petre Aurelian, Greenlake
Residences, Bucharest Sector 1
Tel: +40 21 380 3535
Age range: 1–13
No. of pupils: 139 B70 G69
Curriculum: National, UK
Language instr: English

Lauder Reut Education Complex
15 Iuliu Barasch st, District
3, 030791 Bucharest
Tel: +40 31 805 57 72
Age range: 4–18

Liceul Teoretic Scoala Europeana Bucuresti
33 Baiculesti st., 013913 Bucharest
Tel: +40 21 3117 770
Curriculum: IBDP
Language instr: English

Little London International Academy
Strada Erou Iancu Nicolae 65,
Pipera, 077190 Voluntari, Ilfov
Tel: +40 721 689 762
Curriculum: IBPYP
Language instr: English

Lycée Français Anna de Noailles
160A, Soseaua Bucuresti-Ploiesti,
Sector 1, 015016 Bucharest
Tel: +40 212 125 893
Age range: 4–18
No. of pupils: 934

Mark Twain International School
25 Erou Iancu Nicolae Street,
077190 Voluntari, Ilfov
Tel: +40 73 500 0160
Age range: 2–19 years
No. of pupils: 600
Curriculum: IBDP, IBMYP, IBPYP
Language instr: English, Romanian

Nikolaus-Lenau-Lyzeum Timisoara
Strada Gheorge Lazar nr.
2, 300078 Timisoara
Tel: +40 256 290987
Age range: 11–18
No. of pupils: 1300

Olga Gudynn Bilingual High School - Oxford Gardens
Bulevardul Pipera No.
141, Voluntari, Ilfov
Tel: +40 72 627 7487
Curriculum: IBDP, IBMYP
Language instr: English, Romanian

Olga Gudynn International School - Cotroceni
Str. Fagaras No. 6, Bucharest
Tel: +40 73 441 1332
Language instr: English, Romanian

Olga Gudynn International School - Floreasca
Str. Ancuta Baneasa No. 8, Bucharest
Tel: +40 73 441 1359
Language instr: English, Romanian

Olga Gudynn International School - Pipera
Str. Erou Iancu Nicolae No.
82-84, Voluntari, Ilfov
Tel: +40 31 717 2724
Language instr: English, Romanian

Paradis International School
Str. Iancu Flondor, Nr. 2 M, Lasi
Tel: +40 722133091
Curriculum: UK

Pick Me Academy
Nr. 9, Dragos Voda Street district 2,
Tel: +40 726 000 640
Curriculum: UK

Royal School in Transylvania
44-46 Henri Barbusse
Street, Cluj-Napoca
Tel: +40 770 103 108
Curriculum: IGCSE, ALevs

Seven Hills International School
Str. Palas nr 5B, United Business
Centre 2, Etaj 3, 700051 Iasi
Tel: +40 770 687 719

Transylvania College
Aleea Baisoara 2A,
400445 Cluj-Napoca
Tel: +40 (0) 264 418 990
Age range: 2–18
Curriculum: UK, IGCSE, ALevs
Language instr: English, Romanian

Verita International School
Soldat Gheorghe Pripu Street
22A, 1st District, Bucharest
Tel: +40 21 311 8811
Curriculum: IBDP
Language instr: English

RUSSIAN FEDERATION

Alabuga International School
Nord Drive, Building 1,
Yelabuga, Tatarstan 423600
Tel: +7 855 575 3405
Curriculum: IBMYP, IBPYP
Language instr: English, Russian

British School St Petersburg
Zhdanovskaya Ulitsa, 45,
St. Petersburg 197110
Tel: +7 812 46 777 46
Curriculum: UK

Brookes Moscow
Lazorevyy Proezd, 7, Moscow 129323
Tel: +7 (499) 110 70 01
Age range: 2–18 years
No. of pupils: 550
Curriculum: IBDP, IBMYP, IBPYP
Language instr: English

Brookes Saint Petersburg
Tatarskiy Pereulok, 3-5, Saint
Petersburg 197198
Tel: +7 (812) 320 89 25
Age range: 3–18 years
No. of pupils: 120

CET International Primary School
Vodoprovodnaya 2, Tyumen 625002
Tel: +7 3452 63 10 55
Age range: 3–11
Curriculum: IPC, UK
Language instr: English

CIS Russia - Festivalnaya Campus
Festivalnaya Street, 7A, 125565
Tel: +7 (903) 281 2720
Age range: 3–13
Curriculum: UK
Language instr: English

CIS Russia - Skolkovo Senior Campus
Odintsovo District, Zarechye,,
Berezovaya Str., 1A, Moscow 143085
Tel: +7 903 726 2811
Curriculum: IGCSE, ALevs
Language instr: English, Russian

Europe

CIS Russia - St Petersburg Campus
Ulitsa Mebelnaya 11A, St. Petersburg 197345
Tel: +7 812 604 33 22
Age range: 3–18
No. of pupils: 175
Language instr: English

Deutsche Schule Moskau
Prospekt Wernadskogo 103/5, Moscow 119526
Tel: +7 495 434 31 25

'Education through Dialogue' School
Nekrasova Street, 19, St. Petersburg 191014
Tel: +7 812 272 0360
Language instr: English

European Gymnasium
Sokolnichesky Val., d.28, Sokolniki, Moscow 107113
Tel: +7 985 795 4273
Age range: 4–18
Curriculum: IBDP, IBMYP, IBPYP
Language instr: Russian, English

International School in Novie Veshki
p. Veshki, residential complex Novie Veshki, Green Boulevard, VL.86, Mytishchi district, Moscow 141031
Tel: +7 499 707 8899
Curriculum: IBPYP
Language instr: English

International School of Herzen University
Vosstania str., 8 B, St. Petersburg
Tel: +7 812 275 7684
Age range: 6–18
No. of pupils: 115
Curriculum: IBDP, IBMYP
Language instr: English, Russian

International School of Kazan
5 Mavlyutova St., Kazan
Tel: +7 843 204 12 82
Curriculum: IBDP, IBMYP, IBPYP
Language instr: English, Russian
(CIS)

International School of Samara
ul. Kyibysheva, Building 32, Samara 443099
Tel: +7 846 332 2880
Curriculum: IBPYP
Language instr: English, French, Russian

Istochnik International School
62 Tsentralnaya St., Leninsky Village of Ulyanovsk 432067
Tel: +7 8422 260417

Kaluga International School
Lunacharskogo 16, Kaluga
Tel: +7 4843 400444
Age range: 3–15
No. of pupils: 50
Curriculum: IBPYP
Language instr: English

Khoroshevskaya Shkola
45 Marshala Tukhachevskogo St., appt. 2, Moscow 123154
Tel: +7 (499) 401 02 71
Curriculum: IBDP
Language instr: English, Russian

Letovo School
35 Valovaya str., Moscow
Tel: +7 8 800 100 51 15
Curriculum: IBDP, IBMYP
Language instr: English, Russian

Lycée Français de Moscou Alexandre-Dumas
7A Milioutinsky per, Moscow 101000
Tel: +7 495 514 15 46
Curriculum: FrenchBacc

Lyceum-Boarding School No. 2 - Municipal Autonomous Educational Institution
11 Shamil Usmanov Street, Kazan 420095
Tel: +7 8435 543234
Language instr: English, Russian

Moscow Economic School, Odintsovo Branch
1-A, Zaitsevo Village, Odintsovo Region, Moscow Oblast 143020
Tel: +7 495 780 5230
Age range: 3–16 years
No. of pupils: 620
Curriculum: IBDP, IBMYP, IBPYP
Language instr: Russian, English
(ECIS)

Moscow Economic School, Presnya Campus
29 Zamorenova Street, Moscow 123022
Tel: +7 499 255 55 66
Age range: 3–18
No. of pupils: B324 G293 VIth29
Curriculum: IBDP, IBMYP, IBPYP
Language instr: English, Russian
(CEE) (CIS) (ECIS)

Moscow International Gymnasia
111123 3rd Vladimirskaya Str, House 5, Moscow
Tel: +7 (095) 304 3794
Age range: 6–10
No. of pupils: 65 B30 G35

President School
Ilyinsky Pod, 2, bld. 1 (in the village of ParkVille Zhukovka), Zhukovka village, Odintsovo district, Moscow Region 143082
Tel: +7 495 955 0000
Age range: 4–18
No. of pupils: 442
Curriculum: IBDP
Language instr: Russian, English

Private Lomonosov School Nizhny Novgorod
Gogol Street, 62, Nizhny Novgorod 603109
Tel: +7 831 430 08 63
Curriculum: IBDP, IBMYP, IBPYP
Language instr: Russian

Russian International School
Domodedevo, Moscow Oblast, Moscow
Tel: +7 (495) 974 04 55
Age range: 5–18
No. of pupils: 300
Curriculum: National

The Anglo-American School of Moscow
1 Beregovaya Street, Moscow 125367
Tel: +7 (495) 231 44 88
Age range: 5–18
No. of pupils: 1111 B595 G580
Curriculum: ACT, AP, IBDP, IBPYP, SAT
Language instr: English
(CEE) (CIS) (ECIS)

The British International School, Moscow
Novoyasenevsky prospekt 19/5, Moscow 117593
Tel: +7 495 425 51 00
Age range: 3–18
No. of pupils: 1200 B650 G550
Curriculum: IBDP, National, UK, ALevs
Language instr: English
(CIS) (COB) (ECIS)

The English International School Moscow
Zeleny prospect 66-a, Moscow 111396
Tel: +7 495 301 2104
Age range: 3–18
Curriculum: UK, IGCSE, ALevs
(COB)

The International Gymnasium of the Skolkovo Innovation Center
Skolkovo Innovation Center, Zvorykin Street 7, Moscow 143026
Tel: +7 (495) 956 00 33
Curriculum: IBDP, IBMYP, IBPYP
Language instr: English

The International School of Moscow
Buildings 5 & 6, Krylatskaya Street 12, Krylatskoe, Moscow 121552
Tel: +7 499 922 4400
Age range: 2–13
No. of pupils: 890 B437 G453
Curriculum: UK, IGCSE, ALevs
Language instr: English
(COB)

Vnukovo International School
Pervomaiskoe, Rogozinino Lugovaya Street 20b, Moscow 108808
Tel: +7 (495) 431 70 70
Curriculum: IBDP
Language instr: Russian

W.I.D.E. School
11a Rimskogo-Korsakova Street, Moscow 127566
Tel: +7 495 999 06 80
Age range: 2–18 years
Curriculum: IBDP
Language instr: English, Russian

XXI Century Integration International Secondary School
16 Marshala Katukova St., Building 3, Moscow 123592
Tel: +7 495 750 3102
Age range: 5–18 years
No. of pupils: 180
Curriculum: IBDP, IBMYP, IBPYP
Language instr: English, Russian

SERBIA

British International School Belgrade
Radoja Dakica 44, 11000 Belgrade
Tel: +381 113 066 096
Age range: 4–18
No. of pupils: 230
(COB) (ECIS)

Chartwell International School
Teodora Drajzera 38, 11000 Belgrade
Tel: +381 113 675 340
Age range: 2–14
(COB)

Crnjanski High School
Djordja Ognjanovica 2, 11030 Belgrade
Tel: +381 112 398 388
Age range: 14–19
Curriculum: IBDP, IGCSE
Language instr: English

International School
45 Sumatovacka Street, Belgrade
Tel: +381 (0)11 4011 220
Age range: 11–19 years
No. of pupils: 250
Curriculum: IBDP
Language instr: English

International School of Belgrade
Temisvarska 19, 11040 Belgrade
Tel: +381 112 069 999
Age range: 4–18
No. of pupils: 364
Curriculum: IBDP, IBMYP, IBPYP, SAT
Language instr: English
(CEE) (CIS) (ECIS)

PRIMA International School
Dragana Mancea Street, Senjak, Belgrade
Tel: +381 113 690 825
Curriculum: UK, IGCSE, ALevs
(COB)

Ruder Bo kovic
Kneza Vi eslava 17, 11000 Belgrade
Tel: +381 113 540 786
Curriculum: IBDP, IBMYP, IBPYP, IGCSE
Language instr: English

Europe

SLOVAKIA

Cambridge International School Bratislava
Úprkova 3, Bratislava 81104
Tel: +421 2 207 206 79
Age range: 2–18
No. of pupils: 450
Curriculum: UK, IGCSE, ALevs
Language instr: English

English International School of Bratislava (EISB)
Radničné námestie 4,
821 05 Bratislava
Tel: +421 91 5832076
Age range: 3–18 years
Curriculum: IBDP, IBMYP, IBPYP
Language instr: English, Slovak

Košice International School (KEIS)
Polná 1, 040 14 Košice
Tel: +421 90 7976444
Curriculum: IBPYP
Language instr: English, Slovak

LEAF Academy (Akadémia LEAF)
Sasinkova 13, 811 08 Bratislava
DIC: 2120216010
Tel: +421 949 443 573
Age range: 14–19 years
No. of pupils: 130
Language instr: English

QSI International School of Bratislava
Záhradnicka 1006/2, Samorin 93101
Tel: +421 903 704 436
Age range: 3–18 years
No. of pupils: 233
Curriculum: AP, IBDP, SAT, USA
Language instr: English

Súkromná spojená skola
Starozagorská 8, 040 23 Košice
Curriculum: IBPYP
Language instr: English, Slovak

Súkromné Bilingválne Gymnázium Ceská
Ceská 10, 831 03 Bratislava
Tel: +421 2 44450733
Curriculum: IBDP
Language instr: English, Slovak

The British International School, Bratislava
J. Valačana Dolinského 1
(Pekníkova 6), Bratislava 841 02
Tel: +421 2 6930 7081
Age range: 2–18
Curriculum: IBDP, UK, ALevs
Language instr: English
(COB)

SLOVENIA

British International School of Ljubljana
Podmilscakova ulica 18, 1000 Ljubljana
Tel: +386 40 486 548
Age range: 3–18
No. of pupils: 70 B36 G34
Curriculum: IPC, SAT, UK, IGCSE, ALevs
Language instr: English
(COB)

ERUDIO International School
Litostrojska cesta 40, 1000 Ljubljana
Tel: +386 15 142 808
Age range: 14–19 years
Curriculum: IBDP, IBMYP
Language instr: English, Slovene

Gimnazija Bezigrad
Periceva 4, 1000 Ljubljana
Tel: +386 13 000 400
Age range: 14–19
No. of pupils: 74
Curriculum: IBDP, IBMYP, National
Language instr: English
(ECIS)

Ljubljana International School
Campus S20, Selanova ulica 20, 1000 Ljubljana
Tel: +386 12 007 870
Age range: 4–18 years
Curriculum: IBPYP, USA
Language instr: English

QSI International School of Ljubljana
Dolgi most 6A, 1000 Ljubljana
Tel: +386 1 244 1750
Age range: 3–17
No. of pupils: 108
Curriculum: AP, SAT, USA

Vector International Academy
Stula 23, 1000 Ljubljana
Tel: +386 40 862 445
Curriculum: IBDP
Language instr: English, French

SPAIN

AGORA BARCELONA INTERNATIONAL SCHOOL
For further details see p. 93
Carrer Puig de Mira, Sant Esteve Sesrovires, 08635
Barcelona, Catalonia
Tel: +34 93 779 89 28
Email: admissions@agoraisbarcelona.edu.es
Website: www.agorabarcelona.com
Headmaster: Marc Andreu
No. of pupils: 500
Curriculum: IBDP
Language instr: English, Spanish, Catalan, French/German
(ISA)

AGORA GRANADA COLLEGE INTERNATIONAL SCHOOL
For further details see p. 94
Urbanización Llanos de Silva, 18230 Atarfe, Granada, Andalusia
Tel: +34 958 499 009
Email: admissions@granadacollege.es
Website: www.agoragranadacollege.com
Head of School: Javier Jiménez Ortiz
Age range: 0–18 years
No. of pupils: 1050
Curriculum: IBDP, IBPYP
Language instr: English, Spanish

AGORA LLEDÓ INTERNATIONAL SCHOOL
For further details see p. 95
Camino Caminàs, 175, Castelló de la Plana, 12003 Castelló, Valencia
Tel: +34 964 72 31 70
Email: admissions@lledo.edu.es
Website: www.agoralledo.com
Headmaster: Luis Madrid
No. of pupils: 850
Curriculum: IBDP, IBMYP, IBPYP
Language instr: English, Spanish
(ISA)

AGORA MADRID INTERNATIONAL SCHOOL
For further details see p. 96
Calle Duero, 35, Villaviciosa de Odón, 28670 Madrid
Tel: +34 91 616 71 25
Email: admissions@agoraism.com
Website: www.agoramadrid.com
Headmaster: Daniel García
No. of pupils: 600
Curriculum: IBDP
Language instr: English, Spanish

Agora Patufet Infant School
C/ Sant Jordi 22, Sant Cugat del Vallés, 08172 Barcelona, Catalonia
Tel: +34 93 674 12 39
Age range: 0–6 years

AGORA PORTALS INTERNATIONAL SCHOOL
For further details see p. 97
Carretera Vella Palma-Andratx, s/n, Portals Nous, 07181 Mallorca, Balearic Islands
Tel: +34 964 72 31 70
Email: admissions@agoraportals.edu.es
Website: www.agoraportals.com
Headmaster: Rafael Barea
No. of pupils: 1000
Curriculum: IBDP, IBPYP
Language instr: English, Spanish

AGORA PRINCESS MARGARET INTERNATIONAL SCHOOL
For further details see p. 98
Passeig de la Fond d'en Fargas 15-17, 8032 Barcelona, Catalonia
Tel: +34 934 290 313
Email: admissions@agoraprincessmargaret.com
Website: www.agoraprincessmargaret.com
Headmaster: Alex Cerdá
Age range: 3–15 years
No. of pupils: 300
Curriculum: IBMYP, IBPYP
Language instr: English, Spanish

AGORA SANT CUGAT INTERNATIONAL SCHOOL
For further details see p. 99
Carrer Ferrer i Guàrdia, s/n, Sant Cugat del Vallès, 08174 Barcelona, Catalonia
Tel: +34 93 590 26 00
Email: ruth.sale@agorasantcugat.edu.es
Website: www.agorasantcugat.com
Headmaster: Jordi Ros
Age range: 1–18 years
No. of pupils: 1800
Curriculum: IBDP, IBMYP, IBPYP, National
Language instr: English, Spanish, Catalan
(ISA)

Almunecar International School
Calle Pinariego, Los Pinos, 18690 Almuñecar, Granada, Andalusia
Tel: +34 9586 35911
Age range: 3–18
No. of pupils: 280
Curriculum: UK, IGCSE

Aloha College Marbella
Urbanización el Angel, 29660 Marbella, Málaga, Andalusia
Tel: +34 95 281 41 33
Age range: 3–18
No. of pupils: 800
Curriculum: IBDP, SAT, UK, IGCSE, ALevs
Language instr: English, Spanish
(COB) (ECIS)

American School of Barcelona
Calle Balmes 7, Esplugues de Llobregat, 08950 Barcelona, Catalonia
Tel: +34 93 371 4016
Age range: 3–18
No. of pupils: 850
Curriculum: IBDP, National, SAT
Language instr: English
(ECIS)

American School of Bilbao
Soparda Bidea 10, 48640 Berango, Biscay, Basque Country
Tel: +34 94 668 0860
Age range: 2–18
No. of pupils: 375 B185 G190 VIth35
Curriculum: IBDP, IBMYP, IBPYP, IGCSE
Language instr: English
(CIS) (ECIS)

Europe

American School of Las Palmas
Carretera de los Hoyos, Km 1.7, 35017 Las Palmas de Gran Canaria, Las Palmas, Can+
Tel: +34 928 430 023
Age range: 3–18
Curriculum: AP, USA

American School of Madrid
Apartado 80, 28080 Madrid
Tel: +34 91 740 19 00
Age range: 3–18
No. of pupils: 900
Curriculum: IBDP, SAT, USA
Language instr: English
(ECIS)

American School of Valencia
Urbanización Los Monasterios, Apartado de Correos 9, 46530 Puzol, Valencia
Tel: +34 96 140 5412
Age range: 2–18
No. of pupils: 792 VIth104
Curriculum: ACT, IBDP, National, SAT, USA
Language instr: English, Spanish, Valencia
(ECIS)

Angel de la Guarda
Calle Andalucía 17-20, 03016 Alicante, Valencia
Tel: +34 9652 61899
Curriculum: IBDP
Language instr: English, Spanish

Aquinas American School
Calle Transversal Cuatro, 4, Urbanización Monte Alina, Pozuelo de Alarcon, 28223 Madrid
Tel: +34 91 352 31 20
Age range: 3–18
No. of pupils: 650
Curriculum: AP, IBDP, SAT, USA
Language instr: English

Areteia School
C/ Salvia 24 Urb. La Moraleja, 28109 Alcobendas, Madrid
Tel: +34 91 650 74 08
Age range: 3–20

Atlas American School of Málaga
Calle Monda No. 2, Selwo Hills, 29689 Estepona, Málaga, Andalusia
Tel: +34 952 938 155
Curriculum: IBDP
Language instr: English, Spanish

Aula Escola Europea
Avinguda Mare de, Déu de Lorda, 34-36, 08034 Barcelona, Catalonia
Tel: +34 93 203 03 54
No. of pupils: 1250
Curriculum: IBDP
Language instr: Catalan

Baleares International College, Mallorca, Sa Porrassa
Crta. Cala Figuera, 3A, Sa Porassa, 07181 Calvia, Balearic Islands
Tel: +34 971 133167
Age range: 3–18
No. of pupils: 230
Curriculum: AP, SAT, TOEFL, ALevs
(COB)

Baleares International College, Mallorca, San Augustin Campus
Calle de Marià Villangómez, 17, Palma De Mallorca, 07015 Sant Agusti, Balearic Islands
Tel: +34 9 7140 3161
Curriculum: UK
(COB)

Bell-lloc Del Pla
Carrer de Can Pau Birol, 2, 17005 Girona, Catalonia
Tel: +34 972 232 111
Curriculum: IBDP
Language instr: Spanish

Bellver International College
Calle Jose Costa Ferrer No 5, Palma de Mallorca, 07015 Marivent, Balearic Islands
Tel: +34 971 401679
Age range: 3–18
No. of pupils: 300 B153 G147
Curriculum: UK, IGCSE, ALevs
Language instr: English

Benjamin Franklin International School
Martorell i Pena 9, 08017 Barcelona, Catalonia
Tel: +34 93 434 2380
Age range: 3–18
Curriculum: ACT, IBDP, National, SAT, TOEFL, USA
Language instr: English
(ECIS)

Brains International School, Conde de Orgaz
Calle Frascuelo 2, 28043 Madrid
Tel: +34 913 889 355
Curriculum: IBPYP
Language instr: English, Spanish

Brains International School, La Moraleja
Calle Salvia No. 48, 28109 Alcobendas, Madrid
Tel: +34 916 504 300
Curriculum: IBDP, IBPYP
Language instr: English

Brains International School, Las Palmas
Paseo Tomás Morales 111, 35004 Las Palmas, Canary Islands
Tel: +34 928 296 444

Brains International School, Telde
Camino Angostura 2, 35213 La Pardilla, Las Palmas, Canary Islands
Tel: +34 928 506 114

Brewster Madrid
Calle Eloy Gonzalo, 3-5Chamberí, 28010 Madrid
Tel: +34 663 319 387
Curriculum: IBDP
Language instr: English, Spanish

British College La Cañada
Calle 299, No 25, La Canada, Paterna, 46182 Valencia
Tel: +34 96 132 40 40
Age range: 3–18
No. of pupils: 50

British College of Gavà
Carrer de Josep Lluís Sert 32, 08850 Gavà, Barcelona, Catalonia
Tel: +34 932 777 899
Age range: 3–18 years
Curriculum: IBDP, IBCP
Language instr: English, Spanish

British Council School
Calle Solano,5-7, Pozuelo de Alarcón, 28223 Madrid
Tel: +34 91 337 3612
Age range: 2–18 years
No. of pupils: 1955 B969 G986 VIth225
Curriculum: National, SAT, UK, IGCSE
Language instr: English, Spanish
(ECIS)

British School Alzira
Ctra. Alzira a Tavernes km. 11, La Barraca de Aguas Vivas, 46792 Valencia
Tel: +34 902 123 883
Age range: 1–18
Curriculum: UK

British School of Córdoba
Calle México 4, 14012 Córdoba, Andalusia
Tel: +34 957 767 048
Age range: 3–18 years
Curriculum: IBDP, UK
Language instr: English, Spanish

British School of Gran Canaria
Apartado 11, Tafira Alta, 35017 Las Palmas de Gran Canaria, Las Palmas, Can+
Tel: +34 9 28 351167
Age range: 3–18
No. of pupils: 569
Curriculum: UK, ALevs
Language instr: English
(COB)

British School of Lanzarote
Calle, 1 Juan Echevarria 10, 35509 Tahiche, Lanzarote, Canary Islands
Tel: +34 928 810085
Age range: 4–16
No. of pupils: 200 B100 G100

British School of Málaga
Avenida Centaurea 8, Cerrado de Calderón 29018, Málaga, Andalusia
Tel: +34 952 290 149
Age range: 3–18
No. of pupils: 675
Curriculum: National, IGCSE, ALevs
Language instr: English

British School of Tenerife
Ctra. de La Luz, s/n, 38300 La Orotava, Tenerife, Canary Islands
Tel: +34 922 33 69 29

British School of Valencia
Calle Filipinas 37, 46006 Valencia
Tel: +34 963 742 930
Age range: 2–18 years
Curriculum: UK, IGCSE, ALevs
Language instr: English

C.E. Punta Galea
Urbanización Punta Galea Playa del Sardinero, 1, 28290 Las Rozas, Madrid
Tel: +34 91 630 26 41
Curriculum: IBDP
Language instr: Spanish

Calpe School
Los Eucaliptos 60, Urbanazacion Linda Vista Baja, San Pedro de Alcantara, 29670 Málaga, Andalusia
Tel: +34 952 786 029
Age range: 2–11
No. of pupils: 100
Curriculum: SAT, UK

CAMBRIDGE HOUSE BRITISH INTERNATIONAL SCHOOL
For further details see p. 105
Calle Profesorado Espanol 1, Santa Barbara, 46111 Rocafort, Valencia
Tel: +34 96 390 5019
Email: info@cambridgehouse.es
Website: www.cambridgehouse.es
Executive Head: Harry Ainscough
No. of pupils: 1700
Curriculum: National, UK
Language instr: English, Spanish

Campus Politécnico Aceimar
Av. da Ponte 80, Cabral, 36318 Vigo, Pontevedra, Galicia
Tel: +34 986 251 511
Language instr: Spanish

Canterbury School
San Lorenzo Campus, 35018 San Lorenzo, Las Palmas, Canary Islands
Tel: +34 828 11 34 00
Age range: 18 months–18 years
Curriculum: IBDP, UK, IGCSE
Language instr: English, Spanish

Casvi International American School
C/ Gavilán, 2, Tres Cantos, 28760 Madrid
Tel: +34 91 804 02 12
Age range: 0–18 years
No. of pupils: 380
Curriculum: IBDP, IBMYP, IBPYP
Language instr: English

Caxton College
C/ Mas de León, 5, 46530 Puzol, Valencia
Tel: +34 96 142 4500
Age range: 1–18 years
No. of pupils: 1595
Curriculum: UK, IGCSE, ALevs
Language instr: English

Europe

Centro de Estudios Ibn Gabirol Colegio Estrella Toledano
Paseo de Alcobendas 7 (La Moraleja), 28109 Alcobendas, Madrid
Tel: +34 916 50 12 29
Curriculum: IBDP
Language instr: English

Centro Educativo Agave
Camino de la Gloria no 17, 04230 Huercal de Almería, Almería, Andalusia
Tel: +34 9503 01026
Curriculum: IBDP
Language instr: English

Chester College International School
Travesía de Montouto 2, 15894 Santiago de Compostela, A Coruña, Galicia
Tel: +34 981 819 160
Curriculum: USA
Language instr: English, Spanish

Colegio Adharaz
Urb. La Vina. C/ Garnacha 1, 41807 Espartinas, Seville, Andalusia
Tel: +34 955 713 820
Curriculum: IBMYP, IBPYP
Language instr: English, Spanish

Colegio Alameda de Osuna
Paseo de la Alameda de Osuna, 60, 28042 Madrid
Tel: +34 91 742 70 11
Curriculum: IBDP, IBMYP, IBPYP
Language instr: English, Spanish

Colegio Alauda
Cerillo 6, 14014 Córdoba, Andalusia
Tel: +34 957 40 55 07
Curriculum: IBDP
Language instr: English

Colegio Alegra
Calle de Sorolla 4, 28222 Majadahonda, Madrid
Tel: +34 916 39 79 03
Curriculum: IBDP, IBMYP
Language instr: English, Spanish

Colegio Alemán Alberto Durero de Sevilla
Avda. Cueva de Altamira s/n, 41020 Seville, Andalusia
Tel: +34 954 999 509
Curriculum: UK

Colegio Altaduna
Ctra. de Alicún KM. 8, 04740 Roquetas de Mar, Almería, Andalusia
Tel: +34 950 559 500
Curriculum: IBPYP
Language instr: English, Spanish

Colegio Altasierra
Urb. La Viña. C/ Garnacha 2., 41807 Espartinas, Seville, Andalusia
Tel: +34 954 614 760
Curriculum: IBMYP, IBPYP
Language instr: English, Spanish

Colegio Altocastillo
Ctra. de Córdoba s/n, 23005 Jaén, Andalusia
Tel: +34 953 296 910
Curriculum: IBPYP
Language instr: English, Spanish

Colegio Arcangel Rafael
Calle Maqueda no. 4, 28024 Madrid
Tel: +34 91 711 93 00
Curriculum: IBDP, IBMYP, IBPYP
Language instr: English, Spanish

Colegio Arenas
Llano de Los Tarahales, 76, 35013 Las Palmas de Gran Canaria, Las Palmas, Can+
Tel: +34 928 41 59 96
Language instr: Spanish

Colegio Arenas Atlántico
Paseo San Patricio, No 20, 35413 Trasmontaña, Las Palmas, Canary Islands
Tel: +34 928 629 140
Age range: 3–18
No. of pupils: 306 B179 G127
Curriculum: IBDP, IBMYP, National
Language instr: Spanish

Colegio Arenas Internacional
Avenida del Mar 37, Lanzarote, 35509 Costa Teguise, Las Palmas, Canary Islands
Tel: +34 928 590 835
Curriculum: IBDP, IBMYP, IBPYP
Language instr: Spanish

Colegio Arenas Sur
Las Margaritas s/n, 35290 San Agustín, Las Palmas, Canary Islands
Tel: +34 928 765 934
No. of pupils: 620
Curriculum: IBDP
Language instr: Spanish

Colegio Arturo Soria
C. Duque de Tamames 4, Cdad. Lineal, 28043 Madrid
Tel: +34 914 157 295
Curriculum: IBPYP
Language instr: English, Spanish

Colegio Atalaya
Calle Pico Alcazaba 24-28, Urbanización El Marqués, 29680 Estepona, Málaga
Tel: +34 952 003 171
Curriculum: IBDP
Language instr: English, Spanish

Colegio Base
Calle del Camino Ancho 10, La Moraleja, 28109 Alcobendas, Madrid
Tel: +34 916 500 313
Age range: 1–18 years
Curriculum: IBDP, IBPYP
Language instr: Spanish

Colegio Brains Maria Lombillo
Calle Maria Lombillo 5, 28027 Madrid
Tel: +34 917 421 060
Age range: 6–18 years
Curriculum: IBDP, IBMYP, IBPYP
Language instr: English, Spanish

Colegio Camarena Canet
C/ De la Rosa s/n, 46529 Canet d'en Berenguer, Valencia
Tel: +34 960 609 036
Curriculum: IBDP, IBMYP, IBPYP
Language instr: English, Spanish

Colegio Camarena Valterna
Calle Carlina s/n 46980, Valterna, Urb. Lloma Llarga, Paterna, Valencia
Tel: +34 961 381 898
Curriculum: IBPYP
Language instr: English, Spanish

Colegio Cervantes
Avda. de la Fuensanta, 37, 14010 Córdoba, Andalusia
Tel: +34 957 255150
Curriculum: IBDP
Language instr: Spanish

Colegio CEU San Pablo Montepríncipe
Avda. Montepríncipe, s/n, 28668 Boadilla del Monte, Madrid
Tel: +34 91 352 05 23
No. of pupils: 1200
Curriculum: IBDP, IBPYP
Language instr: Spanish, English

Colegio CEU San Pablo Sanchinarro
Niceto Alcalá Zamora, 43, 28050 Madrid
Tel: +34 91 392 34 40/41
Curriculum: IBDP
Language instr: English

Colegio CEU San Pablo Valencia
Edificio Seminario Metropolitano, 46113 Moncada, Valencia
Tel: +34 961 36 90 14
Curriculum: IBDP, IBPYP
Language instr: Spanish

Colegio Compañía de María - Almería
Rambla Obispo Orberá 35, 04001 Almería, Andalusia
Tel: +34 950 235 422
Curriculum: IBDP
Language instr: Spanish

Colegio Compañía de María - La Enseñanza - Valladolid
C/ Juan Mambrilla 17, 47003 Valladolid, Castile & León
Tel: +34 983 291 400
Age range: 0–18 years
Curriculum: IBDP
Language instr: Spanish

Colegio de San Francisco de Paula
C/ Santa Angela de la Cruz, 11, 41003 Seville, Andalusia
Tel: +34 95 422 4382
Age range: 3–18
Curriculum: IBDP, IBMYP, IBPYP, National
Language instr: Spanish, English

Colegio Ecos
C/ Velázquez, 7. Urb. Elvira, La Mairena, Ojén, 29612 Marbella, Málaga, Andalusia
Tel: +34 952 831 027
Curriculum: IBMYP, IBPYP
Language instr: English, Spanish

Colegio El Planet
Partida Planet 71, 03590 Altea, Alicante, Valencia
Tel: +34 965 844 224
Language instr: English

Colegio El Romeral
Calle De Eolo 2, 29010 Málaga, Andalusia
Tel: +34 952 070 370
Curriculum: IBMYP, IBPYP
Language instr: English, Spanish

Colegio El Tomillar
C/ Pantano de la Serena, 48. Las Vaguadas, 06010 Badajoz, Extremadura
Tel: +34 924 268 807
Curriculum: IBPYP
Language instr: English, Spanish

Colegio El Valle Alicante
Avda. Condomina 65, 03540 Alicante, Valencia
Tel: +34 965 155 619
Curriculum: IBDP, IBMYP, IBPYP
Language instr: English, Spanish

Colegio El Valle II - Sanchinarro
Calle Ana De Austria, 60, 28050 Madrid
Tel: +34 91 7188426
Curriculum: IBDP

Colegio Entrepinos
C/ Escultor León Ortega s/n, Bellavista, 21110 Aljaraque, Huelva, Andalusia
Tel: +34 959 319 125
Curriculum: IBPYP
Language instr: English, Spanish

Colegio Europeo de Madrid
Calle Cólquide 14, Las Rozas de Madrid, 28231 Madrid
Tel: +34 687 521 151
Age range: 1–18 years
Curriculum: IBPYP, National
Language instr: English, Spanish

Colegio Grazalema
C/ Caracola, 2. Urb. Valdelagrana, 11500 El Puerto de Santa María, Cádiz, Andalusia
Tel: +34 956 561 542
Curriculum: IBMYP, IBPYP
Language instr: English, Spanish

Colegio Guadalete
C/ Ubrique, 36. Urb. Valdelagrana, 11500 El Puerto de Santa María, Cádiz, Andalusia
Tel: +34 956 561 646
Curriculum: IBMYP, IBPYP
Language instr: English, Spanish

Europe

Colegio Guadalimar
Ctra. de Córdoba s/n,
23005 Jaén, Andalusia
Tel: +34 953 295 083
Curriculum: IBPYP
Language instr: English, Spanish

Colegio Heidelberg
Apartado de Correos 248, Barranco
Seco 15, 35090 Las Palmas de
Gran Canaria, Las Palmas, Can+
Tel: +34 928 350 462
Age range: 3–18
Curriculum: IBDP, IBMYP
Language instr: Spanish

**Colegio HH. Maristas
Sagrado Corazón Alicante**
Calle de la Isla de Corfú, 5,
03005 Alicante, Valencia
Tel: +34 965 130 941
Curriculum: IBDP
Language instr: Spanish

**Colegio Hispano Inglés
de Las Palmas**
(Secondary & Bachillerato),
Bandama Country, Finca
Los Fierros, Tafira Alta, Las
Palmas, Canary Islands
Tel: +34 928 25 16 16
Curriculum: UK, IGCSE

**Colegio Inglés English
School of Asturias**
Finca La Llosona s/n, 33192
Pruvia, Asturias
Tel: +34 985 237 171
Age range: 2–18 years
Curriculum: IBDP, UK
Language instr: English, Spanish

Colegio Inglés Zaragoza
Av. de Movera 147, 50194
Zaragoza, Aragon
Tel: +34 976 573 030
Age range: 3–16 years
Language instr: English, Spanish

**Colegio Internacional
Ausiàs March**
Urbanización Residencial Tancat de
l'Alter s/n, 46220 Picassent, Valencia
Tel: +34 961 230 566
Curriculum: IBDP, IBMYP
Language instr: English, Spanish

**Colegio Internacional
de Levante**
Río Jalón 25 Urbanización
Calicanto, 46370 Valencia
Tel: +34 961980650
Curriculum: IBDP, IBMYP
Language instr: Spanish

**Colegio Internacional
Jesuitinas Miralba**
Avda Gran Vía 164, 36211
Vigo, Pontevedra, Galicia
Tel: +34 986 213 047
Curriculum: IBDP, IBPYP
Language instr: Spanish, Galician

Colegio Internacional Meres
Camino del Colegio,
33199 Meres, Asturias
Tel: +34 985 792 427
Age range: 3–18 years
Curriculum: IBDP, IBMYP,
IBPYP, National
Language instr: Spanish

**Colegio Internacional
Peñacorada**
Calle Bandonilla 32, CP Armunia,
24009 León, Castile & León
Tel: +34 987 202352
Language instr: Spanish

**Colegio Internacional
Pureza de María
Los Realejos**
C/ Ciudad Jardín 16. La Montañeta,
Los Realejos, 38419 Santa Cruz de
Tenerife, Tenerife, Canary Is+
Tel: +34 922 340 550
Curriculum: IBDP
Language instr: English, Spanish

**Colegio Internacional
SEK Eirís**
C Castaño de Eirís, 1, 15009
A Coruña, Galicia
Tel: +34 981 28 44 00
Age range: 3–18 years
No. of pupils: 720 B360 G360 VIth30
Curriculum: IBDP, National
Language instr: Spanish, English

**Colegio Internacional
Torrequebrada**
C/ Ronda del Golf Este, 7-11,
Urbanización Torrequebrada, 29639
Benalmádena, Málaga, Andalusia
Tel: +34 952 57 60 65
Age range: 2–18
Curriculum: IBDP, IBMYP, IBPYP
Language instr: English, Spanish

**Colegio International
de Valladolid**
Av. El Norte de Castilla 40-42,
47008 Valladolid, Castile & León
Tel: +34 983 458 267
Age range: 1–18 years
Curriculum: UK, IGCSE
Language instr: English, Spanish

**Colegio Jesuitinas
Stella Maris**
Av de Federico García Lorca
22, 04004 Almería, Andalusia
Tel: +34 950 250 388
Curriculum: IBDP
Language instr: Spanish

Colegio Joyfe
Calle de Vital Aza 65, 28017 Madrid
Tel: +34 914 082 263
Language instr: English, Spanish

Colegio Juan de Lanuza
Crta Areopuerto 275, 50011
Zaragoza, Aragon
Tel: +34 976 300 336
Curriculum: IBPYP
Language instr: English, Spanish

Colegio Las Chapas
Urb. Las Chapas s/n, 29604
Marbella, Málaga, Andalusia
Tel: +34 952 831 616
Curriculum: IBDP, IBMYP, IBPYP
Language instr: English, Spanish

Colegio Legamar
Ctra. Leganés-Fuenlabrada Km.
1.5, 28914 Leganés, Madrid
Tel: +34 916 933 812
Curriculum: IBDP
Language instr: English, Spanish

Colegio Liceo Europeo
C/ Camino Sur 10, 28100
Alcobendas, Madrid
Tel: +34 91 650 00 00
Curriculum: IBDP, IBMYP, IBPYP
Language instr: English, Spanish

Colegio Logos
Urbanización Molino de la Hoz c/,
Sacre 2, 28232 Las Rozas, Madrid
Tel: +34 91 630 34 94
Curriculum: IBDP
Language instr: English

**Colegio Los Sauces
La Moraleja**
C. del Camino Ancho 83,
28109 Alcobendas, Madrid
Age range: 0–18 years
Curriculum: IBDP
Language instr: English, Spanish

**Colegio Los Sauces
Pontevedra**
Carretera de Campaño a Cabaleiro,
36157 Pontevedra, Galicia
Age range: 3–18 years
Curriculum: IBDP
Language instr: English, Spanish

**Colegio Los Sauces
Torrelodones**
Lake Avenue 27, Los
Peñascales Urbanization,
28250 Torreldones, Madrid
Age range: 1–18 years
Curriculum: IBDP
Language instr: English, Spanish

Colegio Los Sauces Vigo
As Pereiras Pardellas Cela, 36419
Vigo, Pontevedra, Galicia
Age range: 3–18 years
Curriculum: IBDP
Language instr: English, Spanish

Colegio Madrid
Avda. del Comandante
Franco 8, 28016 Madrid
Tel: +34 910 572 501
Curriculum: IBDP
Language instr: Spanish

Colegio Manuel Peleteiro
Monte Redondo - Castiñeiriño,
15702 Santiago de Compostela,
A Coruña, Galicia
Tel: +34 98 1591475

Colegio Mater Salvatoris
Calle Valdesquí no. 4, 28023 Madrid
Tel: +34 91 307 1243
Curriculum: IBDP
Language instr: Spanish

Colegio Monaita
C/ Acequia de la Madraza s/n,
18015 Granada, Andalusia
Tel: +34 958 806 940
Curriculum: IBMYP, IBPYP
Language instr: English, Spanish

Colegio Montecalpe
Urb. San García, C/ La Carpa s/n,
11207 Algeciras, Cádiz, Andalusia
Tel: +34 956 605 888
Curriculum: IBPYP
Language instr: English, Spanish

Colegio Montserrat
Av Vallvidrera, 68, 08017
Barcelona, Catalonia
Tel: +34 932 038 800
Curriculum: IBDP, IBMYP
Language instr: English, Spanish

Colegio Mulhacén
Ctra. Pinos Puente 10, 18015
Granada, Andalusia
Tel: +34 958 806 800
Curriculum: IBMYP, IBPYP
Language instr: English, Spanish

**Colegio Nuestra
Señora de Europa**
C/ Estrada de Goñi, 3, 48993
Getxo, Biscay, Basque Country
Tel: +34 94 491 03 92
Age range: 3–18
No. of pupils: 750
Language instr: Spanish

**Colegio Nuestra Señora
de Schoenstatt**
Camino de Alcorcón 17, 28223
Pozuelo de Alarcón, Madrid
Tel: +34 917 159 226
Curriculum: IBDP
Language instr: English, Spanish

**Colegio Nuestra Señora
del Recuerdo**
Plaza Duque de Pastrana
5, 28036 Madrid
Tel: +34 91 3022640
Age range: 3–18
Curriculum: IBDP
Language instr: Spanish, English

Colegio Obradoiro
Rua Obradoiro 49, 15190
A Coruña, Galicia
Tel: +34 981 281 888
Curriculum: IBDP, IBMYP, IBPYP
Language instr: English, Spanish

Colegio Parque
Calle Piamonte, 19 Urbanización
Parquelagos, La Navata,
28420 Galapagar, Madrid
Tel: +34 918 590 630
Curriculum: IBDP
Language instr: English, Spanish

Europe

Colegio Puertapalma
Avda. de las Vaguadas 44,
06010 Badajoz, Extremadura
Tel: +34 924 267 763
Curriculum: IBPYP
Language instr: English, Spanish

Colegio Puertoblanco
Calle Goleta 2, 11207 Algeciras,
Cádiz, Andalusia
Tel: +34 956 604 422
Curriculum: IBPYP
Language instr: English, Spanish

Colegio Retamar
Madrid España, c/ Pajares
22, 28223 Madrid
Tel: +34 91 714 10 22
Age range: B6–18
No. of pupils: 2100
Curriculum: IBDP
Language instr: Spanish

Colegio Sagrada Familia Jesuitinas
Carretera de Segovia 1, 47012
Valladolid, Castile & León
Tel: +34 983 230 412
Curriculum: IBDP
Language instr: English, Spanish

Colegio Saladares
Ctra. de Alicún. KM. 10300,
04721 El Parador de las
Hortichuelas, Almería, An+
Tel: +34 950 559 644
Curriculum: IBPYP

Colegio San Cayetano
Av. Picasso 21, 07014 Palma De
Mallorca, Balearic Islands
Tel: +34 971 220 575
Curriculum: IBDP
Language instr: English, Spanish

Colegio San Cristóbal
Calle San Jorge del Maestrazgo,
2, 12003 Castellón de la Plana,
Castellón, Valencia
Tel: +34 964 228 758
Curriculum: IBDP, IBMYP, IBPYP
Language instr: English, Spanish

Colegio San Fernando
Avenida San Agustín, s/n,
33400 Avilés, Asturias
Tel: +34 985 565 745
Curriculum: IBDP, IBMYP, IBPYP

Colegio San Jorge
Soc. Coop. Enseñanza la
Alcayna. CIF: F30410328, Avda.
Picos de Europa s/n, 30507
Molina de Segura, Murcia
Tel: +34 968 430 711
Curriculum: IBDP
Language instr: English, Spanish

Colegio San José Estepona
Avd. Litoral 22, 29680 Estepona,
Málaga, Andalusia
Tel: +34 952 800 148
Age range: 3–18 years
No. of pupils: 755
Curriculum: IBDP
Language instr: Spanish

COLEGIO SAN PATRICIO EL SOTO
For further details see p. 107
Calle Jazmin 148, El Soto
de la Moraleja, 28109
Alcobendas, Madrid
Tel: +34 916 500 602
Email: infosoto@colegiosanpatricio.es
Website: www.colegiosanpatriciomadrid.com
Head of School: Borja Díaz
Age range: 12–18 years
Curriculum: IBDP, IBMYP
Language instr: English, Spanish

Colegio San Patricio La Moraleja
Paseo de Alcobendas 9, La Moraleja,
28109 Alcobendas, Madrid
Tel: +34 916 500 791
Age range: 2–11 years

Colegio San Patricio Serrano
Calle Serrano 200, 28002 Madrid
Tel: +34 915 638 420
Age range: 2–11 years

Colegio Santa María del Camino
C/ Peguerinos 13, Puerta de
Hierro, 28035 Madrid
Tel: +34 913 161 347
Curriculum: IBDP, IBMYP, IBPYP
Language instr: English, Spanish

Colegio Sierra Blanca
Avenida de Plutarco 34,
29010 Málaga, Andalusia
Tel: +34 952 070 650
Curriculum: IBMYP, IBPYP
Language instr: English, Spanish

Colegio Suizo de Madrid
Carretera de Burgos km 14,
28108 Alcobendas, Madrid
Tel: +34 91 650 58 18
Age range: 3–18
No. of pupils: 600

Colegio Tierrallana
C/ Abeto, s/n. Urb.Dehesa Golf,
21110 Aljaraque, Huelva, Andalusia
Tel: +34 959 522 810
Curriculum: IBPYP
Language instr: English, Spanish

Colegio Timon
Rusia 11, 28022 Madrid
Tel: +34 91 5346935
Age range: 2–15
No. of pupils: 150

Colegio Valdefuentes
Ana de Austria 6, Sanchinarro,
28050 Madrid
Tel: +34 917 188 229
Curriculum: IBDP
Language instr: English, Spanish

Colegio Virgen de Europa
C/ Valle de Santa Ana No.
1, Las Lomas, 28669 Boadilla
del Monte, Madrid
Tel: +34 91 633 0155
Curriculum: IBDP, IBMYP, IBPYP
Language instr: English, Spanish

Colegios Ramón Y Cajal
C/ Arturo Soria, 206, 28043 Madrid
Tel: +34 91 413 56 31
Curriculum: IBDP, IBMYP, IBPYP
Language instr: English

College Saint-Exupery
Camino Ancho 85, 28109
Alcobendas, Madrid
Tel: +34 91 650 70 19

Complejo Educativo Mas Camarena
C/ 1 Urbanización, Mas Camarena,
46117 Bétera, Valencia
Tel: +34 961687535
Age range: 6–18
No. of pupils: 2500
Curriculum: IBDP, IBMYP,
IBPYP, IBCP, USA
Language instr: English, Spanish

Cooperativa de Enseñanza San Cernin
Avenida de Barañain 3, 31011
Pamplona, Navarre
Tel: +34 948 176 288
Curriculum: IBDP
Language instr: English, Spanish

CORUÑA BRITISH INTERNATIONAL SCHOOL (A CORUÑA)
For further details see p. 109
Rúa Roma 1, 15008 A
Coruña, Galicia
Tel: +34 981 28 67 99
Email: admissions@biscoruna.com
Website: www.biscoruna.com
Head of School: Dominic Abbott
No. of pupils: 450
Curriculum: National, UK
Language instr: English,
Spanish, French, Galician

Costa Blanca International College
Av. Del Albir s/n, (partida Sanz),
03503 Benidorm, Alicante, Valencia
Tel: +34 96 680 34 11
Age range: 3–18
No. of pupils: 300
Curriculum: UK
Language instr: Spanish, English

Deutsche Schule in der provinz Malaga - Coleg
Apartado de Correos 318, 29600
Marbella, Málaga, Andalusia
Tel: +34 952 831 417

Deutsche Schule Madrid
Colegio Alemán de Madrid,
Calle Monasterio de
Guadalupe 7, 28049 Madrid
Tel: +34 91 558 02 00

Deutsche Schule Valencia - Colegio Alemán Valencia
Jaime Roig 14-16, 46010 Valencia
Tel: +34 96 3690100

École Française Bel Air
Caretera C-246 KM 42, 8810 Saint
Pere de Ribes, Barcelona, Catalonia
Tel: +34 938 962267
Age range: 4–16
No. of pupils: 740

Ecole Saint-Louis des Français
Calle Portugalete 1, Pozuelo
de Alarcón, 28223 Madrid
Tel: +34 91 352 05 17
Age range: 4–18
No. of pupils: 100
Curriculum: National

El Centro Ingles
Apartado Correos 85, Carretera
Fuentebravia KM1.2, 11500 Puerto
de Santa Maria, Cádiz, Andalusia
Tel: +34 956 850560
Age range: 2–18
No. of pupils: 805 B404 G401 VIth77

El Limonar International School (ELIS) Murcia
Colonia Buenavista s/n,
30120 El Palmar, Murcia
Tel: +34 968 882 818
Age range: 3–18 years
Curriculum: National,
UK, IGCSE, ALevs
Language instr: English, Spanish

El Limonar International School (ELIS) Villamartin
c/ Filipinas, 15 - Urb. Blue
Lagoon, 03193 San Miguel de
Salinas, Alicante, Valencia
Tel: +34 966 722 821
Age range: 3–18 years
Curriculum: National,
UK, IGCSE, ALevs
Language instr: English, Spanish

El Plantío International School of Valencia
Calle 233 No36 Urb El Plantío, La
Cañada, 46182 Paterna, Valencia
Tel: +34 96 132 14 10
Age range: 2–18
No. of pupils: 650
Curriculum: IBDP, National, UK, IGCSE
Language instr: English, Spanish

Elian's British School of La Nucía
Av. El Copet 5, 03530 La
Nucía, Alicante, Valencia
Tel: +34 966 877 055
Age range: 3–18 years
Curriculum: IBDP
Language instr: English, Spanish

Engage Independent School
Calle Mar Egeo 32,
Majadahonda, 28220 Madrid
Tel: +34 916 380 196
Age range: 1–18 years
Language instr: English, Spanish

English Academy Santa Claus
Carrer Lleó XIII, No 12, 08022
Barcelona, Catalonia
Tel: +34 93 417 18 47
Age range: 3–12
No. of pupils: 100
Curriculum: USA

English School Los Olivos
Avda Los Almendros 13, Valencia
Tel: +34 963 631 409
Age range: 3–18
Curriculum: National,
UK, IGCSE, ALevs

ES AMERICAN SCHOOL
For further details see p. 114
Autovia de Castelldefels C-31
Km 191, El Prat de Llobregat,
08820 Barcelona, Catalonia
Tel: +34 93 479 1611
Email: admin@es-school.com
Website: www.es-school.com
Head of School: Melanie Rose
Age range: 6–18 years
No. of pupils: 140
Fees: Day €12,020–€20,485
Curriculum: AP, IBPYP, SAT, USA
Language instr: English

Escola Frederic Mistral Tècnic Eulàlia
Pere II de Montcada 8, 08034
Barcelona, Catalonia
Tel: +34 932 031 280
Curriculum: IBDP
Language instr: English, Spanish

Escola Internacional del Camp
Salvador Espiriu s/n, 43840
Salou, Tarragona, Catalonia
Tel: +34 977325620
Age range: 1–19
No. of pupils: 560 B280 G280 VIth45
Curriculum: IBDP, National
Language instr: English, Spanish, Catalan

Escola Pia Sabadell
Carrer Escola Pia 92, 08201
Sabadell, Barcelona, Catalonia
Tel: +34 93 748 44 30
Curriculum: USA

Escuela Ideo
Highway from Colmenar
to Alcobendas, Km.
0.500, 28049 Madrid
Tel: +34 917 523 343
Age range: 1–18 years
No. of pupils: 1244
Curriculum: IBDP
Language instr: English, Spanish

Escuela Suiza de Barcelona
Alfonso XII 95-105, 08006
Barcelona, Catalonia
Tel: +34 932 096544
Age range: 3–18
No. of pupils: 640

Eurocolegio Casvi Boadilla
C/ Miguel Ángel Cantero Oliva,
13, Boadilla del Monte, Madrid
Tel: +34 91 632 96 53
Curriculum: IBMYP, IBPYP
Language instr: Spanish

Eurocolegio Casvi Villaviciosa
Avenida de Castilla, 27, Villaviciosa
de Odón, 28670 Madrid
Tel: +34 91 616 22 18
Age range: 1–18 years
No. of pupils: 1090
Curriculum: IBDP, IBMYP, IBPYP
Language instr: Spanish

European International School of Barcelona
Av. Pla del Vinyet 110, 08172
Sant Cugat del Vallés
Barcelona, Catalonia
Tel: +34 935 898 420
Curriculum: IBDP
Language instr: English, Spanish

Everest School Monteclaro
C/Rosas s/n, Urb Monteclaro, Urb
Monteclaro, 28223 Madrid
Tel: +34 91 799 48 88
Age range: 3–18
No. of pupils: 1000
Curriculum: IGCSE

Fundacion Privada Oak House School
Sant Pere Claver 12-18, 08017
Barcelona, Catalonia
Tel: +34 932 524 020
Age range: 3–17
Curriculum: IBDP, UK
Language instr: English

Green Valley School
Cami de la Vileta 210, Son Puig, 07011
Palma De Mallorca, Balearic Islands
Tel: +34 971 160 817
Curriculum: IBDP
Language instr: English

Greenleaves Montessori International School
Avenida Victoria 73,
Moncloa-Aravaca, 28023
Majadahonda, Madrid
Tel: +34 913 077 935
Curriculum: IBPYP
Language instr: English, Spanish

GRESOL International-American School
Ctra. Sabadell a Matadepera,
(BV-1248) km. 6, 08227 Terrassa,
Barcelona, Catalonia
Tel: +34 937 870 158
Age range: 4–18 years
Curriculum: IBDP, USA
Language instr: English

GSD International School Buitrago
Av. de Madrid 16, 28730
Buitrago del Lozoya, Madrid
Tel: +34 918 680 200
Age range: 5–18 years
No. of pupils: 1500
Curriculum: IBDP
Language instr: English, Spanish

GSD Las Rozas
C/ Clara Campoamor 1,
28232 Las Rozas, Madrid
Tel: +34 916 408 923
Age range: 0–18 years
Curriculum: IBDP, National
Language instr: Spanish

HAMELIN-LAIE INTERNATIONAL SCHOOL BARCELONA
For further details see p. 116
178-180 Ronda 8 de Març, 08390
Montgat, Barcelona, Catalonia
Tel: +34 935 55 67 17
Email: admissions@hamelinschool.com
Website: www.hamelinschool.com
Principal: Sarah Osborne-James
Age range: 4 months–18 years
No. of pupils: 1475
Curriculum: IBDP, National
Language instr: English, Spanish, Catalan

Hastings School, Azulinas
Azulinas 8, 28036 Madrid
Tel: +34 910 107 060
Age range: 9–10 years
Curriculum: UK
Language instr: English

Hastings School, Bendición de Campos
Bendición de Campos
5, 28036 Madrid
Tel: +34 910 107 062
Age range: 6–8 years
Curriculum: UK
Language instr: English

Hastings School, Lorenzo Solano Tendero
Calle Lorenzo Solano Tendero
11, 28043 Madrid
Tel: +34 918 316 318
Age range: 3–18 years
Curriculum: National, UK, IGCSE
Language instr: English

Hastings School, Manuel Marañón
Calle Manuel Maranon
8, 28043 Madrid
Tel: +34 918 337 790
Age range: 7–18 years
Curriculum: IBDP, UK, IGCSE
Language instr: English, Spanish

Hastings School, Paseo de la Habana
Paseo de la Habana
204, 28036 Madrid
Tel: +34 913 590 621
Age range: 3–5 years
Curriculum: UK
Language instr: English

Hastings School, Sobradiel
Ronda de Sobradiel 31-
33, 28043 Madrid
Tel: +34 918 316 198
Age range: 3–7 years
Curriculum: UK
Language instr: English

Holy Mary British Catholic School
Calle Cinca 20, 28002 Madrid
Tel: +34 91 287 2752
Age range: 2–18
No. of pupils: 575
Curriculum: UK, GCSE, ALevs
Language instr: English

I.E.S. Clot de la Illot
Avinguda els Furs 4, Campello,
3560 Alicante, Valencia
Tel: +34 965 632 854
Age range: 4–19

Iale International School, L'Eliana
Calle Campoamor, 24,
46183 L'Eliana, Valencia
Tel: +34 962 740 272
Age range: 4–19

Institucion Educativa SEK (San Estenislao de Kostka)
Ciudalcampo Urb. San Sebastian
de los Reyes, 28707 Madrid
Tel: +34 91 659 63 00
Language instr: Spanish

Instituto Saudi de Madrid
Avenida de Ahones,11, 28043 Madrid
Tel: +34 9138 84406
Language instr: English

Internacional Aravaca
Calle Santa Bernardita
3, 28023 Madrid
Tel: +34 913 571 256
Curriculum: IBDP, IBMYP, IBPYP
Language instr: English, Spanish

International College Spain
C/Vereda Norte, 3, La Moraleja,
28109 Alcobendas, Madrid
Tel: +34 91 650 2398
Age range: 3–18 years
Curriculum: IBDP, IBMYP, IBPYP
Language instr: English

International English School of Castellón
Ronda Circunvalación 346-
348, 12004 Castellón de la
Plana, Castellón, Valencia
Tel: +34 964 261 241
Age range: 3–18 years
Language instr: English, Spanish

International School Andalucía
Carretera Sevilla-Huelva s/n, 41800
Sanlúcar La Mayor, Seville, Andalusia
Tel: +34 955 702 430
Curriculum: IBDP
Language instr: English, Spanish

International School of Barcelona
Passeig Isaac Albeniz s/n, Vallpineda,
08870 Sitges, Barcelona, Catalonia
Tel: +34 93 894 20 40
Age range: 2–18
Curriculum: IBDP, National, SAT, UK
Language instr: English

International School of Catalunya (ISCAT)
Manuel Raspall 8, 08530 La
Garriga, Barcelona, Catalonia
Tel: +34 93 841 4077
Age range: 3–18
Curriculum: UK
Language instr: English

Europe

INTERNATIONAL SCHOOL OF MADRID
For further details see p. 140
Calle Rosa Jardón 3, 28016 Madrid
Tel: +34 91 359 21 21
Email: info@internationalschoolofmadrid.com
Website: www.internationalschoolofmadrid.com
Heads of School: Mr. Rich Cook & Mr. Tom Davidson
Age range: 2–18 years
No. of pupils: 920 B433 G487 VIth130
Curriculum: UK, IGCSE, ALevs
Language instr: English, Spanish

INTERNATIONAL SCHOOL SAN PATRICIO TOLEDO
For further details see p. 148
Juan de Vergara, 1, Urbanización La Legua, Toledo, Castilla-La Mancha 45005
Tel: +34 925 280 363
Email: infotoledo@colegiosanpatricio.es
Website: colegiosanpatriciotoledo.com/en
Head of School: Simon Hatton-Burke
Age range: 1–18 years
No. of pupils: 510
Curriculum: IBDP, IBMYP, IBPYP
Language instr: English, Spanish

Irabia-Izaga Colegio
Calle Cintruénigo, 31015 Pamplona, Navarre
Tel: +34 948 12 62 22
Curriculum: IBDP, IBMYP
Language instr: English, Spanish

Jesuitinas Donostia, Nuestra Señora de Aranzazu
Paseo de Errondo 121, Aiete, 20009 Donostia-San Sebastian, Gipuzkoa, Basque Co+
Tel: +34 943 212 307
Curriculum: IBDP
Language instr: English, Spanish

KENSINGTON SCHOOL
For further details see p. 153
Avenida de Bularas No. 2, Pozuelo de Alarcón, 28224 Madrid
Tel: +34 91 7154 699
Email: kensington@kensingtonschool.net
Website: www.kensington-school.es
Head of School: Paul Murphy
Age range: 18 months–18 years
No. of pupils: 1300
Fees: Day €6,875–€9,245
Curriculum: IBDP, UK
Language instr: English, Spanish

Kensington School Barcelona
Carrer Dels Cavaller 31-33, 08034 Barcelona, Catalonia
Tel: +34 93 203 5457
Age range: 3–18
No. of pupils: 240
Curriculum: UK, IGCSE, ALevs
Language instr: English

King Richard III College
Calle Oratorio 4, Portals Nous, 07181 Calvià, Mallorca, Balearic Islands
Tel: +34 971 675 850/1
Age range: 2–18
No. of pupils: 350 B190 G160
Curriculum: National, UK, IGCSE, ALevs
Language instr: English

King's College School Alicante
Glorieta del Reino Unido No. 5, 03008 Alicante, Valencia
Tel: +34 96 510 6351
Age range: 2–18 years
No. of pupils: 1280
Curriculum: IBDP, UK, IGCSE, ALevs
Language instr: English, Spanish

KING'S COLLEGE SCHOOL MURCIA
For further details see p. 154
Calle Pez Volador s/n, Urbanización La Torre Golf Resort, 30709 Roldán, Murcia
Tel: +34 968 032 500
Email: murcia.info@kings.education
Website: www.murcia.kingscollegeschools.org
Head of School: Dawn Akyurek
Age range: 18 months–18 years
No. of pupils: 522
Curriculum: IBDP, UK, GCSE, ALevs
Language instr: English, Spanish

King's College School, The British School of Madrid (La Moraleja)
Paseo de Alcobendas 5, La Moraleja, 28109 Alcobendas, Madrid
Tel: +34 916 585 540
Age range: 1–16 years
Curriculum: UK, IGCSE, ALevs
Language instr: English

KING'S COLLEGE SOTO DE VIÑUELAS
For further details see p. 156
Paseo de los Andes 35, Soto de Viñuelas, 28760 Madrid
Tel: +34 918 034 800
Email: kc.admissions@kingscollegeschools.org
Website: madrid-soto.kingscollegeschools.org
Headteacher: Chris Ramsey
Age range: 0 months–18 years
No. of pupils: 1300
Fees: Day €2,600–€6,630 FB €32,940–€39,390
Curriculum: IBDP, UK, GCSE, IGCSE, ALevs
Language instr: English, Spanish

King's Infant School, The British School of Madrid (Chamartín)
Prieto Urena 9E, 28016 Chamartín, Madrid
Tel: +34 913 505 843
Age range: 18 months–7 years
Language instr: English

La Dehesa de Humanes
Av. de los Deportes 8, 28970 Humanes de Madrid, Madrid
Tel: +34 916 049 002
Curriculum: IBDP
Language instr: English, Spanish

LA MIRANDA - THE GLOBAL QUALITY SCHOOL
For further details see p. 159
Carrer del Canigó 15, 08960 Sant Just Desvern, Barcelona, Catalonia
Tel: +34 93 371 73 58
Email: info@lamiranda.eu
Website: www.lamiranda.eu
Head of School: Debra Gregory
Age range: 0–18 years
No. of pupils: 1210
Curriculum: IBDP, IBMYP
Language instr: English, Spanish

LADY ELIZABETH SCHOOL
For further details see p. 160
Entrada Norte Cumbre del Sol s/n, 03726 Benitachell, Alicante, Valencia
Tel: +34 671 698 769
Email: info@les.edu.es
Website: ladyelizabethschool.com
Principal: Chris Akin
Age range: 3–18 years
Fees: Day €6,580–€14,900 WB €32,511–€34,801 FB €38.010–€40,300
Curriculum: UK, GCSE, ALevs
Language instr: English, Spanish

Laude Colegio Palacio de Granda
C/ El Llugarín, 4, 33199 Granda, Siero, Asturias
Tel: +34 985 792 031
Age range: 1–18 years
No. of pupils: 530
Language instr: English, Spanish

Laude El Altillo School
C/ Santiago de Chile, s/n, 11407 Jerez de la Frontera, Cádiz, Andalusia
Tel: +34 956 302 400
Age range: 2–18 years
No. of pupils: 1120
Curriculum: IBDP, IBMYP, National
Language instr: English, Spanish, French

Laude Fontenebro School
C/ Colonia del Redondillo, 8 Moralzarzal, 28411 Madrid
Tel: +34 91 857 89 42
Age range: 1–18 years
No. of pupils: 500
Language instr: English, Spanish

Laude Newton College
Camino Viejo de Elche-Alicante Km, 3, Alicante, Valencia
Tel: +34 96 545 14 28
Age range: 1–18 years
No. of pupils: 1306
Curriculum: IBDP, IBMYP
Language instr: Spanish, English

Laude San Pedro International College
Urb. Nueva Alcántara, Avda. La Coruña, 2, 29670 San Pedro de Alcántara, Málaga, Andalusia
Tel: +34 952 799 900
Age range: 3–18 years
No. of pupils: 850
Language instr: English, Spanish

Laude The British School of Vila-real
Ctra. Vila-real a Burriana 3o Sedeny, 12540 Vila-real, Castellón, Valencia
Tel: +34 964 500 155
Age range: 2–18 years
No. of pupils: 610
Curriculum: IPC, UK, GCSE, IGCSE, ALevs
Language instr: English, Spanish

Les Alzines
La Creu de Palau 2, 17003 Girona, Catalonia
Tel: +34 972 212162
Age range: G0–18
Curriculum: IBDP
Language instr: Spanish

Lestonnac L'Ensenyança
Carrer Arc de Sant Llorenç, 2, 43003 Tarragona, Catalonia
Tel: +34 977 23 25 19
Curriculum: IBDP
Language instr: English

Liceo Sorolla c
Avda. Bularas 4, 28224 Pozuelo de Alarcón, Madrid
Tel: +34 91 715 04 99
Curriculum: IBDP
Language instr: English

Lycée Français de Palma
Calle Salud 4, 7014 Palma De Mallorca, Balearic Islands
Tel: +34 971 739260
Age range: 4–18
No. of pupils: 550

Lycée Français Molière
Calle Cristo 27, 28691 Villanueva de la Canada, Madrid
Tel: +34 91 815 50 00
Curriculum: FrenchBacc

Lycée Français Murcie
Avenida del Golf, 107 Urbanización Altorreal, Apartado de correos 133, 30506 Molina de Segura, Murcia
Tel: +34 968 64 80 65
No. of pupils: 650
Curriculum: FrenchBacc

Lycée Français Renée-Verneau de Gran Canaria
Carretera de Taliarte s/n, 35214 Telde, Gran Canaria, Canary Islands
Tel: +34 928 576 091
No. of pupils: 388

Europe

Lycée International Barcelona - Bon Soleil
Camí de la Pava, no. 15, Gavà, 08850 Barcelona, Catalonia
Tel: +34 93 633 13 58
Age range: 3–18 years
No. of pupils: 1412
Curriculum: IBDP
Language instr: English, French, Spanish

Maristes Sants Les Corts
C/Vallespir 160, 08014 Barcelona, Catalonia
Tel: +34 934 908 625
Age range: 16–18 years
No. of pupils: 45
Curriculum: IBDP
Language instr: Catalan, Valencian, Spanish

Mayfair International Academy
Avda. De Las Golondrinas, Atalaya Park, Estepona, 29680 Málaga, Andalusia
Tel: +34 952 78 49 23
Age range: 14–19
Curriculum: UK, ALevs

MIRABAL INTERNATIONAL SCHOOL
For further details see p. 168
Calle Monte Almenara, s/n, 28660 Boadilla del Monte, Madrid
Tel: +34 916 331 711
Email: mirabal@colegiomirabal.com
Website: www.colegiomirabal.com
Head of School: Rosario de la Cruz López
Age range: 0–18 years
No. of pupils: 1678
Curriculum: IBDP, IBMYP
Language instr: English, Spanish

Mirasur School
Calle Pablo Gargallo 1, 28320 Pinto, Madrid
Tel: +34 640 783 768
Age range: 1–18 years
Curriculum: IBPYP, National
Language instr: English, Spanish

Montessori British School, Murcia
c/ Ermita Vieja, 26B, 30006 Murcia
Tel: +34 868 86 34 16
Age range: 1–12 years
Curriculum: SAT

Montessori School La Florida
Calle de Motrico 3, Urb. La Florida, 28023 Madrid
Tel: +34 918 579 304
Curriculum: IBDP
Language instr: English, Spanish

Montessori School Los Fresnos Mataespesa
Calle Navacerrada 13, 28430 Alpedrete, Madrid
Tel: +34 91 857 1743
Age range: 11–18
No. of pupils: 200

Montjuïc Girona International School
C/ Bellpuig, N° 8-10, 17007 Girona, Catalonia
Tel: +34 972 212 838
Age range: 0 years–18 years
No. of pupils: 250
Language instr: Spanish, Catalan, English, French

Morna International College
Apartado 333, Santa Gertrudis, 07814 Ibiza, Balearic Islands
Tel: +34 971 19 76 72
Age range: 3–18
Curriculum: UK, IGCSE, ALevs
Language instr: English

New Castelar College
Las Palmas S/N 30740, San Pedro del Pinatar, Murcia
Tel: +34 968 178 276
Language instr: English, Spanish

Novaschool Sunland International
Cartera Cartama-Pizarra, Nueva Aljaima, Cartama Estacion, Málaga, Andalusia
Tel: +34 952 42 4253
Age range: 3–18
No. of pupils: 180 B90 G90
Curriculum: National, UK

Numont School
C/ Parma, 16, 28043 Madrid
Tel: +34 913 002 431
Age range: 3–11
No. of pupils: 320

NYsKOOL
C/O Preiskel & Co Llp, 4 King's Bench Walk, London EC4Y 7DL, UK
Tel: +34 676 29 53 96
Age range: 6–11 years

O CASTRO BRITISH INTERNATIONAL SCHOOL (VIGO)
For further details see p. 172
Camiño San Cosme 1, 36419 San Pedro de Cela (Mos), Pontevedra, Galicia
Tel: +34 986 20 00 28
Email: admissions@bisocastro.com
Website: www.bisocastro.com
Executive Head: Chis Long
Age range: 3–18 years
No. of pupils: 700
Curriculum: National, UK
Language instr: English, Spanish, French, Galician

Oakley College
Calle Zuloaga, 17, Tafira Alta, 35017 Las Palmas de Gran Canaria, Las Palmas, Can+
Tel: +34 928 354247
Age range: 2–18 years
No. of pupils: 550
Curriculum: UK, GCSE, IGCSE, ALevs

Phoenix International School
Calle Albacete, Urb Las Comunicaciones, 03193 San Miguel de Salinas, Valencia
Tel: +34 965 720 785
Age range: 1–18
No. of pupils: 130

Queen's College
Juan de Saridakis 64, 07015 Palma de Mallorca, Balearic Islands
Tel: +34 971 401 011
Age range: 3–18 years
Curriculum: IBDP, National, UK, GCSE, IGCSE, ALevs
Language instr: English, Spanish

Richmond International School
Rambla del Garraf 14-16, 08810 Sant Pere de Ribes, Barcelona, Catalonia
Tel: +34 93 893 67 12
Age range: 3–18
Curriculum: UK, IGCSE
Language instr: English

Runnymede College
c/Salvia 30, La Moraleja, 28109 Alcobendas, Madrid
Tel: +34 916 508 302
Age range: 3–18
No. of pupils: 702 B361 G341
Curriculum: UK, IGCSE, ALevs
Language instr: English

Santa Clara International School
Carrer de Pomaret 17-19, 08017 Barcelona, Catalonia
Tel: +34 93 212 35 93

Scandinavian School of Madrid
Camino Ancho 14, La Moraleja, 28109 Alcobendas, Madrid
Tel: +34 91 650 01 27
Age range: 2–18
Curriculum: National

Schellhammer International School
Calle Flaminio 2, Urb. Valle Romano, 29680 Estepona, Málaga, Andalusia
Tel: +34 952 907 892
Age range: 16–18
Curriculum: ALevs

SEK INTERNATIONAL SCHOOL ALBORÁN
For further details see p. 180
C/ Barloveno 141, Urb. Almerimar, El Ejido, 04711 Almería, Andalusia
Tel: +34 900 87 87 98
Email: sek-alboran@sek.es
Website: alboran.sek.es
Principal: Guadalupe Sánchez Ruiz
Age range: 4 months–18 years
No. of pupils: 735
Curriculum: IBDP, IBMYP, IBPYP
Language instr: English, Spanish

SEK INTERNATIONAL SCHOOL ATLÁNTICO
For further details see p. 181
Rúa Illa de Arousa 4, Boavista. A Caeira, Poio, 36005 Pontevedra, Galicia
Tel: +34 900 87 87 98
Email: sek-atlantico@sek.es
Website: atlantico.sek.es
Principal: Jacobo Olmedo
Age range: 4 months–18 years
No. of pupils: 735
Curriculum: IBDP, IBMYP, IBPYP
Language instr: Spanish, English

SEK INTERNATIONAL SCHOOL CATALUNYA
For further details see p. 182
Av. del Tremolencs, 24, La Garriga, 08530 Barcelona, Catalonia
Tel: +34 900 87 87 98
Email: sek-catalunya@sek.es
Website: catalunya.sek.es
Principal: David Bauzá-Capart
Age range: 4 months–18 years
No. of pupils: 1040
Curriculum: IBDP, IBMYP, IBPYP
Language instr: English, Spanish, Catalan

SEK INTERNATIONAL SCHOOL CIUDALCAMPO
For further details see p. 183
Urb. Ciudalcampo, Paseo de las Perdices, 2, San Sebastián de los Reyes, 28707 Madrid
Tel: +34 900 87 87 98
Email: sek-ciudalcampo@sek.es
Website: ciudalcampo.sek.es
Principal: Cecilia Villavicencio
Age range: 4 months–18 years
No. of pupils: 1400
Curriculum: IBDP, IBMYP, IBPYP
Language instr: English, Spanish

SEK INTERNATIONAL SCHOOL EL CASTILLO
For further details see p. 185
Urb. Villafranca del Castillo, Castillo de Manzanares, s/n, Villanueva de la Cañada, 28692 Madrid
Tel: +34 900 87 87 98
Email: sek-castillo@sek.es
Website: madrid.sekinternationalschools.com
Head of School: Elvira Chiquero
Age range: 4 months–18 years
No. of pupils: 1150
Curriculum: IBDP, IBMYP, IBPYP
Language instr: English, Spanish

SEK INTERNATIONAL SCHOOL GLOBAL CAMPUS
For further details see p. 186
Urb. Villafranca del Castillo, Castillo de Manzanares, s/n, 28707 Ciudalcampo, Madrid
Email: sek-globalcampus@sek.online
Website: sek.es/l/colegio-internacional/online
Head of School: Ana Karina
Age range: 16–19 years
Curriculum: IBDP
Language instr: English

SEK INTERNATIONAL SCHOOL SANTA ISABEL
For further details see p. 188
Calle San Ildefonso, 18, 28012 Madrid
Tel: +34 900 87 87 98
Email: sek-santaisabel@sek.es
Website: santaisabel.sek.es
Head of School: Nilce Morales
Age range: 3–12 years
No. of pupils: 324
Curriculum: IBPYP
Language instr: English, Spanish

Europe

Shoreless Lake School
Apdo 239, 30850 Totana, Murcia
Tel: +34 968 424 386
Age range: 14–18
No. of pupils: 200
Curriculum: AP, USA

Sierra Bernia School
San Rafael S/N, Alfaz del Pi,
03580 Alicante, Valencia
Tel: +34 96 687 5149
Age range: 3–18
No. of pupils: 100 B50 G50
Curriculum: UK, GCSE, IGCSE, ALevs
Language instr: English

SOTOGRANDE INTERNATIONAL SCHOOL
For further details see p. 192
Avenida La Reserva
SN, Sotogrande, Cádiz,
Andalusia 11310
Tel: +34 956 795 902
Email: info@sis.ac
Website: www.sis.ac
Head of School: Rachel Dent
Age range: 4 months–18 years
No. of pupils: 1300
Fees: €901–€2,595
Curriculum: IBDP, IBMYP, IBPYP, National
Language instr: English, Spanish

St George's English Academy Bilbao
Alameda Urquijo 100, 48013
Bilbao, Biscay, Basque Country
Tel: +34 944 772 989

St Paul's School
Avenida Pearson 39-45, C/
Joan d'Alòs 19 · 21, 08034
Barcelona, Catalonia
Tel: +34 932 030 500
Age range: 3–18
No. of pupils: 670
Curriculum: UK

St Peter's School Barcelona
C/Eduard Toldrà, 18, 08034
Barcelona, Catalonia
Tel: +34 93 204 36 12
Age range: 1–18
Curriculum: IBDP, IBMYP, IBPYP
Language instr: English, Spanish

St. Anne's School
Av. de Alfonso XIII 162, 28016 Madrid
Tel: +34 913 459 060
Curriculum: IBDP
Language instr: English

St. Anthony's College
Camino de Coin KM 5,25, Mijas
Costa, 29649 Málaga, Andalusia
Tel: +34 952 47 31 66
Age range: 3–18
No. of pupils: 400
Curriculum: IGCSE

St. George, The British School Madrid
Calle Padres Dominicos
1, 28050 Madrid
Tel: +34 916 508 440
Age range: 2–18 years
Curriculum: IBDP, UK, IGCSE
Language instr: English, Spanish

St. George, The British School of Catalunya
Paseo de la Reina Elisenda
de Montcada 18, 08034
Barcelona, Catalonia
Tel: +34 931 293 024
Age range: 2–18 years
Curriculum: IBDP, UK, IGCSE
Language instr: English, Spanish

ST. GEORGE'S BRITISH INTERNATIONAL SCHOOL (BILBAO)
For further details see p. 196
Artazagane 51, 48940 Leioia,
Biscay, Basque Country
Tel: +34 94 4633692
Email: admissions@bisstgeorges.com
Website: www.bisstgeorges.com
Head of School: Chris Long
No. of pupils: 330
Curriculum: National, UK, IGCSE
Language instr: English, Spanish, French, Basque

St. Michael's - El Parque
C/ Río Guadiana 2, 28669
Boadilla del Monte, Madrid
Tel: +34 91 633 00 78

St. Michael's - Escorial
C/Udala 13, Urb la Pizarra,, San
Lorenzo de El Escorial, 28200 Madrid
Tel: +34 91 896 21 69
Age range: 6–18
No. of pupils: 300
Curriculum: UK

St. Michael's - Las Lomas
C/Valle de Bielsa 4, 28669
Boadilla del Monte, Madrid
Tel: +34 91 307 71 74
Age range: 6–18
No. of pupils: 300
Curriculum: UK

Stella Maris College & Prep School
Valdesquí 16, 28023 Madrid
Tel: +34 910 882 353
Curriculum: IBDP
Language instr: English, Spanish

Sunny View School
c/ Tereul No 32, Cerro de Toril, 29620
Torremolinos, Málaga, Andalusia
Tel: +34 952 383164
Age range: 4–18
No. of pupils: 300
Curriculum: ALevs

Swans International Primary School
Urbanizacion El Capricho s/n, 29602
Marbella, Málaga, Andalusia
Tel: +34 952 773 248
Age range: 3–11
No. of pupils: 250
Curriculum: IPC

Swans International Secondary School
C/Lago de los Cisnes, s/n, Urb.
Sierra Blanca, 29602 Marbella,
Málaga, Andalusia
Tel: +34 952 902 755
Age range: 3–18 years
Curriculum: IBDP, National, UK, GCSE, IGCSE
Language instr: English, Spanish

Thames British School Madrid Campus
Calle Barbero de Sevilla 16,
28222 Majadahonda, Madrid
Tel: +34 915 790 147
Age range: 1–18 years
Curriculum: IBDP, UK, IGCSE, ALevs
Language instr: English, Spanish

The Academy International School
Camí de Son Ametler Vell, 250,
07141 Marratxí, Balearic Islands
Tel: +34 971 605008
Age range: 2–19 years
Curriculum: IBDP, UK, IGCSE
Language instr: English

The Benalmádena International College
Clle Catamaran s/n, Nueva
Torrequebrada, 29630
Benalmádena, Málaga, Andalusia
Tel: +34 952 561 666
Age range: 4–19
No. of pupils: 300
Curriculum: UK

The British College
Urbanización Torremuelle, C/ Paseo
del Genil s/n, 29630 Benalmádena
Costa, Málaga, Andalusia
Tel: +34 952 44 22 15
Age range: 1–18
Curriculum: National, UK, IGCSE, ALevs

The British International School of Marbella
Calle Jacinto Benavente S/N, 29601
Marbella, Málaga, Andalusia
Tel: +34 952 779 264
Age range: 2–12
Curriculum: UK
Language instr: English

The British School of Almeria
Calle de Alemania 28, Roquetas
De Mar 04740, Almeria, Andalusia
Tel: +34 950 338 860
Age range: 3–18
Curriculum: UK, IGCSE
Language instr: English

The British School of Aragon
Calle Valencia, KM 8,500, 50410
Cuarte de Huerva, Zaragoza
Tel: +34 976 50 52 23
Curriculum: IBDP, IBPYP
Language instr: English, Spanish

The British School of Barcelona (BSB) Castelldefels
Carrer Ginesta 26, 08860
Castelldefels, Barcelona, Catalonia
Tel: +34 93 665 1584
Age range: 3–16 years
Curriculum: National, UK, IGCSE
Language instr: English

The British School of Barcelona (BSB) City Foundation Campus
Carrer de l'Esperança 32,
08017 Barcelona, Catalonia
Tel: +34 93 665 1584
Age range: 3–18 years
Curriculum: National, UK, IGCSE, ALevs
Language instr: English

The British School of Barcelona (BSB) City Main Campus
Carrer Lucà 1, 08022
Barcelona, Catalonia
Tel: +34 93 665 1584
Age range: 2–18 years
Curriculum: IBDP, National, UK, IGCSE, ALevs
Language instr: English

The British School of Barcelona (BSB) Nexus
Carrer Ginesta 2-10, 08860
Castelldefels, Barcelona, Catalonia
Tel: +34 93 665 1584
Age range: 16–18 years
Curriculum: National, UK, ALevs
Language instr: English

The British School of Barcelona (BSB) Sitges
Passeig Isaac Albéniz s/n, 08870
Sitges, Barcelona, Catalonia
Tel: +34 93 811 0305
Age range: 2–10 years
Curriculum: National, UK
Language instr: English

The British School of Navarra
Camino Ardanaz 4, 31620
Pamplona, Navarre
Tel: +34 948 242 826
Age range: 2–18 years
Curriculum: IBDP, UK, IGCSE, ALevs
Language instr: English, Spanish

The British School of Seville
Urbanizacion Pinar de la Juliana,
Bollullos de la Mitacion, Seville
Tel: +34 902 024 890
Age range: 5–16
Curriculum: UK, IGCSE
Language instr: English, Spanish

The English International College
Urb Ricmar, Crtr de Cádiz Km 189.5,
29600 Marbella, Málaga, Andalusia
Tel: +34 952 83 1058/9
Age range: 3–18
No. of pupils: 500
Curriculum: SAT, UK, GCSE, IGCSE, ALevs
Language instr: English

Europe

The English Montessori School
C/ Auriga 3, 28023 Aravaca, Madrid
Tel: +34 913 572 667
Age range: 3–18 years
Curriculum: National, UK, IGCSE, ALevs
Language instr: English

The English School
Calle Pintor Gisbert, 3, Mutxamel, 3110 Alicante, Valencia
Tel: +34 965 95 10 17
Curriculum: UK
Language instr: English, Spanish

THE GLOBAL COLLEGE
For further details see p. 211
C. de Castellón de la Plana 8, 28006 Madrid
Tel: +34 915 689 937
Email: info@theglobalcollege.com
Website: theglobalcollege.com
Principal: Barry Cooper
Age range: 15–18 years
Curriculum: IBDP
Language instr: English

The International School Estepona
Centro Commercial La Zarza Calle Azahar, Urbanisation El Paraiso, 29688 Estepona, Málaga, Andalusia
Tel: +34 952 88 47 89
Age range: 2–12
Curriculum: SAT, UK

The Olive Tree School
C/ Modistes, 8 Sant Pere de Ribes, 08812 Barcelona, Catalonia
Tel: +34 931 886 215
Age range: 3–16 years
No. of pupils: 200
Curriculum: UK, IGCSE

Willow International School
Pueblo Bravo, Av. del Mar, 2b, 03170 Ciudad Quesada, Alicante, Valencia
Tel: +34 602 490 917
Age range: 6–18
Curriculum: UK
Language instr: English

Wingate School
Mirador de la Cumbrita, 10, Cabo Blanco, Arona, Tenerife, Canary Islands
Tel: +34 922 720 102
Curriculum: UK, IGCSE, ALevs

Xàbia International School (Primary)
Ctra Portitxol 70, Alicante, Valencia
Tel: +34 96 647 21 21
Age range: 2–11
No. of pupils: 160
Curriculum: UK

Xàbia International School (Secondary)
Apartado de Correos 311, 03730 Jávea, Alicante, Valencia
Tel: +34 96 647 1785
Age range: 12–18
No. of pupils: 130
Curriculum: UK, ALevs
Language instr: English, Spanish, German, French

Yago School Sevilla
Avda. Antonio Mairena 54, 41950 Castilleja de la Cuesta, Seville, Andalusia
Tel: +34 955 51 1234
Age range: 0–18 years
No. of pupils: 945
Curriculum: IBDP, IBPYP
Language instr: English, Spanish, Chinese

Zürich Schule Barcelona
73 Pearson Avenue, 08034 Barcelona, Catalonia
Tel: +34 932 037 606
Curriculum: IBMYP, IBPYP
Language instr: German, Spanish

SWEDEN

Aranäsgymnasiet
Gymnasiegatan 44, 434 42 Kungsbacka, Halland
Tel: +46 300 83 40 00
No. of pupils: 1400
Curriculum: IBDP
Language instr: English

Bladins International School of Malmö
Box 20093, Själlandstorget 1, 200 74 Malmö, Skåne
Tel: +46 40 987970
Age range: 1–19 years
Curriculum: IBMYP, IBPYP
Language instr: English

British International School of Stockholm
Östrka Valhallavagen 17, 182 68 Djursholm, Stockholm
Tel: +46 8 755 2375
Age range: 3–16
No. of pupils: 334 B183 G151
Curriculum: IBDP, SAT, UK
Language instr: English

Dibber International School Sollentuna
Lindvägen 16, 192 70 Sollentuna, Stockholm
Tel: +46 73 3350916
Curriculum: IBMYP, IBPYP
Language instr: English, Swedish

Engelska Skolan Norr
Roslagstullsbacken 4, Stockholm
Curriculum: UK

Europaskolan in Södermalm
Gotlandsgatan 43, 116 65 Stockholm
Tel: +46 8 335054
Curriculum: IBMYP, IBPYP

Futuraskolan International School of Stockholm
Erik Dahlbergsgatan 58, 115 57 Stockholm
Tel: +46 736 001 314
Language instr: English, Swedish

International IT College of Sweden
Halsobrunnsgatan 6, 104 30 Stockholm
Tel: +46 8 704 22 15
Age range: 16–19

International Pre School of Lund
Warholmsvag 2, 224 65 Lund, Skåne
Tel: +46 46140767
Age range: 3–6
No. of pupils: 30

International School of Helsingborg
Östra Vallgatan 9, 254 37 Helsingborg, Skåne
Tel: +46 42 105 705
Age range: 3–20
No. of pupils: 450
Curriculum: IBDP, IBMYP, IBPYP, SAT
Language instr: English

International School of the Gothenburg Region (ISGR)
Molinsgatan 6, 411 33 Göteborg, Västra Götaland
Tel: +46 31 708 92 00
Age range: 5–18
No. of pupils: 831
Curriculum: IBMYP, IBPYP
Language instr: English

Internationella Engelska Skolan
Ostgotagatan 12, 582 32 Linköping, Östergötland
Tel: +46 13 35 5680
Age range: 4–19
No. of pupils: 800

Internationella Engelska Skolan Orebro
Hagmarksgatan 39, Örebro
Tel: +46 19 2652240
Age range: 6–9
No. of pupils: 480

Internationella Engelska Skolan Taby (Junior School)
Nytorpsvägen 36, 183 53 Taby, Stockholm
Tel: +46 8 120 457 66
No. of pupils: 1120
Curriculum: National

Kungsholmen's Gymnasium, International Section
Hantverkargatan 67-69, PO Box 12601, 112 92 Stockholm
Tel: +46 8 508 38 006
Age range: 16–20
No. of pupils: 450 B175 G275
Language instr: English

Lund International School
Warholmsväg 3, 224 65 Lund, Skåne
Tel: +46737087926
Age range: 3–13
No. of pupils: 170 B85 G85
Curriculum: IBMYP, IBPYP
Language instr: English

Lycée Français Saint Louis de Stockholm
Essingestråket 24, 112 66 Stockholm
Tel: +46 8 4413030
Age range: 6–18
No. of pupils: 600

Mälardalen International School
Hydrovägen 3, 721 36 Västerås
Tel: +46 10 498 4301
Curriculum: IBPYP
Language instr: English

Malmö Borgarskola
Box 17029, 200 10 Malmö, Skåne
Tel: +46 4034 1000
Age range: 16–19
No. of pupils: 240 B90 G150
Curriculum: IBDP, IBCP
Language instr: English

Malmö International School
Packhusgatan 2, 205 80 Malmö, Skåne
Tel: +46 (0)733 23 70 37
Age range: 6–16
No. of pupils: 360
Curriculum: IBMYP, IBPYP
Language instr: English

Sigtunaskolan Humanistiska Läroverket
Box 508, 193 28 Sigtunase, Stockholm
Tel: +46 8 592 571 00
Age range: 13–19
Curriculum: IBDP, IBMYP, IBCP
Language instr: English, Swedish

Stockholm International School
Johannesgatan 18, 111 38 Stockholm
Tel: +46 8 412 40 00
Age range: 3–18 years
Curriculum: IBDP, IBMYP, IBPYP
Language instr: English

Uppsala International School - Kvarngärdesskolan
Thunmansgatan 47, 754 21 Uppsala
Tel: +46 18 727 5900
Age range: 6–16
No. of pupils: 104 B32 G52

SWITZERLAND

academia College
Lagerstrasse 1, 8004 Zürich ZH
Tel: +41 58 440 90 21

Europe

ACADEMIA SCHOOLS
For further details see p. 90
Academia Group Switzerland AG,
Binzmühlestrasse 15, 8050 Zürich ZH
Tel: +41 61 260 20 80
Email: info@academia-group.ch
Website:
www.academia-schools.ch
**Co-CEOs Academia
Schools:** Ludovic Allenspach,
Roman Meier & Peter Petrin
Age range: 3–18 years
Curriculum: National, IGCSE, ALevs
Language instr: English, German

Aiglon College
Avenue Centrale 61, 1885 Chesières
Tel: +41 (0)24 496 6177
Age range: 7–18 years
No. of pupils: 460
Curriculum: IBDP, SAT, UK, IGCSE
Language instr: English

Bilingual School Terra Nova
Florastr 19, 8700 Küsnacht ZH
Tel: +41 44 910 43 00
Age range: 4–14
No. of pupils: 200 B102 G98
Curriculum: National
Language instr: German, English

BKA International School
Gellertstrasse 25, 4052 Basel BS
Tel: +41 61 311 76 62
Curriculum: IBPYP
Language instr: English, German

Brillantmont International School
Avenue Secrétan 16,
1005 Lausanne VD
Tel: +41 21 310 04 00
Age range: 11–18
No. of pupils: 140
Curriculum: AP, SAT, UK,
USA, IGCSE, ALevs
Language instr: English

British School of Geneva
Avenue de Châtelaine 95A,
Châtelaine, 1219 Geneva GE
Tel: +41 22 795 75 10
Age range: 4–18
Curriculum: UK, IGCSE, ALevs
Language instr: English

Buissonnets Montani
Rue Saint-Guérin 26, 1950 Sion VS
Tel: +41 27 322 00 80

Campus Muristalden Gymnasium
Muristrasse 8, 3000 Bern BE
Tel: +41 31 350 42 50

Collège Alpin Beau Soleil
Route du Village 1, 1884
Villars-sur-Ollon
Tel: +41 24 496 26 26
Age range: 11–18 years
Curriculum: IBDP, IBMYP, National,
FrenchBacc, SAT, TOEFL, UK, IGCSE
Language instr: English, French

Collège Champittet, Pully
Chemin de Champittet
1, 1009 Pully VD
Tel: +41 21 721 05 05
Age range: 3–18 years
No. of pupils: 700
Curriculum: IBDP, National,
FrenchBacc
Language instr: French, English

Collège du Léman
74, route de Sauverny, 1290 Versoix GE
Tel: +41 22 775 56 56
Age range: 2–18 years
(boarding from 10)
Curriculum: AP, IBDP, IBCP,
IPC, National, FrenchBacc,
SAT, IGCSE, ALevs
Language instr: English, French

Collège et Lycée St-Charles
Route de Belfort 10,
2900 Porrentruy JU
Tel: +41 32 466 11 57
Curriculum: IBDP, IBMYP
Language instr: English

Copperfield Verbier
Rue de la Bérarde 10, Le
Hameau, 1936 Verbier VS
Tel: +41 27 520 61 00
Age range: 4–18 years
No. of pupils: 70
Curriculum: IBDP, IBPYP
Language instr: English

Ecole des Arches
Rue Pépinet, 1003 Lausanne VD
Tel: +41 21 311 09 69
Age range: 16–18+ years
Curriculum: National
Language instr: French

Ecole d'Humanité
Gmeindi 318b, 6085
Hasliberg Goldern BE
Tel: +41 33 972 9292
Age range: 12–19 years
No. of pupils: 120
Curriculum: AP, USA
Language instr: German, English

Ecole française de Bâle - Section Elémentaire
Engelgasse 103, 4052 Basel BS
Tel: +41 61 311 07 30
Age range: 6–11
No. of pupils: 100

Ecole Francaise de Berne
Sulgenrain 11, 3007 Bern BE
Tel: +41 31 376 17 57
No. of pupils: 150
Curriculum: National

Ecole française de Lausanne Valmont
Route d'Oron 47, 1010 Lausanne VD
Tel: 41 (0)21 652 37 33
Curriculum: FrenchBacc

Ecole Mosaic
23, avenue Dumas, 1206 Geneva GE
Tel: +41 22 346 21 69
Age range: 3–12
No. of pupils: 250
Curriculum: UK
Language instr: English, French

Ecole Moser Genève
81 Chemin De-La-Montagne,
1224 Chêne-Bougeries GE
Tel: +41 (0)22 860 80 80
Curriculum: IBDP
Language instr: English, French

Ecole Moser Nyon
4-6 Avenue Reverdil, 1260 Nyon VD
Tel: +41 (0)22 593 88 88
Curriculum: IBDP
Language instr: English, French

Ecole Nouvelle de la Suisse Romande - Lausanne
Chemin de Rovéréaz 20,
CP 161, 1012 Lausanne
Tel: +41 21 654 65 00
Age range: 2.5–18 years
No. of pupils: 550
Curriculum: IBDP
Language instr: French, English

École Primaire Française de Genève
3 Chemin des Vergers,
1208 Geneva GE
Tel: +41 22 735 60 20
Age range: 5–11

Ecole Riviera
Avenue des Planches 25, Case
Postale 1347, 1820 Montreux VD
Tel: +41 21 961 18 72
Age range: 3 months–12 years

ELA Basel
Gartenstrasse 93, 4052 Basel BS
Tel: +41 61 313 05 80
Curriculum: UK
Language instr: English

Four-Forest Bilingual International School – LMS
Maihofstrasse 95a, 6006 Luzern LU
Age range: 15–16 years
Curriculum: UK
Language instr: German

Four-Forest Bilingual International School – Luzern
Maihofstrasse 95a, 6006 Luzern LU
Tel: +41 41 320 25 31
Age range: 3–15 years
Curriculum: National
Language instr: English, German

Four-Forest Bilingual International School – Zug
Chollerstrasse 23, 6312
Zug-Steinhausen ZG
Tel: +41 41 783 27 27
Age range: 3–11 years
Curriculum: National
Language instr: English, German

Freies Gymnasium Zürich
Arbenzstrasse 19, 8034 Zürich ZH
Tel: +41 43 456 77 77
Age range: 11–14
Language instr: English, German

Geneva English School
36 Route de Malagny,
1294 Genthod GE
Tel: +41 22 775 0440
Age range: 3–18 years
No. of pupils: 350
Curriculum: UK, GCSE, IGCSE, ALevs
Language instr: English, French

Gymnasium, Wirtschafts- und Fachmittelschule Thun
Seestrasse 66, 3604 Thun BE
Tel: +41 (0)33 359 58 58
Age range: 14–19
Curriculum: National

HAUT-LAC INTERNATIONAL BILINGUAL SCHOOL
For further details see p. 118
Ch. de Pangires 26, St-Légier-
la Chiésaz CH-1806
Tel: +41 (0)21 555 51 29
Email: admissions@haut-lac.ch
Website: www.haut-lac.ch
**Infant & Primary
Head:** Renaud Milhoux
Age range: 18 months–18 years
No. of pupils: 650
Fees: Day CHF24,900–CHF36,100
FB CHF72,000–CHF88,000
Curriculum: IBDP, IBMYP, USA

Hochalpines Institut Ftan (HIF)
Chalchera 154, 7551 Ftan GR
Tel: +41 81 861 22 11
Age range: 12–18 years
No. of pupils: 70
Curriculum: IBDP, IGCSE
Language instr: English, German

Hull's School
Falkenstrasse 28a, 8008 Zürich ZH
Tel: +41 44 254 30 40
Age range: 16–19
Curriculum: GCSE, ALevs

Institut auf dem Rosenberg
Hohenweg 60, 9000 St Gallen SG
Tel: +41 71 277 77 77
Age range: 7–19
No. of pupils: 150 B90 G60
Curriculum: IBDP
Language instr: English, German

Institut Florimont
37 Avenue du Petit-Lancy,
1213 Petit-Lancy GE
Tel: +41 22 879 0000
Age range: 3–18 years
No. of pupils: 1705
Curriculum: IBDP,
FrenchBacc, SAT, IGCSE
Language instr: English, French

Europe

Institut International de Lancy
24, avenue Eugène-Lance, Grand-Lancy CH-1212
Tel: +41 22 794 2620
Age range: 3–19 years
No. of pupils: 1500
Curriculum: IBDP, FrenchBacc, IGCSE
Language instr: English, French

INSTITUT LE CHÂTELARD
For further details see p. 127
Route des Narcisses 80, 1833 Les-Avants-sur-Montreux
Tel: +41 21 989 8000
Email: info@lechatelard.com
Website: www.ecolechatelard.ch
Head of School: Federica Páez
Age range: G13–17 (annual) & 12–15 (summer camps)
Fees: FB CHF107,550–CHF124,400
Language instr: French

Institut Le Rosey
Château du Rosey, 1180 Rolle VD
Tel: +41 21 822 5500
Age range: 8–18 years
No. of pupils: 460
Curriculum: IBDP, FrenchBacc
Language instr: English, French

INSTITUT MONTANA SWITZERLAND
For further details see p. 128
Schönfels 5, 6300 Zug ZG
Tel: +41 41 729 11 77
Email: admissions@montana-zug.ch
Website: www.montana-zug.ch
Director: Collective Leadership Model
Age range: 6–19 years
No. of pupils: 360
Fees: Day CHF32,900–CHF36,800 FB CHF70,400–CHF72,800
Curriculum: IBDP, National, UK, IGCSE
Language instr: English, German

Institut Monte Rosa
Avenue de Chillon 57, 1820 Montreux VD
Tel: +41 21 965 4545
Age range: 8–20
No. of pupils: 70 B45 G25
Curriculum: AP, SAT, TOEFL, USA
Language instr: English

Institut Villa Pierrefeu
Route de Caux 28, 1823 Glion Sur Montreux VD
Tel: +41 21 963 73 11
Age range: G15–30+
No. of pupils: 30

INTER-COMMUNITY SCHOOL ZURICH
For further details see p. 129
Strubenacher 3, 8126 Zumikon
Tel: +41 44 919 8300
Email: contact@icsz.ch
Website: www.icsz.ch
Age range: 24 months–18 years
No. of pupils: 800
Fees: Day CHF12,600–CHF39,700
Curriculum: IBDP, IBMYP, IBPYP
Language instr: English

International School Altdorf
St. Josefsweg 15, 6460 Altdorf UR
Tel: +41 41 874 0000
Age range: 13–19 years
No. of pupils: 100
Curriculum: IBDP, IBMYP, IBCP, IGCSE
Language instr: English

International School Basel
Fleischbachstrasse 2, 4153 Reinach
Tel: +41 61 715 33 33
Age range: 3–19 years
No. of pupils: 1300
Curriculum: IBDP, IBMYP, IBPYP, SAT
Language instr: English, German

International School of Berne
Allmendingenweg 9, 3073 Gümligen, Bern
Tel: +41 (0)31 959 10 00
Age range: 3–19 years
No. of pupils: 276
Curriculum: IBDP, IBMYP, IBPYP
Language instr: English

International School of Geneva (Campus des Nations)
11 route des Morillons, 1218 Grand Saconnex GE
Tel: +41 22 770 4700
Age range: 3–11
No. of pupils: 963
Curriculum: IBDP, IBMYP, IBPYP, IBCP
Language instr: English, French

International School of Geneva (La Châtaigneraie Campus)
2 chemin de la Ferme, 1297 Founex VD
Tel: +41 22 960 9111
Age range: 3–19
No. of pupils: 1538
Curriculum: IBDP, IBPYP, IGCSE
Language instr: English, French

International School of Geneva (La Grande Boissière Campus)
62, route de Chêne, 1208 Geneva GE
Tel: +41 22 787 2400
Age range: 3–19
No. of pupils: 4438 B2326 G2112 VIth320
Curriculum: IBDP
Language instr: English, French

International School of Kreuzlingen Konstanz
Hauptstrasse 27, 8280 Kreuzlingen TG
Tel: +41 71 672 2727
Age range: 3–19 years
Language instr: English, German, French

INTERNATIONAL SCHOOL OF LAUSANNE
For further details see p. 139
Chemin de la Grangette 2, 1052 Le Mont-sur-Lausanne VD
Tel: +41 21 560 02 02
Email: admissions@isl.ch
Website: www.isl.ch
Director: Frazer Cairns
Age range: 3–18 years
No. of pupils: 860
Fees: Day CHF14,600–CHF38,600
Curriculum: IBDP, IBMYP, IBPYP, SAT
Language instr: English

International School of Rheinfelden
Zürcherstrasse 9, Drei Könige, 4310 Rheinfelden AG
Tel: +41 61 831 06 06
Age range: 2–14
No. of pupils: 80
Curriculum: IBPYP
Language instr: English, German

International School of Schaffhausen
Mühlentalstrasse 280, 8200 Schaffhausen SH
Tel: +41 52 624 1707
Age range: 3 months–18 years
No. of pupils: 300
Curriculum: IBDP, IBPYP
Language instr: English

INTERNATIONAL SCHOOL OF TICINO SA
For further details see p. 147
Via Ponteggia, 23, Cadempino, 6814 Lugano
Tel: +41 919710344
Email: frontoffice@isticino.com
Website: www.isticino.com
Head of School: Mark Waldron
Age range: 3–18 years
No. of pupils: 280
Curriculum: IBDP, IBMYP, IBPYP
Language instr: English, Italian

International School of Zug & Luzern, Riverside Campus
Rothusstrasse 4b, 6331 Hünenberg ZG
Tel: +41 41 768 2950
Age range: 12–18
Curriculum: AP, IBDP, IBMYP, IBPYP, SAT, TOEFL
Language instr: English

International School of Zug & Luzern, Zug Campus
Walterswil, 6340 Baar ZG
Tel: +41 41 768 29 00
Age range: 3–18
No. of pupils: 1250
Curriculum: UK, USA
Language instr: English

International School Rheintal
Werdenbergstrasse 17, 9470 Buchs SG
Tel: +41 81 750 6300
Age range: 3–19 years
No. of pupils: 200
Curriculum: IBDP, IBMYP, IBPYP
Language instr: English

INTERNATIONAL SCHOOL ZURICH NORTH (ISZN)
For further details see p. 150
Industriestrasse 50, 8304 Wallisellen ZH
Tel: +41 44 830 70 00
Email: info@iszn.ch
Website: www.iszn.ch
Headmaster: James Stenning
Age range: 3 months–18 years
No. of pupils: 240
Fees: Day CHF17,316–CHF38,280
Curriculum: IBPYP, IGCSE, ALevs
Language instr: English

International School Zurich West
Unterrohrstrasse 3, 8952 Schlieren ZH
Tel: +41 44 433 3000
Age range: 3–11

ISCS – The British School of Zug
Lorzenparkstrasse 8, 6330 Cham ZG
Tel: +41 41 781 44 44
Age range: 3–19 years
No. of pupils: 200
Curriculum: IGCSE, ALevs
Language instr: English

John F. Kennedy International School
8 Chilchgasse, 3792 Saanen BE
Tel: +41 (0) 33 755 15 74
Age range: 2.5–14 years
No. of pupils: 100
Curriculum: IPC
Language instr: English, French

Juventus Schule Zürich
Lagerstrasse 45, Postfach 3021, Zürich 8021
Tel: +41 43 268 25 11
Age range: 16–21
No. of pupils: 1000 B500 G500
Language instr: English, German, French, Italian

Kantonsschule Baden
Seminarstrasse 3, 5400 Baden AG
Tel: +41 056 200 04 44

Kantonsschule Kusnacht
village Strasse 30, 8700 Kusnacht ZH
Tel: +41 44 913 1717

Kumon Leysin Academy of Switzerland
1854 Leysin VD
Tel: +41 24 4935 335
Age range: 16–19
No. of pupils: 182 B85 G97
Curriculum: AP, SAT, TOEFL

Europe

La Côte International School Aubonne
Chemin de Clamogne 8,
1170 Aubonne VD
Tel: +41 (0)22 823 26 26
Age range: 3–18 years
No. of pupils: 430
Curriculum: IBDP, IPC, National, UK, IGCSE
Language instr: English, French

La Garenne International School
Chemin des Chavasses 23,
1885 Chesières-Villars VD
Tel: +41 (0)24 495 24 53
Age range: 4–18 years
No. of pupils: 170
Curriculum: IBDP, IBMYP, IPC, USA
Language instr: English

Lakeside School Horgen
Alte Landstrasse 33-35,
8810 Horgen ZH
Tel: +41 43 244 00 70
Curriculum: National
Language instr: English, German

Lakeside School Küsnacht
Seestrasse 5, 8700 Kusnacht ZH
Tel: +41 44 914 2050
Age range: 3–12
Curriculum: National
Language instr: English, German

Le Régent International School
Rue du Zier 4, CH-3963 Crans-Montana
Tel: +41 (0)27 480 3201
Age range: 4–18 years
Curriculum: IBDP
Language instr: English, French

Lemania College Lausanne
Chemin de Préville 3,
1003 Lausanne VD
Tel: +41 21 320 15 01
Age range: 15–20 years
No. of pupils: 30
Curriculum: IBDP
Language instr: English

Leysin American School in Switzerland
3 Chemin de la Source,
1854 Leysin VD
Tel: +41 24 493 4878
Age range: 12–18 years
No. of pupils: 300
Curriculum: AP, IBDP, USA
Language instr: English

Lyceum Alpinum Zuoz
Lyceum Alpinum 12, 7524 Zuoz GR
Tel: +41 81 851 30 00
Age range: 12–19 years
No. of pupils: 340
Curriculum: IBDP
Language instr: English, German

Montreux International School
Avenue de Chillon 60,
1820 Montreux VD
Tel: +41 79 596 29 06
Language instr: English

Mutuelle d'études secondaires
7 bis Boulevard Carl Vogt,
1205 Geneva GE
Tel: +41 (0)22 741 00 01
Age range: 15–22
No. of pupils: 60
Curriculum: IBDP
Language instr: French

Neuchâtel Junior College
Cret Taconnet 4, 2002 Neuchatel NE
Tel: +41 (0)32 722 1860
Age range: 16–18 years
No. of pupils: 75
Curriculum: AP, SAT
Language instr: English

Obersee Bilingual School (OBS)
Sihleggstrasse 9, 8832 Wollerau SZ
Tel: +41 55 511 38 00
Age range: 1–18 years
Curriculum: IBDP, IPC, National
Language instr: English, German

Rudolf Steiner Schule Oberaargau
Ringstrasse 30, 4900 Langenthal BE
Tel: +41 (0)62 922 69 05
Curriculum: IBDP
Language instr: English, German

Scuola Rudolf Steiner ii Lugano Origlio
via ai Magi 4, 6945 Origlio TI
Tel: +41 (0)91 966 29 62
Curriculum: IBDP
Language instr: English, Italian

SIS Swiss International School Basel
Erlenstrasse 15, 4058 Basel BS
Tel: +41 61 683 71 40
Age range: 3–18 years
Curriculum: IBDP, National
Language instr: English, German

SIS Swiss International School Basel-Allschwil
Hegenheimermattweg 167c, 4123 Allschwil BL
Tel: +41 61 486 38 00
Age range: 3–12 years
Curriculum: National
Language instr: English, German

SIS Swiss International School Männedorf-Zürich
Seestrasse 57, 8708 Männedorf ZH
Tel: +41 44 921 50 50
Age range: 3–12 years
Language instr: English, German

SIS Swiss International School Päffikon-Schwyz
Eichenstrasse 5, 8808 Pfäffikon SZ
Tel: +41 55 415 44 00
Age range: 3–18 years
Language instr: English, German

SIS Swiss International School Rotkreuz-Zug
Suurstoffi 41c, 6343 Rotkreuz ZG
Tel: +41 41 757 57 11
Age range: 3–16 years
Language instr: English, German

SIS Swiss International School Schönenwerd
Schachenstrasse 24, 5012 Schönenwerd SO
Tel: +41 62 312 30 30
Age range: 3–12 years
Language instr: English, German

SIS Swiss International School Zürich
Seidenstrasse 2, 8304 Wallisellen ZH
Tel: +41 44 388 99 44
Age range: 3–18 years
Curriculum: IBDP
Language instr: English, German

SIS Swiss International School Zürich-Wollishofen
Seestrasse 271, 8038 Zürich ZH
Tel: +41 43 399 88 44
Age range: 3–12 years
Language instr: English, German

ST. GEORGE'S INTERNATIONAL SCHOOL, SWITZERLAND
For further details see p. 197
Chemin de St. Georges 19,
CH-1815 Clarens/Montreux
Tel: +41 21 964 3411
Email: admissions@stgeorges.ch
Website: www.stgeorges.ch
Head of School: Ruth Norris
Age range: 1.5–18 years
No. of pupils: 400
Curriculum: IBDP, SAT, TOEFL, USA, IGCSE
Language instr: English, French

Stiftsschule Engelberg
Benediktinerkloster 5, Engelberg 6390
Tel: +41 41 639 61 00
Age range: 12–19 years
No. of pupils: 120
Curriculum: IBDP, National
Language instr: German, English

Surval Montreux
Route de Glion 56, 1820 Montreux VD
Tel: +41 21 966 16 16
Language instr: English

Tandem IMS (International Multilingual School)
Zurich Campus, Seefeldstrasse 111, 8008 Zürich ZH
Tel: +41 43 500 10 30
Curriculum: UK

TASIS THE AMERICAN SCHOOL IN SWITZERLAND
For further details see p. 202
Via Collina d'Oro 15, 6926 Montagnola-Lugano
Tel: +41 91 960 5151
Email: admissions@tasis.ch
Website: www.tasis.ch
Head of School: Christopher Nikoloff
Age range: 3–19 years
No. of pupils: 730
Fees: Day CHF54,500 FB CHF104,500
Curriculum: ACT, AP, IBDP, SAT, USA
Language instr: English

The Bell Language School
12 Chemin des Colombettes,
1202 Geneva GE
Tel: +41 22 749 16 00
Age range: 2–17
No. of pupils: 345

The British School, Bern
Sperlisacher 2, 3075 Rüfenacht BE
Tel: +41 31 952 7555
Age range: 3–12
No. of pupils: 100 B50 G50
Curriculum: UK
Language instr: English

Verbier International School
Route de Verbier Station 88, 1936 Verbier VS
Tel: +41 27 565 26 56
Age range: 2–16 years
No. of pupils: 120
Curriculum: IBDP, IGCSE
Language instr: English, French

Zurich International School
Steinacherstrasse 140,
8820 Wädenswil ZH
Tel: +41 58 750 2500
Age range: 3–18 years
No. of pupils: 1300
Curriculum: AP, IBDP, SAT
Language instr: English

TÜRKIYE

ABC Okullari Göksu Kampüsü
Göksu Mahallesi 93, Cadde No. 6/1A, Eryaman, Ankara, Central Anatolia
Tel: +90 312 444 2221
Curriculum: IBDP, IBPYP
Language instr: English, Turkish

Açi Schools
Bahçeköy Valide Sultan Cad Su Kemeri Mevkii No:2, Sariyer, 34473 Istanbul, Marmara
Tel: +90 212 349 07 00
Age range: 3–17
Curriculum: National, IGCSE, ALevs

Europe

Acibadem Schools - Acibadem Campus
Acibadem Mah. Cecen Sok. No:48 Ic Kapi No:1, Üsküdar, 34730 Istanbul, Marmara
Tel: +90 216 510 52 32
Curriculum: IBPYP
Language instr: Turkey

Aka School
Radyum Sok No 21 Basin Sitesi, Bahcelievler, Istanbul, Marmara
Tel: +90 212 557 27 72
Age range: 5–18
No. of pupils: 503 B238 G265
Curriculum: IBDP, National
Language instr: Turkish, English

AlJazari International School of Science & Technology
Atakent Mah. 242nd Street, No. 4-3 A Block, Küçükçekmece, 34307 Istanbul, Marmara
Tel: +90 530 930 33 20
Curriculum: IBDP, IBPYP
Language instr: English, Arabic

ALKEV Schools
Alkent 2000 Mah. Mehmet Yesilgül Cd. No: 7, Büyükcekmece, 34535 Istanbul, Marmara
Tel: +90 212 886 88 40
Curriculum: IBDP
Language instr: English, German

Antalya College
Bayindir Mah 333 Sok, PK 545, Antalya, Mediterranean
Tel: +90 242 238 23 00
Age range: 5–17
No. of pupils: 1600
Curriculum: IGCSE

AREL Schools (Kindergarten/Primary/Middle/High)
Merkez Mah, Selahattin Pinar Sok, No:3 Yenibosna Bahcelievler, 34197 Istanbul, Marmara
Tel: +90 212 550 49 30
Age range: 3–18
No. of pupils: 1030 B520 G510
Curriculum: IBMYP, IBPYP
Language instr: Turkish, English

Avrupa Koleji
Prof Muammer Ahsoy Cad No 10, Zeytinburnu, Istanbul, Marmara
Tel: +90 212 547 80 10
Age range: 5–19
No. of pupils: 508
(ECIS)

Balikesir Aci College
Cayirhisar Mah. Yeni Izmir yolu Cad. 3B, 10185 Balikesir, Marmara
Tel: +90 266 239 85 85
Curriculum: IBDP
Language instr: English, Turkish

Batikent ABC Anaokulu
Yenibati Mahallesi 2398, Sok. No. 15, Batikent, Ankara, Central Anatolia
Tel: +90 312 256 12 22
Curriculum: IBPYP
Language instr: English, Turkish

Beykoz Doga Campus
Fener Yolu Cad. No:6 Dereseki, Akbaba, Beykoz, 81650 Istanbul, Marmara
Tel: +90 216 320 52 00
Curriculum: IBPYP
Language instr: English

Bilkent Laboratory & International School
East Campus, 06800 Ankara, Central Anatolia
Tel: +90 312 290 53 61
Age range: 4–18
No. of pupils: 575 B264 G311
Curriculum: IBDP, IBMYP, IBPYP, National, SAT, UK
Language instr: English, Turkish
(CIS) (ECIS)

BJK - Kabatas Vakfi Özel Okullari
Camlica Mahallesi, Seker Maslak Sk. No. 11, Üsküdar, Istanbul, Marmara
Tel: +90 216 326 19 03
Curriculum: IBDP
Language instr: English, Turkish

Bodrum Marmara Elementary School
Cumhuriyet Avenue No. 2, 48420 Bodrum, Aegean
Tel: +90 252 358 61 13
Curriculum: IBPYP
Language instr: English, Turkish

Bodrum Marmara Private College
Cumhuriyet Avenue No. 2, 48420 Bodrum, Aegean
Tel: +90 252 358 61 13
Curriculum: IBDP
Language instr: English, Turkish

British Embassy School Ankara
Sehit Ersan Caddesi 46/A, Cankaya, 06680 Ankara, Central Anatolia
Tel: +90 312 468 65 63
Age range: 3–13
No. of pupils: 200
Curriculum: IPC, SAT, UK
Language instr: English
(COB)

British International School Istanbul - Zekeriyaköy
Zekeriyaköy Mahallesi, Kilyos Caddesi No. 227/12, Sariyer, Istanbul, Marmara
Tel: +90 212 202 70 27
Age range: 2.5–18 years
Curriculum: IBDP
Language instr: English

Cakir Schools
Orhaneli Yolu, Egitimciler Cd 15, Nilüfer, Bursa, Marmara
Tel: +90 224 451 93 30
Curriculum: IBDP, IBMYP, IBPYP
Language instr: Turkish

Çanakkale Özel Ilkokulu
Izmir Yolu 12. Km Güzelyali, Güzelyali, 17100 Canakkale, Marmara
Tel: +90 286 232 86 86
Curriculum: IBPYP
Language instr: English, Turkish

Darussafaka Schools
B.dere cad. Derbent Mevkii, Sariyer, 34457 Istanbul, Marmara
Tel: +90 212 286 22 00

Deutsche Schule Istanbul – Özel Alman Lisesi
Sahkulu Bostani Sokak No. 10, Beyoglu, 34420 Istanbul, Marmara
Tel: +90 212 245 13 90

Deutsche Schule Izmir
Kuscular Cad. No. 82, Kuscular Köyü, Urla, 35430 Izmir, Aegean
Tel: +90 232 234 75 07
Age range: 2–19
No. of pupils: 157
Curriculum: IBDP
Language instr: German, English

Edirne Beykent Schools
Ayse Kadin Tren Gari Yani, 22100 Edirne, Marmara
Tel: +90 506 301 70 73

Egitmen Koleji
Istasyon Mah. Fevzi Çakmak Cad. No: 123, Tuzla, 34940 Istanbul, Marmara
Tel: +90 216 446 48 46
Curriculum: IBPYP
Language instr: Turkish

Emine Ornek Schools
Bademli Mah, Egitim Cad 12 Sokak No 2, 16940 Bursa, Marmara
Tel: +90 224 549 16 00
Language instr: English, Turkish
(CIS) (ECIS)

Enka Schools - Adapazari Campus
Dagdibi Mahallesi, Enka Yolu Caddesi, No. 66/A, Adapazari, Marmara
Tel: +90 264 323 37 74
Curriculum: IBMYP, IBPYP
Language instr: English, Turkish

Enka Schools - Istanbul Campus
Sadi Gülcelik Spor Sitesi, Istinye, 34460 Istanbul, Marmara
Tel: +90 212 705 65 00
Curriculum: IBDP, IBMYP, IBPYP, National, IGCSE
Language instr: English, Turkish
(CIS) (ECIS) (RS)

Ernst-Reuter-Schule
Tunus Cad 56, Kavaklidere, 06690 Ankara, Central Anatolia
Tel: +90 312 426 63 82
No. of pupils: 184
Curriculum: IBDP
Language instr: English, German

Eskisehir Gelisim Okullari
Asagi Söğütönü Mah. 993, Sokak No. 14, Tepebasi, 26200 Eskisehir, Central Anatolia
Tel: +90 222 313 01 01
Curriculum: IBDP
Language instr: English, Turkish

Eyüboglu Atasehir Primary School
2 Cadde 59 Ada Manolya 4, Bloklari yani No 6, Atasehir, 34758 Istanbul, Marmara
Tel: +90 216 522 12 22
Curriculum: IBPYP

Eyüboglu Kemerburgaz Middle School
Mithatpasa Mah. Pirinccikoy Yolu, 34075 Istanbul, Marmara
Tel: +90 216 522 12 72
Curriculum: IBMYP
Language instr: English, Turkish

Eyüboglu Kemerburgaz Preschool & Primary School
Mithatpasa Mah. Pirinccikoy Yolu, 34075 Istanbul, Marmara
Tel: +90 216 522 12 72
Language instr: English

Eyüboglu Schools
Esenevler Mah, Dr Rüstem Eyüboglu sok 3, Ümraniye, 34762 Istanbul, Marmara
Tel: +90 216 522 12 12
Age range: 3–18 years
No. of pupils: 2988
Curriculum: IBDP, IBMYP, IBPYP, National
Language instr: Turkish, English
(CIS)

Ezgililer Private Primary School
Kusculu Mah. 1728 Sok. No.6, Ilkadim, Samsun, Black Sea
Tel: +90 362 233 21 22
Curriculum: IBPYP
Language instr: English

Feyziye Mektepleri Vakfi Isik Okullari
Tesvikiye Cad. No:06, Nisantasi, 34365 Istanbul, Marmara
Tel: +90 212 233 12 03
Age range: 3–18
No. of pupils: 3947
(CIS)

FMV Ayazaga Isik High School
Maslak Mah. Büyükdere Cad. No:106, Sisli, Sariyer, 34460 Istanbul, Marmara
Tel: +90 212 286 11 30
Curriculum: IBDP
Language instr: English, Turkish

FMV Ayazaga Isik Primary & Middle School
Maslak Mah. Büyükdere Cad. No:106, Sisli, Sariyer, 34460 Istanbul, Marmara
Tel: +90 212 286 11 30
Curriculum: IBPYP
Language instr: English, Turkish

FMV Erenköy Isik High School
Sinan Ercan Cad. No:19, Erenköy, 34736 Istanbul, Marmara
Tel: +90 216 385 31 47
Curriculum: IBDP
Language instr: English, Turkish

Europe

FMV Erenköy Isik Primary & Middle School
Sinan Ercan Cad. No:19, Erenköy, 34736 Istanbul, Marmara
Tel: +90 216 385 31 47
Curriculum: IBPYP
Language instr: English, Turkish

FMV Isik High School
Tesvikiye Cad. No:6 Nisantasi, 34365 Istanbul, Marmara
Tel: +90 212 233 12 03
Curriculum: IBDP
Language instr: English, Turkish

FMV Isik Primary & Middle School
Tesvikiye Cad. No:06, Nisantasi, 34365 Istanbul, Marmara
Tel: +90 212 233 12 03
Curriculum: IBPYP
Language instr: English, Turkish

FMV Ispartakule Isik High School
Tahtakale Mah. Gaffar Okkan Cad. No: 5/7 Blok No: 1, Avcilar, 34325 Istanbul, Marmara
Tel: +90 212 648 09 75
Curriculum: IBDP
Language instr: English, Turkish

FMV Ispartakule Isik Primary & Middle School
Tahtakale Mah. Gaffar Okkan Cad. No: 5/7 Blok No: 1, Avcilar, 34325 Istanbul, Marmara
Tel: +90 212 648 09 75
Curriculum: IBPYP
Language instr: English, Turkish

Gazi University Foundation Private High School
Ali Suavi Street, Eti Quarter No 15, Maltepe, 06570 Ankara, Central Anatolia
Tel: +90 312 232 28 12
Curriculum: IBDP

Gaziantep Kolej Vakfi Cemil Alevli College
Guvenevler Mah., Hoca Ahmet Yesevi Caddesi, No. 2, Sehitkamil, 27060 Gaziantep, Southeastern Anatolia
Tel: +90 342 321 01 00
Age range: 4–17 years
No. of pupils: 1350
Curriculum: IBDP
Language instr: English

Gökkusagi Koleji - Bahçelievler
Eski Londra Asfalti No: 15 Haznedar, Bahcelievler, 34180 Istanbul, Marmara
Tel: +90 212 644 59 00
No. of pupils: 200
Curriculum: IBDP
Language instr: English, Turkish

Gökkusagi Koleji - Bahçesehir
Orhan Gazi Mah, 1654 sk. No. 40, Esenyurt, Istanbul, Marmara
Tel: +90 212 672 84 26
Curriculum: IBPYP
Language instr: English, Turkish

Gökkusagi Koleji - Beylikdüzü
Adnankahveci Mh. Fabrikalar Cd. No. 4, Beylikdüzü, Istanbul, Marmara
Tel: +90 212 855 89 04 07

Gökkusagi Koleji - Ümraniye
Inkilap Mh. Alemdag Cd. Üntel Sk. No. 30, Ümraniye, Istanbul, Marmara
Tel: +90 216 634 60 60
Curriculum: IBPYP
Language instr: English

Hisar School
Göktürk Merkez Mahallesi Istanbul Caddesi No. 3, Eyüp, Kemerburgaz, 34077 Istanbul, Marmara
Tel: +90 212 364 00 00
Age range: 4–17
No. of pupils: 1248 B661 G587
Curriculum: AP, National, SAT
Language instr: Turkish

IDV Özel Bilkent High School
IDV Özel Bilkent Ilkokulu, Ortaokulu ve Lisesi Universiteler Mah 1600, Cad. No. 6, Dogu Kampus, 06800 Ankara, Central Anatolia
Tel: +90 312 290 89 39
Age range: 4–18
No. of pupils: 325
Curriculum: IBDP, National
Language instr: English, Turkish

IDV Özel Bilkent Middle School
IDV Özel Bilkent Ilkokulu, Ortaokulu ve Lisesi, Universiteler Mah 1600, Cad. No. 6, Dogu Kampus, 06800 Ankara, Central Anatolia
Tel: +90 312 290 54 40
No. of pupils: 325

IDV Özel Bilkent Primary School
IDV Özel Bilkent Ilkokulu, Ortaokulu ve Lisesi, Universiteler Mah 1600, Cad. No. 6, Dogu Kampus, 06800 Ankara, Central Anatolia
Tel: +90 312 290 54 40
No. of pupils: 400

IELEV Private High School
Ensar Cad. No:4/3 Nisantepe Mah. B Blok, Çekmeköy, 34794 Istanbul, Marmara
Tel: +90 216 304 30 92
Age range: 14–19
No. of pupils: 381
Curriculum: IBDP
Language instr: English, German, Turkish

International Pre-School PLUS
Bagdat Cad. Kadıköy., Istanbul, Marmara
Tel: +90 216 350 06 06
Language instr: English, German, French

Irmak Schools
Cemil Topuzlu Caddesi No. 100, Caddebostan P.K. 34728, Kadıköy, Istanbul, Marmara
Tel: +90 216 411 39 23
Age range: 4–18 years
Curriculum: IBDP, IBMYP, IBPYP, National, SAT
Language instr: English, Turkish

Isikkent Egitim Kampusu
6240/5 Sokak No. 3, Karacaoglan Mah., Yesilova, Bornova, 35070 Izmir, Aegean
Tel: +90 232 462 71 00
Age range: 3–18
No. of pupils: 745 B400 G345
Curriculum: IBDP, IBMYP, IBPYP, National
Language instr: Turkish, English

Istanbul Beykent Schools
Gurpinar E-5 Yol Ayrimi, Beykent Büyükçekmece, 34500 Istanbul, Marmara
Tel: +90 212 872 64 32

Istanbul Coskun College
Sema Egitim Hiz. A.S, Zümrütevler Mah. Emek Cad. Maltepe, 34852 Istanbul, Marmara
Tel: +90 216 370 55 55
Language instr: English

Istanbul International Community School
Karaagac Koyu Mahallesi, Kahraman Caddesi, 27/1, Buyukcekmece, 34500 Istanbul, Marmara
Tel: +90 212 857 82 64
Age range: 3–18 B3–18 G3–18
No. of pupils: 600
Curriculum: IBDP, IBMYP, IBPYP
Language instr: English

Istanbul International School
Turistik Camilica Cad. No. 12 Büyük Camilica, Istanbul, Marmara
Tel: +90 216 335 00 55
Age range: 3–18
Curriculum: IGCSE
Language instr: English, Turkish

Istanbul Marmara Private College
Marmara Egitim Köyü, Maltepe, 34857 Istanbul, Marmara
Tel: +90 216 626 10 00
Curriculum: IBDP, IBPYP
Language instr: English, Turkish

ISTEK 1915 Canakkale Schools
Ismetpasa Mah. 55 Sok. No. 2/1, Merkez, Canakkale, Marmara
Tel: +90 286 501 18 81
Language instr: English, Turkish

ISTEK Acibadem Schools
Acibadem Mah. Bag Sok. No. 6, Kadıköy, 34718 Istanbul, Marmara
Tel: +90 216 325 30 75
Curriculum: IBDP, IBPYP
Language instr: English, Turkish

ISTEK Afyon Schools
Selcuklu Mah. 1523, Sokak Uydukent, Afyonkarahisar, Aegean
Tel: +90 272 214 51 51
Language instr: English, Turkish

ISTEK Ankara Schools
Yasamkent, 3222/1. Cadde, No. 9, Cankaya, 06810Ankara, Central Anatolia
Language instr: English, Turkish

ISTEK Antalya Konyaalti Schools
Uncali Mah. 1257 Sk. No. 3, Konyaalti, Antalya, Mediterranean
Tel: +90 242 229 30 80
Curriculum: IBPYP
Language instr: English, Turkish

ISTEK Antalya Lara Schools
2421 Sok. No. 1 Güzeloba Mah., Muratpasa, Antalya, Mediterranean
Tel: +90 242 502 36 46
Curriculum: IBDP, IBPYP
Language instr: English, Turkish

ISTEK Atanur Oguz Schools
Balmumcu Mah. Gazi Umurpasa Sk. No. 26, Balmumcu, 34349 Istanbul, Marmara
Tel: +90 212 211 34 60
Curriculum: IBDP, IBPYP
Language instr: English, Turkish

ISTEK Bandirma Schools
600 Evler Mah. Atatürk Cad. No. 157, 10200 Bandirma, Marmara
Tel: +90 266 714 36 42
Language instr: English, Turkish

ISTEK Baris Schools
Bagdat Cad. No. 238/1, Ciftehavuzlar, Kadıköy, 34730 Istanbul, Marmara
Tel: +90 216 360 12 18
Age range: 3–11 years
No. of pupils: 580
Curriculum: IBPYP
Language instr: Turkish, English

ISTEK Belde Schools
Kuzguncuk Mah. Rasimaga Sok. No. 7/4, Üsküdar, 34664 Istanbul, Marmara
Tel: +90 216 495 96 23
Curriculum: IBPYP
Language instr: English, Turkish

ISTEK Bilge Kagan Schools
Senlikköy Mah. Florya Cad. No. 2 Florya, Bakırköy, 34153 Istanbul, Marmara
Tel: +90 212 663 29 71
Curriculum: IBPYP
Language instr: English, Turkish

ISTEK Denizli Schools
Sirinköy Mah. Sehit Ögretmen Yusuf Batur Cad. 52. Sk., Merkezefendi, 20030 Denizli, Aegean
Tel: +90 258 257 19 19
Curriculum: IBPYP
Language instr: English, Turkish

ISTEK Izmir Schools
Mavisehir Mah. 2040 Sok. No. 13, Karsiyaka, Izmir, Aegean
Tel: +90 232 324 05 05
Curriculum: IBPYP
Language instr: English, Turkish

Europe

ISTEK Kasgarli Mahmut Schools
Eski Edirne Asfalti No. 512, Sultangazi, 34110 Istanbul, Marmara
Tel: +90 212 594 26 11/12
Age range: 3–11 years
No. of pupils: 340
Curriculum: IBPYP
Language instr: English, Turkish

ISTEK Kemal Atatürk Schools (Kindergarten & Primary School)
Tarabya Bayiri Cad. No. 60, Tarabya/Sariyer, 34457 Istanbul, Marmara
Tel: +90 212 262 75 75
Age range: 3–10 years
Curriculum: IBPYP
Language instr: English, Turkish

ISTEK Kusadasi Schools
Türkmen Mah. Hülya Koçyigit Bulv. Yali Evleri Sitesi A Blok No. 1, Bagimsiz Bölüm No. 1 Blok 1, Kusadasi, 09400 Aydin, Aegean
Tel: +90 256 988 02 56
Language instr: English, Turkish

ISTEK Kütahya Schools
Osmangazi Mah. Tavsanli Karayolu Bulvari üzeri No 33, Kütahya, Aegean
Tel: 0274 666 0 777

ISTEK Lüleburgaz Schools
Atatürk Mah. Istanbul Asfalti Yolu No. 11, Lüleburgaz, Kirklareli, Marmara
Tel: +90 288 412 12 00
Language instr: English, Turkish

ISTEK Mersin Schools
Gökçebelen Mah. Gökçebelen Cad. 33195 Sk. No. 1/A, Yenisehir, 33115 Mersin, Mediterranean
Tel: +90 324 473 24 21
Curriculum: IBPYP
Language instr: English, Turkish

ISTEK Osmaniye Schools
Fakiusagi Mah. 54005 sok. No. 14, Osmaniye, Mediterranean
Tel: +90 328 888 00 33
Language instr: English, Turkish

ISTEK Özel Gaziantep Schools
Osmangazi Mah. 56077 Nolu cad. No. 8A/1, Sehitkamil, Gaziantep, Southeastern Anatolia
Tel: +90 0850 677 27 00
Language instr: English, Turkish

ISTEK Semiha Sakir Schools
Caddebostan Mah. Bagdat Cad. No. 238/1, Kadiköy, 34730 Istanbul, Marmara
Tel: +90 216 360 12 18
Language instr: English, Turkish

ISTEK Ulugbey Schools
Atalar Mah. Akgün Sok. No. 23, Kartal, 34862 Istanbul, Marmara
Tel: +90 216 488 13 08
Curriculum: IBPYP
Language instr: English, Turkish

ITÜ ETA Vakfi Doga Koleji
Barbaros Mah. Halk Cad. Kardelen Sok. N.:2 Incity C Blok, Atasehir, Istanbul, Marmara
Tel: +90 216 4853580
Curriculum: IBDP
Language instr: English

ITU Gelistirme Vakfi Özel Ekrem Elginkan Lisesi
ITU Ayazaga Kampusu, Maslak, 34469 Istanbul, Marmara
Tel: +90 212 367 1300
Curriculum: IBDP
Language instr: English

Izmir SEV Schools
77 Sokak No. 45, Göztepe, 35290 Izmir, Aegean
Tel: +90 232 355 04 44
Curriculum: USA
(CIS)

Jale Tezer Educational Institutions
Jale Tezer Primary & Secondary Schools (Gazi Osman Pasa Campus), Bagcilar Mahallesi Acin Caddesi No:7, Cankaya, 06670 Ankara, Central Anatolia
Tel: +90 312 447 49 49
Age range: 3–18 years
Curriculum: AP, SAT, UK, USA, IGCSE, ALevs
Language instr: English, Turkish

Keystone International Schools
Küçük Çamlica Mahallesi Gülhan Sk. No.1/1-2 PK, Üsküdar, 34660 Istanbul, Marmara
Tel: +90 216 370 49 51

Kirmizi Cizgi Schools
Fener Mah.1964 Sok. Yaliyar Si?t. No : 30/C-D, 07060 Antalya, Mediterranean
Tel: +90 242 242 99 98
Curriculum: IBDP
Language instr: English, Turkish

Kocaeli Marmara Private College
Dumlupinar Mah. Sehit Turgut Cicek Cad. No. 47, 41250 Kartepe, Marmara
Tel: +90 262 373 1313
Curriculum: IBDP
Language instr: English, Turkish

Kultar Koleji
Atakoy 9-10, Ataköy, 34156 Istanbul, Marmara
Tel: +90 212 559 04 88
No. of pupils: 332
Language instr: English

Kültür2000 College
Karaagac Mah., Sirtköy Bulvari No. 2, Büyükcekmece, 34500 Istanbul, Marmara
Tel: +90 212 850 81 81
Age range: 11–18
No. of pupils: 148
Curriculum: IBDP, IBMYP
Language instr: English, Turkish

Maya Schools Antalya
Demircikara Mah. 1436. Sk. No:6 Muratpasa, Antalya, Mediterranean 07100
Tel: +90 (242) 242 62 92
Curriculum: IBDP, IBPYP
Language instr: English, Turkish

MBA Schools - Istanbul Atasehir Campus
Küçükbakkalköy Mahallesi Basar Sokak, No. 7, Atasehir, Istanbul, Marmara
Tel: +90 216 970 76 22
Curriculum: IBPYP
Language instr: English, Turkish

MBA Schools - Istanbul Camlica Campus
Küçük Çamlica Mahallesi Libadiye Caddesi, No. 30, Üsküdar, Istanbul, Marmara
Tel: +90 216 970 66 22
Curriculum: IBPYP
Language instr: English, Turkish

MEF International Schools, Istanbul - Ulus High
Ulus Mah. Leylak Sok. No. 22, Ulus, Besiktas, 34340 Istanbul, Marmara
Tel: +90 212 362 26 33 (Ext:1340)
Age range: 11–18 years
Curriculum: IBDP, IGCSE
Language instr: English
(CIS) (ECIS)

MEF International Schools, Istanbul - Ulus Primary
Ulus Mah. Leylak Sok. No. 22, Ulus, Besiktas, 34340 Istanbul, Marmara
Tel: +90 212 362 26 33 (Ext:1340)
Age range: 3–11 years
Curriculum: IBPYP
Language instr: English
(CIS) (ECIS)

MEF International Schools, Izmir
Dokuz Eylül Mah. 699. Sokak No. 2, Gaziemir, Izmir, Aegean
Tel: +90 232 274 74 74
Age range: 3–18 years
Curriculum: IBDP, IGCSE
Language instr: English
(CIS)

Minecan Okullari
Karsli mah 82064 sok. No. 12-14, Cukurova, 010101 Adana, Mediterranean
Tel: +90 322 233 30 45
Curriculum: IBPYP
Language instr: English, Turkish

Muruvvet Evyap Schools
Maden District Bakir Street, No. 2A/2B/2C, Sariyer, 34450 Istanbul, Marmara
Tel: +90 212 342 43 33
Age range: 3–18 years
Curriculum: IBPYP
Language instr: English, Turkish

Nesibe AYDIN Educational Institutions (Ankara)
Haymana Yolu 5. Km, Karsiyaka Mahallesi 577, Sokak No. 1, Gölbasi, 06830 Ankara, Central Anatolia
Tel: +90 312 498 25 25
Curriculum: IBDP, IBPYP
Language instr: English

Nesibe AYDIN Educational Institutions (Antalya)
Altinova Sinan Mah. Bilgin Sk. No. 1, Kepez, 07170 Antalya, Mediterranean
Tel: +90 242 504 12 50
Curriculum: IBPYP
Language instr: Turkish

Nesibe AYDIN Educational Institutions (Diyarbakir)
Mezopotamya Mah. 301, Sok. No. 8, Kayapinar (DicleKent/Kent Meydani Bitimi), 21070 Diyarbakir, Southeastern Anatolia
Tel: +90 412 257 00 05

Nesibe AYDIN Educational Institutions (Gaziantep)
15 Temmuz Mah. 148063, Cadde No. 15, Sehitkamil, 27560 Gaziantep, Southeastern Anatolia
Tel: +90 342 999 41 05
Curriculum: IBPYP
Language instr: Turkish

Nesibe AYDIN Educational Institutions (Kocaeli)
Dumlupinar Mah. Sakip Sabanci Cad. No 130, Kartepe, 41050 Kocaeli, Marmara
Tel: +90 262 311 59 46

Nesibe AYDIN Educational Institutions (Konya)
Beyhekim Mh. Darülhilafet Sk. No. 1, Selcuklu, 42130 Konya, Central Anatolia
Tel: +90 332 320 85 11
Curriculum: IBPYP
Language instr: Turkish

Nesibe AYDIN Educational Institutions (Mersin)
Egricam Mh. Gazi Mustafa Kemal Bulvari Sahin Tower Sit. A Blok No. 52+, Yenisehir, 33160 Mersin, Mediterranean
Tel: +90 324 325 63 25

NUN Middle & High School
Elmali Mahallesi, Beykoz Elmali Yolu Sokak No. 5/1, Beykoz, Istanbul, Marmara
Tel: +90 216 686 16 86
Curriculum: IBDP, IBMYP
Language instr: English, Turkish

NUN Primary School
Burhaniye Mahallesi Haci Resit Pasa Sk. No. 18, Üsküdar, Istanbul, Marmara
Tel: +90 216 686 16 86
Curriculum: IBPYP
Language instr: English

Özel Antalya Toplum Koleji Anadolu Lisesi
Altinkale, Palmiye Cd. No 10/A, 07192 Dösemealti, Antalya, Mediterranean
Tel: +90 242 443 30 80
Curriculum: IBDP
Language instr: English, Turkish

Europe

Özel Ari Anadolu Lisesi
Ögretmenler cad. No. 16/ C 100,
Yil Cukurambar, Çankaya, 06530
Ankara, Central Anatolia
Tel: +90 312 286 85 85
Curriculum: IBDP, IBPYP
Language instr: English, Turkish

Özel Atayurt Ilkokulu
Yukari Sögütönü Mah., Bursa Yolu
10.km. 951 sokak No. 146, 26563
Eskisehir, Central Anatolia
Tel: +90 222 315 03 60
Curriculum: IBPYP
Language instr: Turkish

Özel Ay Egitim Kurumlari
Barbaros Hayrettin Pasa Mahallesi,
1058. Sk. No. 40, Gaziosmanpasa,
34250 Istanbul, Marmara
Tel: +90 212 609 26 08
Curriculum: IBPYP
Language instr: English, Turkish

Özel Büyük Kolej
Baglar Caddesi No 184, Hulya
Sokak No. 7, Gaziosmanpasa,
06700 Ankara, Central Anatolia
Tel: +90 312 446 66 76
Age range: 5–17
No. of pupils: 1859 B947 G912

Özel Çag Lisesi
Yasar Baybogan Kampüsü, Adana-
Mersin Karayolu Üzeri, Yenice, Tarsus,
33800 Mersin, Mediterranean
Tel: +90 324 651 33 86
Age range: 6–17
No. of pupils: 510 B270 G240
Curriculum: National

Özel Egeberk Anaokulu
Özlüce Mah. Hazal Sk. No:3
Nilüfer, 16010 Bursa, Marmara
Tel: +90 533 593 92 90
Curriculum: IBPYP
Language instr: English

Ozel Ilk Cizgi Kindergarten
Nilüfer Hatun Caddesi, ilk
Cizgi Sokak, No:5, Osmangazi,
16265 Bursa, Marmara
Tel: +90 224 244 91 91
Curriculum: IBPYP
Language instr: English, Turkish

Ozel Istanbul Akademik Sistem Okullari
Basaksehir Mah. Yücelen Sok. No.
5, Basaksehir, Istanbul, Marmara
Curriculum: IBDP
Language instr: English, Turkish

Özel Kariyer Ilkokulu
Turgut Özal Mh. 2212.Sk No:4,
Cakirlarciftligi/Batikent, 06370
Ankara, Central Anatolia
Tel: +90 312 566 22 32
Curriculum: IBPYP
Language instr: Turkish

Özel Rüzgar Fen Lisesi
Bagcilar Mahallesi 1105, Sokak No. 7
Bagimsiz Bölüm No. 11, Baglar, 21090
Diyarbakir, Southeastern Anatolia
Tel: +90 412 503 19 79
Curriculum: IBDP
Language instr: English, Turkish

Özel Yönder Ilkokulu
Atatürk mah. Girne cad. 6-6/1,
Atasehir, 34758 Istanbul, Marmara
Tel: +90 216 455 07 07
Language instr: Turkish

Pakistan Embassy International Study Group
2119 Sok, No. 11, Musafa Kemal Mah,
Cankaya, Ankara, Central Anatolia
Tel: +90 312 219 43 56
Age range: 4–18
No. of pupils: 280
Curriculum: IGCSE

Private ALEV Schools
Kadirova Cad. 52/3, Ömerli Mah.
Cekmeköy, 34797 Istanbul, Marmara
Tel: +90 216 435 83 50
Age range: 3–19
No. of pupils: 910
Curriculum: IBDP
Language instr: Turkish, German, English

Private Kocaeli Bahcesehir Anatolian High School
Fatih Mah, Demokrasi Cad No.8 B.K.3,
Köseköy, 41135 Kartepe, Marmara
Tel: +90 262 373 69 69
Curriculum: IBDP
Language instr: English, Turkish

Private Sahin Schools
Prof. Dr. Sabahattin Zaim Bulvari
Karaman Yolu 4., Km Karakamis
Mah., 54100 Adapazari, Marmara
Tel: +90 264 777 17 00
Curriculum: IBPYP
Language instr: Turkish

Private Sanko Schools
Pancarli District Kültür Street
No. 10, 27060 Sehitkamil,
Southeastern Anatolia
Tel: +90 342 211 55 00
Curriculum: IBPYP
Language instr: English, Turkish

Robert College of Istanbul
Kurucesme Cad No 87, Arnavutkoy,
34345 Istanbul, Marmara
Tel: +90 212 359 22 22
Age range: 14–19
No. of pupils: 997 B499 G498
Curriculum: AP, National, SAT, USA
Language instr: English, Turkish

SEV American College
Nisantepe Mah. Kerem Sok.
76, No. 5-9, Cekmeköy, 34794
Istanbul, Marmara
Tel: +90 216 625 27 22
Curriculum: IBDP
Language instr: English

Tarabya British Schools
Salcikir Caddesi No. 44, Tarabya,
34457 Istanbul, Marmara
Tel: +90 212 223 86 46
Curriculum: IGCSE, ALevs
Language instr: English, Turkish

Tarsus American School
Cengiz Topel Caddesi, Caminur
Mahallesi No. 66, Tarsus, 33440
Mersin, Mediterranean
Tel: +90 324 241 81 81
Age range: 5–18
No. of pupils: 551 B287 G264
Curriculum: IBDP, SAT, TOEFL
Language instr: English

Tas Private Elementary School
Cevizlik Mah. Hallac Hüseyin, Sk. No.
11, Bakirköy, 34142 Istanbul, Marmara
Tel: +90 212 543 60 00
Curriculum: IBPYP
Language instr: Turkish, English

TED Ankara College Foundation High School
Golbasi Taspinar Koyu
Yumrubel, Mevkii No. 310, 06830
Ankara, Central Anatolia
Tel: +90 312 586 90 00
Age range: 5–18
No. of pupils: 1499
Curriculum: IBDP, National
Language instr: English

TED Bursa College
21 Yüzyil Cad Mürsel, Köyü Mevkii,
Bademli, Bursa, Marmara
Tel: +90 224 549 21 00
Curriculum: IBDP
Language instr: English

TED Istanbul College Foundation
Cavusbasi Acarkent D Girisi,
81686 Istanbul, Marmara
Tel: +90 216 485 03 33
Age range: 4–18
No. of pupils: 1311 B671 G640

Terakki Foundation - Levent Campus
Ebulula Mardin Cad. Öztürk Sok No.
2, Levent, 34335 Istanbul, Marmara
Tel: +90 212 351 00 60
Curriculum: IBDP, IBPYP
Language instr: English, Turkish

Terakki Foundation - Tepeoren Campus
Medeniyet Blv. No. 55L, Tuzla,
34959 Istanbul, Marmara
Tel: +90 216 709 18 77
Curriculum: IBDP, IBPYP
Language instr: English, Turkish

Tev Inanc Turkes High School For Gifted Students
Muallimköy Mah. 4126, Sok. No.
25/A, 41490 Gebze, Marmara
Tel: +90 262 679 36 36
Language instr: English

The British International School Istanbul - Etiler
Etiler Mahallesi Cengiz Topel
Caddesi Tugcular Sokak No. 27,
Besiktas, 34337 Istanbul, Marmara
Tel: +90 212 202 70 27
Age range: 2.5–11 years

The Koç School
Tepeören Mahallesi, Eski
Ankara Asfalti Caddesi No. 60,
34941 Istanbul, Marmara
Tel: +90 216 585 62 00
Age range: 5–18
No. of pupils: 2197
Curriculum: IBDP, National, SAT
Language instr: Turkish, English

The Sezin School
Ulubatli Hasan Caddesi No:18,
Cekmeköy, 34782 Istanbul, Marmara
Tel: +90 216 642 00 10
Curriculum: IBDP
Language instr: English, Turkish

Üsküdar American Academy
Vakif Sokak No. 1 Baglarbasi,
Üsküdar, 34664 Istanbul, Marmara
Tel: +90 216 333 11 00
Age range: 4–18 years
Curriculum: IBDP
Language instr: English

Yeni Yol Schools
Yeniakcayir Mahallesi No. 551,
Tepebasi, Eskisehir, Central Anatolia
Tel: +90 222 230 39 00
Curriculum: IBDP, IBPYP
Language instr: English, Turkish

YTÜ Schools (YTÜ Okullari)
Çifte Havuzlar Mah.Eski Londra
Asfalti Cad., Idari Bina Dis Kapi
No. 151/1L Iç Kapi No. 1, Esenler,
34220 Istanbul, Marmara
Tel: +90 212 223 19 11
Curriculum: IBPYP
Language instr: English, Turkish

YUCE Schools
Ozel YUCE Okullari, Zuhtu Tigrel
Caddesi, Ismet Eker Sok No 5,
Oran, 06450 Ankara, Central Anatolia
Tel: +90 312 490 02 02
Curriculum: IBDP, IBMYP, IBPYP
Language instr: English

Zafer Koleji
Eskisehir Yolu, Baglica Kavsagi
No. 461, Cayyolu, 06790
Ankara, Central Anatolia
Tel: +90 312 444 55 12
Curriculum: IBDP
Language instr: English

UK

Abbotsholme School
Rocester, Uttoxeter,
Staffordshire ST14 5BS
Tel: 01889 590217
Age range: 2–18 years
No. of pupils: 285
Curriculum: GCSE, IGCSE, ALevs
Language instr: English

Europe

Abingdon School
Park Road, Abingdon,
Oxfordshire OX14 1DE
Tel: +44 (0)1235 849029
Age range: B11–18 years
Language instr: English

Ackworth School
Pontefract Road, Ackworth,
Pontefract, West Yorkshire WF7 7LT
Tel: 01977 233600
Age range: 2.5–18 years
(boarding from 11)
No. of pupils: 430
Curriculum: GCSE, ALevs
Language instr: English

ACS Cobham International School
Heywood, Portsmouth Road,
Cobham, Surrey KT11 1BL
Tel: +44 (0) 1932 867251
Age range: 2–18 years
Curriculum: IBDP
Language instr: English

ACS Egham International School
London Road, Egham,
Surrey TW20 0HS
Tel: +44 (0) 1784 430800
Age range: 4–18 years
Curriculum: IBDP, IBMYP, IBPYP, IBCP
Language instr: English

ACS Hillingdon International School
108 Vine Lane, Hillingdon,
Uxbridge, Middlesex UB10 0BE
Tel: +44 (0) 1895 259771
Age range: 4–18 years
Curriculum: IBDP, IBCP
Language instr: English

Adcote School for Girls
Little Ness, Shrewsbury,
Shropshire SY4 2JY
Tel: 01939 260202
Age range: G7–18 years
(boarding from 7)

Aldenham School
Elstree, Hertfordshire WD6 3AJ
Tel: 01923 858122
Age range: 3–18 years
Language instr: English

Ampleforth College
York, North Yorkshire YO62 4ER
Tel: 01439 766000
Age range: 11–18 years

Ardingly College
College Road, Ardingly, Haywards
Heath, West Sussex RH17 6SQ
Tel: +44 (0)1444 893320
Age range: 13–18 years
Curriculum: IBDP, UK,
GCSE, IGCSE, ALevs
Language instr: English

Ashford School
East Hill, Ashford, Kent TN24 8PB
Tel: +44 (0)1233 625171
Age range: 3 months–18
years (boarding from 11)
No. of pupils: 1034 B536 G498 VIth140
Curriculum: GCSE, ALevs
Language instr: English

Ashville College
Green Lane, Harrogate,
North Yorkshire HG2 9JP
Tel: +44 (0)1423 566358
Age range: 2–18 years
Language instr: English

Atelier 21 Future School
Broadfield Park, Crawley,
West Sussex RH11 9RZ
Tel: 01293 265 417
Age range: 4–16 years
Curriculum: IBMYP
Language instr: English

Badminton School
Westbury Road, Westbury-on-
Trym, Bristol, Bristol BS9 3BA
Tel: 0117 905 5200
Age range: G3–18 years
(boarding from 9)
Curriculum: GCSE, IGCSE, ALevs
Language instr: English

Bales College
2 Kilburn Lane, London,
London W10 4AA
Tel: 020 8960 5899
Age range: 11–18 years
Curriculum: GCSE, IGCSE, ALevs

Barnard Castle Senior School
Barnard Castle, Durham DL12 8UN
Tel: +44 (0)1833 696030
Age range: 4–18 years
No. of pupils: 723
Curriculum: GCSE, IGCSE, ALevs
Language instr: English

Bath Academy
27 Queen Square, Bath, Bath &
North-East Somerset BA1 2HX
Tel: 01225 334577
Age range: 14–19+ years
Curriculum: GCSE, IGCSE, ALevs

Battle Abbey School
High Street, Battle, East
Sussex TN33 0AD
Tel: 01424 772385
Age range: 3 months–18
years (boarding from 11)
Curriculum: GCSE, ALevs

Bedales School
Church Road, Steep, Petersfield,
Hampshire GU32 2DG
Tel: 01730 300100
Age range: 13–18 years

Bede's Senior School
Upper Dicker, Hailsham,
East Sussex BN27 3QH
Tel: 01323 356609
Age range: 13–18 years
(boarding from 13)
No. of pupils: 802
Curriculum: GCSE, IGCSE, ALevs

Bedford Girls' School
Cardington Road, Bedford,
Bedfordshire MK42 0BX
Tel: 01234 361900
Age range: G7–18 years
Curriculum: IBDP, GCSE, ALevs
Language instr: English

Bedford School
De Parys Avenue, Bedford,
Bedfordshire MK40 2TU
Tel: 01234 362200
Age range: B7–18 years
Curriculum: IBDP, GCSE, IGCSE, ALevs
Language instr: English

Bedstone College
Bedstone, Bucknell,
Shropshire SY7 0BG
Tel: 01547 530303
Age range: 4–18 years
Curriculum: IBCP
Language instr: English

Benenden School
Cranbrook, Kent TN17 4AA
Tel: 01580 240592
Age range: G11–18 years
(boarding from 11)
Language instr: English

Berkhamsted School
Overton House, 131 High Street,
Berkhamsted, Hertfordshire HP4 2DJ
Tel: 01442 358001
Age range: 3–18 years
No. of pupils: 1994 VIth462
Curriculum: GCSE, ALevs

Bethany School
Curtisden Green, Goudhurst,
Cranbrook, Kent TN17 1LB
Tel: 01580 211273
Age range: 11–18 years
No. of pupils: 354 B232 G122 VIth84
Curriculum: GCSE, ALevs
Language instr: English

Bishop's Stortford College
School House, Maze Green
Road, Bishop's Stortford,
Hertfordshire CM23 2PQ
Tel: +44 (0)1279 838575
Age range: 13–18 years
Language instr: English

Bishop's Stortford College Prep School
School House, Maze Green
Road, Bishop's Stortford,
Hertfordshire CM23 2PQ
Tel: +44 (0)1279 838583
Age range: 4–13 years
Language instr: English

Bishopstrow College
Barrow House, Bishopstrow
Road, Bishopstrow, Warminster,
Wiltshire BA12 9HU
Tel: +44 (0)1985 219210
Age range: 7–17 years
Language instr: English

Bloxham School
Bloxham, Banbury,
Oxfordshire OX15 4PE
Tel: 01295 720222
Age range: 11–18 years

Blundell's School
Tiverton, Devon EX16 4DN
Tel: 01884 252543
Age range: 11–18 years

Bootham School
York, North Yorkshire YO30 7BU
Tel: 01904 623261
Age range: 11–18 years

Box Hill School
London Road, Mickleham,
Dorking, Surrey RH5 6EA
Tel: 01372 373382
Age range: 11–18 years
No. of pupils: 410
Curriculum: IBDP, GCSE, IGCSE
Language instr: English

Bradfield College
Bradfield, Berkshire RG7 6AU
Tel: 0118 964 4516
Age range: 13–18 years
No. of pupils: 850
Curriculum: IBDP, UK,
GCSE, IGCSE, ALevs
Language instr: English

Brentwood School
Middleton Hall Lane,
Brentwood, Essex CM15 8EE
Tel: 01277 243243
Age range: 3–18 years
No. of pupils: 1920
Curriculum: IBDP, GCSE, IGCSE, ALevs
Language instr: English

Brighton College
Eastern Road, Brighton,
East Sussex BN2 0AL
Tel: 01273 704200
Age range: 3–18 years
Curriculum: GCSE, IGCSE, ALevs

Europe

Brighton International School
5 Old Steine, Brighton,
East Sussex BN1 1EJ
Tel: 07796 997780
Age range: 15–17 years

Bristol Grammar School
University Road, Bristol, Bristol BS8 1SR
Tel: 0117 973 6006
Age range: 4–18 years
Curriculum: IBDP, GCSE, IGCSE, ALevs
Language instr: English

Brockwood Park School
Brockwood Park, Bramdean,
Alresford, Hampshire SO24 0LQ
Tel: +44 (0)1962 771744
Age range: 14–19 years
Language instr: English

Bromsgrove School
Worcester Road, Bromsgrove,
Worcestershire B61 7DU
Tel: +44 (0)1527 579679
Age range: 7–18 years (boarding from 7)
No. of pupils: 1650
Curriculum: IBDP, ALevs
Language instr: English

Brooke House College
12 Leicester Road, Market Harborough, Leicestershire LE16 7AU
Tel: 01858 462452
Age range: 11–19 years

Bryanston School
Blandford Forum, Dorset DT11 0PX
Tel: 01258 484633
Age range: 3–18 years
No. of pupils: 806
Curriculum: IBDP, IBCP, GCSE, ALevs
Language instr: English

Buckswood School
Broomham Hall, Rye Road, Guestling, Hastings, East Sussex TN35 4LT
Tel: 01424 813 813
Age range: 10–19 years
Curriculum: IBDP, UK, GCSE, IGCSE, ALevs

Burgess Hill Girls
Keymer Road, Burgess Hill,
West Sussex RH15 0EG
Tel: 01444 241050
Age range: B2.5–4 years G2.5–18 years
No. of pupils: 503 B19 G484 VIth59
Curriculum: UK, GCSE, ALevs
Language instr: English

Cambridge International School
Cherry Hinton Road, Cambridge,
Cambridgeshire CB1 8DW
Tel: +44 (0) 1223 416938
Age range: 2–11 years
Curriculum: IPC, UK

Campbell College
Belmont Road, Belfast,
County Antrim BT4 2ND
Tel: 028 9076 3076
Age range: B11–18 years
Curriculum: GCSE, ALevs

Canford School
Canford Magna, Wimborne,
Dorset BH21 3AD
Tel: 01202 841254
Age range: 13–18 years
Curriculum: GCSE, IGCSE, ALevs
Language instr: English

Cardiff Academy
Harlech Court, Bute Terrace,
Cardiff, Glamorgan CF10 2FE
Tel: 02920 318 318
Age range: 16–19 years
Curriculum: ALevs

Cardiff Sixth Form College
1-3 Trinity Court, 21-27 Newport
Road, Cardiff CF24 0AA
Tel: +44 (0)29 2049 3121
Age range: 15–18 years

Cardiff Sixth Form College, Cambridge
89 Regent Street, Cambridge,
Cambridgeshire CB2 1AW
Tel: +44 (0)1223 903080
Age range: 15–18 years

Carfax College
39-42 Hythe Bridge Street,
Oxford, Oxfordshire OX1 2EP
Tel: +44 (0)1865 200676
Age range: 11–21 years
No. of pupils: 24
Curriculum: GCSE, ALevs

Caterham School
Harestone Valley Road,
Caterham, Surrey CR3 6YA
Tel: 01883 343028
Age range: 3–18 years
Curriculum: UK, GCSE, IGCSE, ALevs
Language instr: English

CATS Cambridge
Elizabeth House, 1 High Street,
Chesterton, Cambridge,
Cambridgeshire CB4 1NQ
Tel: +44 (0)1223 314431
Age range: 14–19+ years
Curriculum: UK, GCSE, ALevs

Centre Academy London
92 St John's Hill, Battersea,
London, London SW11 1SH
Tel: 020 7738 2344
Age range: 9–19 years
Language instr: English

Charterhouse
Godalming, Surrey GU7 2DX
Tel: +44 (0)1483 291501
Age range: B13–18 years (boarding from 13) G16–18 years
No. of pupils: 1005
Curriculum: IBDP, National, UK, GCSE, IGCSE, ALevs
Language instr: English

Chase Grammar School International Study Centre
Convent Close, Cannock,
Staffordshire WS11 0UR
Tel: +44 (0)1543 501800
Age range: 9–19 years

Cheltenham College
Bath Road, Cheltenham,
Gloucestershire GL53 7LD
Tel: 01242 265600
Age range: 13–18 years
Curriculum: GCSE, IGCSE, ALevs

Cheltenham Ladies' College
Bayshill Road, Cheltenham,
Gloucestershire GL50 3EP
Tel: +44 (0)1242 520691
Age range: G11–18 years (boarding from 11)
No. of pupils: 862
Curriculum: IBDP, GCSE, IGCSE, ALevs
Language instr: English

Chetham's School of Music
Long Millgate, Manchester,
Greater Manchester M3 1SB
Tel: 0161 834 9644
Age range: 8–18 years
No. of pupils: 300
Curriculum: GCSE, IGCSE, ALevs

Chigwell School
High Road, Chigwell, Essex IG7 6QF
Tel: 020 8501 5700
Age range: 4–18 years
No. of pupils: 1111 B597 G514
Curriculum: GCSE, ALevs

Christ College
Brecon, Powys LD3 8AF
Tel: 01874 615440
Age range: 7–18 years
No. of pupils: 370
Curriculum: GCSE, ALevs
Language instr: English

Christ's Hospital
Horsham, West Sussex RH13 0LJ
Tel: 01403 211293
Age range: 11–18 years
Curriculum: National, GCSE, IGCSE, ALevs

City of London Freemen's School
Ashtead Park, Ashtead,
Surrey KT21 1ET
Tel: +44 (0)1372 822400
Age range: 7–18 years
Curriculum: GCSE, ALevs

Clayesmore School
Blandford Road, Iwerne Minster, Dorset DT11 8LL
Tel: 01747 813111
Age range: 3–18 years
Curriculum: GCSE, IGCSE, ALevs
Language instr: English

Clifton College
32 College Road, Clifton,
Bristol, Bristol BS8 3JH
Tel: 0117 315 7000
Age range: 13–18 years (boarding from 13)
Curriculum: ALevs

Clifton College Preparatory School
The Avenue, Clifton,
Bristol, Bristol BS8 3HE
Tel: +44 (0)117 315 7502
Age range: 2–13 years (boarding from 8)

Cobham Hall School
Brewers Road, Cobham,
Kent DA12 3BL
Tel: 01474 823371
Age range: 11–19 years (boarding from 11)
No. of pupils: 130
Curriculum: UK, GCSE, IGCSE
Language instr: English

COLLÈGE FRANÇAIS BILINGUE DE LONDRES (CFBL)
For further details see p. 108
87 Holmes Road, Kentish Town,
London, London NW5 3AX
Tel: 020 7993 7400
Email: info@cfbl.org.uk
Website: www.cfbl.org.uk
Head of School: David Gassian
Age range: 3–15 years
No. of pupils: 700
Fees: £15,440
Curriculum: FrenchBacc
Language instr: French, English

Collegiate School, Bristol
Stapleton, Bristol, Bristol BS16 1BJ
Tel: 0117 965 5207
Age range: 3–18 years
No. of pupils: 816
Curriculum: ALevs

Collingham College
23 Collingham Gardens,
London, London SW5 0HL
Tel: 020 7244 7414
Age range: 13–19 years
Curriculum: GCSE, ALevs

Europe

Concord College
Acton Burnell Hall, Acton Burnell,
Shrewsbury, Shropshire SY5 7PF
Tel: +44 (0)1694 731631
Age range: 13–18 years
No. of pupils: 600
Curriculum: UK, GCSE, ALevs

Cranleigh School
Horseshoe Lane, Cranleigh,
Surrey GU6 8QQ
Tel: +44 (0) 1483 273666
Age range: 7–18 years
(including Prep School)
No. of pupils: 695 B407 G288 VIth281
Curriculum: GCSE, IGCSE, ALevs

Culford School
Bury St Edmunds, Suffolk IP28 6TX
Tel: +44 (0)1284 728615
Age range: 1–18 years
Curriculum: GCSE, IGCSE, ALevs
Language instr: English

Dauntsey's
High Street, West Lavington,
Devizes, Wiltshire SN10 4HE
Tel: 01380 814500
Age range: 11–18 years
(boarding from 11)
No. of pupils: 840
Curriculum: GCSE, ALevs
Language instr: English

Dean Close School
Shelburne Road, Cheltenham,
Gloucestershire GL51 6HE
Tel: +44 (0)1242 258000
Age range: 13–18 years
(boarding from 13)
No. of pupils: 490
Curriculum: GCSE, IGCSE, ALevs
Language instr: English

Deenway Montessori School & Unicity College
3-5 Sidmouth Street, Reading,
Berkshire RG1 4QX
Tel: 0118 9574737
Age range: 3–18+ years

Denstone College
Uttoxeter, Staffordshire ST14 5HN
Tel: 01889 590484
Age range: 4–18 years
(boarding from 7)
No. of pupils: 750 VIth200
Curriculum: GCSE, IGCSE, ALevs

Deutsche Schule London
Douglas House, Petersham Road,
Richmond, Surrey TW10 7AH
Tel: +44 (0)20 8940 2510
Age range: 3–18 years
Curriculum: Abitur, IBDP, National
Language instr: English, German

Didac School
16 Trinity Trees, Eastbourne,
East Sussex BN21 3LE
Tel: +44 1323 417276
Age range: 16–18 years

DLD College London
199 Westminster Bridge Road,
London, London SE1 7FX
Tel: +44 (0)20 7935 8411
Age range: 13–19 years
No. of pupils: 418
Curriculum: GCSE, IGCSE, ALevs
Language instr: English

Dover College
Effingham Crescent,
Dover, Kent CT17 9RH
Tel: 01304 205969
Age range: 3–18 years
Language instr: English

d'Overbroeck's
333 Banbury Road, Oxford,
Oxfordshire OX2 7PL
Tel: 01865 688 600
Age range: 11–18 years
Curriculum: GCSE, IGCSE, ALevs
Language instr: English

Downe House School
Downe House, Cold Ash, Thatcham,
West Berkshire RG18 9JJ
Tel: +44 (0)1635 200286
Age range: G11–18 years
(boarding from 11)
No. of pupils: 580
Curriculum: GCSE, IGCSE, ALevs
Language instr: English

Downside School
Stratton-on-the-Fosse,
Radstock, Bath, Bath & North-
East Somerset BA3 4RJ
Tel: 01761 235100
Age range: 11–18 years
No. of pupils: 360
Curriculum: GCSE, IGCSE, ALevs
Language instr: English

Duke of Kent School
Peaslake Road, Ewhurst,
Surrey GU6 7NS
Tel: 01483 277313
Age range: 3–16 years
No. of pupils: 316
Curriculum: GCSE

Dulwich College
Dulwich Common, London,
London SE21 7LD
Tel: 020 8693 3601
Age range: B6 months–18 years G6 months–7 years
Curriculum: National, GCSE, IGCSE, ALevs
Language instr: English

Durham School
Quarryheads Lane, Durham,
Durham DH1 4SZ
Tel: +44 (0)191 731 9270
Age range: 11–18 years

Dwight School London
6 Friern Barnet Lane, London,
London N11 3LX
Tel: 020 8920 0600
Age range: 2–18 years
Curriculum: IBDP, IBMYP, IBPYP, GCSE
Language instr: English

Earlscliffe
29 Shorncliffe Road,
Folkestone, Kent CT20 2NB
Tel: 01303 253951
Age range: 15–19 years
No. of pupils: 140
Curriculum: ALevs

Eastbourne College
Old Wish Road, Eastbourne,
East Sussex BN21 4JX
Tel: 01323 452323 (Admissions)
Age range: 13–18 years
No. of pupils: 622
Curriculum: GCSE, IGCSE, ALevs

Ecole Française de Bristol
Stanton Road, Southmead,
Bristol, Bristol BS10 5SJ
Tel: +44 (0)117 9692410
Age range: 3–16 years

Ecole Française de Londres Jacques Prévert
59 Brook Green, Hammersmith,
London, London W6 7BE
Tel: 020 7602 6871
Age range: 4–11 years
Language instr: English, French

École Primaire Marie D'Orliac
60 Clancarty Road, London,
London SW6 3AA
Tel: +44 (0)20 7736 5863
Age range: 4–11 years
Curriculum: National

EF Academy Oxford
Cotuit Hall, Pullens Lane, Headington,
Oxford, Oxfordshire OX3 0DA
Tel: +44 (0)1865 759667
Age range: 16–19 years
No. of pupils: 70
Curriculum: IBDP, ALevs
Language instr: English

EIFA International School
36 Portland Place, London,
London W1B 1LS
Tel: +44 (0)20 7637 5351
Age range: 21 months–18 years
Curriculum: IBDP, IGCSE
Language instr: English, French

Ellesmere College
Ellesmere, Shropshire SY12 9AB
Tel: 01691 622321
Age range: 7–18 years
(boarding from 12)
No. of pupils: 600
Curriculum: IBDP, UK, GCSE, ALevs
Language instr: English

Elmhurst Ballet School
249 Bristol Road, Edgbaston,
Birmingham, West Midlands B5 7UH
Tel: +44 (0)1214 726655
Age range: 11–19 years
(boarding from 11)
Curriculum: National, UK, GCSE, ALevs
Language instr: English

Embley
Embley Park, Romsey,
Hampshire SO51 6ZE
Tel: 01794 512206
Age range: 2–18 years
No. of pupils: 600
Language instr: English

Epsom College
College Road, Epsom,
Surrey KT17 4JQ
Tel: 01372 821000
Age range: 11–18 years
(boarding from 13)
No. of pupils: 1143
Curriculum: GCSE, IGCSE, ALevs
Language instr: English

Eton College
Windsor, Berkshire SL4 6DW
Tel: +44 (0)1753 370 611
Age range: B13–18 years
No. of pupils: 1342
Curriculum: GCSE, IGCSE, ALevs
Language instr: English

Fairview International School, Bridge of Allan
52 Kenilworth Road, Bridge
of Allan, Stirling FK9 4RY
Tel: +44 (0)1786 231952
Age range: 5–18 years
No. of pupils: 86
Curriculum: IBDP, IBMYP, IBPYP
Language instr: English

Farlington School
Strood Park, Horsham,
West Sussex RH12 3PN
Tel: 01403 282573
Age range: 6 months–18 years
No. of pupils: 473
Curriculum: SAT, GCSE, IGCSE, ALevs
Language instr: English

Farringtons School
Perry Street, Chislehurst, Kent BR7 6LR
Tel: 020 8467 0256
Age range: 3–18 years
No. of pupils: 700 B366 G334 VIth100
Curriculum: National, GCSE, IGCSE, ALevs
Language instr: English

Felixstowe International College
Maybush House, Maybush Lane,
Felixstowe, Suffolk IP11 7NA
Tel: +44 (0)1394 282388
Age range: 9–19 years
Curriculum: GCSE, ALevs

Europe

Felsted School
Felsted, Great Dunmow,
Essex CM6 3LL
Tel: +44 (0)1371 822600
Age range: 4–18 years
Curriculum: IBDP, UK, GCSE, IGCSE, ALevs
Language instr: English

Fettes College
Carrington Road, Edinburgh,
Edinburgh EH4 1QX
Tel: 0131 332 2281
Age range: 5–18 years
No. of pupils: 730
Curriculum: IBDP, UK, GCSE, IGCSE, ALevs, Scot Nat
Language instr: English

Finborough School
The Hall, Great Finborough,
Stowmarket, Suffolk IP14 3EF
Tel: +44 (0)1449 773600
Age range: 2–18 years
Curriculum: GCSE, ALevs
Language instr: English

Framlingham College
Framlingham, Suffolk IP13 9EY
Tel: +44 (0)1728 723789
Age range: 2–18 years
No. of pupils: 600
Curriculum: GCSE, IGCSE, ALevs
Language instr: English

Frensham Heights
Rowledge, Farnham, Surrey GU10 4EA
Tel: 01252 792561
Age range: 3–18 years (boarding from 11)
Curriculum: GCSE, ALevs

Fulham School
1-3 Chesilton Road, London,
London SW6 5AA
Tel: 020 8154 6751
Age range: 3–18 years
No. of pupils: 600
Curriculum: GCSE, ALevs
Language instr: English

Fulneck School
Fulneck, Pudsey, Leeds,
West Yorkshire LS28 8DS
Tel: +44 (0)113 257 0235
Age range: 3–18 years (boarding from 11)
No. of pupils: 245 B116 G129 VIth22
Curriculum: UK, GCSE, ALevs

Fyling Hall School
Robin Hood's Bay, Whitby,
North Yorkshire YO22 4QD
Tel: 01947 880353
Age range: 4–18 years

George Watson's College
69-71 Colinton Road, Edinburgh,
Edinburgh EH10 5EG
Tel: 0131 446 6000
Age range: 3–18 years
Curriculum: ALevs, Scot Nat, SVQ, CSFS
Language instr: English

Giggleswick School
Settle, North Yorkshire BD24 0DE
Tel: 01729 893000
Age range: 2–18 years (boarding from 8)
Curriculum: GCSE, ALevs
Language instr: English

Glenalmond College, Perth
Glenalmond, Perth, Perth & Kinross PH1 3RY
Tel: 01738 842000
Age range: 12–18 years
Curriculum: GCSE, IGCSE, ALevs

Godolphin and Latymer School
Iffley Road, Hammersmith,
London, London W6 0PG
Tel: +44 (0)20 8741 1936
Age range: G11–18 years
No. of pupils: 800
Curriculum: IBDP, GCSE, IGCSE, ALevs
Language instr: English

Godolphin School
Milford Hill, Salisbury, Wiltshire SP1 2RA
Tel: 01722 430545
Age range: G11–18 years (boarding from 11)
Curriculum: GCSE, IGCSE, ALevs

Gordonstoun
Elgin, Moray IV30 5RF
Tel: 01343 837837
Age range: 4.5–18 years (Boarding from age 8)
No. of pupils: 515
Curriculum: SAT, GCSE, ALevs

Gosfield School
Cut Hedge Park, Halstead Road,
Gosfield, Halstead, Essex CO9 1PF
Tel: 01787 474040
Age range: 2–18 years

Grantham Preparatory International School
Gorse Lane, Grantham,
Lincolnshire NG31 7UF
Tel: +44 (0)1476 593293
Age range: 3–11 years
Language instr: English

Greene's College Oxford
45 Pembroke Street, Oxford,
Oxfordshire OX1 1BP
Tel: 01865 664400
Age range: 16–18 years
No. of pupils: VIth60
Curriculum: GCSE, ALevs

Greenfields Independent Day & Boarding School
Priory Road, Forest Row,
East Sussex RH18 5JD
Tel: +44 (0)1342 822189
Age range: 2–18 years (boarding from 10)
Curriculum: GCSE, ALevs

Gresham's Nursery and Pre-Prep School
Market Place, Holt, Norfolk NR25 6BB
Tel: 01263 714575
Age range: 2–7 years

Gresham's Prep School
Holt, Norfolk NR25 6EY
Tel: 01263 714600
Age range: 7–13 years
Language instr: English

Gresham's Senior School
Cromer Road, Holt, Norfolk NR25 6EA
Tel: 01263 714500
Age range: 13–18 years
No. of pupils: 540
Curriculum: IBDP, UK, GCSE, IGCSE, ALevs
Language instr: English

Guildhouse School
43-45 Bloomsbury Square,
London, London WC1A 2RA
Tel: +44 (0)1223 341300
Age range: 15–24 years
Curriculum: UK, ALevs

HAILEYBURY
For further details see p. 115
Haileybury, Hertford,
Hertfordshire SG13 7NU
Tel: +44 (0)1992 706353
Email: admissions@haileybury.com
Website: www.haileybury.com
The Master: Eugene du Toit
Age range: 11–18 years AGE1
*** DESCRIPTION REQUIRED (entry at 11+, 13+, 14+ and 16+)
No. of pupils: 925 B476 G449 VIth400
Fees: £56,796
Curriculum: IBDP, GCSE, IGCSE, ALevs
Language instr: English

Halcyon London International School
33 Seymour Place, London,
London W1H 5AU
Tel: +44 (0)20 7258 7785
Age range: 11–18 years
No. of pupils: 170
Curriculum: IBDP, IBMYP
Language instr: English

Harrogate Ladies' College
Clarence Drive, Harrogate,
North Yorkshire HG1 2QG
Tel: 01423 504543
Age range: G11–18 years (boarding from 11)

Headington Rye Oxford
Headington Road, Oxford,
Oxfordshire OX3 7TD
Tel: +44 (0)1865 759100
Age range: G11–18 years
Curriculum: GCSE, ALevs
Language instr: English

Heathfield School
London Road, Ascot,
Berkshire SL5 8BQ
Tel: 01344 898343
Age range: G11–18 years (boarding from 11)
Curriculum: GCSE, IGCSE, ALevs
Language instr: English

Hill House
17 Hans Place, Chelsea,
London, London SW1X 0EP
Tel: 020 7584 1331
Age range: 4–13 years

HOCKERILL ANGLO-EUROPEAN COLLEGE
For further details see p. 120
Dunmow Road, Bishops Stortford,
Hertfordshire CM23 5HX
Tel: 01279 658451
Email: admissions@hockerill.com
Website: www.hockerill.com
Principal: Alasdair Mackenzie
Age range: 11–18 years
No. of pupils: 920
Fees: £15,279
Curriculum: IBDP, IBMYP, GCSE
Language instr: English

Hurst College
College Lane, Hurstpierpoint,
West Sussex BN6 9JS
Tel: 01273 833636
Age range: 4–18 years (boarding from 13)
No. of pupils: 1295
Curriculum: GCSE, ALevs

ICS LONDON
For further details see p. 122
7B Wyndham Place, London,
London W1H 1PN
Tel: +44 (0)20 729 88800
Email: admissions@icslondon.co.uk
Website: www.icslondon.co.uk
Head of School: Mona Taybi
Age range: 3–18 years
No. of pupils: 150
Fees: Day £22,890–£34,200
Curriculum: IBDP, IBMYP, IBPYP, IGCSE
Language instr: English

Europe

IMPINGTON INTERNATIONAL COLLEGE
For further details see p. 125
New Road, Impington, Cambridge, Cambridgeshire CB24 9LX
Tel: 01223 200402
Email: international@ivc.tmet.org.uk
Website: www.impingtoninternational.org.uk
College Principal: Johanna Sale
Age range: 16–19 years
No. of pupils: 250
Curriculum: IBDP, IBMYP
Language instr: English

Instituto Español Vicente Cañada Blanch
317 Portobello Road, London, London W10 5SZ
Tel: +44 (0) 20 8969 2664
Age range: 3–18 years
Language instr: English, Spanish

International School of Aberdeen
Pitfodels House, North Deeside Road, Pitfodels, Cults, Aberdeen, Aberdeen AB15 9PN
Tel: 01224 730300
Age range: 3–18 years
Curriculum: ACT, IBDP, SAT, IGCSE
Language instr: English

International School of Creative Arts (ISCA)
Framewood Road, Wexham, Buckinghamshire SL2 4QS
Tel: +44 (0)1753 208820
Age range: 15–19 years
No. of pupils: 85
Language instr: English

International School of London (ISL)
139 Gunnersbury Avenue, London, London W3 8LG
Tel: +44 (0)20 8992 5823
Age range: 3–18 years
No. of pupils: 420
Curriculum: IBDP, IBMYP, IBPYP
Language instr: English & home language programme

Ipswich School
Henley Road, Ipswich, Suffolk IP1 3SG
Tel: 01473 408300
Age range: 0–18 years
Curriculum: GCSE, IGCSE, ALevs
Language instr: English

JEANNINE MANUEL SCHOOL
For further details see p. 152
Bloomsbury, London, London WC1B 3DN
Tel: 020 3829 5970
Email: admissions@jmanuel.uk.net
Website: www.ecolejeanninemanuel.org.uk
Head of School: Pauline Prévot
Age range: 3–18 years
No. of pupils: 700
Fees: Day £24,780–£35,208
Curriculum: IBDP, FrenchBacc, IGCSE
Language instr: English, French

Kensington Park School
40-44 Bark Place, Bayswater, London, London W2 4AT
Tel: +44 (0)20 7616 4400
Age range: 11–18 years
Curriculum: GCSE, ALevs

Kensington Wade School
Fulham Palace Road, London, London W6 9ER
Tel: 020 3096 2888
Age range: 3–11 years
No. of pupils: 135

Kent College Pembury
Old Church Road, Pembury, Tunbridge Wells, Kent TN2 4AX
Tel: +44 (0)1892 822006
Age range: B3–11 years G3–18 years (boarding from 11)
No. of pupils: 500
Curriculum: GCSE, ALevs
Language instr: English

Kent College, Canterbury
Whitstable Road, Canterbury, Kent CT2 9DT
Tel: +44 (0)1227 763 231
Age range: 3 months–18 years (boarding from 10 years) *Garden Cottage Nursery* 3 months–3 years
No. of pupils: 820
Curriculum: IBDP, UK, GCSE, IGCSE, ALevs
Language instr: English

Kimbolton School
Kimbolton, Huntingdon, Cambridgeshire PE28 0EA
Tel: 01480 860505
Age range: 4–18 years
Curriculum: GCSE, ALevs
Language instr: English

King Edward's School
Edgbaston Park Road, Birmingham, West Midlands B15 2UA
Tel: 01214 721672
Age range: B11–18
No. of pupils: 885 VIth221
Curriculum: IBDP, GCSE, IGCSE
Language instr: English

King Edward's Witley
Petworth Road, Godalming, Surrey GU8 5SG
Tel: 01428 686735
Age range: 11–18 years
No. of pupils: 476
Curriculum: UK, GCSE, IGCSE, ALevs
Language instr: English

King William's College
Castletown, Isle of Man IM9 1TP
Tel: +44 (0)1624 820110
Age range: 11–18 years
No. of pupils: 290
Curriculum: IBDP, GCSE, IGCSE
Language instr: English

Kingham Hill School
Kingham, Chipping Norton, Oxfordshire OX7 6TH
Tel: 01608 658999
Age range: 11–18 years
No. of pupils: 370
Curriculum: GCSE, ALevs
Language instr: English

Kings Bournemouth
58 Braidley Road, Bournemouth, Dorset BH2 6LD
Tel: +44 (0)1202 293535
Age range: 14–25 years
Curriculum: GCSE, ALevs

Kings Brighton
27-33 Ditchling Road, Brighton, East Sussex BN1 4SB
Tel: +44 (0)1273 443403
Age range: 14–25 years
Curriculum: GCSE, ALevs

King's Bruton
The Plox, Bruton, Somerset BA10 0ED
Tel: 01749 814200
Age range: 13–18 years
No. of pupils: 360
Curriculum: GCSE, IGCSE, ALevs

King's College
South Road, Taunton, Somerset TA1 3LA
Tel: 01823 328204
Age range: 13–18 years
No. of pupils: 490

King's College School, Wimbledon
Southside, Wimbledon Common Wimbledon, London, London SW19 4TT
Tel: 020 8255 5300
Age range: B7–18 years G16–18 years
No. of pupils: 1510
Curriculum: IBDP, GCSE, ALevs
Language instr: English

King's Ely
Ely, Cambridgeshire CB7 4EW
Tel: 01353 660707
Age range: 2–18 years
No. of pupils: 1148
Curriculum: GCSE, IGCSE, ALevs
Language instr: English

KING'S INTERHIGH
For further details see p. 158
3 Burlington Gardens, London, London W1S 3EP
Tel: +44 (0)1873 777 444
Email: contact@kingsinterhigh.co.uk
Website: www.kingsinterhigh.co.uk
Headteacher: Catriona Olsen
Age range: 7–19 years
No. of pupils: 6350
Fees: £4,040
Curriculum: National, UK, IGCSE, ALevs

Kings London
25 Beckenham Road, Beckenham, Kent BR3 4PR
Tel: +44 (0)2086 505891
Age range: 14–25 years
Curriculum: GCSE, ALevs

Kings Oxford
Temple Road, Oxford, Oxfordshire OX4 2UJ
Tel: +44 (0)1865 711829
Age range: 14–25 years
Curriculum: GCSE, ALevs

King's School Rochester
Satis House, Boley Hill, Rochester, Kent ME1 1TE
Tel: 01634 888555
Age range: 3–18 years
No. of pupils: 680 VIth105
Curriculum: GCSE, IGCSE, ALevs

Kingsley School
Northdown Road, Bideford, Devon EX39 3LY
Tel: 01237 426200
Age range: 0–18 years (boarding from 9)
No. of pupils: 395
Curriculum: GCSE, ALevs

Kingswood School
Lansdown Road, Bath, Bath & North-East Somerset BA1 5RG
Tel: 01225 734200
Age range: 9 months–18 years
Curriculum: GCSE, ALevs
Language instr: English

Kirkham Grammar School
Ribby Road, Kirkham, Preston, Lancashire PR4 2BH
Tel: 01772 684264
Age range: 3–18 years
No. of pupils: 820
Curriculum: GCSE, ALevs
Language instr: English

La Petite Ecole Française
73 Saint Charles Square, London, London W10 6EJ
Tel: +44 (0)20 8960 1278
Age range: 3–11 years
Language instr: English, French

Europe

Lancing College
Lancing, West Sussex BN15 0RW
Tel: 01273 465805
Age range: 13–18 years
No. of pupils: 612
Curriculum: GCSE, IGCSE, ALevs
Language instr: English

Landmark International School
The Old Rectory, 9 Church Lane, Fulbourn, Cambridge, Cambridgeshire CB21 5EP
Tel: 01223 755100
Age range: 4–16 years
No. of pupils: 120
Curriculum: IBPYP, IGCSE
Language instr: English

Langley Senior School & Sixth Form
Langley Park, Loddon, Norwich, Norfolk NR14 6BJ
Tel: 01508 520210
Age range: 10–18 years

Leighton Park School
Shinfield Road, Reading, Berkshire RG2 7ED
Tel: 0118 987 9600
Age range: 11–18 years
No. of pupils: 560
Curriculum: IBDP, UK, GCSE, IGCSE, ALevs
Language instr: English

Leweston Senior School
Sherborne, Dorset DT9 6EN
Tel: 01963 210691
Age range: 11–18 years
No. of pupils: 344
Curriculum: GCSE, ALevs

Lichfield Cathedral School
The Palace, The Close, Lichfield, Staffordshire WS13 7LH
Tel: 01543 306170
Age range: 2.5–18 years

Lime House School
Holm Hill, Dalston, Carlisle, Cumbria CA5 7BX
Tel: 01228 710225
Age range: 7–18 years
No. of pupils: 168
Curriculum: GCSE, IGCSE, ALevs

Lincoln Minster School
The Prior Building, Upper Lindum Street, Lincoln, Lincolnshire LN2 5RW
Tel: 01522 551300
Age range: 4–18 years
No. of pupils: 450
Curriculum: UK
Language instr: English

Llandovery College
Queensway, Llandovery, Carmarthenshire SA20 0EE
Tel: +44(0)1550 723000
Age range: 3–18 years
Curriculum: GCSE, IGCSE, ALevs

Lomond School
10 Stafford Street, Helensburgh, Argyll & Bute G84 9JX
Tel: +44 (0)1436 672476
Age range: 3–18 years
No. of pupils: 320
Curriculum: IBDP, IBCP
Language instr: English

Longridge Towers School
Longridge Towers, Berwick-upon-Tweed, Northumberland TD15 2XQ
Tel: 01289 307584
Age range: 3–19 years
No. of pupils: 350

Lord Wandsworth College
Long Sutton, Hook, Hampshire RG29 1TA
Tel: 01256 862201
Age range: 11–18 years
No. of pupils: 700
Curriculum: GCSE, IGCSE, ALevs
Language instr: English

LORETTO SCHOOL
For further details see p. 162
Linkfield Road, Musselburgh, East Lothian EH21 7RE
Tel: +44 (0)131 653 4455
Email: admissions@loretto.com
Website: www.loretto.com
Head of School: Pete Richardson
Age range: 3–18 years
No. of pupils: 480
Fees: Day £3,733–£11,274
WB £12,333–£15,226
FB £13,460–£16,544
£10,825–£13,909
Curriculum: SAT, GCSE, IGCSE, ALevs, Scot Nat

Loughborough Grammar School
Buckland House, Burton Walks, Loughborough, Leicestershire LE11 2DU
Tel: 01509 233233
Age range: B10–18 years
No. of pupils: 856
Curriculum: GCSE, IGCSE, ALevs
Language instr: English

Luckley House School
Luckley Road, Wokingham, Berkshire RG40 3EU
Tel: 0118 978 4175
Age range: 11–18 years
Curriculum: GCSE, ALevs

Lucton School
Lucton, Herefordshire HR6 9PN
Tel: 01568 782000
Age range: 6 months–18 years (boarding from 7)
No. of pupils: 300
Curriculum: National, IGCSE, ALevs
Language instr: English

LVS Ascot
London Road, Ascot, Berkshire SL5 8DR
Tel: 01344 882770
Age range: 4–19 years
No. of pupils: 787
Curriculum: GCSE, ALevs

Lycée Français Charles de Gaulle de Londres
35 Cromwell Road, London, London SW7 2DG
Tel: 020 7584 6322
Age range: 3–18 years
No. of pupils: 3450
Language instr: French, English

Lycée International de Londres Winston Churchill
54 Forty Lane, Wembley, Middlesex HA9 9LY
Tel: +44 (0)203 824 4900
Age range: 3–18 years
Curriculum: IBDP, FrenchBacc
Language instr: English, French

Malvern College
College Road, Malvern, Worcestershire WR14 3DF
Tel: +44 (0)1684 581515
Age range: 13–18 years
No. of pupils: 650
Curriculum: IBDP, GCSE, IGCSE, ALevs
Language instr: English

Malvern St James School
15 Avenue Road, Great Malvern, Worcestershire WR14 3BA
Tel: 01684 892288
Age range: 3–18 years (boarding from 7)
Curriculum: GCSE, IGCSE, ALevs

Manchester High School for Girls
Grangethorpe Road, Manchester, Greater Manchester M14 6HS
Tel: 0161 224 0447
Age range: G4–18 years
No. of pupils: 1000
Curriculum: GCSE, ALevs
Language instr: English

Marlborough College
Bath Road, Marlborough, Wiltshire SN8 1PA
Tel: 01672 892200
Age range: 13–18 years
No. of pupils: 1011 B566 G445
Language instr: English

Marymount International School London
George Road, Kingston upon Thames, Surrey KT2 7PE
Tel: +44 (0)20 8949 0571
Age range: G11–18 years
No. of pupils: 248
Curriculum: IBDP, IBMYP
Language instr: English

Mayfield School
The Old Palace, Mayfield, East Sussex TN20 6PH
Tel: 01435 874642
Age range: G11–18 years (boarding from 11)
No. of pupils: 425
Curriculum: GCSE, IGCSE, ALevs

MERCHISTON CASTLE SCHOOL
For further details see p. 165
294 Colinton Road, Edinburgh, Edinburgh EH13 0PU
Tel: 0131 312 2200
Email: admissions@merchiston.co.uk
Website: www.merchiston.co.uk
Headmaster: Huw Jones
Age range: B3–18 years (boarding 12–18) G3–9 years
No. of pupils: 350
Fees: Day £18,000–£36,774
FB £23,205–£48,276
Curriculum: GCSE, IGCSE, ALevs, Scot Nat
Language instr: English

Methodist College
1 Malone Road, Belfast, County Antrim BT9 6BY
Tel: 028 9020 5205
Age range: 4–18 years

Michael Hall School
Kidbrooke Park, Priory Road, Forest Row, East Sussex RH18 5JA
Tel: 01342 822275
Age range: 0–19 years
Language instr: English

Mill Hill International
Milespit Hill, London, London NW7 2RX
Tel: +44 (0)20 3826 33
Age range: 13–18 years
No. of pupils: 120
Curriculum: UK, GCSE, IGCSE

Mill Hill School
The Ridgeway, Mill Hill Village, London, London NW7 1QS
Tel: 020 8959 1176
Age range: 13–18 years (boarding from 13)
No. of pupils: 893
Curriculum: TOEFL, UK, GCSE, ALevs

Millfield School
Butleigh Road, Street, Somerset BA16 0YD
Tel: 01458 442291
Age range: 13–18 years
No. of pupils: 1330
Curriculum: GCSE, IGCSE, ALevs

Milton Abbey School
Blandford Forum, Dorset DT11 0BZ
Tel: 01258 880484
Age range: 13–18 years
Curriculum: GCSE, ALevs
Language instr: English

Europe

Monkton Senior School
Monkton Combe, Bath, Bath & North-East Somerset BA2 7HG
Tel: 01225 721133
Age range: 13–18 years (boarding from 13)
No. of pupils: 365 B201 G164 VIth152
Curriculum: GCSE, IGCSE, ALevs

Monmouth School for Boys
Almshouse Street, Monmouth, Monmouthshire NP25 3XP
Tel: 01600 713143
Age range: B7–18 years
No. of pupils: 645
Language instr: English

Monmouth School for Girls
Hereford Road, Monmouth, Monmouthshire NP25 5XT
Tel: 01600 711100
Age range: G7–18 years
No. of pupils: 600

Moreton Hall
Weston Rhyn, Oswestry, Shropshire SY11 3EW
Tel: +44 (0)1691 773671
Age range: G11–18 years
Curriculum: GCSE, ALevs

Mount Kelly
Parkwood Road, Tavistock, Devon PL19 0HZ
Tel: +44 (0)1822 813100
Age range: 4–18 years
Curriculum: UK, GCSE, IGCSE, ALevs

Mount St Mary's College
College Road, Spinkhill, Near Sheffield, Derbyshire S21 3YL
Tel: 01246 433388
Age range: 11–18 years
No. of pupils: 350
Curriculum: GCSE, IGCSE, ALevs
Language instr: English

Moyles Court School
Moyles Court, Ringwood, Hampshire BH24 3NF
Tel: 01425 472856
Age range: 2–16 years

New Hall School
The Avenue, Boreham, Chelmsford, Essex CM3 3HS
Tel: 01245 467588
Age range: 1–19 years (boarding from 7)
No. of pupils: 1339
Curriculum: UK, GCSE, ALevs
Language instr: English

North London Collegiate School
Canons, Canons Drive, Edgware, Middlesex HA8 7RJ
Tel: +44 (0)20 8952 0912
Age range: G4–18 years
No. of pupils: 1080
Curriculum: IBDP, GCSE, IGCSE, ALevs
Language instr: English

Norwich School
71a The Close, Norwich, Norfolk NR1 4DD
Tel: 01603 728430
Age range: 4–18 years
No. of pupils: 1198 VIth341

Oakham School
Chapel Close, Oakham, Rutland LE15 6DT
Tel: 01572 758758
Age range: 11–18 years
No. of pupils: 950
Curriculum: IBDP, GCSE, IGCSE, ALevs
Language instr: English

Oswestry School
Upper Brook Street, Oswestry, Shropshire SY11 2TL
Tel: 01691 655711
Age range: 4–18 years
Language instr: English

Oundle School
The Great Hall, New Street, Oundle, Northamptonshire PE8 4GH
Tel: 01832 277122
Age range: 11–18 years
Language instr: English

Oxford International College
1 London Place, Oxford, Oxfordshire OX4 1BD
Tel: +44 (0)1865 203988
Age range: 14–19 years

Padworth College
Sopers Lane, Reading, Berkshire RG7 4NR
Tel: 0118 983 2644
Age range: 14–19 years
Curriculum: GCSE, IGCSE, ALevs

Pangbourne College
Pangbourne, Reading, Berkshire RG8 8LA
Tel: 0118 984 2101
Age range: 11–18 years
No. of pupils: 410
Curriculum: ALevs
Language instr: English

Plymouth College
Ford Park, Plymouth, Devon PL4 6RN
Tel: 01752 505100
Age range: 3–18 years
No. of pupils: 569 B329 G240
Curriculum: UK, GCSE, IGCSE, ALevs
Language instr: English

Pocklington School
West Green, Pocklington, York, North Yorkshire YO42 2NJ
Tel: 01759 321200
Age range: 2–18 years
No. of pupils: 741 B369 G372 VIth165
Curriculum: GCSE, IGCSE, ALevs
Language instr: English

Prior Park College
Ralph Allen Drive, Bath, Bath & North-East Somerset BA2 5AH
Tel: +44 (0)1225 835353
Age range: 11–18 years
Curriculum: GCSE, ALevs

Prior's Field
Priorsfield Road, Godalming, Surrey GU7 2RH
Tel: 01483 810551
Age range: G11–18 years (boarding from 11)
Curriculum: GCSE, IGCSE, ALevs

Queen Anne's School, Caversham
6 Henley Road, Caversham, Reading, Berkshire RG4 6DX
Tel: 01189187333
Age range: G11–18 years (boarding from 11)
Curriculum: GCSE, IGCSE, ALevs

QUEEN ETHELBURGA'S
For further details see p. 175
Thorpe Underwood Estate, York, North Yorkshire YO26 9SS
Tel: +44 (0)1423 33 33 30
Email: admissions@qe.org
Website: www.qe.org
Principal: Daniel Machin
Age range: 3 months–19 years (boarding from 7)
No. of pupils: 1100
Fees: £23,330
Curriculum: National, UK, GCSE, IGCSE, ALevs
Language instr: English

Queen Margaret's School
Escrick Park, York, North Yorkshire YO19 6EU
Tel: 01904 727600
Age range: G11–18 years (boarding from 11)

Queen Mary's School
Baldersby Park, Topcliffe, Thirsk, North Yorkshire YO7 3BZ
Tel: 01845 575000
Age range: B4–7 years G4–16 years (boarding from 7)

Queen Victoria School
Dunblane, Perthshire FK15 0JY
Tel: 01786 822288
Age range: 11–18 years
Curriculum: Scot Nat, SVQ, CSFS

Queen's College
Trull Road, Taunton, Somerset TA1 4QS
Tel: +44 (0)1823 272559
Age range: 3 months–18 years

Radley College
Radley, Abingdon, Oxfordshire OX14 2HR
Tel: 01235 543000
Age range: B13–18 years

Ratcliffe College
Fosse Way, Ratcliffe on the Wreake, Leicester, Leicestershire LE7 4SG
Tel: +44 (0)1509 817000
Age range: 3–18 years (boarding from 11)
Language instr: English

REDDAM HOUSE BERKSHIRE
For further details see p. 176
Bearwood Road, Sindlesham, Wokingham, Berkshire RG41 5BG
Tel: +44 (0)118 974 8300
Email: registrar@reddamhouse.org.uk
Website: www.reddamhouse.org.uk
Principal: Rick Cross
Age range: 3 months–18 years
No. of pupils: 785
Fees: Day £13,026–£20,883 WB £32,769–£36,558 FB £34,578–£38,310
Curriculum: UK, GCSE, ALevs
Language instr: English

Redmaids' High School Senior & Sixth Form
Westbury Road, Westbury-on-Trym, Bristol, Bristol BS9 3AW
Tel: 0117 962 2641
Age range: G11–18 years
Curriculum: IBDP, GCSE, IGCSE, ALevs
Language instr: English

Reed's School
Sandy Lane, Cobham, Surrey KT11 2ES
Tel: 01932 869001
Age range: B11–18 years (boarding from 11) G16–18 years
Curriculum: GCSE, IGCSE, ALevs
Language instr: English

Rendcomb College
Rendcomb, Cirencester, Gloucestershire GL7 7HA
Tel: 01285 831213
Age range: 3–18 years

Repton School
The Hall, Repton, Derbyshire DE65 6FH
Tel: 01283 559200
Age range: 13–18 years
Curriculum: GCSE, IGCSE, ALevs

Europe

Rikkyo School in England
Guildford Road, Rudgwick,
Horsham, West Sussex RH12 3BE
Tel: +44 (0)1403 822107
Age range: 10–18 years

Rishworth School
Oldham Road, Sowerby Bridge,
Halifax, West Yorkshire HX6 4QA
Tel: 01422 822217
Age range: 3–18 years
(boarding from 11)
No. of pupils: 408
Curriculum: GCSE, ALevs

Rochester Independent College
254 St Margaret's Banks,
Rochester, Kent ME1 1HY
Tel: +44 (0)163 482 8115
Age range: 11–18 years

Rockport School
15 Rockport Road, Craigavad,
Holywood, County Down BT18 0DD
Tel: 028 9042 8372
Age range: 3–18 years
Curriculum: GCSE, ALevs

Roedean School
Roedean Way, Brighton,
East Sussex BN2 5RQ
Tel: 01273 667500
Age range: G11–18 years
No. of pupils: 620 VIth180
Curriculum: GCSE, IGCSE, ALevs
Language instr: English

Rookwood School
Weyhill Road, Andover,
Hampshire SP10 3AL
Tel: 01264 325900
Age range: 2–18 years
(boarding from 7)

Rossall School
Broadway, Fleetwood,
Lancashire FY7 8JW
Tel: +44 (0)1253 774201
Age range: 0–18 years
No. of pupils: 843 B488 G367 VIth220
Curriculum: IBDP, National, GCSE, IGCSE, ALevs
Language instr: English

ROYAL HIGH BATH
For further details see p. 178
Lansdown Road, Bath, Bath & North-East Somerset BA1 5SZ
Tel: +44 (0)1225 313877
Email: admissions@rhsb.gdst.net
Website: www.royalhighbath.gdst.net
Head: Heidi-Jayne Boyes
Age range: G3–18 years
(boarding from 11)
No. of pupils: 580
Fees: Day £6,592
WB £13,549 FB £15,073
Curriculum: IBDP, National, GCSE, ALevs
Language instr: English

Royal Russell School
Coombe Lane, Croydon,
Surrey CR9 5BX
Tel: +44 (0)20 8657 4433
Age range: 11–18 years
Curriculum: GCSE, ALevs

Rugby School
Lawrence Sheriff Street, Rugby,
Warwickshire CV22 5EH
Tel: 01788 556155
Age range: 13–18 years
(boarding from 13)
No. of pupils: 870
Curriculum: IBDP, UK, GCSE, IGCSE, ALevs

Ruthin School
Mold Road, Ruthin,
Denbighshire LL15 1EE
Tel: 01824 702543
Age range: 11–18 years
Curriculum: GCSE, ALevs

Rydal Penrhos Senior School
Pwllycrochan Avenue, Colwyn
Bay, Clwyd LL29 7BT
Tel: +44 (0)1492 530155
Age range: 11–18 years
Curriculum: IGCSE, ALevs
Language instr: English

Ryde School with Upper Chine
Queen's Road, Ryde, Isle of Wight PO33 3BE
Tel: 01983 562229
Age range: 2–18 years
(boarding from 11)
No. of pupils: 720
Curriculum: IBDP, IBCP, National, GCSE, ALevs
Language instr: English

Saint Felix School
Halesworth Road, Southwold,
Suffolk IP18 6SD
Tel: +44 (0)15027 22175
Age range: 2–18 years
(boarding from 7)
Language instr: English

Scarborough College
Filey Road, Scarborough,
North Yorkshire YO11 3BA
Tel: +44 (0)1723 360620
Age range: 3–18 years
(boarding from 11)
No. of pupils: 528
Curriculum: IBDP, GCSE, IGCSE
Language instr: English

Seaford College
Lavington Park, Petworth,
West Sussex GU28 0NB
Tel: 01798 867392
Age range: 5–18 years
No. of pupils: 943 B560 G383 VIth264
Curriculum: National, GCSE, IGCSE, ALevs
Language instr: English

Sedbergh School
Station Road, Sedbergh,
Cumbria LA10 5HG
Tel: 015396 20535
Age range: 3–19 years
Curriculum: GCSE, IGCSE, ALevs

SEVENOAKS SCHOOL
For further details see p. 189
High Street, Sevenoaks,
Kent TN13 1HU
Tel: +44 (0)1732 455133
Email: admissions@sevenoaksschool.org
Website: www.sevenoaksschool.org
Head of School: Jesse R Elzinga
Age range: 11–18 years
No. of pupils: 1245
Fees: Day: £35,925–£41,514,
Full boarding: £58,770–£64,257
Curriculum: IBDP, National, GCSE, IGCSE
Language instr: English

Shebbear College
Shebbear, Beaworthy,
Devon EX21 5HJ
Tel: 01409 282000
Age range: 4–18 years
Curriculum: GCSE, ALevs
Language instr: English

Sherborne Girls
Bradford Road, Sherborne,
Dorset DT9 3QN
Tel: 01935 812245
Age range: G11–18 years
(boarding from 11)
Curriculum: GCSE, IGCSE, ALevs
Language instr: English

Sherborne International
Newell Grange, Newell,
Sherborne, Dorset DT9 4EZ
Tel: +44 (0)1935 814743
Age range: 8–17 years
Curriculum: National, GCSE, IGCSE
Language instr: English

Sherborne School
Abbey Road, Sherborne,
Dorset DT9 3LF
Tel: +44 (0)1935 812249
Age range: B13–18 years
Curriculum: GCSE, IGCSE, ALevs
Language instr: English

Sherfield School
South Drive, Sherfield-on-Loddon,
Hook, Hampshire RG27 0HU
Tel: 01256 884800
Age range: 3 months–18 years (boarding from 9)
No. of pupils: 609
Curriculum: GCSE, IGCSE, ALevs
Language instr: English

Shiplake College
Henley-on-Thames,
Oxfordshire RG9 4BW
Tel: +44 (0)1189 402455
Age range: 11–18 years
No. of pupils: 540 B424 G116 VIth202
Curriculum: GCSE, IGCSE, ALevs
Language instr: English

Shrewsbury School
The Schools, Shrewsbury,
Shropshire SY3 7BA
Tel: 01743 280552
Age range: 13–18 years
No. of pupils: 825
Curriculum: GCSE, IGCSE, ALevs
Language instr: English

SIAL.school
154-156 Holland Park Avenue,
London, London W11 4UH
Tel: +44 (0)20 7603 5353
Age range: 3–11 years
Language instr: English, Italian

Sibford School
Sibford Ferris, Banbury,
Oxfordshire OX15 5QL
Tel: 01295 781200
Age range: 3–18 years
Language instr: English

Sidcot School
Oakridge Lane, Winscombe,
Somerset BS25 1PD
Tel: 01934 843102
Age range: 3–18 years
(boarding from 11)
No. of pupils: 620
Curriculum: IBDP, GCSE, ALevs
Language instr: English

Slindon College
Slindon House, Top Road, Slindon,
Arundel, West Sussex BN18 0RH
Tel: 01243 814320
Age range: B8–18 years
(boarding from 11)
No. of pupils: 107
Curriculum: UK, GCSE, IGCSE, ALevs
Language instr: English

Southbank International School - Hampstead
16 Netherhall Gardens,
London, London NW3 5TH
Tel: 020 3890 1969
Age range: 2–11 years
Curriculum: IBPYP
Language instr: English

SOUTHBANK INTERNATIONAL SCHOOL - KENSINGTON
For further details see p. 190
36-38 Kensington Park Road,
London, London W11 3BU
Tel: 020 3890 1969
Email: admissions@southbank.org
Website: www.southbank.org
Head of School: David MacMorran
Age range: 2–18 years
Fees: £6,724–£10,721
Curriculum: IBPYP
Language instr: English

Europe

Southbank International School - Westminster
63-65 Portland Place, London, London W1B 1QR
Tel: 020 3890 1969
Age range: 11–18 years
Curriculum: IBDP, IBMYP
Language instr: English

St Andrew's College Cambridge
13 Station Road, Cambridge, Cambridgeshire CB1 2JB
Tel: +44 (0)1223 903048
Age range: 14–19 years

St Catherine's, Bramley
Station Road, Bramley, Guildford, Surrey GU5 0DF
Tel: 01483 899609
Age range: G4–18 years (boarding from 11)
Curriculum: UK, GCSE, IGCSE, ALevs

St Christopher School
Barrington Road, Letchworth Garden City, Hertfordshire SG6 3JZ
Tel: 01462 650 850
Age range: 3–18 years

St Clare's, Oxford
139 Banbury Road, Oxford, Oxfordshire OX2 7AL
Tel: +44 (0)1865 552031
Age range: 15–19 years
No. of pupils: 290
Curriculum: IBDP
Language instr: English

St David's College
Gloddaeth Hall, Llandudno, Clwyd LL30 1RD
Tel: 01492 875974
Age range: 9–19 years
No. of pupils: 270
Curriculum: GCSE, ALevs

St Dunstan's College
Stanstead Road, London, London SE6 4TY
Tel: 020 8516 7200
Age range: 3–18 years
Language instr: English

St Edmund's College & Prep School
Old Hall Green, Nr Ware, Hertfordshire SG11 1DS
Tel: 01920 824247
Age range: 3–18 years (boarding from 11)

St Edmund's School
St Thomas Hill, Canterbury, Kent CT2 8HU
Tel: 01227 475601
Age range: 2–18 years (boarding from 11)
No. of pupils: 602
Curriculum: National, GCSE, ALevs

St Edward's, Oxford
Woodstock Road, Oxford, Oxfordshire OX2 7NN
Tel: +44 (0)1865 319200
Age range: 13–18 years
No. of pupils: 810
Curriculum: IBDP, GCSE, IGCSE, ALevs
Language instr: English

St Francis' College
Broadway, Letchworth Garden City, Hertfordshire SG6 3PJ
Tel: 01462 670511
Age range: B3–11 years G3–18 years (boarding from 10)
Language instr: English

St George's Ascot
Wells Lane, Ascot, Berkshire SL5 7DZ
Tel: 01344 629900
Age range: G11–18 years (boarding from 11)
No. of pupils: 250
Curriculum: GCSE, ALevs
Language instr: English

St George's School for Girls
Garscube Terrace, Edinburgh, Edinburgh EH12 6BG
Tel: 0131 311 8000
Age range: B3–5 years G3–18 years (boarding from 10)
Curriculum: UK, GCSE, IGCSE, ALevs, Scot Nat, CSFS
Language instr: English

St George's School Windsor Castle
Windsor Castle, Windsor, Berkshire SL4 1QF
Tel: 01753 865553
Age range: 3–13 years (boarding from 8)
Curriculum: IBPYP
Language instr: English

St Helen's School
Eastbury Road, Northwood, Middlesex HA6 3AS
Tel: +44 (0)1923 843210
Age range: G3–18 years
No. of pupils: 1150
Language instr: English

St James Senior Boys' School
Church Road, Ashford, Surrey TW15 3DZ
Tel: 01784 266930
Age range: B11–18 years
Curriculum: GCSE, IGCSE, ALevs

St James Senior Girls' School
Earsby Street, London, London W14 8SH
Tel: 02073 481777
Age range: G11–18 years
Curriculum: GCSE, IGCSE, ALevs

St John's School
Broadway, Sidmouth, Devon EX10 8RG
Tel: 01395 513984
Age range: 2–18 years (boarding from 8)
Curriculum: GCSE, IGCSE

St John's School
Epsom Road, Leatherhead, Surrey KT22 8SP
Tel: 01372 373000
Age range: 11–18 years (boarding from 11)
Curriculum: UK, GCSE, ALevs
Language instr: English

St Joseph's College
Belstead Road, Ipswich, Suffolk IP2 9DR
Tel: +44 (0)1473 690281
Age range: 2–18 years
Curriculum: GCSE, ALevs

St Lawrence College
College Road, Ramsgate, Kent CT11 7AE
Tel: 01843 572931
Age range: 3–18 years
No. of pupils: 501
Curriculum: GCSE, ALevs
Language instr: English

St Leonards School
South Street, St Andrews, Fife KY16 9QJ
Tel: 01334 472126
Age range: 5–18 years (boarding from 10)
No. of pupils: 570
Curriculum: IBDP, IBMYP, IBPYP, IBCP, GCSE, IGCSE
Language instr: English

St Margaret's School, Bushey
Merry Hill Road, Bushey, Hertfordshire WD23 1DT
Tel: +44 (0)20 8416 4400
Age range: 2–18 years
No. of pupils: 830
Curriculum: GCSE, IGCSE, ALevs

St Mary's Calne
Curzon Street, Calne, Wiltshire SN11 0DF
Tel: 01249 857200
Age range: G11–18 years (boarding from 11)
No. of pupils: 350 VIth120
Curriculum: GCSE, IGCSE, ALevs
Language instr: English

St Mary's Music School
Coates Hall, 25 Grosvenor Crescent, Edinburgh, Edinburgh EH12 5EL
Tel: 0131 538 7766
Age range: 9–19 years
Curriculum: IGCSE, ALevs, Scot Nat, CSFS

St Mary's School Ascot
St Mary's Road, Ascot, Berkshire SL5 9JF
Tel: 01344 296614
Age range: G11–18 years (boarding from 11)
Curriculum: GCSE, IGCSE, ALevs
Language instr: English

St Mary's School, Cambridge
Bateman Street, Cambridge, Cambridgeshire CB2 1LY
Tel: +44 (0)1223 224167
Age range: G3–18 years (boarding from 9)
No. of pupils: 630
Curriculum: GCSE, ALevs

St Paul's School
Lonsdale Road, Barnes, London, London SW13 9JT
Tel: 020 8748 9162
Age range: B7–18 years
Curriculum: UK, IGCSE, ALevs

St Peter's 13-18
Clifton, York, North Yorkshire YO30 6AB
Tel: 01904 527300
Age range: 13–18 years
Curriculum: National, UK
Language instr: English

St Swithun's School
Alresford Road, Winchester, Hampshire SO21 1HA
Tel: 01962 835703
Age range: G11–18 years
No. of pupils: 508 VIth138
Curriculum: GCSE, ALevs

St Teresa's Effingham (Senior School)
Effingham, Surrey RH5 6ST
Tel: +44 (0)1372 452037
Age range: G11–18 years (boarding from 11)
Curriculum: GCSE, ALevs

St. James School
22 Bargate, Grimsby, North-East Lincolnshire DN34 4SY
Tel: 01472 503260
Age range: 11–18 years
Language instr: English

Stamford High School
St. Martin's Street, Stamford, Lincolnshire PE9 2LL
Tel: 01780 484200
Age range: G11–18 years (boarding from 11)
Curriculum: GCSE, ALevs

Europe

Stamford School
Southfields House, Stamford,
Lincolnshire PE9 2BQ
Tel: 01780 750300
Age range: B11–18 years
(boarding from 11)
Curriculum: GCSE, IGCSE, ALevs

Stanborough Secondary School
Stanborough Park, Garston,
Watford, Hertfordshire WD25 9JT
Tel: 01923 673268
Age range: 11–18 years
Language instr: English

Stephen Perse Sixth Form
Bateman Street, Cambridge,
Cambridgeshire CB2 1NA
Tel: 01223 454700 (Ext: 3000)
Age range: 16–18 years
Curriculum: GCSE, IGCSE, ALevs
Language instr: English

Stewart's Melville College
Queensferry Road, Edinburgh,
Edinburgh EH4 3EZ
Tel: +44 (0)131 311 1000
Age range: B12–18 years
Curriculum: National, Scot Nat, CSFS

Stoke College
Ashen Lane, Stoke by Clare,
Sudbury, Suffolk CO10 8JE
Tel: +44 (0)1787 278141
Age range: 11–18 years

Stonar School
Cottles Park, Atworth,
Melksham, Wiltshire SN12 8NT
Tel: 01225 701740
Age range: 2–18 years
(boarding from 10)
Curriculum: GCSE, IGCSE, ALevs

Stonyhurst College
Stonyhurst, Clitheroe,
Lancashire BB7 9PZ
Tel: 01254 827073
Age range: 3–18 years
(boarding from 9)
No. of pupils: 658
Curriculum: IBDP, GCSE, ALevs

Stover School
Stover, Newton Abbot,
Devon TQ12 6QG
Tel: +44 (0)1626 354505
Age range: 3–18 years

Stowe School
Buckingham, Buckinghamshire
MK18 5EH
Tel: 01280 818000
Age range: 13–18 years
Curriculum: UK, GCSE, IGCSE, ALevs
Language instr: English

Strathallan School
Forgandenny, Perth, Perth
& Kinross PH2 9EG
Tel: 01738 812546
Age range: 7–18 years
No. of pupils: 545
Curriculum: GCSE, ALevs, Scot Nat

Sutton Valence School
North Street, Sutton Valence,
Kent ME17 3HL
Tel: 01622 845200
Age range: 11–18 years
(boarding from 11)
No. of pupils: 557
Curriculum: UK, GCSE, IGCSE, ALevs
Language instr: English

Talbot Heath
Rothesay Road, Talbot Woods,
Bournemouth, Dorset BH4 9NJ
Tel: 01202 761881
Age range: G3–18 years
(boarding from 11)
Curriculum: GCSE, ALevs

TASIS ENGLAND
For further details see p. 201
Coldharbour Lane, Thorpe,
Surrey TW20 8TE
Tel: +44 (0)1932 582316
Email: ukadmissions@tasisengland.org
Website: www.tasisengland.org
Head of School: Bryan Nixon
Age range: 4–18 years
(boarding from 13)
No. of pupils: 650
Fees: Day £15,600–
£35,740 FB £66,970
Curriculum: ACT, AP,
IBDP, SAT, TOEFL, USA
Language instr: English

Taunton School
Staplegrove Road, Taunton,
Somerset TA2 6AD
Tel: +44 (0)1823 703703
Age range: 0–18 years
No. of pupils: 1182
Curriculum: IBDP, UK,
GCSE, IGCSE, ALevs
Language instr: English

Taunton School International
206-216 Greenway Road,
Taunton, Somerset TA2 6LJ
Tel: 01823 703200
Age range: 8–18 years
No. of pupils: 145

Teikyo School UK
Framewood Road, Wexham,
Buckinghamshire SL2 4QS
Tel: 01753 663711
Age range: 15–18 years
Curriculum: IBDP

Tettenhall College
Wood Road, Tettenhall,
Wolverhampton, West
Midlands WV6 8QX
Tel: 01902 751119
Age range: 2–18 years
(boarding from 10)
No. of pupils: 521
Curriculum: National, UK,
GCSE, IGCSE, ALevs

The Abbey School
Kendrick Road, Reading,
Berkshire RG1 5DZ
Tel: 0118 987 2256
Age range: G3–18 years
No. of pupils: 987
Curriculum: IBDP, IBPYP,
GCSE, IGCSE, ALevs
Language instr: English

The American School in London
One Waverley Place, London,
London NW8 0NP
Tel: +44 (0)20 7449 1200
Age range: 4–18 years
Language instr: English

The Chalfonts Independent Grammar School
19 London Road, High Wycombe,
Buckinghamshire HP11 1BJ
Tel: +44 (0)1494 875502
Age range: 11–18 years
Curriculum: IBDP, IBMYP, UK

The Hammond School
Mannings Lane, Chester,
Cheshire CH2 4ES
Tel: 01244 305350
Age range: 11–19+ years

The King's School, Canterbury
Lattergate Office, 25 The Precincts,
Canterbury, Kent CT1 2ES
Tel: 01227 595501
Age range: 13–18 years
Curriculum: GCSE, IGCSE, ALevs
Language instr: English

The Leys School
Trumpington Road, Cambridge,
Cambridgeshire CB2 7AD
Tel: 01223 508900
Age range: 11–18 years
No. of pupils: 570
Curriculum: GCSE, ALevs, CSFS

The Manchester Grammar School
Old Hall Lane, Fallowfield,
Manchester, Greater
Manchester M13 0XT
Tel: 0161 224 7201
Age range: B7–18 years
Language instr: English

The Mary Erskine School
Ravelston, Edinburgh,
Edinburgh EH4 3NT
Tel: +44 (0)131 347 5700
Age range: G12–18 years
Curriculum: Scot Nat, CSFS

The Mount School York
Dalton Terrace, York, North
Yorkshire YO24 4DD
Tel: 01904 667500
Age range: G3–18 years
(boarding from 11)

The Oratory School
Woodcote, Reading,
Berkshire RG8 0PJ
Tel: 01491 683500
Age range: 11–18 years
Curriculum: UK, GCSE, ALevs
Language instr: English

The Peterborough School
Thorpe Road, Peterborough,
Cambridgeshire PE3 6AP
Tel: 01733 343357
Age range: 6 weeks–18 years
No. of pupils: 500
Curriculum: GCSE, ALevs

The Portsmouth Grammar School
High Street, Portsmouth,
Hampshire PO1 2LN
Tel: +44 (0)23 9236 0036
Age range: 2.5–18 years
Language instr: English

The Purcell School, London
Aldenham Road, Bushey,
Hertfordshire WD23 2TS
Tel: 01923 331100
Age range: 10–18 years

The Read School
Drax, Selby, North Yorkshire YO8 8NL
Tel: 01757 618248
Age range: 4–18 years
(boarding from 8)
Language instr: English

The Roche School
11 Frogmore, London,
London SW18 1HW
Tel: 020 8877 0823
Age range: 2–11 years
No. of pupils: 282 B126 G156
Language instr: English, Spanish

The Royal Hospital School
Holbrook, Ipswich, Suffolk IP9 2RX
Tel: 01473 326136
Age range: 11–18 years
No. of pupils: 730
Curriculum: GCSE, ALevs
Language instr: English

Europe

THE ROYAL MASONIC SCHOOL FOR GIRLS
For further details see p. 213
Rickmansworth Park, Rickmansworth, Hertfordshire WD3 4HF
Tel: 01923 725354
Email: admissions@rmsforgirls.com
Website: www.rmsforgirls.com
Headmaster: Kevin Carson
Age range: B2–3 years G2–18 years (boarding from 8)
No. of pupils: 901
Fees: Day £5,685–£9,674
WB £12,776–£16,135
FB £14,050–£17,340
Language instr: English

The Royal School, Dungannon
2 Ranfurly Road, Dungannon, County Tyrone BT71 6EG
Tel: 02887 722710
Age range: 11–18 years (boarding from 11)
Language instr: English

The Royal School, Haslemere
Farnham Lane, Haslemere, Surrey GU27 1HQ
Tel: 01428 605805
Age range: 10–18 years (boarding from 10+)
No. of pupils: 140
Language instr: English

The Stewart Bilingual School
90 Oxford Gardens, London, London W10 5UW
Tel: +44 (0)20 8960 2725
Age range: 2–11 years
Language instr: English, French

The Worthgate School
68 New Dover Road, Canterbury, Kent CT1 3LQ
Tel: +44 (0)1227 866510
Age range: 13–21 years
No. of pupils: 450
Curriculum: IBDP, UK, GCSE, ALevs
Language instr: English

Thornton College
College Lane, Thornton, Milton Keynes, Buckinghamshire MK17 0HJ
Tel: 01280 812610
Age range: G3–18 years (boarding from 8)
No. of pupils: 367
Curriculum: GCSE, ALevs

Tonbridge School
High Street, Tonbridge, Kent TN9 1JP
Tel: 01732 304297
Age range: B13–18 years
No. of pupils: 807
Curriculum: GCSE, IGCSE, ALevs

Total French School, Aberdeen
c/o Albyn School, 17-23 Queen's Road, Aberdeen, Aberdeenshire AB15 4PB
Tel: +44 (0)1224 329884
Age range: 2–18 years

Trent College and The Elms
Derby Road, Long Eaton, Nottingham, Nottinghamshire NG10 4AD
Tel: 0115 8494949
Age range: 0–18 years
No. of pupils: 1121
Curriculum: GCSE, IGCSE, ALevs

Tring Park School for the Performing Arts
Mansion Drive, Tring, Hertfordshire HP23 5LX
Tel: 01442 824255
Age range: 8–19 years
No. of pupils: 370 B112 G258 VIth171
Curriculum: National, GCSE, IGCSE, ALevs
Language instr: English

Trinity School
Buckeridge Road, Teignmouth, Devon TQ14 8LY
Tel: 01626 774138
Age range: 3–18 years (boarding from 9)
Language instr: English

Truro School
Trennick Lane, Truro, Cornwall TR1 1TH
Tel: 01872 272763
Age range: 3–18 years
Curriculum: National, GCSE, IGCSE, ALevs
Language instr: English

Tudor Hall School
Wykham Park, Banbury, Oxfordshire OX16 9UR
Tel: 01295 263434
Age range: G11–18 years (boarding from 11)
Language instr: English

Uppingham School
Uppingham, Rutland LE15 9QE
Tel: +44 (0)1572 822216
Age range: 13–18 years

UWC Atlantic
St Donat's Castle, St Donat's, Llantwit Major, Glamorgan CF61 1WF
Tel: +44 (0)1446 799000
Age range: 16–19 years
No. of pupils: 350
Curriculum: IBDP
Language instr: English

Warminster School
Church Street, Warminster, Wiltshire BA12 8PJ
Tel: +44 (0)1985 210100
Age range: 2–18 years (boarding from 7)
No. of pupils: 551
Curriculum: IBDP, IBCP, GCSE, ALevs
Language instr: English

Warwick School
Myton Road, Warwick, Warwickshire CV34 6PP
Tel: 01926 776400
Age range: B7–18 years

Wellington College
Duke's Ride, Crowthorne, Berkshire RG45 7PU
Tel: +44 (0)1344 444013
Age range: 13–18 years
No. of pupils: 1140 B594 G546 VIth510
Curriculum: IBDP, UK, GCSE, IGCSE, ALevs
Language instr: English

Wellington School
South Street, Wellington, Somerset TA21 8NT
Tel: 01823 668800
Age range: 3–18 years
Language instr: English

Wells Cathedral School
The Liberty, Wells, Somerset BA5 2ST
Tel: +44 (0)1749 834200
Age range: 2–18 years

West Buckland School
Barnstaple, Devon EX32 0SX
Tel: 01598 760000
Age range: 3–18 years
Curriculum: IBCP
Language instr: English

Westbourne School
Hickman Road, Penarth, Glamorgan CF64 2AJ
Tel: 029 2070 5705
Age range: 2–18 years
No. of pupils: 302
Curriculum: IBDP, GCSE, IGCSE
Language instr: English

Westfield School
Oakfield Road, Gosforth, Newcastle upon Tyne, Tyne & Wear NE3 4HS
Tel: 01912 553980
Age range: G3–18 years

Westminster School
17A Dean's Yard, Westminster, London, London SW1P 3PB
Tel: 020 7963 1000
Age range: B13–18 years G16–18 years
Curriculum: GCSE, IGCSE, ALevs

Westonbirt School
Westonbirt, Tetbury, Gloucestershire GL8 8QG
Tel: 01666 880333
Age range: 11–18 years
Language instr: English

Whitgift School
Haling Park, South Croydon, Surrey CR2 6YT
Tel: +44 20 8633 9935
Age range: B10–18 years (boarding from 13)
No. of pupils: 1550
Curriculum: IBDP, UK, GCSE, IGCSE, ALevs
Language instr: English

Winchester College
College Street, Winchester, Hampshire SO23 9NA
Tel: 01962 621100
Age range: B13–18 years (boarding from 13)
Language instr: English

Windermere School
Patterdale Road, Windermere, Cumbria LA23 1NW
Tel: 015394 46164
Age range: 3–18 years (boarding from 8)
No. of pupils: 300
Curriculum: IBDP, IBCP, GCSE, IGCSE
Language instr: English

Woldingham School
Marden Park, Woldingham, Surrey CR3 7YA
Tel: 01883 349431
Age range: G11–18 years (boarding from 11)
No. of pupils: 550
Curriculum: GCSE, ALevs

Wolsey Hall Oxford
Midland House, West Way, Oxford, Oxfordshire OX2 0PH
Tel: 0800 622 6599
Age range: 4–18 years
Curriculum: IGCSE, ALevs

Woodbridge School
Burkitt Road, Woodbridge, Suffolk IP12 4JH
Tel: +44 (0)1394 615000
Age range: 4–18 years
Curriculum: GCSE, IGCSE, ALevs
Language instr: English

Woodhouse Grove School
Apperley Bridge, Bradford, West Yorkshire BD10 0NR
Tel: 0113 250 2477
Age range: 2–18 years (boarding from 11)
No. of pupils: 1048 B578 G470 VIth212
Curriculum: GCSE, IGCSE, ALevs

Europe

Worksop College
Cuthbert's Avenue, Worksop,
Nottinghamshire S80 3AP
Tel: 01909 537100
Age range: 11–18 years
Language instr: English

Worth School
Paddockhurst Road, Turners Hill,
Crawley, West Sussex RH10 4SD
Tel: +44 (0)1342 710200
Age range: 11–18 years
(boarding from 13)
Curriculum: IBDP, National, GCSE, IGCSE, ALevs
Language instr: English

Wotton House International School
Wotton House, Horton Road,
Gloucester, Gloucestershire GL1 3PR
Tel: +44 (0)1452 764248
Age range: 7–16 years
Curriculum: IBMYP
Language instr: English

Wrekin College
Wellington, Shropshire TF1 3BH
Tel: +44 (0)1952 265600
Age range: 11–18 years
Language instr: English

Wychwood School
74 Banbury Road, Oxford,
Oxfordshire OX2 6JR
Tel: +44 (0)18655 57976
Age range: 11–18 years
(boarding from 11)
Language instr: English

Wycliffe College
Bristol Road, Stonehouse,
Gloucestershire GL10 2AF
Tel: 01453 822432
Age range: 3–19 years
(boarding from 7)
No. of pupils: 696
Curriculum: GCSE, IGCSE, ALevs

Wycombe Abbey
Frances Dove Way, High Wycombe,
Buckinghamshire HP11 1PE
Tel: +44 (0)1494 520381
Age range: G11–18 years
No. of pupils: 660
Curriculum: GCSE, IGCSE, ALevs

Yehudi Menuhin School
Cobham Road, Stoke d'Abernon,
Cobham, Surrey KT11 3QQ
Tel: 01932 864739
Age range: 8–19 years
Curriculum: GCSE, IGCSE, ALevs
Language instr: English

UKRAINE

Brookes CIL International School
Parus Business Center, 2
Mechnikov Street, Kyiv 01023
Tel: +38 44 333 77 73
Curriculum: AP

Gymnasium A+
Berezneva Street 14, Kyiv 02160
Tel: +38 44 363 14 03
Curriculum: IBDP
Language instr: English, Ukrainian

International American School & University (AISU)
Street Dragomanova 1-V, Kyiv 02068
Tel: +38 44 333 88 14
Curriculum: IBDP
Language instr: English, Ukrainian

Meridian International School
Kvitnevy Provulok 5A, Kyiv 04108
Tel: +380 44 484 77 39
Age range: 3–18
No. of pupils: 315

Pechersk School International Kyiv
7a Victora Zabily, Kyiv 03039
Tel: +380 44 377 52 92
Age range: 3–19 years
No. of pupils: 96
Curriculum: IBDP, IBMYP, IBPYP
Language instr: English

Prime Innovative Private Lviv Lyceum (PIPL Lyceum)
5a Naukova Street, Lviv 79060
Tel: +38 67 408 16 55
Curriculum: IBDP
Language instr: English, Ukrainian

QSI Kyiv International School
3A Svyatoshinsky Provuluk, Kyiv 03115
Tel: +38 (044) 452 27 92
Age range: 3–18 years
No. of pupils: 225
Curriculum: AP, IBDP, USA
Language instr: English

Simferopol International School
Barrikadnaya Street 59A,
Simferopol 95000
Tel: +7 3652 54 06 06
Age range: 2–17
No. of pupils: 185 B125 G60
Curriculum: National, UK
Language instr: Russian, Ukrainian, English

The British International School Ukraine (Nivki Campus)
45 Tolbukhina Street, Kyiv 03190
Tel: +38 44 502 39 09
Age range: 3–18 years
Curriculum: UK, IGCSE, ALevs
Language instr: English

The British International School Ukraine (Pechersk Campus)
1 Dragomirova Street, Kyiv 01103
Tel: +38 44 596 18 28
Age range: 3–18 years
Curriculum: IBDP, UK, IGCSE, ALevs
Language instr: English

International schools in North America

Schools ordered A–Z by Country

Key to directory

Country

Name of school or college

Indicates that this school has a profile

Address and contact number

Head's name

Age range

Number of pupils.
B = boys G = girls VIth = sixth form

Fees per annum.
Day = fees for day pupils.
WB = fees for weekly boarders.
FB = fees for full boarders.

Curriculum

Language of instruction

Memberships/Accreditation

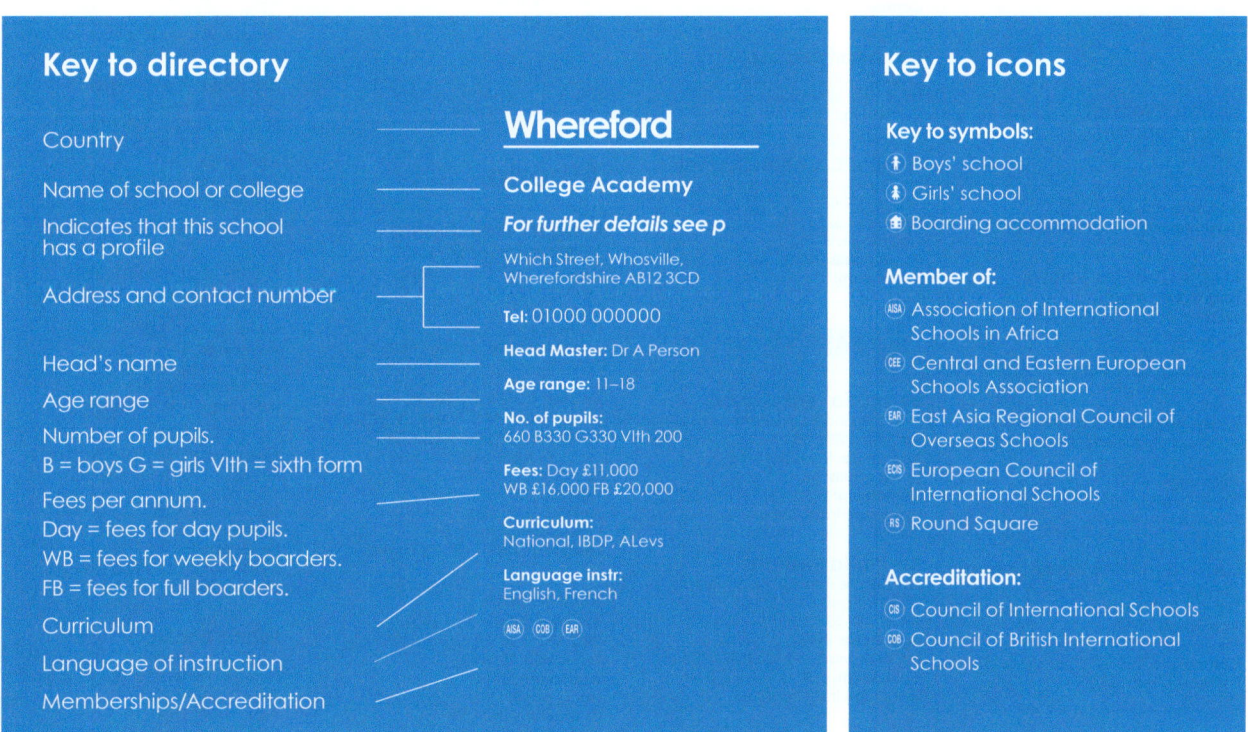

Whereford

College Academy

For further details see p

Which Street, Whosville,
Wherefordshire AB12 3CD

Tel: 01000 000000

Head Master: Dr A Person

Age range: 11–18

No. of pupils:
660 B330 G330 VIth 200

Fees: Day £11,000
WB £16,000 FB £20,000

Curriculum:
National, IBDP, ALevs

Language instr:
English, French

(AISA) (COB) (EAR)

Key to icons

Key to symbols:
- Boys' school
- Girls' school
- Boarding accommodation

Member of:
- (AISA) Association of International Schools in Africa
- (CEE) Central and Eastern European Schools Association
- (EAR) East Asia Regional Council of Overseas Schools
- (ECIS) European Council of International Schools
- (RS) Round Square

Accreditation:
- (CIS) Council of International Schools
- (COB) Council of British International Schools

Please note: Schools are coeducational day schools unless otherwise indicated

North America

ANGUILLA

Omololu International School
P.O Box 703, The Valley BWI, AI2640
Tel: +1 264 497 5430
Curriculum: IBPYP
Language instr: English

ANTIGUA

Island Academy International School
Oliver's Estate, PO Box W1884, St John's
Tel: +1 268 460 1094
Age range: 3–18
No. of pupils: 270
Curriculum: IBDP, National
Language instr: English

Soufriere Primary
St Mark
Tel: +1 767 448 0373

ARUBA

International School of Aruba
Wayaca 238A, Oranjestad
Tel: +297 583 5040
Age range: 3–19
No. of pupils: 190
Curriculum: AP, SAT, TOEFL, USA
Language instr: English

BAHAMAS

Aquinas College
PO Box N-7540, Nassau 7540
Tel: + 1 242 361 5534

Bishop Michael Eldon School
East Sunrise Highway, PO Box 40667, Freeport
Tel: +1 242 373 3579
Age range: 4–18
Curriculum: ACT, AP, SAT, GCSE

King's College School, The Bahamas
Western Road, Nassau, New Providence
Tel: +1 242 820 0976
Age range: 4–12 years

Kingsway Academy
PO Box N 4378, Bernard Road, Nassau
Tel: +1 242 324 5049
Age range: 4–18
No. of pupils: 1005
Curriculum: AP, USA

Lucaya International School
Chesapeake Drive, Freeport
Tel: +1 242 373 4004
Age range: 3–18
No. of pupils: 200
Curriculum: ACT, IBDP, IBPYP, IGCSE
Language instr: English

Lyford Cay International School
Lyford Cay Drive, PO Box N-7776, Nassau NB
Tel: +1 242 362 4774
Age range: 3–18
No. of pupils: 273 B133 G140
Curriculum: IBDP, IBMYP, IBPYP, IBCP, National, SAT, UK, USA
Language instr: English

St Andrew's International School
PO Box EE 17340, Yamacraw Hill Road, Nassau, NP
Tel: +1 242 677 7800
Age range: 4–18
Curriculum: AP, IBDP, IBPYP, SAT, UK, USA
Language instr: English

St Johns College
PO Box N 4858, Nassau NP
Tel: +1 242 322 3249
Age range: 4–17
No. of pupils: 1015
Curriculum: SAT

St. Andrews Anglican School
P.O. Box EX-29093, Georgetown, Exuma
Tel: +1 242 336 4130

St. Anne's School
P.O. Box SS-6256, Nassau
Tel: +1 242 324 1203

Summit Academy
PO Box EE-17972, Nassau
Tel: +1 242 394 4781
Curriculum: IPC

Tambearly School
P.O. Box N-4284, Nassau
Tel: +1 242 327 5965
Curriculum: USA

Temple Christian School
4th Terrace Collins Avenue, Nassau N-1566
Tel: +1 242 325 1119
Age range: 3–18
No. of pupils: 1240
Curriculum: USA

BERMUDA

Bermuda High School
19 Richmond Road, Pembroke HM08
Tel: +441 295 6153
Age range: B16–18 G4–18
No. of pupils: 640
Curriculum: IBDP, SAT, GCSE, IGCSE
Language instr: English

Bermuda Institute
234 Middle Road (P. O. Box SN 114), Southampton SN BX
Tel: +1 441 238 1566
Age range: 4–18
No. of pupils: 241 B120 G121
Curriculum: USA
Language instr: English

Chatmore British International School
Rockmore Estate, 9 St Marks Road, Smiths FL06
Tel: +1 441 236 3339
Curriculum: IPC, UK, IGCSE
Language instr: English

Saltus Grammar School
PO Box HM 2224, Hamilton HM JX
Tel: +1 441 292 6177
Age range: 5–18
No. of pupils: 1022 B613 G409
Curriculum: AP, SAT

Somersfield Academy
107 Middle Road, Devonshire DV 06
Tel: +1 441 236 9797
Age range: 3–18 years
No. of pupils: 529
Curriculum: IBDP, IBMYP
Language instr: English

Warwick Academy
117 Middle Road, Warwick PG01
Tel: +1 441 236 1917/239 9452
Age range: 4–18
No. of pupils: 830
Curriculum: IBDP, IBCP, UK, IGCSE
Language instr: English

BRITISH VIRGIN ISLANDS

Cedar International School
Waterfront Drive, Kingston
Tel: +1 284 494 5262
Age range: 3–18
No. of pupils: 240 B120 G120
Curriculum: IBDP, IBMYP, IBPYP
Language instr: English

CANADA

Alberta

Calgary French and International School
700-77th Street SW, Calgary AB Alberta T3H 5R1
Tel: +1 403 240 1500
Curriculum: IBDP, IBPYP
Language instr: English, French

Lycee Louis Pasteur The International French School
4099 Garrison Boulevard SW, Calgary AB Alberta T2T 6G2
Tel: +1 403 243 5420
Age range: 3–17
No. of pupils: 380
Curriculum: FrenchBacc
Language instr: French, English

Strathcona-Tweedsmuir School
RR 2, Okotoks AB Alberta T1S 1A2
Tel: +1 403 938 4431
Age range: 5–18
No. of pupils: 700
Curriculum: IBDP, IBMYP, IBPYP, FrenchBacc
Language instr: English

British Columbia

Alexander Academy
200-688 West Hastings Street, Vancouver BC British Columbia V6B 1P1
Tel: +1 604 687 8832
Curriculum: IBDP
Language instr: English, French

Aspengrove School
7660 Clark Drive, Lantzville BC British Columbia V0R 2H0
Tel: +1 250 390 2201
Age range: 3–18 years
Curriculum: IBDP, IBMYP, IBPYP
Language instr: English

Bodwell High School
955 Harbourside Drive North, Vancouver BC British Columbia V7P 3S4
Tel: +1 604 998 1000
Curriculum: IBMYP
Language instr: English

Brentwood College School
2735 Mount Baker Road, Mill Bay BC British Columbia V0R 2P1
Tel: +1 250 743 5521
Age range: 14–18
No. of pupils: 435 B226 G109
Curriculum: AP, National

Brockton School
3467 Duval Road, North Vancouver BC British Columbia V7J 3E8
Tel: +1 604 929 9201
Age range: 5–18
Curriculum: IBDP, IBMYP, IBPYP, IBCP, National
Language instr: English

Brookes Westshore
1939 Sooke Road, Victoria BC British Columbia V9B 1W2
Tel: +1 250 929 0506
Age range: 11–18
Curriculum: IBDP, IBMYP
Language instr: English

Fraser Valley School
19533 64th Avenue, Surrey BC British Columbia V3S 4J3
Tel: +1 604 427 2282
Age range: 5–13
No. of pupils: 129
Curriculum: IBPYP
Language instr: English

Glenlyon Norfolk School
801 Bank Street, Victoria BC British Columbia V8S 4A8
Tel: +1 250 370 6801
Age range: 4–18 years
No. of pupils: 690
Curriculum: IBDP, IBMYP, IBPYP
Language instr: English

Island Pacific School
671 Carter Road, Box 128, Bowen Island BC British Columbia V0N 1G0
Tel: +1 604 947 9311
Age range: 11–14
Curriculum: IBMYP
Language instr: English

North America

Lowell High School
750 Hamilton Street, Suite 210, Vancouver BC British Columbia V6B 2R5
Tel: +1 604 336 0456
Curriculum: IBDP
Language instr: English, Chinese

Meadowridge School
12224 240th Street, Maple Ridge BC British Columbia V4R 1N1
Tel: +1 604 467 4444
Age range: 4–18 years
No. of pupils: 665
Curriculum: IBDP, IBMYP, IBPYP
Language instr: English

MULGRAVE SCHOOL, THE INTERNATIONAL SCHOOL OF VANCOUVER
For further details see p. 227
2330 Cypress Bowl Lane, West Vancouver BC British Columbia V7S 3H9
Tel: +1 604 922 3223
Email: admissions@mulgrave.com
Website: www.mulgrave.com
Head of School: Craig Davis
Age range: 3–18 years
No. of pupils: 1030
Fees: Day CND$28,850–CND$32,560
Curriculum: ACT, IBDP, IBMYP, IBPYP
Language instr: English

Pacific Academy
10238 168th Street, Surrey BC British Columbia V4N 1Z4
Tel: +1 604 581 5353
Age range: 5–18
No. of pupils: 1400
Curriculum: IBDP
Language instr: English

Pearson College UWC
650 Pearson College Drive, Victoria BC British Columbia V9C 4H7
Tel: +1 250 391 2411
Age range: 16–19
No. of pupils: 200
Curriculum: IBDP, IBCP, SAT
Language instr: English

SenPokChin School
1156 SenPokChin Boulevard, Oliver BC British Columbia V0H 1T8
Tel: +1 250 498 2019
Age range: 4–12 years
Curriculum: IBPYP
Language instr: English, nsyilxcen

Shawnigan Lake School
1975 Renfrew Road, Postal Bag 2000, Shawnigan Lake BC British Columbia V0R 2W1
Tel: +1 250 743 5516
Age range: 13–18
No. of pupils: 493
Language instr: English

Southpointe Academy
1900 56th Street, Tsawwassen BC British Columbia V4L 2B1
Tel: +1 604 948 8826
Curriculum: AP, IBDP, IBMYP, IBPYP
Language instr: English

Southridge School
2656 160th Street, Surrey BC British Columbia V3S 0B7
Tel: +1 604 535 5056
Age range: 4–17
No. of pupils: 667
Curriculum: AP, IBMYP, IBPYP
Language instr: English

St. John's Academy Shawnigan Lake
2371 Shawnigan Lake Road, Shawnigan Lake BC British Columbia V0R 2W5
Tel: +1 250 220 4888
Age range: 9–18 years (boarding from 11)
Curriculum: IBDP, IBMYP
Language instr: English

St. Margaret's School
1080 Lucas Avenue, Victoria BC British Columbia V8X 3P7
Tel: +1 250 479 7171
Age range: G1–18 years (boarding from 12)
Curriculum: IBDP
Language instr: English

STRATFORD HALL
For further details see p. 231
3000 Commercial Drive, Vancouver BC British Columbia V5N 4E2
Tel: +1 604 436 0608
Email: info@stratfordhall.ca
Website: www.stratfordhall.ca
Head of School: Richard Kassissieh
Age range: 5–18 years
No. of pupils: 545
Fees: Day CAD$29,490–CAD$34,450
Curriculum: IBDP, IBMYP, IBPYP
Language instr: English

The High School at Vancouver Island University
Nanaimo (Main Campus), 900 Fifth Street, Nanaimo BC British Columbia V9R 5S5
Tel: +1 250 753 3245
Curriculum: IBDP
Language instr: English

Unisus School (Lower)
7808 Pierre Drive, Summerland BC British Columbia V0H 1Z2
Tel: +1 250 404 3232
Curriculum: IBPYP
Language instr: English

Unisus School (Upper)
7808 Pierre Drive, Summerland BC British Columbia V0H 1Z2
Tel: +1 250 404 3232
Curriculum: IBDP
Language instr: English

White Rock Christian Academy
2265 -152nd Street, Surrey BC British Columbia V4A 4P1
Tel: +1 604 531 9186
Curriculum: IBDP, IBMYP, IBPYP
Language instr: English

Whole Education Academy
10019 Granville Avenue, Richmond BC British Columbia V6Y 1R5
Tel: +1 236 454 1520
Curriculum: IBDP
Language instr: English

Windsor Hall
11295 Mellis Drive, Richmond BC British Columbia V6X 1L8
Tel: +1 604 285 7766
Curriculum: IBMYP
Language instr: English, French

New Brunswick

Eastgate Academy
200 Karolie Road, Riverview NB New Brunswick E1B 1R1
Tel: +1 506 830 6929
Curriculum: IBPYP
Language instr: English, French

Rothesay Netherwood School
40 College Hill Road, Rothesay NB New Brunswick E2E 5H1
Tel: +1 506 847 8224
Age range: 11–18
Curriculum: IBDP
Language instr: English

Newfoundland and Labrador

Lakecrest Independent School
58 Patrick Street, St. John's NL Newfoundland and Labrador A1E 2S7
Tel: +1 709 738 1212
Curriculum: IBPYP
Language instr: English

Nova Scotia

Halifax Grammar School
945 Tower Road, Halifax NS Nova Scotia B3H 2Y2
Tel: +1 902 423 9312
Age range: 3–18
No. of pupils: 500 *B*283 G242
Curriculum: IBDP
Language instr: English

King's-Edgehill School
11 King's-Edgehill Lane, Windsor NS Nova Scotia B0N 2T0
Tel: +1 902 798 2278
Age range: 11–19
No. of pupils: 350
Curriculum: IBDP
Language instr: English

Munro Academy
2 School Street, Sydney Mines NS Nova Scotia B1V 1R3
Tel: +1 902 241 5090
Curriculum: IBCP
Language instr: English, French

Sacred Heart School of Halifax
5820 Spring Garden Rd, Halifax NS Nova Scotia B3H 1X8
Tel: +1 902 422 4459

Ontario

Académie de la Capitale
1010 Morrison Dr Suite 200, Ottawa ON Ontario K2H 8K7
Tel: +1 613 721 3872
Curriculum: IBPYP
Language instr: French, English

Académie Ste Cécile International School
925 Cousineau Road, Windsor ON Ontario N9G 1V8
Tel: +1 519 969 1291
Age range: 5–19
No. of pupils: 260
Curriculum: AP, IBDP, IBMYP, National, SAT
Language instr: English

Albert College
160 Dundas Street West, Belleville ON Ontario K8P 1A6
Tel: +1 613 968 5726
Age range: 2.5–18

Appleby College
540 Lakeshore Road West, Oakville ON Ontario L6K 3P1
Tel: +1 905 845 4681 ext. 200
Age range: 12–18

Ashbury College
362 Mariposa Avenue, Ottawa ON Ontario K1M 0T3
Tel: +1 613 749 5954
Age range: 9–18
No. of pupils: 700
Curriculum: IBDP
Language instr: English

Ashwood Glen
3430 Fairview Street, Burlington ON Ontario L7N 2R5
Tel: +1 905 320 1272
Curriculum: IBPYP
Language instr: English, French

Bayview Glen
275 Duncan Mill Road, Toronto ON Ontario M3B 3H9
Tel: +1 416 443 1030

Branksome Hall
10 Elm Avenue, Toronto ON Ontario M4W 1N4
Tel: +1 416 920 9741
Age range: AGE1 *** DESCRIPTION REQUIRED 4–17 (Residence from Grade 7+)
No. of pupils: 900
Curriculum: IBDP, IBMYP, IBPYP
Language instr: English

North America

Bronte College
88 Bronte College Court, 1444 Dundas Cres, Mississauga ON Ontario L5C 1E9
Tel: +1 905 270 7788
Curriculum: IBDP
Language instr: English

Crescent School for Boys
2365 Bayview Avenue, Toronto ON Ontario M2L 1A2
Tel: +1 416 449 2556
Age range: B8–18
No. of pupils: 725
Language instr: English

Elmwood School
261 Buena Vista Road, Ottawa ON Ontario K1M 0V9
Tel: +1 613 749 6761
Age range: G3–18
No. of pupils: 360
Curriculum: IBDP, IBMYP, IBPYP
Language instr: English

Fern Hill School
801 North Service Road, Burlington ON Ontario L7P 5B6
Tel: +1 905 634 8652
Language instr: English

German International School Toronto
25 Burnhamthorpe Road, Toronto ON Ontario M9A 1G9
Tel: +1 416 922 6413
Curriculum: IBDP
Language instr: English, German

Kempenfelt Bay School
576 Bryne Drive, Barrie ON Ontario L4N 9P6
Tel: +1 705 739 4731
Language instr: English

Khalsa School Malton
7280 Airport Road, Mississauga ON Ontario L4T 2H3
Tel: +1 905 671 2010
Language instr: English

King Heights Academy
28 Roytec Road, Woodbridge ON Ontario L4L 8E4
Tel: +1 905 652 1234
Curriculum: IBPYP
Language instr: English

La Citadelle International Academy of Arts & Science
36 Scarsdale Road, North York, Toronto ON Ontario M3B 2R7
Tel: +1 416 385 9685
Age range: 2–18 years
No. of pupils: 180
Curriculum: AP, IBMYP
Language instr: English, French

Lakefield College School
4391 County Road 29, Lakefield ON Ontario K0L 2H0
Tel: +1 705 652 3324
Language instr: English

Lauremont School
500 Elgin Mills Road East, Richmond Hill ON Ontario L4C 5G1
Tel: +1 905 889 6882
Curriculum: IBDP, IBMYP
Language instr: English

London International Academy
361-365 Richmond Street, London, ON Ontario N6A 3C2
Tel: +1 519 433 3388
Age range: 13–18 years
No. of pupils: 200
Curriculum: IBDP
Language instr: English, Spanish, Mandarin

Lynn-Rose Heights Private School
7215 Millcreek Drive, Mississauga ON Ontario L5N 3R3
Tel: +1 905 567 3553
Curriculum: IBMYP, IBPYP
Language instr: English

MacLachlan College
337 Trafalgar Road, Oakville ON Ontario L6J 3H3
Tel: +1 905 844 0372
Age range: 3–11
No. of pupils: 200
Curriculum: AP, IBPYP
Language instr: English

Matthews Hall
1370 Oxford Street West, London ON Ontario N6H 1W2
Tel: +1 519 471 1506
Age range: 4–14
No. of pupils: B126 G111
Curriculum: National
Language instr: English

NOIC Academy
50 Featherstone Avenue, Markham ON Ontario L3S 2H4
Tel: +1 905 472 2002
Age range: 15–19
No. of pupils: 250
Curriculum: IBDP
Language instr: English

Richland Academy
11570 Yonge Street, Richmond Hill, ON Ontario L4E 3N7
Tel: +1 905 224 5600
Curriculum: IBPYP
Language instr: English, French

Ridley College
PO Box 3013, 2 Ridley Road, St Catharines ON Ontario L2R 7C3
Tel: +1 905 684 1889
Age range: 4–18 years
No. of pupils: 840
Curriculum: IBDP, IBMYP, IBPYP, National
Language instr: English

Southern Ontario Collegiate
28 Rebecca Street, Hamilton ON Ontario L8R 1B4
Tel: +1 905 546 1500

St Andrew's College
15800 Yonge Street, Aurora ON Ontario L4G 3H7
Tel: +1 905 727 3178
Age range: B10–18
No. of pupils: 650

St Clement's School
21 St. Clements Avenue, Toronto ON Ontario M4R 1G8
Tel: +1 416 483 4835
Language instr: English

St John's - Kilmarnock School
2201 Shantz Station Road, Box 179, Breslau (Waterloo Region) ON Ontario N0B 1M0
Tel: +1 519 648 2183
Age range: 4–18
No. of pupils: 400
Curriculum: IBDP, IBMYP, IBPYP
Language instr: English

St Jude's Academy
2150 Torquay Mews, Mississauga ON Ontario L5N 2M6
Tel: +1 905 814 0202
Curriculum: IBDP, IBMYP, IBPYP

St Mildred's Lightbourn School
1080 Linbrook Road, Oakville ON Ontario L6J 2L1
Tel: +1 905 845 2386
Language instr: English

Sunnybrook School
469 Merton Street, Toronto ON Ontario M4S 1B4
Tel: +1 416 487 5308
Curriculum: IBPYP

Tall Pines School
8525 Torbram Road, Brampton ON Ontario L6T 5K4
Tel: +2 905 458 6770
Curriculum: IBMYP, IBPYP
Language instr: English, French

TFS - CANADA'S INTERNATIONAL SCHOOL
For further details see p. 232
306 Lawrence Avenue East, Toronto ON Ontario M4N 1T7
Tel: +1 416 484 6533
Email: admissions@tfs.ca
Website: www.tfs.ca
Head of School: Norman Gaudet
Age range: 2–18 years
No. of pupils: 1500
Fees: Day CAD$24,230–CAD$40,830
Curriculum: IBDP, IBMYP, IBPYP
Language instr: French, English

The Leo Baeck Day School
501 Arlington Avenue, Toronto ON Ontario M6C 3A4
Tel: +1 416 787 9899
Curriculum: IBMYP, IBPYP

The York School
1320 Yonge Street, Toronto ON Ontario M4T 1X2
Tel: Admissions: +1 416 646 5275 Switchboard: +1 416 926 1325
Age range: 4–18
No. of pupils: 700
Curriculum: IBDP, IBMYP, IBPYP
Language instr: English

Toronto Academy of EMC
10 Gurney Crescent, Toronto ON Ontario M6B 1S8
Tel: +1 647 667 2479
Curriculum: IBDP
Language instr: English

Town Centre Montessori Private Schools
155 Clayton Drive, Markham ON Ontario L3R 7P3
Tel: +1 905 470 1200
Curriculum: IBDP, IBMYP, IBPYP
Language instr: English

Upper Canada College
200 Lonsdale Road, Toronto ON Ontario M4V 1W6
Tel: +1 416 488 1125
Curriculum: IBDP, IBMYP, IBPYP
Language instr: English

USCA Academy
2187 Dunwin Drive, Mississauga ON Ontario L5L 1X2
Tel: +1 905 232 0411
Age range: 6–18 years

Walden International School
1030 Queen Street West, Brampton ON Ontario L6X 0B2
Tel: +1 905 338 6236
Curriculum: IBMYP, IBPYP
Language instr: English, French

Wheatley School
497 Scott Street, St Catharines ON Ontario L2M 3X3
Tel: +1 905 641 3012
No. of pupils: 180
Curriculum: IBMYP
Language instr: English

Quebec

Académie Antoine-Manseau
20 rue St Charles Borromée Sud, CP 410, Joliette QC Quebec J6E 3Z9
Tel: +1 450 753 4271
No. of pupils: 612
Language instr: French

Académie François-Labelle
1227 rue Notre Dame, Repentigny QC Quebec J5Y 3H2
Tel: +1 450 582 2020
Curriculum: IBPYP

Académie Lafontaine
2171 boulevard Maurice, Saint-Jérôme, Québec QC Quebec J7Z 4M7
Tel: +1 450 431 3733
No. of pupils: 1293
Language instr: French

North America

Alexander von Humboldt Schule
216, rue Victoria, Baie d'Urfé
QC Quebec H9X 2H9
Tel: +1 514 457 2886

Bishop's College School
80 Moulton Hill Road, PO Box 5001, Station Lennoxville, Sherbrooke
QC Quebec J1M 1Z8
Tel: +1 819 566 0227
Age range: 13–18
No. of pupils: 246 B148 G98 VIth68
Curriculum: IBDP
Language instr: English, French

Campus Notre-Dame-de-Foy
5000 rue Clement-Lockquell,
St-Augustin-de-Desmaures
QC Quebec G3A 1B3
Tel: +1 418 872 8041

Centennial Academy
3641 Prud'homme Avenue,
Montréal QC Quebec H4A 3H6
Tel: +1 514 486 5533
No. of pupils: 225
Language instr: English

Collège Charlemagne
5000 rue Pilon, Pierrefonds,
Montréal QC Quebec H9K 1G4
Tel: +1 514 626 7060
No. of pupils: 1235
Curriculum: IBMYP
Language instr: French

Collège Charles-Lemoyne - Campus Longueuil
901, chemin Tiffin, Longueuil
QC Quebec J4P 3G6
Tel: +1 514 875 0505
Curriculum: IBMYP, IBPYP
Language instr: English, French

Collège de l'Assomption
270 boulevard de l'Ange-Gardien, L'Assomption, Montréal
QC Quebec J5Y 3R7
Tel: +1 450 589 5621
No. of pupils: 1336
Curriculum: IBMYP
Language instr: French

Collège de Lévis
9 rue Mgr Gosselin, Levis
QC Quebec G6V 5K1
Tel: +1 418 833 1249
Language instr: French

Collège du Mont-Sainte-Anne
2100 Chemin de Sainte-Catherine,
Sherbrooke QC Quebec J1N 3V5
Tel: +1 819 823 3003
Age range: B12–17
No. of pupils: 260
Language instr: French

Collège Esther-Blondin
101 rue Sainte-Anne, Saint-Jacques QC Quebec J0K 2R0
Tel: +1 450 839 3672
Age range: 12–17
Curriculum: IBMYP
Language instr: French

Collège François-de-Laval
6 rue de la Vieille-Université,
Québec QC Quebec G1R 5X8
Tel: +1 418 694 1020
Age range: 12–18
No. of pupils: 810

Collège Jean-de-Brebeuf
3200, chemin de la Côte-Sainte-Catherine, Montréal
QC Quebec H3T 1C1
Tel: +1 514 342 9342
Age range: 13–18 years
Curriculum: IBDP, IBMYP
Language instr: French

Collège Jésus-Marie de Sillery
2047 chemin Saint-Louis, Québec City QC Quebec G1T 1P3
Tel: +1 418 687 9250
Age range: B5,6,7 & 12+G5–17
No. of pupils: 1000
Curriculum: IBMYP
Language instr: French

Collège Laflèche
1687 boulevard du Carmel, Trois-Rivières QC Quebec G8Z 3R8
Tel: +1 819 375 7346
Language instr: French

Collège Laurentien
1200, 14th Avenue, Val-Morin
QC Quebec J0T 2R0
Tel: +1 819 322 2913
Age range: 11–18 years
Language instr: French

Collège Marie-de-l'Incarnation
725 rue Hart, Trois-Rivières
QC Quebec G9A 4R9
Tel: +1 819 379 3223

Collège Mont Notre-Dame de Sherbrooke
114 rue Cathédrale, Sherbrooke
QC Quebec J1H 4MI
Tel: +1 819 563 4104
No. of pupils: 573
Curriculum: IBMYP
Language instr: French

Collège Notre-Dame-de-Lourdes
845 chemin Tiffin, Longueuil
QC Quebec J4P 3G5
Tel: +1 450 670 4740
Age range: 12–17
No. of pupils: 960
Curriculum: IBMYP
Language instr: French

Collège Saint-Bernard
25 avenue des Frères de la Charité, Drummondville QC Quebec J2B 6A2
Tel: +1 819 478 3330 (Ext: 230)
Age range: 3–18 years
Language instr: French

Collège Saint-Joseph de Hull
174 rue Notre-Dame-de-l'île,
Gatineau QC Quebec J8X 3T4
Tel: +1 819 776 3123
Language instr: French

Collège Saint-Maurice
630 rue Girouard Ouest, Saint-Hyacinthe QC Quebec J2S 2Y3
Tel: +1 450 773 7478 Ext:222
Age range: G12–17
No. of pupils: 700
Curriculum: IBMYP, National
Language instr: French

Collège Saint-Paul
235 rue Sainte-Anne, Varennes
QC Quebec J3X 1P9
Tel: +1 450 652 2941
Language instr: French

Collège Ville-Marie
2850 rue Sherbrooke Est, Montréal
QC Quebec H2K 1H3
Tel: +1 514 525 2516
Language instr: French

École de la Synergie
2255 Cavendish Boulevard,
Montréal QC Quebec H4B 2L4
Tel: +1 514 484 5084
Curriculum: IBMYP
Language instr: English, French

Ecole Internationale de Montreal Primaire
5010 Avenue Coolbrook,
Montreal QC Quebec H3X 2K9
Tel: +1 514 596 5721
Age range: 4–11

École Internationale des Apprenants
4505 Boul Henri-Bourassa O, Saint-Laurent QC Quebec H4L 1A5
Tel: +1 514 334 4153
Curriculum: IBPYP
Language instr: French

École Les Mélèzes
393 de Lanaudière, Joliette
QC Quebec J6E3L9
Tel: +1 450 752 4433
Curriculum: IRPYP
Language instr: French

École Marie-Clarac
3530 Boul Gouin Est, Montréal-Nord QC Quebec H1H 1B7
Tel: +1 514 322 1160
Curriculum: IBMYP
Language instr: French

École Plein Soleil (Association Coopérative)
300, rue de Montréal, Sherbrooke
QC Quebec J1H 1E5
Tel: +1 819 569 8359
Age range: 4–12
No. of pupils: 205
Curriculum: IBPYP, National
Language instr: French

École secondaire Saint-Joseph de Saint-Hyacinthe
2875 avenue Bourdages Nord, Saint-Hyacinthe QC Quebec J2S 5S3
Tel: +1 450 774 3775
Curriculum: IBMYP
Language instr: French

L'École des Ursulines de Québec
4 rue du Parloir, CP 820, Haute - Ville,
Québec QC Quebec G1R 4S7
Tel: +1 418 692 2612
Curriculum: IBPYP

Lower Canada College
4090, avenue Royal, Montréal
QC Quebec H4A 2M5
Tel: +1 514 482 9916
Age range: 5–18 years
No. of pupils: 850
Curriculum: IBDP, IBMYP, SAT
Language instr: English, French

Miss Edgar's & Miss Cramp's School
525 Mount Pleasant Road,
Westmount QC Quebec H3Y 3H6
Tel: +1 514 935 6357
Age range: G5–18
No. of pupils: G300
Language instr: English, French

Pensionnat du Saint-Nom-de-Marie
628 chemin de la Côte, St Catherine,
Outremont QC Quebec H2V 2C5
Tel: +1 514 735 5261
No. of pupils: 1030
Curriculum: IBMYP
Language instr: French

Selwyn House School
95, chemin Côte St-Antoine,
Westmount QC Quebec H3Y 2H8
Tel: +1 514 931 9481
Age range: 5–17
No. of pupils: 540
Language instr: English, French

Stanstead College
450 Duferin Street, Stanstead
QC Quebec J0B 3E0
Tel: +1 819 876 2702
Age range: 11–18
No. of pupils: 200

The Sacred Heart School of Montreal
3635 Atwater Ave., Montreal
QC Quebec H3H 1Y4
Tel: +1 514 937 2845
Age range: G12–17 years
No. of pupils: 250

North America

Saskatchewan

Athol Murray College of Notre Dame
PO Box 100, Wilcox SK
Saskatchewan S0G 5E0
Tel: +1 306 732 1203
Age range: 14–18 years

LCBI High School
700 Ash Street, Box 459, Outlook
SK Saskatchewan S0L 2N0
Tel: +1 306 867 8971
Age range: 14–18
No. of pupils: 80
Language instr: English

Luther College High School
1500 Royal Street, Regina SK
Saskatchewan S4T 5A5
Tel: +1 306 791 9150
Age range: 16–18
No. of pupils: 450
Curriculum: IBDP
Language instr: English

CAYMAN ISLANDS

Cayman International School
P.O. Box 31364, 95 Minerva Drive, Camana Bay, Grand Cayman KY1-1206
Tel: +1 345 945 4664
Age range: 3–18
Curriculum: IBDP
Language instr: English

Cayman Prep & High School
PO Box 10013, Grand Cayman KY1-1001
Tel: +1 345 949 9115
Curriculum: UK, IGCSE, ALevs

Grace Christian Academy
21 Crescent Close, Grand Cayman
Tel: +1 345 945 0899
Curriculum: USA

St Ignatius Catholic School
PO Box 2638, 597 Walkers Road, Grand Cayman KY1-1102
Tel: +1345 949 9250
Curriculum: UK, IGCSE, ALevs

Triple C School
P.O. Box 10498, 74 Fairbanks Road, George Town, Grand Cayman KY1-1005
Tel: + 1 345 949 6022
Curriculum: USA

COSTA RICA

American International School of Costa Rica
Ciudad Cariari, La Asuncion, Belen, Heredia
Tel: +506 2293 2567
Age range: 4–18
No. of pupils: 170 B90 G80
Curriculum: AP, SAT

Anglo American School
La Unión, 1 Km al norte de Sub Estación Electríca del ICE, Provincia de Cartago, Tres Rios, San Jose
Tel: +506 2279 2626
Age range: 3–11
Curriculum: IBDP, USA

Blue Valley School
From Multiplaza, 1.2 Km. northwest, right hand side of the road, Guachipelín, Escazú, San José
Tel: +506 2215 2204
Age range: 2–18 years
No. of pupils: 769
Curriculum: IBDP
Language instr: English, Spanish

Centro Educativo Futuro Verde
1 km este del Banco Nacional, Cóbano, Puntarenas 60111
Tel: +506 2642 0291
Curriculum: IBDP
Language instr: English, Spanish

Centro Educativo Nueva Generacion
Sn Rafael de Heredia Del parqu 1 km al norte, Heredia 24-3015
Tel: +506 2237 8927
Curriculum: IBDP
Language instr: English

Colegio Humboldt
Contiguo a la Iglesia Nuestra Señora de Loreto, Pavas, San José
Tel: +506 2 232 1455

Colegio Internacional SEK Costa Rica
Cipreses de Curridabat, San José 963 2050
Tel: +506 2 272 5464
Curriculum: IBDP
Language instr: Spanish, English

Colegio Iribó
Lomas de Ayarco sur, segunda entrada, 800 mts. sur, Curridabat, San José
Tel: +506 4000 8989
Curriculum: IBDP
Language instr: Spanish

Colegio Metodista de Costa Rica
Sabanilla de Montes de Oca, San José 11502
Tel: +506 4036 3100
Curriculum: IBDP
Language instr: English, Spanish

Colegio Miravalle
800m al sur de la esquina sureste de los Tribunales de Justicia, Cartago
Tel: +506 2552 7378
Curriculum: IBDP
Language instr: English, Spanish

Colegio Saint Francis
San Vicente, Moravia, San José
Tel: +506 2430 7639
Curriculum: IBDP
Language instr: English, Spanish

Colegio Santa María de Guadalupe
Calle 7, Damasco Villalobos, Santo Domingo, Heredia
Tel: +506 2244 0739
Curriculum: IBDP

Colegio Yorkín
Lomas de Ayarco sur, segunda entrada, 800 mts. sur y 200 mts. este, Curridabat, San José
Tel: +506 4000 8900
Curriculum: IBDP
Language instr: Spanish

Costa Rica International Academy
500 mts sur del Hotel Westin Conchal, Brasilito, Guanacaste
Tel: +506 2654 5042
Age range: 2–19
No. of pupils: 320 B160 G160
Curriculum: ACT, AP, SAT, USA
Language instr: English

Country Day School
Apartado 1139-1250, Escazú, San José
Tel: +506 2289 0919
Age range: 2–19
No. of pupils: 844 B424 G420
Curriculum: AP, SAT

Del Mar Academy
P.O. Box: 130, Nosara, Nicoya, Guanacaste 5233
Tel: +506 2682 1211
Curriculum: IBDP
Language instr: English

European School
Heredia, San Pablo, P.O. Box: 177, Heredia
Tel: +506 2261 0717
Age range: 4–18
No. of pupils: 518
Curriculum: IBDP
Language instr: English

Falcon International School
Herradura Beach, Puntarenas
Tel: +506 2637 7400
Curriculum: USA

Franz Liszt Schule
800 metros al sur de la gasolinera, Hermanos Montes a mano izq, Santa Ana, San José 10901
Tel: +506 2203 8128
Curriculum: IBDP
Language instr: English, German

Golden Valley School
Del Lubricentro San Francisco 800 mts. Suroeste, Portones azules grandes a mano derecha, San Isidro, Heredia 40604
Tel: +506 2268 9114
Curriculum: IBDP
Language instr: English, Spanish

GSD International School Costa Rica
Ciudad Hacienda Los Reyes, La Guácima, Alajuela
Tel: +506 2201 9467
Curriculum: IBDP
Language instr: English, Spanish

Instituto Dr. Jaim Weizman
100 norte, 100 oeste Compañía Nacional de Fuerza y Luz, Carretera Anonos, Mata Redonda, San José 4114-100
Tel: +506 2220 1050
No. of pupils: 300
Curriculum: IBDP, IBMYP, IBPYP
Language instr: English, Spanish

International Christian School
San Miguel de Santo Domingo, Heredia
Tel: +506 22411445
Age range: 15–18 years
Curriculum: IBDP, National, USA
Language instr: English, Spanish

Journey School of Costa Rica
900 metros norte gasolinera JSM, Tamarindo, Guanacaste 50309
Tel: +506 8728 2178
Curriculum: IBDP
Language instr: English, Spanish

La Paz Community School
500 metros sur de la ferreteria, Buenaventura, Flamingo, Guanacaste 50309
Tel: +506 2654 4532
Curriculum: IBDP
Language instr: English

Liceo Bilingüe Experimental José Figueres Ferrer
Via 219, Cartago
Tel: +506 2537 2425
Curriculum: IBDP
Language instr: English, Spanish

Lighthouse International School
1 km north of the Guachipelin Tunnel, Escazú, San José 29028
Tel: +506 2215 2390
Age range: 3–18 years
No. of pupils: 210
Curriculum: IBDP, USA
Language instr: English, Spanish

Lincoln School
Barrio Socorro, Santo Domingo de Heredia
Tel: +506 2247 6600
Age range: 4–19
No. of pupils: 632 VIth632
Curriculum: ACT, IBDP, IBMYP, IBPYP, National, SAT, USA
Language instr: English

Los Angeles School
Calle Luisa, San José
Tel: +506 2232 0122
Curriculum: IBDP
Language instr: English

Marian Baker School
PO Box 4269-1000, San José 1000
Tel: +506 2273 0024
Age range: 3–18
No. of pupils: 199
Curriculum: AP, IBDP, USA
Language instr: English, Spanish

North America

Mount View School
Guachipelín de Escazú,
De ConstruPlaza 2kms al
norte, San José 10203
Tel: +506 2215 1154
Age range: 1 year 3 months–18 years
Curriculum: IBDP
Language instr: English, Spanish

Olmos Preescolar
Lomas de Ayarco sur, second
entrance, 800 mts. sur,
Curridabat, San José
Tel: +506 7284 0052
Language instr: Spanish

PAN-AMERICAN SCHOOL
For further details see p. 229
632-4005 San Antonio
de Belen, Heredia
Tel: +506 2298 5700
Email: info@panam.ed.cr
Website: www.panam.ed.cr
Head of School: Alan Wrafter
Age range: 6 months–18 years
No. of pupils: 512
Fees: *Day* US$10,200–US$20,250
Curriculum: IBDP, IBMYP, IBPYP
Language instr: English, Spanish

Saint Gregory School
San Juan de La Unión, Cartago
Tel: +1 506 2279 4444
Curriculum: IBDP
Language instr: English, Spanish

Saint Mary School
Apartado 1471, Escazu 1250,
San José Escazú 1250
Tel: +506 4036 6010
Curriculum: IBDP
Language instr: Spanish

Saint Paul College
San Rafael, Alajuela
Tel: +506 2438 0824 (Ext:108)
Curriculum: IBDP
Language instr: English, Spanish

Sistema Educativo Saint Clare
900m E & 200m S of Curridabat
Walmart, San Juan de
La Unión, Cartago
Tel: +506 2278 9300
Curriculum: IBDP
Language instr: English, Spanish

St. Jude School
1.5 Kilometros al Oeste de
Davivienda, Santa Ana,
San José 488-6150
Tel: +506 2203 6474
Curriculum: IBDP
Language instr: Spanish

The British School of Costa Rica
PO Box 8184, San José 1000
Tel: +506 2220 0131
Age range: 4–18
Curriculum: IBDP, National, UK
Language instr: English, Spanish

UWC Costa Rica
De la esquina sureste de la
Iglesia Católica, 400m al norte,
Santa Ana, San José 10901
Tel: +506 22825609
Age range: 16–19
No. of pupils: 204
Curriculum: IBDP
Language instr: English, Spanish

CUBA

Ecole Française de la Havane
Calle 15 N° 18004 entre 180
y 182, Siboney, Havana
Tel: +53 7 273 62 64
Age range: 4–18
No. of pupils: 184
Curriculum: FrenchBacc

International School of Havana
115 Calle 22 entre, Avenida
1ra y 3ra, Miramar, Havana
Tel: +53 7214 0773
Age range: 2 1/2–17 years
No. of pupils: 330
Curriculum: IBDP, IPC, IGCSE
Language instr: English

DOMINICA

Dominica Seventh-Day Adventist Secondary School
Chambers Street,
Glanvillia, Portsmouth
Tel: +1 767 445 5152

Newtown Primary School
Victoria Street, Newtown, Roseau
Tel: +1 767 448 0287
Age range: 4–11

DOMINICAN REPUBLIC

Abraham Lincoln School
Central Romana Corporation
Ltd, La Romana 22000
Tel: +1 809 723 2055
Age range: 4–18
No. of pupils: 450
Curriculum: UK, IGCSE, ALevs
Language instr: English

American School of Santo Domingo
Calle C #7, Cuesta Hermosa III,
Arroyo Hondo, Santo Domingo
Tel: +001 809 567 6824
Age range: 5–18
Curriculum: AP, National, USA
Language instr: English, Spanish

Ashton School
Jacinto Mañón #16, Ensanche
Paraíso, Santo Domingo 11105
Tel: +1 809 562 0891
Curriculum: USA

Babeque Secundaria
Roberto Pastoriza #329, Ens.
Naco, Distrito Nacional,
Santo Domingo 10124
Tel: +1 809 567 9647
Curriculum: IBDP
Language instr: Spanish

Cap Cana Heritage School
Ciudad Las Canas, Cap Cana,
Tel: +1 809 695 5519
Curriculum: USA

Carol Morgan School
Avenida Sarasota, Apartado
1169, Santo Domingo
Tel: +1 809 947 1005/6
Age range: 4–18
No. of pupils: 1100 B506 G594
Curriculum: IBDP
Language instr: English

Cathedral International School
Juan Goico Alix #1, Ensanche
Ozama, Santo Domingo
Tel: +1 809 592 9997

Colegio Bilingue New Horizons Santo Domingo
Ave. Sarasota 51, Bella
Vista, Santo Domingo
Tel: +1 809 5334915

Colegio Internacional SEK Las Américas
C/ El Altar y Rep. de Colombia,
Arroyo Hondo II, Santo Domingo
Tel: +1 809 2380737
Language instr: Spanish

Comunidad Educativa Conexus
Máximo Avilés Blonda 34,
Evaristo, Santo Domingo
Tel: +1 809 334 5634
Curriculum: IBDP
Language instr: English, Spanish

Comunidad Educativa Lux Mundi
Av. Gustavo Mejía Ricart No. 87,
Ens. Piantini, Santo Domingo
Tel: +1 829 520 7947
Curriculum: IBDP
Language instr: English, Spanish

Garden Kids School
Calle Los Pinos, No 4 La Mulata, Sosua
Tel: +1809 571 2857
Curriculum: National, USA

Instituto Cultural Domínico-Americano
Ave. Abraham Lincoln
21, Santo Domingo,
Tel: +1 809 535 0665
Curriculum: IBCP, USA

Instituto Iberia
José Giménez Miralles 12, Santiago
De Los Caballeros 51054
Tel: +1 809 736 9111
Curriculum: IBDP
Language instr: English, Spanish

Instituto Leonardo Da Vinci
Carretera Don Pedro Km 1, Esq. Calle
El Guano, Santiago de los Caballeros
Tel: +1 809 734 1535
Curriculum: IBDP
Language instr: English, Spanish

Lycée Alexandre Dumas
Rue Marcadieu Bourdon,
BP 2213, Port Au Prince
Tel: +509 29 40 61 42
Curriculum: FrenchBacc

Lycée Français de Saint Domingue
Rafael Damirón Esq. Jimenez
Moya, Centro de los Heroes,
Saint Domingue
Tel: +1 809 638 7021

Notre Dame School
Manuel de Jesus Troncoso 52,
Ensanche Paraiso Z-7, Santo Domingo
Tel: +1 809 565 2511
Age range: 4–18
No. of pupils: 441 B223 G218
Curriculum: National, USA
Language instr: English

Puntacana International School
Punta Cana Village, Across from
Puntacana Int'l Airport, Punta Cana
Tel: +1 809 959 3382
Age range: 2–18

Saint George School
C/ Porfirio Herrera #6, Ens.
Piantini, Santo Domingo
Tel: +1 809 562 5262
Age range: 2–18
Curriculum: IBDP
Language instr: English, Spanish

Saint Joseph School
Ave. Pedro H. Ureña No. 95, Ens.
La Esperilla, Santo Domingo
Tel: +1 809 540 8992
Curriculum: USA

Saint Thomas School
Juan Tomas Mejia y Cotes #43,
Arroyo Hondo Viejo, Santo Domingo
Tel: +1 809.732.5870
Curriculum: USA

Santiago Christian School
Autopista Duarte Km 5 1/2,
Sabaneta La Palomas, Santiago
Tel: +1 809 570 6140
Age range: 3–18
No. of pupils: 470
Curriculum: AP, USA

St. Michael's School
Héctor Inchaustegui #8,
Piantini, Santo Domingo
Tel: +1 809 563 1707
Curriculum: USA

St. Patrick School
Calle Jose A. Aybar Castellanos
No.163, La Esperilla, Santo Domingo
Tel: +1 809 338 5995
Curriculum: USA

North America

The Americas Bicultural School
Calle Fernando Valerio No. 2, Ensanche La Julia, Santo Domingo
Tel: +1 809 535 3371
Language instr: English, French, Spanish, Mandarin
(ISA)

The Community for Learning
Carretera La Isabela No. 101 La Meseta Arroyo Hondo, Santo Domingo
Tel: +1 809 563 2708

The International School of Sosua
La Mulata 1, El Batey, Puerto Plata
Tel: +1 809 571 3271
Age range: 3–16
No. of pupils: 125
Curriculum: USA

DUTCH CARIBBEAN

Caribbean International Academy
#4 Tigris Road, Cupecoy, St Maarten
Tel: +1 721 545 3871
Age range: 3–18 years

ECUADOR

Academia Cotopaxi American International School
PO Box 17-11-6510, Quito, Pichincha
Tel: +593 (0)2 382 3270
Age range: 3–17
No. of pupils: B348 G293
Curriculum: IBDP, IBPYP
Language instr: English

Academia Naval Almirante Illingworth
Ave José Gómez Gault KM 8 1/2, Vía Daule, Guayaquil, Guayas
Tel: +593 (0)4 3703300
Curriculum: IBDP

Alliance Academy International
Juan José Villalengua 789 & 10 de Agosto Ave., Quito, Pichincha
Tel: +593 2 393 3800
Age range: 3–18 years
Curriculum: USA
Language instr: English

Atenas Unidad Educativa
Calle Gabriel Roman y Av. Pedro Vasconez, Yacupamba, Izamba, Ambato, Tungurahua EC 180156
Tel: +593 3 285 4297
Curriculum: IBDP
Language instr: English

Centro Educativo La Moderna
Km 2,5 Vía a Samborondón, Guayaquil, Guayas
Tel: +593 42830581
Curriculum: IBDP
Language instr: English

Centro Educativo Naciones Unidas
Samborondón Km. 1 detrás del C.C. La Piazza, Samborondón, Guayas EC 092301
Tel: +593 (0)4 6018560
Curriculum: IBDP, IBMYP, IBPYP
Language instr: English, Spanish

Colegio Alemán Humboldt - DS Samborondón
Av. Ing. León Febres-Cordero #4571, Ciudad Celeste, Samborondón, Guayas EC 090902
Tel: +593 (4) 259 7800
Curriculum: IBDP
Language instr: Spanish, German

Colegio Alemán Humboldt de Guayaquil
Ciudadela Los Ceibos, Dr. Héctor Romero 216 y Av. Dr. José M. García Moreno, Guayaquil, Guayas EC 090904
Tel: +593 (0)4 2850260
Curriculum: IBDP
Language instr: Spanish, German, English

Colegio Alemán Quito - Deutsche Schule Quito
Calle Alfonso Lamiña S6-120, vía a Lumbisí - Cumbayá, Quito, Pichincha
Tel: +593 (0)2 3560124

Colegio Alemán Stiehle Cuenca Ecuador
Autopista Cuenca - Azogues, Km 11,5, Sector Challuabamba, Cuenca, Azuay
Tel: +593 (0)7 4075646
Curriculum: IBDP
Language instr: Spanish

Colegio Americano De Guayaquil
Direccion General, Casilla 3304, Guayaquil, Guayas
Tel: +593 (0)4 3082 020
Curriculum: IBDP, IBPYP
Language instr: English, Spanish

Colegio Americano de Quito
Casilla 17-01-157, Quito, Pichincha
Tel: +593 (0)2 3976 300
Age range: 4–18
No. of pupils: 2806
Curriculum: AP, IBDP, IBMYP, IBPYP, SAT, TOEFL
Language instr: English

Colegio Balandra Cruz del Sur
Perimeter Road, The Prosperina, Guayaquil, Guayas
Tel: +593 (0)4 285 0020
Curriculum: IBDP
Language instr: Spanish

Colegio Becquerel
Tulipanes E12-50 y Los Rosales, Quito, Pichincha
Tel: +593 (0)2 2257896
Curriculum: IBDP

Colegio Católico José Engling
Calle Juan Montalvo s/n, Barrio La Dolorosa, Tumbaco, Quito, Pichincha EC 17172010
Tel: +593 (0)2 237 4329
Curriculum: IBDP
Language instr: English, Spanish

Colegio Experimental Británico Internacional
Amagasí del Inca, Calle de las Nueces E18-21, y Las Camelias, Quito, Pichincha
Tel: +593 (0)2 3261254
Age range: 2–18
Curriculum: IBDP, IBMYP, IBPYP
Language instr: Spanish, English

Colegio Internacional Rudolf Steiner
Calle Francisco Montalvo Nro 212, y Av Mariscal Sucre, (Av Occidental), Sector Cochabampa, Quito, Pichincha
Tel: +593 2244 3315
Age range: 3–18 years
No. of pupils: 475
Curriculum: IBDP, IBMYP, IBPYP
Language instr: Spanish

Colegio Internacional SEK Ecuador
De los Guayacanes N51-69 y Carmen Olmo Mancebo, San Isidro de El Inca, Quito, Pichincha
Tel: +593 2 2401 896
Age range: 3–18
No. of pupils: 1630 B831 G799 VIth95
Curriculum: IBDP, IBMYP, IBPYP
Language instr: English, Spanish
(ISA)

Colegio Internacional SEK Guayaquil
Vía Salinas Km. 20.5, Guayaquil, Guayas EC 11373
Tel: +593 987 917 164
Age range: 2–18
No. of pupils: 299 B152 G147
Curriculum: IBDP, IBPYP
Language instr: Spanish, English

Colegio Internacional SEK Los Valles
Eloy Alfaro S8-48 y De los Rosales, San Juan de Cumbayá, Quito, Pichincha EC 1717933
Tel: +593 2 3566220
Curriculum: IBDP, IBMYP, IBPYP
Language instr: English, Spanish

Colegio Intisana
Avenida Occidental 5329, y Marcos Joffre, Quito, Pichincha
Tel: +593 2 2440 128
Curriculum: IBDP
Language instr: Spanish

Colegio Letort
Los Guayabos Nro E 13-05 y Farsalias, San Isidro del Inca, Quito, Pichincha
Tel: +593 2 326 0202
No. of pupils: 572
Curriculum: IBDP, IBMYP, IBPYP
Language instr: Spanish

Colegio Los Pinos
Calle Agustín Zambrano entre Vicente Pajuelo y Tomás Chariove, Quito, Pichincha EC 170104
Tel: +593 2 246 3189
Age range: G4–18
No. of pupils: 987
Curriculum: IBDP, TOEFL
Language instr: Spanish, English, French

Colegio Menor Campus Samborondon
Km. 8 Vía Samborondón, Guayaquil, Guayas
Tel: +59 34 5000250
Age range: 5–18
Curriculum: USA

Colegio Menor San Francisco de Quito
Juan Montalvo N2-168 y Manuela Sáenz, Cumbayá, Quito, Pichincha
Tel: +59 32 4008100
Curriculum: National, USA

Colegio Pachamama
Via Ilalo S/N, San José de Rumihuaico-Tumbaco, Quito, Pichincha EC 170157
Tel: +593 2 382 3210
Curriculum: IBDP
Language instr: English, Spanish

Colegio Séneca
Calle Juan Díaz y Paseo de la Universidad # 20, Urb. Iñaquito Alto, Quito, Pichincha EC 170523
Tel: +593 22 922 544
Curriculum: IBDP

Colegio Stella Maris
Avenida 6 y Calle 14, Manta, Manabí
Tel: +593 5 2611352
Curriculum: IBDP
Language instr: Spanish

EducaMundo
Km 12 Av. León Febres-Cordero, Urb. Villa Club, entre las etapas Aura y Doral, Guayaquil, Guayas
Tel: +593 4372 5860
Curriculum: IBDP
Language instr: English, Spanish

El Sauce School
Via Interoceánica Km. 12, Junto al Club El Nacional, Tumbaco, Quito, Pichincha EC 170184
Tel: +593 237 4684/5/6
Curriculum: IBDP
Language instr: English, Spanish

EMDI School
EMDI sector B, Parroquia Alangasi, Valle de los Chilos, Quito, Pichincha
Tel: +593 2278 8652
Curriculum: IBDP
Language instr: English, Spanish

Escuela Particular Liceo Panamericano - Sede Centenario
Dolores Sucre 302 y Nicolás Augusto González, Guayaquil
Tel: +593 (0)4 3707888
Curriculum: IBDP, IBMYP, IBPYP
Language instr: English, Spanish

North America

Gutenberg Schule
Esmeraldas y Chillo Jijón, Sector El Dean Bajo Conocoto, Valle de Los Chillos, Quito, Pichincha EC 170805
Curriculum: IBDP
Language instr: English, Spanish

Inter-American Academy Guayaquil
Puerto Azul, 10.5 via a la costa, Guayaquil, Guayas
Tel: +593 4 3713360
Age range: 2–18
No. of pupils: 260 B130 G130
Curriculum: ACT, AP, SAT, USA

ISM Academy Quito
San Miguel de Anagaes, Quito, Pichincha EC 170124
Tel: +593 2 2414 198
Curriculum: IBDP, IBMYP, IBPYP
Language instr: Spanish

ISM International Academy
Calle Unión 886 y Ave Geovanny Calle, Sector Calderon, Quito, Pichincha
Tel: +593 2 282 0549
Curriculum: IBDP, IBMYP, IBPYP
Language instr: English, Spanish

JESSS - International Christian Academy
Pasaje E18 No 52-120 y, De los Nogales, Quito, Pichincha EC 170124
Tel: +593 9 9901 9696
Curriculum: IBPYP
Language instr: English, Spanish

La Salle Conocoto
Av. Abdón Calderón S18 - 104, Conocoto, Quito, Pichincha EC 170156
Tel: +593 2 234 2115
Curriculum: IBDP
Language instr: English, Spanish

La Salle Latacunga
Calle Quijano y Ordoñez 532, Y Av. General Maldonado, Latacunga, Cotopaxi EC 050104
Tel: +593 32 807 884 / +593 32 801 333
Curriculum: IBDP
Language instr: English

Liceo del Valle
km 1 vía a Pintag, Valle de los Chillos, Quito, Pichincha
Tel: +593 2 2330703
Age range: 3–18
Curriculum: IBDP, IBMYP, IBPYP
Language instr: Spanish

Liceo José Ortega y Gasset
Calle de los Cipreses N64-332 y Manuel Ambrosi, Quito, Pichincha EC 170309
Tel: +593 22482976
Curriculum: IBDP
Language instr: Spanish

Liceo Panamericano Internacional
Km 3.5 vía Samborondón, Samborondon, Guayas
Tel: +593 04 3707888
Curriculum: IBDP, IBMYP, IBPYP
Language instr: English, Spanish

Logos Academy
Km 14.5 Via a la Costa, Guayaquil, Guayas
Tel: +59 34 390 0125
Curriculum: IBDP, National
Language instr: Spanish, English

Ludoteca Elementary & High School, Padre Victor Grados
Av Simón Bolívar y Camino de los Incas # 5-6, Nueva Vía Oriental, Quito, Pichincha
Tel: +593 2 268 8142
Curriculum: IBDP, IBMYP, IBPYP
Language instr: English, Spanish

Lycée La Condamine
Calle Japón Y Naciones Unidas, Quito, Pichincha
Tel: +593 2 292 10 90
Age range: 4–18
No. of pupils: 1255
Curriculum: FrenchBacc

Martim Cererê Unidad Educativa Particular Bilingüe
De Los Guayacanes N51-01, y Los Álamos, Quito, Pichincha EC 170150
Tel: +593 2 380 2980
Curriculum: IBDP
Language instr: English, Spanish

The British School Quito
Via Cununyacu, Km 2.5 Tumbaco, PO Box 17-21-52, Quito, Pichincha
Tel: +593 2 2 374 649
Age range: 3–19
No. of pupils: 218 B132 G86
Curriculum: IBDP, SAT, UK, USA
Language instr: English

Uk School
Campus Macasto, Calle Sn y Av. Teniente Hugo Ortiz, Ambato
Tel: +593 3 370 0820
Age range: 4–16 years
Curriculum: IBDP, IBMYP
Language instr: English, Spanish

Unidad Educativa Alberto Einstein
Av Diego Vásquez de Cepeda N77-157 y Alberto Einstein, Casilla Postal 17-11-5018, Quito, Pichincha
Tel: +593 2 393 2570
Age range: 3–18
No. of pupils: 700 B350 G350 Vlth90
Curriculum: IBDP, IBMYP, IBPYP
Language instr: Spanish, English

Unidad Educativa Bilingüe Delta
Kilómetro 12.5 Vía Puntilla-Samborondón, Guayaquil, Guayas
Tel: +593 4 251 1266
Curriculum: IBDP
Language instr: English

Unidad Educativa Bilingüe Hontanar
Calle El Canelo E17-121 y Las Nueces, Sector Amagasí del Inca., Quito
Tel: +593 2 3261 264
Curriculum: IBDP
Language instr: English, Spanish

Unidad Educativa Bilingüe Mixta Sagrados Corazones
El Oro 1219 y Avenida Quito, Guayaquil, Guayas
Tel: +593 04 2440087
Curriculum: IBDP, IBMYP

Unidad Educativa Bilingüe Nueva Semilla
Barrio Centenario Calle D and Argüelles, Guayaquil, Guayas
Tel: +593 4 2441174
Curriculum: IBDP
Language instr: English

Unidad Educativa Bilingüe Nuevo Mundo
Calle Celeste Blacio de Rendón #112, y Km. 2,5 Vía Samborondón, Guayaquil, Guayas
Tel: +593 4 2 830 095
Curriculum: IBDP, IBMYP, IBPYP
Language instr: English

Unidad Educativa Bilingüe Torremar
Km 14.5 via La Puntilla, La Aurotra (Perimetral), Al lado de Parques de la Paz, Guayaquil, Guayas
Tel: +59 34 251 2512
Language instr: Spanish

Unidad Educativa Bilingüe William Caxton College
Moises Luna Andrade y Calle 6, Quito, Pichincha EC 170144
Tel: +593 2 340 6309
Curriculum: IBDP
Language instr: English, Spanish

Unidad Educativa 'Cap. Edmundo Chiriboga G.'
Av 9 de Octubre y Garcia Moreno, Riobamba, Chimborazo
Tel: +593 (0)3 294 0845
Language instr: Spanish

Unidad Educativa Cristo Rey
Calle Cristo Rey entre Sucre y Baquerizo Moreno, Portoviejo, Manabí EC 13010014
Tel: +593 052632558
Curriculum: IBDP
Language instr: Spanish

Unidad Educativa 'Émile Jaques-Dalcroze'
Av. Ilaló y Río Pastaza No. 777, Valle de Los Chillos, Quito, Pichincha
Tel: +593 2 2861 500
Curriculum: IBDP, IBMYP

Unidad Educativa Isaac Newton
Guayabos N50-120 y Los Álamos, Quito, Pichincha EC 170149
Tel: +593 22405001
Curriculum: IBDP
Language instr: Spanish

Unidad Educativa Juan León Mera La Salle
Av. Los Chasquis y Rio Guayabamba, Ambato, Tungurahua EC 180102
Tel: +593 3 284 1007
Curriculum: IBDP
Language instr: English, Spanish

Unidad Educativa 'Julio Verne'
De Los Nopales #58 Y De Los Helechos, Quito, Pichincha EC 170150
Tel: +593 2280 7117
Curriculum: IBDP
Language instr: English, Spanish

Unidad Educativa Maurice Ravel
Av. Cantabria OE2-18 y Av. Cacha, (Sector San José de Morán), Quito, Pichincha EC 170155
Tel: +593 2 202 3508
Curriculum: IBDP
Language instr: Spanish

Unidad Educativa Monte Tabor Nazaret
Km 13.5 Via Samborondón, Guayaquil, Guayas
Tel: +593 4 259 0370
Curriculum: IBDP, IBMYP, IBPYP
Language instr: Spanish, English, German

Unidad Educativa Particular Bilingüe Ecomundo
Av. Juan Tanca Marengo Km 2, Guayaquil, Guayas EC 90112
Tel: +593 4 3703700 (Ext:115-118)
Curriculum: IBDP, IBMYP

Unidad Educativa Particular Bilingüe Leonardo da Vinci
Vía a San Mateo Km. 2.4, a 100 metros de la Urbanización Ciudad del Mar, Manta, Manabí EC 130802
Tel: +593 5 3 700 865
Curriculum: IBDP
Language instr: Spanish

Unidad Educativa Particular Bilingüe Principito y Marcel Laniado de Wind
Avenida Luis Ángel León Roman y 1era Avenida 5ta, Machala, El Oro EC 0701835
Tel: +593 72981881
Curriculum: IBDP, IBMYP, IBPYP
Language instr: English

Unidad Educativa Particular Bilingüe Santiago Mayor
Urb. Torres del Salado Km 11.5 vía a la costa, Guayaquil, Guayas
Tel: +593 4 380 3770
Age range: 4–18 years
Curriculum: IBDP
Language instr: English, Spanish

Unidad Educativa Particular Bilingüe Santo Domingo de Guzmán
Calle 5ta # 608 y Las Monjas (URDESA), Guayaquil, Guayas
Tel: +593 2 882 561
Curriculum: IBDP
Language instr: Spanish

Unidad Educativa Particular Hermano Miguel De La Salle
Av. Solano 7-01 y Luis Moreno Mora, Cuenca, Azuay
Tel: +593 7 281 0349
Curriculum: IBDP
Language instr: English, Spanish

North America

Unidad Educativa Particular Javier
Km 5.5 vía a la Costa, Guayaquil, Guayas
Tel: +593 4 2001590/3520/0724
Age range: 2–18
No. of pupils: 1500
Curriculum: IBDP
Language instr: Spanish

Unidad Educativa Particular Politécnico
Campus Politécnico 'Gustavo Galindo Velasco', Km. 30.5 vía Perimetral, contiguo a Ceibos Norte, Guayaquil, Guayas
Tel: +593 4 226 9654
Age range: 3–18
Curriculum: IBDP, IBMYP, IBPYP
Language instr: Spanish

Unidad Educativa Particular Redemptio
10 de Agosto 701 entre Colón y Juan Montalvo, Jipijapa, Manabí
Tel: +593 5 2 600 475
Curriculum: IBDP
Language instr: English, Spanish

Unidad Educativa Particular 'Rosa de Jesús Cordero'
Parroquia Ricaurte, Sector el Tablón, Cuenca, Azuay EC 010162
Tel: +593 7 2890503
Curriculum: IBDP
Language instr: Spanish

Unidad Educativa Paul Dirac
Av. Pedro Vicente Maldonado y la Cocha, Quito, Pichincha EC 170146
Tel: +593 2 691 241 (Ext:1)
Curriculum: IBDP
Language instr: English, Spanish

Unidad Educativa Saint Dominic School
César Davila N10-222 y Charles Darwin, Quito, Pichincha
Tel: +593 (0)2 3959960
Curriculum: IBDP
Language instr: Spanish

Unidad Educativa Salesiana Cardenal Spellman
Mercadillo OE340 y Ulloa, Quito, Pichincha EC 1703125
Tel: +593 2 3560 001/2/3
Curriculum: IBDP, IBMYP
Language instr: Spanish

Unidad Educativa Salinas Innova
Av. Carlos Espinoza Larrea via a salinas, Junto al centro de atención ciudadana, Salinas, Santa Elena EC 241550
Tel: +593 4 277 5954
Language instr: Spanish

Unidad Educativa San Francisco de Sales
Av. Cristobal Colón E10-07 y Tamayo, Quito, Pichincha
Tel: +593 98 394 3560
Curriculum: IBDP
Language instr: English, Spanish

Unidad Educativa San Jose La Salle
Tomás Martínez 501 y Baquerizo Moreno, Guayaquil, Guayas EC 090150
Tel: +593 4 25 631 37
Curriculum: IBDP
Language instr: Spanish

Unidad Educativa Santana
Av. los Cerezos S/N y vía a Racar, Cuenca, Azuay
Tel: +593 7 4121879
Age range: 3–18
No. of pupils: 800
Curriculum: IBDP
Language instr: Spanish

Unidad Educativa Terranova
Calle De Los Rieles 507, y Ave Simón Bolívar, San Juan Alto de Cumbayá, Quito, Pichincha
Tel: +593 2 356 4000
Curriculum: IBDP, IBMYP, IBPYP
Language instr: English, Spanish, French

Unidad Educativa Theodore W. Anderson
Av. Gaspar de Villarroel E5-35 e Isla Isabela, Quito, Pichincha EC 170104
Tel: +593 2 2604 4738
Language instr: Spanish

Unidad Educativa Tomás Moro
Av De Las Orquideas E13-120, y De Los Guayacanes, Quito, Pichincha
Tel: +593 2 392 2618
Curriculum: IBDP, IBMYP, IBPYP
Language instr: Spanish

Unidad Educativo Bilingüe CEBI
Calle Modesto Chacón y Av. Pedro Vásconez Sevilla, Parroquia Izamba, Ambato, Tungurahua
Tel: +593 3 373 0370
Curriculum: IBDP, IBMYP, IBPYP
Language instr: Spanish

Victoria Bilingual Christian Academy
Melchor de Valdez Oe-9240, Pbx: 253-6116, Quito, Pichincha EC 170528
Tel: +593 (0)2 2536116
Curriculum: IBDP
Language instr: Spanish

Young Living Academy
Km. 24 vía a la Costa, Chongoncito, Guayaquil, Guayas
Tel: +593 9965 4897
Curriculum: IBDP
Language instr: English, Spanish

EL SALVADOR

Academia Britanica Cuscatleca
KM 10.5 Carretera a Santa Tecla, Santa Tecla, La Libertad
Tel: +503 2201 6200
Age range: 2–18 years
No. of pupils: 1300
Curriculum: IBDP, IBMYP, IPC, IGCSE
Language instr: English, Spanish

Colegio Internacional de San Salvador
Apartado 05-15, San Salvador
Tel: +503 2224 1330
Age range: 4–19
No. of pupils: 318 B154 G164
Curriculum: ACT, AP, National, SAT, USA

Colegio La Floresta
Estamos en el Km. 13 1/2, Carretera al Puerto de La Libertad,
Tel: +503 2534 8800
Age range: G6–17
No. of pupils: 642
Curriculum: IBDP
Language instr: Spanish

Colegio Lamatepec
Carretera al Puerto de La Libertad Km 12.5, Calle Nueva a Comasauga Santa Tecla, La Libertad, San Salvador
Tel: +503 2534 8900
Age range: B6–18
No. of pupils: 655
Curriculum: IBDP
Language instr: Spanish, English

Colegio Maya
7a calle poniente Bis #4925, Colonia Escalón, San Salvador
Tel: +503 2263 2358
Age range: 4–19
Curriculum: National, USA

Colegio Salvadoreño Inglés
No 113, 85 Avenida Norte, Colonia Escalón, San Salvador
Tel: +503 2263 7586
Curriculum: UK

Deutsche Schule - Escuela Alemana San Salvador
Calle del Mediterráneo, Jardines de Guadalupe, Antiguo Cuscatlán, San Salvador CA
Tel: +503 2243 4898
No. of pupils: 588
Curriculum: IBDP
Language instr: Spanish

Escuela Americana
VIPSAL #1352, PO Box 025364, Miami FL 33102-5364, USA
Tel: +503 2528 8300
Age range: 4–18
Curriculum: USA
Language instr: English

Escuela Bilingüe Maquilishuat
Boulevard del Hipodromo No. 540, Colonia San Benito, San Salvador
Tel: +503 2132 8700
Curriculum: IBPYP
Language instr: English, Spanish

Escuela Panamericana
Final Pje Union, Calle El Carmen #1348, Colonia Esculon, San Salvador
Tel: +503 2505 7558
Age range: 4–19
No. of pupils: 435 B220 G215
Curriculum: National, SAT, USA
Language instr: English, Spanish

Lycée Français de San Salvador Antoine et Consuelo de Saint-Exupéry
km 10 1/2 carretera a Santa Tecla, La Libertad, San Salvador
Tel: +503 22 280615
Curriculum: FrenchBacc

GUATEMALA

American School of Guatemala
11 Calle 15-79 Zona 15 Vista Hermosa III, Guatemala
Tel: +502 2500 9595
Age range: 4–18
Curriculum: National, USA
Language instr: Spanish, English

Antigua Green School
Calle del Portal No. 11, Finca Azotea, Antigua
Tel: +502 4060 0023

Antigua International School
Km 74.8, Ruta Nacional 14, Ciudad Vieja, Sacatepequez
Tel: +502 4138 3110
Age range: 4–18
No. of pupils: 300
Curriculum: AP, SAT, USA
Language instr: English, Spanish

Centro Escolar Campoalegre
35 Calle and 12 Av Final, Zona 11, Código 01011
Tel: +502 2380 3900
Age range: G7–18
Curriculum: IBDP
Language instr: Spanish

Centro Escolar 'El Roble'
11 Avenida Sur Final Zona 11, Guatemala City 01011
Tel: +502 2387 7000
Curriculum: IBDP
Language instr: Spanish

Centro Escolar Entrevalles
Km. 16.8 Antigua Carretera a El Salvador, Santa Catarina Pinula
Tel: +502 6685 4700
Curriculum: IBDP
Language instr: Spanish, English

North America

Centro Escolar Solalto
Km. 22.5 Carretera a
Fraijanes, Fraijanes,
Tel: +502 6686 0500
Age range: B7–18
No. of pupils: 369 B369
Curriculum: IBDP
Language instr: English, Spanish

Christian American School
8va. Avenida 9-41, zona 8 de
Mixco, Sector A-10 Finca Santa
Barbará, San Cristóbal
Tel: +502 2218 1100
Curriculum: USA

Colegio Decroly Americano
11 Calle 6-47, Finca El Naranjo,
Zona 4 de Mixco, Guatemala City
Tel: +502 23802380 (Ext:4014/4020)
Age range: 15 months–18
No. of pupils: 994 B491 G503
Curriculum: AP, SAT, USA
Language instr: English, Spanish

Colegio Interamericano
Boulevard La Montana, Finca
El Socorro, Zona 16 1016
Tel: +502 2200 2990
No. of pupils: 1200
Curriculum: USA

Colegio Internacional SEK Guatemala
Km.20.5 carretera Brisas Pavón,
carretera a Lo de Diéguez, Fraijanes
Tel: +502 66 70 26 00

Colegio Julio Verne
1a Avenida 2-62 Zona1, Aldea
Don Justo Km. 18.5 a San Jose
Pinula, 01062 Fraijanes
Tel: +502 6661 1800/4
Curriculum: National, FrenchBacc

Colegio Maya - The American International School of Guatemala
Km 12.5 Carretera a El Salvador,
Santa Catarina Pinula 1051
Tel: +502 6644 1200
Age range: 3–18
No. of pupils: 372
Curriculum: AP, USA

Equity American School
15 Avenida A 21-00, Zona 13,
Guatemala City 01013
Tel: +502 2390 6800
Curriculum: USA

Inter-American School
0 Avenida 1-43 Zona 6,
Quetzaltenango
Tel: +502 7761 4080
Curriculum: USA

QSI International School of Belize
11/13 Dean Crescent, University
Heights, University Heights,
Cayo District Belize
Tel: +501 832 2666
Age range: 4–12
Curriculum: USA

Village School
Km 25.5 Carretera a El Salvador,
Finca Labor El Rosario, Villa Canales
Tel: +502 6643 6300
Age range: 4–18
No. of pupils: 680
Curriculum: USA

HAITI

Union School Haiti
Route du Canape-Vert, Petion Ville
Tel: +509 2943 4923
Curriculum: USA
Language instr: English, French

JAMAICA

American International School of Kingston
2 College Green Avenue, Kingston
Tel: +1 876 702 2070
Age range: 3–18
No. of pupils: 277 B147 G130
Curriculum: IBDP
Language instr: English

Hillel Academy
PO Box 2687, 51 Upper
Mark Way, Kingston 8
Tel: +1 876 925 1980
Age range: 3–19 years
No. of pupils: 702
Curriculum: IBDP, IGCSE
Language instr: English

MÉXICO

Alexander Bain Colegio
Barranca de Pilares 29,
Colonia Tlacopac, San Angel,
México D.F. C.P. 01040
Tel: +52 55 5595 0493
Age range: 3–12
Curriculum: IBPYP
Language instr: Spanish

American Institute of Monterrey - APS Campus
La República No. 300, Col.
La Aurora, Santa Catarina,
Nuevo León C.P. 66378
Tel: +52 81 8048 3700
Age range: 11–18 years
Language instr: English, Spanish

American Institute of Monterrey - San Pedro Campus
Perseverancia 100, Col. Balcones
del Valle, San Pedro Garza
García, Nuevo León C.P. 66220
Tel: +52 81 8174 3700
Age range: 2–11 years
Language instr: English, Spanish

American Institute of Monterrey - Valle Oriente Campus
Ave. Humberto Junco Voigt No. 2305,
Col. Valle Oriente, San Pedro Garza
García, Nuevo León C.P. 66260
Tel: +52 81 1958 9800
Age range: 2–16 years
Language instr: English, Spanish

American School Foundation of Chiapas
Blvd. Belisario Dominguez 5588-F,
Fraccion Las Cinco Plumas, Terán,
Tuxtla Gutierrez, Chiapas C.P. 29052
Tel: +52 961 346 4840
Curriculum: IBPYP
Language instr: English, Spanish

American School Foundation of Guadalajara
Colomos 2100, Col. Providencia,
Guadalajara, Jalisco C.P. 44630
Tel: +52 33 3648 0299
Age range: 3–18
No. of pupils: 1400 B700 G700
Curriculum: AP, National,
SAT, TOEFL, USA
Language instr: English, Spanish

American School Foundation of Monterrey
Ave. Ignacio Morones Prieto
No. 1500, Col. San Isidro, Santa
Catarina, Nuevo León C.P. 66190
Tel: +52 81 5000 4400
Age range: 3–18
No. of pupils: 561

American School of Pachuca
Blvd Valle de Anáhuac s/n, Col San
Javier, Pachuca, Hidalgo C.P. 42086
Tel: +52 771 713 1058
Age range: 4–14
No. of pupils: 830
Curriculum: USA

American School of Puerto Vallarta
Albatros 129, Col. Marina Vallarta,
Puerto Vallarta, Jalisco C.P. 48335
Tel: +52 322 226 7670
Age range: 3–18
No. of pupils: 348
Curriculum: AP, SAT

Avalon International School
Av. San Jerónimo 1135, San
Jerónimo de Lídice La Magdalena
Contreras, Mexico D.F. C.P. 10200
Tel: +52 555 595 5582
Curriculum: IBPYP
Language instr: English, Spanish

Bachillerato Alexander Bain, SC
Las Flores 497, Tlacopac, San Ángel,
Ciudad de México C.P. 01049
Tel: +52 (55) 5683 2911
Age range: 12–18
No. of pupils: 610
Curriculum: IBDP, IBMYP
Language instr: Spanish, English

Bosques International School
Prol. Zaragoza No. 701,
Fracc. Valle de las Trojes,
Aguascalientes C.P. 20115
Tel: +52 449 300 9903
Age range: 4–18 years
Curriculum: IBMYP, IBPYP, IBCP
Language instr: English, Spanish

British American School S.C.
Fuente del Niño #16 Col.
Tecamachalco, Naucalpan de
Juárez, Estado de México C.P. 53950
Tel: +55 52 94 37 21
Curriculum: IBPYP
Language instr: English

Centro de Enseñanza Técnica y Superior - Campus Mexicali
Calzada del Cetys S/N,
Colonia Rivera, Mexicali,
Baja California C.P. 21259
Tel: +52 686 567 3704
Curriculum: IBDP

Centro de Ensenanza Tecnica y Superior - Campus Tijuana
Av. CETYS Universidad, No. 4
Fracc. El Lago, Tijuana, Baja
California C.P. 22210
Tel: +52 664 903 1800
No. of pupils: 608
Curriculum: IBDP
Language instr: Spanish

Centro Educativo Alexander Bain Irapuato
Enrique del Moral Domínguez
335, Ejido Lo de Juárez, 36630,
Irapuato, Guanajuato
Tel: +52 462 114 2246
Age range: 3–19
No. of pupils: 391
Curriculum: IBDP, IBMYP, IBPYP
Language instr: Spanish, English

Centro Educativo CRECER AC
Calle del Vecino No 3,
Atlihuetzia, Yahuquehmecan,
Tlaxcala C.P. 90459
Tel: +52 24 646 13 148
Curriculum: IBMYP, IBPYP

Centro Escolar Instituto La Paz, SC
Av Plan de San Luis 445, Col
Nueva Santa María, Ciudad
de México C.P. 02800
Tel: +52 55 55 56 66 46
Age range: 3–15
No. of pupils: 1200
Curriculum: IBMYP, IBPYP, National
Language instr: Spanish, English

Churchill College
Moctezuma 125, Colonia San
Pablo Tepetlapa, Ciudad
de México C.P. 04620
Tel: +52 55 56 19 82 43
Curriculum: IBDP, National, UK, IGCSE
Language instr: Spanish, English

Colegio Álamos
Acceso al Aeropuerto 1000,
Colonia Arboledas, Santiago de
Querétaro, Querétaro C.P. 76940
Tel: +52 442 182 0222
Language instr: Spanish

North America

Colegio Alemán de Guadalajara
Av Bosques de los Cedros No. 32, Las Cañadas, Zapopan, Jalisco C.P. 45132
Tel: +52 33 3685 0136
Age range: 16–19 years
Curriculum: IBDP
Language instr: Spanish, German

Colegio Alerce
Blvd. Juan Navarrete No. 631, Col. Obispos Residencial, Hermosillo, Sonora C.P. 83210
Tel: +52 66 2260 7770
Curriculum: IBPYP
Language instr: English, Spanish

Colegio Alfonsino de San Pedro AC
Galeana 257 Pte, San Pedro, Garza Garcia, Nuevo León C.P. 68230
Tel: +52 81 8338 3818
Age range: 1–16

Colegio Americano de Durango
Francisco Sarabia 416 Pte, Apartado Postal 495, Durango C.P. 34000
Tel: +52 618 811 5098
Age range: 2–18
No. of pupils: 475 B240 G235
Curriculum: National, SAT, USA
Language instr: English, Spanish

Colegio Americano de San Carlos
Blvd. Luis Encinas S/N, esquina Faustino Félix, Colonia Miramar, Guaymas, Sonora C.P. 85450
Tel: +52 622 221 2551
Curriculum: IBMYP, IBPYP
Language instr: English, Spanish

Colegio Americano de Torreón
Paso del Algodón #500, Fraccionamiento Los Viñedos, Torreón, Coahuila C.P. 27019
Tel: +871 222 51 00
Age range: 3–18
Curriculum: ACT, AP, National, SAT, TOEFL, USA, ALevs
Language instr: English

Colegio Anglo
Av. 5 de Febrero 1007, Valle del Tecnológico, Lázaro Cárdenas, Michoacán C.P. 60950
Tel: +52 753 537 7274
Curriculum: IBPYP
Language instr: English, Spanish

Colegio Anglo Mexicano de Chiapas
Av Pmarrosa No 239, Colonia Pomarosa, Tuxtla Gutiérrez, Chiapas
Tel: +52 961 60 232274
Language instr: English

Colegio Arji
Avenida México # 2, esquina Periférico, Colonia del Bosque, Villahermosa, Tabasco C.P. 86160
Tel: +52 993 3 510 250
Age range: 3–18
No. of pupils: 1200 B600 G600 VIth80
Curriculum: IBDP, IBMYP, IBPYP
Language instr: English, Spanish

Colegio Atid AC
Av. Carlos Echanove #224, Col. Vista Hermosa Cuajimalpa, Ciudad de México C.P. 05100
Tel: +52 55 5814 0800
Age range: 4–18
Curriculum: IBDP, IBMYP, IBPYP, IBCP
Language instr: English, Spanish

Colegio Bilingüe Carson de Ciudad Delicias
Ave 50 Aniversario 1709, Delicias, Chihuahua C.P. 33058
Tel: +52 (639) 472 9340
Curriculum: IBPYP

Colegio Británico
Calle Pargo # 24, S.M. 3, Cancun, Quintana Roo C.P. 77500
Tel: +52 (998) 884 1295
No. of pupils: 370 B120 G250
Curriculum: IBDP, IBPYP
Language instr: English, Spanish

Colegio Buena Tierra SC
Camino Viejo a San Mateo 273, San Salvador Tizatlalli, Metepec, Estado de México C.P. 52172
Tel: +52 722 271 2500
Language instr: English, Spanish

Colegio Celta Internacional
Libramiento Sur-Poniente Km 4+200, Colonia Los Olvera, Villa Corregidora, Querétaro C.P. 76902
Tel: +52 442 227 3600
Curriculum: IBMYP, IBPYP, IBCP
Language instr: English, Spanish

Colegio Ciudad de Mexico - Contadero
Calle de la Bolsa 456, El Contadero, Cuajimalpa, Ciudad de México C.P. 05500
Tel: +52 555 812 0610
Curriculum: IBPYP
Language instr: Spanish

Colegio Ciudad de México - Polanco
Campos Eliseos 139, Polanco, Ciudad de México C.P. 11560
Tel: +52 555 203 7894
Curriculum: IBDP, IBMYP, IBPYP
Language instr: Spanish

Colegio Columbia
Poza Rica #507, Col Petrolera, Tampico, Tamaulipas C.P. 89110
Tel: +52 833 213 0054/1045
Age range: 2–15
No. of pupils: 820 B429 G391
Curriculum: National

Colegio Discovery
Circuito Interior Norte Socorro Romero, Sánchez, No. 3525, Col. San Lorenzo, Tehuacán, Puebla
Tel: +52 238 3820005
Curriculum: IBDP
Language instr: English, Spanish

Colegio El Camino
Callejon del Jornongo #210, Colonia El Pedregal, Cabo San Lucas, B.C.S. C.P. 23453
Tel: +52 624 143 2100 (Ext:112)
Age range: 3–18 years
Curriculum: IBDP, IBMYP, IBPYP
Language instr: English, Spanish

Colegio Euroamericano de Monterrey
Blvd Diaz Ordaz 250 Ote, Colonia Santa Maria, Monterrey, Nuevo León C.P. 64650
Tel: +52 81 8248 8400
Age range: 2–15
No. of pupils: 1321 B691 G630
Curriculum: National, USA
Language instr: English, Spanish, German

Colegio Fontanar
Camino al Fraccionamiento, Vista Real 119, Corregidora, Querétaro C.P. 76900
Tel: +52 442 228 13 65
No. of pupils: 630
Curriculum: IBDP
Language instr: Spanish

Colegio Hebreo Maguen David
Antiguo Camino a Tecamachalco #370, Lomas de Vista Hermosa, Ciudad de México
Tel: +52 (55) 52 46 26 00
Age range: 2–18 years
No. of pupils: 1194
Curriculum: IBDP, IBMYP, IBPYP, National, TOEFL
Language instr: Spanish, Hebrew, English

Colegio Hebreo Monte Sinai AC
Av Loma de la Palma 133, Col Vista Hermosa, Cuajimalpa, Ciudad de México C.P. 05109
Tel: +52 55 52 53 01 68
Curriculum: IBDP, IBMYP, IBPYP
Language instr: Spanish, English

Colegio Hebreo Tarbut
Av. Loma del Parque 216, Colonia Lomas de Vista Hermosa, Ciudad de México C.P. 05100
Tel: +52 55 5814 0500
Language instr: Spanish, English, Hebrew

Colegio Inglés
Real San Agustin #100, Col San Agustin Campestre, Garza Garcia, Nuevo León C.P. 66270
Tel: +52 81 8133 1700
Age range: 4–16
Curriculum: National

Colegio Internacional de México
Río Magdalena 263, Colonia Tizapan San Ángel, Álvaro Obregón, Ciudad de México D.P. 01090
Tel: +52 55 55 50 01 01
Age range: 3–18
Curriculum: IBMYP, IBPYP
Language instr: English, Spanish

Colegio Internacional SEK Guadalajara
Daniel Comboni #850, Colonia Jardines de Guadalupe, Zapopan Jalisco C.P 45030
Tel: +52 33 36202423
Curriculum: IBDP
Language instr: English, Spanish

Colegio Internacional Terranova
Av Palmira No. 705, Privadas del Pedregal, San Luis Potosí C.P. 78295
Tel: +52 444 8 41 64 22
Curriculum: IBDP, IBMYP, IBPYP

Colegio La Paz de Chiapas
Carretera Tuxtla, Villaflores N° 1170, Tuxtla Gutiérrez, Chiapas C.P. 29089
Tel: +52 961 663 7000
Curriculum: IBDP, IBMYP
Language instr: Spanish

Colegio Laureles IAP
Inzancanac s/n esq Jugueteros y Canteros, Barrio Tlatel Xochitenco, Chimalhuacan, Estado de México C.P. 56330
Tel: +52 5 55852 9002
Language instr: English, Spanish

Colegio Linares AC
Marina Silva de Rodriguez 1301 Pte, Colonia centro Linares, Nuevo León C.P. 67700
Tel: +52 821 212 0269
Curriculum: IBDP

Colegio Madison Chihuahua
Fuente Trevi #7001, Fracc. Puerta de Hierro, Chihuahua C.P. 31205
Tel: +52 614 430 1464
Age range: 3–15
No. of pupils: 475
Curriculum: IBMYP, IBPYP
Language instr: English, Spanish

Colegio Madison Torreón
Blvd. De la Senda #321, Fracc. Residencial Senderos, Torreón, Coahuila C.P. 27018
Tel: +52 87 1193 4400

Colegio Maria Montessori de Monclova
Blvd Harold R Pape Nro 2002, Col Jardines del Valle, Monclova, Coahuila C.P. 25730
Tel: +52 866 633 2993
Curriculum: IBDP

Colegio Merici
Granjas 45, Col Palo Alto, Cuajimalpa, Ciudad de México C.P. 05110
Tel: +52 55 55703183

Colegio Monteverde
Av Santa Lucia No 260, Col Prados de la Montaña, Cualjimalpa, Ciudad de México C.P. 05610
Tel: +52 55 50819700
Age range: B2–6 years G2–19 years
Curriculum: UK
Language instr: Spanish, English

Colegio Nuevo Continente
Nicolás San Juan 1141, Colonia Del Valle, Ciudad de México C.P. 03100
Tel: +52 55 5575 4066
Curriculum: IBDP
Language instr: English, Spanish

North America

Colegio Olinca, Altavista
Av. Altavista No. 130, San Ángel, Álvaro Obregón, Ciudad de México C.P. 01060
Tel: +52 55 5616 0216/+52 55 5550 4083
Age range: 1.5–18 years
Curriculum: National
Language instr: English, Spanish

Colegio Olinca, Periférico
Periférico Sur No. 5170, Col. Pedregal de Carrasco, Coyoacán, Ciudad de México C.P. 04700
Tel: +52 55 5606 3113/+52 55 5606 3371
Age range: 1.5–18 years
Curriculum: IBDP, IBMYP, IBPYP, National
Language instr: English, French, Spanish

Colegio Simón Bolivar
Av. Río Mixcoac No.125, Col. Insurgentes, Mixcoac, Ciudad de México C.P. 03920
Tel: +52 55 55 63 6300
No. of pupils: 626

Colegio Springfield, SC
Isidro Fabela Nte 1061, Col Tres Caminos, Toluca, Estado de México C.P. 50020
Tel: +52 722 272 0586
Language instr: Spanish

Colegio Suizo de México - Campus Cuernavaca
Calle Amates s/n, Col. Lomas de Ahuatlán, Cuernavaca, Morelos C.P. 62130
Tel: +52 777 323 5252
Curriculum: IBDP
Language instr: English

Colegio Suizo de México - Campus México DF
Nicolás San Juan 917, Col del Valle, Ciudad de México C.P. 03100
Tel: +52 55 55 43 78 62
Age range: 3–19
No. of pupils: 726
Curriculum: IBDP
Language instr: English

Colegio Suizo de México - Campus Querétaro
Circ. La Cima 901, Fracc. La Cima, Santiago de Querétaro, Querétaro C.P. 76146
Tel: +52 442 254 3390
Age range: 3–19
No. of pupils: 305
Curriculum: IBDP
Language instr: Spanish, German, English

Colegio Vista Hermosa
Bachillerato, Av Loma de Vista Hermosa 221, Cuajimalpa, Ciudad de México C.P. 05100
Tel: +52 55 50914630
Age range: 13–18
No. of pupils: 900 B400 G500
Curriculum: IBDP, IBMYP, TOEFL
Language instr: Spanish

Colegio Williams
Mixcoac Campus, Empresa 8, Col Mixcoac, Alcaldía Benito Juárez, Ciudad de México C.P. 03910
Tel: +52 55 1087 9797
Curriculum: IBDP, IBMYP, IBPYP
Language instr: Spanish

Colegio Williams de Cuernavaca
Luna #32, Jardines de Cuernavaca, Cuernavaca, Morelos C.P. 62360
Tel: +52 (777) 3223640
Age range: 1–19
No. of pupils: 850 B460 G390
Curriculum: IBDP, IBMYP, IBPYP, National, TOEFL
Language instr: English, Spanish

Colegio Williams Unidad San Jerónimo
Presa Reventada No 53, Col San Jerónimo Lídice, Del. Magdalena Contreras, Ciudad de México C.P. 10400
Tel: +52 55 1087 9797
Language instr: Spanish, English

Colegio Xail
Calle Xail No 10, Col. Lázaro Cárdenas, San Francisco de Campeche, Campeche C.P. 24520
Tel: +52 981 813 0322
Curriculum: IBMYP, IBPYP

Discovery School
Chilpancingo No 102, Colonia Vista Hermosa, Cuernavaca, Morelos C.P. 62290
Tel: +52 777 318 5721
Curriculum: IBPYP
Language instr: English

Educare Centro de Servicios Educativos S.C.
Norte 26 #498, Orizaba, Veracruz C.P. 94300
Tel: +52 272 7241194
Language instr: Spanish

Escuela Alexander Bain SC
Barranca de Pilares 4, Tlacopac, San Ángel, Ciudad de México C.P. 01049
Tel: +52 56 833 255
Age range: 3–12
Language instr: Spanish

Escuela Ameyalli SC
Calzada de las Águilas 1972, Axomiatla, Ciudad de México C.P. 01820
Tel: +52 55 12 85 70 20
Age range: 2–18
Curriculum: IBMYP, IBPYP
Language instr: Spanish, English

Escuela Bancaria y Comercial, SC
Paseo de la Reforma No 202 Edif E 3er piso, Col Juárez, Del Cuauhtemoc, Ciudad de México C.P. 06600
Tel: +52 (55) 91 49 20 79
Language instr: Spanish

Escuela John F. Kennedy
Av Sabinos 272, Jurica, Querétaro C.P. 76100
Tel: +52 442 218 0075
Age range: 3–19
No. of pupils: 1444 B751 G693
Curriculum: IBDP, IBMYP, IBPYP
Language instr: English, Spanish

Escuela Lomas Altas S.C.
Montañas Calizas #305, Lomas de Chapultepec, Ciudad de México C.P. 11000
Tel: +52 55 55 20 53 75/20 37 25
Age range: 1 –13
No. of pupils: 260 B124 G136
Curriculum: IBPYP
Language instr: English, Spanish

Escuela Mexicana Americana, A. C.
Gabriel Mancera 1611, Col. Del Valle, Ciudad de México C.P. 03100
Tel: +52 55 240214
Curriculum: IBDP
Language instr: English, Spanish

Escuela Secundaria y Preparatoria de la Ciudad de Mexico
Campos Eliseos # 139, Col Polanco, Ciudad de México C.P. 11560
Tel: +52 5545 5761
Curriculum: IBCP

Eton, SC
Domingo García Ramos s/n, Col. Prados de la Montaña, Santa Fe, Cuajimalpa, Ciudad de México C.P. 05619
Tel: +52 5 261 5800
Age range: 2–18
Curriculum: IBDP, IBMYP
Language instr: Spanish, English

Foresta International School
Calle Publico los Gallos #3, Rancho Blanco, Espiritu Santo, Jilotzingo, Estado de México C.P. 54570
Tel: +52 55 5308 4236
Curriculum: IBPYP
Language instr: English, Spanish

Formus
Cañon de la Mesa 6745, Monterrey, Nuevo León C.P. 64898
Tel: +52 8317 8560
Curriculum: IBMYP
Language instr: Spanish

Fundación Colegio Americano de Puebla
Av 9 Pte 2709, La Paz, Puebla C.P. 72160
Tel: +52 22 2303 0400
Age range: 6 months–19 years
Curriculum: IBDP, IBMYP, IBPYP, IBCP
Language instr: Spanish, English

GREENGATES SCHOOL
For further details see p. 222
Av. Circunvalación Pte. 102, Balcones de San Mateo, Naucalpan, Estado de México C.P. 53200
Tel: +52 55 5373 0088
Email: admissions@greengates.edu.mx
Website: www.greengates.edu.mx
General Director: Eamonn Mullally
Age range: 3–18 years
No. of pupils: 1200
Curriculum: IBDP, IPC, UK, IGCSE
Language instr: English

Greenville International School
Prolongación Avenida Paseo Usumacinta 2122, Ría. Lázaro Cárdenas 2a Sección, Villahermosa, Tabasco C.P. 86287
Tel: +52 (993) 310 8060
Age range: 2–18 years
No. of pupils: 936
Curriculum: IBDP, IBMYP, IBPYP
Language instr: English

Harmony School
Mariano Narváez 414, Col. Los Alpes Norte, Saltillo, Coahuila C.P 25253
Tel: +52 84 4485 5598
Curriculum: IBPYP
Language instr: English, Spanish

Humanitree
725 Sierra Madre, Lomas de Chapultepec, Miguel Hidalgo, Ciudad de México C.P. 11000
Tel: +52 55 8620 7301
Curriculum: IBDP
Language instr: English, Spanish

Instituto Alexander Bain SC
Cascada 320, Jardines del Pedregal, Ciudad de México
Tel: +52 55 5595 6579
Age range: 2–13
No. of pupils: B381 G382
Curriculum: IBMYP, IBPYP, National
Language instr: Spanish, English

Instituto Anglo Británico Campus Cumbres
Paseo de los leones 7001, Avenida Bosque de las Lomas, Valle de Cumbres, García, Nuevo León C.P. 66035
Tel: +52 81 8526 2222
Age range: 1–15
No. of pupils: 428
Curriculum: IBMYP, IBPYP
Language instr: English, Spanish

Instituto Anglo Británico Campus La Fe
Av. Isidoro Sepúlveda #555, Col. La Encarnación, Apodaca, Nuevo León C.P. 66633
Tel: +52 8183 21 5000
Age range: 1–15
Curriculum: IBMYP, IBPYP
Language instr: English, Spanish

Instituto Bilingüe Rudyard Kipling
Cruz de Valle Verde No 25, Santa Cruz del Monte, Naucalpan, Estado de México C.P. 53110
Tel: +52 55 5572 6282
Age range: 3–18
Curriculum: IBDP, IBMYP, IBPYP
Language instr: Spanish, English

Instituto Bilingüe Victoria A.C.
Vicente Suárez No. 9, Barrio de la Magdalena, Tequisquiapan, Querétaro C.P. 76750
Tel: +52 414 273 3739
Age range: 3–18
No. of pupils: 528
Curriculum: IGCSE

North America

Instituto Cervantes, A.C.
Prol. León García # 2355,
Col. General I. Martínez, San
Luis Potosí C.P. 78360
Tel: +52 444 815 91 50
Age range: 2 1/2–15 years
No. of pupils: 1370
Curriculum: IBMYP, IBPYP
Language instr: Spanish

Instituto D'Amicis, AC
Camino a Morillotla s/n, Colonia
Bello Horizonte, Puebla C.P. 72170
Tel: +52 222 303 2618
Curriculum: AP, IBDP,
IBMYP, IBPYP, IBCP
Language instr: Spanish

Instituto Internacional Octavio Paz
Calle Internacional 63 Fracc. Las
Brisas el Jaguey, Col. Las Redes,
Chapala, Jalisco C.P. 45903
Tel: +52 376 766 0903
Curriculum: IBDP

Instituto Kipling de Irapuato
Villa Mirador 5724, Villas de Irapuato,
Irapuato, Guanajuato C.P. 36670
Tel: +52 462 6230165
Age range: 2–18
No. of pupils: B611 G687
Curriculum: IBMYP, IBPYP
Language instr: Spanish, English

Instituto Ovalle Monday - Plantel Secundaria
Guillermo Massieu Helguera 265,
Col. Residencial La Escalera,
Del. Gustavo A. Madero,
Ciudad de México C.P. 07320
Tel: +52 5586 0316 (Ext:101)
Curriculum: IBMYP
Language instr: Spanish

Instituto para la Educación Integral del Bachiller (INEDIB)
Calle 20 de Noviembre No. 310,
San Mateo Oxtotitlán, Toluca,
Estado de México C.P. 50100
Tel: +52 722 278 10 40
Language instr: Spanish

Instituto Piaget
Nubes 413, Col Jardines del Pedregal,
Ciudad de México C.P. 01900
Tel: +52 555568 8881
Age range: 2–18
No. of pupils: 550
Curriculum: IBPYP
Language instr: English, Spanish

Instituto Tecnológico Sanmiguelense de Estudios Superiores
Calle Escuadrón 201, No. 10 Palmita
de Landeta Km. 0.5, San Miguel de
Allende, Guanajuato C.P. 37748
Tel: +52 415 154 8484
Age range: 15–18 years
No. of pupils: 210
Curriculum: IBDP
Language instr: Spanish

Instituto Thomas Jefferson, Campus Santa Monica
Gardenia 5, Ex-hacienda de Santa
Monica, Tlalnepantla de Baz,
Ciudad de México C.P. 54050
Tel: +52 55 4160 2000
Curriculum: IBDP
Language instr: English, Spanish

Instituto Thomas Jefferson, Campus Zona Esmeralda
Av. Jorge Jiménez Cantu 1, Hacienda
de Valle Escondido, 52937 Ciudad
López Mateos, Estado de México
Tel: +52 55 4162 2100
Curriculum: IBDP
Language instr: English, Spanish

Kinder Kri-Kri
Circuito Puericultores No 6,
Ciudad Satélite, Naucalpan,
Estado de México C.P. 53100

Kipling Esmeralda
Av. Parque de los Ciervos No.1,
Hacienda de Valle Escondido, Zona
Esmeralda, Atizapan de Zaragoza,
EEstado de México C.P. 52937
Tel: +52 55 55726282
Curriculum: IBDP, IBMYP, IBPYP
Language instr: Spanish

Kipling Satélite
Cruz de Valle Verde No 25, Sta.
Cruz del Monte, Naucalpan,
Estado de México C.P. 53110

La Escuela de Lancaster A.C.
Av Insurgentes sur 3838, Tlalpan,
Ciudad de México C.P. 14000
Tel: +52 5556 6697 96
Curriculum: IBDP, IBPYP
Language instr: English, Spanish

Liceo de Apodaca Centro Educativo
Ave. Virrey de Velazco No. 500,
Apodaca, Nuevo León C.P. 66606
Tel: +52 81 83862089
Curriculum: IBMYP, IBPYP
Language instr: English

Liceo de Monterrey Blueridge
Av Insurgentes 2000, La Escondida,
Monterrey, Nuevo Leon C.P. 64640
Tel: +52 81 8221 9800
Curriculum: IBDP, IBMYP, IBPYP
Language instr: English, Spanish

Liceo de Monterrey Redwood
Humberto Junco Voigt 400, Zona
Loma Larga Oriente, San Pedro
Garza García, Nuevo León C.P. 66266
Tel: +52 81 8221 9800
Curriculum: IBDP, IBMYP, IBPYP
Language instr: English, Spanish

Liceo de Monterrey Rosemont
Av San Jerónimo 201, San Jerónimo,
Monterrey, Nuevo Leon C.P. 64640
Tel: +52 81 8221 9800
Language instr: English, Spanish

Liceo Federico Froebel de Oaxaca
Ajusco No. 100, Colonia
Volcanes, Oaxaca C.P. 68020
Tel: +52 951 5200 675
Age range: 15–18 years
No. of pupils: 100
Curriculum: IBDP
Language instr: Spanish

Lomas Hill
Av. Veracruz 158, Cuajimalpa,
Ciudad de México C.P. 05000
Tel: +52 55 5812 0818
Curriculum: IBPYP
Language instr: English, Spanish

Madison Campus Monterrey
Marsella #3055, Col. Alta Vista,
Monterrey, Nuevo León C.P. 64840
Tel: +52 81 8359 0627
Age range: 2–15 years
Curriculum: IBMYP, IBPYP
Language instr: English, Spanish

Madison International School
Camino Real #100, Col. El Uro,
Monterrey, Nuevo León C.P. 64986
Tel: +52 81 8218 7909
Age range: 1–15 years
No. of pupils: 964
Curriculum: IBMYP, IBPYP
Language instr: English, Spanish

Madison International School Campus Country-Mérida
Calle 24776 s/n, Chablekal,
Merida, Yucatán C.P. 97300
Tel: +52 99 9611 9053
Curriculum: IBDP, IBMYP, IBPYP
Language instr: English, Spanish

Montessori Sierra Madre
Avenida Licenciado Benito Juárez
Sur 250, Centro de San Pedro
Garza García, San Pedro Garza
García, Nuevo León C.P. 66200
Tel: +52 81 8124 6400
Age range: 3–15

Noordwijk International College
Blvd. del Mar #491, Fracc. Costa de
Oro, Boca del Río, Veracruz C.P. 94299
Tel: +52 229 130 0714
Age range: 3–15
No. of pupils: 500
Curriculum: IBDP, IBMYP, IBPYP
Language instr: English, Spanish

Nuevo Colegio Israelita de Monterrey
Preescolar y Primaria, Canadá
#207, Col Vista Hermosa - CP
64620, Monterrey, NL C.P. 64620
Tel: +52 81 8346 9677
No. of pupils: 110

Orbis International School
Km 3.5 Carretera Aeropuerto
#551, Colonia Rivera, Mexicali,
Baja California C.P. 21220
Tel: +52 686 565 0877
Language instr: English

Pan American School - Campus Monterrey
Hidalgo No 656 Pte Col
Centro, Apartado Postal 474,
Monterrey C.P. 64000
Tel: +52 81 8342 0778
Age range: 2–15
No. of pupils: 554
Curriculum: USA

Peterson School - Cuajimalpa
Huizachito 80, Lomas de
Vista Hermosa, Chajimalpa,
Mexico City C.P. 05720
Tel: +52 55 5813 0114

Peterson School - Lomas
Monte Himalaya 615, Lomas de
Chapultepec, Miguel Hidalgo,
México D.F. C.P. 11000
Tel: +52 5520 2213
Age range: 17–19
Curriculum: IBDP
Language instr: Spanish

Peterson School - Pedregal
Rocío 142, Jardines del
Pedregal, Álvaro Obregón,
México D.F. C.P. 01900
Tel: +52 5568 3139

Peterson School Tlalpan
Carretera Federal a
Cuernavaca, Km. 24 No. 6871,
San Andrés Totoltepec, Tlalpan,
México D.F. C.P. 14400
Tel: +52 55 5849 1885
Language instr: Spanish

Prepa UNI
Carretera Panamerican Km 269,
Celaya, Guanajuato C.P. 38080
Tel: +52 461 61 39099
Curriculum: IBDP
Language instr: Spanish

Prepa UPAEP Angelópolis
Gustavo Díaz Ordaz 1547, Real
de Santa Clara II, San Andrés
Cholula, Puebla C.P. 72160
Tel: +52 222 225 7024
Curriculum: IBDP, IBCP
Language instr: English, Spanish

Prepa UPAEP Atlixco
Camino a la Uvera No.
2004, San Diego la Blanca,
Atlixco, Puebla C.P. 74365
Tel: +52 244 445 1991
Curriculum: IBCP
Language instr: English, Spanish

Prepa UPAEP Cholula
Blvd. Forjadores de Puebla
1804, Barrio de Jesús Tlatempa,
Cholula, Puebla C.P. 72760
Tel: +52 222 403 7373
Curriculum: IBDP, IBCP
Language instr: English, Spanish

North America

Prepa UPAEP Huamantla
Carrt. Fed Mex-Ver Km 147.5
Col. Sta. Clara, Huamantla,
Tlaxcala C.P. 90500
Tel: +52 247 472 2550
Curriculum: IBCP
Language instr: Spanish

Prepa UPAEP Lomas
Circuito Molina No. 15, Lomas
de Angelópolis, Tlaxcalancingo,
Puebla C.P. 72828
Tel: +52 222 582 2102
Curriculum: IBDP, IBCP
Language instr: English, Spanish

Prepa UPAEP San Martín
C/ Lardizabal s/n Col. La
Purisima, San Martín Texmelucan,
Puebla C.P. 74030
Tel: +52 248 484 4142
Curriculum: IBCP
Language instr: English, Spanish

Prepa UPAEP Santa Ana
Avenida Tecpanxochitl 52 A, San
Pedro Tlalcuapan, Chiautempan,
Tlaxcala C.P. 90845
Tel: +52 246 464 9633
Curriculum: IBCP
Language instr: English, Spanish

Prepa UPAEP Santiago
Av 9 Pte 1508, Barrio de
Santiago, Puebla C.P. 72160
Tel: +52 222 232 7740
Curriculum: IBDP, IBCP
Language instr: English, Spanish

Prepa UPAEP Sur
Calle Independencia No. 6339, El
Patrimonio, Puebla C.P. 72470
Tel: +52 222 710 7455
Curriculum: IBDP, IBCP
Language instr: English, Spanish

Prepa UPAEP Tehuacán
Boulevard Tehuacán, San Marcos
#1700, Col. Nueva España,
Tehuacán, Puebla C.P. 75859
Tel: +52 238 380 2258
Curriculum: IBCP
Language instr: English, Spanish

Rootland School
Hortensia 6, Florida, Álvaro Obregón,
Ciudad de México C.P. 01030
Tel: +52 55 9211 6920
Curriculum: IBPYP
Language instr: English, Spanish

San Roberto International School
Av Real San Agustín #4, Garza
García, NL C.P. 66260
Tel: +52 81 8625 1500
Age range: 1–15
Language instr: English, Spanish

Tecnológico de Monterrey
Ave Eugenio Garza Sada
2501, Sur Col Tecnológico,
Monterrey, NL C.P. 64849
Tel: +52 81 8358 2000

Tecnológico de Monterrey - Campus Cuernavaca
Autopista del Sol Km 104, Colonia
Real del Puente, Xochitepec,
Morelos, Cuernavaca C.P. 62790
Tel: +52 (77) 7362 0832
Language instr: Spanish

Tecnológico de Monterrey - Campus Puebla
Vía Atlixcáyotl 5718, Col
Reserva Territorial Atlixcayotl,
Puebla C.P. 72453
Age range: 15–18
No. of pupils: 1000
Language instr: Spanish, English

Tecnológico de Monterrey - Campus San Luis Potosí
Av Eugenio Garza Sada No 300,
Fraccionamiento Lomas del
Tecnológico, San Luis Potosi C.P. 78211
Tel: +52 44 4834 1000
Language instr: English

Tecnológico de Monterrey - PrepaTec Ciudad de México
Calle del Puente #222, Col.
Ejidos de Huipulco, Tlalpan,
Distrito Federal C.P. 14380
Tel: +52 (55) 5483 2110
Curriculum: IBDP
Language instr: Spanish

Tecnológico de Monterrey - PrepaTec Cumbres
Linces #1000, Col. Cumbres Elite,
Monterrey, Nuevo León C.P. 64639
Tel: +52 (81) 8158 4622
Curriculum: IBDP
Language instr: Spanish, English

Tecnológico de Monterrey - PrepaTec Esmeralda
Fracc. Conjunto Urbano, Col.
Bosque Esmeralda, Manzana 7
Lote 1 y 2, Atizapán de Zaragoza,
Estado de México C.P. 52930
Tel: +52 (55) 5864 5370 (Ext:2903)
Curriculum: IBDP
Language instr: Spanish

Tecnológico de Monterrey - PrepaTec Estado de México
Carretera Lago de Guadalupe,
Km 3.5, Col. Margarita Maza de
Juárez, Atizapán de Zaragoza,
Estado de México C.P. 52926
Tel: +52 (55) 5864 5714
Curriculum: IBDP
Language instr: Spanish, English

Tecnológico de Monterrey - PrepaTec Eugenio Garza Lagüera
Topolobampo #4603, Valle
de las Brisas, Monterrey,
Nuevo León C.P. 64790
Tel: +52 (81) 8155 4490
Curriculum: IBDP
Language instr: Spanish

Tecnológico de Monterrey - PrepaTec Eugenio Garza Sada
Dinamarca #451 Sur Col Del Carmen,
Monterrey, Nuevo León C.P. 64710
Tel: +52 (81) 8151 4264
Language instr: Spanish, English

Tecnológico de Monterrey - PrepaTec Metepec
Av. Las Torres 1957 Ote., San Salvador
Tizatlali, Metepec C.P. 52172
Tel: +52 (722) 271 5977
Language instr: Spanish, English

Tecnológico de Monterrey - PrepaTec Querétaro
Av. Epigmenio González #500,
Fracc. San Pablo, Santiago
de Querétaro C.P. 76130
Tel: +52 (442) 238 3208
Curriculum: IBDP
Language instr: Spanish

Tecnológico de Monterrey - PrepaTec Santa Catarina
Morones Prieto No 290 Pte., Col
Jesús M. Garza, Santa Catarina,
Nuevo León C.P. 66180
Tel: +52 (81) 8153 4045
Curriculum: IBDP
Language instr: English, Spanish

Tecnológico de Monterrey - PrepaTec Santa Fe
Av Carlos Lazo #100, Santa
Fe, Delegación Alvaro
Obregón C.P. 01389
Tel: +52 (55) 9177 8130
Curriculum: IBDP
Language instr: Spanish, English

Tecnológico de Monterrey - PrepaTec Valle Alto
Carretera Nacional #8002
Km. 267.7, Col. La Estanzuela,
Monterrey, N.L C.P. 64986
Tel: +52 (81)8228 5310
Curriculum: IBDP
Language instr: Spanish, English

The American School Foundation, A.C.
Bondojito 215, Colonia Las Americas,
Ciudad de México C.P. 01120
Tel: +52 55 5227 4900
Age range: 3–18 years
Curriculum: AP, IBDP,
IBPYP, National, USA
Language instr: English, Spanish

The American School of Tampico
Calle Hidalgo #100, Colonia
Tancol, Tampico C.P. 89320
Tel: +52 833 2 27 20 80
Age range: 3–20
No. of pupils: 733
Curriculum: AP, USA

The Churchill School
Felipe Villanueva No. 24, Col.
Guadalupe Inn, Mexico City
Tel: +52 55 50288800
Age range: 2–16
No. of pupils: B547 G482
Curriculum: IBMYP, IBPYP
Language instr: English, Spanish

The Edron Academy
Calz. Desierto de los Leones
#5578, Col Olivar de Los Padres,
Ciudad de México C.P. 1740
Tel: +52 55 5585 1920
Age range: 2–18 years
Curriculum: IBDP
Language instr: English, Spanish

THE WINGATE SCHOOL
For further details see p. 238
Carr. Huixquilucan Río Hondo
Km 14, Col. San Bartolomé
Coatepec, Huixquilucan,
Estado de México C.P. 52770
Tel: +52 55 8288 0982
Email: office@wingate.edu.mx
Website: www.wingate.edu.mx
Head Teacher: Tom Wingate
Age range: 2–18 years
Curriculum: IBDP, IPC, UK, IGCSE
Language instr: English, Spanish

Tomás Alva Edison
Heriberto Frías 1401 Colonia del
Valle, Benito Juárez, Ciudad
de México C.P. 03100
Tel: +52 55 5604 0314
Curriculum: IBDP
Language instr: English, Spanish

Universidad de Monterrey Unidad Valle Alto
Carretera Nacional Salida
Valle Alto Km1, Colonia Valle
Alto, Monterrey, NL C.P. 64989
Curriculum: IBDP, IBCP
Language instr: English, Spanish

Universidad Internacional Jefferson
Boulevard Jefferson No 666,
Morelia, Michoacán C.P. 58090
Tel: +52 44 3680 5333
Curriculum: IBDP, National
Language instr: Spanish

University of Monterrey
Av. Ignacio Morones Prieto 4500,
Pte., 66238, San Pedro Garza
García, Nuevo León C.P. 66238
Tel: +52 81 8215 1010
Curriculum: IBDP, IBCP
Language instr: Spanish

Westhill Institute
Domingo Garcia Ramos No. 56, Col.
Prados de la Montaña, Santa Fe,
Cuajimalpa, Mexico City C.P. 05610
Tel: +52 55 8851 7000
Curriculum: IBDP, IBMYP, IBPYP
Language instr: English,
Spanish, French

Westhill Institute - Carpatos
Monte Carpatos 940, Lomas de
Chapultepec, México D.F. C.P. 11000
Tel: +52 55 88517067
Language instr: English, Spanish

Winpenny School
José María Castorena 318, Colonia
Cuajimalpa, México D. F. C.P. 05000
Tel: +52 55 8000 6100
Curriculum: IBDP
Language instr: Spanish

MONTSERRAT

St Augustine Primary
PO Box 192, Palm Loop
Tel: +1 664 491 4768

North America

NICARAGUA

American Nicaraguan School
Frente al Club de Lomas de Montserrat, P.O. Box 2670, Managua
Tel: +505 2278 0029
Age range: 3–18
No. of pupils: 970
Curriculum: USA

Colegio Alemán Nicaragüense
Apartado 1636, Managua
Tel: +505 2265 8449
No. of pupils: 479
Curriculum: IBDP
Language instr: Spanish

Lincoln International Academy
Las Colinas Sur, Managua
Tel: +505 2276 3000

Notre Dame International School
Km 8.5 Carretera a Masaya, Managua
Tel: +505 2276 0353 54
Age range: 2–19
Curriculum: IBDP, IBMYP, IBPYP
Language instr: English

PUERTO RICO

Academia del Perpetuo Socorro
704 Calle Martí, Miramar, San Juan 907
Tel: +1 787 724 1447
Curriculum: USA

Caribbean School
Urb La Rambla, 1689 Calle Navarra, Ponce 00730-4043
Tel: +1 787 843 2048
Age range: 4–18
No. of pupils: 640
Curriculum: ACT, AP, SAT, TOEFL, USA

Commonwealth-Parkville School
PO BOX 70177, SAN JUAN, PR 00936-8177
Tel: +1 787 720 3992

Robinson School
5 Nairn Street, San Juan 00907
Tel: +1 787 999 4600
Curriculum: IBDP, IBMYP, IBPYP
Language instr: English

St John's School
1454 Ashford Avenue, San Juan 00907 1560
Tel: +1 787 728 5256

The Baldwin School of Puerto Rico
PO Box 1827, Bayamón 00960-1827
Tel: +1 787 720 2421
Age range: 3–18 years
No. of pupils: 820
Curriculum: ACT, AP, IBDP, IBMYP, IBPYP, SAT, USA
Language instr: English

SAINT LUCIA

International School of Saint Lucia
PO Box RB 2701, Rodney Bay, Gros Islet, Saint Lucia
Tel: +1 758 458 0989

TRINIDAD & TOBAGO

Maple Leaf International School
Alyce Heights Drive, Alyce Glen, Petit Valley
Tel: +1 868 632 9578
Age range: 4–19 years
No. of pupils: 300
Language instr: English

QSI International School of Trinidad
74 Long Circular Road, Port of Spain
Tel: +1 868 465 6198

The British Academy
23 Alexandra Street, St Clair, Port of Spain
Tel: +1 868 622 4285
Age range: 4–19
No. of pupils: 144 B85 G59 VIth23
Curriculum: UK, IGCSE, ALevs
Language instr: English

The International School of Port of Spain
1 International Drive, Westmoorings, Port of Spain
Tel: +1 868 633 4777
Age range: 4–19
No. of pupils: 452 B245 G207 VIth101
Curriculum: ACT, AP, IBMYP, IBPYP, SAT
Language instr: English

TURKS AND CAICOS ISLANDS

British West Indies Collegiate
PO Box 338, 51 Venetian Road, Providenciales TKCA 1ZZ
Tel: +1 649 941 3333

International School Turks and Caicos
P.O. Box 278, Leeward, Providenciales
Tel: +1 649 946 5523
Curriculum: UK

Providenciales Primary School
PO Box 329, Providenciales
Tel: +1 649 333 5638
Age range: 2–11
Curriculum: UK

The Ashcroft School
PO Box 278, Governor's Road, Leeward, Providenciales
Tel: +1 649 94 65523
Age range: 2–13
No. of pupils: 124

USA

Alabama

Cornerstone Schools of Alabama
118 55th Street North, Birmingham Alabama AL 35212
Tel: +1 205 591 7600
Age range: 4–11
No. of pupils: 305
Curriculum: IBPYP
Language instr: English

Arizona

Desert Garden Montessori
5130 E. Warner Rd., Phoenix Arizona AZ 85044
Tel: +1 480 496 9833
Curriculum: IBMYP
Language instr: English

International School of Arizona
9522 E. San Salvador Drive, Scottsdale Arizona AZ 85258
Tel: +1 480 874 2326
Age range: 18 months–14 years
No. of pupils: 305
Curriculum: USA

International School of Tucson
1701 East Seneca Street, Tucson Arizona AZ 85719
Tel: +1 520 406 0552
Age range: 6 months–14 years
No. of pupils: 230
Language instr: English

Maple Bear Tempe
1255 W. Elliot Road, Suite 20, Tempe Arizona AZ 85284
Tel: +1 480 474 4455

Rancho Solano Preparatory School
9180 E. Via de Ventura, Scottsdale Arizona AZ 85258
Tel: +1 480 646 8200
Age range: 4–18
Curriculum: IBDP
Language instr: English

Verde Valley School
3511 Verde Valley School Road, Sedona Arizona AZ 86351
Tel: +1 928 284 2272
No. of pupils: 135
Curriculum: IBDP
Language instr: English

Arkansas

Mount Saint Mary Academy
3224 Kavanaugh Blvd, Little Rock Arkansas AR 72205
Tel: +1 501 664 8006
Age range: G14–18
No. of pupils: 537
Language instr: English

California

Al-Arqam Islamic School & College Preparatory
6990 65th Street, Sacramento California CA 95823
Tel: +1 916 391 3333
Curriculum: IBDP
Language instr: English

Alto International School
475 Pope St, Menlo Park California CA 94025
Tel: +1 650 324 8617
Age range: 3–14
No. of pupils: 250
Curriculum: IBDP, IBMYP, IBPYP
Language instr: German, English

American University Research Academy (AURA Academy)
1600 E Hill Street, Signal Hill California CA 90755
Tel: +1 562 800 0249
Curriculum: IBDP
Language instr: English

Cate School
1960 Cate Mesa Road, Carpinteria California CA 93013
Tel: +1 805 684 4127
Language instr: English

Damien High School
2280 Damien Avenue, La Verne California CA 91750
Tel: +1 909 596 1946
Age range: B13–19
No. of pupils: 922
Curriculum: IBCP
Language instr: English

East Bay German International School
1070 41st Street, Emeryville California CA 94608
Tel: +1 510 380 0301
Curriculum: IBDP
Language instr: English, German

Ecole Bilingue de Berkeley
1009 Heinz Aveunue, Berkeley California CA 94710
Tel: +1 510 549 3867
Age range: 2–14
No. of pupils: 460
Curriculum: USA
Language instr: French, English

EF Academy Pasadena
1539 E Howard St., Pasadena California CA 91104
Tel: +1 626 507 9223
Age range: 14–19 years
Curriculum: USA, IGCSE

Escuela Bilingüe Internacional
410 Alcatraz Avenue, Oakland California CA 94609
Tel: +1 510 653 3324
Curriculum: IBMYP, IBPYP

North America

Fairmont Private School of Fresno
435 W. Fairmont, Fresno California CA 93705
Tel: +1 559 226 2347
Curriculum: IBPYP
Language instr: English, Spanish

Fairmont Private Schools - Anaheim Hills Campus
5300 E La Palma Avenue, Anaheim California CA 92807
Tel: +1 714 693 3812

Fairmont Private Schools - Historic Anaheim Campus
1557 W. Mable Street, Anaheim California CA 92805
Tel: +1 714 563 4050
Curriculum: IBMYP, IBPYP
Language instr: English

Fairmont Private Schools - North Tustin Campus
12421 Newport Avenue, North Tustin California CA 92705
Tel: +1 714 832 4867

Fairmont Private Schools - Preparatory Academy
2200 West Sequoia Avenue, Anaheim California CA 92801
Tel: +1 714 999 5055
Age range: 13–19
No. of pupils: 450
Curriculum: AP, IBDP, USA
Language instr: English

French American International School & International High School
150 Oak Street, San Francisco California CA 94102-5812
Tel: +1 415 558 2000
Age range: 4–18
Curriculum: IBDP
Language instr: English

French-American School of Silicon Valley
1522 Lewiston Drive, Sunnyvale California CA 94087
Tel: +1 408 746 0460
Curriculum: USA

GISSV German International School of Silicon Valley
Mountain View Campus, 310 Easy Street, Mountain View California CA 94043
Tel: +1 650 254 0748

Golden Hills School
1060 Suncast Lane, El Dorado Hills California CA 95762
Tel: +1 916 933 0100
Curriculum: IBMYP
Language instr: English

Granada Preparatory School
10400 Zelzah Avenue, Northridge California CA 91326
Tel: +1 818 368 7254
Curriculum: IBMYP, IBPYP
Language instr: English

Guide Academy
121 S. Citron Street, Anaheim California CA 92805
Tel: +1 714 603 7811
Curriculum: IBMYP
Language instr: English, Arabic

INTERNATIONAL SCHOOL OF LOS ANGELES
For further details see p. 225
1105 W. Riverside Drive, Burbank California CA 91506
Tel: +1 626 695 5159
Email: admissions@lilaschool.com
Website: www.internationalschool.la
Head of School: Anneli Harvey
Age range: 2–18 years
No. of pupils: 1060
Fees: Day $22,925–$31,580
Curriculum: AP, IBDP, FrenchBacc, SAT
Language instr: English, French

La Scuola International San Francisco
K-8 Campus, 735 Fell Street, San Francisco California CA 94117
Tel: +1 415 551 0000
Curriculum: IBPYP

La Scuola International School
3250 18th Street, San Francisco California CA 94110
Tel: +1 415 551 0000
Age range: 2–14 years
No. of pupils: 440
Curriculum: IBMYP, IBPYP
Language instr: English

LE LYCÉE FRANÇAIS DE LOS ANGELES
For further details see p. 226
3261 Overland Avenue, Los Angeles California CA 90034
Tel: +1 310 836 3464
Email: generalinfo@LyceeLA.org
Website: www.lyceela.org
President: Clara-Lisa Kabbaz
Age range: 2–18 years
No. of pupils: 680 B300 G380
Fees: Day $22,000–$40,780
Curriculum: ACT, AP, National, FrenchBacc, SAT, USA
Language instr: English, French

Lycée Français de San Francisco
1201 Ortega Street, San Francisco California CA 94122
Tel: +1 415 661 5232
Curriculum: FrenchBacc

Monte Vista Christian School
2 School Way, Watsonville California CA 95076
Tel: +1 831 722 8178
Curriculum: IBDP, IBMYP
Language instr: English

New Covenant Academy
3119 W 6th Street, Los Angeles California CA 90020
Tel: +1 213 487 5437
Age range: 6–19
No. of pupils: 137 B83 G55
Curriculum: ACT, IBDP, SAT, USA
Language instr: English

Pacific Rim International School
454 Peninsula Avenue, San Mateo California CA 94401
Tel: +1 650 685 1881
Language instr: English

Quarry Lane School
6363 Tassajara Road, Dublin California CA 94568
Tel: +1 925 829 8000
Curriculum: IBDP
Language instr: English

San Diego French-American School
6550 Soledad Mountain Road, La Jolla California CA 92037
Tel: +1 858 456 2807
Age range: 2–13

San Gabriel Mission High School
254 South Santa Anita Street, San Gabriel California CA 91776
Tel: +1 626 282 3181
Language instr: English

Santa Margarita Catholic High School
22062 Antonio Parkway, Rancho Santa Margarita California CA 92688
Tel: +1 949 766 6000
Curriculum: IBDP
Language instr: English

Schools of the Sacred Heart
2222 Broadway, San Francisco California CA 94115
Tel: +1 415 563 2900
Curriculum: IBDP
Language instr: English

Shu Ren International School
2125 Jefferson Avenue, Berkeley California CA 94703
Tel: +1 510 841 8899
Curriculum: IBPYP
Language instr: English, Mandarin

Silicon Valley International School
151 Laura Lane, Palo Alto California CA 94303
Tel: +1 650 251 8522
Age range: 3 1/2–14 years
Curriculum: USA
Language instr: English, Chinese

St. Francis of Assisi Elementary School
2500 K Street, Sacramento California CA 95816
Tel: +1 916 442 5494
Curriculum: IBMYP, IBPYP
Language instr: English

St. Mary's School
7 Pursuit, Aliso Viejo California CA 92656
Tel: +1 949 448 9027
Curriculum: IBMYP, IBPYP
Language instr: French

Stanford Online High School
Academy Hall, Floor 2 8853, 415 Broadway, Redwood City California CA 94063
Age range: 12–18 years

The Healdsburg School
33H Healdsburg Avenue, Healdsburg California CA 95448
Tel: +1 707 433 4847
Curriculum: IBPYP
Language instr: English

THINK GLOBAL SCHOOL
For further details see p. 236
960 Madison Avenue Fifth Floor, New York California NY 10021
Tel: +1 646 504 6924
Email: info@thinkglobalschool.org
Website: thinkglobalschool.org
Principal: Jen Buchanan
Age range: 16–18 years
No. of pupils: 31
Fees: FB $94,000

Valley Preparatory School
1605 Ford Street, Redlands California CA 92373
Tel: +1 909 793 3063
Curriculum: IBPYP
Language instr: English, Spanish

Villanova Preparatory School
12096 N. Ventura Avenue, Ojai California CA 93023
Tel: +1 805 646 1464
Curriculum: IBDP
Language instr: English

Vistamar School
737 Hawaii Street, El Segundo California CA 90245
Tel: +1 310 643 7377
Age range: 13–19
No. of pupils: 176 B90 G86
Curriculum: USA
Language instr: English

Yew Chung International School of Silicon Valley
310 Easy Street, Mountain View California CA 94043
Tel: +1 650 903 0986
Age range: 2–14 years
Curriculum: USA
Language instr: English, Mandarin

Colorado

Boulder Country Day School
4820 Nautilus Court North, Boulder Colorado CO 80301
Tel: +1 303 527 4931
Curriculum: IBMYP
Language instr: English

Dos Rios Elementary School
2201 34th Street, Evans Colorado CO 80620
Tel: +1 970 348 1309
Curriculum: IBPYP
Language instr: English

North America

Fountain Valley School of Colorado
6155 Fountain Valley School Rd,
Colorado Springs Colorado CO 80911
Tel: +1 719 390 7035
Language instr: English

INTERNATIONAL SCHOOL OF DENVER
For further details see p. 224
7701 E. 1st Pl, Unit C, Denver
Colorado CO 80230
Tel: +1 303 340 3647
Email: info@isdenver.org
Website: www.isdenver.org
Head of School: Roberto d'Erizans
Age range: 3–15 years
No. of pupils: 679
Fees: US$28,100
Curriculum: IBMYP, IBPYP
Language instr: Chinese, English, French, Spanish

Mackintosh Academy Boulder
6717 S. Boulder Road, Boulder
Colorado CO 80303
Tel: +1 303 554 2011
Curriculum: IBMYP, IBPYP
Language instr: English

Mackintosh Academy Littleton
7018 S. Prince Street, Littleton
Colorado CO 80120
Tel: +1 303 794 6222
Curriculum: IBMYP, IBPYP
Language instr: English

Telluride Mountain School
Lawson Hill, 200 San Miguel River
Dr., Telluride Colorado CO 81435
Tel: +1 970 728 1969
Curriculum: IBDP
Language instr: English

Connecticut

Cheshire Academy
10 Main Street, Cheshire
Connecticut CT 06410
Tel: +1 203 272 5396
Curriculum: IBDP, National

Notre Dame High School
One Notre Dame Way, West
Haven Connecticut CT 06516
Tel: +1 203 933 1673
Curriculum: IBDP
Language instr: English, Spanish

Notre Dame High School, Fairfield
220 Jefferson Street, Fairfield
Connecticut CT 06825
Tel: +1 203 372 6521
Curriculum: IBDP
Language instr: English

The Hotchkiss School
11 Interlaken Road, Lakeville
Connecticut CT 06039-2141
Tel: +1 860 435 2591
Language instr: English

Whitby School
969 Lake Avenue, Greenwich
Connecticut CT 06831
Tel: +1 203 302 3900
Age range: 18 months–14 years
No. of pupils: 290
Curriculum: IBMYP, IBPYP
Language instr: English

Delaware

Wilmington Friends School
101 School Road, Wilmington
Delaware DE 19803
Tel: +1 302 576 2900
Age range: 2–19
Curriculum: AP, IBDP, SAT
Language instr: English

District of Columbia

Archbishop Carroll High School
4300 Harewood Road
NE, Washington District of
Columbia DC 20017
Tel: +1 202 529 0900 Ext:135
No. of pupils: 545
Language instr: English

British International School of Washington
2001 Wisconsin Avenue
NW, Washington District of
Columbia DC 20007
Tel: +1 202 829 3700
Age range: 2–18
No. of pupils: 450
Curriculum: IBDP, UK, IGCSE
Language instr: English

Creative Minds International Public Charter School
Sherman Building, 3700 N Capitol
Street NW #217, Washington District
of Columbia DC 20011-8400
Tel: +1 202 588 0370
Curriculum: IPC

Washington International School
3100 Macomb Street NW, Washington
District of Columbia DC 20008
Tel: +1 202 243 1800
Age range: 4–18
Curriculum: IBDP, IBPYP
Language instr: English, French, Spanish, Dutch, Chinese

Florida

American Youth Academy
5905 E. 130th Avenue,
Tampa Florida FL 33617
Tel: +1 813 987 9282
Age range: 3–18 years
Curriculum: IBDP, IBMYP
Language instr: English, Arabic

Arthur I. Meyer Jewish Academy
5225 Hood Rd, Palm Beach
Gardens Florida FL 33418
Tel: +1 561 686 6520
Curriculum: IBMYP

Bhaktivedanta Academy
17414 NW 112th Blvd, Alachua
Florida FL 32615
Tel: +1 386 462 2886
Curriculum: IBMYP
Language instr: English

Boca Prep International School
10333 Diego Drive South, Boca
Raton Florida FL 33428
Tel: +1 561 765 6079
Age range: 3–18 years
Curriculum: IBDP, IBMYP, IBPYP
Language instr: English

Brandon Academy
801 Limona Road, Brandon
Florida FL 33510
Tel: +1 813 689 1952
Language instr: English

Cardinal Newman High School
512 Spencer Drive, West Palm
Beach Florida FL 33409
Tel: +1 561 683 6266
Language instr: English

Carrollton School of the Sacred Heart
3747 Main Highway, Miami
Florida FL 33133
Tel: +1 305 446 5673
Curriculum: IBDP
Language instr: English

Carrollwood Day School
1515 W. Bearss Avenue,
Tampa Florida FL 33613
Tel: +1 813 920 2288
Age range: 2–18
Curriculum: IBDP, IBMYP, IBPYP
Language instr: English

Clearwater Central Catholic High School
2750 Haines Bayshore Road,
Clearwater Florida FL 33760
Tel: +1 727 531 1449
Curriculum: IBDP
Language instr: English

Corbett Preparatory School of IDS
12015 Orange Grove Drive,
Tampa Florida FL 33618
Tel: +1 813 961 3087
Curriculum: IBMYP, IBPYP
Language instr: English

Cornerstone Learning Community
2524 Hartsfield Road,
Tallahassee Florida FL 32303
Tel: +1 850 386 5550
Curriculum: IBMYP
Language instr: English

Creation Village Preparatory School
599 Celebration Place,
Celebration Florida FL 34747
Tel: +1 407 900 7708
Curriculum: IBMYP, IBPYP
Language instr: English

French American International School of Boca Raton
2500 NW 5th Avenue, Boca
Raton Florida FL 33431
Tel: +1 561 479 8266
Curriculum: IBPYP
Language instr: English, French

Gulliver Academy Middle School
12595 Red Road, Coral
Gables Florida FL 33156
Tel: +1 305 665 3593
Curriculum: IBMYP

Gulliver Preparatory School
6575 North Kendall Drive,
Miami Florida FL 33156
Tel: +1 305 666 6333
Age range: 2–18 years
No. of pupils: 2200
Curriculum: AP, IBDP
Language instr: English

International School of Broward - Charter School
3100 N. 75th Avenue,
Hollywood Florida FL 33024
Tel: +1 954 987 2026

New Gate School
5237 Ashton Road, Sarasota
Florida FL 34233
Tel: +1 941 922 4949
Age range: 2–18
No. of pupils: 175 B84 G91
Curriculum: IBDP, USA
Language instr: English

North Broward Preparatory School
7600 Lyons Road, Coconut
Creek Florida FL 33073
Tel: +1 954.247.0011
Age range: 3–18 years
Curriculum: ACT, AP, IBDP, SAT, USA
Language instr: English

Palmer Trinity School
7900 SW 176th Street, Miami
Florida FL 33157
Tel: +1 305 251 2230
Curriculum: IBDP
Language instr: English

North America

Saint John Paul II Catholic School
4341 W Homosassa Trail,
Lecanto Florida FL 34461
Tel: +1 352 746 2020
Curriculum: IBMYP
Language instr: English

Scheck Hillel Community School
19000 NE 25th Avenue, North Miami Beach Florida FL 33180
Tel: +1 305 931 2831

Score Academy
2900 SW 28th Lane, Miami Florida FL 33133
Tel: +1 844 438 1600
Age range: 11–18 years

St Andrew's School
3900 Jog Road, Boca Raton Florida FL 33434
Tel: +1 561 210 2000
Curriculum: IBDP, IBMYP, IBPYP
Language instr: English

St Ann Catholic School
324 North Olive Avenue, West Palm Beach Florida FL 33401
Tel: +1 561 832 3676
Curriculum: IBMYP, IBPYP
Language instr: English

St. Cecelia Interparochial Catholic School
1350 Court Street, Clearwater Florida FL 33756
Tel: +1 727 461 1200
Curriculum: IBMYP, IBPYP
Language instr: English

St. Thomas the Apostle Catholic School
7303 S.W. 64th Street, Miami Florida FL 33143
Tel: +1 305 661 8591
Age range: 2–14
No. of pupils: 512
Curriculum: USA
Language instr: English

THE BILTMORE SCHOOL
For further details see p. 233
1600 S. Red Road, Miami Florida FL 33155
Tel: +1 305 266 4666
Email: info@biltmoreschool.com
Website: www.biltmoreschool.com
Principal: Gina C. Duarte-Romero
Age range: 1–14 years
No. of pupils: 200
Fees: US$18,575–US$29,575
Curriculum: IBPYP

The Discovery School
102 15th Street South, Jacksonville Beach Florida FL 32250
Tel: +1 904 247 4577
Curriculum: IBPYP
Language instr: English

The French American School of Tampa Bay
2100 62nd Avenue N, St. Petersburg Florida FL 33702
Tel: +1 727 800 2159
Curriculum: IBPYP
Language instr: English, French

The Rock School
Suite B, 9818 SW 24th Avenue, Gainesville Florida FL 32607
Tel: +1 352 331 7625
Age range: 1–18 years
Curriculum: IBDP, IBMYP
Language instr: English

The Roig Academy
8000 SW 112 St, Miami Florida FL 33156
Tel: +1 305 235 1313
Curriculum: IBPYP
Language instr: English, Spanish

Trinity Catholic School
706 E. Brevard Street, Tallahassee Florida FL 32308
Tel: +1 850 222 0444
Curriculum: IBMYP
Language instr: English, Spanish

Windermere Preparatory School
6189 Winter Garden Vineland Road, Windermere Florida FL 34786
Tel: +1 407 905 7737
Age range: 3–18 years
No. of pupils: 1508
Curriculum: IBDP
Language instr: English

Georgia

Atlanta International School
2890 North Fulton Drive, Atlanta Georgia GA 30305
Tel: +1 404 841 3840
Age range: 3–18 years
No. of pupils: 1345
Curriculum: IBDP, IBMYP, IBPYP, IBCP
Language instr: English, Chinese, French, German, Spanish

Brandon Hall School
1701 Brandon Hall Drive, Atlanta Georgia GA 30350
Tel: +1 770 394 8177
Curriculum: IBDP
Language instr: English

Endeavor International School
48 Perimeter Center East, Atlanta Georgia GA 30346
Tel: +1 770 637 4737
Curriculum: IBMYP
Language instr: English, Spanish

High Meadows School
1055 Willeo Road, Roswell Georgia GA 30188
Tel: +1 770 993 2940
Age range: 3–14
No. of pupils: 387
Curriculum: IBPYP
Language instr: English

Montessori Academy Sharon Springs
2830 Old Atlanta Road, Cumming Georgia GA 30041
Tel: +1 770 205 6277
Curriculum: IBDP
Language instr: English, Spanish

Notre Dame Academy, GA
4635 River Green Parkway, Duluth Georgia GA 30096
Tel: +1 678 387 9385
Age range: 2–18 years
Curriculum: AP, IBDP, IBMYP, IBPYP
Language instr: English

St Andrew's School
601 Penn Waller Road, Savannah Georgia GA 31410
Tel: +1 912 897 4941
Age range: 3–18
Curriculum: IBDP
Language instr: English

Hawaii

Island Pacific Academy
909 Haumea Street, Kapolei Hawaii HI 96707
Tel: +1 808 674 3523
Age range: 4–18 years
Language instr: English

Le Jardin Academy
917 Kalanianaole Highway, Kailua Hawaii HI 96734
Tel: +1 808 261 0707
Age range: 3–17
No. of pupils: 800
Curriculum: IBDP, IBMYP, IBPYP, SAT
Language instr: English, French, Spanish, Japanese, Chinese

Mid-Pacific Institute
2445 Kaala Street, Honolulu Hawaii HI 96822
Tel: +1 808 973 5020
Age range: 4–18
No. of pupils: 1500
Curriculum: IBDP, SAT, TOEFL
Language instr: English

Punahou School
1601 Punahou Street, Honolulu Hawaii HI 96822-3336
Tel: +1 808 944 5711
Age range: 4–18 years
Curriculum: USA

Idaho

Riverstone International School
5521 Warm Springs Avenue, Boise Idaho ID 83716
Tel: +1 208 424 5000
Age range: 5–19
No. of pupils: 330
Curriculum: AP, IBDP, IBMYP, IBPYP, SAT
Language instr: English

Illinois

Beacon Academy
622 Davis St., Evanston Illinois IL 60201
Tel: +1 224 999 1177
Curriculum: IBDP
Language instr: English

BRITISH INTERNATIONAL SCHOOL OF CHICAGO, LINCOLN PARK
For further details see p. 220
814 & 821 W Eastman Street, Chicago Illinois IL 60642
Tel: +1 773 907 5000
Email: admissions@bischicagolp.org
Website: www.bischicagolp.org
Principal: John Biggs
Age range: 15 months–11 years
No. of pupils: 675
Fees: Day $11,380–$38,400
Language instr: English

British International School of Chicago, South Loop
161 W. 9th Street, Chicago Illinois IL 60605
Tel: +1 773 599 2472
Age range: 3–18
No. of pupils: 651
Curriculum: IBDP
Language instr: English

Daystar Academy
1550 S. State St., Chicago Illinois IL 60605
Tel: +1 312 791 0001
Curriculum: IBDP, IBMYP, IBPYP
Language instr: English, Spanish

DePaul College Prep
3633 North California Avenue, Chicago Illinois IL 60618
Tel: +1 773 539 3600
Curriculum: IBDP
Language instr: English

EFAC French-American School of Chicago
615 W Kemper Place, Chicago Illinois IL 60614
Tel: +1 773 800 2728
Curriculum: FrenchBacc, USA

GEMS World Academy Chicago
350 E. South Water Street, Chicago Illinois IL 60601
Tel: +1 312 809 8900
Age range: 3–18 years
No. of pupils: 450
Curriculum: IBDP, IBMYP, IBPYP
Language instr: English

German International School Chicago
1447 West Montrose Ave, Chicago Illinois IL 60613
Tel: +1 773 880 8812
Curriculum: IBPYP
Language instr: English

North America

Josephinum Academy
1501 North Oakley Boulevard,
Chicago Illinois IL 60622
Tel: +1 773 276 1261
No. of pupils: 189 G189
Curriculum: ACT
Language instr: English

Lincoln Park High School
2001 North Orchard Street,
Chicago Illinois IL 60614
Tel: +1 773 534 8149
Age range: 13–19 years
No. of pupils: 2055
Curriculum: IBDP, IBMYP, IBCP
Language instr: English

Lycée Français de Chicago
1929 W Wilson Ave, Chicago
Illinois IL 60640
Tel: +1 773 665 0066
Age range: 2–18
No. of pupils: 820
Curriculum: IBDP, IBMYP,
National, FrenchBacc
Language instr: English, French

Peoria Academy
2711 West Willow Knolls Drive,
Peoria Illinois IL 61614
Tel: +1 309 692 7570
Age range: 3–13 years
Curriculum: IBMYP, IBPYP
Language instr: English, Spanish

St. Laurence High School
5556 West 77th Street,
Burbank Illinois IL 60459
Tel: +1 708 458 6900
Curriculum: IBDP
Language instr: English, Spanish

St. Matthias School
4910 N. Claremont Ave,
Chicago Illinois IL 60625
Tel: +1 773 784 0999
Curriculum: IBMYP, IBPYP
Language instr: English

Trinity College Preparatory High School
7574 West Division Street, River
Forest Illinois IL 60305
Tel: +1 708 771 8383
Curriculum: IBDP
Language instr: English

Indiana

Cathedral High School
5225 East 56th Street, Indianapolis
Indiana IN 46226
Tel: +1 317 542 1481
Language instr: English

Guerin Catholic High School
15300 Gray Road, Noblesville
Indiana IN 46062
Tel: +1 317 582 0120
Curriculum: IBDP
Language instr: English

International School of Indiana
4330 N. Michigan Road,
Indianapolis Indiana IN 46208
Tel: +1 317 923 1951
Age range: 3–18
No. of pupils: 600
Curriculum: AP, IBDP,
IBMYP, IBPYP, SAT, USA
Language instr: English,
French, Spanish, Mandarin

Kentucky

Sacred Heart Academy
3175 Lexington Road, Louisville
Kentucky KY 40206
Tel: +1 502 897 6097
Age range: G14–18
Curriculum: ACT, AP, IBDP,
IBMYP, SAT, USA
Language instr: English

Sacred Heart Model School
3107 Lexington Road, Louisville
Kentucky KY 40206
Tel: +1 502 896 3931
Language instr: English

Louisiana

Audubon Charter School - Upper School
1111 Milan Street, New Orleans
Louisiana LA 70115
Tel: +1 504 324 7110

Kehoe-France Northshore
25 Patricia Drive, Covington
Louisiana LA 70433
Tel: +1 985 892 4415
Age range: 8 weeks–13 years
Curriculum: IBMYP, IBPYP
Language instr: English

Kehoe-France School
720 Elise Avenue, Metairie
Louisiana LA 70003
Tel: +1 504 733 0472
Curriculum: IBMYP, IBPYP
Language instr: English, Spanish

St. Frederick High School
3300 Westminster Avenue,
Monroe Louisiana LA 71201
Tel: +1 318 323 9636
Curriculum: IBMYP
Language instr: English, Spanish

Maine

Academia Fórum
3 Canal Plaza, Suite 600,
Portland Maine ME 04101
Tel: +1 207 553 2327
Language instr: Spanish

Foxcroft Academy
975 West Main Street, Dover-
Foxcroft Maine ME 04426
Tel: +1 207 564 8351
Age range: 14–19 years
No. of pupils: 420
Curriculum: IBDP
Language instr: English

L'Ecole Francaise du Maine
P.O. Box 737, 99 South Freeport Road,
South Freeport Maine ME 04078
Tel: +1 207 865 3308
Age range: 3–11 years
Curriculum: IBPYP
Language instr: English, French

Maryland

Archbishop Spalding High School
8080 New Cut Road, Severn
Maryland MD 21144
Tel: +1 410 969 9105
Curriculum: IBDP
Language instr: English

German International School Washington D.C.
8617 Chateau Drive, Potomac
Maryland MD 20854
Tel: +1 301 767 3800

Maryland International School
6135 Old Washington Road,
Elkridge Maryland MD 21075
Tel: +1 410 220 3792
Age range: 6–18 years
No. of pupils: 215
Curriculum: IBDP, IBMYP, IBPYP
Language instr: English

Mercy High School Baltimore
1300 East Northern Parkway,
Baltimore Maryland MD 21239
Tel: +1 410 433 8880
Curriculum: IBDP, IBMYP
Language instr: English, Spanish

Our Lady of Good Counsel High School
17301 Old Vic Boulevard,
Olney Maryland MD 20832
Tel: +1 240 283 3200
Age range: 14–18 years
Curriculum: AP, IBDP, SAT
Language instr: English

> **ROCHAMBEAU, THE FRENCH INTERNATIONAL SCHOOL**
> *For further details see p. 230*
> 9600 Forest Road, & 9650
> Rockville Pike, Bethesda
> Maryland MD 20814
> **Tel:** +1 301 530 8260
> **Email:** admissions@rochambeau.org
> **Website:** www.rochambeau.org
> **Head of School:** Xavier Jacquenet
> **Age range:** 2–18 years
> **No. of pupils:** 1272
> **Fees:** US$26,890
> **Curriculum:** IBDP, FrenchBacc, USA
> **Language instr:** English, French

Saint James Academy
3100 Monkton Road, Monkton
Maryland MD 21111
Tel: +1 410 771 4816
Age range: 5–14
No. of pupils: 296 B151 G145
Language instr: English

Sandy Spring Friends School
16923 Norwood Rd, Sandy
Spring Maryland MD 20860
Tel: +1 301 774 7455
Age range: 3–18

Seneca Academy
15601 Germantown Road,
Darnestown Maryland MD 20874
Tel: +1 301 869 3728
Age range: 2–12
Curriculum: IBPYP
Language instr: English

Springdale Preparatory School
1000 Green Valley Rd, New
Windsor Maryland MD 21776
Tel: +1 443 671 0072
Curriculum: IBDP
Language instr: English

St. Francis of Assisi
3617 Harford Rd, Baltimore
Maryland MD 21218
Tel: +1 410 467 1683
Curriculum: IBMYP
Language instr: English

St. Timothy's School
8400 Greenspring Ave, Stevenson
Maryland MD 21153
Tel: +1 410 486 7400
No. of pupils: 200
Curriculum: IBDP, IBMYP
Language instr: English

Tarbiyah Academy
6785 Business Pky, Elkridge
Maryland MD 21075
Tel: +1 844 827 2492
Curriculum: IBPYP
Language instr: English

The Academy of the Holy Cross
4920 Strathmore Avenue,
Kensington Maryland MD 20895
Tel: +1 301 929 6459
Language instr: English

The Boys' School of St Paul's Parish
PO Box 8100, Brooklandville
Maryland MD 21022-8100
Tel: +1 410 825 4400
Curriculum: IBDP
Language instr: English

North America

The Calverton School
300 Calverton School Rd,
Huntingtown Maryland MD 20639
Tel: +1 410 535 0216
Age range: 14–18
No. of pupils: 140 B70 G70
Curriculum: IBDP
Language instr: English

Massachusetts

**British International
School of Boston**
416 Pond Street, Boston
Massachusetts MA 02130
Tel: +1 617 522 2261
Age range: 2–18 years
No. of pupils: 445
Curriculum: IBDP, IPC, UK, IGCSE
Language instr: English

CATS Academy Boston
2001 Washington Street, Braintree
Massachusetts MA 02184
Tel: +1 857 400 9700
Age range: 13–18 years
Curriculum: USA

**Chamberlain
International School**
1 Pleasant Street, PO Box 778,
Middleboro Massachusetts MA 02346
Tel: +1 508 946 9348
Age range: 11–22 years
Language instr: English

Deerfield Academy
7 Boyden Lane, P.O. Box 87, Deerfield
Massachusetts MA 01342
Tel: +1 413 772 0241
Age range: 14–19
No. of pupils: 650
Curriculum: AP, USA
Language instr: English

Eagle Hill School
242 Old Petersham Road, P.O. Box 116,
Hardwick Massachusetts MA 01037
Tel: +1 413 477 6000
Age range: 13–18
No. of pupils: 220
Curriculum: IBDP
Language instr: English

**German International
School Boston**
57 Holton Street, Boston
Massachusetts MA 02134
Tel: +1 617 783 2600
Age range: 3–18
No. of pupils: 285
Language instr: English, German

**International School
of Boston**
45 Matignon Road, Cambridge
Massachusetts MA 02140
Tel: +1 617 499 1451
Age range: 2–18 years
No. of pupils: 580
Curriculum: IBDP, FrenchBacc, USA
Language instr: English,
French, Spanish, Chinese

Notre Dame Academy, MA
1073 Main Street, Hingham
Massachusetts MA 02043-3996
Tel: +1 781 749 5930
Age range: G11–18 years
Language instr: English

**Pope Francis
Preparatory School**
134 Springfield St, Chicopee
Massachusetts MA 01013
Tel: +1 413 331 2480
Language instr: English

Stoneleigh-Burnham School
574 Bernardston Road, Greenfield
Massachusetts MA 01301
Tel: +1 413 774 2711
Age range: G11–20
No. of pupils: 137
Curriculum: IBDP, USA
Language instr: English

The Newman School
247 Marlborough Street, Boston
Massachusetts MA 02116
Tel: +1 617 267 4530
Age range: 12–19 years
No. of pupils: 250
Curriculum: IBDP, IBMYP
Language instr: English

Michigan

Coit Creative Arts Academy
617 Coit Ave NE, Grand Rapids
Michigan MI 49503
Tel: +1 616 819 2390
Curriculum: IBPYP
Language instr: English

Detroit Country Day School
22305 West 13 Mile Road, Beverly
Hills Michigan MI 48025
Tel: +1 248 646 7717
Age range: 3–18 years
No. of pupils: 650
Curriculum: AP, IBDP, SAT
Language instr: English

French School of Detroit
Meadow Lake Center, 7100
Lindenmere Drive, Bloomfield
Hills Michigan MI 48301
Tel: +1 248 203 5703

Genesee Academy
9447 Corunna Road, Swartz
Creek Michigan MI 48473
Tel: +1 810 250 7557
Age range: 4–18
No. of pupils: 265 B127 G138
Curriculum: AP, IBMYP, SAT
Language instr: English

Huda School and Montessori
32220 Franklin Road, Franklin
Michigan MI 48025
Tel: +1 248 626 0900
Curriculum: IBMYP

**Notre Dame Preparatory
School & Marist Academy**
1300 Giddings Road, Pontiac
Michigan MI 48340
Tel: +1 248 373 5300
Age range: 3–18
No. of pupils: 1081 B520 G561
Curriculum: ACT, AP, IBDP,
IBMYP, IBPYP, SAT, USA

Minnesota

**Annunciation
Catholic School**
525 W 54th St, Minneapolis
Minnesota MN 55419
Tel: +1 612 823 4394
Curriculum: IBPYP
Language instr: English

**Rochester Arts and
Sciences Academy**
400 5th Avenue SW, Rochester
Minnesota MN 55902
Tel: +1 507 206 4646
Age range: 3–12
No. of pupils: 72
Curriculum: IBPYP, USA
Language instr: English

Rochester Montessori School
5099 7th Street NW, Rochester
Minnesota MN 55901
Tel: +1 507 288 8725
Curriculum: IBMYP

**Saint John's
Preparatory School**
1857 Watertower Road, Collegeville
Minnesota MN 56321
Tel: +1 320 363 3315
Language instr: English

**The International
School of Minnesota**
6385 Beach Road, Eden Prairie
Minnesota MN 55344
Tel: +1 952 918 1800
Age range: 4–18 years
Curriculum: ACT, AP, SAT

Missouri

MAP St. Louis
3840 Washington Boulevard,
St. Louis Missouri MO 63108
Tel: +1 314 391 2994
Age range: 12–18 years
Curriculum: IBDP
Language instr: English

Montana

**Missoula International
School**
1100 Harrison Street, Missoula
Montana MT 59802
Tel: +1 406 542 9924
Age range: 3–14
No. of pupils: 190
Curriculum: IBMYP, IBPYP
Language instr: Spanish, English

New Hampshire

New Hampton School
70 Main Street, New Hampton
New Hampshire NH 03256
Tel: +1 603-677-3400
Age range: 14–19 years
No. of pupils: 330
Curriculum: IBDP
Language instr: English

New Jersey

**All Saints Episcopal
Day School**
707 Washington Street, Hoboken
New Jersey NJ 07030
Tel: +1 201 792 0736
Age range: 4–13 years
Curriculum: IBMYP, IBPYP
Language instr: English

Donovan Catholic
711 Hooper Ave, Toms River
New Jersey NJ 08753
Tel: +1 732 349 8801
Curriculum: IBDP
Language instr: English

**French American
School of Princeton**
75 Mapleton Road, Princeton
New Jersey NJ 08540
Tel: +1 609 430 3001
Age range: 3–13 years

Learning Ladders
35 Hudson Street, Jersey City
New Jersey NJ 07302
Tel: +1 201 885 2960
Curriculum: IBPYP
Language instr: English

Newark Academy
91 South Orange Avenue,
Livingston New Jersey NJ 07039
Tel: +1 973 992 7000
Age range: 11–18
No. of pupils: 582
Curriculum: AP, IBDP
Language instr: English

Princeton Junior School
90 Fackler Road, Princeton
New Jersey NJ 08540
Tel: +1 609 924 8126
Curriculum: IBPYP
Language instr: English

Princeton Montessori School
487 Cherry Valley Road, Princeton
New Jersey NJ 08540
Tel: +1 609 924 4594
Curriculum: IBMYP
Language instr: English

Rutgers Preparatory School
1345 Easton Avenue, Somerset
New Jersey NJ 08873
Tel: +1 732 545 5600
Age range: 3–18
No. of pupils: 640
Curriculum: AP

North America

New Jersey

Solomon Schechter Day School of Bergen County
275 McKinley Avenue, New Milford New Jersey NJ 07646
Tel: +1 201 262 9898
Age range: 4–14 years
Language instr: English

St Dominic Academy
2572 Kennedy Boulevard, Jersey City New Jersey NJ 07304
Tel: +1 201 434 5938
No. of pupils: 525
Curriculum: AP
Language instr: English

Tessa International School
720 Monroe Street, Hoboken New Jersey NJ 07030
Tel: +1 201 755 5585
Curriculum: IBPYP
Language instr: French, Spanish

The Red Oaks School
340 Speedwell Ave., Morristown New Jersey NJ 07960
Tel: +1 973 998 9424
Curriculum: IBMYP
Language instr: English

Waldo International School
110 1st Street, Jersey City New Jersey NJ 07302
Tel: +1 201 721 6000
Age range: 4 months–13 years
Curriculum: IBPYP
Language instr: English

Waterfront Montessori
150 Warren St., Suite 108, Jersey City New Jersey NJ 7302
Tel: +1 201 333 5600
Curriculum: IBMYP
Language instr: English

YingHua International School
25 Laurel Avenue, Kingston New Jersey NJ 08528
Tel: +1 609 375 8015
Age range: 18 months–13 years
No. of pupils: 80
Curriculum: IBPYP
Language instr: English, Chinese

New Mexico

New Mexico International School
8650 Alameda Blvd NE, Albuquerque New Mexico NM 87122
Tel: +1 505 503 7670
Curriculum: IBPYP
Language instr: English

UWC-USA
State Rte 65, Montezuma New Mexico NM 87731
Tel: +1 505 454 4252
Age range: 17–19
No. of pupils: 235
Curriculum: IBDP
Language instr: English

New York

Archbishop Walsh Academy
208 North 24th Street, Olean New York NY 14760
Tel: +1 716 372 8122
Age range: 3–18 years
No. of pupils: 155

Aurora Waldorf School
525 West Falls Road, West Falls New York NY 14170
Tel: +1 716 655 2029
Age range: 3–13 years

Bishop Ludden Junior Senior High School
815 Fay Road, Syracuse New York NY 13219
Tel: +1 315 468 2591
Curriculum: IBDP
Language instr: English

Brooklyn Friends School
375 Pearl Street, Brooklyn, New York City New York NY 11201
Tel: +1 718 852 1029
Age range: 3–18 years
Curriculum: IBDP
Language instr: English

Buffalo Academy of the Sacred Heart
3860 Main Street, Buffalo New York NY 14226
Tel: +1 716 834 2101
Curriculum: IBDP
Language instr: English

Convent of the Sacred Heart
1 East 91 Street, New York City New York NY 10128
Tel: +1 212 722 4745
Age range: G3–18 years

DWIGHT SCHOOL
For further details see p. 221
291 Central Park West, New York New York NY 10024
Tel: +1 212 724 6360
Email: admissions@dwight.edu
Website: dwight.edu/newyork
Chancellor: Stephen H. Spahn
Age range: 2–18 years
No. of pupils: 910
Fees: US$63,900
Curriculum: ACT, IBDP, IBMYP, IBPYP, SAT, TOEFL
Language instr: English

EF Academy New York
582 Columbus Avenue, Thornwood New York NY 10594
Tel: +1 914 495 6056
Age range: 13–18 years
Curriculum: IBDP, National
Language instr: English

French-American School of New York
320 East Boston Post Road, Mamaroneck New York NY 10543
Tel: +1 914 250 0000
Age range: 3–18 years
No. of pupils: 750
Curriculum: AP, IBDP, National, FrenchBacc, SAT
Language instr: English, French

Hackley School
293 Benedict Ave, Tarrytown New York NY 10591
Tel: +1 914 631 0128
Language instr: English

International School of Brooklyn
477 Court Street, Brooklyn, New York New York NY 11231
Tel: +1 718 369 3023
Age range: 3–14 years
No. of pupils: 358
Curriculum: IBMYP, IBPYP
Language instr: English, French, Spanish

Kennedy International School
225 East 43rd Street, New York New York NY 10017
Tel: +1 212 681 1877
Age range: 3–18 years
Curriculum: IBDP
Language instr: English, French

La Scuola d'Italia Guglielmo Marconi
12 East 96th Street, New York New York NY 10128
Tel: +1 212 369 3290
Age range: 2–18 years
No. of pupils: 170
Curriculum: IBDP
Language instr: English, Italian

Léman Manhattan Preparatory School
41 Broad Street, New York New York NY 10004
Tel: +1 212 232 0266
Age range: 16 months–18 years
No. of pupils: 900
Curriculum: IBDP
Language instr: English

Lycée Français de New York
505 East 75th Street, New York New York NY 10021
Tel: +1 212 439 3890
Age range: 4–17
No. of pupils: 1350
Curriculum: National, FrenchBacc
Language instr: French, English

NORD ANGLIA INTERNATIONAL SCHOOL, NEW YORK
For further details see p. 228
111 E 22nd Street, New York New York NY 10010
Tel: +1 212 600 2010
Email: info@ny.nae.school
Website: www.naisny.com
Principal: Jimmy Frawley
Age range: 2–14 years
No. of pupils: 150
Fees: US$49,100
Curriculum: IPC, UK

Pine Street School
25 Pine Street, New York New York NY 10005
Tel: +1 212 235 2325
Age range: 2–9
No. of pupils: 150
Curriculum: IBPYP
Language instr: English, Spanish, Mandarin

Portledge School
355 Duck Pond Road, Locust Valley New York NY 11560-2499
Tel: +1 516 750 3100
Curriculum: IBDP
Language instr: English

Saint Edmund Preparatory High School
2474 Ocean Avenue, Brooklyn, New York New York NY 11229
Tel: +1 718 743 6100
Curriculum: IBDP
Language instr: English

The British International School of New York
20 Waterside Plaza, New York New York NY 10010
Tel: +1 212 481 2700
Age range: 3–14
No. of pupils: 290
Curriculum: IBMYP, IBPYP, SAT, UK
Language instr: English

THE ÉCOLE
For further details see p. 234
115 East 22nd Street, New York New York NY 10010
Tel: +1 646 410 2238
Email: bonjour@theEcole.org
Website: www.theecole.org
Head of School: Jean-Yves Vesseau
Age range: 2–14 years
No. of pupils: 360
Fees: Day $44,700

United Nations International School
24-50 Franklin D Roosevelt Drive, New York New York NY 10010
Tel: +1 212 684 7400
Age range: 5–18
No. of pupils: 1573 B763 G778
Curriculum: IBDP
Language instr: English

York Prep School
40 West 68th Street, New York New York NY 10023
Tel: +1 212 362 0400
Age range: 11–18 years
Curriculum: USA
Language instr: English

North Carolina

Charlotte Country Day School
1440 Carmel Road, Charlotte North Carolina NC 28226
Tel: 0017049434500
Age range: 4–18
No. of pupils: 1634
Curriculum: AP, IBDP
Language instr: English

Hickory Day School
2535 21st Ave NE, Hickory North Carolina NC 28601
Tel: +1 828 256 9492
Age range: 4–13
Curriculum: IBPYP
Language instr: English

North America

Morganton Day School
305 West Concord Street, Morganton
North Carolina NC 28655
Tel: +1 828 437 6782
Age range: 4–13
No. of pupils: 100 B45 G55
Curriculum: IBPYP
Language instr: English

The British International School of Charlotte
7000 Endhaven Lane, Charlotte
North Carolina NC 28277
Tel: +1 704 341 3236
Age range: 1.5–18
No. of pupils: 187
Curriculum: IBDP, UK

The Montessori School of Raleigh
408 Andrews Chapel Road,
Durham North Carolina NC 27703
Tel: +1 919 848 1545
Curriculum: IBDP
Language instr: English, Spanish

Ohio

Central Catholic High School
2550 Cherry Street, Toldeo
Ohio OH 43608
Tel: +1 419 255 2280
Age range: 13–18
Language instr: English

Discovery School
855 Millsboro Rd, Mansfield
Ohio OH 44903
Tel: +1 419 756 8880
Curriculum: IBPYP
Language instr: English

Kent State University Child Development Center
775 Loop Rd., Kent Ohio OH 44242
Tel: +1 330 672 2559
Age range: 18 months–6 years
No. of pupils: 150
Curriculum: IBPYP
Language instr: English

Notre Dame Academy, OH
3535 W Sylvania Avenue,
Toledo Ohio OH 43623
Tel: +1 419 475 9359
Curriculum: IBDP
Language instr: English

Purcell Marian High School
2935 Hackberry Street,
Cincinnati Ohio OH 45206
Tel: +1 513 751 1230
Curriculum: IBDP
Language instr: English

St Edward High School
13500 Detroit Avenue,
Lakewood Ohio OH 44107
Tel: +1 216 221 3776
Age range: B14–18
No. of pupils: 945
Curriculum: IBDP, IBMYP
Language instr: English

Oregon

French International School of Oregon
8500 NW Johnson Street,
Portland Oregon OR 97229
Tel: +1 503 292 7776
Curriculum: IBMYP, IBPYP
Language instr: English, French

German International School of Portland
3900 SW Murray Blvd, Beaverton
Oregon OR 97005
Tel: +1 503 626 9089
Curriculum: IBPYP
Language instr: German, English

International School of Portland
025 SW Sherman Street,
Portland Oregon OR 97210
Tel: +1 503 226 2496
Age range: 3–11
Curriculum: IBPYP
Language instr: Chinese, Japanese, Spanish

Seven Peaks School
19660 SW Mountaineer Way,
Bend Oregon OR 97702
Tel: +1 541 382 7755
Curriculum: IBMYP, IBPYP
Language instr: English

Pennsylvania

French International School of Philadelphia EFIP
Upper School, 23 City Avenue, Bala
Cynwyd Pennsylvania PA 19004
Tel: +1 610 667 1284

George School
1690 Newtown Langhorne Rd,
Newtown Pennsylvania PA 18940-2414
Tel: +1 215 579 6500
Age range: 13–19 years
Curriculum: ACT, AP, IBDP, SAT
Language instr: English

Harrisburg Academy
10 Erford Road, Wormleysburg
Pennsylvania PA 17043
Tel: +1 717 763 7811
Age range: 3–18 years
Curriculum: IBDP, IBMYP, IBPYP
Language instr: English

Mercyhurst Preparatory School
538 East Grandview Boulevard,
Erie Pennsylvania PA 16504
Tel: +1 814 824 2323
Age range: 13–18 years
No. of pupils: 441
Curriculum: ACT, IBDP, SAT, USA
Language instr: English

Westtown School
975 Westtown Rd, West Chester
Pennsylvania PA 19382
Tel: +1 610 399 0123
Language instr: English

Rhode Island

Prout School
4640 Tower Hill Road, Wakefield
Rhode Island RI 02879
Tel: +1 401 789 9262
Age range: 14–18
No. of pupils: 647
Curriculum: IBDP
Language instr: English

St. Andrew's School (RI)
63 Federal Road, Barrington
Rhode Island RI 02806
Tel: +1 401 246 1230
Curriculum: IBDP, IBMYP
Language instr: English

The French American School of Rhode Island
75 John Street, Providence
Rhode Island RI 02906
Tel: +1 401 274 3325
Age range: 4–13 years

South Carolina

Christ Church Episcopal School
245 Cavalier Drive, Greenville
South Carolina SC 29607
Tel: +1 864 299 1522
Age range: 5–19
No. of pupils: 1093
Curriculum: IBDP, IBPYP
Language instr: English

Christ Our King-Stella Maris School
1183 Russell Drive, Mt Pleasant
South Carolina SC 29464
Tel: +1 843 884 4721

Spartanburg Day School
1701 Skylyn Drive, Spartanburg
South Carolina SC 29307
Tel: +1 864 582 7539
No. of pupils: 500
Curriculum: IBPYP
Language instr: English

Tennessee

Lausanne Collegiate School
1381 West Massey Road,
Memphis Tennessee TN 38120
Tel: +1 901 474 1001
Curriculum: IBDP, IBMYP, IBPYP
Language instr: English

Texas

Alcuin School
6144 Churchill Way, Dallas
Texas TX 75230
Tel: +1 972 239 1745
Age range: 18 months–18 years
No. of pupils: 537 B247 G290
Curriculum: IBDP, IBMYP, SAT
Language instr: English

Austin Eco Bilingual School (Austin EBS) USA
8707 Mountain Crest Dr,
Austin Texas TX 78735
Tel: +1 512 299 5731
Curriculum: IBPYP
Language instr: English

Brighter Horizons Academy
3145 Medical Plaza Dr.,
Garland Texas TX 75044
Tel: +1 972 675 2062
Curriculum: IBPYP
Language instr: English

British International School of Houston
2203 North Westgreen Boulevard,
Katy Texas TX 77449
Tel: +1 713 290 9025
Age range: 3–18
No. of pupils: 1200
Curriculum: IBDP, IBCP, UK, GCSE, IGCSE
Language instr: English

CC Mason Elementary
1501 N. Lakeline Blvd, Cedar
Park Texas TX 78613
Tel: +1 512 570 5500
Curriculum: IBPYP
Language instr: English

Cunae International School LLC
5655 Creekside Forest Drive,
Spring Texas TX 77389
Tel: +1 281 516 3770
Curriculum: IBDP, IBPYP

Dallas International School
17811 Waterview Pkwy,
Dallas Texas TX 75252
Tel: +1 469 250 0001
Curriculum: IBDP, FrenchBacc, SAT
Language instr: English, French

Esprit International School
4890 W Panther Creek Dr, The
Woodlands Texas TX 77381
Tel: +1 281 298 9200
Curriculum: IBPYP
Language instr: English

International School of Texas
4402 Hudson Bend, Austin
Texas TX 78734
Tel: +1 512 351 3403
Curriculum: IBMYP, IBPYP
Language instr: English, Spanish

Lincoln Middle School
500 Mulberry Ave., El
Paso Texas TX 79932
Tel: +1 915 236 3400
Curriculum: IBMYP
Language instr: English, Spanish

Lycée International de Houston
15950 Park Row, Houston
Texas TX 77084
Tel: +1 832 474 1013
Curriculum: IBDP
Language instr: English, French

North America

Magellan International School
7938 Great Northern Boulevard, Austin Texas TX 78757
Tel: +1 512 782 2327
Age range: 3–14
No. of pupils: 465
Curriculum: IBMYP, IBPYP
Language instr: English, Spanish, Mandarin

St. Stephens Episcopal School Houston
1800 Sul Ross Street, Houston Texas TX 77098
Tel: +1 713 821 9100
Language instr: English

Temple Emanu-El
8500 Hillcrest Road, Dallas Texas TX 75225
Tel: +1 214 706 0000
Curriculum: IBPYP
Language instr: English

The Awty International School
7455 Awty School Lane, Houston Texas TX 77055
Tel: +1 713 686 4850
Age range: 3–18 years
Curriculum: IBDP, FrenchBacc
Language instr: English, French

The Clariden School
100 Clariden Ranch Road, Southlake Texas TX 76092
Tel: +1 682 237 0400
Curriculum: IBDP
Language instr: English

The Post Oak School
4600 Bissonnet Street, Bellaire Texas TX 77401
Tel: +1 713 661 6688
Age range: 14 months–18 years
No. of pupils: 502
Curriculum: IBDP
Language instr: English

THE VILLAGE SCHOOL
For further details see p. 235
13051 Whittington Drive, Houston Texas TX 77077
Tel: +1 281 496 7900
Email: admissions@thevillageschool.com
Website: www.thevillageschool.com
Head of School: Bill Delbrugge
Age range: 2–18 years
Curriculum: AP, IBDP, USA
Language instr: English

The Westwood School
14340 Proton Road, Dallas Texas TX 75244
Tel: +1 972 239 8598
Age range: 1–19
No. of pupils: 280
Curriculum: IBDP
Language instr: English

The Woodlands Preparatory School
27440 Kuykendahl Road, Tomball Texas TX 77375
Tel: +1 936 548 9442
Language instr: English

Westlake Academy
2600 J.T. Ottinger Road, Westlake Texas TX 76262
Tel: +1 817 4905757
Age range: 5–18 years
No. of pupils: 879
Curriculum: ACT, AP, IBDP, IBMYP, IBPYP, SAT, USA
Language instr: English

Yorkshire Academy
14120 Memorial Drive, Houston Texas TX 77079
Tel: +1 281 531 6088
Curriculum: USA

Vermont

Long Trail School
1045 Kirby Hollow Road, Dorset Vermont VT 05251
Tel: +1 802 867 5717
Age range: 10–19
Curriculum: IBDP
Language instr: English

Virginia

Carlisle School
PO Box 5388, Martinsville Virginia VA 24115
Tel: +1 276 632 7288
Age range: 3–19
No. of pupils: 430
Curriculum: AP, SAT
Language instr: English

K12 International Academy
2300 Corporate Park Drive, Herndon Virginia VA 20171
Tel: +1 877 512 7748

King Abdullah Academy
2949 Education Dr, Herndon Virginia VA 20171
Tel: +1 571 351 5520
Curriculum: IBDP, IBMYP, IBPYP
Language instr: Arabic, English

Mary Passage Middle School
400 Atkinson Way, Newport News Virginia VA 23608
Tel: +1 757 886 7600
Language instr: English

Massanutten Military Academy
614 South Main Street, Woodstock Virginia VA 22664
Tel: +1 540 459 2167
Language instr: English

Millwood School
15100 Millwood School Lane, Midlothian Virginia VA 23112
Tel: +1 804 639 3200
Age range: 4–18 years
Curriculum: IBMYP
Language instr: English

Norfolk Academy
1585 Wesleyan Drive, Norfolk Virginia VA 23502
Tel: +1 757 461 6236

Saint Mary's Catholic School
9501 Gayton Road, Richmond Virginia VA 23229
Tel: +1 804 740 1048
No. of pupils: 140
Curriculum: IBMYP
Language instr: English

Strelitz International Academy
5000 Corporate Woods Driv, Suite 180, Virginia Beach Virginia VA 23462
Tel: +1 757 424 4327
Curriculum: IBPYP
Language instr: English, Hebrew

The Hague School
739 Yarmouth St., Norfolk Virginia VA 23510
Tel: +1 757 317 3033
Curriculum: IBDP
Language instr: English, French

Trinity Episcopal School
3850 Pittaway Road, Richmond Virginia VA 23235
Tel: +1 804 272 5864
Age range: 13–18
No. of pupils: 503
Curriculum: AP, IBDP
Language instr: English

Trinity Lutheran School
6812 River Road, Newport News Virginia VA 23607
Tel: +1 757 245 2576
Language instr: English

Williamsburg Christian Academy
101 School House Lane, Williamsburg Virginia VA 23188
Tel: +1 757 568 9322
Age range: 14–19 years
No. of pupils: 200
Curriculum: IBDP, IBMYP, IBPYP
Language instr: English, Spanish

Washington

Annie Wright Schools
827 N Tacoma Avenue, Tacoma Washington WA 98403
Tel: +1 253 272 2216
Age range: 3–18 years
Curriculum: IBDP, IBMYP, IBPYP
Language instr: English

Bellevue Children's Academy
14600 NE 24th St., Bellevue Washington WA 98007
Tel: +1 425 649 0791
Curriculum: IBPYP
Language instr: English

Forest Ridge School of the Sacred Heart
4800 139th Avenue SE, Bellevue Washington WA 98006
Tel: +1 425 641 0700

French American School of Puget Sound
3795 East Mercer Way, Mercer Island Washington WA 98040
Tel: +1 206 275 3533
Curriculum: IPC

Saint George's School
2929 W. Waikiki Road, Spokane Washington WA 99208
Tel: +1 509 466 1636 Ext:331
Curriculum: IBDP
Language instr: English

Soundview School
6515 196th Street SW, Lynnwood Washington WA 98036
Tel: +1 425 778 8572
Curriculum: IBMYP, IBPYP
Language instr: English

St. Luke School
17533 St Luke Place N, Shoreline Washington WA 98133
Tel: +1 206 542 1133
Curriculum: IBMYP, IBPYP
Language instr: English

Washington Preparatory School
18323 Bothell-Everett Highway, Suite 220, Bothell Washington WA 98012
Tel: +1 425 892 8669
Curriculum: IBDP
Language instr: English

West Sound Academy
16571 Creative Drive NE, Poulsbo Washington WA 98370
Tel: +1 360 598 5954
Curriculum: IBDP

Willows Preparatory School
12280 NE Woodinville-Redmond Rd, Redmond Washington WA 98052
Tel: +1 425 649 0791
Curriculum: IBDP, IBMYP
Language instr: English

North America

Wisconsin

Catholic Memorial High School
601 East College Avenue, Waukesha Wisconsin WI 53186
Tel: +1 262 542 7101
No. of pupils: 750
Curriculum: IBDP, IBCP
Language instr: English

Holy Family School
1204 S. Fisk Street, Green Bay Wisconsin WI 54304
Tel: +1 920 494 1931
Curriculum: IBMYP
Language instr: English

Madison Country Day School
5606 River Road, Waunakee Wisconsin WI 53597
Tel: +1 608 850 6000
Age range: 4–19
No. of pupils: 456
Curriculum: IBDP, IBMYP, IBPYP
Language instr: English, Spanish

Notre Dame de la Baie Academy
610 Maryhill Drive, Green Bay Wisconsin WI 54303
Tel: +1 920 429 6100
Age range: 14–18
No. of pupils: 731 B377 G354
Curriculum: ACT, IBDP, IBCP, USA
Language instr: English

St. Joan Antida High School
1341 N. Cass Street, Milwaukee Wisconsin WI 53202
Tel: +1 414 272 8423
Language instr: English

Wyoming

Mountain Academy
700 Coyote Canyon Road, Jackson Wyoming WY 83001
Tel: +1 307 733 3729
Age range: 4–18 years
Curriculum: IBDP
Language instr: English

VIRGIN ISLANDS (US)

Antilles School
7280 Frenchman's Bay, St Thomas 802
Tel: +1 340 776 1600
Age range: 2–17/18
No. of pupils: 500
Curriculum: USA

Good Hope Country Day School
Rt 1 Box 6199, Kings Hill VI 00850
Tel: +1 340 778 1974

Virgin Islands Montessori School & Peter Gruber International Academy
6936 Vessup Lane, St Thomas VI 00802
Tel: +1 340 775 6360
Curriculum: IBDP, IBMYP
Language instr: English

International schools in South America

Schools ordered A–Z by Country

Key to directory

Country

Name of school or college

Indicates that this school has a profile

Address and contact number

Head's name

Age range

Number of pupils.
B = boys G = girls VIth = sixth form

Fees per annum.
Day = fees for day pupils.
WB = fees for weekly boarders.
FB = fees for full boarders.

Curriculum

Language of instruction

Memberships/Accreditation

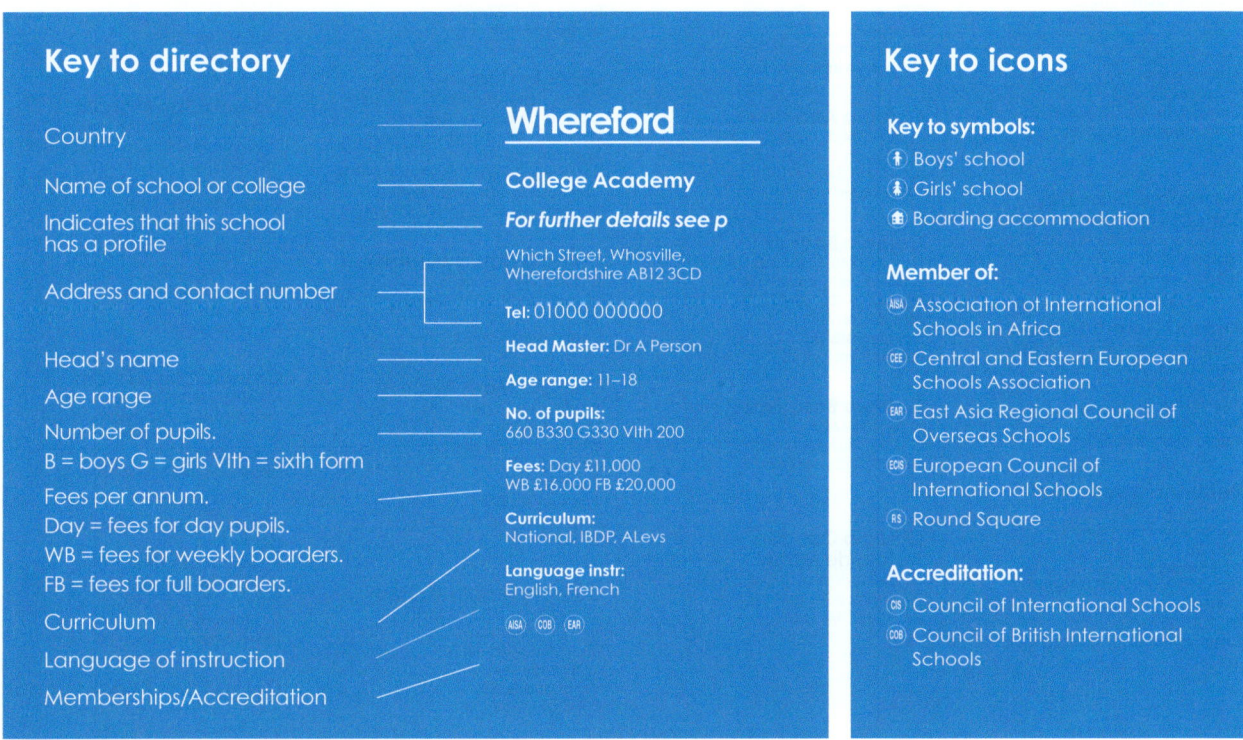

Whereford

College Academy

For further details see p

Which Street, Whosville,
Wherefordshire AB12 3CD

Tel: 01000 000000

Head Master: Dr A Person

Age range: 11–18

No. of pupils:
660 B330 G330 VIth 200

Fees: Day £11,000
WB £16,000 FB £20,000

Curriculum:
National, IBDP, ALevs

Language instr:
English, French

(AISA) (COB) (EAR)

Key to icons

Key to symbols:
- Boys' school
- Girls' school
- Boarding accommodation

Member of:
- (AISA) Association of International Schools in Africa
- (CEE) Central and Eastern European Schools Association
- (EAR) East Asia Regional Council of Overseas Schools
- (ECIS) European Council of International Schools
- (RS) Round Square

Accreditation:
- (CIS) Council of International Schools
- (COB) Council of British International Schools

Please note: Schools are coeducational day schools unless otherwise indicated

D425

South America

ARGENTINA

Aberdare College
Av. Francia 1245, Bella Vista,
1661 San Miguel, Buenos Aires
Tel: +54 11 4666 8813
Curriculum: IGCSE

Academia Arguello
Avda Rafael Nunez 5675,
Arguello, 5021 Córdoba
Tel: +54 3543 421010/420387
Age range: 4–16
No. of pupils: 300
Curriculum: IGCSE

Asociación Cultural Pestalozzi
R Freire 1882, 1428 Ciudad
de Buenos Aires
Tel: +54 11 4555 3688
Age range: 2–18
No. of pupils: 346
Curriculum: IBDP
Language instr: Spanish, German

Asociación Escuelas Lincoln
Andres Ferreyra 4073, 1637
La Lucila, Buenos Aires
Tel: +54 11 4851 1700
Age range: 4–18
No. of pupils: 702 B347 G355
Curriculum: ACT, IBDP, SAT, USA
Language instr: English, Spanish

Austin Eco Bilingual School (Austin EBS) Argentina
Porto 463, Campana, Buenos Aires
Tel: +54 3489 462203/4
Curriculum: IBDP
Language instr: Spanish, English

Barker College
Mitre 131, 1832 Lomas de
Zamora, Buenos Aires
Tel: +54 11 4292 1107
Age range: 2–18
No. of pupils: 600
Curriculum: IGCSE, ALevs
Language instr: Spanish,
English, French

Bartolome Mitre Day School - Moreno
Padre Fahy and Miero, 1744
Moreno, Buenos Aires
Tel: +54 237 4623698

Bede's Grammar School
Alejandro Korn y Panama, 1667
Tortuguitas, Buenos Aires
Tel: +54 348 4477 355
Age range: 3–18
No. of pupils: 420
Curriculum: IGCSE

Belgrano Day School
Juramento 3035, 1428
Ciudad de Buenos Aires
Tel: +54 11 4781 6011
Age range: 2–18
No. of pupils: 1160 B612 G548
Curriculum: National,
UK, IGCSE, ALevs
Language instr: Spanish, English
(RS)

Boston College (Childrens School)
Primario / EGB - Secundario, Charcas
3949, 1425 Ciudad de Buenos Aires
Tel: +54 11 4833 2607
Curriculum: National, UK, IGCSE

British School Cordoba-Cerro de las Rosas
Jose Roque Funes 1511, Córdoba
Tel: + 54 351 4812104

Buenos Aires International Christian Academy
1646 San Fernando, Buenos Aires
Tel: +54 11 4549 1300
Age range: 2–18
No. of pupils: 170
Curriculum: AP, USA

Cardinal Newman College
Eliseo Reclus 1133, 1609 Boulogne
Sur Mer, Buenos Aires
Tel: +54 11 4737 0042
Age range: 14–18
Curriculum: IGCSE

Caxton School (Escuela William Caxton)
José María Paz 3540, 1636
Olivos, Buenos Aires
Tel: +54 11 4799 6424

Chaltel College
Lucio Melendez 1617, 1611 Don
Torcuato, Buenos Aires
Tel: +54 11 4748 3153
Age range: 4–17
Curriculum: IGCSE

Colegio Alemán Córdoba
Recta Martinoli 6230 (Esq. Neper),
5021 Argüello, Córdoba
Tel: +54 35 4342 0834
Curriculum: IBDP, IBPYP
Language instr: Spanish

Colegio Arrayanes
Mateo Churich y Salvo s/n,
1619 Garín, Buenos Aires
Tel: +54 (0)348 4471283
Curriculum: National

Colegio Bayard
Castex 3348, Salguero, 2969
Ciudad de Buenos Aires
Tel: +54 11 4803 0902
Age range: 4–19
No. of pupils: 200
Curriculum: IGCSE

Colegio Bosque del Plata
Calle 501 e/ 28 y 30,
Gonnet, Buenos Aires
Tel: +54 (0)221 4845997
(symbol)

Colegio Carmen Arriola de Marin
Av del Libertador 17.115, 1642
San Isidro, Buenos Aires
Tel: +54 11 4743 0028

Colegio Confluencia
Dr. Luis Federico Leloir
210, 8300 Neuquén
Tel: +54 299 442 2417
Age range: 4–19
No. of pupils: 300
Curriculum: IGCSE

Colegio De La Salle
Ayacucho 665, 1025 Ciudad
de Buenos Aires
Tel: +54 011 4374 6449
No. of pupils: 286
Curriculum: IBDP
Language instr: Spanish

Colegio de Todos Los Santos
Thames 798, Villa Adelina, 1607
San Isidro, Buenos Aires
Tel: +54 114 766 3878
Age range: 2–18
No. of pupils: 700
Curriculum: IBDP
Language instr: Spanish, English

Colegio El Buen Ayre
Av. Uruguay 2820, Beccar,
Buenos Aires
Tel: +54 11 4723 0088
Curriculum: National, IGCSE
(symbol)

Colegio Esquiú
11 de Septiembre 1240, 1426
Ciudad de Buenos Aires
Tel: +54 11 4784 3222
Age range: 4–19
No. of pupils: 300
Curriculum: IGCSE

Colegio Franco Argentino
Lavalle 1067, Acassuso, 1641
San Isidro, Buenos Aires
Tel: +54 11 4792 4628
Language instr: Spanish

Colegio Lincoln
Olleros 2283, Belgrano,
Ciudad de Buenos Aires
Tel: +54 11 4772 0108
Age range: 2–18
No. of pupils: 800 B400 G400 VIth35
Curriculum: IBDP, National, UK
Language instr: Spanish, English

Colegio Maria Montessori
Segurola 949, Turdera, 1833
Ciudad de Buenos Aires
Tel: +54 11 4294 2068
Curriculum: National, UK

Colegio Mark Twain
José Roque Funes 1525,
5009 Córdoba
Tel: +54 351 432 3847
Age range: 3–17
No. of pupils: VIth25
Curriculum: IBDP
Language instr: Spanish
(symbol)

Colegio Martin Y Omar
25 de Mayo 170, 1642 San
Isidro, Buenos Aires
Tel: +54 11 4743 6888
Age range: 4–19
No. of pupils: 500
Curriculum: IGCSE

Colegio Montessori de Luján
Mitre 1247, Lujan, Buenos Aires
Tel: +51 23 2343 3981
Curriculum: IBDP
Language instr: English, Spanish

Colegio Padre Luis Maria Etcheverry Boneo
Juncal 2131, 1125 Ciudad
de Buenos Aires
Tel: +54 11 4822 3687
Language instr: Spanish
(symbol)

Colegio Palermo Chico
Thames 2037/41, 1425
Ciudad de Buenos Aires
Tel: +54 114 774 3975
Curriculum: IBDP
Language instr: Spanish

Colegio Patris
Calle 146 entre 446 y Arroyo
Carnaval, City Bell, 1896
La Plata, Buenos Aires
Tel: +54 221 475 1091
Age range: 4–19
No. of pupils: 300
Curriculum: IGCSE

Colegio San Ignacio
Guardias Nacionales 1400,
5806 Río Cuarto, Córdoba
Tel: +54 (358) 464 8484/0802
Age range: 12–18
No. of pupils: 125 B60 G65
Curriculum: IBDP, IGCSE
Language instr: Spanish, English
(symbol)

Colegio San Jorge
Godoy Cruz, Pedro J Godoy
1191, 5547 Mendoza
Tel: +54 2 614 287 247
Curriculum: IBDP
Language instr: Spanish

Colegio San Marcos
Nivel Secundario, Jorge Miles 153,
1842 Monte Grande, Buenos Aires
Tel: +54 11 4296 3138
Curriculum: IBDP, National, UK, IGCSE
Language instr: Spanish

Colegio San Pablo
25 de Mayo 430 E, 5400 San Juan
Tel: +54 264 421 9948
Age range: 5–19
No. of pupils: 475

Colegio San Patricio
Moreno y Las Higueritas, 4107
Yerba Buena, Tucumán
Tel: +54 381 4250 708
Curriculum: IBDP
Language instr: Spanish

Colegio San Patricio de Luján
Acceso Oeste 2145,
Lujan, Buenos Aires
Tel: +54 23 2343 7998
Curriculum: IBDP
Language instr: Spanish

Colegio San Pedro Apostol
Av. Piamonte s/n, B. Chateau
Carreras, 5016 Córdoba
Tel: +54 351 484 6584

South America

Colegio Santa María
Coronel Suárez 453, 4400 Salta
Tel: +54 387 421 3127
Curriculum: IBDP
Language instr: Spanish

Colegio Tarbut
Rosales 3019, 1636 Olivos, Buenos Aires
Tel: +54 11 4794 3444
Curriculum: IBDP, IGCSE
Language instr: Spanish

Deutsche Schule Temperley
Av. Fernández 27, 1834
Temperley, Buenos Aires
Tel: +54 114244 2832
Curriculum: IBDP
Language instr: English, Spanish

Dover High School
San Martín y Ruta 26, 1623
Maschwitz, Buenos Aires
Tel: +54 93488 441106
Curriculum: IBDP
Language instr: English, Spanish

Escuela Goethe Rosario
España 440, 2000 Rosario, Santa Fe
Tel: +54 34 1426 3024
Age range: 2–18
No. of pupils: 80 B30 G50
Curriculum: IBDP
Language instr: Spanish

Escuela Privada Ranelagh
Avenida Eva Perón (ex Sevilla) 3842, 1886 Ranelagh, Buenos Aires
Tel: +54 11 4258 8509

Escula Argentina Modelo - Sede EAM / Sede NORTE
Riobamba 1059, Ciudad de Buenos Aires
Tel: + 54 11 4811 2705
Curriculum: National, IGCSE

Florida Day School
Gral. Justo José de Urquiza 2151, Florida, 1602 Ciudad de Buenos Aires
Tel: +54 11 4796 1122
Curriculum: National, IGCSE

Godspell College
Autopista Panamericana, KM 41 - Ramal Rilar, The Marigolds, 2600 Tortugitas, Buenos Aires
Tel: +54 2320 407676
Age range: 2–17
No. of pupils: 800
Curriculum: USA

Goethe Schule
Reclus 2250, 1609 Boulogne
Buenos Aires
Tel: +54 11 4513 7700

Holmberg Schule
Sarmiento 679, Quilmes, Buenos Aires
Tel: +54 11 4254 8583
Curriculum: IBDP
Language instr: German, Spanish

Hölters Schule Villa Ballester
Calle 65 No 5886, Ciudad de Buenos Aires
Tel: +54 11 4768 0480

Holy Trinity College
Gascón 544, 7600 Mar del Plata, Buenos Aires
Tel: +54 223 486 3471
Age range: 2–18
No. of pupils: 637 B328 G309
Curriculum: IBDP
Language instr: English, Spanish

Instituto Ballester
Calle 69 N° 5140 (ex San Martín 444), 1653 Villa Ballester, Buenos Aires
Tel: +54 11 4768 0760
No. of pupils: 1583
Curriculum: IBDP
Language instr: Spanish, German

Instituto Santa Brígida
Av Gaona 2068, 1416
Ciudad de Buenos Aires
Tel: +54 1 145 811 268
No. of pupils: B150 G141
Curriculum: IBDP
Language instr: Spanish

Instituto Wolfsohn
2972, AEB, Amenábar, 1429
Ciudad de Buenos Aires
Tel: +54 11 4545 6020
Curriculum: IBDP
Language instr: English, Spanish

Islands International School
Amenábar St. 1840, 1428
Ciudad de Buenos Aires
Tel: +54 11 4787 2294
Age range: 2–18 years
Curriculum: IBDP
Language instr: Spanish, English, Italian, Portuguese

Kindergarten Manantiales
Cabello 3735, 1425 Ciudad de Buenos Aires
Tel: +54 11 4806 3939
Age range: 4–11
No. of pupils: 200

Limerick Bilingual School
José Bonifacio 2560, Ciudad de Buenos Aires
Tel: +54 11 4612 3833
Curriculum: National, UK

Lomas High School
Lomas De Zamora, Buenos Aires
Tel: +54 11 4244 6555
Curriculum: IPC, IGCSE, ALevs

Lycée Franco-Argentin Jean Mermoz
Ramsay 2131, Ciudad de Buenos Aires
Tel: +54 11 47 81 16 00
Curriculum: FrenchBacc

Modern School
Enrique del Valle Iberlucea 3952, 1826 Remedios de Escalada, Buenos Aires
Tel: + 54 11 4241 2570
Curriculum: National, UK, IGCSE

New Model International School
El Salvador 3952, 1175
Ciudad de Buenos Aires
Tel: +54 11 4825 2900
Language instr: Spanish

Northern International School
Ruote 8 Km 61.5., 1633.
Pilar, Buenos Aires
Tel: +54 2322 49 1208
Age range: 2–18 years
Curriculum: IBDP
Language instr: Spanish, English, Italian, Portuguese

Northlands School
Olivos Site: Roma 1248,
Olivos, Buenos Aires
Tel: +54 11 4711 8400
Age range: 2–18 years
No. of pupils: 1828
Curriculum: IBDP, IBPYP, National, IGCSE
Language instr: English, Spanish

Northlands School Nordelta
Nordelta site: Av de los Colegios 590, Nordelta, Buenos Aires B1670NNN
Tel: +54 11 4871 2668/9
Curriculum: IBDP, IBPYP, National, IGCSE
Language instr: English, Spanish

Orange Day School
Av. San Martín 1651/7, 1657
Ramos Mejia, Buenos Aires
Tel: +54 11 4464 7014
Age range: 14–19
No. of pupils: 300
Curriculum: IBDP, IGCSE
Language instr: English, Spanish

Poplars School
Estrada 335, 9400 Río Gallegos, Santa Cruz
Tel: +54 29 6642 5703
Curriculum: IBDP
Language instr: English, Spanish

Quilmes High School
Rivadavia 460, 1878
Quilmes, Buenos Aires
Tel: +54 11 4253 0123
Age range: 1–15
No. of pupils: 900 B500 G400 VIth50
Curriculum: IGCSE, ALevs
Language instr: Spanish

Saint Alban's College, Lomas de Zamora
Ramon Falcon 250, 1832 Lomas de Zamora, Buenos Aires
Tel: +54 11 4244 8060

Saint Mary of the Hills School
Xul Solar 6650, 1646 San Fernando, Buenos Aires
Tel: +54 11 4714 0330
No. of pupils: 850
Curriculum: AP, IBDP, IPC, IGCSE
Language instr: Spanish, English

Saint Mary of the Hills School Sede Pilar
Ruta 25 y Caamaño, 1644 Pilar, Buenos Aires
Tel: +54 2304 458181
Curriculum: IBDP
Language instr: Spanish

Saint Matthews College
Roque Sáenz Peña 1855, 1636 Olivos, Buenos Aires
Tel: +54 11 4790 8211
Age range: 4–19
No. of pupils: 380
Curriculum: IGCSE, ALevs
Language instr: Spanish, English

Saint Patrick College
Av. Maipú 3187, Corrientes
Curriculum: IBDP
Language instr: English, Spanish

SGS Loma Verde Bilingual School
Leguizamo 1174, 1625 Belén de Escobar, Buenos Aires
Tel: +54 348 449 3376
Curriculum: National, IGCSE, ALevs

Southern International School
Freeway Buenos Aires - La Plata Km 34., 1884 Hudson, Buenos Aires
Tel: +54 11 4215 3636
Age range: 2–18 years
Curriculum: IBDP
Language instr: Spanish, English, Italian, Portuguese

St George's College
Guido 800, 1878 Quilmes, Buenos Aires
Tel: +54 (11) 4350 7900
Age range: 3–18
No. of pupils: 859 B451 G408 VIth49
Curriculum: IBDP, IBPYP, National, UK, IGCSE
Language instr: English, Spanish

St George's College North
Mosconi 3500 y Don Bosco s/n, 1613 Los Polvorines, Buenos Aires
Tel: +54 (11) 4663 2494
Age range: 2–18
No. of pupils: 640 B340 G300 VIth82
Curriculum: IBDP, IBPYP, National, IGCSE
Language instr: English, Spanish

St Lukes College
Miguel de Azcuénaga 2340, 1636 Olivos, Buenos Aires
Tel: +54 11 4799 5922
Age range: 2–18
No. of pupils: 600
Curriculum: UK, IGCSE

St Margarets School
Marsical Antonio Jose de Sucre 3668, 1430 Ciudad de Buenos Aires
Tel: +54 11 4551 2942
Age range: 4–18
No. of pupils: 300
Curriculum: IGCSE

St Mark's College
M. Alegre 325, 1842 Monte Grande, Buenos Aires
Tel: +54 11 4296 5045

St Mary's International College
Martin Garcia 1435/1236/1501, 1804 Ezeiza, Buenos Aires
Tel: +54 11 5075 0370
No. of pupils: 870
Curriculum: IBDP
Language instr: English, Spanish

South America

St Matthew's College - Sede Fundadora
Moldes 1469, 1426 Ciudad de Buenos Aires
Tel: +54 11 4783 1110
Age range: 2–18
No. of pupils: 650
Curriculum: IBDP, National, IGCSE
Language instr: Spanish, English

St Matthew's College - Sede Norte
Caamano 493, 1631 Pilar, Buenos Aires
Tel: +54 230 4693600
Age range: 2–18
No. of pupils: 1365
Curriculum: IBDP, IGCSE
Language instr: English, Spanish

St Patrick's School
Nahuel Huapí 4134/40, 1430 Ciudad de Buenos Aires
Tel: +54 11 4545 7746
Age range: 4–19
No. of pupils: 800
Curriculum: UK

St Xavier's College
José Antonio Cabrera 5901, 1414 Ciudad de Buenos Aires
Tel: +54 114 777 5011/14
Curriculum: IBDP
Language instr: English

St. Andrew's Scots School
Roque Saenz Peña 601, 1636 Olivos, Buenos Aires
Tel: +54 11 4846 6500
Age range: 3–18
No. of pupils: 1866 B950 G916
Curriculum: IBDP, National, IGCSE
Language instr: English, Spanish

St. Catherine's Moorlands - Belgrano
Carbajal 3250, 1426 Ciudad de Buenos Aires
Tel: +54 11 4552 4353
Age range: 3–18
Curriculum: IBDP, IBMYP, National, UK
Language instr: English, Spanish

St. Catherine's Moorlands - Tortuguitas
Ruta Panamericana Km 38 Ramal Pilar, 1667 Tortuguitas, Buenos Aires
Tel: +54 348 463 9001/2
Age range: 3–18
Curriculum: IBMYP, National, UK, IGCSE
Language instr: English

St. John's School - Beccar
España 348/370, 1643 Beccar, Buenos Aires
Tel: +54 11 4513 4400
Curriculum: IBDP
Language instr: English, Spanish

St. John's School - Escobar
Av de los Colegios 385, 1625 Puertos Escobar, Buenos Aires
Tel: +54 03484 268118

St. John's School - Martínez
General Pueyrredón 1499, 1640 Martinez, Buenos Aires
Tel: +54 11 4580 3500
Age range: 6–16
No. of pupils: 1330
Curriculum: IGCSE

St. John's School - Pilar
Panamericana Km. 48.800, 1629 Pilar, Buenos Aires
Tel: +54 23 0466 7667
Curriculum: IBDP
Language instr: English, Spanish

St. Nicholas' School
Guillermo Rawson 2625, 1636 Olivos, Buenos Aires
Tel: +54 11 4799 5254
Curriculum: National

St. Paul's College
El Cardenal 950, 1686 Hurlingham, Buenos Aires
Tel: +54 11 4665 3309
Age range: 2–18 years
No. of pupils: 550
Language instr: English, Spanish, French

Sunrise School
Chacra 116 Colonia Lucinda, 8324 Cipolletti, Río Negro
Tel: +54 299 4786590
No. of pupils: 400
Curriculum: IBDP
Language instr: Spanish

Sworn College S.A. Moreno
Ruta 24 entre Gral. Savio y Puerto Madryn, Barrio Santa Ana, Francisco Alvarez, 1744 Moreno, Buenos Aires
Tel: +54 237 483 1552
Curriculum: IGCSE

Sworn Junior College
Viceroy del Pino 3299, 1426 Ciudad de Buenos Aires
Tel: +54 11 4552 2498
Age range: 14–19
No. of pupils: 1000
Curriculum: UK, ALevs

United High School
Montañeses 2434, 1428 Ciudad de Buenos Aires
Tel: +54 11 4783 3006
Curriculum: AICE, IGCSE

Villa Devoto School
Pedro Morán 4441, 1419 Ciudad de Buenos Aires
Tel: +54 114 501 9419
Curriculum: IBDP
Language instr: English, Spanish

Washington School
Av. Federico Lacroze 1973/2012, 1426 Ciudad de Buenos Aires
Tel: +54 11 4772 8131
Curriculum: IBDP
Language instr: English, Spanish

Wellspring School
Las Camelias 3883, 1669 Del Viso, Ciudad de Buenos Aires
Tel: +54 (0)23 20 300100
Curriculum: AICE, IGCSE, ALevs

Woodville School
Av. Los Pioneros km 2,900, 8400 San Carlos de Bariloche, Río Negro
Tel: +54 2944 44 11 33
Age range: 16–18
No. of pupils: 169 B83 G86 VIth45
Curriculum: IBDP, IGCSE
Language instr: Spanish, English

BARBADOS

The Codrington School
St John BB 20008
Tel: +1 246 423 2570
Age range: 3–18
No. of pupils: 140 B80 G60
Curriculum: IBDP, IBMYP, IBPYP
Language instr: English

The Lester Vaughan School
Cane Garden
Tel: +1 246 535 6030
Age range: 11–17 years

BOLIVIA

American Cooperative School
c/o American Embassy, La Paz
Tel: +591 2 279 2302
Age range: 4–18

American International School of Bolivia
Casilla 5309, Cochabamba
Tel: +591 4 428 8577
Age range: 3–18
No. of pupils: 240
Curriculum: IBDP
Language instr: English

British Bolivian School
Av Cristo Redentor Km 6 1/2, (Entre 7 y 8 anillos), Santa Cruz de la Sierra
Tel: +591 3 311 1669
Curriculum: IBDP
Language instr: English, Spanish

Cambridge College
Av. Banzer Carretera al norte, km 8 1/2 (frente a La Chonta), Santa Cruz
Tel: +591 3 343 4653
Age range: 3–18 years
No. of pupils: 1200

Cochabamba Co-Operative School
Avenida Circunvalacion, s/n Zona Mesadilla, Cochabamba
Tel: + 591 4 4490 605

Colegio Alemán Santa Cruz
Casilla 624, Av San Martin s/n, Santa Cruz
Tel: +591 3 3326820
Age range: 4–18
No. of pupils: 1400
Curriculum: IBDP, IBMYP
Language instr: Spanish

Deutsche Schule La Paz - Colegio Alemán 'Mariscal Braun'
Avenida Alexander # 100 Achumani, Casilla 605 - 4442, La Paz
Tel: +591 2 2710812

Highlands International School
Urbanizacion Valle Del Sol, Ex Fabrica de Ladrillos, Mallasilla, La Paz
Tel: +591 2745113
Curriculum: National, USA

Lycée Franco Bolivien Alcide d'Orbigny - La Paz
Av. Francia s/n, Achumani, Casilla postal 6547, La Paz
Tel: +591 2 2793370
Curriculum: FrenchBacc

Saint Andrew's School
Casilla 1679, Av Las Retamas s/n La Florida, La Paz
Tel: +591 22 79 24 84
Curriculum: IBDP, IBMYP, IBPYP
Language instr: English, Spanish

Santa Cruz Cooperative School
Barrio Las Palmas, Calle Barcelona #1, Santa Cruz 753
Tel: +591 3 353 0808
Age range: 3–18
Curriculum: AP, SAT

Santa Cruz International School
PO Box 4640, Santa Cruz de la Sierra, Santa Cruz 4640
Tel: +591 3 353 5035
Age range: 3–18
No. of pupils: 360
Curriculum: USA, ALevs

BRAZIL

ABA Global School
Av. Rosa e Silva, 1510, Aflitos, Recife, Pernambuco PE 52050-245
Tel: +55 81 3427 8800
Curriculum: IBPYP
Language instr: English

Amazon Valley Academy
Rodovia BR 316 - Km 3, Tv.Tenri, n132 Guanabara, Ananindeua, Pará PA 67113-120
Tel: +55 91 3245 2566
Age range: 4–18
No. of pupils: 89
Curriculum: ACT, SAT, USA
Language instr: English

American School of Brasilia
SGAS 605, Conjunto E, Lotes 34/37, Brasília DF 70200-650
Tel: +55 61 3442 9700
Age range: 3–19
No. of pupils: 569 B262 G307
Curriculum: IBDP, USA
Language instr: English

American School of Campinas - Escola Americana de Campinas
Rua Cajamar, #35, Campinas, São Paulo SP 13090-860
Tel: +55 19 21021006
Age range: 3–18
No. of pupils: 444 B219 G225
Curriculum: ACT, IBDP, IBPYP, SAT

South America

American School of Recife
Street Sa e Souza, Boa Viagem,
Recife, Pernambuco PE 51030-065
Tel: +55 81 3341 4716
Curriculum: USA
Language instr: English

Associação Educacional Luterana Bom Jesus / IELUSC
Rua Princesa Isabel, 438, Joinville,
Santa Catarina SC 89201-270
Tel: +55 47 3026 8000
Curriculum: IBDP

Beacon School
Rua Mergenthaler 1138, Vila
Leopoldina, São Paulo SP 05311-030
Tel: +55 11 3643 6900
Age range: 2–17 years
No. of pupils: 1400
Curriculum: IBDP, IBMYP, IBPYP
Language instr: English, Portuguese

Brasilia International School
SGAS 914 Conjunto C Lotes
67/68, Brasília DF 70390-140
Tel: +55 (61) 3346 1200
Age range: 3
Curriculum: USA

Bright School
R. Anfrisio Lobao 2024, Sao Cristovao,
Teresina, Piauí PI 64051-152
Tel: +55 86 3233 1839
Curriculum: IBDP, IBMYP, IBPYP
Language instr: English, Portuguese

Centro Internacional de Educacao Integrada
Estrada do Pontal 2093,
Recreio dos Bandeirantes, Rio
de Janeiro RJ 22790-877
Tel: +55 21 2490 1673
Curriculum: IBDP, IBPYP
Language instr: English

Chapel School – The American International School of Brazil
Rua Vigário João de Pontes,
537, Chácara Flora, São
Paulo SP 04748-000
Tel: +55 11 2101 7400
No. of pupils: 700
Curriculum: ACT, IBDP, SAT, TOEFL
Language instr: English

Colégio 7 de Setembro
R. Henriqueta Galeno, 1011, Dionísio
Torres, Fortaleza, Ceará CE 60135-420
Tel: +55 85 4006 7777
Curriculum: IBDP
Language instr: English, Portuguese

Colegio Bonja
84 Mafra Street, Saguaçu, Santa
Catarina SC 89221-665
Tel: +55 47 3026 8000
Curriculum: IBPYP
Language instr: English, Portuguese

Colégio Humboldt
Av. Eng. Alberto Kuhlmann 525,
Interlagos, São Paulo SP 04784-010
Tel: +55 11 5686 4055

Colégio Maxi
Av. Duque de Caxias 1589,
Jardim Petrópolis, Londrina,
Paraná PR 86015-000
Tel: +55 43 3372 5555
Age range: 3–18 years
Curriculum: National
Language instr: Portuguese

Colégio Miguel de Cervantes
Avenida Jorge João Saad, 905,
São Paulo, Morumbí SP 05618-001
Tel: +55 11 3779 1800
No. of pupils: 1500
Curriculum: IBDP
Language instr: Portuguese, Spanish, English

Colegio Positivo Internacional
Professor Pedro Viriato de Souza St
5300, Curitiba, Paraná PR 81280-330
Tel: +55 (41) 3335 3535
Age range: 3–17 years
No. of pupils: 917
Curriculum: IBDP, IBMYP, IBPYP
Language instr: Portuguese, English

Colegio Sao Luis
Av. Dr. Dante Pazzanese, 295, Vila
Mariana, São Paulo SP 04012-180
Curriculum: IBDP
Language instr: English, Portuguese

Colégio Sidarta
Estrada Fernando Nobre,
1332, Granja Viana, Cotia,
São Paulo SP 06705-490
Tel: +55 11 4612 2711
(ISA)

Colégio Soka do Brasil
Avenida Cursino, 362,
Saúde SP 04132-000
Tel: +55 11 5060 3300
Curriculum: IBDP
Language instr: English, Portuguese

Colégio Suíço-Brasileiro de Curitiba
Rua Wanda dos Santos
Mallmann, 537, Jardim Pinhais,
Pinhais, Paraná PR 83323-400
Tel: +55 41 3525 9100
Curriculum: IBDP
Language instr: English

Corce International School
R. Gothard Kaesemodel 961,
Anita Garibaldi, Joinville, Santa
Catarina SC 89203-522
Tel: +55 47 3121 6700
Age range: 6–18
No. of pupils: 220
Curriculum: IBDP, IBMYP, IBPYP

Cultura Inglesa - Filial Cabral
Rua Moyses Marcondes 625, Cabral,
Curitiba, Paraná PR 80030-410
Tel: +55 41 3254 7239
Age range: 4–18

Dual International School Blumenau
Rua Pandiá Calógeras 272,
Jardim Blumenau, Blumenau,
Santa Catarina SC 89010-350
Tel: +55 47 3285 3586
Curriculum: IBDP, IBPYP
Language instr: English, Portuguese

Dual International School Florianopolis
Rua Salvatina Feliciana dos Santos
525, Itacorubi, Florianópolis,
Santa Catarina SC 88034-600
Tel: +55 48 3030 6100
Curriculum: IBDP, IBPYP
Language instr: English, Portuguese

Escola Alemã Corcovado
Rua São Clemente 388, Botafogo,
Rio de Janeiro RJ 22260-000
Tel: +55 (21) 2528 0400

Escola Americana de Belo Horizonte
Av. Professor Mario Werneck,
3002, Bairro Buritis, Belo Horizonte,
Minas Gerais MG 30575-180
Tel: +55 31 3378 6700
Age range: 3–18
No. of pupils: 180 B95 G85
Curriculum: IBMYP, IBPYP
Language instr: English, Portuguese

Escola Americana do Rio de Janeiro - Barra da Tijuca
Rua Colbert Coelho 155, Barra da
Tijuca, Rio de Janeiro RJ 22793-313
Tel: +55 21 3747 2000
Curriculum: IBDP, IBMYP, IBPYP
Language instr: English

Escola Americana do Rio de Janeiro - Gávea
Estrada da Gávea 132, Gávea,
Rio de Janeiro RJ 22451-263
Tel: +55 21 2125 9000
Age range: 3–18 years
No. of pupils: 1300
Curriculum: IBDP, IBMYP, IBPYP, National, USA
Language instr: English

Escola Beit Yaacov
Av Marques de Sao Vicente no 1748,
Barra Funda, São Paulo SP 01139-002
Tel: +55 11 3611 0600
Curriculum: IBDP, IBPYP
Language instr: English

Escola Bilíngue Pueri Domus - Aclimação Campus
Rua Muniz de Sousa 1051, Aclimação,
São Paulo SP 01534-020
Tel: +55 11 3478 7701
Curriculum: IBDP
Language instr: English, Portuguese

Escola Bilíngue Pueri Domus - Itaim Campus
Rua Itacema 214, Itaim Bibi,
São Paulo SP 04530-050
Tel: +55 11 3078 6999
Curriculum: IBDP
Language instr: English, Portuguese

Escola Bilíngue Pueri Domus - Perdizes Campus
Rua Ministro Godói 1697, Perdizes,
São Paulo SP 05015-001
Tel: +55 11 3803 4240
Curriculum: IBDP
Language instr: English, Portuguese

Escola Bilíngue Pueri Domus - Verbo Divino Campus
Rua Verbo Divino 993-A, Chacara
Sto. Antonio, São Paulo SP 04719-001
Tel: +55 11 3512 2222
Curriculum: IBDP
Language instr: English, Portuguese

Escola Canadense de Brasilia
SIG Quadra 8, Lote 2225, Parte
F, Brasília DF 70610-480
Tel: +55 61 3961 4350
Age range: 2–18 years
Curriculum: IBPYP
Language instr: English, Portuguese

Escola Castanheiras
Alameda Castanheiras, 250,
Res. Tres (Tambore), Santana de
Parnaíba, São Paulo SP 06543-510
Tel: +55 114 152 4600
Curriculum: IBDP
Language instr: English

ESCOLA DO FUTURO - SÃO PAULO
For further details see p. 240
R. Dr. Francisco Pati 40,
Cidade São Francisco,
São Paulo SP 05352-120
Tel: +55 (11) 2168 4100
Email: visitas@escoladofuturo.com.br
Website: www.escoladofuturo.com.br
Headmaster: Ivonne Betsabé Muniz
Age range: 2–18 years
No. of pupils: 600

Escola Eleva - Barra da Tijuca
Av. José Silva de Azevedo
Neto 309, Barra da Tijuca, Rio
de Janeiro RJ 22775-056
Tel: +55 21 3094 5020
Age range: 2–18 years
No. of pupils: 1200
Curriculum: IBDP
Language instr: English, Portuguese

Escola Eleva - Urca
Avenida João Luiz Alves 13, Urca,
Rio de Janeiro RJ 22291-090
Tel: +55 21 3528 4370
Age range: 14–18 years
No. of pupils: 285
Curriculum: IBDP
Language instr: English, Portuguese

Escola Francesa de Natal
Rua Pastor Gabino Brelaz, 1470 -
Capim Macio, Natal RN 59082-010
Tel: +55 (84) 3217 4558

South America

Escola Internacional de Alphaville
Av. Copacabana, 624, Cond. Empresarial 18 do Forte, Alphaville, Barueri SP 06472-001
Tel: +55 11 4134 6686
Curriculum: IBDP, IBMYP, IBPYP
Language instr: English

Escola Internacional Nova Geração
EING - Portaria de alunos, Rua Washington, 264, Vila Maia, Guarujá, São Paulo SP 11410-150
Tel: +55 (13) 3384-3009
Curriculum: National, USA

Escola Lourenco Castanho - Alto da Boa Vista
Rua Comendador Elias Zarzur 301, Alto da Boa Vista, São Paulo SP 04736-000
Tel: +55 11 4118 4365
Curriculum: IBDP
Language instr: English, Portuguese

Escola Lourenco Castanho - Vila Nova Conceição
Av. Antônio Joaquim de Moura Andrade 731, Vila Nova Conceição, São Paulo SP 04506-000
Tel: +55 11 3090 1290
Curriculum: IBDP
Language instr: English, Portuguese

Escola Nova by SIS Swiss International School
Rua Major Rubens Vaz 392, Gávea, Rio de Janeiro RJ 22470-070
Tel: +55 21 3875 9898
Age range: 3–18 years
Curriculum: IBDP
Language instr: English, Portuguese

Escola Suíço-Brasileira (ESB) Rio de Janeiro by SIS Swiss International School
Rua Corréa de Araújo 81, Barra da Tijuca, Rio de Janeiro RJ 22611-060
Tel: +55 21 3389 2089
Age range: 3–18 years
Curriculum: IBDP, IBMYP, IBPYP
Language instr: English, Portuguese

Escola Suíço-Brasileira de São Paulo
Rua Visconde de Porto Seguro 391, Alto da Boa Vista, São Paulo SP 04642-000
Tel: +55 11 5682 2140
Curriculum: IBDP, National
Language instr: German, English, Portuguese

Escola Villare
Rua José Benedetti 55, Bairro Santo Antônio, São Caetano do Sul, São Paulo SP 09531-000
Tel: +55 11 4225 5500
Age range: 1–18 years
Curriculum: National, TOEFL
Language instr: English, Portuguese

GIS SP - The International School of São Paulo
Alameda dos Jurupis 485, Moema, São Paulo SP 04088-000
Tel: +55 11 3900 8931
Age range: 1.5–11 years
No. of pupils: 60
Curriculum: IBPYP
Language instr: English, Portuguese

Graded - The American School of São Paulo
Av. José Galante, 425, São Paulo SP 05642-000
Tel: +55 11 3747 4800
Age range: 2–18
No. of pupils: 1246
Curriculum: ACT, IBDP, SAT, USA
Language instr: English

Great International School
Av. Nossa Senhora de Fátima 1000, Jóquei, Teresina, Piauí PI 64048-185
Tel: +55 86 2222 4000
Curriculum: IBDP
Language instr: English, Portuguese

Instituto GayLussac
R. Maria Caldas 35, São Francisco, Niterói, Rio de Janeiro RJ 24365-050
Tel: +55 21 2612 4000
Age range: 2–18 years
Curriculum: IPC, National, SAT, IGCSE
Language instr: English, Portuguese

International School of Curitiba
Ave. Eugenio Bertolli, 3900, Sta. Felicidade, Curitiba, Paraná PR 82410-530
Tel: +55 41 3525 7400
Age range: 3–19
No. of pupils: 681
Curriculum: IBDP, SAT, USA
Language instr: English

Land School
R. José Wilson de Vasconcelos 05, Federação, Salvador, Bahia BA 40230-102
Tel: +55 71 3368 8400
Age range: 2–18 years
No. of pupils: 1200
Curriculum: IBDP, IBMYP
Language instr: English, Portuguese

Liceu Albert Sabin
Rua José Curvelo da Silveira Jr. 110, Ribeirão Preto, São Paulo
Tel: +55 16 3602 8200
Curriculum: IBDP
Language instr: English, Portuguese

Lighthouse Ensino Bilíngue
Av. dos Expedicionários, 3548, Moradias Bom Jesus, Campo Largo, Paraná PR 83604-360
Tel: +55 (41) 3032 1222

Lycée Français François Mitterrand
SHIS QI 21 Bloco D, Lago Sul, Brasília DF 71655-580
Tel: +55 (61) 3246 9763
Curriculum: FrenchBacc

Lycée Pasteur (Lycée français de São Paulo / Unité Vergueiro)
Rua Vergueiro, 3799 - Vila Mariana, São Paulo SP 04101-300
Tel: +55 (11) 5904 7822
Curriculum: FrenchBacc

Maple Bear Barra da Tijuca
Rua Martinho de Mesquita 136, Barra da Tijuca, Rio de Janeiro RJ 22630-220
Tel: +55 21 3486 6466
Curriculum: IBDP
Language instr: English, Portuguese

Maxi Global School
Av. Maringá 1700, Jardim Presidente, Vitoria, Londrina, Paraná PR 86060-000
Tel: +55 43 3376 1700
Age range: 11–18 years
Curriculum: National
Language instr: English, Portuguese

Pan American Christian Academy
Rua Cássio de Campos Nogueira, 393, São Paulo SP 04829-310
Tel: +55 11 5929 9500
Age range: 5–18
No. of pupils: 350
Curriculum: USA

Pan American School of Bahia
Av Ibirapitanga, Loteamento Patamares, s/n, Salvador, Bahia BA 41680-060
Tel: +55 71 3368 8400
Curriculum: IBDP, IBPYP

Pan American School of Porto Alegre
Av. João Obino 110, Petrópolis, Porto Alegre, Rio Grande do Sul RS 90470-150
Tel: +55 513 334 5866
Age range: 3–18
No. of pupils: 391 B191 G200
Curriculum: ACT, AP, IBMYP, IBPYP, National, SAT, USA
Language instr: English, Portuguese

Pingo de Gente & Laviniense
Rua Galícia No. 34, Adrianópolis, Manaus, Amazonas AM 69060-625
Tel: +55 92 3236 0000
Age range: 2–17 years
Curriculum: National
Language instr: Portuguese

PlayPen Escola Cidade Jardim
Praça Professor Américo de Moura 101, São Paulo SP 05670-060
Tel: +55 11 3812 9122
Age range: 1–17 years
Curriculum: IBPYP, IPC, National
Language instr: English, Portuguese

Red House International School - Campus Higienópolis
Rua Albuquerque Lins 773, Higienópolis, São Paulo SP 01230-001
Age range: 4–11 years
Curriculum: IBMYP, IBPYP
Language instr: English, Portuguese

Red House International School - Campus Perdizes
Rua Ministro Godói 301, Perdizes, São Paulo SP 05015-000
Age range: 11–18 years
Curriculum: IBDP
Language instr: English, Portuguese

Rio International School
Avenida Prefeito Dulcidio Cardoso, 4351, Barra da Tijuca, Rio de Janeiro RJ 22793-011
Tel: +55 (21) 97945 0088
Curriculum: USA

Sant'Anna International School
Av. Independência, 5588, Aquário, Vinhedo SP 13280-000
Tel: +55 19 3113 3777
Age range: 2–18
Curriculum: SAT, USA
Language instr: Portuguese

School of the Nations
SHIS QI 21 Área Especial Conjunto C1, Brasilia DF 71655-600
Tel: +55 61 3366 1800
Age range: 2–18 years
Curriculum: AP, IBDP, IBPYP, National, USA
Language instr: English, Portuguese

SIS Swiss International School Brasília
SGA/SUL, Quadra 905, cj B, Brasília DF 70390-050
Tel: +55 61 3443 4145
Age range: 3–18 years
Curriculum: IBDP, IBMYP, IBPYP
Language instr: English, Portuguese

Sphere International School
Av Anchieta, 908 - Jardim Nova Europa, Sao José dos Campos, São Paulo SP 12242-280
Tel: +55 11 9 7279 4340
Age range: 2–16 years
No. of pupils: 410
Curriculum: IBDP, IBMYP, IBPYP
Language instr: Portuguese, English

St. Francis College, Brazil
Rua Joaquim Antunes 678, Pinheiros, São Paulo SP 05415-001
Tel: +55 11 3728 8053
Age range: 3–18 years
No. of pupils: 918
Curriculum: IBDP, IBMYP, IBPYP, SAT, IGCSE
Language instr: English, Portuguese

St. Nicholas School - Alphaville
Av. Honório Álvares Penteado 5463, Tamboré, Santana de Parnaíba SP 06543-320
Tel: +55 11 3465 9658; +55 11 3465 9697
Age range: 18 months–16 years
No. of pupils: 510
Curriculum: IBDP, IBMYP, IBPYP
Language instr: English, Portuguese

South America

St. Nicholas School - Pinheiros
Rua do Emissário 333, Pinheiros,
São Paulo SP 05423-070
Tel: +55 11 3465 9650; +55 11 3465 9666
Age range: 18 months–18 years
No. of pupils: 650
Curriculum: IBDP, IBMYP, IBPYP, IGCSE
Language instr: English, Portuguese

St. Paul's School
Rua Juquiá 166, Jardim Paulistano,
São Paulo SP 01440-903
Tel: +55 11 3087 3399
Age range: 3–18 years
Curriculum: IBDP, UK, IGCSE
Language instr: English

THE BRITISH COLLEGE OF BRAZIL
For further details see p. 242
Rua Álvares de Azevedo,
50, Chácara Flora, São
Paulo SP 04671-040
Tel: +55 11 5547 3030
Email: admissions-bcb@britishcollegebrazil.org
Website: www.britishcollegebrazil.org
Headteacher: Maurice Hartnett
Age range: 2–18 years
No. of pupils: 600
Fees: 92,000–138,000
Curriculum: IBDP, UK, IGCSE
Language instr: English

The British School of Brasilia
SHIS EQI 7/9, Lote F, Lago Sul,
Brasília DF 71615-370
Tel: +55 61 3248 3694
Age range: 2–18 years
Curriculum: IBDP, UK
Language instr: English, Portuguese

THE BRITISH SCHOOL, RIO DE JANEIRO
For further details see p. 243
Rua Real Grandeza 99, Botafogo,
Rio de Janeiro RJ 22281-030
Tel: +55 21 2539 2717
Email: edu@britishschool.g12.br
Website: www.britishschool.g12.br
Directors: Steve Lang, Fernanda Reis & Isadora Guise
Age range: 2–18 years
No. of pupils: 2300 B1100 G1200
Fees: *Day* R115,000
Curriculum: IBDP, IPC, UK, IGCSE
Language instr: English

The British School, Rio de Janeiro - Barra Site
Rua Mario Autuori, 100, Barra
da Tijuca, RJ 22793
Tel: +55 21 3329 2854
Curriculum: IBDP

Valley International School
Av. Osvaldo Reis, 2000 Praia Brava,
Itajai, Santa Catarina SC 88306-600
Tel: +55 47 3349 0969
Curriculum: IBDP, IBPYP
Language instr: English, Portuguese

Villa Global Education, Campus Litoral Norte
Rod BA 099, Estrada do Coco,
s/n lote 08 09 11 GL 11 Camacari,
Salvador, Bahia BA 42825-001
Tel: +55 71 99678 8035
Curriculum: IBDP
Language instr: English, Portuguese

Villa Global Education, Campus Paralela
Avenida Luis Viana 7731, Paralela,
Salvador, Bahia BA 41745-130
Tel: +55 71 99939 3875
Curriculum: IBDP
Language instr: English, Portuguese

CHILE

American British School
Avenida Walker Martinez No.
2972, La Florida, Santiago
Tel: +56 2 2605 9010
Age range: 3–18 years
Curriculum: National, UK, IGCSE, ALevs
Language instr: English, Spanish

Andrée English School
Avenida Principe de Gales
7605, La Reina, Santiago
Tel: +56 22 273 1027
Age range: 5–13
No. of pupils: 300

Antofagasta International School
Avenida Jaime Guzmán Errázuriz
04300, Antofagasta
Tel: +56 55 694900
Language instr: English

Bradford School
Avada Luis Pateur 6335,
Vitacura, Santiago
Tel: +56 (2) 29 12 31 40
Age range: 4–18
Curriculum: IBDP, UK

Caernarfon College
Fundo Mundo Nuevo, Ruta 68,
Km. 65, Casablanca, Valparaíso
Tel: +56 (32) 2215 6193
Curriculum: IGCSE

Colegio Alemán Chicureo
Av. Alemania 170, Piedra
Roja, Chicureo, Santiago
Tel: +56 223078962
Curriculum: IBDP, IBMYP, IBPYP
Language instr: Spanish

Colegio Alemán de Concepción
Camino El Venado 1075,
Andalué, San Pedro de la
Paz, Concepción, Biobío
Tel: +56 41 2140000
No. of pupils: 1080
Curriculum: IBDP
Language instr: Spanish

Colegio Alemán de San Felipe de Aconcagua
60 CH Nº 501 Panquehue,
San Felipe, Valparaíso
Tel: +56 34 2 59 11 71
Age range: 3–17
No. of pupils: 343 B173 G170
Curriculum: IBDP
Language instr: Spanish

Colegio Alemán De Santiago
Nuestra Señora del Rosario
850, Las Condes, Santiago
Tel: +56 (2) 24246100

Colegio Alemán de Temuco
Avenida Holandesa 0855,
Temuco, Araucanía
Tel: +56 45 963000
Curriculum: IBDP, IBMYP

Colegio Alemán de Valparaiso
Alvarez 2950, El Salto, Viña
del Mar, Valparaíso
Tel: +56 32 216 1531
No. of pupils: 1252
Curriculum: IBDP
Language instr: Spanish

Colegio Alemán La Serena
Avda. Cuatro Esquinas s/n, El Milagro,
401346 La Serena, Coquimbo
Tel: +56 512 294 703
Curriculum: IBDP
Language instr: German, Spanish

Colegio Alemán Los Angeles
Casilla 367, Av. Gabriela Mistral
1360 (ex 1751), Los Ángeles, Biobío
Tel: +56 43 2521111
Curriculum: IBDP

Colegio Alemán Puerto Varas
KM1, 4 Camino Ensenada,
Puerto Varas, Los Lagos
Tel: +56 65 223 0450
Curriculum: IBMYP, IBPYP
Language instr: Spanish, German

Colegio Alemán St Thomas Morus
Avenida Pedro de Valdivia
320, Providencia, Santiago
Tel: +56 2 2729 1600
Curriculum: IBDP

Colegio Inglés de Talca
No. 5766 Avenida San
Miguel, Talca, Maule
Tel: +56 71 2247 832
Curriculum: IBDP
Language instr: Spanish

Colegio Internacional SEK Chile
Avd Los Militares 6640, Las
Condes, Santiago
Tel: +56 2 2127116
Curriculum: IBDP
Language instr: Spanish

Colegio Internacional SEK Pacifico
San Estanislao 50, Lomas de
Montemar, Concón, Valparaíso
Tel: +56 32 2275700
Age range: 3–18 years
Curriculum: IBDP, IBPYP
Language instr: English, Spanish

Colegio 'La Maisonnette'
Avda Luis Pasteur 6076,
Vitacura, Santiago
Tel: +56 2 228162945
Curriculum: IBDP
Language instr: Spanish

Colegio Manquecura - Ciudad de Los Valles
Av. Del Canal 19877,
Pudahuel, Santiago
Tel: +56 2 2605 9014
Age range: 3–18 years
Curriculum: National
Language instr: Spanish

Colegio Manquecura - Ciudad del Este
Diego Portales 7045,
Puente Alto, Santiago
Tel: +56 2 2605 9013
Age range: 3–18 years
Curriculum: National
Language instr: Spanish

Colegio Manquecura - Valle lo Campino
Camino del Cerro 2700,
Quilicura, Santiago
Tel: +56 2 2605 9015
Age range: 3–18 years
Curriculum: National
Language instr: Spanish

Colegio Manquecura Ñuñoa
Irarrázaval No. 5310, Ñuñoa, Santiago
Tel: +56 2 2605 9016
Age range: 4–18 years
Curriculum: National, UK, IGCSE, ALevs
Language instr: English, Spanish

Colegio Pumahue - Chicauma
Camino La Siembra 5605, Chicauma
Ciudad Parque, Lampa, Santiago
Tel: +56 2 2605 9007
Age range: 3–18 years
Curriculum: National
Language instr: Spanish

Colegio Pumahue - Chicuero
Sta. Elena 215, Colina, Santiago
Tel: +56 2 2605 9001
Age range: 3–18 years
Curriculum: National
Language instr: Spanish

Colegio Pumahue - Curauma
Nudo Curauma 495,
Placilla, Valparaíso
Tel: +56 2 2605 9002
Age range: 3–18 years
Curriculum: National
Language instr: Spanish

South America

Colegio Pumahue - Huechuraba
Av. Sta. Rosa de Huechuraba 7201, Huechuraba, Santiago
Tel: +56 2 2605 9003
Age range: 3–18 years
Curriculum: National
Language instr: Spanish

Colegio Pumahue - Peñalolén
Av. Quilín 8200, Peñalolén, Santiago
Tel: +56 2 2605 9005
Age range: 3–18 years
Curriculum: National
Language instr: Spanish

Colegio Pumahue - Puerto Montt
Volcán Puntiagudo 1700, Puerto Montt, Los Lagos
Tel: +56 2 2605 9004
Age range: 3–18 years
Curriculum: National
Language instr: Spanish

Colegio Pumahue - Temuco
Av. Martin Lutero 03015, Temuco, Araucanía
Tel: +56 2 2605 9006
Age range: 3–18 years
Curriculum: National
Language instr: Spanish

Colegio San Francisco Javier Huechuraba
Los Cedros 7550, Huechuraba, Santiago
Tel: +56 2 2753 9600
Age range: 2–18 years
Curriculum: National
Language instr: Spanish

Craighouse School
Casilla 20 007, Correo 20., Santiago
Tel: +56 2 227560218
Age range: 3–18
No. of pupils: 1877
Curriculum: IBDP, IBMYP, IBPYP
Language instr: English, Spanish

Dunalastair Chicureo
Camino del Solar 9300, Colina, Santiago
Tel: +56 2 2673 6097
Age range: 3–18 years
Curriculum: IBDP, National, IGCSE, ALevs
Language instr: English, Spanish

Dunalastair Las Condes
Av. Las Condes 11.931, Las Condes, Santiago
Tel: +56 2 2495 6600
Age range: 3–18 years
Curriculum: IBDP, National, IGCSE, ALevs
Language instr: English, Spanish

Dunalastair Peñalolén
Av. Quilín 8669, Peñalolén, Santiago
Tel: +56 2 2592 0240
Age range: 3–18 years
Curriculum: IBDP, National, IGCSE, ALevs
Language instr: English, Spanish

Instituto Alemán Carlos Anwandter
Los Laureles 050, Casilla 2-D, Valdivia, Los Ríos
Tel: +56 63 2471100
Curriculum: IBDP
Language instr: Spanish

Instituto Alemán de Osorno
Los Carreras 818, Osorno, Los Lagos
Tel: +56 64 233 1800/1805
Curriculum: IBDP, IBMYP, IBPYP
Language instr: Spanish

Instituto Alemán Puerto Montt
Bernardo Phillipi #350, Sector Seminario, 5480000 Puerto Montt, Los Lagos
Tel: +56 65 2 252560
Curriculum: IBMYP, IBPYP
Language instr: Spanish

Instituto Chileno Britanico de Cultura
Santa Lucia 124, Santiago
Tel: +56 2 241 320 00
Age range: 6–19

International Preparatory School
PO Box 20015, Las Condes, Santiago
Tel: +56 2 321 5800
Age range: 3–18
No. of pupils: 141 B83 G58
Curriculum: UK
(COB)

International School Nido de Aguilas
Av. El Rodeo 14200, Lo Barnechea, Santiago
Tel: +56 2 2339 8100
Age range: 3–18 years
No. of pupils: 1440
Curriculum: ACT, IBDP, SAT, USA
Language instr: English, Spanish

Lincoln International Academy, Chicureo
Seaquist No. 100, Chicureo, Santiago
Tel: +56 2 2496 7650
Curriculum: IBDP
Language instr: English, Spanish

Lincoln International Academy, Lo Barnechea
Av. Las Condes No. 13.150, Lo Barnechea, Santiago
Tel: +562 2 496 7600
Curriculum: IBDP
Language instr: English, Spanish

Lycée Antoine-de-Saint-Exupéry
Av. Luis Pasteur 5418, Vitacura, Santiago
Tel: +56 2 28 27 82 00
Curriculum: FrenchBacc

Lycée Charles de Gaulle
Colo Colo 51, Concepción, Biobío
Tel: +56 41 262 7000

Lyceé Claude Gay
Las Quemas S/N Loteo 4A, Osorno, Los Lagos
Tel: +56 (64) 454 811

Lycée Jean d'Alembert
Avenida Las Perdices No 450, Reñaca, Viña del Mar, Valparaíso
Tel: +56 32 251 2000

Mackay School
Vicuña Mackenna 700, Viña del Mar, Valparaíso
Tel: +56 32 2386614
Age range: B4–18
No. of pupils: 880
Curriculum: IBDP, IBMYP, IBPYP, National
Language instr: Spanish, English

Redland School
Camino El Alba 11357, Las Condes, 7600022 Santiago
Tel: +56 2 29598500
Age range: 4–18
No. of pupils: 842 B420 G422
Curriculum: IBDP, IBMYP, IBPYP
Language instr: Spanish

Saint Gabriel's School
Avda Fco Bilbao 3070, Providencia, Santiago
Tel: +56 22 462 5400
Age range: 4–18
Curriculum: IBDP, National, IGCSE
Language instr: English, Spanish (5th–12th grade)

SANTIAGO COLLEGE
For further details see p. 241
Av. Camino Los Trapenses 4007, Lo Barnechea, Santiago
Tel: +56 2 27338800
Email: master@scollege.cl
Website: www.scollege.cl
Head of School: Alan Lorenzini
Age range: 4–18 years
No. of pupils: 2044
Curriculum: IBDP, IBMYP, IBPYP
Language instr: Spanish, English
(CIS) (ECIS)

St John's School
Fundo el Venado, San Pedro de la Paz, Concepción, Biobío
Tel: +56 41 2466440
Age range: 4–18
No. of pupils: 1348
Curriculum: IBDP, IBMYP, IBPYP, National, IGCSE
Language instr: English, Spanish

St Margaret's British School For Girls
Casilla 392, Viña del Mar, Valparaíso
Tel: +56 3 2245 1701
Curriculum: IBDP
Language instr: Spanish, English

St Paul's School
Merced Oriente 54, Viña del Mar, Valparaíso
Tel: (56 32) 314 2200
Curriculum: IBPYP
Language instr: English, Spanish

St Peter's School
Av. Libertad 575, Viña del Mar, Valparaíso
Tel: +56 32 238 1400
Curriculum: UK

The American School
Michimahuida 301 Volcano, Volcanoes Valle, Puerto Montt, Los Lagos
Tel: +56 652 252 170
Age range: 4–18
Curriculum: SAT, USA

The Antofagasta British School
Pedro León Gallo 723, Antofagasta
Tel: +55 2 598 950
Curriculum: IBDP, IBMYP, IBPYP
Language instr: English, Spanish

The British School - Punta Arenas
Waldo Seguel 454, Punta Arenas, Magallanes
Tel: +56 61 2 22 33 81
Age range: 4–18
No. of pupils: 600
Curriculum: IBDP, IBMYP, IBPYP
Language instr: Spanish, English

The Grange School
Príncipe de Gales 6154, La Reina, Santiago
Tel: +56 2 2598 1500
Age range: 4–18
Curriculum: National, UK, IGCSE, ALevs
Language instr: English, Spanish

The Greenland School
Av. Oceánica 6300, Estación Central, 9190793 Santiago
Tel: +56 2 2605 9017
Age range: 3–18 years
Curriculum: National
Language instr: Spanish

The Mayflower School
Avda Las Condes 12 167, Las Condes, Santiago
Tel: +56 22 3523100
Age range: 4–18
Curriculum: IBDP, IBMYP, IBPYP, ALevs
Language instr: Spanish

The Wessex School
Granada 314-A, Vilumanque, 4081022 Concepción, Biobío
Tel: +56 41 333 2150
Age range: 3–18
No. of pupils: 695 B345 G350
Language instr: English (Junior), Spanish (Senior)

Trebulco School
Camino Carampangue 550, Talagante, Santiago
Tel: +56 2 815 7550
Age range: 3–17
Language instr: English

Wenlock School
Casilla 27169, Correo 27, Santiago
Tel: +56 223631803
Age range: 3–18
No. of pupils: 780 B390 G390
Curriculum: IBDP, National, UK, IGCSE
Language instr: Spanish

COLOMBIA

Altamira International School
Km 10 Autopista, Puerto, Atlántico
Tel: +57 (5) 385 35 77
Age range: 4–18
No. of pupils: 650
Curriculum: SAT, USA

Asociación Colegio Granadino
AA 2138, Manizales, Caldas
Tel: +57 (6) 874 57 74
Age range: 3–18
No. of pupils: 600 B295 G305
Language instr: English, Spanish

Aspaen Gimnasio Iragua
Av. Calle 170, No. 76-55, Barrio San José de Bavaria, Bogotá, D.C.
Tel: +57 (1) 667 95 00
Curriculum: IBDP
Language instr: Spanish

Aspaen Liceo Tacuri
Callejon de la Viga Pance, Cll 22 and 23, Cali, Valle del Cauca
Tel: +57 (2) 555 75 02
Age range: 4–18
No. of pupils: 184

British International School
Cra 30 # 2 - 906, Puerto Colombia, Atlantico
Tel: +57 6053854411
Age range: 3–18 years
No. of pupils: 1104
Curriculum: IBDP, IBMYP
Language instr: English, Spanish, French

Buckingham School
Cra 52 No 214 - 55, Bogotá, D.C.
Tel: +57 (1) 676 08 12
Age range: 3–17
Curriculum: IBDP, IBMYP, IBPYP, National
Language instr: English, Spanish

Bureche School
Troncal del Caribe Km2 vía Gaira, Santa Marta, Magdalena
Tel: +57 315 389 98 77
Age range: 1–17 years
Curriculum: IBDP, National, USA
Language instr: English, Spanish

CAS Colombo American School
Carrera 73 No. 214-53, Bogotá, D.C.
Curriculum: IBDP
Language instr: English, Spanish

CIEDI - Colegio Internacional de Educación Integral
Km 3 vía Suba-Cota, Bogotá, D.C.
Tel: +57 (1) 683 06 04
Curriculum: IBDP, IBMYP, IBPYP
Language instr: Spanish, English

Colegio Abraham Lincoln
Av. Calle 170 # 65 31, Bogotá, D.C.
Tel: +57 (1) 742 31 66
Curriculum: IBDP
Language instr: Spanish

Colegio Albania
Calle 15 3-00, Campamento de Mushaisa, Cerrejón La Mina, La Guajira
Tel: +57 (5) 350 56 48
Curriculum: IBDP, IBMYP, IBPYP
Language instr: Spanish, English

Colegio Alemán
Autopista al Mar poste 89 Electricaribe, Baranquilla, Atlántico
Tel: +57 (5) 359 85 20
No. of pupils: 1000
Curriculum: IBDP
Language instr: Spanish

Colegio Americano
Carrera 89 No 4c-35B Melendez, Cali, Valle del Cauca
Tel: +57 (2) 332 58 40
Curriculum: USA

Colegio Andino - Deutsche Schule
Cra 51 No 218-85, Bogotá, D.C.
Tel: +57 (1) 668 42 50

Colegio Anglo-Colombiano
Apartado Aéreo 253393, Avenida 19 N° 152A-48, Santa Fé, Bogotá, D.C.
Tel: +57 (1) 259 57 00
Age range: 4–18
Curriculum: IBDP, IBMYP, IBPYP, National, UK
Language instr: Spanish, English

Colegio Bilingüe Santa Marta
Troncal del Caribe Urb. San Francisco, 470004 Santa Marta, Magdalena
Tel: +57 605 420 96 44
Curriculum: IBMYP, IBPYP
Language instr: English, Spanish

Colegio Bolivar
Calle. 5 #122-21, Cali, Valle del Cauca
Tel: +57 (2) 485 50 50
Curriculum: USA

Colegio Británico - The British School
Call 18 # 142-255 (Esquina), La Viga, Pance, Cali, Valle del Cauca
Tel: +57 (2) 555 75 45
Curriculum: IBDP

Colegio Británico de Cartagena
Anillo Vial Km. 12, 130001 Cartagena, Bolívar
Tel: +57 5 693 09 82
Age range: 1–17 years
Curriculum: IBDP, National, USA
Language instr: English, Spanish

Colegio Británico de Montería
Calle 65 No. 9-100, Montería
Tel: +57 3 227 71 82 91
Curriculum: IBPYP
Language instr: English, Spanish

Colegio Cambridge
Sede Cajicá, Kilómetro 2 Vía Cajicá, Chía Vereda El Canelón, Cajicá, Cundinamarca
Tel: +1 601 746 4737
Curriculum: IBDP
Language instr: English, Spanish

Colegio Canadiense
Carrera 51 # 97 Sur 137, Sector Sierra Morena, Itagüi, Antioquia
Tel: +57 (4) 279 88 48

Colegio Colombo Británico
Avenida La Maria 69, Pance, Cali, Valle del Cauca
Tel: +57 2 555 53 85
Age range: 2–18
No. of pupils: 1260 B634 G626
Curriculum: IBDP, IBMYP, IBPYP, IBCP
Language instr: English, Spanish

Colegio Colombo Británico de Envigado (IED)
Transversal 29 Sur Diagonal 32 B-97, Envigado, Antioquia
Tel: +57 604 590 33 22
Curriculum: IBDP
Language instr: English, Spanish

Colegio Colombo Gales
Avenida Guaymaral, Costado sur Aeropuerto, Bogotá, D.C.
Tel: +57 (1) 668 49 10
No. of pupils: 808
Curriculum: IBDP, IBPYP

Colegio de Cambridge (Cambridge International School)
Vereda La Aurora, Municipio La Calera, Bogotá, D.C.
Tel: +57 (1) 593 18 90
Curriculum: IBDP
Language instr: Spanish

Colegio de Inglaterra - The English School
Calle 170 #15-68, Bogotá, D.C.
Tel: +57 601 676 77 00
Age range: 2–18 years
Curriculum: IBDP, IBMYP, IBPYP, IBCP
Language instr: English, Spanish

Colegio Domingo Savio
Calle 24 Sur #24 f-16, Bogotá, D.C.
Tel: +57 366 61 63
Curriculum: IBMYP
Language instr: English, Spanish

Colegio Gimnasio Internacional de Medellín
Calle 73 sur #64-23, La Estrella, 055468 Medellín, Antioquia
Curriculum: IBDP
Language instr: English, Spanish

Colegio Gran Bretaña
Carrera 51 No 215-20, Bogotá, D.C.
Tel: +57 (1) 676 03 91
Age range: 3–18
No. of pupils: 535 B265 G270
Curriculum: IBDP, IPC, National, UK, IGCSE
Language instr: English

Colegio Hacienda Los Alcaparros
Vía Bogotá La Calera, Vereda el Salitre, km 3, Bogotá, D.C.
Tel: +57 (1) 592 22 66
Age range: 3–18
Curriculum: USA
Language instr: English, Spanish, Portuguese

Colegio Helvetia
Calle 128 no 71A-91, Santa Fé, Bogotá, D.C.
Tel: +57 (1) 624 73 74
Age range: 4–19

Colegio Inglés de los Andes
Km 4 Vía Cali Puerto Tejada, Cali, Valle del Cauca
Tel: +57 550 43 11
Curriculum: UK, IGCSE

Colegio Internacional de Bogota
Carrera 49 no 202-85, Apartado Aereo 103314, Bogotá, D.C.
Tel: +57 (1) 676 22 00
Language instr: English

Colegio Internacional Los Cañaverales
Carrera 29 No 10-500, Arroyohonfo, Vía Dapa Km 1 Yumbo, Yumbo, Valle del Cauca
Tel: +57 (2) 658 28 18
Curriculum: IBDP
Language instr: English

Colegio Jordán de Sajonia
Cra. 1 Nro 68-50 Rosales, Bogotá, D.C.
Tel: +57 1 756 10 11
Curriculum: IBDP
Language instr: English, Spanish

Colegio Karl C. Parrish
Km. 2 Antigua Via a Puerto Colombia, Barranquilla, Atlántico
Tel: +57 (5) 359 89 29

Colegio La Arboleda
Carrera 125 No. 2, Avenida La Maria 80, Pance, Cali, Valle del Cauca
Tel: +57 2 555 34 05
Age range: 1–17 years
Curriculum: IBDP, National, USA
Language instr: English, Spanish

Colegio Los Ángeles Tunja
Calle 73A No. 2-02 E, Altos de la Arboleda, Tunja, Boyacá
Tel: +57 304 380 8353
Curriculum: IBDP
Language instr: English, Spanish

Colegio Los Nogales
Calle 202 # 56 - 50, Bogotá, D.C.
Tel: +57 (1) 676 11 28
Age range: 4–18
No. of pupils: B451 G517
Curriculum: AP, National, SAT, USA
Language instr: English, Spanish

South America

Colegio Los Tréboles
Vereda cerca de Piedra, Finca
Santa Elena, Chía, Cundinamarca
Tel: +57 (1) 862 48 30
Age range: 4–18
No. of pupils: 250
Curriculum: IBDP
Language instr: Spanish

Colegio Marymount Barranquilla
Km. 5, Via a Sabanilla,
Barranquilla, Atlántico
Tel: +57 (5) 388 50 20
Age range: 3–18
No. of pupils: 986
Curriculum: National
Language instr: Spanish, English

Colegio Mayor de los Andes
Kilómetro 3 vía Chía, Cajicá,
Cundinamarca
Curriculum: IBDP, IBPYP
Language instr: Spanish

Colegio Nueva Granada
Cra 2 Este # 70-20, Bogotá, D.C.
Tel: +57 (1) 212 35 11
Language instr: English

Colegio Nueva Inglaterra (New England School)
Calle 218, No. 50-60, Bogotá, D.C.
Tel: +57 (1) 676 07 88
Curriculum: IBDP
Language instr: Spanish

Colegio Nueva York
Calle 227, No. 49-64 Urbanización
El Jardín, Bogotá, D.C.
Tel: +57 1 668 48 90
Age range: 4–18 years
Curriculum: IBDP, IBPYP
Language instr: English, Spanish

Colegio Panamericano
Calle 34 No. 8 -73 Cañaveral
Alto, Floridablanca,
Bucaramanga, Santander
Tel: +57 (7) 638 62 13
Curriculum: National

Colegio San Mateo
Calle 215 #50-24, Bogotá, D.C.
Tel: +57 1 676 08 85
Age range: 4–18 years
Language instr: English, Spanish

Colegio San Viator - Sede Bogotá
Autopista Norte 209-51, Bogotá, D.C.
Tel: +57 (1) 676 09 97
Curriculum: IBDP, IBMYP, IBPYP
Language instr: English

Colegio San Viator - Sede Tunja
Av Universitaria 62 - 100,
Tunja, Boyacá
Curriculum: IBDP
Language instr: English, Spanish

Colegio Santa Francisca Romana
Calle 151 No. 16-40, Bogotá, D.C.
Tel: +57 601 580 44 44
Age range: 3–17 years
Curriculum: IBDP, National
Language instr: English, Spanish

Colegio Santa Maria
Carrera 11 #185B-17, Bogotá, D.C.
Tel: +57 (1) 671 44 40
Age range: G4–18
No. of pupils: 1000

Colegio Santo Tomás de Aquino
Cra 21 No. 132-46, Bogotá, D.C.
Curriculum: IBDP
Language instr: English, Spanish

Colegio Tilatá
Kilómetro 9 vía La Calera,
Bogotá, D.C.
Tel: +57 (1) 592 14 14
Curriculum: IBDP, IBMYP, IBPYP

Deutsche Schule - Cali / Kolumbien
Avenida Guali N° 31, Barrio Ciudad
Jardín, Cali, Valle del Cauca
Tel: +57 (2) 685 89 00
Curriculum: IBDP
Language instr: German, Spanish

Deutsche Schule Medellín
Cra 61, No. 34-62, Itagüi, Antioquia
Tel: +57 (604) 2818811 (Ext:100)
Curriculum: IBDP
Language instr: Spanish

El Camino Academy
Calle 221 #52-30, Bogotá, D.C.
Tel: +57 (1) 742 23 30
Curriculum: National, USA

Fundacion Gimnasio Ingles de Armenia (GI SCHOOL)
KM.3 Via Armenia-Circasia,
630007 Salento, Quindío
Tel: +57 6 749 51 11
Curriculum: IBDP, IBPYP, National, USA
Language instr: English, Spanish

Fundación Gimnasio Los Portales
Calle 212 No. 77- 20, Bogotá, D.C.
Tel: +57 (1) 676 40 55
Curriculum: IBDP, IBMYP, IBPYP
Language instr: English, Spanish

Fundacion Liceo Ingles (Pereira)
Km 5 Via Cerritos Entrada
17, Pereira, Risaralda
Tel: +57 (6) 320 55 63
Age range: 2–18
No. of pupils: 680
Curriculum: SAT, USA

Fundación Nuevo Marymount
Calle 169B, No 74A-02, Bogotá, D.C.
Tel: +57 (1) 669 90 77
Age range: G3–18
Curriculum: IBDP
Language instr: Spanish

GCB - Bilingüe Internacional
Costado Sur - Occidental Aeropuerto
Guaymaral, Bogotá, D.C.
Tel: +57 1 668 39 99
Curriculum: IBDP
Language instr: English, Spanish

George Washington School
Apartado Aereo 2899,
Cartagena, Bolívar
Tel: +57 (5) 665 31 36
Age range: 4–18
No. of pupils: 523 B257 G266
Curriculum: AP, SAT

Gimnasio Británico
Calle 21 No 9A-58, Avenida
Chilacos, Chía, Cundinamarca
Tel: +57 (1) 861 50 84
Age range: 2–16
No. of pupils: 1500
Curriculum: IBDP
Language instr: Spanish, English, French

Gimnasio Campestre la Fontana
Km 4 Vereda El Amor, Vía Multf.
Centauros, Villavicencio, Meta
Tel: +57 314 279 7928
Language instr: English, Spanish

Gimnasio Campestre Los Cerezos
Vereda Canelón, Cajicá,
Cundinamarca
Tel: +57 866 26 79
Curriculum: IBDP, IBPYP

Gimnasio Campestre Montería
Calle 78 Vereda Sevilla,
Montería, Córdoba
Tel: +57 4 791 46 00
Curriculum: IBDP
Language instr: Spanish

Gimnasio Campestre San Rafael
Sede Campestre, Km 6 vía
Siberia, Tenjo, Cundinamarca
Tel: +57 593 30 40
Curriculum: IBDP
Language instr: Spanish

Gimnasio Cantillana
Vereda La Mata, Menzuly Sector,
Highway Piedecuesta, Floridablanca,
Bucaramanga, Santander
Tel: +57 (7) 655 91 01
Curriculum: UK

Gimnasio Contemporaneo
Cra. 6 #29 Norte-648 a 29
Norte-1034, Salento, Quindío
Tel: +57 310 4322191
Curriculum: IBDP
Language instr: English, Spanish

Gimnasio de Los Cerros
Calle 119 N° 0-68, Usaquén,
Santa Fé, Bogotá, D.C.
Tel: +57 (1) 657 60 00
Curriculum: IBDP
Language instr: Spanish

Gimnasio del Norte
Calle 207 No.70-50, Bogotá, D.C.
Tel: +57 601 745 10 00
Age range: 1–17 years
Curriculum: IBDP, IBMYP, IBPYP, National, USA
Language instr: English, Spanish

Gimnasio El Hontanar
Cra. 76 No. 150-26, Bogotá, D.C.
Tel: +57 (1) 681 52 87
Curriculum: IBDP
Language instr: English, Spanish

Gimnasio Femenino
K7 #128-40, Bogotá, D.C.
Tel: +57 (1) 657 84 20
Age range: G4–19
No. of pupils: 600
Curriculum: IBDP, IBMYP, IBPYP
Language instr: Spanish, English

Gimnasio Fontana
Calle 221#108-20, Guaymaral,
Bogotá, D.C.
Tel: +57 (1) 742 03 03 (Ext:122-123)
Age range: 4–18
No. of pupils: 922 B465 G457
Curriculum: National, TOEFL
Language instr: Spanish, English, French

Gimnasio Los Alcázares
Calle 63 Sur No 41-05 Sabaneta,
Medellín, Antioquia
Tel: +57 (4) 305 40 00
Curriculum: IBDP
Language instr: Spanish

Gimnasio Los Pinares
Carrera 35 No. 9 sur 160,
Medellín, Antioquia
Tel: +57 (4) 268 60 34
Curriculum: National, UK, IGCSE

Gimnasio Los Pinos
Calle 193 #38-20, Bogotá, D.C.
Tel: +57 1 670 00 08
Curriculum: IBDP, IBMYP, IBPYP
Language instr: English, Spanish

Gimnasio Vermont
Cl 195 No 54-75, Bogotá, D.C.
Tel: +57 (1) 674 80 70
Age range: 4–18
No. of pupils: 1577
Curriculum: IBDP
Language instr: Spanish

International Berckley School
Km 5 - Vía al Mar, Poste 115,
Barranquilla, Atlántico
Tel: +575 354 81 31
Curriculum: IBDP
Language instr: Spanish

Jardín Infantil Stanford
Calle 134A No. 16-39, Bogotá, D.C.
Curriculum: IBPYP
Language instr: English, Spanish

Jardín Infantil Tía Nora y Liceo Los Alpes
Av 8 Norte, No. 66-05 Urbanización
Menga, Cali, Valle del Cauca
Tel: +57 (2) 665 41 20
Curriculum: IBDP, IBMYP, IBPYP
Language instr: English, Spanish

South America

Knightsbridge Schools International Bogotá (KSI Bogotá)
Calle 221 No. 115-51, Vereda Recodo de Guaymaral, 111176 Bogotá, D.C.
Tel: +57 60 1 745 62 15
Age range: 4–18 years
No. of pupils: 130
Curriculum: IBDP, IBPYP
Language instr: English, Spanish

La Colina School
Km 9.5 Via La Calera Vda Salitre, Bogotá, D.C.
Tel: +57 (1) 439 13 74
Age range: 4–18
No. of pupils: 800
Curriculum: USA
Language instr: Spanish

La Sierra International School
KM 2.5 Vía Los Besotes Después, del Seminario Juan Pablo II, Valledupar, Cesar
Tel: +57 314 501 76 48
Curriculum: USA

Liceo de Cervantes
Carrera 51B, No. 87-99, 080001 Barranquilla, Atlántico
Tel: +57 378 41 72
Curriculum: IBDP
Language instr: English, Spanish

Liceo Francés de Pereira
Kilometro 5 vía Armenia, Pereira, Risaralda
Tel: +57 (6) 315 23 55
Curriculum: National

Liceo Pino Verde
Kilometro 5 Vía Cerritos Entrada 16, El Tigre, Pereira, Risaralda
Tel: +57 322 269 69 51
Curriculum: IBDP, IBMYP, IBPYP
Language instr: English, Spanish

Lycée Français Louis Pasteur
Calle 87 #7-77, Bogotá, D.C.
Tel: +57 (1) 796 50 40

Lycée français Paul-Valéry
Calle 50 N #4AN-56, Cali, Valle del Cauca
Tel: +57 (2) 485 58 50
Curriculum: National, FrenchBacc, UK

Marymount School - Medellín
Calle 7 No 25-64, Medellín, Antioquia
Tel: +57 (4) 266 15 55
Age range: G3–18
No. of pupils: 950
Curriculum: National
Language instr: Spanish, English

Montessori British School, Bogota
Calle 128 #72-80 Calatrava, Bogotá, D.C.
Tel: +57 (1) 652 85 85

Neil Armstrong School
Dir. Cr 44 Cl 14 El Buque, Villavicencio
Curriculum: IBDP
Language instr: English, Spanish

New Cambridge School Bucaramanga - Sede Cabecera
Cra. 39 No. 44-72, Bucaramanga, Santander
Tel: +57 7 638 61 52
Age range: 1–17 years
Curriculum: National, USA
Language instr: English, Spanish

New Cambridge School Bucaramanga - Sede Cañaveral
Calle 32 No. 22-140, Floridablanca, Bucaramanga, Santander
Tel: +57 7 638 61 52
Age range: 1–17 years
Curriculum: IBDP, National, USA
Language instr: English, Spanish

New Cambridge School Cali
Cra 125 No. 12-20, Barrio Pance, Cali, Valle del Cauca
Tel: +57 2 386 59 80
Age range: 1–17 years
Curriculum: IBDP, National, USA
Language instr: English, Spanish

Newport School
Ruitoque Bajo, Km3 vía Acapulco Ramal, Hacienda Trinitarios 600m adentro, Floridablanca, Santander
Tel: +57 7 618 50 11 (Ext: 1416-1401)
Age range: 1–14 years
Curriculum: National, USA
Language instr: English, Spanish

Nuevo Gimnasio School
Kilometro 1 Autopista, Villavicencio, Meta
Tel: +57 310 801 52 83
Curriculum: IBDP
Language instr: English, Spanish

Still I Rise International School - Bogotá
Cra. 17d No. 65 Sur-70, Ciudad Bolivar, Bogotá, D.C.
Language instr: English, Spanish

The Columbus School
Vda. El Penasco, Envigado, Antioquia
Tel: +57 604 403 30 00
Curriculum: National, USA

The Victoria School
Calle 215 N° 50-60, Bogotá, D.C.
Tel: +57 (1) 676 15 03
Age range: 3–18
No. of pupils: 510
Curriculum: IBDP, IBMYP, IBPYP
Language instr: English, Spanish

Vermont School Medellín
Avenida Las Palmas Indiana Mall Km. 2 Vía La Fe, El Retiro, Antioquia
Tel: +57 4 520 60 60
Age range: 1–17 years
Curriculum: IBDP, National, USA
Language instr: English, Spanish

CURAÇAO

International School of Curaçao
PO Box 3090, Koninginnelaan z/n, Emmastad
Tel: +599 9 737 3633
Age range: 2–19
No. of pupils: 375
Curriculum: ACT, AP, IBDP, IBMYP, SAT, TOEFL, USA
Language instr: English

The Curacao American Preparatory School
Erosweg 69, Willemstad
Tel: +599 9 736 8674
Curriculum: USA

GUYANA

Georgetown International Academy
9-10 Delhi Street, Prashbad Nagar, Georgetown
Tel: +592 226 1595
Age range: 4–18
No. of pupils: 64 B31 G33
Curriculum: AP, SAT

HONDURAS

Academia Los Pinares
KM 10 El Hatillo, Apartado 3250, Tegucigalpa
Tel: +504 2211 8231
No. of pupils: 729
Curriculum: USA

Albert Einstein International School
2 Calle, 11-12 Avenida NO, Los Andes #88, San Pedro Sula Cortes 21102
Tel: +504 2550 4622
Curriculum: National, USA

DelCampo School
P.O. Box 2100, Tegucigalpa
Tel: +504 2268 1820
Curriculum: USA

Discovery School
Zona El Molinón, Anillo Poriférico, Sulida a Valle de Angeles, Tegucigalpa
Tel: +504 2221 7790

Escuela Internacional Sampedrana
Col. Gracias a Dios, 500 metros arriba Blvd Hospital Catarino Rivas, San Pedro Sula
Tel: + 504 2540 2722
Age range: 4–18
Curriculum: USA

Happy Days School & Freedom High School
Km 2 carretera al Zapotal, San Pedro Sula
Tel: +504 2551 1501
Age range: 4–18
Curriculum: National, USA
Language instr: English, Spanish

Lycee Franco Hondurien
Col. las colinas, Boulevard francia calle principal, 11101 Tegucigalpa, Francisco Morazan
Tel: +504 2231 1472
Curriculum: FrenchBacc

Mazapan School
La Ceiba
Tel: +1 504 443 2716
Age range: 3–17
Curriculum: USA

The American School of Tegucigalpa
P.O. Box 2134, Tegucigalpa
Tel: +504 2276 8400
Age range: 3–18 years
No. of pupils: 1117
Curriculum: IBDP, USA
Language instr: English

PANAMA

Academia Integral San Lucas
Alto Bonito, Nuevo Emperador, Arraiján
Tel: +507 241 0597
Curriculum: IBPYP
Language instr: English, Spanish

Academia Internacional Arabe Panamena
Naciones Unidas Street, Colon
Tel: +507 474 071 3/4/5
Age range: 4–18
Language instr: English

Balboa Academy
Jorge Gil 100, City of Knowledge, Panama City
Tel: +507 302 0035
Age range: 3–18 years
No. of pupils: 905
Curriculum: AP, National, USA
Language instr: English

Boston School International
Avenida Paseo del Mar con Calle Vista del Pacífico, Edificio H-51, Costa del Este, Panama City
Tel: +507 833 8888
Age range: 3–18 years
Curriculum: IBDP, IBMYP, IBPYP
Language instr: English, Spanish

Caribbean International School
Box 0301 03289, Cristobel, Colon
Tel: +507 445 0933/0961
Age range: 3–18
No. of pupils: 672
Curriculum: AP, National, USA

Centro Bilingüe Vista Alegre
Calle Omega, Vista Alegre
Tel: +506 251 5236
Curriculum: IBDP
Language instr: English, Spanish

Colegio Isaac Rabin
Edificio 130, Ciudad del Saber
Tel: +507 3170059
Curriculum: IBDP, IBMYP, IBPYP
Language instr: Spanish

South America

Instituto Alberto Einstein
Via Israel, in front of
Multiplaza, Panamá City
Tel: +507 270 2266
Curriculum: IBMYP
Language instr: English, Spanish

**International School
of Panama**
P.O. Box 0819-02588, Cerro
Viento Rural, Panama City
Tel: +507 293 3000
Age range: 3–18
No. of pupils: 1262
Curriculum: ACT, IBDP,
National, SAT, USA
Language instr: English

Jacarandá School
Calle Arnulfo Arias Madrid, Ancón,
Edificio 841 a un lado del MEDUCA,
Edificio del teatro+, Panamá City
Tel: +507 6554 0231
Age range: 3–13 years

**King's College
School Panama**
Av. Demetrio B. Lakas,
Clayton, Panama City
Tel: +507 282 3300
Age range: 2–18 years
Curriculum: IBDP, UK, IGCSE, ALevs
Language instr: English, Spanish

**Metropolitan School
of Panama**
Green Valley, Panama
Norte, Panama City
Tel: +507 317 1130
Age range: 3–18 years
No. of pupils: 800
Curriculum: IBDP, IBMYP,
IBPYP, National
Language instr: English

Oxford International School
74th East Street and Via España,
Carrasquilla, Panama City
Tel: +507 308 7100
Age range: 4–18
No. of pupils: 1264
Language instr: English

**Panama Prep
International School**
Camino al nuevo Club de Golf,
Brisas del Golf, Panama
Tel: +507 220 2520
Age range: 3–11 years

**SABIS International
School - Costa Verde**
Paseo de los Guayacanes y Av.
Circunvalación, Costa Verde
Tel: +507 209 2606
Age range: 4–18 years
Curriculum: AP, SAT, UK,
USA, IGCSE, ALevs

The Casco School
Calle 2a, entre Avenida A y Av.
Central España, Panamá City
Tel: +507 6644 2413
Age range: 2–18 years
Curriculum: UK
Language instr: English, Spanish

The Oxford School
Edison Park, Via Simon Bolivar,
Apartado 6-7247, El Dorado
Tel: +507 321 3800
Age range: 4–18

PARAGUAY

**American School
of Asunción**
Avenida España 1175, PO
Box 10093, Asunción
Tel: +595 21 236 4000
Age range: 4–18
No. of pupils: 640
Curriculum: National, USA

**Asuncion Christian
Academy**
Avenida Santísimo Sacramento
1181, Casilla 1562, Asuncion 1209
Tel: +595 (21) 612-477
Curriculum: USA

Centro Educativo Arambé
Santísima Trinidad No 3.211, c/
Avda. Ita Ybaté (Zona Brítez
Cue), Luque, Asunción
Tel: +595 21 694 662
Curriculum: IBDP
Language instr: Spanish

Colegio Goethe Asunción
Cnl Silva esq Tte Rocholl,
Asuncion 232
Tel: +595 21 606860
Curriculum: IBDP

**Colegio International
SEK Paraguay**
C/Mercedes Grau-Parques del
Yacht y Golf Club, Asunción
Tel: +595 21 907650
Curriculum: IBDP
Language instr: English, Spanish

Colegio San Andrés
Avenue General Sanrtos 567 Esp,
Juan de Salazar, Asuncion
Tel: +595 21 221 647
Curriculum: UK, IGCSE, ALevs

Faith Christian School
Del Maestro 3471 c/ Soriano
González, Barrio Herrera, Asunción
Tel: +595 21 620 5024
Curriculum: IBDP
Language instr: English, Spanish

**Lycée Français d'Asunción
Marcel Pagnol**
Enrique Solano López 1139,
Calle Concordia, Asuncion
Tel: 00 595 21 207083
Curriculum: FrenchBacc

**Pan American
International School**
Calle América esq. 2da Capital de la
República, Urb. Loma Merlo, Luque
Tel: +595 21 645 470
Age range: 4–18
No. of pupils: 200
Curriculum: USA

Santa Teresa de Jesús
Avda. Mcal. López 237 c/
Brasil, Asunción 927
Tel: +595 21 224683
Language instr: English

St Anne's School
Tte. Manuel Pino Gonzalez y
Eulalio Facetti, Asunción
Tel: +595 21 295649
Age range: 4–18
No. of pupils: 600 B300 G300
Curriculum: IBDP
Language instr: English, Spanish

PERU

American School
Av. Larco Nro 288, Urb. San Andrés,
Trujillo, La Libertad 13008
Tel: +51 44 612370
Curriculum: IBDP
Language instr: English, Spanish

**Andino Cusco
International School**
Km 10.5 Carretera, Chinchero
Distrito de Cachimayo, Cusco
Tel: +51 84 275135
Curriculum: IBDP, IBPYP
Language instr: English, Spanish

Cambridge College Lima
Av. Alameda de los Molinos
728-730, La Encantada de
Villa, Chorrillos, Lima 15067
Tel: +51 12 540107
Age range: 2–18 years
No. of pupils: 1108
Curriculum: IBDP
Language instr: English, Spanish

**Casuarinas International
College**
Av Jacarandá 391, Valle
Hermoso, Monterrico, Santiago
de Surco, Lima 15023
Tel: +51 13 444040
Age range: 4–17
No. of pupils: 881
Curriculum: IBDP, IBMYP, IBPYP, IBCP
Language instr: Spanish, English,
French, Portuguese, Mandarin

**Centro Educativo Particular
San Francisco de Borja**
San Borja, Lima
Curriculum: IBDP
Language instr: English, Spanish

Clemente Althaus
Prolongación Jirón Cuzco
360, San Miguel - Alt. Cdra. 12
Av. La Marina, Lima 15086
Tel: +51 14 194700
Curriculum: IBDP
Language instr: Spanish

Colegio Alpamayo
Calle Bucaramanga 145, Urb
Mayorazgo, Lima 15026
Tel: +51 13 490111
Age range: B5–17
Curriculum: IBDP
Language instr: Spanish, English

Colegio Altair
Av. La Arboleda 385, Urb. Sirius,
La Molina, Lima 15024
Tel: +51 13 650298
Age range: 2–18 years
No. of pupils: 900
Curriculum: IBDP, IBMYP, IBPYP
Language instr: Spanish, English

Colegio Champagnat
Paseo de la República 7930,
Santiago de Surco, Lima 15049
Tel: +51 15 1905000
Curriculum: IBDP, IBMYP, IBPYP
Language instr: Spanish

**Colegio Franklin
Delano Roosevelt**
Av. Las Palmeras 325,
Camacho, Lima 15023
Tel: +51 14 350890
Age range: 3–18
No. of pupils: 1218 B687 G531
Curriculum: AP, IBDP, SAT
Language instr: English, Spanish

Colegio Hipólito Unanue
Sector 2, Grupo 25, Mz M Lote
3, Villa el Salvador, Lima
Tel: +51 947 242115
Curriculum: IBDP
Language instr: English, Spanish

Colegio La Unión
Av. Cipriano Dulanto 1950,
Pueblo Libre, Lima 15084
Tel: +51 12 610533
Curriculum: IBDP
Language instr: English

Colegio León Pinelo
Calle Maimónides 610 (ex Los
Manzanos), San Isidro, Lima 15076
Tel: +51 12 183040
Age range: 3–17
Curriculum: IBDP, IBMYP, IBPYP, IGCSE
Language instr: Spanish

Colegio Los Álamos
Calle Estados Unidos 731,
Jesús María, Lima 15701
Tel: +51 14 631044
Curriculum: IBDP

Colegio Magister
Calle Francisco de Cuéllar 686,
Monterrico, Santiago de Surco, Lima
Tel: +51 14 363063
Age range: 3–17
Curriculum: IBDP, National, TOEFL
Language instr: Spanish

Colegio Mater Admirabilis
Av. Arica 898, San Miguel, Lima
Curriculum: IBMYP
Language instr: Spanish

Colegio Max Uhle
Av. Fernandini s/n, Sachaca,
Arequipa 04013
Tel: +51 54 232921
No. of pupils: 1165
Curriculum: IBDP
Language instr: Spanish

South America

Colegio Montealto
Los Eucaliptos 491, San Isidro, Lima
Tel: +51 441 2685
Curriculum: IBDP
Language instr: Spanish

Colegio Nuestra Señora del Pilar
Av. Virgen del Pilar 1711, Cercado, Arequipa
Tel: +51 54 226262
Curriculum: IBDP

Colegio Peruano - Alemán Reina del Mundo
Avenida Rinconada del Lago 675, La Molina, Lima
Tel: +51 14 792191
Age range: 2–17
No. of pupils: 771
Curriculum: IBDP
Language instr: Spanish

Colegio Peruano Alemán Beata Imelda
Carretera Central Km 29 s/n, Lurigancho-Chosica, Lima
Tel: +51 13 603119
Curriculum: IBDP

Colegio Peruano Británico
Av. Vía Láctea 445, Monterrico, Santiago de Surco, Lima 15023
Tel: +51 14 360151
Curriculum: IBDP
Language instr: Spanish, English

Colegio Peruano Norteamericano Abraham Lincoln
Av. José Antonio 475, Urb. Parque de Monterico, La Molina, Lima 15023
Tel: +51 16 174500
Age range: 3–17
Curriculum: IBDP, IBMYP, IBPYP, National
Language instr: Spanish, English

Colegio Pestalozzi (Colegio Suizo del Peru)
Casilla 18-1027, Aurora-Miraflores, Lima
Tel: +51 16 178600
Age range: 4–18
No. of pupils: 574 B282 G292
Curriculum: IBDP
Language instr: Spanish

Colegio Sagrados Corazones 'Recoleta'
Av. Circunvalación del Golf 368, La Molina, Lima 15023
Tel: +51 17 022500
Age range: 4–18 years
Curriculum: IBDP
Language instr: Spanish

Colegio Salcantay
Av. Pío XII 261, Monterrico, Santiago de Surco, Lima 15023
Tel: +51 14 359224
Curriculum: IBDP
Language instr: Spanish

Colegio San Agustín
Av. Javier Prado Este 980, Urb. El Palomar, San Isidro, Lima
Tel: +51 16 164242
Curriculum: IBDP, IBPYP

Colegio San Agustín de Chiclayo
Km. 8 Carretera Pimentel S/N, Pimentel, Chiclay, Lambayeque
Tel: +51 74 208173
Age range: B4–17 G4–16
No. of pupils: VIth110
Curriculum: IBDP
Language instr: Spanish

Colegio San Ignacio de Recalde
Calle Géminis 251, San Borja, Lima 15037
Tel: +51 12 119430
Curriculum: IBDP, IBPYP
Language instr: English

Colegio San Pedro
Calle Hurón 409, Rinconada del Lago, La Molina, Lima 15026
Tel: +51 16 149500
Curriculum: IBDP
Language instr: English, Spanish

Colegio Santa Úrsula
Av. Nicolas de Rivera 132, San Isidro, Lima 15073
Tel: +51 12 027430
Curriculum: IBDP

Colegio Santísimo Nombre de Jesús
Urbanización Chacarilla del Estanque Calle Mayorazgo 176, San Borja, Lima
Tel: +51 13 721655
Curriculum: IBDP
Language instr: English, Spanish

Colegio Villa Caritas
Calle Hurón 409, Rinconada del Lago, La Molina, Lima 15026
Tel: +51 16 149500
Curriculum: IBDP
Language instr: English, Spanish

Colegio Villa Maria
Av. La Laguna 280, La Planicie, La Molina, Lima 15026
Tel: +51 947 316 465
Curriculum: IBDP
Language instr: English, Spanish

Colegio Virgen Inmaculada de Monterrico
Av. Morro Solar No. 110, Santiago de Surco, Lima 15039
Tel: +51 13 726499
Curriculum: IBDP
Language instr: English, Spanish

Collège André Malraux
Calle Batallón Concepción 245, Urb. Sta. Teresa, Santiago de Surco, Lima
Tel: +51 12 754937
Curriculum: IBDP
Language instr: English

Davy College
Av. Hoyos Rubio 2684, Cajamarca 06001
Tel: +51 76 367501
Age range: 2–18
No. of pupils: B359 G418 VIth8
Curriculum: IBDP
Language instr: Spanish, English

El Pinar College
Calle los Quenuales 205, Urbanización El Pinar, Huaraz, Ancash 02002
Tel: +51 1 43 452000
Curriculum: IBDP
Language instr: English, Spanish

Euroamerican College
Fundo Casablanca, Pachacamac, Lima
Tel: +51 12 311617
Age range: 3–18
No. of pupils: 490 B245 G245
Curriculum: IBDP, IBPYP
Language instr: Spanish, English

Fleming College
Av América Sur 3701, Trujillo, La Libertad 13008
Tel: +51 44 284440
Age range: 2–18 years
No. of pupils: 600 B300 G300
Curriculum: IBDP, IBPYP, National, IGCSE
Language instr: Spanish, English

Hiram Bingham, The British International School of Lima
Av. Paseo la Castellana 919, Urbanización La Castellana, Santiago de Surco, Lima 15048
Tel: +51 27 19880
Age range: 3–17 years
No. of pupils: 660
Curriculum: IBDP, IBMYP, IBPYP
Language instr: English, Spanish

IE Pedro Ruiz Gallo
Av. Cdra 2 S/N Costado de la Clinica Maison de Sante Chorrillos, Chorrillos, Lima
Tel: +51 16 802673
Curriculum: IBDP, IBMYP, IBPYP
Language instr: English, Spanish

Institución Educativa Particular San Antonio de Padua
Av. Estados Unidos 569, Jesús Maria, Lima
Tel: +51 16 143600
Curriculum: IBDP
Language instr: Spanish

Institución Educativa Privada Lord Byron
Calle Grande 250, Sr. de la Caña, Cayma, Arequipa
Tel: +51 54 255038
Curriculum: IBDP
Language instr: Spanish

Lima Villa College
Av. Alameda Don Alfonso 125, Los Huertos de Villa, Chorrillos, Lima
Tel: +51 12 553232
Curriculum: IBPYP
Language instr: English, Spanish

Lord Byron School
Jr. Viña del Mar 375 - 379, Sol de la Molina, Lima 15026
Tel: +51 14 791717
Curriculum: IBDP, IBMYP, IBPYP
Language instr: English, Spanish

Lycée Franco-Péruvien
Jr. Morro Solar 550, Santiago de Surco, Lima 15039
Tel: +51 16 267800
Curriculum: FrenchBacc

Markham College - Peru
Calle Augusto Angulo 291, San Antonio, Miraflores, Lima 15048
Tel: +51 13 156750 (Ext: 1325)
Age range: 3–18 years
No. of pupils: 2000
Curriculum: IBDP
Language instr: English, Spanish

Montessori International College
Maz. A Sub Lote 01A, Urb. Tecsup, Distrito Víctor Larco Herrera, Trujillo, La Libertad 13009
Tel: +51 44 340000
Curriculum: IBDP, IBPYP
Language instr: English, Spanish

Newton College
Av. Ricardo Elías Aparicio 240, Lima 15026
Tel: +51 12 079900
Age range: 2–18
Curriculum: IBDP, IBMYP, IBPYP
Language instr: English

San Francisco College
Urb. El Oasis II, Calle Costa del Sol Mz 'D' Lote 14, (Pista Camino a Huacachina), Ica 11004
Tel: +51 95 6298110
Curriculum: IBDP, IBPYP
Language instr: Spanish

San Silvestre School
Av. Santa Cruz 1251, Miraflores, Lima 15074
Tel: +51 12 413334
Age range: G3–18
No. of pupils: 1180
Curriculum: IBDP
Language instr: English

St. George's College - Sede Senior
Alameda Don Augusto Mz- D-1 Lote 15, Urb. Los Huertos de Villa, Chorrillos
Tel: +51 17 197390
Age range: 11–18 years
Curriculum: IBDP, IBCP
Language instr: English, Spanish

Villa Alarife School
Jr. Alameda Don Augusto Mz. D Lt. 5, Urb. Los Huertos de Villa, Chorrillos, Lima 15067
Tel: +51 12 346969
Curriculum: IBDP

Weberbauer School
Calle Pio XII 123, Santiago de Surco, Lima 15023
Tel: +51 14 366212
Curriculum: IBDP
Language instr: German, Spanish

South America

SURINAME

International Academy of Suriname
Lawtonlaan 20, Paramaribo
Tel: +597 499 461
Age range: 3–18
No. of pupils: 103
Curriculum: USA

URUGUAY

Colegio Stella Maris
Máximo Tajes 7357/7359, CP 11500 Montevideo 11500
Tel: +598 2 600 0702
Age range: 4–17
No. of pupils: 1086 B576 G510
Curriculum: IBDP, IGCSE
Language instr: Spanish, English

Escuela Integral Hebreo Uruguaya
Jose Benito Lamas 2835, Montevideo 11300
Tel: +598 2 708 1712
Curriculum: IBDP, IBPYP
Language instr: Spanish

Escuela y Liceo Elbio Fernandez
Maldonado 1381, Montevideo 11200
Tel: +598 2901 1254
Curriculum: IBDP, IBMYP
Language instr: English, Spanish

International College
Blvr Artigas y Avda del Mar, Punta del Este, Maldonado
Tel: +598 42 228 888
Curriculum: IBDP
Language instr: English, Spanish

St Brendan's School
Av Rivera 2314, Montevideo CP 11200
Tel: +598 2409 4939
Age range: 3–17
Curriculum: IBDP, IBMYP, IBPYP, IBCP
Language instr: English, Spanish

St Clare's College
California y los Médanos, Punta del Este, San Rafael 20000
Tel: +598 42 490200
Curriculum: IBDP, ALevs
Language instr: Spanish, English

St Patrick's College
Camino Gigantes 2735, Montevideo 12100
Tel: +598 2 601 3474
Age range: 3–18
Curriculum: IBMYP
Language instr: Spanish

St. George's School
Juana Pereyra 1, Entre José Batlle y Ordoñez y Manuel Espinosa, Montevideo
Tel: +598 2613 5338
Curriculum: IBMYP, UK
Language instr: English, Spanish

The Anglo School
Sede Carrasco, Saldún de Rodríguez 2195, Montevideo 11500
Tel: +598 2600 6452
Curriculum: National

The British Schools, Montevideo
Máximo Tajes 6400, esq Havre, Montevideo 11500
Tel: +598 2 600 3421
Age range: 4–18
No. of pupils: B720 G750
Curriculum: IBDP, IBPYP, National
Language instr: English, Spanish

Uruguayan American School
Saldún de Rodríguez 2375, Montevideo 11500
Tel: + (598) 2600 7681
Curriculum: IBDP
Language instr: English

Woodlands School
San Carlos de Bolivar s/n entre Havre y Cooper, Montevideo 11500
Tel: +598 2601 4602
Curriculum: IBMYP, IGCSE
Language instr: Spanish

Woodside School
Mercedes y Louvre. Barrio Cantegril, 20100 Punta del Este, Maldonado
Tel: +598 4223 2298
Age range: 2–18
No. of pupils: 578 B295 G283
Curriculum: IBDP, National, UK, IGCSE, ALevs
Language instr: English, Spanish

VENEZUELA

Centro Educativo Internacional Anzoátegui (CEIA)
Av José Antonio Anzoátegui km 98, Anaco
Tel: +58 282 4222683
Age range: 3–18
No. of pupils: 78
Curriculum: USA

Colegio Bellas Artes
Avenida 3F con calle 71, Maracaibo 4002
Tel: +58 261 7911175
No. of pupils: 897
Language instr: Spanish

Colegio Guayamuri
Av. Luisa Cáceres de Arismendi, Atamo Norte, La Asunción 6311
Tel: +58 295 2423048
Curriculum: IBDP
Language instr: English, Spanish

Colegio Humboldt Caracas
Prolongación Av. El Estanque Urb. Ávila, Norte del Country Club, Caracas
Tel: +58 212 7311195

Colegio Integral El Avila
Centro de Artes Integradas, Urb. Terrazas del Avila, La Urbina Norte, Caracas 1073
Tel: +58 500 3528452
Curriculum: IBDP
Language instr: Spanish

Colegio Integral El Manglar
Carrera No. 41 S/N Sector Nueva Barcelona, Barcelona 6001
Tel: +58 281 3172170
Curriculum: IBDP
Language instr: English, Spanish

Colegio Internacional de Caracas
Calle el Colegio Americano Entre Samanes y Minas, Baruta, Caracas 1080
Tel: +58 212 9450708
Age range: 3–19 years
No. of pupils: 180
Curriculum: ACT, IBDP, IBMYP, SAT, USA
Language instr: English, Spanish

Colegio Los Arcos
Calle Los Arcos, Caracas 1080
Tel: +58 212 9453344
Curriculum: IBDP
Language instr: English, Spanish

Colegio Los Campitos
Urbanización Los Campitos, Ruta C, Caracas 1080
Tel: +58 212 9771695
Curriculum: IBDP
Language instr: Spanish

Colegio Moral y Luces 'Herzl-Bialik'
Final Av. Principal de Los Chorros, Caracas 1071
Tel: +58 212 2736894
Curriculum: IBDP

Colegio San Agustín El Paraíso
Av. E, El Pinar El Paraíso Urbanization, Caracas 1020
Curriculum: IBDP
Language instr: English, Spanish

Colegio Valle Abierto
Calle Loma Azul, Urb San Luis, El Cafetal, Caracas 1061
Tel: +58 424 2401430
Age range: 1–18
No. of pupils: B189 G151
Curriculum: National
Language instr: Spanish

Escuela Bella Vista
67th Street between Av. 3D and 3E, La Lago sector, Maracaibo 4001
Tel: +58 261 7940000
Curriculum: IBDP
Language instr: English

Escuela Campo Alegre
Final Calle La Cinta, Las Mercedes, Caracas 1080
Tel: +58 212 9933922
Age range: 3–18
No. of pupils: 300 B153 G147
Curriculum: ACT, IBDP, SAT, USA
Language instr: English

Instituto Educacional Juan XXIII
Calle San Enrique No 85-70, Trigal Centro, Valencia 2002
Tel: +58 241 8425732
Age range: 1–18
No. of pupils: 1500 B750 G750
Curriculum: IBDP, IBCP
Language instr: Spanish

International School of Monagas
Km 1 Carretera via a la Toscana, Maturin 6201
Tel: +58 291 3150011
Age range: 3–19
No. of pupils: 243
Curriculum: SAT, USA

Le Lycée Français de Caracas - Colegio Francia
Av.D de Campo Claro, Caracas 1071
Tel: +58 212 2375959
Curriculum: FrenchBacc

Liceo Los Robles
Urb. El Doral Norte, Calle 34. Esquina con Avenida Fuerzas Armadas, Edificio Liceo Los Robles, Maracaibo
Tel: +58 261 7421833
Language instr: Spanish

QSI International School of El Tigre
Avenida Intercomunal, (detras de C.C. El Roble), El Tigre
Tel: +58 424 8111336
Age range: 4–16
No. of pupils: 74
Curriculum: USA
Language instr: English

The British School Caracas
Transversal 9 Este Av. Luis Roche, Quinta DAMI Urbanización Altamira, Caracas 1060
Tel: +58 212 917 6450
Age range: 3–18 years
Curriculum: IBDP, UK, IGCSE

Washington Academy
Calle C, Urb. Colinas de Valle Arriba, Caracas 1080
Tel: +58 212 9757777
Age range: 4–18 years
No. of pupils: 523
Curriculum: IBDP, IBMYP
Language instr: Spanish, English

International school associations

International school associations

THE ACCREDITING COMMISSION FOR SCHOOLS, WESTERN ASSOCIATION FOR SCHOOLS AND COLLEGES (ACS WASC)

ACS WASC works closely with the Office of Overseas Schools under the U.S. Department of State. ACS WASC provides assistance to schools worldwide, primarily in California, Hawaii, Guam, Asia, the Pacific Region, the Middle East, Africa, and Europe.

The Accrediting Commission for Schools, WASC, extends its services to over 5,000 public, independent, church-related, and proprietary Pre-K–12 and adult schools, works with 18 associations in joint accreditation processes, and collaborates with other organizations such as the California Department of Education (CDE).

ACS, WASC, Northern California Office, 533 Airport Boulevard, Suite 200, Burlingame, CA 94010-2009, USA
Tel: +1 650 696-1060
Email: mail@acswasc.org
Website: www.acswasc.org

THE ALLIANCE FOR INTERNATIONAL EDUCATION (AIE)

The Alliance for International Education is committed to promoting international learning in any context. Its aim is always to balance theoretical discourse and research with practical action. Its conferences and activities bring together mainstream international schools with universities, researchers, providers of curriculum, resources and training, and representatives from state and private educational systems who are keen to internationalise learning in their own schools. Besides its 'world conferences' the AIE supports regional initiatives in several parts of the world – and in line with its vision that international education should be available to every child, it operates as an open access, open source organization where there are no membership fees for becoming a partner or for accessing resources. For more information about the AIE, contact:
Email: vicki.aie.bath@gmail.com
Website: www.intedalliance.com

AMERICAN INTERNATIONAL SCHOOLS IN THE AMERICAS (AMISA)

AMISA, formerly the Associationof American Schools in South America, has more than 65 world-class member schools in 25 countries, namely: Argentina, Aruba, Bolivia, Brazil, Chile, Cayman Islands, Colombia, Costa Rica, Curacao, Dominican Republic, Ecuador, El Salvador, Guatemala, Guyana, Haiti, Honduras, Jamaica, Mexico, Panama, Paraguay, Peru, Trinidad & Tobago, USA, Uruguay and Venezuela. Its mission is to provide and promote programmes and services to their members, all of whom offer an American international education. AMISA's mission statement says their mission is to enhance the quality of education in American/international member schools.

Various services are provided for member schools including: a purchasing service; a recruiting fair in Central America and the Caribbean; four annual professional development conferences; a payroll processing service; awards to AMISA Heads; annual salary and benefits survey; and a quarterly newsletter.

AMISA member schools are all private institutions offering a mainly American curriculum; the language of instruction is English. Each of the schools combines US and host country courses of study, and many grant both host country and US diplomas. Some schools also offer the IB, Advanced Placement (AP) courses, and English as a Second Language (ESL).

AMISA schools who hold full membership are: elementary and/or secondary schools; have English as the primary language of instruction; are accredited by a recognised organization such as CIS or the IB; and agree to follow the principles, purposes and objectives of AMISA.
3105 NW 107th Avenue, Suite 400-S5,
Doral, FL 33172, USA
Tel: +1 954 436 4034
Website: www.amisa.us

ASSOCIATION FOR THE ADVANCEMENT OF INTERNATIONAL EDUCATION (AAIE)

AAIE is a non-profit, membership-based international organization that partners with educational institutions and associations worldwide to exchange international ideas, resources and research that help develop and improve international education, to diversify and expand school leadership capacity.

Its mission global community that connects diverse people, ideas and resources, AAIE helps international educators lead with vision, wisdom, courage and integrity.
AAIE 15 Roszel Road
Princeton NJ 08540
Phone: +1 609-716-7441
www.aaie.org

ASSOCIATION OF AMERICAN SCHOOLS OF CENTRAL AMERICA (AASCA)

The Association of American Schools of Central America (AASCA) was formed to support and encourage academic, artistic, athletic and cultural interaction between international schools that offer a US type education in Central America. It believes that through the organization and sponsorship of these types of activities that all young people involved will be exposed to and benefit from the multicultural interaction. It is the desire of AASCA to promote a better understanding of multiculturalism among all races of young people through these events.

AASCA also supports the continuing education of its member teachers and administrators through facilitating workshops and conferences that focus on the latest educational ideas and teaching methods from the United States. AASCA aims to improve the quality of all education in the countries in which they reside and create a greater awareness and appreciation for cultural diversity through the programs they sponsor.

AASCA has schools in the following countries: Guatemala, El Salvador, Honduras, Nicaragua, Costa Rica and Panama. Any Central American school that provides a US curriculum is eligible to join this association.
President: Lilliana Jenkins (ljenkins@amschool.org)
Secretary: Adolfo González (adolfo@lincoln.edu.ni)
Website: www.aascaonline.net

ASSOCIATION OF BRITISH SCHOOLS IN CHILE (ABSCH)

Founded in 1977 with just seven schools, this association now has 22 member schools, in Santiago, Viña del Mar, Casablanca, Concepción, Punta Arenas and Antofagasta. Its schools offer education for pupils aged four to 18 and all schools are bilingual with similar aims and practices. It believes in ongoing training for teaching staff and its mission is to 'encourage and support member schools in its endeavour to provide an education of quality that reflects the best of British practice, in co-operation with one another, and with Chilean and British educational authorities'.
ABSCH, Apoquindo 7935, oficina 404
A, Las Condes, Santiago, Chile
Tel: +56 2 2121 953
Email: asistente@absch.cl
Website: www.absch.cl

ASSOCIATION OF CHINA AND MONGOLIA INTERNATIONAL SCHOOLS (ACAMIS)

Founded to promote and support the building of international schools in China and Mongolia, ACAMIS now has a membership that includes more than 90 of the 150+ international schools operating within China, Hong Kong, Macao, Taiwan and Mongolia.

The association hosts various student activities, professional development workshops for teachers and networking opportunities for Heads of schools, and other educational personnel within member schools. There is an annual meeting for ACAMIS Heads.

The association's aims are: to widen and evolve the curriculum of ACAMIS schools; to encourage the professional development of staff within their schools; to facilitate communication between member schools; to promote understanding and international friendship; to co-operate with others pursuing the same objectives; to encourage student exchanges; to collaborate on professional development; and to support national and regional networking.
ACAMIS, 33 Wai Man Road, Sai Kung, Hong Kong
Email: operations@acamis.org
Website: www.acamis.org

ASSOCIATION OF COLOMBIAN-CARIBBEAN AMERICAN SCHOOLS (ACCAS)

ACCAS is one of the regional associations affiliated with the Tri-Association.

It has 27 schools offering an American education in the Colombian and Caribbean region. Its core values include: school improvement and ongoing staff development.

All member schools must be US accredited candidates for accreditation.

Currently it has schools in the Dominican Republic, Ecuador, Haiti, Jamaica and Colombia.
Email: contact@tri-association.org
Website: www.tri-association.org

ASSOCIATION OF GERMAN INTERNATIONAL SCHOOLS (AGIS)

The Association of German International Schools (AGIS) represents and supports the educational and public interest of member schools and their communities by promoting and improving international education. It currently has 22 members.
AGIS, Bruchmeisterallee 6, 30169 Hannover, Germany
Tel: +49 0511 10532406
Email: julia@agis-schools.org
Website: www.agis-schools.org

ASSOCIATION OF INTERNATIONAL SCHOOLS IN AFRICA (AISA)

AISA represents international schools on the continent of Africa. Its schools range in size from 20 to 2000+ students. AISA schools tend to have an American or British-based curriculum; others have an eclectic mix but all have an international focus.

The association's goal is to serve the varying needs of its students, teachers and administrators. Its mission is to increase school effectiveness and inspire student learning by promoting communication, collaboration, and professional development.

AISA's objectives are: to enhance the quality of learning by promoting effective practice; foster intercultural and international understanding; promote an appreciation and understanding of Africa; support professional development within member schools; collate, analyse, and distribute information to help guide member schools; enable collaboration and networking between members; and to develop and maintain partnerships with organisations and institutions that complement the association's values and mission.
AISA, PO Box 14103-00800, Nairobi, Kenya
Tel: +254 (0) 20 269 7442/8076067
Email: info@aisa.or.ke
Website: www.aisa.or.ke

International school associations

ASSOCIATION OF AMERICAN SCHOOLS IN MEXICO (ASOMEX)
ASOMEX is a member of the Tri-Association (www.tri-association.org).

It was founded in 1957 and originally included eight American schools. Today, it is made up of 19 member schools throughout Mexico. These schools are private, non-profit establishments ranging in size from 42 to over 3000 students. It is committed to offering an American style curriculum, whilst meeting the criteria set down by the Mexican Secretariat of Education.

ASOMEX's main aims are: to develop a closer union of the American schools in Mexico; seek to resolve common problems of member schools; advance ideals and standards; assist member schools in establishing and maintaining high standards; encourage and enhance the multicultural/bilingual aspects of member schools; provide qualified consultants to teachers and administrators; select and procure quality educational materials and equipment; and develop communications and relations amongst member schools.

There are a wide variety of annual ASOMEX activities for members, including athletic tournaments, teacher and student workshops, model UN, and art and musical festivals.
Website: www.asomex.org

BRITISH ASSOCIATION OF INDEPENDENT SCHOOLS WITH INTERNATIONAL STUDENTS (BAISIS)
The British Association of Independent Schools with International Students (BAISIS) is a group of educational centres which provide a full academic curriculum in the United Kingdom to students from other countries.

Members are drawn from independent schools, study centres and colleges. Originally founded in 1997 by Bedford, Rossall, Sherborne and Taunton Schools, membership has grown steadily and today the association is an influential organisation which occupies, and speaks for, an important niche sector in international education in the UK.

The Association exists to provide help in the form of training, development, and mutual support to its members and for quality assurance purposes. This is achieved through regular meetings, training from inside and outside the Association and through a bespoke annual conference. All member institutions provide a supportive pastoral framework and quality academic environment for international students.The Association also represents the interests of schools and colleges with international students in the UK at the national level.
Website: www.baisis.org.uk

BRITISH SCHOOLS IN THE MIDDLE EAST (BSME)
BSME has more than 150 member schools and over 90 supporting members.

It provides a quality-assured network of schools helping Heads and Teachers share best practice and keep abreast of the latest educational developments. BSME runs its own Accreditation System, Annual Headteachers' Conferences and Continuing Professional Development (CPD) programme of conferences, courses and webinars.

All members schools are: an English Medium, essentially British Curriculum School in which the Principal/Head Teacher and the majority of teachers (apart from those teaching local languages) have qualifications recognised by the UK Department for Education.

Each year BSME holds a conference to discuss and learn about developments in UK education and school leadership and management issues.
BSME FZE, DSO HQ, D-309, Dubai Silicon Oasis, Dubai, UAE
Email: business@bsme.org.uk
Website: www.bsme.org.uk

CENTRAL & EASTERN EUROPEAN SCHOOLS ASSOCIATION (CEESA)
The Central & Eastern European Schools Association (CEESA) was founded as a result of the growth of American and International Schools in Central and Eastern Europe. In many cases, the schools were geographically isolated from each other and from the main stream of American and International Education.

CEESA was formed to broaden the horizons of schools and to promote professional growth. In addition to the CEESA Annual Conference in March, CEESA sponsors regional workshops, institutes and meetings to foster professionalism, scholarship, and a deeper understanding of improvements for leading, teaching and learning.

CEESA also sponsors student activities, focusing on a variety of academic and non-academic areas, and a full schedule of sports events.
Executive Director: Kathy Stetson
CEESA, Ul. Damira Tomljanovića 3, 10020, Zagreb, Croatia
Tel: +385 91 181 7921
Email: office@ceesa.org
Website: www.ceesa.org

International school associations

COGNIA
Cognia, previously known as AdvancED, is a non-profit, non-partisan organization that conducts rigorous, on-site external reviews of Pre-K-12 schools and school systems to ensure that all learners realize their full potential.

Combining 'the knowledge and expertise of a research institute, the skills of a management consulting firm and the passion of a grassroots movement for educational change', Cognia serves as a partner to 40,000 schools and school systems across 90+ countries. Cognia was created through a 2006 merger of the Pre-K-12 divisions of the North Central Association Commission on Accreditation and School Improvement (NCA CASI) and the Southern Association of Colleges and Schools Council on Accreditation and School Improvement (SACS CASI) — and expanded through the addition of the Northwest Accreditation Commission (NWAC) in 2012.
Cognia, Alpharetta, GA 30009, USA
Tel: +1 888 413 3669
Website: www.cognia.org

COUNCIL OF BRITISH INTERNATIONAL SCHOOLS (COBIS)
COBIS is a membership association of British schools of quality worldwide and is committed to a stringent process of quality assurance for all its member schools.

Founded more than 30 years ago, it is governed by an elected board of Headteachers and Governors from member schools worldwide. COBIS hosts a range of conferences and professional development events for teachers, middle leaders, support staff throughout the year plus an annual conference in London in May for school leaders and Governors

COBIS represents its members with the British Government, educational bodies, the corporate sector and Ministries of Education worldwide. It is a member of the Independent Schools Council (ISC) of the United Kingdom.
CEO: Colin Bell (ceo@cobis.org.uk)
COBIS, 55-56 Russell Square, London WC1B 4HP
Tel: +44 (0) 20 3826 7190
Website: www.cobis.org.uk

COUNCIL OF INTERNATIONAL SCHOOLS (CIS)
CIS is a not-for-profit organisation committed to supporting its member schools and colleges in achieving and delivering the highest standards of international education.

CIS provides accreditation to schools, teacher and leader recruitment and best practice development. CIS Higher Education assists member colleges and universities in recruiting a diverse profile of qualified international students.
Executive Director: Jane Larsson
CIS, Schipholweg 113, 2316 XC Leiden, The Netherlands
Tel: +31 71 524 3300
Email: info@cois.org
Website: www.cois.org

EAST ASIA REGIONAL COUNCIL OF OVERSEAS SCHOOLS (EARCOS)
The East Asia Regional Council of Schools is an organization of 200+ member schools in East Asia. These schools have a total of more than 164,022 pre-K to 12th grade students. EARCOS also has 150 associate members – textbook and software publishers and distributors, universities, financial planners, architectural firms, insurance companies, youth organizations, etc – and 41 individual members.

The Council has a vision that includes: developing collaborative educational partnerships worldwide; providing professional development opportunities for members; connecting schools, communities, and individuals through the use of technology; understanding, and access to broader educational opportunities; engaging all in learning activities that will promote friendship, understanding and global citizenship.
Executive Director: Dr. Edward Greene
EARCOS, Brentville subdivision, Barangay Mamplasan, Biñan, Laguna, 4024, Philippines
Tel: +63 (02) 8779-5147
Fax: +63 (49) 511 4694
Email: info@earcos.org
Website: www.earcos.org

ECIS
A network of schools and companies committed to promoting international education. Founded in 1965, ECIS is made up of regular member schools, affiliate members who provide services such as professional development for teachers, supporting members made up of commercial companies who supply/service the international schools market, and individual members.
Executive Director: Kam Chohan
ECIS, 24 Greville Street, London, EC1N 8SS, United Kingdom
Tel: +44 (0)203 963 5229
Email: ecis@ecis.org
Website: www.ecis.org

International school associations

FEDERATION OF BRITISH INTERNATIONAL SCHOOLS IN ASIA (FOBISIA)

FOBISIA is a regional federation of the leading British international schools in Asia. Member schools have to meet a range of quality standards in order to be accepted into the federation and to retain membership.

Additionally, affiliate membership of FOBISIA is open to reputable educational organisations and suppliers whose services and products are of interest to member schools.

FOBISIA hosts a range of student events including the FOBISIA Games, a music festival, drama festivals, gamelan festivals, community and environmental conferences, model united nations conferences, as well as a range of other events around the subject areas of maths, science, DT and English.

It also organises conferences and workshops where teachers from across the region can meet to share good practice, swap ideas and receive professional training from invited university lecturers and consultants from around the world.

Chief Operating Officer:
John Gwyn Jones MBE
39/4 Todsamon Clubhouse Building
M Fl, Soi Lasalle 39/1, Sukhumvit 105, Bangna
Bangkok, Thailand 10260
Tel: +66 2744 4070
Website: www.fobisia.org

INTERNATIONAL SCHOOLS ASSOCIATION (ISA)

The ISA is based in Geneva, with offices in India and the USA, and was established in Paris in 1951 as an international organisation for the development of co-operation among its member schools and with all those interested in promoting international understanding.

The ISA was instrumental in the development of the International Baccalaureate Organization and in creating a programme for middle schools, which later developed into the IBMYP. It publishes Internationalism in Schools – a Self-Study Guide for schools and sponsors an annual 'Youth Encounter' for students from member and non-member schools. A biannual World Conference is organized around a theme dealing with international education and the association sponsors oral English examinations.
International Schools Association, 3 rue Schaub
CH 1202 Geneva, Switzerland
Email: info@isaschools.org
Website: www.isaschools.org

INTERNATIONAL SCHOOLS ASSOCIATION OF THAILAND (ISAT)

This association was established in 1994 principally to act as a link between its member international schools, the Ministry of Education and the Office of the Private Education Commission. It is now involved in the joint marketing of international education both in Thailand and overseas.

ISAT has over 75 schools offering a range of curricula: American, British and international systems. They are committed to the promotion of the Thai language and culture in international schools along with support for culture and sporting links between international schools in Thailand and worldwide. ISAT member schools are accredited by WASC, NEASC and CIS.
ISAT, 39/7 Soi Nichada Thani, Samakee Road,
Pakkret, Nonthaburi, Thailand 11120
Tel: +66 (0)2 960 4101
Email: isat@isat.or.th
Website: www.isat.or.th

MEDITERRANEAN ASSOCIATION OF INTERNATIONAL SCHOOLS (MAIS)

The Mediterranean Association of International Schools strives to improve the quality of education in its member schools. It promotes the professional development of faculty, administrators, and school board members, effective communication and interchange, and creates international understanding.

MAIS serves as a liaison between its 42 Member Schools, 30 Associate Member organizations as well as other regional, professional, and in-service organizations. Presently, MAIS is composed of schools from 16 different countries, including Austria, Cyprus, Egypt, France, Greece, Italy, Lebanon, Morocco, Oman, Portugal, Saudi Arabia, Spain, Tunisia, Turkey, United Arab Emirates and the United Kingdom. In addition, several associate members, such as schools outside the Mediterranean region, colleges, businesses, and interested individuals, support MAIS endeavors and have joined the organization.
Tel: +34 91 352 0678
Email: contact@mais-web.org
Website: www.mais-web.org

International school associations

MIDDLE STATES ASSOCIATION OF COLLEGES AND SCHOOLS

The MSA's Commissions on Elementary and Secondary Schools accredit early-childhood through post-secondary, non-degree granting public, private, faith-based educational institutions including special purpose schools, supplementary education centers, learning services providers, and distance education institutions.

Historically, MSA-CESS has operated in the mid-Atlantic region (Delaware, Maryland, New Jersey, New York, Pennsylvania, and the District of Columbia); with its cooperative partners, it has expanded its scope to include schools and institutions seeking accreditation throughout the United States. The Commissions also award accreditation to member institutions in more than 110 countries around the world.

The Commissions on Elementary and Secondary Schools are affiliated with the United States State Department's Office of Overseas Schools and provide accreditation services to American and international style schools attended by members of the US foreign service and US citizens working for non-government agencies and multi-national corporations. The Commission on Secondary Schools is also recognized by the U.S. Department of Education as a gatekeeper for eligibility for Title IV funding for post secondary non-degree granting institutions and distance education.

The Commissions on Elementary and Secondary Schools are founding members of the International Alliance of Accrediting Associations which includes the major regional, national and international accrediting agencies.
St. Leonard's Court 3819-33 Chestnut Street,
Suite 310 | Philadelphia, PA 19104-3171
Tel: +1 267-284-5000
Email: info@msa-cess.org
Website: www.msa-cess.org

NATIONAL ASSOCIATION OF BRITISH SCHOOLS IN SPAIN (NABSS)

The National Association of British Schools in Spain (NABSS) was founded in 1978 to promote, uphold and defend British education in Spain. The only schools permitted to be members of NABSS are those that are fully authorised British schools, recognised as such by the British Council and its official inspectorate.

NABSS insists on regular inspection of member schools, provides professional training for Heads and teachers and organises an annual conference with workshops.

The association aims to maintain contact with the British Council and the Spanish educational authorities as per the requirements of legislation referring to foreign schools in Spain.

NABSS's website lists all member schools. These schools follow the British National Curriculum and employ fully qualified staff. They range in age from early years to 16 and offer a broad selection of GCSE, AS and A level courses and generally administer UCAS entry to universities in the UK. Spanish authorities give full recognition to A levels and grant automatic access to Spanish universities for NABSS A level students.
NABSS, Calle de Ferraz, 85, 28008 Madrid, Spain
Tel: +34 91 550 0123
Email: nabss@acade.es
Website: www.nabss.org

NEAR EAST SOUTH ASIA COUNCIL OF OVERSEAS SCHOOLS (NESA)

NESA began informally in the early 1960s and has evolved into a world class organisation that serves more than 100 American international schools. The association promotes links between educators working in private, independent international schools in the Near East and South Asia region. Regular membership of the association is open to any American overseas or international overseas school located in the Near East South Asia geographical area, as long as they share the objectives and purposes of NESA and are accredited by a recognized agency.
NESA, Gravias 6, Aghia Paraskevia 153 42, Athens, Greece
Email: nesa@nesacenter.org
Website: www.nesacenter.org

International school associations

NEW ENGLAND ASSOCIATION OF SCHOOLS AND COLLEGES (NEASC)

NEASC is an independent, voluntary, nonprofit membership organization which connects and serves over 2,000 public and independent schools, technical/career institutions, colleges and universities in New England plus International Schools in more than 65 nations worldwide. A globally recognized standard of excellence, NEASC Accreditation attests to a school's high quality and integrity. NEASC is comprised of four commissions which decide matters of accreditation in the context of research-driven standards reviewed by their membership.
NEASC, 1115 Westford Street, Third Floor,
Lowell, MA, 01851 USA
Tel: +1 781-425-7700
Email: info@neasc.org
Website: www.neasc.org

NORDIC NETWORK OF INTERNATIONAL SCHOOLS

Organisation that serves English speaking schools in the Nordic and Baltic regions. Originally founded by five international schools from Denmark, Norway and Sweden, it now offers membership to other schools in the region who provide an international education in English.
NNIS, c/o ISGR, Molinsgatan 6,
411 33 Göteborg, Sweden
Tel: + 46 738509782
Email: nordicnetworkonline@gmail.com
Website: www.nordicnetworkonline.net

ROUND SQUARE INTERNATIONAL SCHOOLS (RSIS)

Round Square is a world-wide association of schools on five continents. Students attending Round Square schools make a strong commitment, beyond academic excellence, to personal development and responsibility.

The Round Square approach promotes six IDEALS of learning: Internationalism, Democracy, Environment, Adventure, Leadership and Service. These are incorporated into the curriculum throughout all member schools.

Access to the Round Square network affords member schools the opportunity to arrange local and international student and teacher exchanges on a regular basis between their schools. Pupils also have the opportunity to participate in local and international community service projects and conferences

Tasks tackled through the community projects include building schools, classrooms and community centres; building clean water systems for remote hill-tribes or creating and maintaining trails in National Parks. Local materials are used, and teams always work with local people ensuring that they take ownership of the work once it has been completed
Round Square, First Floor, Morgan House,
Madeira Walk, Windsor, SL4 1EP, United Kingdom
Website: www.roundsquare.org

SWISS GROUP OF INTERNATIONAL SCHOOLS (SGIS)

The Swiss Group of International Schools (SGIS) is a non-profit organization. It exists to: promote closer links between the teachers, administrators, and students of its member schools and professional development; provide opportunities for arranging educational, cultural and sporting activities; represent the concerns of Swiss international schools; and co-operate and maintain professional contacts with other regional and international educational bodies and associations.

Each year it holds conferences and workshops, promote inter-school sports competitions at all levels, and hold an AGM that all members are encouraged to attend.
Website: www.sgischools.com

THE TRI-ASSOCIATION – THE ASSOCIATION OF AMERICAN SCHOOLS OF CENTRAL AMERICA, COLOMBIA-CARIBBEAN AND MEXICO

Name of the joint association for AASCA, ACCAS and ASOMEX – see those entries for more information.
Executive Director:
Michael W. Adams, Ed.D.
2637 Ascot Dr., Florence, SC 29501, USA
Tel: +1 843 799 5754
Website: www.tri-association.org

Ministries of Education worldwide

Ministries of Education

Please note: every effort has been made to obtain information about all the Ministries of Education worldwide. However, some countries do not publish this information, others either do not have a specific education department or provide this information freely.

Most schools now refer to Years or Grades when talking about a specific age group. As a general guide the charts below outlines which Year/Grade denotes which age group.

UK SYSTEM

Year	Age
1	5-6
2	6-7
3	7-8
4	8-9
5	9-10
6	10-11
7	11-12
8	12-13
9	13-14
10	14-15
11	15-16
12	16-17
13	17-18

USA SYSTEM

Grade	Age
Preschool	
Pre-kindergarten	4-6
Elementary School	
Kindergarten	5-6
1st Grade	6-7
2nd Grade	7-8
3rd Grade	8-9
4th Grade	9-10
5th Grade	10-11
Middle School	
6th Grade	11-12
7th Grade	12-13
8th Grade	13-14
High School	
9th Grade – Freshman	14-15
10th Grade – Sophomore	15-16
11th Grade – Junior	16-17
12th Grade – Senior	17-18

Ministries of Education

ANGOLA
Angola Ministry of Education, Avenue Comandante Gika, Luanda
Tel: +244 222 320 582
Primary school, ages 6-14
Secondary school, ages 14-19

ANTIGUA AND BARBUDA
Ministry of Education, Sports, Youth and Gender Affairs, Government Office Complex, St John's, Antigua
Tel: +1 268 462 0192/3
Website: www.education.gov.ag
Primary school, ages 5-12
Secondary school, ages 12-16
Post-16 education available at three colleges

ARGENTINA
Ministry of Education, Pizzurno 935, Ciudad Autónoma de Buenos Aires C1020ACA
Tel: +54 11 4129 1000
Website: www.argentina.gob.ar/educacion
Primary - Educación General Básica (EGB I), ages 6-8
Primary - Educación General Básica (EGB II), ages 9-11
Secondary - Educación General Básica (EGB III), ages 12-14
Secondary - Polimodal, ages 15-17
Other: some areas of Argentina have different names and criteria for secondary education.

ARMENIA
The Ministry of Education, Science, Culture and Sports, Vazgen Sargsyan 3, 0010 Yerevan
Tel: +374 (10) 52 6602
Website: https://escs.am/am
Elementary, ages 7-9
Basic secondary, ages 10-14
High school, ages 15-16
Post-16 education available in technical secondary colleges, universities

AUSTRALIA
Department of Education, Skills and Employment, GPO Box 9880, Canberra, ACT 2601
Tel: +61 1300 566 046
Website: https://www.dese.gov.au
Compulsory education:
- Lower primary level education, ages 5-9
- Upper primary level education, ages 9-13
- Lower secondary phase education, ages 11-16
- Upper secondary level education, ages 16-18

Other: each state and territory in Australia has the responsibility for their own schools, including enrolment policies, curriculum content, course accreditation and certification, as well as the methods of assessment used. Australia also has part-time, pre-schools, which are available for up to two years before the age of six. However, during the second pre-school year there is the option to go full-time; this year is known as the preparatory year.
Post-16 education in Australia is available in the form of secondary schools, technical or vocational colleges, senior colleges or rural training schools.

AUSTRIA
Federal Ministry of Education, Science and Research, Minoritenplatz 5, A-1010 Vienna
Tel: +43 (0)1 53120 0
Website: https://www.bmbwf.gv.at/en
Pre-school, age 5
Primary, ages 6-9
Lower secondary, ages 10-13
Upper secondary, ages 14-17
Vocational, ages 14-18

AZERBAIJAN REPUBLIC
Ministry of Education, 49 Khatai Avenue, Baku, AZ-1008
Tel: +994 12 599 1155
Website: www.edu.gov.az
Primary, ages 6-10
Basic, ages 10-15
Secondary, ages 15-17

Ministries of Education

THE BAHAMAS
Ministry of Education, Thompson Boulevard, Nassau
Tel: +1 242 502 2700
Website: www.ministryofeducationbahamas.com
Nursery/kindergarten, ages 3-5
Primary, ages 5-11
Secondary, ages 12-15
Senior high school, ages 16-18

KINGDOM OF BAHRAIN
Ministry of Education, PO Box 43, Manama
Tel: +973 1727 8999
Website: www.moe.gov.bh
Primary, ages 6-11
Intermediate, 12-14
Secondary, ages 15-17
Other: state run schools tend to be single sex, whereas private education offers coeducational schools.

BANGLADESH
Ministry of Education, Building 6, Floor 17th & 18th, Bangladesh Secretariat, Dhaka-1000
Tel: +88 02 7167577
Website: www.moedu.gov.bd
Pre-primary, ages 3-6
Primary, ages 6-10
Secondary, ages 11-17

BARBADOS
Ministry of Education, Technological and Vocational Training, Elsie Payne Complex, St Michael, West Indies
Tel: +1 246 535 0600
Website: www.mes.gov.bb
Primary, ages 5-11
Secondary, ages 11-16
Other: some private secondary schools are government assisted.

REPUBLIC OF BELARUS
Ministry of Education, 9 Sovetskaya Street, 220010, Minsk
Tel: +375 (017) 327 47 36
Website: www.edu.gov.by
Primary, ages 6-10
Basic, ages 10-15
General secondary, ages 15-17
Specialised secondary, ages 15-19
Vocational secondary, ages 15-18
Other: secondary education lasts between two and four years, depending on which type the student enrols for.

BELGIUM
Flemish Ministry of Education and Training, Koning Albert II-laan 15, 1210 Brussels
Tel: +32 2 553 6601
Website: www.vlaanderen.be/en
Pre-primary, ages 2-6
Primary, ages 6-11
Secondary, ages 12-18
Other: VGO schools, which are privately owned and either religious (Catholic, Jewish etc) or method (Steiner, Freinet, Montessori); these schools are funded by the government.

BELIZE
Ministry of Education, Culture, Science & Technology, West Block Building 3rd Floor, Belmopan, Cayo
Tel: +501 822 2380/3315
Website: www.moe.gov.bz
Primary, ages 5-13
Secondary, ages 13-17
Other: Church-run schools. Secondary education in Belize is not free and students from many low-income families leave school before the age of 15.

BERMUDA
Ministry of Education, 44 Church Street, Hamilton, Bermuda, HM 12
Tel: +1 (441) 278 3300
Website: www.moed.bm
Pre-school, ages 4-5
Primary, ages 5-11
Middle, ages 11-14
Secondary, ages 14-18

BHUTAN
Ministry of Education, PO Box 112, Thimphu
Tel: +975 32 53 25
Website: www.education.gov.bt
Primary, ages 6-12
Secondary, ages 12-16
Other: Monastic schools.

BOLIVIA
Ministry of Education, Avenida Arce No 2147, PO Box 3116, La Paz
Tel: +591 2244 2144
Website: www.minedu.gob.bo
Pre-primary, ages 4-6
Primary, ages 6-13
Secondary, ages 14-17

Ministries of Education

BOSNIA AND HERZEGOVINA
Federal Ministry of Education and Science, dr. Ante Starčevića bb., Sarajevo
Tel: +387 036 355 700
Website: www.fmon.gov.ba
Pre-school, ages 3-5
Elementary, ages 6-15
Secondary, ages 15-19

BOTSWANA
Ministry of Education and Skills Development, Private bag 005, Block 6 Building, Government Enclave, Gaborone
Tel: +267 365 5400
Website: www.gov.bw
Primary, ages 5-12
Junior secondary, ages 13-15
Senior secondary, ages 16-18

BRAZIL
Ministry of Education, Esplanada dos Ministeries, Bloeo L. Brasilia DF, 70047-900
Tel: +55 (61) 410 0444
Website: www.gov.br/mec/pt-br
Pre-school, ages 4-6
Fundamental, ages 7-14
Intermediate, ages 15-18

BRITISH VIRGIN ISLANDS
Ministry of Education, Culture, Youth Affairs, Fisheries and Agriculture, 33 Admin Drive, Wickhams Cay 1, Road Town, Tortola
Tel: +1 284 468 3701
Website: www.bvi.gov.vg/content/ministry-education-and-culture
Pre-primary, ages 3-5
Primary, ages 5-12
Secondary, ages 13-17

BRUNEI DARUSSALAM
Ministry of Education, Old Airport Road, Berakas BB3510
Tel: +673 2381133
Website: www.moe.gov.bn
Pre-school, age 5
Primary, ages 6-13
Secondary, ages 13-17

BULGARIA
Ministry of Education and Science, 2A Knyaz Dondukov Blvd, 1000 Sofia
Tel: +359 921 7799
Website: www.mon.bg
Primary, ages 7-10
Lower secondary, ages 10-14
Upper secondary, ages 15-19
Vocational secondary, ages 15-19
Professional secondary, ages 15-19
Other: time spent in secondary education depends on which secondary school is attended.

BURMA
Ministry of Education, Theinbyu Street, Botahtaung Township, Yangon
Tel: +95 1 503 141
Website: https://myanmar.gov.mm/en/ministry-of-education
Pre-school, ages 2-4
Kindergarten, age 5
Primary, ages 6-11
Middle, ages 12-16
Secondary, ages 17-19

CAMBODIA
Ministry of Education, Youth and Sport, 80 Norodom Blvd, Phnom Penh
Tel: +855 23 219 285
Website: www.moeys.gov.kh
Primary, ages 6-11
Secondary, ages 12-17

CAMEROON
Ministry of Education, Yaounde
Tel: +237 22 22 26 716
Website: www.minedub.cm
Primary, ages 5-11
Secondary, ages 11-18
Other: primary schools are free but parents must pay for books and uniforms.

Ministries of Education

CANADA
New Brunswick Department of Education and Early Childhood Development, Place 2000, P.O. Box 6000 Fredericton, New Brunswick E3B 5H1
Tel: +1 506 453 3678
Website: www.gnb.ca/education

Newfoundland and Labrador Department of Education and Early Childhood Development, P.O. Box 8700, Confederation Building St. John's, Newfoundland and Labrador A1B 4J6
Tel: +1 709 729 5097
Website: https://www.gov.nl.ca/education

Northwest Territories Department of Education, Culture and Employment, P.O. Box 1320, Public Affairs Yellowknife, Northwest Territories X1A 2L9
Tel: + 1 867 920 6222
Website: www.ece.gov.nt.ca

Nova Scotia Department of Education and Early Childhood Development, P.O. Box 578, 2021 Brunswick Street, Halifax, Nova Scotia B3J 2S9
Tel: +1 902 424 5168
Website: https://beta.novascotia.ca/government/education-and-early-childhood-development

Nunavut Department of Education, P.O. Box 1000, Station 900 Iqaluit, Nunavut X0A 0H0
Tel: +1 867 975 5600
Website: www.gov.nu.ca/education

Ontario Ministry of Education, 900 Bay Street, 14th Floor, Mowat Block, Toronto, Ontario M7A 1L2
Tel: +1 416 325 2929
Website: https://www.ontario.ca/page/ministry-education

Prince Edward Island Department of Education and Lifelong Learning, 101-250 Water Street, Holman Centre Summerside, Prince Edward Island C1N 1B6
Tel: +1 902 438 4854
Website: https://www.princeedwardisland.ca/en/topic/education-and-lifelong-learning

Quebec - Ministère de l'Éducation et de l'Enseignement supérieur du Québec, 1035, rue De La Chevrotière, 28e étage, Québec, Quebec G1R 5A5
Tel: +1 418 643 7095
Website: www.education.gouv.qc.ca

Manitoba Department of Education and Training, 1181 Portage Avenue, Winnipeg, Manitoba R3G 0T3
Tel: +1 204 945 0746
Website: www.edu.gov.mb.ca

Alberta Education, 7th Floor, Commerce Place, 10155-102 Street Edmonton, Alberta T5J 4L5
Tel: +1 780 427 7219
Website: https://www.alberta.ca/education.aspx

Saskatchewan Ministry of Education, 6th Floor, 2220 College Avenue, Regina, Saskatchewan S4P 4V9
Tel: +1 306-787-6089
Website: www.saskatchewan.ca/government/government-structure/ministries/education

Yukon Department of Education, Box 2703 Whitehorse, Yukon Y1A 2C6
Tel: +1 867 667 5141
Website: https://yukon.ca/en/education-and-schools

British Columbia Ministry of Education, PO Box 9150, Stn Prov Govt Victoria, British Columbia V8W 9H1
Tel: +1 250 387 6121
Website: www.gov.bc.ca/bced

Primary education, ages 6-13, Grade 1-8.
Secondary education, ages 14-18, or Grade 9-12.
Each territory or province in Canada has control over their own School system. Most Local Authorities offer publicly-funded kindergarten classes from age five.

CAYMAN ISLANDS
Ministry of Education, Youth, Sports, Agriculture, and Lands, 5th Floor, Government Administration Building, 133 Elgin Avenue, George Town, Grand Cayman,
Tel: +1 345 244 2417
Website: www.gov.ky/education
Primary, ages 4-10
Secondary, ages 11-16

CHILE
Ministry of Education, Av. Libertador Bernardo O'Higgins, 1371 Santiago
Tel: +56 2 2406 6000
Website: www.mineduc.cl
Pre-school, ages up to 6
Primary, ages 6-13
Secondary, ages 13-18
Other: some private schools are subsidised by the government.

PR CHINA
Ministry of Education for PR of China, 37 Damucang Hutong, Xidan, Beijing 100816
Tel: +86 10 660 961 14
Website: www.moe.gov.cn
Pre-school or Kindergarten, ages 3-6
Elementary/primary school, ages 6-12
Junior middle school (secondary), ages 12-15
Senior middle school (secondary), ages 15-18

Ministries of Education

COLOMBIA
Ministry of Education, Calle 43 No 57-14, Bogota
Tel: +57 1222 2800
Website: www.mineducacion.gov.co
Primary, ages 6-11
Secondary (lower), ages 11-15
Secondary (vocational), ages 15-18
Other: there are non-profit schools that are not state run and do not charge fees they are largely funded by resources from outside Colombia from countries such as the US.

COOK ISLANDS
Ministry of Education, PO Box 97,
Rarotonga, Cook Islands
Tel: +68 229 357
Website: www.education.gov.ck
Preschool, ages 3-5
Primary, ages 5-11
Secondary, ages 11-16

COSTA RICA
Ministry of Education, PO Box 10087-1000, San Jose
Tel: +506 2256 8132
Primary, ages 6-13
Secondary, ages 13-18
Other: Catholic schools

CROATIA
Ministry of Science and Education, Donje Svetice 38, 10000 Zagreb
Tel: +385 1 4569 000
Website: www.mzo.hr/en
Pre-school, ages 6m-6
Elementary, ages 6-14
Secondary, ages 14-18

CUBA
Ministry of Education of the Republic of Cuba, Calle 17 y O, Vedado, Havana, Cuba
Tel: +53 7832 8077
Website: www.mined.gob.cu
Primary, ages 6-11
Secondary, ages 12-15

CYPRUS
Ministry of Education, Culture, Sports and Youth, Corner of Kimonos and Thucydides, Acropolis, 1434 Nicosia
Tel: +357 2280 0600
Website: www.moec.gov.cy
Pre-school, ages 3-6
Primary, ages 6-12
Secondary, ages 12-18

CZECH REPUBLIC
Ministry of Education, Youth and Sport, Karmelitská 529/5, 118 12, Praha 1
Tel: +42 0234 811 111
Website: www.msmt.gov.cz
Pre-school, ages 2-5
Primary, ages 6-11
Secondary, ages 12-16

DENMARK
Ministry of Children and Education, Frederiksholms Kanal 21, 1220 Copenhagen K
Tel: +45 3392 5000
Website: https://www.eng.uvm.dk
Primary school, grades 1-6, ages 7-12
Lower secondary, grades 7-10, ages 13-16
Upper secondary, ages 16-19, consists of either general education towards higher education or vocational/technical training.
Other: production schools, which are independent schools approved and partially funded by the Local Authority; they have representatives on their school board from the local employers.

DOMINICAN REPUBLIC
Ministry of Education, Avenida Máximo Gómez esq. Santiago, No. 02, Gazcue, Distrito Nacional
Tel: +1 809 688 9700
Website: http://education.gov.dm
Pre-school, ages 3-6
Elementary, ages 6-14
High School, ages 14-18

EGYPT
Ministry of Education, 12 El-Falaky Street, Cairo
Tel: +20 27963273
Website: www.moe.gov.eg
Kindergarten, ages 2-4
Primary, ages 4-10
Preparatory, ages 11-14
Secondary, ages 15-17

EL SALVADOR
Ministry of Education, Buildings A, Master Plan, Government Centre, Alameda Juan Pablo II & Calle Guadalupe, 503
Tel: +503 2537 2122
Website: www.mined.gob.sv
Pre-school, ages up to 6
Basic, ages 7-15
Middle, ages 15-18

Ministries of Education

EQUATORIAL GUINEA
Ministry of Education and Sciences
Website: www.guineaecuatorialpress.com
Preschool, ages 3-6
Primary, ages 6-12
Lower Secondary, ages 13-17
Upper Secondary, ages 17-19
Other: education in Equatorial Guinea is very basic and not enforced, particularly for females.

ESTONIA
Ministry of Education and Research, Munga Street 18, 50088 Tartu
Tel: +372 735 0222
Website: www.hm.ee
Preschool, ages 1-7
Basic, ages 7-16
General secondary, ages 16-19

ESWATINI
Ministry of Education and Training, P.O. Box 39, Mbabane
Tel: +268 241 62 407
Website: www.gov.sz
Early childhood care and development, ages up to 8
Primary, ages 6-13
Secondary, ages 14-19

ETHIOPIA
Ministry of Education, PO Box 1367, Addis Ababa
Tel: 00251 11 155 3133
Website: www.moe.gov.et
Elementary, ages 5-11
Junior elementary, ages 11-13
Senior secondary, ages 13-16

FIJI
Ministry of Education, Head Quarters Senikau House, Gordon Street, Government Building, Suva
Tel: +679 331 4477
Website: www.education.gov.fj
Pre-school/kindergarten, ages 3-5
Primary, ages 6-14
Secondary, ages 14-18
Other: church run schools.

FINLAND
Ministry of Education and Culture, PO Box 29, FI - 00023 Government
Tel: +358 2953 16001
Website: www.okm.fi/en
Pre-primary, age 6
Primary or basic, ages 7-16
General upper secondary, ages 16-19
Other: most private schools follow the Finnish National Curriculum. However, Steiner schools and those offering education in languages other than Finnish, tend to follow their own curriculums.

FRANCE
Ministry of Education, 110 rue de Grenelle, 75357 Paris SP07
Tel: +33 01 5555 1080
Website: www.education.gouv.fr
Elementary school (école élémentaire), ages 6-11
Lower secondary school (college), ages 11-15
Lycée (general/technical or vocational) (lycée d'enseignement général et technologique, LEGT, or lycée professionnel, LP), ages 15-16
Other: the majority of the private fee-paying schools are Catholic schools. Some of these independent schools receive funding from the state to pay salaries and training costs and, in return, the schools must follow the same timetables and curriculum as the state schools.
There are state-funded kindergartens available, for ages 2-6, called école maternelle or classe enfantine. There are also private pre-schools, which are fee paying. All pre-schools follow a National Curriculum.
Post-16 education is covered by a lycée général et technologique, LEGT or a lycée d'enseignement professionnel, LP. Although the final year of compulsory state education (15-16 years old) usually takes place in a lycée.

GEORGIA
Ministry of Education, Science, Culture And Sport of Georgia, 0102 Tbilisi, Dimitri Uznadze N52
Tel: +995 32 2 200 220
Website: www.mes.gov.ge
Elementary, ages 6-12
Basic, ages 13-15
Secondary, ages 16-18

GERMANY
Federal Ministry of Education and Research
Tel: +49 228 99570
Website: www.bmbf.de/en
Each state controls its own school system.
Compulsory education:
Primary education, aged 6-10 (12 in Berlin and Brandenburg)
Lower secondary education, ages 10-16 (12-16)
Upper secondary education, ages 15-19
Other: private schools receive some government funding and are therefore subject to some state supervision.
Kindergärten is available for children between the ages of 3-6. All such schools, whether state maintained or private, are supervised by the state. There is also a National Curriculum now for all pre-schools.
Post-16 education is compulsory in Germany up to the age of 18; 19 in some areas.

Ministries of Education

GHANA
Ministry of Education, PO Box M45, Accra, Greater Accra
Tel: +233 302 683627
Website: www.moe.gov.gh
Kindergarten, ages 4-6
Primary, ages 6-11
Secondary, ages 12-15

GIBRALTAR
Ministry of Education, Suite 771 europort
Tel: +350 200 79336
Website: www.gibraltar.gov.gi
Pre-school, ages 3-4
Primary, ages 4-11
Secondary, ages 12-16

GREECE
Greek Ministry of Education, Religious Affairs and Sport, Andrea Papandreou 37, Marousi 15180
Tel: +30 210 344 2000
Website: www.minedu.gov.gr
Kindergarten, ages 2.5-5
Primary (Dimotiko), ages 6-12
Middle School (Gymnasio), ages 12-15
Secondary (Lykeio), ages 15-17
Other: private schools are supervised by the Ministry of Education.

GRENADA
Ministry of Education and Human Resource Development, Botanical Gardens, Tanteen St George's, West Indies
Tel: +1 473 440 2737
Website: https://www.gov.gd/moe
Primary, ages 5-11
Secondary, ages 12-16

GUATEMALA
Ministry of Education, 6a calle 1-87 zona 10, 01010, Guatemala, CA
Tel: +502 2411 9595
Website: www.mineduc.gob.gt
Primary, ages 7-13
Middle, ages 13-16
Secondary, ages 16-18
Other: faith schools.

GUYANA
Ministry of Education, 26 Brickdam, Georgetown, 413722 Demerara – Mahaica
Tel: +592 223 7900
Website: www.education.gov.gy
Primary, ages 5-11
Secondary, ages 12-16

HONDURAS
Ministry of Education, 1a Avenida Entre 2a y 3a calle, Comayagüela, MDC
Tel: +504 2220 5583
Website: https://www.se.gob.hn
Primary, ages 6-12
Middle, ages 12-15
Secondary, ages 15-18

HONG KONG
Education Bureau, 15/F, Wu Chung House, 213 Queen's Road East, Wan Chai, Hong Kong (SAR)
Tel: +852 2891 0088
Website: www.edb.gov.hk/en
Kindergarten, ages 3-6
Primary, ages 6-12
Junior secondary, ages 12-15
Senior secondary, ages 15-17
Other: state schools are divided into three groups: government schools, subsidised schools (usually charities), and private schools run by organisations. Private, international schools tend to offer the IB. It is rare for an international student to take Hong Kong qualifications, particularly since they switched from the British to Chinese system.

HUNGARY
Ministry of National Resources, 1055 Budapest, Szalay u. 10-14
Tel: +36 1 795 1200
Website: http://www.nefmi.gov.hu/english
Pre-primary (Óvoda), ages 5-6
General school (Általános iskola), aged 6-14
General lower and upper secondary grammar school (Gimnázium), aged 10-19
Secondary or training school, ages 14-18
Other: for children aged 3-6 kindergarten is available and the final year is compulsory (for children aged 6). Post-16 education is compulsory in Hungary up to the age of 18.

ICELAND
The Ministry of Education, Science and Culture, Solvholsgata 4, 101 Reykjavik
Tel: +354 545 9500
Website: https://www.government.is/ministries/ministry-of-education-science-and-culture/
Pre-primary, ages 1-6
Compulsory schools, ages 6-16
Upper secondary, ages 16-20

INDIA
Ministry of Human Resource Development, Shastri Bhawan, New Delhi-110001
Tel: +91 11 2338 3936
Website: https://www.education.gov.in
Primary, ages 6-14
Secondary, ages 14-18

Ministries of Education

INDONESIA
Ministry of Education, Culture, Research, and Technology, Jalan Jenderal Sudirman Senayan, Jakarta 10270
Tel: +62 21 5790 3020 ext. 2115
Website: www.partnership.kemdikbud.go.id
Kindergarten, ages 3-5
Elementary, ages 6-11
Middle school, ages 12-15
High school, ages 15-18

IRAN
Ministry of Education
Tel: +98 8889 4024 021
Website: www.irangov.ir
Pre-school, age 5-6
Primary, ages 6-12
Lower Secondary, ages 12-16
Upper Secondary, ages 15-18

IRAQ
Ministry of Higher Education and Scientific Research
Pre-school, ages 4-5
Elementary, ages 6-11
Intermediate, ages 12-15
Secondary, ages 15-18

IRELAND
Department of Education and Youth, Marlborough Street, Dublin 1, D01 RC96
Tel: +353 1 8896 400
Website: www.education.ie
Primary level, ages 6-12
Second level (junior cycle), ages 12-16
Other: there are privately owned schools, usually by religious communities, which are state funded for the purposes of salaries and running costs.
From the age of four, children can be enrolled in infant classes in primary schools. There is also a pre-school year for children aged from 39 months.
Post-16 education for children aged 15-19 is called the second-level senior cycle and usually lasts two years. If they wish, students can opt for a further year of education, called a transition year, or undertake a two-year leaving certificate programme.

ISRAEL
Ministry of Education, Dvora Hanevia 2, Jerusalem 9510402
Tel: +972 1 800 25 00 25
Website: https://www.gov.il/en/departments/ministry_of_education
Kindergarten, ages 3-5
Primary, ages 6-12
Middle school, ages 12-15
High school, ages 15-18
Other: faith schools (Orthodox Jewish), and Arab schools.

ITALY
Ministry of Education, Universities and Research, Sede Viale Trastevere, 76A 00153 Roma
Tel: +39 065849 2377
Website: www.mim.gov.it
Primary education, ages 6-11
Lower secondary education, ages 11-14
Upper secondary education, ages 14-19
Other: there are private schools in Italy who are not bound by the same rules and who issue qualifications that are not legally recognised.
Pre-schools/nurseries are available from the age of three.
Upper secondary education is covered by the liceo classico, (general academic), liceo scientifico (sciencies), liceo artistico or istituti d'arte (art), and istituti professionali (technical/vocational).

JAMAICA
Ministry of Education, Skills, Youth & Information, 2-4 National Heroes Circle, Kingston
Tel: +1 876 922 14009
Website: www.moey.gov.jm
Early childhood, ages 3-5
Primary, ages 5-12
Secondary, ages 12-17
Other: independent education is strictly monitored and has its own department at the ministry: The Independent Schools Section. The schools are also required to be registered and regularly inspected.

JAPAN
Ministry of Education, Culture, Sports, Science and Technology (MEXT), 3-2-2 Kasumigaseki, Chiyoda-ku, Tokyo 100-8959
Tel: +81 03 5253 4111
Website: www.mext.go.jp/en
Kindergarten, ages 3-6
Elementary school, ages 6-12
Lower secondary school, ages 12-15
Upper secondary school, ages 15-18
Other: private schools receive public funding and they tend to follow the National Curriculum. The major difference between the state and private sectors are that the private schools tend to include religious education.

JORDAN
Ministry of Education, PO Box 1646, Amman
Tel: +962 6 5607 331
Website: www.moe.gov.jo
Basic, ages 6-16
Secondary/vocational, ages 16-18

Ministries of Education

KAZAKHSTAN
Ministry of Education and Science, 01000 Astana, Orenburgskaya St
Tel: +7 (7172) 74 23 62
Website: www.edu.gov.kz
Kindergarten, ages 5-6
Primary, ages 6-10
Basic, ages 10-15
General secondary, ages 15-17

KENYA
State Department of Education, Jogoo House B, Harambee Avenue, PO Box 30040-00100, Nairobi
Tel: +254 20 3318581
Website: www.education.go.ke
Preschool, age 5
Primary, ages 6-14
Secondary, ages 14-18

DEMOCRATIC PEOPLE'S REPUBLIC OF KOREA
Department of Education
Kindergarten, ages 4-6
Primary, ages 6-9
Senior middle school, ages 10-15

SOUTH KOREA
The Ministry of Education, Government Complex-Sejong, 408 Galmae-Ro, Sejong 30119,
Tel: +82 2 6222 6060
Website: www.english.moe.go.kr
Primary school, ages 7-12
Junior high school, ages 13-15
Senior high school, ages 16-18
Other: parents are expected to pay fees if their child goes to senior high school. Private fee-paying schools follow the National Curriculum.
Kindergartens are available for children aged 4-6. They too follow a National Curriculum.

KOSOVO
Ministry of Education, Science and Technology, Rruga, Agim Ramadani, 10000 Prishtine
Tel: +381 038 213 327
Website: masht.rks-gov.net/en
Pre-school, age 5
Primary school, ages 6-11
Lower secondary, ages 12-15
Upper secondary, ages 16-18

KUWAIT
Ministry of Education, PO Box 7, Shuwaikh, Building No. 1, Al-Safat 13001
Website: www.moe.edu.kw
Tel: +965 483 5721
Primary, ages 6-11
Intermediate, ages 11-16
Secondary, ages 16-19

KYRGYZSTAN
Ministry of Education and Science, 720040 Biskek, Tynystanou St, 257, Bishkek
Tel: +996 312 62 05 19
Website: www.chea.org
Pre-school, ages 3-6
Primary, ages 6-10
Secondary, ages 10-15
High school, ages 15-17

LAO
Ministry of Education and Sports, (PO Box. 67 Free) Lan Xang Road No. 1, The Vientiane, Laos
Tel: +856 21 215 161
Website: www.moes.edu.la
Primary, ages 6-10
Secondary, ages 11-17

LATVIA
Ministry of Education and Science, Valnu Street 2, Riga, LV-1050
Tel: +371 6722 6209
Website: www.izm.gov.lv/en/
Pre-school, ages up to 5
Primary, ages 5-7
Basic, ages 7-16
Secondary, ages 16-19

LEBANON
Ministry of Education and Higher Education, P.O. Box 55264 Dekwaneh, Beirut
Tel: +961 1 683 202
Website: www.crdp.org
Elementary, ages 6-11
Intermediate, ages 12-14
Secondary, ages 15-18

LESOTHO
Ministry of Education and Training, Constitution Rd, Maseru
Tel: +266 222 144 00
Website: www.gov.ls
Pre-primary, up to age 6
Primary, ages 6-13
Secondary, ages 13-18

LIBYA
National Commission for Education, Science and Culture, PO Box 1091, Tripoli
Tel: +218 21 362 0602
Primary, ages 6-12
Secondary, ages 12-15
Specialised Secondary, ages 15-19

Ministries of Education

LITHUANIA
**Ministry of Education, Science and Sport,
A Volano str 2/7, LT-01516, Vilnius**
Tel: +370 5219 1190
Website: https://www.smsm.lrv.lt/lt
Primary, ages 6-11
Lower secondary, ages 10-17
Senior secondary, ages 16-19

LUXEMBOURG
**Ministry of National Education, Children and Youth, 33,
Rives de Clausen, L-2165**
Tel: +352 2478 5100
Website: www.men.public.lu
Pre-elementary, ages 4-6
Primary, ages 6-12
Secondary, ages 12-19

MACAU
**Ministry of Education, Public Information Centre –
Rua do Campo, nos. 188-198, Vicky Plaza, 26 andar.**
Tel: +853 8866 8866
Website: www.gov.mo/en/
Primary, ages 6-12
Secondary, ages 12-18
Other: Macau does not have its own educational system at present. Different schools follow the Chinese, British and Portuguese systems and most schools are private or heavily subsidised schools. Therefore the years spent in each type of school will depend on which system the school follows. The Chinese and British schools have similar periods of attendance, the Portuguese schools tend to allow less time in primary, and more time in secondary and high school.

NORTH MACEDONIA
**Ministry of Education and Science,
ul. St. Cyril and Methodius no. 54, 1000 Skopje**
Tel: +389 2 3117 896
Website: www.mon.gov.mk
Elementary, ages 7-15
General secondary, ages 15-19

MALAYSIA
**Ministry of Education, No. 2, Menara 2, Jalan P5/6, Presint 5,
Pusat Pentadbiran Kerajaan Persekutuan, 62200 Putrajaya,**
Tel: +60 38 870 6000
Website: www.moe.gov.my
Pre-school, ages 4-6
Primary, ages 7-13
Secondary, ages 13-19

REPUBLIC OF THE MALDIVES
Ministry of Education, Velaanaage, 8th Floor, Ameer Ahmed Magu, 20096, Malé, Republic of Maldives
Tel: +960 332 3262
Website: www.moe.gov.mv
Primary, ages 5-10
Middle school, ages 11-15
Secondary, ages 15-17
Other: some private schools, called Makthab, are traditional Islamic schools.

MALI
Ministry of Education, Place de la Liberté, Bamako
Tel: +223 223 1036
Primary, ages 7-13
Secondary, ages 13-19

MALTA
Ministry for Education, Sport, Youth, Research and Innovation, Great Siege Road, Floriana, VLT2000
Tel: +356 2598 0000
Website: www.education.gov.mt
Pre-primary, ages 3-5
Primary, ages 5-11
Secondary, ages 11-16
Other: Malta also has Church schools.

MAURITIUS
**Ministry of Education, Tertiary Education, Science and Technology
IVTB House Pont Fer, Phoenix**
Tel: +230 601 5200
Website: https://education.govmu.org
Pre-primary, ages 3-5
Primary, ages 5-11
Secondary, ages 12-18

MOLDOVA
**Ministry of Education, Culture and Research, MD-2033,
Chisinau mun., Great National Assembly Square 1**
Tel: +373 22 22 76 20
Website: www.mecc.gov.md
Kindergarten, ages 3-6
Primary, ages 6-10
Gymnasium, ages 10-15
Lyceum, ages 15-18

Ministries of Education

MONACO
Education, Youth and Sports, Lycée Technique, Avenue de l'Annonciade, MC – 98000
Tel: +377 9898 8305
Website: https://en.gouv.mc/Government-Institutions/The-Government/Ministry-of-Interior/Department-of-Education-Youth-and-Sport
Elementary school (école élémentaire), ages 6-11
Lower secondary school (college), ages 11-15
Lycée (general/technical or vocational) (lycée d'enseignement général et technologique, LEGT, or lycée professionnel, LP), ages 15-18
Other: the majority of the private fee-paying schools are Catholic schools. Some of these independent schools receive funding from the state to pay salaries and training costs and in return the schools must follow the same timetables and curriculum as the state schools.
There are state-funded kindergartens available, for ages 3-6, called école maternelle or classe enfantine. There are also private pre-schools, which are fee paying.
Post-16 education is covered by a lycée général et technologique, LEGT or a lycée d'enseignement professionnel, LP. Although the final year of compulsory state education (15-16 years old) usually takes place in a lycée.

MONTENEGRO
Ministry of Education and Science, Vaka Durovica, 81000 Podgorica
Tel: +382 20 410 100
Website: www.gov.me/en/mps
Elementary, ages 6-14
Secondary, ages 14-18

MOROCCO
Ministry of National Education, Preschool and Sports, 29 Avenue d'Alger, 10000, Rabat
Tel: +212 5 3777 1822
Website: www.men.gov.ma
Pre-school, ages 4-6
Primary, ages 6-12
Secondary, ages 12-18
Other: Morocco has three systems of education: a continuation of the French system; Islamic; and technical, skills and vocational training.

MOZAMBIQUE
Ministry of Education, Avenida 24 de Julho, No 167, PO Box 34, Maputo
Tel: +258 21 490 677
Website: www.mined.gov.mz
Pre-primary, ages up to 6
Primary, ages 6-13
Secondary, ages 13-18
Other: missionary schools.

NAMIBIA
Ministry of Education, Arts and Culture, Government Office Park (Luther Street), Private Bag 13186, Windhoek
Tel: +264 61 293 3111
Website: www.moe.gov.na
Primary, ages 6-13
Secondary, ages 13-18

NEPAL
Ministry of Education, Science and Technology, Sanothimi, Bhaktapur, Nepal
Tel: +977 1 4200340/390
Website: www.doe.gov.np
Pre-primary, ages 4-6
Primary, ages 6-11
Secondary, ages 11-18
Other: schools run by the local people that receive no grants or financial support.

NETHERLANDS
Ministry of Education, Culture and Science, Rijnstraat 50, 2515 XP The Hague
Tel: +31 (0)70 412 34 56
Website: www.government.nl/ministries/ministry-of-education-culture-and-science
Primary school, ages 4-12
Secondary school, ages 12-18
Other: private schools receive funding from the state and have to meet and maintain certain conditions to retain their funding, although they are allowed to set their own curriculum.
Pre-school is available for children between 2.5 and 4, the cost is split between the parents and the government.

NEW ZEALAND
The Ministry of Education, PO Box 1666, Wellington 6140
Tel: +64 (04) 463 8000
Website: www.govt.nz/browse/education/
Primary school, ages 4-10
Middle school, ages 10-12, Forms 1-2.
Secondary school, ages 12-18, Forms 3-7.
Other: integrated schools: private schools that have been integrated into the state system and are therefore state funded. These are usually religious schools. Kindergarten/pre-school education is available for children ages 3-4.

NIGERIA
Federal Ministry of Education, Federal Secretarial Phase III, FCT, Abuja
Tel: +234 903 0009 912
Website: www.education.gov.ng
Basic, ages 6-12
Secondary, ages 12-18

Ministries of Education

NORWAY
Ministry of Education and Research,
Postboks 8119 Dep, 0032 Oslo
Tel: +47 2224 9090
Website: www.regjeringen.no
Primary and lower secondary, ages 6-16
Upper secondary, ages 16-19

OMAN
Ministry of Education, PO Box 3, Muscat 113
Website: https://home.moe.gov.om
Tel: +968 24255552
Primary, ages 6-12
Preparatory, ages 12-15
Secondary, ages 15-18

PAKISTAN
Ministry of Federal Education and Professional Training
Tel: +92 51 92 11 622
Website: http://www.mofept.gov.pk
Pre-school, ages 3-5
Primary, ages 6-11
Middle, ages 11-14
High, ages 14-16
Intermediate, ages 16-18

PALAU
Ministry of Education, PO Box 6051, Koror
Tel: +680 767 2403
Website: www.palaumoe.net
Elementary, ages 6-12
Middle school, ages 13-15
High school, ages 15-19

PALESTINE
Ministry of Education and Higher Education
Tel: +970 22983200
Website: www.moehe.gov.ps
Pre-primary, ages 4-6
Primary, ages 7-15
Secondary, ages 15-18

PANAMA
Ministry of Education, PO Box 0816-04049,
Villa Cárdenas, Ancón
Tel: +507 511 4400
Primary, ages 6-12
Middle school, ages 12-15
Secondary, ages 15-18

PARAGUAY
Ministry of Education and Sciences, Chile 849, Asunción
Tel: +595 21 452 440
Website: www.mec.gov.py
Pre-school, ages 3-6
Elementary, ages 6-15
High school, ages 15-18

PERU
Ministry of Education, Calle Del Comercio 193
San Borja, Lima - 15021
Tel: +51 1 615 5800
Website: www.gob.pe/minedu
Primary, ages 6-12
Secondary, ages 13-18

PHILIPPINES
Department of Education
Tel: +63 633 7208
Website: www.deped.gov.ph
Elementary, ages 4-12
Junior high, ages 12-16
Senior high, ages 16-18

POLAND
Ministry of National Education,
al. J Ch Szucha 25, 00-918 Warsaw
Tel: +48 22 34 74 100
Website: www.gov.pl/web/edukacja
Kindergarten, ages 6-7
Primary, ages 7-15
Secondary, ages 15-19

PORTUGAL
Ministry of Education, Avenida 5 de Outubro, 107 1069-018,
Lisboa
Tel: +351 217 811 800
Website: www.portugal.gov.pt
Pre-primary, ages 3-5
Basic, ages 6-14
Secondary, ages 15-17

PUERTO RICO
Department of Education,
PO Box 190759, San Juan, PR 00919-0759
Tel: +787 759 2000
Website: www.de.pr.gov
Primary, ages 6-12
Intermediate, ages 12-15
High school, ages 15-18

QATAR
Ministry of Education
Website: www.edu.gov.qa
Elementary, ages 6-12
Preparatory, ages 13-15
Secondary, ages 16-18

ROMANIA
Ministry of National Education, Str Gen Berthelot 28-30,
Sector 1, 010168, Bucharest
Tel: +40 21 405 6200
Website: www.edu.ro
Kindergarten, ages 3-6
Elementary, ages 6-14
High school, ages 15-19

Ministries of Education

RUSSIA
The Ministry of Education of the Russian Federation
Website: http://government.ru/en/department/390
Pre-school, ages up to 6 years
Primary school, ages 6-10
Middle school, ages 10-15
Secondary school, ages 15-17

RWANDA
Ministry of Education, PO Box 622, Kigali
Tel: +250 737 093 807
Website: www.mineduc.gov.rw
Primary, ages 6-12
Secondary, ages 12-18

SAUDI ARABIA
Ministry of Education, King Abdullah Road, Riyadh 12435
Tel: +966 11 4753 000
Website: www.moe.gov.sa
Kindergarten, ages 3-5
Primary, ages 6-12
Intermediate, ages 13-16
High school, ages 17-19

SENEGAL
**Ministry of Education,
Rue Alpha Hachamiyou TALL, BP 4025**
Tel: +221 33 849 54 54
Primary, ages 7-12
Secondary, ages 13-19
Other: Islamic schools.

SERBIA
Ministry of Education, Science and Technological Development, 24 Nemanjina Street, Belgrade 11 000
Tel: +381 11 3613 734
Website: www.mpn.gov.rs
Pre-primary, age 6
Primary, ages 7-14
High school, ages 15-19

SEYCHELLES
Ministry of Education and Human Resource Development, Mont Fleuri, PO Box 48
Tel: +248 4283283
Website: www.edu.gov.sc
Primary, ages 7-12
Secondary, ages 12-18

SIERRA LEONE
Ministry Of Basic And Senior Secondary Education, New England, Freetown, Sierra Leone
Website: https://mbsse.gov.sl
Primary, ages 6-12
Junior secondary, 12-15
Senior secondary, 15-18

SINGAPORE
Ministry of Education, 1 North Buona Vista Drive, Singapore 138675
Tel: +65 6872 2220
Website: www.moe.gov.sg
Primary school, ages 7-13
Secondary school, ages 14-17
Other: there are also government-aided schools (formerly privately owned by churches or other organisations), who receive most of their funding from the state. Kindergarten (ages 3-6) is also available. These are privately run establishments, which have to be registered with the Ministry of Education.

SLOVAKIA
Ministry of Education, Science, Research and Sport, Stromová 1, 813 30, Bratislava
Tel: +421 2593 74111
Website: www.minedu.sk
Nursery, ages 3-6
First stage, ages 6-10
Second stage (primary), ages 10-15
Secondary, ages 15-19

SLOVENIA
Ministry of Education, Science and Sport, Masarykova 16, SI-1000 Ljubljana
Tel: +386 1 400 52 00
Website: https://www.gov.si/drzavni-organi/ministrstva/ministrstvo-za-izobrazevanje-znanost-in-sport/
Pre-school, ages 1-6
Basic, ages 6-15
Secondary, ages 15-18

SOMALIA
Ministry of Education and Higher Education of Puntland
Website: www.moehe.pl.so

Somaliland Ministry of Education and Science
Website: moe.govsomaliland.org

Early childhood, ages up to 6
Elementary, ages 6-10
Intermediate, ages 11-14
Secondary, ages 15-18

Ministries of Education

SOUTH AFRICA
Department of Basic Education, Sol Plaatje House, 222 Struben Street, Pretoria
Tel: +27 012 357 3000
Website: www.education.gov.za
Pre-primary, ages birth to 5
Reception, Grade R, ages 5-6
Primary, Grades 1-6, ages 7-12
Secondary, Grades 7-9, ages 12-15
Post secondary, Grades 10-12, ages 16-18
Other: South Africa runs a state school system that is unique. Schools are divided into five categories determined by the level of wealth in a particular area; the poorer schools are allocated larger funding than wealthier schools. Only the poorest state schools are completely free and entirely government funded, most charge some form of fee to top up their funding.

SPAIN
The Ministry of Education and Vocational Training, Calle de los Madrazo, 15 Madrid
Tel: +34 910 837 937
Website: www.educacionyfp.gob.es
Primary school, ages 6-12
Lower secondary school, ages 12-16
Other: there are also private schools that receive state funding and are therefore under the control of the state. Spain also offers pre-school education for children from birth to age six, which is free from the age of three. Post-16 education consists of either general upper secondary school or intermediate vocational training; both take place up to the age of 18. State colleges are free to students but parents are expected to pay for additional items such as meals, transport and various materials needed for their child's coursework.

SRI LANKA
Ministry of Education, Isurupaya, Pelawatta, Battaramulla
Tel: +94 112 785141 50
Website: www.moe.gov.lk
Primary, ages 6-11
Junior, ages 12-14
Senior secondary, ages 15-16
Post secondary, ages 17-18
Other: pirivenas (schools for Buddhist priests).

ST LUCIA
Ministry of Education, 4th Floor, Francis Compton Building, Waterfront Castries
Tel: +1 758 468 5202
Website: www.education.gov.lc
Preschools, ages 3-5
Primary, ages 5-13
Secondary, ages 13-18

SUDAN
Ministry of Education, PO Box 284, Sudan Khartoum, Alneel Avenue
Tel: +24 9122 838 009
Website: www.moe.gov.sd
Kindergarten, ages 3-5
Primary, ages 6-13
Secondary, ages 14-17

SWEDEN
National Ministry of Education and Research, SE-103 33, Stockholm
Tel: +46 8 405 1000
Website: www.government.se
Other: independent schools receive grants from the NAE for each registered student, but they are essentially fee-paying. Compulsory education runs from age 6-16 and takes place in all-through schools, which are coeducational and non-selective. There are several varieties of pre-schools available for children from birth to ages seven. These are: Daghem (day nursery/pre-school), Familjedaghem (registered childminders), Deltidsgrupp (part-time group), Oppen förskola (pre-school/parent and toddler groups), and Förskoleklass (pre-school for ages 6-7). Post-16 is not compulsory but such education available is for students, should they want it, up to the age of 20.

SWITZERLAND
State Secretariat for Education, Research and Innovation SERI Einsteinstrasse 2, CH-3003 Bern
Tel: +41 58 462 21 29
Website: www.sbfi.admin.ch
Pre-school/kindergarten, ages 4-6
Primary, ages 6-12
Secondary I, ages 12-16
Secondary II, ages 16-20
Other: tertiary education is either general or professional education. Professional education applies to universities or occupational qualifications; the latter tend to be supported/sponsored by the relevant association (medical, law, etc) who are also responsible for setting the examinations.

Ministries of Education

TAIWAN
Ministry of Education, No 5 Zhongshan S Road, Zhongzheng District, Taipei City 10051
Tel: +886 2773 66666
Website: english.moe.gov.tw
Preschool, ages 3-6
Primary, ages 6-12
Junior high, ages 12-15
Senior secondary, ages 15-18

TAJIKISTAN
Ministry of Education and Science, 734024, Dushanbe, Nisor Muhammad St, 13a
Tel: +992 3772 221 4605
Website: www.maorif.tj
Pre-school, ages 3-6
Primary, ages 7-11
Secondary, ages 11-18

TANZANIA
Ministry of Education, Science and Technology, PO Box 10, Dodoma
Tel: +255 26 296 3533
Website: www.moe.go.tz
Pre-primary, ages 3-4
Primary, ages 5-11
Secondary, ages 12-16

THAILAND
Ministry of Education, Bangkok 10300
Tel: +66 228 198 09
Website: www.en.moe.go.th
Pre-school, ages 4-6
Elementary, ages 7-12
Secondary, ages 13-18

TIMOR-LESTE
Ministry of Education
Website: www.moe.gov.tl

TRINIDAD AND TOBAGO
Ministry of Education, No 5 St Vincent Street, Port of Spain
Tel: +1 868 622 2181
Website: www.moe.gov.tt
Pre-school, ages 3-5
Primary, ages 5-11
Secondary, ages 12-16
Other: religious schools.

TUNISIA
Ministry of Education, 60 Boulevard Bab Bnet, 1030 Tunis
Tel: +216 71 833 800
Website: www.education.gov.tn
Pre-school, ages 3-6
Primary, ages 6-12
Preparatory, ages 13-16
Secondary, ages 16-20

TURKEY
Ministry of National Education, Devlet Mahallesi, Atatürk Blv No 98, 06420 Çankaya/Ankara
Tel: +90 312 4132680
Website: www.meb.gov.tr
Pre-school, ages 3-6
Primary, ages 6-14
Secondary, ages 15-17

TURKS AND CAICOS ISLANDS
Department of Education (Zone I) Mission Folly, Grand Turk
Tel: +1 649 9462319
Website: www.gov.tc/education
Primary, ages 5-11
Secondary, ages 12-16

UGANDA
Ministry of Education and Sports, PO Box 7063, Kampala
Tel: +256 414 259 338
Website: www.education.go.ug
Primary, ages 7-13
Secondary, ages 14-17

UK – ENGLAND
Department for Education, Piccadilly Gate, Store Street Manchester M1 2WD
Tel: 0370 000 2288
Website: https://www.gov.uk/government/organisations/department-for-education
Pre-school, ages 3-5
Primary/preparatory, ages 5-11 (or 13 in private preparatory schools)
Secondary/senior, ages 11-16
Sixth form, ages 16-18
Other: faith schools, free schools, and academies.

UK – NORTHERN IRELAND
Department of Education, Rathgael House, Balloo Road, Rathgill, Bangor, BT19 7PR
Tel: 028 9127 9279
Website: www.education-ni.gov.uk
Primary, ages 4-11
Secondary, ages 11-16
Sixth form, ages 16-18
Other: faith schools.

UK – SCOTLAND
Education and Skills, Denholm House, Almondvale Business Park, Almondvale Way, Livingston, EH54 6GA
Tel: 0300 244 4000
Website: www.education.gov.scot
Primary, ages 4-11
Secondary, ages 11-18
Other: faith schools.

Ministries of Education

UK – WALES
Department for Education and Skills, Cathays Park, Cardiff, CF10 3NQ
Tel: 0300 060 4400
Website: www.gov.wales/education-skills
Pre-school, ages 3-4
Primary/preparatory, ages 5-11 (or 13 in private preparatory schools)
Secondary/senior, ages 11-16
Sixth form, ages 16-18
Other: Welsh-speaking only schools.

UKRAINE
Ministry of Education and Science, 01135, Kyiv, prospect Peremohy, 10
Tel: +380 044 481 32 21
Website: www.mon.gov.ua
Primary, ages 6-10
Basic general secondary, ages 10-15
Complete general secondary, ages 15-18

UNITED ARAB EMIRATES
Ministry of Education
Tel: +971 8005 1115
Website: www.moe.gov.ae
Primary, ages 6-12
Middle, ages 12-15
Secondary, ages 15-18

UNITED STATES OF AMERICA
Department of Education, 400 Maryland Avenue, SW, Washington, DC 20202
Tel: +1 800 872 5327
Website: www.ed.gov
Pre-school, ages 4-5
Kindergarten, ages 5-6
Elementary, ages 6-11, 1st-5th grade
Middle/junior high, ages 11-14, 6th-8th grade
High school, ages 14-18, 9th-12th grade
Other: in high school, ninth graders are called 'freshmen', tenth graders 'sophomores', eleventh graders 'juniors' and twelfth graders 'seniors'.

VIRGIN ISLANDS
The Ministry of Education, Culture, Youth Affairs, Fisheries and Agriculture, 33 Admin Drive, Wickhams Cay 1, Road Town, Tortola
Tel: +1 284 468-3701
Website: http://www.bvi.gov.vg/content/ministry-education-and-culture
Junior high, ages 5-12
Senior high, ages 13-17

UZBEKISTAN
Ministry of Education, 120100, Syrdarya region, Gulistan city, Peoples' Friendship street, 30th building
Tel: +998 71 241 01 86
Website: www.uzedu.uz
Primary, ages 6-10
Secondary, ages 10-15
Upper secondary, ages 15-17

VENEZUELA
Ministry of Education
Preschool, ages up to 6
Primary, ages 6-11
Secondary, ages 11-17

VIETNAM
Ministry of Education and Training, 35 Dai Co Viet Street, Hanoi
Tel: +84 43869 5144
Website: en.moet.gov.vn
Pre-school, ages 3-6
Primary, ages 6-11
Lower secondary, ages 12-15
Upper secondary, ages 16-18

ZAMBIA
Ministry of General Education, PO Box 50093, Lusaka
Tel: +260 211 250 855
Website: www.moge.gov.zm
Primary, ages 6-13
Junior secondary, 13-15
Upper secondary, ages 15-18

ZIMBABWE
Ministry of Primary and Secondary Education, Head Office, PO Box CY 121, Causeway, Harare
Tel: +263 4 705153
Website: http://mopse.co.zw
Primary, ages 6-13
Secondary, ages 13-16
High schools, ages 17-19

Curricula, examinations and tests

Curricula, examinations and tests

INTERNATIONAL QUALIFICATIONS

THE CAMBRIDGE PATHWAY

The Cambridge Pathway gives students a clear path through education from age 3 to 19. It has five stages: Cambridge Early Years, Cambridge Primary, Cambridge Lower Secondary, Cambridge Upper Secondary and Cambridge Advanced. Schools can offer all the stages, or just some of them. Every stage helps learners to thrive in and outside the classroom, so that they are ready for the world.

CAMBRIDGE EARLY YEARS

Cambridge Early Years is a new programme for 3-6 year olds. It gives young learners the best start in life, helping them to meet key early milestones and thrive in and outside of school. Cambridge Early Years is the first stage in the Cambridge Pathway.

The programme is child-centred and play-based and helps young learners to develop at their own pace. It encourages them to act independently, make their own choices and discover feelings of self-worth.

It includes everything schools need for high-quality learning: a holistic, balanced curriculum, engaging classroom resources, professional development and assessment approaches to help measure learners' progress.

The curriculum is made up of six areas:
- communication and literacy
- creative expression
- mathematics
- physical development
- personal, social and emotional development
- understanding the world.

Cambridge Early Years supports learners, whatever their level of English when they begin the programme. Cambridge also help schools offer a bilingual or multilingual approach if learners have a home language other than English
Website: www.cambridgeinternational.org/earlyyears

CAMBRIDGE PRIMARY

Cambridge Primary is typically for learners aged 5 to 11 years. It develops learner skills and understanding in 11 subjects: English as a first or second language, mathematics, science, art & design, computing, digital literacy, music, physical education, wellbeing and Cambridge Global Perspectives. Subjects can be offered in any combination and adapted to suit the school's context, culture and school ethos.

The flexible curriculum frameworks include optional assessment tools to help schools monitor learners' progress and give detailed feedback to parents. At the end of Cambridge Primary, schools can enter students for Cambridge Primary Checkpoint tests which are marked in Cambridge. Website: www.cambridgeinternational.org/primary

CAMBRIDGE LOWER SECONDARY

Cambridge Lower Secondary is typically for learners aged 11 to 14 years. It develops learner skills and understanding in 11 subjects: English, English as a second language, mathematics, science, art & design, computing, digital literacy, music, physical education, wellbeing, and Cambridge Global Perspectives. Subjects can be offered in any combination and adapted to suit the school's context, culture and school ethos.

The programme includes a range of optional assessments to help measure students' potential and progress. At the end of Cambridge Lower Secondary, schools can enter students for Cambridge Lower Secondary Checkpoint tests which are marked in Cambridge and provide an external international benchmark for student performance. Website: www.cambridgeinternational.org/lowersecondary

CAMBRIDGE IGCSE (CAMBRIDGE UPPER SECONDARY STAGE)

Cambridge IGCSE is the world's most popular international qualification for 14 to 16 year olds. It develops skills in creative thinking, enquiry and problem solving, in preparation for the next stage in a student's education. Cambridge IGCSE is taken in over 150 countries, and is widely recognised by employers and higher education institutions worldwide.

Cambridge IGCSE is graded from A*-G and the standards are aligned to the GCSE qualification taken in England. It can be used as preparation for Cambridge International A & AS Levels, UK A and AS levels, IB or AP and gives schools flexibility to build a curriculum that meets their students' needs. Cambridge IGCSE First Language English and Cambridge IGCSE English Language qualifications are recognised by a significant number of UK universities as evidence of competence in the language for university entrance.

Subjects: available in over 70 subjects including accounting, Afrikaans – first language, Afrikaans – second language, agriculture, Arabic – first language, Arabic – foreign language, art and design, Baha Indonesia, Bangladesh studies, biology, business studies, chemistry, child development, Chinese – first language, Chinese – second language, Chinese (Mandarin) – foreign language, computer studies, Czech – first language, design and technology, development studies, drama, Dutch – first language, Dutch – foreign language, economics, English – additional language, English – first language, English – literature, English – second language, enterprise, environmental management, food and nutrition, French – first language, French – foreign language, geography, German – first language, German – foreign language, global perspectives, Greek – foreign language, Hindi as a second language, Italian – foreign language, history, India studies, Indonesian – foreign language, information and

Curricula, examinations and tests

communication technology, IsiZulu as a second language, Japanese – first language, Japanese – foreign language, Kazakh as a second language, Korean (first language), Latin, Malay – first language, Malay – foreign language, mathematics, mathematics – additional, international mathematics, music, Pakistan studies, physical education, physical science, physics, Portuguese – first language, Portuguese – foreign language, religious studies, Russian – first language, science – combined, sciences – co-ordinated (double), sociology, Spanish – first language, Spanish – foreign language, Spanish – literature, Thai – first language, travel and tourism, Turkish – first language, Urdu – second language, world literature.
Website: www.cambridgeinternational.org/igcse

CAMBRIDGE ICE (CAMBRIDGE UPPER SECONDARY STAGE)

The Cambridge International Certificate of Education (ICE) is the group award of Cambridge IGCSE (see above). In order to be awarded a Cambridge ICE certificate, a student must obtain at least grade G in seven subjects from five subject groups. They must take two different languages and one subject from each of the other groups: humanities and social sciences, sciences, mathematics, and creative and professional. The seventh subject can be taken from any of the five subject groups.

The certificates are awarded in the following levels:
- Distinction – student must obtain grade A or above in five subjects and grade C or above in two further subjects.
- Merit – student must obtain grade C or above in five subjects and grade F or above in two further subjects.
- Pass – student must obtain grade G or above in seven subjects.

CAMBRIDGE INTERNATIONAL AS & A LEVEL (CAMBRIDGE ADVANCED STAGE)

Cambridge International AS & A Level is an internationally recognised qualification, taught in over 130 countries worldwide. It is typically for learners aged 16 to 19 years who need advanced study to prepare for university. Like Cambridge IGCSE, it has been created specifically for an international audience and the content has been designed to be accessible and fair to students whose first language is not English and avoid any cultural bias.

Cambridge International A Level is typically a two-year course, and Cambridge International AS Level is typically one year. Some subjects can be started as a Cambridge International AS Level and extended to a Cambridge International A Level. Students can either follow a broad course of study, or specialise in one particular subject area.

Learners use Cambridge International AS & A Levels to gain places at leading universities worldwide, including the UK, Ireland, USA, Canada, Australia, New Zealand, India, Singapore, Egypt, Jordan, South Africa, the Netherlands, Germany and Spain. In places such as the US and Canada, good grades in carefully chosen Cambridge International A Level subjects can result in up to one year of university course credit.

Assessment options:
Cambridge International AS & A Levels have a linear structure with exams at the end of the course. Students can choose from a range of assessment options:
Option 1: take Cambridge International AS Levels only. The Cambridge International syllabus content is half a Cambridge International A Level.
Option 2: staged assessment, which means taking the Cambridge International AS Level in one exam session and the Cambridge International A Level at a later session. However, this route is not possible in all subjects.
Option 3: take all Cambridge International A Level papers in the same examination session, usually at the end of the course.

Grades and subjects
Cambridge International A Levels are graded from A* to E. Cambridge International AS Levels are graded from A to E.

Subjects: available in 55 subjects including accounting, Afrikaans, Afrikaans – first language (AS only), Afrikaans language (AS only), applied information and communication technology, Arabic, Arabic language (AS only), art and design, biology, business, chemistry, Chinese, Chinese language (AS only), classical studies, computing, design and technology, design and textiles, digital media & design, divinity, economics, English language, English literature, environmental management, food studies, French, French language (AS only), French literature (AS only), general paper, geography, German, German language (AS only), Global Perspectives & Research, Hindi, Hindi language (AS only), Hindi literature (AS only), Hinduism, history, Islamic studies, Japanese language (AS only), English language and literature (AS only), law, Marathi, Marathi language (AS only), marine science, mathematics, further mathematics, media studies, music, physical education, physical science, physics, Portuguese, Portuguese language (AS only), Portuguese literature (AS only), psychology, sociology, Spanish, Spanish first language (AS only), Spanish language (AS only), Spanish literature (AS only), Tamil, Tamil language (AS only), Telugu, Telugu language (AS only), thinking skills, travel and tourism, Urdu, Urdu language (AS only).
Website: www.cambridgeinternational.org/alevel

CAMBRIDGE AICE DIPLOMA (CAMBRIDGE ADVANCED STAGE)

The Cambridge Advanced International Certificate of Education (AICE) Diploma prepares students for honours degree programmes. It is made up of individual Cambridge International AS & A Levels, and requires the study of subjects drawn from three curriculum areas within an international curriculum framework: mathematics and sciences; languages; and arts and humanities.

To achieve the Diploma, all learners also need to study and pass a compulsory core subject: Cambridge

International AS Level Global Perspectives & Research. This is a cross-curricular skills-based course.

In order to receive a Cambridge AICE Diploma, a candidate must earn a minimum of seven credits (including Cambridge International AS Level Global Perspectives & Research), with at least one credit coming from each of the three curriculum areas. The remaining credits can come from any of the curriculum areas, including an optional group of interdisciplinary subjects (Group 4).

A Cambridge International AS Level is awarded one credit, and a Cambridge International A Level is awarded two credits.

Learners who pass the Cambridge International A Level in Global Perspectives & Research meet the compulsory requirement of the core group and also have one credit which may then be included in Group 4 to contribute to the overall requirement of seven credits.

Grading and points system
Cambridge International AS Level subjects – candidates are graded A to E.
Cambridge International A Level subjects – candidates are graded A* to E.
The Cambridge AICE Diploma is awarded on the basis of a points system:

Two credits study (A Levels)

Grade	Points
A*	140
A	120
B	100
C	80
D	60
E	40

One credit study (AS Levels)

Grade	Points
A	60
B	50
C	40
D	30
E	20

Candidates who meet the requirements will receive a Cambridge AICE Diploma at one of three levels – pass, merit or distinction – on the basis of their overall AICE diploma score:

Cambridge AICE Diploma with Distinction: awarded to students with a score of 360 points or above. The maximum Diploma score is 420 points.
Cambridge AICE Diploma with Merit: awarded to students with between 250 and 359 points.
Cambridge AICE Diploma at Pass level: awarded to students with between 140 and 249 points.
The maximum number of Cambridge AICE Diploma points is capped at 420.

Subjects
Group 1: Mathematics and sciences. Subjects available include biology, chemistry, computing, design and technology, environmental management, mathematics, physics and psychology.
Group 2: Languages. Subjects available include English language, Afrikaans, Chinese, Portuguese, Spanish, French, German, Urdu.
Group 3: Arts and humanities. Subjects available include accounting, art and design, business studies, economics, geography, history, English literature, French literature, Portuguese literature, Spanish literature, music, psychology, sociology.
Group 4: Interdisciplinary subjects (optional). Subjects include a general paper and thinking skills.
Core: Cambridge Global Perspectives. It is compulsory for all learners to study Cambridge International AS Level Global Perspectives & Research.
Website: www.cambridgeinternational.org/aice

EDEXCEL INTERNATIONAL GCSES

Pearson's Edexcel International GCSEs are academic qualifications aimed at learners aged 14 to 16. They're equivalent to a UK General Certificate of Secondary Education (GCSE), and are the main requirement for Level 3 studies, including progression to GCE AS or A levels, BTECs or employment. International GCSEs are linear qualifications, meaning that students take all of the exams at the end of the course. They are available at Level 1 and Level 2. There are currently more than 100,000 learners studying Edexcel International GCSEs, in countries throughout Asia, Africa, Europe, the Middle East and Latin America. Developed by subject specialists and reviewed regularly, many of Pearson's Edexcel International GCSEs include specific international content to make them relevant to students worldwide.

International GCSEs are offered in over 30 subjects. Subject areas include: Art and Design, Business & Economics, English, Humanities, Information and Communication Technology, Languages, Mathematics, Sciences. Note that the subject areas highlighted in bold are also available as part of the Edexcel Certificate qualification suite.

EUROPEAN BACCALAUREATE (EB)

Not to be confused with the International Baccalaureate (IB) or the French Baccalaureate, this certificate is available in European schools and recognised in all EU countries.

To obtain the baccalaureate, a student must obtain a minimum score of 50%, which is made up from: coursework, oral participation in class and tests (50%); five written examinations (35%) – mother-tongue, first foreign language and maths are compulsory for all candidates; three oral examinations (15%) – mother tongue and first foreign language are compulsory (history or geography may also be compulsory here, dependant on whether the candidate has taken a written examination in these subjects).

Subjects taught in different languages have the same syllabi, regardless of the language, and the same

Curricula, examinations and tests

is valid for examinations – the content is simply translated into different languages. In case of languages, the syllabi vary, but nevertheless, they are harmonized and the examinations have to follow an agreed structure. The EB has been specifically designed to meet, at the very least, the minimum qualification requirements of each member state.

Study for the EB begins at nursery stage (age 4) and progresses through primary (age six) and on into secondary school (age 12).

Syllabus
Languages: Bulgarian, Czech, Danish, Dutch, English, Estonian, Finnish, Finnish as a second national language, French, Gaelic as other national language German, Greek, Hungarian, Italian, Latvian, Lithuanian, Maltese as other national language, Polish, Portuguese, Romanian, Slovak, Slovenian, Spanish, Swedish, Swedish for Finnish pupils.

Literary: art education, non-confessional ethics, geography, ancient Greek, history, human sciences, Latin, music, philosophy, physical education.

Sciences: biology, chemistry, economics, ICT, mathematics, physics.

For more information, contact:
Office of the Secretary-General of the European Schools
Rue de la Science 23, B-1040 Bruxelles
Tel: +32 2295 3745; Fax: +32 2298 6298
Website: www.eursc.eu

FRENCH BACCALAUREATE

The French Baccalauréat or 'le bac', is an academic qualification taken at the end of the lycée (secondary education), usually when the student is 18. It is the required qualification in France for those students wishing to carry on their studies at university. Students not wishing to go on to higher education can, in theory, opt out of taking the baccalaureate and those who do not have one can instead take the higher education entrance exam, which leads to its own diploma.

There are three main types of baccalaureate in France:
- the baccalauréat général (general);
- the baccalauréat professionnel (professional);
- the baccalauréat technologique (technological).

General Baccalaureate
The new bac général, introduced in 2021, includes six obligatory core subjects: French, history-geography, two foreign languages, sport, and a new subject called humanités scientifiques et numériques, which covers science and technology.

In the second year of lycée, students can choose three speciality subjects. In the third year, they continue with two speciality subjects.

Five exams, including an oral exam, will account for 60% of the overall mark. Continued assessment will account for 40% (of which 30% from set tests, and 10% from term grades).

Students will take the French exam (written and oral) at the end of the second year, as philosophy lessons replace French lessons in the final year. They will then sit the exam for each of the two speciality subjects immediately after the spring school holiday in the final year, and finally the philosophy and oral exam at the end of the summer term.

Option Internationale du Baccalauréat
This is an additional option to the general baccalaureate and offers further subjects. Extra exams are offered in literature, history and geography allowing a higher grade to be achieved towards the final baccalaureate mark. In general, this option is taken by students wishing to study at overseas universities.

Grades
Students need a total combined mark of 50% or above to pass their brévet and baccalauréat exams in France. Accreditations, known as mentions ('assez bien', 'bien', 'très bien'), are awarded for achieving certain percentage thresholds above the median.

THE INTERNATIONAL BACCALAUREATE (IB)

The International Baccalaureate (IB) offers four challenging and high quality educational programmes for a worldwide community of schools, aiming to develop internationally minded people who, recognizing their common humanity and shared guardianship of the planet, help to create a better, more peaceful world.

The IB works with schools around the world (both state and privately funded) that share the commitment to international education to deliver these programmes.

Schools that have achieved the high standards required for authorization to offer one or more of the IB programmes are known as IB World Schools. There are over half a million students attending more than 5400 IB World Schools in 153 countries and this number is growing annually.

The Primary Years, Middle Years and Diploma Programmes share a common philosophy and common characteristics. They develop the whole student, helping students to grow intellectually, socially, aesthetically and culturally. They provide a broad and balanced education that includes science and the humanities, languages and mathematics, technology and the arts. The programmes teach students to think critically, and encourage them to draw connections between areas of knowledge and to use problem-solving techniques and concepts from many disciplines. They instil in students a sense of responsibility towards others and towards the environment. Lastly, and perhaps most importantly, the programmes give students an awareness and understanding of their own culture and of other cultures, values and ways of life.

A fourth programme called the IB Career Related Certificate (IBCC) became available to IB World Schools from September 2012.

All IB programmes include:
- a written curriculum or curriculum framework;
- student assessment appropriate to the age range;

- professional development and networking opportunities for teachers;
- support, authorization and programme evaluation for the school.

The IB Primary Years Programme
The IB Primary Years Programme (PYP), for students aged three to 12, focuses on the development of the whole child as an inquirer, both in the classroom and in the world outside. It is a framework consisting of five essential elements (concepts, knowledge, skills, attitude, action) and guided by six trans-disciplinary themes of global significance, explored using knowledge and skills derived from six subject areas (language, social studies, mathematics, science and technology, arts, and personal, social and physical education) with a powerful emphasis on inquiry-based learning.

The most significant and distinctive feature of the PYP is the six trans-disciplinary themes. These themes are about issues that have meaning for, and are important to, all of us. The programme offers a balance between learning about or through the subject areas, and learning beyond them. The six themes of global significance create a trans-disciplinary framework that allows students to 'step up' beyond the confines of learning within subject areas:
- Who we are.
- Where we are in place and time.
- How we express ourselves.
- How the world works.
- How we organize ourselves.
- Sharing the planet.

The PYP exhibition is the culminating activity of the programme. It requires students to analyse and propose solutions to real-world issues, drawing on what they have learned through the programme. Evidence of student development and records of PYP exhibitions are reviewed by the IB as part of the programme evaluation process.

Assessment is an important part of each unit of inquiry as it both enhances learning and provides opportunities for students to reflect on what they know, understand and can do. The teacher's feedback to the students provides the guidance, the tools and the incentive for them to become more competent, more skilful and better at understanding how to learn.

The IB Middle Years Programme (MYP)
The Middle Years Programme (MYP), for students aged 11 to 16, comprises eight subject groups:
- Language acquisition
- Language and literature
- Individuals and societies
- Sciences
- Mathematics
- Arts
- Physical and health education
- Design

The MYP requires at least 50 hours of teaching time for each subject group in each year of the programme. In years 4 and 5, students have the option to take courses from six of the eight subject groups within certain limits, to provide greater flexibility in meeting local requirements and individual student learning needs.

Each year, students in the MYP also engage in at least one collaboratively planned interdisciplinary unit that involves at least two subject groups.

MYP students also complete a long-term project, where they decide what they want to learn about, identify what they already know, discovering what they will need to know to complete the project, and create a proposal or criteria for completing it.

The MYP aims to help students develop their personal understanding, their emerging sense of self and their responsibility in their community.

The MYP allows schools to continue to meet state, provincial or national legal requirements for students with access needs. Schools must develop an inclusion/special educational needs (SEN) policy that explains assessment access arrangements, classroom accommodations and curriculum modification that meet individual student learning needs.

The IB Diploma Programme (IBDP)
The IB Diploma Programme, for students aged 16 to 19, is an academically challenging and motivating curriculum of international education that prepares students for success at university and in life beyond studies.

DP students choose at least one course from six subject groups, thus ensuring depth and breadth of knowledge and experience in languages, social studies, the experimental sciences, mathematics, and the arts. With more than 35 courses to choose from, students have the flexibility to further explore and learn subjects that meet their interest. Out of the six courses required, at least three and not more than four must be taken at higher level (240 teaching hours), the others at standard level (150 teaching hours). Students can take examinations in English, French or Spanish.

In addition, three unique components of the programme – the DP core – aim to broaden students' educational experience and challenge them to apply their knowledge and skills. The DP core – the extended essay (EE), theory of knowledge (TOK) and creativity, activity, service (CAS) – are compulsory and central to the philosophy of the programme.

The IB uses both external and internal assessment to measure student performance in the DP. Student results are determined by performance against set standards, not by each student's position in the overall rank order. DP assessment is unique in the way that it measures the extent to which students have mastered advanced academic skills not what they have memorized. DP assessment also encourages an international outlook and intercultural skills, wherever appropriate.

The IB diploma is awarded to students who gain at least 24 points out of a possible 45 points, subject to

Curricula, examinations and tests

certain minimum levels of performance across the whole programme and to satisfactory participation in the creativity, activity, and service requirement.

Recognized and respected by leading universities globally, the DP encourages students to be knowledgeable, inquiring, caring and compassionate, and to develop intercultural understanding, open-mindedness and the attitudes necessary to respect and evaluate a range of viewpoints.

The IB Career Related Programme (IBCP)

The IB Career-related Programme, for students aged 16 to 19, offers an innovative educational framework that combines academic studies with career-related learning. Through the CP, students develop the competencies they need to succeed in the 21st century. More importantly, they have the opportunity to engage with a rigorous study programme that genuinely interests them while gaining transferable and lifelong skills that prepares them to pursue higher education, apprenticeships or direct employment.

CP students complete four core components – language development, personal and professional skills, service learning and a reflective project – in order to receive the International Baccalaureate Career-related Programme Certificate. Designed to enhance critical thinking and intercultural understanding, the CP core helps students develop the communication and personal skills, as well as intellectual habits required for lifelong learning.

Schools that choose to offer the CP can create their own distinctive version of the programme and select career pathways that suit their students and local community needs. The IB works with a variety of CRS providers around the world and schools seeking to develop career pathways with professional communities can benefit from our existing collaborations. All CRS providers undergo a rigorous curriculum evaluation to ensure that their courses align with the CP pedagogy and meet IB quality standards. The flexibility to meet the needs, backgrounds and contexts of learners allows CP schools to offer an education that is relevant and meaningful to their students.

Launched in 2012, there are more than 400 CP schools to date. Many schools with the IB Diploma Programme (DP) and the Middle Years Programme (MYP) have chosen the CP as an alternative IB pathway to offer students. CP schools often report that the programme has helped them raise student aspiration, increase student engagement and retention and encouraged learners to take responsibility for their own actions, helping them foster high levels of self-esteem through meaningful achievements.
For more information, visit: www.ibo.org

THE INTERNATIONAL EARLY YEARS CURRICULUM (IEYC)

The International Early Years Curriculum is a research-based programme that incorporates international best practices in the developmental needs of 2-5 year olds, and can be easily extended to include older children in settings and countries where early years education goes beyond the age of five. It is also a perfect tool for the transition between early and formal education.

The IEYC is designed around eight learning principles, each conveying a belief considered essential to children's learning and development, and are intrinsically linked to a unique IEYC Process of Learning.

The IEYC Process of Learning

The IEYC Process of Learning provides a strong implementation structure, sequencing each unit. The process of learning captures children's natural curiosity as a starting point and, within an enabled environment, balances child-initiated and teacher-led learning. Each element of the Process of Learning is linked to the eight Learning Principles, ensuring the IEYC beliefs about children's learning and development are connected to all practices.

The IEYC Learning Strands

Underpinning all learning and development, are the IEYC Learning Strands:
- Independence and Interdependence
- Communicating
- Enquiring
- Healthy Living and Physical Wellbeing

Each unit has been carefully designed around a central theme, holistically linking all four Learning Strands to relevant and engaging activities that can be adapted and extended to meet individual needs.

For more details on the IEYC visit: fieldworkeducation.com/curriculums/early-years

Curricula, examinations and tests

THE INTERNATIONAL MIDDLE YEARS CURRICULUM (IMYC)

The International Middle Years Curriculum (IMYC) provides an enriching, engaging and rigorous learning experience for 11-14 year olds. It is practical for the school to deliver, and inspiring and relevant for students, preparing them well for the next stage in their learning.

The IMYC is a curriculum that makes meaning, connects learning and develops minds. It delivers rigorous and transformational knowledge, skills and understanding of all subjects, linking all learning to a conceptual theme. The IMYC creates a challenging, student-led learning environment preparing students well for iGCSE, A levels and IB Diploma.

Each IMYC unit guides students to make meaning of the conceptual theme through a personal and global perspective which they represent at the end of their unit learning through a media project. Within each IMYC unit there is a learning process designed to engage and inspire teenagers, helping them to become confident, independent learners.

IMYC member schools and students are part of a worldwide IMYC community through which they share learning experiences, ideas and resources.

The IMYC is part of Fieldwork Education which, since 1984, has been helping schools around the world to develop children's learning. For more information about the IMYC visit fieldworkeducation.com/curriculums/middle-years

THE INTERNATIONAL PRIMARY CURRICULUM (IPC)

The International Primary Curriculum (IPC) is one of the only comprehensive curricula in the world equally committed to improving learning and developing international mindedness. It focuses on developing knowledge, skills and understanding of subjects set within child-friendly, relevant, cross-curricular thematic units of work that are creative and challenging for children of all abilities. The IPC has over 140 different thematic units of learning; all modern-day topics appealing to all ages of primary children. This enables young children to remain motivated through the learning of science, geography, history and so on.

Within each theme, the IPC suggests many ideas for collaborative learning, for active learning, for learning outside the classroom, for role play, and for children learning from each other. The IPC's engaging approach also encourages parental involvement through a range of initiatives.

Each IPC unit incorporates most of the core subjects including science, history, geography, ICT, art and PE and provides opportunities to incorporate language arts and mathematics. Each subject then has a number of learning tasks to help teachers to help their children meet a range of learning goals set out in the curriculum. These learning goals are deliberately explicit, designed to make sure that teachers distinguish clearly between children's learning of knowledge, skills and understanding.

Each IPC unit has embedded within it learning-focused activities that help young children to start developing a global awareness and gain an increasing sense of the 'other'. Every unit creates opportunities to look at learning of the theme through a local perspective, a national perspective and an international perspective.

With schools in over 90 countries learning with the IPC, there are opportunities for children to share their local experiences related to an IPC unit with children in dramatically different environments.

Each IPC unit has a very structured yet flexible teaching framework providing teachers with a series of learning tasks. These are designed to achieve the learning goals through creative, meaningful and memorable learning activities that appeal to all learning styles and are relevant for all children of all abilities. However, the learning tasks are purely a guide and provide plenty of scope for creative teaching, personalisation to the class and locality, and development on the theme as well as linking with other schools learning with the IPC. With IPC member schools in countries as diverse as Swaziland, Malaysia, Qatar, and Japan, this sharing of learning opportunities ensures that no school, however remote, feels isolated.

The IPC is part of Fieldwork Education. For more information about the IPC visit fieldworkeducation.com/curriculums/primary-years

Curricula, examinations and tests

UK SYSTEM

WHAT IS COMMON ENTRANCE?

The Common Entrance examinations are used in UK independent schools (and some independent schools overseas) for transfer from junior to senior schools at the ages of 11+ and 13+. They were first introduced in 1904 and are internationally recognised as being a rigorous form of assessment following a thorough course of study. The examinations are produced by the Independent Schools Examinations Board and backed by HMC (Headmasters' and Headmistresses' Conference), GSA (Girls' Schools Association), and IAPS (Independent Association of Prep Schools) which together represent the leading independent schools in the UK, and many overseas.

Common Entrance is not a public examination as, for example, GCSE, and candidates may normally be entered only in one of the following circumstances:

a) they have been offered a place at a senior school subject to their passing the examination, or

b) they are entered as a 'trial run', in which case the papers are marked by the junior school concerned. Candidates normally take the examination in their own junior or preparatory schools, either in the UK or overseas.

How does Common Entrance fit into the progression to GCSEs?

Rapid changes in education nationally and internationally have resulted in regular reviews of the syllabuses for all the Common Entrance examinations. Reviews of the National Curriculum, in particular, have brought about a number of changes, with the Board wishing to ensure that it continues to set high standards. It is also a guiding principle that Common Entrance should be part of the natural progression from 11-16, and not a diversion from it.

Common Entrance at 11+

At 11+, the examination consists of papers in English, mathematics and science. It is designed so that it can be taken by candidates either from independent preparatory schools or by candidates from schools in the maintained sector or overseas who have had no special preparation. The examination is normally taken in January for entrance to senior schools in the following September.

Common Entrance at 13+

At 13+, most candidates come from independent preparatory schools. The compulsory subjects are English, mathematics and science. Papers in French, geography, German, Classical Greek, history, Latin, religious studies and Spanish are also available and candidates usually offer as many subjects as they can. In most subjects, papers are available at more than one level to cater for candidates of different abilities. There are three examination sessions each year, with the majority of candidates sitting in the summer prior to entry to their senior schools in September.

Marking and grading

The papers are set centrally but the answers are marked by the senior school for which a candidate is entered. Mark schemes are provided by the Board but senior schools are free to set their own grade boundaries. Results are available within two weeks of the examinations taking place.

Pre-Testing and the ISEB Common Pre-Tests

A number of senior independent schools 'pre-test' pupils for entry, prior to them taking their main entrance examinations at a later date. Usually, these pre-tests take place when a pupil is in Year 6 or Year 7 of his or her junior school and will then be going on to sit Common Entrance in Year 8. The tests are designed to assess a pupil's academic potential and suitability for a particular senior school so that the child, the parents and the school know well in advance whether he/she is going to be offered a place at the school, subject to a satisfactory performance in the entrance examinations. The tests enable senior schools to manage their lists and help to ensure that pupils are not entered for examinations in which they are unlikely to be successful. In short, it reduces uncertainty for all concerned.

Pre-tests may be written specifically for the senior school for which the candidate is entered but a growing number of schools are choosing to use the Common Pre-Tests provided by the Independent Schools Examinations Board. These online tests are usually taken in the candidate's own junior school and one of their main advantages is that a pupil need sit the tests only once, with the results then made available to any senior school which wishes to use them. The multiple-choice tests cover verbal reasoning, non-verbal reasoning, English and mathematics, with the results standardised according to the pupil's age when they are taken. Further information is available on the ISEB website at www.iseb.co.uk.

Parents are advised to check the entrance requirements for senior schools to see if their child will be required to sit a pre-test.

Further information

Details of the Common Entrance examinations and how to register candidates are available on the ISEB website www.iseb.co.uk. Copies of past papers and a wide range of textbooks and other resources can be purchased from Galore Park Publishing Ltd at www.galorepark.co.uk. Support materials are also available from Hodder Education and other publishers; see the Resources section of the ISEB website for details.

Independent Schools Examinations Board
Endeavour House, Crow Arch Lane,
Ringwood, Hampshire BH24 1HP

Telephone: 01425 470555
Email: enquiries@iseb.co.uk
Web: www.iseb.co.uk

GENERAL CERTIFICATE OF SECONDARY EDUCATION (GCSE)

What are the GCSE qualifications?
GCSE qualifications were first introduced in 1986 and are the principal means of assessment at Key Stage 4 across a range of academic subject areas. They command respect and have status not only in the UK but worldwide.

Main features of the GCSE
There are four unitary awarding organisations for GCSEs in England. WJEC and CCEA also offer GCSE qualifications in Wales and Northern Ireland. Each examining group designs its own specifications but they are required to conform to set criteria. For some aspects of the qualification system, the exam boards adopt common ways of working. When the exam boards work together in this way they generally do so through the Joint Council of Qualifications (JCQ). The award of a grade is intended to indicate that a candidate has met the required level of skills, knowledge and understanding.

New, reformed GCSEs have been introduced in recent years. Assessment in these reformed GCSEs consists primarily of formal examinations taken at the end of the student's two-year course. Other types of assessment, non-exam assessment (NEA), is used where there are skills and knowledge which cannot be assessed through exams. Ofqual have set the percentage of the total marks that will come from NEA.

The reformed GCSEs feature new and more demanding content, as required by the government and developed by the exam boards. Courses are designed for two years of study (linear assessment) and no longer divided into different modules.

Exams can only be split into 'foundation tier' and 'higher tier' if one exam paper does not give all students the opportunity to show their knowledge and their abilities. Such tiering is only available in maths, science and modern foreign languages; other subjects do not have tiers. Resit opportunities will only be available each November in English language and maths, and then only for students who have turned 16 by the 31st of August in the year of the November assessment.

Summer 2022 marked the return of exams for the first time since 2019. Exams in 2020 and 2021 were replaced by alternatives due to constraints imposed following the pandemic. Grades were awarded through teachers' assessments based on mock exams, coursework and other available evidence.

Grading
The basic principle that exam boards follow when setting grade boundaries is that if the group of students (the cohort) taking a qualification in one year is of similar ability to the cohort in the previous year then the overall results (outcomes) should be comparable.

The reformed exams taken in summer 2017 were the first to show a new grading system, with the A* to G grades being phased out.

The grading system is 9 to 1, with 9 being the top grade. Ofqual says this allows greater differentiation between students. It expects that broadly the same proportion of students will achieve a grade 4 and above as currently achieve a grade C and above, that broadly the same proportion of students will achieve a grade 7 and above as currently achieve a grade A and above. There are three anchor points between the new grading system and the old one: the bottom of the new 1 grade is the same as the bottom of the old G grade, the bottom of the new 4 grade is the bottom of the old C grade, and the bottom of the 7 grade is the same as the bottom of the old A grade. Grade 9 will be set using the tailored approach formula in the first award.

Grades 2, 3, 5 and 6 will be awarded arithmetically so that the grade boundaries are equally spaced in terms of marks from neighbouring grades.

The government's definition of a 'strong pass' will be set at grade 5 for reformed GCSEs. A grade 4 – or 'standard pass' – will continue to be a level 2 achievement. The DfE does not expect employers, colleges or universities to raise the bar to a grade 5 if a grade 4 would meet their requirements.

Can anyone take GCSE qualifications?
GCSEs are intended mainly for 16-year-old pupils, but are open to anyone of any age, whether studying full-time or part-time at a school, college or privately. There are no formal entry requirements.

Students normally study up to ten subjects over a two-year period. Short course GCSEs are available in some subjects (including PE and religious studies) – these include half the content of a full GCSE, so two short course GCSEs are equivalent to one full GCSE.

The English Baccalaureate
The English Baccalaureate (EBacc) is a school performance measure. It allows people to see how many pupils get a grade C or above (current grading) in the core academic subjects at Key Stage 4 in any government-funded school. The DfE introduced the EBacc measure in 2010.

Curricula, examinations and tests

GENERAL CERTIFICATE OF EDUCATION (GCE) ADVANCED LEVEL (A LEVEL)

Typically, A level qualifications are studied over a two-year period. There are no lower or upper age limits. Schools and colleges usually expect students aged 16-18 to have obtained grades A*-C (grade 5 in the new criteria) in five subjects at GCSE level before taking an advanced level course. This requirement may vary between centres and according to which specific subjects are to be studied. Mature students may be assessed on different criteria as to their suitability to embark on the course.

GCE Qualifications

Over the past few years, AS level and A level qualifications have been in a process of reform. New subjects have been introduced gradually, with the first wave taught from September 2015. Subjects that have not been reformed are no longer available for teaching.

GCE qualifications are available at two levels: the Advanced Subsidiary (AS), which is generally delivered over one year and is seen as half an A level; and the A level (GCE). Nearly 70 titles are available, covering a wide range of subject areas, including humanities, sciences, language, business, arts, mathematics and technology.

One of the major reforms is that AS level results no longer count towards an A level (they previously counted for 50%). The two qualifications are linear, with AS assessments typically taking place after one year and A levels after two.

Some GCE AS and A levels, particularly the practical ones, contain a proportion of coursework. All GCE A levels that contain one or more types of assessment will have an element of synoptic assessment that tests students' understanding of the whole specification. GCE AS are graded A-E and A levels are graded A*-E.

Overall the amount of coursework at A level has been reduced in the reforms. In some subjects, such as the sciences, practical work will not contribute to the final A level but will be reported separately in a certificate of endorsement. In the sciences, students will do at least 12 practical activities, covering apparatus and techniques. Exam questions about practical work will make up at least 15% of the total marks for the qualification and students will be assessed on their knowledge, skills and understanding of practical work.

US SYSTEM PROGRAMS AND TESTS

THE ADVANCED PLACEMENT (AP) PROGRAM

The Advanced Placement (AP) program provides an opportunity for willing and academically prepared students to take rigorous university-level courses that help them develop the skills necessary for success in university and their future careers. Over 600 universities in more than 60 countries recognize successful AP Exam scores in the admission process.

Additionally, students who succeed on AP Exams have the opportunity to earn university credit and/or advanced placement, particularly in the US and Canada, helping them to reduce tuition costs and offering more time and flexibility to double major, study abroad, complete an internship or graduate earlier.

AP courses and exams are designed by secondary school teachers and university professors to match the rigor of university courses and exams. The program allows students to develop a global perspective, as well as skills such as critical thinking and problem solving. For each course, there is a standardized university-level exam that tests the skills and knowledge addressed in the course. AP Exams are administered in May of every year and are scored by AP teachers and university professors from around the world. Hence, a student's score on an AP Exam gives universities a globally recognized validation of their mastery of university-level content.

The College Board continues to innovate and ensure that the AP program provides equitable access to high quality education that prepares students for an ever-changing and increasingly global world.

Beginning in the 2023-24 school year, the College Board will launch the AP Precalculus course university-level mathematics and science courses. The course teaches content and skills common to university precalculus courses that are foundational for careers in mathematics, physics, biology, health science, social science, and data science.

Students and parents: To find schools that offer AP around the world, visit: apcourseaudit.inflexion.org/ledger and begin the search by entering a country in the 'Ledger Search' area. The AP Course Ledger is the official record of schools with authorized AP courses.

Educators: For more information, visit https://apcentral.collegeboard.org/.

AP CAPSTONE

AP Capstone™ is an innovative diploma program that provides students with an opportunity to engage in rigorous scholarly practice of the core academic skills necessary for successful university completion.

AP Capstone is built on the foundation of two courses – AP Seminar and AP Research. These two AP Capstone courses, with their associated performance tasks, assessments, and application of research methodology, complement the rigor of AP courses and exams by equipping students with the power to analyze and evaluate information with accuracy and precision in order to craft and communicate evidence-based arguments.

Students who earn scores of 3 or higher in AP Seminar, AP Research, and four additional AP exams of their choosing receive the AP Capstone Diploma™. This signifies their outstanding academic achievement and attainment of university-level academic and research skills. Students who earn scores of 3 or higher in both AP Seminar and AP Research but not on four additional AP exams receive the AP Seminar and Research Certificate™.

AP Capstone was developed in response to feedback from higher education and is easily implemented, affordable, and flexible. It has the potential to differentiate and transform high schools and their students by elevating the learning environment through a challenging university-level program with high standards of assessment.

For more information, visit collegeboard.org/apcapstone or email apcapstone@collegeboard.org.

ADVANCED PLACEMENT INTERNATIONAL DIPLOMA (APID)

The Advanced Placement International Diploma (APID) is a globally recognized credential for students who embrace an international outlook. The APID also challenges a student to display exceptional achievement across several disciplines. Universities worldwide utilize the APID in admissions.

The APID is available to students attending secondary schools outside the United States and to US resident students applying to universities outside the country. The APID is not a substitute for a high school diploma, but provides additional recognition of outstanding academic excellence.

In addition, for students attending schools within the United States to be eligible for the APID scholar award, they must send their official AP score report to a university outside the United States. For a list of universities outside the US that recognize AP, visit: international.collegeboard.org/students/ap/find-universities-recognize-ap

In order to earn the APID, students must earn scores of 3 or higher on five or more total AP Exams, based on the exam criteria requirements listed within each of the following content areas:

Curricula, examinations and tests

a. Two AP Exams from two different languages, either one selected from English and one from another world language OR two different world languages other than English: AP Chinese Language and Culture, AP English Language and Composition, AP English Literature and Composition, AP French Language and Culture, AP German Language and Culture, AP Spanish Language and Culture, AP Italian Language and Culture, and AP Japanese Language and Culture.
b. One AP Exam offering a global perspective: AP Art History, AP Comparative Government and Politics, AP Environmental Science, AP Human Geography, AP Macroeconomics and AP World History.
c. c) One AP Exam from the sciences or mathematics and computer science content areas: AP Biology, AP Calculus AB, AP Calculus BC, AP Chemistry, AP Computer Science A, AP Environmental Science, AP Physics C: Electricity and Magnetism, AP Physics C: Mechanics, AP Physics 1: Algebra-based, AP Physics 2: Algebra-based and AP Statistics.
d. d) One additional exam from among any content areas except English and world languages, excluding Latin. These include the content areas already described as well as AP Capstone, history and social science, and arts: AP Seminar, AP Research, AP Art History, AP European History, AP Latin, AP Macroeconomics, AP Microeconomics, AP Music Theory, AP Psychology, AP Studio Art: Drawing, AP Studio Art: 2-D Design, AP Studio Art: 3-D Design, AP US Government and Politics, AP US History and AP World History.

AMERICAN HIGH SCHOOL DIPLOMA

The American High School Diploma is a certificate awarded to students when they complete high school. Students generally study for the diploma for four years, from the 9th to 12th grade.

There is no national curriculum in the US, although states, school districts and national associations do recommend that certain standards are met and guidelines followed.

Each state sets the requirements for the high school diploma. Students are assessed throughout each semester with tests, exams, essays, homework assignments, classroom preparation, group work, projects and attendance, and given a final 'grade' for each course at the end of the semester.

Parents are sent a 'report card' with the grades achieved in each subject at the end of each quarter, semester or year. They will also ultimately receive a 'transcript' – an overview of their academic history, produced by the school – which will be requested by universities upon application.

Marks are given as letters (A+, A, B+ etc.) or a percentage. These marks will result in a Grade Point Average (GPA). The grading system is not standardised across school districts. However, in general they are:
A grade – excellent level – 4 points
B grade – above average – 3 points
C grade – average – 2 points
D grade – below average – 1 point
F – failure – 0 points (Note: a student that fails a required course must take it again.)

A student's high school GPA represents their accumulated grades throughout high school. It is calculated by adding the total of all points earned for each course, then dividing the total points by the total number of courses taken. Additional points may be awarded for extra work done in honors, AP or IB courses.

When applying for university, a student's GPA is taken into consideration and there are also admissions tests, such as the SAT and the ACT.

UNIVERSITY ADMISSIONS TESTS AND PROGRAMS

AMERICAN COLLEGE TESTING (ACT)

The ACT test is a curriculum-based achievement test, meaning it measures what students have learned in school, and tests them on the knowledge and skills they should have prior to pursuing a college or career path.

The ACT is not an aptitude or IQ test, it is a standardized achievement test, used for admissions purposes, scholarship eligibility, course placement, remediation, and retention.

Composite scores range from one to 36; and each section test (English, math, reading, science) is also scored on a scale from 1–36. The composite score given to each student is the average of the four tests added together, rounded to the nearest whole number. Students taking the optional writing test can score from two to 12.

The ACT is offered in the US on seven national test dates in September, October, December, February, April, June and July. ACT testing is also administered internationally on five international test dates, and on school days in the US. in select states and school districts that pay for their students to test.

Contact ACT for further information or to register for a test, via their website: www.act.org.

See how ACT scores compare to SATs: www.act.org/content/dam/act/unsecured/documents/ACT-SAT-Concordance-Tables.pdf

SAT (USA)

The SAT®, which is now offered digitally, is taken by millions of students each year and helps them achieve their dreams of studying in the US and elsewhere. The SAT measures the skills that students develop in secondary school.

The SAT is designed to predict a student's likely academic performance at a particular university in their first year and beyond. The SAT covers content areas deemed critical for success in university and SAT performance data illustrate that success on the SAT is linked to the type and rigor of course work completed during high school.

Over four million students take the SAT each academic year via nearly 7,000 test centers in more than 180 countries and territories. SAT questions are prescreened on students from around the world to ensure fairness. Before any test question appears on a scored section of the SAT, it is included on one of the unscored test forms that are included in every SAT administration. By pretesting questions in this way, College Board researchers can be sure that each question is fair and valid for all students regardless of gender, race, ethnicity, country of origin or socio-economic status. The SAT is the only university entrance exam that prescreens test questions on a global population of test-takers. The SAT is currently offered seven times a year outside the United States.

Dates for international test administrations, registrations requirements and deadlines can be found at: sat.org/international.

The SAT Suite of Assessments

The full SAT® Suite of Assessments (SAT, PSAT/NMSQT, PSAT 10, PSAT 8/9) is in the process of transition to be delivered digitally. The SAT exam is currently digital when taken outside the United States.

While the transition to digital will bring numerous student- and educator-friendly changes, many important features of the SAT Suite will stay the same.

- The SAT Suite will continue to measure the knowledge and skills that students are learning in high school and that matter most for university and career readiness.
- The SAT continues to be scored on a 1600 scale, and educators and students can continue to track growth across the suite over time.
- The digital SAT continues to be administered in a school or in a test center with a proctor present—not at home.
- Practice resources are even more closely linked to the test day experience. Students will still have access to free practice resources on Khan Academy, plus new practice resources are available directly on the digital testing application, Bluebook.
- Students can still connect directly to scholarships and the College Board National Recognition Programs.
- College Board continues to support all students, including those who receive accommodations on test day.

College Board made the transition from paper and pencil to digital at international SAT test centers beginning in March 2023. U.S. schools and test centers will go digital in March 2024.

- Most students who take the SAT for the first time do so in the spring of their junior year. (For students testing internationally, those in the class of 2024 will be the first to take the digital SAT. In the U.S., students in the high school class of 2025 will be the first class to take the digital test.)
- All students will take the digital PSAT 8/9 and PSAT/NMSQT starting in fall 2023, followed by the digital PSAT 10 in spring 2024.

What's new?

- The digital SAT Suite is shorter, about two hours instead of three, with more time per question.
- Reading and Writing passages will be shorter, with one question tied to each.
  - College Board's intention is to create a test experience that is less stressful for all students, particularly English learners.
  - More than 80% of students who participated in the recent digital SAT pilot said the test experience was less stressful than the paper-and-pencil test.

Curricula, examinations and tests

- Students and educators will see scores in a matter of days: Students get the information they need to make key university decisions, and educators get the information they need to support students and inform instruction.

The digital SAT Suite is more secure.
Previously, if one paper-and-pencil test is compromised, it can mean canceling scores for whole groups of students. The digital SAT allows College Board to give every student a virtually unique test form, so it will be practically impossible to share answers.

The SAT is more relevant for students.
- Students are now doing more of their learning and testing digitally, and taking the SAT shouldn't be the exception.
  - A digital test means no more bubble sheets and no more #2 pencils.
  - Calculators are allowed in the entire Math section. A graphing calculator and other tools are built into the digital testing application, or students can bring their own calculator.
- Featuring many shorter Reading and Writing passages instead of a few long texts means students see a wider range of topics that represent the works they read in university.
- The digital SAT is a useful tool for more students as the digital SAT score reports will connect students to information and resources about local two-year university and workforce training programs.

PSAT 8/9
PSAT™ 8/9 can be administered in the fall or spring of U.S.-equivalent eighth and/or ninth grade, depending on the goals of districts and schools. The test serves as a foundation for understanding student progress as they enter secondary school and ensuring that they are on target for being university and career ready by the time they leave secondary school.

PSAT 10 and PSAT/NMSQT
Both exams cover the same content domain and serve as a "check-in" on student progress and pinpoint areas for focused practice. Students can take the PSAT/NMSQT in the fall of U.S.-equivalent tenth and/or eleventh grade (though only eleventh graders who are U.S. citizens are eligible for the National Merit Scholarship Program). Instead of delivering the PSAT/NMSQT to tenth graders in the fall, some schools may instead deliver the PSAT™ 10 in the spring.

PRELIMINARY SAT/NATIONAL MERIT SCHOLARSHIP QUALIFYING TEST (PSAT/NMSQT ®)

The Preliminary SAT/National Merit Scholarship Qualifying Test (PSAT/NMSQT®) is a standardized test that measures the skills that students will need for higher education and careers after secondary school. Like the SAT, the digital PSAT/NMSQT measures the skills and knowledge that are essential for university readiness and success. For more information visit: http://sat.org/digital

STUDENT SEARCH SERVICE®

The College Board's Student Search Service is a free, voluntary program that connects students with information about educational and financial aid opportunities from more than 1,500 eligible universities, and over $300 million in scholarship and other educational programs.

When students take the SAT, PSAT/NMSQT, and PSAT 10, they're asked if they want to participate. Students can also opt in online at any time. By opting in, they give the College Board permission to share their names and limited information with university and scholarship programs looking for students like them.

Learn more about Student Search Service here: https://bigfuture.collegeboard.org/student-search-service

Index

Index

10X International School, India ... D284
1st International School of Ostrava, Czech Republic ... D349
2 Spoleczne Liceum Ogolnoksztalcace STO im. Pawla Jasienicy (2SLO), Poland ... D365

A

A'Soud Global School, Oman ... D312
A'Takamul International School, Kuwait ... D305
Aalesund International School, Norway ... D364
Aalto University School of Business, Finland ... D351
Aarhus International School, Denmark ... D350
Aarth Universal School, India ... D284
ABA Global School, Brazil ... D428
ABA Oman International School, Oman ... D311
Abbotsholme School, UK ... D386
ABC International School, Japan ... D299
ABC Okullari Göksu Kampüsü, Türkiye ... D382
Abdul Hamid Sharaf School, Jordan ... D303
Abdul Kadir Molla International School, Bangladesh ... D268
Abdul Rahman Kanoo International School, Bahrain ... D268
Abdulaziz International School - Al Sulaimaniah, Saudi Arabia ... D318
Abdulaziz International School - Al Wadi, Saudi Arabia ... D318
Aberdare College, Argentina ... D426
Abingdon School, UK ... D387
ABQ Azzan Bin Qais International School, Oman ... D312
Abraham Lincoln School, Dominican Republic ... D405
Abroad International School - Okayama, Japan ... D299
Abroad International School - Osaka, Japan ... D299
Abu Dhabi International (Pvt) School, United Arab Emirates ... D327
Abuja Capital International College, Nigeria ... D258
Abundant Life International School, Cambodia ... D270
Acacia School, Zambia ... D265
Academia Arguello, Argentina ... D426
Academia Britanica Cuscatleca, El Salvador ... D408
academia College, Switzerland ... D379
Academia Cotopaxi American International School, Ecuador ... D406
Academia del Perpetuo Socorro, Puerto Rico ... D414
Academia Fórum, USA ... D418
Academia Integral San Lucas, Panama ... D435
Academia Internacional Arabe Panamena, Panama ... D435
Academia Los Pinares, Honduras ... D435
Academia Naval Almirante Illingworth, Ecuador ... D406
Academia Private School, South Africa ... D262
Academia Schools, Switzerland ... 90, D380
Academic International School, Tanzania ... D263
Academic School of Excellence, Cameroon ... D248
Académie Antoine-Manseau, Canada ... D402
Académie de la Capitale, Canada ... D401
Académie François-Labelle, Canada ... D402
Académie Lafontaine, Canada ... D402
Académie Ste Cécile International School, Canada ... D401
accadis International School Bad Homburg, Germany ... 91, D354
Access International Academy Ningbo, China ... D270
Access International School, Nigeria ... D258
Accra Grammar School, Ghana ... D253
ACE Leadership School, Bonaberi Campus, Cameroon ... D248
ACE Leadership School, Midrand Campus, South Africa ... D262
ACG Parnell College, New Zealand ... D343
ACG Penguins Early Learning, New Zealand ... D343
ACG Queenstown Early Learning, New Zealand ... D343
ACG Remuera Early Learning, New Zealand ... D343
ACG School Jakarta, Indonesia ... 44, D295
ACG Strathallan, New Zealand ... D343
ACG Sunderland, New Zealand ... D343
ACG Tauranga, New Zealand ... D343
Achieve Xiamen International School (AXIS School), China ... D270
Açi Schools, Türkiye ... D382
Acibadem Schools - Acibadem Campus, Türkiye ... D383
Ackworth School, UK ... D387
Acorn International School, Italy ... D358
Acorns and Oaks Academy, Nigeria ... D258
Acorns British Style Nursery, Romania ... D367
Acorns International School, Uganda ... 40, D265
ACS (International), Singapore, Singapore ... D321
ACS Cobham International School, UK ... D387
ACS Doha International School, Qatar ... D315
ACS Egham International School, UK ... D387
ACS Hillingdon International School, UK ... D387
ACS Jakarta, Indonesia ... D295
Adani International School, India ... D284
Adcote School for Girls, UK ... D387
Adelaide High School, Australia ... D338
Adelaide Secondary School of English, Australia ... D338
Aditya Birla World Academy, India ... D284
Adria International School, Croatia ... D349
Adriatic College, Montenegro ... D363
Aduvie International School, Nigeria ... D258
Advanced Generations School - Elementary Boys, Saudi Arabia ... D318
Advanced Generations School - Elementary Girls, Saudi Arabia ... D318
Advanced Learning Schools, Saudi Arabia ... D318
Adventist International School, Sri Lanka ... D323
Affiliated School of JNU for Hong Kong and Macao Students - Dongguan, China ... D270
Affiliated School of JNU for Hong Kong and Macao Students - Guangzhou, China ... D270
AFNORTH International School, Netherlands ... D363
African American Academy, Bonanjo Campus, Cameroon ... D248
African American Academy, Ouagadougou Campus, Burkina Faso ... D248
Agnès School, Belgium ... D347
Agora Andorra International School, Andorra ... 92, D346
Agora Barcelona International School, Spain ... 93, D370
Agora Granada College International School, Spain ... 94, D370
Agora Lledó International School, Spain ... 95, D370
Agora Madrid International School, Spain ... 96, D370
Agora Patufet Infant School, Spain ... D370
Agora Portals International School, Spain ... 97, D370
Agora Princess Margaret International School, Spain ... 98, D370
Agora Sant Cugat International School, Spain ... 99, D370
Ahlcon Public School, India ... D284
Ahlia School, Bahrain ... D268
Ahliah School, Lebanon ... D306
Ahliyyah & Mutran, Jordan ... D303
Ahmedabad International School, India ... D284
AIC World College of Hiroshima Elementary School, Japan ... D299
Aichi International School, Japan ... D299
AICJ Junior & Senior High School, Japan ... D299
AIE International High School, Japan ... D299
Aiglon College, Switzerland ... D380
AISB-Hope International, China ... D270
AISL Harrow Haikou, China ... D270
AISL Harrow School Beijing, China ... D270
AIT International School, Thailand ... D324
Aitchison College, Pakistan ... D312
Ajial Aseer International School, Saudi Arabia ... D318
Ajman Academy, United Arab Emirates ... D327
Ajman Modern School, United Arab Emirates ... D328
Ajmera Global School, India ... D284
Ajyal International School, United Arab Emirates ... D328
Aka School, Türkiye ... D383
Akademeia High School in Warsaw, Poland ... D365
Akal Academy Baru Sahib, India ... D284
Akosombo International School, Ghana ... D253
Akshar Árbol International School - ECR Campus, India ... D284
Al Adab Iranian Private School for Boys, United Arab Emirates ... D328
Al Adhwa Private School, United Arab Emirates ... D328
Al Afak Al Gadeda International School, Egypt ... D249
Al Ain American School, United Arab Emirates ... D328
Al Ain British Academy, United Arab Emirates ... D328
Al Ain English Speaking School, United Arab Emirates ... D328
Al Ain International School, United Arab Emirates ... D328
Al Akhawayn School of Ifrane (ASI), Morocco ... D257
Al Alia International Indian School, Saudi Arabia ... D318
Al Amal Indian School, Kuwait ... D305
Al Amana Private School, United Arab Emirates ... D328
Al Andalus Private Schools, Saudi Arabia ... D318
Al Anjal Private School, Saudi Arabia ... D318
Al Ansar International School, United Arab Emirates ... D328
Al Assriya Schools, Jordan ... D303
Al Bashaer International School, Egypt ... D249
Al Basma British School, United Arab Emirates ... D328
Al Batinah International School, Oman ... D312
Al Bayan Educational Complex for Girls, Qatar ... D315
Al Bayan Model School Girls, Saudi Arabia ... D319
Al Bustan Private School, United Arab Emirates ... D328
Al Dhafra Private School, United Arab Emirates ... D328
Al Diyafah High School, United Arab Emirates ... D328
Al Fajr International School, India ... D284
Al Faris International School, Saudi Arabia ... D319
Al Firdaus World Class Islamic School, Indonesia ... D295
Al Ghanim Bilingual School, Kuwait ... D305
Al Hekma International School, Bahrain ... D268
Al Hussan International Academy, Saudi Arabia ... D319
Al Hussan International Grammar School, Saudi Arabia ... D319
Al Hussan International School Jubail, Saudi Arabia ... D319
Al Hussan International School Riyadh, Saudi Arabia ... D319
Al Hussan International School Yanbu, Saudi Arabia ... D319
Al Injaz International Private School, Oman ... D312

Index

Al Isra International School, Saudi Arabia D319
Al Ittihad International School, Jordan D303
Al Ittihad Private School Jumeirah, United Arab Emirates D328
Al Ittihad Private School Mamzar, United Arab Emirates D328
Al Jabr Islamic School, Indonesia D295
Al Jazeera Academy, Qatar D315
Al Kawthar International Schools, Saudi Arabia D319
Al Khor International School, Qatar D315
Al Ma'Arifa Private School, United Arab Emirates D328
Al Maali International School, United Arab Emirates D328
Al Maaref Private School, United Arab Emirates D328
Al Maharat Private School, United Arab Emirates D328
Al Mahd School, Riffa, Bahrain D268
Al Mahd School, Saar, Bahrain D268
Al Mahd School, Samaheej, Bahrain D268
Al Majd International School, Saudi Arabia D319
Al Manhal International School, United Arab Emirates D328
Al Mawakeb School - Al Barsha, United Arab Emirates D328
Al Mawakeb School - Al Garhoud, United Arab Emirates D328
Al Muntazir Schools, Tanzania D264
Al Murooj English School, United Arab Emirates D328
Al Murooj Scientific Private School, United Arab Emirates D328
Al Mustaqbal School, Palestine D314
Al Nahda International Schools, United Arab Emirates D328
Al Nahda National Schools, United Arab Emirates D328
Al Najah Private School (ANPS), United Arab Emirates D328
Al Noor International School, Bahrain D268
Al Omam International School, Saudi Arabia D319
Al Qamar Academy, India D284
Al Rabeeh School, United Arab Emirates D328
Al Raja School, Bahrain D268
Al Rawabi School, Bahrain D268
Al Reeyada International School, Saudi Arabia D319
Al Resalah School of Science, United Arab Emirates D328
Al Rissalah International School, Saudi Arabia D319
Al Ru'ya Bilingual School, Kuwait D305
Al Sahwa Schools, Oman D312
Al Salam Private School and Nursery, United Arab Emirates D328
Al Sanawbar School, United Arab Emirates D328
Al Shohub School, United Arab Emirates D328
Al Shomoukh International School, Oman D312
Al Waha International School, Saudi Arabia D319
Al Yasat Private School, United Arab Emirates D328
Al Zahra College, Australia D338
Al-Afaq International School, Saudi Arabia D319
Al-Arqam Islamic School & College Preparatory, USA D414
Al-Bassam International School, Saudi Arabia D319
Al-Bassam School - Girls Section, Saudi Arabia D319
Al-Bayan Bilingual School, Kuwait D305
Al-Faisal International School, Saudi Arabia D319
Al-Hayat International School, Lebanon D306
Al-Mizhar American Academy for Girls, United Arab Emirates D328
Al-Oruba International School, Saudi Arabia D319
Al-Ra'ed Al-Arabi School, Jordan D303
Al-Rayan International School, Ghana D253
Al-Rowad International Schools, Saudi Arabia D319
Alabuga International School, Russian Federation D368
Albanian College Durres, Albania D346
Albert College, Canada D401
Albert Einstein International School, Honduras D435
Alcanta International College, China D270
Alcuin School, USA D421
Aldenham Prep Riyadh, Saudi Arabia D319
Aldenham School, UK D387
Alexander Academy, Canada D400
Alexander Bain Colegio, México D409
Alexander von Humboldt Schule, Canada D403
Alexandra House School, Mauritius D256
Alexandria House of English, Egypt D249
Alexandria International Academy, Egypt D249
Alice Smith School, Malaysia D308
AlJazari International School of Science & Technology, Türkiye D383
ALKEV Schools, Türkiye D383
All Saints Episcopal Day School, USA D419
All Saints' College, Australia D338
All Saints' College, India D285
Alliance Academy International, Ecuador D406
Alliance World School, India D285
Alma Mater International School, South Africa D262
Almunecar International School, Spain D370
Aloha College Marbella, Spain D370
Aloisiuskolleg, Germany D354
Alotau International School, Papua New Guinea D344
Alpha Beta Education Centres - Pre-School, Primary & Christian College, Ghana D253
Alpha Cambridge School, Qatar D315
aLphabet School, India D285
Alrashid School, Kuwait D305
Altamira International School, Colombia D433
Alto International School, USA D414
Alwaha Schools, Egypt D249
AMADEUS International School Vienna, Austria D346
Amal Language Schools, Egypt D249
Amazing Grace Private School, South Africa D262
Amazon Valley Academy, Brazil D428
Ambassador International Academy, United Arab Emirates D328
Ambassador School, United Arab Emirates D328
Ambatovy International School, Madagascar D256
Ambrit International School, Italy D358
Ambrosoli International School, Uganda D265
American Academy Casablanca, Morocco D257
American Academy Larnaca, Cyprus D349
American Academy Primary School, Cyprus D349
American Academy Secondary School, Cyprus D349
American Baccalaureate School, Kuwait D305
American British School, Chile D431
American Christian Academy, Nigeria D258
American City International School, Egypt D249
American College Arcus, Bulgaria D348
American College of Sofia, Bulgaria D348
American Community School Amman, Jordan D303
American Community School Beirut, Lebanon D306
American Community School of Abu Dhabi, United Arab Emirates D328
American Community Schools of Athens, Greece D357
American Cooperative School, Bolivia D428
American Cooperative School of Tunis, Tunisia D264
American Creativity Academy, Kuwait D305
American Elementary School, Poland D365
American Embassy School, India D285
American English Academy Sofia, Bulgaria D348
American Farm School, Greece D357
American Gulf School, United Arab Emirates D328
American High School Skopje, Macedonia D362
American Institute of Monterrey - APS Campus, México D409
American Institute of Monterrey - San Pedro Campus, México D409
American Institute of Monterrey - Valle Oriente Campus, México D409
American International School, Ghana D253
American International School - Chennai, India D285
American International School - Riyadh, Saudi Arabia D319
American International School – Salzburg, Austria D346
American International School Dubai, United Arab Emirates D328
American International School Hong Kong, Hong Kong, China D281
American International School in Abu Dhabi, United Arab Emirates D328
American International School in Cyprus, Cyprus D349
American International School in Egypt - Main Campus, Egypt D249
American International School in Egypt - West Campus, Egypt D249
American International School Libreville, Gabon D253
American International School of Abuja, Nigeria D258
American International School of Bamako, Mali D256
American International School of Bolivia, Bolivia D428
American International School of Brazzaville, Republic of the Congo D261
American International School of Bucharest, Romania D368
American International School of Budapest, Hungary D358
American International School of Cape Town, South Africa D262
American International School of Conakry, Guinea D254
American International School of Costa Rica, Costa Rica D404
American International School of Freetown, Sierra Leone D261
American International School of Guangzhou, China D270
American International School of Jeddah, Saudi Arabia D319
American International School of Johannesburg, South Africa D262
American International School of Kingston, Jamaica D409
American International School of Kuwait, Kuwait D305
American International School of Lagos, Nigeria D258
American International School of Lesotho, Lesotho D256
American International School of Lomé, Togo D264
American International School of Lusaka, Zambia D265
American International School of Monrovia, Liberia D256
American International School of Mozambique, Mozambique D257
American International School of Niamey, Niger D258
American International School of Nouakchott, Mauritania D256
American International School of Vietnam, Vietnam D334
American International School of Zagreb, Croatia D349
American International School Vienna, Austria 100, D346
American International School, Dhaka, Bangladesh D269
American Nicaraguan School, Nicaragua D414
American Overseas School of Rome, Italy 101, D359
American Pacific International School, Thailand D324

Index

American School, Peru ... D436
American School Beverly Hills Cairo, Egypt ... D249
American School Dhahran, Saudi Arabia ... D319
American School Foundation of Chiapas, México ... D409
American School Foundation of Guadalajara, México ... D409
American School Foundation of Monterrey, México ... D409
American School Hong Kong, Hong Kong, China ... D281
American School in Taichung, Taiwan ... D323
American School of Alexandria, Egypt ... D249
American School of Asunción, Paraguay ... D436
American School of Bahrain, Bahrain ... D268
American School of Barcelona, Spain ... D370
American School of Bilbao, Spain ... D370
American School of Bombay, India ... D285
American School of Brasilia, Brazil ... D428
American School of Campinas - Escola Americana de Campinas, Brazil ... D428
American School of Doha, Qatar ... D315
American School of Douala, Cameroon ... D248
American School of Dubai, United Arab Emirates ... D328
American School of Guatemala, Guatemala ... D408
American School of Las Palmas, Spain ... D371
American School of Madrid, Spain ... D371
American School of Marrakesh, Morocco ... D257
American School of Milan, Italy ... D359
American School of Pachuca, México ... D409
American School of Paris, France ... D351
American School of Puerto Vallarta, México ... D409
American School of Recife, Brazil ... D429
American School of Santo Domingo, Dominican Republic ... D405
American School of Tangier, Morocco ... D257
American School of The Hague, Netherlands ... D363
American School of Ulaanbaatar, Mongolia ... D310
American School of Valencia, Spain ... D371
American School of Warsaw, Poland ... D365
American School of Wroclaw, Poland ... D365
American School of Yaoundé, Cameroon ... D248
American Standard International School, Bangladesh ... D269
American United School, Kuwait ... D305
American University of Nigeria Schools, Nigeria ... D258
American University Research Academy (AURA Academy), USA ... D414
American Youth Academy, USA ... D416
Amgad International School, Egypt ... D249
Amity Global School, Gurgaon, India ... D285
Amity Global School, Noida, India ... D285
Amity International School Amsterdam, Netherlands ... D363
Amity International School Saket, India ... D285
Amman Academy, Jordan ... D303
Amman Baccalaureate School, Jordan ... D303
Amman Baptist School, Jordan ... D304
Amman National School, Jordan ... D304
Amnuay Silpa School, Thailand ... D324
Ampleforth College, UK ... D387
Amrita International Vidyalayam, India ... D285
Amsterdam International Community School, Netherlands ... D363
Amsterdam Liberal Arts & Sciences Academy (ALASCA), Netherlands ... D363
Anatolia High School, Greece ... D357
Andalus International School, Jeddah, Saudi Arabia ... D319
Andalus International School, Mecca, Saudi Arabia ... D319
Andersen International School, Italy ... D359
Andinet International School, Ethiopia ... D253
Andino Cusco International School, Peru ... D436
Andrée English School, Chile ... D431
Anfield School, Hong Kong, China ... D281
Angel de la Guarda, Spain ... D371
Angel Kindergarten, Japan ... D299
Angels International College, Pakistan ... D312
Anglican Church Grammar School, Australia ... D338
Anglican International School Jerusalem, Israel ... D299
Anglo American School, Costa Rica ... D404
Anglo American School of Sofia, Bulgaria ... D348
Anglo Singapore International School, Thailand ... D324
Anglo-Chinese School (Independent), Singapore ... D321
Annesley Junior School, Australia ... D338
Annie Wright Schools, USA ... D422
Annunciation Catholic School, USA ... D419
Antalya College, Türkiye ... D383
Antigua Green School, Guatemala ... D408
Antigua International School, Guatemala ... D408
Antilles School, Virgin Islands (US) ... D423
Antofagasta International School, Chile ... D431
Anton Bruckner International School (ABIS), Austria ... D346
Antonia International School (École Antonia), France ... D351
Antonine International School, Lebanon ... D306
Antwerp International School, Belgium ... D347
Aoba-Japan Bilingual Preschool - Harumi Campus, Japan ... D299
Aoba-Japan Bilingual Preschool - Mitaka Campus, Japan ... D300
Aoba-Japan Bilingual Preschool - Nakano Campus, Japan ... D300
Aoba-Japan Bilingual Preschool - Shimomeguro Campus, Japan ... D300
Aoba-Japan Bilingual Preschool - Waseda Campus, Japan ... D300
Aoba-Japan International School, Japan ... D300
Apeejay School International, South Delhi, India ... D285
Apex2100 Academy, France ... D351
APL Global School, India ... D285
Apple International School, United Arab Emirates ... D328
Appleby College, Canada ... D401
Aqaba International School, Jordan ... D304
Aqeeq International Academy, Saudi Arabia ... D319
Aquinas American School, Spain ... D371
Aquinas College, Australia ... D338
Aquinas College, Bahamas ... D400
Arab International Academy, Qatar ... D315
Arab Unity School, United Arab Emirates ... D328
Arabian Pearl Gulf (APG) School, Bahrain ... D268
Aranäsgymnasiet, Sweden ... D379
Arc-en-Ciel International School, Togo ... D264
Arcadia Academy, Montenegro ... D363
Arcadia School, United Arab Emirates ... D328
Archbishop Carroll High School, USA ... D416
Archbishop Spalding High School, USA ... D418
Archbishop Walsh Academy, USA ... D420
Ardingly College, UK ... D387
Ardingly College Zhongshan Kindergarten, China ... D270
AREL Schools (Kindergarten/Primary/Middle/High), Türkiye ... D383
Arendal International School, Norway ... D364
Areteia School, Spain ... D371
Arthur I. Meyer Jewish Academy, USA ... D416
Asahijuku Secondary School, Japan ... D300
Asamiah International School, Jordan ... D304
Ascend International School, India ... D285
Ascensia International School, Singapore ... D321
Ascham School, Australia ... D338
Ascot International School, Thailand ... D324
Ashbury College, Canada ... D401
Ashford School, UK ... D387
Ashton School, Dominican Republic ... D405
Ashville College, UK ... D387
Ashwood Glen, Canada ... D401
Asia Pacific International School, Republic of Korea ... D317
Asia Pacific International School, Malaysia ... D308
Asian Hope International School, Cambodia ... D270
Asian International Private School - Madinat Zayed (Western Zone), United Arab Emirates ... D329
Asian International Private School - Ruwais (Western Zone), United Arab Emirates ... D329
Asian International School Primary School, Vietnam ... D334
ASIS Chennai, India ... D285
Asmara International Community School (AICS), Eritrea ... D253
Asociación Colegio Granadino, Colombia ... D433
Asociación Cultural Pestalozzi, Argentina ... D426
Asociación Escuelas Lincoln, Argentina ... D426
Aspaen Gimnasio Iragua, Colombia ... D433
Aspaen Liceo Tacuri, Colombia ... D433
Aspee Nutan Academy, India ... D285
Aspen Heights British School, United Arab Emirates ... D329
Aspengrove School, Canada ... D400
Aspiration International School, Malaysia ... D308
Assafwah Private School, Oman ... D312
Associação Educacional Luterana Bom Jesus / IELUSC, Brazil ... D429
Association International School, Ghana ... D253
Assumption College San Lorenzo, Philippines ... D314
Assumption Commercial College, Thailand ... D324
Astana Garden School, Kazakhstan ... D304
Asuncion Christian Academy, Paraguay ... D436
ATEA College, New Zealand ... D343
Atelier 21 Future School, UK ... D387
Atenas Unidad Educativa, Ecuador ... D406
Atherton International School (AIS) Geoje, Republic of Korea ... D317
Athol Murray College of Notre Dame, Canada ... D404
Atlanta International School, USA ... D417
Atlantic Hall School, Nigeria ... D258
Atlas American School of Málaga, Spain ... D371
Attwool School, Nigeria ... D258
ATUT Bilingual Primary School, Poland ... D365
Audentes School, Estonia ... D351
Audubon Charter School - Upper School, USA ... D418
Aula Escola Europea, Spain ... D371

Index

Aurora International School, Bangladesh D269
Aurora Waldorf School, USA D420
Austin Eco Bilingual School (Austin EBS) Argentina, Argentina D426
Austin Eco Bilingual School (Austin EBS) USA, USA D421
Australian Independent School, Bali, Indonesia D295
Australian Independent School, Jakarta, Indonesia D296
Australian International Academy - Caroline Springs Campus, Australia D338
Australian International Academy - Kellyville Campus, Australia D338
Australian International Academy - King Khalid Coburg Campus, Australia D338
Australian International Academy - Strathfield Campus, Australia D338
Australian International Academy of Education, Australia D338
Australian International School, United Arab Emirates D329
Australian International School (AIS), Vietnam 45, D335
Australian International School Hong Kong, Hong Kong, China D281
Australian International School Malaysia, Malaysia D308
Australian International School Phnom Penh, Cambodia D270
Australian International School, Dhaka, Bangladesh D269
Australian International School, Manila, Philippines D314
Australian International School, Singapore, Singapore D321
Australian School of Abu Dhabi, United Arab Emirates D329
Avalon International School, México D409
Aves International Academy, Ghana D253
Avi-Cenna International School, Nigeria D258
Avrupa Koleji, Türkiye D383
Awfaz Global School, Qatar D316
AWSAJ Academy, Qatar D316
Ayeyarwaddy International School, Myanmar D310
Azerbaijan British College, Azerbaijan D347

B

Babeque Secundaria, Dominican Republic D405
Bachillerato Alexander Bain, SC, México D409
Bade Intercultural Academy, Chengdu, China D271
Badminton School, UK D387
Bahan International Science Academy, Myanmar D310
Bahrain Bayan School, Bahrain D268
Bahrain Capital School, Bahrain D268
Bahrain School, Bahrain D268
Baku International Education Complex, Azerbaijan D347
Baku Modern Educational Complex, Azerbaijan D347
Baku Talents Education Complex, Azerbaijan D347
Balboa Academy, Panama D435
Baldwin Boys' High School, India D285
Baleares International College, Mallorca, Sa Porrassa, Spain D371
Baleares International College, Mallorca, San Augustin Campus, Spain D371
Bales College, UK D387
Bali Island School, Indonesia D296
Balikesir Aci College, Türkiye D383
Ballarat Grammar, Australia D338
Bambino Schools, Malawi D256
Banani International School, Zambia D265
Bandung Alliance Intercultural School, Indonesia D296
Bandung Independent School, Indonesia D296
Bangalore International School, India D285
Bangkok Adventist International School, Thailand D324
Bangkok Christian College, Thailand D324
Bangkok Christian International School, Thailand D324
Bangkok Grace International School, Thailand D324
Bangkok Patana School, Thailand 46, D324
Bangkok Prep International School, Thailand D324
Bangladesh International School, Jeddah (Bangla Section), Saudi Arabia D319
Bangladesh International School, Jeddah (Bangla Section) Riyadh, Saudi Arabia D319
Bangladesh International Tutorial School, Bangladesh D269
Bangladesh School Muscat, Oman D312
Banjul American International School, The Gambia D264
Banksia Park International High School, Australia D338
Bannister Academy, Philippines D314
Baobab College, Zambia D265
Baowei Kindergarten, China D271
Baraem RAIS - Dhahran - Al-Dana, Saudi Arabia D319
Baraem RAIS - Riyadh - Al-Sahafa, Saudi Arabia D319
Barker College, Argentina D426
Barker College, Australia D338
Barnard Castle Senior School, UK D387
Bartolome Mitre Day School - Moreno, Argentina D426
Bateen World Academy, United Arab Emirates D329
Bath Academy, UK D387
Batikent ABC Anaokulu, Türkiye D383
Battle Abbey School, UK D387
Bava International School, Papua New Guinea D344
Bavarian International School gAG (BIS) - City Campus, Germany D354
Bavarian International School gAG (BIS) - Haimhausen Campus, Germany D354
Bayan Gardens School, Saudi Arabia D319
Bayview Glen, Canada D401
BBIS Berlin Brandenburg International School, Germany D354
BD Somani International School, India D285
Beacon Academy, Indonesia D296
Beacon Academy, USA D417
Beacon International School, Ghana D253
Beacon Private School, Bahrain D268
Beacon School, Brazil D429
Beaconhouse College Campus Gulberg, Pakistan D312
Beaconhouse Newlands Islamabad, Pakistan D312
Beaconhouse Newlands Lahore, Pakistan D312
Beaconhouse Newlands Multan, Pakistan D312
Beaconhouse School System, Clifton Campus, Pakistan D312
Beaconhouse School System, Defence Campus, Pakistan D312
Beaconhouse School System, Margalla Campus, Pakistan D312
Beaconhouse School System, PECHS Campus, Pakistan D312
Beaconhouse Yamssard International School - Pattankarn, Thailand D324
Beaconhouse-Newlands, Kuala Lumpur International School, Malaysia D308
Beanstalk International Bilingual School (BIBS) - Changying, China D271
Beanstalk International Bilingual School (BIBS) - Chengdu, China D271
Beanstalk International Bilingual School (BIBS) - Haidian Academy, China D271
Beanstalk International Bilingual School (BIBS) - Huairou, China D271
Beanstalk International Bilingual School (BIBS) - Kunming, China D271
Beanstalk International Bilingual School (BIBS) - Shunyi, China D271
Beanstalk International Bilingual School (BIBS) - Upper East Side, China D271
Beanstalk International Bilingual School (BIBS) - Weihai, China D271
Bedales School, UK D387
Bedayia International School, Egypt D249
Bede's Grammar School, Argentina D426
Bede's Senior School, UK D387
Bedford Girls' School, UK D387
Bedford School, UK D387
Bedstone College, UK D387
Beijing Bacui Bilingual School, China D271
Beijing BISS International School, China D271
Beijing Chaoyang KaiWen Academy, China D271
Beijing City International School, China D271
Beijing Concord College of Sino-Canada, China D271
Beijing Enlighten School, China D271
Beijing Haidian Foreign Languages Tengfei School, China D271
Beijing Huijia Kindergarten, Beiou Campus, China D271
Beijing Huijia Kindergarten, Wanquan Campus, China D271
Beijing Huijia Kindergarten, Xibahe Dongli Campus, China D271
Beijing Huijia Private School, China D271
Beijing Hurston Kindergarten, China D271
Beijing International Bilingual Academy, China D271
Beijing Royal Foreign Language School, China D271
Beijing Royal Kindergarten, China D271
Beijing Royal School, China D271
Beijing Shuren-Ribet Private School, China D271
Beijing World Youth Academy, China D271
Beijing Xin Fuxue International Academy, China D271
Beijing Zhongshan International School, China D271
Belgrano Day School, Argentina D426
Bell-lloc Del Pla, Spain D371
Bellevue Children's Academy, USA D422
Bellver International College, Spain D371
Bendigo Senior Secondary College, Australia D338
Bendigo South East College, Australia D338
Benedictine International School, Philippines D314
Benenden School, UK D387
Benga Riverside International School, Mozambique D257
Benghazi European School, Libya D256
Benjamin Franklin International School, Spain D371
BEPS International School, Belgium 102, D347
Berkeley International School, Thailand D325
Berkhamsted School, UK D387
Berlin British School, Germany D354
Berlin Cosmopolitan School, Germany D354
Berlin International School, Germany D354
Berlin Metropolitan School, Germany D354
Bermuda High School, Bermuda D400
Bermuda Institute, Bermuda D400
Bernadotte Skolen, Denmark D350

Index

Bertolt-Brecht-Gymnasium Dresden, Germany D354
Beta Cambridge School, Qatar D316
Bethany School, UK D387
Beykoz Doga Campus, Türkiye D383
Beyondia International School Ikebukuro, Japan D300
BGS International Academia School, India D285
Bhaktivedanta Academy, USA D416
Bilingual British School, Italy D359
Bilingual European School, Italy 103, D359
Bilingual School Terra Nova, Switzerland D380
Bilkent Laboratory & International School, Türkiye D383
Billabong High International (Santa Cruz), India D285
Billabong High International School, Republic of Maldives D318
Billanook College, Australia D338
Bina Bangsa School, Indonesia D296
Bingham Academy, Ethiopia D253
Binus School Bekasi, Indonesia D296
Binus School Semarang, Indonesia D296
Binus School Serpong, Indonesia D296
Binus School Simprug, Indonesia D296
Birla Open Minds International School, India D285
Birralee International School, Norway D364
Bishkek International School, Kyrgyzstan D306
Bishop Cotton School, India D285
Bishop Ludden Junior Senior High School, USA D420
Bishop Mackenzie International School, Malawi D256
Bishop Michael Eldon School, Bahamas D400
Bishop's College School, Canada D403
Bishop's Stortford College, UK D387
Bishop's Stortford College Prep School, UK D387
Bishops Diocesan College, South Africa D262
Bishopstrow College, UK D387
BJK - Kabatas Vakfi Özel Okullari, Türkiye D383
Bjorn's International School, Denmark D350
BKA International School, Switzerland D380
Black Forest Academy, Germany D354
Bladins International School of Malmö, Sweden D379
BLiSS Edify International School, Pune, India D285
Bloom World Academy, United Arab Emirates D329
Bloomfield Hall Schools, Pakistan D312
Bloomingdale International School, India D285
Bloomsbury International School Hatyai, Thailand D325
Blossom International School, Indonesia D296
Blouberg International School, South Africa D262
Bloxham School, UK D387
Blue Valley School, Costa Rica D404
Bluebells School International, India D285
Bluebird British International School, Cambodia D270
Blundell's School, UK D387
BME International Secondary School, Hungary D358
Boca Prep International School, USA D416
Bodhi International School, India D285
Bodrum Marmara Elementary School, Türkiye D383
Bodrum Marmara Private College, Türkiye D383
Bodwell High School, Canada D400
Bogaerts International School - North Campus, Belgium D347
Bogaerts International School - South Campus, Belgium D347
Bombay International School, India D285
Bonn International School e.V., Germany D354
Bootham School, UK D387
Bordeaux International School, France 104, D351
Boren Sino Canadian School, China D271
Bosques International School, México D409
Boston College (Childrens School), Argentina D426
Boston International School, China D271
Boston School International, Panama D435
Boulder Country Day School, USA D415
Box Hill School, UK D387
Boya International Academy - Kindergarten, China D271
Bradenton Preparatory Academy, United Arab Emirates D329
Bradfield College, UK D387
Bradford School, Chile D431
Braeburn Dar es Salaam International School, Tanzania D264
Braeburn Garden Estate School, Kenya D254
Braeburn Imani International School, Kenya D254
Braeburn International School Arusha, Tanzania D264
Braeburn Kisumu International School, Kenya D254
Braeburn Mombasa International School, Kenya D254
Braeburn Nanyuki International School, Kenya D254
Braeburn School, Kenya D254
Braeside School, Kenya D254
Brains International School, Conde de Orgaz, Spain D371
Brains International School, La Moraleja, Spain D371
Brains International School, Las Palmas, Spain D371
Brains International School, Telde, Spain D371
Brainworks Total International Schools Yangon, Myanmar D310
Brandon Academy, USA D416
Brandon Hall School, USA D417
Branksome Hall, Canada D401
Branksome Hall Asia, Republic of Korea D317
Brasilia International School, Brazil D429
Brent International School Baguio, Philippines D314
Brent International School Manila, Philippines D314
Brent International School Subic, Philippines D314
Brentwood College of Asia International School, Philippines D314
Brentwood College School, Canada D400
Brentwood School, UK D387
Brewster Madrid, Spain D371
Bribie Island State High School, Australia D338
Bridge House College, Nigeria D258
Bridge House School, South Africa D262
Bright Academy, China D271
Bright Horizons - International School of Zagreb, Croatia D349
Bright Jigsaw International School, Brunei Darussalam D269
Bright Kids Garden International School Kokura, Japan D300
Bright Life International School, Saudi Arabia D319
Bright Minds International School, Saudi Arabia D319
Bright School, Brazil D429
Bright Start Fellowship International School, India D285
Brighter Horizons Academy, USA D421
Brighton College, UK D387
Brighton College Abu Dhabi, United Arab Emirates D329
Brighton College Al Ain, United Arab Emirates D329
Brighton College International School Bangkok, Thailand D325
Brighton College Signapore, Singapore D321
Brighton Grammar School, Australia D338
Brighton International School, UK D388
Brighton International School (BIS), Malaysia D308
Brillantmont International School, Switzerland D380
Brilliant International School, China D271
Brisbane Grammar School, Australia D338
Bristol Grammar School, UK D388
BRITANICA Park School, Bulgaria D348
Britannia International School of Rome, Italy D359
Britannica International School, Hungary D358
Britesparks International School, Philippines D314
British Academy of Tunis, Tunisia D265
British American School S.C., México D409
British Bolivian School, Bolivia D428
British College La Cañada, Spain D371
British College of Gavà, Spain D371
British Columbia Canadian International School - East, Egypt D249
British Columbia Canadian International School - West, Egypt D249
British Columbia International School, Thailand D325
British Council School, Spain D371
British Education Korea, Republic of Korea D317
British Embassy School Ankara, Türkiye D383
British Georgian Academy, Georgia D354
British International Academy, Republic of Korea D317
British International Academy (BIA), Jordan D304
British International College - Bryanston, South Africa D262
British International College - Pretoria, South Africa D262
British International Preparatory School, South Africa D262
British International School, Colombia D433
British International School and Montessori Education Freetown, Sierra Leone D261
British International School Belgrade, Serbia D369
British International School Classic, Bulgaria D348
British International School Ho Chi Minh City, Vietnam D335
British International School Istanbul - Zekeriyaköy, Türkiye D383
British International School Nigeria, Nigeria D258
British International School of Al Khobar, Saudi Arabia D319
British International School of Boston, USA D419
British International School of Casablanca, Morocco D257
British International School of Chicago, Lincoln Park, USA 220, D417
British International School of Chicago, South Loop, USA D417
British International School of Cracow, Poland D365
British International School of Houston, USA D421
British International School of Ljubljana, Slovenia D370
British International School of Stavanger (BISS) Gausel, Norway D364
British International School of Stockholm, Sweden D379
British International School of Tbilisi, Georgia D354
British International School of the University of Lodz, Poland D365
British International School of Timisoara, Romania D368
British International School of Tunis, Tunisia D265
British International School of Washington, USA D416
British International School of Zagreb, Croatia D349
British International School Riyadh, Saudi Arabia D319

Index

British International School Wroclaw, Poland D365
British International School, Addis Ababa, Ethiopia D253
British International School, Hanoi, Vietnam D335
British International School, Phuket, Thailand D325
British International Schools in Kurdistan, Iraq D299
British Nigerian Academy, Nigeria D258
British Oak Tree Nursery, India D285
British Overseas School, Pakistan D313
British Primary School of Wilanow, Poland D365
British School Alzira, Spain D371
British School Bangkok Ltd, Thailand D325
British School Cordoba-Cerro de las Rosas, Argentina D426
British School Genova, Italy D359
British School in Baku, Azerbaijan D347
British School in Colombo, Sri Lanka D323
British School Jakarta, Indonesia D296
British School Manila, Philippines D314
British School Muscat - BSM, Oman D312
British School of Beijing, Shunyi, China D272
British School of Bucharest, Romania D368
British School of Córdoba, Spain D371
British School of Geneva, Switzerland D380
British School of Gran Canaria, Spain D371
British School of Lanzarote, Spain D371
British School of Málaga, Spain D371
British School of Sofia, Bulgaria D348
British School of Tenerife, Spain D371
British School of Ulaanbaatar, Mongolia D310
British School of Valencia, Spain D371
British School Salalah - BSS, Oman D312
British School St Petersburg, Russian Federation D368
British Standard School, Bangladesh D269
British Vietnamese International School, Hanoi, Vietnam D335
British Vietnamese International School, Ho Chi Minh City, Vietnam D335
British West Indies Collegiate, Turks And Caicos Islands D414
Britus International School, Al Olaya, Saudi Arabia D319
Britus International School, Bahrain, Bahrain D268
Broadhurst Primary School, Botswana D248
Brockton School, Canada D400
Brockwood Park School, UK D388
Bromsgrove International School Early Years Campus, Thailand D325
Bromsgrove International School Primary and Secondary Campus, Thailand D325
Bromsgrove School, UK D388
Bronte College, Canada D402
Brooke House College, UK D388
Brookes CIL International School, Ukraine D398
Brookes Moscow, Russian Federation D368
Brookes Saint Petersburg, Russian Federation D368
Brookes Westshore, Canada D400
Brookhouse School, Karen, Kenya D254
Brookhouse School, Runda, Kenya D255
Brooklyn Friends School, USA D420
Brookstone School International, Nigeria D258
Brummana High School, Lebanon D306
Brussels International Catholic School, Belgium D347
Bryanston School, UK D388
BTB School (Sekolah Bina Tunas Bangsa), Indonesia D296
Bubble Kingdom International Kindergarten, China D272
Bucharest - Beirut International School, Romania D368
Buckingham School, Colombia D433
Buckswood International School Tbilisi, Georgia D354
Buckswood School, UK D388
Buckswood School Nigeria, Nigeria D258
Budapest British International Academy, Hungary D358
Budapest British International School, Hungary D358
Buddhi School, India D285
Buena Vista Concordia International School, China D272
Buenos Aires International Christian Academy, Argentina D426
Buffalo Academy of the Sacred Heart, USA D420
Buissonnets Montani, Switzerland D380
Bulgarsko Shkolo Private Secondary School, Bulgaria D348
Bunda Mulia School, Indonesia D296
Bunts Sangha's S.M. Shetty International School & Jr. College, India D285
Bureche School, Colombia D433
Burgess Hill Girls, UK D388
Busan Foreign School, Republic of Korea D317
BXCL International School Penang, Malaysia D308
Byron College, Greece D357

C

C P Goenka International School - Borivali, India D285
C P Goenka International School - Oshiwara, India D285
C P Goenka International School - Pune, India D285
C P Goenka International School - Thane, India D285
C P Goenka International School - Ulwe, India D286
C P Goenka's Spring Buds International Preschool - Juhu, India D286
C P Goenka's Spring Buds International Preschool - Lamington Road, India D286
C.E. Punta Galea, Spain D371
Cabella International Sahaja School CISS, Italy D359
Cade International Kindergarten, China D272
Cadmous College, Lebanon D306
Caernarfon College, Chile D431
Cairo American College, Egypt D249
Cairo Covenant School, Egypt D249
Cairo English School, Egypt D249
Cairo Modern International School, Egypt D249
Cakir Schools, Türkiye D383
Calcutta International School, India D286
Caleb British International School, Nigeria D258
Caledonian International School, India D286
Calgary French and International School, Canada D400
California Prep International School (CPIS), Thailand D325
California School, Hong Kong, China D281
Calorx Olive International School, India D286
Calpe School, Spain D371
Camberwell Grammar School, Australia D338
Cambridge College, Bolivia D428
Cambridge College Lima, Peru D436
Cambridge High School, Jordan D304
Cambridge House British International School, Spain 105, D371
Cambridge International School, India D286
Cambridge International School, Sri Lanka D323
Cambridge International School, UK D388
Cambridge International School - Bahry, Sudan D263
Cambridge International School - Khartoum, Sudan D263
Cambridge International School - Omdurman, Sudan D263
Cambridge International School Bratislava, Slovakia D370
Cambridge International School for Girls, Qatar D316
Cambridge International School, Dasuya, India D286
Cambridge Primary School, Australia D338
Cambridge School of Bucharest, Romania D368
Cambridge School of Constanta, Romania D368
Campbell College, UK D388
Campion International School, India D286
Campion School Athens, Greece D357
Campus Muristalden Gymnasium, Switzerland D380
Campus Notre-Dame-de-Foy, Canada D403
Campus Politécnico Aceimar, Spain D371
Campus Wien West, Austria D346
Canada British Columbia International Schools - Hefei, China D272
Canadian Academy, Japan D300
Canadian Academy of Libya, Libya D256
Canadian College Italy (CCI - The Renaissance School), Italy D359
Canadian Foreign Language School-Cambridgeshire, China D272
Canadian International School, India D286
Canadian International School - Amman, Jordan D304
Canadian International School - Erbil, Iraq D299
Canadian International School - Vietnam, Vietnam D335
Canadian International School Abu Dhabi, United Arab Emirates D329
Canadian International School Bangladesh, Bangladesh D269
Canadian International School of Beijing, China D272
Canadian International School of Beijing - Jianguomen DRC Campus, China D272
Canadian International School of Guangzhou, China D272
Canadian International School of Hefei, China D272
Canadian International School of Hong Kong, Hong Kong, China D281
Canadian International School of Phnom Penh, Cambodia D270
Canadian International School of Shenyang, China D272
Canadian International School of Thailand, Thailand D325
Canadian International School Tokyo, Japan D300
Canadian International School, Lakeside Campus, Singapore D321
Canadian School of Florence, Italy 106, D359
Canadian School of Milan, Italy D359
Çanakkale Özel ilkokulu, Türkiye D383
Canberra Girls Grammar School, Australia D338
Canberra Grammar School, Australia D338
Candor International School, India D286
Canford School, UK D388
Canggu Community School, Indonesia D296
Canon Andrea Mwaka School, Tanzania D264
Canterbury School, Spain D371
Cap Cana Heritage School, Dominican Republic D405
Capital School, United Arab Emirates D329
Cardiff Academy, UK D388
Cardiff International School, Qatar D316

Index

Cardiff Sixth Form College, UK	D388
Cardiff Sixth Form College, Cambridge, UK	D388
Cardinal Newman College, Argentina	D426
Cardinal Newman High School, USA	D416
Carey Baptist Grammar School, Australia	D338
Carfax College, UK	D388
Caribbean International Academy, Dutch Caribbean	D406
Caribbean International School, Panama	D435
Caribbean School, Puerto Rico	D414
Carleton College International School, Egypt	D249
Carlisle School, USA	D422
Carlucci American International School of Lisbon, Portugal	D366
Carmel School, Hong Kong, China	D282
Carol Morgan School, Dominican Republic	D405
Carrollton School of the Sacred Heart, USA	D416
Carrollwood Day School, USA	D416
CAS Colombo American School, Colombia	D433
Casablanca American School, Morocco	D257
Castelli International School, Italy	D359
Castle Park School, Ireland	D358
Casuarinas International College, Peru	D436
Casvi International American School, Spain	D371
Cate School, USA	D414
Caterham School, UK	D388
Cathedral High School, USA	D418
Cathedral International School, Dominican Republic	D405
Catholic Memorial High School, USA	D423
CATS Academy Boston, USA	D419
CATS Cambridge, UK	D388
CATS College China, China	D272
Caulfield Grammar School - Caulfield Campus, Australia	D338
Caulfield Grammar School - Malvern Campus, Australia	D338
Caulfield Grammar School - Wheelers Hill Campus, Australia	D338
Caulfield Junior College, Australia	D338
Causeway Bay Victoria International Kindergarten, Hong Kong, China	D282
Cavina School, Kenya	D255
Caxton College, Spain	D371
Caxton School (Escuela William Caxton), Argentina	D426
Cayman International School, Cayman Islands	D404
Cayman Prep & High School, Cayman Islands	D404
CBIS Bilingual School, China	D272
CC Mason Elementary, USA	D421
Cebu International School, Philippines	D314
Cecilien Gymnasium, Germany	D354
Cedar Court British International School, Nigeria	D258
Cedar International School, British Virgin Islands	D400
Cedars Interdisciplinary School, Iraq	D299
Cedarwood School, Nigeria	D258
CEDEC International Schools, Nigeria	D258
Cempaka International Ladies' College, Malaysia	D308
Cempaka International School, Malaysia	D308
Centennial Academy, Canada	D403
Central Catholic High School, USA	D421
Central School Dubai, United Arab Emirates	D329
Centre Academy London, UK	D388
Centro Bilingüe Vista Alegre, Panama	D435
Centro de Enseñanza Técnica y Superior - Campus Mexicali, México	D409
Centro de Enseñanza Tecnica y Superior - Campus Tijuana, México	D409
Centro de Estudios Ibn Gabirol Colegio Estrella Toledano, Spain	D372
Centro Educativo Agave, Spain	D372
Centro Educativo Alexander Bain Irapuato, México	D409
Centro Educativo Arambé, Paraguay	D436
Centro Educativo CRECER AC, México	D409
Centro Educativo Futuro Verde, Costa Rica	D404
Centro Educativo Internacional Anzoátegui (CEIA), Venezuela	D438
Centro Educativo La Moderna, Ecuador	D406
Centro Educativo Naciones Unidas, Ecuador	D406
Centro Educativo Nueva Generacion, Costa Rica	D404
Centro Educativo Particular San Francisco de Borja, Peru	D436
Centro Escolar 'El Roble', Guatemala	D408
Centro Escolar Campoalegre, Guatemala	D408
Centro Escolar Entrevalles, Guatemala	D408
Centro Escolar Instituto La Paz, SC, México	D409
Centro Escolar Solalto, Guatemala	D409
Centro Internacional de Educacao Integrada, Brazil	D429
Centrul Gifted Education, Romania	D368
CET Gunar - Baku Oxford School, Azerbaijan	D347
CET International Primary School, Russian Federation	D368
CGK International School, Japan	D300
Chadwick International, Republic of Korea	48, D317
Chaltel College, Argentina	D426
Chaman Bhartiya School, India	D286
Chamberlain International School, USA	D419
Champs International School, Fiji	D343
Changchun American International School, China	D272
Changsha WES (Bilingual) Academy, China	D272
Changsha WES Academy, China	D272
Changwai Bilingual School, China	D272
Changzhou Wujin Qingying Foreign Language School, China	D272
Chapel School – The American International School of Brazil, Brazil	D429
Charles Campbell College, Australia	D338
Charlotte Country Day School, USA	D420
Charter College International High School, South Africa	D262
Charter International School, Thailand	D325
Charterhouse, UK	D388
Charterhouse Malaysia, Malaysia	D308
Charterhouse Schools, South Africa	D262
Chartwell International School, Serbia	D369
Chase Grammar School International Study Centre, UK	D388
Chatmore British International School, Bermuda	D400
Chatrabhuj Narsee School, India	D286
Chatsworth International School, Singapore	D321
Chatsworth International School - Orchard Campus, Singapore	D321
Chavagnes International College, France	D351
Cheka School, Tanzania	D264
Cheltenham College, UK	D388
Cheltenham Ladies' College, UK	D388
Chengdu International School, China	D272
Chengdu Jinjiang Jiaxiang Foreign Languages High School, China	D272
Chengdu Meishi International School, China	D272
Chengdu Parkview PYP Kindergarten, China	D272
Chenshan School, China	D272
Cheshire Academy, USA	D416
Chester College International School, Spain	D372
Chetham's School of Music, UK	D388
Chiang Kai Shek College, Philippines	D314
Chiang Mai International School, Thailand	D325
Chigwell School, UK	D388
Children's Academy International School, India	D286
Children's International School, Nigeria	D258
Children's International School Fredrikstad, Norway	D364
Children's International School Moss, Norway	D364
Children's International School Sarpsborg, Norway	D364
Chilton Saint James School, New Zealand	D343
China World Academy Changsu, China	D272
Chinese International School, Hong Kong, China	D282
Chinese International School Manila, Philippines	D314
Chinmaya International Residential School, India	D286
Chinmaya International Vidyalaya, India	D286
CHIREC International, India	D286
Chittagong Grammar School (CGS), Bangladesh	D269
Chittagong Grammar School (CGS) Dhaka, Bangladesh	D269
Chiway Repton School Xiamen, China	D272
Choithram International, India	D286
Chongqing Bachuan International High School, China	D272
Chongqing Nankai Liangjiang Secondary School, China	D272
Chrisland Schools, Nigeria	D258
Christ Church Episcopal School, USA	D421
Christ Church Grammar School, Australia	D338
Christ Church School, India	D286
Christ College, UK	D388
Christ Junior College, India	D286
Christ Junior College - Residential, India	D286
Christ Our King-Stella Maris School, USA	D421
Christ's Hospital, UK	D388
Christian Academy in Japan, Japan	D300
Christian Alliance International School, Hong Kong, China	D282
Christian American School, Guatemala	D409
Christian German School Chiangmai, Thailand	D325
Christian International School of Prague (CISP), Czech Republic	D349
Christian Teaching Institute (CTI), Lebanon	D306
Chung Nam Samsung Academy, Republic of Korea	D317
Chuo International School, Japan	D300
Churchill College, México	D409
CIA FIRST International School, Cambodia	D270
CIE British School, Philippines	D314
CIEDI - Colegio Internacional de Educación Integral, Colombia	D433
CIS Russia - Festivalnaya Campus, Russian Federation	D368
CIS Russia - Skolkovo Senior Campus, Russian Federation	D368
CIS Russia - St Petersburg Campus, Russian Federation	D369
Cistercian College, Ireland	D358
Cita Hati Christian School - East Campus, Indonesia	D296
Cita Hati Christian School - Samarinda Campus, Indonesia	D296
Cita Hati Christian School - West Campus, Indonesia	D296
Cite Scolaire Internationale de Lyon, France	D351
City Impact Church School, New Zealand	D343
City of Knowledge Academy, Nigeria	D259

Index

City of London Freemen's School, UK D388
Clarion School, United Arab Emirates D329
Clavis International Primary School, Mauritius D256
Clayesmore School, UK D388
Clearwater Central Catholic High School, USA D416
Clemente Althaus, Peru D436
CLIB - The Braga International School, Portugal D366
Clifford School, China D272
Clifton College, UK D388
Clifton College Preparatory School, UK D388
CLIP - Oporto International School, Portugal D366
Coast Academy, Kenya D255
Cobham Hall School, UK D388
Cochabamba Co-Operative School, Bolivia D428
Cochin International School, India D286
Cogdel Cranleigh School, Changsha, China D272
Cogdel Cranleigh School, Wuhan, China D272
Coit Creative Arts Academy, USA D419
Colegio 'La Maisonnette', Chile D431
Colégio 7 de Setembro, Brazil D429
Colegio Abraham Lincoln, Colombia D433
Colegio Adharaz, Spain D372
Colegio Alameda de Osuna, Spain D372
Colegio Álamos, México D409
Colegio Alauda, Spain D372
Colegio Albania, Colombia D433
Colegio Alegra, Spain D372
Colegio Alemán, Colombia D433
Colegio Alemán Alberto Durero de Sevilla, Spain D372
Colegio Alemán Chicureo, Chile D431
Colegio Alemán Córdoba, Argentina D426
Colegio Alemán de Concepción, Chile D431
Colegio Alemán de Guadalajara, México D410
Colegio Alemán de San Felipe de Aconcagua, Chile D431
Colegio Alemán De Santiago, Chile D431
Colegio Alemán de Temuco, Chile D431
Colegio Alemán de Valparaiso, Chile D431
Colegio Alemán Humboldt - DS Samborondón, Ecuador D406
Colegio Alemán Humboldt de Guayaquil, Ecuador D406
Colegio Alemán La Serena, Chile D431
Colegio Alemán Los Angeles, Chile D431
Colegio Alemán Nicaragüense, Nicaragua D414
Colegio Alemán Puerto Varas, Chile D431
Colegio Alemán Quito - Deutsche Schule Quito, Ecuador D406
Colegio Alemán Santa Cruz, Bolivia D428
Colegio Alemán St Thomas Morus, Chile D431
Colegio Alemán Stiehle Cuenca Ecuador, Ecuador D406
Colegio Alerce, México D410
Colegio Alfonsino de San Pedro AC, México D410
Colegio Alpamayo, Peru D436
Colegio Altaduna, Spain D372
Colegio Altair, Peru D436
Colegio Altasierra, Spain D372
Colegio Altocastillo, Spain D372
Colegio Americano, Colombia D433
Colegio Americano de Durango, México D410
Colegio Americano De Guayaquil, Ecuador D406
Colegio Americano de Quito, Ecuador D406
Colegio Americano de San Carlos, México D410
Colegio Americano de Torreón, México D410
Colegio Andino - Deutsche Schule, Colombia D433
Colegio Anglo, México D410
Colegio Anglo Mexicano de Chiapas, México D410
Colegio Anglo-Colombiano, Colombia D433
Colegio Arcangel Rafael, Spain D372
Colegio Arenas, Spain D372
Colegio Arenas Atlántico, Spain D372
Colegio Arenas Internacional, Spain D372
Colegio Arenas Sur, Spain D372
Colegio Arji, México D410
Colegio Arrayanes, Argentina D426
Colegio Arturo Soria, Spain D372
Colegio Atalaya, Spain D372
Colegio Atid AC, México D410
Colégio Atlântico, Portugal D366
Colegio Balandra Cruz del Sur, Ecuador D406
Colegio Base, Spain D372
Colegio Bayard, Argentina D426
Colegio Becquerel, Ecuador D406
Colegio Bellas Artes, Venezuela D438
Colegio Bilingüe Carson de Ciudad Delicias, México D410
Colegio Bilingue New Horizons Santo Domingo, Dominican Republic D405
Colegio Bilingüe Santa Marta, Colombia D433
Colegio Bolivar, Colombia D433
Colegio Bonja, Brazil D429
Colegio Bosque del Plata, Argentina D426
Colegio Brains Maria Lombillo, Spain D372
Colegio Británico, México D410
Colegio Británico - The British School, Colombia D433
Colegio Británico de Cartagena, Colombia D433
Colegio Británico de Montería, Colombia D433
Colegio Buena Tierra SC, México D410
Colegio Camarena Canet, Spain D372
Colegio Camarena Valterna, Spain D372
Colegio Cambridge, Colombia D433
Colegio Canadiense, Colombia D433
Colegio Carmen Arriola de Marin, Argentina D426
Colegio Católico José Engling, Ecuador D406
Colegio Celta Internacional, México D410
Colegio Cervantes, Spain D372
Colegio CEU San Pablo Montepríncipe, Spain D372
Colegio CEU San Pablo Sanchinarro, Spain D372
Colegio CEU San Pablo Valencia, Spain D372
Colegio Champagnat, Peru D436
Colegio Ciudad de Mexico - Contadero, México D410
Colegio Ciudad de México - Polanco, México D410
Colegio Colombo Británico, Colombia D433
Colegio Colombo Británico de Envigado (IED), Colombia D433
Colegio Colombo Gales, Colombia D433
Colegio Columbia, México D410
Colegio Compañía de María - Almería, Spain D372
Colegio Compañía de María - La Enseñanza - Valladolid, Spain D372
Colegio Confluencia, Argentina D426
Colegio de Cambridge (Cambridge International School), Colombia D433
Colegio de Inglaterra - The English School, Colombia D433
Colegio De La Salle, Argentina D426
Colegio de San Francisco de Paula, Spain D372
Colegio de Todos Los Santos, Argentina D426
Colegio Decroly Americano, Guatemala D409
Colegio Discovery, México D410
Colegio Domingo Savio, Colombia D433
Colegio Ecos, Spain D372
Colegio El Buen Ayre, Argentina D426
Colegio El Camino, México D410
Colegio El Planet, Spain D372
Colegio El Romeral, Spain D372
Colegio El Tomillar, Spain D372
Colegio El Valle Alicante, Spain D372
Colegio El Valle II - Sanchinarro, Spain D372
Colegio Entrepinos, Spain D372
Colegio Esquiú, Argentina D426
Colegio Euroamericano de Monterrey, México D410
Colegio Europeo de Madrid, Spain D372
Colegio Experimental Británico Internacional, Ecuador D406
Colegio Fontanar, México D410
Colegio Franco Argentino, Argentina D426
Colegio Franklin Delano Roosevelt, Peru D436
Colegio Gimnasio Internacional de Medellín, Colombia D433
Colegio Goethe Asunción, Paraguay D436
Colegio Gran Bretaña, Colombia D433
Colegio Grazalema, Spain D372
Colegio Guadalete, Spain D372
Colegio Guadalimar, Spain D373
Colegio Guayamuri, Venezuela D438
Colegio Hacienda Los Alcaparros, Colombia D433
Colegio Hebreo Maguen David, México D410
Colegio Hebreo Monte Sinai AC, México D410
Colegio Hebreo Tarbut, México D410
Colegio Heidelberg, Spain D373
Colegio Helvetia, Colombia D433
Colegio HH. Maristas Sagrado Corazón Alicante, Spain D373
Colegio Hipólito Unanue, Peru D436
Colegio Hispano Inglés de Las Palmas, Spain D373
Colegio Humboldt, Costa Rica D404
Colégio Humboldt, Brazil D429
Colegio Humboldt Caracas, Venezuela D438
Colegio Inglés, México D410
Colegio Inglés de los Andes, Colombia D433
Colegio Inglés de Talca, Chile D431
Colegio Inglés English School of Asturias, Spain D373
Colegio Inglés Zaragoza, Spain D373
Colegio Integral El Avila, Venezuela D438
Colegio Integral El Manglar, Venezuela D438
Colegio Interamericano, Guatemala D409
Colegio Internacional Ausiàs March, Spain D373
Colegio Internacional de Bogota, Colombia D433
Colegio Internacional de Caracas, Venezuela D438
Colegio Internacional de Levante, Spain D373

Index

Colegio Internacional de México, México D410
Colegio Internacional de San Salvador, El Salvador D408
Colégio Internacional de Vilamoura (Vilamoura International School), Portugal D366
Colegio Internacional Jesuitinas Miralba, Spain D373
Colegio Internacional Los Cañaverales, Colombia D433
Colegio Internacional Meres, Spain D373
Colegio Internacional Peñacorada, Spain D373
Colegio Internacional Pureza de María Los Realejos, Spain D373
Colegio Internacional Rudolf Steiner, Ecuador D406
Colegio Internacional SEK Chile, Chile D431
Colegio Internacional SEK Costa Rica, Costa Rica D404
Colegio Internacional SEK Ecuador, Ecuador D406
Colegio Internacional SEK Eirís, Spain D373
Colegio Internacional SEK Guadalajara, México D410
Colegio Internacional SEK Guatemala, Guatemala D409
Colegio Internacional SEK Guayaquil, Ecuador D406
Colegio Internacional SEK Las Américas, Dominican Republic D405
Colegio Internacional SEK Los Valles, Ecuador D406
Colegio Internacional SEK Pacifico, Chile D431
Colegio Internacional Terranova, México D410
Colegio Internacional Torrequebrada, Spain D373
Colegio International de Valladolid, Spain D373
Colegio International SEK Paraguay, Paraguay D436
Colegio Intisana, Ecuador D406
Colegio Iribó, Costa Rica D404
Colegio Isaac Rabin, Panama D435
Colegio Jesuitinas Stella Maris, Spain D373
Colegio Jordán de Sajonia, Colombia D433
Colegio Joyfe, Spain D373
Colegio Juan de Lanuza, Spain D373
Colegio Julio Verne, Guatemala D409
Colegio Karl C. Parrish, Colombia D433
Colegio La Arboleda, Colombia D433
Colegio La Floresta, El Salvador D408
Colegio La Paz de Chiapas, México D410
Colegio La Unión, Peru D436
Colegio Lamatepec, El Salvador D408
Colegio Las Chapas, Spain D373
Colegio Laureles IAP, México D410
Colegio Legamar, Spain D373
Colegio León Pinelo, Peru D436
Colegio Letort, Ecuador D406
Colegio Liceo Europeo, Spain D373
Colegio Linares AC, México D410
Colegio Lincoln, Argentina D426
Colegio Logos, Spain D373
Colegio Los Álamos, Peru D436
Colegio Los Ángeles Tunja, Colombia D433
Colegio Los Arcos, Venezuela D438
Colegio Los Campitos, Venezuela D438
Colegio Los Nogales, Colombia D433
Colegio Los Pinos, Ecuador D406
Colegio Los Sauces La Moraleja, Spain D373
Colegio Los Sauces Pontevedra, Spain D373
Colegio Los Sauces Torrelodones, Spain D373
Colegio Los Sauces Vigo, Spain D373
Colegio Los Tréboles, Colombia D434
Colégio Luso-Internacional do Centro, Portugal D366
Colegio Madison Chihuahua, México D410
Colegio Madison Torreón, México D410
Colegio Madrid, Spain D373
Colegio Magister, Peru D436
Colegio Manquecura - Ciudad de Los Valles, Chile D431
Colegio Manquecura - Ciudad del Este, Chile D431
Colegio Manquecura - Valle lo Campino, Chile D431
Colegio Manquecura Ñuñoa, Chile D431
Colegio Manuel Peleteiro, Spain D373
Colegio Maria Montessori, Argentina D426
Colegio Maria Montessori de Monclova, México D410
Colegio Mark Twain, Argentina D426
Colegio Martin Y Omar, Argentina D426
Colegio Marymount Barranquilla, Colombia D434
Colegio Mater Admirabilis, Peru D436
Colegio Mater Salvatoris, Spain D373
Colegio Max Uhle, Peru D436
Colégio Maxi, Brazil D429
Colegio Maya, El Salvador D408
Colegio Maya - The American International School of Guatemala, Guatemala D409
Colegio Mayor de los Andes, Colombia D434
Colegio Menor Campus Samborondon, Ecuador D406
Colegio Menor San Francisco de Quito, Ecuador D406
Colegio Merici, México D410
Colegio Metodista de Costa Rica, Costa Rica D404
Colégio Miguel de Cervantes, Brazil D429
Colégio Mira Rio, Portugal D366
Colegio Miravalle, Costa Rica D404
Colegio Monaita, Spain D373
Colegio Montealto, Peru D437
Colegio Montecalpe, Spain D373
Colegio Montessori de Luján, Argentina D426
Colegio Monteverde, México D410
Colegio Montserrat, Spain D373
Colegio Moral y Luces 'Herzl-Bialik', Venezuela D438
Colegio Mulhacén, Spain D373
Colegio Nuestra Señora de Europa, Spain D373
Colegio Nuestra Señora de Schoenstatt, Spain D373
Colegio Nuestra Señora del Pilar, Peru D437
Colegio Nuestra Señora del Recuerdo, Spain D373
Colegio Nueva Granada, Colombia D434
Colegio Nueva Inglaterra (New England School), Colombia D434
Colegio Nueva York, Colombia D434
Colegio Nuevo Continente, México D410
Colegio Obradoiro, Spain D373
Colegio Olinca, Altavista, México D411
Colegio Olinca, Periférico, México D411
Colegio Pachamama, Ecuador D406
Colegio Padre Luis Maria Etcheverry Boneo, Argentina D426
Colegio Palermo Chico, Argentina D426
Colegio Panamericano, Colombia D434
Colegio Parque, Spain D373
Colegio Patris, Argentina D426
Colegio Peruano - Alemán Reina del Mundo, Peru D437
Colegio Peruano Alemán Beata Imelda, Peru D437
Colegio Peruano Británico, Peru D437
Colegio Peruano Norteamericano Abraham Lincoln, Peru D437
Colegio Pestalozzi (Colegio Suizo del Peru), Peru D437
Colegio Planalto, Portugal D366
Colegio Positivo Internacional, Brazil D429
Colegio Puertapalma, Spain D374
Colegio Puertoblanco, Spain D374
Colegio Pumahue - Chicauma, Chile D431
Colegio Pumahue - Chicuero, Chile D431
Colegio Pumahue - Curauma, Chile D431
Colegio Pumahue - Huechuraba, Chile D432
Colegio Pumahue - Peñalolén, Chile D432
Colegio Pumahue - Puerto Montt, Chile D432
Colegio Pumahue - Temuco, Chile D432
Colegio Retamar, Spain D374
Colegio Sagrada Familia Jesuitinas, Spain D374
Colegio Sagrados Corazones 'Recoleta', Peru D437
Colegio Saint Francis, Costa Rica D404
Colegio Saladares, Spain D374
Colegio Salcantay, Peru D437
Colegio Salvadoreño Inglés, El Salvador D408
Colegio San Agustín, Peru D437
Colegio San Agustín de Chiclayo, Peru D437
Colegio San Agustín El Paraíso, Venezuela D438
Colegio San Andrés, Paraguay D436
Colegio San Cayetano, Spain D374
Colegio San Cristóbal, Spain D374
Colegio San Fernando, Spain D374
Colegio San Francisco Javier Huechuraba, Chile D432
Colegio San Ignacio, Argentina D426
Colegio San Ignacio de Recalde, Peru D437
Colegio San Jorge, Argentina D426
Colegio San Jorge, Spain D374
Colegio San José Estepona, Spain D374
Colegio San Marcos, Argentina D426
Colegio San Mateo, Colombia D434
Colegio San Pablo, Argentina D426
Colegio San Patricio, Argentina D426
Colegio San Patricio de Luján, Argentina D426
Colegio San Patricio El Soto, Spain 107, D374
Colegio San Patricio La Moraleja, Spain D374
Colegio San Patricio Serrano, Spain D374
Colegio San Pedro, Peru D437
Colegio San Pedro Apostol, Argentina D426
Colegio San Viator - Sede Bogotá, Colombia D434
Colegio San Viator - Sede Tunja, Colombia D434
Colegio Santa Francisca Romana, Colombia D434
Colegio Santa Maria, Colombia D434
Colegio Santa María, Argentina D427
Colegio Santa María de Guadalupe, Costa Rica D404
Colegio Santa María del Camino, Spain D374
Colegio Santa Úrsula, Peru D437
Colégio Santiago Internacional, Portugal D366

Index

Colegio Santísimo Nombre de Jesús, Peru	D437
Colegio Santo Tomás de Aquino, Colombia	D434
Colegio Sao Luis, Brazil	D429
Colegio Séneca, Ecuador	D406
Colegio Sidarta, Brazil	D429
Colegio Sierra Blanca, Spain	D374
Colegio Simón Bolivar, México	D411
Colégio Soka do Brasil, Brazil	D429
Colegio Springfield, SC, México	D411
Colegio Stella Maris, Uruguay	D438
Colegio Stella Maris, Ecuador	D406
Colégio Suíço-Brasileiro de Curitiba, Brazil	D429
Colegio Suizo de Madrid, Spain	D374
Colegio Suizo de México - Campus Cuernavaca, México	D411
Colegio Suizo de México - Campus México DF, México	D411
Colegio Suizo de México - Campus Querétaro, México	D411
Colegio Tarbut, Argentina	D427
Colegio Tierrallana, Spain	D374
Colegio Tilatá, Colombia	D434
Colegio Timon, Spain	D374
Colegio Valdefuentes, Spain	D374
Colegio Valle Abierto, Venezuela	D438
Colegio Villa Caritas, Peru	D437
Colegio Villa Maria, Peru	D437
Colegio Virgen de Europa, Spain	D374
Colegio Virgen Inmaculada de Monterrico, Peru	D437
Colegio Vista Hermosa, México	D411
Colegio Williams, México	D411
Colegio Williams de Cuernavaca, México	D411
Colegio Williams Unidad San Jerónimo, México	D411
Colegio Xail, México	D411
Colegio Yorkín, Costa Rica	D404
Colegios Ramón Y Cajal, Spain	D374
Colegiul German Goethe, Romania	D368
Collège Alpin Beau Soleil, Switzerland	D380
Collège Anatole France, Morocco	D257
Collège André Malraux, Peru	D437
Collège Champittet, Pully, Switzerland	D380
Collège Charlemagne, Canada	D403
Collège Charles-Lemoyne - Campus Longueuil, Canada	D403
Collège de l'Assomption, Canada	D403
Collège De La Salle Frères, Jordan	D304
Collège de Lévis, Canada	D403
Collège de Niki de St Phalle - Anglophone Section, France	D351
College Den Hulster, Netherlands	D363
Collège des Frères Maristes Champville, Lebanon	D307
Collège du Léman, Switzerland	D380
Collège du Mont-Sainte-Anne, Canada	D403
Collège Esther-Blondin, Canada	D403
Collège et Lycée St-Charles, Switzerland	D380
Collège Français Bilingue de Londres (CFBL), UK	108, D388
Collège Français de Tel-Aviv Marc Chagall, Israel	D299
Collège François-de-Laval, Canada	D403
College Hauts Grillets, France	D351
College International de Fontainebleau, France	D351
Collège Jean-de-Brebeuf, Canada	D403
Collège Jésus-Marie de Sillery, Canada	D403
Collège Laflèche, Canada	D403
Collège Laurentien, Canada	D403
College Marcel Roby (American Section), France	D351
Collège Marie-de l'Incarnation, Canada	D403
Collège Mont Notre-Dame de Sherbrooke, Canada	D403
Collège Notre Dame de Nazareth, Lebanon	D307
Collège Notre Dame des Soeurs Antonines (Hazmieh-Jamhour), Lebanon	D307
Collège Notre-Dame de Jamhour, Lebanon	D307
Collège Notre-Dame-de-Lourdes, Canada	D403
Collège Protestant Français, Lebanon	D307
Collège Protestant Français Montana, Lebanon	D307
Collège Saint Marc, Alexandria, Egypt	D249
Collège Saint-Bernard, Canada	D403
College Saint-Exupery, Spain	D374
Collège Saint-Joseph de Hull, Canada	D403
Collège Saint-Maurice, Canada	D403
Collège Saint-Paul, Canada	D403
College Sainte Clotilde, France	D351
Collège Ville-Marie, Canada	D403
Collège-Lycée Saint François-Xavier, France	D352
Collegiate International School, United Arab Emirates	D329
Collegiate School, Bristol, UK	D388
Collegio San Carlo, Italy	D359
Collingham College, UK	D388
Cologne International School, Germany	D354
Colombo International School, Sri Lanka	D323
Colombo International School Kandy, Sri Lanka	D323
Columbia International School, Japan	D300
Commonwealth-Parkville School, Puerto Rico	D414
Compass International School Doha, Gharaffa, Qatar	D316
Compass International School Doha, Madinat Khalifa, Qatar	D316
Compass International School Doha, Themaid, Qatar	D316
Complejo Educativo Mas Camarena, Spain	D374
Complexe Scolaire Les Calinours, Democratic Republic of the Congo	D249
Comunidad Educativa Conexus, Dominican Republic	D405
Comunidad Educativa Lux Mundi, Dominican Republic	D405
Concord College, UK	D389
Concordia College, Concordia Campus - Highgate, Australia	D338
Concordia College, St Peter's Campus - Blackwood, Australia	D338
Concordia International School, Hong Kong, China	D282
Concordia International School Hanoi, Vietnam	D335
Concordia International School Shanghai, China	D272
Concordian International School, Thailand	D325
Confluence International School of Khartoum, Sudan	D263
Connie's Academy International British Primary School, Republic of the Congo	D261
Contofield International School, Tajikistan	D324
Convent of the Sacred Heart, USA	D420
Cooperativa de Enseñanza San Cernin, Spain	D374
Copenhagen International School, Denmark	D350
Copperfield Verbier, Switzerland	D380
Coral International School, Saudi Arabia	D319
Corbett Preparatory School of IDS, USA	D416
Core International School, Italy	D359
Coree International School, Brazil	D429
Cornerstone International Academy, Ghana	D253
Cornerstone Learning Community, USA	D416
Cornerstone Schools of Alabama, USA	D414
Cornish College, Australia	D339
Cornwall Hill College, South Africa	D262
Corona School Gbagada, Nigeria	D259
Corona School Ikoyi, Nigeria	D259
Corona School Lekki, Nigeria	D259
Corona School Victoria Island, Nigeria	D259
Coruña British International School (A Coruña), Spain	109, D374
Cosmos International College, Nepal	D311
Costa Blanca International College, Spain	D374
Costa Rica International Academy, Costa Rica	D404
Costeas-Geitonas School, Greece	D357
Country Day School, Costa Rica	D404
Country Garden Silver Beach School, China	D272
Cours Lumière, Togo	D264
Cours Moliere, France	D352
Cours Sainte Marie de Hann, Senegal	D261
Courtney House International School, South Africa	D262
CPS Global School - Anna Nagar Campus, India	D286
CPS Global School - Thirumazhisai Campus, India	D286
Cradle to Crayon School, Nigeria	D259
Craighouse School, Chile	D432
Cranbrook School, Australia	D339
Cranleigh Abu Dhabi, United Arab Emirates	D329
Cranleigh School, UK	D389
Crans-Montana International School, Bangladesh	D269
Crawford International Bedfordview, South Africa	D262
Crawford International Bryanston, South Africa	D262
Crawford International Fourways, South Africa	D262
Crawford International La Lucia, South Africa	D262
Crawford International Lonehill, South Africa	D262
Crawford International North Coast, South Africa	D262
Crawford International Pretoria, South Africa	D262
Crawford International Ruimsig, South Africa	D262
Crawford International Sandton, South Africa	D262
Creation Village Preparatory School, USA	D416
Creative International School, Egypt	D249
Creative Minds International Public Charter School, USA	D416
Creative Primary School, Hong Kong, China	D282
Creativity Private School, Bahrain	D268
Creek Street Christian College, Australia	D339
Crescent English High School Dubai, United Arab Emirates	D329
Crescent International School, Thailand	D325
Crescent School for Boys, Canada	D402
Crnjanski High School, Serbia	D369
Crossroads International School, India	D286
CTC International School, Nigeria	D259
Cubahiro International School, Rwanda	D261
Culford School, UK	D389
Cultura Inglesa - Filial Cabral, Brazil	D429
Cunae International School LLC, USA	D421
Cygnus World School, India	D286

Index

D

D Y Patil International College, India	D286
D Y Patil International School, Lohagaon, India	D286
D Y Patil International School, Nagpur, India	D286
D Y Patil International School, Nerul, India	D286
D Y Patil International School, Worli, India	D286
D-Ivy College, Nigeria	D259
D-PREP International School, Thailand	D325
d'Overbroeck's, UK	D389
Da Vinci International School Antwerp, Belgium	D347
Da Vinci School International Duhok, Iraq	D299
Da Vinci School International Erbil, Iraq	D299
Da Vinci's International Schools, Poland	D365
Daegu Daegun Middle School, Republic of Korea	D318
Daegu International School (DIS), Republic of Korea	D318
Dainfern College, South Africa	D262
Dakar Academy, Senegal	D261
Dalat International School, Malaysia	D308
Dalian American International School, China	D272
Dalian Maple Leaf Foreign Nationals School, China	D273
Dalian Maple Leaf International High School, China	D273
Dallas International School, USA	D421
Daly College, India	D286
Damien High School, USA	D414
Danah Universal School of Kuwait, Kuwait	D305
Danube International School Vienna, Austria	D346
Dar Al Fikr Schools, Saudi Arabia	D319
Dar Al Marefa Private School, United Arab Emirates	D329
Dar El Tarbiah - IGCSE Agouza, Egypt	D249
Dar El Tarbiah - IGCSE Zamalek, Egypt	D249
Dar es Salaam Independent School, Tanzania	D264
Dar es Salaam International Academy, Tanzania	D264
Dar Essalaam American School, Morocco	D257
Dar Jana International School-Rawda Campus, Saudi Arabia	D319
Darussafaka Schools, Türkiye	D383
Dasman Bilingual School, Kuwait	D305
Datus International School, Ghana	D253
Dauntsey's, UK	D389
Davy College, Peru	D437
Dawha High School, United Arab Emirates	D329
Day Waterman College, Nigeria	D259
Dayspring International Academy, Ghana	D254
Daystar Academy, China	D273
Daystar Academy, USA	D417
Daystar Academy Sanlitun, China	D273
Daystar Primary School, Botswana	D248
De Paul International Residential School, India	D286
Dean Close School, UK	D389
Debiruss School, Nigeria	D259
Deenway Montessori School & Unicity College, UK	D389
Deerfield Academy, USA	D419
Dehong Beijing International Chinese School, China	D273
Dehong Shanghai International Chinese School, China	D273
Deira International School, United Arab Emirates	D329
Deira Private School, United Arab Emirates	D329
Del Mar Academy, Costa Rica	D404
DelCampo School, Honduras	D435
Deledda International School, Italy	D359
Delhi Private School (DPS) International Ghana, Ghana	D254
Delhi Private School Dubai, United Arab Emirates	D329
Delhi Private School Sharjah, United Arab Emirates	D329
Delhi Public School - BPKIHS, Nepal	D311
Delhi Public School Bangalore East (DPSBE), India	D287
Delhi Public School Bangalore North (DPSBN), India	D287
Delhi Public School Bangalore South (DPSBS), India	D287
Delhi Public School Ghaziabad (DPSG) International, India	D287
Delhi Public School Ghaziabad (DPSG) Meerut Road, India	D287
Delhi Public School Ghaziabad (DPSG) Palam Vihar, India	D287
Delhi Public School Ghaziabad (DPSG) Vasundhara, India	D287
Delia School Of Canada, Hong Kong, China	D282
Delightsome Land School, Nigeria	D259
Delta American School, Egypt	D249
Delta English School, United Arab Emirates	D329
Delta Waters International School, Botswana	D248
Denstone College, UK	D389
DePaul College Prep, USA	D417
Desert Garden Montessori, USA	D414
Destiny Academy, Malaysia	D308
Destiny School, New Zealand	D343
Detroit Country Day School, USA	D419
Deutsche Botschaftsschule Peking, China	D273
Deutsche Evangelische Oberschule Kairo, Egypt	D249
Deutsche Höhere Privatschule Windhoek, Namibia	D258
Deutsche Internationale Schule Den Haag, Netherlands	D363
Deutsche Internationale Schule Doha, Qatar	D316
Deutsche Internationale Schule Jeddah, Saudi Arabia	D319
Deutsche Schule - Cali / Kolumbien, Colombia	D434
Deutsche Schule - Escuela Alemana San Salvador, El Salvador	D408
Deutsche Schule Abuja, Nigeria	D259
Deutsche Schule Athen, Greece	D357
Deutsche Schule Beverly Hills Kairo, Egypt	D249
Deutsche Schule Budapest Thomas Mann Gymnasium, Hungary	D358
Deutsche Schule der Borromäerinnen Alexandria, Egypt	D249
Deutsche Schule der Borromäerinnen Kairo, Egypt	D249
Deutsche Schule Erbil, Iraq	D299
Deutsche Schule Genua, Italy	D359
Deutsche Schule Helsinki, Finland	D351
Deutsche Schule Hurghada, Egypt	D249
Deutsche Schule in der provinz Malaga - Coleg, Spain	D374
Deutsche Schule Istanbul – Özel Alman Lisesi, Türkiye	D383
Deutsche Schule Izmir, Türkiye	D383
Deutsche Schule Jakarta, Indonesia	D296
Deutsche Schule Kobe International (DSKI), Japan	D300
Deutsche Schule Kuala Lumpur, Malaysia	D308
Deutsche Schule La Paz - Colegio Alemán 'Mariscal Braun', Bolivia	D428
Deutsche Schule London, UK	D389
Deutsche Schule Madrid, Spain	D374
Deutsche Schule Mailand, Italy	D359
Deutsche Schule Medellín, Colombia	D434
Deutsche Schule Moskau, Russian Federation	D369
Deutsche Schule New Delhi, India	D287
Deutsche Schule Oslo - Max Tau, Norway	D364
Deutsche Schule Prag, Czech Republic	D350
Deutsche Schule Shanghai Pudong, China	D273
Deutsche Schule Temperley, Argentina	D427
Deutsche Schule Thessaloniki - DST, Greece	D357
Deutsche Schule Tokyo Yokohama, Japan	D300
Deutsche Schule Toulouse, France	D352
Deutsche Schule Valencia - Colegio Alemán Valencia, Spain	D374
Dhahran Ahliyya Schools, Saudi Arabia	D319
Dhahran British Grammar School, Saudi Arabia	D320
Dhahran Elementary/Middle School, Saudi Arabia	D320
Dhirubhai Ambani International School, India	D287
Diamond International School, Laos	D306
Diamond Stone International School, India	D287
Dibber International School Sollentuna, Sweden	D379
Didac School, UK	D389
Digital Private School, Oman	D312
Dili International School, East Timor	D281
Dino High School s.r.o., Czech Republic	D350
Diocesan Boys' School, Hong Kong, China	D282
Diocesan School for Girls, New Zealand	D343
Discover (Otkrivatel) Montessori School, Bulgaria	D348
Discovery Bay International School, Hong Kong, China	49, D282
Discovery Mind Primary School - Discovery Bay Campus, Hong Kong, China	D282
Discovery Mind Primary School - Tung Chung Campus, Hong Kong, China	D282
Discovery Montessori Academy, Hong Kong, China	D282
Discovery School, México	D411
Discovery School, USA	D421
Discovery School, Honduras	D435
DISTED College, Malaysia	D308
Divaris Makaharis, Zimbabwe	D266
Divine Royal International College, Nigeria	D259
DLD College London, UK	D389
Doha British School - Ain Khaled, Qatar	D316
Doha British School - Al Wakrah, Qatar	D316
Doha British School - Rawdat Al Hamama, Qatar	D316
Doha College, Qatar	D316
Doha English Speaking School (DESS), Qatar	D316
Doha Modern Indian School, Qatar	D316
Dominica Seventh-Day Adventist Secondary School, Dominica	D405
Dominican International School, Taiwan	D323
Domuschola International School, Philippines	D314
Don Bosco International School, India	D287
Don Bosco Landser, France	D352
Dongguan Hanlin Experimental School, China	D273
Donovan Catholic, USA	D419
Doregos Private Academy, Nigeria	D259
Dos Rios Elementary School, USA	D415
Doshisha International Academy (DIA) Elementary School, Japan	D300
Doshisha International School, Kyoto, Japan	D300
Dostyk American International School, Kazakhstan	D304
Dover College, UK	D389
Dover Court International School Singapore, Singapore	D321
Dover High School, Argentina	D427

Index

Dover International School, Egypt D250
Dowen College, Nigeria D259
Downe House School, UK D389
Downside School, UK D389
DPS International School, Singapore D321
DPS International, Gurgaon, India D287
DPS International, Saket, India D287
Dr Pillai Global Academy, India D287
Dr Pillai Global Academy, New Panvel, India D287
Dr. Nermien Ismail Schools (NIS) - 6th of October City, Egypt D250
Dr. Nermien Ismail Schools (NIS) - El Shorouk City, Egypt D250
Dr. Nermien Ismail Schools (NIS) - First Settlement, Egypt D250
Dr. Nermien Ismail Schools (NIS) - Nasr City, Egypt D250
Dr. Nermien Ismail Schools (NIS) - New Capital All Girls International School, Egypt D250
Dr. Nermien Ismail Schools (NIS) - New Capital National School, Egypt D250
Dr. Nermien Ismail Schools (NIS) - Porto Said, Egypt D250
Dream International School, Egypt D250
Dresden International School e.V, Germany D354
DRS International School, India D287
DSB International School, India D287
Dual International School Blumenau, Brazil D429
Dual International School Florianopolis, Brazil D429
Dubai British Foundation, United Arab Emirates D329
Dubai British School, United Arab Emirates D329
Dubai British School Jumeirah Park, United Arab Emirates D329
Dubai Carmel School, United Arab Emirates D329
Dubai College, United Arab Emirates D329
Dubai English Speaking College, United Arab Emirates D329
Dubai English Speaking School, United Arab Emirates D329
Dubai International Academy, Al Barsha, United Arab Emirates D329
Dubai International Academy, Emirates Hills, United Arab Emirates D329
Dubai International School - Al Garhoud, United Arab Emirates D329
Dubai International School - Al Qouz Branch, United Arab Emirates D329
Dubai Modern Education School, United Arab Emirates D329
Dubai National School - Al Barsha Branch, United Arab Emirates D329
Dubai Scholars Private School, United Arab Emirates D329
Duke of Kent School, UK D389
Dukhan English Speaking School, Qatar D316
Dulwich College, UK D389
Dulwich College (Singapore), Singapore 50, D321
Dulwich College Beijing, China D273
Dulwich College Kindergarten, Shanghai, China D273
Dulwich College Seoul, Republic of Korea D318
Dulwich College Shanghai Pudong, China D273
Dulwich College Shanghai Puxi, China D273
Dulwich College Suzhou, China D273
Dulwich International High School Suzhou, China D273
Dulwich International High School Zhuhai, China D273
Dunalastair Chicureo, Chile D432
Dunalastair Las Condes, Chile D432
Dunalastair Peñalolén, Chile D432
Dunecrest American School, United Arab Emirates D329
Dunes International School, Saudi Arabia D320
Dunya School, Azerbaijan D347
Durham School, UK D389
Dushanbe International School, Tajikistan D324
Dwarkibai Gangadhar Khetan International School, India D287
Dwight School, USA 221, D420
Dwight School Dubai, United Arab Emirates D329
Dwight School Hanoi, Vietnam 51, D335
Dwight School London, UK D389
Dwight School Seoul, Republic of Korea D318

E

E.S.C.O.L.A. - English School Community of Luanda, Angola, Angola 41, D248
Eagle Hill School, USA D419
Eaglebridge International School, China D273
Earlscliffe, UK D389
East Bay German International School, USA D414
East West International School & College, Bangladesh D269
East-West International School, Cambodia D270
Eastbourne College, UK D389
Eastern Public School, India D287
Eastgate Academy, Canada D401
Eastwood College Kafarshima, Lebanon D307
Eastwood International School Beirut, Lebanon D307
Eastwood International School Erbil, Iraq D299
Eaton International School, Malaysia D308
Ebenezery Heights International Schools, Nigeria D259
Ecole Active Bilingue, France D352
Ecole André Chénier, Morocco D257
École at Montessori - Babylone, France D352
École at Montessori - Ranelagh, France D352
Ecole Bilingue de Berkeley, USA D414
École Canadienne de Tunis, Tunisia D265
Ecole d'Humanité, Switzerland D380
École de la Synergie, Canada D403
Ecole des Arches, Switzerland D380
Ecole des Francs Bourgeois, France D352
Ecole Des Roches, France D352
École du Centre - Collège Pierre Poivre, Mauritius D257
Ecole du Nord, Mauritius D257
Ecole Élémentaire Franco-Allemande de Stuttgart - Sillenburch, Germany D354
Ecole Européenne de Strasbourg, France D352
Ecole Français Jules Verne, Finland D351
École française Arthur Rimbaud de Dar es Salaam, Tanzania D264
École Française Bel Air, Spain D374
Ecole française de Bâle - Section Elémentaire, Switzerland D380
École Française de Banjul, The Gambia D264
Ecole Francaise de Berne, Switzerland D380
École Française de Bristol, UK D389
École Française de Kano, Nigeria D259
École Française de la Havane, Cuba D405
Ecole française de Lausanne Valmont, Switzerland D380
Ecole Française de Londres Jacques Prévert, UK D389
Ecole Française de Naples Alexandre Dumas, Italy D359
École française de Sarrebruck et Dilling, Germany D354
École Française de Téhéran, Iran D298
Ecole Francaise Internationale de Canton, China D273
École Française Internationale de Katmandou, Nepal D311
École francaise internationale de Wuhan, China D273
École Française Internationale de Zagreb, Croatia D349
École Française Les Grands Lacs, Uganda D265
École Française Marcel Pagnol d'Abuja, Nigeria D259
École française Pierre et Marie Curie, Germany D354
école Franco-Chypriote, Cyprus D349
École Grundschule Voltaire, Germany D354
Ecole Internationale Arc de Triomphe, Saudi Arabia D320
Ecole Internationale Bilingue Le Cartésien (EIBC), Democratic Republic of the Congo D249
Ecole Internationale de Montreal Primaire, Canada D403
École Internationale des Apprenants, Canada D403
Ecole Jeannine Manuel - Lille, France 110, D352
Ecole Jeannine Manuel - Paris, France 111, D352
Ecole Les Lutins, Mali D256
École Les Mélèzes, Canada D403
École Marie-Clarac, Canada D403
Ecole Mondiale World School, India D287
École Montessori Bilingue de Levallois-Perret, France D352
Ecole Mosaic, Switzerland D380
Ecole Moser Genève, Switzerland D380
Ecole Moser Nyon, Switzerland D380
Ecole Nouvelle de la Suisse Romande - Lausanne, Switzerland D380
Ecole Oasis Internationale, Egypt D250
Ecole Paul Cézanne, Morocco D257
École Pilote Innovante Alpha, Togo D264
École Plein Soleil (Association Coopérative), Canada D403
École Primaire Française de Genève, Switzerland D380
École Primaire Marie D'Orliac, UK D389
Ecole Privée Bilingue Internationale, France D352
Ecole Privee Over the Rainbow, Luxembourg D362
Ecole Privée Val Saint André, France D352
Ecole Riviera, Switzerland D380
École Robert Desnos, Tunisia D265
Ecole Saint-Louis des Français, Spain D374
École secondaire Saint-Joseph de Saint-Hyacinthe, Canada D403
Écoles Al Madina, Site Ain Sebaa, Morocco D257
Écoles Al Madina, Site Californie, Morocco D257
Écoles Al Madina, Site Polo, Morocco D257
Eden Christian Academy, New Zealand D343
Edgewood College, Nigeria D259
Edirne Beykent Schools, Türkiye D383
Edison Primary School, Poland D365
Edubridge International School, India D287
EducaMundo, Ecuador D406
Educare Centro de Servicios Educativos S.C., México D411
Education Castle International School, Saudi Arabia D320
Education City High School, Qatar D316
Education Gate International School, Al Murraba, Saudi Arabia D320
Education Gate International School, Al Rawdah, Saudi Arabia D320
'Education through Dialogue' School, Russian Federation D369
Eerde International Boarding School Netherlands, Netherlands D363
EF Academy New York, USA D420
EF Academy Oxford, UK D389
EF Academy Pasadena, USA D414

Index

EFAC French-American School of Chicago, USA ... D417
EFE Montaigne, Benin ... D248
EFID - French International School of Dhaka, Bangladesh ... D269
Egitmen Koleji, Türkiye ... D383
Egypt British International School (EBIS), Egypt ... D250
Egyptian American International School (EAIS) 6th October, Egypt ... D250
Egyptian American International School (EAIS) El Shorouk, Egypt ... D250
Egyptian American International School (EAIS) New Cairo, Egypt ... D250
Egyptian American School, Egypt ... D250
Egyptian British International School (EBIS) 6th October, Egypt ... D250
Egyptian British International School (EBIS) El Shorouk, Egypt ... D250
Egyptian British International School (EBIS) New Cairo, Egypt ... D250
Egyptian English Language Schools (EELS), Egypt ... D250
Egyptian Language School (ELS) New Cairo, Egypt ... D250
EIB de La Jonchère, France ... D352
EIB Etoile High School, France ... D352
EIB Grenelle, France ... D352
EIB Lamartine, France ... D352
EIB Monceau Middle School (Collège EIB Monceau), France ... D352
EIB Monceau Primary School, France ... D352
EIFA International School, UK ... D389
Eisugakkan School, Japan ... D300
Ekamai International School, Thailand ... D325
El Alsson British and American International Schools - NewGiza, Egypt ... D250
El Camino Academy, Colombia ... D434
El Centro Ingles, Spain ... D374
EL Genesis Kindergarten, China ... D273
El Gouna International School, Egypt ... D250
El Limonar International School (ELIS) Murcia, Spain ... D374
El Limonar International School (ELIS) Villamartin, Spain ... D374
El Mokatam International Language School, Egypt ... D250
El Pinar College, Peru ... D437
El Plantío International School of Valencia, Spain ... D374
El Rowad College, Egypt ... D250
El Sauce School, Ecuador ... D406
El-Fouad International School, Egypt ... D250
El-Massira Integrated School, Egypt ... D250
El-Quds Language Schools, Egypt ... D250
ELA Basel, Switzerland ... D380
Ela Green School, India ... D287
Ela Murray International School, Papua New Guinea ... D344
elc International School, Malaysia ... D308
ELC International School Cyberjaya, Malaysia ... D308
ELCHK Lutheran Academy, Hong Kong, China ... D282
Elckerlyc International School, Netherlands ... 112, D363
Elian's British School of La Nucía, Spain ... D374
Elite English School, United Arab Emirates ... D329
Elite International School, Egypt ... D250
Elite Private School, United Arab Emirates ... D329
Elizabeth Moir School, Sri Lanka ... D323
Ellesmere College, UK ... D389
Ellesmere Muscat, Oman ... D312
Ellipse Montessori Academy, France ... D352
Elmhurst Ballet School, UK ... D389
Elmwood School, Canada ... D402
Elonera Montessori School, Australia ... D339
Elpro International School, India ... D287
Elyon Christian School, Indonesia ... D296
Embley, UK ... D389
EMDI School, Ecuador ... D406
Emerald Schools, Nigeria ... D259
Emine Ornek Schools, Türkiye ... D383
Emirates Future International Academy, United Arab Emirates ... D329
Emirates International School - Jumeirah, United Arab Emirates ... D330
Emirates International School - Meadows, United Arab Emirates ... D330
Emirates National School - Abu Dhabi City Campus, United Arab Emirates ... D330
Emirates National School - Al Ain City Campus, United Arab Emirates ... D330
Emirates National School - Branch 3, United Arab Emirates ... D330
Emirates National School - Dubai Campus, United Arab Emirates ... D330
Emirates National School - Mohammed Bin Zayed Campus, United Arab Emirates ... D330
Emirates National School - Ras Al Khaimah Campus, United Arab Emirates ... D330
Emirates National School - Sharjah Campus, United Arab Emirates ... D330
Emirates Private School Abu Dhabi, United Arab Emirates ... D330
Emirates Private School Al Ain, United Arab Emirates ... D330
EMS High School, Pakistan ... D313
Encounter Lutheran College, Australia ... D339
Endeavor International School, USA ... D417
Engage Independent School, Spain ... D374
Engelska Skolan Norr, Sweden ... D379
English Academy Santa Claus, Spain ... D374
English French School (EFS), Vietnam ... D335
English Gate School, Italy ... 113, D359
English International School, Benin ... D248
English International School of Bratislava (EISB), Slovakia ... D370
English School in Kalba, United Arab Emirates ... D330
English School Los Olivos, Spain ... D374
English Talents School, Jordan ... D304
English-Speaking School of Lubumbashi, Democratic Republic of the Congo ... D249
Enishi International School, Japan ... D300
Enka Schools - Adapazari Campus, Türkiye ... D383
Enka Schools - Istanbul Campus, Türkiye ... D383
Enko Bamako International School, Mali ... D256
Enko Bonanjo International School, Cameroon ... D248
Enko Botho International School, Botswana ... D248
Enko Keur Gorgui International School, Senegal ... D261
Enko La Gaiete International School, Cameroon ... D248
Enko Ouaga International School, Burkina Faso ... D248
Enko Riverside International School, Mozambique ... D258
Enko Riviera International School, Cote d'Ivoire ... D248
Enko Sekeleka International School, Mozambique ... D258
Enko Waca International School, Senegal ... D261
Epsom College, UK ... D389
Epsom College in Malaysia, Malaysia ... D308
Equity American School, Guatemala ... D409
Erasmus International School, Germany ... D354
Ermitage International School, France ... D352
Ernst-Reuter-Schule, Türkiye ... D383
ERUDIO International School, Slovenia ... D370
Erudito Licejus, Kaunas, Lithuania ... D362
Erudito Licejus, Vilnius, Lithuania ... D362
ES American School, Spain ... 114, D375
Esbjerg International School, Denmark ... D350
Escola Alemã Corcovado, Brazil ... D429
Escola Americana de Belo Horizonte, Brazil ... D429
Escola Americana do Rio de Janeiro - Barra da Tijuca, Brazil ... D429
Escola Americana do Rio de Janeiro - Gávea, Brazil ... D429
Escola Beit Yaacov, Brazil ... D429
Escola Bilíngue Pueri Domus - Aclimação Campus, Brazil ... D429
Escola Bilíngue Pueri Domus - Itaim Campus, Brazil ... D429
Escola Bilíngue Pueri Domus - Perdizes Campus, Brazil ... D429
Escola Bilíngue Pueri Domus - Verbo Divino Campus, Brazil ... D429
Escola Canadense de Brasilia, Brazil ... D429
Escola Castanheiras, Brazil ... D429
Escola da APEL, Portugal ... D366
Escola do Futuro - São Paulo, Brazil ... 240, D429
Escola Eleva - Barra da Tijuca, Brazil ... D429
Escola Eleva - Urca, Brazil ... D429
Escola Francesa de Natal, Brazil ... D429
Escola Frederic Mistral Tècnic Eulàlia, Spain ... D375
Escola Internacional de Alphaville, Brazil ... D430
Escola Internacional del Camp, Spain ... D375
Escola Internacional Nova Geração, Brazil ... D430
Escola Lourenco Castanho - Alto da Boa Vista, Brazil ... D430
Escola Lourenco Castanho - Vila Nova Conceição, Brazil ... D430
Escola Nova by SIS Swiss International School, Brazil ... D430
Escola Pia Sabadell, Spain ... D375
Escola Suíço-Brasileira (ESB) Rio de Janeiro by SIS Swiss International School, Brazil ... D430
Escola Suíço-Brasileira de São Paulo, Brazil ... D430
Escola Villare, Brazil ... D430
Escuela Alexander Bain SC, México ... D411
Escuela Americana, El Salvador ... D408
Escuela Ameyalli SC, México ... D411
Escuela Bancaria y Comercial, SC, México ... D411
Escuela Bella Vista, Venezuela ... D438
Escuela Bilingüe Internacional, USA ... D414
Escuela Bilingüe Maquilishuat, El Salvador ... D408
Escuela Campo Alegre, Venezuela ... D438
Escuela Goethe Rosario, Argentina ... D427
Escuela Ideo, Spain ... D375
Escuela Integral Hebreo Uruguaya, Uruguay ... D438
Escuela Internacional Sampedrana, Honduras ... D435
Escuela John F. Kennedy, México ... D411
Escuela Lomas Altas S.C., México ... D411
Escuela Mexicana Americana, A. C., México ... D411
Escuela Panamericana, El Salvador ... D408
Escuela Particular Liceo Panamericano - Sede Centenario, Ecuador ... D406
Escuela Privada Ranelagh, Argentina ... D427
Escuela Secundaria y Preparatoria de la Ciudad de Mexico, México ... D411
Escuela Suiza de Barcelona, Spain ... D375
Escuela y Liceo Elbio Fernandez, Uruguay ... D438
Escula Argentina Modelo - Sede EAM / Sede NORTE, Argentina ... D427
ESF Abacus International Kindergarten, Hong Kong, China ... D282
ESF Beacon Hill School, Hong Kong, China ... D282

Index

ESF Bradbury School, Hong Kong, China D282
ESF Clearwater Bay School, Hong Kong, China D282
ESF Discovery College, Hong Kong, China D282
ESF Glenealy School, Hong Kong, China D282
ESF Hillside International Kindergarten, Hong Kong, China D282
ESF Island School, Hong Kong, China D282
ESF Jockey Club Sarah Roe School, Hong Kong, China D282
ESF Kennedy School, Hong Kong, China D282
ESF King George V School, Hong Kong, China D282
ESF Kowloon Junior School, Hong Kong, China D282
ESF Peak School, Hong Kong, China D282
ESF Quarry Bay School, Hong Kong, China D282
ESF Renaissance College, Hong Kong, China D282
ESF Sha Tin College, Hong Kong, China D282
ESF Sha Tin Junior School, Hong Kong, China D282
ESF South Island School, Hong Kong, China D282
ESF Tsing Yi International Kindergarten, Hong Kong, China D283
ESF Tung Chung International Kindergarten, Hong Kong, China D283
ESF West Island School, Hong Kong, China D283
ESF Wu Kai Sha International Kindergarten, Hong Kong, China D283
Eskisehir Gelisim Okullari, Türkiye D383
Esprit International School, USA D421
Eton College, UK D389
Eton International School, Philippines D314
Eton, SC, México D411
EtonHouse International School Suzhou, China D273
EtonHouse International School Times Residence, Chengdu, China D273
EtonHouse International School, Broadrick, Singapore D321
EtonHouse International School, Claymore, Singapore D321
EtonHouse International School, Foshan, China D273
EtonHouse International School, Islander, Singapore D321
EtonHouse International School, Mountbatten 223, Singapore D321
EtonHouse International School, Mountbatten 717, Singapore D321
EtonHouse International School, Mountbatten 718, Singapore D321
EtonHouse International School, Nanjing, China D273
EtonHouse International School, Newton, Singapore D322
EtonHouse International School, Orchard, Singapore D322
EtonHouse International School, Riverside, China D273
EtonHouse International School, Robertson Walk, Singapore D322
EtonHouse International School, Sentosa, Singapore D322
Etonhouse International School, Thomson, Singapore D322
EtonHouse International School, Upper Bukit Timah, Singapore D322
EtonHouse International School, Vanda, Singapore D322
EtonHouse International School, Zhong Hua, Singapore D322
Etqan Global Academy, Qatar D316
Etu King's Kindergarten of Wuhan, China D273
Eurecole, France D352
Euroamerican College, Peru D437
Eurocolegio Casvi Boadilla, Spain D375
Eurocolegio Casvi Villaviciosa, Spain D375
Europa-Schule Kairo, Egypt D250
Europaskolan in Södermalm, Sweden D379
European Azerbaijan School, Azerbaijan D347
European Gymnasium, Russian Federation D369
European High School BRG 15, Austria D346
European Interactive School (DES), Greece D357
European International School, India D287
European International School HCMC, Vietnam 52, D335
European International School of Barcelona, Spain D375
European Middle School, Austria D346
European School, Costa Rica D404
European School, Georgia D354
European School Bergen, Netherlands D363
European School Brussels I, Belgium D347
European School Brussels II, Belgium D347
European School Brussels III, Belgium D347
European School Karlsruhe, Germany D354
European School Munich, Germany D354
European School of Bruxelles-Argenteuil, Belgium D347
European School of Frankfurt, Germany D354
European School of Helsinki, Finland D351
European School of Luxembourg, Luxembourg D362
European School of Mol, Belgium D347
European School of Varese, Italy D359
European School RheinMain gGmbH, Germany D354
Everest International School, Japan, Japan D300
Everest School Monteclaro, Spain D375
Evolution International School, Egypt D250
Excelsior American School, India D287
Exploratory Model Primary School, China D273
Exupery International School, Latvia D361
Eyüboglu Atasehir Primary School, Türkiye D383
Eyüboglu Kemerburgaz Middle School, Türkiye D383
Eyüboglu Kemerburgaz Preschool & Primary School, Türkiye D383
Eyüboglu Schools, Türkiye D383
Ezgililer Private Primary School, Türkiye D383

F

Fahaheel Al Watanieh Indian Private School, Kuwait D305
Fairgreen International School, United Arab Emirates D330
Fairmont Private School of Fresno, USA D415
Fairmont Private Schools - Anaheim Hills Campus, USA D415
Fairmont Private Schools - Historic Anaheim Campus, USA D415
Fairmont Private Schools - North Tustin Campus, USA D415
Fairmont Private Schools - Preparatory Academy, USA D415
Fairview International School Ipoh (FISI), Malaysia D308
Fairview International School Johor Bahru (FISJB), Malaysia D308
Fairview International School Kuala Lumpur (FISKL), Malaysia D308
Fairview International School Penang (FISP), Malaysia D308
Fairview International School Subang Jaya (FISJ), Malaysia D308
Fairview International School, Bridge of Allan, UK D389
Faith Academy, Philippines D314
Faith Christian School, Paraguay D436
Faith Lutheran College, Australia D339
Falcon College, Zimbabwe D266
Falcon International School, Costa Rica D404
FAMAKS British Schools, Nigeria D259
Far Eastern Private School, United Arab Emirates D330
Farlington School, UK D389
Farringtons School, UK D389
Fazlani L'Académie Globale, India D287
Felixstowe International College, UK D389
Felsted School, UK D390
Fern Hill School, Canada D402
FES Futures British School, Egypt D250
FES Futures International School, Egypt D250
FES L'Ecole de l'Avenir, Egypt D250
Fettes College, UK D390
Fettes College Guangzhou, China D273
Feyziye Mektepleri Vakfi Isik Okullari, Türkiye D383
Feza Schools, Tanzania D264
Finborough School, UK D390
Finland International School (FIS) Thane, India D287
Finnish Schools International, Kosovo D361
Fintona Girls' School, Australia D339
Firbank Grammar School - Brighton Campus, Australia D339
Firbank Grammar School - Sandringham Campus, Australia D339
First Steps School and Nursery, United Arab Emirates D330
FirstSteps School, India D287
Fleming College, Peru D437
Florence Bilingual School, Italy D359
Florida Day School, Argentina D427
FLS Personalized Innovative Education Preschool, China D273
FMV Ayazaga Isik High School, Türkiye D383
FMV Ayazaga Isik Primary & Middle School, Türkiye D383
FMV Erenköy Isik High School, Türkiye D383
FMV Erenköy Isik Primary & Middle School, Türkiye D384
FMV Isik High School, Türkiye D384
FMV Isik Primary & Middle School, Türkiye D384
FMV Ispartakule Isik High School, Türkiye D384
FMV Ispartakule Isik Primary & Middle School, Türkiye D384
Foley's Grammar and Junior School, Cyprus D349
Footprints International School, Cambodia D270
Foremarke School Dubai, United Arab Emirates D330
Forest International School, France D352
Forest Ridge School of the Sacred Heart, USA D422
Foresta International School, México D411
Formus, México D411
Forum Private Institute and Language Centre, Cyprus D349
Fosco International School (FIS), Vietnam D335
Foundation Public School, Pakistan D313
Foundation Public School - O Level Defence Campus, Pakistan D313
Fountain International School, Philippines D314
Fountain Valley School of Colorado, USA D416
Fountainhead School, India D287
Four-Forest Bilingual International School – LMS, Switzerland D380
Four-Forest Bilingual International School – Luzern, Switzerland D380
Four-Forest Bilingual International School – Zug, Switzerland D380
Foxcroft Academy, USA D418
Fräi-Ëffentlech Waldorfschoul Lëtzebuerg, Luxembourg D362
Framlingham College, UK D390
Franconian International School, Germany D354
Frankfurt International School, Germany D355
Frankfurt International School (Wiesbaden Campus), Germany D355
Franklin St Louis De Gonzague, France D352
Franz Liszt Schule, Costa Rica D404
Fraser Valley School, Canada D400

Index

Fravashi International Academy, India ...D287
Freies Gymnasium Zürich, Switzerland ...D380
French American International School & International High School, USA ...D415
French American International School of Boca Raton, USA ...D416
French American School of Princeton, USA ...D419
French American School of Puget Sound, USA ...D422
French International High School Vientiane, Laos ...D306
French International School, Hong Kong, China ...D283
French international School of Amman, Jordan ...D304
French International School of Oregon, USA ...D421
French International School of Philadelphia EFIP, USA ...D421
French School of Detroit, USA ...D419
French-American School of New York, USA ...D420
French-American School of Silicon Valley, USA ...D415
Frensham Heights, UK ...D390
Froebel's International School, Pakistan ...D313
Fujairah Private Academy, United Arab Emirates ...D330
Fukuoka Daiichi High School, Japan ...D300
Fukuoka International School, Japan ...D300
Fulham School, UK ...D390
Fulneck School, UK ...D390
Fundación Colegio Americano de Puebla, México ...D411
Fundacion Gimnasio Ingles de Armenia (GI SCHOOL), Colombia ...D434
Fundación Gimnasio Los Portales, Colombia ...D434
Fundacion Liceo Ingles (Pereira), Colombia ...D434
Fundación Nuevo Marymount, Colombia ...D434
Fundacion Privada Oak House School, Spain ...D375
Funful Sear Rogers International School, Hong Kong, China ...D283
Funtaj International School, Nigeria ...D259
Futuraskolan International School of Stockholm, Sweden ...D379
Future Bilingual Schools, Kuwait ...D305
Future International Academy, United Arab Emirates ...D330
Fuzhou International Preschool @ 1 Park Avenue, China ...D273
Fuzhou Lakeside International School, China ...D273
Fyling Hall School, UK ...D390

G

G D Goenka Global School, India ...D287
G D Goenka World School, India ...D287
G Global School, India ...D287
G. T. (Ellen Yeung) College, Hong Kong, China ...D283
Gaborone International School, Botswana ...D248
Galaxy International School, Ghana ...D254
Galaxy International School, Kazakhstan ...D304
Galaxy International School Uganda, Uganda ...D265
Galilee International School, Hong Kong, China ...D283
Gandaki Boarding School, Nepal ...D311
Gandhi Memorial Intercontinental School, Bali, Indonesia ...D296
Gandhi Memorial Intercontinental School, Jakarta, Indonesia ...D296
Garden International School, Malaysia ...D308
Garden International School (Bangkok campus), Thailand ...D325
Garden International School (Rayong Campus), Thailand ...D325
Garden International School Kuantan, Malaysia ...D308
Garden Kids School, Dominican Republic ...D405
Garodia International Centre for Learning, India ...D287
Gateway College Colombo, Sri Lanka ...D323
Gateway College Dehiwala, Sri Lanka ...D323
Gateway College Kandy, Sri Lanka ...D323
Gateway College Negombo, Sri Lanka ...D323
Gateway International Montessori School, Egypt ...D250
Gateway International School, India ...D287
Gazi University Foundation Private High School, Türkiye ...D384
Gaziantep Kolej Vakfi Cemil Alevli College, Türkiye ...D384
GCB - Bilingüe Internacional, Colombia ...D434
GDQ International Christian School, Albania ...D346
GDUFS International School Guangzhou, China ...D273
Geelong Grammar School - Bostock House, Australia ...D339
Geelong Grammar School - Corio Campus, Australia ...D339
Geelong Grammar School - Timbertop, Australia ...D339
Geelong Grammar School - Toorak Campus, Australia ...D339
Geitonas School, Greece ...D357
GEMS Academy Alexandria, Egypt ...D250
GEMS Akademia International School, India ...D288
GEMS Al Barsha National School, United Arab Emirates ...D330
GEMS Al Khaleej International School, United Arab Emirates ...D330
GEMS American Academy - Abu Dhabi, United Arab Emirates ...D330
GEMS American Academy - Qatar, Qatar ...D316
GEMS British International School - Madinaty, Egypt ...D250
GEMS British School - Al Rehab, Egypt ...D250
GEMS Cambridge International Private School - Sharjah, United Arab Emirates ...D330
GEMS Cambridge International School - Abu Dhabi, United Arab Emirates ...D330
GEMS Cambridge International School - Dubai, United Arab Emirates ...D330
GEMS Cambridge International School - Kampala, Uganda ...D265
GEMS Cambridge International School, Batala, India ...D288
GEMS Cambridge International School, Hoshiarpur, India ...D288
GEMS Dubai American Academy, United Arab Emirates ...D330
GEMS FirstPoint School, United Arab Emirates ...D330
GEMS Founder School - Mizhar, United Arab Emirates ...D330
GEMS Founders School - Dubai, United Arab Emirates ...D330
GEMS Genesis International School, India ...D288
GEMS International School - Al Khail, United Arab Emirates ...D330
GEMS International School - Cairo, Egypt ...D250
GEMS International School, Gurgaon, India ...D288
GEMS Jumeirah College, United Arab Emirates ...D330
GEMS Jumeirah Primary School, United Arab Emirates ...D330
GEMS Legacy School, United Arab Emirates ...D330
GEMS Metropole School - Al Waha, United Arab Emirates ...D330
GEMS Metropole School - Dubai, United Arab Emirates ...D330
GEMS Millennium School - Sharjah, United Arab Emirates ...D330
GEMS Modern Academy - Dubai, United Arab Emirates ...D330
GEMS Modern Academy - Kochi, India ...D288
GEMS Modern Academy, Gurgaon, India ...D288
GEMS New Millennium School - Al Khail, United Arab Emirates ...D330
GEMS Our Own English High School - Al Ain, United Arab Emirates ...D330
GEMS Our Own English High School - Boys, United Arab Emirates ...D330
GEMS Our Own English High School - Dubai, United Arab Emirates ...D331
GEMS Our Own English High School - Girls, United Arab Emirates ...D331
GEMS Our Own High School - Al Warqa'a, United Arab Emirates ...D331
GEMS Our Own Indian School - Dubai, United Arab Emirates ...D331
GEMS Royal Dubai School, United Arab Emirates ...D331
GEMS United Indian School, United Arab Emirates ...D331
GEMS Wellington Academy - Al Khail, United Arab Emirates ...D331
GEMS Wellington Academy - Silicon Oasis, United Arab Emirates ...D331
GEMS Wellington International School, United Arab Emirates ...D331
GEMS Wellington School - Qatar, Qatar ...D316
GEMS Westminster School - Ras Al Khaimah, United Arab Emirates ...D331
GEMS Westminster School - Sharjah, United Arab Emirates ...D331
GEMS Winchester School - Abu Dhabi, United Arab Emirates ...D331
GEMS Winchester School - Dubai, United Arab Emirates ...D331
GEMS Winchester School - Fujairah, United Arab Emirates ...D331
GEMS World Academy - Abu Dhabi, United Arab Emirates ...D331
GEMS World Academy - Dubai, United Arab Emirates ...D331
GEMS World Academy Chicago, USA ...D417
Genazzano FCJ College, Australia ...D339
Genesee Academy, USA ...D419
Genesis College, Romania ...D368
Genesis Global School, India ...D288
Genesis International Schools, Egypt ...D250
Genesis Schools, Tanzania ...D264
Geneva English School, Switzerland ...D380
Genius School Lalitpur, Nepal ...D311
George School, USA ...D421
George Washington Academy, Morocco ...D257
George Washington School, Colombia ...D434
George Watson's College, UK ...D390
Georgetown International Academy, Guyana ...D435
Geraldton Grammar School, Australia ...D339
German Embassy School Addis Ababa, Ethiopia ...D253
German Embassy School Tehran (DBST), Iran ...D298
German European School Manila, Philippines ...D314
German European School Singapore (GESS), Singapore ...D322
German International School Accra, Ghana ...D254
German International School Beirut, Lebanon ...D307
German International School Boston, USA ...D419
German International School Chennai, India ...D288
German International School Chicago, USA ...D417
German International School Dubai, United Arab Emirates ...D331
German International School of Portland, USA ...D421
German International School Sharjah, United Arab Emirates ...D331
German International School Sydney, Australia ...D339
German International School Toronto, Canada ...D402
German International School Washington D.C., USA ...D418
German School Abu Dhabi, United Arab Emirates ...D331
German School Nairobi (Michael Grzimek Schule), Kenya ...D255
German School of Rome, Italy ...D359
German Swiss International School, Hong Kong, China ...D283
Ghana Christian International High School, Ghana ...D254
Ghana International School, Ghana ...D254
Gifted Minds International School, Netherlands ...D363
Giggleswick School, UK ...D390
Gimnasio Británico, Colombia ...D434
Gimnasio Campestre la Fontana, Colombia ...D434

Index

Gimnasio Campestre Los Cerezos, Colombia D434
Gimnasio Campestre Montería, Colombia D434
Gimnasio Campestre San Rafael, Colombia D434
Gimnasio Cantillana, Colombia D434
Gimnasio Contemporaneo, Colombia D434
Gimnasio de Los Cerros, Colombia D434
Gimnasio del Norte, Colombia D434
Gimnasio El Hontanar, Colombia D434
Gimnasio Femenino, Colombia D434
Gimnasio Fontana, Colombia D434
Gimnasio Los Alcázares, Colombia D434
Gimnasio Los Pinares, Colombia D434
Gimnasio Los Pinos, Colombia D434
Gimnasio Vermont, Colombia D434
Gimnazija Bezigrad, Slovenia D370
Girne American University, Cyprus D349
GIS SP - The International School of São Paulo, Brazil D430
GIS The International School of Monza srl, Italy D359
GISSV German International School of Silicon Valley, USA D415
Gjøvikregionen International School, Norway D364
GJR International School, India D288
Glenalmond College, Perth, UK D390
Glendale Academy, Sun City, India D288
Glendale International School, Tellapur, India D288
Glenlyon Norfolk School, Canada D400
Glisten International Academy, Nigeria D259
Global Academy International, Qatar D316
Global City International School, India D288
Global English School - Calicut, India D288
Global Indian International School (GIIS) Uppal Campus, India D288
Global Indian International School (GIIS) Abu Dhabi Campus, United Arab Emirates D331
Global Indian International School (GIIS) Ahmedabad Campus, India D288
Global Indian International School (GIIS) Balewadi Campus, India D288
Global Indian International School (GIIS) Bangkok Campus, Thailand D325
Global Indian International School (GIIS) Bannerghatta Campus, India D288
Global Indian International School (GIIS) Dubai Campus, United Arab Emirates D331
Global Indian International School (GIIS) East Coast Campus, Singapore D322
Global Indian International School (GIIS) Hadapsar Campus, India D288
Global Indian International School (GIIS) Higashi Kasai Campus, Japan D300
Global Indian International School (GIIS) Kuala Lumpur Campus, Malaysia D308
Global Indian International School (GIIS) Nishi Kasai Campus, Japan D300
Global Indian International School (GIIS) Noida Campus, India D288
Global Indian International School (GIIS) Seishincho Campus, Japan D300
Global Indian International School (GIIS) SMART Campus, Singapore D322
Global Indian International School (GIIS) Surat Campus, India D288
Global Indian International School (GIIS) Vietnam Campus, Vietnam D335
Global Indian International School (GIIS) Whitefield Campus, India D288
Global Indian School, Ajman, United Arab Emirates D331
Global International Secondary School & College, Nigeria D259
Global Jaya School, Indonesia D296
Global Paradigm Baccalaureate School, Egypt D250
Global Paradigm International School, Egypt D251
Global Sevilla - Pulo Mas Campus, Indonesia D296
Global Sevilla - Puri Indah Campus, Indonesia D296
Global United School, Iraq D299
Godolphin and Latymer School, UK D390
Godolphin School, UK D390
Godspell College, Argentina D427
Goethe Schule, Argentina D427
Gökkusagi Koleji - Bahçelievler, Türkiye D384
Gökkusagi Koleji - Bahçesehir, Türkiye D384
Gökkusagi Koleji - Beylikdüzü, Türkiye D384
Gökkusagi Koleji - Ümraniye, Türkiye D384
Goldcrest International, India D288
Golden Apple International Preschool and Kindergarten, China D273
Golden Apple Jincheng No. 1 Secondary School, China D273
Golden Apple New Montessori Kindergarten (Jincheng Lake), China D273
Golden Apple Tianfu International Preschool and Kindergarten, China D274
Golden Gate American School, Cambodia D270
Golden Grove Lutheran Primary School, Australia D339
Golden Hills School, USA D415
Golden Valley School, Costa Rica D404
Gonzaga International School, Italy D359
Good Hope Country Day School, Virgin Islands (US) D423
Good News Lutheran College, Australia D339
Good Shepherd International School, India D288
Good Shepherd Lutheran College - Howard Springs Campus, Australia D339
Good Shepherd Lutheran College - Leanyer Campus, Australia D339
Good Shepherd Lutheran College - Noosa, Australia D339
Good Shepherd Lutheran College - Palmerston Campus, Australia D339
Good Shepherd Lutheran School - Angaston, Australia D339
Goodwill Children Private School, United Arab Emirates D331
Gordon International School, Papua New Guinea D344
Gordonstoun, UK D390
Goroka International School, Papua New Guinea D344
Gosfield School, UK D390
GPS Brookes Kochi, India D288
Grace Christian Academy, Cayman Islands D404
Grace Christian College, Australia D339
Grace International School, Bangladesh D269
Grace International School, Thailand D325
Graded - The American School of São Paulo, Brazil D430
Gradinita BritAcademy Sector 2, Romania D368
Granada Preparatory School, USA D415
Grand Canadian Academy (GCA Jiaxing), China D274
Grand Lycée Franco-Libanais Beyrouth, Lebanon D307
Grandeur International School, Mozambique D258
Grange School, Nigeria D259
Grantham Preparatory International School, UK D390
Grassroots Global School, India D288
Great International School, Brazil D430
Greater Grace International School of Budapest, Hungary D358
Green Heights International School, Egypt D251
Green Hills Academy, Rwanda D261
Green Hills Elementary School/Junior High School, Japan D300
Green Hills International School, Saudi Arabia D320
Green Land - Pré Vert International Schools - GPIS-Egypt, Egypt D251
Green Oasis School, China D274
Green School Bali, Indonesia D296
Green Valley School, Spain D375
Greene's College Oxford, UK D390
Greene's College Oxford, Estoril, Portugal D366
Greenfield College, Lebanon D307
Greenfield International School, United Arab Emirates D331
Greenfields Independent Day & Boarding School, UK D390
Greengates School, México 222, D411
Greenleaves Montessori International School, Spain D375
Greenoak International School, Nigeria D259
Greensprings School, Lagos, Nigeria D259
Greensteds International School, Kenya D255
Greenville International School, México D411
Greenwood Bay College, South Africa D262
Greenwood Garden School, Italy D359
Greenwood High International School, India D288
Greenwood International School, United Arab Emirates D331
GREGG International School, Japan D300
Grenville Primary School, Nigeria D259
Grenville Secondary School, Nigeria D259
Gresham's Nursery and Pre-Prep School, UK D390
Gresham's Prep School, UK D390
Gresham's Senior School, UK D390
GRESOL International-American School, Spain D375
Groupe Scolaire Al Karaouiyine, Morocco D257
Groupe Scolaire International Les Nouvelles Générations, Tunisia D265
Groupe Scolaire Jean de la Fontaine, Germany D355
Groupe Scolaire L'Ardoise, Cote d'Ivoire D248
Groupe Scolaire La Résidence, Morocco D257
GSD International School Buitrago, Spain D375
GSD International School Costa Rica, Costa Rica D404
GSD Las Rozas, Spain D375
Guangdong Country Garden School, China D274
Guangdong Shunde Desheng School, China D274
Guangzhou Huamei International School, China D274
Guangzhou International Kindergarten Huangpu ZWIE, China D274
Guangzhou International Middle School Huangpu ZWIE, China D274
Guangzhou International Primary School Baiyun ZWIE, China D274
Guangzhou International Primary School Huangpu ZWIE, China D274
Guangzhou SCA School, China D274
Guerin Catholic High School, USA D418
Guide Academy, USA D415
Guildhouse School, UK D390
Guiyang Huaxi Country Garden International School, China D274
Gulf Asian English School, United Arab Emirates D331

Index

Gulf British Academy, Kuwait D305
Gulf English School, Kuwait....D305
Gulf Model School, United Arab Emirates D331
Gulliver Academy Middle School, USA D416
Gulliver Preparatory School, USA D416
Gunma Kokusai Academy, Japan D300
Gutenberg Schule, Ecuador....D407
Gyeonggi Academy of Foreign Languages, Republic of Korea....D318
Gyeonggi Suwon International School, Republic of Korea D318
Gyeongnam International Foreign School, Republic of Korea D318
Gymnasium A+, Ukraine D398
Gymnasium Evolution, Czech Republic....D350
Gymnasium im Stift Neuzelle, Germany....D355
Gymnasium, Wirtschafts- und Fachmittelschule Thun, Switzerland D380
Gymnázium Duhovka, Czech Republic....D350

H

H-FARM International School, Italy 119, D359
H-International School Rosà, Italy....D359
H-International School Vicenza, Italy....D359
Hackley School, USA....D420
Hadhramaut International Schools, Yemen D336
HAEF, Athens College, Greece....D357
HAEF, Athens College Elementary, Greece....D357
HAEF, John M. Carras Kindergarten, Greece D357
HAEF, Psychico College, Greece....D357
HAEF, Psychico College Elementary, Greece D357
Haileybury, Australia....D339
Haileybury, UK 115, D390
Haileybury Almaty, Kazakhstan....D304
Haileybury Astana, Kazakhstan....D304
Haileybury Rendall School, Australia D339
Hailiang Foreign Language School, China....D274
Hainan Micro-City Future School, China D274
Hala International School, Saudi Arabia....D320
Halcyon London International School, UK....D390
Halifax Grammar School, Canada D401
Halifield Schools, Nigeria....D259
Hamelin-Laie International School Barcelona, Spain 116, D375
Hamilton Hill International Kindergarten, Hong Kong, China....D283
Hamilton International School, Qatar....D316
Han Academy, Hong Kong, China....D283
Hangzhou Binjiang Wickham Kindergarten, China....D274
Hangzhou Dipont School of Arts and Science, China D274
Hangzhou Future Sci-Tech City Wickham Kindergarten, China....D274
Hangzhou Greentown Yuhua Qinqin School, China....D274
Hangzhou Greentown Yuhua School, China D274
Hangzhou Huamei Wickham Kindergarten, China....D274
Hangzhou International School, China....53, D274
Hangzhou Shanghai World Foreign Language School, China....D274
Hangzhou Victoria Kindergarten (Jiarun), China....D274
Hangzhou Victoria Kindergarten (Landscape Bay), China....D274
Hangzhou Weiyou Guotai Preschool, China D274
Hangzhou Wesley School (Binjiang Campus), China D274
Hangzhou Wesley School (Early Education Center), China D274
Hangzhou Wesley School (Gongshu/Blue Peacock Campus), China D274
Hangzhou Wesley School (Shangcheng/Jianggan Campus), China D274
Hangzhou Wickham International School, China....D274
Hangzhou World Foreign Language School, China....D274
Hanoi Academy, Vietnam....D335
Hanoi International School, Vietnam....D335
Hansa-Gymnasium, Hamburg-Bergedorf, Germany D355
Happy Days School & Freedom High School, Honduras D435
Happy Home School- O Level Maryam Faruqi Campus, Pakistan D313
Happykids Kindergarten, China....D274
Harare International School, Zimbabwe....D266
Harfa International School, Croatia D349
Hariri High School II, Lebanon D307
Harmony School, México D411
Harrisburg Academy, USA....D421
Harrogate Ladies' College, UK D390
Harrow Innovation Leadership Academy Chongqing, China D274
Harrow Innovation Leadership Academy Nanning, China....D275
Harrow Innovation Leadership Academy Zhuhai (Hengqin), China....D275
Harrow International School Appi, Japan....D300
Harrow International School Bangkok, Thailand D325
Harrow International School Bengaluru, India D288
Harrow International School Hong Kong, Hong Kong, China D283
Harrow International School Shanghai, China....D275
Harrow International School Shenzhen (Qianhai), China D275
Hartland International School, United Arab Emirates D331
Harvest International School, India D288
Harvest International School, India D288
Hastings School, Azulinas, Spain D375
Hastings School, Bendición de Campos, Spain....D375
Hastings School, Lorenzo Solano Tendero, Spain D375
Hastings School, Manuel Marañón, Spain....D375
Hastings School, Paseo de la Habana, Spain....D375
Hastings School, Sobradiel, Spain....D375
Hattemer Bilingue Paris 16e, France....D352
Hattemer Bilingue Paris 8e, France....D352
Haut-Lac International Bilingual School, Switzerland....118, D380
Haven of Peace Academy, Tanzania....D264
Hawar International School, Bahrain....D268
Hay Al Sharooq International School, Oman D312
Hayah International Academy, Egypt....D251
Hayat Universal School (HUBS), Qatar....D316
HD Beijing School, China....D275
Headfort School, Ireland....D358
Headington Rye Oxford, UK....D390
Headstart School, Kuri Campus, Pakistan....D313
Healthy-Mind International School, Ghana....D254
Heathfield International School, Thailand....D325
Heathfield School, UK....D390
Hebron School, India....D288
Hefei Run'an Boarding School, China D275
Hefei Shanghai World Foreign Language School, China....D275
Hefei Xinhua Academy, China....D275
Heidelberg International School, Germany D355
Helderberg International School, South Africa D262
HELP International School HIS, Malaysia D308
Helsingin Suomalainen Yhteiskoulu, Finland....D351
Henan Jianye Little Harvard Bilingual School, China D275
Hengyang Royal Kindergarten, China....D275
Heritage International School, Egypt....D251
Heritage Xperiential Learning School, Gurgaon, India D288
Herlufsholm Skole, Denmark....D350
Hermann Oberth International German School, Romania....D368
HFS International Powai, India D288
HH Shaikh Rashid Al Maktoum Pakistan School, Dubai, United Arab Emirates....D331
HIBISCUS International School, Malaysia D308
Hickory Day School, USA D420
High Meadows School, USA D417
Highgate Private School, Cyprus D349
Highlands International School, Bolivia....D428
Highlands Lutheran International School, Papua New Guinea D344
Hilal International Academy, Somalia....D262
Hill House, UK....D390
Hill Spring International School, India D288
Hillcrest Preparatory School, Kenya D255
Hillcrest School, Indonesia D296
Hillcrest School (Jos), Nigeria....D259
Hillcrest Secondary School, Kenya D255
Hillel Academy, Jamaica....D409
Hills Grammar, Australia....D339
Hills International College, Australia....D339
Hillside Academy, India....D288
Hillview International School, Malawi....D256
Hilton College, South Africa D262
Himalayan International Residential School, India D288
Himalayan WhiteHouse IB World School, Nepal....D311
Himali Boarding School, India....D288
Hindustan International School, India D288
Hiram Bingham, The British International School of Lima, Peru D437
Hiroshima International School, Japan D300
Hisar School, Türkiye....D384
HKCA Po Leung Kuk School, Hong Kong, China D283
HKMA David Li Kwok Po College, Hong Kong, China D283
HLC International - Chennai, India D289
Hochalpines Institut Ftan (HIF), Switzerland....D380
Hockerill Anglo-European College, UK 120, D390
Hoi An International School, Vietnam 54, D335
Hokkaido International School, Japan....D300
Hokkaido International School, Niseko, Japan D300
Hollandse School Singapore, Singapore D322
Holmberg Schule, Argentina....D427
Hölters Schule Villa Ballester, Argentina D427
Holy Family School, USA....D423
Holy Mary British Catholic School, Spain....D375
Holy Trinity College, Argentina D427
Holy Trinity Primary School, Australia....D339
Hong Kong Academy, Hong Kong, China 55, D283
Hong Kong International School, Hong Kong, China D283
Hong Qiao International School, China....D275
Hong Wen Senior High School, Taiwan....D323
Hongwen School, Qingdao Campus, China D275

Index

Hongwen School, Shanghai Campus, China D275
Hope Academy, Indonesia D296
Hope Academy of Bishkek, Kyrgyzstan D306
Hope Christian High School, Philippines D314
HOPE International School, Cambodia D270
Hope International School, Tanzania D264
Horizon Academy Sendai Campus, Japan D300
Horizon English School, United Arab Emirates D331
Horizon High School, South Africa D262
Horizon International Bilingual School - Hanoi Campus, Vietnam D335
Horizon International Bilingual School - HCMC Campus, Vietnam D335
Horizon International School, Saudi Arabia D320
Horizon International School, United Arab Emirates D331
Horizon Japan International School, Japan D300
Hosei University Kokusai High School, Japan D301
Houssam Eddine Hariri High School, Lebanon D307
Hout Bay International School, South Africa D262
HPC International School, Germany D355
Hsinchu International School, Taiwan D323
HSV International Primary School - KSS Location, Netherlands D363
HSV International Primary School - NSL Location, Netherlands D363
HSV International Primary School - VNS Location, Netherlands D363
Hua Hin International School, Thailand D325
Huanan Country Garden International Kindergarten, China D275
Huanui College, New Zealand D343
Huawai-Tongman Foreign Language School (SCNUFL-TM), China D275
Hübschmann Zhan International School, China D275
Huda School and Montessori, USA D419
Huili School Shanghai, China D275
Hull's School, Switzerland D380
Human International School, Mongolia D310
Humanitas High School, Australia D339
Humanitree, México D411
Hunter Valley Grammar School, Australia D339
Hurdco International School, Bangladesh D269
Hurst College, UK D390
HUS International School, India D289
HVB Global Academy, India D289
Hwa Chong International School, Singapore D322
HWA International School, Singapore D322
Hyundai Foreign School, Republic of Korea D318

I

I-Shou International School, Taiwan D323
I.E.S. Clot de la Illot, Spain D375
I.M. Panagiotopoulos School, Greece D357
Iale International School, L'Eliana, Spain D375
Ibadan International School, Nigeria D259
Ibn Khuldoon National School, Bahrain D268
IBN Rushd National Academy, Jordan D304
IBSM - International Bilingual School Munich gGmbH, Germany D355
iCademy Middle East, United Arab Emirates D331
iCAN British International School, Cambodia D270
Ichthus School - West Campus, Indonesia D296
ICS Côte d'Azur, France 121, D352
ICS London, UK 122, D390
ICS Milan, Italy 123, D359
ICS Paris, France 124, D352
Ideal Education School, Kuwait D305
Idrak Lyceum, Azerbaijan D347
IDV Özel Bilkent High School, Türkiye D384
IDV Özel Bilkent Middle School, Türkiye D384
IDV Özel Bilkent Primary School, Türkiye D384
IE Pedro Ruiz Gallo, Peru D437
IELEV Private High School, Türkiye D384
IES College, Australia D339
IGB International School, Malaysia D308
Ikuei Nishi Jr. & Sr. High School, Japan D301
ILBC IGCSE & A Level School, Myanmar D310
Ilma International Girl's School, Sri Lanka D323
Ilmesters Academy, Pakistan D313
Immaculate Conception Academy, Philippines D314
Immanuel College, Australia D339
Immanuel Gawler, Australia D339
Immanuel Primary School, Australia D339
Impington International College, UK 125, D391
Independent Bonn International School, Germany D355
Independent School Seychelles, Seychelles D261
India International School, India D289
India International School, India D289
India International School in Japan, Japan D301
India Kids School, India D289
Indian Central School, Kuwait D305
Indian Educational School, Kuwait D305
Indian High School, United Arab Emirates D331
Indian School Al Buraimi, Oman D312
Indian School Al Ghubra, Oman D312
Indian School Muscat, Oman D312
Indian School Ras Al Khaimah, United Arab Emirates D331
Indian School Rustaq, Oman D312
Indian School Thumrait, Oman D312
Indus International Primary School, India D289
Indus International School (Bangalore), India D289
Indus International School, Hyderabad, India D289
Indus International School, Pune, India D289
Innova Early Years Center, Yizhuang Campus, China D275
Inspire Academy, Nigeria D259
Institución Educativa Particular San Antonio de Padua, Peru D437
Institución Educativa Privada Lord Byron, Peru D437
Institucion Educativa SEK (San Estenislao de Kostka), Spain D375
Institut auf dem Rosenberg, Switzerland D380
Institut Aurora, Democratic Republic of the Congo D249
Institut Florimont, Switzerland D380
Institut Français de Thessalonique, Greece D357
Institut International de Lancy, Switzerland D381
Institut International Saint-Dominique, Italy 126, D359
Institut Le Châtelard, Switzerland 127, D381
Institut Le Rosey, Switzerland D381
Institut Montana Switzerland, Switzerland 128, D381
Institut Monte Rosa, Switzerland D381
Institut Sankt Joseph, Denmark D350
Institut Scolaire les Palmiers, Morocco D257
Institut Villa Pierrefeu, Switzerland D381
Institute of Applied Technology, United Arab Emirates D331
Institution Bilingue Montessori, Senegal D261
Institution El Yakada, Morocco D257
Instituto Alberto Einstein, Panama D436
Instituto Alemán Carlos Anwandter, Chile D432
Instituto Alemán de Osorno, Chile D432
Instituto Alemán Puerto Montt, Chile D432
Instituto Alexander Bain SC, México D411
Instituto Anglo Británico Campus Cumbres, México D411
Instituto Anglo Británico Campus La Fe, México D411
Instituto Ballester, Argentina D427
Instituto Bilingüe Rudyard Kipling, México D411
Instituto Bilingüe Victoria A.C., México D411
Instituto Cervantes, A.C., México D412
Instituto Chileno Britanico de Cultura, Chile D432
Instituto Cultural Domínico-Americano, Dominican Republic D405
Instituto D'Amicis, AC, México D412
Instituto Dr. Jaim Weizman, Costa Rica D404
Instituto Educacional Juan XXIII, Venezuela D438
Instituto Español Vicente Cañada Blanch, UK D391
Instituto GayLussac, Brazil D430
Instituto Iberia, Dominican Republic D405
Instituto Internacional Octavio Paz, México D412
Instituto Kipling de Irapuato, México D412
Instituto Leonardo Da Vinci, Dominican Republic D405
Instituto Ovalle Monday - Plantel Secundaria, México D412
Instituto para la Educación Integral del Bachiller (INEDIB), México D412
Instituto Piaget, México D412
Instituto Santa Brígida, Argentina D427
Instituto Saudi de Madrid, Spain D375
Instituto Tecnológico Sanmiguelense de Estudios Superiores, México D412
Instituto Thomas Jefferson, Campus Santa Monica, México D412
Instituto Thomas Jefferson, Campus Zona Esmeralda, México D412
Instituto Wolfsohn, Argentina D427
Insworld Institute, Singapore D322
Integrated Thebes American College in Cairo (ITACC), Egypt D251
Inter-American Academy Guayaquil, Ecuador D407
Inter-American School, Guatemala D409
Inter-Community School Zurich, Switzerland 129, D381
Internacional Aravaca, Spain D375
International Academic School, United Arab Emirates D331
International Academy of Kuwait, Kuwait D305
International Academy of Suriname, Suriname D438
International American School, Poland D365
International American School & University (AISU), Ukraine D398
International American School of Alexandria, Egypt D251
International Arab Egyptian School, Egypt D251
International Berckley School, Colombia D434
International Bilingual School of Provence, France 130, D352
International British Academy, Philippines D315
International British School, Kuwait D305
International British School of Bucharest, Romania D368
International British School Vocandus, Poland D365
International Christian School, Hong Kong, China D283

Index

International Christian School, Costa Rica D404
International Christian School Nonthaburi (ICSN), Thailand D325
International Christian School of Budapest, Hungary D358
International Christian School of Cascais, Portugal D366
International Christian School of Lomé, Togo D264
International Christian School of Vienna, Austria D346
International Christian School Pyeongtaek, Republic of Korea D318
International Christian School Uijeongbu, Republic of Korea D318
International College, Uruguay D438
International College Hong Kong, Hong Kong, China D283
International College Hong Kong - Hong Lok Yuen, Hong Kong, China D283
International College Lebanon, Ain Aar, Lebanon D307
International College Lebanon, Ras Beirut, Lebanon D307
International College of Continuous Education, Almaty, Kazakhstan D304
International College of Continuous Education, Astana, Kazakhstan D304
International College Spain, Spain D375
International College University School (ICUS) Baghdad, Iraq D299
International Community College, Ghana D254
International Community School, Jordan D304
International Community School, Thailand D325
International Community School, Singapore 56, D322
International Community School (ICS) Al Falah, United Arab Emirates D331
International Community School (ICS) City Centre, United Arab Emirates D331
International Community School (ICS) Khalidiya, United Arab Emirates D331
International Community School (ICS) Khalifa, United Arab Emirates D331
International Community School (ICS) Mushrif, United Arab Emirates D331
International Community School Ghana - Accra, Ghana D254
International Community School Ghana - Kumasi, Ghana D254
International Community School of Abidjan, Cote d'Ivoire D249
International Community School of Addis Ababa, Ethiopia D253
International Community School, Abuja, Nigeria D259
International Concept for Education (ICE Dubai), United Arab Emirates D331
International English School of Castellón, Spain D375
International European School Warsaw, Poland D365
International Fateh Academy, India D289
International French School of Amsterdam, Netherlands 131, D363
International German School HCMC, Vietnam D335
International Gymnasium Geithain, Germany D355
International Gymnasium Reinsdorf, Germany D355
International High School of Wroclaw, Poland D365
International Highschool Herzogberg, Austria D346
International Independent Schools IIS, Jordan D304
International Indian School - Jeddah, Saudi Arabia D320
International Islamic School, Malaysia D308
International IT College of Sweden, Sweden D379
International Kids Campus, Germany D355
International Learning Group School - ILG School, Kosovo D361
International Maarif Schools Erbil, Iraq D299
International Metropolitan School, Greece D357
International Montessori School, Belgium 132, D347
International Montessori School of Beijing, China D275
International Montessori School of Prague, Czech Republic D350
International New Future School (Neue Deutsche Schule Alexandria), Egypt D251
International Pioneers School, Thailand D325
International Pre School of Lund, Sweden D379
International Pre-School PLUS, Türkiye D384
International Preparatory School, Chile D432
International Preparatory School, Mauritius D257
International Primary School, Poland D365
International Primary School GSV, Netherlands D363
International Programs School, Saudi Arabia D320
International School, Serbia D369
International School 33, France D352
International School Aamby, India D289
International School Altdorf, Switzerland D381
International School Andalucía, Spain D375
International School Augsburg (ISA), Germany D355
International School Bangkok, Thailand D325
International School Basel, Switzerland D381
International School Benghazi, Libya D256
International School Braunschweig-Wolfsburg, Germany D355
International School Brescia, Italy D359
International School Brunei, Brunei Darussalam 57, D269
International School Carinthia, Austria D346
International School Cygnaeus, Finland D351
International School Delft, Netherlands D363
International School Dhaka (ISD), Bangladesh D269
International School Eastern Seaboard, Thailand D325
International School Edward Steichen, Luxembourg 133, D362
International School Eindhoven, Netherlands D363
International School Ghent, Belgium D347
International School Hannover Region, Germany D355
International School Ho Chi Minh City (ISHCMC), Vietnam 60, D335
International School Ho Chi Minh City (ISHCMC) - American Academy, Vietnam D335
International School Ikast-Brande, Denmark D350
International School in Novie Veshki, Russian Federation D369
International School Kashmir (ISK), India D289
International School Kufstein Tirol, Austria D346
International School Leiden, Netherlands 134, D363
International School Mainfranken e.V., Germany D355
International School Manila, Philippines D315
International School Maximilian, Macedonia D362
International School Nadi, Fiji D343
International School Nido de Aguilas, Chile D432
International School of Aarhus, Denmark D350
International School of Aberdeen, UK D391
International School of Accra, Ghana D254
International School of Africa, Ethiopia D253
International School of Ahafo, Ghana D254
International School of Almaty, Kazakhstan D305
International School of Amsterdam, Netherlands D363
International School of Arizona, USA D414
International School of Aruba, Aruba D400
International School of Astana, Kazakhstan D305
International School of Athens, Greece D357
International School of Barcelona, Spain D375
International School of Béarn, France D352
International School of Beijing-Shunyi, China D275
International School of Belgium, Belgium D347
International School of Belgrade, Serbia D369
International School of Bergamo, Italy 135, D359
International School of Bergen, Norway D364
International School of Berne, Switzerland D381
International School of Billund, Denmark D350
International School of Bologna, Italy D360
International School of Boston, USA D419
International School of Bremen, Germany D355
International School of Brno, Czech Republic D350
International School of Brooklyn, USA D420
International School of Broward - Charter School, USA D416
International School of Bucharest, Romania D368
International School of Budapest, Hungary D358
International School of Busan, Republic of Korea D318
International School of Cape Town, South Africa D262
International School of Carthage, Tunisia D265
International School of Catalunya (ISCAT), Spain D375
International School of Chonburi, Thailand D325
International School of Como, Italy 136, D360
International School of Creative Arts (ISCA), UK D391
International School of Creative Science, United Arab Emirates D332
International School of Curaçao, Curaçao D435
International School of Curitiba, Brazil D430
International School of Dakar, Senegal D261
International School of Debrecen (ISD), Hungary D358
International School of Denver, USA 224, D416
International School of Dongguan, China D275
International School of Dublin, Ireland D358
International School of Düsseldorf e.V., Germany 137, D355
International School of Elite Education, Egypt D251
International School of Estonia, Estonia D351
International School of Flanders, Belgium 138, D347
International School of Flanders (Tervuren Campus), Belgium D347
International School of Florence, Italy D360
International School of Gdansk, Poland D365
International School of Geneva (Campus des Nations), Switzerland D381
International School of Geneva (La Châtaigneraie Campus), Switzerland D381
International School of Geneva (La Grande Boissière Campus), Switzerland D381
International School of Hamburg, Germany D355
International School of Havana, Cuba D405
International School of Hellerup, Denmark D350
International School of Helsingborg, Sweden D379
International School of Helsinki, Finland D351
International School of Herzen University, Russian Federation D369
International School of Hyderabad, India D289
International School of Iceland, Iceland D358
International School of Indiana, USA D418
International School of Islamabad, Pakistan D313
International School of Kazan, Russian Federation D369
International School of Kenya, Kenya D255

Index

International School of Kigali, Rwanda	D261
International School of Krakow, Poland	D365
International School of Kreuzlingen Konstanz, Switzerland	D381
International School of Kuantan, Malaysia	D308
International School of Lago Patria, Italy	D360
International School of Larissa, Greece	D357
International School of Latvia, Latvia	D361
International School of Lausanne, Switzerland	139, D381
International School of Leuven, Belgium	D347
International School of London (ISL), UK	D391
International School of London (ISL) Qatar, Qatar	D316
International School of Los Angeles, USA	225, D415
International School of Lusaka, Zambia	D265
International School of Luxembourg, Luxembourg	D362
International School of Lyon, France	D352
International School of Madrid, Spain	140, D376
International School of Marseille, France	D353
International School of Milan, Italy	141, D360
International School of Modena, Italy	142, D360
International School of Monaco, Monaco	D362
International School of Monagas, Venezuela	D438
International School of Monza, Italy	143, D360
International School of Morocco, Morocco	D257
International School of Myanmar, Myanmar	D310
International School of Nagano, Japan	D301
International School of Nanshan Shenzhen, China	D275
International School of Neustadt, Germany	144, D355
International School of Nice, France	145, D353
International School of Ouagadougou, Burkina Faso	D248
International School of Palmela, Portugal	D366
International School of Panama, Panama	D436
International School of Paris, France	D353
International School of Phnom Penh, Cambodia	D270
International School of Piraeus, Greece	D357
International School of Portland, USA	D421
International School of Poznan, Poland	D365
International School of Prague, Czech Republic	D350
International School of Prishtina, Kosovo	D361
International School of Qingdao, China	D275
International School of Rheinfelden, Switzerland	D381
International School of Riga, Latvia	D361
International School of Rimini, Italy	D360
International School of Saint Lucia, Saint Lucia	D414
International School of Samara, Russian Federation	D369
International School of Schaffhausen, Switzerland	D381
International School of Siem Reap, Cambodia	D270
International School of Siena, Italy	146, D360
International School of South Africa, South Africa	D262
International School of Stavanger, Norway	D364
International School of Stuttgart, Degerloch Campus, Germany	D355
International School of Stuttgart, Sindelfingen Campus, Germany	D355
International School of Talents - Multicampus (IST), Italy	D360
International School of Tallinn, Estonia	D351
International School of Tanganyika, Tanzania	D264
International School of Texas, USA	D421
International School of the Gothenburg Region (ISGR), Sweden	D379
International School of the Sacred Heart, Japan	D301
International School of Tianjin, China	D275
International School of Ticino SA, Switzerland	147, D381
International School of Toulouse, France	D353
International School of Trieste, Italy	D360
International School of Tucson, USA	D414
International School of Turin, Italy	D360
International School of Uganda, Uganda	D265
International School of Ulaanbaatar, Mongolia	D310
International School of Ulm/Neu Ulm, Germany	D355
International School of Vantaa, Finland	D351
International School of Venice, Italy	D360
International School of Verona, Italy	D360
International School of Vietnam, Vietnam	D335
International School of Western Australia, Australia	84, D339
International School of Zanzibar, Tanzania	D264
International School of Zug & Luzern, Riverside Campus, Switzerland	D381
International School of Zug & Luzern, Zug Campus, Switzerland	D381
International School Olomouc, Czech Republic	D350
International School Premjers, Latvia	D361
International School Rheintal, Switzerland	D381
International School Ruhr, Germany	D355
International School Saigon Pearl, Vietnam	D335
International School San Patricio Toledo, Spain	148, D376
International School Seychelles, Seychelles	D261
International School Strasbourg, France	D353
International School Suva, Fiji	D343
International School Telemark, Norway	D364
International School The Rijnlands Lyceum Oegstgeest, Netherlands	D363
International School Turks and Caicos, Turks And Caicos Islands	D414
International School Twente, Netherlands	D363
International School Utrecht, Netherlands	D363
International School Westpfalz, Germany	149, D355
International School Zurich North (ISZN), Switzerland	150, D381
International School Zurich West, Switzerland	D381
International Schools Group (ISG) Dammam, Saudi Arabia	D320
International Schools Group (ISG) Jubail, Saudi Arabia	D320
International Schools of Egypt - Alexandria, Egypt	D251
International Schools of Kenana - American Division, Egypt	D251
International Schools of North America, Vietnam	D335
International Sharing School - Madeira, Portugal	D366
International Sharing School - Taguspark, Portugal	D367
International Talent Academy, Uzbekistan	D334
International University Demonstration School (IUDS), Cote d'Ivoire	D249
International Village School Chennai, India	D289
Internationale Deutsche Schule Brüssel, Belgium	D348
Internationale Deutsche Schule Paris (iDSP), France	D353
Internationales Stiftungsgymnasium Magdeburg, Germany	D355
Internationella Engelska Skolan, Sweden	D379
Internationella Engelska Skolan Orebro, Sweden	D379
Internationella Engelska Skolan Taby (Junior School), Sweden	D379
INVENTO the Uzbek International School, Uzbekistan	D334
Inventure Academy, India	D289
Invictus Horizon Hills, Malaysia	D308
Invictus International School Phnom Penh, Cambodia	D270
Invictus School Hong Kong, Hong Kong, China	D283
Invictus Secondary School, Hong Kong, China	D283
Ionios School, Greece	D357
IPEKA Integrated Christian School, Indonesia	D296
IPS Cascais, Portugal	151, D367
IPS Macedonia, Macedonia	D362
Ipswich School, UK	D391
IQRA Bilingual Academy, Senegal	D261
Iqra English Girls School, Qatar	D316
Iqra'a Bilingual School, Kuwait	D305
Iqraa International School, United Arab Emirates	D332
Irabia-Izaga Colegio, Spain	D376
Iringa International School, Tanzania	D264
Irish School Cairo, Egypt	D251
Irmak Schools, Türkiye	D384
ISA International Academy, China	D275
ISA Liwan International School, China	D275
ISA Science City International School, China	D275
ISA Tianhe International School, China	D275
ISA Wenhua International Centre for A Level, China	D275
ISA Wenhua Liwan School, China	D275
ISA Wenhua Wuhan School, China	D275
ISA Wuhan International School, China	D275
Isamilo International School Mwanza, Tanzania	D264
ISCS - The British School of Zug, Switzerland	D381
ISE Kiddy English, Italy	D360
ISF International School Frankfurt Rhein-Main, Germany	D355
Isikkent Egitim Kampusu, Türkiye	D384
Islamic College of Melbourne (ICOM), Australia	D340
Islamic Educational College, Jordan	D304
Islamic Village School, Indonesia	D296
Island Academy International School, Antigua	D400
Island Christian Academy, Hong Kong, China	D283
Island Pacific Academy, USA	D417
Island Pacific School, Canada	D400
Islands International School, Argentina	D427
ISM Academy Quito, Ecuador	D407
ISM International Academy, Ecuador	D407
ISM International School, Libya	D256
ISR International School on the Rhine - NRW, Germany	D355
ISS International School, Singapore	D322
Istak Lyceum, Azerbaijan	D347
Istanbul Beykent Schools, Türkiye	D384
Istanbul Coskun College, Türkiye	D384
Istanbul International Community School, Türkiye	D384
Istanbul International College, Türkiye	D384
Istanbul Marmara Private College, Türkiye	D384
ISTEK 1915 Canakkale Schools, Türkiye	D384
ISTEK Acibadem Schools, Türkiye	D384
ISTEK Afyon Schools, Türkiye	D384
ISTEK Ankara Schools, Türkiye	D384
ISTEK Antalya Konyaalti Schools, Türkiye	D384
ISTEK Antalya Lara Schools, Türkiye	D384
ISTEK Atanur Oguz Schools, Türkiye	D384
ISTEK Bandirma Schools, Türkiye	D384
ISTEK Baris Schools, Türkiye	D384
ISTEK Belde Schools, Türkiye	D384

Index

ISTEK Bilge Kagan Schools, Türkiye D384
ISTEK Denizli Schools, Türkiye D384
ISTEK Izmir Schools, Türkiye D384
ISTEK Kasgarli Mahmut Schools, Türkiye D385
ISTEK Kemal Atatürk Schools (Kindergarten & Primary School), Türkiye D385
ISTEK Kusadasi Schools, Türkiye D385
ISTEK Kütahya Schools, Türkiye D385
ISTEK Lüleburgaz Schools, Türkiye D385
ISTEK Mersin Schools, Türkiye D385
ISTEK Osmaniye Schools, Türkiye D385
ISTEK Özel Gaziantep Schools, Türkiye D385
ISTEK Semiha Sakir Schools, Türkiye D385
ISTEK Ulugbey Schools, Türkiye D385
Istochnik International School, Russian Federation D369
Italian School, Saudi Arabia D320
Ithaka International School, India D289
ITÜ ETA Vakfi Doga Koleji, Türkiye D385
ITU Gelistirme Vakfi Özel Ekrem Elginkan Lisesi, Türkiye D385
Ivanhoe Grammar School, Australia D340
Ivy Academy, China D276
Ivy Collegiate Academy, Taiwan D323
IVY Kindergarten of Tongzhou District, Beijing, China D276
Ivy World Play School, Jalandhar, India D289
Ivy World School, Jalandhar, India D289
Izmir SEV Schools, Türkiye D385

J

Jacaranda Academy, South Africa D262
Jacarandá School, Panama D436
Jain International Residential School, India D289
Jakarta Intercultural School, Indonesia D296
Jakarta Montessori School, Indonesia D296
Jakarta Multicultural School, Indonesia D296
Jakarta Nanyang School, Indonesia D296
Jale Tezer Educational Institutions, Türkiye D385
James Hope College, Nigeria D259
Jamnabai Narsee International School, India D289
Jana Dan International School, Egypt D251
Japanese International School, Hong Kong, China D283
Japanese School, United Arab Emirates D332
Japanese School in Dubai, United Arab Emirates D332
Jardín Infantil Stanford, Colombia D434
Jardín Infantil Tía Nora y Liceo Los Alpes, Colombia D434
Jay Pritzker Academy, Cambodia D270
Jayshree Periwal High School, India D289
Jayshree Periwal International School, India D289
JBCN International School - Borivali, India D289
JBCN International School - Chembur, India D289
JBCN International School - Oshiwara, India D289
JBCN International School - Parel, India D289
Jeannine Manuel School, UK 152, D391
Jebel Ali School, United Arab Emirates D332
Jeddah International Academy, Saudi Arabia D320
Jeddah Knowledge International School, Saudi Arabia D320
Jeddah Prep and Grammar School, Saudi Arabia D320
Jeddah Private International School, Saudi Arabia D320
Jennings International College, Sri Lanka D323
Jerudong International School, Brunei Darussalam 58, D269
Jerusalem American International School, Israel D299
JESSS - International Christian Academy, Ecuador D407
Jesuitinas Donostia, Nuestra Señora de Aranzazu, Spain D376
Jesus & Mary School, Lebanon D307
Jewels International School of Kinshasa, Democratic Republic of the Congo D249
JG International School, India D289
Jianye International School, China D276
Jianye Xie He Cheng Bang Kindergarten, China D276
Jinan Tianshan Experimental School, China D276
John Dewey School de Sousse, Tunisia D265
John F. Kennedy International School, Switzerland D381
John Paul College, Australia D340
John Scottus School, Ireland D358
John Wollaston Anglican Community School, Australia D340
Johnson Grammar School ICSE&IBDP, India D289
Jordanian International Schools, Jordan D304
Josef-Schwarz-Schule (JSS), Germany D355
Josephinum Academy, USA D418
Journey School of Costa Rica, Costa Rica D404
Joy to the World American International School, Japan D301
JSS International School, United Arab Emirates D332
Jubail International School, Saudi Arabia D320
Jubilee Institute, Jordan D304
Jumeira Baccalaureate School, United Arab Emirates D332
Jumeirah English Speaking School (JESS), Arabian Ranches, United Arab Emirates D332
Jumeirah English Speaking School (JESS), Jumeirah, United Arab Emirates D332
Junior High School Neue Mittelschule, Austria D346
Juntou International School, Taiwan D323
Jurong Country Garden School, China D276
Juventus Schule Zürich, Switzerland D381
Jyotirmay International School, India D289

K

K. International School Tokyo (KIST), Japan D301
K.R. Mangalam Global School, India D289
K.R. Mangalam Global School, Gurugram, India D289
K12 International Academy, USA D422
KAD Academy, Nigeria D259
Kaduna International School, Nigeria D259
Kagoshima Shugakukan Junior & Senior High School, Japan D301
Kai Early Years, India D289
Kaichi Junior & Senior High School, Japan D301
Kaichi Nihonbashi Gakuen Junior & Senior High School, Japan D301
Kaichi Nozomi Primary & Secondary School, Japan D301
KAIS International School, Japan D301
Kaluga International School, Russian Federation D369
Kamarau International School, Papua New Guinea D344
Kambala, Australia D340
Kämmer International Bilingual School, Germany D356
Kampala International School Uganda (KISU), Uganda D265
Kamuzu Academy, Malawi D256
Kanaan Global School, Indonesia D296
Kanakia International School Chembur, India D289
Kang Chiao International School (East China Campus), China D276
Kang Chiao International School, Xiugang Campus, Taiwan D323
Kansai Christian School, Japan D301
Kansai International Academy, Japan D301
Kantonsschule Baden, Switzerland D381
Kantonsschule Kusnacht, Switzerland D381
Kaohsiung American School, Taiwan D324
Karachi American School, Pakistan D313
Kardinia International College, Australia D340
Karugamo English School, Japan D301
Kaspi International School, Azerbaijan D347
Kathmandu Euro School, Nepal D311
Kathmandu International Study Centre (KISC), Nepal D311
Katoh Gakuen Gyoshu Junior & Senior High School, Japan D301
Kaumeya Language School, Egypt D251
Kaunas Jesuit High School, Lithuania D362
Kazakhstan International School, Kazakhstan D305
KC High, India D290
Kehoe-France Northshore, USA D418
Kehoe-France School, USA D418
Keiki Intercultural Preschool, Japan D301
Kelantan International School, Malaysia D308
Kelem International School, Ethiopia D253
Kellett School, Hong Kong, China D283
Kempenfelt Bay School, Canada D402
Kendale International Primary School, Italy D360
Kennedy High - The Global School, India D290
Kennedy House International School, Tanzania D264
Kennedy International School, USA D420
Kensington Park School, UK D391
Kensington School, Spain 153, D376
Kensington School, Japan D301
Kensington School Barcelona, Spain D376
Kensington Wade School, UK D391
Kent College Dubai, United Arab Emirates D332
Kent College Pembury, UK D391
Kent College, Canterbury, UK D391
Kent State University Child Development Center, USA D421
Kenton College Preparatory School, Kenya D255
KES School of Languages, Cyprus D349
Kevalee International School, Thailand D325
Keys School Manila, Philippines D315
Keystone Academy, China D276
Keystone International Schools, Türkiye D385
Kgaswe International School, Botswana D248
Khalifa School, Kuwait D305
Khalil Gibran School, Morocco D257
Khalsa School Malton, Canada D402
Khartoum American School, Sudan D263
Khartoum International Community School, Sudan D263
Khoroshevskaya Shkola, Russian Federation D369
Kiangsu & Chekiang Primary School, Hong Kong, China D283

Index

Kiangsu-Chekiang College, International Section, Hong Kong, China ... D283
Kiddykare International Kindergarten, Thailand ... D325
Kids 'R' Kids Nanjing, China ... D276
Kids Academy International Pre-School, Thailand ... D325
Kids International Learning Academy, Philippines ... D315
Kids Tairiku Frontown Ikuta, Japan ... D301
Kiettisack International School, Laos ... D306
Kigali International Community School, Rwanda ... D261
KiiT International School, India ... D290
Kimbe International School, Papua New Guinea ... D344
Kimbolton School, UK ... D391
Kinabalu International School, Malaysia ... D308
Kincaid International School of Bangkok, Thailand ... D326
Kindai University High School, Japan ... D301
Kinder College, Italy ... D360
Kinder Kri-Kri, México ... D412
Kindergarten & Primary School 'Yllka', Kosovo ... D361
Kindergarten Manantiales, Argentina ... D427
Kinderstation Primary, Indonesia ... D297
KinderWorld International Kindergarten (KIK) @ Hanoi Towers, Vietnam ... D335
KinderWorld International Kindergarten (KIK) @ The Manor (Hanoi), Vietnam ... D335
KinderWorld International Kindergarten (KIK) @ The Manor (HCMC), Vietnam ... D335
King Abdulaziz School, Saudi Arabia ... D320
King Abdullah Academy, USA ... D422
King Edward's School, UK ... D391
King Edward's Witley, UK ... D391
King Faisal Boys School, Saudi Arabia ... D320
King Faisal Girls School, Saudi Arabia ... D320
King Heights Academy, Canada ... D402
King Henry VIII College - Malaysia, Malaysia ... D308
King Richard III College, Spain ... D376
King Solomon School, Israel ... D299
King William's College, UK ... D391
King's Academy, Jordan ... D304
King's Bruton, UK ... D391
King's College, UK ... D391
King's College India, India ... D290
King's College School Alicante, Spain ... D376
King's College School Murcia, Spain ... 154, D376
King's College School Panama, Panama ... D436
King's College School, Cascais, Portugal ... 155, D367
King's College School, The Bahamas, Bahamas ... D400
King's College School, The British School of Madrid (La Moraleja), Spain ... D376
King's College School, Wimbledon, UK ... D391
King's College Soto de Viñuelas, Spain ... 156, D376
King's College, Auckland, New Zealand ... D343
King's College, Doha, Qatar ... D316
King's College, The British School of Latvia, Latvia ... 157, D362
King's Ely, UK ... D391
King's Infant School, The British School of Madrid (Chamartín), Spain ... D376
King's InterHigh, UK ... 158, D391
King's Kindergarten Shenzhen, China ... D276
King's Oak British International School, Romania ... D368
King's School Rochester, UK ... D391
King's School The Crown, Egypt ... D251
King's-Edgehill School, Canada ... D401
Kingdom Schools, Saudi Arabia ... D320
Kingham Hill School, UK ... D391
Kings Bournemouth, UK ... D391
Kings Brighton, UK ... D391
Kings London, UK ... D391
Kings Oxford, UK ... D391
Kings' School Al Barsha, United Arab Emirates ... D332
Kings' School Dubai, United Arab Emirates ... D332
Kings' School Nad Al Sheba, United Arab Emirates ... D332
Kingsley International School, Malaysia ... D308
Kingsley School, UK ... D391
Kingston College, Pakistan ... D313
Kingston International Kindergarten, Hong Kong, China ... D283
Kingston International School, Hong Kong, China ... D283
Kingston School, Indonesia ... D297
Kingsway Academy, Bahamas ... D400
Kingswood College, Australia ... D340
Kingswood School, UK ... D391
Kipling Esmeralda, México ... D412
Kipling Satélite, México ... D412
Kirkham Grammar School, UK ... D391
Kirmizi Cizgi Schools, Türkiye ... D385
KIS International School, Thailand ... D326
Kiunga International School, Papua New Guinea ... D344
Klaipeda Universa Via International School, Lithuania ... D362
Knightsbridge Schools International Bogotá (KSI Bogotá), Colombia ... D435
Knightsbridge Schools International Montenegro (KSI Montenegro), Montenegro ... D363
Knowledge Gate International School, Oman ... D312
Knowledgeum Academy, India ... D290
Ko ice International School (KEIS), Slovakia ... D370
Kobe Bilingual School, Japan ... D301
Kocaeli Marmara Private College, Türkiye ... D385
Kodaikanal International School, India ... D290
Kohinoor American School, India ... D290
Kolegium Europejskie, Poland ... D365
Kolej Tuanku Ja'afar, Malaysia ... D308
Kolej Yayasan UEM, Malaysia ... D309
Kopano School, Botswana ... D248
Korea Foreign School, Republic of Korea ... D318
Korea International School, Republic of Korea ... D318
Korea International School, Japan ... D301
Korea Kent Foreign School, Republic of Korea ... D318
Koroboro International School, Papua New Guinea ... D344
Kotkansaari School, Finland ... D351
Kouhoku School Corporation - Certified Child Center Ainosato, Japan ... D301
Krabi International School, Thailand ... D326
Kristiansand International School, Norway ... D364
Kristin School, New Zealand ... D343
Kultar Koleji, Türkiye ... D385
Kültür2000 College, Türkiye ... D385
Kumamoto International School, Japan ... D301
Kumon Leysin Academy of Switzerland, Switzerland ... D381
Kundiawa International School, Papua New Guinea ... D344
Kungsholmen's Gymnasium, International Section, Sweden ... D379
Kunming International Academy, China ... D276
Kunming World Youth Academy, China ... D276
Kunskapsskolan Gurgaon, India ... D290
Kuwait American School, Kuwait ... D305
Kuwait Bilingual School, Kuwait ... D305
Kuwait English School, Kuwait ... D305
Kuwait International English School, Kuwait ... D305
Kuwait National English School, Kuwait ... D306
Kwangju Foreign School, Republic of Korea ... D318
Kwanza International School, Tanzania ... D264
Kyoto International School, Japan ... D301

L

L'École des Ursulines de Québec, Canada ... D403
L'Ecole Francaise du Maine, USA ... D418
L'Ecole Française Internationale de Bombay, India ... D290
L'école Mondiale, Pakistan ... D313
L'École Trilingue, Portugal ... D367
La Citadelle International Academy of Arts & Science, Canada ... D402
La Colina School, Colombia ... D435
La Côte International School Aubonne, Switzerland ... D382
La Dehesa de Humanes, Spain ... D376
La Escuela de Lancaster A.C., México ... D412
La Garenne International School, Switzerland ... D382
La Joconde de Carthage, Tunisia ... D265
La Miranda The Global Quality School, Spain ... 159, D376
La Paz Community School, Costa Rica ... D404
La Petite Ecole Française, UK ... D391
La Salle Beit Hanina, Israel ... D299
La Salle Conocoto, Ecuador ... D407
La Salle Green Hills, Philippines ... D315
La Salle Latacunga, Ecuador ... D407
La Scuola d'Italia Guglielmo Marconi, USA ... D420
La Scuola International San Francisco, USA ... D415
La Scuola International School, USA ... D415
La Sierra International School, Colombia ... D435
La Villa Blanche - Notre Dame du Sacre Coeur, France ... D353
Laar & Berg, Netherlands ... D363
Lab School Paris, France ... D353
Labuan International School, Malaysia ... D309
LACAS School - Gujranwala Campus, Pakistan ... D313
Lady Andal Venkatasubba Rao Matriculation School, India ... D290
Lady Eleanor Holles International School Foshan (LEH Foshan), China ... D276
Lady Elizabeth School, Spain ... 160, D376
Ladybird International Kindergarten, Thailand ... D326
Lae International School, Papua New Guinea ... D344
Lagos Preparatory & Secondary School, Nigeria ... D260
Lahore American School, Pakistan ... D313

Index

Lahore Grammar School Defence (Phase 1), Pakistan	D313
Lahore Grammar School Defence (Phase V), Pakistan	D313
Lahore Grammar School International, Pakistan	D313
Lahore Grammar School Islamabad, Pakistan	D313
Lahore Grammar School Johar Town International, Pakistan	D313
Lakecrest Independent School, Canada	D401
Lakefield College School, Canada	D402
Lakeside School Horgen, Switzerland	D382
Lakeside School Küsnacht, Switzerland	D382
Lakshmipat Singhania Academy, India	D290
Lalaji Memorial Omega International School, India	D290
Lale Youth International School, Republic of Maldives	D318
Lampiri Schools, Greece	D357
Lancers International School, India	D290
Lancing College, UK	D392
Land School, Brazil	D430
Landmark International School, UK	D392
Langley Senior School & Sixth Form, UK	D392
Lanna International School Thailand, Thailand	D326
Lantau International School - Pui O Campus, Hong Kong, China	D283
Lanzhou Country Garden School, China	D276
Latifa School for Girls, United Arab Emirates	D332
Laude Colegio Palacio de Granda, Spain	D376
Laude El Altillo School, Spain	D376
Laude Fontenebro School, Spain	D376
Laude Newton College, Spain	D376
Laude San Pedro International College, Spain	D376
Laude The British School of Vila-real, Spain	D376
Lauder Reut Education Complex, Romania	D368
Launceston Church Grammar School, Australia	D340
LauraStephens School, Nigeria	D260
Laureate International School, Tanzania	D264
Lauremont School, Canada	D402
Lauriston Girls' School, Australia	D340
Lausanne Collegiate School, USA	D421
Lawrence College, Pakistan	D313
LCBI High School, Canada	D404
Le Bocage International School, Mauritius	D257
Le Collège Bilingue de Dakar, Senegal	D261
Le Jardin Academy, USA	D417
Le Lycée Français de Caracas - Colegio Francia, Venezuela	D438
Le Lycée Français de Los Angeles, USA	226, D415
Le Petit Lotus Bleu, China	D276
Le Régent International School, Switzerland	D382
Le Verseau International School, Belgium	D348
Lead British International School, Nigeria	D260
Lead-Forte Gate Schools, Nigeria	D260
Leaders International College, Egypt	D251
Leaders Private School, United Arab Emirates	D332
LEAF Academy (Akadémia LEAF), Slovakia	D370
Learners International School, India	D290
Learning Alliance, Pakistan	D313
Learning Caravan International School, Saudi Arabia	D320
Learning Ladders, USA	D419
Learning Links Academy, Philippines	D315
Learning Oasis International National School, Saudi Arabia	D320
Learning Panorama School, India	D290
Learning Skills International School, Ghana	D254
Learning Tree International School, Japan	D301
Lechwe School, Zambia	D265
Legacy School, Bangalore, India	D290
Legae Academy, Botswana	D248
Leibniz Privatschule Elmshorn, Germany	D356
Leighton Park School, UK	D392
Leila C. Saad SABIS School El-Metn, Lebanon	D307
Leipzig International School, Germany	D356
Lekki British School, Nigeria	D260
Léman International School Chengdu, China	61, D276
Léman Manhattan Preparatory School, USA	D420
Lemania College Lausanne, Switzerland	D382
Lennen Bilingual School - Primary Campus, France	D353
Leonardo da Vinci Academy, Czech Republic	D350
Leonardo Da Vinci Campus, Germany	D356
Lertlah School, Phetkasem Road, Thailand	D326
Les Alzines, Spain	D376
Les écoles Idéales - Lycee Nabeul, Tunisia	D265
Les écoles Idéales - Primaire/Maternelle Nabeul, Tunisia	D265
Les Petits Polyglottes, France	D353
Lestonnac L'Ensenyança, Spain	D376
Letovo School, Russian Federation	D369
Leweston Senior School, UK	D392
Leysin American School in Switzerland, Switzerland	D382
Liberty American School (LAS), Ghana	D254
Liberty International School, Japan	D301
Liceo Bilingüe Experimental José Figueres Ferrer, Costa Rica	D404
Liceo de Apodaca Centro Educativo, México	D412
Liceo de Cervantes, Colombia	D435
Liceo de Monterrey Blueridge, México	D412
Liceo de Monterrey Redwood, México	D412
Liceo de Monterrey Rosemont, México	D412
Liceo del Valle, Ecuador	D407
Liceo Federico Froebel de Oaxaca, México	D412
Liceo Francés de Pereira, Colombia	D435
Liceo José Ortega y Gasset, Ecuador	D407
Liceo Los Robles, Venezuela	D438
Liceo Panamericano Internacional, Ecuador	D407
Liceo Pino Verde, Colombia	D435
Liceo Sorolla c, Spain	D376
Liceu Albert Sabin, Brazil	D430
Liceul Teoretic Scoala Europeana Bucuresti, Romania	D368
Lichfield Cathedral School, UK	D392
Life Academy International, Philippines	D315
Lifeforte International Schools, Nigeria	D260
Lifespring Montessori School, Nigeria	D260
Light Academy Mombasa, Kenya	D255
Light International School - Malindi, Kenya	D255
Light International School - Mombasa, Kenya	D255
Light International School - Nairobi, Kenya	D255
Lighthouse Ensino Bilíngue, Brazil	D430
Lighthouse International School, Costa Rica	D404
Lihir International School/School to Mine, Papua New Guinea	D344
Lilima Montessori High School, Eswatini	D253
Lima Villa College, Peru	D437
Lime House School, UK	D392
Limerick Bilingual School, Argentina	D427
Lincoln Community School, Ghana	D254
Lincoln International Academy, Nicaragua	D414
Lincoln International Academy, Chicureo, Chile	D432
Lincoln International Academy, Lo Barnechea, Chile	D432
Lincoln Middle School, USA	D421
Lincoln Minster School, UK	D392
Lincoln Park High School, USA	D418
Lincoln School, Nepal	D311
Lincoln School, Costa Rica	D404
Linden Hall High School, Japan	D301
Lindenwood International School, France	D353
Links School, Pakistan	D313
Lisbon Montessori School, Portugal	D367
Little Genius International, Italy	D360
Little Land Nursery & Montessori Centre, Kuwait	D306
Little London International Academy, Romania	D368
Livorno Elementary/Middle School, Italy	D360
Liwa International School, United Arab Emirates	D332
Ljubljana International School, Slovenia	D370
Llandovery College, UK	D392
Lodge Group of Schools, Malaysia	D309
Logos Academy, Ecuador	D407
Logos Academy, Hong Kong, China	D283
Logos School of English Education, Cyprus	D349
Lomas High School, Argentina	D427
Lomas Hill, México	D412
Lomond School, UK	D392
Lonati Anglo American School, Italy	D360
London International Academy, Canada	D402
Long Trail School, USA	D422
Longridge Towers School, UK	D392
Lord Byron School, Peru	D437
Lord Wandsworth College, UK	D392
Loreto College, Australia	D340
Loreto Convent School, Gibraltar	D357
Loretto School, UK	162, D392
Los Angeles School, Costa Rica	D404
Loughborough Grammar School, UK	D392
Lowell High School, Canada	D401
Lower Canada College, Canada	D403
Loydence Academy, Qatar	D316
Loyola International School, Qatar	D316
Luanda International School, Angola	D248
Lucaya International School, Bahamas	D400
Luckley House School, UK	D392
Lucton School, UK	D392
Ludoteca Elementary & High School, Padre Victor Grados, Ecuador	D407
Lumbini International College, Nepal	D311
Lumio Private School, Cyprus	D349
Lund International School, Sweden	D379
Lusaka International Community School, Zambia	D265
Luther College High School, Canada	D404
LVS Ascot, UK	D392

Index

LWIS DT Beirut-City International School, Lebanon D307
LWIS Keserwan-Adma International School, Lebanon D307
LWIS Koura-Universal School of Lebanon, Lebanon D307
Lycée Abdallah Rassi, Lebanon D307
Lycée Albert 1er, Monaco D362
Lycée Alexandre Dumas, Dominican Republic D405
Lycée Antoine-de-Saint-Exupéry, Chile D432
Lycée Antoine-de-Saint-Exupéry de Hambourg, Germany D356
Lycée Billes, Senegal D261
Lycée Bonaparte, Qatar D316
Lycée Charles de Gaulle, Chile D432
Lycée Chateaubriand de Rome, Italy D360
Lyceé Claude Gay, Chile D432
Lycée Condorcet - The International French School of Sydney, Australia D340
Lycee de Sevres, International Sections, France D353
Lycée Enoch Olinga, Niger D258
Lycée Français, Germany D356
Lycée Français Alexandre Yersin, Vietnam D335
Lycée Français Alioune Blondin Beye, Angola D248
Lycée Français Anna de Noailles, Romania D368
Lycée Français Charles de Gaulle de Londres, UK D392
Lycée Français d'Asunción Marcel Pagnol, Paraguay D436
Lycée Français d'Irlande - Collège et Lycée, Ireland D358
Lycée Français de Bali, Indonesia D297
Lycée Français de Chicago, USA D418
Lycée français de Düsseldorf, Germany D356
Lycée Français de Jérusalem, Israel D299
Lycee Francais De Koweit, Kuwait D306
Lycée Français de Kuala Lumpur, Malaysia D309
Lycée Français de Moscou Alexandre-Dumas, Russian Federation D369
Lycée Français de New York, USA D420
Lycée Français de Palma, Spain D376
Lycée français de Pondichéry, India D290
Lycée Français De Prague, Czech Republic D350
Lycée Français de Saint Domingue, Dominican Republic D405
Lycée Français de San Francisco, USA D415
Lycée Français de San Salvador Antoine et Consuelo de Saint-Exupéry, El Salvador D408
Lycee Français de Shanghai-Qingpu Campus, China D276
Lycée Français de Sofia Victor Hugo, Bulgaria D348
Lycée français de Varsovie (French School in Warsaw), Poland 163, D365
Lycèe Français de Vienne, Austria D346
Lycée Français du Caire - Maadi, Egypt D251
Lycée Français du Caire - Mearag, Egypt D251
Lycée Français du Caire - New Cairo, Egypt D251
Lycée Français du Caire - Zamalek, Egypt D251
Lycée Français François Mitterrand, Brazil D430
Lycée Français Guy de Maupassant, Morocco D257
Lycee Francais International, United Arab Emirates D332
Lycée Français International Anvers, Belgium D348
Lycée Français International Charles de Gaulle de Pekin, China D276
Lycée Français International de Bahreïn, Bahrain D268
Lycee Francais International de Bangkok, Thailand D326
Lycée français international de Kyoto, Japan D301
Lycée Français International de Porto, Portugal D367
Lycée français international de Tokyo, Japan D301
Lycée Français International Denis Diderot, Kenya D255
Lycée Français International Elite, Lebanon D307
Lycée Français International Georges Pompidou - École de Sharjah, United Arab Emirates D332
Lycée Français International Gustave Eiffel, Mozambique D258
Lycée Français International Institut Moderne du Liban, Lebanon D307
Lycée Français International Jacques Prévert d'Accra, Ghana D254
Lycée français Jean Giono de Turin, Italy D360
Lycee Francais Jean Monnet, Belgium D348
Lycée Français Jean Renoir, Germany D356
Lycèe Français Libertè de Bamako, Mali D256
Lycée Français Louis Pasteur, Nigeria D260
Lycée Français Louis Pasteur, Colombia D435
Lycée Français Louis-Charles Damais, Indonesia D297
Lycée Français Molière, Spain D376
Lycée Français Murcie, Spain D376
Lycée Français of Lusaka (LFL), Zambia D265
Lycée français Paul-Valéry, Colombia D435
Lycée Français Prins Henrik, Denmark D350
Lycée Français René Cassin, Norway D364
Lycée Français René Descartes, Cambodia D270
Lycée Français Renée-Verneau de Gran Canaria, Spain D376
Lycée Français Saint Louis de Stockholm, Sweden D379
Lycée Français Théodore Monod, Mauritania D256
Lycée Français Victor Hugo, Germany D356
Lycée français Victor-Hugo, Germany D356
Lycee Francais Vincent Van Gogh, Netherlands D363
Lycée Franco Bolivien Alcide d'Orbigny - La Paz, Bolivia D428
Lycee Franco Hondurien, Honduras D435
Lycée Franco-Argentin Jean Mermoz, Argentina D427
Lycée Franco-Britannique Ecole Internationale, Gabon D253
Lycée Franco-Éthiopien Guébré-Mariam, Ethiopia D253
Lycée Franco-Hellénique Eugène Delacroix, Greece D357
Lycée Franco-Libanais Abdel Kader, Lebanon D307
Lycée Franco-Libanais Alphonse De Lamartine, Lebanon D307
Lycée Franco-Libanais Habbouche-Nabatieh, Lebanon D307
Lycée Franco-Libanais Nahr Ibrahim, Lebanon D307
Lycée Franco-Libanais Verdun, Lebanon D307
Lycée Franco-Péruvien, Peru D437
Lycee Franco-Qatarien Voltaire, Qatar D316
Lycée International Balzac, Egypt D251
Lycée International Barcelona - Bon Soleil, Spain D377
Lycée International de Houston, USA D421
Lycée International de Londres Winston Churchill, UK D392
Lycée International de Saint Germain-en-Laye, American Section, France D353
Lycee International Des Pontonniers, France D353
Lycee International François 1ER, France D353
Lycee Internationale de Saint Germain-en-Leye - British Section, France D353
Lycée Jean d'Alembert, Chile D432
Lycée Jules Verne, South Africa D262
Lycée La Bourdonnais, Mauritius D257
Lycée La Condamine, Ecuador D407
Lycee Libanais Francophone Prive, United Arab Emirates D332
Lycee Louis de Foix, France D353
Lycee Louis Massignon, United Arab Emirates D332
Lycee Louis Pasteur The International French School, Canada D400
Lycée Lyautey, Morocco D257
Lycée Montaigne, Lebanon D307
Lycee Notre Dame, France D353
Lycee Notre Dame du Grandchamp, France D353
Lycée Pasteur (Lycée français de São Paulo / Unité Vergueiro), Brazil D430
Lycee Pierre de Coubertin, France D353
Lycée Pierre Mendès France, Tunisia D265
Lycée Victor Hugo, Italy D360
Lyceum Alpinum Zuoz, Switzerland D382
Lyceum School Nurorda, Kazakhstan D305
Lyceum-Boarding School No. 2 - Municipal Autonomous Educational Institution, Russian Federation D369
Lyford Cay International School, Bahamas D400
Lynn-Rose Heights Private School, Canada D402

M

M Ct M Chidambaram Chettyar International School, India D290
M-PESA Foundation Academy, Kenya D255
Maadi British International School, Egypt D251
Maadi Community Study Centre (MCSC), Egypt D251
Maarif Schools of Sarajevo, Bosnia & Herzegovina D348
Maartenscollege & International School Groningen, Netherlands D363
Macau Anglican College, China D276
Machabeng College, International School of Lesotho, Lesotho D256
Machhapuchchhre School, Nepal D311
Machida Kobato Kindergarten, Japan D301
Mackay School, Chile D432
Mackintosh Academy Boulder, USA D416
Mackintosh Academy Littleton, USA D416
MacLachlan College, Canada D402
MADAC Schools, Saudi Arabia D320
Madang International School, Papua New Guinea D344
Madania, Indonesia D297
MADAR International School, United Arab Emirates D332
Madinat Al Sultan Qaboos Private School (MSQPS), Oman D312
Madinaty Integrated Language Schools (MILS), Egypt D251
Madinaty Language School, Egypt D251
Madison Campus Monterrey, México D412
Madison Country Day School, USA D423
Madison International School, México D412
Madison International School Campus Country-Mérida, México D412
Madrasah Aljunied Al-Islamiah, Singapore D322
Magellan International School, USA D422
Magic Years International School, Thailand D326
Mahatma Gandhi International School, India D290
Mahindra International School, India D290
Main Taunus International School, Germany D356
Mainadevi Bajaj International School, India D290
Majesty International Schools, Egypt D251
Makassar Independent School, Indonesia D297
Makuhari International School, Japan D301
Malacca Expatriate School, Malaysia D309

Index

Mälardalen International School, Sweden	D379
Malherbe International School, France	D353
Mallya Aditi International School, India	D290
Malmö Borgarskola, Sweden	D379
Malmö International School, Sweden	D379
Malpi International College (MIC), Nepal	D311
Malvern College, UK	D392
Malvern College Chengdu, China	D276
Malvern College Egypt, Egypt	D251
Malvern College Hong Kong, Hong Kong, China	D283
Malvern College Qingdao, China	D276
Malvern College Tokyo, Japan	D301
Malvern St James School, UK	D392
Mamoura British Academy, United Arab Emirates	D332
Manado Independent School, Indonesia	D297
Manarat El Mostaqbal International School, Egypt	D251
Manarat Jeddah International School - Boys, Saudi Arabia	D320
Manarat Jeddah International School - Girls, Saudi Arabia	D320
Manarat School - Kuwait (MSK), Kuwait	D306
Manaret Heliopolis International School, Egypt	D251
Manav Rachna International School, India	D290
Manchester High School for Girls, UK	D392
Manchester International School, India	D290
Mandalay International Science Academy, Myanmar	D311
Manila Xiamen International School, China	D276
Manor House American & IGCSE School, Egypt	D251
Manor House American School, Egypt	D251
Manor House International School - British Division, Egypt	D251
Mansfield Steiner School, Australia	D340
Mansoura College, Egypt	D251
Manthan International School Kompally, India	D290
Manukau Christian School, New Zealand	D343
MAP St. Louis, USA	D419
Maple Bear Barra da Tijuca, Brazil	D430
Maple Bear Canadian School, India	D290
Maple Bear Tempe, USA	D414
Maple Leaf International School, Trinidad & Tobago	D414
Maputo International School, Mozambique	D258
Mar Qardakh School, Iraq	D299
Marcanti College, Netherlands	D364
Marian Baker School, Costa Rica	D404
Marie Jahoda School Vienna, Austria	D346
Marina International School, The Gambia	D264
Marist Brothers International School, Japan	D301
Maristes Sants Les Corts, Spain	D377
Mark Twain International School, Romania	D368
Markham College - Peru, Peru	D437
Marlborough College, UK	D392
Marlborough College Malaysia, Malaysia	62, D309
Martim Cererê Unidad Educativa Particular Bilingüe, Ecuador	D407
Martin House Trust School, Zambia	D265
Maru-a-Pula School, Botswana	D248
Mary N. Raptou School SA, Greece	D357
Mary Passage Middle School, USA	D422
Maryland International School, USA	D418
Marymount International School London, UK	D392
Marymount International School Paris, France	D353
Marymount International School Rome, Italy	164, D360
Marymount School - Medellín, Colombia	D435
Maseru Preparatory School, Lesotho	D256
Mashrek International School, Jordan	D304
Massanutten Military Academy, USA	D422
Massillon - Ecole Bilingue Internationale, France	D353
Mater Christi College, Australia	D340
Matrix Global Schools, Malaysia	D309
Matsumoto Kokusai High School, Japan	D301
Matthews Hall, Canada	D402
Maunula Primary School, Finland	D351
Maxi Global School, Brazil	D430
Maya Schools Antalya, Türkiye	D385
Mayfair International Academy, Spain	D377
Mayfield School, UK	D392
Mayo College, India	D290
Mayo College Girls' School, India	D290
MAZ International School, Malaysia	D309
Mazapan School, Honduras	D435
MBA Schools - Istanbul Atasehir Campus, Türkiye	D385
MBA Schools - Istanbul Camlica Campus, Türkiye	D385
Meadow Hall Education, Nigeria	D260
Meadowridge School, Canada	D401
Medan Independent School, Indonesia	D297
MEF International Schools, Istanbul - Ulus High, Türkiye	D385
MEF International Schools, Istanbul - Ulus Primary, Türkiye	D385
MEF International Schools, Izmir, Türkiye	D385
Mehmet Akif College - Gjakova, Kosovo	D361
Mehmet Akif College - Lipjan, Kosovo	D361
Mehmet Akif College - Prizren, Kosovo	D361
Mehr-e-Taban International School, Iran	D298
Meikei High School, Japan	D301
Melbourne Grammar School, Australia	D340
Melbourne Grammar School - Grimwade House, Australia	D340
Melbourne Montessori School, Australia	D340
Meltho International School, Iraq	D299
Meluha International School, India	D290
Memorial International School of Tirana, Albania	D346
Memphis International School, Egypt	D251
Mentari Intercultural School Bintaro, Indonesia	D297
Mentari Intercultural School Jakarta, Indonesia	D297
Mentone Girls' Grammar School, Australia	D340
Mercedes College, Australia	D340
Merchiston Castle School, UK	165, D392
Mercy High School Baltimore, USA	D418
Mercyhurst Preparatory School, USA	D421
Merici College, Australia	D340
Meridian 22 Private High School, Bulgaria	D348
Meridian International School, Ukraine	D398
Meridian International School, Czech Republic	D350
Meridian School, Banjara Hills, India	D290
Meridian School, Madhapur, India	D290
Merton International School, Ghana	D254
MET Rishikul Vidyalaya - Bhujbal Knowledge Centre, Mumbai, India	D290
Methodist College, Malaysia	D309
Methodist College, UK	D392
Methodist Ladies' College (MLC), Australia	D340
Metro Delhi International School, India	D290
Metropolitan International School (MIS Heidelberg), Germany	D356
Metropolitan International School (MIS Mannheim), Germany	D356
Metropolitan International School (MIS Viernheim), Germany	D356
Metropolitan School Frankfurt, Germany	D356
Metropolitan School of Panama, Panama	D436
MGC New Life Christian Academy, Philippines	D315
MGD Girls' School, India	D290
Michael Hall School, UK	D392
Michaelhouse, South Africa	D263
Mid-Pacific Institute, USA	D417
Middle East International School, Qatar	D316
Mill Hill International, UK	D392
Mill Hill School, UK	D392
Millfield School, UK	D392
Millwood School, USA	D422
Milton Abbey School, UK	D392
Minecan Okullari, Türkiye	D385
Mingdao High School, Taiwan	D324
Mirabal International School, Spain	168, D377
Miras International School, Almaty, Kazakhstan	D305
Miras International School, Astana, Kazakhstan	D305
Mirasur School, Spain	D377
Mirdif American School, United Arab Emirates	D332
Miri Piri Academy, India	D290
Misr Language Schools, Egypt	D251
Miss Edgar's & Miss Cramp's School, Canada	D403
Missoula International School, USA	D419
MIT International School, Philippines	D315
Miura Gakuen High School, Japan	D301
Mizuho School, Japan	D302
MLC School, Australia	D340
MM International School, India	D290
MM International School, India	D290
Modern American School, Jordan	D304
Modern Education Schools, Egypt	D251
Modern English School Cairo, Egypt	D251
Modern High School for Girls, India	D291
Modern Indian School, Nepal	D311
Modern International School, Tajikistan	D324
Modern International School Bangkok, Thailand	D326
Modern Knowledge Schools, Bahrain	D268
Modern Montessori School, Jordan	D304
Modern Public School, India	D291
Modern School, India	D291
Modern School, Argentina	D427
Mody School, India	D291
MOK Kindergarten, China	D276
Mokopane Destiny Academy, South Africa	D263
Mombasa Academy, Kenya	D255
Monkton Senior School, UK	D393
Monmouth School for Boys, UK	D393
Monmouth School for Girls, UK	D393
Monnet International School, Poland	D365

Index

Monsif International School, Lebanon D307
Mont'Kiara International School, Malaysia D309
Montalvo International School, Portugal 166, D367
Monte Sant' Angelo Mercy College, Australia D340
Monte Vista Christian School, USA D415
Montessori Academy Sharon Springs, USA D417
Montessori British School, Bogota, Colombia D435
Montessori British School, Murcia, Spain D377
Montessori International College, Peru D437
Montessori International College, Australia D340
Montessori Lyceum Amsterdam, Netherlands D364
Montessori School La Florida, Spain D377
Montessori School Los Fresnos Mataespesa, Spain D377
Montessori Sierra Madre, México D412
Montfort International College, Thailand D326
Montgomery International School - Brussels, Belgium 169, D348
Montjuïc Girona International School, Spain D377
Montreux International School, Switzerland D382
Moraitis School, Greece D357
Moreton Bay Boys' College, Australia D340
Moreton Bay College, Australia D340
Moreton Hall, UK D393
Morgan Henry Bilingual Kindergarten, China D276
Morgan International Community School, Ghana D254
Morganton Day School, USA D421
Morna International College, Spain D377
Morogoro International School, Tanzania D264
Morrison Academy Kaohsiung, Taiwan D324
Morrison Academy Taichung, Taiwan D324
Morrison Academy Taipei, Taiwan D324
Moscow Economic School, Odintsovo Branch, Russian Federation D369
Moscow Economic School, Presnya Campus, Russian Federation D369
Moscow International Gymnasia, Russian Federation D369
Mosman Church of England Preparatory School, Australia D340
Mother Goose Lipa, Philippines D315
Motilal Nehru School of Sports, India D291
Mougins British International School, France 170, D353
Mount Abu Public School, India D291
Mount Hagen International School, Papua New Guinea D344
Mount Kelly, UK D393
Mount Litera School International (MLSI), India D291
Mount Saint Mary Academy, USA D414
Mount Scopus Memorial College, Australia D340
Mount St Mary's College, UK D393
Mount View School, Costa Rica D405
Mountain Academy, USA D423
Mountainview Christian School, Indonesia D297
Moyles Court School, UK D393
MSB Private School, United Arab Emirates D332
Mt Zaagkam School, Indonesia D297
Mulberry House International Pre-school, Thailand D326
Mulgrave School, The International School of Vancouver, Canada 227, D401
Multinational School - Riyadh, Saudi Arabia D320
Multiple Intelligence International School, Philippines D315
Muna British Academy, United Arab Emirates D332
Munich International School e.V., Germany D356
Munro Academy, Canada D401
Muruvvet Evyap Schools, Türkiye D385
Musashino University Chiyoda High School, Japan D302
Muscat International School, Oman D312
Musikili Primary School, Zambia D265
Mussalon ala-asta, Finland D351
Mussoorie International School, India D291
Mustard Seed International Schools, Kenya D255
Mutiara Harapan Islamic School, Indonesia D297
Mutiara International Grammar School, Malaysia D309
Mutuelle d'études secondaires, Switzerland D382
Myanmar International School, Myanmar D311
Myanmar International School Yangon (MISY) Mandalay, Myanmar D311
Myanmar International School Yangon (MISY) Yangon, Myanmar D311
Myllytullin Koulu, Finland D351
MySchool Oman, Oman D312
Mzuzu International Academy, Malawi D256

N

Nada International School, Saudi Arabia D320
Nadeen School Bahrain, Bahrain D268
Nagano Nihon University School of Education, Japan D302
Nagoya International School, Japan D302
Nahar International School, India D291
Nairobi Jaffery Academy, Kenya D255
Nairobi Waldorf School, Kenya D255
Naisula School, Kenya D255
Najd International School, Saudi Arabia D320
Nakornpayap International School (NIS), Thailand D326
Namsung Elementary School, Republic of Korea D318
Nanchang International School, China D276
Nanjing Eternal Sea Kindergarten, China D276
Nanjing International School, China D276
Nansha College Preparatory Academy, China D276
Nanshan Chinese International College Immersion, China D276
Nantong Stalford International School, China D276
Narmer American College, Egypt D252
Naseem International School, Bahrain D268
Nassa School, Indonesia D297
National Centre for Excellence - CV Raman Nagar, India D291
National Orthodox School Shmaisani, Jordan D304
Navigator College, Australia D340
Navrachana International School, India D291
Nay Pyi Taw International Science Academy, Myanmar D311
Neerja Modi School, India D291
Neev Academy - North Campus, India D291
Neev Academy - Yemalur Campus, India D291
Nefertari International School, Egypt D252
Nefertari International School - 6th of October, Egypt D252
Neil Armstrong School, Colombia D435
NEOM Community School, Saudi Arabia D320
NES International School Dombivli, India D291
NES International School Mumbai, India D291
Nesibe AYDIN Educational Institutions (Ankara), Türkiye D385
Nesibe AYDIN Educational Institutions (Antalya), Türkiye D385
Nesibe AYDIN Educational Institutions (Diyarbakir), Türkiye D385
Nesibe AYDIN Educational Institutions (Gaziantep), Türkiye D385
Nesibe AYDIN Educational Institutions (Kocaeli), Türkiye D385
Nesibe AYDIN Educational Institutions (Konya), Türkiye D385
Nesibe AYDIN Educational Institutions (Mersin), Türkiye D385
Netherlands International School Lagos (NISL), Nigeria D260
Netzaberg Middle School, Germany D356
Neuchâtel Junior College, Switzerland D382
New Academy School, United Arab Emirates D332
New Cairo British International School, Egypt D252
New Cambridge School Bucaramanga - Sede Cabecera, Colombia D435
New Cambridge School Bucaramanga - Sede Cañaveral, Colombia D435
New Cambridge School Cali, Colombia D435
New Castelar College, Spain D377
New Castle International School, Egypt D252
New Covenant Academy, USA D415
New Covenant American School International, Benin D248
New England Girls' School, Australia D340
New English School, Kuwait D306
New English School, Jordan D304
New Future International School, Egypt D252
New Gate School, USA D416
New Generation International Schools, Egypt D252
New Hall School, UK D393
New Hampton School, USA D419
New Horizon International School, Egypt D252
New Indian Model School, United Arab Emirates D332
New Indian Model School (Dubai), United Arab Emirates D332
New International School of Japan, Japan D302
New Mexico International School, USA D420
New Middle East International School, Saudi Arabia D320
New Model International School, Argentina D427
New Oriental Academy, China D276
New Oriental Stars Kindergarten, China D276
New Pakistan International School, Kuwait D306
New Ramses College, Egypt D252
New Sathorn International School, Thailand D326
New School, International School of Georgia, Georgia D354
New Vision International Schools, Egypt D252
New World International School, Saudi Arabia D320
New World Private School, United Arab Emirates D332
New Zealand Independent School, Indonesia D297
Newark Academy, USA D419
Newington College - Lindfield, Australia D340
Newington College - Stanmore, Australia D340
Newport School, Colombia D435
Newton British Academy AlDafna, Qatar D316
Newton British Academy Barwa City, Qatar D316
Newton British School Al Waab, Qatar D316
Newton College, Peru D437
Newton Free School, Georgia D354
Newton International School, Morocco D257
Newton International School, Qatar D316
Newton International School Lagoon, Qatar D316

Index

Newton International School West Bay, Doha, Qatar D316
Newtown Primary School, Dominica D405
NEXT School, India D291
Nexus International School (Singapore), Singapore D322
Nexus International School Malaysia, Malaysia D309
Nexus Preschool, China D276
Nga Tawa Diocesan School, New Zealand D343
NICE International School, Sri Lanka D323
Nigerian Tulip International College - Abuja, Nigeria D260
Nigerian Tulip International College - Kaduna, Nigeria D260
Nigerian Tulip International College - Kano, Nigeria D260
Nigerian Tulip International College - Lagos, Nigeria D260
Nigerian Tulip International College - Ogun, Nigeria D260
Nigerian Tulip International College - Yobe, Nigeria D260
Nikolaus-Lenau-Lyzeum Timisoara, Romania D368
Nile International College, Egypt D252
Ningbo Huamao International School, China D276
Ningbo Zhicheng School, China D277
Niraj International School, India D291
Nishimachi International School, Japan D302
NIST International School, Thailand 63, D326
Niva International School, Thailand D326
Nobel Algarve British International School - Almancil, Portugal D367
Nobel Algarve British International School - Lagoa, Portugal 171, D367
Noble Hall Leadership Academy for Girls, Nigeria D260
Nobles International School, Saudi Arabia D320
Noblesse International School, Philippines D315
NOIC Academy, Canada D402
Noor Al Khaleej International School, Qatar D316
Noordwijk International College, México D412
Nord Anglia Chinese International School, Shanghai, China D277
Nord Anglia International School Dublin, Ireland D358
Nord Anglia International School Manila, Philippines D315
Nord Anglia International School Rotterdam, Netherlands D364
Nord Anglia International School Shanghai, Pudong, China D277
Nord Anglia International School, Al Khor, Qatar D317
Nord Anglia International School, Dubai, United Arab Emirates D332
Nord Anglia International School, Hong Kong, Hong Kong, China 64, D283
Nord Anglia International School, New York, USA 228, D420
Nord Anglia School Beijing, Fangshan, China D277
Nord Anglia School Foshan, China D277
Nord Anglia School Jakarta, Indonesia D297
Nord Anglia School Jiaxing, China D277
Nord Anglia School Nantong, China D277
Nord Anglia School Ningbo, Fenghua, China D277
Nord Anglia School Suzhou, Xiangcheng, China D277
Norfolk Academy, USA D422
Norlights International School, Norway D364
North American International School, South Africa D263
North Broward Preparatory School, USA D416
North Jakarta Intercultural School, Indonesia D297
North London Collegiate School, UK D393
North London Collegiate School Dubai, United Arab Emirates D332
North London Collegiate School Jeju, Republic of Korea D318
North London Collegiate School Singapore, Singapore D322
North Zealand International School, Denmark D351
Northbridge International School Cambodia, Cambodia D270
Northern International School, Argentina D427
Northfields International School, Mauritius D257
Northlands School, Argentina D427
Northlands School Nordelta, Argentina D427
Northside Primary School, Botswana D248
Norwegian International School, Nigeria D260
Norwegian International School Hong Kong, Hong Kong, China D283
Norwich International School, Bangkok, Thailand D326
Norwich School, UK D393
Norwood International High School, Australia D340
Notion International School, Egypt D252
Notre Dame Academy, GA, USA D417
Notre Dame Academy, MA, USA D419
Notre Dame Academy, OH, USA D421
Notre Dame de la Baie Academy, USA D423
Notre Dame High School, USA D416
Notre Dame High School, Fairfield, USA D416
Notre Dame International High School, France D353
Notre Dame International School, Nicaragua D414
Notre Dame Preparatory School & Marist Academy, USA D419
Notre Dame School, Dominican Republic D405
NOVA International Schools, Macedonia D362
Novaschool Sunland International, Spain D377
Novel Academy, Nepal D311
NPS International School, Singapore D322
NUCB International College, Japan D302
NUCB International Junior & Senior High School, Japan D302
Nuevo Colegio Israelita de Monterrey, México D412
Nuevo Gimnasio School, Colombia D435
Numont School, Spain D377
Nün Academy, Saudi Arabia D320
NUN Middle & High School, Türkiye D385
NUN Primary School, Türkiye D385
Nymphenburger Schulen, Germany D356
NYsKOOL, Spain D377

O

O Castro British International School (Vigo), Spain 172, D377
O.M.C. - Collegio Vescovile Pio X, Italy D360
Oak International School, Benin D248
Oakham School, UK D393
Oakland International British School, Nigeria D260
Oakleigh Grammar, Australia D340
Oakley College, Spain D377
Oakridge International School, Bachupally, India D291
Oakridge International School, Bengaluru, India D291
Oakridge International School, Gachibowli, India D291
Oakridge International School, Mohali, India D291
Oakridge International School, Visakhapatnam, India D291
Oasis International School, India D291
Oberoi International School, India D291
Oberoi International School - JVLR Campus, India D291
Obersee Bilingual School (OBS), Switzerland D382
OBS Dubbeldam, Netherlands D364
Ocean Crest School, Nigeria D260
Ocean of Light International School, Tonga D344
Odyssey International School, Vietnam D335
Odyssey The Global Preschool - Dempsey Campus, Singapore D322
Odyssey The Global Preschool - Fourth Avenue Campus, Singapore D322
Odyssey The Global Preschool - Loyang Campus, Singapore D322
Odyssey The Global Preschool - Orchard Campus, Singapore D322
Odyssey The Global Preschool - Still Road Campus, Singapore D322
Odyssey The Global Preschool - Wilkinson Campus, Singapore D322
Oeiras International School, Portugal D367
Ohanyan Educational Complex, Armenia D346
Okayama University of Science High School, Japan D302
Okinawa Christian School International, Japan D302
Okinawa International School, Japan D302
Okinawa Shogaku School, Japan D302
Olashore International School, Nigeria D260
Olga Gudynn Bilingual High School - Oxford Gardens, Romania D368
Olga Gudynn International School - Cotroceni, Romania D368
Olga Gudynn International School - Floreasca, Romania D368
Olga Gudynn International School - Pipera, Romania D368
Olive International School - Doha, Qatar D317
Olive Tree International Academy, BFSU, China D277
Olmos Preescolar, Costa Rica D405
Olonlog Academy, Mongolia D310
Ombrosa, Lycée Multilingue de Lyon, France D353
Omololu International School, Anguilla D400
ONE International School Philippines, Philippines D315
One Planet International School, Ethiopia D253
One World International School (OWIS) Digital Campus Punggol, Singapore D322
One World International School (OWIS) Nanyang, Singapore D322
One World International School (OWIS) Osaka, Japan D302
One World International School (OWIS) Riyadh, Saudi Arabia D320
One World International School (OWIS) Sarjapur, India D291
One World International School (OWIS) Suntec, Singapore D322
One World International School (OWIS) Tsukuba, Japan D302
One World International School (OWIS) Whitefield, India D291
Open Future International School, Poland D365
Open Gate School, Czech Republic D350
Oporto British School, Portugal D367
Orange Day School, Argentina D427
Orbis International School, México D412
Orbit International School Khobar, Saudi Arabia D320
Orchlon International School, Mongolia D310
Orient College, Nepal D311
Oriental Cambridge International School (Shenyang/Benxi Campus), China D277
Oriental English College, Shenzhen, China D277
Orouba Language School - Dokki, Egypt D252
Orouba Language School - Maadi, Egypt D252
Oryx International School, Qatar D317
Osaka International High School, Japan D302
Osaka International School of Kwansei Gakuin, Japan D302
Osaka Jogakuin Senior High School, Japan D302
Osaka YMCA International School, Japan D302
Oshwal Academy Mombasa, Kenya D255

Index

Oshwal Academy Nairobi, Kenya ... D255
Oslo International School, Norway ... D364
Ostrcilova International School, Czech Republic ... D350
Oswestry School, UK ... D393
OTR International School Luxembourg, Luxembourg ... D362
Oujing International Kindergarten, China ... D277
Oulu International School, Finland ... D351
Oundle School, UK ... D393
Our Lady of Good Counsel High School, USA ... D418
Our Lady of Grace International School, Liberia ... D256
Our Lady of the Nativity, Australia ... D340
Our Lady of Victories Catholic School of Quezon City, Philippines ... D315
Our Own English High School - Fujairah, United Arab Emirates ... D332
Our Saviour Lutheran School, Australia ... D340
OurPlanet International School Muscat, Oman ... D312
Overseas Chinese Academy Suzhou, China ... D277
Overseas Family School, Singapore ... D322
Own Heliopolis Schools, Egypt ... D252
Oxbridge International School, Uzbekistan ... D334
Oxbridge Tutorial College, Nigeria ... D260
Oxford Academy, Kuwait ... D306
Oxford International College, UK ... D393
Oxford International College, Chengdu, China ... D277
Oxford International School, Panama ... D436
Oxford International School, Kyrgyzstan ... D306
Oxford International School - Banasree Campus, Bangladesh ... D269
Oxford International School - Dhamnondi Main Campus, Bangladesh ... D269
Oxford International School - Gulshan Campus, Bangladesh ... D269
Oxford International School - Old Dhaka Campus, Bangladesh ... D269
Oxford International School - Uttara Campus, Bangladesh ... D269
Oxford Schools, Jordan ... D304
Oxstand International School, Shenzhen, China ... D277
Özel Antalya Toplum Koleji Anadolu Lisesi, Türkiye ... D385
Özel Ari Anadolu Lisesi, Türkiye ... D386
Özel Atayurt Ilkokulu, Türkiye ... D386
Özel Ay Egitim Kurumlari, Türkiye ... D386
Özel Büyük Kolej, Türkiye ... D386
Özel Çag Lisesi, Türkiye ... D386
Özel Egeberk Anaokulu, Türkiye ... D386
Ozel Ilk Cizgi Kindergarten, Türkiye ... D386
Ozel Istanbul Akademik Sistem Okullari, Türkiye ... D386
Özel Kariyer Ilkokulu, Türkiye ... D386
Özel Rüzgar Fen Lisesi, Türkiye ... D386
Özel Yönder Ilkokulu, Türkiye ... D386

P

P P Savani Cambridge International School, India ... D291
Pacific Academy, Canada ... D401
Pacific American School, Taiwan ... D324
Pacific Harbour Multi-Cultural School, Fiji ... D343
Pacific Rim International School, USA ... D415
Paderewski Private Grammar School, Poland ... D365
Padworth College, UK ... D393
Pak Shamaa School, Qatar ... D317
Pak Turk International School - Islamabad Girls Campus, Pakistan ... D313
Pakistan Education Academy, United Arab Emirates ... D332
Pakistan Embassy International Study Group, Türkiye ... D386
Pakistan International School (English Section) Jeddah, Saudi Arabia ... D320
Pakistan International School (English Section) Riyadh, Saudi Arabia ... D320
Pakistan International School Cairo, Egypt ... D252
Pakistan International School of Damascus, Syrian Arab Republic ... D323
Pakistan Islamia Higher Secondary School, United Arab Emirates ... D332
Pakistan School Muscat, Oman ... D312
Palmer Trinity School, USA ... D416
Pampers Private School Lekki, Nigeria ... D260
Pampers Private School Surulere, Nigeria ... D260
Pan American Christian Academy, Brazil ... D430
Pan American International School, Paraguay ... D436
Pan American School - Campus Monterrey, México ... D412
Pan American School of Bahia, Brazil ... D430
Pan American School of Porto Alegre, Brazil ... D430
Pan-American School, Costa Rica ... 229, D405
Pan-Asia International School, Thailand ... D326
Panama Prep International School, Panama ... D436
Panbai International School, India ... D291
Pangbourne College, UK ... D393
Panyaden International School, Thailand ... D326
Panyathip International School, Laos ... D306
Paradis International School, Romania ... D368
Paragon International School Cambodia - Primary Campus, Cambodia ... D270
Paragon International School Cambodia - Secondary Campus, Cambodia ... D270
Park House English School, Qatar ... D317
PaRK International School, Portugal ... 173, D367
PaRK International School - Cascais, Portugal ... D367
PaRK International School - Praça de Espanha, Portugal ... D367
PaRK International School - Restelo, Portugal ... D367
Park Lane International School - Prague 1, Czech Republic ... D350
Park Lane International School - Prague 6, Czech Republic ... D350
Parkview International Pre-school, Hong Kong, China ... D284
Parkview International Pre-School (Kowloon), Hong Kong, China ... D284
PASCAL Private English School - Larnaka, Cyprus ... D349
PASCAL Private English School - Lefkosia, Cyprus ... D349
Patanadek School, Thailand ... D326
Pathways School Gurgaon, India ... D291
Pathways School Noida, India ... D291
Pathways World School, Gurgaon, India ... D291
PDO School, Oman ... D312
Pearl British Academy, United Arab Emirates ... D332
Pearl International Academy, Jordan ... D304
Pearling Season International School of Doha, Qatar ... D317
Pearson College UWC, Canada ... D401
Pechersk School International Kyiv, Ukraine ... D398
Pegasus International College - Da Nang, Vietnam ... D335
Pegasus International College - Hanoi, Vietnam ... D335
Pegasus International College (Singapore), Singapore ... D322
Pegasus Schools, Eket, Nigeria ... D260
Pelangi School (Yayasan Cahaya Pelangi Bali), Indonesia ... D297
Pembroke House School, Kenya ... D255
Pembroke School, Australia ... D340
Penabur Secondary Tanjung Duren (PSTD), Indonesia ... D297
Penrhos College, Australia ... D341
Penrith Anglican College, Australia ... D341
Penryn College, South Africa ... D263
Pensionnat du Saint-Nom-de-Marie, Canada ... D403
Peoria Academy, USA ... D418
Peponi House, Kenya ... D255
Peponi School, Kenya ... D255
Pestalozzi Education Centre, Zambia ... D265
Peterhouse Boys School, Zimbabwe ... D266
Peterhouse Girls School, Zimbabwe ... D266
Peterhouse Group of Schools, Zimbabwe ... D266
Peterson School - Cuajimalpa, México ... D412
Peterson School - Lomas, México ... D412
Peterson School - Pedregal, México ... D412
Peterson School Tlalpan, México ... D412
PeyJoy Kindergarten, China ... D277
Philadelphia Private School Dubai, United Arab Emirates ... D332
Philippine School Doha, Qatar ... D317
Phoenix City International Kindergarten, China ... D277
Phoenix City International School, China ... D277
Phoenix House International School, Japan ... D302
Phoenix International School, Spain ... D377
Phorms Campus Berlin Mitte, Germany ... D356
Phorms Campus Berlin Süd, Germany ... D356
Phorms Campus Hamburg, Germany ... D356
Phorms Campus Munich, Germany ... D356
Phorms Frankfurt City, Germany ... D356
Phorms Taunus Campus, Germany ... D356
Phuket Thaihua ASEAN Wittaya School, Thailand ... D326
Pick Me Academy, Romania ... D368
Pierce - The American College of Greece, Greece ... D357
Pine Street School, USA ... D420
Pinefield School, Nigeria ... D260
Pinehurst School, New Zealand ... D343
Pinewood American International School, Greece ... D357
Pingo de Gente & Laviniense, Brazil ... D430
Pingtan Saier Bilingual School, China ... D277
Pinnacle High International School, India ... D291
Pioneers International School, Egypt ... D252
Planete Montessori International School, Morocco ... D257
Platon School, Greece ... D357
PlayPen Escola Cidade Jardim, Brazil ... D430
Pledge Harbor International School, Bangladesh ... D269
Plenty Valley Christian College, Australia ... D341
Plymouth College, UK ... D393
Po Leung Kuk Choi Kai Yau School, Hong Kong, China ... D284
Pocklington School, UK ... D393
Podar International School, India ... D291
Podar International School (Kalyan), India ... D292
Podar O.R.T International School, Worli, India ... D292
Polish British Academy of Warsaw, Poland ... D365
Pope Francis Preparatory School, USA ... D419
Poplars School, Argentina ... D427

Index

Popondetta International School, Papua New Guinea D344
PORG International School - Ostrava, Czech Republic D350
PORG International School - Prague, Czech Republic D350
Port Moresby Grammar School, Papua New Guinea D344
Port Moresby International School, Papua New Guinea D344
Port Said International Schools, Egypt D252
Port Vila International School, Fiji D343
Portledge School, USA D420
Poznan British International School, Poland D365
Prague British International School, Czech Republic D350
Prälat-Diehl-Schule Oberstufe, Germany D356
Prem Tinsulanonda International School, Thailand D326
Premier Academy, Kenya D255
Premier International School, Nepal D311
Premier International School, Nigeria D260
Premiere Academy, Nigeria D260
Prepa UNI, México D412
Prepa UPAEP Angelópolis, México D412
Prepa UPAEP Atlixco, México D412
Prepa UPAEP Cholula, México D412
Prepa UPAEP Huamantla, México D413
Prepa UPAEP Lomas, México D413
Prepa UPAEP San Martín, México D413
Prepa UPAEP Santa Ana, México D413
Prepa UPAEP Santiago, México D413
Prepa UPAEP Sur, México D413
Prepa UPAEP Tehuacán, México D413
Presbyterian Ladies' College - Perth, Australia D341
Presbyterian Ladies' College Melbourne, Australia D341
Preshil - The Margaret Lyttle Memorial School, Australia D341
President School, Russian Federation D369
Pride International School Myanmar (PISM), Myanmar D311
PRIGO Language and Humanities Grammar School, Czech Republic D350
PRIMA International School, Serbia D369
Prime Innovative Private Lviv Lyceum (PIPL Lyceum), Ukraine D398
Prime School Estoril, Portugal 174, D367
Prime School Lisbon, Portugal D367
Prime School São Pedro do Estoril, Portugal D367
Prime School Sintra, Portugal D367
Primegate Academy, Nigeria D260
Primus Public School, India D292
Prince Alfred College, Australia D341
Prince of Wales Island International Primary School (POWIIS Primary), Malaysia D309
Prince of Wales Island International School (POWIIS), Malaysia D309
Princeton International School, Egypt D252
Princeton Junior School, USA D419
Princeton Montessori School, USA D419
Princeton SkyLake International Kindergarten, China D277
Prior Park College, UK D393
Prior Park School, Gibraltar D357
Prior's Field, UK D393
Pristine Private School, United Arab Emirates D332
Private ALEV Schools, Türkiye D386
Private Herder-Schule, Germany D356
Private High School Gaudium et Studium, Poland D365
Private Kocaeli Bahcesehir Anatolian High School, Türkiye D386
Private Lomonosov School Nizhny Novgorod, Russian Federation D369
Private Primary School 'Progressive Education'-Sofia, Bulgaria D348
Private Primary School 97, Poland D365
Private Sahin Schools, Türkiye D386
Private Sanko Schools, Türkiye D386
Prometheus School, India D292
Prout School, USA D421
Providence English Private School, United Arab Emirates D332
Providenciales Primary School, Turks And Caicos Islands D414
Prywatne Liceum Ogolnokształcace im.M.Wankowicza, Poland D365
PSKD Mandiri, Indonesia D297
Pukekohe Christian School, New Zealand D343
Punahou School, USA D417
Punjab Public School, India D292
Puntacana International School, Dominican Republic D405
Purcell Marian High School, USA D421

Q

Qatar Academy Al Khor, Qatar D317
Qatar Academy Al Wakra, Qatar D317
Qatar Academy Doha, Qatar D317
Qatar Academy Msheireb, Qatar D317
Qatar Academy Sidra, Qatar D317
Qatar International School, Qatar D317
Qatar Leadership Academy, Qatar D317
Qingdao Academy, China D277
Qingdao Amerasia International School, China D277
Qingdao Chaoyin Primary School, China D277
Qingdao MINGDE School, China D277
Qingdao No.1 International School of Shangdong Province (QISS), China D277
Qodrat Alajyal School, Saudi Arabia D320
QSI Almaty International School, Kazakhstan D305
QSI Ashgabat International School, Turkmenistan D327
QSI Baku International School, Azerbaijan D347
QSI International School of Astana, Kazakhstan D305
QSI International School of Atyrau, Kazakhstan D305
QSI International School of Belize, Guatemala D409
QSI International School of Benin, Benin D248
QSI International School of Bishkek, Kyrgyzstan D306
QSI International School of Bratislava, Slovakia D370
QSI International School of Brindisi, Italy D360
QSI International School of Chengdu, China D277
QSI International School of Chisinau, Moldova D362
QSI International School of Dili, East Timor D281
QSI International School of Djibouti, Ethiopia D253
QSI International School of Dongguan, China D277
QSI International School of Dushanbe, Tajikistan D324
QSI International School of El Tigre, Venezuela D438
QSI International School of Haiphong, Vietnam D335
QSI International School of Kosovo, Kosovo D361
QSI International School of Ljubljana, Slovenia D370
QSI International School of Malta, Malta D362
QSI International School of Minsk, Belarus D347
QSI International School of Montenegro, Montenegro D363
QSI International School of Münster, Germany D356
QSI International School of Pápa, Hungary D358
QSI International School of Phuket, Thailand D326
QSI International School of Sarajevo, Bosnia & Herzegovina D348
QSI International School of Shenyang, China D277
QSI International School of Shenzhen, China D277
QSI International School of Skopje, Macedonia D362
QSI International school of Tbilisi, Georgia D354
QSI International School of Trinidad, Trinidad & Tobago D414
QSI International School of Yerevan, Armenia D346
QSI International School of Zhuhai, China D277
QSI Kyiv International School, Ukraine D398
QSI Tirana International School, Albania D346
Quality Education School, Bahrain D268
Quantum College, Armenia D346
Quarry Lane School, USA D415
Queen Anne's School, Caversham, UK D393
Queen Elizabeth's School, Portugal D367
Queen Ethelburga's, UK 175, D393
Queen Margaret College, New Zealand D343
Queen Margaret's School, UK D393
Queen Mary's School, UK D393
Queen Mira International School, India D292
Queen Victoria School, UK D393
Queen's College, Spain D377
Queen's College, UK D393
Queenwood, Australia D341
Quilmes High School, Argentina D427
Qurtubah Private Schools, Saudi Arabia D321

R

R.E.A.L Schools, Cheras Campus, Malaysia D309
R.E.A.L Schools, Johor Bahru Campus, Malaysia D309
R.E.A.L Schools, Shah Alam Campus, Malaysia D309
RA International School (RAIS), Nigeria D260
Rabat American School, Morocco D257
Rabaul International School, Papua New Guinea D344
Radford College, Australia D341
Radhwa International School Yanbu, Saudi Arabia D321
Radley College, UK D393
Raffles American School Bangkok, Thailand D326
Raffles American School Johor, Malaysia D309
Raffles Christian School, Indonesia D297
Raffles International School, United Arab Emirates D332
Raffles World Academy, United Arab Emirates D332
Rafflesia International School Kajang Campus, Malaysia D309
Rafflesia International School Puchong Campus, Malaysia D309
Rafic Hariri High School, Lebanon D307
Raha International School - Gardens Campus, United Arab Emirates D332
Raha International School - Khalifa City Campus, United Arab Emirates D332
Rahn Schulen Kairo, Egypt D252
Rain Forest International School, Cameroon D248
Rainbow College, Nigeria D260
Rainbow International School Uganda, Uganda D265

Index

Rainbow Schools, Botswana D248
RAIS - Dammam - AlZahour for Boys, Saudi Arabia D321
RAIS - Dammam - AlZahour for Girls, Saudi Arabia D321
RAIS - Dammam - Hamra International for Girls, Saudi Arabia D321
RAIS - Jeddah - Abhor for Girls, Saudi Arabia D321
RAIS - Riyadh - Mogharazat for Boys, Saudi Arabia D321
RAIS - Riyadh - Mogharazat for Girls, Saudi Arabia D321
RAIS - Riyadh - Qurtoba for Girls, Saudi Arabia D321
Rajac Language Schools, Egypt D252
Rajagiri International School, United Arab Emirates D332
Rajala School, Finland D351
Rajkumar College Raipur, India D292
Rama School, Indonesia D297
Ramallah Friends School (Lower School), Palestine D314
Ramallah Friends School (Upper School), Palestine D314
Ramkhamhaeng Advent International School, Thailand D326
RAMS (Rawdat Al-Maaref Schools & College), Jordan D304
Ranches Primary School, United Arab Emirates D333
Rancho Solano Preparatory School, USA D414
Rand International School, Saudi Arabia D321
Ranum Efterskole College, Denmark D351
Ras Al Khaimah Academy, United Arab Emirates D333
Ras Al Khaimah American Academy, United Arab Emirates D333
Rasami British International School, Thailand D326
Rasbihari International School, India D292
Rashid School for Boys, United Arab Emirates D333
Ratcliffe College, UK D393
Rato Bangala School, Nepal D311
Ravenswood, Australia D341
RBK International School, Bhayandar, India D292
RC International School, Thailand D326
REAL School Budapest, Hungary D358
Reborn Kids Education Academy (RKEA), Kuwait D306
Red House International School - Campus Higienópolis, Brazil D430
Red House International School - Campus Perdizes, Brazil D430
Redbridge International Academy, India D292
Reddam ELS Lindfield, Australia D341
Reddam ELS St Leonards, Australia D341
Reddam ELS Woollahra, Australia D341
Reddam House Atlantic Seaboard, South Africa D263
Reddam House Ballito, South Africa D263
Reddam House Bedfordview, South Africa D263
Reddam House Berkshire, UK 176, D393
Reddam House Constantia, South Africa D263
Reddam House Durbanville, South Africa D263
Reddam House Helderfontein, South Africa D263
Reddam House Sydney, Australia D341
Reddam House Umhlanga, South Africa D263
Reddam House Waterfall, South Africa D263
Reddford House Blue Hills, South Africa D263
Reddford House Northcliff, South Africa D263
Reddford House The Hills, South Africa D263
Redeemer Lutheran School, Nuriootpa, Australia D341
Redeemer's International School, Nigeria D260
Redhill School, South Africa D263
Redland School, Chile D432
Redlands, Australia D341
Redmaids' High School Senior & Sixth Form, UK D393
Redwood Center of Excellence, United Arab Emirates D333
Reed's School, UK D393
Reedley International School, Philippines D315
Regent British School - New Mansoura, Egypt D252
Regent British School - West, Egypt D252
Regent International School, United Arab Emirates D333
Regents International School Pattaya, Thailand 66, D326
Renaissance International School Saigon, Vietnam D336
Rendcomb College, UK D393
Repton Abu Dhabi, United Arab Emirates D333
Repton Al Barsha, United Arab Emirates D333
Repton Dubai, United Arab Emirates D333
Repton International School (Invictus Spring Hills), Malaysia D309
Repton School, UK D393
Richland Academy, Canada D402
Richmond International School, Spain D377
Richmond Park International School, Bihac, Bosnia & Herzegovina D348
Richmond Park International School, Sarajevo, Bosnia & Herzegovina D348
Richmond Park International School, Tuzla, Bosnia & Herzegovina D348
Ridley College, Canada D402
Riffa Views International School, Bahrain D268
Rift Valley Academy, Kenya D255
Rikkyo School in England, UK D394
RIMS International School and Junior College, India D292
Rio International School, Brazil D430
RIS Rome International School, Italy 177, D360
RIS Swiss Section-Deutschsprachige Schule Bangkok, Thailand D326
RISE Royal Institute of Smart Education, Bangladesh D269
Rishworth School, UK D394
Ritsumeikan Uji Junior and Senior High School, Japan D302
Rivercrest Christian College, Australia D341
Rivers International School Arnhem, Netherlands D364
Riverside International School, Czech Republic D350
Riverside International School, India D292
Riverstone International School, USA D417
Riyadh Schools, Saudi Arabia D321
Robert College of Istanbul, Türkiye D386
Robinson School, Puerto Rico D414
Rochambeau, The French International School, USA 230, D418
Rochester Arts and Sciences Academy, USA D419
Rochester Independent College, UK D394
Rochester Montessori School, USA D419
Rockport School, UK D394
Rockwell International School, India D292
Roedean School, South Africa D263
Roedean School, UK D394
Rookwood School, UK D394
Roong Aroon International School, Thailand D326
Rootland School, México D413
Roots International Schools Islamabad Pakistan, Pakistan D313
Roots IVY International School - Chaklala Campus, Pakistan D313
Roots Ivy International School - DHA Phase V Lahore, Pakistan D313
Roots IVY International School - Faisalabad Campus, Pakistan D313
Roots IVY International School - Riverview Campus, Pakistan D313
Roots Millennium Schools, Flagship Campus, Pakistan D313
Roots Millennium Schools, One World Campus, Pakistan D313
Rosary Sisters School - Aqaba, Jordan D304
Rosemount International School, Singapore D322
Roseville College, Australia D341
Rossall School, UK D394
Rosslyn Academy, Kenya D255
Rothesay Netherwood School, Canada D401
Rotterdam International Secondary School, Netherlands D364
Rousseau International School, Cameroon D248
Royal British International School Yangon, Myanmar D311
Royal Canadian School - Cairo, Egypt D252
Royal Flight School, Oman D312
Royal High Bath, UK 178, D394
Royal Institute International School, Sri Lanka D323
Royal Russell School, UK D394
Royal School in Transylvania, Romania D368
RTU International School of Science & Technology, Latvia D362
Ruamrudee International School, Thailand D326
Ruder Bo kovic, Serbia D369
Rudolf Steiner Schule Oberaargau, Switzerland D382
Rugby School, UK D394
Rugby School Japan, Japan D302
Ruh Continuum School, India D292
Rungta International School, India D292
Runnymede College, Spain D377
Rupani Academy, Pakistan D313
Rusinga Schools, Kenya D255
Russian International School, Russian Federation D369
Russian International School Galaxy, Cameroon D248
Rutgers Preparatory School, USA D419
Ruthin School, UK D394
Ruzawi School, Zimbabwe D266
Ryan Global School, Andheri, India D292
Ryan Global School, Chembur, India D292
Ryan Global School, Kharghar, India D292
Ryan Global School, Kundalahalli, India D292
Rydal Penrhos Senior School, UK D394
Ryde School with Upper Chine, UK D394
Rygaards School, Denmark D351

S

Saad National School, Saudi Arabia D321
SABIS International School - Adma, Lebanon D307
SABIS International School - Aljada, United Arab Emirates D333
SABIS International School - Costa Verde, Panama D436
SABIS International School - Runda, Kenya D255
SABIS International School - Ruwais, United Arab Emirates D333
SABIS International School - Yas Island, United Arab Emirates D333
SABIS SUN International School - Baku, Azerbaijan D347
Sacred Heart Academy, USA D418
Sacred Heart College Geelong, Australia D341
Sacred Heart Model School, USA D418
Sacred Heart Primary School, Nigeria D260
Sacred Heart School, Bahrain D268

Index

Sacred Heart School of Halifax, Canada D401
Sadiq Public School, Pakistan D313
Safa British School, United Arab Emirates D333
Safa Community School, United Arab Emirates D333
Sagesse High School, Lebanon D307
Sai International School, India D292
Sai Sishya International School, Japan D302
Saigon South International School, Vietnam D336
Saint Alban's College, Lomas de Zamora, Argentina D427
Saint Andrew's School, Bolivia D428
Saint Dominic's International School, Portugal, Portugal D367
Saint Edmund Preparatory High School, USA D420
Saint Felix School, UK D394
Saint Gabriel's School, Chile D432
Saint George School, Dominican Republic D405
Saint George's School, USA D422
Saint Gregory School, Costa Rica D405
Saint James Academy, USA D418
Saint John Paul II Catholic School, USA D417
Saint John's Preparatory School, USA D419
Saint Joseph School, Dominican Republic D405
Saint Joseph School, Lebanon D307
Saint Jude Catholic School, Philippines D315
Saint Kentigern Boys' School, New Zealand D343
Saint Kentigern College, New Zealand D343
Saint Kentigern Girls' School, New Zealand D343
Saint Marcel Academy International School, Democratic Republic of the Congo D249
Saint Mary of the Hills School, Argentina D427
Saint Mary of the Hills School Sede Pilar, Argentina D427
Saint Mary School, Costa Rica D405
Saint Mary's Catholic School, USA D422
Saint Matthews College, Argentina D427
Saint Maur International School, Japan D302
Saint Patrick College, Argentina D427
Saint Paul American School, China D277
Saint Paul College, Costa Rica D405
Saint Peter's School, Indonesia D297
Saint Thomas School, Dominican Republic D405
Sainte Victoire International School, France 179, D353
Saipal Academy, Nepal D311
Salahaldin International School, Egypt D252
Salmiya School, Kuwait D306
Saltus Grammar School, Bermuda D400
Salwa School, Kuwait D306
SAMA International School, Egypt D252
Sampoerna Academy, Jakarta Campus, Indonesia D297
Sampoerna Academy, Medan Campus, Indonesia D297
San Andrea School, Malta D362
San Anton School, Malta D362
San Diego French-American School, USA D415
San Francisco College, Peru D437
San Gabriel Mission High School, USA D415
San Roberto International School, México D413
San Silvestre School, Peru D437
Sana'a British School, Yemen D336
Sanatan High School, India D292
Sancta Maria International School - Faridabad, India D292
Sancta Maria International School - Hyderbad, India D292
Sandford International School, Ethiopia D253
Sandford Park School, Ireland D358
Sandpiper International School, Kenya D255
Sands International School, Saudi Arabia D321
Sandy Spring Friends School, USA D418
Sangam School of Excellence, India D292
Sanjay Ghodawat International School, India D292
Sankt Petri Skole, Denmark D351
Sanskar School, India D292
Sant'Anna International School, Brazil D430
Santa Clara International School, Spain D377
Santa Cruz Cooperative School, Bolivia D428
Santa Cruz International School, Bolivia D428
Santa Margarita Catholic High School, USA D415
Santa Maria College, Australia D341
Santa Sabina College, Australia D341
Santa Teresa de Jesús, Paraguay D436
Santiago Christian School, Dominican Republic D405
Santiago College, Chile 241, D432
Sanya Foreign Language School, China D277
Sanya Foreign Language School Kindergarten (SLSK), China D278
Sanya Overseas Chinese School - Nanxin Campus, China D278
Sapporo Nihon University High School, Japan D302
Sarala Birla Academy, India D292
Sarasas Extra School, Thailand D326
Satit Bilingual School of Rangsit University, Thailand D326
Satya School, India D292
Saud International School, Saudi Arabia D321
Saudi School in Paris, France D353
Saudi School in Rabat, Morocco D257
Sayfol International School, Malaysia D309
SCAD World School, India D292
Scandinavian School of Madrid, Spain D377
Scarborough College, UK D394
Scheck Hillel Community School, USA D417
Schellhammer International School, Spain D377
Schloss Krumbach International School, Austria D346
Scholars Indian School RAK, United Arab Emirates D333
Scholars International Academy, United Arab Emirates D333
Scholastica Schools, Bangladesh D269
Schole International Academy, Pakistan D313
School of Modern Skills, United Arab Emirates D333
School of the Nations, China D278
School of the Nations, Brazil D430
Schools of the Sacred Heart, USA D415
Schule Birklehof, Germany D356
Schule Schloss Salem, Germany D356
Schutz American School, Egypt D252
Scindia Kanya Vidyalya, India D292
Score Academy, USA D417
Scotch College, Australia D341
Scotch Oakburn College, Australia D341
Scots College, New Zealand D343
Scottish High International School, India D292
Scuola Rudolf Steiner ii Lugano Origlio, Switzerland D382
Scuola Svizzera di Catania, Italy D360
Scuola Svizzera di Milano, Italy D360
SDK BPK Penabur Banda, Indonesia D297
Seaford College, UK D394
Sections Internationales de Sèvres, France D353
Sedbergh School, UK D394
Seedling International Academy, India D292
Seirei Gakuen, Japan D302
Seisen International School, Japan D302
SEK Budapest International School, Hungary D358
SEK International School Alborán, Spain 180, D377
SEK International School Atlántico, Spain 181, D377
SEK International School Catalunya, Spain 182, D377
SEK International School Ciudalcampo, Spain 183, D377
SEK International School Dublin, Ireland 184, D358
SEK International School El Castillo, Spain 185, D377
SEK International School Global Campus, Spain 186, D377
SEK International School Les Alpes, France 187, D353
SEK International School Qatar, Qatar 67, D317
SEK International School Riyadh, Saudi Arabia 68, D321
SEK International School Santa Isabel, Spain 188, D377
Sekolah Bogor Raya, Indonesia D297
Sekolah Buin Batu, Indonesia D297
Sekolah Cikal Jakarta, Indonesia D297
Sekolah Cikal Lebak Bulus, Indonesia D297
Sekolah Cikal Surabaya, Indonesia D297
Sekolah Ciputra, Surabaya, Indonesia D297
Sekolah Cita Buana, Indonesia D297
Sekolah Djuwita Batam, Indonesia D297
Sekolah Global Indo-Asia, Indonesia D297
Sekolah Monte Sienna, Indonesia D297
Sekolah Mutiara Nusantara, Indonesia D297
Sekolah Paradisa Cendekia, Indonesia D297
Sekolah Pelita Harapan, Kemang Village, Indonesia D297
Sekolah Pelita Harapan, Lippo Cikarang, Indonesia D298
Sekolah Pelita Harapan, Lippo Village, Indonesia D298
Sekolah Pelita Harapan, Sentul City, Indonesia D298
Sekolah Pilar Indonesia, Indonesia D298
Sekolah Sri KDU (Kota Damansara), Malaysia D309
Sekolah Tunas Bangsa, Indonesia D298
Sekolah Victory Plus, Indonesia D298
SelaQui International School, India D292
Selwyn House School, New Zealand D344
Selwyn House School, Canada D403
Semarang Multinational School, Indonesia D298
Sendai Ikuei Gakuen High School, Japan D302
Seneca Academy, USA D418
SenPokChin School, Canada D401
Senri International School of Kwansei Gakuin, Japan D302
Sentinel Kabitaka School, Zambia D265
Seoul Foreign British School, Republic of Korea D318
Seoul Foreign School, Republic of Korea D318
Seoul International School, Republic of Korea D318
Seri Mulia Sarjana International School, Brunei Darussalam D270

Index

Serpell Primary School, Australia ... D341
Seta International School, Japan ... D302
SEV American College, Türkiye ... D386
Seven Hills International School, Romania ... D368
Seven Peaks School, USA ... D421
Seven Star Kindergarten Xiamen, China ... D278
Sevenoaks School, UK ... 189, D394
Seymour College, Australia ... D341
SGIS International School, Cambodia ... D270
SGS Loma Verde Bilingual School, Argentina ... D427
Shahid Mahdavi Educational Foundation, Iran ... D299
Shaikha Hessa Girls' School, Bahrain ... D268
Shambhu Dayal Global School, India ... D292
Shanghai American School (Pudong Campus), China ... D278
Shanghai American School (Puxi Campus), China ... D278
Shanghai Arete Bilingual Kindergarten, China ... D278
Shanghai Arete Bilingual School, China ... D278
Shanghai BeiBeiJia Olion Kindergarten, China ... D278
Shanghai Changning International School, China ... D278
Shanghai Community International School - Hongqiao Campus, China ... 69, D278
Shanghai Community International School - Pudong Campus, China ... D278
Shanghai Ivy School, China ... D278
Shanghai Liaoyuan Bilingual School, China ... D278
Shanghai Livingston American School, China ... D278
Shanghai Pinghe School, China ... D278
Shanghai Qibao Dwight High School, China ... D278
Shanghai Qingpu World Foreign Language Kindergarten, China ... D278
Shanghai Qingpu World Foreign Language School, China ... D278
Shanghai Shangde Experimental School, China ... D278
Shanghai Singapore International School, China ... D278
Shanghai United International School, Gubei/Hongqiao Campus, China ... D278
Shanghai United International School, Jiaoke, China ... D278
Shanghai United International School, Pudong, China ... D278
Shanghai United International School, Shangyin, China ... D278
Shanghai United International School, Wanyuan, China ... D278
Shanghai United International School, Wenzhou, China ... D278
Shanghai United International School, Xiamen, China ... D278
Shanghai Victoria Kindergarten (Gumei), China ... D278
Shanghai Victoria Kindergarten (Pudong), China ... D278
Shanghai Victoria Kindergarten (Qibao), China ... D278
Shanghai Victoria Kindergarten (Xuhui), China ... D278
Shanghai World Foreign Language Middle School, China ... D278
Shanghai World Foreign Language Primary School, China ... D278
Shantiniketan International School, India ... D292
Shape International School, Belgium ... D348
Sharanya Narayani International School, India ... D293
Sharjah American International School, United Arab Emirates ... D333
Sharjah British International School, United Arab Emirates ... D333
Sharjah English School, United Arab Emirates ... D333
Sharjah Public School, United Arab Emirates ... D333
Sharm International British School, Egypt ... D252
Shawnigan Lake School, Canada ... D401
Shebbear College, UK ... D394
Sheikh Zayed International Academy, Pakistan ... D313
Shekou International School, China ... D278
Shen Wai International School, China ... D279
Sheng Kung Hui Choikou School, China ... D279
Shenghua Zizhu Academy, China ... D279
Shenyang No.2 Sino-Canadian High School, China ... D279
Shenzhen American International School, China ... D279
Shenzhen College of International Education, China ... 72, D279
Shenzhen Concord College of Sino-Canada, China ... D279
Shenzhen Elite International Academy, China ... D279
Shenzhen Foreign Languages GBA Academy, China ... D279
Shenzhen Futian Funful Bilingual School, China ... D279
Sheraton Heliopolis Language Schools, Egypt ... D252
Sherborne Girls, UK ... D394
Sherborne International, UK ... D394
Sherborne Qatar, Qatar ... D317
Sherborne School, UK ... D394
Sherfield School, UK ... D394
Shigally Hill International Academy, India ... D293
Shiloh Bilingual Education Centre (SBEC) International School, The Gambia ... D264
Shinagawa International School, Japan ... D302
Shine Ue School, Mongolia ... D310
Shiplake College, UK ... D394
Shirakatsy Lyceum International Scientific-Educational Complex, Armenia ... D346
Shirley Boys' High School, New Zealand ... D344
Shiv Nadar School Chennai, India ... D293
Shiv Nadar School Faridabad, India ... D293
Shiv Nadar School Gurgaon, India ... D293
Shiv Nadar School Noida, India ... D293
Shizuoka Salesio School, Japan ... D302
Shkolla Udha e Shkronjave, Albania ... D346
Shohei Junior & Senior High School, Japan ... D302
Shoreless Lake School, Spain ... D378
Shree Swaminarayan Gurukul Vishwavidya Pratishthanam SGVP, India ... D293
Shrewsbury International School, Thailand ... D326
Shrewsbury International School Hong Kong, Hong Kong, China ... D284
Shrewsbury School, UK ... D394
Shu Ren International School, USA ... D415
Shukou Junior High School, Japan ... D302
SIAL.school, UK ... D394
Siam International School, Thailand ... D327
Sias International School, China ... D279
Sibford School, UK ... D394
SICAS DHA Phase VI, Pakistan ... D313
Sidcot School, UK ... D394
Sierra Bernia School, Spain ... D378
Sifundzani School, Eswatini ... D253
Sigtunaskolan Humanistiska Läroverket, Sweden ... D379
Silicon Valley International School, USA ... D415
Silk Road International School, Kyrgyzstan ... D306
Silver Fern International School, Thailand ... D327
Silver Oaks International, South Africa ... D263
Silver Oaks International School, Hyderabad, India ... D293
Silver Oaks International School, Visakhapatnam, India ... D293
Simba International School, Zambia ... D265
Simeon Radev School, Bulgaria ... D348
Simferopol International School, Ukraine ... D398
Sinarmas World Academy, Indonesia ... D298
Sinarmas World Academy Thamrin, Indonesia ... D298
Singapore American School, Singapore ... D322
Singapore Chinese Girls School, Singapore ... D322
Singapore International School (Hong Kong) - Preparatory Years & Primary Section, Hong Kong, China ... D284
Singapore International School (Hong Kong) - Secondary Section, Hong Kong, China ... D284
Singapore International School (SIS) @ BDNC, Vietnam ... D336
Singapore International School (SIS) @ Can Tho, Vietnam ... D336
Singapore International School (SIS) @ Ciputra, Vietnam ... D336
Singapore International School (SIS) @ Da Nang, Vietnam ... D336
Singapore International School (SIS) @ Gamuda Gardens, Vietnam ... D336
Singapore International School (SIS) @ Ha Long, Vietnam ... D336
Singapore International School (SIS) @ Saigon South, Vietnam ... D336
Singapore International School (SIS) @ Van Phuc, Vietnam ... D336
Singapore International School (SIS) @ Vung Tau, Vietnam ... D336
Singapore International School of Bangkok, Thailand ... D327
Singapore International School, Mumbai, India ... D293
Singapore Korean School, Singapore ... D322
Singapore School Cebu, Philippines ... D315
Singapore School Clark, Philippines ... D315
Singapore School Manila, Philippines ... D315
Singapore School Manila Green Campus, Philippines ... D315
Singapore Vietnam International School (SVIS) @ Nha Trang, Vietnam ... D336
Sir Harry Johnston International School, Malawi ... D256
Sir Manasseh Meyer International School, Singapore ... D322
SIS Cilegon, Indonesia ... D298
SIS Gwangju, Republic of Korea ... D318
SIS Kelapa Gading, Indonesia ... D298
SIS Medan, Indonesia ... D298
SIS Palembang, Indonesia ... D298
SIS Pantai Indah Kapuk, Indonesia ... D298
SIS Semarang, Indonesia ... D298
SIS South Jakarta, Indonesia ... D298
SIS Swiss International School Basel, Switzerland ... D382
SIS Swiss International School Basel-Allschwil, Switzerland ... D382
SIS Swiss International School Berlin, Germany ... D356
SIS Swiss International School Brasília, Brazil ... D430
SIS Swiss International School Frankfurt, Germany ... D356
SIS Swiss International School Friedrichshafen, Germany ... D356
SIS Swiss International School Ingolstadt, Germany ... D356
SIS Swiss International School Kassel, Germany ... D356
SIS Swiss International School Männedorf-Zürich, Switzerland ... D382
SIS Swiss International School Milano-Basiglio, Italy ... D360
SIS Swiss International School Päffikon-Schwyz, Switzerland ... D382
SIS Swiss International School Regensburg, Germany ... D356
SIS Swiss International School Rotkreuz-Zug, Switzerland ... D382
SIS Swiss International School Schönenwerd, Switzerland ... D382
SIS Swiss International School Stuttgart-Fellbach, Germany ... D356
SIS Swiss International School Zürich, Switzerland ... D382

515

Index

SIS Swiss International School Zürich-Wollishofen, Switzerland D382
SIS Yangon, Myanmar D311
Sistema Educativo Saint Clare, Costa Rica D405
Skagerak International School, Norway D364
SKBZ Bangladesh Islamia School & College, United Arab Emirates D333
Skill Stork International School, India D293
SKILLS - Suad Kafafi International Language Learning Schools, Egypt D252
SKT International College, Myanmar D311
Skt. Josef's International School, Denmark D351
Slindon College, UK D394
SMA Islam Al-Azhar 3 Jakarta, Indonesia D298
SMA Pradita Dirgantara, Indonesia D298
Smart International Schools, Egypt D252
Smart School, Uzbekistan D334
SMIC Private School, China D279
Smiling International School, Italy D361
Smt. Sulochanadevi Singhania School, India D293
Sokrates International High School, Poland D365
Solomon Schechter Day School of Bergen County, USA D420
Somerset College, Australia D341
Somersfield Academy, Bermuda D400
Sønderborg International School, Denmark D351
Soochow Foreign Language School, China D279
Soodeh Educational Complex, Iran D299
Soong Ching Ling School, China D279
Sophia Mundi Steiner School, Australia D341
SOS-Hermann Gmeiner International College, Ghana D254
Sotogrande International School, Spain 192, D378
Soufriere Primary, Antigua D400
Soundview School, USA D422
South City International School, India D293
Southbank International School - Hampstead, UK D394
Southbank International School - Kensington, UK 190, D394
Southbank International School - Westminster, UK D395
Southend Secondary School, Malawi D256
Southern Christian College, Australia D341
Southern International School, Argentina D427
Southern Ontario Collegiate, Canada D402
Southpointe Academy, Canada D401
Southridge School, Canada D401
Southville International School & Colleges (SISC), Philippines D315
Spartanburg Day School, USA D421
Spectrum International School, Kazakhstan D305
Sphere International School, Brazil D430
Split International School, Croatia D349
Springbank School, New Zealand D344
Springboard International Bilingual School, China D279
Springdale Indian School, United Arab Emirates D333
Springdale International School, Bangladesh D269
Springdale Preparatory School, USA D418
Springfield Public School & College, Pakistan D313
Springfield School - Permata Buana 1 Campus, Indonesia D298
Springvale House, Zimbabwe D266
Sreenidhi International School, India D293
Sri Ara International School, Malaysia D309
Sri Emas International School, Malaysia D309
Sri KDU International School (Klang), Malaysia D309
Sri KDU International School (Kota Damansara), Malaysia D309
Sri KDU International School (Subang Jaya), Malaysia D309
Sri Kuala Lumpur School, Malaysia D309
Srithammarat Suksa School, Thailand D327
SRV International School, India D293
St Andrew's Cathedral School, Australia 85, D341
St Andrew's College, Ireland 193, D358
St Andrew's College, South Africa D263
St Andrew's College, Canada D402
St Andrew's College Cambridge, UK D395
St Andrew's International High School, Malawi D256
St Andrew's International Primary School, Malawi D256
St Andrew's International School, Bahamas D400
St Andrew's School, Australia D341
St Andrew's School, USA D417
St Andrew's School, USA D417
St Andrew's Turi Prep School, Kenya D255
St Andrew's Turi Senior School, Kenya D255
St Andrews International School Bangkok, Thailand D327
St Andrews International School, Dusit Campus, Thailand D327
St Andrews International School, Green Valley Campus, Thailand D327
St Andrews International School, Sathorn Campus, Thailand D327
St Andrews International School, Sukhumvit Campus, Thailand D327
St Andrews Lutheran College, Australia D341
St Andrews Samakee International School, Thailand D327
St Ann Catholic School, USA D417
St Anne's Middle School, Gibraltar D357
St Anne's School, Paraguay D436
St Augustine Primary, Montserrat D413
St Bees Dongguan, China D279
St Bees Shijiazhuang, China D279
St Brendan's School, Uruguay D438
St Brigid's College, Australia D341
St Catherine's British School, Greece D357
St Catherine's, Bramley, UK D395
St Christopher School, UK D395
St Christopher's International Primary School, Malaysia D309
St Christopher's School, Bahrain D268
St Clare's College, Uruguay D438
St Clare's, Oxford, UK D395
St Clement's School, Canada D402
St Columba's College, Ireland D358
St Cuthbert's College, New Zealand D344
St Cyprian's School, South Africa D263
St David's College, UK D395
St Dominic Academy, USA D420
St Dominic's Priory College, Australia D341
St Dunstan's College, UK D395
St Edmund's College & Prep School, UK D395
St Edmund's School, UK D395
St Edward High School, USA D421
St Edward's College, Malta, Malta 194, D362
St Edward's, Oxford, UK D395
St Francis Methodist School, Singapore D322
St Francis' College, UK D395
St George's Ascot, UK D395
St George's British Georgian School, Georgia D354
St George's British International School, Rome, Italy 195, D361
St George's College, Argentina D427
St George's College, Zimbabwe D266
St George's College North, Argentina D427
St George's Diocesan School, Namibia D258
St George's English Academy Bilbao, Spain D378
St George's International School Luxembourg, Luxembourg D362
St George's School for Girls, UK D395
St George's School Windsor Castle, UK D395
St Gregory's College Campbelltown, Australia D341
St Helen's School, UK D395
St Ignatius Catholic School, Cayman Islands D404
St James Senior Boys' School, UK D395
St James Senior Girls' School, UK D395
St James' Primary School, Portugal D367
St John's - Kilmarnock School, Canada D402
St John's Anglican College, Australia D341
St John's College, Zimbabwe D266
St John's College, South Africa D263
St John's Lutheran School, Eudunda, Inc., Australia D341
St John's Preparatory School, Zimbabwe D266
St John's School, Chile D432
St John's School, Puerto Rico D414
St John's School, UK D395
St John's School, UK D395
St Johns College, Bahamas D400
St Joseph's College, UK D395
St Joseph's International Catholic College, Papua New Guinea D344
St Jude's Academy, Canada D402
St Julian's School, Portugal D367
St Lawrence College, Greece D358
St Lawrence College, UK D395
St Leonard's College, Australia D341
St Leonards School, UK D395
St Lukes College, Argentina D427
St Margaret's Berwick Grammar, Australia D341
St Margaret's British School For Girls, Chile D432
St Margaret's College, New Zealand D344
St Margaret's School, Bushey, UK D395
St Margarets School, Argentina D427
St Mark's College, Argentina D427
St Mark's International School, Thailand D327
St Mark's School, New Zealand D344
St Mary Star of the Sea College, Australia D341
St Mary's Academy, Pakistan D313
St Mary's Calne, UK D395
St Mary's Catholic High School, United Arab Emirates D333
St Mary's Catholic High School, United Arab Emirates D333
St Mary's International College, Argentina D427
St Mary's Music School, UK D395
St Mary's School Ascot, UK D395
St Mary's School, Cambridge, UK D395
St Matthew's College - Sede Fundadora, Argentina D428
St Matthew's College - Sede Norte, Argentina D428

Index

St Michael's International School, Japan ... D302
St Michael's Lutheran School, Australia ... D342
St Mildred's Lightbourn School, Canada ... D402
St Patrick's College, Uruguay ... D438
St Patrick's School, Argentina ... D428
St Patrick's Silverstream, New Zealand ... D344
St Paul's College, Namibia ... D258
St Paul's Collegiate School, New Zealand ... D344
St Paul's Grammar School, Australia ... D342
St Paul's School, UK ... D395
St Paul's School, Chile ... D432
St Paul's School, Spain ... D378
St Paul's School Brisbane, Australia ... D342
St Peter's 13-18, UK ... D395
St Peter's Anglican Primary School, Australia ... D342
St Peter's College, Australia ... D342
St Peter's College, New Zealand ... D344
St Peter's Girls' School, Australia ... D342
St Peter's School, Chile ... D432
St Peter's School Barcelona, Spain ... D378
St Peter's School, Cambridge, New Zealand ... D344
St Peter's Woodlands Grammar School, Australia ... D342
St Peters Lutheran College, Australia ... D342
St Philips College, Australia, Australia ... D342
St Saviour's School, Nigeria ... D260
St Stephen's International School, Thailand ... D327
St Stephen's International School, Khao Yai, Thailand ... D327
St Stithians College, South Africa ... D263
St Swithun's School, UK ... D395
St Teresa's Effingham (Senior School), UK ... D395
St Ursula's College Kingsgrove, Australia ... D342
St Xavier's College, Argentina ... D428
St. Andrew's School (RI), USA ... D421
St. Andrew's Scots School, Argentina ... D428
St. Andrews Anglican School, Bahamas ... D400
St. Anne's School, Bahamas ... D400
St. Anne's School, Spain ... D378
St. Anthony's College, Spain ... D378
St. Austin's Academy, Kenya ... D255
St. Bernadette School Akoka, Nigeria ... D260
St. Bernadette School Ipaja, Nigeria ... D260
St. Catherine's Moorlands - Belgrano, Argentina ... D428
St. Catherine's Moorlands - Tortuguitas, Argentina ... D428
St. Cecelia Interparochial Catholic School, USA ... D417
St. Christopher's Schools, Kenya ... D255
St. Constantine's International School, Tanzania ... D264
St. Fatima Schools - Badr, Egypt ... D252
St. Fatima Schools - Nasr City, Egypt ... D252
St. Francis College, Brazil, Brazil ... D430
St. Francis International School, Italy ... D361
St. Francis of Assisi, USA ... D418
St. Francis of Assisi Elementary School, USA ... D415
St. Frederick High School, USA ... D418
St. George International School and Preschool, Bulgaria ... D348
St. George, The British School Madrid, Spain ... D378
St. George, The British School of Catalunya, Spain ... D378
St. George's British International School (Bilbao), Spain ... 196, D378
St. George's College - Sede Senior, Peru ... D437
St. George's International School, Switzerland, Switzerland ... 197, D382
St. George's School, Uruguay ... D438
St. George's The British International School Cologne, Germany ... D356
St. George's The British International School Munich, Germany ... D356
St. George's The British International School, Düsseldorf Rhein-Ruhr, Germany ... D357
St. Gilgen International School GmbH, Austria ... D346
St. James School, UK ... D395
St. Joan Antida High School, USA ... D423
St. John American School, Egypt ... D252
St. John's Academy Shawnigan Lake, Canada ... D401
St. John's International School, Belgium ... 198, D348
St. John's School, Guam ... D343
St. John's School - Beccar, Argentina ... D428
St. John's School - Escobar, Argentina ... D428
St. John's School - Martínez, Argentina ... D428
St. John's School - Pilar, Argentina ... D428
St. Joseph's Institution International, Singapore ... D322
St. Joseph's Institution International School Malaysia (Tropicana PJ Campus), Malaysia ... D309
St. Joseph's International School, Egypt ... D252
St. Joseph's Junior High & Senior High School, Japan ... D302
St. Joseph's Primary School, Japan ... D303
St. Jude School, Costa Rica ... D405
St. Laurence High School, USA ... D418
St. Louis Archinto, Italy ... D361
St. Louis Colonna, Italy ... D361
St. Louis School, Italy ... 199, D361
St. Luke School, USA ... D422
St. Margaret's School, Canada ... D401
St. Mary's International School, Japan ... D303
St. Mary's School, USA ... D415
St. Mary's School - Nairobi, Kenya ... D255
St. Matthias School, USA ... D418
St. Michael's - El Parque, Spain ... D378
St. Michael's - Escorial, Spain ... D378
St. Michael's - Las Lomas, Spain ... D378
St. Michael's School, Dominican Republic ... D405
St. Nicholas School - Alphaville, Brazil ... D430
St. Nicholas School - Pinheiros, Brazil ... D431
St. Nicholas' School, Argentina ... D428
St. Patrick School, Dominican Republic ... D405
St. Paul American School Hanoi, Vietnam ... D336
St. Paul's Co-educational College, Hong Kong, China ... D284
St. Paul's College, Argentina ... D428
St. Paul's School, Brazil ... D431
St. Peter's International School, Portugal ... 200, D367
St. Peter's School, Egypt ... D252
St. Stephen's School, Italy ... D361
St. Stephens Episcopal School Houston, USA ... D422
St. Thomas the Apostle Catholic School, USA ... D417
St. Thomas's International School, Italy ... D361
St. Timothy's School, USA ... D418
St. Xavier's High School, India ... D293
Stafford International School, Sri Lanka ... D323
Stafford Sri Lankan School Doha, Qatar ... D317
Stamford American International School, Singapore ... D323
Stamford American School Hong Kong, Hong Kong, China ... D284
Stamford High School, UK ... D395
Stamford School, UK ... D396
Stanborough Secondary School, UK ... D396
Stanford Lake College, South Africa ... D263
Stanford Online High School, USA ... D415
Stanstead College, Canada ... D403
Star College Bridgetown, South Africa ... D263
Star College Cape Town, South Africa ... D263
Star College Durban Boys High, South Africa ... D263
Star College Durban Girls High, South Africa ... D263
Star College Durban Primary, South Africa ... D263
Star College Pretoria, South Africa ... D263
Star International School, United Arab Emirates ... D333
Star International School, Mirdif, United Arab Emirates ... D333
Starlight International Kindergarten - Feng Yuan Campus, Taiwan ... D324
Starlight International Kindergarten - Hui Wen Campus, Taiwan ... D324
Stars College, Lebanon ... D307
Start-Rite International School, Nigeria ... D260
Stedelijk Gymnasium Nijmegen, Netherlands ... D364
Stella Maris College & Prep School, Spain ... D378
Stella Maris Medan Damansara, Malaysia ... D309
Stella Maris School, Indonesia ... D298
Step by Step School, India ... D293
Step One International School, Qatar ... D317
Stephen Perse Sixth Form, UK ... D396
Stewart's Melville College, UK ... D396
Stiftsschule Engelberg, Switzerland ... D382
Stiftung Landheim Schondorf am Ammersee, Germany ... D357
Stiftung Louisenlund, Germany ... D357
Still I Rise International School - Bogotá, Colombia ... D435
Still I Rise International School - Mumbai, India ... D293
Still I Rise International School - Nairobi, Kenya ... D255
Stockholm International School, Sweden ... D379
Stoke College, UK ... D396
Stonar School, UK ... D396
Stonehill International School, India ... 70, D293
Stoneleigh-Burnham School, USA ... D419
Stonyhurst College, UK ... D396
Stonyhurst Southville International School - Batangas City Campus, Philippines ... D315
Stonyhurst Southville International School - Malarayat Campus, Philippines ... D315
Stover School, UK ... D396
Stowe School, UK ... D396
Straits International School, Malaysia ... D309
Stratford Hall, Canada ... 231, D401
Strathallan School, UK ... D396
Strathcona-Tweedsmuir School, Canada ... D400
Strawberry Fields High School, India ... D293
Strelitz International Academy, USA ... D422
Strothoff International School Rhein-Main Campus Dreieich, Germany ... D357

Index

Súkromná spojená skola, Slovakia D370
Súkromné Bilingválne Gymnázium Ceská, Slovakia D370
Summerhill International School, Japan D303
Summit Academy, Bahamas D400
Sunbeam Kindergarten, Qatar D317
Suncity School, India D293
Sunflower English School, India D293
Sunmarke School, United Arab Emirates D333
Sunny Canadian International School, Czech Republic D350
Sunny View School, Spain D378
Sunnybrook School, Canada D402
Sunnydale School, Bangladesh D269
Sunnyside International School, Japan D303
Sunrise English Private School, United Arab Emirates D333
Sunrise International School, Egypt D252
Sunrise School, Argentina D428
Sunshine Grammar School and College, Bangladesh D269
Sunshine Kids Academy, Japan D303
Sunshine Worldwide Secondary School, India D293
Sunway International School, Bandar Sunway, Malaysia D309
Sunway International School, Sunway Iskandar, Malaysia D309
Surabaya European School, Indonesia D298
Surabaya Intercultural School, Indonesia D298
Surefoot International School, Nigeria D261
Surval Montreux, Switzerland D382
Sutton Park School, Ireland D358
Sutton Valence School, UK D396
Suzhou Foreign Language School, China D279
Suzhou Industrial Park Foreign Language School, China D279
Suzhou Innovation Academy, China D279
Suzhou North America High School, China D279
Suzhou Science and Technology Town Foreign Language School, China D279
Suzhou Singapore International School, China D279
Suzhou Victoria Kindergarten, China D279
SVKM JV Parekh International School, India D293
Swami Vivekanand International School - Gorai, India D293
Swami Vivekanand International School - Kandivali, India D293
Swans International Primary School, Spain D378
Swans International Secondary School, Spain D378
Swiss International School Qatar, Qatar D317
Swiss International Scientific School in Dubai, United Arab Emirates D333
Swiss School in Singapore, Singapore D323
Sworn College S.A. Moreno, Argentina D428
Sworn Junior College, Argentina D428
Swostishree Gurukul, Nepal D311
Sylhet Khananchibari International School and College, Bangladesh D269
Symbiosis International School, India D293
Szczecin International School, Poland D366
Szczecinska Szkola Witruwianska SVS, Poland D366
Szeged International Primary School, Hungary D358
Szkola Europejska - Gimnazjum / Liceum, Poland D366

T

Taaleem, United Arab Emirates D333
Tabeetha School, Israel D299
Tabubil International School, Papua New Guinea D344
Taejon Christian International School, Republic of Korea D318
Tai Kwong Hilary College (TKHC), Hong Kong, China D284
Taichung City Starlight Experimental Education, Taiwan D324
Taipei Adventist American School, Taiwan D324
Taipei American School, Taiwan D324
Taipei European School, Taiwan D324
Taipei Kuei Shan School, Taiwan D324
Taiwan Adventist International School, Taiwan D324
Takoradi International School, Ghana D254
Taktse International School, India D293
Talbot Heath, UK D396
Talent International & The Infant School (Manama Branch), Bahrain D268
Talent International & The Infant School (Riffa Branch), Bahrain D268
Talitha Kumi School, Israel D299
Tall Pines School, Canada D402
Tallinn European School, Estonia D351
Tallinna Saksa Gümnaasium, Estonia D351
Tamagawa Academy K-12 & University, Japan D303
Taman Rama School, Indonesia D298
Tambearly School, Bahamas D400
Tanarata International Schools, Malaysia D309
Tandem IMS (International Multilingual School), Switzerland D382
Tanglin Trust School in Singapore, Singapore 73, D323
Tara Anglican School for Girls, Australia D342
Tarabya British Schools, Türkiye D386
Tarbiyah Academy, USA D418
Tariq Bin Ziad School, Qatar D317
Tarsus American School, Türkiye D386
Tartu International School, Estonia D351
Tas Private Elementary School, Türkiye D386
Tashkent International School, Uzbekistan D334
Tashkent Ulugbek International School, Uzbekistan D334
TASIS England, UK 201, D396
TASIS Portugal, Portugal D367
TASIS The American School in Switzerland, Switzerland 202, D382
Taunggyi International School, Myanmar D311
Taunton School, UK D396
Taunton School International, UK D396
Taunus International Montessori School, Germany D357
Taylor's College Sri Hartamas, Malaysia D310
Taylor's College Subang Jaya, Malaysia D310
Taylor's International School, Kuala Lumpur, Malaysia D310
TCIS, India D293
Te Hihi School, New Zealand D344
Tecnológico de Monterrey, México D413
Tecnológico de Monterrey - Campus Cuernavaca, México D413
Tecnológico de Monterrey - Campus Puebla, México D413
Tecnológico de Monterrey - Campus San Luis Potosí, México D413
Tecnológico de Monterrey - PrepaTec Ciudad de México, México D413
Tecnológico de Monterrey - PrepaTec Cumbres, México D413
Tecnológico de Monterrey - PrepaTec Esmeralda, México D413
Tecnológico de Monterrey - PrepaTec Estado de México, México D413
Tecnológico de Monterrey - PrepaTec Eugenio Garza Lagüera, México D413
Tecnológico de Monterrey - PrepaTec Eugenio Garza Sada, México D413
Tecnológico de Monterrey - PrepaTec Metepec, México D413
Tecnológico de Monterrey - PrepaTec Querétaro, México D413
Tecnológico de Monterrey - PrepaTec Santa Catarina, México D413
Tecnológico de Monterrey - PrepaTec Santa Fe, México D413
Tecnológico de Monterrey - PrepaTec Valle Alto, México D413
TED Ankara College Foundation High School, Türkiye D386
TED Bursa College, Türkiye D386
TED Istanbul College Foundation, Türkiye D386
Teda International School, China D279
Teikyo School UK, UK D396
Teikyo University Kani Junior & Senior High School, Japan D303
Telluride Mountain School, USA D416
Tema International School, Ghana D254
Temple Christian School, Bahamas D400
Temple Emanu-El, USA D422
Temple Primary School, Nigeria D261
Temple Secondary School, Nigeria D261
Tenby Schools Ipoh, Malaysia D310
Tenby Schools Miri, Malaysia D310
Tenby Schools Penang, Malaysia D310
Tenby Schools Setia Eco Gardens, Malaysia D310
Tenby Schools Setia Eco Hill, Malaysia D310
Tenby Schools Setia Eco Park, Malaysia D310
Terakki Foundation - Levent Campus, Türkiye D386
Terakki Foundation - Tepeoren Campus, Türkiye D386
Tesla Education - Tan Binh Campus, Vietnam D336
Tessa International School, USA D420
Tettenhall College, UK D396
Tev Inanc Turkes High School For Gifted Students, Türkiye D386
TFS - Canada's International School, Canada 232, D402
TH School, Vietnam D336
Thai Sikh International School, Thailand D327
Thai-Chinese International School, Thailand D327
Thakur International School, India D293
Thalun International School, Myanmar D311
Thamer International School, Saudi Arabia D321
Thames British School Madrid Campus, Spain D378
Thames British School Mokotów High School Campus, Poland 203, D366
Thames British School Mokotów Primary Campus, Poland 204, D366
Thames British School Ochota Campus, Poland 205, D366
Thames British School Wlochy Campus, Poland 206, D366
The Abbey School, UK D396
The ABC International School, Vietnam D336
The Academy International School, Spain D378
The Academy of the Holy Cross, USA D418
The Affiliated International School of Shenzhen University, China D279
The Aga Khan Academy Dhaka, Bangladesh D269
The Aga Khan Academy Hyderabad, India D293
The Aga Khan Academy Maputo, Mozambique D258
The Aga Khan Academy Mombasa, Kenya D255
The Aga Khan Academy, Nairobi, Kenya D255
The Aga Khan High School, Kampala, Uganda D265
The Aga Khan High School, Nairobi, Kenya D256
The Aga Khan Mzizima Secondary School, Dar es Salaam, Tanzania D264
The Aga Khan Nursery and Primary School, Dar es Salaam, Tanzania D264

Index

The Aga Khan Nursery School, Nairobi, Kenya..................D256
The Aga Khan Primary School, Kampala, Uganda..................D265
The Aga Khan School, Dhaka, Bangladesh..................D269
The American Academy for Girls, Kuwait..................D306
The American Academy Nicosia, Cyprus..................D349
The American International School in Gaza, Palestine..................D314
The American International School of Muscat (TAISM), Oman..................D312
The American International School of Vilnius, Lithuania..................D362
The American School, Chile..................D432
The American School Foundation, A.C., México..................D413
The American School in Japan, Japan..................D303
The American School in London, UK..................D396
The American School of Antananarivo, Madagascar..................D256
The American School of Bangkok - Green Valley Campus, Thailand..................D327
The American School of Bangkok - Sukhumvit Campus, Thailand..................D327
The American School of Kinshasa, Democratic Republic of the Congo..................D249
The American School of Kuwait, Kuwait..................D306
The American School of Tampico, México..................D413
The American School of Tegucigalpa, Honduras..................D435
The Americas Bicultural School, Dominican Republic..................D406
The Anglo School, Uruguay..................D438
The Anglo-American School of Moscow, Russian Federation..................D369
The Anglo-Italian School, Montessori Division, Italy..................D361
The Antofagasta British School, Chile..................D432
The Aquila School, United Arab Emirates..................D333
The Arbor School, United Arab Emirates..................D333
The Armidale School, Australia..................D342
The Ashcroft School, Turks And Caicos Islands..................D414
The Asian International School, Vietnam..................D336
The Asian School, Bahrain..................D268
The Assam Valley School, India..................D293
The Australian International School, Laos..................D306
The Australian International School (AISPNG), Papua New Guinea..................D344
The Avicenna School - Tipu Sultan Road (Girls Campus), Pakistan..................D313
The Avicenna School - Tipu Sultan Road Campus (Boys and Girls), Pakistan..................D313
The Awty International School, USA..................D422
The Baldwin School of Puerto Rico, Puerto Rico..................D414
The Banda School, Kenya..................D256
The Beacon Academy, Philippines..................D315
The Beacon School, Philippines..................D315
The Bell Language School, Switzerland..................D382
The Benalmádena International College, Spain..................D378
The Bilingual Montessori School of Paris - Auteuil, France..................D353
The Bilingual Montessori School of Paris - George V, France..................D353
The Bilingual Montessori School of Paris - Orsay, France..................D353
The Biltmore School, USA..................233, D417
The Bombay Suburban Grain Dealers' Junior College of Commerce, Arts & Science, India..................D293
The Boys' School of St Paul's Parish, USA..................D418
The Bridge International School, Cameroon..................D248
The British Academy, Trinidad & Tobago..................D414
The British College, Spain..................D378
The British College of Andorra, Andorra..................D346
The British College of Brazil, Brazil..................242, D431
The British International School, Hungary..................D358
The British International School Istanbul - Etiler, Türkiye..................D386
The British International School of Brussels, Belgium..................D348
The British International School of Charlotte, USA..................D421
The British International School of Jeddah, Saudi Arabia..................D321
The British International School of Kuala Lumpur, Malaysia..................D310
The British International School of Marbella, Spain..................D378
The British International School of New York, USA..................D420
The British International School of Northern Thailand, Thailand..................D327
The British International School Shanghai, Puxi, China..................D279
The British International School Ukraine (Nivki Campus), Ukraine..................D398
The British International School Ukraine (Pechersk Campus), Ukraine..................D398
The British International School, Abu Dhabi, United Arab Emirates..................D333
The British International School, Bratislava, Slovakia..................D370
The British International School, Cairo, Egypt..................D252
The British International School, Moscow, Russian Federation..................D369
The British Junior Academy of Brussels, Belgium..................D348
The British Preparatory School, Bahrain..................D268
The British School, India..................D293
The British School - Al Khubairat, United Arab Emirates..................D333
The British School - Punta Arenas, Chile..................D432
The British School Caracas, Venezuela..................D438
The British School in Cairo, Egypt..................D253
The British School in the Netherlands - Leidschenveen, Netherlands..................D364
The British School in the Netherlands - Vlaskamp, Netherlands..................D364
The British School in the Netherlands - Voorschoten, Netherlands..................D364
The British School in Tokyo, Japan..................D303
The British School Kathmandu, Nepal..................D311

The British School of Almeria, Spain..................D378
The British School of Amsterdam, Netherlands..................207, D364
The British School of Aragon, Spain..................D378
The British School of Bahrain, Bahrain..................D268
The British School of Barcelona (BSB) Castelldefels, Spain..................D378
The British School of Barcelona (BSB) City Foundation Campus, Spain..................D378
The British School of Barcelona (BSB) City Main Campus, Spain..................D378
The British School of Barcelona (BSB) Nexus, Spain..................D378
The British School of Barcelona (BSB) Sitges, Spain..................D378
The British School of Beijing, Sanlitun, China..................74, D279
The British School of Benghazi, Libya..................D256
The British School of Brasilia, Brazil..................D431
The British School of Brussels (BSB), Belgium..................208, D348
The British School of Costa Rica, Costa Rica..................D405
The British School of Egypt, Egypt..................D253
The British School of Guangzhou, China..................D279
The British School of Kuwait, Kuwait..................D306
The British School of Lisbon, Portugal..................D367
The British School of Lomé, Togo..................D264
The British School of Milan (Sir James Henderson), Italy..................209, D361
The British School of Nanjing, China..................D279
The British School of Navarra, Spain..................D378
The British School of Paris, France..................D354
The British School of Seville, Spain..................D378
The British School of Tashkent, Uzbekistan..................D334
The British School of Vilnius, Lithuania..................D362
The British School Quito, Ecuador..................D407
The British School Warsaw, Poland..................210, D366
The British School Yangon, Myanmar..................D311
The British School, Alexandria, Egypt..................D253
The British School, Bern, Switzerland..................D382
The British School, Rio de Janeiro, Brazil..................243, D431
The British School, Rio de Janeiro - Barra Site, Brazil..................D431
The British School, Sector 8, Panchkula, India..................D293
The British Schools, Montevideo, Uruguay..................D438
The Calverton School, USA..................D419
The Cambridge High School - Abu Dhabi, United Arab Emirates..................D333
The Cambridge School, Qatar..................D317
The Cambridge School, India..................D294
The Canadian School of Warsaw, Poland..................D366
The Casco School, Panama..................D436
The Cathedral & John Connon School, India..................D294
The Centagon International School, Nigeria..................D261
The Chalfonts Independent Grammar School, UK..................D396
The Children's Academy, Bahrain, Bahrain..................D268
The Children's House, Norway..................D365
The Childville, Nigeria..................D261
The Choice School, Tripunithura, India..................D294
The Churchill School, México..................D413
The City School, Thailand..................D327
The City School - A Level Campus, Pakistan..................D313
The City School, Capital Campus Islamabad, Pakistan..................D314
The City School, Kohat Campus, Pakistan..................D314
The Clariden School, USA..................D422
The Codrington School, Barbados..................D428
The Columbus School, Colombia..................D435
The Community for Learning, Dominican Republic..................D406
The Courtyard International School of Tervuren, Belgium..................D348
The Curacao American Preparatory School, Curaçao..................D435
The Democratic School, Pakistan..................D314
The Discovery School, USA..................D417
The Doon School, India..................D294
The École, USA..................234, D420
The Edron Academy, México..................D413
The Educational World (FB Area Senior Chapter), Pakistan..................D314
The Emerald Heights International School, India..................D294
The English Academy, Kuwait..................D306
The English College, United Arab Emirates..................D333
The English International College, Spain..................D378
The English International School Moscow, Russian Federation..................D369
The English International School of Padua, Italy..................D361
The English Learning Centre, Cyprus..................D349
The English Modern School, Qatar..................D317
The English Montessori School, Spain..................D379
The English School, Spain..................D379
The English School, Finland..................D351
The English School Fahaheel, Kuwait..................D306
The English School for Girls, Kuwait..................D306
The English School of Kyrenia, Cyprus..................D349
The English School of Mongolia, Mongolia..................D310
The English School, Cyprus, Cyprus..................D349
The English School, Kuwait, Kuwait..................D306
The English Speaking Community School of Guinea, Guinea..................D254

Index

The Essington School, Australia D342
The Falcon School, Cyprus D349
The French American School of Rhode Island, USA D421
The French American School of Tampa Bay, USA D417
The Friends' School, Australia 86, D342
The G C School of Careers, Cyprus D349
The Galaxy School, India D294
The Garden International School, China D279
The Gaudium School, India D294
The Giving Tree International School, Cambodia D270
The Global College, Spain 211, D379
The Grammar School Limassol, Cyprus D349
The Grammar School Limassol - Junior School, Cyprus D349
The Grammar School, Nicosia, Cyprus D349
The Grange School, Chile D432
The Greenland School, Chile D432
The Gulf English School, Qatar D317
The Hague School, USA D422
The Hammond School, UK D396
The Harbour School, Hong Kong, China D284
The Healdsburg School, USA D415
The Heritage Private School, Cyprus D349
The Heritage School Zimbabwe, Zimbabwe D266
The Heritage School, Kolkata, India D294
The High School at Vancouver Island University, Canada D401
The Hilltop International British School of Kumasi, Ghana D254
The Hotchkiss School, USA D416
The Hutchins School, Australia 87, D342
The Illawarra Grammar School, Australia D342
The Independent School Batam, Indonesia D298
The Independent Schools Foundation Academy, Hong Kong, China D284
The Indian Academy, Dubai, United Arab Emirates D333
The Indian Community School Kuwait, Kuwait D306
The Indian School, Bahrain D268
The Intercultural School of Bogor, Indonesia D298
The International Academy - Amman, Jordan 76, D304
The International Gymnasium of the Skolkovo Innovation Center, Russian Federation D369
The International School (TIS), Pakistan D314
The International School @ Park City Hanoi, Vietnam D336
The International School @ Park City Kuala Lumpur, Malaysia D310
The International School Bangalore, India D294
The International School Estepona, Spain D379
The International School in Genoa, Italy D361
The International School of Azerbaijan, Baku, Azerbaijan D347
The International School of Brussels (ISB), Belgium D348
The International School of Choueifat - Abu Dhabi, United Arab Emirates D333
The International School of Choueifat - Abu Dhabi Khalifa City, United Arab Emirates D334
The International School of Choueifat - Ajman, United Arab Emirates D334
The International School of Choueifat - Al Ain, United Arab Emirates D334
The International School of Choueifat - Amman, Jordan D304
The International School of Choueifat - Cairo, Egypt D253
The International School of Choueifat - Choueifat, Lebanon D307
The International School of Choueifat - City of 6 October, Egypt D253
The International School of Choueifat - Damascus, Syrian Arab Republic D323
The International School of Choueifat - Doha, Qatar D317
The International School of Choueifat - Dream City, Iraq D299
The International School of Choueifat - Dubai, United Arab Emirates D334
The International School of Choueifat - Dubai Investments Park, United Arab Emirates D334
The International School of Choueifat - Erbil, Iraq D299
The International School of Choueifat - Koura, Lebanon D307
The International School of Choueifat - Lahore, Pakistan D314
The International School of Choueifat - Manama, Bahrain D268
The International School of Choueifat - Muscat, Oman D312
The International School of Choueifat - Ras Al Khaimah, United Arab Emirates D334
The International School of Choueifat - Sharjah, United Arab Emirates D334
The International School of Choueifat - Sulaimani, Iraq D299
The International School of Choueifat - Umm Al Quwain, United Arab Emirates D334
The International School of Egypt, Egypt D253
The International School of Gabon Ruban Vert, Gabon D253
The International School of IITA, Nigeria D261
The International School of Kuala Lumpur (ISKL), Malaysia 77, D310
The International School of Macao, China D279
The International School of Minnesota, USA D419
The International School of Moscow, Russian Federation D369
The International School of Naples, Italy D361
The International School of Paphos, Cyprus D349
The International School of Penang (Uplands), Malaysia D310
The International School of Port of Spain, Trinidad & Tobago D414
The International School of Samui, Thailand D327
The International School of Sosua, Dominican Republic D406
The International School of The Hague, Netherlands D364
The International School of Walvis Bay, Namibia D258
The International School Yangon, Myanmar D311
The Island Private School of Limassol, Cyprus D349
The Italian School of Lusaka, Zambia D266
The Junior & Senior School, Cyprus D349
The KAUST School, Saudi Arabia D321
The Kindergarten of Hefei Run'an Boarding School, China D279
The King's Hospital, Ireland D358
The King's School, Australia D342
The King's School, Canterbury, UK D396
The King's School, Tudor House, Australia D342
The Koç School, Türkiye D386
The Latham School, Tanzania D264
The Lawrence School, India D294
The Learning Tree, Pakistan D314
The Leo Baeck Day School, Canada D402
The Lester Vaughan School, Barbados D428
The Leys School, UK D396
The Little Academy, Jordan D304
The Little Skool-House International (By-the-Vista), Singapore D323
The Lyceum School, Pakistan D314
The MacDuffie School, Shanghai, China D280
The Manchester Grammar School, UK D396
The Manila Times College of Subic, Philippines D315
The Mary Erskine School, UK D396
The Mayflower School, Chile D432
The Mervyn Academy, Nigeria D261
The Millennium School - Dubai, United Arab Emirates D334
The Model School, United Arab Emirates D334
The Montessori School Kingsley, Australia D342
The Montessori School of Raleigh, USA D421
The Montessori School of Tokyo, Japan D303
The Mount School York, UK D396
The Mountain Cambridge School, South Africa D263
The Nairobi Academy, Kenya D256
The Nazareth Middle and High School in Warsaw, Poland D366
The NEST School, India D294
The New School Rome, Italy 212, D361
The New Tulip International School, India D294
The Newman School, USA D419
The Olive Tree School, Spain D379
The Olympia Schools, Vietnam D336
The Oratory School, UK D396
The Ostrava International School, Czech Republic D350
The Overseas School of Colombo, Sri Lanka D323
The Owl's Nest International School (ONIS), Ghana D254
The Oxford School, Panama D436
The Oxford School Dubai, United Arab Emirates D334
The Peace Attitude Schools, Pakistan D314
The Pearl School, Qatar D317
The Peterborough School, UK D396
The Portsmouth Grammar School, UK D396
The Post Oak School, USA D422
The Prague British School - Kamyk Site, Czech Republic D350
The Prague British School - Vlastina Site, Czech Republic D350
The Priory Preparatory School, Nigeria D261
The Pupil, Saveetha Eco School, India D294
The Purcell School, London, UK D396
The Rajkumar College Rajkot, India D294
The Read School, UK D396
The Red Oaks School, USA D420
The Regent Primary School, Abuja, Nigeria D261
The Regent Secondary School, Abuja, Nigeria D261
The Regent's School, Bangkok, Thailand D327
The RiverBank School, Nigeria D261
The Riverina Anglican College, Australia D342
The Riverside School, India D294
The Roche School, UK D396
The Rock School, USA D417
The Roig Academy, USA D417
The Roman Ridge School, Ghana D254
The Royal Grammar School Guildford, Doha, Qatar D317
The Royal Grammar School Guildford, Dubai, United Arab Emirates D334
The Royal Grammar School Guildford, Nanjing, China D280
The Royal Hospital School, UK D396
The Royal Masonic School for Girls, UK 213, D397
The Royal School, Dungannon, UK D397

Index

The Royal School, Haslemere, UK D397
The Sacred Heart School of Montreal, Canada D403
The Sanskaar Valley School, India D294
The Scholars' International School, Qatar D317
The School of Research Science, United Arab Emirates D334
The Scindia School, India D294
The Scots College, Australia D342
The Scots School Albury, Australia D342
The Senior School, Cyprus D349
The Sezin School, Türkiye D386
The Sheffield Private School, United Arab Emirates D334
The Sheikh Zayed Private Academy for Boys, United Arab Emirates D334
The Sheikh Zayed Private Academy for Girls, United Arab Emirates D334
The Shri Ram Academy, India D294
The Shri Ram School, India D294
The Shriram Millennium School, Faridabad, India D294
The Shriram Millennium School, Gurugram, India D294
The Shriram Millennium School, Noida, India D294
The Southport School, Australia D342
The Sri Lankan School Muskat, Oman D312
The Stewart Bilingual School, UK D397
The Sultan's School, Oman D312
The Universal School, India D294
The Vale School Muthaiga, Kenya D256
The Victoria School, Colombia D435
The Village School, USA 235, D422
The WellSpring School, United Arab Emirates D334
The Wessex School, Chile D432
The Westminster School - Dubai, United Arab Emirates D334
The Westwood School, USA D422
The White School International, India D294
The Winchester School - Dubai, United Arab Emirates D334
The Wingate School, México 238, D413
The Woodlands Preparatory School, USA D422
The World Academy, Saudi Arabia D321
The Worthgate School, UK D397
The York School, Canada D402
Theodore International Startup Academy (TISA) Leiden, Netherlands D364
Theodore International Startup Academy (TISA) Lisbon, Portugal D367
Theresa Nuzzo (Marsa) School, Malta D362
Theresianische Foundation Academy, Austria D346
Think and Grow, Pakistan D314
THINK Global School, USA 236, D415
Think International School, Hong Kong, China D284
Thomas Adewumi International College (TAICO), Nigeria D261
Thomas Mitchell Primary School, Australia D342
Thornhill Primary School, Botswana D248
Thornton College, UK D397
Tianjin International School, China D280
Tianjin Yinghua International School, China D280
Tien Shan International School, Kazakhstan D305
Times College, China D280
TIPS Bengaluru, India D294
TIPS Chennai, India D294
TIPS Coimbatore, India D294
TIPS Erode, India D294
TIPS Karur, India D294
TIPS Kochi, India D294
TIPS Kuala Lumpur, Malaysia D310
TIPS Madurai, India D294
TIPS Salem, India D294
TIPS Tirupur, India D294
TIPS Trichy, India D294
TLC International School, Mauritania D256
TNS Beaconhouse Defence, Pakistan D314
TNS Beaconhouse Gulberg, Pakistan D314
Tohoku International School, Japan D303
Tokai Gakuen High School, Japan D303
Tokyo International School, Japan D303
Tokyo West International School, Japan D303
Tomás Alva Edison, México D413
Tonbridge School, UK D397
Tongwen School, Jiaxing, China D280
Toorak College, Australia D342
Torisawa Kindergarten, Japan D303
Toronto Academy of EMC, Canada D402
Total French School, Aberdeen, UK D397
Towarzystwo Edukacyjne Vizja, Poland D366
Towheed Iranian School, United Arab Emirates D334
Town Centre Montessori Private Schools, Canada D402
Townshend International School, Czech Republic D350
Townsville Grammar School, Australia D342
Traill International School, Thailand D327
Transylvania College, Romania D368
Treamis, India D294
Trebulco School, Chile D432
TreeHouse International School (T.H.I.S.), Israel D299
Treetops Montessori School, Australia D342
Trent College and The Elms, UK D397
Trident College Solwezi, Zambia D265
Trident Prep School, Zambia D266
Trillium International School, France D354
Tring Park School for the Performing Arts, UK D397
Trinity Anglican School, Australia D342
Trinity Catholic School, USA D417
Trinity College Preparatory High School, USA D418
Trinity Episcopal School, USA D422
Trinity Grammar School Preparatory School, Australia D342
Trinity Grammar School, Kew, Australia D342
Trinity Grammar School, Sydney, Australia D342
Trinity International School, India D294
Trinity Lutheran College, Australia D342
Trinity Lutheran College, Australia D342
Trinity Lutheran School, USA D422
Trinity School, UK D397
Trio World Academy, India D294
Triple C School, Cayman Islands D404
Trivandrum International School, India D294
Tromsø International School, Norway D365
Truro School, UK D397
Tsinghua International School, China D280
Tsukuba International School, Japan D303
Tudor Hall School, UK D397
Tunas Muda School Kedoya, Indonesia D298
Tunas Muda School Meruya, Indonesia D298
Tunas Unggul, Indonesia D298
Tung Der High School, Taiwan D324
Tungwah Wenzel International School, China D280
Tunku Putra School, Malaysia D310
Tzu Chi School, Pantai Indah Kapuk, Indonesia D298

U

UCSI International School, Malaysia D310
Udgam School for Children, India D294
Udine International School, Italy D361
Udon Thani International School (UDIS), Thailand D327
UFS International, Eswatini D253
UIA International School of Tokyo, Japan D303
Uk School, Ecuador D407
Ukarumpa International School, Papua New Guinea D344
Ulaanbaatar Elite International School, Mongolia D310
ULink College Guangzhou, China D280
Ulink College of Shanghai, China D280
Ullens School, Nepal D311
UNICOSMOS School, India D295
Unidad Educativa 'Cap. Edmundo Chiriboga G.', Ecuador D407
Unidad Educativa 'Émile Jaques-Dalcroze', Ecuador D407
Unidad Educativa 'Julio Verne', Ecuador D407
Unidad Educativa Alberto Einstein, Ecuador D407
Unidad Educativa Bilingüe Delta, Ecuador D407
Unidad Educativa Bilingüe Hontanar, Ecuador D407
Unidad Educativa Bilingüe Mixta Sagrados Corazones, Ecuador D407
Unidad Educativa Bilingüe Nueva Semilla, Ecuador D407
Unidad Educativa Bilingüe Nuevo Mundo, Ecuador D407
Unidad Educativa Bilingüe Torremar, Ecuador D407
Unidad Educativa Bilingüe William Caxton College, Ecuador D407
Unidad Educativa Cristo Rey, Ecuador D407
Unidad Educativa Isaac Newton, Ecuador D407
Unidad Educativa Juan León Mera La Salle, Ecuador D407
Unidad Educativa Maurice Ravel, Ecuador D407
Unidad Educativa Monte Tabor Nazaret, Ecuador D407
Unidad Educativa Particular 'Rosa de Jesús Cordero', Ecuador D408
Unidad Educativa Particular Bilingüe Ecomundo, Ecuador D407
Unidad Educativa Particular Bilingüe Leonardo da Vinci, Ecuador D407
Unidad Educativa Particular Bilingüe Principito y Marcel Laniado de Wind, Ecuador D407
Unidad Educativa Particular Bilingüe Santiago Mayor, Ecuador D407
Unidad Educativa Particular Bilingüe Santo Domingo de Guzmán, Ecuador D407
Unidad Educativa Particular Hermano Miguel De La Salle, Ecuador D407
Unidad Educativa Particular Javier, Ecuador D408
Unidad Educativa Particular Politécnico, Ecuador D408
Unidad Educativa Particular Redemptio, Ecuador D408
Unidad Educativa Paul Dirac, Ecuador D408
Unidad Educativa Saint Dominic School, Ecuador D408
Unidad Educativa Salesiana Cardenal Spellman, Ecuador D408

Index

Unidad Educativa Salinas Innova, Ecuador D408
Unidad Educativa San Francisco de Sales, Ecuador D408
Unidad Educativa San Jose La Salle, Ecuador D408
Unidad Educativa Santana, Ecuador D408
Unidad Educativa Terranova, Ecuador D408
Unidad Educativa Theodore W. Anderson, Ecuador D408
Unidad Educativa Tomás Moro, Ecuador D408
Unidad Educativo Bilingüe CEBI, Ecuador D408
Union School Haiti, Haiti D409
Unison World School, India D295
Unisus School (Lower), Canada D401
Unisus School (Upper), Canada D401
United High School, Argentina D428
United International Private School, United Arab Emirates D334
United Kids International Montenegro, Montenegro D363
United Lisbon International School, Portugal 214, D367
United Nations International School, USA D420
United Nations International School of Hanoi, Vietnam D336
United World Academy (UWA), India D295
Unity College Murraylands, Australia D342
Unity High School, Sudan D263
Universal American School, Kuwait D306
Universal American School, Dubai, United Arab Emirates D334
Universal College - Aley, Lebanon D307
Universidad de Monterrey Unidad Valle Alto, México D413
Universidad Internacional Jefferson, México D413
University of Monterrey, México D413
UPBEAT International School - Atsuta Campus, Japan D303
UPBEAT International School - Nakagawa Campus, Japan D303
UPBEAT International School - Tempaku Campus, Japan D303
Upper Canada College, Canada D402
Uppingham School, UK D397
Uppsala International School - Kvarngärdesskolan, Sweden D379
Uptown International School, United Arab Emirates D334
Uptown International School, Egypt D253
Urawagakuin High School, Japan D303
Uruguayan American School, Uruguay D438
USCA Academy, Canada D402
Üsküdar American Academy, Türkiye D386
Utahloy International School Guangzhou (UISG), China D280
Utahloy International School Zengcheng (UISZ), China D280
Utpal Shanghvi Global School, India D295
Uttpal Shanghvi School, India D295
UWC Adriatic, Italy 215, D361
UWC Atlantic, UK D397
UWC Changshu China, China D280
UWC Costa Rica, Costa Rica D405
UWC Dilijan, Armenia D346
UWC East Africa, Arusha Campus, Tanzania D264
UWC East Africa, Moshi Campus, Tanzania D264
UWC ISAK Japan, Japan D303
UWC Maastricht, Netherlands 216, D364
UWC Mahindra College, India D295
UWC Mostar, Bosnia & Herzegovina D348
UWC Red Cross Nordic, Norway D365
UWC Robert Bosch College, Germany D357
UWC South East Asia, Dover Campus, Singapore D323
UWC South East Asia, East Campus, Singapore D323
UWC Thailand International School, Thailand D327
UWC-USA, USA D420
Uwekind International School, Bulgaria D348

V

Vaels International School, India D295
Vale Verde International School, Portugal D367
Valley International School, Brazil D431
Valley Preparatory School, USA D415
Vanke Bilingual School, China D280
Vanke School Pudong, China D280
Varee Chiangmai International School, Thailand D327
VAUBAN, Ecole et Lycée Français de Luxembourg, Luxembourg D362
VBS Vienna Bilingual School, Austria D346
Vector International Academy, Slovenia D370
Vedanya International School, India D295
Verbier International School, Switzerland D382
Verdala International School, Malta D362
Verde Valley School, USA D414
Verita International School, Romania D368
Vermont School Medellín, Colombia D435
Vibgyor High School, Pune (NIBM Road), India D295
Vibgyor High, Mumbai (Goregagon), India D295
Vibgyor High, Vadodara, India D295
Victoria (Belcher) International Kindergarten, Hong Kong, China D284
Victoria (Harbour Green) International Kindergarten, Hong Kong, China D284
Victoria (Homantin) International Nursery, Hong Kong, China D284
Victoria (South Horizons) International Kindergarten, Hong Kong, China D284
Victoria Academy, Taiwan D324
Victoria Bilingual Christian Academy, Ecuador D408
Victoria English School, United Arab Emirates D334
Victoria International School of Sharjah, United Arab Emirates D334
Victoria Kindergarten, Hong Kong, China D284
Victoria Kindergarten Shenzhen (Futian), China D280
Victoria Kindergarten Shenzhen (Le Parc), China D280
Victoria Kindergarten Shenzhen (Lilin), China D280
Victoria Kindergarten Shenzhen (Shenzhen Bay), China D280
Victoria Nursery, Hong Kong, China D284
Victoria Park Academy, China D280
Victoria Shanghai Academy (VSA), Hong Kong, China D284
Victorious Kidss Educares, India D295
Victory Christian International School, Philippines D315
Victory Heights Primary School, United Arab Emirates D334
Vidhyashram International School, India D295
Vidya Global School, India D295
Vidyanjali International School, India D295
Vienna International School, Austria D346
Vientiane International School, Laos D306
Vietnam-Finland International School, Vietnam D336
VIII Prywatne Akademickie Liceum Ogólnokształcace, Poland D366
Vijay International School, Seychelles D261
Vikaasa World School, India D295
Vilac International School, Ghana D254
Villa Alarife School, Peru D437
Villa Devoto School, Argentina D428
Villa Global Education, Campus Litoral Norte, Brazil D431
Villa Global Education, Campus Paralela, Brazil D431
Villa Grimani International School, Italy D361
Village School, Guatemala D409
Villanova Preparatory School, USA D415
Villiers School, Ireland D358
Vilniaus Karalienes Mortos mokykla, Lithuania D362
Vilnius International Meridian School (VIMS), Lithuania D362
Vilnius International School, Lithuania D362
Vilnius Private Gymnasium, Lithuania D362
Violenschool International Primary School - Frans Hals Location, Netherlands D364
Virgin Islands Montessori School & Peter Gruber International Academy, Virgin Islands (US) D423
Vishwashanti Gurukul, India D295
Vision International School - Qatar, Qatar D317
Vista International School, India D295
Vistamar School, USA D415
Vittoria International School, Italy 217, D361
VIVA The School, India D295
Vivek High School, India D295
Vivian Fowler Memorial College for Girls, Nigeria D261
Vnukovo International School, Russian Federation D369
Vosiq International School, Uzbekistan D334
VpR International, Denmark D351

W

W.I.D.E. School, Russian Federation D369
Waad Academy, Saudi Arabia D321
Wadi Sofia College, Malaysia D310
Wahaha International School, China D280
Waikerie Lutheran Primary School, Australia D342
Wakakusa Kindergarten, Japan D303
Walden International School, Canada D402
Waldo International School, USA D420
Walford Anglican School for Girls, Australia D342
Walton Foreign Language School, Taicang, China D280
Walworth Barbour American International School, Israel D299
Warminster School, UK D397
Warsaw Montessori High School, Poland D366
Warwick Academy, Bermuda D400
Warwick School, UK D397
Washington Academy, Venezuela D438
Washington International School, USA D416
Washington Preparatory School, USA D422
Washington School, Argentina D428
Waterford Kamhlaba UWC of Southern Africa, Eswatini D253
Waterfront Montessori, USA D420
Weberbauer School, Peru D437
Weihai IVY International School, China D280
Weihai Zhongshi International School (WZIS), China D280

Index

Welham Boys' School, India D295
Wellington College, UK D397
Wellington College International Hangzhou, China D280
Wellington College International School Bangkok, Thailand.... 78, D327
Wellington College International Shanghai, China D280
Wellington College International Tianjin, China D280
Wellington School, UK D397
Wells Cathedral School, UK....D397
Wells International School - Bang Na Campus, Thailand D327
Wells International School - On Nut Campus, Thailand D327
Wellspring International Bilingual School - Hanoi, Vietnam....D336
Wellspring Learning Community, Lebanon.... 80, D307
Wellspring Saigon International Bilingual School, Vietnam D336
Wellspring School, Argentina....D428
Wenlock School, Chile D432
Wenona School, Australia....D342
Wentworth College & Primary, New Zealand D344
Wesgreen International School - Sharjah, United Arab Emirates D334
Wesley College Melbourne - Elsternwick Campus, Australia....D343
Wesley College Melbourne - Glen Waverley Campus, Australia....D343
Wesley College Melbourne - St Kilda Road Campus, Australia....D343
Wesley School, Indonesia....D298
West Buckland School, UK....D397
West Nairobi School, Kenya....D256
West Sound Academy, USA....D422
Westbourne College Singapore, Singapore D323
Westbourne School, UK D397
Westcoast International Primary School, Mauritius....D257
Westcoast International Secondary School, Mauritius D257
Western Academy Of Beijing, China D280
Western Australian Primary and High School, Vietnam D336
Western International School, Cambodia....D270
Western International School of Shanghai (WISS), China 81, D280
Westfield School, UK D397
Westfields International School, Philippines D315
Westhill Institute, México....D413
Westhill Institute - Carpatos, México D413
Westlake Academy, USA....D422
Westlake International School, Malaysia....D310
Westlink International School, Vietnam....D336
Westminster Canadian Academy, Republic of Korea D318
Westminster School, UK....D397
Westminster School, Adelaide, Australia D343
Westonbirt School, UK D397
Westtown School, USA D421
Westwood International School, Botswana D248
Wewak International School, Papua New Guinea D344
Wheatley School, Canada....D402
Whitby School, USA....D416
White Rock Christian Academy, Canada D401
Whiteplains British School, Nigeria D261
Whitgift School, UK D397
Whitman Academy, Jordan....D304
Whittle School & Studios - Shenzhen Campus, China D280
Whole Education Academy, Canada D401
William Carey Academy, Bangladesh D269
Williamsburg Christian Academy, USA D422
Willow International School, Spain D379
Willowbrook International School, Japan D303
Willows Preparatory School, USA....D422
Wilmington Friends School, USA D416
Winchester College, UK....D397
Windermere Preparatory School, USA....D417
Windermere School, UK....D397
Windhoek International School, Namibia D258
Windrose Academy, Egypt....D253
Windsor Hall, Canada....D401
Wingate School, Spain....D379
Winpenny School, México D413
Wisdom High International School, India....D295
Wisdomland Diamond Island, Vietnam....D336
Witty International School Bhilwara, India....D295
Witty International School Malad, India D295
Witty International School Udaipur, India....D295
Witty World Goregaon, India....D295
Wockhardt Global School, India....D295
Woldingham School, UK....D397
Wolsey Hall Oxford, UK D397
Woodbridge School, UK D397
Woodcroft College, Australia D343
Woodford International School, Solomon Islands D344
Woodhouse Grove School, UK....D397
Woodlands International School, Malaysia D310
Woodlands School, Uruguay D438
Woodleigh School, Australia D343
Woodside School, Uruguay....D438
Woodstock School, India 82, D295
Woodville School, Argentina....D428
Worksop College, UK....D398
World Academy of Tirana, Albania....D346
World International School of Torino, Italy D361
Worth School, UK D398
Wotton House International School, UK....D398
Wrekin College, UK....D398
Wroclaw International School, Poland....D366
Wuhan Aoxin Elite School, China D280
Wuhan Britain-China School, China D280
Wuhan Yangtze International School, China D280
Wuxi Dipont School of Arts and Science, China D280
Wuxi Foreign Language School, China....D281
Wuxi United International School, China D281
Wycherley International School Gampaha, Sri Lanka....D323
Wychwood School, UK....D398
Wycliffe College, UK D398
Wycombe Abbey, UK....D398
Wycombe Abbey International School, China....D281

X

X.L.X. Kindergarten (Qingcheng Campus), China D281
X.L.X. Kindergarten (Tangzhen Campus), China D281
Xàbia International School (Primary), Spain D379
Xàbia International School (Secondary), Spain....D379
Xavier College, Kostka Hall Campus, Australia D343
Xavier College, Senior Campus, Australia D343
Xavier School, Philippines....D315
XCL World Academy, Singapore D323
Xenion Education, Cyprus D349
Xi'an Hanova International School, China D281
Xi'an Liangjiatan International School (XLIS), China D281
Xiamen Flair Kindergarten, China D281
Xiamen International School, China D281
Xiaomiao Kindergarten (Luoxiu Campus), China D281
Xiaomiao Kindergarten (Xinsong Campus), China D281
Xining International Academy, China....D281
XXI Century Integration International Secondary School, Russian Federation D369
XXI Century International Education and Innovation Center, Azerbaijan D347

Y

Yadavindra Public School, India....D295
Yago School Sevilla, Spain D379
Yamanashi Gakuin School, Japan D303
Yamata Kindergarten, Japan....D303
Yang Guang Qing School of Beijing, China D281
Yangon Academy International School, Myanmar.... D311
Yangon American International School, Myanmar.... D311
Yangon International School, Myanmar.... D311
Yantai American School, China....D281
Yantai Huasheng International School, China D281
Yas American Academy, United Arab Emirates D334
Yasmina British Academy, United Arab Emirates....D334
Yehudi Menuhin School, UK....D398
Yeni Yol Schools, Türkiye....D386
Yew Chung International School of Beijing, China D281
Yew Chung International School of Chongqing, China....D281
Yew Chung International School of Hong Kong, Hong Kong, China D284
Yew Chung International School of Hong Kong - Early Childhood Education, Hong Kong, China D284
Yew Chung International School of Hong Kong - Primary Section, Hong Kong, China D284
Yew Chung International School of Qingdao, China....D281
Yew Chung International School of Shanghai - Century Park Campus, China D281
Yew Chung International School of Shanghai - Gubei Campus, China D281
Yew Chung International School of Shanghai - Hongqiao Campus, China D281
Yew Chung International School of Shanghai - Regency Park Campus, China....D281
Yew Chung International School of Silicon Valley, USA.... D415
YIES Your Italian English School, Italy D361
YingHua International School, USA....D420
YK Pao School, China....D281
YMCA of Hong Kong Christian College, Hong Kong, China....D284

Index

Yogyakarta Independent School, Indonesia D298
Yokohama International School, Japan D303
Yongsan International School of Seoul, Republic of Korea..............................D318
York Prep School, USA..D420
Yorkshire Academy, USA D422
Young Living Academy, Ecuador D408
Yoyogi International School, Japan...D303
YPJ School Kuala Kencana, Indonesia D298
YPJ School Tembagapura, Indonesia..D298
YTÜ Schools (YTÜ Okullari), Türkiye D386
YUCE Schools, Türkiye D386
Yuwen Princeton Kindergarten, China...D281

Z

Zafer Koleji, Türkiye D386
Zahrat Al Sahraa International School, Saudi Arabia D321
Zakladni Skola a Materska Skola Klas s.r.o, Czech Republic D350
Zakladni Skola Buresova, Czech Republic...D350
Zenith International School, Malaysia..D310
Zespól Szkól Ogólnoksztalcacych im. Pawla z Tarsu, Poland..........................D366
Zhuhai International School, China..D281
Ziling Changxing Kindergarten, China...D281
Zlatarski International School, Bulgaria D348
Zurich International School, Switzerland D382
Zürich Schule Barcelona, Spain...D379